A TOPICAL BIBLIOGRAPHY OF COMPUTER(-AIDED) TRANSLATION

A Topical Bibliography of Computer(-aided) Translation

Chan Sin-wai

The Chinese University Press

A Topical Bibliography of Computer(-aided) Translation
Chan Sin-wai

ISBN: 978–962–996–330–9

THE CHINESE UNIVERSITY PRESS
The Chinese University of Hong Kong
SHA TIN, N.T., HONG KONG
Fax: +852 2603 6692
+852 2603 7355
E-mail: cup@cuhk.edu.hk
Web-site: www.chineseupress.com

Printed in Hong Kong

For my mother

獻給母親賴梅蓮女士

❖ CONTENTS ❖

❖ INTRODUCTION ❖

Introductory Remarks

As a result of the rapid advances in information technology, computer (-aided) translation has become a major part of translation studies and practice in recent decades. As far as we know, of the 193 countries in the world, 30 have conducted research on computer(-aided) translation, 9 actively. During the ten years from 1993 to 2003, for example, 26 conferences on computer translation and its related areas were held, second only to translation studies in terms of number. In the area of publication, we know that of the 1,000 books that have been published in either English or Chinese since the beginning of translation in the very ancient period, those on computer translation, totalling 169 entries, are again second to translation studies in terms of volume. All these indicate that computer(-aided) translation is a very important area of research and publication for translation scholars, computer scientists, and linguists. The need of a topical bibliography to provide information on the literature in the field is therefore necessary, important, and in fact, overdue.

This bibliography contains 8,363 entries of works written either in English or Chinese by 5,404 authors between 1948 and 2006, a period of 58 years. It is a collection of journal articles, conference papers, book chapters, project reports, software reviews, and newsletter features on or about documentary and speech computer(-aided) translation. These entries have been grouped alphabetically into 39 categories or parts, based on their relationship with computer(-aided) translation. Entries in each part have also been put alphabetically according to the names of the authors in their original pronunciations or transliterations. This bibliography should serve as a guide to the literature on the various aspects of computer(-aided) translation, especially in the contemporary period.

Rationales for Categorization

To facilitate a better understanding of the rationales of categorization, detailed explanations on all the parts may be in order. Part 1, to begin with, is "Alignment," which is "a process of matching up a source text and the target text segment by segment into translation pairs" (Chan 2004: 8) as units of translation memory in computer-aided translation. Apart from the general topic of "Alignment (33)," [hereafter the figures in brackets indicate the number of entries in the book] it also includes "Aligner," "Alignment Technology," and "Alignment Template." Entries in Alignment have been grouped technically into "Automatic Alignment," "Fuzzy Alignment," and "Statistical Alignment," and linguistically into "Lexical Alignment," "Terminology Alignment," "Word Alignment," "Phrase Alignment," "Clause Alignment," "Sentence Alignment," and "Text Alignment." Of all these alignments, "Word Alignment (65)" and "Sentence Alignment (25)" have the largest numbers of entries. It is also found that the algorithm, methods, techniques, and other practical issues in the automatic or statistical alignment of parallel or comparative texts are the subjects of examination in a large number of articles in this part.

Part 2 is about ambiguity and disambiguation, which is the removal of ambiguities. As computer translation is context-insensitive, the existence of ambiguity, which refers to expressions with more than one meaning, causes problems to computer translation systems. Resolving translation ambiguity is therefore a central issue in most of the articles in "Ambiguity (23)," which is divided into "Lexical Ambiguity (3)" and "Syntactical Ambiguity (3)." "Disambiguation (29)," on the other hand, is to establish a single interpretation or meaning for easier computer processing. "Word Sense Disambiguation (119)" figures prominently in this area. It has been proposed by some authors that monolingual, bilingual, or even multilingual word sense disambiguation can be resolved through conceptual density, probabilistic models, knowledge sources, neural networks, domain information, ontological knowledge, similarity-based methods, corpus statistics, wordnet relations, sense examples, and syntactic dependency.

Part 3 is "Analysis (9)." It goes without saying that analysis is important in both human and computer translation. Generally and computationally, it is necessary to conduct "Source Analysis (5)," "Text Analysis (11)," "Natural Language Analysis (4)," and "Translation Analysis (4)." More specifically and linguistically, we need to have "Linguistic Analysis (7)," including "Morphological Analysis (13)," "Semantic Analysis (16)," "Syntactical Analysis (14)," or "Sentence

Analysis (7)." Automatic linguistic analysis is generally considered as a basis for quality translation. What needs to be studied are the units and tools of analysis.

Part 4 covers all types of checkers, which are translation tools used in both computer and computer-aided translation. Six types of checkers have been identified, including the "Controlled Language Checker (1)" for the proper usage of controlled language text, "Grammar Checker (10)" for grammatical accuracy, "Spelling Checker (6)" for spelling correctness, "Style Checker (2)" for stylistic reproduction, and "Syntax Checker (2)" for syntactical well-formedness. "Translatability Checker (1)" is a tool for users to decide whether computer translation is needed for text generation, while "TransCheck (3)" is an aid for automatic validation of human and computer translation.

Part 5 is related to computers and translation. It includes entries on "Computer (5)," and the subheadings of "Interface (11)," "Storage (9)," "Usability (4)," and "User-friendliness (1)." Other topics in this part are wider in scope and therefore have more entries. "Computer Applications in Translation" has 86 entries, "Computer Aid," 12, "Computer Learning," 31, and "Computer Translatability," 11. What deserves special mention is the literature on practical experience in the application of computer (-aided) translation systems for translating domain-specific texts, such as scientific writings, and for office automation at large corporations. The issue of improving the machine translatability of certain texts is also noteworthy.

Part 6 is about "Computer-aided Translation," totalling 60 entries. Central concepts in this areas, such as "Productivity (10)," "Reusability (4)," and "Similarity (15)," have been included. Also included are the history, systems, system evaluation, teaching, and tools of computer-aided translation. A total of 164 entries have been recorded. Some genuine issues in computer-aided translation have been raised and discussed by works in this part, which include the selection, use, and evaluation of computer-aided translation systems, the treatment of repeated structures, the reusability of linguistic resources, the training of computer-aided translators, the increase in translation productivity, and the importance of making the most out of textual similarity. Also of considerable interest are articles on hands-on experience in the operation of computer-aided systems, the strengths and weaknesses of some language-specific systems, and the teaching of computer-aided translation at vocational and tertiary institutions.

Part 7 is on "Computer/Machine Translation," which forms the main core of this bibliography, with a total of 2,013 entries. It has 24 headings. "Computer Translation" alone has 174 entries. 25 approaches to computer translation have been included, with "Example-based Computer translation (131)" and "Statistical Computer Translation (140)" having the largest numbers of entries. There are 8 subheadings for "Computer Translation Evaluation," and entries have also been included for 8 factors of evaluation criteria. Also covered in this part are the various aspects of computer translation, including its history, industry, market, methodology, process, programming, projects, and research. A total of 53 computer translation systems have been included, with most entries on popular systems. Relating to translation systems are entries on system customization, design, and evaluation. Entries have also been included on computer translation teaching, 13 types of computer translation, computer translation users, and computer translators.

Part 8 is on "Concordancing," which is an effective way of analyzing the source text. This part has entries on 3 different concordancers: Multiconcord, ParaConc, and WordSmith, and also 3 types of linguistic concordancers: Bilingual, Multilingual, and Parallel. Concordancing is the first stage of the technology-oriented translation procedure where statistical and lexical information of the source text is given in a systematic manner.

Part 9 is about "Controlled Language," which is a type of natural language with restrictive grammars and vocabularies so as to reduce or eliminate ambiguity and complexity, and to make it easier for computer processing. It has been suggested that if control can be exerted on the three stages of translation process, namely, source analysis, transfer, and text generation, then quality translation can be produced. Included in this part are entries on "Controlled Authoring (16)," "Controlled Language (68)," "Controlled Translation (5)," and "Controlled Vocabulary (4)." Authors in this part rightly point out that there are advantages of controlled language translation, including improved consistency, more reusability, easier processing, greater standardization, and increased translatability. But at the same time, the disadvantages of time-consuming authoring, restrictive checking process, high maintenance cost, and expensive system construction, have also been noted.

Part 10 is about "Corpus," which is "a body of written or verbal data collected for linguistic analysis or some specific purpose, such as dictionary-making and machine translation." (Chan 2004: 46) This explains why there are three subheadings for this part: "Corpus," "Data," and "Dictionary." "Corpus" has 274 entries on corpus annotation, monolingual, bilingual, and multilingual corpora, text corpus, speech corpus, translation corpus, and web corpus. Attention is drawn to the acquisition and alignment of comparative bilingual corpora, and the use of these corpora for translator training. There are also articles on the role of parallel corpora in translation and multilingual lexicography. "Data," on the other hand, has 13 entries on "Data Bank," "Data Collection," "Data Management," and "Data Processing." And lastly, the part on "Dictionary" has 81 entries on "Bilingual Dictionary," "Electronic Dictionary," and "Translation Dictionary."

The next part, Part 11, lists 30 domains to which computer translation has been applied. These domains include "Advertisement," "Appointment Scheduling," "The Bible," "Braille," "Broadcasting," "Business," "Caption," "Culture," "Flight Information," "Food," "Industry," "Law," "Literature," "Manual," "Mathematics," "Medicine," "Navigation," "News," "Patent," "Safety," "Science," "Speech," "Subtitle," "Technology," "Telephone," "Title," "Travel," "War," and "Weather." These domains show very clearly which areas or fields are most suitable for computer translation. And it has also been shown that considerable success has been achieved with the translation of "Weather" bulletins. Statistically speaking, most of the entries in Part 11 are on "Telephone (10)," "Medicine (17)," and "News (25)."

Entries on editing make up Part 12. Editing is divided into "Pre-editing (11)" and "Post-editing (44)." Pre-editing is to "prepare a source text for translation in a machine translation system" (Chan 2004: 178) while post-editing is defined as "an activity undertaken for the purpose of rendering a machine output text suitable for use." (Chan 2004: 175) There are 76 entries on "Editing." To edit machine outputs into acceptable and usable translations would be essential training for translation editors.

Part 13 contains 157 entries on "Grammar (68)" and 89 entries on 9 different grammatical systems which have been applied to computer translation. Some of the entries in this part explore the usefulness of some grammars, such as dependency grammar and stochastic grammar, in computer translation, and the creation of machine grammar.

Part 14 brings in "Human Translation (41)" to contrast it with "Human-aided Computer Translation," to illustrate its interaction with computer translation, and to discuss its role in computer translation. Questions that have been asked center around the value of human-man interaction, the cooperation of translators and computers, and comparisons between human translation and computer translation.

Part 15 is about "Information (206)" in the context of computer translation. Computer translation is actually the use of "Information Technology (8)" to do "Information Processing (30)," involving "Information Extraction (53)," "Information Management (4)," and "Information Retrieval (60)." Some articles point out the need of information-based computer translation, and the importance of extracting information from the web. Others discuss principles of information retrieval and skills in cross-lingual search.

Part 16 is on "Inputting (40)," which is the act of entering the source text into the computer for machine processing. Various aspects of inputting, such as the "Dictation Machine," "Optical Character Recognition," "Proof-reading," and issues relating to "Punctuation," are covered in this part. It should be realized that computer translation is a global activity and the skills of inputting different languages into the computer are essential for computer translation.

Part 17 is a collection of entries on "Interpreting (14)." Figures in this part show that very little has been done on this area. One of the issues raised in interpreting is whether example-based incremental transfer can be effectively used in simultaneous interpreting.

Part 18 is a much studied area, involving the application of knowledge to computer translation systems. It has 97 entries on "Knowledge Acquisition," "Knowledge Bank," "Knowledge Extraction," and the lexical, linguistic, semantic, syntactic, terminological, and translation knowledge that has been used in computer processing.

Part 19 is a large area, containing 861 entries on "Languages and Translation." Apart from topics such as "Language Features," "Language Functions," "Language Learning," and "Language Modelling," the greater parts of this area are on the translation of 50 national or regional languages and the translation of 80 language pairs. Of all the languages, Spanish (31), Arabic (19), English (19), Russian (33), Chinese (44), Japanese (42) are much studied. As far as language-pair translation is concerned, Chinese-English (42) and English-Chinese (31), Japanese-English (32) and English-Japanese (14), English-Korean (13) and Korean-English (14) have the highest number of entries.

Part 20 has 71 entries on "Lexicography," which is essential knowledge for anyone interested in computer translation. Articles have been written on "Computational Lexicography (12)" and "Corpus Lexicography (1)." "Lexicon (42)" is also studied from the perspectives of "Lexical Acquisition (6)," "Phrasal Lexicon (1)," and "Translation Lexicon (3)."

Part 21 is on "Linguistics (320)," one of the most important areas in computer translation. Entries on "Chinese Linguistics (3)," "Computational Linguistics (23)," "Contrastive Linguistics (1)," and "Corpus Linguistics (7)" have been included. Also included are entries on some sub-areas of linguistics, such as "Discourse (25)," "Morphology (37)," "Pragmatics (4)," "Semantics (69)," "Stylistics (1)," and "Syntax (37)."

Part 22 goes into "Localization (87)," an area which is gaining increasing attention in the field of computer translation. Localization, which is defined as "taking a product and making it linguistically, technically and culturally appropriate to the target locale where it will be used and sold," (Lisa) is often interchangeable with "Globalization (21)" and "Internationalization (7)." Entries on 6 different types of localization systems have also been included. Articles in this part examine the teaching of localization in universities, cost and quality of localization, and workflow in the localization process.

Part 23 puts together entries on the development of computer translation in different countries and regions. As mentioned before, there are 30 countries or places in the world where research and development of computer translation is active. France (15), China (16), Japan (25), Russia (26), Europe (37), and the United States (51) have the largest numbers of entries. It is obvious that the Western countries in America and Europe are dominant in the research and development of computer translation.

Part 24 is about "Natural Language (314)" and its understanding, processing, and generation. Under the topic of "Natural Language Processing," there are entries on related issues, such as "Finite State Transducer," "Maximum Entropy," "N-gram," and "Tokenization." Under "Natural Language Understanding," there are also entries on "Artificial Intelligence" and "Hierarchical Networks of Concepts." It is common knowledge that the application of computational linguistics in computer translation is natural language processing. The more one studies it, the better it will be in performance. That explains, at least partly, why so many works have been written on this area.

Part 25 has 59 entries on "Online Translation," which is the translation of texts by a computer translation system that is available at all times on demand from users. There are 21 entries on "Internet," 20 entries on "Online Translation," and 18 entries on "Web Translation." In the terminology of computer translation, "Online Translation" is actually synonymous with "Web Translation."

Part 26 is about "Parsing (251)," which is the process of recognizing the grammatical function of each word or groups of words in the sentence for use in computer translation. Included in this part are 30 entries on "Parser," 169 entries on "Parsing," and 38 entries on "Dependency Parsing," "Robust Parsing," "Semantic Parsing," "Sentence Parsing," "Shallow Parsing," and "Statistical Parsing."

Part 27 includes articles and works on "Parts of Speech (165)." It is important, as we know, to know the functions of different parts of speech in a computer translation system to ensure that the output is of good quality. Entries on "Adjective," "Adverb," "Article," "Classifier," "Conjunction," "Measure Word," "Noun," "Preposition," "Pronoun," and "Verb," have been collected in this part.

Part 28 contains biographical sketches of eminent scholars and experts in the field of computer translation. A total of 26 entries have been included in "Profiles," paying tribute to 17 personalities. Most of the entries are attributable to the book edited by John Hutchins. The articles reveal the efforts made by pioneers in the early years of computer translation. (Hutchins 2000)

Part 29 is about "Segmentation (63)," which is sentence separation in machine translation. Some languages are easier to be segmented; others are not. Chinese, which has no interval marks, or word boundaries, between two successive characters or phrases in a Chinese sentence, is difficult for segmentation. That explains why most entries in "Automatic Segmentation (6)" are related to Chinese. Segmentation can also be done statistically. Segmentation has been divided into "Word Segmentation (21)," "Sentence Segmentation (3), and "Text Segmentation (9)."

Part 30 focuses on the "Sentence (51)," which is the level at which computer translation works. There are entries on "Sentence Boundary," "Sentence Generation," "Sentence Length," "Sentence Pattern," "Sentence Splitting," "Sentence Structure," with "Sentence Translation (17)" having the largest number of entries.

Part 31 is on "Speech (478)," covering "Dialogue" and "Speech." The

Dialogue part covers "Dialogue-based Computer Translation," "Dialogue Processing," "Dialogue Translation," and "Dialogue Translation System." The success of speech translation is related to "Speech Recognition" through the use of "Speech Technology" and some "Speech Recognition Systems." It also hinges on "Speech Processing," "Speech Synthesis," and "Speech Generation." The entire process of translating a spoken text from one language into another is "Speech Translation," which requires the use of "Speech Translation Systems" and entries on evaluations of these systems have also been included.

Part 32 is "Tagging (85)," which is to give each word in a sentence a grammatical category, such as noun or adjective, so that its syntactical structure can be shown and properly used in computer translation. The entries of this part are in the areas of "Part-of-speech Tagging (36)," the "Taggers (9)" available, and "Tagging (40)" itself.

Part 33 is about "Terminology (151)." In computer translation, terminology is the study of the body of specialized words relating to a particular subject which are processed electronically. This part includes the various aspects of terminology and computer translation, such as "Terminology Recognition," "Terminology Acquisition," "Terminology Extraction," the creation of "Terminology Bank," "Terminology Processing," "Terminology Management," and the systems used for terminology management. All these are constituent parts of "Terminology Translation."

Part 34 is a list of articles on the "Text," which is the basic unit of documentary computer translation. Several types of texts have been included, such as "Bilingual Text," "Bitext," "Colloquial Text," "Comparative Text," "Parallel Text," and "Source Text." Also included are the different ways texts are treated in computer translation, known as "Text Processing," such as "Text Categorization," "Text Chunking," "Text Clustering," "Text Generation," "Text Abstracting," and "Text Summarization."

Part 35 goes into the core concept of "Translation (358)" in the context of computer translation. There are 26 subheadings of "Translation," all of which have been studied from the perspective of computer translation. "Translation Quality (56)," for example, refers to entries on quality in computer translation but not human translation.

Part 36 is "Translation Memory (91)," which is singled out for more focused treatment. It includes 4 topics: "Translation Memory," covering both "Matching" and "Fuzzy Match," "Translation Memory Database," "Translation Memory System," and "Translation Memory Exchange," which is about an agreement to allow translation memory databases developed from one product to be imported into another. (Chan 2004: 251–252.)

Part 37 is the domain of "Translator's Workstation," which is an integrated system for professional translators. Included in this part are entries on "Translator's Workstation (22)," and its synonym, "Translator's Workbench (13)."

Part 38 is about "Transliteration (111)." It covers different issues in "Transliteration" and problems of "Name Entity." It should be pointed out that one of the most thorny issues in computer translation is the treatment of proper names. Articles collected in this part discuss, among others, the detection, recognition, extraction, and disambiguation of name entities. Also important are the transliteration and translation of bilingual and multilingual name entities, and the creation of name entity corpora and taggers in computer translation systems.

The last part, Part 39, is all about "Words (135)," generally considered as the smallest translation unit in computer translation. It covers the topics of "Collocation (35)," "Context (25)," "Neologism (1)," "Synonym (4)," and "Unknown Word (15)." Prominent issues in this part include the retrieval and extraction of lexical and grammatical collocations from corpora in computer translation, the recognition of context at the extrasentential level to produce quality computer translation, and the detection and translation of unknown words. Also included are entries on "Word Order," "Word Processing," "Word Processor," "Word Recognition," "Word-reordering Rule," "Word Selection," "Word Sense," and "Word Translation."

Concluding Remarks

The rapid growth of computer translation in recent decades has brought major changes to the world of translation. It challenges traditional concepts, enrichs translation vocabulary, and widens the role of the professional translator. We have witnessed a drastic proliferation of all kinds of publications on computer(-aided) translation. The following table lists the quantity of annual publications from 1948 to 2006.

【1948】(1)	【1949】(0)	【1950】(1)	【1951】(4)	【1952】(15)
【1953】(9)	【1954】(13)	【1955】(35)	【1956】(47)	【1957】(30)
【1958】(32)	【1959】(16)	【1960】(20)	【1961】(54)	【1962】(60)
【1963】(19)	【1964】(19)	【1965】(18)	【1966】(16)	【1967】(34)
【1968】(11)	【1969】(5)	【1970】(13)	【1971】(13)	【1972】(17)
【1973】(24)	【1974】(24)	【1975】(24)	【1976】(31)	【1977】(30)
【1978】(35)	【1979】(49)	【1980】(44)	【1981】(54)	【1982】(70)
【1983】(54)	【1984】(99)	【1985】(64)	【1986】(135)	【1987】(197)
【1988】(163)	【1989】(147)	【1990】(144)	【1991】(104)	【1992】(202)
【1993】(210)	【1994】(270)	【1995】(288)	【1996】(304)	【1997】(383)
【1998】(344)	【1999】(340)	【2000】(650)	【2001】(447)	【2002】(447)
【2003】(415)	【2004】(389)	【2005】(378)	【2006】(352)	

What is clearly observable from the above table is the huge increase in the number of publications on computer(-aided) translation. From 1948 to 1952, for example, the number of works on computer translation in the first five years of its development is 21. In the last five years, from 2002 to the first half of 2006, the total number of works on computer translation stands at 1981, and this is a 94-fold increase of the first period. This trend, we suspect, will continue for a long time to come. With computer(-aided) translation gaining more and more interest and attention, an increasing number of academic programmes in this area will be established. It is also expected that more scholars will be able to look into the possibility of putting translation theories into practice through computer translation. And it is genuinely hoped that this topical bibliography would serve as a foundation for further and faster growth of computer(-aided) translation.

References

Chan, Sin-wai (2004). *A Dictionary of Translation Technology*. Hong Kong: The Chinese University Press.

——, ed. (2004). *Translation and Bilingual Dictionaries*. Tubingen: Max Niemeyer Verlag.

Hutchins, W. John, ed. (2000). *Early Years in Machine Translation: Memoirs and Biographies of Pioneers*. Amsterdam and Philadelphia: John Benjamins Publishing Company.

* Acknowledgement is given to Mr Zheng Hongbo who prepared partly the Title Index and wholly the Author Index.

❖ PART 1 ❖

Alignment

Alignment

Ayan, Necip Fazil, Bonnie J. Dorr, and Nizar Habash (2004). "Multi-align: Combining Linguistic and Statistical Techniques to Improve Alignments for Adaptable MT." In Robert E. Frederking and Kathryn B. Taylors, eds., *Machine Translation: From Real Users to Research*. Berlin: Springer Verlag, pp. 17–26.

Ayan, Necip Fazil, Bonnie J. Dorr, and Christof Monz (2005). "Alignment Link Projection Using Transformation-based Learning." *Proceedings of Human Language Technology Conference and Conference on Empirical Methods in Natural Language Processing* (*HLT/EMNLP-2005*), Vancouver, BC, Canada.

Barzilay, Regina and Lillian Lee (2003). "Learning to Paraphrase: An Unsupervised Approach Using Multiple-sequence Alignment." *Proceedings of the Human Language Technology and North American Chapter of Association of Computational Linguistics 2003* (*HLT/NAACL-2003*), Edmonton, Alberta, Canada.

Bender, Oliver, Richard Zens, Evgeny Matusov, and Hermann Ney (2004). "Alignment Templates: The RWTH SMT System." *Proceedings of the International Workshop on Spoken Language Translation* (*IWSLT-2004*), Kyoto, Japan, pp. 79–84.

Chen, Kuang-Hua and Chen Hsin-Hsi (1995). "Aligning Bilingual Corpus: Especially for Language Pairs from Different Families." *Information Sciences*, Vol. 4, No. 2, pp. 57–81.

Collier, Nigel, Hideki Kirakawa, and Akira Kumano (1998). "Machine Translation vs. Dictionary Term Translation—A Comparison for English-Japanese News Article Alignment." *Proceedings of the 36th Annual Meeting of the Association for Computational Linguistics and 17th International Conference on Computational Linguistics* (*COLING-ACL-98*), Montreal, Quebec, Canada.

Eisenstein, Jacob and C. Mario Christoudias (2004). "A Salience-based Approach to Gesture-speech Alignment." *Proceedings of the Human Language Technology Conference/North American Chapter of the Association for Computational Linguistics Annual Meeting* (*HLT/NAACL-2004*), Boston, MA, USA.

Fung, Pascale and Kenneth W. Church (1994). "K-vec: A New Approach for Aligning Parallel Texts." *Proceedings of the 15th International Conference on Computational Linguistics* (*COLING-94*), Kyoto,

Japan, pp. 1096–1102.

Fung, Pascale and Kathleen R. McKeown (1994). "Aligning Noisy Parallel Corpora across Language Groups: Word Pair Feature Matching by Dynamic Time Warping." *Technology Partnerships for Crossing the Language Barrier: Proceedings of the 1st Conference of the Association for Machine Translation in the Americas*, Columbia, Maryland, USA, pp. 81–87.

Giguet, Emmanuel (2005). "Multi-grained Alignment of Parallel Texts with Endogenous Resources." In Walther van Hahn, John Hutchins, and Cristina Vertan, eds., *Proceedings of the International Workshop on Modern Approaches in Translation Technologies*, Borovets, Bulgaria.

Haruno, Masahiko and Takefumi Yamazaki (1997). "High-performance Bilingual Text Alignment Using Statistical and Dictionary Information." *Natural Language Engineering*, Vol. 3, pp. 1–14.

Kay, Martin and Martin Röscheisen (1993). "Text-translation Alignment." *Computational Linguistics*, Vol. 19, No. 1, pp. 121–142.

Kay, Martin (2004). "Substring Alignment Using Suffix Trees." *Proceedings of the 5th International Conference on Intelligent Text Processing and Computational Linguistics (CICLing-2004)*, Chung-Ang University, Seoul, Korea, pp. 271–279.

Kondrak, Grzegorz (2000). "A New Algorithm for the Alignment of Phonetic Sequences." *Proceedings of the 1st Meeting of the North American Chapter of the Association for Computational Linguistics*, Seattle, Washington, DC, USA, pp. 288–295.

Langlais, Philippe, Michel Simard, and Jean Veronis (1998). "Methods and Practical Issues in Evaluating Alignment Techniques." *Proceedings of the 36th Annual Meeting of the Association for Computational Linguistics*, Montreal, Quebec, Canada.

Macklovitch, Elliott and Marie-Louise Hannan (1998). "Line 'Em Up: Advances in Alignment Technology and Their Impact on Translation Support Tools." *Machine Translation*, Vol. 13, No. 1, pp. 41–57.

McEnery, Tony, Scott Piao, and Xu Xin (2000). "Parallel Alignment in English and Chinese." In Simon Philip Botley, Anthony Mark McEnery, and Andrew Wilson, eds., *Multilingual Corpora in Teaching and Research*. Amsterdam: Rodopi, pp. 177–191.

Melamed, I. Dan (2001). "Application: Alignment." *Empirical Methods for Exploiting Parallel Texts*. Cambridge, MA: MIT Press, pp. 35–40.

Menezes, Arul and Stephen D. Richardson (2001). "A Best-first Alignment Algorithm for Automatic Extraction of Transfer Mappings from Bilingual Corpora." *Proceedings of the Association for Computational Linguistics 39th Annual Meeting and 10th Conference of the European Chapter: Data-driven Machine Translation (ACL-EACL-2001)*, Toulouse, France, pp. 39–46.

Menezes, Arul and Stephen D. Richardson (2003). "A Best-first Alignment Algorithm for Automatic Extraction of Transfer Mappings from Bilingual Corpora." In Michael Carl and Andy Way, eds., *Recent Advances in Example-based Machine Translation*. Dordrecht: Kluwer Academic Publishers, pp. 421–442.

Meyers, Adam, Roman Yangarber, and Ralph Grishman (1996). "Alignment of Shared Forests for Bilingual Corpora." *Proceedings from the 16th International Conference on Computational Linguistics (COLING-96)*. Copenhagen, Denmark, pp. 459–465.

Och, Franz Josef, Christoph Tillmann, and Hermann Ney (1999). "Improved Alignment Models for Statistical Machine Translation." *Proceedings of the Joint SIGDAT Conference on Empirical Methods in NLP and Very Large Corpora (EMNLP/VLC-99)*, University of Maryland, College Park, MD, USA.

Och, Franz Josef and Hermann Ney (2000). "Improved Statistical Alignment Models." *Proceedings of the 38th Annual Meeting of the Association for Computational Linguistics (ACL-2000)*, Hong Kong, pp. 440–447.

Papageorgiou, Harris V., Lambros Cranias, and Stelios Piperidis (1994). "Automatic Alignment in Parallel Corpora." *Proceedings of the 32nd Annual Meeting of the Association for Computational Linguistics (ACL-94)*, Las Cruces, New Mexico, USA.

Papageorgiou, Harris V. (1997). "Clause Recognition in the Framework of Alignment." In Ruslan Mitkov and Nicolas Nicolov, eds., *Recent Advances in Natural Language Processing*. Amsterdam and Philadelphia: John Benjamins Publishing Company, pp. 417–425.

Pohl, Gábor (2005). "English-Hungarian NP Alignment in MetaMorpho TM." *Proceedings of the 11th Workshop of the European Association for Machine Translation: Machine Translation/Translation Aids—Tools to Increase Quality and to Save Money*, the University of Oslo, Oslo, Norway.

Ribeiro, António, Gabriel Lopes, and Joao Mexia (2000). "A Self-learning

Method of Parallel Texts Alignment." In John S. White, ed., *Envisioning Machine Translation in the Information Future*. Berlin: Springer Verlag, pp. 30–39.

Ribeiro, António, Gaël Dias, Gabriel Lopes, and João Mexia (2001). "Cognates Alignment." In Bente Maegaard, ed., *Proceedings of MT Summit VIII: Machine Translation in the Information Age*, Santaigo de Compostela, Spain.

Senellart, Jean, Mirko Plitt, Christophe Bailly, and Francoise Cardoso (2001). "Resource Alignment for Machine Translation or Implicit Transfer." In Bente Maegaard, ed., *Proceedings of MT Summit VIII: Machine Translation in the Information Age*, Santiago de Compostela, Spain.

Tan, Chew Lim and Makato Nagao (1995). "Automatic Alignment of Japanese-Chinese Bilingual Texts." *IEICE Transactions on Information and Systems*, E78-D.1, pp. 68–76.

Wu, Dekai (1994). "Aligning Parallel English-Chinese Text Statistically with Lexical Criteria." *Proceedings of the 32nd Annual Meeting of the Association for Computational Linguistics* (*ACL-94*), Las Cruces, New Mexico, USA, pp. 80–87.

Wu, Dekai (2000). "Alignment." In Robert Dale, Hermann Moisl, and Harold L. Somers, eds., *Handbook of Natural Language Processing*. New York: Marcel Dekker, pp. 415–458.

Xu, Donghua and Chew Lim Tan (1999). "Alignment and Matching of Bilingual English-Chinese News Texts." *Machine Translation*, Vol. 14, No. 1, pp. 1–33.

Aligner

Deng, Yonggang and William Byrne (2006). "MTTK: An Alignment Toolkit for Statistical Machine Translation." *Proceedings of the Human Language Technology Conference—Annual Meeting of the North American Chapter of the Association for Computational Linguistics* (*HLT-NAACL-2006*), New York, USA.

Ittycheriah, Abraham and Salim Roukos (2005). "A Maximum Entropy Word Aligner for Arabic-English Machine Translation." *Proceedings of Human Language Technology Conference and Conference on Empirical Methods in Natural Language Processing* (*HLT/EMNLP-2005*), Vancouver, BC, Canada.

Ma, Xiaoyi (2006). "Champollion: A Robust Parallel Text Sentence Aligner." *Proceedings of the 5th International Conference on Language Resources and Evaluation* (*LREC-2006*), Genoa, Italy.

Zhang, Yujie, Ma Qing, and Hitoshi Isahara (2005). "A Multi-aligner for Japanese-Chinese Parallel Corpora." *Proceedings of MT Summit X*, Phuket, Thailand.

Alignment Technology

Langlais, Philippe, Michel Simard, and Jean Véronis (1998). "Methods and Practical Issues in Evaluating Alignment Techniques." *Proceedings of the 36th Annual Meeting of the Association for Computational Linguistics and 17th International Conference on Computational Linguistics* (*COLING-ACL-98*), Montreal, Quebec, Canada.

Macklovitch, Elliott and Marie-Louise Hannan (1996). "Line 'em up: Advances in Alignment Technology and Their Impact on Translation Support Tools." *Proceedings of the 2nd Conference of the Association for Machine Translation in the Americas: Expanding MT Horizons* (*AMTA-2*), Montreal, Quebec, Canada, pp. 145–156.

Alignment Template

Bender, Oliver, Klaus Macherey, Franz Josef Och, and Hermann Ney (2003). "Comparison of Alignment Templates and Maximum Entropy Models for Natural Language Understanding." *Proceedings of the 10th Conference of the European Chapter of the Association of Computational Linguistics* (*EACL-2003*), Budapest, Hungary.

Bender, Oliver, Richard Zens, Evgeny Matusov, and Hermann Ney (2004). "Alignment Templates: The RWTH SMT System." *Proceedings of the International Workshop on Spoken Language Translation* (*IWSLT-2004*), Kyoto, Japan.

Kumar, Shankar and William Byrne (2003). "A Weighted Finite State Transducer Implementation of the Alignment Template Model for Statistical Machine Translation." *Proceedings of the Human Language Technology and North American Chapter of Association of Computational Linguistics 2003* (*HLT/NAACL-2003*), Edmonton, Alberta, Canada.

Lin, Dekang and Colin Cherry (2003). "ProAlign: Shared Task System

Description." *Proceedings of the Human Language Technology and North American Chapter of Association of Computational Linguistics 2003* (*HLT/NAACL-2003*), Edmonton, Alberta, Canada.

Automatic Alignment

Macdonald, K. (2001). "Improving Automatic Alignment for Translation Memory Creation." In *Translating and the Computer 23*. London: The Association for Information Management.

Moirón, Begoña Villada and Jörg Tiedemann (2006). "Identifying Idiomatic Expressions Using Automatic Word-alignment." *Proceedings of the 11th Conference of the European Chapter of the Association for Computational Linguistics* (*EACL-2006*), Trento, Italy.

Papageorgiou, Harris, Lambros Cranias, and Stelios Piperidis (1994). "Automatic Alignment in Parallel Corpora." *Proceedings of the 32nd Annual Meeting of the Association for Computational Linguistics* (*ACL-94*), Las Cruces, New Mexico, USA, pp. 80–87.

Clause Alignment

Boutsis, Sotiris and Stelios Piperidis (1998). "Aligning Clauses in Parallel Texts." *Proceedings of the 3rd Conference on Empirical Methods in Natural Language Processing*, Granada, Spain.

Wang, Xiaojie and Fuji Ren (2005). "Chinese-Japanese Clause Alignment." *Proceedings of the 6th International Conference on Intelligent Text Processing and Computational Linguistics* (*CICLing-2005*), Mexico City, Mexico, pp. 391–401.

Fuzzy Alignment

Foster, George, Philippe Langlais, and Guy Lapalme (2002). "Text Prediction with Fuzzy Alignments." In Stephen D. Richardson, ed., *Machine Translation: From Research to Real Users*. Berlin and New York: Springer Verlag, pp. 44–53.

Lexical Alignment

Tufis, Dan, Radu Ion, Alexandru Ceausu, and Dan Stefanescu (2006).

"Improved Lexical Alignment by Combining Multiple Reified Alignments." *Proceedings of the 11th Conference of the European Chapter of the Association for Computational Linguistics* (*EACL-2006*), Trento, Italy.

Phrase Alignment

de Gispert, Adria, Jose B. Marino, and Josep Maria Crego (2004). "Phrase-based Alignment Combining Corpus Cooccurrences and Linguistic Knowledge." *Proceedings of the International Workshop on Spoken Language Translation* (*IWSLT-2004*), Kyoto, Japan.

Deng, Yonggang and William Byrne (2005). "HMM Word and Phrase Alignment for Statistical Machine Translation." *Proceedings of Human Language Technology Conference and Conference on Empirical Methods in Natural Language Processing* (*HLT/EMNLP-2005*), Vancouver, BC, Canada.

Imamura, Kenji (2001). "A Hierarchical Phrase Alignment from English and Japanese Bilingual Text." *Proceedings of the 2nd International Conference on Intelligent Text Processing and Computational Linguistics* (*CICLing-2001*), Mexico City, Mexico.

Ion, Radu, Alexandru Ceauşu, and Dan Tufiş (2006). "Dependency-based Phrase Alignment." *Proceedings of the 5th International Conference on Language Resources and Evaluation* (*LREC-2006*), Genoa, Italy.

Kim, Seonho, Juntae Yoon, and Dong-Yul Ra (2004). "Two-level Alignment by Words and Phrases Based on Syntactic Information." *Proceedings of the 5th International Conference on Intelligent Text Processing and Computational Linguistics* (*CICLing-2004*), Chung-Ang University, Seoul, Korea, pp. 306–317.

Watanabe, Taro, Kenji Imamura, and Eiichiro Sumita (2002). "Statistical Machine Translation Based on Hierarchical Phrase Alignment." *Proceedings of the 9th International Conference on Theoretical and Methodological Issues in Machine Translation* (*TMI-2002*), Keihanna, Japan, pp. 188–198.

Zhang, Ying and Stephan Vogel (2005). "An Efficient Phrase-to-phrase Alignment Model for Arbitrarily Long Phrase and Large Corpora." *Proceedings of the 10th Workshop of the European Association for Machine Translation: Practical Applications of Machine Translation*, Budapest, Hungary, pp. 294–301.

Sentence Alignment

Andriamanankasina, Tantely, Kenji Araki, and Koji Tochinai (1999). "Sub-sentential Alignment Method by Analogy." *Proceedings of the 13th Pacific Asia Conference on Language, Information and Computation (PACILIC-13)*, Taipei, Taiwan, pp. 277–284.

Barzilay, Regina and Noemie Elhadad (2003). "Sentence Alignment for Monolingual Comparable Corpora." *Proceedings of the 41st Annual Meeting of the Association for Computational Linguistics (ACL-2003)*, Sapporo, Japan.

Blank, I. (1995). "Sentence Alignment: Methods and Implementation." *Traitement automatique des langues: Traitements probabilistes et corpus*, numéro spécial, pp. 81–89.

Boutsis, Sotiris and Stelios Piperidis (1998). "OK with Alignment of Sentences. What about Clauses?" *Proceedings of the Panhellenic Conference on New Information Technology (NIT-98)*, Athens, Greece, pp. 288–297.

Brown, Peter F., Jennifer C. Lai, and Robert L. Mercer (1991). "Aligning Sentences in Parallel Corpora." *Proceedings of the 29th Annual Meeting of the Association for Computational Linguistics*, Berkeley, CA, USA, pp. 169–176.

Casillas, Arantza, Idoia Fernández, and Raquel Martínez (2004). "Sentence Alignment for Spanish-Basque Bitexts: Word Correspondences vs. Markup Similarity." *Proceedings of the 5th International Conference on Intelligent Text Processing and Computational Linguistics (CICLing-2004)*, Chung-Ang University, Seoul, Korea, pp. 302–305.

Chen, Stanley F. (1993). "Aligning Sentences in Bilingual Corpora Using Lexical Information." *Proceedings of the 31st Annual Conference of the Association for Computational Linguistics*, Columbus, Ohio, USA, pp. 9–16.

Chuang, Thomas C., G. N. You, and Jason S. Chang (2002). "Adaptive Bilingual Sentence Alignment." In Stephen D. Richardson, ed., *Machine Translation: From Research to Real Users*. Berlin and New York: Springer Verlag, pp. 11–30.

Collier, Nigel, Hideki Hirakawa, and Akira Kumano (1998). "An Experiment in Hybrid Dictionary and Statistical Sentence Alignment." *Proceedings of the 36th Annual Meeting of the Association for*

Computational Linguistics and 17th International Conference on Computational Linguistics (*COLING-ACL-98*), Montreal, Quebec, Canada, pp. 268–274.

Fattah, Mohamed Abdel, Fuji Ren, and Shingo Kuroiwa (2006). "Probabilistic Neural Network Based English-Arabic Sentence Alignment." *Proceedings of the 7th International Conference on Intelligent Text Processing and Computational Linguistics* (*CICLing-2006*), Mexico City, Mexico.

Gale, William A. and Kenneth W. Church (1991). "A Program for Aligning Sentences in Bilingual Corpora." *Proceedings of the 29th Annual Meeting of the Association for Computational Linguistics*, Berkeley, CA, USA, pp. 177–184.

Gale, William A. and Kenneth W. Church (1993). "A Program for Aligning Sentences in Bilingual Corpora." *Computational Linguistics*, Vol. 19, No. 1, pp. 75–102.

Grishman, Ralph (1999). "Iterative Alignment of Syntactic Structures for a Bilingual Corpus." In Susan Armstrong, Kenneth W. Church, Pierre Isabelle, Sandra Manzi, Evelyne Tzoukermann, and David Yarowsky, eds., *Natural Language Processing Using Very Large Corpora*. Dordrecht: Kluwer Academic Publishers, pp. 225–234.

Hofland, Knut (1995). "A Program for Aligning English and Norwegian Sentences." *Proceedings of the Association for Computers in the Humanities/Association for Literary and Linguistic Computing Conference*, Santa Barbara, USA.

Lü, Xueqiang 吕學強, Li Qingyin 李清隱, Ren Feiliang 任飛亮, and Yao Tianshun 姚天順 (2002).〈基於統計的漢英句子對齊研究〉(Alignment of Single Source Words and Target Multi-word Units from Parallel Corpus).《第一屆學生計算語言學研討會論文集》(*SWCL2002: First Students' Workshop on Computational Linguistics: Proceedings*). Beijing: Institute of Computational Linguistics, Peking University, p. 328.

McEnery, Anthony M., Michael P. Oakes, and Roger G. Garside (1994). "The Use of Approximate String Matching Techniques in the Alignment of Sentences in Parallel Corpora." *Machine Translation—Ten Years On: Proceedings of the 2nd International Conference Organised by Cranfield University*, Cranfield, England.

Meyers, Adam, Michiko Kosaka, and Ralph Grishman (1998). "A Multilingual Procedure for Dictionary-based Sentence Alignment." In

David L. Farwell, Laurie Gerber, and Eduard Hovy, eds., *Machine Translation and the Information Soup*. Berlin: Springer Verlag, pp. 187–198.

Moore, Robert C. (2002). "Fast and Accurate Sentence Alignment of Bilingual Corpora." In Stephen D. Richardson, ed., *Machine Translation: From Research to Real Users*. Berlin and New York: Springer Verlag, pp. 135–144.

Nelken, Rani and Stuart M. Shieber (2006). "Towards Robust Context-sensitive Sentence Alignment for Monolingual Corpora." *Proceedings of the 11th Conference of the European Chapter of the Association for Computational Linguistics* (*EACL-2006*), Trento, Italy.

Nightingale, Stephen and Hideki Tanaka (2003). "Comparing the Sentence Alignment Yield from Two News Corpora Using a Dictionary-based Alignment System." *Proceedings of the Human Language Technology and North American Chapter of Association of Computational Linguistics 2003* (*HLT/NAACL-2003*), Edmonton, Alberta, Canada.

Pang, Bo, Kevin Knight, and Daniel Marcu (2003). "Syntax-based Alignment of Multiple Translations: Extracting Paraphrases and Generating New Sentences." *Proceedings of the Human Language Technology and North American Chapter of Association of Computational Linguistics 2003* (*HLT/NAACL-2003*), Edmonton, Alberta, Canada, pp. 102–109.

Simard, Michel, George Foster, and Pierre Isabelle (1992). "Using Cognates to Align Sentences in Bilingual Corpora." *Proceedings of the 4th International Conference on Theoretical and Methodological Issues in Machine Translation of Natural Languages: Empiricist vs. Rationalist Methods in MT* (*TMI-92*), Montreal, Quebec, Canada, pp. 67–81.

Simard, Michel and Pierre Plamondon (1996). "Bilingual Sentence Alignment: Balancing Robustness and Accuracy." *Proceedings of the 2nd Conference of the Association for Machine Translation in the Americas: Expanding MT Horizons* (*AMTA-2*), Montreal, Quebec, Canada, pp. 135–144.

Simard, Michel and Pierre Plamondon (1998). "Bilingual Sentence Alignment: Balancing Robustness and Accuracy." *Machine Translation*, Vol. 13, No. 1, pp. 59–80.

Zhao, Bing, Klaus Zechner, Stephen Vogel, and Alex H. Waibel (2003). "Efficient Optimization for Bilingual Sentence Alignment Based on

Linear Regression." *Proceedings of the Human Language Technology and North American Chapter of Association of Computational Linguistics 2003* (*HLT/NAACL-2003*), Edmonton, Alberta, Canada.

Statistical Alignment

Och, Franz Josef, Christoph Tillmann, and Hermann Ney (1999). "Improved Alignment Models for Statistical Machine Translation." *Proceedings of the Conference on Empirical Methods in Natural Language Processing and Very Large Corpora,* University of Maryland, College Park, MD, USA, pp. 20–28.

Och, Franz Josef and Hermann Ney (2000). "Improved Statistical Alignment Models." *Proceedings of the 38th Annual Meeting of the Association for Computational Linguistics* (*ACL-2000*), Hong Kong, pp. 440–447.

Och, Franz Josef and Hermann Ney (2003). "A Systematic Comparison of Various Statistical Alignment Models." *Computational Linguistics*, Vol. 29, No. 1, pp. 19–51.

Simard, Michel and Philippe Langlais (2003). "Statistical Translation Alignment with Compositionality Constraints." *Proceedings of the Human Language Technology and North American Chapter of Association of Computational Linguistics 2003* (*HLT/NAACL-2003*), Edmonton, Alberta, Canada.

Toutanova, Kristina, H. Tolga Ilhan, and Christopher D. Manning (2002). "Extensions to Hmm-based Statistical Word Alignment Models." *Proceedings of the Conference on Empirical Methods in Natural Language Processing*, Philadelphia, PA, USA.

Varea, Ismael García, Franz J. Och, Hermann Ney, and Francisco Casacuberta (2002). "Efficient Integration of Maximum Entropy Lexicon Models within the Training of Statistical Alignment Models." In Stephen D. Richardson, ed., *Machine Translation: From Research to Real Users*. Berlin and New York: Springer Verlag, pp. 54–63.

Wu, Hua, Haifeng Wang, and Zhanyi Liu (2006). "Boosting Statistical Word Alignment Using Labeled and Unlabeled Data." *Proceedings of the Joint Conference of the International Committee on Computational Linguistics and the Association for Computational Linguistics* (*COLING/ACL-2006*), Sydney, Australia.

Terminology Alignment

Hull, David A. (1998). "A Practical Approach to Terminology Alignment." *Proceedings of Computerm '98 (First Workshop on Computational Terminology)*, Montreal, Quebec, Canada, pp. 1–7.

Hull, David A., Gaussier, Eric, and Salah Ait-Mokhtar (1999). "Term Alignment in Use: Machine-aided Human Translation." Meylan: Xerox Research Centre Europe.

Text Alignment

Fung, Pascale and Kenneth W. Church (1994). "K-vec: A New Approach for Aligning Parallel Texts." *Proceedings of the 15th International Conference on Computational Linguistics (COLING-94)*, Kyoto, Japan, pp. 1096–1102.

Haruno, Masahiko and Takefumi Yamazaki (1996). "High-performance Bilingual Text Alignment Using Statistical and Dictionary Information." *Proceedings of the 34th Annual Conference of the Association for Computational Linguistics*, Santa Cruz, CA, USA, pp. 131–138.

Kay, Martin and Martin Röscheisen (1993). "Text-translation Alignment." *Computational Linguistics*, Vol. 19, No. 1, pp. 121–142.

Oakes, Michael and Tony McEnery (2000). "Bilingual Text Alignment—An Overview." In Simon Philip Botley, Anthony Mark McEnery, and Andrew Wilson, eds., *Multilingual Corpora in Teaching and Research*. Amsterdam-Atlanta: Rodopi, pp. 1–37.

Ribeiro, António, José Gabriel Pereira Lopes, and João Mexia (2000). "A Self-learning Method of Parallel Texts Alignment." *Proceedings of the Conference of the Association for Machine Translation in the Americas: Envisioning Machine Translation in the Information Future (AMTA-2000)*, Cuernavaca, Mexico City, Mexico, pp. 30–39.

Ribeiro, António, Gabriel Lopes, and João Mexia (2000). "Using Confidence Bands for Parallel Texts Alignment." *Proceedings of the 38th Annual Meeting of the Association for Computational Linguistics (ACL-2000)*, Hong Kong.

Simard, Michel (1999). "Text-translation Alignment: Three Languages Are Better Than Two." *Proceedings of the Joint SIGDAT Conference on Empirical Methods in NLP and Very Large Corpora (EMNLP/VLC-99)*, University of Maryland, College Park, MD, USA.

Simard, Michel, George Foster, Marie-Louise Hannan, Elliott Macklovitch, and Pierre Plamondon (2000). "Bilingual Text Alignment —Where Do We Draw the Line?" In Simon Philip Botley, Anthony Mark McEnery, and Andrew Wilson, eds., *Multilingual Corpora in Teaching and Research*. Amsterdam: Rodopi, pp. 38–64.

Somers, Harold L. (1998). "Further Experiments in Bilingual Text Alignment." *International Journal of Corpus Linguistics*, Vol. 3, pp. 115–150.

Word Alignment

Ahrenberg, Lars, Magnus Merkel, Anna Sågvall Hein, and Jörg Tiedemann (2000). "Evaluation of Word Alignment Systems." *Proceedings of the 2nd International Conference on Linguistic Resources and Evaluation* (*LREC-2000*), Athens, Greece, Vol. 3, pp. 1255–1261.

Ayan, Necip Fazil, Bonnie J. Dorr, and Christof Monz (2005). "NeurAlign: Combining Word Alignments Using Neural Networks." *Proceedings of Human Language Technology Conference and Conference on Empirical Methods in Natural Language Processing* (*HLT/EMNLP-2005*), Vancouver, BC, Canada.

Ayan, Necip Fazil and Bonnie J. Dorr (2006). "A Maximum Entropy Approach to Combining Word Alignments." *Proceedings of the Human Language Technology Conference—Annual Meeting of the North American Chapter of the Association for Computational Linguistics* (HLT-NAACL-2006), New York, USA.

Ayan, Necip Fazil and Bonnie J. Dorr (2006). "Going Beyond AER: An Extensive Analysis of Word Alignments and Their Impact on MT." *Proceedings of the Joint Conference of the International Committee on Computational Linguistics and the Association for Computational Linguistics* (*COLING/ACL-2006*), Sydney, Australia.

Bridget Thomson and Ted Pedersen (2003). "The Duluth Word Alignment System." *Proceedings of the Human Language Technology and North American Chapter of Association of Computational Linguistics 2003* (*HLT/NAACL-2003*), Edmonton, Alberta, Canada.

Carl, Michael and Sisay Fissaha (2003). "Phrase-based Evaluation of Word-to-word Alignments." *Proceedings of the Human Language Technology and North American Chapter of Association of*

Computational Linguistics 2003 (*HLT/NAACL-2003*), Edmonton, Alberta, Canada.

Casillas, Arantza and Raquel Martínez (2002). "Aligning Multiword Terms Using a Hybrid Approach." *Proceedings of the 3rd International Conference on Intelligent Text Processing and Computational Linguistics* (*CICLing-2002*), Mexico City, Mexico.

Chang, Jyun-Sheng and Huey-Chyun Chen (1994). "Using Partial Aligned Parallel Text and Part-of-speech Information in Word Alignment." *Proceedings of the 1st Conference of the Association for Machine Translation in the Americas: Technology Partnerships for Crossing the Language Barrier* (*AMTA-1*), Columbia, Maryland, USA, pp. 16–23.

Chatterjee, Niladri and Saumya Agrawal (2006). "Word Alignment in English-Hindi Parallel Corpus Using Recency-vector Approach: Some Studies." *Proceedings of the Joint Conference of the International Committee on Computational Linguistics and the Association for Computational Linguistics* (*COLING/ACL-2006*), Sydney, Australia.

Chen, Boxing 陳博興 and Du Limin 杜利民 (2002).〈基於雙語語料的單個源語詞匯和目標語多詞單元的對齊〉(Alignment of Single Source Words and Target Multi-word Units from Parallel Corpus).《第一屆學生計算語言學研討會論文集》(*SWCL2002: First Students' Workshop on Computational Linguistics: Proceedings*). Beijing: Institute of Computational Linguistics, Peking University, pp. 318–327.

Chen, Mathis H., Jason S. Chang, Sue J. Ker, and Jen-Nan Chen (1997). "TopAlign: Word Alignment for Bilingual Corpora Based on Topical Clusters of Dictionary Entries and Translations." *Proceedings of the 7th International Conference on Theoretical and Methodological Issues in Machine Translation* (*TMI-97*), St. John's College, Santa Fe, New Mexico, USA.

Cherry, Colin and Dekang Lin (2003). "A Probability Model to Improve Word Alignment." *Proceedings of the 41st Annual Meeting of the Association for Computational Linguistics* (*ACL-2003*), Sapporo, Japan, pp. 88–95.

Cherry, Colin and Dekang Lin (2006). "A Comparison of Syntactically Motivated Word Alignment Spaces." *Proceedings of the 11th Conference of the European Chapter of the Association for Computational Linguistics* (*EACL-2006*), Trento, Italy.

Cherry, Colin and Dekang Lin (2006). "Soft Syntactic Constraints for Word Alignment through Discriminative Training." *Proceedings of the*

Joint Conference of the International Committee on Computational Linguistics and the Association for Computational Linguistics (*COLING/ACL-2006*), Sydney, Australia.

Church, Kenneth W. (1993). "Char-align: A Program for Aligning Parallel Texts at the Character Level." *Proceedings of the 31st Annual Meeting of the Association for Computational Linguistics* (*ACL-93*), Columbus, Ohio, USA, pp. 1–8.

Corston-Oliver, Simon and Michael Gamon (2004). "Normalizing German and English Inflectional Morphology to Improve Statistical Word Alignment." In Robert E. Frederking and Kathryn B. Taylors, eds., *Machine Translation: From Real Users to Research*. Berlin: Springer Verlag, pp. 48–57.

Dagan, Ido, Kenneth W. Church, and William A. Gale (1993). "Robust Bilingual Word Alignment for Machine Aided Translation." *Proceedings of the Workshop on Very Large Corpora: Academic and Industrial Perspectives*, Columbus, Ohio, USA, pp. 1–9.

Dagan, Ido, Kenneth W. Church, and William A. Gale (1999). "Robust Bilingual Word Alignment for Machine Aided Translation." In Susan Armstrong, Kenneth W. Church, Pierre Isabelle, Sandra Manzi, Evelyne Tzoukermann, and David Yarowsky, eds., *Natural Language Processing Using Very Large Corpora*. Dordrecht: Kluwer Academic Publishers, pp. 209–224.

Debili, Faith, Elybs Sammouda, and Adnane Zribi (1994). "Using Syntactic Dependencies for Word Alignment." *Proceedings of the 4th Conference on Applied Natural Language Processing* (*ANLP-94*), Stuttgart, Germany, pp. 188–189.

Dejean, Herve, Eric Gaussier, Cyril Goutte, and Kenji Yamada (2003). "Reducing Parameter Space for Word Alignment." *Proceedings of the Human Language Technology and North American Chapter of Association of Computational Linguistics 2003* (*HLT/NAACL-2003*), Edmonton, Alberta, Canada, pp. 23–26.

Deng, Yonggang and William Byrne (2005). "HMM Word and Phrase Alignment for Statistical Machine Translation." *Proceedings of Human Language Technology Conference and Conference on Empirical Methods in Natural Language Processing* (*HLT/EMNLP-2005*), Vancouver, BC, Canada.

Ding, Yuan, Daniel Gildea, and Martha Palmer (2003). "An Algorithm for Word-level Alignment of Parallel Dependency Trees." *Proceedings of*

MT Summit IX, New Orleans, Louisiana, USA.

Dorr, Bonnie J., Lisa Pearl, Rebecca Hwa, and Nizar Habash (2002). "DUSTer: A Method for Unraveling Cross-language Divergences for Statistical Word-level Alignment." In Stephen D. Richardson, ed., *Machine Translation: From Research to Real Users*. Berlin and New York: Springer Verlag, pp. 31–43.

Fraser, Alexander and Daniel Marcu (2006). "Semi-supervised Training for Statistical Word Alignment." *Proceedings of the Joint Conference of the International Committee on Computational Linguistics and the Association for Computational Linguistics* (*COLING/ACL-2006*), Sydney, Australia.

Gaussier, Eric (1998). "Flow Network Models for Word Alignment and Terminology Extraction from Bilingual Corpora." *Proceedings of the 36th Annual Meeting of the Association for Computational Linguistics and 17th International Conference on Computational Linguistics* (*COLING-ACL-98*), Montreal, Quebec, Canada, pp. 444–450.

Goutte, Cyril, Kenji Yamada, and Eric Gaussier (2004). "Aligning Words Using Matrix Factorisation." *Proceedings of the 42nd Annual Meeting of the Association for Computational Linguistics* (*ACL-2004*), Barcelona, Spain, pp. 502–509.

Henderson, John C. (2003). "Word Alignment Baselines." *Proceedings of the Human Language Technology and North American Chapter of Association of Computational Linguistics 2003* (*HLT/NAACL-2003*), Edmonton, Alberta, Canada.

Hou, Hongxu, Dan Deng, Gang Zou, Hongkui Yu, Yang Liu, Deyi Xiong, and Qun Liu (2004). "An EBMT System Based on Word Alignment." *Proceedings of the International Workshop on Spoken Language Translation* (*IWSLT-2004*), Kyoto, Japan.

Kashioka, Hideki (2005). "Word Alignment Viewer for Long Sentences." *Proceedings of MT Summit X*, Phuket, Thailand.

Ker, Sue J. and Jason S. Chang (1997). "A Class-based Approach to Word Alignment." *Computational Linguistics*, Vol. 23, No. 2, pp. 313–343.

Kim, Seonho, Juntae Yoon, and Dong-Yul Ra (2004). "Two-level Alignment by Words and Phrases Based on Syntactic Information." *Proceedings of the 5th International Conference on Intelligent Text Processing and Computational Linguistics* (*CICLing-2004*), Chung-Ang University, Seoul, Korea, pp. 306–317.

Kondrak, Grzegorz (2005). "Cognates and Word Alignment in Bitexts."

Proceedings of MT Summit X, Phuket, Thailand.
Kumar, Shankar and William Byrne (2002). "Minimum Bayes-risk Word Alignments of Bilingual Texts." *Proceedings of the 2002 Conference on Empirical Methods in Natural Language Processing* (*EMNLP-2002*), University of Pennsylvania, Philadelphia, PA, USA.
Lacoste-Julien, Simon, Ben Taskar, Dan Klein, and Michael I. Jordan (2006). "Word Alignment via Quadratic Assignment." *Proceedings of the Human Language Technology Conference—Annual Meeting of the North American Chapter of the Association for Computational Linguistics* (*HLT-NAACL-2006*), New York, USA.
Liang, Percy, Ben Taskar, and Dan Klein (2006). "Alignment by Agreement." *Proceedings of the Human Language Technology Conference—Annual Meeting of the North American Chapter of the Association for Computational Linguistics* (*HLT-NAACL-2006*), New York, USA.
Lin, Dekang and Colin Cherry (2003). "Word Alignment with Cohesion Constraint." *Proceedings of the Human Language Technology and North American Chapter of Association of Computational Linguistics 2003* (*HLT/NAACL-2003*), Edmonton, Alberta, Canada.
Liu, Yang, Qun Liu, and Shouxun Lin (2005). "Log-linear Models for Word Alignment." *Proceedings of the 43rd Annual Meeting of the Association of Computational Linguistics* (*ACL-2005*), Ann Arbor, Michigan, USA.
Lopez, Adam and Philip Resnik (2006). "Word-based Alignment, Phrase-based Translation: What's the Link?" *Proceedings of the 7th Biennial Conference of the Association for Machine Translation in the Americas* (*AMTA-2006*)*: Visions for the Future of Machine Translation*, Boston Marriott, Cambridge, Massachusetts, USA.
Lü, Yajuan 呂雅娟, Zhao Tiejun 趙鐵君, Li Sheng 李生, and Yang Muyun 楊沐昀 (2001). 〈統計和詞典方法相結合的雙語語料庫詞對齊〉(Word Alignment Based on Statistics and Lexicon). In Huang Changning 黃昌寧 and Zhang Pu 張普, eds.,《自然語言理解與機器翻譯》(*Natural Language Understanding and Machine Translation*). Beijing: Tsinghua University Press 清華大學出版社, pp. 108–115.
McInnes, Bridget Thomson and Ted Pedersen (2003). "The Duluth Word Alignment System." *Proceedings of the Human Language Technology and North American Chapter of Association of Computational Linguistics 2003* (*HLT/NAACL-2003*), Edmonton, Alberta, Canada.

Mihalcea, Rada F. and Ted Pedersen (2003). "An Evaluation Exercise for Word Alignment." *Proceedings of the Human Language Technology and North American Chapter of Association of Computational Linguistics 2003* (*HLT/NAACL-2003*), Edmonton, Alberta, Canada.

Moore, Robert C. (2004). "Improving IBM Word Alignment Model 1." *Proceedings of the 42nd Annual Meeting of the Association for Computational Linguistics* (*ACL-2004*), Barcelona, Spain, pp. 518–525.

Moore, Robert C. (2005). "A Discriminative Framework for Bilingual Word Alignment." *Proceedings of Human Language Technology Conference and Conference on Empirical Methods in Natural Language Processing* (*HLT/EMNLP-2005*), Vancouver, BC, Canada.

Sun, Le, Youbing Jin, Lin Du, and Yufang Sun (2000). "Word Alignment of English-Chinese Bilingual Corpus Based on Chunks." *Proceedings of the Joint Sigdat Conference on Empirical Methods in Natural Language Processing and Very Large Corpora* (*EMNLP/VLC-2000*), Hong Kong University of Science and Technology, Hong Kong, pp. 110–116.

Taskar, Ben, Lacoste-Julien Simon, and Klein Dan (2005). "A Discriminative Matching Approach to Word Alignment." *Proceedings of Human Language Technology Conference and Conference on Empirical Methods in Natural Language Processing* (*HLT/EMNLP-2005*), Vancouver, BC, Canada.

Tiedemann, Jörg (2003). "Combining Clues for Word Alignment." *Proceedings of the 10th Conference of the European Chapter of the ACL* (*EACL*), Budapest, Hungary.

Toutanova, Kristina, H. Tolga Ilhan, and Christopher Manning (2002). "Extensions to HMM-based Statistical Word Alignment Models." *Proceedings of the 2002 Conference on Empirical Methods in Natural Language Processing* (*EMNLP-2002*), University of Pennsylvania, Philadelphia, PA, USA.

Tufis, Dan, Ana-Maria Barbu, and Radu Ion (2003). "TREQ-AL: A Word Alignment System with Limited Language Resources." *Proceedings of the Human Language Technology and North American Chapter of Association of Computational Linguistics 2003* (*HLT/NAACL-2003*), Edmonton, Alberta, Canada.

van der Plas, Lonneke and Joerg Tiedemann (2006). "Finding Synonyms Using Automatic Word Alignment and Measures of Distributional

Similarity." *Proceedings of the Joint Conference of the International Committee on Computational Linguistics and the Association for Computational Linguistics* (*COLING/ACL-2006*), Sydney, Australia.

Vogel, Stephan, Hermann Ney, and Christoph Tillmann (1996). "Hmm-based Word Alignment in Statistical Translation." *Proceedings from the 16th International Conference on Computational Linguistics* (*COLING-96*). Copenhagen, Denmark, pp. 836–841.

Wang, Bin 王斌, Liu Qun 劉群, and Zhang Xiang 張祥 (1999).〈漢英雙語庫詞匯對齊研究〉(Word Alignment on Chinese-English Bilingual Corpora). In Huang Changning 黃昌寧 and Dong Zhendong 董振東, eds.,《計算機語言學文集》(*Essays on Computational Linguistics*). Beijing: Tsinghua University Press, pp. 123–128.

Wang, Haifeng, Hua Wu, and Zhanyi Liu (2006). "Word Alignment for Languages with Scarce Resources Using Bilingual Corpora of Other Language Pairs." *Proceedings of the Joint Conference of the International Committee on Computational Linguistics and the Association for Computational Linguistics* (*COLING/ACL-2006*), Sydney, Australia.

Wu, Dekai (1994). "Aligning a Parallel English-Chinese Corpus Statistically with Lexical Criteria." *Proceedings of the 32nd Annual Meeting of the Association for Computational Linguistics* (*ACL-94*), New Mexico State University, Las Cruces, New Mexico, USA, pp. 80–87.

Wu, Dekai (1995). "An Algorithm for Simultaneously Bracketing Parallel Texts by Aligning Words." *Proceedings of the 33rd Annual Meeting of the Association of Computational Linguistics* (*ACL-95*), Cambridge, MA, USA, pp. 244–251.

Wu, Hua and Haifeng Wang (2004). "Improving Domain-specific Word Alignment with a General Bilingual Corpus." In Robert E. Frederking and Kathryn B. Taylors, eds., *Machine Translation: From Real Users to Research*. Berlin: Springer Verlag, pp. 262–271.

Wu, Hua, Haifeng Wang, and Zhanyi Liu (2005). "Alignment Model Adaptation for Domain-specific Word Alignment." *Proceedings of the 43rd Annual Meeting of the Association of Computational Linguistics* (*ACL-2005*), Ann Arbor, Michigan, USA.

Wu, Hua and Haifeng Wang (2005). "Boosting Statistical Word Alignment." *Proceedings of MT Summit X*, Phuket, Thailand.

Wu, Hua, Haifeng Wang, Zhanyi Liu, and Kai Tang (2005). "Improving

Translation Memory with Word Alignment Information." *Proceedings of MT Summit X*, Phuket, Thailand.

Xu, Donghua and Tan Chew Lim (1999). "Alignment and Matching of Bilingual English-Chinese News Texts." *Machine Translation*, Vol. 14, No. 1, pp. 1–33.

Yang, Muyun, Zhao Tiejun, Liu Haijie, Shi Xiasheng, and Jiang Hongfei (2004). "Auto Word Alignment Based Chinese-English EBMT." *Proceedings of the International Workshop on Spoken Language Translation* (*IWSLT 2004*), Kyoto, Japan.

Zhang, Hao and Daniel Gildea (2006). "Inducing Word Alignments with Bilexical Synchronous Trees." *Proceedings of the Joint Conference of the International Committee on Computational Linguistics and the Association for Computational Linguistics* (*COLING/ACL-2006*), Sydney, Australia.

Zhang, Ruiqiang, Genichiro Kikui, and Eiichiro Sumita (2006). "Subword-based Tagging for Confidence-dependent Chinese Word Segmentation." *Proceedings of the Joint Conference of the International Committee on Computational Linguistics and the Association for Computational Linguistics* (*COLING/ACL-2006*), Sydney, Australia.

Zhao, Bing and Stephan Vogel (2003). "Word Alignment Based on Bilingual Bracketing." *Proceedings of the Human Language Technology and North American Chapter of Association of Computational Linguistics 2003* (*HLT/NAACL-2003*), Edmonton, Alberta, Canada.

Zhao, Bing, Niyu Ge, and Kishore Papineni (2005). "Inner-outer Bracket Models for Word Alignment Using Hidden Blocks." *Proceedings of Human Language Technology Conference and Conference on Empirical Methods in Natural Language Processing* (*HLT/EMNLP-2005*), Vancouver, BC, Canada.

Zhao, Bing and Eric Xing (2006). "BiTAM: Bilingual Topic AdMixture Models for Word Alignment." *Proceedings of the Joint Conference of the International Committee on Computational Linguistics and the Association for Computational Linguistics* (*COLING/ACL-2006*), Sydney, Australia.

❖ PART 2 ❖

Ambiguity and Disambiguation

Ambiguity

Ari-Ben, Danit, Mori Rimon, and Daniel M. Berry (1988). "Translational Ambiguity Rephrased." *Proceedings of the 2nd International Conference on Theoretical and Methodological Issues in Machine Translation of Natural Languages* (*TMI-88*), Carnegie Mellon University, Center for Machine Translation, Pittsburgh, Pennsylvania, USA.

Bernth, Arendse (1998). "EasyEnglish: Addressing Structural Ambiguity." In David L. Farwell, Laurie Gerber, and Eduard Hovy, eds., *Machine Translation and the Information Soup*. Berlin: Springer Verlag, pp. 164–173.

Boguslavsky, Igor M., Leonid L. Iomdin, Alexander V. Lazursky, Leonid G. Mityushin, Victor G. Sizov, Leonid G. Kreydlin, and Alexander S. Berdichevsky (2005). "Interactive Resolution of Intrinsic and Translational Ambiguity in a Machine Translation System." *Proceedings of the 6th International Conference on Intelligent Text Processing and Computational Linguistics* (*CICLing-2005*), Mexico City, Mexico, pp. 379–390.

Chang, Chao-Huang and Gilbert K. Krulee (1991). "Resolution of Ambiguity in Chinese and Its Application to Machine Translation." *Machine Translation*, Vol. 6, No. 4, pp. 279–315.

Doi, Shinichi and Kazunori Muraki (1992). "Translation Ambiguity Resolution Based on Text Corpora of Source and Target Language." *Proceedings of the 14th International Conference of Computational Linguistics* (*COLING-92*), Nantes, France, pp. 525–531.

Dostert, Leon E. (1959). "Approaches to the Reduction of Ambiguity in Machine Translation." *Journal of the Society of Motion Picture and Television Engineers*, Vol. 68, pp. 234–235.

Emele, Martin C. and Michael Dorna (1998). "Ambiguity Preserving Machine Translation Using Packed Representations." *Proceedings of the 36th Annual Meeting of the Association for Computational Linguistics and 17th International Conference on Computational Linguistics* (*COLING-ACL-98*), Montreal, Quebec, Canada, pp. 365–371.

Feng, Zhiwei 馮志偉 (1996).〈論歧義結構的潛在性〉(On the Potentiality of Ambiguity Structures). In Yu Shiwen 俞士汶 and Zhu Xuefeng 朱學鋒, eds.,《計算語言學文集》(*Papers on Computational Linguistics*). Beijing:

Department of Computer Science and Technology 北京大學計算機科學技術系 and Institute of Computational Linguistics 北京大學計算語言學研究所, Peking University, pp. 21–30.

Franz, Alexander (1992). *Ambiguity Resolution in Natural Language Parsing*. Pittsburgh: Center for Machine Translation, Carnegie Mellon University.

Haverkort, Kurt (1990). "Some Reflections on Ambiguity and Its Consequences for MT." In Marcel Thelen and Barbara Leeandowska-Tomaszczyk, eds., *Translation and Meaning, Part 1*. Maastricht: Euroterm, pp. 28–38.

Hwang, Feng-long and Yu Ming-shing (1999). "Resolving Category Ambiguity of Non-text Symbols in Mandarin Text." *Proceedings of MT Summit VII: MT in the Great Translation Era*, Singapore.

Jaspaert, Lieven (1984). "About the Treatment of Ambiguity in Machine Translation." *ITL Review of Applied Linguistics*, No. 64, pp. 1–21.

Kaplan, Abraham (1955). "An Experimental Study of Ambiguity and Context." *Mechanical Translation*, Vol. 2, No. 2, pp. 39–46.

Kikui, Genichiro (1999). "Resolving Translation Ambiguity Using Non-parallel Bilingual Corpora." *Proceedings of the ACL Workshop on Unsupervised Learning in Natural Language Processing*, University of Maryland, College Park, MD, USA.

Lee, Young-Suk, Clifford Weinstein, Stephanie Seneff, and Dinesh Tummala (1997). "Ambiguity Resolution for Machine Translation of Telegraphic Messages." *Proceedings of the 35th Annual Meeting of the Association for Computational Linguistics and 8th Conference of the European Chapter of the Association for Computational Linguistics*, Madrid, Spain, pp. 120–127.

Madhu, Swaminathan and Dean W. Lytle (1965). "A Figure of Merit Technique for the Resolution of Non-grammatical Ambiguity." *Mechanical Translation*, Vol. 8, No. 2, pp. 9–13.

Oepen, Stephan and John B. Carroll (2000). "Ambiguity Packing in Constraint-based Parsing—Practical Results." *Proceedings of the 1st Meeting of the North American Chapter of the Association for Computational Linguistics*, Seattle, Washington, DC, USA, pp. 162–169.

Sammer, Marcus, Kobi Reiter, Stephen Soderland, Katrin Kirchhoff, and Oren Etzioni (2006). "Ambiguity Reduction for Machine Translation: Human-computer Collaboration." *Proceedings of the 7th Biennial Conference of the Association for Machine Translation in the Americas*

(*AMTA-2006*)*: Visions for the Future of Machine Translation*, Boston Marriott, Cambridge, MA, USA.

Yamabana, Kiyoshi, Shin'ichiro Kamei, and Kazunori Muraki (1993). "On Representation of Preference Scores." *Proceedings of the 5th International Conference on Theoretical and Methodological Issues in Machine Translation of Natural Languages: MT in the Next Generation* (*TMI-93*), Kyoto, Japan, pp. 92–101.

Yeh, Ching-Long 葉慶隆 and Hsi-Jian Lee 李錫堅 (1991). "Ambiguity Resolution of Serial Noun Constructions in Chinese Sentences." *Proceedings of the Conference of the Association for Computational Linguistics and Chinese Language Processing* (*ROCLING-IV*), National Chiao-Tung University, Hsin-Chu, Taiwan.

Yeh, Ching-Long and Hsi-jian Lee (1996). "Ambiguity Resolution of Serial Noun Constructions in Chinese Sentences." *Journal of Chinese Linguistics*, Vol. 9, pp. 103–122.

Yoon, Juntae, Seonho Kim, and Mansuk Song (1997). "Ambiguity Resolution Using Lexical Association." *Proceedings of the International Conference on Research in Computational Linguistics* (*ROCLING-X*), Academia Sinica, Taipei, Taiwan.

Zhang, Liangping 張良平 and Chen Shenxin 陳聖信 (1987). 〈英漢機器翻譯中的歧義處理〉 (The Handling of Ambiguity in English-to-Chinese Machine Translation). *Proceedings of the Conference on Translation Today*, Hong Kong.

Lexical Ambiguity

Gonzalo, Julio, Anselmo Penas, and Felisa Verdejo (1999). "Lexical Ambiguity and Information Retrieval Revisited." *Proceedings of the Joint SIGDAT Conference on Empirical Methods in NLP and Very Large Corpora* (*EMNLP/VLC-99*), University of Maryland, College Park, MD, USA.

Melinger, Alissa, Sabine Schulte im Walde, and Andrea Weber (2006). "Characterizing Response Types and Revealing Noun Ambiguity in German Association Norms." *Proceedings of the 11th Conference of the European Chapter of the Association for Computational Linguistics* (*EACL-2006*), Trento, Italy.

Pedersen, Bolette Sandford (2000). "Lexical Ambiguity in Machine Translation: Using Frame Semantics for Expressing Regularities in

Polysemy." In Nicolas Nicolov and Ruslan Mitkov, eds., *Recent Advances in Natural Language Processing II*. Amsterdam and Philadelphia: John Benjamins Publishing Company, pp. 207–218.

Syntactical Ambiguity

Koutsoudas, Andreas and A. Humecky (1957). "Ambiguity of Syntactic Function Resolved by Linear Context." *Word*, Vol. 13, No. 3, pp. 403–414.

Kuno, Susumu and Anthony G. Oettinger (1963). "Syntactic Structure and Ambiguity of English." *Proceedings of AFIPS 1963 Fall Joint Computer Conference*. New York: Spartan Books, pp. 397–418.

Pericliev, Vladimir (1984). "Handling Syntactic Ambiguity in Machine Translation." *Proceedings of the 10th International Conference on Computational Linguistics (COLING-84)*, Stanford, California, USA, pp. 521–524.

Disambiguation

Agirre, Eneko and German Rigau (1997). "A Proposal for Word Sense Disambiguation Using Conceptual Distance." In Ruslan Mitkov and Nicolas Nicolov, eds., *Recent Advances in Natural Language Processing*. Amsterdam and Philadelphia: John Benjamins Publishing Company, pp. 161–172.

Boitet, Christian and Mutsuko Tomokiyo (1997). "Ambiguities and Ambiguity Labelling: Towards Ambiguity Data Bases." In Ruslan Mitkov and Nicolas Nicolov, eds., *Recent Advances in Natural Language Processing*. Amsterdam and Philadelphia: John Benjamins Publishing Company, pp. 185–209.

Brown, Peter F., Stephen A. Della Pietra, Vincent J. Della Pietra, and Robert L. Mercer (1991). "Word-sense Disambiguation Using Statistical Methods." *Proceedings of the 29th Annual Meeting of the Association for Computational Linguistics (ACL-91)*, University of California, Berkeley, California, USA.

Brown, Ralf D. (1989). "Augmentation." *Machine Translation*, Vol. 4, No. 2, pp. 129–147.

Buscaldi, Davide, Paolo Rosso, Ferran Pla, Encarna Segarra, and Emilio Sanchis Arnal (2006). "Verb Sense Disambiguation Using Support

Vector Machines: Impact of WordNet-extracted Features." *Proceedings of the 7th International Conference on Intelligent Text Processing and Computational Linguistics* (*CICLing-2006*), Mexico City, Mexico.

Calvo, Hiram and Alexander F. Gelbukh (2004). "Extracting Semantic Categories of Nouns for Syntactic Disambiguation from Human-oriented Explanatory Dictionaries." *Proceedings of the 5th International Conference on Intelligent Text Processing and Computational Linguistics* (*CICLing-2004*), Chung-Ang University, Seoul, Korea, pp. 254–257.

Chen, Gang 陳剛, Yuan Chunfa 苑春法, and Huang Changning 黃昌寧 (1999).〈漢語句法規則的排歧與禁止規則〉(Disambiguation of Chinese Grammar Rules and Forbidden Rules). In Huang Changning 黃昌寧 and Dong Zhendong 董振東, eds.,《計算機語言學文集》(*Essays on Computational Linguistics*). Beijing: Tsinghua University Press, pp. 261–266.

Chen, Jinxiu, Donghong Ji, Chew Lim Tan, and Zhengyu Niu (2006). "Unsupervised Relation Disambiguation Using Spectral Clustering." *Proceedings of the Joint Conference of the International Committee on Computational Linguistics and the Association for Computational Linguistics* (*COLING/ACL-2006*), Sydney, Australia.

Feng, Zhiwei (1995).〈歧義消解策略初探〉(Some Initial Methods of Disambiguation). In《計算語言學進展與應用》(*Developments and Applications in Computational Linguistics*). Beijing: Tsinghua University Press.

Feng, Zhiwei (1996).〈自然語言處理中的歧義消解方法〉(Method of Disambiguation in Natural Language Processing).《語言文字應用》(*Applied Linguistics*), No. 1, pp. 55–60.

Feng, Zhiwei (2001).〈基於集合運算的德語冠詞歧義消解〉(German Article Disambiguation Based on Set Operation). In Huang Changning 黃昌寧 and Zhang Pu 張普, eds.,《自然語言理解與機器翻譯》(*Natural Language Understanding and Machine Translation*). Beijing: Tsinghua University Press, pp. 272–277.

Hou, Min 侯敏 and Sun Jianjun 孫建軍 (1996).〈漢語自動分詞中的歧義問題〉(Disambiguation in the Automatic Segmentation of the Chinese Language).《語言文字應用》(*Applied Linguistics*), No. 1, pp. 68–72.

Hwang, Feng-Long, Ming-Shing Yu, and Min-Jer Wu (2000). "The Improving Techniques for Disambiguating Non-alphabet Sense Categories." *Proceedings of the International Conference on Research in Computational Linguistics* (*ROCLING-XIII*), Taipei, Taiwan.

Jung, Youngim, Aesun Yoon, and Hyuk-Chul Kwon (2006). "Disambiguation Based on Wordnet for Transliteration of Arabic Numerals for Korean TTS." *Proceedings of the 7th International Conference on Intelligent Text Processing and Computational Linguistics* (*CICLing-2006*), Mexico City, Mexico.

Kilgarriff, Adam and David Tugwell (2001). "WASP-Bench: An MT Lexicographers' Workstation Supporting State-of-the-art Lexical Disambiguation." In Bente Maegaard, ed., *Proceedings of MT Summit VIII: Machine Translation in the Information Age*, Santiago de Compostela, Spain.

Li, Hang 李航 (2001). "A Statistical Learning Approach to Lexical Knowledge Acquisition and Structural Disambiguation." In Huang Changning and Zhang Pu, eds.,《自然語言理解與機器翻譯》(*Natural Language Understanding and Machine Translation*). Beijing: Tsinghua University Press, pp. 173–179.

Li, Tangqiu, Xiaofeng Yang, Qingyang Hong, and Shaozi Li (2002). "A Hybrid Method for Syntactic and Semantic Structure Disambiguation of Chinese." In Chan Sin-wai, ed., *Translation and Information Technology*. Hong Kong: The Chinese University Press, pp. 43–55.

Liu, Chao-Lin 劉昭麟, Jing-Shin Chang 張景新, and Keh-Yih Su 蘇克毅 (1990). "The Semantic Score Approach to the Disambiguation of PP Attachment Problem." *Proceedings of the Conference of the Association for Computational Linguistics and Chinese Language Processing* (*ROCLING-III*), Taipei, Taiwan.

Mráková, Eva and Radek Sedláček (2003). "From Czech Morphology through Partial Parsing to Disambiguation." *Proceedings of the 4th International Conference on Intelligent Text Processing and Computational Linguistics* (*CICLing-2003*), Mexico City, Mexico, pp. 129–138.

Olteanu, Marian and Dan Moldovan (2005). "PP-attachment Disambiguation Using Large Context." *Proceedings of Human Language Technology Conference and Conference on Empirical Methods in Natural Language Processing* (*HLT/EMNLP-2005*), Vancouver, BC, Canada.

Park, So-Young, Yong-Jae Kwak, Joon-Ho Lim, and Hae-Chang Rim (2004). "Evaluation of Feature Combination for Effective Structural Disambiguation." *Proceedings of the 5th International Conference on*

Intelligent Text Processing and Computational Linguistics (*CICLing-2004*), Chung-Ang University, Seoul, Korea, pp. 95–98.

Schuetze, Hinrich and Michaela Atterer (2006). "The Effect of Corpus Size in Combining Supervised and Unsupervised Training for Disambiguation." *Proceedings of the Joint Conference of the International Committee on Computational Linguistics and the Association for Computational Linguistics* (*COLING/ACL-2006*), Sydney, Australia.

Shao, Jingmin 邵敬敏 (1986). 〈關於歧義結構的研討〉 (Research on Disambiguation). 《語文導報》 (*Language Bulletin*).

Srinivas, Medimi and Pushpak Bhattacharyya (2004). "Unsupervised PP Attachment Disambiguation Using Semantics." *Proceedings of the International Conference on Natural Language Processing* (*ICON-2004*), International Institute of Information Technology, Hyderabad, India.

Subbarao, Karumuri V. (2004). "The Role of Particles and Clitics in Disambiguation." *Proceedings of the International Conference on Natural Language Processing* (*ICON-2004*), International Institute of Information Technology, Hyderabad, India.

Trujillo, Arturo (1999). "Disambiguation." *Translation Engines: Techniques for Machine Translation*. Berlin and New York: Springer Verlag, pp. 223–250.

Uramoto, Naohiko (1995). "Automatic Learning of Knowledge for Example-based Disambiguation of Attachment." *Proceedings of the 6th International Conference on Theoretical and Methodological Issues in Machine Translation* (*TMI-95*), Leuven, Belgium, pp. 295–302.

Yuan, Chunfa 苑春法 and Kam Fai Wong 黃錦輝 (1999). 〈基於語義知識的漢語句法結構排歧〉 (On Semantic Knowledge in Chinese Syntactical Disambiguation). 《中文信息學報》 (*Journal of Chinese Information Processing*), Vol. 13, No. 1.

Zheng, Xuling 鄭旭鈴, Tangqiu Li 李堂秋, Xiaofeng Yang 楊曉峰, and Yidong Chen 陳毅東 (2001). 〈基於語義規則的漢語短語結構分析排歧初探〉 (Research on Chinese Phrase Structure Disambiguation Based on Semantic Rules). Huang Changning 黃昌寧 and Zhang Pu 張普, eds., 《自然語言理解與機器翻譯》 (*Natural Language Understanding and Machine Translation*). Beijing: Tsinghua University Press, pp. 219–226.

Morphological Disambiguation

Oflazer, Kemal and Gökhan Tur (1996). "Unsupervised Learning in Constraint-based Morphological Disambiguation." *Proceedings of the Conference on Empirical Methods in Natural Language Processing*, University of Pennsylvania, PA, USA.

Smith, Noah A., David A. Smith, and Roy W. Tromble (2005). "Context-based Morphological Disambiguation with Random Fields." *Proceedings of Human Language Technology Conference and Conference on Empirical Methods in Natural Language Processing* (*HLT/EMNLP-2005*), Vancouver, BC, Canada.

Tesprasit, Virongrong, Paisarn Charoenpornsawat, and Virach Sortlertlamvanich (2003). "A Context-sensitive Homograph Disambiguation in Thai Text-to-speech Synthesis." *Proceedings of the Human Language Technology and North American Chapter of Association of Computational Linguistics 2003* (*HLT/NAACL-2003*), Edmonton, Alberta, Canada.

Yuret, Deniz and Ferhan Ture (2006). "Learning Morphological Disambiguation Rules for Turkish." *Proceedings of the Human Language Technology Conference—Annual Meeting of the North American Chapter of the Association for Computational Linguistics* (*HLT-NAACL-2006*), New York, USA.

Semantic Disambiguation

Brown, Ralf D. and Sergei Nirenburg (1990). "Human-computer Interaction for Semantic Disambiguation." *Proceedings of the 13th International Conference on Computational Linguistics* (*COLING-90*), Helsinki, Finland, Vol. 3, pp. 42–47.

Meya, Montserrat (1990). "Semantic Disambiguation for PP-attachment." *Proceedings of the 3rd International Conference on Theoretical and Methodological Issues in Machine Translation of Natural Languages* (*TMI 90*), Linguistics Research Center, University of Texas at Austin, Texas, USA, pp. 271–277.

Pedersen, Ted (2001). "Lexical Semantic Ambiguity Resolution with Bigram-based Decision Trees." *Proceedings of the 2nd International Conference on Intelligent Text Processing and Computational Linguistics* (*CICLing-2001*), Mexico City, Mexico.

Sentence Disambiguation

Galicia-Haro, Sofía N., Alexander F. Gelbukh, and Igor A. Bolshakov (2001). "Three Mechanisms of Parser Driving for Structure Disambiguation." *Proceedings of the 2nd International Conference on Intelligent Text Processing and Computational Linguistics* (*CICLing-2001*), Mexico City, Mexico.

Lin, Ssu-Liang and Von-Wun Soo (1991). "Training a Recurrent Neural Network to Parse Syntactically Ambiguous and Ill-formed Sentences." *Proceedings of the Conference of the Association for Computational Linguistics and Chinese Language Processing* (*ROCLING-IV*), National Chiao-Tung University, Hsin-Chu, Taiwan.

Rivera, Miguel Angel Ibarra, Aurelio López López, and Jesús Favela Vara (2000). "Sentence Disambiguation Using a Restricted Spanish Lexicon Extracted from WordNet." *Proceedings of the 1st International Conference on Intelligent Text Processing and Computational Linguistics* (*CICLing-2000*), Mexico City, Mexico.

Tomita, Masaru (1986). "Sentence Disambiguation by Asking." *Computers and Translation*, Vol. 1, No. 1, pp. 39–51.

Word Sense Disambiguation

Agirre, Eneko and German Rigau (1996). "Word Sense Disambiguation Using Conceptual Density." *Proceedings from the 16th International Conference on Computational Linguistics* (*COLING-96*), Copenhagen, Denmark, pp. 16–22.

Agirre, Eneko and German Rigau (1997). "A Proposal for Word Sense Disambiguation Using Conceptual Distance." In Ruslan Mitkov and Nicolas Nicolov, eds., *Recent Advances in Natural Language Processing*. Amsterdam and Philadelphia: John Benjamins Publishing Company, pp. 161–172.

Ahlswede, Thomas E. and David Lorand (1993). "Word Sense Disambiguation by Human Subjects: Computational and Psycholinguistic Applications." In Branimir K. Boguraev and James Pustejovsky, eds., *Proceedings of a Workshop Sponsored by the SIGLEX of the ACL*, Ohio State University, Ohio, USA.

Arranz, Victoria M., Jordi Atserias, and Mauro Castillo (2005). "Multiwords and Word Sense Disambiguation." *Proceedings of the*

6th International Conference on Intelligent Text Processing and Computational Linguistics (*CICLing-2005*), Mexico City, Mexico, pp. 244–255.

Banerjee, Satanjeev and Ted Pedersen (2002). "An Adapted Lesk Algorithm for Word Sense Disambiguation Using WordNet." *Proceedings of the 3rd International Conference on Intelligent Text Processing and Computational Linguistics* (*CICLing-2002*), Mexico City, Mexico.

Barrett, Leslie, Anthony R. Davis, and Bonnie J. Dorr (2001). "Interpretation of Compound Nominals Using WordNet." *Proceedings of the 2nd International Conference on Intelligent Text Processing and Computational Linguistics* (*CICLing-2001*), Mexico City, Mexico.

Batori, Istvan S. (1969). "Disambiguation Verbs with Multiple Meaning in the MT System of IBM Germany." *Review of the Institute of Applied Linguistics*, Vol. 5, pp. 5–16.

Bhattacharya, Indrajit, Lise Getoor, and Yoshua Benjio (2004). "Unsupervised Sense Disambiguation Using Bilingual Probabilistic Models." *Proceedings of the 42nd Annual Meeting of the Association for Computational Linguistics* (*ACL-2004*), Barcelona, Spain, pp. 287–294.

Bickel, Daniel (2000). "A Statistical Model for Parsing and Word-sense Disambiguation." *Proceedings of the 38th Annual Meeting of the Association for Computational Linguistics* (*ACL-2000*), Hong Kong.

Bordag, Stefan (2003). "Sentence Co-occurrences as Small-world Graphs: A Solution to Automatic Lexical Disambiguation." *Proceedings of the 4th International Conference on Intelligent Text Processing and Computational Linguistics* (*CICLing-2003*), Mexico City, Mexico, pp. 331–334.

Bruce, Rebecca and Janyce Wiebe (1994). "Word-sense Disambiguation Using Decomposable Models." *Proceedings of the 32nd Annual Meeting of the Association for Computational Linguistics* (*ACL-94*), Las Cruces, New Mexico, USA, pp. 139–145.

Bruce, Rebecca and Janyce Wiebe (1998). "Word-sense Distinguishability and Inter-coder Agreement." *Proceedings of the 3rd Conference on Empirical Methods in Natural Language Processing*, Granada, Spain.

Buscaldi, Davide, Paolo Rosso, and Manuel Montes-y-Gómez (2005). "Context Expansion with Global Keywords for a Conceptual Density-based WSD." *Proceedings of the 6th International Conference on*

Intelligent Text Processing and Computational Linguistics (*CICLing-2005*), Mexico City, Mexico, pp. 256–259.

Carpuat, Marine and Dekai Wu (2005). "Word Sense Disambiguation vs. Statistical Machine Translation." *Proceedings of the 43rd Annual Meeting of the Association of Computational Linguistics* (*ACL-2005*), Ann Arbor, Michigan, USA.

Chan, Yee Seng and Hwee Tou Ng (2006). "Estimating Class Priors in Domain Adaptation for Word Sense Disambiguation." *Proceedings of the Joint Conference of the International Committee on Computational Linguistics and the Association for Computational Linguistics* (*COLING/ACL-2006*), Sydney, Australia.

Chang, Jason S., Jen-Nan Chen, Huei-Hong Sheng, and Sur-Jin Ker (1996). "Combining Machine Readable Lexical Resources and Bilingual Corpora for Broad Word Sense Disambiguation." *Proceedings of the 2nd Conference of the Association for Machine Translation in the Americas: Expanding MT Horizons* (*AMTA-2*), Montreal, Quebec, Canada, pp. 115–124.

Chen, Jen-Nan and Jason S. Chang (1998). "Concept-based Adaptive Approach to Word Sense Disambiguation." *Proceedings of the 36th Annual Meeting of the Association for Computational Linguistics and 17th International Conference on Computational Linguistics* (*COLING-ACL-98*), Montreal, Quebec, Canada, pp. 237–243.

Chen, Jinying, Andrew Schein, Lyle Ungar, and Martha Palmer (2006). "An Empirical Study of the Behavior of Active Learning for Word Sense Disambiguation." *Proceedings of the Human Language Technology Conference—Annual Meeting of the North American Chapter of the Association for Computational Linguistics* (*HLT-NAACL-2006*), New York, USA.

Cheung, Percy and Pascale Fung (2004). "Translation Disambiguation in Mixed Language Queries." *Machine Translation*, Vol. 18, No. 4, pp. 251–273.

Chung, You-Jin, Sin-Jae Kang, Kyong-Hi Moon, and Jong-Hyeok Lee (2002). "Word Sense Disambiguation in a Korean-to-Japanese MT System Using Neural Networks." *Proceedings of COLING-2002 Workshop on Machine Translation in Asia,* Taipei, Taiwan.

Chung, You-Jin and Jong-Hyeok Lee (2005). "Practical Word-sense Disambiguation Using Co-occurring Concept Codes." *Machine Translation*, Vol. 19, No. 1, pp. 59–82.

Cowie, Jim, Yevgeny Ludovik, and Sergei Nirenburg (1999). "Using a Target Language Model for Domain Independent Lexical Disambiguation." *Proceedings of MT Summit VII: MT in the Great Translation Era*, Singapore.

Cucerzan, Silviu and David Yarowsky (2002). "Augmented Mixture Models for Lexical Disambiguation." *Proceedings of the 2002 Conference on Empirical Methods in Natural Language Processing* (*EMNLP-2002*), University of Pennsylvania, Philadelphia, PA, USA.

Dagan, Ido, and Alon Itai (1994). "Word Sense Disambiguation Using a Second Language Monolingual Corpus." *Computational Linguistics*, Vol. 20, pp. 564–596.

Dagan, Ido, Lillian Lee, and Fernando Pereira (1997). "Similarity-based Methods for Word Sense Disambiguation." *Proceedings of the 35th Annual Meeting of the Association for Computational Linguistics and 8th Conference of the European Chapter of the Association for Computational Linguistics*, Madrid, Spain, pp. 56–63.

Diab, Mona (2004). "Relieving the Data Acquisition Bottleneck in Word Sense Disambiguation." *Proceedings of the 42nd Annual Meeting of the Association for Computational Linguistics* (*ACL-2004*), Barcelona, Spain, pp. 303–310.

Dinh, Dien (2002). "Building a Training Corpus for Word Sense Disambiguation in English-to-Vietnamese Machine Translation." *Proceedings of COLING-2002 Workshop on Machine Translation in Asia,* Taipei, Taiwan.

Escudero, Gerard, Lluis Marquez, and German Rigau (2000). "An Empirical Study of the Domain Dependence of Supervised Word Sense Disambiguation Systems." *Proceedings of the Joint Sigdat Conference on Empirical Methods in Natural Language Processing and Very Large Corpora* (*EMNLP/VLC-2000*), Hong Kong University of Science and Technology, Hong Kong.

Feng, Zhiwei (2004). 〈詞義排歧方法〉 (Method of Word Sense Disambiguation). In《機器翻譯研究》(*Studies on Machine Translation*). Beijing: China Translation and Publishing Corporation 中國對外翻譯出版公司, pp. 566–595.

Florian, Radu and David Yarowsky (2002). "Modeling Consensus: Classifier Combination for Word Sense Disambiguation." *Proceedings of the 2002 Conference on Empirical Methods in Natural Language*

Processing (*EMNLP-2002*), University of Pennsylvania, Philadelphia, PA, USA.

Gale, William A., Kenneth W. Church, and David Yarowsky (1992). "Estimating Upper and Lower Bounds on the Performance of Word-sense Disambiguation Programs." *Proceedings of the 30th Conference of the Association for Computational Linguistics*, Association for Computational Linguistics, Newark, Delaware, USA, pp. 249–256.

Gale, William A., Kenneth W. Church, and David Yarowsky (1992). "Using Bilingual Materials to Develop Word Sense Disambiguation Methods." *Proceedings of the 4th International Conference on Theoretical and Methodological Issues in Machine Translation of Natural Languages: Empiricist vs. Rationalist Methods in MT* (*TMI-92*), Montreal, Quebec, Canada, pp. 101–112.

Gale, William A., Kenneth W. Church, and David Yarowsky (1992). "Work on Statistical Methods for Word Sense Disambiguation." *Proceedings of the 10th National Conference on Artificial Intelligence* (*AAAI-92*), San Jose, California, USA.

Gale, William A., Kenneth W. Church, and David Yarowsky (1993). "A Method for Disambiguating Word Senses in a Large Corpus." *Computers and Humanities*, Vol. 26, pp. 415–439.

Giuliano, Claudio, Alfio Gliozzo, and Carlo Strapparava (2006). "Syntagmatic Kernels: A Word Sense Disambiguation Case Study." *Proceedings of the 11th Conference of the European Chapter of the Association for Computational Linguistics* (*EACL-2006*), Trento, Italy.

Gliozzo, Alfio, Claudio Giuliano, and Carlo Strapparava (2005). "Domain Kernels for Word Sense Disambiguation." *Proceedings of the 43rd Annual Meeting of the Association of Computational Linguistics* (*ACL-2005*), Ann Arbor, Michigan, USA.

Gliozzo, Alfio Massimiliano, Marcello Ranieri, and Carlo Strapparava (2005). "Crossing Parallel Corpora and Multilingual Lexical Databases for WSD." *Proceedings of the 6th International Conference on Intelligent Text Processing and Computational Linguistics* (*CICLing-2005*), Mexico City, Mexico, pp. 236–239.

Ide, Nancy and Jean Veronis (1991). "Introduction to the Special Issue on Word Sense Disambiguation: The State of the Art." *Computational Linguistics*, Vol. 24, No. 1, pp. 1–41.

Inkpen, Diana Zaiu and Graeme Hirst (2003). "Automatic Sense Disambiguation of the Near-synonyms in a Dictionary Entry."

Proceedings of the 4th International Conference on Intelligent Text Processing and Computational Linguistics (*CICLing-2003*), Mexico City, Mexico, pp. 260–269.

Kang, Sin-Jae, Li Hui-Feng, and Lee Jong-Hyeok (2001). "Semi-automatic Construction of Language Independent and Practical Ontology for Word Senses Disambiguation." In Bente Maegaard, ed., *Proceedings of MT Summit VIII: Machine Translation in the Information Age*, Santiago de Compostela, Spain.

Karov, Yael and Shimon Edelman (1998). "Similarity-based Word Sense Disambiguation." *Computational Linguistics*, Vol. 24, pp. 41–59.

Kilgarriff, Adam (1997). "What Is Word Sense Disambiguation Good for?" *NLP Pacific Rim Symposium '97*, Phuket, Thailand.

Kilgarriff, Adam and Rob Koeling (2003). "An Evaluation of a Lexicographer's Workbench Incorporating Word Sense Disambiguation." *Proceedings of the 4th International Conference on Intelligent Text Processing and Computational Linguistics* (*CICLing-2003*), Mexico City, Mexico, pp. 227–242.

Kohomban, Upali Sathyajith and Wee Sun Lee (2005). "Learning Semantic Classes for Word Sense Disambiguation." *Proceedings of the 43rd Annual Meeting of the Association of Computational Linguistics* (*ACL-2005*), Ann Arbor, Michigan, USA.

Leacock, Claudia, Martin Chodorow, and George A. Miller (1998). "Using Corpus Statistics and WordNet Relations for Sense Identification." *Computational Linguistics*, Vol. 24, pp. 147–165.

Lee, Changki, Geunbae Lee, and Seo Jung Yun (2000). "Automatic WordNet Mapping Using Word Sense Disambiguation." *Proceedings of the Joint Sigdat Conference on Empirical Methods in Natural Language Processing and Very Large Corpora* (*EMNLP/VLC-2000*), Hong Kong University of Science and Technology, Hong Kong.

Lee, Hian-Beng (1999). "Article Selection Using Probabilistic Sense Disambiguation." *Proceedings of MT Summit VII: MT in the Great Translation Era*, Singapore.

Lee, Ho, Dae-Ho Baek, and Hae-Chang Rim (1997). "Word Sense Disambiguation Based on the Information Theory." *Proceedings of the International Conference on Research in Computational Linguistics* (*ROCLING-X*), Academia Sinica, Taipei, Taiwan.

Lee, Yoong Keok and Hwee Tou Ng (2002). "An Empirical Evaluation of Knowledge Sources and Learning Algorithms for Word Sense

Disambiguation." *Proceedings of the 2002 Conference on Empirical Methods in Natural Language Processing* (*EMNLP-2002*), University of Pennsylvania, Philadelphia, PA, USA.
Legrand, Steve (2006). "Word Sense Disambiguation with Basic-level Categories." In Alexander F. Gelbukh, ed., *Advances in Natural Language Processing*, Special Issue of *Research in Computing Science*, No. 18, pp. 71–82.
Levin, Esther, Mehrbod Sharifi, and Jerry Ball (2006). "Evaluation of Utility of LSA for Word Sense Discrimination." *Proceedings of the Human Language Technology Conference—Annual Meeting of the North American Chapter of the Association for Computational Linguistics* (*HLT-NAACL-2006*), New York, USA.
Lin, Dekang (1997). "Using Syntactic Dependency as Local Context to Resolve Word Sense Ambiguity." *Proceedings of the 35th Annual Meeting of the Association for Computational Linguistics and 8th Conference of the European Chapter of the Association for Computational Linguistics*, Madrid, Spain, pp. 64–71.
Li, Hui-Feng, Namwon Heo, Kyoung-Hi Moon, Jong-Hyeok Lee, and Gary Geunbae Lee (2000). "Lexical Transfer Ambiguity Resolution Using Automatically-extracted Concept Co-occurrence Information." *International Journal of Computer Processing of Oriental Languages*, Vol. 13, No. 1, pp. 53–68.
Li, Juanzi 李涓子 and Huang Changning 黃昌寧 (1999).〈一種無指導的詞義排歧模型〉(An Unsupervised Word-sense Disambiguation Model). In Huang Changning 黃昌寧 and Dong Zhendong 董振東, eds.,《計算機語言學文集》(*Essays on Computational Linguistics*). Beijing: Tsinghua University Press, pp. 229–234.
Liu, Xiaoyong Mary, Ted Diamond, and Anne R. Diekema (2000). "Word Sense Disambiguation for Cross-language Information Retrieval." *Proceedings of the ANLP-NAACL 2000, Student Research Workshop*, Seattle, Washington, DC, USA, pp. 35–40.
Lu, Zhimao, Haifeng Wang, Jianmin Yao, Ting Liu, and Sheng Li (2006). "Equivalent Pseudoword for Unsupervised Chinese Word Sense Disambiguation." *Proceedings of the Joint Conference of the International Committee on Computational Linguistics and the Association for Computational Linguistics* (*COLING/ACL-2006*), Sydney, Australia.
Luk, Alpha K. (1995). "Statistical Sense Disambiguation with Relatively

Small Corpora Using Dictionary Definitions." *Proceedings of the 33rd Annual Meeting of the Association for Computational Linguistics*, Columbus, Ohio, USA, pp. 181–188.

Magnini, Bernardo, Carlo Strapparava, Giovanni Pezzulo, and Alfio Gliozzo (2002). "The Role of Domain Information in Word Sense Disambiguation." *Natural Language Engineering*, Vol. 8, pp. 359–373.

Mahesh, Kavi, Sergei Nirenburg, and Stephen Beale (1997). "If You Have It, Flaunt It: Using Full Ontological Knowledge for Word Sense Disambiguation." *International Conference, Recent Advances in Natural Language Processing*, Tzigov Chark, Bulgaria, pp. 8–15.

Mahesh, Kavi, Sergei Nirenburg, and Stephen Beale (1997). "If You Have It, Flaunt It: Using Full Ontological Knowledge for Word Sense Disambiguation." *Proceedings of the 7th International Conference on Theoretical and Methodological Issues in Machine Translation* (*TMI-97*), St. John's College, Santa Fe, New Mexico, USA.

Mahesh, Kavi, Sergei Nirenburg, Stephen Beale, Evelyne Viegas, Victor Raskin, and Boyan Onyshkevych (1997). "Word Sense Disambiguation: Why Statistics When We Have These Numbers?" *Proceedings of the 7th International Conference on Theoretical and Methodological Issues in Machine Translation* (*TMI-97*), St. John's College, Santa Fe, New Mexico, USA.

Mahesh, Kavi, Sergei Nirenburg, and Stephen Beale (2000). "Toward Full-text Ontology-based Word Sense Disambiguation." In Nicolas Nicolov and Ruslan Mitkov, eds., *Recent Advances in Natural Language Processing II*. Amsterdam and Philadelphia: John Benjamins Publishing Company, pp. 131–142.

McCarthy, Diana, Rob Koeling, Julie Weeds, and John B. Carroll (2004). "Finding Predominant Word Senses in Untagged Text." *Proceedings of the 42nd Annual Meeting of the Association for Computational Linguistics* (*ACL-2004*), Barcelona, Spain, pp. 279–286.

McCarthy, Diana (2006). "Relating WordNet Senses for Word Sense Disambiguation." *Proceedings of the 11th Conference of the European Chapter of the Association for Computational Linguistics* (*EACL-2006*), Trento, Italy.

McRoy, Susan W. (1992). "Using Multiple Knowledge Sources for Word Sense Discrimination." *Computational Linguistics*, Vol. 18, No. 1, pp. 1–30.

Mezquita, Yoel Ledo, Grigori Sidorov, and Alexander F. Gelbukh (2003).

"Tool for Computer-aided Spanish Word Sense Disambiguation." *Proceedings of the 4th International Conference on Intelligent Text Processing and Computational Linguistics* (*CICLing-2003*), Mexico City, Mexico, pp. 279–282.

Miangah, Tayebeh Mosavi, and Ali Delavar Khalafi (2004). "Statistical Analysis of Target Language Corpus for Word Sense Disambiguation in a Machine Translation System." *Proceedings of the 9th Workshop of the European Association for Machine Translation: Broadening Horizons of Machine Translation and Its Applications*, Foundation for International Studies, Malta, pp. 129–137.

Mihalcea, Rada F. (2005). "Unsupervised Large-vocabulary Word Sense Disambiguation with Graph-based Algorithms for Sequence Data Labeling." *Proceedings of Human Language Technology Conference and Conference on Empirical Methods in Natural Language Processing* (*HLT/EMNLP 2005*), Vancouver, BC, Canada.

Mihalcea, Rada F. and Ted Pedersen (2005). "Advances in Word Sense Disambiguation." *Proceedings of the 43rd Annual Meeting of the Association of Computational Linguistics* (*ACL-2005*), Ann Arbor, Michigan, USA.

Miháltz, Márton (2005). "Towards a Hybrid Approach to Word-sense Disambiguation in Machine Translation." In Walther van Hahn, John Hutchins, and Cristina Vertan, eds., *Proceedings of the International Workshop on Modern Approaches in Translation Technologies*, Borovets, Bulgaria.

Montoyo, Andrés and Manuel Palomar (2001). "Specification Marks for Word Sense Disambiguation: New Development." *Proceedings of the 2nd International Conference on Intelligent Text Processing and Computational Linguistics* (*CICLing-2001*), Mexico City, Mexico.

Montoyo, Andrés, Armando Suárez, and Manuel Palomar (2002). "Combining Supervised-unsupervised Methods for Word Sense Disambiguation." *Proceedings of the 3rd International Conference on Intelligent Text Processing and Computational Linguistics* (*CICLing-2002*), Mexico City, Mexico.

Mooney, Raymond J. (1996). "Comparative Experiments on Disambiguating Word Senses: An Illustration of the Role of Bias in Machine Learning." *Proceedings of the Conference on Empirical Methods in Natural Language Processing*, University of Pennsylvania, PA, USA.

Navigli, Roberto (2006). "Meaningful Clustering of Senses Helps Boost Word Sense Disambiguation Performance." *Proceedings of the Joint Conference of the International Committee on Computational Linguistics and the Association for Computational Linguistics (COLING/ACL-2006)*, Sydney, Australia.

Navigli, Roberto (2006). "Online Word Sense Disambiguation with Structural Semantic Interconnections." *Proceedings of the 11th Conference of the European Chapter of the Association for Computational Linguistics (EACL-2006)*, Trento, Italy.

Ng, Hwee Tou and Hian Beng Lee (1996). "Integrating Multiple Knowledge Sources to Disambiguate Word Sense: An Exemplar-based Approach." *Proceedings of the 34th Annual Meeting of the Association for Computational Linguistics*, Santa Cruz, CA, USA, pp. 40–47.

Nica, Iulia, Mª. Antónia Martí, Andrés Montoyo, and Sonia Vázquez (2004). "Combining EWN and Sense-untagged Corpus for WSD." *Proceedings of the 5th International Conference on Intelligent Text Processing and Computational Linguistics (CICLing-2004)*, Chung-Ang University, Seoul, Korea, pp. 185–197.

Niu, Zhengyu and Donghong Ji (2004). "Feature Selection for Chinese Character Sense Discrimination." *Proceedings of the 5th International Conference on Intelligent Text Processing and Computational Linguistics (CICLing-2004)*, Chung-Ang University, Seoul, Korea, pp. 198–205.

Niu, Zhengyu, Donghong Ji, and Chew Lim Tan (2005). "A Semi-supervised Feature Clustering Algorithm with Application to Word Sense Disambiguation." *Proceedings of Human Language Technology Conference and Conference on Empirical Methods in Natural Language Processing (HLT/EMNLP-2005)*, Vancouver, BC, Canada.

Niu, Zhengyu, Donghong Ji, Chew-Lim Tan, and Lingpeng Yang (2005). "Word Sense Disambiguation by Semi-supervised Learning." *Proceedings of the 6th International Conference on Intelligent Text Processing and Computational Linguistics (CICLing-2005)*, Mexico City, Mcxico, pp. 232–235.

Niu, Zhengyu, Donghong Ji, and Chew-Lim Tan (2005). "Word Sense Disambiguation Using Label Propagation Based Semi-supervised Learning." *Proceedings of the 43rd Annual Meeting of the Association of Computational Linguistics (ACL-2005)*, Ann Arbor, Michigan, USA.

Pancardo-Rodríguez, Aarón, Manuel Montes-y-Gómez, Luis Villaseñor-

Pineda, and Paolo Rosso (2005). "A Mapping between Classifiers and Training Conditions for WSD." *Proceedings of the 6th International Conference on Intelligent Text Processing and Computational Linguistics* (*CICLing-2005*), Mexico City, Mexico, pp. 240–243.

Park, Seong-Bae, Byoung-Tak Zhang, and Yung Taek Kim (2000). "Word Sense Disambiguation by Learning from Unlabeled Data." *Proceedings of the 38th Annual Meeting of the Association for Computational Linguistics* (*ACL-2000*), Hong Kong.

Patwardhan, Siddharth, Satanjeev Banerjee, and Ted Pedersen (2003). "Using Measures of Semantic Relatedness for Word Sense Disambiguation." *Proceedings of the 4th International Conference on Intelligent Text Processing and Computational Linguistics* (*CICLing-2003*), Mexico City, Mexico, pp. 243–259.

Pedersen, Ted, Rebecca Bruce, and Janyce Wiebe (1997). "Sequential Model Selection for Word Sense Disambiguation." *Proceedings of the 5th Conference on Applied Natural Language Processing*, Seattle, Washington, DC, USA.

Pedersen, Ted (2000). "A Simple Approach to Building Ensembles of Naive Bayesian Classifiers for Word Sense Disambiguation." *Proceedings of the 1st Meeting of the North American Chapter of the Association for Computational Linguistics*, Seattle, Washington, DC, USA, pp. 63–69.

Pedersen, Ted (2000). "An Ensemble Approach to Corpus-based Word Sense Disambiguation." *Proceedings of the 1st International Conference on Intelligent Text Processing and Computational Linguistics* (*CICLing-2000*), Mexico City, Mexico.

Pedersen, Ted (2002). "A Baseline Methodology for Word Sense Disambiguation." *Proceedings of the 3rd International Conference on Intelligent Text Processing and Computational Linguistics* (*CICLing-2002*), Mexico City, Mexico.

Pedersen, Ted, Amruta Purandare, and Anagha Kulkarni (2005). "Name Discrimination by Clustering Similar Contexts." *Proceedings of the 6th International Conference on Intelligent Text Processing and Computational Linguistics* (*CICLing-2005*), Mexico City, Mexico, pp. 220–231.

Peh, Li Shiuan and Hwee Tou Ng (1997). "Domain-specific Semantic Class Disambiguation Using WordNet." *Proceedings of the 5th Workshop on Very Large Corpora*, Beijing and Hong Kong, pp. 56–64.

Rapp, Reinhard (2003). "Word Sense Discovery Based on Sense Descriptor Dissimilarity." *Proceedings of MT Summit IX*, New Orleans, Louisiana, USA.

Resnik, Philip (1997). "Selectional Preference and Sense Disambiguation." *Proceedings of the ACL SIGLEX Workshop on Tagging Text with Lexical Semantics: Why, What, and How?*, Seattle, Washington, DC, USA, pp. 52–57.

Resnik, Philip and David Yarowsky (1997). "A Perspective on Word Sense Disambiguation Methods and Their Evaluation." *Proceedings of the ACL SIGLEX Workshop on Tagging Text with Lexical Semantics: Why, What, and How?*, Seattle, Washington, DC, USA.

Rosso, Paolo, Francesco Masulli, Davide Buscaldi, Ferran Pla, and Antonio Molina (2003). "Automatic Noun Sense Disambiguation." *Proceedings of the 4th International Conference on Intelligent Text Processing and Computational Linguistics (CICLing-2003)*, Mexico City, Mexico, pp. 275–278.

Rosso, Paolo, Manuel Montes-y-Gómez, Davide Buscaldi, Aarón Pancardo-Rodríguez, and Luis Villaseñor Pineda (2005). "Two Web-based Approaches for Noun Sense Disambiguation." *Proceedings of the 6th International Conference on Intelligent Text Processing and Computational Linguistics (CICLing-2005)*, Mexico City, Mexico, pp. 260–271.

Sanfilippo, Antonio, Stephen Tratz, and Michelle Gregory (2006). "Word Domain Disambiguation via Word Sense Disambiguation." *Proceedings of the Human Language Technology Conference—Annual Meeting of the North American Chapter of the Association for Computational Linguistics (HLT-NAACL-2006)*, New York, USA.

Savova, Guergana, Terry Therneau, and Christopher Chute (2006). "Cluster Stopping Rules for Word Sense Discrimination." *Proceedings of the 11th Conference of the European Chapter of the Association for Computational Linguistics (EACL-2006)*, Trento, Italy.

Schuetze, Hinrich (1998). "Automatic Word Sense Discrimination." *Computational Linguistics*, Vol. 24, No. 1, pp. 97–124.

Seo, Hee-Cheol, Young-Sook Hwang, and Hae-Chang Rim (2004). "Word Sense Disambiguation Based on Weight Distribution Model with Multiword Expression." *Proceedings of the 5th International Conference on Intelligent Text Processing and Computational*

Linguistics (*CICLing-2004*), Chung-Ang University, Seoul, Korea, pp. 173–184.

Şerban, Gabriela and Doina Tătar (2003). "Word Sense Disambiguation for Untagged Corpus: Application to Romanian Language." *Proceedings of the 4th International Conference on Intelligent Text Processing and Computational Linguistics* (*CICLing-2003*), Mexico City, Mexico, pp. 270–274.

Shirai, Kiyoaki (2002). "Japanese Word Sense Disambiguation." In Yu Shiwen, ed., *Proceedings of the Second China-Japan Natural Language Processing Joint Research Promotion Conference* (*CJNLP-2002*). Beijing: Institute of Computational Linguistics, Peking University, China, pp. 183–188.

Soler, Susana and Andrés Montoyo (2002). "A Proposal for WSD Using Semantic Similarity." *Proceedings of the 3rd International Conference on Intelligent Text Processing and Computational Linguistics* (*CICLing-2002*), Mexico City, Mexico.

Specia, Lucia, Maria das Graças Volpe Nunes, Mark Stevenson, Gabriela Castelo, and Branco Ribeiro (2006). "Multilingual versus Monolingual WSD." *Proceedings of the 11th Conference of the European Chapter of the Association for Computational Linguistics* (*EACL-2006*), Trento, Italy.

Stevenson, Mark and Yorick Wilks (1999). "Combining Weak Knowledge Sources for Sense Disambiguation." *Proceedings of the 16th International Joint Conference on Artificial Intelligence* (*IJCAI-99*), Stockholm, Sweden.

Suárez, Armando and Manuel Palomar (2002). "Feature Selection Analysis for Maximum Entropy-based WSD." *Proceedings of the 3rd International Conference on Intelligent Text Processing and Computational Linguistics* (*CICLing-2002*), Mexico City, Mexico.

Vaidyaraman, Srinivasan (2001). "Word-sense Disambiguation through Visual Thought Analysis." *International Journal of Translation*, Vol. 13, Nos. 1–2, pp. 147–158.

Vázquez, Sonia, Estela Saquete, Andrés Montoyo, Patricio Martínez-Barco, and Rafael Muñoz (2004). "The Role of Temporal Expressions in Word Sense Disambiguation." *Proceedings of the 5th International Conference on Intelligent Text Processing and Computational Linguistics* (*CICLing-2004*), Chung-Ang University, Seoul, Korea, pp. 206–209.

Vickrey, David, Luke Biewald, Marc Teyssier, and Daphne Koller (2005). "Word-sense Disambiguation for Machine Translation." *Proceedings of Human Language Technology Conference and Conference on Empirical Methods in Natural Language Processing* (*HLT/EMNLP-2005*), Vancouver, BC, Canada.

Wang, Xinglong and John Carroll (2005). "Word Sense Disambiguation Using Sense Examples Automatically Acquired from a Second Language." *Proceedings of Human Language Technology Conference and Conference on Empirical Methods in Natural Language Processing* (*HLT/EMNLP-2005*), Vancouver, BC, Canada.

Wang, Xinglong and David Martinez (2006). "Word Sense Disambiguation Using Automatically Translated Sense Examples." *Proceedings of the 11th Conference of the European Chapter of the Association for Computational Linguistics* (*EACL-2006*), Trento, Italy.

Wilks, Yorick and Mark Stevenson (1997). "Combining Independent Knowledge Sources for Word Sense Disambiguation." *Proceedings of the Conference on Recent Advances in Natural Language Processing*, Tzigov Chark, Bulgaria, pp. 1–7.

Wilks, Yorick and Mark Stevenson (2000). "Combining Independent Knowledge Sources for Word Sense Disambiguation." In Nicolas Nicolov and Ruslan Mitkov, eds., *Recent Advances in Natural Language Processing II*. Amsterdam and Philadelphia: John Benjamins Publishing Company, pp. 117–130.

Wu, Dekai, Weifeng Su, and Marine Carpuat (2004). "A Kernel PCA Method for Superior Word Sense Disambiguation." *Proceedings of the 42nd Annual Meeting of the Association for Computational Linguistics* (*ACL-2004*), Barcelona, Spain, pp. 637–644.

Yang, Dongqiang and David Powers (2006). "Word Sense Disambiguation Using Lexical Cohesion in the Context." *Proceedings of the Joint Conference of the International Committee on Computational Linguistics and the Association for Computational Linguistics* (*COLING/ACL-2006*), Sydney, Australia.

Yang, Erhong 楊爾弘, Mi Liping 米麗萍, and Hao Xiulan 郝秀蘭 (2001). 〈基於「知網」的詞義排歧方法〉 (The Word Sense Disambiguation Method Based on HOWNET). 《輝煌二十年——中國中文信息學會二十周年學術會議》 (*Proceedings of Conference of the 20th Anniversary of CIPSC*). Beijing: Tsinghua University Press, pp. 179–185.

Yang, Xiaofeng 楊曉峰, Li Tangqiu 李堂秋, and Hong Qingyang 洪青陽

(2001).〈漢英機器翻譯系中的一種詞義排歧方法〉(Word Sense Disambiguation Method in Chinese-English Machine Translation System). In Huang Changning 黃昌寧 and Zhang Pu 張普, eds.,《自然語言理解與機器翻譯》(*Natural Language Understanding and Machine Translation*). Beijing: Tsinghua University Press, pp. 300–305.

Yarowsky, David (1992). "Word Sense Disambiguation Using Statistical Models of Roget's Categories Trained on Large Corpora." *Proceedings of the 14th International Conference of Computational Linguistics* (*COLING-92*), Nantes, France, pp. 415–439.

Yarowsky, David (1993). "One Sense Per Collocation." *Proceedings of DARPA Workshop on Human Language Technology*, Princeton, New Jersey, USA, pp. 266–271.

Yarowsky, David (1995). "Unsupervised Word Sense Disambiguation Rivaling Supervised Methods." *Proceedings of the 33rd Annual Meeting of the Association for Computational Linguistics* (*ACL-95*), Cambridge, MA, USA, pp. 189–196.

❖ PART 3 ❖

Analysis

Analysis

Brown, Peter F., Stephen A. Della Pietra, Vincent J. Della Pietra, John D. Lafferty, and Robert L. Mercer (1992). "Analysis, Statistical Transfer, and Synthesis in Machine Translation." *Proceedings of the 4th International Conference on Theoretical and Methodological Issues in Machine Translation of Natural Languages: Empiricist vs. Rationalist Methods in MT (TMI-92)*, Montreal, Quebec, Canada, pp. 83–100.

Ceccato, Silvio (1967). "Correlational Analysis and Mechanical Translation." In Andrew D. Booth, ed., *Machine Translation*. Amsterdam: North-Holland Publishing Company, pp. 77–135.

Colbath, Sean and Francis Kubala (2003). "TAP-XL: An Automated Analyst's Assistant." *Proceedings of the Human Language Technology and North American Chapter of Association of Computational Linguistics 2003 (HLT/NAACL-2003)*, Edmonton, Alberta, Canada.

Gates, Donna, Koichi Takeda, Teruko Mitamura, Lori S. Levin, and Marion Kee (1989). "Analysis and Generation Grammars." *Machine Translation*, Vol. 4, No. 1, pp. 53–66.

Hutchins, W. John and Harold L. Somers (1992). "Analysis." *An Introduction to Machine Translation*. London: Academic Press, pp. 81–97.

Morrisson, Stephen, Marion Kee, and Kenneth Goodman (1989). "Analysis." *Machine Translation*, Vol. 4, No. 2, pp. 113–128.

Straub, J. R. and C. A. Rogers (1979). "Computer Analysis of Basic English as a First Step in Machine Translation." In R. Trappl, F. Hanika, and F. R. Pichler, eds., *Progress in Cybernetics and Systems Research*, Vol. 5, pp. 491–494.

Varga, Dániel (1967). "Towards a New System of Automatic Analysis." *Computational Linguistics*, Vol. 6, pp. 123–136.

Weissenborn, Jürgen (1977). "The Role and Form of Analysis in Machine Translation: The Automatic Analysis of French at Saarbrücken." *Overcoming the Language Barrier: Third European Congress on Information Systems and Networks*. Munchen: Verlag Dokumentation, pp. 593–611.

Linguistic Analysis

Ceccato, Silvio (1961). *Linguistic Analysis and Programming for Mechanical Translation*. Milan: University of Milan.

Chen, Guanghuo 陳光火 (2000).〈語言分析〉(Linguistic Analysis).《電子翻譯》(*Electronic Translation*). Tianjin: Tianjin University Press 天津大學出版社, pp. 63–71.

Feng, Zhiwei 馮志偉 (1994).〈語言的自動分析和生成技術〉(Automatic Analysis and Generation Technology of Languages). In《自然語言機器翻譯新論》(*New Essays on Machine Translation of Natural Languages*). Beijing: Language Press 語文出版社, pp. 79–121.

Garvin, Paul L. (1962). "Automatic Linguistic Analysis—A Heuristic Problem." In National Physical Laboratory, ed., *1961 International Conference on Machine Translation of Languages and Applied Language Analysis: Proceedings of the Conference Held at the National Physical Laboratory, Teddington, Middlesex, on 5th, 6th, 7th and 8th September*. London: Her Majesty's Stationery Office, Vol. 1, pp. 656–669.

Hutchins, W. John (1984). "Elements of Linguistic Methods of Analysis." *Proceedings of the International Conference on the Methodology and Techniques of Machine Translation*, Cranfield Institute of Technology, England.

Zarechnak, Michael (1962). "A Fourth Level of Linguistic Analysis." In National Physical Laboratory, ed., *1961 International Conference on Machine Translation of Languages and Applied Language Analysis, Proceedings of the Conference Held at the National Physical Laboratory, Teddington, Middlesex, on 5th, 6th, 7th, and 8th September*. London: Her Majesty's Stationery Office, Vol. 1, pp. 160–173.

Zarechnak, Michael (1959). "Three Levels of Linguistic Analysis in Machine Translation." *Journal of the Association for Computing Machinery*, Vol. 6, No. 1, pp. 24–32.

Morphological Analysis

Asahara, Masayuki and Yuji Matsumoto (2003). "Japanese Named Entity Extraction with Redundant Morphological Analysis." *Proceedings of the Human Language Technology and North American Chapter of Association of Computational Linguistics 2003* (*HLT/NAACL-2003*), Edmonton, Alberta, Canada.

Berri, Jawad, Hamza Zidoum, and Yacine Atif (2001). "Web-based Arabic Morphological Analyzer." *Proceedings of the 2nd International*

Conference on Intelligent Text Processing and Computational Linguistics (*CICLing-2001*), Mexico City, Mexico.

Choi, Ho-cheol and Sang-yong Han (2005). "Korma 2003: Newly Improved Korean Morpheme Analysis Module for Reducing Terminological and Spacing Errors in Document Analysis." *Proceedings of the 6th International Conference on Intelligent Text Processing and Computational Linguistics* (*CICLing-2005*), Mexico City, Mexico, pp. 192–195.

Garrido-Alenda, Alicia, Mikel L. Forcada, and Rafael C. Carrasco (2002). "Incremental Construction and Maintenance of Morphological Analysers Based on Augmented Letter Transducers." *Proceedings of the 9th International Conference on Theoretical and Methodological Issues in Machine Translation* (*TMI-2002*), Keihanna, Japan, pp. 53–63.

Gelbukh, Alexander F. and Grigori Sidorov (2003). "Approach to Construction of Automatic Morphological Analysis Systems for Inflective Languages with Little Effort." *Proceedings of the 4th International Conference on Intelligent Text Processing and Computational Linguistics* (*CICLing-2003*), Mexico City, Mexico, pp. 217–222.

Goldwater, Sharon and David McClosky (2005). "Improving Statistical MT through Morphological Analysis." *Proceedings of Human Language Technology Conference and Conference on Empirical Methods in Natural Language Processing* (*HLT/EMNLP-2005*), Vancouver, BC, Canada.

Habash, Nizar and Owen Rambow (2005). "Tokenization, Morphological Analysis, and Part-of-speech Tagging for Arabic in One Fell Swoop." *Proceedings of the 43rd Annual Meeting of the Association of Computational Linguistics* (*ACL-2005*), Ann Arbor, Michigan, USA.

Habash, Nizar and Owen Rambow (2006). "Magead: A Morphological Analyzer and Generator for the Arabic Dialects." *Proceedings of the Joint Conference of the International Committee on Computational Linguistics and the Association for Computational Linguistics* (*COLING/ACL-2006*), Sydney, Australia.

Nagata, Masaaki (2000). "Synchronous Morphological Analysis of Grapheme and Phoneme for Japanese OCR." *Proceedings of the 38th Annual Meeting of the Association for Computational Linguistics* (*ACL-2000*), Hong Kong.

Niessen, Sonja and Hermann Ney (2001). "Morpho-syntactic Analysis for

Reordering in Statistical Machine Translation." In Bente Maegaard, ed., *Proceedings of MT Summit VIII: Machine Translation in the Information Age*, Santiago de Compostela, Spain.

Tablan, Valentin, Wim Peters, Diana Maynard, and Hamish Cunningham (2006). "Creating Tools for Morphological Analysis of Sumerian." *Proceedings of the 5th International Conference on Language Resources and Evaluation* (*LREC-2006*), Genoa, Italy.

Tatsuo, Yamashita and Yuji Matsumoto (2000). "Language Independent Morphological Analysis." *Proceedings of the 6th Applied Natural Language Processing Conference*, Seattle, USA, pp. 232–238.

Yarowsky, David and Richard Wicentowski (2000). "Minimally Supervised Morphological Analysis by Multimodal Alignment." *Proceedings of the 38th Annual Meeting of the Association for Computational Linguistics* (*ACL-2000*), Hong Kong.

Natural Language Analysis

Chen, Hsin-Hsi, Jiunn-Liang Leu, and Yue-Shi Lee (1992). "A Parallel Augmented Context-free Parsing System for Natural Language Analysis." *Proceedings of the Conference of the Association for Computational Linguistics and Chinese Language Processing* (*ROCLING-V*), National Taiwan University, Taipei, Taiwan.

Ishikawa, Masahiko and Ryoichi Sugimura (1992). "Natural Language Analysis Using a Network Model—Modification Deciding Network." *Proceedings of the 4th International Conference on Theoretical and Methodological Issues in Machine Translation of Natural Languages: Empiricist vs. Rationalist Methods in MT* (*TMI-92*), Montreal, Quebec, Canada, pp. 55–66.

Wasyliw, Boh and Douglas Clarke (1994). "Natural Language Analysis and Machine Translation in Pilot-ATC Communication." *Machine Translation—Ten Years On: Proceedings of the 2nd International Conference Organised by Cranfield University*, Cranfield, England.

Woods, William (1970). "Transition Network Grammars for Natural Language Analysis." *Communications of the ACM*, Vol. 13, pp. 591–606.

Semantic Analysis

Atserias, Jordi, Irene Castellón, Montse Civit, and German Rigau (2000).

"Semantic Analysis Based on Verbal Subcategorization." *Proceedings of the 1st International Conference on Intelligent Text Processing and Computational Linguistics* (*CICLing-2000*), Mexico City, Mexico.

Bestgen, Yves (2006). "Improving Text Segmentation Using Latent Semantic Analysis." *Computational Linguistics*, Vol. 32, No. 1, pp. 5–12.

Choi, Freddy Y. Y., Peter Wiemer-Hastings, and Johanna D. Moore (2001). "Latent Semantic Analysis for Text Segmentation." *Proceedings of the 2001 Conference on Empirical Methods in Natural Language Processing* (*EMNLP-2001*), Carnegie Mellon University, Pittsburgh, PA, USA.

Farahat, Ayman and Francine Chen (2006). "Improving Probabilistic Latent Semantic Analysis with Principal Component Analysis." *Proceedings of the 11th Conference of the European Chapter of the Association for Computational Linguistics* (*EACL-2006*), Trento, Italy.

Feng, Zhiwei 馮志偉 (2004).〈語義自動分析〉(Automatic Semantic Analysis). In《機器翻譯研究》(*Studies on Machine Translation*). Beijing: China Translation and Publishing Corporation 中國對外翻譯出版公司, pp. 467–565.

Guo, Yanhui 郭燕慧, Liu Jianyi 劉建毅, Yao Junyong 姚均勇, and Zhong Yixin 鍾義信 (2002).〈語義分析在 Internet 文件分類和過濾中的應用〉(Application of Semantic Analysis in Internet Document Categorization and Filtering). In Yu Shiwen, ed., *Proceedings of the 2nd China-Japan Natural Language Processing Joint Research Promotion Conference* (*CJNLP-2002*). Beijing: Institute of Computational Linguistics, Peking University, China, pp. 232–235.

Laffling, John (1991). "Configuration and Operation of the Analyser." In *Towards High-precision Machine Translation: Based on Contrastive Textology*. Berlin and New York: Foris Publications.

Lu, Jianming 陸儉明 (1996).〈關於語義指向分析〉(On the Analysis of the Direction of Semantic Indication). In Yu Shiwen 俞士汶 and Zhu Xuefeng 朱學鋒, eds.,《計算語言學文集》(*Papers on Computational Linguistics*). Beijing: Department of Computer Science and Technology and Institute of Computational Linguistics, Peking University, pp. 8–20.

Nastase, Vivi and Stan Szpakowicz (2005). "Customisable Semantic Analysis of Texts." *Proceedings of the 6th International Conference on Intelligent Text Processing and Computational Linguistics* (*CICLing-2005*), Mexico City, Mexico, pp. 303–314.

Paolillo, John (2004). "Latent Structure Analysis: Semantic or Syntactic?" *Proceedings of the International Conference on Natural Language Processing* (*ICON-2004*), International Institute of Information Technology, Hyderabad, India.

Reeder, Florence M. (2006). "Measuring MT Adequacy Using Latent Semantic Analysis." *Proceedings of the 7th Biennial Conference of the Association for Machine Translation in the Americas* (*AMTA-2006*): *Visions for the Future of Machine Translation*, Boston Marriott, Cambridge, MA, USA.

Serafin, Riccardo, Barbara Di Eugenio, and Michael Glass (2003). "Latent Semantic Analysis for Dialogue Act Classification." *Proceedings of the Human Language Technology and North American Chapter of Association of Computational Linguistics 2003* (*HLT/NAACL-2003*), Edmonton, Alberta, Canada.

Serafin, Riccardo and Barbara Di Eugenio (2004). "FLSA: Extending Latent Semantic Analysis with Features for Dialogue Act Classification." *Proceedings of the 42nd Annual Meeting of the Association for Computational Linguistics* (*ACL-2004*), Barcelona, Spain, pp. 692–699.

Tribble, Alicia, Alon Lavie, and Lori S. Levin (2002). "Rapid Adaptive Development of Semantic Analysis Grammars." *Proceedings of the 9th International Conference on Theoretical and Methodological Issues in Machine Translation* (*TMI-2002*), Keihanna, Japan, pp. 178–187.

Wilks, Yorick (1968). "On-line Semantic Analysis of English Texts." *Mechanical Translation*, Vol. 11, Nos. 3–4, pp. 59–72.

Zarechnak, Michael and Edward J. Coyne (1976). "Semantic Analysis of Natural Language Statements." *Linguistics*, Vol. 182, pp. 73–81.

Sentence Analysis

Lee, Bing-Huang 李炳煌, Chuei-Feng Chiou 邱垂豐, and Wei-Chuan Lee 黎偉權 (1989). 〈超長句之剖析〉 (Analysis of Superlong Sentences). *Proceedings of the Conference of the Association for Computational Linguistics and Chinese Language Processing* (*ROCLING-II*), Taipei, Taiwan.

Lee, Chun-Hsiao 李俊曉 and Hsi-Jian Lee 李錫堅 (1989). "Computer Interpretation of Chinese Declarative Sentences Based on Situation Semantics." *Proceedings of the Conference of the Association for*

Computational Linguistics and Chinese Language Processing (*ROCLING-II*), Taipei, Taiwan.

Mathews, G. H. (1962). "Analysis by Synthesis of Sentences of Natural Languages." In National Physical Laboratory, ed., *1961 International Conference on Machine Translation of Languages and Applied Language Analysis: Proceedings of the Conference Held at the National Physical Laboratory, Teddington, Middlesex, on 5th, 6th, 7th and 8th September*. London: Her Majesty's Stationery Office, Vol. 2, pp. 532–540.

Nagao, Makoto (1989). "Methods of Analysis of Sentence Structure." In Norman D. Cook, trans., *Machine Translation: How Far Can It Go?* London: Oxford University Press, pp. 83–104.

Plath, Warren J. (1962). "Automatic Sentence Diagramming." In National Physical Laboratory, ed., *1961 International Conference on Machine Translation of Languages and Applied Language Analysis: Proceedings of the Conference Held at the National Physical Laboratory, Teddington, Middlesex, on 5th, 6th, 7th and 8th September*. London: Her Majesty's Stationery Office, Vol. 1, pp. 176–191.

Serutla, Lebelo and Derrick Kourie (1998). "Sentence Analysis Using a Concept Lattice." In David L. Farwell, Laurie Gerber, and Eduard Hovy, eds., *Machine Translation and the Information Soup*. Berlin: Springer Verlag, pp. 225–235.

Tang, Li, Donghong Ji, Yu Nie, and Lingpeng Yang (2004). "An Application of a Semantic Framework for the Analysis of Chinese Sentences." *Proceedings of the 5th International Conference on Intelligent Text Processing and Computational Linguistics* (*CICLing-2004*), Chung-Ang University, Seoul, Korea, pp. 41–44.

Source Analysis

Bernth, Arendse and Michael C. McCord (2000). "The Effect of Source Analysis on Translation Confidence." In John S. White, ed., *Envisioning Machine Translation in the Information Future*. Berlin: Springer Verlag, pp. 89–99.

Feng, Zhiwei 馮志偉 and Yang Ping 楊平 (1987).〈原語自動分析〉(Automatic Source Language Analysis). In《自動翻譯》(*Automatic Translation*). Shanghai: Knowledge Press 知識出版社, pp. 269–291.

Mitamura, Teruko, Kathryn Baker, David Svoboda, and Eric H. Nyberg

(2003). "Source Language Diagnostics for MT." *Proceedings of MT Summit IX*, New Orleans, Louisiana, USA.

Nirenburg, Sergei, Jaime G. Carbonell, Masaru Tomita, and Kenneth Goodman (1992). "Source Language Analysis." *Machine Translation: A Knowledge-based Approach.* San Matero, California: Morgan Kaufmann, pp. 117–134.

Nyberg, Eric H., Teruko Mitamura, David Svoboda, Jeongwoo Ko, Kathryn Baker, and Jeffrey Micher (2003). "An Integrated System for Source Language Checking, Analysis and Term Management." *Proceedings of MT Summit IX*, New Orleans, Louisiana, USA.

Syntactical Analysis

Aduriz, Itziar, Maxux J. Aranzabe, Jose Mari Arriola, Arantza Díaz de Ilarraza, Koldo Gojenola, Maite Oronoz, and Larraitz Uria (2004). "A Cascaded Syntactic Analyser for Basque." *Proceedings of the 5th International Conference on Intelligent Text Processing and Computational Linguistics* (*CICLing-2004*), Chung-Ang University, Seoul, Korea, pp. 121–131.

Gelbukh, Alexander F., Grigori Sidorov, Sang-Yong Han, and Erika Hernández-Rubio (2004). "Automatic Syntactic Analysis for Detection of Word Combinations." *Proceedings of the 5th International Conference on Intelligent Text Processing and Computational Linguistics* (*CICLing-2004*), Chung-Ang University, Seoul, Korea, pp. 240–244.

Kuno, Susumu and Anthony G. Oettinger (1963). "Multiple-path Syntactic Analyzer." *Information Processing 1962: Proceedings of IFIP Congress 62*. Amsterdam: Harth-Holland, pp. 306–311.

Lai, Tom B. Y. and Huang Changning (2000). "Dependency-based Syntactic Analysis of Chinese and Annotation of Parsed Corpus." *Proceedings of the 38th Annual Meeting of the Association for Computational Linguistics* (*ACL-2000*), Hong Kong.

Lamb, Sydney M. (1962). "On the Mechanization of Syntactic Analysis." In National Physical Laboratory, ed., *1961 International Conference on Machine Translation of Languages and Applied Language Analysis: Proceedings of the Conference Held at the National Physical Laboratory, Teddington, Middlesex, on 5th, 6th, 7th and 8th September.* London: Her Majesty's Stationery Office, pp. 673–686.

Oettinger, Anthony G. (1961). "Automatic Syntactic Analysis and the Pushdown Store." *Structure of Language and Its Mathematical Aspects: Proceedings of Symposium in Applied Mathematics*. Providence, RI: American Mathematical Society, pp. 104–129.

Oettinger, Anthony G. and Murray E. Sherry (1961). "Current Research on Automatic Translation at Harvard University and Predictive Syntactic Analysis." In Harold P. Edmundson, ed., *Proceedings of the National Symposium on Machine Translation*. London: Prentice-Hall, pp. 173–182.

Okumura, Akitoshi, Kazunori Muraki, and Kiyoshi Yamabana (1992). "A Pattern-learning Based, Hybrid Model for the Syntactic Analysis of Structural Relationships among Japanese Clauses." *Proceedings of the 4th International Conference on Theoretical and Methodological Issues in Machine Translation of Natural Languages: Empiricist vs. Rationalist Methods in MT* (*TMI-92*), Montreal, Quebec, Canada, pp. 45–54.

Paolillo, John (2004). "Latent Structure Analysis: Semantic or Syntactic?" *Proceedings of the International Conference on Natural Language Processing* (*ICON-2004*), International Institute of Information Technology, Hyderabad, India.

Petrick, Stanley R. (1971). "Syntactic Analysis for Transformational Grammars." In Winfred P. Lehmann and Rolf A. Stachowitz, eds., *Feasibility Study on Fully Automatic High Quality Translation*. Griffiss AFB: Rome Air Development Center, pp. 325–342.

Rhodes, Ida (1959). *A New Approach to the Mechanical Syntactic Analysis of Russian*. Washington, DC: National Bureau of Standards.

Rhodes, Ida (1961). "A New Approach to the Mechanical Syntactic Analysis of Russian." *Mechanical Translation*, Vol. 6, pp. 33–50.

Sherry, Murray E. and Anthony G. Oettinger (1961). "A New Model of Natural Language for Predictive Syntactic Analysis." In Colin Cherry, ed., *Information Theory*. London: Butterworths, pp. 458–468.

Sherry, Murray E. (1962). "The Identification of Nested Structures in Predictive Syntactic Analysis." In National Physical Laboratory, ed., *1961 International Conference on Machine Translation of Languages and Applied Language Analysis: Proceedings of the Conference Held at the National Physical Laboratory, Teddington, Middlesex, on 5th, 6th, 7th and 8th September*. London: Her Majesty's Stationery Office, Vol. 1, pp. 144–155.

Text Analysis

Gerloff, Pamela (1987). "Identifying the Unit of Analysis in Translation." In Claus Færch and Gabriele Kasper, eds., *Introspection in Second Language Research*. Clevedon: Multilingual Matters, pp. 135–158.

Giguet, Emmanuel, Nadine Lucas, and Grégoire Cousin (2000). "Document Structure Identification as a Means for Relevant Indexation." *Proceedings of the 1st International Conference on Intelligent Text Processing and Computational Linguistics* (*CICLing-2000*), Mexico City, Mexico.

Hoppe, Alfred (1984). "Communicative Grammar and Machine-assisted Text Contents Analysis." *International Classification*, Vol. 11, No. 1, pp. 9–12.

Hou, Min 侯敏 (2001).〈漢語自動分析中的若干問題與對策〉(Some Problems and Countermeasures in Automatic Chinese Analysis). In Huang Changning 黃昌寧 and Zhang Pu 張普, eds.,《自然語言理解與機器翻譯》(*Natural Language Understanding and Machine Translation*). Beijing: Tsinghua University Press, pp. 204–210.

Levison, Michael (1962). "The Mechanical Analysis of Language." In National Physical Laboratory, ed., *1961 International Conference on Machine Translation of Languages and Applied Language Analysis: Proceedings of the Conference Held at the National Physical Laboratory, Teddington, Middlesex, on 5th, 6th, 7th and 8th September*. London: Her Majesty's Stationery Office, Vol. 2, pp. 562–575.

Serutla, Lebelo and Derrick Kourie (1998). "Sentence Analysis Using a Concept Lattice." In David L. Farwell, Laurie Gerber, and Eduard Hovy, eds., *Machine Translation and the Information Soup*. Berlin: Springer Verlag, pp. 225–235.

Straub, J. R. and C. A. Rogers (1979). "Computer Analysis of Basic English as a First Step in Machine Translation." *Progress in Cybernetics*, Vol. 5, pp. 491–494.

Taylor, Chris and Anthony Baldry (2001). "Computer Assisted Text Analysis and Translation: A Functional Approach in the Analysis and Translation of Advertising Texts." In Erich H. Steiner and Colin Yallop, eds., *Exploring Translation and Multilingual Text Production: Beyond Content*. Berlin and New York: Mouton de Gruyter, pp. 277–305.

Wilks, Yorick (1975). "An Intelligent Analyzer and Understander of

English." *Communications of the ACM*, Vol. 18, No. 5, pp. 264–274.
Wonsever, Dina and Jean-Luc Minel (2001). "Contextual Rules for Text Analysis." *Proceedings of the 2nd International Conference on Intelligent Text Processing and Computational Linguistics* (*CICLing-2001*), Mexico City, Mexico.
Yarowsky, David, Grace Ngai, and Richard Wicentowski (2001). "Introducing Multilingual Text Analysis Tools via Robust Projection across Aligned Corpora." *Proceedings of the Human Language Technology Conference* (*HLT-2001*), San Diego, California, USA, pp. 109–116.

Translation Analysis

Garvin, Paul L. (1957). "Linguistic Analysis and Translation Analysis." In Leon Dostert, ed., *Research in Machine Translation: Report of the 8th Annual Round Table Meeting on Linguistics and Language Studies*. Washington, DC: Georgetown University Press, pp. 19–38.
Isabelle, Pierre, Marc Dymetman, George Foster, Jean-Marc Jutras, Elliott Macklovitch, François Perrault, Ren Xiaobo, and Michel Simard (1993). "Translation Analysis and Translation Automation." *Proceedings of the 5th International Conference on Theoretical and Methodological Issues in Machine Translation of Natural Languages: MT in the Next Generation* (*TMI-93*), Kyoto, Japan, pp. 201–217.
Isabelle, Pierre (1993). "Translation Analysis and Translation Support Tools." *Proceedings of the 13th International Conference on Artificial Intelligence, Expert Systems and Natural Language*, Avignon, France.
Landsbergen, Jan (1994). "A Compositional Definition of the Translation Relation." In M. T. Rosetta, *Compositional Translation*. Dordrecht: Kluwer Academic Publishers, pp. 15–33.

❖ PART 4 ❖

Checker

Controlled Language Checker

Karkaletsis, Vangelis, Georgios Samaritakis, Georgios Petasis, Dimitra Farmakiotou, Ion Androutsopoulos, Stella Markantonatou, and Constantine Spyropoulos (2001). "A Controlled Language Checker Based on the Ellogon Text Engineering Platform." *Proceedings of the 2nd Meeting of the North American Chapter of the Association for Computational Linguistics: Language Technologies 2001* (*NAACL-2001*), Pittsburgh, PA, USA.

Grammar Checker

Adriaens, Geert and Dirk Schreurs (1992). "From Cogram to Alcogram: Toward a Controlled English Grammar Checker." *Proceedings of the 14th International Conference of Computational Linguistics* (*COLING-92*), Nantes, France, pp. 595–601.

Chodorow, Martin and Claudia Leacock (2000). "An Unsupervised Method for Detecting Grammatical Errors." *Proceedings of the 1st Meeting of the North American Chapter of the Association for Computational Linguistics*, Seattle, Washington, DC, USA, pp. 140–147.

Hamon, Olivier and Martin Rajman (2006). "X-Score: Automatic Evaluation of Machine Translation Grammaticality." *Proceedings of the 5th International Conference on Language Resources and Evaluation* (*LREC-2006*), Genoa, Italy.

Hashemi, Sylvana Sofkova, Robin Cooper, and Robert Andersson (2003). "Positive Grammar Checking: A Finite State Approach." *Proceedings of the 4th International Conference on Intelligent Text Processing and Computational Linguistics* (*CICLing-2003*), Mexico City, Mexico, pp. 637–648.

Holan, Tomas, Vladimir Kubon, and Martin Platek (1997). "A Prototype of Grammar Checker for Czech." *Proceedings of the 5th Conference on Applied Natural Language Processing*, Seattle, Washington, DC, USA.

Kambhatla, Nanda and Wlodek Zadrozny (2000). "A Tool for Automated Revision of Grammars for NLP Systems." *Proceedings of the 6th Applied Natural Language Processing Conference*, Seattle, Washington, DC, USA, pp. 210–217.

Liu, Yuan-Ling, Shih-ping Wang, and Keh-Yih Su (1993). "Corpus-based Automatic Rule Selection in Designing a Grammar Checker."

Proceedings of the Conference of the Association for Computational Linguistics and Chinese Language Processing (*ROCLING-VI*), Nantou, Taiwan.

Oliva, Karel (1997). "Techniques for Accelerating a Grammar Checker." *Proceedings of the 5th Conference on Applied Natural Language Processing*, Seattle, Washington, DC, USA.

Paggio, Patrizia (2000). "Spelling and Grammar Correction for Danish in SCARRIE." *Proceedings of the 6th Applied Natural Language Processing Conference*, Seattle, Washington, DC, USA, pp. 255–261.

Thurmair, Gregor (1995). "Grammar and Style Checkers." In Marianne Kugler, Khurshid Ahmad, and Gregor Thurmair, eds., *Translator's Workbench*. Berlin: Springer Verlag, pp. 117–127.

Spelling Checker

Bustamante, Flora Ramírez, Alfredo Arnaiz, and Mar Ginés (2006). "A Spell Checker for a World Language: The New Microsoft's Spanish Spell Checker." *Proceedings of the 5th International Conference on Language Resources and Evaluation* (*LREC-2006*), Genoa, Italy.

Ghneim, Nada and Veronique Auberge (1995). "Optimising Tools for the French Letter-to-phone Grammar TOPH with a View to Phonographic Spelling Correction." *Proceedings of the Conference of the Association for Computational Linguistics and Chinese Language Processing* (*ROCLING-VIII*), Yuan-Ze Institute of Technology Chung-Li, Taiwan.

Huang, Hai 黃海, Luo Zhensheng 羅振聲, and Cheng Musheng 程慕勝 (1999). "Automatic Spelling Check of English Texts Based on Corpus Statistics." In Huang Changning 黃昌寧 and Dong Zhendong 董振東, eds.,《計算機語言學文集》(*Essays on Computational Linguistics*). Beijing: Tsinghua University Press, pp. 222–228.

Meya, Montserrat (1995). "Word- and Context-based Spell Checkers." In Marianne Kugler, Khurshid Ahmad, and Gregor Thurmair, eds., *Translator's Workbench*. Berlin: Springer Verlag, pp. 110–116.

Paggio, Patrizia (2000). "Spelling and Grammar Correction for Danish in SCARRIE." *Proceedings of the 6th Applied Natural Language Processing Conference*, Seattle, Washington, DC, USA, pp. 255–261.

Pollock, Joseph J. and Antonio Zamora (1984). "Automatic Spelling Correction in Scientific and Scholarly Text." *Communication of ACM*, Vol. 27, No. 4, pp. 358–368.

Style Checker

Genzel, Dmitriy (2005). "A Paragraph Boundary Detection System." *Proceedings of the 6th International Conference on Intelligent Text Processing and Computational Linguistics (CICLing-2005)*, Mexico City, Mexico, pp. 804–814.

Thurmair, Gregor (1995). "Grammar and Style Checkers." In Marianne Kugler, Khurshid Ahmad, and Gregor Thurmair, eds., *Translator's Workbench*. Berlin: Springer Verlag, pp. 117–127.

Syntax Checker

Gojenola, Koldo and Maite Oronoz (2000). "Corpus-based Syntactic Error Detection Using Syntactic Patterns." *Proceedings of the ANLP-NAACL 2000, Student Research Workshop*, Seattle, Washington, DC, USA, pp. 24–29.

Hellwig, Peter (1995). "Automatic Syntax Checking." In Marianne Kugler, Khurshid Ahmad, and Gregor Thurmair, eds., *Translator's Workbench*. Berlin: Springer Verlag, pp. 128–144.

Translatability Checker

Underwood, Nancy and Bart Jongejan (2001). "Translatability Checker: A Tool to Help Decide Whether to Use MT." In Bente Maegaard, ed., *Proceedings of MT Summit VIII: Machine Translation in the Information Age*, Santiago de Compostela, Spain, pp. 363–368.

TransCheck

Jutras, Jean-Marc (2000). "An Automatic Reviser: The TransCheck System." *Proceedings of the 6th Applied Natural Language Processing Conference*, Seattle, Washington, DC, USA, pp. 127–134.

Macklovitch, Elliott (1994). "Using Bi-textual Alignment for Translation Validation: The TransCheck System." *Proceedings of the 1st Conference of the Association for Machine Translation in the Americas: Technology Partnerships for Crossing the Language Barrier (AMTA-1)*, Columbia, Maryland, USA, pp. 157–168.

Macklovitch, Elliott (1995). "TransCheck—Or the Automatic Validation of Human Translations." *Proceedings of MT Summit V: Machine Translation Conference, Exhibition and Tutorial*, Luxembourg.

❖ PART 5 ❖

Computer

Computer

Dreyfus, Hubert L. (1992). *What Computers Still Can't Do: A Critique of Artificial Reason*. Cambridge, MA: MIT Press.

Gregoire, Jean-Francois (1980). "Translating and the Computing." *Meta*, Vol. 25, pp. 360–367.

Lawson, Veronica (1979). "Tigers and Polar Bears, Or: Translating and the Computer." *The Incorporated Linguist*, Vol. 18, pp. 81–85.

Lewis, Derek (2001). "PC-based Machine Translation: An Illustration of Capabilities in Response to Submitted Test Sentences." *Machine Translation Review*, No. 12, pp. 36–47.

Liro, Joseph (1987). "On Computers, Translation, and Stanislaw Lem." *Computers and Translation*, Vol. 2, No. 2, pp. 89–104.

Interface

Cohen, Philip, David McGee, and Josh Clow (2000). "The Efficiency of Multimodal Interaction for a Map-based Task." *Proceedings of the 6th Applied Natural Language Processing Conference*, Seattle, Washington, DC, USA, pp. 331–338.

de Gregorio-Godeo, Eduardo and Silvia Molina-Plaza (2006). "Exploring the Culture-technology Interface in the Design of Translation Tools: Creating an English-Spanish/Spanish-English Dictionary of Phaseological Units." *Proceedings of the 6th Portsmouth Translation Conference: Translation Technologies and Culture,* School of Languages and Area Studies, University of Portsmouth, England.

Divi, Vijay, Clifton Forlines, Jan Van Gemert, Bhiksha Raj, Bent Schmidt-Nielsen, Kent Wittenburg, Joseph Woelfel, and Zhang Fangfang (2004). "A Speech-in List-out Approach to Spoken User Interfaces." *Proceedings of the Human Language Technology Conference/North American Chapter of the Association for Computational Linguistics Annual Meeting* (*HLT/NAACL-2004*), Boston, MA, USA.

Dowding, John and James Hieronymus (2003). "A Spoken Dialogue Interface to a Geologist's Field Assistant." *Proceedings of the Human Language Technology and North American Chapter of Association of Computational Linguistics 2003* (*HLT/NAACL-2003*), Edmonton, Alberta, Canada.

Johnson, Heidi M., Yukiko Sekine, John S. White, and Gil C. Kim (1988).

"Application of Natural Language Interface to a Machine Translation Problem." *Proceedings of the 2nd International Conference on Theoretical and Methodological Issues in Machine Translation of Natural Languages* (*TMI-88*), Carnegie Mellon University, Center for Machine Translation, Pittsburgh, Pennsylvania, USA.

Marcus, Richard S. and J. Francis Reintjes (1981). "A Translating Computer Interface for End-user Operation of Heterogeneous Retrieval Systems, I: Evaluations." *Journal of the American Society for Information Science*, Vol. 32, No. 4, pp. 287–303.

Marcus, Richard S. and J. Francis Reintjes (1981). "A Translating Computer Interface for End-user Operation of Heterogeneous Retrieval Systems, II: Design." *Journal of the American Society for Information Science*, Vol. 32, No. 4, pp. 304–317.

Montoro, Germán, Xavier Alamán, and Pablo A. Haya (2004). "A Plug and Play Spoken Dialogue Interface for Smart Environments." *Proceedings of the 5th International Conference on Intelligent Text Processing and Computational Linguistics* (*CICLing-2004*), Chung-Ang University, Seoul, Korea, pp. 355–365.

Moser-Mercer, Barbara (1987). "Man/Machine Interface in Translation and Terminology." *Meta*, Vol. 32, No. 2, pp. 156–163.

Sheremetyeva, Svetlana (2003). "Towards Designing Natural Language Interfaces." *Proceedings of the 4th International Conference on Intelligent Text Processing and Computational Linguistics* (*CICLing-2003*), Mexico City, Mexico, pp. 479–491.

Somers, Harold L. (1987). "Some Thoughts on Interface Structures." In Wolfram Wilss and Klaus-Dirk Schmitz, eds., *Maschinelle Übersetzung—Methoden and Werkzeuge*. Tubingen: Max Niemeyer Verlag, pp. 81–99.

Tang, Lappoon R. and Raymond J. Mooney (2000). "Automated Construction of Database Interfaces: Integrating Statistical and Relational Learning for Semantic Parsing." *Proceedings of the Joint Sigdat Conference on Empirical Methods in Natural Language Processing and Very Large Corpora* (*EMNLP/VLC-2000*), Hong Kong University of Science and Technology, Hong Kong.

Thurmair, Gregor (1997). "Exchange Interfaces for Translation Tools." *Machine Translation Summit VI*, San Diego, CA, USA, pp. 74–93.

Vainio-Larsson, Arja (1990). "Evaluating the Usability of User Interfaces: Research in Practice." In Dan Diaper, David J. Gilmore, Gilbert

Cockton, and Brian Shackel, eds., *Human Computer Interaction—INTERACT '90*. Amsterdam: Elsevier, pp. 323–328.

Whittaker, Edward, Joanna Mrozinski, and Sadaoki Furui (2006). "Question Answering with Web, Mobile and Speech Interfaces." *Proceedings of the Human Language Technology Conference—Annual Meeting of the North American Chapter of the Association for Computational Linguistics* (*HLT-NAACL-2006*), New York, USA.

Yu, Hong and Minsuk Lee (2006). "BioEx: A Novel User-interface that Accesses Images from Abstract Sentences." *Proceedings of the Human Language Technology Conference—Annual Meeting of the North American Chapter of the Association for Computational Linguistics* (*HLT-NAACL-2006*), New York, USA.

Zárate M., J. Antonio, Rodolfo A. Pazos R., Alexander F. Gelbukh, and J. Isabel Padrón C. (2003). "A Portable Natural Language Interface for Diverse Databases Using Ontologies." *Proceedings of the 4th International Conference on Intelligent Text Processing and Computational Linguistics* (*CICLing-2003*), Mexico City, Mexico, pp. 496–507.

Storage

Booth, Andrew D. (1952). "A Survey of Memory Devices Suitable for MT." *Proceedings of the M.I.T. Conference on Mechanical Translation,* Massachusetts Institute of Technology, Cambridge, MA, USA.

Booth, Andrew D. (1955). "Storage Devices." In William N. Locke and Andrew D. Booth, eds., *Machine Translation of Languages: Fourteen Essays.* Cambridge, MA: Technology Press of the Massachusetts Institute of Technology, pp. 119–123.

Chen, Hsin-Hsi and Yue-Shi Lee (1993). "A Storage Reduction Method for Corpus-based Language Models." *Proceedings of the Conference of the Association for Computational Linguistics and Chinese Language Processing* (*ROCLING-VI*), Nantou, Taiwan.

Forrester, Jay (1952). "Problems of Storage and Cost." *Proceedings of the M.I.T. Conference on Mechanical Translation,* Massachusetts Institute of Technology, Cambridge, MA, USA.

King, Gilbert W., George W. Brown, and Louis N. Ridenour (1953). "Photographic Techniques for Information Storage." *Proceedings of the IRE* (*Institute of Radio Engineers*), Vol. 41, pp. 1421–1428.

King, Gilbert W. (1955). "A New Approach to Information Storage." *Control Engineering*, Vol. 2, pp. 48–53.

King, Gilbert W. (1957). "The Requirements of Lexical Storage." In Leon Dostert, ed., *Report of the 8th Annual Round Table Meeting on Linguistics and Language Studies*. Washington, DC: Georgetown University Press, pp. 79–87.

Meyer, E. (1976). "The Storage and Retrieval of Alpha-numeric Information." *Rechentechnische Datenverarbeitung*, Vol. 13, No. 5, pp. 43–47.

Rodes, Ida (1967). "The Importance of the Glossary Storage in Machine Translation." In Andrew D. Booth, ed., *Machine Translation*. Amsterdam: North-Holland Publishing Company, pp. 429–449.

Usability

Barrett, Leslie and Robert Levin (2005). "Usability Considerations for a Cellular-based Text Translator." *Proceedings of MT Summit X*, Phuket, Thailand.

Bevan, Nigel and Ian Curson (1997). "Methods of Measuring Usability." *Proceedings of the 6th IFIP Conference on Human-computer Interaction*, Sydney, Australia.

Dray, Susan M. (2003). "Cross-cultural Usability and Localization: Partners in Making Products, Documentation and Web Sites Usable around the World." *Proceedings of the Localization World Conference 2003*, Seattle, Washington, DC, USA.

Gaspari, Federico (2004). "Controlled Language, Web Usability and Machine Translation Services on the Internet." *International Journal of Translation*, Vol. 16, No. 1, pp. 41–54.

User-friendliness

Farwell, David L. and Stephen Helmreich (1997). "User-friendly Machine Translation: Alternate Translations Based on Differing Beliefs." *Proceedings of MT Summit VI*, San Diego, California, USA.

Computer Aid

Arthern, Peter J. (1981). "Aids Unlimited: The Scope for Machine Aids in a Large Organization." *Aslib Proceedings*, Vol. 33, Nos. 7–8, pp. 309–319.

Clark, Robert M. (1981). "Machine Aids: A Small User's Reaction." *Aslib Proceedings*, Vol. 33, Nos. 7–8, pp. 278–289.

Karlgren, Hans (1981). "Computer Aids in Translation." *Studia Linguistica*, Vol. 35, pp. 86–101.

King, Margaret (1998). "Workflow, Computer Aids and Organisational Issues." *Proceedings of the 1998 EAMT Workshop, Translation Technology: Integration in the Workflow Environment*, Geneva, Switzerland, pp. 29–39.

Knowles, Francis E. (1990). "Machine Aids for Translators: What Does the Future Betoken?" In Pamela Mayorcas, ed., *Translating and the Computer 10*. London: The Association of Information Management, pp. 125–135.

Lippmann, Edward O. (1976). "Experimental On-line Computer Aids for the Human Translator." *American Journal of Computational Linguistics* (2, microfiche 46), pp. 11–13.

Lippmann, Edward O. (1977). "Computer Aids for the Human Translator." *Proceedings of the 8th World Congress of FIT*, Montreal, Quebec, Canada.

Lippmann, Edward O. (1980). "Human Factors in the Design of Computer Aids for Translators." *ATA Chronicle*, Vol. 9, No. 6, p. 5.

Schneider, Thomas (1983). "Some Notes on Machine Aids for Translators." *Meta*, Vol. 28, No. 4, pp. 344–351.

Stiegler, A. D. (1981). "Machine Aids for Translators: A Review." *Aslib Proceedings*, Vol. 33, Nos. 7-8, pp. 268–277.

Tanke, Eberhard (1979). "Implementing Machine Aids to Translation." In Barbara M. Snell, ed., *Translating and the Computer*. Amsterdam: North-Holland Publishing Company, pp. 45–69.

Zachary, Wayne W. (1978). "Machine Aids to Translation: A Concise State-of-the-art Bibliography." *American Journal of Computational Linguistics*, Vol. 3, pp. 34–40.

Computer Applications in Translation

Allen, Jeffrey (2004). "Case Study: Implementing MT for the Translation of Pre-sales Marketing and Post-sales Software Deployment Documentation at Mycom International." In Robert E. Frederking and

Kathryn B. Taylors, eds., *Machine Translation: From Real Users to Research*. Berlin: Springer Verlag, pp. 1–6.
Arnold, Doug J. (2003). "Why Translation Is Difficult for Computers?" In Harold L. Somers, ed., *Computers and Translation: A Translator's Guide*. Amsterdam and Philadelphia: John Benjamins Publishing Company, pp. 119–142.
Arnold, Doug J., Lorna Balkan, R. Lee Humphreys, Seity Meijer, and Louisa Sadler (1994). "Machine Translation in Practice." *Machine Translation: An Introductory Guide*. Manchester and Oxford: NCC Blackwell, pp. 19–35.
Arntz, Reiner (1989). "Practical Experience in the Application of MT Systems." In Christian Rohrer, ed., *Proceedings of MT Summit II*, Munich, Germany, pp. 42–43.
Arthern, Peter J. (1980). "Machine Translation—A Translator's Viewpoint." *Lebenden Sprachen*, No. 1, pp. 9–14.
Austermühl, Frank (2001). "A Translator's Sword of Damocles? An Introduction to Machine Translation." In *Electronic Tools for Translators*. Manchester: St. Jerome Publishing Company, pp. 153–176.
Bech, Annelise (1996). "Building Term Dictionaries for Machine Translation in Practice: A User Experience." *Proceedings of the 1st Workshop of the European Association for Machine Translation (TKE-96): Language Resources, Terminology, Economics, and User Needs*, Vienna, Austria, pp. 45–50.
Bech, Annelise (1997). "MT from an Everyday User's Point of View." *Proceedings of MT Summit VI*, San Diego, California, USA.
Bernhard, Ursula (1995). "Machine Translation: Success or Failure—Using MT in an IT Research and Development Environment." In *Translating and the Computer 17*. London: The Association for Information Management.
Bezhanova, Olga (1997). "Translating Scientific Texts Using MT and MAT Systems: Practical Experience of a Professional Translator." *Proceedings of MT Summit VI*, San Diego, California, USA.
Boitet, Christian (1990). "Towards Personal MT: General Design, Dialogue Structure, Potential Role of Speech, Text Encoding." *Proceedings of the Conference of the Association for Computational Linguistics and Chinese Language Processing (ROCLING-III)*, Taipei, Taiwan.

Brundage, Jennifer A. (2001). "Machine Translation: Evolution Not Revolution." In Bente Maegaard, ed., *Proceedings of MT Summit VIII: Machine Translation in the Information Age*, Santiago de Compostela, Spain.

Choi, Key-Sun (1995). "Machine Translation for the Office Automation." *Proceedings of MT Summit V: Machine Translation Conference, Exhibition and Tutorial*, Luxembourg.

Church, Kenneth W. and Eduard H. Hovy (1993). "Good Applications for Crummy Machine Translation." *Machine Translation*, Vol. 1, pp. 239–258.

Clarke, Anthony, Elisabeth Maier, and Hans-Udo Stadler (2002). "A Report on the Experiences of Implementing an MT System for Use in a Commercial Environment." In Stephen D. Richardson, ed., *Machine Translation: From Research to Real Users*. Berlin and New York: Springer Verlag, pp. 187–194.

Cremers, Lou and Christine Kamprath (1997). "Using MT in a Corporate Setting." *Proceedings of MT Summit VI*, San Diego, California, USA.

Datta, Jean (1988). "MT in Large Organizations: Revolution in the Workplace." In Muriel Vasconcellos, ed., *Technology as Translation Strategy*. New York: State University of New York at Binghamton, pp. 167–173.

Day, Joan M. (1990). "CD-ROM: What Can It Offer the Translator?" In Catriona Picken, ed., *Translating and the Computer 11: Preparing for the Next Decade*. London: The Association for Information Management, pp. 75–78.

Deschamps, Rene (1986). "Computerized Translation: Judging the Promise against the Reality." In Karl Kummer, ed., *Building Bridges: Proceedings of the 27th Annual Conference of the American Translators Association*. Medford, New Jersey: Learned Information Inc., pp. 151–156.

Dessau, Ralph B. and George Mallard (1986). "Automated Language Translation for Personal Computers." In Karl Kummer, ed., *Building Bridges: Proceedings of the 27th Annual Conference of the American Translators Association*. Medford, New Jersey: Learned Information Inc., pp. 125–128.

Downs, Linn Hedwig (1985). "Installation of MT at Burroughs Corporation: The First Year." In Patricia E. Newman, ed., *American*

Translators Association Conference—1985. Medford, New Jersey: Learned Information, Inc., pp. 127–133.
Eng, Dawn (1988). "MT in a Service Bureau: Its Uses and Limitations." In Muriel Vasconcellos, ed., *Technology as Translation Strategy*. New York: State University of New York at Binghamton, pp. 174–177.
Freibott, Gerhard (1989). "Practical Experience in the Application of MT Systems." In Christian Rohrer, ed., *Proceedings of MT Summit II*, Munich, Germany, pp. 58–59.
Gross, Alex, Claude Bédard, Harald Hille, Martin Kay, Frederick Klein, and Sergei Nirenburg (1993). "Translators and MT?" In Sergei Nirenburg, ed., *Progress in Machine Translation*. Amsterdam: IOS and Tokyo: Ohmsha, pp. 253–266.
Gurina, Tatyana M. (2001). "Educational Applications of a Machine Translation System." *International Journal of Translation*, Vol. 13, Nos. 1–2, pp. 189–193.
Hatley, John (1995). "Some Practical Suggestions for Implementing Machine Translation." In *Translating and the Computer 17*. London: The Association for Information Management.
Hutchins, W. John and Harold L. Somers (1992). "The Practical Use of MT Systems." *An Introduction to Machine Translation*. London: Academic Press, pp. 147–159.
Jaekel, Gary (1995). "In the Balance—Ericsson Language Services." In *Translating and the Computer 17*. London: The Association for Information Management.
Johnson, Ian (1997). "Personal Translation Applications." In *Translating and the Computer 19*. London: The Association for Information Management.
Johnson, Roderick L. and Peter J. Whitelock (1987). "Machine Translation as an Expert Task." In Sergei Nirenburg, ed., *Machine Translation: Theoretical and Methodological Issues*. Cambridge: Cambridge University Press, pp. 136–144.
Jones, Malcolm (1988). "New Ways to Communicate: Services Provided by British Telecom." In Catriona Picken, ed., *Translating and the Computer 9: Potential and Practice*. London: The Association for Information Management, pp. 56–68.
Kawasaki, Zenshiro (1993). "Organizational Use of Machine Translation Systems." In Sergei Nirenburg, ed., *Progress in Machine Translation*. Amsterdam: IOS and Tokyo: Ohmsha, pp. 217–224.
Kopris, Craig (2004). "Rapid MT Experience in an LCTL (Pashto)." In

Robert E. Frederking and Kathryn B. Taylors, eds., *Machine Translation: From Real Users to Research*. Berlin: Springer Verlag, pp. 130–133.

Környei, Tibor (2001). "Using MS Word's Advanced Find and Replace Function." *Translation Journal*, Vol. 5, No. 1.

Kulagina, Olga S. (1963). "The Use of Computers in Machine Translation." In C. M. Popplewell, ed., *Information Processing 62: Proceedings of IFIP Congress 62*. Amsterdam: Horth-Holland, pp. 301–303.

Lawson, Veronica (1981). "Introduction: Help from the Computer—Machine Aids for Translators." *Aslib Proceedings*, Vol. 33, Nos. 7–8, pp. 265–267.

Lawson, Veronica (1982). "Machine Translation and People." In Veronica Lawson, ed., *Practical Experience of Machine Translation.* Amsterdam: North-Holland Publishing Company, pp. 3–9.

Lawson, Veronica, ed. (1982). *Practical Experience of Machine Translation.* Amsterdam: North-Holland Publishing Company.

Lawson, Veronica (1984). "A Basic Survey of Practical MT." *Proceedings of the International Conference on the Methodology and Techniques of Machine Translation*, Cranfield Institute of Technology, England.

Lewis, Terence and Rudolf Meier (2005). "The MT Developer/Provider and the Global Corporation." *Proceedings of the 10th Annual Conference of the European Association for Machine Translation (EAMT-2005*), Budapest, Hungary.

Liu, Zhuo 劉倬 and Jiang Yiping 姜一平 (1983).〈電腦翻譯的研究與應用〉(The Study and Application of Computer Translation). In China Translation and Publishing Corporation 中國對外翻譯出版公司, ed.,《外國翻譯理論評介文集》(*Review Essays on Foreign Translation Theories*). Beijing: China Translation and Publishing Corporation, pp. 118–126.

Lueke, Dirk (1995). "MT at SAP—A Successful Integration." In *Translating and the Computer 17*. London: The Association for Information Management.

Macklovitch, Elliott (1989). "Recent Canadian Experience in Machine Translation." In Ian D. K. Kelly, ed., *Progress in Machine Translation: Natural Language and Personal Computers*. Wilmslow: Sigma Press, pp. 59–67.

Masterman, Margaret (1982). "The Limits of Innovation in Machine

Translation." In Veronica Lawson, ed., *Practical Experience of Machine Translation*. Amsterdam: North-Holland Publishing Company, pp. 163–186.

Meek, Brian L., ed. (1986). *Computers and Their Applications*. New York: Halsted Press.

Melby, Alan K. (1987). "Creating an Environment for the Translator." In Margaret King, ed., *Machine Translation Today: The State of the Art*. Edinburgh: Edinburgh University Press, pp. 124–132.

Melby, Alan K. (1996). "Building Machine Translation on a Firm Foundation." In *Translating and the Computer 18*. London: The Association for Information Management.

Morland, Verne (2002). "Getting the Message in: A Global Company's Experience with the New Generation of Low-cost, High Performance Machine Translation Systems." In Stephen D. Richardson, ed., *Machine Translation: From Research to Real Users*. Berlin and New York: Springer Verlag, pp. 195–206.

Newton, John (1987). "An Insider's View of Machine Translation." *The Linguist*, Vol. 26, No. 1, pp. 21–24.

Newton, John (1992). "The Perkins Experience." In John Newton, ed., *Computers in Translation: A Practical Appraisal*. London and New York: Routledge, pp. 46–57.

Nirenburg, Sergei, Rod Johnson, Richard Kitteredge, Lori S. Levin, Hiroshi Uchida, Steven Weinstein, Yorick Wilks, and Stephen Richardson (1993). "Applications of MT Technology." In Sergei Nirenburg, ed., *Progress in Machine Translation*. Amsterdam: IOS and Tokyo: Ohmsha, pp. 285–296.

O'Brien, Sharon (1998). "Practical Experience of Computer-aided Translation Tools in the Localization Industry." In Lynne Bowker, Michael Cronin, Dorothy Kenny, and Jennifer Pearson, eds., *Unity in Diversity? Current Trends in Translation Studies*. Manchester: St. Jerome Publishing, pp. 115–122.

Peterson-Boogaard, Jill E. (1988). "Deciding on the Level of Computer Participation in Translation." In Muriel Vasconcellos, ed., *Technology as Translation Strategy*. New York: State University of New York at Binghamton, pp. 217–222.

Pigott, Ian M. (1986). "Machine Translation as an Integral Part of the Electronic Office Environment." In Catriona Picken, ed., *Translating and the Computer 7*. London: The Association for Information

Management, pp. 144–151.

Rangan, K. (1988). "Communicating with Machine: Moment of Joy and Frustration." In K. Karunakaran and M. Jayakumar, eds. *Translation as Synthesis: A Search for a New Gestalt*. New Delhi: Bahri Publications Private Limited, pp. 91–104.

Rico Pérez, Celia (2001). "From Novelty to Ubiquity: Computers and Translation at the Close of the Industrial Age." *Translation Journal*, 11 July.

Rolling, Loll (1989). "Practical Experience in the Application of MT Systems." In Christian Rohrer, ed., *Proceedings of MT Summit II*, Munich, Germany, pp. 123–124.

Ruffino, J. Richard (1982). "Coping with Machine Translation." In Veronica Lawson, ed., *Practical Experience of Machine Translation*. Amsterdam: North-Holland Publishing Company, pp. 57–60.

Ryan, Joann P. (1993). "Machine Translation: Matching Reality to Expectations." In Sergei Nirenburg, ed., *Progress in Machine Translation*. Amsterdam: IOS and Tokyo: Ohmsha, pp. 225–235.

Rychtyckyj, Nestor (2002). "An Assessment of Machine Translation for Vehicle Assembly Process Planning at Ford Motor Company." In Stephen D. Richardson, ed., *Machine Translation: From Research to Real Users*. Berlin and New York: Springer Verlag, pp. 207–215.

Sakurai, Keizou, Masahiko Ozeki, and Yoshiyuki Nishihara (1993). "MT Application for the Translation Agency." In Sergei Nirenburg, ed., *Progress in Machine Translation*. Amsterdam: IOS and Tokyo: Ohmsha, pp. 237–242.

Santangelo, Susana (1988). "Making an MT System Work: Perspective of a Translator." In Muriel Vasconcellos, ed., *Technology as Translation Strategy*. New York: State University of New York at Binghamton, pp. 133–139.

Santos, Diana (1999). "Toward Language-dependent Applications." *Machine Translation*, Vol. 14, No. 2, pp. 83–112.

Sato, Shigeru (1989). "Practical Experience in the Application of MT Systems." In Christian Rohrer, ed., *Proceedings of MT Summit II*, Munich, Germany, pp. 125–127.

Schäler, Reinhard (1998). "The Problem with Machine Translation." In Lynne Bowker, Michael Cronin, Dorothy Kenny, and Jennifer Pearson, eds., *Unity in Diversity? Current Trends in Translation Studies*. Manchester: St. Jerome Publishing, pp. 151–156.

Sereda, Stanley P. (1982). "Practical Experience of Machine Translation." In Veronica Lawson, ed., *Practical Experience of Machine Translation*. Amsterdam: North-Holland Publishing Company, pp. 119–123.

Shaefer, Leonard A. (1988). "MT and the Independent Translator." In Muriel Vasconcellos, ed., *Technology as Translation Strategy*. New York: State University of New York at Binghamton, pp. 190–197.

Shaefer, Leonard A. (1989). "PC-based Machine Translation: To Buy or Not to Buy." In Deanna Lindberg Hammond, ed., *Coming of Age: Proceedings of the 30th Annual Conference of the American Translators Association*. Medford, New Jersey: Learned Information, Inc., pp. 503–512.

Sharp, Randall and Oliver Streiter (1992). "Simplifying the Complexity of Machine Translation." *Meta*, Vol. 37, No. 4, pp. 681–692.

Shih, Chung-ling (2002). "Complimentary Relevance of MT to HT." In *The English Teaching and Learning*. Taibei: The Crane Publishing Co. Ltd., pp. 85–114.

Shih, Chung-ling 史宗玲 (2004).〈開發機器翻譯新航道〉(Opening Up a New Path in Machine Translation). In《電腦輔助翻譯》(*MT and TM*). Taipei: The Bookman Press 書林出版有限公司, pp. 1–22.

Smith, Kim L. (1988). "Nuts and Bolts for Translators: How Do I Get ã on This #$&*@* Computer?" In Muriel Vasconcellos, ed., *Technology as Translation Strategy*. New York: State University of New York at Binghamton, pp. 25–28.

Smith, Raoul N. (1984). "On Personal Translation." In William Frawley, ed., *Translation: Literary, Linguistic, and Philosophical Perspectives*. Cranbury, New Jersey: University of Delaware Press, pp. 150–158.

Sokolova, Svetlana (1996). "Users' Experiences with a Set of Domain-specific Dictionaries for the Stylus Machine Translation System." *Proceedings of the 1st Workshop of the European Association for Machine Translation* (*TKE-96*): *Language Resources, Terminology, Economics, and User Needs*, Vienna, Austria, pp. 37–44.

Somers, Harold L. (1998). "Machine Translation: Applications." In Mona Baker, ed., *Routledge Encyclopedia of Translation Studies*. London and New York: Routledge, pp. 136–153.

Spalink, Karin and Muriel Vasconcellos (1995). "Using MT in Practice—Helpful Hints and Advice." *Proceedings of MT Summit V: Machine Translation Conference, Exhibition and Tutorial*, Luxembourg.

Su, Keh-Yih and Jing-Shin Chang (1992). "Why MT Systems Are Still Not

Widely Used." *Machine Translation*, Vol. 7, No. 4, pp. 285–291.
Theologitis, Dimitrios and J. Ross (1997). "Production MT in the Public Agencies." *Proceedings of MT Summit VI*, San Diego, California, USA.
Trang, Claire (1987). "Translating by Computer: Critique and Reality." In Karl Kummer, ed., *Across the Language Gap: Proceedings of the 28th Annual Conference of the American Translators Association*. Medford, New Jersey: Learned Information, Inc., pp. 445–451.
T'sou, Benjamin K. Y. 鄒嘉彥 (1986).〈翻譯、機器、人〉(Translation, Machines, and People). In Liu Ching-chih 劉靖之, ed.,《翻譯叢論一九八六》(*Essays on Translation—1986*). Hong Kong: The Commercial Press 商務印書館, pp. 48–61.
Vasconcellos, Muriel (1989). "Long-term Data for an MT Policy." *Literary and Linguistic Computing*, Vol. 4, No. 3, pp. 203–213.
Vasconcellos, Muriel and Dale A. Bostad (1992). "Machine Translation in a High-volume Translation Environment." In John Newton, ed., *Computers in Translation: A Practical Appraisal*. London and New York: Routledge, pp. 58–77.
Vasconcellos, Muriel, Bernard Scott, John Chandioux, and Hideki Tanaka (1993). "MT User Experience." In Sergei Nirenburg, ed., *Progress in Machine Translation*. Amsterdam: IOS and Tokyo: Ohmsha, pp. 243–252.
Wheeler, Peter (1994). "The Errant Avocado Returns—A Personal Odyssey." *Machine Translation—Ten Years On: Proceedings of the 2nd International Conference Organised by Cranfield University*, Cranfield, England.
Widmann, R. L. (1975). "Trends in Computer Applications to Literature." *Computers and the Humanities*, Vol. 9, No. 5, pp. 231–235.
Willson, A. Leslie (1989). "Remember Johnny Appleseed." In Deanna Lindberg Hammond, ed., *Coming of Age: Proceedings of the 30th Annual Conference of the American Translators Association*. Medford, New Jersey: Learned Information, Inc., pp. 513–516.

Computer Learning

Alegria, Iñaki, Bertol Arrieta, Arantza Diaz de Ilarraza, Elisabete Izagirre, and Montse Maritxalar (2006). "Using Machine Learning Techniques to Build a Comma Checker for Basque." *Proceedings of the Joint Conference of the International Committee on Computational*

Linguistics and the Association for Computational Linguistics (COLING/ACL-2006), Sydney, Australia.

Alm, Cecilia Ovesdotter, Dan Roth, and Richard Sproat (2005). "Emotions from Text: Machine Learning for Text-based Emotion Prediction." *Proceedings of Human Language Technology Conference and Conference on Empirical Methods in Natural Language Processing (HLT/EMNLP-2005)*, Vancouver, BC, Canada.

Chrupa, Grzegorz and Josef van Genabith (2006). "Using Machine-learning to Assign Function Labels to Parser Output for Spanish." *Proceedings of the Joint Conference of the International Committee on Computational Linguistics and the Association for Computational Linguistics (COLING/ACL-2006)*, Sydney, Australia.

Gamon, Michael, Hisami Suzuki, and Simon Corston-Oliver (2001). "Using Machine Learning for System-internal Evaluation of Transferred Linguistic Representations." In Bente Maegaard, ed., *Proceedings of MT Summit VIII: Machine Translation in the Information Age*, Santiago de Compostela, Spain.

Gamon, Michael, Eric K. Ringger, Simon Corston-Oliver, and Robert C. Moore (2002). "Machine-learned Contexts for Linguistic Operations in German Sentence Realization." *Proceedings of the 40th Annual Meeting of the Association for Computational Linguistics*, Philadelphia, PA, USA, pp. 25–32.

Hatzivassiloglou, Vasileios, Judith L. Klavans, and Eleazar Eskin (1999). "Detecting Text Similarity over Short Passages: Exploring Linguistic Feature Combinations via Machine Learning." *Proceedings of the Joint SIGDAT Conference on Empirical Methods in NLP and Very Large Corpora (EMNLP/VLC-99)*, University of Maryland, College Park, MD, USA.

Joachims, Thorsten (1999). "Making Large-scale Support Vector Machine Learning Practical." In Bernhard Schölkopf, Christopher J. C. Burges, and Alexander J. Smola, eds., *Advances in Kernel Methods—Support Vector Machines*, Cambridge, MA: The MIT Press, pp. 41–56.

Joshi, Aravind K. and Sriram Venkatapathy (2004). "Recognition of Multi-word Expressions Using Machine Learning Techniques: A Study of Verb-noun (V-N) Collocations." *Proceedings of the International Conference on Natural Language Processing (ICON-2004)*, International Institute of Information Technology, Hyderabad, India.

Jung, Sung-Won and Hyuk-Chul Kwon (2006). "A Machine Learning Based Approach for Separating Head from Body in Web-tables." *Proceedings of the 7th International Conference on Intelligent Text Processing and Computational Linguistics* (*CICLing-2006*), Mexico City, Mexico.

Li, Wenjie, Kam-fai Wong, Guihong Cao, and Chunfa Yuan (2004). "Applying Machine Learning to Chinese Temporal Relation Resolution." *Proceedings of the 42nd Annual Meeting of the Association for Computational Linguistics* (*ACL-2004*), Barcelona, Spain, pp. 582–588.

Mani, Inderjeet, Marc Verhagen, Ben Wellner, and James Pustejovsky (2006). "Machine Learning of Temporal Relations." *Proceedings of the Joint Conference of the International Committee on Computational Linguistics and the Association for Computational Linguistics* (*COLING/ACL-2006*), Sydney, Australia.

Marquez, Lluis, Horacio Rodriguez, Josep Carmona, and Josep Montolio (1999). "Improving POS Tagging Using Machine-learning Techniques." *Proceedings of the Joint SIGDAT Conference on Empirical Methods in NLP and Very Large Corpora* (*EMNLP/VLC-99*), University of Maryland, College Park, MD, USA.

Menezes, Arul (2002). "Better Contextual Translation Using Machine Learning." In Stephen D. Richarson, ed., *Machine Translation: From Research to Real Users*. Berlin and New York: Springer Verlag, pp. 124–134.

Moschitti, Alessandro (2006). "Syntactic Kernels for Natural Language Learning: The Semantic Role Labeling Case." *Proceedings of the Human Language Technology Conference—Annual Meeting of the North American Chapter of the Association for Computational Linguistics* (*HLT-NAACL-2006*), New York, USA.

Murata, Masaki, Kiyotaka Uchimoto, Qing Ma, and Hitoshi Isahara (2001). "A Machine-learning Approach to Estimating the Referential Properties of Japanese Noun Phrases." *Proceedings of the 2nd International Conference on Intelligent Text Processing and Computational Linguistics* (*CICLing-2001*), Mexico City, Mexico.

Murata, Masaki, Masao Utiyama, Kiyotaka Uchimoto, Qing Ma, and Hitoshi Isahara (2002). "Correction of Errors in a Modality Corpus Used for Machine Translation Using Machine-learning." *Proceedings of the 9th International Conference on Theoretical and Methodological*

Issues in Machine Translation (*TMI-2002*), Keihanna, Japan, pp. 125–134.

Murata, Masaki and Hitoshi Isahara (2003). "Conversion of Japanese Passive/Causative Sentences into Active Sentences Using Machine Learning." *Proceedings of the 4th International Conference on Intelligent Text Processing and Computational Linguistics* (*CICLing-2003*), Mexico City, Mexico, pp. 118–128.

Ng, Hwee Tou, Leong Hwee Teo, and Jennifer Lai Pheng Kwan (2000). "A Machine Learning Approach to Answering Questions for Reading Comprehension Tests." *Proceedings of the Joint Sigdat Conference on Empirical Methods in Natural Language Processing and Very Large Corpora* (*EMNLP/VLC-2000*), Hong Kong University of Science and Technology, Hong Kong.

Ng, Vincent and Claire Gardent (2002). "Improving Machine Learning Approaches to Coreference Resolution." *Proceedings of the 40th Annual Meeting of the Association for Computational Linguistics*, Philadelphia, PA, USA, pp. 104–111.

Ng, Vincent (2005). "Machine Learning for Coreference Resolution: From Local Classification to Global Ranking." *Proceedings of the 43rd Annual Meeting of the Association of Computational Linguistics* (*ACL-2005*), Ann Arbor, Michigan, USA.

Niu, Zhengyu, Donghong Ji, and Chew-Lim Tan (2004). "Learning Word Sense with Feature Selection and Order Identification Capabilities." *Proceedings of the 42nd Annual Meeting of the Association for Computational Linguistics* (*ACL-2004*), Barcelona, Spain, pp. 629–636.

Oflazer, Kemal, Sergei Nirenburg, and Marjorie McShane (2001). "Bootstrapping Morphological Analyzers by Combining Human Elicitation and Machine Learning." *Computational Linguistics*, Vol. 27, pp. 59–85.

Pang, Bo, Lillian Lee, and Shivakumar Vaithyanathan (2002). "Thumbs up? Sentiment Classification Using Machine Learning Techniques." *Proceedings of the 2002 Conference on Empirical Methods in Natural Language Processing* (*EMNLP-2002*), University of Pennsylvania, Philadelphia, PA, USA.

Quinlan, J. Ross (1993). *Programs for Machine Learning*. San Mateo, CA: Morgan Kaufmann.

Ridenour, Louis N. (1952). "Learning Machines." *Proceedings of the*

M.I.T. Conference on Mechanical Translation, Massachusetts Institute of Technology, Cambridge, MA, USA.

Rieser, Verena and Oliver Lemon (2006). "Using Machine Learning to Explore Human Multimodal Clarification Strategies." *Proceedings of the Joint Conference of the International Committee on Computational Linguistics and the Association for Computational Linguistics* (*COLING/ACL-2006*), Sydney, Australia.

Suzuki, Yasuhiro, Hiroya Takamura, and Manabu Okumura (2006). "Application of Semi-supervised Learning to Evaluative Expression Classification." *Proceedings of the 7th International Conference on Intelligent Text Processing and Computational Linguistics* (*CICLing-2006*), Mexico City, Mexico.

Tinker, John F. (1963). "Learning and Translating by Machines." *Mechanical Translation*, Vol. 7, No. 2, pp. 47–49.

Tsuchiya, Masatoshi, Takao Shime, Toshihiro Takagi, Takehito Utsuro, Kiyotaka Uchimoto, Suguru Matsuyoshi, Satoshi Sato, and Seiichi Nakagawa (2006). "Chunking Japanese Compound Functional Expressions by Machine Learning." *Proceedings of the 11th Conference of the European Chapter of the Association for Computational Linguistics* (*EACL-2006*), Trento, Italy.

Vu, Huyen-Trang and Patrick Gallinari (2006). "A Machine Learning-based Approach to Evaluating Retrieval Systems." *Proceedings of the Human Language Technology Conference—Annual Meeting of the North American Chapter of the Association for Computational Linguistics* (*HLT-NAACL-2006*), New York, USA.

Yamada, Setsuo, Masaaki Nagata, and Kenji Yamada (2003). "Improving Translation Models by Applying Asymmetric Learning." *Proceedings of MT Summit IX*, New Orleans, Louisiana, USA.

Computer Translatability

Bernth, Arendse and Claudia Gdaniec (2001). "MTranslatability." *Machine Translation*, Vol. 16, No. 3, pp. 175–218.

Dillinger, Mike (2006). "Tools and Techniques for Translatable Content." *Proceedings of the 7th Biennial Conference of the Association for Machine Translation in the Americas (AMTA-2006): Visions for the Future of Machine Translation*, Boston Marriott, Cambridge, MA, USA.

Kumhyr, David, Carla Merrill, and Karin Spalink (1994). "Internationalization and Translatability." *Proceedings of the 1st Conference of the Association for Machine Translation in the Americas: Technology Partnerships for Crossing the Language Barrier (AMTA-1)*, Columbia, Maryland, USA, pp. 142–148.

Malpas, Jeff E. (1989). "The Intertranslatability of Natural Languages." *Synthese*, Vol. 78, pp. 233–264.

O'Brien, Sharon (2004). "Machine Translatability and Post Editing Effort: How Do They Relate?" In *Translating and the Computer 26*. London: The Association for Information Management.

O'Brien, Sharon (2005). "Methodologies for Measuring the Correlations between Post-editing Effort and Machine Translatability." *Machine Translation*, Vol. 19, No. 1, pp. 37–58.

Schmandt, Linda (1997). "Improving the Translatability of Technical Documents: The Logica Carnegie Group ClearCheck Approach." (http://www.cgi.com/web2/cis/ccwhite.html)

Sheremetyeva, Svetlana (2006). "Handling Low Translatability in Machine Translation of Long Sentences." *Proceedings of the 11th Workshop of the European Association for Machine Translation: Machine Translation/Translation Aids—Tools to Increase Quality and to Save Money*, the University of Oslo, Oslo, Norway.

Uchimoto, Kiyotaka, Naoko Hayashida, Toru Ishida, and Hitoshi Isahara (2005). "Automatic Rating of Machine Translatability." *Proceedings of MT Summit X*, Phuket, Thailand.

Underwood, Nancy and Bart Jongejan (2001). "Translatability Checker: A Tool to Help Decide Whether to Use MT." *Machine Translation Summit VIII*, Santiago de Compostela, Spain, pp. 363–368.

Wells-Akis, Jennifer and William R. Sisson (2002). "Improving Translatability—A Case Study at Sun Microsystems Inc." *The LISA Newsletter: Globalization Insider*, Vol. 4, No. 5.

❖ PART 6 ❖

Computer-aided Translation

Computer-aided Translation

Barnes, Janet (1987). "A User Perspective on Computer-assisted Translation for Minority Languages." *Computers and Translation*, Vol. 2, No. 3, pp. 131–134.

Boitet, Christian (1995). "Machine-aided Human Translation." *Survey of the State of the Art in Human Language Technology*. Grenoble.

Boitet, Christian (1996). "Machine-aided Human Translation." In Ronald Cole, Joseph Mariani, Hans Uszkoreit, Annie Zaenen, and Victor Zue, eds., *Survey of the State of the Art in Human Language Technology*. (http://www.cse.ogi.edu/CSLU/HLTsurvey/, Section 8.4)

Booth, Kathleen H. V. (1967). "Machine Aided Translation with a Post-editor." In Andrew D. Booth, ed., *Machine Translation*. Amsterdam: North-Holland Publishing Company, pp. 51–76.

Bowker, Lynne (2002). *Computer-aided Translation Technology: A Practical Introduction*. Ottawa: University of Ottawa Press.

Brinkmann, Karl-Heinz (1974). "On the Development and Operation of Terminology Data Banks as a Requirement for Machine-aided Translation." *Nachrichten fuer Dokumentation*, Vol. 25, No. 3, pp. 99–104.

Bruderer, Herbert E. (1976). "A Register of Machine Translation and Machine-aided Translation Projects." *Computers and the Humanities*, Vol. 10, No. 1, p. 45.

Carl, Michael, Andy Way, and Reinhard Schäler (2002). "Toward a Hybrid Integrated Translation Environment." In Stephen D. Richardson, ed., *Machine Translation: From Research to Real Users*. Berlin and New York: Springer Verlag, pp. 11–20.

Carter-Sigglow, Janet (2004). "Who's Afraid of CAT—Redefining the Boundaries of Translation." In *Translating and the Computer 26*. London: The Association for Information Management.

Champollion, Yves (2003). "Convergence in CAT: Blending MT, TM, OCR and SR to Boost Productivity." In *Translating and the Computer 25*. London: The Association for Information Management.

Clark, Robert (1994). "Computer-assisted Translation: The State of the Art." In Cay Dollerup and Annette Lindegaard, eds., *Teaching Translation and Interpreting 2: Insights, Aims, Visions*. Amsterdam and Philadelphia: John Benjamins Publishing Company, pp. 301–308.

Coughlin, Josette M. (1990). "MT or CAT: Criteria for the Independent

Translator to Select a Computerized System." *Meta*, Vol. 35, No. 2, pp. 455–457.
Craciunescu, Olivia, Constanza Gerding-Salas, and Susan Stringer-O'Keeffe (2004). "Machine Translation and Computer-assisted Translation: A New Way of Translating?" *Translation Journal*, Vol. 8, No. 3.
Dagan, Ido, Kenneth W. Church and William A. Gale (1993). "Robust Bilingual Word Alignment for Machine Aided Translation." *Proceedings of the Workshop on Very Large Corpora: Academic and Industrial Perspectives*, Columbus, Ohio, USA, pp. 1–9.
Dagan, Ido, Kenneth W. Church, and William A. Gale (1999). "Robust Bilingual Word Alignment for Machine Aided Translation." In Susan Armstrong, Kenneth W. Church, Pierre Isabelle, Sandra Manzi, Evelyne Tzoukermann, and David Yarowsky, eds., *Natural Language Processing Using Very Large Corpora*. Dordrecht: Kluwer Academic Publishers, pp. 209–224.
DeCesaris, Janet Ann (1996). "Computerized Translation Managers as Teaching Aids." In Cay Dollerup and Vibeke Appel, eds., *Teaching Translation and Interpreting 3: New Horizons*. Amsterdam and Philadelphia: John Benjamins Publishing Company, pp. 263–269.
Dyson, Mary C. and Jean Hannah (1987). "Towards a Methodology for the Evaluation of Machine-assisted Translation Systems." *Computers and Translation*, Vol. 2, pp. 163–176.
Ebermann, Basle Martha (1996). "Use and Value of Computer-assisted Translation in the Central Translation Service of Coop Switzerland, Basle." *Proceedings of the 1st Workshop of the European Association for Machine Translation* (*TKE-96*): *Language Resources, Terminology, Economics, and User Needs*, Vienna, Austria, pp. 89–94.
Eggermont, Carmen and Karel van der Eynde (1990). "A Pronominal Basis for Computer Assisted Translation: The Proton Project." In Marcel Thelen and Barbara Leeandowska-Tomaszczyk, eds., *Translation and Meaning, Part 1*. Maastricht: Euroterm, pp. 1–14.
Elliston, John S. G. (1979). "Computer Aided Translation: A Business Viewpoint." In Barbara M. Snell, ed., *Translating and the Computer*. Amsterdam: North-Holland Publishing Company, pp. 149–158.
Freigang, Karl-Heinz (1998). "Machine-aided Translation." In Mona Baker, ed., *Routledge Encyclopedia of Translation Studies*. London and New York: Routledge, pp. 134–136.

Gaspari, Federico (2003). "Relevance of Parallel Corpora to the Latest Developments of Machine Translation and Computer-assisted Translation." *International Journal of Translation*, Vol. 15, No. 1, pp. 27–41.

Gaussier, Eric, David A. Hull, and Salah Ait-Mokhtar (1999). "Term Alignment in Use: Machine-aided Human Translation." Meylan: Xerox Research Centre Europe.

Gordon, Ian (1996). "Letting the CAT out of the Bag—Or Was It MT?" In *Translating and the Computer 18*. London: The Association for Information Management.

Greenfield, Concetta C. and Daniel Serain (1977). *Machine-aided Translation: From Terminology Banks to Interactive Translation Systems*. Pittsburgh, Pennsylvania: Department of Computer Science, Carnegie-Mellon University; and Paris, France: Institut de Recherche en Informatique et Automatique.

Gui, Wen 桂文 (1992).〈提高翻譯效率的一種新途徑：用計算機輔助翻譯〉(A New Way of Raising the Efficiency of Translation: Machine-aided Translation).《中國翻譯》(*Chinese Translators Journal*), No. 1, pp. 53–54.

Hasan, Sasa, Shahram Khadivi, Richard Zens, and Hermann Ney (2006). "A Flexible Architecture for CAT Applications." *Proceedings of the 11th Workshop of the European Association for Machine Translation: Machine Translation/Translation Aids—Tools to Increase Quality and to Save Money*, the University of Oslo, Oslo, Norway.

Hays, David G. (1976). "Machine (Aided) Translation: Generalities and Guides to Action." *American Journal of Computational Linguistics*, Vol. 46, pp. 84–88.

Heyn, Matthias (1995). "Key Technologies. Impacts of Neural Network Technology on Computer Aided Translation." *Proceedings of the 3rd TermNet Symposium: Terminology in Advanced Microcomputer Applications* (*TAMA-94*), Vienna, Austria, pp. 71–84.

Hutchins, W. John (1978). "Progress in Documentation: Machine Translation and Machine-aided Translation." *Journal of Documentation*, Vol. 34, No. 2, pp. 119–159.

Hutchins, W. John (1999). "Retrospect and Prospect in Computer-based Translation." *Proceedings of MT Summit VII: MT in the Great Translation Era*, Singapore.

Isabelle, Pierre (1993). "Machine-aided Human Translation and the

Paradigm Shift." *Proceedings of MT Summit IV: International Cooperation for Global Communication*, Kobe, Japan, pp. 177–179.

Khadivi, Shahram, Richard Zens, and Hermann Ney (2006). "Integration of Speech to Computer-assisted Translation Using Finite-state Automata." *Proceedings of the Joint Conference of the International Committee on Computational Linguistics and the Association for Computational Linguistics* (*COLING/ACL-2006*), Sydney, Australia.

Knowles, Francis E. (1984). "Machine-aided Translation and Lexical Strategies." *Proceedings of the International Conference on the Methodology and Techniques of Machine Translation*, Cranfield Institute of Technology, England.

Langé, Jean-Marc, Éric Gaussier, and Béatrice Daille (1997). "Bricks and Skeletons: Some Ideas for the Near Future of MAHT." *Machine Translation*, Vol. 12, Nos. 1–2, pp. 39–51.

Langlais, Philippe, George Foster, and Guy Lapalme (2000). "Unit Completion for a Computer-aided Translation Typing System." *Machine Translation*, Vol. 15, No. 4, pp. 267–294.

Lessard, Gregory and Jean-Jacques Hamm (1991). "Computer-aided Analysis of Repeated Structures: The Case of Stendahl's Armance." *Literary and Linguistic Computing*, Vol. 6, No. 4, pp. 246–252.

Lewis, Terence (1999). "The Best of Both Worlds—Or Will Two Mongrels Ever Make a Pedigree." In *Translating and the Computer 21*. London: The Association for Information Management.

Lippmann, Erhard O. (1971). "An Approach to Computer-aided Translation." *IEEE Transactions on Engineering Writing and Speech*, Vol. 14, No. 1, pp. 10–33.

Lippmann, Erhard O. (1974). "On Computational Linguistics and Computer-aided Translation." *ATA Chronicle*, Vol. 3, No. 5, pp. 7–8.

Mathias, J. (1973). "Some Computer Functions for Machine-aided Translation." In S. Gould, ed., *Proceedings of the 1st International Symposium on Computers and the Chinese Input-output Systems*, Taipei, Taiwan: Academia Sinica, Vol. 13, pp. 589–592.

Melby, Alan K. (1987). "Creating an Environment for the Translator." In Margaret King, ed., *Machine Translation Today: The State of the Art*. Edinburgh: Edinburgh University Press, pp. 124–132.

Merkel, Magnus (1992). *Recurrent Patterns in Technical Documentation*. Department of Computer and Information Science, Linköping University, Sweden.

Merkel, Magnus (1993). "When and Why Should Translations Be Reused." *Papers from the XIII AAKKI Symposium*, Vaasa, Finland, pp. 139–149.

Neubert, Albrecht (1991). "Computer-aided Translation: Where Are the Problems?" *Target*, Vol. 3, No. 1, pp. 55–64.

Nirenburg, Sergei, Jaime G. Carbonell, Masaru Tomita, and Kenneth Goodman (1992). "Machine-aided Translation." In *Machine Translation: A Knowledge-based Approach*. San Matero, California: Morgan Kaufmann, pp. 191–204.

Scherf, Willi G. (1990). "Computer Assisted Translation, the Workstation and the Translator." In Hans Czap and Wolfgang Nedobity, eds., *Proceedings of the Conference on Terminology and Knowledge Engineering* (*TKE-90*). Frankfurt: INDEKS Verlag, pp. 574–578.

Shih, Chung-ling 史宗玲 (2004).〈結論與展望〉(Conclusions and Prospective).《電腦輔助翻譯》(*MT and TM*). Taipei: The Bookman Press, pp. 211–284.

Shih, Chung-ling (2004).《電腦輔助翻譯》(*MT and TM*). Taipei: The Bookman Press.

Shreve, Gregory M. (1990). "Requirements Analysis, Empirical Research and Prototyping in the Software Engineering of Workstations for Computer Assisted Translation." In Hans Czap and Wolfgang Nedobity, eds., *Proceedings of the Conference on Terminology and Knowledge Engineering* (*TKE-90*). Frankfurt: INDEKS Verlag, pp. 553–564.

Sinha, R. Mahesh K. (2005). "Integrating CAT and MT in AnglaBharti-II Architecture." *Proceedings of the 10th Workshop of the European Association for Machine Translation: Practical Applications of Machine Translation*, Budapest, Hungary, pp. 235–244.

St-Pierre, Paul (1990). "Computer-assisted Translator Training." In Marcel Thelen and Barbara Leeandowska-Tomaszczyk, eds., *Translation and Meaning*, *Part 1*. Maastricht: Euroterm, pp. 90–97.

Strossa, Petr (1994). "Machine Assisted Translation from English to a Slavic Language: What Linguistics and Programming Methodologies Can Do for It." *Machine Translation*, Vol. 9, No. 1, pp. 61–80.

Taylor, Chris and Anthony Baldry (2001). "Computer Assisted Text Analysis and Translation: A Functional Approach in the Analysis and Translation of Advertising Texts." In Erich H. Steiner and Colin Yallop, eds., *Exploring Translation and Multilingual Text Production:*

Beyond Content. Berlin and New York: Mouton de Gruyter, pp. 277–305.

Tomás, Jesús and Francisco Casacuberta (2006). "Statistical Phrase-based Models for Interactive Computer-assisted Translation." *Proceedings of the Joint Conference of the International Committee on Computational Linguistics and the Association for Computational Linguistics (COLING/ACL-2006)*, Sydney, Australia.

van Hahn, Walther and Galia Angelova (1994). "Providing Factual Information in MAT." *Machine Translation—Ten Years On: Proceedings of the 2nd International Conference Organised by Cranfield University*, Cranfield, England.

van Hahn, Walther (1997). "Knowledge Based Machine Aided Translation." *Proceedings of the 2nd Workshop of the European Association for Machine Translation: Language Technology in Your Organization?* University of Copenhagen, Copenhagen, Denmark, pp. 79–90.

Vauquois, Bernard (1983). "Automatic Computer Aided Translation and the Arabic Languages." *First Arab School on Science and Technology: Applied Arabic Linguistics and Signal and Information Processing*, Rabat, Morocco.

Warotamasikkhadit, Udom (1986). "Computer Aided Translation Project, University Sains Malaysia, Penang, Malaysia." *Machine Translation*, Vol. 1, No. 2, p. 113.

Wyckoff, S.K. (1979). "Computer-assisted Translation: Mainframe to Microprocessor." *Proceedings of the 19th IEEE Computer Society International Conference (COMPCON-79)*, Seattle, Washington, DC, USA, pp. 472–476.

Productivity

Bowker, Lynne (2005). "Productivity vs. Quality? A Pilot Study on the Impact of Translation Memory Systems." *Localization Focus*, Vol. 4, No. 1, pp. 13–20.

Champollion, Yves (2003). "Convergence in CAT: Blending MT, TM, OCR and SR to Boost Productivity." In *Translating and the Computer 25*. London: The Association for Information Management.

Flanagan, Mary A. and Friederike Bruckert (1997). "MT from the

Production Perspective." *Proceedings of MT Summit VI*, San Diego, California, USA.
Gomez, Pedro, Tom Shapiro, and Jaap van der Meer (2003). "Productivity & ROI: Doing More with Less." *Proceedings of the Localization World Conference 2003*, Seattle, Washington, DC, USA.
Hartmann, Walter K. (1999). "The Next Step: Moving to an Integrated MT System for High-volume Environments." *Proceedings of MT Summit VII: MT in the Great Translation Era*, Singapore.
Langlais, Philippe and Guy Lapalme (2002)."Trans Type: Development-evaluation Cycles to Boost Translator's Productivity." *Machine Translation*, Vol. 17, No. 2, pp. 77–98.
Lawson, Veronica (1984). "Users of Machine Translation System Report Increased Output." *Language Monthly*, Vol. 11, pp. 6–10.
Pym, Anthony (2004). "Quantity Speaks." *The Moving Text: Localization, Translation, and Distribution*. Amsterdam and Philadelphia: John Benjamins Publishing Company, pp. 87–109.
Tsujii, Jun-ichi (1997). "Machine Translation: Productivity and Conventionality of Language." In Ruslan Mitkov and Nicolas Nicolov, eds., *Recent Advances in Natural Language Processing*. Amsterdam and Philadelphia: John Benjamins Publishing Company, pp. 377–392.
Vallianatou, Fotini (2005). "CAT Tools and Productivity: Tracking Words and Hours." *Translation Journal*, Vol. 9, No. 4.

Reusability

Craig, Murray G., Bonnie J. Dorr, Jimmy Lin, Pecina Pavel, and Jan Hajic (2006). "Leveraging Reusability: Cost-effective Lexical Acquisition for Large-scale Ontology Translation." *Proceedings of the Joint Conference of the International Committee on Computational Linguistics and the Association for Computational Linguistics (COLING/ACL-2006)*, Sydney, Australia.
de Ilarraza, Arantxa Diaz, Aingeru Mayor, and Kepa Sarasola (2000). "Reusability of Wide-coverage Linguistic Resources in the Construction of Multilingual Technical Documentation." *Proceedings of the International Conference on Machine Translation and Multilingual Applications in the New Millenium (MT-2000)*, University of Exeter, England.
Grover, Claire and Richard Tobin (2006). "Rule-based Chunking and

Reusability." *Proceedings of the 5th International Conference on Language Resources and Evaluation* (*LREC-2006*), Genoa, Italy.
Merkel, Magnus (1993). "When and Why Should Translations Be Reused." *Papers from the XIII VAAKKI Symposium*, Vaasa, Finland, pp. 139–149.

Similarity

Boisson, Cecile (2000). "Applying Similarity Measures for Management of Textual Templates." *Proceedings of the 38th Annual Meeting of the Association for Computational Linguistics* (*ACL-2000*), Hong Kong.
Carroll, John B. (1990). "Repetitions Processing Using a Metric Space and the Angle of Similarity." Report No. 90/3, Centre for Computational Linguistics, University of Manchester Institute of Science and Technology, Manchester, England.
Chen, Francine, Ayman Farahat, and Thorsten Brants (2004). "Multiple Similarity Measures and Source-pair Information in Story Link Detection." *Proceedings of the Human Language Technology Conference/North American Chapter of the Association for Computational Linguistics Annual Meeting* (*HLT/NAACL-2004*), Boston, MA, USA.
Chotthan, Anirut, Chumsak Siboonr, Jantima Polpini, Rapeeporn Chamc, and Somnuk Puangpro (2004). "Automated Thai Text Summarization Using a Similarity Measure." *Proceedings of the International Conference on Natural Language Processing* (*ICON-2004*), International Institute of Information Technology, Hyderabad, India.
Hatzivassiloglou, Vasileios, Judith L. Klavans, and Eleazar Eskin (1999). "Detecting Text Similarity over Short Passages: Exploring Linguistic Feature Combinations via Machine Learning." *Proceedings of the Joint SIGDAT Conference on Empirical Methods in NLP and Very Large Corpora* (*EMNLP/VLC-99*), University of Maryland, College Park, MD, USA.
Hroza, Jiøí and Jan Žižka (2005). "Selecting Interesting Articles Using Their Similarity Based Only on Positive Examples." *Proceedings of the 6th International Conference on Intelligent Text Processing and Computational Linguistics* (*CICLing-2005*), Mexico City, Mexico, pp. 596–599.
Jiang, Jay J. and David W. Conrath (1997). "Semantic Similarity Based on Corpus Statistics and Lexical Taxonomy." *Proceedings of the*

International Conference on Research in Computational Linguistics (*ROCLING-X*), Academia Sinica, Taipei, Taiwan.

Lyon, Caroline, James Malcolm, and Bob Dickerson (2001). "Detecting Short Passages of Similar Text in Large Document Collections." *Proceedings of the 2001 Conference on Empirical Methods in Natural Language Processing* (*EMNLP-2001*), Carnegie Mellon University, Pittsburgh, PA, USA.

Patel, Agam and Dragomir R. Radev (2006). "Lexical Similarity Can Distinguish between Automatic and Manual Translations." *Proceedings of the 5th International Conference on Language Resources and Evaluation* (*LREC-2006*), Genoa, Italy.

Soler, Susana and Andrés Montoyo (2002). "A Proposal for WSD Using Semantic Similarity." *Proceedings of the 3rd International Conference on Intelligent Text Processing and Computational Linguistics* (*CICLing-2002*), Mexico City, Mexico.

Steinberger, Ralf, Bruno Pouliquen, and Johan Hagman (2002). "Cross-lingual Document Similarity Calculation Using the Multilingual Thesaurus EUROVOC." *Proceedings of the 3rd International Conference on Intelligent Text Processing and Computational Linguistics* (*CICLing-2002*), Mexico City, Mexico.

Tiedemann, Jorg (1999). "Automated Construction of Weighted String Similarity Measures." *Proceedings of the Joint SIGDAT Conference on Empirical Methods in NLP and Very Large Corpora* (*EMNLP/VLC-99*), University of Maryland, College Park, MD, USA.

Utsumi, Akira and Daisuke Suzuki (2006). "Word Vectors and Two Kinds of Similarity." *Proceedings of the Joint Conference of the International Committee on Computational Linguistics and the Association for Computational Linguistics* (*COLING/ACL-2006*), Sydney, Australia.

Wang, Yang 王洋, Qin Bing 秦兵, and Zheng Shifu 鄭實福 (2002).〈句子相似度計算在FAQ中的應用〉(Sentence Similarity for Frequently-asked Questions).《第一屆學生計算語言學研討會論文集》(*SWCL2002: First Students' Workshop on Computational Linguistics: Proceedings*), Institute of Computational Linguistics, Peking University, Beijing, China, pp. 175–181.

Zhou, Lina and James Liu (1997). "Similarity Comparison between Chinese Sentences." *Proceedings of the International Conference on Research in Computational Linguistics* (*ROCLING-X*), Academia Sinica, Taipei, Taiwan.

Computer-aided Translation History

Bruderer, Herbert E. (1975). "The Present State of Machine Translation and Machine-aided Translation." *ALLC Bulletin*, Vol. 3, No. 3, pp. 258–261.

Bruderer, Herbert E. (1977). "The Present State of Machine and Machine-assisted Translation." *Overcoming the Language Barrier*. Munich: Verlag Dokumentation, pp. 529–556.

Heyn, Matthias (1996). "Present and Future Needs in the CAT World." *The Localisation Industry Standards Association Forum Newsletter*, Vol. 5, No. 3, pp. 15–33.

Rolling, Loll (1978). "Computer-aided Translation Today and Tomorrow." *Proceedings of the FID Congress*, Edinburgh, Scotland.

Computer-aided Translation System

Bachut, Daniel and Nelson Verastegui (1984). "Software Tools for the Environment of a Computer Aided Translation System." *Proceedings of the 10th International Conference on Computational Linguistics (COLING-84)*, Stanford University, Stanford, California, USA, pp. 330–333.

Benton, Peter M. (1989). "A Practical Test of Machine Assisted Translation Systems and Agencies." In Deanna Lindberg Hammond, ed., *Coming of Age: Proceedings of the 30th Annual Conference of the American Translators Association*. Medford, New Jersey: Learned Information Inc., pp. 443–448.

Blekhman, Michael S., Maryna Byezhanova, Andrei Kursin, Igor Backlam, Alexander Kazakov, and Vladimir Petrov (1999). "Computer-aided Translation Tools for Russian, Ukrainian, and English." *Proceedings of MT Summit VII: MT in the Great Translation Era*, Singapore.

Boonkwan, Prachya and Asanee Kawtrakul (2002). "Plaesarn: Machine-aided Translation Tool for English-to-Thai." *Proceedings of the Workshop on Machine Translation in Asia (COLING-2002)*, Taipei, Taiwan.

Bowker, Lynne (2002). "Some Commercially Available CAT Tools." In *Computer-aided Translation Technology: A Practical Introduction*. Ottawa: University of Ottawa Press, pp. 157–174.

Gommlich, Klaus (1989). "The Control Potential of a Computer-aided Translation System." *Linguistische Studien*, No. 196, pp. 72–79.

Goto, Isao, Naoto Kato, Noriyoshi Uratani, Terumasa Ehara, Tadashi Kumano, and Hideki Tanaka (2003). "A Multi-language Translation Example Browser." *Proceedings of MT Summit IX*, New Orleans, Louisiana, USA.

Hodász, Gábor and Gábor Pohl (2005). "MetMorpho TM: A Linguistically Enriched Translation Memory." In Walther van Hahn, W. John Hutchins, and Cristina Vertan, eds., *Proceedings of the International Workshop on Modern Approaches in Translation Technologies*, Borovets, Bulgaria.

Hundt, Michael (1982). "Working with the Weidner Machine-aided Translation System." In Veronica Lawson, ed., *Practical Experience of Machine Translation*. Amsterdam: North-Holland Publishing Company, pp. 45–51.

Hutchins, W. John (1996)."Computer-based Translation Systems and Tools." *ELRA Newsletter*, Vol. 1, No. 4.

Kingscott, Geoffrey (1984). "ALPS Moves to Improve European Sales for Computer-aided Translation." *Language Monthly*, Vol. 14, pp. 27–29.

Langlais, Philippe, George Foster, and Guy Lapalme (2000). "Unit Completion for a Computer-aided Translation Typing System." *6th Applied Natural Language Processing Conference and 1st Meeting of the North American Chapter of the Association for Computational Linguistics: Proceedings of the Conferences, and Proceedings of the ANLP-NAACL-2000*, Student Research Workshop, Seattle, Washington, DC, USA, pp. 135–141.

Liu, Ting, Ming Zhou, Jianfeng Gao, Endong Xun, and Changning Huang (2000). "PENS: A Machine-aided English Writing System for Chinese Users." *Proceedings of the 38th Annual Meeting of the Association for Computational Linguistics* (*ACL-2000*), Hong Kong.

Marčuk, Jurij N. (1989). "Machine-aided Translation: A Survey of Current Systems." In Istvan S. Batori, Winfried Lenders, and Wolfgang Putschke, eds., *Computational Linguistics: An International Handbook on Computer-oriented Language Research and Applications*. Berlin and New York: De Gruyter, pp. 682–688.

Melby, Alan K. (1980). "Design and Implementation of a Computer-assisted Translation System." *British Computer Society, Natural Language Translation Specialist Group, Newsletter*, Vol. 9, pp. 7–19.

Melby, Alan K. (1983). "Computer Assisted Translation Systems: The

Standard Design and A Multi-level Design." *Proceedings of the ACL-NRL Conference on Applied Natural Language Processing*, Santa Monica, California, USA, pp. 174–177.
Sinha, R. Mahesh K. and Ajai Jain (2003). "AnglaHindi: An English to Hindi Machine-aided Translation System." *Proceedings of MT Summit IX*, New Orleans, Louisinan, USA.
Sumita, Eiichiro and Yutaka Tsutsumi (1988). "A Translation Aid System Using Flexible Text Retrieval Based on Syntax-matching." *Proceedings of the 2nd International Conference on Theoretical and Methodological Issues in Machine Translation of Natural Languages (TMI-88)*, Carnegie Mellon University, Center for Machine Translation, Pittsburgh, Pennsylvania, USA.
Sun, Le (2006). "A User Adaptive Framework for Computer-aided Translation Systems." *Programme of an International Conference on Computer-aided Translation: Theory and Practice*, Department of Translation, The Chinese University of Hong Kong, Hong Kong.
Zachary, Wayne W. (1979). "A Survey of Approaches and Issues in Machine-aided Translation Systems." *Computers and the Humanities*, Vol. 13, No. 1, pp. 13–28.

Déjà Vu

Austermühl, Frank (2001). "Deja Vu?—Translation Memories and Localization Tools." *Electronic Tools for Translators*. Manchester: St. Jerome Publishing Company, pp. 134–152.
Benis, Michael (1998). "Review of Atril Déjà Vu Version 2: The Happy Hoarder." *Translation Journal*, Vol. 2, No. 1.
Benis, Michael (2003). "Much More Than Memories—Review of Atril Déjà Vu Version 3." *ITI Bulletin*, November–December.
Benito, Daniel and Celia Rico (1999). *Deja Vu. Productivity System for Translators. (Deja Vu Manual)*. Atril Software. (http://www.atril.com/)
Wassmer, Thomas (2003). "Review of Comparative Review of Four Localization Tools: Déjà Vu, MULTILIZER, MultiTrans and TRANS Suite 2000." *Multilingual Computing and Technology*, Vol. 14, No. 3.

IBM Translation Manager

Falcone, Suzanne (1998). "Translation Aid Software: Four Translation

Memory Programs Reviewed." *Translation Journal*, Vol. 2, No. 1.
Jornitz, G. and A. Lüdde (1999). "OTELO WP AP.7. Architecture: Enabling IBM Machine Translation." (http://www-4.ibm.com/software/ad/translat/tm/otelo/lmt1.htm)
Jornitz, G., A. Lüdde, and G. Schmidt (1999). "OTELO WP TM.6. Common TM Interface Format: Integration of IBM Translation Manager with Logos Machine Translation." (http://www-4.ibm.com/software/ad/translat/tm/otelo/lmt2.htm)
Pashley, Joyce (1995). "Using IBM Translation Manager: An SCO Experience." In *Translating and the Computer 17*. London: The Association for Information Management.

OmegaT

Prior, Marc (2003). "Close Windows. Open Doors." *Translation Journal*, Vol. 7, No. 1.

SDL

Hummel, Jochen (2005). "TM, TRADOS and SDL. What's Next?" In *Translating and the Computer 27*. London: The Association for Information Management.
Lawlor, Terry (2006). "SDL International: Optimizing Global Information Flows—Enhance Your Brand, Improve Your Customer's Experience and Shorten Time-to-market." *Proceedings of the Localization World Conference*, Barcelona, Spain.
McClure, Steve (2004). "SDL Crafts a More Complete Solution for Translations." In *Executive Insights*. Framingham, MA: IDC.
Nogueira, Danilo (2005). "From Shoebox to SQL." *Translation Journal*, Vol. 9, No. 1.
Waβmer, Thomas (2003). "SDLX™ Translation Suite 2003." *Translation Journal*, Vol. 7, No. 3.

Trados

Avery, Cate (1999). "Case Study: Trados Software and Trade Mark Translations for the EU." In *Translating and the Computer 21*. London: The Association for Information Management.

Berry, Mark (1996). "Trados Translator's Workbench." *Proceedings of the 2nd Conference of the Association for Machine Translation in the Americas: Expanding MT Horizons (AMTA-2)*, Montreal, Quebec, Canada, pp. 285–289.

Boehme, Ulrich and Svetlana Svetova (2001). "An Integrated Solution: Applying PROMT Machine Translation Technology, Terminology Mining, And TRADOS's TWB Translation Memory to SAP Content Translation." In Bente Maegaard, ed., *Proceedings of MT Summit VIII: Machine Translation in the Information Age*, Santiago de Composetela, Spain.

Carroll, Sarah (2000). "Introducing the TRADOS Workflow Development." In *Translating and the Computer 22*. London: The Association for Information Management.

Garcia, Ignacio and Vivian Stevenson (2005). "TRADOS and the Evolution of Language Tools: The Rise of the De Facto TM Standard —And Its Future with SDL." *Multilingual Computing and Technology*, Vol. 16, No. 7.

Gerasimov, Andrei (2002). "Trados—Is It a Must?" *Translation Journal*, Vol. 6, No. 4.

Hummel, Jochen (2005). "TM, TRADOS and SDL. What's Next?" In *Translating and the Computer 27*. London: The Association for Information Management.

Pym, John (1999). "Report on the Implementation of the TRADOS Workbench Translation Memory System in the CERN Translation Service and Assessment of Results after One Year of Use." European Organization for Nuclear Research, European Laboratory for Particle Physics, CERN.

Qiu, Kerry (2006). "New Features of SDL Trados 2006: A Tutorial." *Programme of an International Conference on Computer-aided Translation: Theory and Practice*, Department of Translation, The Chinese University of Hong Kong, Hong Kong.

Raff, Galina (2000). "Reviews. Translation Tools: TRADOS Translation Solution Freelance Edition." *MultiLingual Computing and Technology*, Vol. 11, No. 1, pp. 25–28.

Raff, Galina (2002). "Review of TRADOS 5.5 Translation Memory Software." *Multilingual Computing and Technology*, Vol. 13, No. 8.

Shih, Chung-ling (2006). "Training in the Use of TRADOS." In *Helpful*

Assistance to Translators: MT & TM. Taipei: Bookman Books Ltd., pp. 152–193.
Shih, Chung-ling (2006). "Using the Tool of Trados WinAlign to Teach the Translation Equivalence Concept." In *Helpful Assistance to Translators: MT & TM*. Taipei: Bookman Books Ltd., pp. 276–298.
Shih, Chung-ling (2006). "Using Trados's WinAlign Tool to Teach the Translation Equivalence Concept." *Translation Journal*, Vol. 10, No. 2.
Shih, Chung-ling (2006). "Using Trados TagEditor in the Teaching of Web Translation." In *Helpful Assistance to Translators: MT & TM*. Taipei: Bookman Books Ltd., pp. 321–343.
Wessel, Rainer (1995). "Trados: MultiTerm for Windows User Report." *Proceedings of the 3rd TermNet Symposium: Terminology in Advanced Microcomputer Applications—Recent Advances and User Reports* (*TAMA-94*), Vienna, Austria, pp. 87–105.

Wordfast

Condak, Milan (2004). "Workflow in Wordfast and Invisible Machine Translator." *International Journal of Translation*, Vol. 16, No. 1, pp. 87–108.
Gerasimov, Andrei (2001). "An Effective and Inexpensive Translation Memory Tool." *Translation Journal*, Vol. 5, No. 3.
Gerasimov, Andrei (2002). "Review of Wordfast (Windows Version)." *Multilingual Computing and Technology*, Vol. 13, No. 1.
Miller, François (2002). "Review of Wordfast (Macintosh Version)." *Multilingual Computing and Technology*, Vol. 13, No. 1.

WordFisher

Környei, Tibor (2000). "WordFisher for MS Word: An Alternative to Translation Memory Programs for Freelance Translators?" *Translation Journal*, Vol. 4, No. 1.

Yaxin

Liu Bin 劉彬 and Tan Waiyuan 譚外元 (2002). 〈雅信CAT和東方快車機器翻譯軟件的分析及建議〉 (Analysis and Suggestions for Yaxin CAT and

Oriental Express).《第一屆學生計算語言學研討會論文集》(*SWCL2002: First Students' Workshop on Computational Linguistics: Proceedings*), Institute of Computational Linguistics, Peking University, Beijing, China, pp. 215–221.

Computer-aided Translation System Evaluation

Arnold, Doug J., Lorna Balkan, R. Lee Humphreys, Seity Meijer, and Louisa Sadler (1994). "Evaluating MT Systems." *Machine Translation: An Introductory Guide*. Manchester and Oxford: NCC Blackwell, pp. 165–181.

Dyson, Mary C. and Jean Hannah (1987). "Towards a Methodology for the Evaluation of Machine-assisted Translation Systems." *Computers and Translation*, Vol. 2, No. 3, pp. 163–176.

Falcone, Suzanne (1998). "Translation Aid Software: Four Translation Memory Programs Reviewed." *Translation Journal*, Vol. 2, No. 1.

Hovy, Eduard H., Margaret King, and Andrei Popescu-Belis (2002). "Computer-aided Specification of Quality Models for MT Evaluation." *LREC 2002: 3rd International Conference on Language Resources and Evaluation*, Las Palmas de Gran Canaria, Spain, pp. 1239–1246.

King, Margaret, Yorick Wilks, Sture Allen, Ulrich Heid, and Doris Albisser (1993). "Evaluation of MT Systems." In Sergei Nirenburg, ed., *Progress in Machine Translation*. Amsterdam: IOS and Tokyo: Ohmsha, pp. 267–282.

Lin Mao-sung 林茂松 and Chen Pin-chi 陳蘋琪 (2006). "An Analysis of Fuzzy Match Function in CAT Software—A Case Study on Three Professional Technical Translators in Taiwan." (電腦輔助翻譯軟體中模糊比對功能之效益評估：以目前台灣翻譯市場專業英中技術文件翻譯者為例). *Proceedings of the 10th Taiwan Symposium on Translator and Interpreter Training: Modelling the Processes of Translation and Interpretation*〈第十屆台灣國際口筆譯教學研討會 · 如何將口筆譯過程模型化〉, Fu Jen University, Taiwan.

Rico Pérez, Celia (2001). "Reproducible Models for CAT Tools Evaluation: A User-oriented Perspective." In *Translating and the Computer 23*. London: The Association for Information Management.

Computer-aided Translation Teaching

Altanero, Tim (2006). "Access to Resources and Accreditation—The Training Providers' View." In *Translating and the Computer 28*. London: The Association for Information Management.

Ball, R. V. (1989). "Computer-assisted Translation and the Modern Languages Curriculum." *The CTISS File* 8, pp. 52–55.

Bowker, Lynne (2003). "Towards a Collaborative Approach to Corpus Building in the Translation Classroom." In Brian James Baer and Geoffrey S. Koby, eds., *Beyond the Ivory Tower: Rethinking Translation Pedagogy*. Amsterdam and Philadelphia: John Benjamins Publishing Company, pp. 193–210.

Kenny, Dorothy and Andy Way (2001). "Teaching Machine Translation and Translation Technology: A Contrastive Study." In Bente Maegaard, ed., *Proceedings of MT Summit VIII: Machine Translation in the Information Age*, Santiago de Compostela, Spain, pp. 13–17.

Kenny, Dorothy and Sharon O'Brien (2001). "In Dublin's Fair City: Teaching Translation Technology at Dublin City University." *Language International*, Vol. 13, No. 5, pp. 20–23.

Koby, Geoffrey S. and Brian James Baer (2003). "Task-based Instruction and the New Technology: Training Translators for the Modern Language Industry." In Brian James Baer and Geoffrey S. Koby, eds., *Beyond the Ivory Tower: Rethinking Translation Pedagogy*. Amsterdam and Philadelphia: John Benjamins Publishing Company, pp. 211–227.

Kosaka, Takashi and Masaki Itagaki (2003). "Building a Curriculum for Japanese Localization Translators." In Brian James Baer and Geoffrey S. Koby, eds., *Beyond the Ivory Tower: Rethinking Translation Pedagogy*. Amsterdam and Philadelphia: John Benjamins Publishing Company, pp. 229–249.

Mata, Pastor M. (2004). "Two Paradoxes and a Few Errors in CAT Training Today: A Realistic Approach." *Proceedings of the International Conference on Translating with Computer-assisted Technology: Changes in Research, Teaching, Evaluation and Practice*, Rome, Italy.

Merten, Pascaline (1998). "Some Reflections on the Teaching of CAT." In *Translating and the Computer 20*. London: The Association for Information Management.

Schäffner, Christina (2004). "Squaring the Circle—The Contribution of Universities to the Needs of the Profession." *Programme of the Annual Conference of the Association of Translation Companies: Getting in Shape for the Future—Working towards a New Environment for the Translation Profession*, School of Oriental and African Studies, University of London, England.

Schellekens, Philida (2004). "Developing a Futurc Translation Workforce." *Programme of the Annual Conference of the Association of Translation Companies: Getting in Shape for the Future—Working towards a New Environment for the Translation Profession*, School of Oriental and African Studies, University of London, England.

Shei, Chi-chiang (2002). "Incorporating Translation Memory System into the Teaching of Translation: CJU Experience." *Proceedings of Twenty-first Century Innovation in Technology: Teaching Translation and Interpretation*. Tainan: CJU, pp. 46–64.

Shei, Chi-chiang (2002). "Teaching MT through Pre-editing: Three Case Studies." *Proceedings of the 6th Workshop of the European Association for Machine Translation: Teaching Machine Translation*, Manchester, England, pp. 89–98.

Shih, Chung-ling (2002). *Theory and Application of MT/MAHT Pedagogy*. Taipei: The Crane Publishing Co. Ltd.

Shih, Chung-ling (2006). "Computer-aided Translation Teaching of the Passive Construction." *Programme of an International Conference on Computer-aided Translation: Theory and Practice*, Department of Translation, The Chinese University of Hong Kong, Hong Kong.

Shuttleworth, Mark (2002). "Combining MT and CAT on a Technology-oriented Translation Masters." *Proceedings of the 6th EAMT Workshop on Teaching Machine Translation*, Manchester, England, pp. 123–130.

Zanettin, Federico (2001). "Machine (Assisted) Translation for Translator Training." *Rassegna Italiana di Linguistica Applicata*, pp. 241–262.

Computer-aided Translation Tool

Blekhman, Michael S., Arndrei Kursin, and Igor Fagradiants (1998). "Machine-aided Translation Tools for Slavonic Languages." *Machine Translation Review*, No. 7, pp. 20–27.

Blekhman, Michael S., Maryna Byezhanova, Andrei Kursin, Igor Backlam, Alexander Kazakov, and Vladimir Petrov (1999).

"Computer-aided Translation Tools for Russian, Ukrainian, and English." *Proceedings of MT Summit VII: MT in the Great Translation Era*, Singapore.

Chang, Baobao, Yu Shiwen, and Kang Byeong-Kwu (2006). "Developing CAT Tools for Translating Chinese Scientific Monographs." *Programme of an International Conference on Computer-aided Translation: Theory and Practice*, Department of Translation, The Chinese University of Hong Kong, Hong Kong.

Drugan, Joanna (2006). "The Effects of Computer-assisted Translation Tools on Translation Quality." *Proceedings of the 6th Portsmouth Translation Conference: Translation Technologies and Culture*, School of Languages and Area Studies, University of Portsmouth, England.

Kenny, Dorothy (1999). "CAT Tools in an Academic Environment: What Are They Good for?" *Target*, Vol. 11, No. 1, pp. 65–82.

Maegaard, Bente (1997). "Evaluation of Language Tools." In *Translating and the Computer 19*. London: The Association for Information Management.

O'Brien, Sharon (1998). "Practical Experience of Computer-aided Translation Tools in the Software Localization Industry." In Lynne Bowker, Michael Cronin, Dorothy Kenny, and Jennifer Pearson, eds., *Unity in Diversity? Current Trends in Translation Studies*. Manchester: St. Jerome Publishing, pp. 115–122.

❖ PART 7 ❖

Computer/Machine Translation

Computer Translation

Arnold, Doug J., Lorna Balkan, R. Lee Humphreys, Seity Meijer, and Louisa Sadler (1994). *Machine Translation: An Introductory Guide*. Manchester and Oxford: NCC Blackwell.

Arnold, Doug Steven Krauwer, Louis des Tombe, and Louisa Sadler (1988). "'Relaxed' Compositionality in Machine Translation." *Proceedings of the 2nd International Conference on Theoretical and Methodological Issues in Machine Translation of Natural Languages (TMI-88)*, Carnegie Mellon University, Center for Machine Translation, Pittsburgh, Pennsylvania, USA.

Bar-Hillel, Yehoshua (1953). "Machine Translation." *Computers and Automation*, Vol. 2, No. 5, pp. 1–6.

Bel'skaya, I. K. (1957). "Machine Translation of Languages." *Research*, Vol. 10, No. 10, pp. 383–389.

Bernhard, Ursula (1995). "Machine Translation—Success or Failure?" In *Translating and the Computer 17*. London: The Association for Information Management.

Blekhman, Michael S. (2001). "General Remarks on Machine Translation." *International Journal of Translation*, Vol. 13, Nos. 1–2, pp. 65–80.

Bond, Francis (2002). "Toward a Science of Machine Translation." *Proceedings of the 9th International Conference on Theoretical and Methodological Issues in Machine Translation (TMI-2002)*, Keihanna, Japan.

Bond, Francis (2002). "Toward a Science of Machine Translating." *Journal of the Asia-Pacific Association for Machine Translation*, No. 32, pp. 12–20.

Booth, Andrew D. (1956). "The Practical Realisation of Machine Translation." *Methodos: Linguaggio e Cibernetica*, Vol. 8, Nos. 29–30, pp. 23–33.

Booth, Andrew D. (1958). *Aspects of Translation*. London: Secker and Warburg.

Booth, Andrew D. (1958). "Progress in Machine Translation." *New Scientist*, Vol. 4, pp. 665–667.

Booth, Andrew D. (1958). "Translating Machines." *International Social Science Bulletin*, Vol. 10, pp. 55–62.

Booth, Andrew D., ed. (1967). *Machine Translation*. Amsterdam: North-Holland Publishing Company.

Brekke, Magnar and Ronald Skarsten (1988). "Machine Translation: A Threat or a Promise?" In Catriona Picken, ed., *Translating and the Computer 9: Potential and Practice*. London: The Association for Information Management, pp. 1–79.

Brinkmann, Karl-Heinz (1978). "Perspectives of Machine Translation." *Nachrichten Für Dokumentation*, Vol. 29, No. 3, pp. 104–108.

Bruderer, Herbert E. (1977). *Handbook of Machine Translation*. Amsterdam: North-Holland Publishing Company.

Bruderer, Herbert E. (1978). *Handbook of Machine Translation and Machine-aided Translation: Automatic Translation of Natural Languages and Multilingual Terminology Data Banks*. Amsterdam: North-Holland Publishing Company.

Bull, William E. (1952). "Frequency Problems in MT." *Proceedings of the M.I.T. Conference on Mechanical Translation,* Massachusetts Institute of Technology, Cambridge, MA, USA.

Carbonell, Jaime G. and Masaru Tomita (1985). *New Approaches to Machine Translation*. Pittsburgh: Carnege-Mellon University.

Carbonell, Jaime G. (1994). "Partnerships in Machine Translation." *Technology Partnerships for Crossing the Language Barrier: 1st Conference of the Association for Machine Translation in the Americas*, Columbia, Maryland, USA.

Chafe, Wallace L. (1974). "An Approach to Verbalization and Translation by Machine." *The Finite String*, Vol. 11, Nos. 3–4, p. 10.

Chan, Sin-wai (2006). "A Review of the Literature on Computer(-aided) Translation: 1948–2006." *Programme of an International Conference on Computer-aided Translation: Theory and Practice*, Department of Translation, The Chinese University of Hong Kong, Hong Kong.

Chandioux, John and Annette Grimaila (1996). "'Specialized' Machine Translation." *Expanding MT Horizons: Proceedings of the 2nd Conference of the Association for Machine Translation in the Americas*, Montreal, Quebec, Canada. Washington, DC: AMTA, pp. 206–211.

Chang, Jason S. (2006). "Machine Translation Fast Forward." *Programme of an International Conference on Computer-aided Translation: Theory and Practice*, Department of Translation, The Chinese University of Hong Kong, Hong Kong.

Chao, Yuen Ren 趙元任 (1964). "Translation without Machine." In Horace G. Lunt, ed., *Proceedings of the 9th International Congress of Linguists*. The Hague: Mouton, pp. 504–510.

Chen, Kuang-hua and Hsin-hsi Chen (1995). "Machine Translation: An Integrated Approach." *Proceedings of the 6th International Conference on Theoretical and Methodological Issues in Machine Translation* (*TMI-95*), Leuven, Belgium, pp. 287–294.

Chen, Mingyuan 陳明遠 (1982). 〈機器翻譯〉 (Machine Translation). 《語言文字的信息處理》 (*Information Processing of Spoken and Written Languages*). Shanghai: Knowledge Press, pp. 126–163.

Chong, Leighton (1994). "Intellectual Property Rights and MT." *Technology Partnerships for Crossing the Language Barrier: 1st Conference of the Association for Machine Translation in the Americas*, Columbia, Maryland, USA.

Connell, Charles (1986). "Machine Translation Poised for Growth." *High Technology*, No. 6, pp. 53–55.

Copeland, Charles, Jacques Durand, Steven Krauwer, and Bente Maergaard (1991). *Studies in Machine Translation and Natural Language Processing*, Vols. 1–2. Luxembourg: Office for Official Publications of the European Community.

Cowie, Jim and Sergei Nirenburg (2002). "Two Experiments in Situated MT." *Proceedings of the 9th International Conference on Theoretical and Methodological Issues in Machine Translation* (*TMI-2002*), Keihanna, Japan, pp. 22–30.

Cullingford, Richard E. and Boyan A. Onyshkevych (1987). "An Experiment in Lexicon-driven Machine Translation." In Sergei Nirenburg, ed., *Machine Translation: Theoretical and Methodological Issues*. Cambridge: Cambridge University Press, pp. 278–301.

de Cea, Guadalupe Aguado and Antonio Pareja-Lora (2000). "A Competition Model for the Generation of Complementation Patterns in Machine Translation." *International Journal of Translation*, Vol. 12, Nos. 1–2, pp. 25–37.

Delavenay, Emile (1960). *An Introduction to Machine Translation.* London: Thames and Hudson.

Ding, Samuel S. Y. 丁紹源 (1991). 〈機器翻譯〉 (Machine Translation). In Liu Ching-chih 劉靖之, ed., 《翻譯工作者手冊》 (*A Translator's Handbook*). Hong Kong: The Commercial Press, pp. 263–297.

Ding, Yuan and Martha Palmer (2006). "Better Learning and Decoding for Machine Translation Using SXYZ." *Proceedings of the 7th Biennial Conference of the Association for Machine Translation in the Americas*

(*AMTA-2006*)*: Visions for the Future of Machine Translation*, Boston Marriott, Cambridge, MA, USA.

Dorr, Bonnie J. (1993). *Machine Translation: A View from the Lexicon*. Cambridge, MA: MIT Press.

Dostert, B. H., et al. (1979). *Machine Translation*. The Hague: Mouton.

Dreyfus, Hubert (1972). *What Computers Can't Do: A Critique of Artificial Reason*. New York: Harper and Row.

Edmundson, Harold P., ed. (1961). *Proceedings of the National Symposium on Machine Translation*. Englewood Cliffs: Prentice-Hall.

Feng, Zhiwei 馮志偉 (1985).〈機器翻譯的困難性和它的工程化〉(The Difficulty and Engineering of Machine Translation).《情報學報》(*Journal of the China Society for Scientific and Technical Information*), Vol. 4, No. 5.

Feng, Zhiwei (1985).〈機器翻譯和它的「代」〉(Machine Translation and Its "Generations").《文字改革》(*Language Reform*), No. 5.

Feng, Zhiwei (1994).〈機器翻譯的工程化〉(The Engineering of Machine Translation). In《自然語言機器翻譯新論》(*New Essays on Machine Translation of Natural Languages*). Beijing: Language Press, pp. 224–242.

Feng, Zhiwei (1994).〈機器翻譯與邏輯〉(Machine Translation and Logic).《自然語言機器翻譯新論》(*New Essays on Machine Translation of Natural Languages*). Beijing: Language Press, pp. 61–78.

Feng, Zhiwei (2004).〈機器翻譯概述〉(Introduction to Machine Translation).《機器翻譯研究》(*Studies on Machine Translation*). Beijing: China Translation and Publishing Corporation, pp. 1–34.

Feng, Zhiwei (2004).《機器翻譯研究》(*Studies on Machine Translation*). Beijing: China Translation and Publishing Corporation.

Garvin, Paul L. (1958). "Machine Translation: Report." *Proceedings of the 8th International Congress of Linguists*. Oslo: Oslo University Press, pp. 502–510.

Garvin, Paul L. (1967). "Machine Translation—Fact or Fancy?" *Datamation*, Vol. 13, No. 4, pp. 29–31.

Garvin, Paul L., ed. (1972). *On Machine Translation: Selected Papers*. The Hague: Mouton.

Gaspari, Federico (2003). "Relevance of Parallel Corpora to the Latest Developments of Machine Translation and Computer-assisted Translation." *International Journal of Translation*, Vol. 15, No. 1, pp. 27–41.

Gerber, Laurie (2001). "Working toward Success in Machine Translation." In Bente Maegaard, ed., *Proceedings of MT Summit VIII: Machine Translation in the Information Age*, Santiago de Compostela, Spain.

Gerber, Laurie (2003). "Recent Evolution in Machine Translation." *Proceedings of the Localization World Conference 2003*, Seattle, Washington, DC, USA.

Gobeil, Fernand (1981). *Machine Translation Feasibility Study*. Ottawa: Translation Bureau, Secretary of State.

Gode, Alexander (1968). "Reflections on Machine Translation." *American Translator*, Vol. 2, No. 4, pp. 4–6.

Goshawke, Walter, Ian D. K. Kelly, and J. David Wigg (1987). *Computer Translation of Natural Language*. Wilmslow: Sigma Press.

Gregoire, Jean-Francois (1981). "Translating and the Computer." *Meta*, Vol. 25, No. 3, pp. 366–367.

Grimaila, Annette (1992). "Made to Measure Solutions." In John Newton, ed., *Computers in Translation: A Practical Appraisal*. London and New York: Routledge, pp. 33–45.

Hacken, Pius Ten (2001). "Has There Been a Revolution in Machine Translation?" *Machine Translation*, Vol. 16, No. 1, pp. 1–19.

Harper, Kenneth E. (1963). "Machine Translation." In Thomas Seboek *et al.*, eds., *Current Trends in Linguistics*. The Hague: Mouton, Vol. 1, pp. 133–142.

Harris, Brian (1975). "Notation and Index for Informative Congruence in Translation." *Meta*, Vol. 20, No. 3, pp. 184–193.

Hatley, John (1995). "Demystifying the Implementation of MT." In *Translating and the Computer 17*. London: The Association for Information Management.

Hayes, John (1988). "The Three Faces of Joyce: Word Processors and Other Hardware Allegedly of Use to Translators." In Catriona Picken, ed., *Translating and the Computer 9: Potential and Practice*. London: The Association for Information Management, pp. 3–10.

Haynes, Colin (1998). "Why Is MT So Important?" *Breaking Down the Language Barriers*. London: The Association for Information Management, pp. 32–44.

Haynes, Colin (1998). *Breaking Down the Language Barriers*. London: The Association for Information Management.

Hays, David G. (1976). "Machine (Aided) Translation: Generalities and

Guides to Action." *American Journal of Computational Linguistics*, Vol. 46, pp. 84–88.

Hays, David G. (1977). "Machine Translation and Abstract Terminology." In P. J. Hopper, ed., *Studies in Descriptive and Historical Linguistics: Festschrift for Winfred P. Lehmann*. Amsterdam and Philadelphia: John Benjamins Publishing Company, pp. 95–108.

Henisz-Dostert, Bozena (1967). "Experimental Machine Translation." In William M. Austin, ed., *Papers in Linguistics in Honor of Léon Dostert*. The Hague: Mouton, pp. 57–91.

Henisz-Dostert, Bozena, R. Ross MacDonald, and Michael Zarechnak (1979). *Machine Translation*. The Hague: Mouton Publishers.

Hovy, Eduard (1997). "A Gentle Introduction to MT: Theory and Current Practice." *Proceedings of MT Summit VI*, San Diego, California, USA.

Hovy, Eduard and Deepak Ravichandran (2003). "Holy and Unholy Grails." *Proceedings of MT Summit IX*, New Orleans, Louisiana, USA.

Huang, Heyan 黃河燕 and Chen Zhaoxiong 陳肇雄 (1997).〈機器翻譯基本問題研究〉(A Study on the Fundamental Issues in Machine Translation).《語言文字應用》(*Applied Linguistics*), No. 3, pp. 101–104.

Huang, Long 黃龍 (1988). "Computerized Translation." *Translatology*. Shanghai: Jiangsu Education Press 江蘇教育出版社, pp. 443–474.

Humphreys, Lee R. (1992). "Is Machine Translation Actually Translation?" *Language International*, Vol. 4, No. 2, pp. 7–11.

Hutchins, W. John (1978). "Progress in Documentation: Machine Translation and Machine-aided Translation." *Journal of Documentation*, Vol. 34, No. 2, pp. 119–159.

Hutchins, W. John (1984). "Machine Translation and Machine-aided Translation." In William Frawley, ed., *Translation: Literary, Linguistic, and Philosophical Perspectives*. Cranbury, New Jersey: University of Delaware Press, pp. 93–149.

Hutchins, W. John (1986). *Machine Translation: Past, Present and Future*. Chichester: Ellis Horwood.

Hutchins, W. John and Harold L. Somers (1992). *An Introduction to Machine Translation*. London: Academic Press.

Hutchins, W. John (1995). "Machine Translation." In Chan Sin-wai and David E. Pollard, eds., *An Encyclopaedia of Translation: Chinese-English. English-Chinese*. Hong Kong: The Chinese University Press, pp. 591–602.

Hutchins, W. John (2003). "Has Machine Translation Improved? Some

Historical Comparisons." *Proceedings of MT Summit IX*, New Orleans, Louisiana, USA, pp. 181–188.

Institute of Scientific and Technical Information of China 中國科學技術信息研究所, ed. (1979).《機器翻譯論文選輯》(*Collected Papers on Machine Translation*). Beijing: Scientific and Technical Documents Publishing House 科學技術文獻出版社.

Isabelle, Pierre (1989). "Towards Reversible MT Systems." In Christian Rohrer, ed., *Proceedings of MT Summit II*, Munich, Germany, pp. 67–68.

Kay, Martin (1982). "Machine Translation." *American Journal of Computational Linguistics*, Vol. 8, No. 2, pp. 74–78.

Kent, Allen (1960). "Machine Literature Search and Translation: An Analytical Review." In Allen Kent, ed., *Information Retrieval and Machine Translation*. New York: Interscience, Vol. 1, pp. 213–226.

King, Margaret, ed. (1987). *Machine Translation Today: The State of the Art.* Edinburgh: Edinburgh University Press.

King, Margaret (1995). "An Introduction to MT." *Proceedings of MT Summit V: Machine Translation Conference, Exhibition and Tutorial*, Luxembourg.

Knowles, Francis E. (1979). "Re-emergence of Interest in Machine Translation (MT)." *Proceedings of the British Computer Society '79*, London, England.

Laffling, John (1991). *Towards High-precision Machine Translation: Based on Contrastive Textology*. Berlin and New York: Foris Publications.

Lamb, Sydney M. (1961). "Advances in Machine Translation." *New Scientist*, Vol. 9, pp. 260–261.

Lamb, Sydney M. (1965). "The Nature of the Machine Translation Problem." *Journal of Verbal Learning and Verbal Behavior*, Vol. 4, pp. 196–210.

Lawson, Veronica (1982). "Machine Translation and People." In Veronica Lawson, ed., *Practical Experience of Machine Translation*. Amsterdam: North-Holland Publishing Company, pp. 3–9.

Lawson, Veronica (1983). "Machine Translation." In Catriona Picken, ed., *The Translator's Handbook*. London: The Association for Information Management, pp. 81–88.

Lawson, Veronica (1985). "Machine Translation in Practice." In Patricia E. Newman, ed., *American Translators Association Conference—1985*. Medford, New Jersey: Learned Information, Inc., p. 125.

Lawson, Veronica (1986). "The Background to Practical Machine Translation." *Computers and Translation*, Vol. 1, No. 2, pp. 109–112.

Lawson, Veronica (1988). "A Translator's Map of Machine Translation." In Muriel Vasconcellos, ed., *Technology as Translation Strategy*. New York: State University of New York at Binghamton, pp. 105–115.

Leermakers, René (1994). "Software Engineering Aspects." In M. T. Rosetta, *Compositional Translation*. Dordrecht: Kluwer Academic Publishers, pp. 417–423.

Lehmann, Winfred P. (1961). "Machine Translation: Agent of the Humanities." *University of Texas Studies in Literature and Language*, Vol. 3, No. 2, pp. 163–170.

Lehmann, Winfred P. (1965). "An Experiment in Machine Translation." *The Graduate Journal*, Vol. 7, No. 1, pp. 111–131.

Lehmann, Winfred P. (1969). "Machine Translation." In Archibald A. Hill, ed., *Linguistics Today*. New York: Basic Books, pp. 188–197.

Lehmann, Winfred P. and Rolf A. Stachowitz (1978). "Machine Translation." In Jack Belzer, Albert G. Holzman, and Allen Kent, eds., *Encyclopedia of Computer Science and Technology*. New York, Basel: Marcel Dekker, Vol. 10, pp. 151–164.

Lehmann, Winfred P. (1987). "Four Decades with the Computer." *IDEAL*, Vol. 2, pp. 5–16.

Lehmann, Winfred P. (1987). "The Context of Machine Translation." *Computers and Translation*, Vol. 2, No. 3, pp. 135–157.

Lehmann, Winfred P. (1989). "Machine Translation: Achievements, Problems, Promise." In James E. Alatis, ed., *Georgetown University Round Table on Languages and Linguistics 1989*. Washington, DC: Georgetown University Press, pp. 385–392.

León, Marjorie (1997). "Making MT Work for You." *Proceedings of MT Summit VI*, San Diego, California, USA.

Levy, M. (1989). "Consolidating a Machine Translation Project at the Post-implementation Stage." In Deanna Lindberg Hammond, ed., *Coming of Age: Proceedings of the 30th Annual Conference of the American Translators Association*. Medford, New Jersey: Learned Information, Inc., pp. 479–488.

Liro, Joseph (1987). "On Computers, Translation, and Stanislaw Lem." *Computers and Translation*, Vol. 2, No. 2, pp. 89–104.

Liu, Shuying 劉淑英 and Zhao Qidi 趙啟迪 (1993).〈機器翻譯的優勢與局

限〉(Advantages and Limitations of Machine Translation).《中國翻譯》(*Chinese Translators Journal*), No. 2, pp. 53–54, 61.

Liu, Yongquan 劉湧泉, Gao Zhushun 高祖舜, and Liu Zhuo 劉倬 (1965).《機器翻譯淺說》(*An Introduction to Machine Translation*). Beijing: Popular Science Press 科普出版社.

Locke, William N. and Andrew D. Booth, eds. (1955). *Machine Translation of Languages: Fourteen Essays*. Cambridge, MA: Technology Press of the Massachusetts Institute of Technology.

Locke, William N. (1956). "Translation by Machine." *Scientific America*, Vol. 194, pp. 29–33.

Locke, William N. (1975). "Machine Translation." In Allen Kent, Harold Lancour, and Jay E. Daily, eds., *Encyclopedia of Library and Information Science*. New York: Marcel Dekker, Vol. 16, pp. 414–444.

Loh, Shiu-chang 樂秀章 (1975).《電腦翻譯》(*Machine Translation*). Hong Kong: The Chinese University of Hong Kong.

Macdonald, Neil (1954). "Language Translation by Machine—A Report of the First Successful Trial." *Computers and Automation*, Vol. 3, No. 2, pp. 6–10.

Maegaard, Bente (1997). "Whither MT?" *Proceedings of MT Summit VI*, San Diego, California, USA.

Masterman, Margaret (1979). "The Essential Skills to Be Acquired for Machine Translation." In Barbara M. Snell, ed., *Translating and the Computer*. Amsterdam: North-Holland Publishing Company, pp. 159–180.

Masterman, Margaret (1982). "The Limits of Innovation in Machine Translation." In Veronica Lawson, ed., *Practical Experience of Machine Translation*. Amsterdam: North-Holland Publishing Company, pp. 163–186.

Maxwell, Dan, Klaus Schubert, and Toon Witkam, eds. (1988). *New Directions in Machine Translation*. Dordrecht-Holland: Foris Publications.

Melamed, I. Dan, Ryan Green, and Joseph P. Turian (2003). "Precision and Recall of Machine Translation." *Proceedings of the Human Language Technology and North American Chapter of Association of Computational Linguistics 2003* (*HLT/NAACL-2003*), Edmonton, Alberta, Canada.

Melby, Alan K. (1995). *The Possibility of Language: A Discussion of the*

Nature of Language, with Implications for Human and Machine Translation. Amsterdam: John Benjamins Publishing Company.
Nagao, Makoto (1979). "Machine Translation." *Information Processing Society of Japan*, Vol. 20, No. 10, pp. 896–902.
Nagao, Makoto (1989). "A Perspective on Machine Translation." In Norman D. Cook, trans., *Machine Translation: How Far Can It Go?* Oxford: Oxford University Press, pp. 49–61.
Nagao, Makoto (1989). *Machine Translation: How Far Can It Go?*, translated by Norman D. Cook. Oxford: Oxford University Press.
Nagao, Makoto (1993). "Machine Translation: What Have We To Do?" *Proceedings of MT Summit IV: International Cooperation for Global Communication*, Kobe, Japan, pp. 3–7.
Nagao, Makoto (2004). "Towards a New MT Paradigm." *AAMT Journal*, No. 36.
National Physical Laboratory, ed. (1962). *1961 International Conference on Machine Translation of Languages and Applied Language Analysis: Proceedings of the Conference Held at the National Physical Laboratory, Teddington, Middlesex, on 5th, 6th, 7th and 8th September*. London: Her Majesty's Stationery Office.
Ney, Hermann (2003). "Have We Found the Holy Grail?" *Proceedings of MT Summit IX*, New Orleans, Louisiana, USA.
Nida, Eugene A. (1964). "Machine Translation." *Toward a Science of Translating*. Leiden: E. J. Brill, pp. 252–264.
Nirenburg, Sergei, ed. (1987). *Machine Translation: Theoretical and Methodological Issues—Studies in Natural Language Processing*. Cambridge: Cambridge University Press.
Nirenburg, Sergei, Jaime G. Carbonell, Masaru Tomita, and Kenneth Goodman (1992). "MT in a Nutshell." *Machine Translation: A Knowledge-based Approach*. San Matero, California: Morgan Kaufmann, pp. 1–39.
Nirenburg, Sergei, Stephen Beale, Stephen Helmreich, Kavi Mahesh, Evelyne Viegas, and Rémi Zajac (1996). "Two Principles and Six Techniques for Rapid MT Development." *Proceedings of the 2nd Conference of the Association for Machine Translation in the Americas (AMTA-96)*. Montreal, Quebec, Canada, pp. 96–105.
Nirenburg, Sergei, Harold L. Somers, and Yorick Wilks, eds. (2003). *Readings in Machine Translation*. Cambridge, MA: The MIT Press.
Oettinger, Anthony G. (1961). "A New Theory of Translation and Its

Application." In Harold P. Edmundson, ed., *Proceedings of the National Symposium on Machine Translation*. London: Prentice-Hall, pp. 363–366.

Perschke, Sergei (1968). "Machine Translation—The Second Phase of Development." *Endeavour*, Vol. 27, pp. 97–100.

Perusse, D. (1983). "Machine Translation." *ATA Chronicle*, Vol. 12, No. 8, pp. 6–8.

Picken, Catriona, ed. (1986). *Translating and the Computer 7*. London: The Association for Information Management.

Picken, Catriona, ed. (1987). *Translating and the Computer 8: A Profession on the Move*. London: The Association for Information Management.

Picken, Catriona, ed. (1988). *Translating and the Computer 9: Potential and Practice*. London: The Association for Information Management.

Picken, Catriona, ed. (1990). *Translating and the Computer 11: Preparing for the Next Decade*. London: The Association for Information Management.

Reifler, Erwin (1962). "Machine Translation." *Bulletin of the Medical Library Association*, Vol. 50, No. 3, pp. 473–480.

Richardson, Steve (2003). "Have We Found the Holy Grail?" *Proceedings of MT Summit IX*, New Orleans, Louisiana, USA.

Rolling, L. N. (1979). "The Second Birth of Machine Translation." *Proceedings of the 7th Cranfield International Conference on Mechanised Information Storage and Retrieval Systems*, Cranfield, England

Rolling, L. N. (1981). "The Second Birth of Machine Translation: A Timely Event for Database Suppliers and Operators." *Electronic Publishing Revue*, Vol. 1, No. 3.

Ruffino, J. Richard (1982). "Coping with Machine Translation." In Veronica Lawson, ed., *Practical Experience of Machine Translation*. Amsterdam: North-Holland Publishing Company, pp. 57–60.

Sabourin, Conrad F. and Laurent R. Bourbeau (1994). *Machine Translation, Aids to Translation, Speech Translation: Bibliography*, 2 Vols. Montreal: Infolingua Inc.

Schütz, Jörg (2001). "Blueprints for MT Evolution: Reflections on 'Elements of Style'." In Bente Maegaard, ed., *Proceedings of MT Summit VIII: Machine Translation in the Information Age*, Santiago de Compostela, Spain.

Shen, Libin, Anoop Sarkar, and Franz Josef Och (2004). "Discriminative Reranking for Machine Translation." *Proceedings of the Human Language Technology Conference/North American Chapter of the Association for Computational Linguistics Annual Meeting (HLT/NAACL-2004)*, Boston, MA, USA.

Shen, Yan 沈艷 (2004). 〈機器翻譯及其與語言障礙的矛盾〉 (Machine Translation and Its Contradiction with Language Barrier). 《外語教學與翻譯》 (*Foreign Languages Teaching and Translating*), Vol. 3, No. 3, p. 111.

Shih, Chung-ling (2006). *Helpful Assistance to Translators: MT & TM*. Taipei: Bookman Books Ltd.

Shih, Chung-ling (2006). "Theoretical Studies of MT and TM." *Helpful Assistance to Translators: MT & TM*. Taipei: Bookman Books Ltd., pp. 2–34.

Slocum, Jonathan (1980). "An Experiment in Machine Translation." *Proceedings of the 18th Annual Meeting of the Association for Computational Linguistics and Parasession on Topics in Interactive Discourse*, University of Pennsylvania, USA, pp. 163–167.

Snell, Barbara M., ed. (1979). *Translating and the Computer*. Amsterdam: North-Holland Publishing Company.

Somers, Harold L. (2000). "Machine Translation." In Russel Dale, Hermann Moisl, and Harold L. Somers, eds., *Handbook of Natural Language Processing*. New York: Marcel Dekker, pp. 329–346.

Somers, Harold L., ed. (2003). *Computers and Translation: A Translator's Guide*. Amsterdam and Philadelphia: John Benjamins Publishing Company.

Somers, Harold L. (2003). "Machine Translation." In Kemal Oflazer, ed., *Language Engineering for Lesser-studied Languages*. Amsterdam: IOS Press, pp. 173–221.

Stachowitz, Rolf A. (1971). "Requirements for Machine Translation: Problems, Solutions, Prospects." In Winfred P. Lehmann and Rolf A. Stachowitz, eds., *Feasibility Study on Fully Automatic High Quality Translation*. New York: Rome Air Development Center, pp. 409–532.

Strauss, S. (1983). "Teaching Computers to Translate Languages." *Toronto Globe and Mail*, Vol. 18, No. 3.

ten Hacken, Pius (1998). "Science and Technology in Machine Translation." *Proceedings of the 10th European Summer School on*

Logic, Linguistics and Information: Workshop on Machine Translation, Saarbrücken, Germany.

Toma, Peter (1974). "Computer Translation: In Its Own Right." *Kommunikationsforschung und Phonetik*, pp. 155–164.

Trujillo, Arturo (1999). "Introduction." *Translation Engines: Techniques for Machine Translation*. Berlin and New York: Springer Verlag, pp. 3–7.

Tucker, Allen B. (1984). "A Perspective on Machine Translation: Theory and Practice." *Communications of the Association for Computing Machinery*, Vol. 27, No. 4, pp. 322–329.

Tucker, Allen B. and Sergei Nirenburg (1984). "Machine Translation: A Contemporary View." *Annual Review of Information Science and Technology*, Vol. 19, pp. 129–160.

Vella, Alfred and Dominic Vella (1994). "The Implications of Machine Translation." *Machine Translation—Ten Years On: Proceedings of the 2nd International Conference Organised by Cranfield University*, Cranfield, England.

Wang, Wei, Kevin Knight, and Daniel Marcu (2006). "Capitalizing Machine Translation." *Proceedings of the Human Language Technology Conference—Annual Meeting of the North American Chapter of the Association for Computational Linguistics* (*HLT-NAACL-2006*), New York, USA.

Wilss, Wolfram (1982). "Machine Translation." *The Science of Translation: Problems and Methods*. Tubingen: Gunter Narr Verlag, pp. 228–250.

Wilss, Wolfram (1993). "Basic Concepts of MT." *Meta*, Vol. 38, No. 3, pp. 403–413.

Wood, Paul F. (2000). "What Do Translators Do? And What Machines Can Not." *The Linguist*, Vol. 39, No. 5, pp. 133–135.

Xiong, Yunxiang 熊允享 (1986).〈機器翻譯縱橫談〉(An Outline of Machine Translation).《上海科技翻譯》(*Shanghai Journal of Translators for Science and Technology*), No. 1, pp. 32, 38.

Zajac, Rémi (1998). "MT Express." *Proceedings of the 10th European Summer School on Logic, Linguistics and Information: Workshop on Machine Translation*, Saarbrücken, Germany.

Zampolli, Antonio (1989). "Introduction to the Special Section on Machine Translation." *Literary and Linguistic Computing*, Vol. 4, No. 3, pp. 182–184.

Zarechnak, Michael (1980). "Machine Translation." *The ATA Chronicle*, Vol. 9, Nos. 3–4, pp. 10–12.
Zetzsche, Jost (2006). "TM and MT." *Proceedings of the 7th Biennial Conference of the Association for Machine Translation in the Americas (AMTA-2006): Visions for the Future of Machine Translation*, Boston Marriott, Cambridge, MA, USA.
Zhang, Hao, Liang Huang, Daniel Gildea, and Kevin Knight (2006). "Synchronous Binarization for Machine Translation." *Proceedings of the Human Language Technology Conference—Annual Meeting of the North American Chapter of the Association for Computational Linguistics* (*HLT-NAACL-2006*), New York, USA.
Zhang, Liangping (1995). "Practical Considerations of Machine Translation." In Chan Sin-wai and David E. Pollard, eds., *An Encyclopaedia of Translation: Chinese-English. English-Chinese*. Hong Kong: The Chinese University Press, pp. 603–609.
Zhao, Tiejun 趙鐵軍 (2000).《機器翻譯原理》(*Principles of Machine Translation*). Harbin: Harbin Institute of Technology Press 哈爾濱工業大學出版社.
Zhuang, Xinglai (2002). "The Emerging Role of Translation Experts in the Coming MT Era." *Translation Journal*, Vol. 6, No. 4.

Computer Translation: Approaches

Bangalore, Srinivas and Giuseppe Riccardi (2001). "A Finite-state Approach to Machine Translation." *Proceedings of the 2nd Meeting of the North American Chapter of the Association for Computational Linguistics: Language Technologies 2001* (*NAACL-2001*), Pittsburgh, PA, USA.
Bernth, Arendse and Michael C. McCord (2003). "A Hybrid Approach to Deriving Selectional Preferences." *Proceedings of MT Summit IX*, New Orleans, Louisiana, USA.
Carbonell, Jaime G. and Masaru Tomita (1985). "New Approaches to Machine Translation." In Sergei Nirenburg, ed., *Proceedings of the Conference on Theoretical and Methodological Issues in Machine Translation of Natural Languages* (*TMI-85*). Hamilton, New York: Colgate University, pp. 59–74.
Chellamuthu, K. C. (1986). "A Practical Approach to Machine Translation

System (Russian to Tamil)." *International Journal of Dravidian Linguistics* (*Trivandrum*), Vol. 15, No. 1, pp. 86–95.

Chen, Kuang-hua and Chen Hsin-hsi (1995). "Machine Translation: An Integration Approach." *Proceedings of the 6th International Conference on Theoretical and Methodological Issues in Machine Translation* (*TMI-95*), Leuven, Belgium, pp. 287–294.

Eberle, Kurt (2001). "FUDR-based MT, Head Switching and the Lexicon." In Bente Maegaard, ed., *Proceedings of MT Summit VIII: Machine Translation in the Information Age*, Santiago de Compostela, Spain.

Garvin, Paul L. (1980). "The Fulcrum Approach—Twelve Years Later." *International Forum on Information and Documentation*, Vol. 5, No. 2, pp. 27–29.

Grishman, Ralph and Michiko Kosaka (1992). "Combining Rationalist and Empiricist Approaches to Machine Translation." *Proceedings of the 4th International Conference on Theoretical and Methodological Issues in Machine Translation of Natural Languages: Empiricist vs. Rationalist Methods in MT* (*TMI-92*), Montreal, Quebec, Canada, pp. 263–274.

Le Feal, Karla Dejean (1990). "A Different Approach to Machine Translation." *Meta*, Vol. 35, No. 4, pp. 710–719.

Liang, Percy, Alexandre Bouchard-Côté, Ben Taskar, and Dan Klein (2006). "An End-to-end Discriminative Approach to Machine Translation." *Proceedings of the Joint Conference of the International Committee on Computational Linguistics and the Association for Computational Linguistics* (*COLING/ACL-2006*), Sydney, Australia.

Mandelblit, Nili (1993). "Machine Translation: A Cognitive Linguistics Approach." *Proceedings of the 5th International Conference on Theoretical and Methodological Issues in Machine Translation of Natural Languages: MT in the Next Generation* (*TMI-93*), Kyoto, Japan, pp. 117–130.

McKinnon, Alastair and Per Bondesen (1978). "Computer Translation: A Different Approach." *Revue de l'organisation Internationale pour l'etude des langues anciennes part ordinateur*, Vol. 2, pp. 37–46.

Proszéky, Gábor (2005). "An Approach to Machine Translation via the Rule-to-rule Hypothesis." *Proceedings of the 10th Annual Conference of the European Association for Machine Translation* (*EAMT-2005*), Budapest, Hungary.

Trujillo, Arturo (1999). "Other Approaches to MT." *Translation Engines:*

Techniques for Machine Translation. Berlin and New York: Springer Verlag, pp. 203–220.
Zajac, Rémi (1990). "A Relational Approach to Translation." *Proceedings of the 3rd International Conference on Theoretical and Methodological Issues in Machine Translation of Natural Languages* (*TMI-90*), Linguistics Research Center, University of Texas at Austin, Austin, Texas, USA, pp. 235–254.

Case-based Computer Translation

Wang, Jiande, Chen Zhaoxiong, and Huang Heyan (2001). "Intelligent Case Based Machine Translation System." *Proceedings of the 2nd International Conference on Intelligent Text Processing and Computational Linguistics* (*CICLing-2001*), Mexico City, Mexico.

Concept-based Computer Translation

Gu, Liang and Gao Yuqing (2004). "On Feature Selection in Maximum Entropy Approach to Statistical Concept-based Speech-to-speech Translation." *Proceedings of the International Workshop on Spoken Language Translation* (*IWSLT 2004*), Kyoto, Japan.
Horiguchi, Atsushi, Seiji Tsuchiya, Kazuhide Kojima, Hirokazu Watabe, and Tsukasa Kawaoka (2002). "Constructing a Sensuous Judgment System Based on Conceptual Processing." *Proceedings of the 3rd International Conference on Intelligent Text Processing and Computational Linguistics* (*CICLing-2002*), Mexico City, Mexico.
Ripplinger, Bärbel (1994). "Concept-based Machine Translation and Interpretation." *Machine Translation—Ten Years On: Proceedings of the 2nd International Conference Organised by Cranfield University*, Cranfield, England.
Zhou, Joe and Liu Weiqian (2000). "A Real-time Integration of Concept-based Search and Summarization of Chinese Websites." *Proceedings of the Joint Sigdat Conference on Empirical Methods in Natural Language Processing and Very Large Corpora* (*EMNLP/VLC-2000*), Hong Kong University of Science and Technology, Hong Kong.

Constraint-based Computer Translation

Arnold, Doug J. and Louisa Sadler (1990). "The Theoretical Basis of MiMo." *Machine Translation*, Vol. 5, No. 3, pp. 195–222.

Eberle, Kurt, Walter Kasper, and Christian Rohrer (1992). "Contextual Constraints for Machine Translation." *Proceedings of the 4th International Conference on Theoretical and Methodological Issues in Machine Translation of Natural Languages* (*TMI-92*), Montreal, Quebec, Canada, pp. 213–224.

Kaplan, Ronald M., Klaus Netter, Jürgen Wedekind, and Annie Zaenen (1989). "Translation by Structural Correspondences." *Proceedings of 4th Conference of the European Chapter of the Association for Computational Linguistics*, Manchester, England, pp. 272–281.

Klein, Ewan (2000). "A Constraint-based Approach to English Prosodic Constituents." *Proceedings of the 38th Annual Meeting of the Association for Computational Linguistics* (*ACL-2000*), Hong Kong.

Maruyama, Hiroshi (1991). "JAUNT: A Constraint Solver for Disjunctive Feature Structures." *Proceedings of the Conference of the Association for Computational Linguistics and Chinese Language Processing* (*ROCLING-IV*), National Chiao-Tung University, Hsin-Chu, Taiwan.

Sadler, Louisa and Doug Arnold (1992). "A Constraint-based Approach to Translating Anaphoric Dependencies." *Proceedings of 14th International Conference on Computational Linguistics* (*COLING-92*), Nantes, France, pp. 728–734.

Context-based Computer Translation

Carbonell, Jaime G., Steve Klein, David Miller, Mike Steinbaum, Tomer Grassiany, and Jochen Frey (2006). "Context-based Machine Translation." *Proceedings of the 7th Biennial Conference of the Association for Machine Translation in the Americas* (*AMTA-2006*)*: Visions for the Future of Machine Translation*, Boston Marriott, Cambridge, MA, USA.

Galley, Michel, Jonathan Graehl, Kevin Knight, Daniel Marcu, Steve DeNeefe, Wei Wang, and Ignacio Thayer (2006). "Scalable Inference and Training of Context-rich Syntactic Translation Models." *Proceedings of the Joint Conference of the International Committee on Computational Linguistics and the Association for Computational Linguistics* (*COLING/ACL-2006*), Sydney, Australia.

Hovy, Eduard, Margaret King, and Andrei Popescu-Belis (2002). "Principles of Context-based Machine Translation Evaluation." *Machine Translation*, Vol. 17, No. 1, pp. 43–75.

Kjærsgaard, Poul Soren (1987). "REFTEX—A Context-based Translation Aid." *Proceedings of the 3rd Conference of the European Chapter of the Association for Computational Linguistics (EACL-87)*, Copenhagen, Denmark, pp. 109–112.

Corpus-based Computer Translation

Carl, Michael (2000). "A Model of Competence for Corpus-based Machine Translation." *Proceedings of the 18th International Conference on Computational Linguistics (COLING-2000)*, Saarbrucken, Germany.

Chang, Jing-Shin and Keh-Yih Su (1993). "A Corpus-based Statistics-oriented Transfer and Generation Model for Machine Translation." *Proceedings of the 5th International Conference on Theoretical and Methodological Issues in Machine Translation of Natural Languages: MT in the Next Generation (TMI-93)*, Kyoto, Japan, pp. 3–14.

Danielsson, Pernilla, and Katarina Mühlenbock (1998). "When Stålhandske Becomes Steelglove: A Corpus Based Study of Names in Parallel Texts." In David L. Farwell, Laurie Gerber, and Eduard Hovy, eds., *Machine Translation and the Information Soup*. Berlin: Springer Verlag, pp. 266–274.

Dash, Niladri Sekhar (2004). "Issues Involved in the Development of a Corpus-based Machine Translation System." *International Journal of Translation*, Vol. 16, No. 2, pp. 57–79.

Güvenir, H. Altay and Aysegul Tunç (1996). "Corpus-based Learning of Generalized Parse Tree Rules for Translation." In Gord McCalla, ed., *New Directions in Artificial Intelligence: Proceedings of the 11th Biennial Conference of the Canadian Society for Computational Studies of Intelligence*. Toronto: Springer Verlag, pp. 121–131.

Juola, Patrick (1994). "A Psycholinguistic Approach to Corpus-based Machine Translation." *CSNLP 1994: 3rd Conference on the Cognitive Science of Natural Language Processing*, Dublin, Ireland.

Juola, Patrick (1997). "Corpus-based Acquisition of Transfer Functions Using Psycholinguistic Principles." In Daniel B. Jones and Harold L. Somers, eds., *New Methods in Language Processing*. London: UCL Press, pp. 207–218.

Kenny, Dorothy (2001). "Turning Corpus Linguistics on Its Head: Corpus-based Translation Studies." *Lexis and Creativity in Translation:*

A Corpus-based Study. Manchester: St. Jerome Publishing, pp. 48–72.

Komatsu, Eiji, Cui Jin, and Hiroshi Yasuhara (1993). "A Mono-lingual Corpus-based Machine Translation of the Interlingua Method." *Proceedings of the 5th International Conference on Theoretical and Methodological Issues in Machine Translation of Natural Languages: MT in the Next Generation* (*TMI-93*), Kyoto, Japan, pp. 24–46.

Langkilde, Irene and Kevin Knight (1998). "Generation that Explores Corpus-based Statistical Knowledge." *Proceedings of the 36th Annual Meeting of the Association for Computational Linguistics and 17th International Conference on Computational Linguistics* (*COLING-ACL-98*), Montreal, Quebec, Canada, pp. 704–710.

Regnier-Prost, Sylvie and Eva Dauphin (1995). "The Prerequisites of MT for an Industrial User: A Corpus-based Approach." *Proceedings of MT Summit V: Machine Translation Conference, Exhibition and Tutorial*, Luxembourg.

Sadler, Victor (1990). "A Corpus-based Measure of Semantic Proximity." In Marcel Thelen and Barbara Leeandowska-Tomaszczyk, eds., *Translation and Meaning, Part 1*. Maastricht: Euroterm, pp. 70–78.

Su, Keh-Yih and Jing-Shin Chang (1992). "Why Corpus-based Statistics-oriented Machine Translation." *Proceedings of the 4th International Conference on Theoretical and Methodological Issues in Machine Translation of Natural Languages: Empiricist vs. Rationalist Methods in MT* (*TMI-92*), Montreal, Quebec, Canada, pp. 249–262.

Su, Keh-Yih, Chang Jing-Shin, and Una Hsu Yu-Ling (1995). "A Corpus-based Two-way Design for Parameterized MT Systems: Rationale, Architecture and Training Issues." *Proceedings of the 6th International Conference on Theoretical and Methodological Issues in Machine Translation* (*TMI-95*), Leuven, Belgium, pp. 334–354.

Wantanabe, Hideo, Sadao Kurohashi, and Eiji Aramak (2000). "Finding Structural Correspondences from Bilingual Parsed Corpus for Corpus-based Translation." *Proceedings of the 18th International Conference on Computational Linguistics* (*COLING-2000*), Saarbrucken, Germany.

Widdows, Dominic and Scott Cederberg (2003). "Monolingual and Bilingual Concept Visualization from Corpora." *Proceedings of the Human Language Technology and North American Chapter of Association of Computational Linguistics 2003* (*HLT/NAACL-2003*), Edmonton, Alberta, Canada.

Data-driven Computer Translation

Hearne, Mary and Andy Way (2003). "Seeing the Wood for the Trees: Data-oriented Translation." *Proceedings of MT Summit IX*, New Orleans, Louisiana, USA, pp. 165–172.

Hearne, Mary and Andy Way (2006). "Disambiguation Strategies for Data-oriented Translation." *Proceedings of the 11th Workshop of the European Association for Machine Translation: Machine Translation/ Translation Aids—Tools to Increase Quality and to Save Money*, the University of Oslo, Oslo, Norway.

Richardson, Stephen D. (2004). "Machine Translation of Online Product Support Articles Using a Data-driven MT System." In Robert E. Frederking and Kathryn B. Taylors, eds., *Machine Translation: From Real Users to Research*. Berlin: Springer Verlag, pp. 246–251.

Example-based Computer Translation

Akiba, Yasuhiro, Megumi Ishii, Hussein Almuallim, and Shigeo Kaneda (1995). "Learning English Verb Selection Rules from Hand-made Rules and Translation Examples." *Proceedings of the 6th International Conference on Theoretical and Methodological Issues in Machine Translation* (*TMI-95*), Leuven, Belgium, pp. 206–220.

Akiba, Yasuhiro, Hiromi Nakaiwa, Satoshi Shirai, and Yoshifumi Ooyama (2000). "Interactive Generalization of a Translation Example Using Queries Based on a Semantic Hierarchy." *Proceedings of the 12th IEEE International Conference on Tools with Artificial Intelligence* (*ICTAI-2000*), Vancouver, BC, Canada.

Al-Adhaileh, Mosleh Hmoud, and Enya Kong Tang (1998). "A Flexible Example-based Parser Based on the SSTC." *Proceedings of the 36th Annual Meeting of the Association for Computational Linguistics and 17th International Conference on Computational Linguistics* (*COLING-ACL-98*), Montreal, Quebec, Canada, pp. 687–693.

Al-Adhaileh, Mosleh Hmoud, and Enya Kong Tang (1999). "Example-based Machine Translation Based on the Synchronous SSTC Annotation Schema." *Proceedings of MT Summit VII: MT in the Great Translation Era*, Singapore, pp. 244–249.

Andriamanankasina, Tantely, Kenji Araki, and Koji Tochinai (1999). "Example-based Machine Translation of Part-of-speech Tagged

Sentences by Recursive Division." *Proceedings of MT Summit VII: MT in the Great Translation Era*, Singapore, pp. 509–517.
Andriamanankasina, Tantely, Kenji Araki, and Koji Tochinai (2003). "EBMT of POS-tagged Sentences via Inductive Learning." In Michael Carl and Andy Way, eds., *Recent Advances in Example-based Machine Translation*. Dordrecht: Kluwer Academic Publishers, pp. 225–252.
Aramaki, Eiji, Sadao Kurohashi, Satoshi Sato, and Hideo Watanabe (2001). "Finding Translation Correspondences from Parallel Parsed Corpus for Example-based Translation." In Bente Maegaard, ed., *Proceedings of MT Summit VIII: Machine Translation in the Information Age*, Santiago de Compostela, Spain, pp. 27–32.
Aramaki, Eiji, Sadao Kurohashi, Hideki Kashioka, and Hideki Tanaka (2003). "Word Selection for EBMT Based on Monolingual Similarity and Translation Confidence." *Proceedings of the Human Language Technology and North American Chapter of Association of Computational Linguistics 2003* (*HLT/NAACL-2003*), Edmonton, Alberta, Canada.
Aramaki, Eiji and Sadao Kurohashi (2004). "Example-based Machine Translation Using Structural Translation Examples." *Proceedings of the International Workshop on Spoken Language Translation* (*IWSLT-2004*), Kyoto, Japan.
Aramaki, Eiji, Sadao Kurohashi, Hideki Kashioka, and Naoto Kato (2005). "Probabilistic Model for Example-based Machine Translation." *Proceedings of MT Summit X*, Phuket, Thailand.
Armstrong, Stephen (2006). "Improving the Quality of Automated DVD Subtitles via Example-based Machine Translation (EBMT)." In *Translating and the Computer 28*. London: The Association for Information Management.
Auerswald, Marko (2000). "Example-based Machine Translation with Templates." In Wolfgang Wahlster, ed., *Verbmobil: Foundations of Speech-to-speech Translation*. Berlin: Springer Verlag, pp. 418–427.
Bandyopadhyay, Sivaji (2000). "An Example Based MT System in News Items Domain from English to Indian Languages." *Proceedings of the International Conference on Machine Translation and Multilingual Applications in the New Millenium* (*MT-2000*), University of Exeter, England.
Bandyopadhyay, Sivaji (2001). "An Example Based MT System in News

Items Domain from English to Indian Languages." *Machine Translation Review*, No. 12, pp. 7–10.
Bond, Francis and Satoshi Shirai (2003). "A Hybrid Rule and Example-based Method for Machine Translation." In Michael Carl and Andy Way, eds., *Recent Advances in Example-based Machine Translation*. Dordrecht: Kluwer Academic Publishers, pp. 211–224.
Brockett, Chris, Takako Aikawa, Anthony Aue, Arul Menezes, Chris Quirk, and Hisami Suzuki (2002). "English-Japanese Example-based Machine Translation Using Abstract Linguistic Representation." *Proceedings of the Workshop on Machine Translation in Asia (COLING-2002)*, Taipei, Taiwan.
Brown, Ralf D. (1996). "Example-based Machine Translation in the Pangloss System." *Proceedings from the 16th International Conference on Computational Linguistics (COLING-96)*. Copenhagen, Denmark, pp. 169–174.
Brown, Ralf D. (1997). "Automated Dictionary Extraction for 'Knowledge-free' Example-based Translation." *Proceedings of the 7th International Conference on Theoretical and Methodological Issues in Machine Translation (TMI-97)*, St. John's College, Santa Fe, New Mexico, USA, pp. 111–118.
Brown, Ralf D. (1999). "Adding Linguistic Knowledge to a Lexical Example-based Translation System." *Proceedings of the 8th International Conference on Theoretical and Methodological Issues in Machine Translation (TMI-99)*, Chester, England, pp. 22–32.
Brown, Ralf D. (2000). "Automated Generalization of Translation Examples." *Proceedings of the 18th International Conference on Computational Linguistics (COLING-2000)*, Saarbrücken, Germany, pp. 125–131.
Brown, Ralf D. (2001). "Transfer-rule Induction for Example-based Translation." In Bente Maegaard, ed., *Proceedings of MT Summit VIII: Machine Translation in the Information Age*, Santiago de Compostela, Spain.
Brown, Ralf D. (2003). "Clustered Transfer Rule Induction for Example-based Translation." In Michael Carl and Andy Way, eds., *Recent Advances in Example-based Machine Translation*. Dordrecht: Kluwer Academic Publishers, pp. 287–305.
Brown, Ralf D. (2004). "A Modified Burrows-Wheeler Transform for Highly Scalable Example-based Translation." In Robert E. Frederking

and Kathryn B. Taylors, eds., *Machine Translation: From Real Users to Research*. Berlin: Springer Verlag, pp. 27–36.

Carl, Michael, Leonid L. Iomdin, and Oliver Streiter (1998). "Towards a Dynamic Linkage of Example-based and Rule-based Machine Translation." *Proceedings of the 10th European Summer School on Logic, Linguistics and Information: Workshop on Machine Translation*, Saarbrücken, Germany.

Carl, Michael (1999). "Inducing Translation Templates for Example-based Machine Translation." *Proceedings of MT Summit VII: MT in the Great Translation Era*, Singapore, pp. 250–258.

Carl, Michael and Silvia Hansen (1999). "Linking Translation Memories with Example-based Machine Translation." *Proceedings of MT Summit VII: MT in the Great Translation Era*, Singapore, pp. 617–624.

Carl, Michael (2000). "Combining Invertible Example-based Machine Translation with Translation Memory Technology." In John S. White, ed., *Envisioning Machine Translation in the Information Future*. Berlin: Springer Verlag, pp. 127–136.

Carl, Michael, Catherine Pease, Leonid L. Iomdin, and Oliver Streiter (2000). "Towards a Dynamic Linkage of Example-based and Rule-based Machine Translation." *Machine Translation*, Vol. 15, No. 3, pp. 223–257.

Carl, Michael (2001). "Recent Research in the Field of Example-based Machine Translation." *Proceedings of the 2nd International Conference on Intelligent Text Processing and Computational Linguistics (CICLing-2001)*, Mexico City, Mexico.

Carl, Michael and Andy Way (2003). "Introduction." In Michael Carl and Andy Way, eds., *Recent Advances in Example-based Machine Translation*. Dordrecht: Kluwer Academic Publishers, pp. xvii–xxxi.

Carl, Michael and Andy Way (2003). *Recent Advances in Example-based Machine Translation*. Dordrecht: Kluwer Academic Publishers.

Carroll, J. J. (1990). *Repetitions Processing Using a Metric Space and the Angle of Similarity*. Report No. 90/3, Centre for Computational Linguistics, University of Manchester Institute of Science and Technology, Manchester, England.

Cavalli-Sforza, Violetta, Ralf D. Brown, Jaime G. Carbonell, Peter J. Jansen, and Jae Dong Kim (2004). "Challenges in Using an Example-based MT System for a Translational Digital Government Project." *Proceedings of the 9th Workshop of the European Association for*

Machine Translation: Broadening Horizons of Machine Translation and Its Applications, Foundation for International Studies, Malta, pp. 33–42.

Chatterjee, Niladri (2001). "A Statistical Approach for Similarity Measurement between Sentences for EBMT." *Proceedings of a Symposium on Translation Support Systems* (*STRANS-2001*), Kanpur, India.

Cicekli, Ilyas and H. Altay Güvenir (2003). "Learning Translation Templates from Bilingual Translation Examples." In Michael Carl and Andy Way, eds., *Recent Advances in Example-based Machine Translation*. Dordrecht: Kluwer Academic Publishers, pp. 255–286.

Collins, Bróna and Pádraig Cunningham (1995). "A Methodology for Example-based Machine Translation." *Proceedings of the 4th Conference on the Cognitive Science of Natural Language Processing* (*CSNLP-95*), Dublin, Ireland.

Collins, Bróna and Pádraig Cunningham (1996). "Adaptation-guided Retrieval in EBMT: A Case-based Approach to Machine Translation." In Ian Smith and Boi Faltings, eds., *Advances in Case-based Reasoning: 3rd European Workshop, EWCBR-96*. Berlin: Springer Verlag, pp. 91–104.

Collins, Bróna, Pádraig Cunningham, and Tony Veale (1996). "An Example-based Approach to Machine Translation." *Proceedings of the 2nd Conference of the Association for Machine Translation in the Americas: Expanding MT Horizons* (*AMTA-2*), Montreal, Quebec, Canada, pp. 1–13.

Collins, Bróna and Pádraig Cunningham (1997). "Adaptation-guided Retrieval: Approaching EBMT with Caution." *Proceedings of the 7th International Conference on Theoretical and Methodological Issues in Machine Translation* (*TMI-97*), St. John's College, Santa Fe, New Mexico, USA, pp. 119–126.

Collins, Bróna (1998). *Example-based Machine Translation: An Adaptation-guided Retrieval Approach*. PhD Thesis, Trinity College, Dublin, Ireland.

Collins, Bróna and Harold L. Somers (2003). "EBMT Seen as Case-based Reasoning." In Michael Carl and Andy Way, eds., *Recent Advances in Example-based Machine Translation*. Dordrecht: Kluwer Academic Publishers, pp. 115–153.

Cranias, Lambros, Harris Papageorgiou, and Stelios Piperidis (1994). "A

Matching Technique in Example-based Machine Translation." *Proceedings of the 15th International Conference on Computational Linguistics* (*COLING-94*), Kyoto, Japan, pp. 100–104.

Cranias, Lambros, Harris Papageorgiou, and Stelios Piperidis (1997). "Example Retrieval from a Translation Memory." *Natural Language Engineering*, Vol. 3, pp. 255–277.

Doi, Takao, Eiichiro Sumita, and Hirofumi Yamamoto (2003). "Adaptation Using Out-of-domain Corpus within EBMT." *Proceedings of the Human Language Technology and North American Chapter of Association of Computational Linguistics 2003* (*HLT/NAACL-2003*), Edmonton, Alberta, Canada.

Dorr, Bonnie J. (1993). "Translation Examples." *Machine Translation: A View from the Lexicon*. Cambridge, MA: MIT Press, pp. 285–317.

Elița, Natalia and Antonina Birladeanu (2005). "An Application Using Example-based Machine Translation." In Walther van Hahn, W. John Hutchins, and Cristina Vertan, eds., *Proceedings of the International Workshop on Modern Approaches in Translation Technologies*, Borovets, Bulgaria.

Furuse, Osamu and Hitoshi Iida (1992). "An Example-based Method for Transfer-driven Machine Translation." *Proceedings of the 4th International Conference on Theoretical and Methodological Issues in Machine Translation of Natural Languages: Empiricist vs. Rationalist Methods in MT* (*TMI-92*), Montreal, Quebec, Canada, pp. 139–150.

Furuse, Osamu and Hitoshi Iida (1992). "Cooperation between Transfer and Analysis in Example-based Framework." *Proceedings of the 14th International Conference of Computational Linguistics* (*COLING-92*), Nantes, France, pp. 645–651.

Furuse, Osamu and Hitoshi Iida (1994). "Constituent Boundary Parsing for Example-based Machine Translation." *Proceedings of the 15th International Conference on Computational Linguistics* (*COLING-94*), Kyoto, Japan, pp. 105–111.

Gangadharaiah, Rashmi, Ralf D. Brown, and Jaime G. Carbonell (2006). "Spectral Clustering for Example Based Machine Translation." *Proceedings of the Human Language Technology Conference—Annual Meeting of the North American Chapter of the Association for Computational Linguistics* (*HLT-NAACL-2006*), New York, USA.

Gough, Nano, Andy Way, and Mary Hearne (2002). "Example-based Machine Translation via the Web." In Stephen D. Richardson, ed.,

Machine Translation: From Research to Real Users. Berlin and New York: Springer Verlag, pp. 74–83.

Gough, Nano and Andy Way (2004). "Example-based Controlled Translation." *Proceedings of the 9th Workshop of the European Association for Machine Translation: Broadening Horizons of Machine Translation and Its Applications*, Foundation for International Studies, Malta, pp. 73–81.

Gough, Nano and Andy Way (2004). "Robust Large-scale EBMT with Marker-based Segmentation." *Proceedings of the 10th Conference on Theoretical and Methodological Issues in Machine Translation* (*TMI-04*), Baltimore, MD, USA, pp. 95–104.

Grefenstette, Gregory (1999). "The World Wide Web as a Resource for Example-based Machine Translation Tasks." In *Translating and the Computer 21*. London: The Association for Information Management.

Gupta, Deepa and Niladri Chatterjee (2003). "Identification of Divergence for English to Hindi EBMT." *Proceedings of MT Summit IX*, New Orleans, Louisiana, USA.

Güvenir, H. Altay and Ilyas Cicekli (1998). "Learning Translation Templates from Examples." *Information Systems*, Vol. 23, pp. 353–363.

Hodász, Gábor, Balázs Kis, and Tamás Gröbler (2004). "Translation Memory as a Robust Example-based Translation System." *Proceedings of the 9th Workshop of the European Association for Machine Translation: Broadening Horizons of Machine Translation and Its Applications*, Foundation for International Studies, Malta, pp. 82–89.

Hou, Hongxu, Deng Dan, Zou Gang, Yu Hongkui, Liu Yang, Xiong Deyi, and Liu Qun (2004). "An EBMT System Based on Word Alignment." *Proceedings of the International Workshop on Spoken Language Translation* (*IWSLT-2004*), Kyoto, Japan.

Iida, Hiroshi, Eiichiro Sumita, and Osamu Furuse (1996). "Spoken Language Translation Method Using Examples." *Proceedings from the 16th International Conference on Computational Linguistics* (*COLING-96*), Copenhagen, Denmark, pp. 1074–1077.

Jain, Renu, R. Mahesh K. Sinha, and Ajai Jain (1995). "Role of Examples in Translation." *Proceedings of the 1995 IEEE International Conference on Systems, Man and Cybernetics*, Vancouver, BC, Canada, pp. 1615–1620.

Jain, Renu, R. Mahesh K. Sinha, and Ajai Jain (2001). "ANUBHARTI:

Using Hybrid Example-based Approach for Machine Translation." *Proceedings of the Symposium on Translation Support Systems* (*STRANS-2001*), Kanpur, India.

Jones, Daniel (1992). "Non-hybrid Example-based Machine Translation Architectures." *Proceedings of the 4th International Conference on Theoretical and Methodological Issues in Machine Translation of Natural Languages: Empiricist vs. Rationalist Methods in MT* (*TMI-92*), Montreal, Quebec, Canada, pp. 163–171.

Kim, Jae Dong, Ralf D. Brown, Peter J. Jansen, and Jaime G. Carbonell (2005). "Symmetric Probabilistic Alignment for Example-based Translation." *Proceedings of the 10th Workshop of the European Association for Machine Translation: Practical Applications of Machine Translation*, Budapest, Hungary, pp. 153–159.

Kit, Chunyu, Pan Haihua, and Jonathan J. Webster (2002). "Example-based Machine Translation: A New Paradigm." In Chan Sin-wai, ed., *Translation and Information Technology*. Hong Kong: The Chinese University Press, pp. 57–78.

Kurohashi, Sadao, Toshiaki Nakazawa, Kauffmann Alexis, and Daisuke Kawahara (2005). "Example-based Machine Translation Pursuing Fully Structural NLP." *Proceedings of the International Workshop on Spoken Language Translation* (*IWSLT-2005*), Pittsburgh, PA, USA.

Langlais, Philippe and Michel Simard (2002). "Merging Example-based and Statistical Machine Translation: An Experiment." In Stephen D. Richardson, ed., *Machine Translation: From Research to Real Users*. Berlin and New York: Springer Verlag, pp. 104–113.

Lepage, Yves and Etienne Denoual (2005). "ALEPH: An EBMT System Based on the Preservation of Proportional Analogies between Sentences across Languages." *Proceedings of the International Workshop on Spoken Language Translation* (*IWSLT-2005*), Pittsburgh, PA, USA.

Li, Yaoyong 李耀勇 (2001).〈利用HNC理論進行基於實例的英漢機器翻譯〉(Example-based English-Chinese Machine Translation by Using HNC Theory). In Huang Changning 黃昌寧 and Zhang Pu 張普, eds.,《自然語言理解與機器翻譯》(*Natural Language Understanding and Machine Translation*). Beijing: Tsinghua University Press, pp. 319–325.

Liu, Zhanyi, Wang Haifeng, and Wu Hua (2005). "Example-based Machine Translation Based on TSC and Statistical Generation." *Proceedings of MT Summit X*, Phuket, Thailand.

Malavazos, Christos and Stelios Piperidis (2000). "Application of Analogical Modelling to Example Based Machine Translation." *Proceedings of the 18th International Conference on Computational Linguistics* (*COLING-2000*), Saarbrucken, Germany, pp. 516–522.

Maruyama, Hiroshi and Hideo Watanebe (1992). "Three Cover Search Algorithm for Example-based Translation." *Proceedings of the 4th International Conference on Theoretical and Methodological Issues in Machine Translation of Natural Languages: Empiricist vs. Rationalist Methods in MT* (*TMI-92*), Montreal, Quebec, Canada, pp. 173–184.

McLean, Ian J. (1992). "Example-based Machine Translation Using Connectionist Matching." *Proceedings of the 4th International Conference on Theoretical and Methodological Issues in Machine Translation of Natural Languages: Empiricist vs. Rationalist Methods in MT* (*TMI-92*), Montreal, Quebec, Canada, pp. 35–43.

McTait, Kevin (2001). "Linguistic Knowledge and Complexity in an EBMT System Based on Translation Patterns." In Bente Maegaard, ed., *Proceedings of MT Summit VIII: Machine Translation in the Information Age*, Santiago de Compostela, Spain.

McTait, Kevin (2003). "Translation Patterns, Linguistic Knowledge and Complexity in An Approach to EBMT." In Michael Carl and Andy Way, eds., *Recent Advances in Example-based Machine Translation*. Dordrecht: Kluwer Academic Publishers, pp. 207–238.

Mellebeek, Bart, Karolina Owczarzak, Declan Groves, Josef Van Genabith, and Andy Way (2006). "Wrapper Syntax for Example-based Machine Translation." *Proceedings of the 7th Biennial Conference of the Association for Machine Translation in the Americas* (*AMTA-2006*)*: Visions for the Future of Machine Translation*, Boston Marriott, Cambridge, Massachusetts, USA.

Murata, Masaki, Qing Ma, Kiyotaka Uchimoto, and Hitoshi Isahara (1999). "An Example-based Approach to Japanese-to-English Translation of Tense, Aspect, and Modality." *Proceedings of the 8th International Conference on Theoretical and Methodological Issues in Machine Translation* (*TMI-99*), Chester, England, pp. 66–76.

Nagao, Makoto (1984). "A Framework of a Mechanical Translation between Japanese and English by Analogy Principle." In Alick Elithorn and Ranan Banerji, eds., *Artificial and Human Intelligence*. Amsterdam: North-Holland Publishing Company, pp. 173–180.

Nagao, Makoto (2005). "An Amorphous Object Must Be Cut by A Blunt

Tool." In Walther van Hahn, W. John Hutchins, and Cristina Vertan, eds., *Proceedings of the International Workshop on Modern Approaches in Translation Technologies*, Borovets, Bulgaria.

Naskar, Sudip Kumar and Sivaji Bandyopadhyay (2005). "A Phrasal EBMT System for Translating English to Bangla." *Proceedings of MT Summit X*, Phuket, Thailand.

Nirenburg, Sergei, Constantine Domashnev, and Dean J. Grannes (1993). "Two Approaches to Matching in Example-based Machine Translation." *Proceedings of the 5th International Conference on Theoretical and Methodological Issues in Machine Translation of Natural Languages: MT in the Next Generation (TMI-93)*, Kyoto, Japan, pp. 47–57.

Nederhof, Mark-Jan (2001). "Approximating Context-free by Rational Transduction for Example-based MT." *Proceedings of the Association for Computational Linguistics 39th Annual Meeting and 10th Conference of the European Chapter: Data-driven Machine Translation (ACL-EACL-2001)*, Toulouse, France, pp. 25–32.

Nirenburg, Sergei, Stephen Beale, and Constantino Domashnev (1994). "A Full-text Experiment in Example-based Machine Translation." *Proceedings of the International Conference on New Methods in Language Processing (NeMLaP)*, Manchester, England, pp. 78–87.

Öz, Zeynep and Ilyas Cicekli (1998). "Ordering Translation Templates by Assigning Confidence Factors." In David L. Farwell, Laurie Gerber, and Eduard Hovy, eds., *Machine Translation and the Information Soup*. Berlin: Springer Verlag, pp. 51–61.

Rapp, Reinhard and Carlos Martin Vide (2006). "Example-based Machine Translation Using a Dictionary of Word Pairs." *Proceedings of the 5th International Conference on Language Resources and Evaluation (LREC-2006)*, Genoa, Italy.

Richardson, Stephen D., Lucy Vanderwende, and William B. Dolan (1993). "Combining Dictionary-based and Example-based Methods for Natural Language Analysis." *Proceedings of the 5th International Conference on Theoretical and Methodological Issues in Machine Translation of Natural Languages: MT in the Next Generation (TMI-93)*, Kyoto, Japan, pp. 69–79.

Richardson, Stephen D., William B. Dolan, Arul Menezes, and Jessie Pinkham (2001). "Achieving Commercial-quality Translation with Example-based Methods." In Bente Maegaard, ed., *Proceedings of MT*

Summit VIII: Machine Translation in the Information Age, Santiago de Compostela, Spain, pp. 293–298.
Richardson, Stephen D., William B. Dolan, Arul Menezes, and Monica Corston-Oliver (2001). "Overcoming the Customization Bottleneck Using Example-based MT." *Proceedings of the Association for Computational Linguistics 39th Annual Meeting and 10th Conference of the European Chapter: Data-driven Machine Translation (ACL-EACL-2001)*, Toulouse, France, pp. 9–16.
Samuelsson, Christer (1997). "Example-based Optimisation of Surface-generation Tables." In Ruslan Mitkov and Nicolas Nicolov, eds., *Recent Advances in Natural Language Processing*. Amsterdam and Philadelphia: John Benjamins Publishing Company, pp. 295–315.
Sato, Satoshi (1992). "CTM: An Example-based Translation Aid System." *Proceedings of the 14th International Conference of Computational Linguistics (COLING-92)*, Nantes, France, pp. 1259–1263.
Sato, Satoshi (1993). "Example-based Translation of Technical Terms." *Proceedings of the 5th International Conference on Theoretical and Methodological Issues in Machine Translation of Natural Languages: MT in the Next Generation (TMI-93)*, Kyoto, Japan, pp. 58–68.
Sato, Satoshi (1995). "MBT2: A Method for Combining Fragments of Examples in Example-based Machine Translation." *Artificial Intelligence*, Vol. 75, pp. 31–49.
Schäler, Reinhard, Andy Way, and Michael Carl (2003). "EBMT in a Controlled Environment." In Michael Carl and Andy Way, eds., *Recent Advances in Example-based Machine Translation*. Dordrecht: Kluwer Academic Publishers, pp. 83–114.
Shimohata, Mitsuo and Eiichiro Sumita (2002). "Identifying Synonymous Expressions from a Bilingual Corpus for Example-based Machine Translation." *Proceedings of the Workshop on Machine Translation in Asia (COLING-2002)*, Taipei, Taiwan.
Shimohata, Mitsuo, Eiichiro Sumita, and Yuji Matsumoto (2003). "Example-based Rough Translation for Speech-to-speech Translation." *Proceedings of MT Summit IX*, New Orleans, Louisiana, USA.
Shimohata, Mitsuo, Eiichiro Sumita, and Yuji Matsumoto (2003). "Retrieving Meaning-equivalent Sentences for Example-based Rough Translation." *Proceedings of the Human Language Technology and North American Chapter of Association of Computational Linguistics 2003 (HLT/NAACL-2003)*, Edmonton, Alberta, Canada.

Simões, Alberto and José João Almeida (2005). "Combinatory Examples Extraction for Machine Translation." *Proceedings of the 11th Workshop of the European Association for Machine Translation: Machine Translation/Translation Aids—Tools to Increase Quality and to Save Money*, the University of Oslo, Oslo, Norway.

Somers, Harold L., Ian McLean, and Daniel Jones (1994). "Experiments in Multilingual Example-based Generation." *Proceedings of the 3rd Conference on the Cognitive Science of Natural Language Processing (CSNLP-94)*, Dublin, Ireland.

Somers, Harold L. (1999). "Review Article: Example-based Machine Translation." *Machine Translation*, Vol. 14, No. 2, pp. 113–157.

Somers, Harold L. (2001). "EBMT Seen as Case-based Reasoning." In Bente Maegaard, ed., *Proceedings of MT Summit VIII: Machine Translation in the Information Age*, Santiago de Compostela, Spain.

Somers, Harold L. (2003). "An Overview of EBMT." In Michael Carl and Andy Way, eds., *Recent Advances in Example-based Machine Translation*. Dordrecht: Kluwer Academic Publishers, pp. 3–57.

Streiter, Oliver (2000). "Reliability in Example-based Parsing." *Proceedings of TAG+5, International Workshop on Tree Adjoining Grammars*, Paris, France, pp. 257–261.

Stroppa, Nicolas, Declan Groves, Andy Way, and Kepa Separasola (2006). "Example-based Machine Translation of the Basque Language." *Proceedings of the 7th Biennial Conference of the Association for Machine Translation in the Americas (AMTA-2006): Visions for the Future of Machine Translation*, Boston Marriott, Cambridge, MA, USA.

Sumita, Eiichiro, Hitoshi Iida, and Hideo Khyama (1990). "Translating with Examples: A New Approach to Machine Translation." *Proceedings of the 3rd International Conference on Theoretical and Methodological Issues in Machine Translation of Natural Languages (TMI-90)*, Linguistics Research Center, University of Texas, Austin, Texas, USA, pp. 203–212.

Sumita, Eiichiro and Hitoshi Iida (1991). "Experiments and Prospects of Example-based Machine Translation." *Proceedings of the 29th Annual Meeting of the Association for Computational Linguistics (COLING-91)*, Berkeley, California, USA, pp. 185–192.

Sumita, Eiichiro, Osamu Furuse, and Hitoshi Iida (1993). "An Example-based Disambiguation of Prepositional Phrase Attachment."

Proceedings of the 5th International Conference on Theoretical and Methodological Issues in Machine Translation of Natural Languages: MT in the Next Generation (*TMI-93*), Kyoto, Japan, pp. 80–91.

Sumita, Eiichiro, Kozo Oi, Osamu Furuse, Hitoshi Iida, Tetsuya Higuchi, Naoto Takahashi, and Hiroaki Kitano (1993). "Example-based Machine Translation on Massively Parallel Processors." *Proceedings of the 13th International Joint Conference on Artificial Intelligence* (*IJCAI-93*), Chambéry, France, pp. 1283–1288.

Sumita, Eiichiro, Naoya Nisiyama, and Hitoshi Iida (1994). "The Relationship between Architectures and Example-retrieval Times." *Proceedings of the 12th National Conference on Artificial Intelligence* (*AAAI-94*), Menlo Park: AAAI Press, pp. 478–483.

Sumita, Eiichiro and Hitoshi Iida (1995). "Heterogeneous Computing for Example-based Translation of Spoken Language." *Proceedings of the 6th International Conference on Theoretical and Methodological Issues in Machine Translation* (*TMI-95*), Leuven, Belgium, pp. 273–286.

Sumita, Eiichiro (2001). "Example-based Machine Translation Using DP-matching between Word Sequences." *Proceedings of the Association for Computational Linguistics 39th Annual Meeting and 10th Conference of the European Chapter: Data-driven Machine Translation* (*ACL-EACL-2001*), Toulouse, France, pp. 1–8.

Sumita, Eiichiro (2003). "An Example-based Machine Translation System Using DP-matching between Word Sequences." In Michael Carl and Andy Way, eds., *Recent Advances in Example-based Machine Translation*. Dordrecht: Kluwer Academic Publishers, pp. 189–209.

Turcato, Davide, Paul McFetridge, Fred Popowich, and Janine Toole (1999). "A Unified Example-based and Lexicalist Approach to Machine Translation." *Proceedings of the 8th International Conference on Theoretical and Methodological Issues in Machine Translation* (*TMI-99*), Chester, England, pp. 33–43.

Turcato, Davide and Fred Popowich (2001). "What Is Example-based Machine Translation?" In Bente Maegaard, ed., *Proceedings of MT Summit VIII: Machine Translation in the Information Age*, Santiago de Compostela, Spain.

Turcato, Davide and Fred Popowich (2003). "What Is Example-based Machine Translation?" In Michael Carl and Andy Way, eds., *Recent Advances in Example-based Machine Translation*. Dordrecht: Kluwer Academic Publishers, pp. 59–81.

Utsuro, Takehito, Kiyotaka Uchimoto, Mitsutaka Matsumoto, and Makoto Nagao (1994). "Thesaurus-based Efficient Example Retrieval by Generating Retrieval Queries from Similarities." *Proceedings of the 15th International Conference on Computational Linguistics (COLING-94)*, Kyoto, Japan, pp. 1044–1048.

Veale, Tony and Andy Way (1997). "*Gaijin*: A Bootstrapping Approach to Example-based Machine Translation." *Proceedings of the International Conference on Recent Advances in Natural Language Processing*, Tzigov Chark, Bulgaria, pp. 239–244.

Vertan, Cristina and Vanessa Espin Martin (2005). "Experiments with Matching Algorithms in Example Based Machine Translation." In Walther van Hahn, W. John Hutchins, and Cristina Vertan, eds., *Proceedings of the International Workshop on Modern Approaches in Translation Technologies*, Borovets, Bulgaria.

Wang, Jiande, Chen Zhaoxiong, and Huang Heyan (2001). "Intelligent Case Based Machine Translation System." *Proceedings of the 2nd International Conference on Intelligent Text Processing and Computational Linguistics (CICLing-2001)*, Mexico City, Mexico.

Watanabe, Hideo (1993). "A Method for Extracting Translation Patterns from Translation Examples." *Proceedings of the 5th International Conference on Theoretical and Methodological Issues in Machine Translation: MT in the Next Generation (TMI-93)*, Kyoto, Japan, pp. 292–301.

Watanabe, Hideo (1994). "A Method for Distinguishing Exceptional and General Examples in Example-based Transfer Systems." *Proceedings of the 15th International Conference on Computational Linguistics (COLING-94)*, Kyoto, Japan, pp. 39–44.

Watanabe, Hideo and Koichi Takeda (1998). "A Pattern-based Machine Translation System Extended by Example-based Processing." *Proceedings of the 36th Annual Meeting of the Association for Computational Linguistics and 17th International Conference on Computational Linguistics (COLING-ACL-98)*, Montreal, Quebec, Canada, pp. 169–173.

Way, Andy (2001). "Translating with Examples." In Bente Maegaard, ed., *Proceedings of MT Summit VIII: Machine Translation in the Information Age*, Santiago de Compostela, Spain.

Way, Andy (2003). "Translating with Examples: The LFG-dot Models of Translation." In Michael Carl and Andy Way, eds., *Recent Advances in*

Example-based Machine Translation. Dordrecht: Kluwer Academic Publishers, pp. 443–472.
Way, Andy and Nano Gough (2003). "*WEBMT*: Developing and Validating an Example-based Machine Translation System Using the World Wide Web." *Computational Linguistics*, Vol. 29, pp. 421–457.
Way, Andy and Nano Gough (2005). "Controlled Translation in an Example-based Environment: What Do Automatic Evaluation Metrics Tell Us?" *Machine Translation*, Vol. 19, No. 1, pp. 1–36.
Webster, Jonathan J., Sin King Kui, and Hu Qinan (2002). "The Application of Semantic Web Technology for Example-based Machine Translation (EBMT)." In Chan Sin-wai, ed., *Translation and Information Technology*. Hong Kong: The Chinese University Press, pp. 79–91.
Wu, Dekai (1995). "Grammarless Extraction of Phrasal Translation Examples from Parallel Texts." *Proceedings of the 6th International Conference on Theoretical and Methodological Issues in Machine Translation of Natural Languages* (*TMI-95*), Leuven, Belgium, pp. 354–372.
Yang, Muyun, Zhao Tiejun, Liu Haijie, Shi Xiasheng, and Jiang Hongfei (2004). "Auto Word Alignment Based Chinese-English EBMT." *Proceedings of the International Workshop on Spoken Language Translation* (*IWSLT-2004*), Kyoto, Japan.
Yasuhara, Hiroshi (1993). "An Example-based Multilingual MT System in a Conceptual Language." *Proceedings of MT Summit IV: International Cooperation for Global Communication*, Kobe, Japan, pp. 147–155.
Zhang, Jie 張傑, Zhang Yue 張躍, and Yao Tianshun 姚天順 (1999).〈面向資料的英漢機譯系統中關於組合基於實例的技術〉(The Example-based Technique in an English-Chinese Machine Translation System).《東北大學學報》(*Northeastern University Bulletin*), Vol. 20, No. 3.
Zhang, Ying, Ralf D. Brown, and Robert E. Frederking (2001). "Adapting an Example-based Translation System to Chinese." In James Allan, ed., *Proceedings of the 1st International Conference on Human Language Technology Research* (*HLT-2001*), Morgan Kaufmann, San Francisco, CA, USA, pp. 7–10.
Zhang, Ying, Ralf D. Brown, Robert Frederking, and Alon Lavie (2001). "Pre-processing of Bilingual Corpora for Mandarin-English EBMT." In Bente Maegaard, ed., *Proceedings of MT Summit VIII: Machine Translation in the Information Age*, Santiago de Compostela, Spain.

Grammar-based Computer Translation

Riezler, Stefan and John T. Maxwell III (2006). "Grammatical Machine Translation." *Proceedings of the Human Language Technology Conference—Annual Meeting of the North American Chapter of the Association for Computational Linguistics* (*HLT-NAACL-2006*), New York, USA.

Interlingua-based Computer Translation

Barnett, James, Inderjeet Mani, Elaine Rich, Chinatsu Aone, Kevin Knight, and Juan Carlos Martinez (1993). "Capturing Language-specific Semantic Distinctions in Interlingua-based MT." In Sergei Nirenburg, ed., *Progress in Machine Translation.* Amsterdam: IOS and Tokyo: Ohmsha, pp. 67–77.

Dave, Shachi, Jignashu Parikh, and Pushpak Bhattacharyya (2001). "Interlingua-based English-Hindi Machine Translation and Language Divergence." *Machine Translation*, Vol. 16, No. 4, pp. 251–304.

Dorr, Bonnie J. (1992). "The Use of Lexical Semantics in Interlingual Machine Translation." *Machine Translation*, Vol. 7, No. 3, pp. 135–193.

Hutchins, W. John and Harold L. Somers (1992). "Problems of Transfer and Interlingua." *An Introduction to Machine Translation*. London: Academic Press, pp. 99–130.

Lee, Young-Suk, Wu Sok Yi, Stephanie Seneff, and Clifford Weinstein (2001). "Interlingua-based Broad-coverage Korean-to-English Translation in CCLINC." *Proceedings of the 1st International Conference on Human Language Technology Research* (*HLT-2001*), Morgan Kaufmann, San Francisco, CA, USA.

Lee, Young-Suk (2001). *Interlingua-based Open Domain Machine Translation: A Case Study from Korean-to-English Translation.* MS-15178, MIT Lincoln Laboratory.

Mitamura, Teruko, Eric H. Nyberg, and Jaime G. Carbonell (1991). "An Efficient Interlingua Translation System for Multi-lingual Document Production." *Machine Translation Summit III*, Seattle, Washington, DC, USA, pp. 15–23.

Mitamura, Teruko, Eric H. Nyberg, and Jaime G. Carbonell (1993). "An Efficient Interlingua Translation System for Multi-lingual Document

Production." In Sergei Nirenburg, ed., *Progress in Machine Translation*. Amsterdam: IOS and Tokyo: Ohmsha, pp. 105–117.
Trujillo, Arturo (1999). "Interlingua Machine Translation." *Translation Engines: Techniques for Machine Translation*. Berlin and New York: Springer Verlag, pp. 167–201.
Whitelock, Peter J. (1989). "Why Transfer and Interlingua Approaches to MT Are Both Wrong: A Position Paper." *Proceedings of the "MT into the '90s" Workshop*, Manchester, England.

Knowledge-based Computer Translation

Asaduzzaman, Mostafa M. and Muhammad Masroor Ali (2003). "A Knowledge Based Approach to Bangla-English Machine Translation for Simple Assertive Sentences." *International Journal of Translation*, Vol. 15, No. 2, pp. 77–97.
Carbonell, Jaime G., Richard E. Cullingford, and Anatole V. Gershman (1978). *Knowledge-based Machine Translation*. New Haven: Department of Computer Science, Yale University.
Carbonell, Jaime G., Richard E. Cullingford, and Anatole V. Gershman (1981). "Steps Toward Knowledge-based Machine Translation." *IEEE Transactions on Pattern Analysis and Machine Intelligence*, Vol. 3, No. 4, pp. 376–392.
Carbonell, Jaime G. and Masaru Tomita (1987). "Knowledge-based Machine Translation, the CMU Approach." In Sergei Nirenburg, ed., *Machine Translation: Theoretical and Methodological Issues*. Cambridge: Cambridge University Press, pp. 68–89.
Carlson, Lynn, Elizabeth Cooper, Ronald Dolan, and Steven Maiorano (1994). "Representing Text Meaning for Multilingual Knowledge-based Machine Translation." *Proceedings of the 1st Conference of the Association for Machine Translation in the Americas: Technology Partnerships for Crossing the Language Barrier (AMTA-1)*, Columbia, Maryland, USA, pp. 8–15.
Davis, Randall, Bruce G. Buchanan, and Edward H. Shortliffe (1977). "Production Rules as a Representation for a Knowledge-based Consultation System." *Artificial Intelligence*, Vol. 8, pp. 15–45.
Dong, Zhendong 董振東 and Dong Qiang 董強 (1999). 〈知網〉 (HowNet—An On-line Knowledge System). In Huang Changning 黃昌寧 and

Dong Zhendong 董振東, eds.,《計算語言學文集》(*Essays on Computational Linguistics*). Beijing: Tsinghua University Press, pp. 58–63.

Galinski, Christian (1988). "Advanced Terminology Banks Supporting Knowledge-based MT: Some Reflections on the Costs for Setting-up and Operating a Terminological Data Bank (TDB)." In Dan Maxwell, Klaus Schubert, and Toon Witkam, eds., *New Directions in Machine Translation*. Dordrecht-Holland: Foris Publications, pp. 167–181.

Goodman, Kenneth and Sergei Nirenburg, eds. (1991). *The KBMT Project: A Case Study in Knowledge-based Machine Translation*. San Mateo, CA: Morgan Kaufmann Publishers.

Knight, Kevin, Ishwar Chander, Matthew Haines, Vasileios Hatzivassiloglou, Eduard Hovy, Masayo Iida, Steve K. Luk, Richard A. Whitney, and Kenji Yamada (1995). "Filling Knowledge Gaps in a Broad-coverage Machine Translation System." *Proceedings of the 14th International Joint Conference on Artificial Intelligence*, Montreal, Quebec, Canada, pp. 1390–1396.

Lenat, Douglas B. and Ramanathan V. Guha (1990). *Building Large Knowledge-based Systems. Representation and Inference in the Cyc Project*. Reading, MA: Addison-Wesley Publishing Company, Inc.

Li, Sheng 李生, Yang Muyun 楊沐昀, Zhao Tiejun 趙鐵軍, and Yu Hao 于浩 (2001).〈機器翻譯系統中的知識工程策略研究〉(Research on Knowledge Engineering Strategy of Machine Translation System).《輝煌二十年—中國中文信息學會二十周年學術會議》(*Proceedings of Conference of the 20th Anniversary of CIPSC*). Beijing: Tsinghua University Press, pp. 258–262.

Li, Tangqiu, Eric H. Nyberg, and Jaime G. Carbonell (1996). *Chinese Sentence Generation in a Knowledge-based Machine Translation System*. Pittsburgh: Center for Machine Translation, Carnegie Mellon University.

Lonsdale, Deryle, Teruko Mitamura, and Eric H. Nyberg (1994). "Acquisition of Large Lexicons for Practical Knowledge-based MT." *Machine Translation*, Vol. 9, Nos. 3–4, pp. 251–283.

Meyer, Ingrid, Boyan Onyshkevych, and Lynn Carlson (1990). *Lexicographic Principles and Design for Knowledge-based Machine Translation*. Pittsburgh: Centre for Machine Translation, Carnegie Mellon University.

Mitamura, Teruko and Eric H. Nyberg (1995). "Controlled English for

Knowledge Based MT: Experience with the KANT System." *Proceedings of the 6th International Conference on Theoretical and Methodological Issues in Machine Translation* (*TMI-95*), Leuven, Belgium, pp. 158–172.

Nirenburg, Sergei, Victor Raskin, and Allen B. Tucker (1986). "On Knowledge-based Machine Translation." *Proceedings of the 11th International Conference on Computational Linguistics* (*COLING-86*), Bonn, Germany, pp. 627–632.

Nirenburg, Sergie (1987). *A Distributed Generation System for Machine Translation: Background, Design, Architecture and Knowledge Structures*. Pittsburgh: Center for Machine Translation, Carnegie Mellon University.

Nirenburg, Sergie (1987). "Knowledge and Choices in Machine Translation." In Sergei Nirenburg, ed., *Machine Translation: Theoretical and Methodological Issues*. Cambridge: Cambridge University Press, pp. 1–21.

Nirenburg, Sergei (1989). "KBMT-89: A Knowledge-based MT Project at Carnegie-Mellon University." In Christian Rohrer, ed., *Proceedings of MT Summit II*, Munich, Germany, pp. 106–112.

Nirenburg, Sergei (1989). "Knowledge-based Machine Translation." *Machine Translation*, Vol. 4, No. 1, pp. 5–24.

Nirenburg, Sergei (1989). "Lexicographic Support for Knowledge-based Machine Translation." *Literary and Linguistic Computing*, Vol. 4, No. 3, pp. 185–190.

Nirenburg, Sergei, Jaime G. Carbonell, Masaru Tomita, and Kenneth Goodman (1992). *Machine Translation: A Knowledge-based Approach*. San Matero, California: Morgan Kaufmann.

Nyberg, Eric H., Teruko Mitamura, and Jaime G. Carbonell (1994). "Evaluation Metrics for Knowledge-based Machine Translation." *Proceedings of the 15th International Conference on Computational Linguistics* (*COLING-94*), Kyoto, Japan, pp. 95–99.

Onyshkevich, Boyan and Sergei Nirenburg (1995). "A Lexicon for Knowledge-based MT." *Machine Translation*, Vol. 10, Nos. 1–2, pp. 5–57.

Pappegaaij, Bart C., Victor Sadler, and A. P. M. Toon Witkam (1986). "Experiments with an MT-directed Lexical Knowledge Bank." *Proceedings of the 11th International Conference on Computational Linguistics* (*COLING-86*), Bonn, Germany, pp. 432–434.

Pappegaaij, Bart C., Victor Sadler, and A. P. M. Toon Witkam, eds. (1986). *Word Expert Semantics: An Interlingual Knowledge-based Approach*. Dordrecht: Reidel.

Schütz, Jörg and Rita Nübel (1998). "Evaluating Language Technologies: The MULTIDOC Approach to Taming the Knowledge Soup." In David L. Farwell, Laurie Gerber, and Eduard Hovy, eds., *Machine Translation and the Information Soup*. Berlin: Springer Verlag, pp. 236–249.

Sta, Jean-David and Chiao Yun-Chuang (2001). "Knowledge Acquisition from a Text by a Linguistic and Statistical Method." *Proceedings of the 7th International Workshop on Parsing Technologies* (*IWPT-2001*). Beijing: Tsinghua University Press, pp. 245–248.

Tomita, Masaru and Jaime G. Carbonell (1986). "Another Stride Towards Knowledge-based Machine Translation." *Proceedings of the 11th International Conference on Computational Linguistics* (*COLING-86*), Bonn, Germany, pp. 633–638.

Tomita, Masaru and Jaime G. Carbonell (1987). *The Universal Parser Architecture for Knowledge-based Machine Translation*. Pittsburgh: Center for Machine Translation, Carnegie Mellon University.

Walker, Donald E. (1987). "Knowledge Resource Tools for Accessing Large Text Files." In Sergei Nirenburg, ed., *Machine Translation: Theoretical and Methodological Issues*. Cambridge: Cambridge University Press, pp. 247–261.

Weischedel, Ralph M. and Lance A. Ramshaw (1987). "Reflections on the Knowledge Needed to Process Ill-formed Language." In Sergei Nirenburg, ed., *Machine Translation: Theoretical and Methodological Issues*. Cambridge: Cambridge University Press, pp. 155–167.

Whitelock, Peter J. and Kieran Kilby (1995). "Knowledge Representation and Parsing." *Linguistic and Computational Techniques in Machine Translation System Design*. London: UCL Press, pp. 30–37.

Zhao, Zhenxi and Gong Yuchang (1990). "A Hierarchical Knowledge Based Method to Understand Chinese." *Computer Processing of Chinese and Oriental Languages*, Vol. 5, No. 1, pp. 43–52.

Lexicon-based Computer Translation

Abeillé, Anne, Yves Schabes, and Aravind K. Joshi (1990). "Using Lexicalized Tags for Machine Translation." *Proceedings of the 13th*

International Conference on Computational Linguistics (*COLING-90*), Helsinki, Finland, pp. 1–6.

Bläser, Brigitte, Ulrike Schwall, and Angelika Storrer (1992). "A Reusable Lexical Database Tool for Machine Translation." *Proceedings of the 14th International Conference on Computational Linguistics* (*COLING-92*), Nantes, France, pp. 510–516.

Dorr, Bonnie J. (1989). "Lexical Conceptual Structure and Generation in Machine Translation." *Proceedings of the 11th Annual Conference of the Cognitive Science Society*, Ann Arbor, Michigan, USA, pp. 74–81.

Dorr, Bonnie J. (1990). "A Cross-linguistic Approach to Machine Translation." *Proceedings of the 3rd International Conference on Theoretical and Methodological Issues in Machine Translation of Natural Languages* (*TMI-90*), Linguistics Research Center, University of Texas, Austin, Texas, USA, pp. 13–32.

Dorr, Bonnie J. (1990). "Solving Thematic Divergences in Machine Translation." *Proceedings of the 28th Annual Meeting of the Association for Computational Linguistics* (*ACL-90*), University of Pittsburgh, Pittsburgh, PA, USA, pp. 127–134.

Dorr, Bonnie J. (1991). "Conceptual Basis of the Lexicon in Machine Translation." In Uri Zernik, ed., *Using On-line Resources to Build a Lexicon*. Hillsdale, New Jersey: Lawrence Erlbaum Associates, pp. 263–307.

Dorr, Bonnie J. (1992). "Machine Translation Divergences: A Lexical-semantic Perspective." *Proceedings of the 2nd Seminar on Computational Lexical Semantics*, Toulouse, France, pp. 169–183.

Dorr, Bonnie J. (1992). "The Use of Lexical Semantics in Interlingual Machine Translation." *Machine Translation*, Vol. 7, No. 3, pp. 135–193.

Farwell, David L. and Yorick Wilks (1991). "ULTRA: A Multi-lingual Machine Translator." *Proceedings of Machine Translation Summit*, Seattle, Washington, DC, USA, pp. 19–24.

Sanfilippo, Antonio, Ted Briscoe, Ann Copestake, Maria Antonia Marti, Mariona Taule, and Antonietta Alonge (1992). "Translation Equivalence and Lexicalization in the ACQUILEX LKB." *Proceedings of the 4th International Conference on Theoretical and Methodological Issues in Machine Translation of Natural Languages* (*TMI-92*), Montreal, Quebec, Canada, pp. 1–11.

Trujillo, Arturo (1992). "Locations in the Machine Translation of

Prepositional Phrases." *Proceedings of the 4th International Conference on Theoretical and Methodological Issues in Machine Translation of Natural Languages* (*TMI-92*), Montreal, Quebec, Canada, pp. 13–20.

Trujillo, Arturo (1995). "Bi-lexical Rules for Multi-lexeme Translation in Lexicalist MT." *Proceedings of the 6th International Conference on Theoretical and Methodological Issues in Machine Translation* (*TMI-95*), Leuven, Belgium, pp. 48–66.

Tsujii, Jun-ichi and Kimikaza Fujita (1991). "Lexical Transfer Based on Bilingual Signs: Towards Interaction during Transfer." *Proceedings of the European Chapter of the Association for Computational Linguistics*, Berlin, Germany, pp. 275–280.

Wilks, Yorick, Dan Fass, Guo Cheng-ming, James E. McDonald, Tony Plate, and Brian M. Slator (1990). "Providing Machine Tractable Dictionary Tools." *Machine Translation*, Vol. 5, No. 2, pp. 99–154.

Linguistics-based Computer Translation

Tsujii, Jun-ichi (1993). "After Linguistics-based MT." *Proceedings of MT Summit IV: International Cooperation for Global Communication*, Kobe, Japan, pp. 197–198.

Memory-based Computer Translation

Hodász, Gábor (2006). "Towards a Comprehensive Evaluation Method of Memory-based Translation Systems." *Proceedings of the 11th Workshop of the European Association for Machine Translation: Machine Translation/Translation Aids—Tools to Increase Quality and to Save Money*, the University of Oslo, Oslo, Norway.

Johansson, Christer and Lars G. Johnsen (2006). "Analogical Modeling with Bias—Allowing Feedback and Centering." In Alexander F. Gelbukh, ed., *Advances in Natural Language Processing*, Special Issue of *Research in Computing Science*, No. 18, pp. 57–70.

Kitano, Hiroaki and Tetsuya Higuchi (1991). "High Performance Memory-based Translation on IXM2 Massively Parallel Associative Memory Processor." *Proceedings of the 9th National Conference on Artificial Intelligence* (*AAAI-91*). Menlo Park: AAAI Press/MIT Press, pp. 149–154.

Kitano, Hiroaki and Tetsuya Higuchi (1991). "Massive Parallel Memory-based Parsing." *Proceedings of the 12th International Joint Conference on Artificial Intelligence* (*IJCAI-91*), Sydney, Australia, pp. 918–924.

Kitano, Hiroaki (1993). "A Comprehensive and Practical Model of Memory-based Machine Translation." In Ruzena Bajcsy, ed., *Proceedings of the 13th International Joint Conference on Artificial Intelligence* (*IJCAI-93*). San Fransisco, CA: Morgan Kaufmann Publishers Inc., Vol. 2, pp. 1276–1282.

Kitano, Hiroaki, Dan Moldovan, and Seungho Cha (1993). "Toward High Performance Machine Translation: Preliminary Results from Massively Parallel Memory-based Translation on SNAP." In Sergei Nirenburg, ed., *Progress in Machine Translation*. Amsterdam: IOS and Tokyo: Ohmsha, pp. 139–152.

Kitano, Hiroaki (1994). *Speech-to-speech Translation: A Massively Parallel Memory-based Approach*. Boston: Kluwer Academic Publishers.

Lee, Miriam (2006). "Career Development: Staying Up-to-date—the Freelancers' View." In *Translating and the Computer 28*. London: The Association for Information Management.

O'Leary, Tara (2000). "Memory-based Translation: Using Translation Memory Tools, from a Freelancer's Perspective." In *Translating and the Computer 22*. London: The Association for Information Management.

Ortíz, Daniel, Ismael García-Varea, Franscisco Casacuberta, Antonio Lagarda, and Jorge González (2003). "On the Use of Statistical Machine Translation Techniques with a Memory-based Translation System (AMETRA)." *Proceedings of MT Summit IX*, New Orleans, Louisiana, USA.

Phaholphinyo, Sitthaa, Teerapong Modhiran, Nattapol Kritsuthikul, and Thepchai Supnithi (2005). "A Practical Memory-based Approach for Improving Accuracy of MT." *Proceedings of MT Summit X*, Phuket, Thailand.

Piperidis, Stelios and Christos Malavazos (1999). "A Multi-level Framework for Memory-based Translation Aid Tools." In *Translating and the Computer 21*. London: The Association for Information Management.

Planas, Emmanuel (1999). "Towards Second Generation Translation Memories." *LISA Newsletter*, Vol. 8, No. 2, pp. 7–11.

Sato, Satoshi and Makoto Nagao (1990). "Toward Memory-based Translation." *Proceedings of the 13th International Conference on Computational Linguists* (*COLING-90*), Helsinki, Finland, Vol. 3, pp. 247–252.

Stanfill, Craig and David Waltz (1986). "Toward Memory-based Reasoning." *Communications of the ACM*, Vol. 29, pp. 185–192.

Tomabechi, Hideto (1987). "Direct Memory Access Translation." *Proceedings of the 10th International Joint Conference on Artificial Intelligence* (*IJCAI-87*), Milan, Italy, pp. 722–725.

Network-based Computer Translation

Castaño, M. Asunción, Francisco Casacuberta, and Enrique Vidal (1997). "Machine Translation Using Neural Networks and Finite-state Models." *Proceedings of the 7th International Conference on Theoretical and Methodological Issues in Machine Translation* (*TMI-97*), St. John's College, Santa Fe, New Mexico, USA.

Ishikawa, Masahiko and Ryoichi Sugimura (1992). "Natural Language Analysis Using a Network Model: Modification Deciding Network." *Proceedings of the 4th International Conference on Theoretical and Methodological Issues in Machine Translation of Natural Languages* (*TMI-92*), Montreal, Quebec, Canada, pp. 55–66.

N-gram-based Computer Translation

Crego, Josep Maria, Adria de Gispert, and Jose B. Marino (2005). "The TALP Ngram-based SMT System for IWSLT '05." *Proceedings of the International Workshop on Spoken Language Translation* (*IWSLT-2005*), Pittsburgh, PA, USA.

Mariño, José B., Rafael E. Banchs, Josep Maria Crego, Adrià de Gispert, Patrik Lambert, José A. R. Fonollosa, and Marta R. Costa-jussà (2006). "N-gram-based Machine Translation." *Computational Linguistics*, Vol. 32, No. 4, pp. 527–549.

Pattern-based Computer Translation

Ayuso, Damaris M. and the PLUM Research Group (1994). "Pattern Matching in a Linguistically-motivated Text Understanding System."

Proceedings of the ARPA Human Language Technology Workshop, Plainsboro, NJ, USA, pp. 182–186.

de Cea, Guadalupe Aguado and Antonio Pareja-Lora (2000). "A Competition Model for the Generation of Complementation Patterns in Machine Translation." *International Journal of Translation*, Vol. 12, Nos. 1–2, pp. 25–37.

Gajer, Mirosław (2002). "The Pattern-based French-to-Polish Machine Translation System." *Machine Translation Review*, No. 13, pp. 6–34.

Imamura, Kenji (2002). "Application of Translation Knowledge Acquired by Hierarchical Phrase Alignment for Pattern-based MT." *Proceedings of the 9th International Conference on Theoretical and Methodological Issues in Machine Translation* (*TMI-2002*), Keihanna, Japan.

Kaplan, Ronald M., Klaus Netter, Jiirgen Wedekind, and Annie Zaenen (1989). "Translation by Structural Correspondences." *Proceedings of the 4th Conference of the European Association for Computational Linguistics*, Manchester, England, pp. 272–281.

Kitamura, Mihoko and Toshiki Murata (2003). "Practical Pattern-based Machine Translation System Allowing Complex Patterns." *Proceedings of MT Summit IX*, New Orleans, Louisiana, USA.

Prószéky, Gábor and László Tihanyi (2002). "MetaMorpho: A Pattern-based Machine Translation System." In *Translating and the Computer 24*. London: The Association for Information Management.

Roh, Yoon-Hyung, Munpyo Hong, Sung-Kwon Choi, Ki-Young Lee, and Sang-Kyu Park (2003). "For the Proper Treatment of Long Sentences in a Sentence Pattern-based English-Korean MT System." *Proceedings of MT Summit IX*, New Orleans, Louisiana, USA.

Sasaki, Miki and Toshiki Murata (2005). "A Pattern-based Machine Translation System—Yakushite Net MT Engine." *Proceedings of the International Workshop on Spoken Language Translation* (*IWSLT-2005*), Pittsburgh, PA, USA.

Takeda, Koichi (1996). "Pattern-based Context-free Grammars for Machine Translation." *Proceedings of the 34th Annual Meeting of the Association for Computational Linguistics* (*ACL-96*), Santa Cruz, CA, USA, pp. 144–151.

Takeda, Koichi (1996). "Pattern-based Machine Translation." *Proceedings of the 16th International Conference on Computational Linguistics* (*COLING-96*). Copenhagen, Denmark, pp. 1155–1158.

Takeda, Koichi (2002). "Sentence Generation for Pattern-based Machine

Translation." *Proceedings of the 9th International Conference on Theoretical and Methodological Issues in Machine Translation* (*TMI-2002*), Keihanna, Japan, pp. 168–177.

Vilares, Manuel, Francisco J. Ribadas, and Victor M. Darriba (2001). "Approximate VLDC Pattern Matching in Shared-forest." *Proceedings of the 2nd International Conference on Intelligent Text Processing and Computational Linguistics* (*CICLing-2001*), Mexico City, Mexico.

Watanabe, Hideo (1993). "A Method for Extracting Translation Patterns from Translation Examples." *Proceedings of the 5th International Conference on Theoretical and Methodological Issues in Machine Translation* (*TMI-93*): *MT in the Next Generation*, Kyoto, Japan, pp. 292–301.

Watanabe, Hideo and Koichi Takeda (1998). "A Pattern-based Machine Translation System Extended by Example-based Processing." *Proceedings of the 36th Annual Meeting of the Association for Computational Linguistics and 17th International Conference on Computational Linguistics* (*COLING-ACL-98*), Montreal, Quebec, Canada, pp. 169–173.

Phrase-based Statistical Computer Translation

Birch, Alexandra, Chris Callison-Burch, and Miles Osborne (2006). "Constraining the Phrase-based, Joint Probability Statistical Translation Model." *Proceedings of the 7th Biennial Conference of the Association for Machine Translation in the Americas* (*AMTA-2006*): *Visions for the Future of Machine Translation*, Boston Marriott, Cambridge, MA, USA.

Brockett, Chris, William B. Dolan, and Michael Gamon (2006). "Correcting ESL Errors Using Phrasal SMT Techniques." *Proceedings of the Joint Conference of the International Committee on Computational Linguistics and the Association for Computational Linguistics* (*COLING/ACL-2006*), Sydney, Australia.

Callison-Burch, Chris, Colin Bannard, and Josh Schroeder (2005). "Scaling Phrase-based Statistical Machine Translation to Larger Corpora and Longer Phrases." *Proceedings of the 43rd Annual Meeting of the Association of Computational Linguistics* (*ACL-2005*), Ann Arbor, Michigan, USA.

Cattoni, Roldano, Nicola Bertoldi, Mauro Cettolo, Boxing Chen, and

Marcello Federico (2006). "A Web-based Demonstrator of a Multi-lingual Phrase-based Translation System." *Proceedings of the 11th Conference of the European Chapter of the Association for Computational Linguistics (EACL-2006)*, Trento, Italy.

Chiang, David (2005). "A Hierarchical Phrase-based Model for Statistical Machine Translation." *Proceedings of the 43rd Annual Meeting of the Association of Computational Linguistics (ACL-2005)*, Ann Arbor, Michigan, USA.

Costa-jussa, Marta R. and Jose A. R. Fonollosa (2005). "Tuning a Phrase-based Statistical Translation System for the IWSLT-2005 Chinese to English and Arabic to English Tasks." *Proceedings of the International Workshop on Spoken Language Translation (IWSLT-2005)*, Pittsburgh, PA, USA.

Crego, Josep Maria, Marta R. Costa-jussa, Jose B. Mario, and Jose A. R. Fonollosa (2005). "Ngram-based versus Phrase-based Statistical Machine Translation." *Proceedings of the International Workshop on Spoken Language Translation (IWSLT-2005)*, Pittsburgh, PA, USA.

Eisele, Andreas (2006). "Parallel Corpora and Phrase-based Statistical Machine Translation for New Language Pairs via Multiple Intermediaries." *Proceedings of the 5th International Conference on Language Resources and Evaluation (LREC-2006)*, Genoa, Italy.

Koehn, Philipp, Franz Josef Och, and Daniel Marcu (2003). "Statistical Phrase-based Translation." *Proceedings of the Human Language Technology and North American Chapter of Association of Computational Linguistics 2003 (HLT/NAACL-2003)*, Edmonton, Alberta, Canada, pp. 127–133.

Koehn, Philipp (2004). "Pharaoh: A Beam Search Decoder for Phrase-based SMT." In Robert E. Frederking and Kathryn B. Taylors, eds., *Machine Translation: From Real Users to Research*. Berlin: Springer Verlag, pp. 115–124.

Langlais, Philippe, Michael Carl, and Oliver Streiter (2004). "Experimenting with Phrase-based Statistical Translation within the IWSLT 2004 Chinese-to-English Shared Translation Task." *Proceedings of the International Workshop on Spoken Language Translation (IWSLT-2004)*, Kyoto, Japan.

Lopez, Adam and Philip Resnik (2006). "Word-based Alignment, Phrase-based Translation: What's the Link?" *Proceedings of the 7th Biennial Conference of the Association for Machine Translation in the Americas*

(*AMTA-2006*): *Visions for the Future of Machine Translation*, Boston Marriott, Cambridge, MA, USA.

Marcu, Daniel and William Wong (2002). "A Phrase-based, Joint Probability Model for Statistical Machine Translation." *Proceedings of the 2002 Conference on Empirical Methods in Natural Language Processing* (*EMNLP-2002*), University of Pennsylvania, Philadelphia, PA, USA.

Nguyen, Thai Phuong and Akira Shimazu (2006). "Improving Phrase-based Statistical Machine Translation with Morpho-syntactic Analysis and Transformation." *Proceedings of the 7th Biennial Conference of the Association for Machine Translation in the Americas* (*AMTA-2006*), Boston Marriott, Cambridge, MA, USA.

Ortiz-Martínez, Daniel, Ismael García-Varea, and Francisco Casacuberta (2005). "Thot: A Toolkit to Train Phrase-based Statistical Translation Models." *Proceedings of MT Summit X*, Phuket, Thailand.

Pang, Wei, Zhendong Yang, Zhenbiao Chen, Wei Wei, Bo Xu, and Chengqing Zong (2005). "The CASIA Phrase-based Machine Translation System." *Proceedings of the International Workshop on Spoken Language Translation* (*IWSLT-2005*), Pittsburgh, PA, USA.

Quirk, Chris, Arul Menezes, and Colin Cherry (2005). "Dependency Treelet Translation: Syntactically Informed Phrasal SMT." *Proceedings of the 43rd Annual Meeting of the Association of Computational Linguistics* (*ACL-2005*), Ann Arbor, Michigan, USA.

Ueffing, Nicola and Hermann Ney (2005). "Word-level Confidence Estimation for Machine Translation Using Phrase-based Translation Models." *Proceedings of Human Language Technology Conference and Conference on Empirical Methods in Natural Language Processing* (*HLT/EMNLP-2005*), Vancouver, BC, Canada.

Watanabe, Taro, Hajime Tsukada, and Hideki Isozaki (2006). "Left-to-right Target Generation for Hierarchical Phrase-based Translation." *Proceedings of the Joint Conference of the International Committee on Computational Linguistics and the Association for Computational Linguistics* (*COLING/ACL-2006*), Sydney, Australia.

Zens, Richard and Hermann Ney (2004). "Improvements in Phrase-based Statistical Machine Translation." *Proceedings of the Human Language Technology Conference / North American Chapter of the Association for Computational Linguistics Annual Meeting* (*HLT/NAACL-2004*), Boston, MA, USA, pp. 257–264.

Zens, Richard, Oliver Bender, Sasa Hasan, Shahram Khadivi, Evgeny Matusov, Jia Xu, Yuqi Zhang, and Hermann Ney (2005). "The RWTH Phrase-based Statistical Machine Translation System." *Proceedings of the International Workshop on Spoken Language Translation (IWSLT-2005)*, Pittsburgh, PA, USA.

Zhao, Bing, Stephan Vogel, and Alex H. Waibel (2004). "Phrase Pair Rescoring with Term Weightings for Statistical Machine Translation." *Proceedings of the 2004 Conference on Empirical Methods in Natural Language Processing (EMNLP-2004)*, Barcelona, Spain, pp. 206–213.

Pragmatics-based Computer Translation

Farwell, David L. and Stephen Helmreich (1993). "Insights into Communicative Intent from Pragmatics Based Translation Equivalence." *Proceedings of the 7th Annual Southwestern Cognitive Science Conference*, Tucson, AZ, USA.

Farwell, David L. and Stephen Helmreich (1995). "This Is Not a Bedroom Farce: Pragmatics and Translation." *Contributed Papers of the 4th International Colloquium on Cognitive Science*, Donostia, Spain, pp. 73–82.

Farwell, David L. and Stephen Helmreich (2001). "Towards Pragmatics-based Machine Translation." In Bente Maegaard, ed., *Proceedings of MT Summit VIII: Machine Translation in the Information Age*, Santiago de Compostela, Spain.

Farwell, David L. and Stephen Helmreich (2006). "Pragmatics-based MT and the Translation of Puns." *Proceedings of the 11th Workshop of the European Association for Machine Translation: Machine Translation/ Translation Aids—Tools to Increase Quality and to Save Money*, the University of Oslo, Oslo, Norway.

Helmreich, Stephen and David L. Farwell (1996). "Translation Differences and Pragmatics-based MT." *Proceedings of the 2nd Conference of the Association for Machine Translation in the Americas: Expanding MT Horizons (AMTA-2)*, Montreal, Quebec, Canada, pp. 43–55.

Helmreich, Stephen and David L. Farwell (1998). "Translation Differences and Pragmatics-based MT." *Machine Translation*, Vol. 13, No. 1, pp. 17–39.

Wilks, Yorick (1990). "A White Paper on Research on Pragmatics-based Machine Translation." *Memoranda in Computer and Cognitive*

Science, MCCS-90-188. Las Cruces, NM: Computer Research Laboratory, New Mexico State University.

Principle-based Computer Translation

Chung, Hee Sung (1988). "A Principle-based Korean/Japanese Machine Translation System: NARA." *Proceedings of the 2nd International Conference on Theoretical and Methodological Issues in Machine Translation of Natural Languages* (*TMI-88*), Carnegie Mellon University, Center for Machine Translation, Pittsburgh, Pennsylvania, USA.

Dorr, Bonnie J. (1987). "A Principle-based Approach to Parsing for Machine Translation." *Proceedings of the 9th Annual Conference of the Cognitive Science Society*, University of Washington, Seattle, Washington, DC, USA, pp. 78–88.

Dorr, Bonnie J. (1987). "UNITRAN: An Interlingual Approach to Machine Translation." *Proceedings of the 6th Conference of the American Association of Artificial Intelligence*, Seattle, Washington, DC, USA, pp. 534–539.

Dorr, Bonnie J. (1990). "Machine Translation: A Principle-based Approach." In Patrick H. Winston and Sarah Shellard, eds., *Artificial Intelligence at MIT: Expanding Frontiers*. Cambridge, MA: MIT Press, pp. 326–361.

Dorr, Bonnie J. (1991). "Principle-based Parsing for Machine Translation." In Robert C. Berwick, Steven P. Abney, and Carol Tenny, eds., *Principle-based Parsing: Computation and Psycholinguistics*. Norwell, MA: Kluwer Academic Publishers, pp. 153–183.

Dorr, Bonnie J. (1992). "Parameterization of the Interlingua in Machine Translation." *Proceedings of the 14th International Conference on Computational Linguistics* (*COLING-92*), Nantes, France, pp. 624–630.

Wehrli, Eric (1992). "The IPS System." *Proceedings of the 14th International Conference on Computational Linguistics* (*COLING-92*), Nantes, France, pp. 870–874.

Rule-based Computer Translation

Brill, Eric and Philip Resnik (1994). "A Rule-based Approach to

Prepositional Phrase Attachment Disambiguation." *Proceedings of the 15th International Conference on Computational Linguistics (COLING-94)*, Kyoto, Japan, pp. 1198–1204.

Carbonell, Jaime G., Katharine Probst, Erik Peterson, Christian Monson, Alon Lavie, Ralf D. Brown, and Lori S. Levin (2002). "Automatic Rule Learning for Resource-limited MT." In Stephen D. Richardson, ed., *Machine Translation: From Research to Real Users*. Berlin and New York: Springer Verlag, pp. 1–10.

Carl, Michael, Leonid L. Iomdin, and Oliver Streiter (1998). "Towards a Dynamic Linkage of Example-based and Rule-based Machine Translation." *Proceedings of the 10th European Summer School on Logic, Linguistics and Information: Workshop on Machine Translation*, Saarbrücken, Germany.

Carl, Michael, Cathrine Pease, Leonid L. Iomdin, and Oliver Streiter (2000). "Towards a Dynamic Linkage of Example-based and Rule-based Machine Translation." *Machine Translation*, Vol. 15, No. 3, pp. 223–257.

Charoenpornsawat, Paisarn, Virach Sornlertlamvanich, and Thatsanee Charoenporn (2002). "Improving Translation Quality of Rule-based Machine Translation." *Proceedings of the Workshop on Machine Translation in Asia (COLING-2002),* Taipei, Taiwan.

Elming, Jakob (2006). "Transformation-based Correction of Rule-based MT." *Proceedings of the 11th Workshop of the European Association for Machine Translation: Machine Translation/Translation Aids—Tools to Increase Quality and to Save Money*, the University of Oslo, Oslo, Norway.

Forcada, Mikel L. (2000). "Learning Machine Translation Strategies Using Commercial Systems: Discovering Word-reordering Rules." *Proceedings of MT 2000: Machine Translation and Multilingual Applications in the New Millennium*, Exeter, England, pp. 7–18.

Forcada, Mikel L. (2001). "Learning Machine Translation Strategies Using Commercial Systems: Discovering Word-reordering Rules." *Machine Translation Review*, No. 12, pp. 5–7.

Matsumoto, Yuji and Mihoko Kitamura (1995). "Acquisition of Translation Rules from Parallel Corpora." In Nicolas Nicolov and Ruslan Mitkov, eds., *Recent Advances in Natural Language Processing: Selected Papers from the Conference*. Amsterdam and Philadelphia: John Benjamins Publishing Company, pp. 405–416.

Park, Seong-Bae and Jeong-Woo Son (2005). "Augmentation of Modality Translation Rules in Korean-to-English Machine Translation by Rule Learning." *Proceedings of MT Summit X*, Phuket, Thailand.

Proszéky, Gábór (2005). "An Approach to Machine Translation via the Rule-to-rule Hypothesis." *Proceedings of the 10th Workshop of the European Association for Machine Translation: Practical Applications of Machine Translation*, Budapest, Hungary, pp. 219–225.

Prószéky, Gábor (2005). "Machine Translation and the Rule-to-rule Hypothesis." In Krisztina Károly and Ágota Fóris, eds., *New Trends in Translation Studies: In Honour of Kinga Klaudy*. Budapest: Akadémiai Kiadó, pp. 207–218.

Streiter, Oliver, Leonid L. Iomdin, Munpyo Hong, and Ute Hauck (1999). "Learning, Forgetting and Remembering: Statistical Support for Rule-based MT." *Proceedings of the 8th International Conference on Theoretical and Methodological Issues in Machine Translation (TMI-99)*, Chester, England, pp. 44–54.

Watanabe, Hideo (1995). "A Model of a Bi-directional Transfer Mechanism Using Rule Combinations." *Machine Translation*, Vol. 10, No. 4, pp. 269–291.

Zhu, Jiang and Wang Haifeng (2005). "The Effect of Adding Rules into the Rule-based MT System." *Proceedings of MT Summit X*, Phuket, Thailand.

Shake and Bake Computer Translation

Beaven, John (1992). "Shake and Bake Machine Translation." *Proceedings of the 14th International Conference on Computational Linguistics (COLING-92)*, Nantes, France, pp. 603–609.

Brew, Chris (1992). "Letting the Cat out of the Bag: Generation for Shake-and-bake MT." *Proceedings of the 14th International Conference on Computational Linguistics (COLING-92)*, Nantes, France, pp. 610–616.

Carl, Michael, Ecaterina Rascu, and Paul Schmidt (2005). "Using Template Grammars for Shake and Bake Paraphrasing." *Proceedings of the 10th Workshop of the European Association for Machine Translation: Practical Applications of Machine Translation*, Budapest, Hungary, pp. 66–72.

Turcato, Davide (1995). "Shake-and-bake MT and Morphology." *Proceedings of the 6th International Conference on Theoretical and*

Methodological Issues in Machine Translation (*TMI-95*), Leuven, Belgium, pp. 319–325.
Whitelock, Peter J. (1992). "Shake-and-bake Translation." *Proceedings of the 14th International Conference on Computational Linguistics* (*COLING-92*), Nantes, France, pp. 784–791.
Whitelock, Peter J. (1994). "Shake and Bake Translation." In Christopher J. Rupp, Michael A. Rosner, and Roderick L. Johnson, eds., *Constraints, Language and Computation*. London: Academic Press, pp. 339–359.

Statistical Computer Translation

Al-Onaizan, Yaser, Jan Curin, Michael Jahr, Kevin Knight, John D. Lafferty, I. Dan Melamed, Franz Josef Och, David Purdy, Noah A. Smith, and David Yarowsky (1999). *Statistical Machine Translation*. Baltimore, MD: CLSP Technical Report.
Al-Onaizan, Yaser and Kishore Papineni (2006). "Distortion Models for Statistical Machine Translation." *Proceedings of the Joint Conference of the International Committee on Computational Linguistics and the Association for Computational Linguistics* (*COLING/ACL-2006*), Sydney, Australia.
Benjamin, Bryce, Kevin Knight, and Daniel Marcu (2002). "Translation by the Numbers: Language Weaver." In Stephen D. Richardson, ed., *Machine Translation: From Research to Real Users*. Berlin and New York: Springer Verlag, pp. 229–231.
Berger, Adam L. and John D. Lafferty (1999). "Information Retrieval as Statistical Translation." *Proceedings of the 22nd Annual International ACM SIGIR Conference on Research and Development in Information Retrieval* (*SIGIR-99*), Berkeley, CA, USA, pp. 222–229.
Bertoldi, Nicola, Roldano Cattoni, Mauro Cettolo, and Marcello Federico (2004). "The ITC-irst Statistical Machine Translation System for IWSLT-2004." *Proceedings of the International Workshop on Spoken Language Translation* (*IWSLT-2004*), Kyoto, Japan.
Brown, Peter F., John Cocke, Stephen A. Della Pietra, Vincent J. Della Pietra, Fredrick Jelinek, Robert L. Mercer, and Paul S. Roossin (1988). "A Statistical Approach to Language Translation." *Proceedings of the 12th International Conference on Computational Linguistics* (*COLING-88*), Budapest, Hungary, pp. 71–76.

Brown, Peter F., John Cocke, Stephen A. Della Pietra, Vincent J. Della Pietra, Fredrick Jelinek, John D. Lafferty, Robert L. Mercer, and Paul S. Roossin (1990). "A Statistical Approach to Machine Translation." *Computational Linguistics*, Vol. 16, No. 2, pp. 79–85.

Brown, Peter F., Stephen A. Della Pietra, Vincent J. Della Pietra, and Robert L. Mercer (1991). "The Mathematics of Statistical Machine Translation: Parameter Estimation." *Computational Linguistics*, Vol. 19, pp. 263–311.

Brown, Peter F., Stephen A. Della Pietra, Vincent J. Della Pietra, John D. Lafferty, and Robert L. Mercer (1992). "Analysis, Statistical Transfer, and Synthesis in Machine Translation." *Proceedings of the 14th International Conference of Computational Linguistics* (*COLING-92*), Nantes, France, pp. 83–100.

Brown, Peter F., Stephen A. Della Pietra, Vincent J. Della Pietra, and Robert L. Mercer (1993). "The Mathematics of Statistical Machine Translation: Parameter Estimation." *Computational Linguistics*, Vol. 19, No. 2, pp. 233–312.

Callison-Burch, Chris, Colin Bannard, and Josh Schroeder (2004). "Improving Statistical Translation through Editing." *Proceedings of the 9th Workshop of the European Association for Machine Translation: Broadening Horizons of Machine Translation and Its Applications*, Foundation for International Studies, Malta, pp. 26–32.

Callison-Burch, Chris, David Talbot, and Miles Osborne (2004). "Statistical Machine Translation with Word- and Sentence-aligned Parallel Corpora." *Proceedings of the 42nd Annual Meeting of the Association for Computational Linguistics* (*ACL-2004*), Barcelona, Spain, pp. 175–182.

Callison-Burch, Chris, Philipp Koehn, and Miles Osborne (2006). "Improved Statistical Machine Translation Using Paraphrases." *Proceedings of the Human Language Technology Conference—Annual Meeting of the North American Chapter of the Association for Computational Linguistics* (*HLT-NAACL-2006*), New York, USA.

Cettolo, Mauro, Marcello Federico, Nicola Bertoldi, Roldano Cattoni, and Boxing Chen (2005). "A Look inside the ITC-irst SMT System." *Proceedings of MT Summit X*, Phuket, Thailand.

Chang, Jason S., David Yu, and Lee Chun-Jen (2001). "Statistical Translation Model for Phrases." *Computational Linguistics and Chinese Language Processing*, Vol. 6, No. 2, pp. 43–64.

Charniak, Eugene, Kevin Knight, and Kenji Yamada (2003). "Syntax-based Language Models for Statistical Machine Translation." *Proceedings of MT Summit IX*, New Orleans, Louisiana, USA.

Chen, Boxing, Roldano Cattoni, Nicola Bertoldi, Mauro Cettolo, and Marcello Federico (2005). "The ITC-irst SMT System for IWSLT-2005." *Proceedings of the International Workshop on Spoken Language Translation* (*IWSLT-2005*), Pittsburgh, PA, USA.

Collins, Michael, Philipp Koehn, and Ivona Kucerova (2005). "Clause Restructuring for Statistical Machine Translation." *Proceedings of the 43rd Annual Meeting of the Association of Computational Linguistics* (*ACL-2005*), Ann Arbor, Michigan, USA.

Crego, Josep Maria, José B. Mariño, and Adrià de Gispert (2005). "Reordered Search and Tuple Unfolding for Ngram-based SMT." *Proceedings of MT Summit X*, Phuket, Thailand.

Crego, Josep Maria and José B. Mariño (2006). "Integration of POStag-based Source Reordering into SMT Decoding by an Extended Search Graph." *Proceedings of the 7th Biennial Conference of the Association for Machine Translation in the Americas* (*AMTA-2006*)*: Visions for the Future of Machine Translation*, Boston Marriott, Cambridge, MA, USA.

de Gispert, Adria (2005). "Phrase Linguistic Classification and Generalization for Improving Statistical Machine Translation." *Proceedings of the 43rd Annual Meeting of the Association of Computational Linguistics* (*ACL-2005*), Ann Arbor, Michigan, USA.

DeNeefe, Steve and Kevin Knight (2005). "ISI's 2005 Statistical Machine Translation Entries." *Proceedings of the International Workshop on Spoken Language Translation* (*IWSLT-2005*), Pittsburgh, PA, USA.

Deng, Yonggang and William Byrne (2005). "HMM Word and Phrase Alignment for Statistical Machine Translation." *Proceedings of Human Language Technology Conference and Conference on Empirical Methods in Natural Language Processing* (*HLT/EMNLP-2005*), Vancouver, BC, Canada.

Dologlou, Yannis, Stella Markantonatou, George Tambouratzis, Olga Yannoutsou, Athanassia Fourla, and Nikos Ioannou (2003). "Using Monolingual Corpora for Statistical Machine Translation: The METIS System." *Proceedings of the Joint Conference Combining the 8th International Workshop of the European Association for Machine Translation and the 4th Controlled Language Applications Workshop:*

Controlled Language Translation (*EAMT-CLAW-03*), Dublin City University, Ireland.

Eck, Matthias, Almut Silja Hildebrand, Stephan Vogel, and Alex H. Waibel (2005). "Adaptation of the Translation Model for Statistical Machine Translation Based on Information Retrieval." *Proceedings of the 10th Annual Conference of the European Association for Machine Translation* (*EAMT-2005*), Budapest, Hungary.

Eck, Matthias, Stephan Vogel, and Alex H. Waibel (2005). "Low Cost Portability for Statistical Machine Translation Based on N-gram Coverage." *Proceedings of MT Summit X*, Phuket, Thailand.

Eck, Matthias, Stephan Vogel, and Alex H. Waibel (2005). "Low Cost Portability for Statistical Machine Translation Based on N-gram and TF-IDF." *Proceedings of the International Workshop on Spoken Language Translation* (*IWSLT-2005*), Pittsburgh, PA, USA.

Foster, George, Simona Gandrabur, Philippe Langlais, Graham Russell, Michel Simard, and Pierre Plamondon (2003). "Statistical Machine Translation: Rapid Development with Limited Resources." *Proceedings of MT Summit IX*, New Orleans, Louisiana, USA.

Fox, Heidi J. (2002). "Phrasal Cohesion and Statistical Machine Translation." *Proceedings of the 2002 Conference on Empirical Methods in Natural Language Processing* (*EMNLP-2002*), University of Pennsylvania, Philadelphia, PA, USA.

Fox, Heidi J. (2005). "Dependency-based Statistical Machine Translation." *Proceedings of the 43rd Annual Meeting of the Association of Computational Linguistics* (*ACL-2005*), Ann Arbor, Michigan, USA.

Garcia-Varea, Ismael and Francisco Casacuberta (1998). "Statistical Translation in Limited Domain Tasks." *Proceedings of the 10th European Summer School on Logic, Linguistics and Information: Workshop on Machine Translation*, Saarbrücken, Germany.

Garcia-Varea, Ismael, Franz Josef Och, Hermann Ney, and Francisco Casacuberta (2001). "Refined Lexicon Models for Statistical Machine Translation Using a Maximum Entropy Approach." *Proceedings of the 39th Annual Meeting of the Association for Computational Linguistics* (*ACL-2001*), Toulouse, France, pp. 204–211.

García-Varea, Ismael and Francisco Casacuberta (2001). "Search Algorithms for Statistical Machine Translation Based on Dynamic Programming and Pruning Techniques." In Bente Maegaard, ed.,

Proceedings of MT Summit VIII: Machine Translation in the Information Age, Santiago de Compostela, Spain.

Garcia-Varea, Ismael, Franz Josef Och, Hermann Ney, and Francisco Casacuberta (2002). "Efficient Integration of Maximum Entropy Lexicon Models within the Training of Statistical Alignment Models." *Proceedings of the 5th Conference of the Association for Machine Translation in the Americas* (*AMTA-2002*), Tiburon, CA, USA.

Garcia-Varea, Ismael, Franz Josef Och, Hermann Ney, and Francisco Casacuberta (2002). "Improving Alignment Quality in Statistical Machine Translation Using Context-dependent Maximum Entropy Models." *Proceedings of International Conference on Computational Linguistics*, Taipei, Taiwan.

Germann, Ulrich (2001). "Building a Statistical Machine Translation System from Scratch: How Much Bang for the Buck Can We Expect?" *Proceedings of the Association for Computational Linguistics 39th Annual Meeting and 10th Conference of the European Chapter: Data-driven Machine Translation* (*ACL-EACL-2001*), Toulouse, France, pp. 63–70.

Germann, Ulrich (2003). "Greedy Decoding for Statistical Machine Translation in Almost Linear Time." *Proceedings of the Human Language Technology and North American Chapter of Association of Computational Linguistics 2003* (*HLT/NAACL-2003*), Edmonton, Alberta, Canada.

Gupta, Deepa and Marcello Federico (2006). "Exploiting Word Transformation in Statistical Machine Translation from Spanish to English." *Proceedings of the 11th Workshop of the European Association for Machine Translation: Machine Translation/ Translation Aids—Tools to Increase Quality and to Save Money*, the University of Oslo, Oslo, Norway.

Habash, Nizar and Bonnie J. Dorr (2002). "Handling Translation Divergences: Combining Statistical and Symbolic Techniques in Generation-heavy Machine Translation." In Stephen D. Richardson, ed., *Machine Translation: From Research to Real Users*. Berlin: Springer Verlag, pp. 84–93.

Habash, Nizar and Fatiha Sadat (2006). "Arabic Preprocessing Schemes for Statistical Machine Translation." *Proceedings of the Human Language Technology Conference—Annual Meeting of the North*

American Chapter of the Association for Computational Linguistics (HLT-NAACL-2006), New York, USA.

Habash, Nizar and Fatiha Sadat (2006). "Combination of Arabic Preprocessing Schemes for Statistical Machine Translation." *Proceedings of the Joint Conference of the International Committee on Computational Linguistics and the Association for Computational Linguistics (COLING/ACL-2006)*, Sydney, Australia.

Hasan, Saša, Anas El Isbihani, and Hermann Ney (2006). "Creating a Large-scale Arabic to French Statistical Machine Translation System." *Proceedings of the 5th International Conference on Language Resources and Evaluation (LREC-2006)*, Genoa, Italy.

Hewavitharana, Sanjika, Stephan Vogel, and Alex H. Waibel (2005). "Augmenting a Statistical Translation System with Translation Memory." *Proceedings of the 10th Workshop of the European Association for Machine Translation: Practical Applications of Machine Translation*, Budapest, Hungary, pp. 126–132.

Hewavitharana, Sanjika, Bing Zhao, Almut Silja Hildebrand, Matthias Eck, Chiori Hori, Stephan Vogel, and Alex H. Waibel (2005). "The CMU Statistical Machine Translation System for IWSLT2005." *Proceedings of the International Workshop on Spoken Language Translation (IWSLT-2005)*, Pittsburgh, PA, USA.

Hildebrand, Almut Silja, Matthias Eck, Stephan Vogel, and Alex H. Waibel (2005). "Adaptation of the Translation Model for Statistical Machine Translation Based on Information Retrieval." *Proceedings of the 10th Workshop of the European Association for Machine Translation: Practical Applications of Machine Translation*, Budapest, Hungary, pp. 133–142.

Huang, Liang, Kevin Knight, and Aravind K. Joshi (2006). "Statistical Syntax-directed Translation with Extended Domain of Locality." *Proceedings of the 7th Biennial Conference of the Association for Machine Translation in the Americas (AMTA-2006): Visions for the Future of Machine Translation*, Boston Marriott, Cambridge, MA, USA.

Hwang, Young-Sook and Yutaka Sasaki (2005). "Context-dependent SMT Model Using Bilingual Verb-noun Collocation." *Proceedings of the 43rd Annual Meeting of the Association of Computational Linguistics (ACL-2005)*, Ann Arbor, Michigan, USA.

Imamura, Kenji, Hideo Okuma, and Eiichiro Sumita (2005). "Practical

Approach to Syntax-based Statistical Machine Translation." *Proceedings of MT Summit X*, Phuket, Thailand.

Kim, Nari (1998). "Statistical Approach for Korean Analysis: A Method Based on Structural Patterns." In David L. Farwell, Laurie Gerber, and Eduard Hovy, eds., *Machine Translation and the Information Soup*. Berlin: Springer Verlag, pp. 308–317.

Kim, Yooyung, Jun Huang, Youssef Billawala, Demitrios Master, and Farzad Ehsani (2005). "Sehda S2MT: Incorporation of Syntax into Statistical Translation System." *Proceedings of the International Workshop on Spoken Language Translation* (*IWSLT-2005*), Pittsburgh, PA, USA.

Knight, Kevin (1998). "Statistical Translation: Where It Went." *Proceedings of the 3rd Conference on Empirical Methods in Natural Language Processing*, Granada, Spain.

Knight, Kevin and Yaser Al-Onaizan (1998). "Translation with Finite-state Devices." In David L. Farwell, Laurie Gerber, and Eduard Hovy, eds., *Machine Translation and the Information Soup*. Berlin: Springer Verlag, pp. 421–437.

Knight, Kevin (2003). "Teaching Statistical Machine Translation." *Proceedings of MT Summit IX*, New Orleans, Louisiana, USA, pp. 17–19.

Knight, Kevin and Philipp Koehn (2003). "What's New in Statistical Machine Translation." *Proceedings of the Human Language Technology and North American Chapter of Association of Computational Linguistics 2003* (*HLT/NAACL-2003*), Edmonton, Alberta, Canada.

Koehn, Philipp, Franz Josef Och, and Daniel Marcu (2003). "Statistical Phrase-based Translation." *Proceedings of the Human Language Technology and North American Chapter of Association of Computational Linguistics 2003* (*HLT/NAACL-2003*), Edmonton, Alberta, Canada.

Koehn, Philipp (2005). "Europarl: A Parallel Corpus for Statistical Machine Translation." *Proceedings of MT Summit X*, Phuket, Thailand.

Kondrak, Grzegorz, Daniel Marcu, and Kevin Knight (2003). "Cognates Can Improve Statistical Translation Models." *Proceedings of the Human Language Technology and North American Chapter of Association of Computational Linguistics 2003* (*HLT/NAACL-2003*), Edmonton, Alberta, Canada.

Kuhn, Roland, Denis Yuen, Michel Simard, Patrick Paul, George Foster, Eric Joanis, and Howard Johnson (2006). "Segment Choice Models: Feature-rich Models for Global Distortion in Statistical Machine Translation." *Proceedings of the Human Language Technology Conference—Annual Meeting of the North American Chapter of the Association for Computational Linguistics* (*HLT-NAACL-2006*), New York, USA.

Kumar, Shankar and William Byrne (2004). "Minimum Bayes-risk Decoding for Statistical Machine Translation." *Proceedings of the Human Language Technology Conference/North American Chapter of the Association for Computational Linguistics Annual Meeting* (*HLT/NAACL-2004*), Boston, MA, USA.

Kumar, Shankar and William Byrne (2005). "Local Phrase Reordering Models for Statistical Machine Translation." *Proceedings of Human Language Technology Conference and Conference on Empirical Methods in Natural Language Processing* (*HLT/EMNLP-2005*), Vancouver, BC, Canada.

Lambert, Patrik and Rafael Banchs (2005). "Data Inferred Multi-word Expressions for Statistical Machine Translation." *Proceedings of MT Summit X*, Phuket, Thailand.

Lambert, Patrik and Rafael Banchs (2006). "Grouping Multi-word Expressions According to Part-of-speech in Statistical Machine Translation." *Proceedings of the 11th Conference of the European Chapter of the Association for Computational Linguistics* (*EACL-2006*), Trento, Italy.

Langlais, Philippe and Michel Simard (2002). "Merging Example-based and Statistical Machine Translation: An Experiment." In Stephen D. Richardson, ed., *Machine Translation: From Research to Real Users*. Berlin and New York: Springer Verlag, pp. 104–113.

Lee, Chun-Jen and Jason S. Chang (2003). "Acquisition of English-Chinese Transliterated Word Pairs from Parallel-aligned Texts Using a Statistical Machine Transliteration Model." *Proceedings of the Human Language Technology and North American Chapter of Association of Computational Linguistics 2003* (*HLT/NAACL-2003*), Edmonton, Alberta, Canada.

Lee, Young-Suk (2004). "Morphological Analysis for Statistical Machine Translation." *Proceedings of the Human Language Technology Conference/North American Chapter of the Association for*

Computational Linguistics Annual Meeting (*HLT/NAACL-2004*), Boston, MA, USA.

Lee, Young-Suk (2005). "IBM Statistical Machine Translation for Spoken Languages." *Proceedings of the International Workshop on Spoken Language Translation* (*IWSLT-2005*), Pittsburgh, PA, USA.

Liu, Yang, Qun Liu, and Shouxun Lin (2006). "Tree-to-string Alignment Template for Statistical Machine Translation." *Proceedings of the Joint Conference of the International Committee on Computational Linguistics and the Association for Computational Linguistics* (*COLING/ACL-2006*), Sydney, Australia.

Macherey, Klaus, Franz Josef Och, and Hermann Ney (2001). "Natural Language Understanding Using Statistical Machine Translation." *Proceedings of the 7th European Conference on Speech Communication and Technology* (*EuroSpeech-2001*), Aalborg, Denmark, pp. 2205–2208.

Maji, Hemanta K. and Raghavendra Udupa U. (2006). "Computational Complexity of Statistical Machine Translation." *Proceedings of the 11th Conference of the European Chapter of the Association for Computational Linguistics* (*EACL-2006*), Trento, Italy.

Majithia, Hemali and Phil Rennert (2005). "Rapid Ramp-up for Statistical Machine Translation: Minimal Training for Maximal Coverage." *Proceedings of MT Summit X*, Phuket, Thailand.

Manning, Christopher D. and Hinrich Schütze (1999). *Foundations of Statistical Natural Language Processing*. Cambridge, MA: MIT Press.

Marcu, Daniel and William Wong (2002). "A Phrase-based, Joint Probability Model for Statistical Machine Translation." *Proceedings of the Conference on Empirical Methods in Natural Language Processing*, Philadelphia, PA, USA.

Mariño, José B., Rafael E. Banchs, Josep Maria Crego, Adrià de Gispert, Patrik Lambert, José A. R. Fonollosa, and Marta Ruiz (2005). "Bilingual N-gram Statistical Machine Translation." *Proceedings of MT Summit X*, Phuket, Thailand.

Matusov, Evgeny, Maja Popovic, Richard Zens, and Hermann Ney (2004). "Statistical Machine Translation of Spontaneous Speech with Scarce Resources." *Proceedings of the International Workshop on Spoken Language Translation* (*IWSLT-2004*), Kyoto, Japan.

Matusov, Evgeny, Stephan Kanthak, and Hermann Ney (2005). "Efficient Statistical Machine Translation with Constrained Reordering."

Proceedings of the 10th Workshop of the European Association for Machine Translation: Practical Applications of Machine Translation, Budapest, Hungary, pp. 181–188.

Mauèec, Mirjam Sepesy and Zdravko Kaèiè (2006). "Statistical Machine Translation Using the IJSELAN Corpus." *Proceedings of the 5th SALTMIL Workshop on Minority Languages and the 5th International Conference on Language Resources and Evaluation (LREC-2006): Strategies for Developing Machine Translation for Minority Languages*, Genoa, Italy, pp. 87–90.

Mauser, Arne, Evgeny Matusov, and Hermann Ney (2006). "Training a Statistical Machine Translation System without GIZA++." *Proceedings of the 5th International Conference on Language Resources and Evaluation (LREC-2006)*, Genoa, Italy.

Melamed, I. Dan (2004). "Statistical Machine Translation by Parsing." *Proceedings of the 42nd Annual Meeting of the Association for Computational Linguistics (ACL-2004)*, Barcelona, Spain, pp. 653–660.

Mellebeek, Bart, Karolina Owczarzak, Declan Groves, Josef Van Genabith, and Andy Way (2006). "A Syntactic Skeleton for Statistical Machine Translation." *Proceedings of the 11th Workshop of the European Association for Machine Translation: Machine Translation/ Translation Aids—Tools to Increase Quality and to Save Money*, the University of Oslo, Oslo, Norway.

Miller, Scott, David Stallard, Robert Bobrow, and Richard Schwartz (1996). "A Fully Statistical Approach to Natural Language Interfaces." *Proceedings of the 34th Annual Meeting of the Association for Computational Linguistics (ACL-96)*, Santa Cruz, CA, USA, pp. 55–61.

Moore, Robert C. (2001). "Towards a Simple and Accurate Statistical Approach to Learning Translation Relationships among Words." *Proceedings of the Association for Computational Linguistics 39th Annual Meeting and 10th Conference of the European Chapter: Data-driven Machine Translation (ACL-EACL-2001)*, Toulouse, France, pp. 79–86.

Niessen, Sonja, Stephan Vogel, Hermann Ney, and Christoph Tillmann (1998). "A DP Based Search Algorithm for Statistical Machine Translation." *Proceedings of the 36th Annual Meeting of the Association for Computational Linguistics and 17th International*

Conference on Computational Linguistics (*COLING-ACL-98*), Montreal, Quebec, Canada, pp. 960–966.

Niessen, Sonja and Hermann Ney (2001). "Morpho-syntactic Analysis for Reordering in Statistical Machine Translation." In Bente Maegaard, ed., *Proceedings of MT Summit VIII: Machine Translation in the Information Age*, Santiago de Compostela, Spain.

Niessen, Sonja and Hermann Ney (2001). "Toward Hierarchical Models for Statistical Machine Translation of Inflected Languages." *Proceedings of the Association for Computational Linguistics 39th Annual Meeting and 10th Conference of the European Chapter: Data-driven Machine Translation* (*ACL-EACL-2001*), Toulouse, France.

Niessen, Sonja and Hermann Ney (2004). "Statistical Machine Translation with Scarce Resources Using Morpho-syntactyic Information." *Computational Linguistics*, Vol. 30, No. 2, pp. 181–204.

Och, Franz Josef and Hans Weber (1998). "Improving Statistical Natural Language Translation with Categories and Rules." *Proceedings of the 36th Annual Meeting of the Association for Computational Linguistics and 17th International Conference on Computational Linguistics* (*COLING-ACL-98*), Montreal, Quebec, Canada, pp. 985–989.

Och, Franz Josef, Christoph Tillmann, and Hermann Ney (1999). "Improved Alignment Models for Statistical Machine Translation." *Proceedings of the Joint SIGDAT Conference on Empirical Methods in NLP and Very Large Corpora* (*EMNLP/VLC-99*), University of Maryland, College Park, MD, USA, pp. 20–28.

Och, Franz Josef and Hermann Ney (2000). "Statistical Machine Translation." *Proceedings of the 5th Workshop of the European Association for Machine Translation: Harvesting Existing Resources*, Lubljana, Slovenia, pp. 39–46.

Och, Franz Josef, Nicola Ueffing, and Hermann Ney (2001). "An Efficient A* Search Algorithm for Statistical Machine Translation." *Proceedings of the Association for Computational Linguistics 39th Annual Meeting and 10th Conference of the European Chapter: Data-driven Machine Translation* (*ACL-EACL-2001*), Toulouse, France, pp. 55–62.

Och, Franz Josef and Hermann Ney (2001). "Statistical Multi-source Translation." In Bente Maegaard, ed., *Proceedings of MT Summit VIII: Machine Translation in the Information Age*, Santiago de Compostela, Spain, pp. 253–258.

Och, Franz Josef and Hermann Ney (2002). "Discriminative Training and

Maximum Entropy Models for Statistical Machine Translation." *Proceedings of the 40th Anniversary Meeting of the Association for Computational Linguistics* (*ACL-2002*), Philadelphia, PA, USA, pp. 295–302.

Och, Franz Josef and Hermann Ney (2003). "Efficient Search for Interactive Statistical Machine Translation." *Proceedings of the 10th Conference of the European Chapter of the Association for Computational Linguistics* (*EACL-2003*), Budapest, Hungary, pp. 387–393.

Och, Franz Josef (2003). "Minimum Classification Error Training for Statistical Machine Translation." *Proceedings of the 41st Annual Meeting of the Association for Computational Linguistics* (*ACL-2003*), Sapporo, Japan.

Och, Franz Josef, Daniel Gildea, Sanjeev Khudanpur, Anoop Sarkar, Kenji Yamada, Alex Fraser, Shankar Kumar, Shen Libin, David Smith, Katherine Eng, Viren Jain, Jin Zhen, and Dragomir Radev (2004). "A Smorgasbord of Features for Statistical Machine Translation." *Proceedings of the Human Language Technology Conference/North American Chapter of the Association for Computational Linguistics Annual Meeting* (*HLT/NAACL-2004*), Boston, MA, USA.

Ohashi, Kazuteru, Kazuhide Yamamoto, Kuniko Saito, and Masaaki Nagata (2005). "NUT-NTT Statistical Machine Translation System for IWSLT 2005." *Proceedings of the International Workshop on Spoken Language Translation* (*IWSLT-2005*), Pittsburgh, PA, USA.

Ortíz, Daniel, Ismael García-Varea, Franscisco Casacuberta, Antonio Lagarda, and Jorge González (2003). "On the Use of Statistical Machine Translation Techniques with a Memory-based Translation System (AMETRA)." *Proceedings of MT Summit IX*, New Orleans, Louisiana, USA.

Parker-Rhodes, Arthur Frederick (1958). "The Use of Statistics in Language Research." *Mechanical Translation*, Vol. 5, No. 2, pp. 67–73.

Patry, Alexandre, Fabrizio Gotti, and Philippe Langlais (2006). "MOOD: A Modular Object-oriented Decoder for Statistical Machine Translation." *Proceedings of the 5th International Conference on Language Resources and Evaluation* (*LREC-2006*), Genoa, Italy.

Popović, Maja and Hermann Ney (2005). "Exploiting Phrasal Lexica and Additional Morpho-syntactic Language Resources for Statistical

Machine Translation with Scarce Training Data." *Proceedings of the 10th Workshop of the European Association for Machine Translation: Practical Applications of Machine Translation*, Budapest, Hungary, pp. 212–228.
Popović, Maja and Hermann Ney (2006). "POS-based Word Reorderings for Statistical Machine Translation." *Proceedings of the 5th International Conference on Language Resources and Evaluation (LREC-2006)*, Genoa, Italy.
Popović, Maja and Hermann Ney (2006)."Statistical Machine Translation with and without a Bilingual Training Corpus." *Proceedings of the 5th SALTMIL Workshop on Minority Languages and the 5th International Conference on Language Resources and Evaluation (LREC-2006): Strategies for Developing Machine Translation for Minority Languages*, Genoa, Italy, pp. 25–30.
Quirk, Chris and Arul Menezes (2006). "Do We Need Phrases? Challenging the Conventional Wisdom in Statistical Machine Translation." *Proceedings of the Human Language Technology Conference—Annual Meeting of the North American Chapter of the Association for Computational Linguistics (HLT-NAACL-2006)*, New York, USA.
Sadat, Fatiha and Nizar Habash (2006). "Combination of Arabic Preprocessing Schemes for Statistical Machine Translation." *Proceedings of the Joint Conference of the Association for Computational Linguistics and International Committee on Computational Linguistics (COLING-ACL-2006)*, Sydney, Australia.
Schwenk, Holger, Daniel Dechelotte, and Jean-Luc Gauvain (2006). "Continuous Space Language Models for Statistical Machine Translation." *Proceedings of the Joint Conference of the International Committee on Computational Linguistics and the Association for Computational Linguistics (COLING/ACL-2006)*, Sydney, Australia.
Smith, David A. and Charles Schafer (2006). "Overview of Statistical Machine Translation." *Proceedings of the 7th Biennial Conference of the Association for Machine Translation in the Americas (AMTA-2006): Visions for the Future of Machine Translation*, Boston Marriott, Cambridge, MA, USA.
Su, Keh-Yih and Jing-Shin Chang (1992). "Why Corpus-based Statistics-oriented Machine Translation." *Proceedings of the 4th International*

Conference on Theoretical and Methodological Issues in Machine Translation of Natural Languages: Empiricist vs. Rationalist Methods in MT (*TMI-92*), Montreal, Quebec, Canada, pp. 249–262.

Tillmann, Christoph, Stephan Vogel, Hermann Ney, and Alex Zubiaga (1997). "A DP Based Search Using Monotone Alignments in Statistical Translation." *Proceedings of the 35th Annual Meeting of the Association for Computational Linguistics and 8th Conference of the European Chapter of the Association for Computational Linguistics*, Madrid, Spain, pp. 289–296.

Tillmann, Christoph, Stephan Vogel, Hermann Ney, and Hassan Sawaf (2000). "Statistical Translation of Text and Speech: First Results with the RWTH System." *Machine Translation*, Vol. 15, Nos. 1–2, pp. 43–73.

Tillmann, Christoph and Fei Xia (2003). "A Phrase-based Unigram Model for Statistical Machine Translation." *Proceedings of the Human Language Technology and North American Chapter of Association of Computational Linguistics 2003* (*HLT/NAACL-2003*), Edmonton, Alberta, Canada.

Tillman, Christoph (2004). "A Unigram Orientation Model for Statistical Machine Translation." *Proceedings of the Human Language Technology Conference/North American Chapter of the Association for Computational Linguistics Annual Meeting* (*HLT/NAACL-2004*), Boston, MA, USA.

Tillmann, Christoph and Tong Zhang (2005). "A Localized Prediction Model for Statistical Machine Translation." *Proceedings of the 43rd Annual Meeting of the Association of Computational Linguistics* (*ACL-2005*), Ann Arbor, Michigan, USA.

Tillmann, Christoph and Tong Zhang (2006). "A Discriminative Global Training Algorithm for Statistical MT." *Proceedings of the Joint Conference of the International Committee on Computational Linguistics and the Association for Computational Linguistics* (*COLING/ACL-2006*), Sydney, Australia.

Tomás, Jesús (2001). "Monotone Statistical Translation Using Word Groups." In Bente Maegaard, ed., *Proceedings of MT Summit VIII: Machine Translation in the Information Age*, Santiago de Compostela, Spain.

Tsukada, Hajime, Taro Watanabe, Jun Suzuki, Hideto Kazawa, and Hideki Isozaki (2005). "The NTT Statistical Machine Translation System for

IWSLT2005." *Proceedings of the International Workshop on Spoken Language Translation* (*IWSLT-2005*), Pittsburgh, PA, USA.

Ueffing, Nicola, Franz Josef Och, and Hermann Ney (2002). "Generation of Word Graphs in Statistical Machine Translation." *Proceedings of the 2002 Conference on Empirical Methods in Natural Language Processing* (*EMNLP-2002*), University of Pennsylvania, Philadelphia, PA, USA, pp. 156–163.

Ueffing, Nicola, Klaus Macherey, and Hermann Ney (2003). "Confidence Measures for Statistical Machine Translation." *Proceedings of MT Summit IX*, New Orleans, Louisiana, USA.

Ueffing, Nicola and Hermann Ney (2005). "Application of Word-level Confidence Measures in Interactive Statistical Machine Translation." *Proceedings of the 10th Workshop of the European Association for Machine Translation: Practical Applications of Machine Translation*, Budapest, Hungary, pp. 262–270.

Venugopal, Ashish R. (2004). "Considerations in Maximum Mutual Information and Minimum Classification Error Training for Statistical Machine Translation." *Proceedings of the International Conference on Natural Language Processing* (*ICON-2004*), International Institute of Information Technology, Hyderabad, India.

Venugopal, Ashish R. and Stephan Vogel (2005). "Considerations in Maximum Mutual Information and Minimum Classification Error Training for Statistical Machine Translation." *Proceedings of the 10th Workshop of the European Association for Machine Translation: Practical Applications of Machine Translation*, Budapest, Hungary, pp. 271–279.

Vilar, David, Evgeny Matusov, Sasa Hasan, Richard Zens, and Hermann Ney (2005). "Statistical Machine Translation of European Parliamentary Speeches." *Proceedings of MT Summit X*, Phuket, Thailand.

Vilar, David, Jia Xu, Luis Fernando D'Haro, and Hermann Ney (2006). "Error Analysis of Statistical Machine Translation Output." *Proceedings of the 5th International Conference on Language Resources and Evaluation* (*LREC-2006*), Genoa, Italy.

Vogel, Stephan, Hermann Ney, and Christoph Tillmann (1996). "HMM-based Word Alignment in Statistical Translation." *Proceedings from the 16th International Conference on Computational Linguistics* (*COLING-96*). Copenhagen, Denmark, pp. 836–841.

Vogel, Stephan, Franz Josef Och, Sonja Nieflen, Hassan Sawaf, Christoph Tillmann, and Hermann Ney (2000). "Statistical Methods for Machine Translation." In Wolfgang Wahlster, ed., *Verbmobil: Foundations of Speech to Speech Translation.* Berlin: Springer Verlag, pp. 377–393.

Vogel, Stephan and Alicia Tribble (2002). "Improving Statistical Machine Translation for a Speech-to-speech Translation Task." *Proceedings of the Workshop on Speech-to-speech Translation at the 7th International Conference on Spoken Language Processing* (*ICSLP 2002/Interspeech 2002*), Boulder, Colorado, USA, pp. 1901–1904.

Vogel, Stephan, Zhang Ying, Huang Fei, Ashish Venugopal, Zhao Bing, Alex Tribble, and Alex H. Waibel (2003). "The CMU Statistical Machine Translation System." *Proceedings of MT Summit IX*, New Orleans, Louisiana, USA.

Vogel, Stephan, Sanjika Hewavitharana, Muntsin Kolss, and Alex H. Waibel (2004). "The ISL Statistical Translation System for Spoken Language Translation." *Proceedings of the International Workshop on Spoken Language Translation* (*IWSLT-2004*), Kyoto, Japan.

Wang, Dah-Yih and Jyun-Sheng Chang (1992). "A Modular and Statistical Approach to Machine Translation." *Proceedings of the Conference of the Association for Computational Linguistics and Chinese Language Processing* (*ROCLING-V*), National Taiwan University, Taipei, Taiwan.

Wang, Ye-Yi and Alex H. Waibel (1997). "Decoding Algorithm in Statistical Machine Translation." *Proceedings of the 35th Annual Meeting of the Association for Computational Linguistics and 8th Conference of the European Chapter of the Association for Computational Linguistics*, Madrid, Spain, pp. 366–372.

Wang, Ye-Yi and Alex H. Waibel (1998). "Fast Decoding for Statistical Machine Translation." *Proceedings of the 5th International Conference on Spoken Language Processing,* (*ICSLP-98*), Sydney, Australia, pp. 2775–2779.

Wang, Ye-Yi (1998). *Grammar Inference and Statistical Machine Translation.* Pittsburgh: Language Technologies Institute, Carnegie Mellon University.

Wang, Ye-Yi and Alex H. Waibel (1998). "Modeling with Structures in Statistical Machine Translation." *Proceedings of the 36th Annual*

Meeting of the Association for Computational Linguistics and 17th International Conference on Computational Linguistics (*COLING-ACL-98*), Montreal, Quebec, Canada, pp. 1357–1363.
Watanabe, Taro, Kenji Imamura, and Eiichiro Sumita (2002). "Statistical Machine Translation Based on Hierarchical Phrase Alignment." *Proceedings of the 9th International Conference on Theoretical and Methodological Issues in Machine Translation* (*TMI-2002*), Keihanna, Japan, pp. 188–198.
Watanabe, Taro and Eiichiro Sumita (2003). "Example-based Decoding for Statistical Machine Translation." *Proceedings of MT Summit IX*, New Orleans, Louisiana, USA.
Wu, Dekai (1996). "A Polynomial-time Algorithm for Statistical Machine Translation." *Proceedings of the 34th Annual Meeting of the Association for Computational Linguistics* (*ACL-96*), Santa Cruz, CA, USA, pp. 152–158.
Xiong, Deyi, Qun Liu, and Shouxun Lin (2006). "Maximum Entropy Based Phrase Reordering Model for Statistical Machine Translation." *Proceedings of the Joint Conference of the International Committee on Computational Linguistics and the Association for Computational Linguistics* (*COLING/ACL-2006*), Sydney, Australia.
Xu, Jia, Evgeny Matusov, Richard Zens, and Hermann Ney (2005). "Integrated Chinese Word Segmentation in Statistical Machine Translation." *Proceedings of the International Workshop on Spoken Language Translation* (*IWSLT-2005*), Pittsburgh, PA, USA.
Yamada, Kenji and Kevin Knight (2001). "A Syntax-based Statistical Translation Model." *Proceedings of the Annual Meeting of the Association for Computational Linguistics* (*ACL-01*), Toulouse, France, pp. 523–530.
Zens, Richard, Franz Josef Och, and Hermann Ney (2002). "Phrase-based Statistical Machine Translation." In Matthias Jarke, Jana Koehler, and Gerhard Lakemeyer, eds., *Proceedings of German Conference on Artificial Intelligence* (*KI-2002*), Aachen, Germany.
Zollmann, Andreas, Venugopal Ashish, and Vogel Stephan (2006). "Bridging the Inflection Morphology Gap for Arabic Statistical Machine Translation." *Proceedings of the Human Language Technology Conference—Annual Meeting of the North American Chapter of the Association for Computational Linguistics* (*HLT-NAACL-2006*), New York, USA.

Syntax-based Computer Translation

Huang, Bryant and Kevin Knight (2006). "Relabeling Syntax Trees to Improve Syntax-based Machine Translation Quality." *Proceedings of the Human Language Technology Conference—Annual Meeting of the North American Chapter of the Association for Computational Linguistics (HLT-NAACL-2006)*, New York, USA.

Text-based Computer Translation

Schütz, Jörg and Bärbel Ripplinger (1994). "Towards Text-based Machine Translation." *Proceedings of the 1st Conference of the Association for Machine Translation in the Americas: Technology Partnerships for Crossing the Language Barrier (AMTA-1)*, Columbia, Maryland, USA, pp. 185–192.

Transfer-based Computer Translation

Alonso, Juan Alberto (1990). "Transfer InterStructure: Designing an 'Interlingua' for Transfer-based MT Systems." *Proceedings of the 3rd International Conference on Theoretical and Methodological Issues in Machine Translation of Natural Languages (TMI-90)*, Linguistics Research Center, University of Texas, Austin, Texas, USA, pp. 189–201.

Ananiadou, Sofia and John McNaught (1990). "Treatment of Compounds in a Transfer-based Machine Translation System." *Proceedings of the 3rd International Conference on Theoretical and Methodological Issues in Machine Translation of Natural Languages (TMI-90)*, Linguistics Research Center, University of Texas at Austin, Austin, Texas, USA, pp. 57–63.

Font-Llitjós, Ariadna, Jaime G. Carbonell, and Alon Lavie (2005). "Introducing a Framework for Interactive and Automatic Refinement of Transfer-based Machine Translation." *Proceedings of the 10th Workshop of the European Association for Machine Translation: Practical Applications of Machine Translation*, Budapest, Hungary, pp. 87–96.

Furuse, Osamu and Hitoshi Iida (1992). "An Example-based Method for Transfer-driven Machine Translation." *Proceedings of the 4th*

International Conference on Theoretical and Methodological Issues in Machine Translation of Natural Languages: Empiricist vs. Rationalist Methods in MT (*TMI-92*), Montreal, Quebec, Canada, pp. 139–150.

Furuse, Osamu (1994). "Transfer-driven Machine Translation." *Proceedings of the 1st Conference of the Association for Machine Translation in the Americas: Technology Partnerships for Crossing the Language Barrier* (*AMTA-1*), Columbia, Maryland, USA, pp. 225–226.

Hutchins, W. John (1986). "Transfer Systems since 1970." *Machine Translation: Past, Present and Future.* Chichester: Ellis Horwood, pp. 224–257.

Kinoshita, Jorge (1998). "An Open Transfer Translation." In David L. Farwell, Laurie Gerber, and Eduard Hovy, eds., *Machine Translation and the Information Soup*. Berlin: Springer Verlag, pp. 510–513.

Lavie, Alon, Stephen Vogel, Lori S. Levin, Erik Peterson, Katharina Probst, Ariadna Font-Llitjós, Rachel Reynolds, Jaime G. Carbonell, and Richard Cohen (2003). "Experiments with a Hindi-to-English Transfer-based MT System under a Miserly Data Scenario." *ACM Transactions on Asian Language Information Processing* (*TALIP*), Vol. 2, No. 2, pp. 143–163.

Lavie, Alon, Katharina Probst, Erik Peterson, Stephan Vogel, Lori S. Levin, Ariadna Font-Llitjos, and Jaime G. Carbonell (2004). "A Trainable Transfer-based Machine Translation Approach for Languages with Limited Resources." *Proceedings of the 9th Workshop of the European Association for Machine Translation: Broadening Horizons of Machine Translation and Its Applications*, Foundation for International Studies, Malta, pp. 116–123.

Matsuda, Junichi and Hiroyuki Kumai (1999). "Transfer-based Japanese-Chinese Translation Implemented on an E-mail System." *Proceedings of MT Summit VII: MT in the Great Translation Era*, Singapore.

Trujillo, Arturo (1999). "Transfer Machine Translation." *Translation Engines: Techniques for Machine Translation*. Berlin and New York: Springer Verlag, pp. 121–166.

Watanabe, Hideo (1992). "A Similarity-driven Transfer System." *Proceedings of the 14th International Conference of Computational Linguistics* (*COLING-92*), Nantes, France, pp. 770–776.

Whitelock, Peter J. (1989). "Why Transfer and Interlingua Approaches to MT Are Both Wrong: A Position Paper." *Proceedings of the MT "into the '90s" Workshop*, Manchester, England.

Computer Translation Business

Bone, Andrew (2003). "Point/Counterpoint: Outsourcing vs. Inhouse." *Proceedings of the Localization World Conference 2003*, Seattle, Washington, DC, USA.

David-Cougler, DeAnn (2006). "Streamline Technical and Marketing Communications: A Case Story—Improve Global Collaboration across Technical and Marketing Departments to Improve Consistency of Communications and Increase Translation Throughput and Quality." *Proceedings of the Localization World Conference*, Barcelona, Spain.

Dias, Denver (2005). "Increasing the Profitability of Your Translation Business." *Programme of the Annual Conference of the Association of Translation Companies: Surviving and Prospering in a Changing Translation Market*, School of Oriental and African Studies, University of London, England.

Garcia-Ochoa, Belen and Steve Hackett (2006). "Vendor Control or Relationship Management: When Metris UK Needed to Ship Their Product to China a Close Collaboration with Their Vendor Was the Only Way to Overcome the Technical Barriers." *Proceedings of the Localization World Conference*, Barcelona, Spain.

O'Hagan, Minako (1996). "The Translation Business and the Impact of MT." *The Coming Industry of Teletranslation: Overcoming Communication Barriers through Telecommunication.* Clevedon: Multilingual Matters Ltd., pp. 14–39.

Meer, Jaap van der (2003). "The Business Case for Machine Translation." In *Translating and the Computer 25*. London: The Association for Information Management.

Schuh, Sarah (2006). "Technology in Translation Businesses: An Industry Opinion." *Proceedings of the 6th Portsmouth Translation Conference: Translation Technologies and Culture*, School of Languages and Area Studies, University of Portsmouth, England.

Computer Translation Evaluation

Ackerman, Frank, Priscilla Fowler, and Robert G. Ebenau (1984). "Software Inspection and the Industrial Production of Software, Software Validation." *Proceedings of the Symposium on Software Validation*, Darmstadt, Germany, pp. 13–40.

Adkins, K. (1988). "Evaluation of Software and Hardware for Multilingual Text Production." In Catriona Picken, ed., *ITI Conference 2: Translators and Interpreters Mean Business*. London: The Association for Information Management, pp. 45–52.

Ahrenberg, Lars and Magnus Merkel (2000). "Correspondence Measures for MT Evaluation." In Bente Maegaard, ed., *Proceedings of the Workshop on Machine Translation Evaluation* (*LREC-2000*), Athens, Greece.

Akiba, Yasuhiro, Eiichiro Sumita, Hiromi Nakaiwa, Seiichi Yamamoto, and Hiroshi G. Okuno (2003). "Experimental Comparison of MT Evaluation Methods: RED versus BLEU." *Proceedings of MT Summit IX*, New Orleans, Louisiana, USA, pp. 1–8.

Albisser, Doris (1993). "Evaluation of MT Systems at Union Bank of Switzerland." *Machine Translation*, Vol. 8, Nos. 1–2, pp. 25–27.

Amigó, Enrique, Jesús Gimenez, and Chiori Hori (2005). "Machine Translation Evaluation Inside QARLA." *Proceedings of the International Workshop on Spoken Language Translation* (*IWSLT-2005*), Pittsburgh, PA, USA.

Amigó, Enrique, Jesús Giménez, Julio Gonzalo, Lluís Màrquez, Núria Castell, and Anselmo Peñas (2006). "MT Evaluation: Human-like vs. Human Acceptable." *Proceedings of the Joint Conference of the International Committee on Computational Linguistics and the Association for Computational Linguistics* (*COLING/ACL-2006*), Sydney, Australia.

Arnold, Doug J., Dave Moffat, Louisa Sadler, and Andy Way (1993). "Automatic Test Suite Generation." *Machine Translation*, Vol. 8, Nos. 1–2, pp. 29–38.

Arnold, Doug J., Louisa Sadler, and R. Lee Humphreys (1993). "Evaluation: An Assessment." *Machine Translation*, Vol. 8, Nos. 1–2, pp. 1–24.

Arnold, Doug J., R. Lee Humphreys, and Louisa Sadler, eds. (1993). "Special Issue on Evaluation of MT Systems." *Machine Translation*, Vol. 8, Nos. 1–2.

Arnold, Doug J., Dave Moffat, Louisa Sadler, and Andrew Way (1993). "Automatic Test Suite Generation." *Machine Translation*, Vol. 8, Nos. 1–2, pp. 29–38.

Babych, Bogdan and Tony Hartley (2004). "Extending the BLEU MT Evaluation Method with Frequency Weightings." *Proceedings of the*

42nd Annual Meeting of the Association for Computational Linguistics (ACL-2004), Barcelona, Spain, pp. 621–628.

Balfour, Richard W. (1986). *Machine Translation: A Technology Assessment.* London: BMT Consultants.

Balkan, Lorna, Mattias Jaeschke, R. Lee Humphreys, Siety Meijer, and Andrew Way (1991). "Declarative Evaluation of an MT System: Practical Experiences." *Applied Computer Translation*, Vol. 1, No. 3, pp. 49–59.

Balkan, Lorna (1994). "Test Suites: Some Issues on Their Use and Design." *Machine Translation—Ten Years On: Proceedings of the 2nd International Conference Organised by Cranfield University*, Cranfield, England.

Belam, Judith (2002). "Teaching MT Evaluation by Assessed Portfolio." *Proceedings of the 6th EAMT Workshop: Teaching Machine Translation*, Manchester, England, pp. 131–136.

Boggio, Giorgio and E. Spachis-Papazois, eds. (1984). *Evaluation of Research and Development. Methodologies for R&D Evaluation in the European Community Member States, the United States of America and Japan.* Dordrecht: D. Reidel Publishing Company.

Boisen, Sean and Madeleine Bates (1992). "A Practical Methodology for the Evaluation of Spoken Language Systems." *Proceedings of the 3rd Conference on Applied Natural Language Processing*, Trento, Italy, pp. 162–169.

Bukowski, J. (1987). "Evaluating Software Test Results: A New Approach." *Proceedings: Annual Reliability and Maintainability Symposium*, Philadelphia, USA, pp. 369–375.

Cavar, Damir, Uwe Küssner, and Dan Tidhar (2000). "From Human Evaluation to Automatic Selection of Good Translations." In Bente Maegaard, ed., *Proceedings of the Workshop on Machine Translation Evaluation (LREC-2000)*, Athens, Greece.

Chen, Kuang Hua and Hsin-Hsi Chen (1994). "Extracting Noun Phrases from Large-scale Texts: A Hybrid Approach and Its Automatic Evaluation." *Proceedings of the 32nd Annual Meeting of the Association for Computational Linguistics (ACL-94)*, Las Cruces, New Mexico, USA, pp. 234–241.

Correa, Nelson (2003). "A Fine-grained Evaluation Framework for Machine Translation System Development." *Proceedings of the 1st Conference of the Association for Machine Translation in the Americas*, Columbia, Maryland, USA.

Crook, Mason N. and Harold P. Bishop (1965). *Evaluation of Machine Translation.* Final Report, Institute of Psychological Research, Tufts University.

Culy, Christopher and Susanne Z. Riehemann (2003). "The Limits of N-gram Translation Evaluation Metrics." *Proceedings of the MT Summit IX*, New Orleans, Louisiana, USA, pp. 133–138.

Dauphin, Eva and Veronika Lux (1996). "Corpus-based Annotated Test Set for Machine Translation Evaluation by an Industrial User." *Proceedings from the 16th International Conference on Computational Linguistics* (*COLING-96*). Copenhagen, Denmark, pp. 1061–1065.

DePalma, Don (2006). "Commonsense Advisory Study—Evaluating MT Prior to Deployment." *Proceedings of the 7th Biennial Conference of the Association for Machine Translation in the Americas* (*AMTA-2006*)*: Visions for the Future of Machine Translation*, Boston Marriott, Cambridge, MA, USA.

Dong, Zhendong 董振東 and Dong Qiang 董強 (2001). 〈機譯研究中的一些誤區—從譯文質量分析看〉 (Some Misunderstandings in MT Research—From an Analysis of MT Translations). In Huang Changning 黃昌寧 and Zhang Pu 張普, eds., 《自然語言理解與機器翻譯》 (*Natural Language Understanding and Machine Translation*). Beijing: Tsinghua University Press, pp. 462–471.

Doyon, Jennifer B., Kathryn B. Taylor, and John S. White (1999). "Task-based Evaluation for Machine Translation." *Proceedings of MT Summit VII: MT in the Great Translation Era*, Singapore.

Duan, Huiming 段慧明 and Yu Shiwen 俞士汶 (1996). 〈關於1995年度機器翻譯評測的總結報告〉 (Final Report on Machine Translation Evaluation in 1995). In Yu Shiwen 俞士汶 and Zhu Xuefeng 朱學鋒, eds., 《計算語言學文集》 (*Papers on Computational Linguistics*). Beijing: Department of Computer Science and Technology and Institute of Computational Linguistics, Peking University, pp. 127–131.

Eck, Matthias, Stephan Vogel, and Alex H. Waibel (2006). "A Flexible Online Server for Machine Translation Evaluation." *Proceedings of the 11th Workshop of the European Association for Machine Translation: Machine Translation/Translation Aids—Tools to Increase Quality and to Save Money*, the University of Oslo, Oslo, Norway.

Elliott, Debbie, Anthony F. Hartley, and Eric Atwell (2003). "Rationale for a Multilingual Corpus for Machine Translation Evaluation."

Proceedings of the International Conference on Corpus Linguistics (CL-2003), Lancaster University, England.

Elliott, Debbie, Anthony F. Hartley, and Eric Atwell (2004). "A Fluency Error Categorization Scheme to Guide Automated Machine Translation Evaluation." In Robert E. Frederking and Kathryn B. Taylors, eds., *Machine Translation: From Real Users to Research*. Berlin: Springer Verlag, pp. 64–73.

Elliott, Debbie, Anthony F. Hartley, and Eric Atwell (2004). "Compiling and Using a Shareable Parallel Corpus for Machine Translation Evaluation." *Proceedings of the Workshop on the Amazing Utility of Parallel and Comparable Corpora, the 4th International Conference on Language Resources and Evaluation (LREC-2004)*, Lisbon, Portugal.

Flanagan, Mary A. (1994). "Error Classification for MT Evaluation." *Proceedings of the 1st Conference of the Association for Machine Translation in the Americas: Technology Partnerships for Crossing the Language Barrier (AMTA-1)*, Columbia, Maryland USA, pp. 65–72.

Fuji, Masaru (1999). "Evaluation Experiment for Reading Comprehension of Machine Translation Outputs." *Proceedings of MT Summit VII: MT in the Great Translation Era*, Singapore, pp. 285–289.

Fuji, Masaru and Hitoshi Isahara (2001). "Evaluation Method for Determining Groups of Users Who Find MT 'Useful'." In Bente Maegaard, ed., *Proceedings of MT Summit VIII: Machine Translation in the Information Age*, Santiago de Compostela, Spain.

Gamon, Michael, Anthony Aue, and Martine Smets (2005). "Sentence-level MT Evaluation without Reference Translations: Beyond Language Modeling." *Proceedings of the 10th Workshop of the European Association for Machine Translation: Practical Applications of Machine Translation*, Budapest, Hungary, pp. 103–111.

Giménez, Jesús and Enrique Amigó (2006). "IQmt: A Framework for Automatic Machine Translation Evaluation." *Proceedings of the 5th International Conference on Language Resources and Evaluation (LREC-2006)*, Genoa, Italy.

Grimaila, Annette and John Chandioux (1992). "Made to Measure Solutions." In John Newton, ed., *Computers in Translation: A Practical Appraisal*. London: Routledge, pp. 33–45.

Guessoum, Ahmed and Rached Zantout (2001). "A Methodology for a Semi-automatic Evaluation of the Lexicons of Machine Translation Systems." *Machine Translation*, Vol. 16, No. 2, pp. 127–149.

Guessoum, Ahmed and Rached Zantout (2001). "Semi-automatic Evaluation of the Grammatical Coverage of Machine Translation Systems." In Bente Maegaard, ed., *Proceedings of MT Summit VIII: Machine Translation in the Information Age*, Santiago de Compostela, Spain.

Guida, Giovanni and Giancarlo Mauri (1984). "A Formal Basis for Performance Evaluation of Natural Language Understanding Systems." *Computational Linguistics*, Vol. 10, No. 1, pp. 15–30.

Guida, Giovanni and Giancarlo Mauri (1986). "Evaluation of Natural Language Processing Systems: Issues and Approaches." *Proceedings of the IEEE*, Vol. 74, No. 7, pp. 1026–1035.

Hamon, Olivier, Andrei Popescu-Belis, Khalid Choukri, Marianne Dabbadie, Anthony F. Hartley, W. Mustafa El Hadi, Martin Rajman, and Ismail Timimi (2006). "CESTA: First Conclusions of the Technolanguage MT Evaluation Campaign." *Proceedings of the 5th International Conference on Language Resources and Evaluation* (*LREC-2006*), Genoa, Italy.

Hartley, Anthony F. and Martin Rajman (2001). "Automatically Predicting MT Systems Rankings Compatible with Fluency, Adequacy or Informativeness Scores." In Bente Maegaard, ed., *Proceedings of MT Summit VIII: Machine Translation in the Information Age*, Santiago de Compostela, Spain, pp. 29–34.

Hartley, Anthony F. (2006). "Evaluating Machine Translation: Challenges and Techniques." *Programme of an International Conference on Computer-aided Translation: Theory and Practice*, Department of Translation, The Chinese University of Hong Kong, Hong Kong.

Hogan, Christopher and Robert E. Frederking (1998). "An Evaluation of the Multi-engine MT Architecture." In David L. Farwell, Laurie Gerber, and Eduard Hovy, eds., *Machine Translation and the Information Soup*. Berlin: Springer Verlag, pp. 113–123.

Holland, Melissa, C. Schlesiger, and Calandra Tate (2000). "Evaluating Embedded Machine Translation in Military Field Exercises." In John S. White, ed., *Envisioning Machine Translation in the Information Future*. Berlin: Springer Verlag, pp. 239–247.

Hovy, Eduard H. (1999). "Toward Finely Differentiated Evaluation Metrics for Machine Translation." *Proceedings of the EAGLES Workshop on Standards and Evaluation*, Pisa, Italy.

Hovy Eduard H., Margaret King, and Andrei Popescu-Belis (2002). "An Introduction to Machine Translation Evaluation." *Proceedings of the Workshop at the LREC 2002 Conference*, Las Palmas, Spain, pp. 1–7.

Hovy, Eduard H., Margaret King, and Andrei Popescu-Belis (2002). "Principles of Context-based Machine Translation Evaluation." *Machine Translation*, Vol. 17, No. 1, pp. 43–75.

Hutchins, W. John (1998). "Evaluation of Machine Translation and Translation Tools." In Giovanni B. Varile and Antonio Zampolli, eds., *Survey of the State of the Art in Human Language Technology*. Cambridge: Cambridge University Press, pp. 418–419.

Hwa, Rebecca, Philip Resnik, Amy Weinberg, and Okan Kolak (2002). "Evaluating Translational Correspondence Using Annotation Projection." *Proceedings of the 40th Annual Meeting of the Association for Computational Linguistics* (*ACL-2002*), Philadelphia, PA, USA, pp. 392–399.

ISO/IEC (1991). *International Standard ISO/IEC 9126 Information Technology: Software Product Evaluation—Quality Characteristics and Guidelines for Their Use*. Geneva: International Organization for Standardization/International Electrotechnical Commission.

ISO/IEC (1998). *International Standard ISO/IEC 14598-5. Software Engineering—Product Evaluation—Part 5: Process for Evaluators*. Geneva: International Organization for Standardization/International Electrotechnical Commission.

ISO/IEC (1999). *International Standard ISO/IEC 14598-2. Information Technology—Software Product Evaluation—Part 1: General Overview*. Geneva: International Organization for Standardization/International Electrotechnical Commission.

ISO/IEC (1999). *International Standard ISO/IEC 14598-4. Software Engineering—Product Evaluation—Part 4: Process for Acquirers*. Geneva: International Organization for Standardization/International Electrotechnical Commission.

ISO/IEC (2000). *International Standard ISO/IEC 14598-2. Software Engineering—Product Evaluation—Part 2: Planning and Management*. Geneva: International Organization for Standardization/International Electrotechnical Commission.

ISO/IEC (2000). *International Standard ISO/IEC 14598-3. Software Engineering—Product Evaluation—Part 3: Process for Developers*. Geneva: International Organization for Standardization/International Electrotechnical Commission.

ISO/IEC (2001). *International Standard ISO/IEC 14598-6. Software Engineering—Product Evaluation—Part 6: Documentation of*

Evaluation Modules. Geneva: International Organization for Standardization/International Electrotechnical Commission.

ISO/IEC (2001). *International Standard ISO/IEC 9126-1. Software Engineering—Product Quality—Part 1: Quality Model*. Geneva: International Organization for Standardization/International Electrotechnical Commission.

Jordan, Pamela W., Bonnie J. Dorr, and John W. Benoit (1993). "A First-pass Approach for Evaluating Machine Translation Systems." *Machine Translation*, Vol. 8, Nos. 1–2, pp. 49–58.

King, Margaret (1989). *A Practical Guide to the Evaluation of Machine Translation Systems*. Geneva: Institute for the Study of Semantics and Cognition.

King, Margaret (1990). "A Workshop on Evaluation: Background Paper." *Proceedings of the 3rd International Conference on Theoretical and Methodological Issues in Machine Translation of Natural Languages (TMI-90)*, Linguistic Research Center, University of Texas, Austin, USA, pp. 255–259.

King, Margaret and Kirsten Falkedal (1990). "Using Test Suites in Evaluation of Machine Translation Systems." *Proceedings of the 13th International Conference on Computational Linguistics* (*COLING-90*), Helsinki, Finland, Vol. 2, pp. 211–216.

King, Margaret (1993). "Panel on Evaluation—MT Summit IV: Introduction." *Proceedings of MT Summit IV: International Cooperation for Global Communication*, Kobe, Japan, pp. 201–203.

King, Margaret (1996). "Validity and Evaluation of MT Systems." In Harold L. Somers, ed., *Terminology, LSP and Translation, Studies in Language Engineering in Honour of Juan C. Sager*. Amsterdam and Philadelphia: John Benjamins Publishing Company, pp. 189–203.

King, Margaret (1997). "Evaluating Translation." In Christa Hauenschild and Susanne Heizmann, eds., *Machine Translation and Translation Theory*. Berlin-New York: Mouton de Gruyter, pp. 251–263.

King, Margaret (1998). "Language Resources and Evaluation." *Proceedings of the International Conference on Natural Language Processing and Industrial Applications* (*NLP+IA/TAL+AI-98*), Moncton, New-Brunswick, Canada.

King, Margaret and Bente Maegaard (1998). "Issues in Natural Language Systems Evaluation." *Proceedings of the 1st International Conference on Language Resources and Evaluation* (*LREC-98*), Granada, Spain.

King, Margaret, Eduard Hovy, Benjamin K. Y. T'sou, John S. White, and Yusoff Zaharin (1999). "MT Evaluation—Panel Discussion." *Proceedings of MT Summit VII: MT in the Great Translation Era*, Singapore.

King, Margaret, Andrei Popescu-Belis, and Eduard Hovy (2003). "FEMTI: Creating and Using a Framework for MT Evaluation." *Proceedings of MT Summit IX*, New Orleans, Louisiana, USA, pp. 224–231.

Klein, Frederick (1988). "Factors in the Evaluation of MT: A Pragmatic Approach." In Muriel Vasconcellos, ed., *Technology as Translation Strategy*. New York: State University of New York at Binghamton, pp. 198–202.

Klein, Frederick (1988). "Factors in the Evaluation of MT: A Pragmatic Approach." In Muriel Vasconcellos, ed., *Technology as Translation Strategy*. New York: State University of New York at Binghamton, pp. 198–202.

Klein, Judith, Sabine Lehmann, Klaus Netter, and Tillman Wegst (1999). "DiET in the Context of MT Evaluation." In Rita Nübel and Uta Seewald-Heeg, eds., *Evaluation of the Linguistic Performance of Machine Translation Systems, Proceedings of the Konvens '98*. St. Augustin: Gardezi Verlag, pp. 107–126.

Kotani, Katsunori, Takehiko Yoshimi, Takeshi Kutsumi, Ichiko Sata, and Hitoshi Isahara (2005). "A Useful-based Evaluation of Reading Support Systems: Comprehension, Reading Speed and Effective Speed." *Proceedings of MT Summit X*, Phuket, Thailand.

Krauwer, Steven (1993). "Evaluation of MT Systems: A Programmatic View." *Machine Translation*, Vol. 8, Nos. 1–2, pp. 59–66.

Kulesza, Alex and Stuart M. Shieber (2004). "A Learning Approach to Improving Sentence-level MT Evaluation." *Proceedings of the 10th Conference on Theoretical and Methodological Issues in Machine Translation* (*TMI-04*), Baltimore, MD, USA, pp. 75–84.

Laoudi, Jamal, Calandra Tate, and Clare R. Voss (2006). "Task-based MT Evaluation: From Who/When/Where Extraction to Event Understanding." *Proceedings of the 5th International Conference on Language Resources and Evaluation* (*LREC-2006*), Genoa, Italy.

Lavie, Alon, Kenji Sagae, and Shyamsundar Jayaraman (2004). "The Significance of Recall in Automatic Metrics for MT Evaluation." In Robert E. Frederking and Kathryn B. Taylors, eds., *Machine Translation: From Real Users to Research*. Berlin: Springer Verlag, pp. 134–143.

Lehrberger, John and Laurent Bourbeau (1987). *Machine Translation: Linguistic Characteristics of MT Systems and General Methodology of Evaluation*. Amsterdam and Philadelphia: John Benjamins Publishing Company.

Lesn, M. (1994). "Results of the Warmup Exercises." In Muriel Vasconcellos, ed., *MT Evaluation: Basis for Future Directions: Proceedings of a Workshop Sponsored by the National Science Foundation*, San Diego, California, USA.

Leusch, Gregor, Nicola Ueffing, and Hermann Ney (2003). "String-to-string Distance Measure with Applications to Machine Translation Evaluation." *Proceedings of MT Summit IX*, New Orleans, Louisiana, USA, pp. 240–247.

Leusch, Gregor, Nicola Ueffing, and Hermann Ney (2006). "CDER: Efficient MT Evaluation Using Block Movements." *Proceedings of the 11th Conference of the European Chapter of the Association for Computational Linguistics* (*EACL-2006*), Trento, Italy.

Lewis, Derek (1997). "MT Evaluation: Science or Art?" *Machine Translation Review*, No. 6, pp. 25–36.

Lewis, Derek (1997). "MT Evaluation: Science or Art?" In *Translating and the Computer 19*. London: The Association for Information Management.

Liu, Ding and Daniel Gildea (2006). "Stochastic Iterative Alignment for Machine Translation Evaluation." *Proceedings of the Joint Conference of the International Committee on Computational Linguistics and the Association for Computational Linguistics* (*COLING/ACL-2006*), Sydney, Australia.

Luo, Airong 羅愛榮 and Duan Huiming 段慧明 (1996).〈機譯評估方法評述及一個基於測試集的自動評估系統——MTE的進展〉(Review of Machine Translation Evaluation Methods and the Progress of an Automatic Evaluation System (MTE) Based on Test Suite). In Yu Shiwen 俞士汶 and Zhu Xuefeng 朱學鋒, eds.,《計算語言學文集》(*Papers on Computational Linguistics*). Beijing: Department of Computer Science and Technology and Institute of Computational Linguistics, Peking University, pp. 121–126.

Masterman, Margaret (1978). "Can We Progress in Determining Criteria for Evaluating Machine Translation?" *Actes du Colloque sur l'evaluation des systemes de traduction automatises*. Luxembourg: Commission of the European Communities.

Maybury, Mark T. (1990). "Evaluation Spaces: A Framework for

Evaluating Natural Language Generation Systems." *Proceedings of the AAAI-90 Workshop in Evaluating Natural Language Generation Systems*, Boston, MA, USA.

Miller, Keith J. and Michelle Vanni (2005). "Inter-rater Agreement Measures and the Refinement of Metrics in the PLATO MT Evaluation Paradigm." *Proceedings of MT Summit X*, Phuket, Thailand, pp. 125–132.

Minnis, Stephen (1993). "Constructive Machine Translation Evaluation." *Machine Translation*, Vol. 8, Nos. 1–2, pp. 67–75.

Minnis, Stephen (1994). "A Simple and Practical Method for Evaluating Machine Translation Quality." *Machine Translation*. Vol. 9, No. 2, pp. 133–149.

Miyazawa, Shinichiro, Shoichi Yokoyama, Masaki Matsudaira, Akira Kumano, Shuji Kodama, Hideki Kashioka, Yoshiko Shirokizawa, and Yasuo Nakajima (1999). "Study on Evaluation of WWW MT Systems." *Proceedings of MT Summit VII: MT in the Great Translation Era*, Singapore, pp. 290–297.

Moré, Joaquim and Salvador Climent (2005). "A Cheap MT-evaluation Method Based on Internet Searches." *Proceedings of the 11th Workshop of the European Association for Machine Translation: Machine Translation/Translation Aids—Tools to Increase Quality and to Save Money*, the University of Oslo, Oslo, Norway.

Mowatt, David and Harold L. Somers (2000). "Is MT Software Documentation Appropriate for MT Users?" In John S. White, ed., *Envisioning Machine Translation in the Information Future*. Berlin: Springer Verlag, pp. 223–238.

Mustafa El Hadi, Widad, Ismail Timimi, and Marianne Dabbadie (2001). "Setting a Methodology for Machine Translation Evaluation." In Bente Maegaard, ed., *Proceedings of MT Summit VIII: Machine Translation in the Information Age*, Santiago de Compostela, Spain.

Nagao, Makoto (1985). "Evaluation of the Quality of Machine-translated Sentences and the Control of Language." *Journal of the Information Processing Society of Japan*, Vol. 26, pp. 1197–1202.

Neal, Jeannette G., Elissa L. Feit, and Christine A. Montgomery (1993). "Benchmark Investigation/Identification Project." *Machine Translation*, Vol. 8, Nos. 1–2, pp. 77–84.

Newton, John (1992). *Computers in Translation: A Practical Appraisal*. London: Routledge.

Niessen, Sonja, Franz Josef Och, Gregor Leusch, and Hermann Ney (2000). "An Evaluation Tool for Machine Translation: Fast Evaluation for MT Research." *Proceedings of the 2nd International Conference on Language Resources and Evaluation* (*LREC-2000*), Athens, Greece, Vol. 1, pp. 39–45.

Nomura, Hirosato (1993). "Evaluation Method of Machine Translation: From the Viewpoint of Natural Language Processing." *Proceedings of MT Summit IV: International Cooperation for Global Communication*, Kobe, Japan, pp. 205–207.

Nübel, Rita and Uta Seewald-Heeg, eds. (1998). *Evaluation of the Linguistic Performance of Machine Translation Systems*. Computerlinguistik und neue Medien. Gardez! Verlag, St. Augustin, Bonn.

Papinini, Kishore, Salim Roukos, Todd Ward, and Wei-jing Zhu (2002). "BLEU: A Method for Automatic Evaluation of Machine Translation." *Proceedings of 40th Annual Meeting of the Association for Computational Linguistics* (*ACL-2002*), Philadelphia, PA, USA, pp. 311–318.

Papinini, Kishore, Salim Roukos, Todd Ward, John Henderson, and Florence Reeder (2002). "Corpus-based Comprehensive and Diagnostic MT Evaluation: Initial Arabic, Chinese, French, and Spanish Results." *Proceedings of the Human Language Technology Conference* (*HLT-2002*), San Diego, CA, USA, pp. 124–127.

Pfafflin, Sheila M. (1965). "Evaluation of Machine Translations by Reading Comprehension Tests and Subjective Judgments." *Mechanical Translation*, Vol. 8, No. 2, pp. 2–8.

Popescu-Belis, Andrei (1999). "Evaluation of Natural Language Processing Systems: A Model for Coherence Verification of Quality Measures." In Marc Blasband and Patrick Paroubek, eds., *A Blueprint for a General Infrastructure for Natural Language Processing Systems Evaluation Using Semi-automatic Quantitative Black Box Approach in a Multilingual Environment*, Deliverable D1.1, Project LE-4-8340, LIMSI-CNRS, Orsay, France.

Popescu-Belis, Andrei, Sandra Manzi, and Margaret King (2001). "Towards a Two-stage Taxonomy for Machine Translation Evaluation." In Bente Maegaard, ed., *Proceedings of MT Summit VIII: Machine Translation in the Information Age*, Santiago de Compostela, Spain, pp. 1–8.

Popescu-Belis, Andrei (2003). "An Experiment in Comparative

Evaluation: Humans vs. Computers." *Proceedings of MT Summit IX*, New Orleans, Louisiana, USA.

Popescu-Belis, Andrei, Paula Estrella, Margaret King, and Nancy Underwood (2006). "A Model for Context-based Evaluation of Language Processing Systems and Its Application to Machine Translation Evaluation." *Proceedings of the 5th International Conference on Language Resources and Evaluation* (*LREC-2006*), Genoa, Italy.

Pugh, Jeanette (1992). "The Story So Far: An Evaluation of Machine Translation in the World Today." In John Newton, ed., *Computers in Translation: A Practical Appraisal*. London and New York: Routledge, pp. 14–32.

Rajman, Martin and Tony Hartley (2002). "Automatic Ranking of MT Systems." *Proceedings of 3rd International Conference on Language Resources and Evaluation* (*LREC*), Las Palmas de Gran Canaria, Spain, Vol. 4, pp. 1247–1253.

Read, Walter, Alex Quilici, John Reeves, Michael Dyer, and Eva Baker (1988). "Evaluating Natural Language Systems: A Sourcebook Approach." *Proceedings of the 12th International Conference on Computational Linguistics* (*COLING-88*), Budapest, Hungary, pp. 530–534.

Reeder, Florence, Keith J. Miller, Jennifer B. Doyon, and John White (2001). "The Naming of Things and the Confusion of Tongues: An MT Metric." In Bente Maegaard, ed., *Proceedings of MT Summit VIII: Machine Translation in the Information Age*, Santiago de Compostela, Spain.

Reeder, Florence (2006). "Direct Application of a Language Learner Test to MT Evaluation." *Proceedings of the 7th Biennial Conference of the Association for Machine Translation in the Americas* (*AMTA-2006*): *Visions for the Future of Machine Translation*, Boston Marriott, Cambridge, MA, USA.

Reiter, Ehud, Chris Mellish, and John Levine (1995). "Automatic Generation of Technical Documentation." *Applied Artificial Intelligence*, Vol. 9, No. 3, pp. 259–287.

Rinsche, Adriane (1993). "Towards a MT Evaluation Methodology." *Proceedings of the 5th International Conference on Theoretical and Methodological Issues in Machine Translation of Natural Languages: MT in the Next Generation* (*TMI-93*), Kyoto, Japan, pp. 266–275.

Rolling, Loll (1993). "Panel Contribution on MT Evaluation." *Proceedings of MT Summit IV: International Cooperation for Global Communication*, Kobe, Japan, pp. 209–210.

Roudaud, Brigitte, Maria Puerta, and Otemea Gamrat (1993). "A Procedure for the Evaluation and Improvement of an MT System by the End-user." *Machine Translation*, Vol. 8, Nos. 1–2, pp. 109–116.

Rushinek, Avi and Sara F. Rushinek (1985). "Accounting and Auditing Software Evaluation with Knowledge Based Expert Systems: An Empirical Multivariate Model." *Proceedings of the 4th Annual International Conference on Computers and Communications*, Scottsdale, Arizona, USA, pp. 250–254.

Sager, Juan C. (1978). "Criteria for Machine Translation Evaluation." *Proceedings of Workshop on Evaluation Problems in Machine Translation*, Luxembourg.

Schütz, Jörg (1997). "Utilizing Evaluation in Networked Machine Translation." *Proceedings of the 7th International Conference on Theoretical and Methodological Issues in Machine Translation (TMI-97)*, St. John's College, Santa Fe, New Mexico, USA.

Schütz, Jörg and Rita Nübel (1998). "Evaluating Language Technologies: The MULTIDOC Approach to Taming the Knowledge Soup." In David L. Farwell, Laurie Gerber, and Eduard Hovy, eds., *Machine Translation and the Information Soup*. Berlin: Springer Verlag, pp. 236–249.

Somers, Harold L. and Elizabeth Wild (2000). "Evaluating Machine Translation: The Cloze Procedure Revisited." In *Translating and the Computer 22: Proceedings of the Twenty-second International Conference on Translating and the Computer*. London: The Association for Information Management.

Soricut, Radu and Eric Brill (2004). "A Unified Framework for Automatic Evaluation Using a 4-gram Co-occurrence Statistics." *Proceedings of the 42nd Annual Meeting of the Association for Computational Linguistics (ACL-2004)*, Barcelona, Spain, pp. 613–620.

Spalink, Karin (1994). "Proposal for a Differentiated Text-related Machine Translation Evaluation Methodology." *MT News International*, p. 9.

Sparck, Jones, K. and Julia R. Galliers (1996). *Evaluating Natural Language Processing Systems*. Tubingen: Springer Verlag.

Steiner, Erich H. (1992). "Producers-users-customers: Towards a Differentiated Evaluation of Research in Machine Translation." *Machine Translation*, Vol. 7, No. 4, pp. 281–284.

Surcin, Sylvain, Olivier Hamon, Anthony F. Hartley, Martin Rajman, Andrei Popescu-Belis, Widad Mustafa El Hadi, Ismaïl Timimi, Marianne Dabbadie, and Khalid Choukri (2005). "Evaluation of Machine Translation with Predictive Metrics beyond BLEU/NIST: CESTA Evaluation Campaign # 1." *Proceedings of MT Summit X*, Phuket, Thailand.

Szanser, A. J. (1967). "Machine Translation—The Evaluation of an Experiment." *The Incorporated Linguist*, Vol. 6, No. 4, pp. 90–95.

Tate, Calandra M. and Clare R. Voss (2006). "Combining Evaluation Metrics via Loss Functions." *Proceedings of the 7th Biennial Conference of the Association for Machine Translation in the Americas (AMTA-2006): Visions for the Future of Machine Translation*, Boston Marriott, Cambridge, MA, USA.

Taylor, Kathryn, and John White (1998). "Predicting What MT Is Good for: User Judgments and Task Performance." In David L. Farwell, Laurie Gerber, and Eduard Hovy, eds., *Machine Translation and the Information Soup*. Berlin: Springer Verlag, pp. 364–373.

Tennant, Harry (1981). "What Makes Evaluation Hard?" *Proceedings of the 19th Annual Meeting of the Association for Computational Linguistics* (*ACL-81*), Stanford University, Stanford, California, USA, pp. 37–38.

Thompson, Bozena Henisz (1981). "Evaluation of Natural Language Interface to Data Base Systems." *Proceedings of the 19th Annual Meeting of the Association for Computational Linguistics* (*ACL-81*), Stanford University, Stanford, California, USA, pp. 39–42.

Thompson, Henry S. (1994). "TEMAA: A Testbed Study of Evaluation Methodologies: Authoring Aids." *Proceedings of the Language Engineering Convention* (*ELSNET*), Paris, France, pp. 147–148.

Thompson, Henry S. and Chris Brew (1996). *Automatic Evaluation of Computer-generated Text: Final Report of the TextEval Project*. Human Communication Research Centre, University of Edinburgh, Scotland.

Torrens, Antonio (1994). "Machine Translation Evaluation and Quality Benchmarks." *Terminologie et Traduction*, No. 1, pp. 375–415.

Trujillo, Arturo (1999). "Evaluation." *Translation Engines: Techniques for Machine Translation*. Berlin and New York: Springer Verlag, pp. 251–266.

Turian, Joseph P., Luke Shen, and I. Dan Melamed (2003). "Evaluation of

Machine Translation and Its Evaluation." *Proceedings of MT Summit IX,* New Orleans, Louisiana, USA, pp. 386–393.

Vanni, Michelle (1998). "Evaluating MT Systems: Testing and Researching the Feasibility of a Task-diagnostic Approach." In *Translating and the Computer 20.* London: The Association for Information Management.

Vanni, Michelle and Florence Reeder (2000). "How Are You Doing? A Look at MT Evaluation." In John S. White, ed., *Envisioning Machine Translation in the Information Future.* Berlin: Springer Verlag, pp. 109–116.

Vanni, Michelle and Keith J. Miller (2002). "Scaling the ISLE Framework: Use of Existing Corpus Resources for Validation of MT Metrics across Languages." *Proceedings of the 3rd International Conference on Language Resources and Evaluation* (*LREC*), Las Palmas de Gran Canaria, Spain, Vol. 4, pp. 1254–1262.

Vasconcellos, Muriel (1988). "Factors in the Evaluation of MT: Formal vs. Functional Approaches." In Muriel Vasconcellos, ed., *Technology as Translation Strategy.* New York: State University of New York at Binghamton, pp. 203–216.

Vasconcellos, Muriel, ed. (1992). *MT Evaluation: Basis for Future Directions—Proceedings of a Workshop Sponsored by the National Science Foundation.* Washington, DC: Association for Machine Translation.

Vasconcellos, Muriel (1993). "Evaluation Method of Machine Translation." *Proceedings of MT Summit IV: International Cooperation for Global Communication*, Kobe, Japan, pp. 211–213.

Volk, Martin (1997). "Probing the Lexicon in Evaluating Commercial MT Systems." *Proceedings of the 35th Annual Meeting of the Association for Computational Linguistics and 8th Conference of the European Chapter of the Association for Computational Linguistics* (*ACL-EACL-97*), Madrid, Spain.

Way, Andy (1991). "A Practical Developer-oriented Evaluation of Two MT Systems." *DLL Working Papers in Language Processing*, Department of Language and Linguistics, University of Essex, Colchester, England, p. 26.

White, John S. and Theresa A. O'Connell (1993). "Evaluation of Machine Translation." *ARPA Workshop on Human Language Technology*, Princeton, New Jersey.

White, John S. and Theresa A. O'Connell (1994). *ARPA Workshops on*

Machine Translation: A Series of Four Workshops on Comparative Evaluation, 1992–1994, McLean, VA: Litton PRC Inc.

White, John S. and Theresa A. O'Connell (1994). "The ARPA MT Evaluation Methodologies: Evolution, Lessons, and Future Approaches." *Technology Partnerships for Crossing the Language Barrier: Proceedings of the 1st Conference of the Association for Machine Translation in the Americas*, Columbia, Maryland, USA, pp. 193–205.

White, John S. (1996). "The Primacy of Core Technology MT Evaluation." *Proceedings of the 2nd Conference of the Association for Machine Translation in the Americas: Expanding MT Horizons (AMTA-2)*, Montreal, Quebec, Canada, pp. 212–218.

White, John S. (1997). "MT Evaluation: Old, New, and Recycled Methods." *Proceedings of MT Summit VI*, San Diego, California, USA.

White, John S. and Kathryn B. Taylor (1998). "A Task-oriented Metric for Machine Translation." *Proceedings of the 1st Language Resources and Evaluation Conference*, Granada, Spain, pp. 21–25.

White, John S. (2000). "Toward an Automated, Task-based MT Evaluation Strategy." In Bente Maegaard, ed., *Proceedings of the Workshop on Machine Translation Evaluation at LREC-2000*, Athens, Greece.

White, John S. (2000). "Contemplating Automatic MT Evaluation." In John S. White, ed., *Envisioning Machine Translation in the Information Future*. Berlin: Springer Verlag, pp. 100–108.

White, John S. (2001). "Predicting Intelligibility from Fidelity in MT Evaluation." In Bente Maegaard, ed., *Proceedings of MT Summit VIII: Machine Translation in the Information Age*, Santiago de Compostela, Spain, pp. 35–38.

White, John S. (2003). "How to Evaluate Machine Translation." In Harold L. Somers, ed., *Computers and Translation: A Translator's Guide*. Amsterdam and Philadelphia: John Benjamins Publishing Company, pp. 211–244.

Yamauchi, Satoshi (1999). "A Method of Evaluation of the Quality of Translated Text." *Proceedings of MT Summit VII: MT in the Great Translation Era*, Singapore.

Yao, Tianshun 姚天順 and Yang Ying 楊瑩 (2001).〈關於機器翻譯的評測問題〉(On the Evaluation of Machine Translation). In Huang Changning 黃昌寧 and Zhang Pu 張普, eds.,《自然語言理解與機器翻譯》(*Natural Language Understanding and Machine Translation*), Beijing: Tsinghua University Press, pp. 472–480.

Yasuda, Keiji, Fumiaki Sugaya, Toshiyuki Takezawa, Seiichi Yamamoto, and Masuzo Yanagida (2001). "An Automatic Evaluation Method of Translation Quality Using Translation Answer Candidates Queried from a Parallel Corpus." In Bente Maegaard, ed., *Proceedings of MT Summit VIII: Machine Translation in the Information Age*, Santiago de Compostela, Spain.

Yokoyama, Shoichi (1992). "Toward a Systematic Evaluation of Machine Translation: From the Viewpoint of Natural Language Processing." *Proceedings of the International Symposium on Neural Information Processing (ISKIT-92)*, Fukuoka, Japan.

Yokoyama, Shoichi (1993). "Evaluation Method of Machine Translation: From the Viewpoint of Natural Language Processing." *Proceedings of MT Summit IV: International Cooperation for Global Communication*, Kobe, Japan, pp. 215–217.

Yokoyama, Shoichi, Akira Kumano, Masaki Matsudaira, Yoshiko Shirokizawa, Mutumi Kawagoe, Shuji Kodama, Hideki Kashioka, Terumasa Ehara, Shinichiro Miyazawa, and Yasuo Nakajima (1999). "Quantitative Evaluation of Machine Translation Using Two-way MT." *Proceedings of MT Summit VII: MT in the Great Translation Era*, Singapore.

Yokoyama, Shoichi, Hideki Kashioka, Akira Kumano, Masaki Matsudaira, Yoshiko Shirokizawa, Shuji Kodama, Terumasa Ehara, Shinichiro Miyazawa, and Yuzo Murata (2001). "An Automatic Evaluation Method for Machine Translation Using Two-way MT." In Bente Maegaard, ed., *Proceedings of MT Summit VIII: Machine Translation in the Information Age*, Santiago de Compostela, Spain.

Yu, Shiwen (1993). "Automatic Evaluation of Output Quality for Machine Translation Systems." *Machine Translation*, Vol. 8, Nos. 1–2, pp. 117–126.

Zhang, Ying and Stephan Vogel (2004). "Measuring Confidence Intervals for the Machine Translation Evaluation Metrics." *Proceedings of the 10th Conference on Theoretical and Methodological Issues in Machine Translation (TMI-04),* Baltimore, MD, USA, pp. 85–94.

Advanced Research Projects Agency (ARPA)

Advanced Research Projects Agency (ARPA) (1993). *Human Language*

Technology: Proceedings of a Workshop, San Matero, California: Morgan-Kaufmann.
O'Connell, Theresa, Francis E. O'Mara, and John S. White (1994). "The ARPA MT Evaluation Methodologies: Evolution, Lessons and Further Approaches." *Proceedings of the 1st Conference of the Association for Machine Translation in the Americas*, Columbia, USA.
White, John S., Theresa A. O'Connell, and Francis E. O'Mara (1994). "The ARPA MT Evaluation Methodologies: Evolution, Lessons, and Future Approaches." *Proceedings of the 1st Conference of the Association for Machine Translation in the Americas: Technology Partnerships for Crossing the Language Barrier (AMTA-1)*, Columbia, Maryland, USA, pp. 193–205.

ALPAC

ALPAC (1966). *Language and Machines: Computers in Translation and Linguistics*. A Report by the Automatic Language Processing Advisory Committee. Division of Behavioral Sciences, National Academy of Sciences, National Research Council, Seattle, Washington, DC, USA.
Corness, Patrick (1985). "The ALPS Computer-assisted Translation System in an Academic Environment." In Catriona Picken, ed., *Translating and the Computer 7*. London: The Association for Information Management, pp. 118–127.
Hutchins, W. John (1996). "ALPAC: The (In)famous Report." *MT News International*, Vol. 14, pp. 9–12.
King, Margaret (1984). "When Is the Next ALPAC Report Due?" *Proceedings of the 10th International Conference on Computational Linguistics (COLING-84)*, Stanford University, Stanford, California, USA, pp. 352–353.
Warwick, Susan (1987). "An Overview of Post-ALPAC Developments." In Margaret King, ed., *Machine Translation Today: The State of the Art*. Edinburgh: Edinburgh University Press, pp. 22–37.

Black-box Evaluation

Dahl, Deborah A., Lynette Hirschman, and Catherine N. Ball (1988). "Black Box Evaluation of PUNDIT." *Workshop on Evaluation of Natural Language Processing Systems*, Wayne, Philadelphia, USA.

White, John S. (1995). "Approaches to Black Box MT Evaluation." *Proceedings of MT Summit V: Machine Translation Conference, Exhibition and Tutorial*, Luxembourg.

Zajac, Rémi, Steven Helmreich, and Karine Megerdoomian (2000). "Black-box/Glass-box Evaluation in Shiraz." In Bente Maegaard, ed., *Proceedings of the Workshop on Machine Translation Evaluation* (*LREC-2000*), Athens, Greece.

DARPA

Doyon, Jennifer B., Kathryn B. Taylor, and John S. White (1998). "The DARPA Machine Translation Evaluation Methodology: Past and Present." *Proceedings of the 3rd Conference of the Association for Machine Translation in the Americas* (*AMTA-98*), Philadelphia, PA, USA.

Kubala, Francis, G., Yen-Lu Chow, M. Derr, Ming-Whei Feng, Owen Kimball, John Makhoul, P. Price, J. Rohlicek, S. Roucos, Richard Schwartz, and Jeffrey Vandegrift (1988). "Continuous Speech Recognition Results of the BYBLOS System on the DARPA 1000-word Resource Management Database." *Proceedings of IEEE International Conference on Acoustics, Speech and Signal Processing* (*ICASSP-88*), New York, USA, pp. 291–294.

White, John S. and Theresa A. O'Connell (1996). "Adaptation of the DARPA Machine Translation Evaluation Paradigm to End-to-end Systems." *Proceedings of the 2nd Conference of the Association for Machine Translation in the Americas: Expanding MT Horizons* (*AMTA-2*), Montreal, Quebec, Canada, pp. 106–114.

EAGLES

Blasband, Marc (1999). "Practice of Validation: The ARISE Application of the Eagles Framework." *Proceedings of the European Evaluation of Language Systems Conference* (*EELS*), Hoevelaken, the Netherlands.

Calzolari, Nicoletta, Antonio Zampolli, and Alessandro Lenci (2002). "Towards a Standard for a Multilingual Lexical Entry: The EAGLES/ISLE Initiative." *Proceedings of the 3rd International Conference on Intelligent Text Processing and Computational Linguistics* (*CICLing-2002*), Mexico City, Mexico.

EAGLES MT Evaluation Working Group, The (1996). *EAGLES Evaluation of Natural Language Processing Systems.* Final Report. EAGLES Document EAG-EWG-PR.2, ISBN 87-90708-00-8. Copenhagen: Center for Sprogteknologi. (http://www.issco.unige.ch/projects/ewg96/)

EAGLES MT Evaluation Working Group, The (1998). *EAGLES Evaluation of Natural Language Processing Systems.* Final Report. Copenhagen: Center for Sprogteknologi.

King, Margaret (1998). "Evaluation Design: The EAGLES Framework." *Proceedings of the Conference on Computers, Linguistics and Phonetics between Language and Speech (KONVENS-98)*, Universität Bonn, Bonn, Germany.

King, Margaret (1999). "The 7-step Recipe." *Working Document of the EAGLES Evaluation Group, EELS Conference*, Hoevelaken, the Netherlands.

Glass-box Evaluation

Zajac, Rémi, Steven Helmreich, and Karine Megerdoomian (2000). "Black-box/Glass-box Evaluation in Shiraz." In Bente Maegaard, ed., *Proceedings of the Workshop on Machine Translation Evaluation (LREC-2000)*, Athens, Greece.

Internal Evaluation

Lange, Elke and Laurie Gerber (1992). "Internal Evaluation: Quality Analysis, an Internal Evaluation Tool at SYSTRAN." *MT Evaluation: Basis for Future Directions. Proceedings of a Workshop Sponsored by the National Science Foundation*, San Diego, California, USA, pp. 55–56.

JEIDA

Isahara, Hitoshi (1995). "JEIDA's Test-sets for Quality Evaluation of MT Systems." *Proceedings of MT Summit V: Machine Translation Conference, Exhibition and Tutorial*, Luxembourg.

Japanese Electronic Industry Development Association (1989). "A Japanese View of Machine Translation in the Light of the

Considerations and Recommendations." Reported by ALPAC, USA. Tokyo: Japan Electronic Industry Development Association.

Japanese Electronic Industry Development Association (1992). *JEIDA Methodology and Criteria on Machine Translation Evaluation.* Tokyo: Japanese Electronic Industry Development Association.

Nomura, Hirosato, ed. (1992). *JEIDA Methodology and Criteria on Machine Translation Evaluation* (JEIDA Report). Tokyo: Japan Electronic Industry Development Association.

Nomura, Hirosato and Hitoshi Isahara (1992). "JEIDA's Criteria on Machine Translation Evaluation." *Proceedings of the International Symposium on Natural Language Understanding and AI* (*NLU & AI*) *as a Part of International Symposia on Information Sciences* (*ISKIT-92*), Iizuka, Fukuoka, Japan, pp. 107–117.

Nomura, Hirosato and Hitoshi Isahara (1992). "JEIDA Report on Machine Translation." *Proceedings of the AMTA Workshop on MT Evaluation*, San Diego, CA, USA.

Computer Translation Evaluation Criteria

Acceptability

Banchs, Rafael, Antonio Bonafonte, and Javier Pérez (2006). "Acceptance Testing of a Spoken Language Translation System." *Proceedings of the 5th International Conference on Language Resources and Evaluation* (*LREC-2006*), Genoa, Italy.

Blache, Philippe, Barbara Hemforth, and Stéphane Rauzy (2000). "Acceptability Prediction by Means of Grammaticality Quantification." *Proceedings of the Joint Conference of the International Committee on Computational Linguistics and the Association for Computational Linguistics* (*COLING/ACL-2006*), Sydney, Australia.

Hui, Bowen (2002). "Measuring User Acceptability of Machine Translations to Diagnose System Errors: An Experience Report." *Proceedings of COLING-2002 Workshop on Machine Translation in Asia,* Taipei, Taiwan.

Accuracy

Naruedomkul, Kanlaya and Nick Cercone (1997). "Steps toward Accurate

Machine Translation." *Proceedings of the 7th International Conference on Theoretical and Methodological Issues in Machine Translation* (*TMI-97*), St. John's College, Santa Fe, New Mexico, USA.

Phaholphinyo, Sitthaa, Teerapong Modhiran, Nattapol Kritsuthikul, and Thepchai Supnithi (2005). "A Practical Memory-based Approach for Improving Accuracy of MT." *Proceedings of MT Summit X*, Phuket, Thailand.

Simard, Michel and Pierre Plamondon (1996). "Bilingual Sentence Alignment: Balancing Robustness and Accuracy." *Proceedings of the 2nd Conference of the Association for Machine Translation in the Americas* (*AMTA-96*), Montreal, Quebec, Canada, pp. 135–144.

Soricut, Radu, Kevin Knight, and Daniel Marcu (2002). "Using a Large Monolingual Corpus to Improve Translation Accuracy." In Stephen D. Richardson, ed., *Machine Translation: From Research to Real Users.* Berlin and New York: Springer Verlag, pp. 155–164.

Comprehensibility

Du, Yongping, Helen Meng, Huang Xuanjing, and Wu Lide (2005). "The Use of Metadata, Web-derived Answer Patterns and Passage Context to Improve Reading Comprehension Performance." *Proceedings of Human Language Technology Conference and Conference on Empirical Methods in Natural Language Processing* (*HLT/EMNLP-2005*), Vancouver, BC, Canada.

Orr, David B. and Victor H. Small (1967). "Comprehensibility of Machine-aided Translations of Russian Scientific Documents." *Mechanical Translation*, Vol. 10, Nos. 1–2, pp. 1–10.

Cost

Bodenkamp, Stephan (1995). "Machine Translation—The Economical Part of Multilingual Information Processing." *Proceedings of MT Summit V: Machine Translation Conference, Exhibition and Tutorial*, Luxembourg.

Booth, Andrew D. (1961). "Syntactic Processing in Machine Translation and Its Implications for Cost and Speed." In Allen Kent, ed., *Information Retrieval and Machine Translation.* New York: Interscience, Vol. 2, pp. 759–763.

Forrester, Jay (1952). "Problems of Storage and Cost." *Proceedings of the M.I.T. Conference on Mechanical Translation,* Massachusetts Institute of Technology, Cambridge, MA, USA.

Fosler-Lussier, Eric and C. Anton Rytting (2005). "A Cost-benefit Analysis of Hybrid Phone-manner Representations for ASR." *Proceedings of Human Language Technology Conference and Conference on Empirical Methods in Natural Language Processing (HLT/EMNLP-2005*), Vancouver, BC, Canada.

Pym, Anthony (2004). "Transaction Costs." *The Moving Text: Localization, Translation, and Distribution.* Amsterdam and Philadelphia: John Benjamins Publishing Company, pp. 133–157.

Rolling, Loll (1980). "Automatic Translation Today and Tomorrow: The Computer Is Cheaper Than Human Translation." *Umsch Wiss. und Tech.,* Vol. 80, No. 11, pp. 333–338.

van Slype, Georges (1982). "Economic Aspects of Machine Translation." In Veronica Lawson, ed., *Practical Experience of Machine Translation.* Amsterdam: North-Holland Publishing Company, pp. 79–93.

Fidelity

Ahrenberg, Lars (2005). "Codified Close Translation as a Standard for MT." *Proceedings of the 10th Annual Conference of the European Association for Machine Translation* (*EAMT-2005*), Budapest, Hungary.

Forner, Monika and John S. White (2001). "Predicting MT Fidelity from Noun-compound Handling." In Bente Maegaard, ed., *Proceedings of MT Summit VIII: Machine Translation in the Information Age*, Santiago de Compostela, Spain, pp. 45–48.

King, Margaret (1995). "Les belles infidhles: Fidelity as a Criterion of Good Translation." In Barbara H. Partee and Petr Sgall, eds., *Discourse and Meaning, Papers in Honor of Eva Hajicova.* Amsterdam and Philadelphia: John Benjamins Publishing Company.

White, John S. and Monika Forner (2001). "Predicting Intelligibility from Fidelity in MT Evaluation." In Bente Maegaard, ed., *Proceedings of MT Summit VIII: Machine Translation in the Information Age*, Santiago de Compostela, Spain, pp. 35–38.

Intelligibility

Reeder, Florence (2004). "Investigation of Intelligibility Judgments." In Robert E. Frederking and Kathryn B. Taylors, eds., *Machine Translation: From Real Users to Research*. Berlin: Springer Verlag, pp. 227–235.

Vauquois, Bernard (1979). "Measurement of Intelligibility of Sentences on Two Scales." In Georges van Slype, ed., *Critical Study of Methods for Evaluating the Quality of Machine Translation, Final Report BR 19142*. Brussels: Bureau Marcel van Dijk.

White, John S. (2001). "Predicting Intelligibility from Fidelity in MT Evaluation." In Bente Maegaard, ed., *Proceedings of MT Summit VIII: Machine Translation in the Information Age*, Santiago de Compostela, Spain, pp. 35–38.

Psychology

Bevan, Nigel (1982). "Psychological and Ergonomic Factors in Machine Translation." In Veronica Lawson, ed., *Practical Experience of Machine Translation*. Amsterdam: North-Holland Publishing Company, pp. 75–78.

Readability

Sinaiko, H. Wallace and George R. Klare (1972). "Further Experiments in Language Translation: Readability of Computer Translations." *ITL* (*Review of Institute of Applied Linguistics, Louvain*), Vol. 15, pp. 1–29.

Sinaiko, H. Wallace and George R. Klare (1973). "Further Experiments in Language Translation: A Second Evaluation of the Readability of Computer Translation." *ITL* (*Review of Institute of Applied Linguistics, Louvain*), Vol. 19, pp. 29–52.

Sinaiko, H. Wallace and Richard W. Brislin (1973). "Evaluating Language Translations: Experiments of Three Assessment Methods." *Journal of Applied Psychology*, Vol. 57, No. 3, pp. 328–334.

Taylor, Wilson L. (1953). "Cloze Procedure: A New Tool for Measuring Readability." *Journalism Quarterly*, Vol. 30, pp. 415–433.

Taylor, Wilson L. (1956). "Recent Developments in the Use of Cloze Procedure." *Journalism Quarterly*, Vol. 33, pp. 42–48, 99.

Computer Translation History

Ananiadou, Sofia and Susan Warwick (1984). "An Overview of Post-ALPAC Developments." *The Institute for the Study of Semantics and Cognition Tutorial on Machine Translation*, Lugano, Switzerland.

Arnold, Doug J. (1992). "Reaction to Somers: Current Research in Machine Translation." *Machine Translation*, Vol. 7, No. 4, pp. 247–251.

Arnold, Doug J., Lorna Balkan, R. Lee Humphreys, Seity Meijer, and Louisa Sadler (1994). "Introduction and Overview." *Machine Translation: An Introductory Guide*. Manchester and Oxford: NCC Blackwell, pp. 1–17.

Arnold, Doug J., Lorna Balkan, R. Lee Humphreys, Seity Meijer, and Louisa Sadler (1994). "New Directions in MT." *Machine Translation: An Introductory Guide*. Manchester and Oxford: NCC Blackwell, pp. 183–206.

Austermühl, Frank (2001). "Translation in the Information Age." *Electronic Tools for Translators*. Manchester: St. Jerome Publishing Company, pp. 1–17.

Bar-Hillel, Yehoshua (1951). "The Present State of Research on Mechanical Translation." *American Documentation*, Vol. 2, pp. 229–237.

Bar-Hillel, Yehoshua (1960). "The Present Status of Automatic Translation of Languages." In Franz L. Alt, ed., *Advances in Computers, Vol. 1*. New York: Academic Press, pp. 91–163.

Bar-Hillel, Yehoshua (1962). "The Future of Machine Translation." *The Times Literary Supplement*, 20 April.

Bar-Hillel, Yehoshua (1971). "Some Reflections on the Present Outlook for High-quality Machine Translation." In Winfred P. Lehmann and Rolf A. Stachowitz, eds., *Feasibility Study on Fully Automatic High Quality Translation*. New York: Rome Air Development Center, pp. 72–76.

Beaven, John (1998). "MT: 10 Years of Development." *Terminologie et Traduction*, Vol. 1, pp. 242–256.

Booth, Andrew D. and William N. Locke (1955). "Historical Introduction." In William N. Locke and Andrew D. Booth, eds., *Machine Translation of Languages: Fourteen Essays*. Cambridge, MA: Technology Press of the Massachusetts Institute of Technology, pp. 1–14.

Booth, Andrew D. and Kathleen H.V. Booth (2000). "The Beginnings of MT." In W. John Hutchins, ed., *Early Years in Machine Translation: Memoirs and Biographies of Pioneers*. Amsterdam and Philadelphia: John Benjamins Publishing Company, pp. 253–261.

Bourbeau, Laurent R. (1992). "Current MT Research Orientation/ Disorientation." *Machine Translation*, Vol. 7, No. 4, pp. 253–258.

Brinkmann, Karl-Heinz (1978). "Perspectives of Machine Translation." *Nachrichten fuer Dokumentation*, Vol. 29, No. 3, pp. 104–108.

Bruderer, Herbert E. (1975). "The Present State of Machine Translation and Machine-aided Translation." *ALLC Bulletin*, Vol. 3, No. 3, pp. 258–261.

Bruderer, Herbert E. (1977). "The Present State of Machine and Machine-assisted Translation." *Overcoming the Language Barrier*. Munich: Verlag Dokumentation, pp. 529–556.

Brundage, Jennifer A. (2001). "Machine Translation: Evolution Not Revolution." *Proceedings of MT Summit VII*, Santiago de Compostela, Spain.

Buchmann, Beat (1984). "Early History of Machine Translation." The Institute for the Study of Semantics and Cognition Tutorial on Machine Translation, Lugano, Switzerland.

Buchmann, Beat (1987). "Early History of Machine Translation." In Margaret King, ed., *Machine Translation Today: The State of the Art*. Edinburgh: Edinburgh University Press, pp. 3–21.

Chan, Sin-wai (2004). "Machine Translation in the World: Major Events and Publications." *A Dictionary of Translation Technology*. Hong Kong: The Chinese University Press, pp. 289–344.

Chang, Baobao 常寶寶 and Zhang Wei 張偉 (1998).〈機器翻譯研究的現狀和發展趨勢〉(The Study of Machine Translation: Present and Future). In Yu Shiwen 俞士汶 and Zhu Xuefeng 朱學鋒, eds.,《計算語言學文集》(*Papers on Computational Linguistics*), Vol. 3. Beijing: Department of Computer Science and Technology and Institute of Computational Linguistics, Peking University, pp. 115–121.

De Roeck, Anne (1987). "Linguistic Theory and Early Machine Translation." In Margaret King, ed., *Machine Translation Today: The State of the Art*. Edinburgh: Edinburgh University Press, pp. 38–57.

Devos, Y. (1970). *Survey of Machine Translation*. Brussels: M. Haps.

Dostert, Leon E. (1957). "Brief History of Machine Translation

Research." *Research in Machine Translation*. Georgetown: Georgetown University Press, pp. 3–10.

Feng, Zhiwei 馮志偉 (1994).〈機器翻譯的新發展〉(New Developments in Machine Translation).《自然語言機器翻譯新論》(*New Essays on Machine Translation of Natural Languages*). Beijing: Language Press, pp. 3–13.

Fenwick, Peter W. (1987). "Recent Developments in IT Standards of Interest to Translators." In Catriona Picken, ed., *Translating and the Computer 8: A Profession on the Move*. London: The Association for Information Management, pp. 31–39.

Flanagan, Mary A. (1997). "MT Today: Emerging Roles, New Successes." *Machine Translation*, Vol. 12, Nos. 1–2, pp. 25–27.

Garvin, Paul L. (1968). "Machine Translation Today: The Fulcrum Approach and Heuristics." *Lingua*, Vol. 21, pp. 162–182.

Garvin, Paul L. (1976). "Machine Translation in the Seventies." In Ferenc Papp and Gyorgy Szepe, eds., *Papers in Computational Linguistics*. The Hague: Mouton, pp. 445–459.

Haynes, Colin (1998). "Interpreting the Future." *Breaking Down the Language Barriers*. London: The Association for Information Management, pp. 25–31.

Hutchins, W. John (1986). "Expectations and Criticisms: The Decade from 1956 to 1966." *Machine Translation: Past, Present and Future*. Chichester: Ellis Horwood, pp. 150–173.

Hutchins, W. John (1986). *Machine Translation: Past, Present and Future*. Chichester: Ellis Horwood.

Hutchins, W. John (1986). "Precursors and Pioneers." *Machine Translation: Past, Present and Future*. Chichester: Ellis Horwood, pp. 21–39.

Hutchins, W. John (1986). "Present Developments and Future Prospects." *Machine Translation: Past, Present and Future*. Chichester: Ellis Horwood, pp. 322–335.

Hutchins, W. John (1988). "Recent Developments in Machine Translation." In Dan Maxwell, Klaus Schubert, and Toon Witkam, eds., *New Directions in Machine Translation*. Dordrecht-Holland: Foris Publications, pp. 7–63.

Hutchins, W. John (1992). "And after the Second Generation...." *Machine Translation*, Vol. 7, No. 4, pp. 259–264.

Hutchins, W. John and Harold L. Somers (1992). "General Introduction and Brief History." *An Introduction to Machine Translation*. London: Academic Press, pp. 1–9.

Hutchins, W. John (1994) "Machine Translation: History and General Principles." In R. E. Asher, ed., *The Encyclopedia of Language and Linguistics*. Oxford: Pergamon Press Ltd., pp. 2322–2332.

Hutchins, W. John (1995). "Reflections on the History and Present State of Machine Translation." *Proceedings of MT Summit V: Machine Translation Conference, Exhibition and Tutorial*, Luxembourg.

Hutchins, W. John (1997). "Fifty Years of the Computer and Translation." *Machine Translation Review*, No. 6, pp. 22–24.

Hutchins, W. John (1997). "Machine Translation: A Brief History." In E. F. K. Koerner and R. E. Asher, eds., *Concise History of the Language Sciences: From the Sumerians to the Cognitivists*. Oxford: Pergamon, pp. 431–445.

Hutchins, W. John (1997). "From First Conception to First Demonstration: The Nascent Years of Machine Translation, 1947–1954: A Chronology." *Machine Translation*, Vol. 12, No. 3, pp. 195–252.

Hutchins, W. John (1998). "Twenty Years of Translating and the Computer." In *Translating and the Computer 20*. London: The Association for Information Management.

Hutchins, W. John (1999). "Retrospect and Prospect in Computer-based Translation" *Proceedings of MT Summit VII: MT in the Great Translation Era*, Singapore, pp. 30–34.

Hutchins, W. John, ed. (2000). *Early Years in Machine Translation: Memoirs and Biographies of Pioneers*. Amsterdam and Philadelphia: John Benjamins Publishing Company.

Hutchins, W. John (2000). "The First Decades of Machine Translation: Overview, Chronology, Sources." In W. John Hutchins, ed., *Early Years in Machine Translation: Memoirs and Biographies of Pioneers*. Amsterdam and Philadelphia: John Benjamins Publishing Company, pp. 1–15.

Hutchins, W. John (2001). "Towards a New Vision for MT." In Bente Maegaard, ed., *Proceedings of MT Summit VIII: Machine Translation in the Information Age*, Santiago de Compostela, Spain.

Isabelle, Pierre (1992). "Current Research in Machine Translation: A Reply to Somers." *Machine Translation*, Vol. 7, No. 4, pp. 265–272.

Jin, Hailin 靳海林 (1987). 〈機器翻譯的歷史與展望〉 (Machine Translation:

Past, Present, and Future).《中國翻譯》(*Chinese Translators Journal*), No. 5, pp. 33–34.

Johnson, Roderick L. (1980). "Contemporary Perspectives in Machine Translation." In Suzanne Hanon and Viggo Hjørnager Pedersen, eds., *Human Translation, Machine Translation*. Odense: Romansk Institut, Odense Universitet, pp. 133–147.

King, Margaret, ed. (1987). *Machine Translation Today: The State of the Art*. Edinburgh: Edinburgh University Press.

King, Margaret (1989). "New Directions in MT Systems: A Change in Paradigm." In Christian Rohrer, ed., *Proceedings of MT Summit II*, Munich, Germany, pp. 95–96.

King, Margaret (1992). "State of the Art and Perspectives." *Machine Translation*, Vol. 7, No. 4, pp. 273–279.

Krauwer, Steven (2002). "Where Do We Stand? MT Summit and TMI Report." *Proceedings of the 9th International Conference on Theoretical and Methodological Issues in Machine Translation* (*TMI-2002*), Keihanna, Japan.

Kulagina, Olga S. (1976). "History and Present State of Machine Translation." *Cybernetics*, Vol. 6, pp. 937–944.

Li, Renzhi 李韧之 (1994).〈機器翻譯進展〉(Advances in Machine Translation). In Li Yashu 李亞舒, Yan Yutang 嚴毓棠, Zhang Ming 張明, and Zhao Lanhui 趙蘭慧, eds.,《科技翻譯論著集萃》(*Collected Essays on Scientific and Technical Translation*). Beijing: Chinese Scientific Technology Press, pp. 496–500.

Loh, Shiu-chang 樂秀章 (1976). "Machine Translation: Past, Present, and Future." *ALLC Bulletin*, Vol. 4, No. 2, pp. 105–114.

Lück, Jens Thomas (1998). "Translation in the Next Century: A Future Vision." In *Translating and the Computer 20*. London: The Association for Information Management.

Macklovitch, Elliott (1995). "The Future of MT Is Now and Bar-Hillel Was (Almost Entirely) Right." *Proceedings of the 4th Bar-Ilan Symposium on the Foundations of Artificial Intelligence*, Ramat Gan, Israel.

Maxwell, Dan, Klaus Schubert, and Toon Witkam (1988). *Recent Developments in Machine Translation*. Dordrecht: Foris.

Mitkov, Ruslan and Johann Haller (1994). "Machine Translation, Ten Years On: Discourse Has Yet to Make a Breakthrough." *Machine Translation—Ten Years On: Proceedings of the 2nd International*

Conference Organised by Cranfield University, Cranfield, England.
Nagao, Makato (1989). "The Dawn of Machine Translation." In Norman D. Cook, trans., *Machine Translation: How Far Can It Go?* Oxford: Oxford University Press, pp. 17–38.
Nagao, Makato (1989). "Japanese View of Future of Machine Translation." *Proceedings of the MT Summit II*, Munich, Germany, pp. 123–140.
Nagao, Makoto (1989). "Revival of Machine Translation." In Norman D. Cook, trans., *Machine Translation: How Far Can It Go?* Oxford: Oxford University Press, pp. 39–48.
Nirenburg, Sergei, Jaime G. Carbonell, Masaru Tomita, and Kenneth Goodman (1992). "The Future of Machine Translation." *Machine Translation: A Knowledge-based Approach*. San Matero, California: Morgan Kaufmann, pp. 95–116.
Perez, Celia Rico and Aurora Martin de Santa Olalla Sanchez (1997). "New Trends in Machine Translation." *Meta*, Vol. 42, No. 4, pp. 605–615.
Plum, T. (1974). "The State of Machine Translation." In *Translators and Translating: Selected Essays from the American Translators Association*. Binghamton, New York: State University of New York, pp. 37–42.
Rolling, Loll (1987). "MT: Recent Developments." In Catriona Picken, ed., *Translating and the Computer 8: A Profession on the Move*. London: The Association for Information Management, pp. 109–113.
Sampson, Geoffrey (1987). "MT: A Nonconformist's View of the State of the Art." In Margaret King, ed., *Machine Translation Today: The State of the Art*. Edinburgh: Edinburgh University Press, pp. 91–108.
Sigurd, Bengt (1978). "Machine Translation—State of the Art." In Grahs Lillebill, Gustav Korlen, and Bertil Malmberg, eds. *Theory and Practice of Translation*. Bern: Peter Lang, pp. 33–47.
Slocum, Jonathan (1985). "A Survey of Machine Translation: Its History, Current Status, and Future Prospects." *Computational Linguistics*, Vol. 11, No. 1, pp. 1–17.
Slocum, Jonathan (1987). "A Survey of Machine Translation: Its History, Current Status, and Future Prospects." In Jonathan Slocum, ed., *Machine Translation Systems*. Cambridge: Cambridge University Press, pp. 1–48.
Somers, Harold L. (1990). "Current Research in Machine Translation."

Proceedings of the 3rd International Conference on Theoretical and Methodological Issues in Machine Translation of Natural Languages (TMI-90), Linguistics Research Center, University of Texas, Austin, Texas, USA, pp. 1–12.

Somers, Harold L. (1992). "A Response to the Comments." *Machine Translation*, Vol. 7, No. 4, pp. 315–322.

Somers, Harold L. (1992). "Current Research in Machine Translation." *Machine Translation*, Vol. 7, No. 4, pp. 231–246.

Somers, Harold L. (1992). "Current Research in Machine Translation." In John Newton, ed. *Computers in Translation: A Practical Appraisal.* London and New York: Routledge, pp. 189–207.

Somers, Harold L. (1995). "Problems with the Second Generation Architecture and New Trends in MT." *Proceedings of MT Summit V: Machine Translation Conference, Exhibition and Tutorial*, Luxembourg.

Somers, Harold L. (1997). "The Current State of Machine Translation." *Proceedings of MT Summit VI*, San Diego, California, USA, pp. 81–99, 115–24.

Somers, Harold L. (1998). "Machine Translation: History." In Mona Baker, ed., *Routledge Encyclopedia of Translation Studies*. London and New York: Routledge, pp. 140–143.

Somers, Harold L. (1998). "'New Paradigms in MT: The State of the Art Now That the Dust Has Settled." In Frank van Eynde, ed., *Proceedings of the Workshop on Machine Translation, 10th European Summer School in Logic, Language and Information*, Saarbrucken, Germany, pp. 22–33.

Somers, Harold L. (2002). "What Are We Celebrating Today?" *Proceedings of the 9th International Conference on Theoretical and Methodological Issues in Machine Translation (TMI-2002)*, Keihanna, Japan.

Tamati, T. (1985). "A Historical Overview of Machine Translation." *Journal of the Information Processing Society of Japan*, Vol. 26, No. 10.

Thouin, Benoit (1979). "The Future of Computer Translation." *Association of IT Professionals Reviews*, Vol. 3, No. 6, pp. 18–19.

Thurmair, Gregor (1991). "Recent Developments in Machine Translation." *Computers and the Humanities*, Vol. 25, pp. 115–128.

Troike, R. C. (1976). "The View from the Center: The Future of MT." *The Linguistic Reporter*, Vol. 18, No. 9, p. 2.

Tsujii, Jun-ichi (1986). "Future Directions of Machine Translation." *Proceedings of the 11th International Conference on Computational Linguistics* (*COLING-86*), Bonn, Germany, pp. 655–668.

Tucker, Allen B. and Sergei Nirenburg (1984). "Machine Translation: A Contemporary View." *Annual Review of Information Science and Technology*, Vol. 19.

Vasconcellos, Muriel (1994). "MT in the 1990s." *Technology Partnerships for Crossing the Language Barrier: 1st Conference of the Association for Machine Translation in the Americas*, Columbia, Maryland, USA.

Vasconcellos, Muriel (1994). "The Current State of MT Usage Or: How Do I Use Thee? Let Me Count the Ways." *The LISA Forum Newsletter*, Vol. 3, pp. 21–29.

Vasconcellos, Muriel (1994). "The Present State of Machine Translation Usage Technology Or: How Do I Use Thee? Let Me Count the Ways." *Proceedings of MT Summit IV: International Cooperation for Global Communication*, Kobe, Japan, pp. 35–46.

Vasconcellos, Muriel and L. Chris Miller (1996). "Recent Trends in Machine Translation." In *Translating and the Computer 18*. London: The Association for Information Management.

Ward, Nigel (2002). "Machine Translation in the Mobile and Wearable Age." *Proceedings of the 9th International Conference on Theoretical and Methodological Issues in Machine Translation* (*TMI-2002*), Keihanna, Japan.

Warwick, Susan (1987). "An Overview of Post-ALPAC Developments." In Margaret King, ed., *Machine Translation Today: The State of the Art*. Edinburgh: Edinburgh University Press, pp. 22–37.

Weaver, Warren (1955). "Translation." In William N. Locke and Andrew D. Booth, eds., *Machine Translation of Languages: Fourteen Essays*. Cambridge, MA: Technology Press of the Massachusetts Institute of Technology, pp. 15–33.

Wheeler, Peter J. (1985). "Update on Machine Translation." In Catriona Picken, ed., *Translation and Communication: Translating and the Computer 6*. London: The Association for Information Management, pp. 39–51.

White, John S. (1992). "Responses to Current Research in Machine Translation by Harold Somers." *Machine Translation*, Vol. 7, No. 4, pp. 303–307.

Wilks, Yorick (1978). "Four Generations of Machine Translation Research and Prospects for the Future." In David Gerver and H. Wallace Sinaiko, eds., *Language, Interpretation and Communication*. New York: Plenum Press, pp. 171–184.

Wilks, Yorick (1992). "Commentary on Somers' Article." *Machine Translation*, Vol. 7, No. 4, pp. 309–314.

Wilks, Yorick (1994). "Some Notes on the State of the Art: Where Are We Now in MT: What Works and What Doesn't? And the Role of MT as an International Collaborative Activity." *Machine Translation—Ten Years On: Proceedings of the 2nd International Conference Organised by Cranfield University*, Cranfield, England.

Yngve, Victor H. (1955). "The Outlook for Mechanical Translation." *Babel*, Vol. 2, No. 3, pp. 99–101.

Zarechnak, Michael (1979). "The History of Machine Translation." In Bozena Henisz-Dostert, R. Ross MacDonald, and Michael Zarechnak, eds., *Machine Translation*. The Hague: Mouton, pp. 20–28.

Zarechnak, Michael (1980). "Machine Translation: Past, Present, and Future." *ATA Chronicle*, Vol. 6, No. 7, pp. 10–12.

Zarechnak, Michael (1988). "Machine Translation: Present Status and Future Outlook in the Global Milieu." In John Lihani, ed., *Proceedings of the Conference on National Language Academies and Their Mission*. Lexington: Kentucky Foreign Language Conference, pp. 151–172.

Computer Translation Industry

Barabé, Donald (2003). "Soaring Demand, Shrinking Supply in Translation: How We Plan to Make Ends Meet." *Proceedings of MT Summit IX*, New Orleans, Louisiana, USA, pp. 23–27.

Bennett, Scott and Laurie Gerber (2003). "Inside Commercial Machine Translation." In Harold L. Somers, ed., *Computers and Translation: A Translator's Guide*. Amsterdam and Philadelphia: John Benjamins Publishing Company, pp. 175–190.

Britton, Natalie and Marina Byezhanova (2003). "Machine Translation Market and the Role of Lingvistica '98: An Attempt of a Critical Analysis." *International Journal of Translation*, Vol. 15, No. 1, pp. 131–141.

Byrne, Jody (2006). "Translation and the Internet: Changing the Face of an Industry." *Proceedings of the 6th Portsmouth Translation Conference:*

Translation Technologies and Culture, School of Languages and Area Studies, University of Portsmouth, England.
Champollion, Yves (2001). "Machine Translation (MT), and the Future of the Translation Industry." *Translation Journal*, Vol. 5, No. 1.
Haynes, Colin (1998). "MT in the Business Environment." *Breaking Down the Language Barriers*. London: The Association for Information Management, pp. 45–66.
Haynes, Colin (1998). "Tips to Achieve Faster, More Accurate Translation —And Ways to Make Money from Your MT Intellectual Property." *Breaking Down the Language Barriers*. London: The Association for Information Management, pp. 115–125.
Marty-Albisser, Doris (1995). "Integration of MT into the Business Process." *Proceedings of MT Summit V: Machine Translation Conference, Exhibition and Tutorial*, Luxembourg.
O'Hagan, Minako (1996). *The Coming Industry of Teletranslation: Overcoming Communication Barriers through Telecommunication.* Clevedon: Multilingual Matters Ltd.
Rolling, Loll (1993). "Panel on International Cooperation." *Proceedings of MT Summit IV: International Cooperation for Global Communication*, Kobe, Japan, pp. 221–222.
Torrejón, Enrique and Celia Rico (2002). "Controlled Translation: A New Teaching Scenario Tailor-made for the Translation Industry." *Proceedings of the 6th Workshop of the European Association for Machine Translation: Teaching Machine Translation*, Manchester, England, pp. 107–116.

Computer Translation Market

Benitatto, Renato S. (2006). "A Global Review of the Translation Market Place." *Programme of the 30th Anniversary Conference of the Association of Translation Companies 30th Anniversary Conference 2006: Building Strong Markets for Translations—Making Links and Seizing Opportunities*, School of Oriental and African Studies, University of London, England.
Bennett, Winfield S. (1995). "Realities of Development in Market-oriented MT." *Proceedings of MT Summit V: Machine Translation Conference, Exhibition and Tutorial*, Luxembourg.
Britton, Natalie and Marina Byezhanova (2003). "Machine Translation

Market and the Role of Lingvistica '98: An Attempt of a Critical Analysis." *International Journal of Translation*, Vol. 15, No. 1, pp. 131–141.

Burgess, Carolyn (2006). "The Customer is King (or Queen)! The Secret of Developing Successful Client-translation Provider Relationships —From the Customer and TC Perspectives." *Programme of the 30th Anniversary Conference of the Association of Translation Companies 30th Anniversary Conference 2006: Building Strong Markets for Translations—Making Links and Seizing Opportunities*, School of Oriental and African Studies, University of London, England.

Miller, L. Chris, Colin Brace, and Y. Shimamoto-Caleo (1997). "The MT Market Perspective." *Proceedings of MT Summit VI*, San Diego, California, USA.

Shih, Don (2006). "Taking Advantage of New Emerging Asian Language Markets and Winning Business." *Programme of the 30th Anniversary Conference of the Association of Translation Companies 30th Anniversary Conference 2006: Building Strong Markets for Translations—Making Links and Seizing Opportunities*, School of Oriental and African Studies, University of London, England.

Sznajder, Monika, Jaroslava Flodrova, and Artem Raksha (2005). "Developing Translation Markets." *Programme of the Annual Conference of the Association of Translation Companies: Surviving and Prospering in a Changing Translation Market*, School of Oriental and African Studies, University of London, England.

van der Meer, Jaap (2003). "At Last Translation Automation Becomes a Reality: An Anthology of the Translation Market." *Proceedings of the Joint Conference Combining the 8th International Workshop of the European Association for Machine Translation and the 4th Controlled Language Applications Workshop: Controlled Language Translation (EAMT-CLAW-03)*, Dublin City University, Dublin, Ireland.

Yamada, Setsuo, Syuuji Kodama, Taeko Matsuoka, Hiroshi Araki, Yoshiaki Murakami, Osamu Takano, and Yoshiyuki Sakamoto (2005). "A Report on the Machine Translation Market in Japan." *Proceedings of MT Summit X*, Phuket, Thailand.

Zilinskiene, Jurga (2004). "Marketing—I Did It My Way." *Programme of the Annual Conference of the Association of Translation Companies: Getting in Shape for the Future—Working towards a New Environment for the Translation Profession*, School of Oriental and African Studies, University of London, England.

Computer Translation Methodology

Beliaeva, Larissa (2001). "Machine Translation Methods: Text Structure and Translator Work." *International Journal of Translation*, Vol. 13, Nos. 1–2, pp. 119–146.

Belskaya, I. K. (1960). "Machine Translation Methods and Their Application to an Anglo-Russian Scheme." *Information Processing: Proceedings of the International Conference on Information Processing*, UNESCO, Paris, France, pp. 197–217.

Edmundson, Harold P. and David G. Hays (1958). "Research Methodology for Machine Translation." *Machine Translation*, Vol. 5, No. 1, pp. 8–15.

Nirenburg, Sergei, ed. (1987). *Machine Translation: Theoretical and Methodological Issues. Studies in Natural Language Processing.* Cambridge: Cambridge University Press.

Rhodes, Ida and Franz L. Alt (1962). "Hindsight Technique in Machine Translation of Natural Languages." *Journal of Research of the National Bureau of Standards*, Vol. 66, No. 2, pp. 47–51.

Richens, Richard H. and Andrew D. Booth (1955). "Some Methods of Mechanized Translation." In William N. Locke and Andrew D. Booth, eds., *Machine Translation of Languages: Fourteen Essays.* Cambridge, MA: Technology Press of the Massachusetts Institute of Technology, pp. 24–46.

Somers, Harold L. (1998). "Machine Translation: Methodology." In Mona Baker, ed., *Routledge Encyclopedia of Translation Studies.* London and New York: Routledge, pp. 143–149.

Steiff, S. (1979). "The Development of the 'Titus' Four-language Automatic Translation Method." *International Forum on Information and Documentation*, Vol. 4, pp. 20–26.

Tombe, des Louis (1997). "Compensation." In Christa Hauenschild and Susanne Heizmann, eds., *Machine Translation and Translation Theory.* Berlin-New York: Mouton de Gruyter, pp. 157–173.

Gisting

Resnik, Philip (1997). "Evaluating Multilingual Gisting of Web Pages."

Proceedings of the AAAI Symposium on Cross-language Text and Speech Retrieval, Stanford University, CA, USA.

Omission

Melamed, I. Dan (1996). "Automatic Detection of Omissions in Translations." *Proceedings from the 16th International Conference on Computational Linguistics (COLING-96)*. Copenhagen, Denmark, pp. 764–769.
Melamed, I. Dan (2001). "Application: Automatic Detection of Omissions in Translations." *Empirical Methods for Exploiting Parallel Texts*. Cambridge, MA: MIT Press, pp. 41–53.

Paraphrase

Barzilay, Regina and Lillian Lee (2003). "Learning to Paraphrase: An Unsupervised Approach Using Multiple-Sequence Alignment." *Proceedings of the Human Language Technology and North American Chapter of Association of Computational Linguistics 2003 (HLT/NAACL-2003)*, Edmonton, Alberta, Canada.
Callison-Burch, Chris, Philipp Koehn, and Miles Osborne (2006). "Improved Statistical Machine Translation Using Paraphrases." *Proceedings of the Human Language Technology Conference—Annual Meeting of the North American Chapter of the Association for Computational Linguistics (HLT-NAACL-2006)*, New York, USA.
Carl, Michael, Ecaterina Rascu, and Paul Schmidt (2005). "Using Template Grammars for Shake and Bake Paraphrasing." *Proceedings of the 10th Workshop of the European Association for Machine Translation: Practical Applications of Machine Translation*, Budapest, Hungary, pp. 66–72.
Culicover, Peter W. (1968). "Paraphrase Generation and Information Retrieval from Stored Text." *Mechanical Translation*, Vol. 11, Nos. 3–4, pp. 78–88.
Duboue, Pablo and Jennifer Chu-Carroll (2006). "Answering the Question You Wish They Had Asked: The Impact of Paraphrasing for Question Answering." *Proceedings of the Human Language Technology Conference—Annual Meeting of the North American Chapter of the*

Association for Computational Linguistics (*HLT-NAACL-2006*), New York, USA.

Kauchak, David and Regina Barzilay (2006). "Paraphrasing for Automatic Evaluation." *Proceedings of the Human Language Technology Conference—Annual Meeting of the North American Chapter of the Association for Computational Linguistics* (*HLT-NAACL-2006*), New York, USA.

Milićević, Jasmina (2000). "Communicative Structure of Sentences as a Means of Controlling the Generation of Paraphrases." *Proceedings of the 1st International Conference on Intelligent Text Processing and Computational Linguistics* (*CICLing-2000*), Mexico City, Mexico.

Muraki, Kazunori (1982). "On a Semantic Model for Multi-lingual Paraphrasing." In Jan Horecky, ed., *Proceedings of the 9th International Conference on Computational Linguistics* (*COLING-82*), Prague, the Czech Republic. Amsterdam: North-Holland Publishing Company, pp. 239–244.

Pang, Bo, Kevin Knight, and Daniel Marcu (2003). "Syntax-based Alignment of Multiple Translations: Extracting Paraphrases and Generating New Sentences." *Proceedings of the Human Language Technology and North American Chapter of Association of Computational Linguistics 2003* (*HLT/NAACL-2003*), Edmonton, Alberta, Canada, pp. 102–109.

Shirai, Satoshi, Yamamoto Kazuhide, and Francis Bond (2001). "Japanese-English Paraphrase Corpus." *Proceedings of the 6th Natural Language Processing Pacific Rim Symposium*, National Center of Sciences, Tokyo, Japan, pp. 23–30.

Stede, Manfred (1996). "Lexical Paraphrases in Multilingual Sentence Generation." *Machine Translation*, Vol. 11, Nos. 1–3, pp. 75–107.

Zhou, Liang, Chin-Yew Lin, Dragos Stefan Munteanu, and Eduard Hovy (2006). "ParaEval: Using Paraphrases to Evaluate Summaries Automatically." *Proceedings of the Human Language Technology Conference—Annual Meeting of the North American Chapter of the Association for Computational Linguistics* (*HLT-NAACL-2006*), New York, USA.

Computer Translation Operation

Huskey, Harry D. (1952). "Basic Machine Operations in MT."

Proceedings of the M.I.T. Conference on Mechanical Translation, Massachusetts Institute of Technology, Cambridge, MA, USA.

Computer Translation Portal

Allen, Jeffrey (2000). "The Value of Internet Translation Portals." *International Journal for Language and Documentation*, Vol. 6, pp. 45–46.

Cleary, Róisín and Reinhard Schäler (2000). "R&D Opens Doors to Translation Portals." *Localization Ireland*, Vol. 4, No. 1, p. 9.

Computer Translation Process

Feng, Zhiwei 馮志偉 (2004).〈機器翻譯的實現過程〉(Machine Translation Process).《機器翻譯研究》(*Studies on Machine Translation*). Beijing: China Translation and Publishing Corporation, pp. 67–102.

Haynes, Colin (1998). "How It Works." *Breaking Down the Language Barriers*. London: The Association for Information Management, pp. 67–84.

Korkas, Vassilis (2006). "The Impact of Technology on Translator Training: Translation Product v. Translation Process." *Proceedings of the 6th Portsmouth Translation Conference: Translation Technologies and Culture*, School of Languages and Area Studies, University of Portsmouth, England.

Landsbergen, Jan and Franciska de Jong (1994). "The Translation Process." In M. T. Rosetta, *Compositional Translation*. Dordrecht: Kluwer Academic Publishers, pp. 57–84.

Nagao, Makoto (1989). "The Process of Machine Translation." In Norman D. Cook, trans., *Machine Translation: How Far Can It Go?* Oxford: Oxford University Press, pp. 62–82.

Robichaud, Benoît and Marie-Claude L'Homme (2003). "Teaching the Automation of the Translation Process to Future Translators." *Proceedings of the MT Summit IX Workshop on Teaching Translation Technologies and Tools*, New Orleans, Louisiana, USA, pp. 27–34.

Transfer

Abb, Bernd, Bianka Buschbeck-Wolf, and Christel Tschernitschek (1996). "Abstraction and Underspecification in Semantic Transfer."

Proceedings of the 2nd Conference of the Association for Machine Translation in the Americas: Expanding MT Horizons (*AMTA-2*), Montreal, Quebec, Canada, pp. 56–65.

Amtrup, Jan W. (1995). "Chart-based Incremental Transfer in Machine Translation." *Proceedings of the 6th International Conference on Theoretical and Methodological Issues in Machine Translation* (*TMI-95*), Leuven, Belgium, pp. 131–136.

Arnold, Doug and Louisa Sadler (1991). "Transfer Formalisms." *Machine Translation*, Vol. 6, No. 3, pp. 193–200.

Buschbeck-Wolf, Bianka and Michael Dorna (2000). "Using Hybrid Methods and Resources in Semantic-based Transfer." In Nicolas Nicolov and Ruslan Mitkov, eds., *Recent Advances in Natural Language Processing II*. Amsterdam and Philadelphia: John Benjamins Publishing Company, pp. 285–302.

Eberle, Kurt (2003). "Coordination, Incorporation and Dynamic Semantic Representation in Transfer." *Proceedings of the Joint Conference Combining the 8th International Workshop of the European Association for Machine Translation and the 4th Controlled Language Applications Workshop: Controlled Language Translation* (*EAMT-CLAW-03*), Dublin City University, Dublin, Ireland.

Emele, Martin C., Michael Dorna, Anke Lüdeling, Heike Zinsmeister, and Christian Rohrer (2000). "Semantic-based Transfer." In Wolfgang Wahlster, ed., *Verbmobil: Foundations of Speech-to-speech Translation*. Berlin: Springer Verlag, pp. 359–376.

Estival, Dominique, Afzal Ballim, Graham Russell, and Susan Warwick (1990). "A Syntax and Semantics for Feature-structure Transfer." *Proceedings of the 3rd International Conference on Theoretical and Methodological Issues in Machine Translation of Natural Languages* (*TMI-90*), Linguistics Research Center, University of Texas at Austin, Austin, Texas, USA, pp. 131–141.

Feng, Zhiwei 馮志偉 and Yang Ping 楊平 (1987).〈原譯語轉換和譯語自動生成〉(Transfer of the Source Language and Automatic Generation of the Target Language).《自動翻譯》(*Automatic Translation*). Shanghai: Knowledge Press, pp. 292–323.

Feng, Zhiwei 馮志偉 (1994).〈詞匯轉換器和形態生成器〉(Transfer and Morphological Generator).《自然語言機器翻譯新論》(*New Essays on Machine Translation of Natural Languages*). Beijing: Language Press, pp. 197–223.

Feng, Zhiwei 馮志偉 (2004).〈機器翻譯中的轉換〉(Transfer in Machine Translation).《機器翻譯研究》(*Studies on Machine Translation*). Beijing: China Translation and Publishing Corporation, pp. 637–678.

Hutchins, W. John and Harold L. Somers (1992). "Problems of Transfer and Interlingua." *An Introduction to Machine Translation*. London: Academic Press, pp. 99–130.

Krauwer, Steven and Louis des Tombe (1984). "Reflections on Transfer in Machine Translation." *Contrastes, Revue de l'Association pour le Development des 'Etudes Contrastives*, January, pp. 69–80.

Krauwer, Steven and Louis des Tombe (1984). "Transfer in a Multilingual MT System." *Proceedings of the 10th International Committee on Computational Linguistics and the 22nd Annual Meeting of the Association for Computational Linguistics*, Stanford University, California, USA, pp. 464–467.

Laffling, John (1991). "Transfer: Theoretical Underpinnings and Practical Application." *Towards High-precision Machine Translation: Based on Contrastive Textology*. Berlin and New York: Foris Publications, pp. 81–105.

Laffling, John (1992). "On Constructing a Transfer Dictionary for Man and Machine." *Target*, Vol. 4, No. 1, pp. 17–31.

Mesli, Nadia (1994). "Interlingua vs. Transfer: Knowledge Sharing across Projects." *Proceedings of the 1st Conference of the Association for Machine Translation in the Americas: Technology Partnerships for Crossing the Language Barrier* (*AMTA-1*), Columbia, Maryland, USA, pp. 169–176.

Schmidt, Paul (1988). "Transfer Strategies in EUROTRA." In Erich H. Steiner, Paul Schmidt, and Cornelia Zelinsky-Wibbelt, eds., *From Syntax to Semantics: Insight from Machine Translation*. London: Pinter Publishers Ltd.

Sumita, Eiichiro (2000). "Lexical Transfer Using a Vector-space Model." *Proceedings of the 38th Annual Meeting of the Association for Computational Linguistics* (*ACL-2000*), Hong Kong.

Sun, Chung-Teng and Jyun-Sheng Chang (1991). "Lexicon-driven Transfer in English-Chinese Machine Translation." *Proceedings of the Conference of the Association for Computational Linguistics and Chinese Language Processing* (*ROCLING-IV*), National Chiao-Tung University, Hsinchu, Taiwan.

Tsujii, Jun-ichi (1982). "The Transfer Phase in an English-Japanese Translation System." In Jan Horecky, ed., *Proceedings of the 9th*

International Conference on Computational Linguistics (*COLING-82*), Prague, the Czech Republic. Amsterdam: North-Holland Publishing Company, pp. 383–390.
Tsujii, Jun-ichi and Kimikaza Fujita (1990). "Lexical Transfer Based on Bilingual Signs—Towards Interaction during Transfer." *Proceedings of the 3rd Conference of the Association for Computational Linguistics and Chinese Language Processing* (*ROCLING-III*), Hsin-Chu, Taiwan, pp. 141–157.
Turcato, Davide, Olivier Laurens, Paul McFetridge, and Fred Popowich (2000). "Inflectional Information in Transfer for Lexicalist Machine Translation." In Nicolas Nicolov and Ruslan Mitkov, eds., *Recent Advances in Natural Language Processing II*. Amsterdam and Philadelphia: John Benjamins Publishing Company, pp. 303–314.
Wang, Ye-yi and Alex Maibel (1997). "Connectionist F-structure Transfer." In Ruslan Mitkov and Nicolas Nicolov, eds., *Recent Advances in Natural Language Processing*. Amsterdam and Philadelphia: John Benjamins Publishing Company, pp. 393–404.
Way, Andy (2002). "Testing Students' Understanding of Complex Transfer." *Proceedings of the 6th Workshop of the European Association for Machine Translation: Teaching Machine Translation*, Manchester, England.
Zhao, Gang and Jun-ichi Tsujii (1999). "Transfer in Experience-guided Machine Translation." *Proceedings of MT Summit VII: MT in the Great Translation Era*, Singapore, pp. 501–508.

Computer Translation Profession

Laska, Keith (2005). "Taking over the World or Rationalising the Translation Profession?" *Programme of the Annual Conference of the Association of Translation Companies: Surviving and Prospering in a Changing Translation Market*, School of Oriental and African Studies, University of London, England.
Lund, Anne Davidson and Chus Fernandez-Prieto (2005). "Developing Tomorrow's Translation Talent for the Benefit of Today's Market Place—Work Placements and Graduate Apprenticeships." *Programme of the Annual Conference of the Association of Translation Companies: Surviving and Prospering in a Changing Translation Market*, School of Oriental and African Studies, University of London, England.

Martin, Sigrid B. (1996). "Professional Translation: Can It Be Taught?" In *Translating and the Computer 18*. London: The Association for Information Management.
Picken, Catriona, ed. (1987). *Translating and the Computer 8: A Profession on the Move*. London: The Association for Information Management.
Schäffner, Christina (2004). "Squaring the Circle—The Contribution of Universities to the Needs of the Profession." *Programme of the Annual Conference of the Association of Translation Companies: Getting in Shape for the Future—Working towards a New Environment for the Translation Profession*, School of Oriental and African Studies, University of London, England.
Sinclair, D. A. (1962). "The Machine Translator and the Translating Profession." *Babel*, Vol. 8, No. 2, pp. 76–78.

Computer Translation Programming

Backus, John (1978). "Can Programming Be Liberated from the von Neumann Style? A Functional Style and Its Algebra of Programs." *Communications of the Association for Computing Machinery*, Vol. 21, No. 8, pp. 613–641.
Brown, Antony F. R. (2000). "Machine Translation: Just a Question of Finding the Right Programming Language?" In W. John Hutchins, ed., *Early Years in Machine Translation: Memoirs and Biographies of Pioneers*. Amsterdam and Philadelphia: John Benjamins Publishing Company, pp. 129–134.
Ceccato, Silvio (1961). *Linguistic Analysis and Programming for Mechanical Translation*. Milan: University of Milan.
Cleave, John P. (1957). "A Type of Program for Mechanical Translation." *Mechanical Translation*, Vol. 4, No. 3, pp. 54–58.
Eisner, Jason, Eric Goldlust, and Noah A. Smith (2005). "Compiling Comp Ling: Weighted Dynamic Programming and the Dyna Language." *Proceedings of Human Language Technology Conference and Conference on Empirical Methods in Natural Language Processing (HLT/EMNLP-2005)*, Vancouver, BC, Canada.
Feng, Zhiwei 馮志偉 and Yang Ping 揚平 (1987).〈自動翻譯中的程序技術〉(Programming Techniques for Automatic Translation).《自動翻譯》(*Automatic Translation*). Shanghai: Knowledge Press, pp. 214–268.

Gal, Annie, Guy Lapalme, Patrick Saint-Dizier, and Harold L. Somers (1991). *Prolog for Natural Language Processing*. Chichester: John Wiley.

Kowalski, Robert (1985). "The Origins of Logic Programming." *Byte*, Vol. 10, No. 8, pp. 192–193.

Krauwer, Steven (1993). "Evaluation of MT Systems: A Programmatic View." *Machine Translation*, Vol. 8, Nos. 1–2, pp. 59–66.

Mersel, Jules (1963). "Programming Aspects of Machine Translation." In Paul L. Garvin, ed., *Natural Language and the Computer*. New York: McGraw-Hill, pp. 233–251.

Nagao, Makoto and Jun-ichi Tsujii (1974). "PLATON: A Programming Language for Natural Language Processing." *Journal of the Information Processing Society of Japan*, Vol. 15, No. 9.

Read, Tim (1997). "Java and Its Role in Natural Language Processing and Machine Translation." *Proceedings of MT Summit VI*, San Diego, California, USA.

Richens, Richard H. (1956). "A General Programme for Mechanical Translation between Two Languages via an Algebraic Interlingua." *Mechanical Translation*, Vol. 3, No. 2, p. 37.

Richens, Richard H. (1956). "Preprogramming for Mechanical Translation." *Mechanical Translation*, Vol. 3, No. 1, pp. 20–27.

Smoke, W. and E. Dubinsky (1961). "A Program for the Machine Translation of Natural Languages." *Mechanical Translation*, Vol. 6, No. 1, pp. 2–10.

Somers, Harold L. (2003). "Prolog Models of Classical Approaches to MT." *Proceedings of the MT Summit IX Workshop on Teaching Translation Technologies and Tools*, New Orleans, Louisiana, USA, pp. 35–43.

Sugimoto, Toru, Noriko Ito, Shino Iwashita, and Michio Sugeno (2004). "Towards Programming in Everyday Language: A Case for Email Management." *Proceedings of the 5th International Conference on Intelligent Text Processing and Computational Linguistics* (*CICLing-2004*), Chung-Ang University, Seoul, Korea, pp. 378–389.

Sun, Bin 孫斌 (2000). 〈對象的雙向派生模型與擴展的面向對象編程〉 (The Theory and Methodology of Extended Object-oriented Programming). In Yu Shiwen 俞士汶 and Zhu Xuefeng 朱學鋒, eds., 《計算語言學文集》 (*Papers on Computational Linguistics*), Vol. 4. Beijing: Department of Computer Science and Technology and Institute of Computational Linguistics, Peking University, pp. 232–254.

Yngve, Victor H. (1958). "A Programming Language for Mechanical Translation." *Mechanical Translation*, Vol. 5, No. 1, pp. 25–41.
Yngve, Victor H. (1962). *An Introduction to COMIT Programming*. Cambridge, MA: MIT Press.
Yngve, Victor H. (1962). *COMIT Programmers' Reference Manual*. Cambridge, MA: MIT Press.
Yngve, Victor H. (1972). *Computer Programming with COMIT II*. Cambridge, MA: MIT Press.

Algorithm

Cuayáhuitl, Heriberto (2004). "A Syllabification Algorithm for Spanish." *Proceedings of the 5th International Conference on Intelligent Text Processing and Computational Linguistics* (*CICLing-2004*), Chung-Ang University, Seoul, Korea, pp. 406–409.
García-Hernández, René A., José Fco. Martínez-Trinidad, and Jesús Ariel Carrasco-Ochoa (2006). "A New Algorithm for Fast Discovery of Maximal Sequential Patterns in a Document Collection." *Proceedings of the 7th International Conference on Intelligent Text Processing and Computational Linguistics* (*CICLing-2006*), Mexico City, Mexico.
Giuliano, Vincent E. (1961). "A Formula Finder for the Automatic Synthesis of Translation Algorithms." *Mechanical Translation*, Vol. 6, No. 1, pp. 11–24.
Jung, Jaeyoung, Maki Miyake, and Hiroyuki Akama (2006). "Markov Cluster Shortest Path Founded upon the Alibi-breaking Algorithm." *Proceedings of the 7th International Conference on Intelligent Text Processing and Computational Linguistics* (*CICLing-2006*), Mexico City, Mexico.
Kanayama, Hiroshi (2002). "An Iterative Algorithm for Translation Acquisition of Adpositions." *Proceedings of the 9th International Conference on Theoretical and Methodological Issues in Machine Translation* (*TMI-2002*), Keihanna, Japan, pp. 85–95.
Kulagina, Olga S. (1962). "Construction of a Textual Analysis Algorithm with the Aid of a Computing Machine." In National Physical Laboratory, ed., *1961 International Conference on Machine Translation of Languages and Applied Language Analysis: Proceedings of the Conference Held at the National Physical*

Laboratory, Teddington, Middlesex, on 5th, 6th, 7th and 8th September. London: Her Majesty's Stationery Office, Vol. 1, pp. 613–614.
Kulagina, Olga S. (1965). "Algorithms of Mechanical Translation." In Wayne A. Kalenich, ed., *Information Processing 65: Proceedings of IFIP Congress 65*. Washington, DC: Spartan Books, Vol. 1, pp. 59–64.
Lovins, Julie Beth (1968). "Development of a Stemming Algorithm." *Mechanical Translation*, Vol. 11, Nos. 1–2, pp. 22–31.
Menezes, Arul and Steve Richardson (2001). "A Best-first Alignment Algorithm for Automatic Extraction of Transfer Mappings from Bilingual Corpora." In Bente Maegaard, ed., *Proceedings of MT Summit VIII: Machine Translation in the Information Age*, Santiago de Compostela, Spain.
Noel, Jacques (1975). "Document Analysis Algorithms and Machine Translation Research." *Revue des Langues Vivantes*, Vol. 41, No. 3, pp. 237–260.
Pigott, Ian M. (1984). "The Difficulty of Developing Logical Algorithms for the Machine Translation of Natural Language." *Proceedings of the International Conference on the Methodology and Techniques of Machine Translation*, Cranfield Institute of Technology, England.
Pigott, Ian M. (1984). "The Difficulty of Developing Logical Algorithms for the Machine Translation of Natural Language." *Terminologie Bulletin*, Vol. 45, pp. 7–19.
Prescher, Detlef (2001). "Inside-outside Estimation Meets Dynamic EM." *Proceedings of the 7th International Workshop on Parsing Technologies* (*IWPT-2001*), Peking University, Beijing, China. Beijing: Tsinghua University Press, pp. 241–244.
Ren, Fuji (2004). "An Algorithm for Determining DingYu Structural Particle Using Grammar Knowledge and Statistical Information." *Proceedings of the 5th International Conference on Intelligent Text Processing and Computational Linguistics* (*CICLing-2004*), Chung-Ang University, Seoul, Korea, pp. 338–349.
Shan, Yongming 單永明 (2001).〈漢語文本的篇章結構及其標引算法的研究〉(Study of Chinese Writings Structure and Its Indexing Algorithm). In Huang Changning 黃昌寧 and Zhang Pu 張普, eds.,《自然語言理解與機器翻譯》(*Natural Language Understanding and Machine Translation*). Beijing: Tsinghua University Press, pp. 227–232.
Surendran, Dinoj (2006). "Automating the Creation of Interactive Glyph-supplemented Scatterplots for Visualizing Algorithm Results."

Proceedings of the Human Language Technology Conference—Annual Meeting of the North American Chapter of the Association for Computational Linguistics (*HLT-NAACL-2006*), New York, USA.

Tillmann, Christoph and Tong Zhang (2006). "A Discriminative Global Training Algorithm for Statistical MT." *Proceedings of the Joint Conference of the International Committee on Computational Linguistics and the Association for Computational Linguistics* (*COLING/ACL-2006*), Sydney, Australia.

Vauquois, Bernard (1968). "A Survey of Formal Grammars and Algorithms for Recognition and Transformation in Machine Translation." *Proceedings of International Federation for Information Processing* (*IFIP*) *Congress-68*, Edinburgh, Scotland, pp. 254–260.

Wang, Suge 王素格, Zhang Yongkui 張永奎, and Liu Kaiying 劉開瑛 (1999). 〈漢詞詞性注中兼類詞排歧算法探討〉 (A Discussion of Ambiguous Algorithm to the Chinese Part-of-speech Tagging). In Huang Changning 黃昌寧 and Dong Zhendong 董振東, eds.,《計算機語言學文集》(*Essays on Computational Linguistics*). Beijing: Tsinghua University Press, pp. 162–166.

Zhang, Ruiqiang, Genichiro Kikui, Hirofumi Yamamoto, and Lo Wai-Kit (2005). "A Decoding Algorithm for Word Lattice Translation in Speech Translation." *Proceedings of the International Workshop on Spoken Language Translation* (*IWSLT-2005*), Pittsburgh, PA, USA.

Zhang, Yansen 張仰森 and Ding Bingqing 丁冰青 (1999).〈基於糾錯候選集和似然匹配的自動糾錯算法〉(An Automatic Correcting Algorithm Based on Correcting Suggestion Sets and Likelihood Match). In Huang Changning 黃昌寧 and Dong Zhendong 董振東, eds.,《計算機語言學文集》(*Essays on Computational Linguistics*). Beijing: Tsinghua University Press, pp. 365–370.

Zhou, Qiang 周強 (1999).〈漢語組塊分析算法〉(The Chunk Parsing Algorithm for the Chinese Language). In Huang Changning 黃昌寧 and Dong Zhendong 董振東, eds.,《計算機語言學文集》(*Essays on Computational Linguistics*). Beijing: Tsinghua University Press, pp. 242–247.

Žižka, Jan, Michal Šrédl, and Aleš Bourek (2003). "Searching for Significant Word Associations in Text Documents Using Genetic Algorithms." *Proceedings of the 4th International Conference on Intelligent Text Processing and Computational Linguistics* (*CICLing-2003*), Mexico City, Mexico, pp. 586–589.

Bootstrapping

Abney, Steven (2002). "Bootstrapping." *Proceedings of the 40th Annual Meeting of the Association for Computational Linguistics* (*ACL-2002*), Philadelphia, PA, USA, pp. 360–367.

Barzilay, Regina and Lillian Lee (2002). "Bootstrapping Lexical Choice via Multiple-sequence Alignment." *Proceedings of the 2002 Conference on Empirical Methods in Natural Language Processing* (*EMNLP-2002*), University of Pennsylvania, Philadelphia, PA, USA.

Bergsma, Shane and Dekang Lin (2006). "Bootstrapping Path-based Pronoun Resolution." *Proceedings of the Joint Conference of the International Committee on Computational Linguistics and the Association for Computational Linguistics* (*COLING/ACL-2006*), Sydney, Australia.

Callison-Burch, Chris and Miles Osborne (2003). "Bootstrapping Parallel Corpora." *Proceedings of the Human Language Technology and North American Chapter of Association of Computational Linguistics 2003* (*HLT/NAACL-2003*), Edmonton, Alberta, Canada.

Chen, Wenliang, Zhu Jingbo, Wu Honglin, and Yao Tianshun (2004). "Automatic Learning Features Using Bootstrapping for Text Categorization." *Proceedings of the 5th International Conference on Intelligent Text Processing and Computational Linguistics* (*CICLing-2004*), Chung-Ang University, Seoul, Korea, pp. 565–574.

Efron, Bradley and Robert Tibshirani (1986). "Bootstrap Methods for Standard Errors, Confidence Intervals, and Other Measures of Statistical Accuracy." *Statistical Science*, Vol. 1, No. 1, pp. 54–77.

Eisner, Jason and Damianos Karakos (2005). "Bootstrapping without the Boot." *Proceedings of Human Language Technology Conference and Conference on Empirical Methods in Natural Language Processing* (*HLT/EMNLP-2005*), Vancouver, BC, Canada.

Gliozzo, Alfio, Carlo Strapparava, and Ido Dagan (2005). "Investigating Unsupervised Learning for Text Categorization Bootstrapping." *Proceedings of Human Language Technology Conference and Conference on Empirical Methods in Natural Language Processing* (*HLT/EMNLP-2005*), Vancouver, BC, Canada.

Ide, Nancy (2006). "Making Senses: Bootstrapping Sense-tagged Lists of Semantically-related Words." *Proceedings of the 7th International*

Conference on Intelligent Text Processing and Computational Linguistics (*CICLing-2006*), Mexico City, Mexico.

Ko, Youngjoong and Jungyun Seo (2004). "Learning with Unlabeled Data for Text Categorization Using a Bootstrapping and a Feature Projection Technique." *Proceedings of the 42nd Annual Meeting of the Association for Computational Linguistics* (*ACL-2004*), Barcelona, Spain, pp. 255–262.

Niu, Cheng, Wei Li, Jihong Ding, and Rohini K. Srihari (2003). "Bootstrapping for Named Entity Tagging Using Concept-based Seeds." *Proceedings of the Human Language Technology and North American Chapter of Association of Computational Linguistics 2003* (*HLT/NAACL-2003*), Edmonton, Alberta, Canada.

Oflazer, Kemal, Sergei Nirenburg, and Marjorie McShane (2001). "Bootstrapping Morphological Analyzers by Combining Human Elicitation and Machine Learning." *Computational Linguistics*, Vol. 27, pp. 59–85.

Thelen, Michael and Ellen Riloff (2002). "A Bootstrapping Method for Learning Semantic Lexicons Using Extraction Pattern Contexts." *Proceedings of the 2002 Conference on Empirical Methods in Natural Language Processing* (*EMNLP-2002*), University of Pennsylvania, Philadelphia, PA, USA.

Tomita, Junji, Stephen Soderland, and Oren Etzioni (2006). "Expanding the Recall of Relation Extraction by Bootstrapping." *Proceedings of the 11th Conference of the European Chapter of the Association for Computational Linguistics* (*EACL-2006*), Trento, Italy.

Triantafyllou, Ioannis, Iason Demiros, Christos Malavazos, and Stelios Piperidis (2000). "An Alignment Architecture for Translation Memory Bootstrapping." *Proceedings of the International Conference on Machine Translation and Multilingual Applications in the New Millenium* (*MT-2000*), University of Exeter, England.

Turcato, Davide, Paul McFetridge, Fred Popowich, and Janine Toole (1999). "A Bootstrap Approach to Automatically Generating Lexical Transfer Rules." *Proceedings of MT Summit VII: MT in the Great Translation Era*, Singapore.

Veale, Tony and Andy Way (1997). "*Gaijin*: A Bootstrapping Approach to Example-based Machine Translation." *International Conference, Recent Advances in Natural Language Processing*, Tzigov Chark, Bulgaria, pp. 239–244.

Weerasinghe, Ruvan (2002). "Bootstrapping the Lexicon Building Process for Machine Translation between 'New' Languages." In Stephen D. Richardson, ed., *Machine Translation: From Research to Real Users*. Berlin and New York: Springer Verlag, pp. 177–186.

Xi, Chenhai and Rebecca Hwa (2005). "A Backoff Model for Bootstrapping Resources for Non-English Languages." *Proceedings of Human Language Technology Conference and Conference on Empirical Methods in Natural Language Processing* (*HLT/EMNLP-2005*), Vancouver, BC, Canada.

Computer Translation Project

Alberti, Gábor and Judit Kleiber (2004). "The GeLexi MT Project." *Proceedings of the 9th Workshop of the European Association for Machine Translation: Broadening Horizons of Machine Translation and Its Applications*, Foundation for International Studies, Malta, pp. 1–10.

Fermandez, Chus (2006). "Developing Tomorrow's Project Managers—Academic Learning Meets Work-base Practice." *Programme of the 30th Anniversary Conference of the Association of Translation Companies 30th Anniversary Conference 2006: Building Strong Markets for Translations—Making Links and Seizing Opportunities*, School of Oriental and African Studies, University of London, England.

Ingram, Claire (2006). "Developing the Role of the Translation Project Manager." *Programme of the 30th Anniversary Conference of the Association of Translation Companies 30th Anniversary Conference 2006: Building Strong Markets for Translations—Making Links and Seizing Opportunities*, School of Oriental and African Studies, University of London, England.

Kaeser, Paul (1998). "Workflow Automation of Translation Projects." *Proceedings of the 3rd Workshop of the European Association for Machine Translation: Translation Technology: Integration in the Workflow Environment*, Geneva, Switzerland, pp. 41–44.

Schütz, Jörg (1998). "The MULTIDOC Project: MULTI-lingual Product DOCumentation." *Proceedings of the 3rd Workshop of the European Association for Machine Translation: Translation Technology: Integration in the Workflow Environment*, Geneva, Switzerland, pp. 55–64.

Speers, d'Armond (1994). "The Klingon Machine Translation Project: The

Klingon Language Analyzer." *Proceedings of the 1st Conference of the Association for Machine Translation in the Americas: Technology Partnerships for Crossing the Language Barrier* (*AMTA-1*), Columbia, Maryland, USA, p. 234.

Weisweber, Wilhelm (1994). "The Experimental MT System of the Project KIT-FAST." *Machine Translation—Ten Years On: Proceedings of the 2nd International Conference Organised by Cranfield University*, Cranfield, England.

Computer Translation Research

Arnold, Doug J. (1992). "Reaction to Somers: Current Research in Machine Translation." *Machine Translation*, Vol. 7, No. 4, pp. 247–251.

Bar-Hillel, Yehoshua (1951). "The Present State of Research on Mechanical Translation." *American Documentation*, Vol. 2, No. 4, pp. 229–237.

Bennett, Winfield S. (1987). "The Proper Place of End-users in MT Research." In Karl Kummer, ed., *Across the Language Gap: Proceedings of the 28th Annual Conference of the American Translators Association*. Medford, New Jersey: Learned Information, Inc., pp. 425–427.

Boitet, Christian (1987). "Research and Development on MT and Related Techniques at Grenoble University (GETA)." In Margaret King, ed., *Machine Translation Today: The State of the Art*. Edinburgh: Edinburgh University Press, pp. 133–153.

Boitet, Christian (1995). "Factors for Success (and Failure) in Machine Translation—Some Lessons of the First 50 Years of R&D." *Proceedings of MT Summit V: Machine Translation Conference, Exhibition and Tutorial*, Luxembourg.

Booth, Andrew D. (1956). "Present Objectives of MT Research in the United Kingdom." *Babel*, Vol. 2, No. 3, pp. 108–110.

Bourbeau, Laurent R. (1992). "Current MT Research Orientation/Disorientation." *Machine Translation*, Vol. 7, No. 4, pp. 253–258.

Callison-Burch, Chris, Miles Osborne, and Philipp Koehn (2006). "Re-evaluating the Role of Bleu in Machine Translation Research." *Proceedings of the 11th Conference of the European Chapter of the Association for Computational Linguistics* (*EACL-2006*), Trento, Italy.

Cambridge Language Research Unit (1956). "Report on Research." *Mechanical Translation*, Vol. 3, No. 2, pp. 36–37.

Delavenay, Emile (1960). "Machine Translation of Languages: Research and Organization Problems." *IMPACT*, Vol. 10, No. 1, pp. 26–44.

Dong, Zhendong (1988). "MT Research in China." In Dan Maxwell, Klaus Schubert, and Toon Witkam, eds. *New Directions in Machine Translation*. Dordrecht-Holland: Foris Publications, pp. 85–91.

Dong, Zhendong 董振東 and Dong Qiang 董強 (2001). 〈機譯研究中的一些誤區——從譯文質量分析看〉 (Some Misunderstandings in MT Research—From an Analysis of MT Translations). In Huang Changning 黃昌寧 and Zhang Pu 張普, eds.,《自然語言理解與機器翻譯》(*Natural Language Understanding and Machine Translation*). Beijing: Tsinghua University Press, pp. 462–471.

Dostert, Leon E. (1957). "Brief History of Machine Translation Research." In Leon E. Dostert, ed., *Research in Machine Translation: Report of the 8th Annual Round Table Meeting on Linguistics and Language Studies*. Washington, DC: Georgetown University Press, pp. 3–10.

Dostert, Leon E. (1957). "Practical Objectives of Machine Translation Research." In Leon E. Dostert, ed., *Research in Machine Translation: Report of the 8th Annual Round Table Meeting on Linguistics and Language Studies*. Washington, DC: Georgetown University Press, pp. 181–186.

Dostert, Leon E., ed. (1957). *Research in Machine Translation: Report of the 8th Annual Round Table Meeting on Linguistics and Language Studies*. Washington, DC: Georgetown University Press.

Du, C. Z. and R. Li (1987). *An Overview of MT Research in China*. Xi'an: Xi'an University.

Farwell, David L. (1992). "In Defense of Rationalist Approaches to MT Research." *Proceedings of the 4th International Conference on Theoretical and Methodological Issues in Machine Translation of Natural Languages: Empiricist vs. Rationalist Methods in MT* (*TMI-92*), Montreal, Quebec, Canada, pp. 185–193.

Farwell, David L. (1996). "Observations Concerning Next Steps in MT Research." *Proceedings of the 2nd Conference of the Association for Machine Translation in the Americas: Expanding MT Horizons* (*AMTA-2*), Montreal, Quebec, Canada, pp. 233–236.

Feng, Zhiwei 馮志偉 (1985). 〈我國機器翻譯研究工作的發展〉 (The Progress

of Research Work on Machine Translation in China).《情報學報》(*Journal of the China Society for Scientific and Technical Information*), Vol. 3, No. 3.

Feng, Zhiwei 馮志偉 (1994).〈我國的機器翻譯研究〉(Studies on Machine Translation in China).《自然語言機器翻譯新論》(*New Essays on Machine Translation of Natural Languages*). Beijing: Language Press, pp. 29–41.

Freigang, Karl-Heinz (1987). "Research on Machine Translation at the University of Saarbrucken." In Catriona Picken, ed., *Translating and the Computer 8: A Profession on the Move*. London: The Association for Information Management, pp. 83–97.

Garvin, Paul L. (1958). *Research in Machine Translation from Russian to English: Fulcrum Approach*. Seminar Work Paper MT-73. Group II, Georgetown University.

Giuliano, Vincent E. and Anthony G. Oettinger (1960). "Research on Automatic Translation of the Harvard Computation Laboratory." *Information Process: Proceedings of the International Conference on Information Processing*. Paris: Unesco, pp. 163–183.

Hajic, Jan, Eva Hajicova, and Alexander Rosen (1992). "Machine Translation Research in Czechoslovakia." *Meta*, Vol. 37, No. 4, pp. 802–816.

Harper, Kenneth E. (1961). "Soviet Research in Machine Translation." In Harold P. Edmundson, ed., *Proceedings of the National Symposium on Machine Translation Held at the University of California Los Angeles*. London: Englewood Cliffs, pp. 2–12.

Hays, David G. (1963). "Research Procedures in Machine Translation." In Paul L. Garvin, ed., *Natural Language and the Computer*. New York: McGraw-Hill, pp. 183–214.

Huang, Heyan 黄河燕, ed. (2002).《機器翻譯研究進展：2002年全國機器翻譯研討會論文集》(*Progress in Research on Machine Translation: Proceedings of the 2002 National Conference on Machine Translation*). Beijing: Publishing House of Electronics Industry.

Hutchins, W. John and Harold L. Somers (1992). "Some Other Systems and Directions of Research." *An Introduction to Machine Translation*. London: Academic Press, pp. 313–333.

Hutchins, W. John (1994). "Research Methods and System Designs in Machine Translation: A Ten-year Review, 1984–1994." *Machine Translation—Ten Years On: Proceedings of the 2nd International Conference Organised by Cranfield University*, Cranfield, England.

Isabelle, Pierre (1992). "Current Research in Machine Translation: A Reply to Somers." *Machine Translation*, Vol. 7, No. 4, pp. 265–272.

Josselson, Harry H. (1961). "Research in Machine Translation." In Harold P. Edmundson, ed., *Proceedings of the National Symposium on Machine Translation*. London: Prentice-Hall, pp. 160–172.

Liu, Zhong 劉忠, Wang Chengdao 王成道, and Chen Jiayu 陳家旭 (2002). 〈關於機器翻譯的研究〉 (About Research on Machine Translation). 《外語教學與翻譯》 (*Foreign Language Teaching and Translation*), Vol. 1, No. 1, pp. 86–90.

Ljudskanov, Alexander (1968). "Is the Generally Accepted Strategy of Machine Translation Research Optimal?" *Mechanical Translation*, Vol. 11, Nos. 1–2, pp. 14–21.

Locke, William N. and Victor H. Yngve (1958). "Research in Translation by Machine at M.I.T." *Proceedings of the 8th International Congress of Linguists*, pp. 510–514.

Luo, Jinde 羅進德 (2004). 《機器翻譯研究》 (*Research on Machine Translation*). Beijing: China Translation and Publishing Corporation.

Murgida, Jackie (1996). "Ten Years' Experience Talks about the Future." *Proceedings of the 2nd Conference of the Association for Machine Translation in the Americas: Expanding MT Horizons* (*AMTA-2*), Montreal, Quebec, Canada, pp. 236–237.

Niessen, Sonja, Franz Josef Och, Gregor Leusch, and Hermann Ney (2000). "An Evaluation Tool for Machine Translation: Fast Evaluation for MT Research." *Proceedings of the 2nd International Conference on Language Resources and Evaluation* (*LREC-2000*), Athens, Greece, Vol. 1, pp. 39–45.

Nirenburg, Sergei (1993). "A Direction of MT Development." *Proceedings of MT Summit IV: International Cooperation for Global Communication*, Kobe, Japan, pp. 189–193.

Noel, Jacques (1975). "Document Analysis Algorithms and Machine Translation Research." *Revue des Langues Vivantes*, Vol. 41, No. 3, pp. 237–260.

Oettinger, Anthony G. and Murray E. Sherry (1961). "Current Research on Automatic Translation at Harvard University and Predictive Syntactic Analysis." In Harold P. Edmundson, ed., *Proceedings of the National Symposium on Machine Translation*. London: Prentice-Hall, pp. 173–182.

Reifler, Erwin (1961). "Current Research at the University of Washington."

H.P. Edmundson, ed., *Proceedings of the National Symposium on Machine Translation*. London: Prentice-Hall, pp. 155–159.
Richardson, Stephen D., ed. (2002). *Machine Translation: From Research to Real Users*. Berlin and New York: Springer Verlag.
Somers, Harold L. (1990). "Current Research in Machine Translation." *Proceedings of the 3rd International Conference on Theoretical and Methodological Issues in Machine Translation of Natural Languages (TMI-90)*, Linguistics Research Center, University of Texas, Austin, Texas, USA, pp. 1–12.
Somers, Harold L. (1992). "Current Research in Machine Translation." *Machine Translation*, Vol. 7, No. 4, pp. 231–246.
Somers, Harold L. (1992). "Current Research in Machine Translation." In John Newton, ed., *Computers in Translation: A Practical Appraisal*. London and New York: Routledge, pp. 189–207.
Steiner, Erich H. (1992). "Producers-users-customers: Towards a Differentiated Evaluation of Research in Machine Translation." *Machine Translation*, Vol. 7, No. 4, pp. 281–284.
Tucker, Allen B. (1987). "Current Strategies in Machine Translation Research and Development." In Sergei Nirenburg, ed., *Machine Translation: Theoretical and Methodological Issues*. Cambridge: Cambridge University Press, pp. 22–41.
White, John S. (1992). "Responses to Current Research in Machine Translation by Harold Somers." *Machine Translation*, Vol. 7, No. 4, pp. 303–307.
Wilks, Yorick (1978). "Four Generations of Machine Translation Research and Prospects for the Future." In David Gerver and H. Wallace Sinaiko, eds., *Language, Interpretation and Communication*. New York: Plenum Press, pp. 171–184.
Yngve, Victor H. (1964). "Implications of Mechanical Translation Research." *Proceedings of the American Philosophical Society*, Vol. 108, No. 4, pp. 275–281.
Yngve, Victor H. (2000). "Early MT Research at M.I.T.: The Search for Context." In David G. Lockwood, Peter H. Fries, and James E. Copeland, eds., *Functional Approaches to Language, Culture and Cognition*. Amsterdam and Philadelphia: John Benjamins Publishing Company, pp. 593–628.
Yngve, Victor H. (2000). "Early Research at M.I.T.: In Search of Adequate Theory." In W. John Hutchins, ed., *Early Years in Machine*

Translation: Memoirs and Biographies of Pioneers. Amsterdam and Philadelphia: John Benjamins Publishing Company, pp. 39–72.
Zarechnack, Michael and Antony F. R. Brown (1961). "Current Research at Georgetown University." In Harold P. Edmundson, ed., *Proceedings of the National Symposium on Machine Translation*. London: Prentice-Hall, pp. 67–87.

Computer Translation System

Abir, Eli, Steve Klein, David Miller, and Michael Steinbaum (2002). "Fluent Machines' EliMT System." In Stephen D. Richardson, ed., *Machine Translation: From Research to Real Users*. Berlin and New York: Springer Verlag, pp. 216–219.
Amano, Shinya, Hideki Hirakawa, and Hiroyasu Nogami (1989). "The TAURAS Design Philosophy." In Christian Rohrer, ed., *Proceedings of MT Summit II*, Munich, Germany, pp. 36–41.
Apresjan, Jurij D., Igor M. Boguslavskij, Leonid L. Iomdin, Alexandre V. Lazurskij, Vladimir Z. Sannikov, and Leonid L. Tsinman (1992). "Etap-2: The Linguistics of a Machine Translation System." *Meta*, Vol. 37, No. 1, pp. 97–112.
Ashizaki, Tatsuo (1989). "Outline of the JICST Machine Translation System." *MT Summit II*, Munich, Germany, pp. 44–49.
Bangalore, Srinivas, German Bordel, and Giuseppe Riccardi (2001). "Computing Consensus Translation from Multiple Machine Translation Systems." *Proceedings of the IEEE Automatic Speech Recognition and Understanding Workshop*, Madonna di Campiglio, Italy, pp. 351–354.
Bender, Howard J. (2002). "Natural Intelligence in a Machine Translation System." In Stephen D. Richardson, ed., *Machine Translation: From Research to Real Users*. Berlin and New York: Springer Verlag, pp. 224–228.
Bernardi, Ulrike, Petra Gieselmann, and Steve McLaughlin (2001). "A Taste of MALT." In Bente Maegaard, ed., *Proceedings of MT Summit VIII: Machine Translation in the Information Age*, Santiago de Compostela, Spain.
Blekhman, Michael S. (1994). "How Lingvistica '93 MT Systems Are Used (1991–1993)." *MT News International*, No. 7.
Boitet, Christian and Rene Gerber (1984). "Expert Systems and Other New

Techiques in MT." *Proceedings of the 10th International Conference on Computational Linguistics* (*COLING-84*), Stanford University, Stanford, CA, USA, pp. 468–471.

Boitet, Christian (1986). "Expert Systems and Other New Techniques in M(a)T." In Istvan S. Batori and Hans Weber, eds., *Neue Ansatze in Maschineller Sprachubersetsung: Wissensreprasentation und Textbezug*. Tubingen: Max Niemeyer Verlag, pp. 103–119.

Bojar, Ondrej, Petr Homola, and Vladislav Kubon (2005). "An MT System Recycled." *Proceedings of MT Summit X*, Phuket, Thailand.

Chan, Jing-Shin and Keh-Yih Su (1988). "Incremental Environment for Scored Machine Translation Systems." *Proceedings of the Conference of the Association for Computational Linguistics and Chinese Language Processing* (*ROCLING-I*), Nantou, Taiwan.

Chiang, David, Adam Lopez, Nitin Madnani, Christof Monz, Philip Resnik, and Michael Subotin (2005). "The Hiero Machine Translation System: Extensions, Evaluation, and Analysis." *Proceedings of Human Language Technology Conference and Conference on Empirical Methods in Natural Language Processing* (*HLT/EMNLP-2005*), Vancouver, BC, Canada.

Civera, Jorge and Alfons Juan (2006). "Mixtures of IBM Model 2." *Proceedings of the 11th Workshop of the European Association for Machine Translation: Machine Translation/Translation Aids—Tools to Increase Quality and to Save Money*, the University of Oslo, Oslo, Norway.

Estival, Dominique (2004). "The Language Translation Interface." *Proceedings of the 10th Workshop of the European Association for Machine Translation: Practical Applications of Machine Translation*, Budapest, Hungary, pp. 1–12.

Ettelaie, Emil, Kevin Knight, Daniel Marcu, Dragos Stefan Munteanu, Franz J. Och, Ignacio Thayer, and Quamrul Tipu (2004). "The ISI/USC MT System." *Proceedings of the International Workshop on Spoken Language Translation* (*IWSLT-2004*), Kyoto, Japan.

Fabricz, Karoly (1989). "Machine Translation. Active Systems—East European Countries." In István S. Batori, Winfried Lenders, and Wolfgang Putschke, eds., *Comparative Linguistics*. Berlin: Walterde Gruyter, pp. 645–652.

Feng, Zhiwei 馮志偉 (1994).〈國外的機器翻譯系統〉(Machine Translation Systems in Foreign Countries).《自然語言機器翻譯新論》(*New Essays*

on Machine Translation of Natural Languages). Beijing: Language Press, pp. 14–28.
Feng, Zhiwei 馮志偉 (2004).〈各種類型的機器翻譯系統〉(Types of Machine Translation Systems).《機器翻譯研究》(*Studies on Machine Translation*). Beijing: China Translation and Publishing Corporation, pp. 35–66.
Fukumochi, Yoji (1995). "A Way of Using a Small MT System in Industry." *Proceedings of MT Summit V: Machine Translation Conference, Exhibition and Tutorial*, Luxembourg.
Gajer, Miroslaw (2001). "Towards a Fully-automatic High-quality Machine Translation System for Unrestricted Text." *Machine Translation Review*, No. 12, pp. 24–35.
Grasmick, Daniel (1995). "Two MT Systems and Still Hungry…." *Proceedings of MT Summit V: Machine Translation Conference, Exhibition and Tutorial*, Luxembourg.
Gurina, Tatyana M. (1997). "Educational Implications of a Machine Translation System." *Machine Translation Review*, No. 6, pp. 6–8.
Hartley, Anthony F., Donia R. Scott, John Bateman, and Danail Dochev (2001). "AGILE—A System for Multilingual Generation of Technical Instructions." In Bente Maegaard, ed., *Proceedings of MT Summit VIII: Machine Translation in the Information Age*, Santiago de Compostela, Spain.
Hauenschild, Christa, Edgar Huckert, and Robert Maier (1979). "SALAT: Machine Translation via Semantic Representation." In Rainier Bäuerle, Urs Egli, and Arnim von Stechow, eds., *Semantics from Different Points of View*. Berlin: Springer Verlag, pp. 324–352.
Haynes, Colin (1998). "Essential Requirements for an MT System." *Breaking Down the Language Barriers*. London: The Association for Information Management, pp. 106–114.
Hein, Anna Sågvall, Eva Forsbom, Per Weijnitz, Ebba Gustavii, and Jörg Tiedemann (2003). "MATS—A Glass Box Machine Translation System." *Proceedings of MT Summit IX*, New Orleans, Louisiana, USA.
Howerton, Paul W. (1961). "The Parameters of an Operational Machine Translation System." *Mechanical Translation*, Vol. 6, pp. 108–111.
Hutchins, W. John (1982). "The Evolution of Machine Translation Systems." In Veronica Lawson, ed., *Practical Experience of Machine Translation*. Amsterdam: North-Holland Publishing Company, pp. 21–37.

Hutchins, W. John (1986). "Other Indirect Systems, 1965–1975." *Machine Translation: Past, Present and Future.* Chichester: Ellis Horwood, pp. 201–208.

Hutchins, W. John and Harold L. Somers (1992). "Some Other Systems and Directions of Research." *An Introduction to Machine Translation.* London: Academic Press, pp. 313–333.

Hutchins, W. John (1999). "The Development and Use of Machine Translation Systems and Computer-based Translation Tools." *Proceedings of an International Conference on Machine Translation and Computer Language Information Processing*, Beijing, China, pp. 1–16.

Hutchins, W. John (2000). "The IAMT Certification Initiative and Defining Translation System Categories." *Proceedings of the 5th Workshop of the European Association for Machine Translation: Harvesting Existing Resources*, Lubljana, Slovenia.

Hutchins, W. John (2003). "The Development and Use of Machine Translation Systems and Computer-based Translation Tools." *International Journal of Translation*, Vol. 15, No. 1, pp. 5–26.

Jelinek, Richard (2004). "Modern MT Systems and the Myth of Human Translation: Real World Status Quo." In *Translating and the Computer 26*. London: The Association for Information Management.

Kay, Martin (1990). "On the Architecture of Machine Translation Systems." *Proceedings of the Conference of the Association for Computational Linguistics and Chinese Language Processing (ROCLING-III)*, Taipei, Taiwan.

King, Gilbert W. (1961). "Functions Required of a Translation System." In Harold P. Edmundson, ed., *Proceedings of the National Symposium on Machine Translation.* Englewood Cliffs: Prentice-Hall, pp. 53–62.

King, Margaret (1989). "New Directions in MT Systems: A Change in Paradigm." *Proceedings of MT Summit II*, Munich, Germany, pp. 78–79.

Lehrberger, John and Laurent Bourbeau (1988). *Machine Translation: Linguistic Characteristics of MT Systems and General Methodology of Evaluation.* Amsterdam and Philadelphia: John Benjamins Publishing Company.

Lewis, Derek (1985). "The Development and Progress of Machine Translation Systems." *Literary and Linguistic Computing*, Vol. 5, Nos. 1–2, pp. 40–52.

Loh, Shiu-chang, H-S. Hung, and Kong Luen (1979). "A Dual Language Translator." In D. E. Ager, Francis E. Knowles, and J. Smith, eds., *Advances in Computer-aided Literary and Linguistic Research*. Birmingham: Aston University Press, pp. 107–115.

Maier, Elisabeth and Anthony Clarke (2003). "Scalability in MT Systems." *Proceedings of MT Summit IX*, New Orleans, Louisiana, USA.

Marcuk, Jurij N. (1980). "Syntactico-semantic Analysis in the AMPAR Machine Translation System." *International Forum on Information and Documentation*, Vol. 5, No. 2, pp. 15–17.

Matusov, Evgeny, Nicola Ueffing, and Hermann Ney (2006). "Computing Consensus Translation from Multiple Machine Translation Systems Using Enhanced Hypotheses Alignment." *Proceedings of the 11th Conference of the European Chapter of the Association for Computational Linguistics (EACL-2006)*, Trento, Italy.

Mellebeek, Bart, Anna Khasin, Josef van Genabith, and Andy Way (2005). "TransBooster: Boosting the Performance of Wide-coverage Machine Translation Systems." *Proceedings of the 10th Workshop of the European Association for Machine Translation: Practical Applications of Machine Translation*, Budapest, Hungary, pp. 189–197.

Menezes, Arul and Chris Quirk (2005). "Microsoft Research Treelet Translation System: IWSLT Evaluation." *Proceedings of the International Workshop on Spoken Language Translation (IWSLT-2005)*, Pittsburgh, PA, USA.

Mitkov, Ruslan (1995). "CAT2: A Unification-based Machine Translation System." *Machine Translation Review*, No. 1, pp. 18–19.

Moore, Isabella (1990). "Criteria for Selecting MT Systems." In Pamela Mayorcas, ed., *Translating and the Computer 10*. London: The Association for Information Management, pp. 18–30.

Murzaku, Alex (1999). "MT Open to Standards." *Proceedings of the 4th Workshop of the European Association for Machine Translation: EU and the New Languages: Translation—Possibilities, Policies and Practicalities*, Prague, the Czech Republic.

Nagao, Makoto (1987). "Role of Structural Transformation in a Machine Translation System." In Sergei Nirenburg, ed., *Machine Translation: Theoretical and Methodological Issues*. Cambridge: Cambridge University Press, pp. 262–277.

Nagao, Makoto (1989). "The Future of Machine Translation Systems." In

Norman D. Cook, trans., *Machine Translation: How Far Can It Go?* Oxford: Oxford University Press, pp. 134–146.
Nagao, Makoto (1989). "Machine Translation Systems." In Norman D. Cook, trans., *Machine Translation: How Far Can It Go?* Oxford: Oxford University Press, pp. 123–133.
Nagao, Makoto (1995). "What Have We to Do for the Future MT Systems?" *Proceedings of MT Summit V: Machine Translation Conference, Exhibition and Tutorial*, Luxembourg.
Nishimura, H. (1970). "The Development of a Machine Translation System." *Researches of the Electrotechnical Laboratory*, No. 705.
Nozay, Philippe and Adriane Rinsche (2003). "LTC Communicator." *Proceedings of MT Summit IX*, New Orleans, Louisiana, USA.
Orasan, Constantin, Ted Marshall, Robert Clark, Le An Ha, and Ruslan Mitkov (2005). "Building a WSD Module within an MT System to Enable Interactive Resolution in the User's Source Language." *Proceedings of the 10th Workshop of the European Association for Machine Translation: Practical Applications of Machine Translation*, Budapest, Hungary, pp. 205–211.
Oubine, Ivan I. and Boris D. Tikhomirov (1982). "Machine Translation Systems and Computer Dictionaries in the Information Service: Ways of Their Development and Operation." In Jan Horecky, ed., *Proceedings of the 9th International Conference on Computational Linguistics (COLING-82)*, Prague. Amsterdam: North-Holland Publishing Company, pp. 289–294.
Pigott, Ian M. (1986). "Essential Requirements for a Large-scale Operational Machine-translation System." *Computers and Translation*, Vol. 1, No. 2, pp. 67–72.
Pyne, Chris (1997). "DoVer: MT Information Translation." In *Translating and the Computer 19*. London: The Association for Information Management.
Reichert, Juergen and Alex H. Waibel (2004). "The ISL EDTRL System." *Proceedings of the International Workshop on Spoken Language Translation (IWSLT-2004)*, Kyoto, Japan.
Rohrer, Christian (1989). "New Directions in MT Systems." In Christian Rohrer, ed., *Proceedings of MT Summit II*, Munich, Germany, pp. 120–122.
Rychtyckyj, Nestor (2004). "Maintenance Issues for Machine Translation Systems." In Robert E. Frederking and Kathryn B. Taylors, eds.,

Machine Translation: From Real Users to Research. Berlin: Springer Verlag, pp. 252–261.

Senellart, Jean, Péter Dienes, and Tamós Váradi (2001). "Development of a New Generation of Translation System." In Bente Maegaard, ed., *Proceedings of MT Summit VIII: Machine Translation in the Information Age*, Santiago de Compostela, Spain.

Shen, Wade, Brian Delaney, and Tim Anderson (2005). "The MIT-LL/AFRL MT System." *Proceedings of the International Workshop on Spoken Language Translation* (*IWSLT-2005*), Pittsburgh, PA, USA.

Shim, Kwangseob and Yung Taek Kim (1993). "Towards a Machine Translation System with Self-critiquing Capability." *Proceedings of the 5th International Conference on Theoretical and Methodological Issues in Machine Translation of Natural Languages: MT in the Next Generation* (*TMI-93*), Kyoto, Japan, pp. 266–275.

Slocum, Jonathan, ed. (1988). *Machine Translation Systems*. Cambridge: Cambridge University Press.

Sokolova, Svetlana (1995). "The Tools for Adapting a Machine Translation System to Individual Needs." In *Translating and the Computer 17*. London: The Association for Information Management.

Somers, Harold L. (1983). "Investigating the Possibility of a Microprocessor-based Machine Translation System." *Proceedings of the Conference on Applied Natural Language Processing*, Santa Monica, California, USA, pp. 149–155.

Spalink, Karin, Claudia Gdaniec, Marjorie Leon, Veronica Lawson, and Muriel Vasconcellos (1994). "Choosing an MT System." *Technology Partnerships for Crossing the Language Barrier: 1st Conference of the Association for Machine Translation in the Americas*, Columbia, Maryland, USA.

Su, Keh-Yih and Chang Jing-Shin (1990). "Some Key Issues in Designing MT Systems." *Machine Translation*, Vol. 5, No. 4, pp. 265–300.

Supnithi, Thepchai, Virach Sornlertlamvanich, and Thatsanee Charoenporn (2002). "A Cross System Machine Translation." *Proceedings of the Workshop on Machine Translation in Asia* (*COLING-2002*), Taipei, Taiwan.

Takeda, Koichi (1993). "An Object-oriented Implementation of Machine Translation Systems." *Proceedings of the 5th International Conference on Theoretical and Methodological Issues in Machine Translation of*

Natural Languages: MT in the Next Generation (*TMI-93*), Kyoto, Japan, pp. 154–167.
Tanaka, Yasuhito 田中康仁 (2001). 〈關於機器翻譯系統未來的方向〉 (Future Direction of Machine Translation System Development). In Huang Changning 黃昌寧 and Zhang Pu 張普, eds., 《自然語言理解與機器翻譯》 (*Natural Language Understanding and Machine Translation*). Beijing: Tsinghua University Press, pp. 292–299.
Thurmair, Gregor and Juan A. Alonso (2003). "The Compendium Translation System." *Proceedings of MT Summit IX*, New Orleans, Louisiana, USA.
Tikhomirov, Boris D. (1984). "Some Specific Features of Software and Technology in the AMPAR and NERPA Systems of Machine Translation." *International Forum on Information and Documentation*, Vol. 9, No. 2, pp. 9–11.
Toma, Peter (1976). "An Operational Machine Translation System." In Richard W. Brislin, ed., *Translation: Applications and Research*. New York: Gardner Press, pp. 247–259.
Wältermann, Dieter (1994). "Machine Translation Systems in a Translation Curriculum." In Cay Dollerup and Annette Lindegaard, eds., *Teaching Translation and Interpreting 2: Insights, Aims, Visions*. Amsterdam and Philadelphia: John Benjamins Publishing Company, pp. 309–317.
Wehrli, Eric (1996). "ITSVOX." *Proceedings of the 2nd Conference of the Association for Machine Translation in the Americas: Expanding MT Horizons* (*AMTA-2*), Montreal, Quebec, Canada, pp. 247–251.
Wehrli, Eric (2003). "Translation of Words in Context." *Proceedings of MT Summit IX*, New Orleans, Louisiana, USA.
Wu, Zhibiao, Loke Soo Hsu, Martha Palmer, and Chew Lim Tan (1993). "Developing a Chinese Module in UNITRAN." *Proceedings of the Conference of the Association for Computational Linguistics and Chinese Language Processing* (*ROCLING-VI*), Nantou, Taiwan.
Yang, Mujun 楊沐昀 and Li Zhisheng 李志升 (2000). 《機器翻譯系統》 (*Machine Translation Systems*). Harbin: Harbin Institute of Technology Press 哈爾濱工業大學出版社.
Yngve, Victor H. (1960). "The COMIT System for Mechanical Translation." *Information Processing: Proceedings of the International Conference on Information Processing*, Unesco, Paris, pp. 183–187.
Yngve, Victor H. (1961). "The COMIT System." In Harold P. Edmundson,

ed., *Proceedings of the National Symposium on Machine Translation*. London: Prentice-Hall, pp. 439–443.
Yngve, Victor H. (1962). "COMIT as an IR Language." *Communications of the Association for Computing Machinery*, Vol. 5, No. 1, pp. 19–28.
Yngve, Victor H. (1976). "COMIT." In Jack Belzer, Albert G. Holzmann, and Allen Kent, eds., *Encyclopedia of Computer Science and Technology*. New York and Basel: Marcel Dekker, Vol. 5, pp. 146–174.
Yu, Shiwen, Jiang Xin, and Zhu Xuefeng (1991). "An Automatic System for Evaluating Machine Translation." *Proceedings of the International Symposium on Multilingual Translation* (*MMT-91*), Beijing, China, pp. 57–58.
Zajac, Remi (1999). "A Multilevel Framework for Incremental Development of MT Systems." *Proceedings of MT Summit VII: MT in the Great Translation Era*, Singapore.

ArchTran

Chen, Shu-chuan, Chang Jing-shin, Wang Jong-nae, and Su Keh-yih (1993). "ArchTran: A Corpus-based Statistics-oriented English-Chinese Machine Translation System." In Sergei Nirenburg, ed., *Progress in Machine Translation*. Amsterdam: IOS and Tokyo: Ohmsha, pp. 87–98.

Ariane

Boitet, Christian, Pierre Guillaume, and Maurice Quezel-Ambrunaz (1982). "Implementation and Conversational Environment of ARIANE-78.4, An Integrated System for Automated Translation and Human Revision." In Jan Horecky, ed., *Proceedings of the 9th International Conference on Computational Linguistics* (*COLING-82*), Prague. Amsterdam: North-Holland Publishing Company, pp. 19–27.
Boitet, Christian, Pierre Guillaume, and Maurice Quezel-Ambrunaz (1985). "A Case Study in Software Evolution: From ARIANE-78 to ARIANE-85." In Sergei Nirenburg, ed., *Proceedings of the Conference on Theoretical and Methodological Issues in Machine Translation of Natural Languages* (*TMI-85*). Hamilton, New York: Colgate University.
Hutchins, W. John and Harold L. Somers (1992). "Ariane." *An*

Introduction to Machine Translation. London: Academic Press, pp. 221–238.

Atlas

Schrader, Bettina (2006). "ATLAS—A New Text Alignment Architecture." *Proceedings of the Joint Conference of the International Committee on Computational Linguistics and the Association for Computational Linguistics* (*COLING/ACL-2006*), Sydney, Australia.

Uchida, Hiroshi (1986). "Fujitsu Machine Translation System ATLAS." *Future Generation Computer Systems*, Vol. 2, pp. 95–100.

Uchida, Hiroshi (1988). "ATLAS II: A Machine Translation System Using Conceptual Structures as an Interlingua." *Proceedings of the 2nd International Conference on Theoretical and Methodological Issues in Machine Translation of Natural Languages* (*TMI-88*), Carnegie Mellon University, Center for Machine Translation, Pittsburgh, Pennsylvania, USA.

Uchida, Hiroshi (1989). "ATLAS." In Christian Rohrer, ed., *Proceedings of MT Summit II*, Munich, Germany, pp. 152–157.

Uchida, Hiroshi (1989). "ATLAS-II: A Machine Translation System Using Conceptual Structure as an Interlingua." In Makoto Nagao, ed., *Machine Translation Summit*. Tokyo: Ohmsha, pp. 93–100.

Visser, Eric M., Masaru Fuji, and Makoto Shiotsu (1995). "The World on Your Shoulders: The Development of ATLAS." *Proceedings of MT Summit V: Machine Translation Conference, Exhibition and Tutorial*, Luxembourg.

BABEL

Crawford T. D. (1974). "Machine Translation: The Development of BABEL Program." *Letters*, Vol. 8, pp. 54–60.

Crawford, T. D. (1974). "Project BABEL: Machine Translation with English as the Target Language." In Antonio Zampolli, ed., *Computational and Mathematical Linguistics*. Cardiff.

Crawford, T. D. (1980). "Review of the Cardiff Machine Translation Project." In Antonio Zampolli and Nicoletta Calzolari, eds., *Computational and Mathematical Linguistics*. Firenze: Olschki, pp. 761–771.

Babelfish

Allen, Jeffrey, Violetta Cavalli-Sforza, and Robert Frederking (1998). "Review of AltaVista Babelfish Machine Translation Online System." Internal Technical Report, Center for Machine Translation, Carnegie Mellon University.

Bennett, Winfield S. (2000). "Taking the Babble out of Babel Fish." *Language International*, Vol. 12, No. 3, pp. 20–21.

Yang, Jin and Elke Lange (1998). "Systran on Alta Vista: A User Study on Real-time Machine Translation on the Internet." In David L. Farwell, Laurie Gerber, and Eduard Hovy, eds., *Machine Translation and the Information Soup*. Berlin: Springer Verlag, pp. 275–285.

Yang, Jin and Elke Lange (2003). "Going Live on the Internet." In Harold L. Somers, ed., *Computers and Translation: A Translator's Guide*. Amsterdam and Philadelphia: John Benjamins Publishing Company, pp. 191–210.

BehaviorTran

Hsu, Yu-Ling Una and Keh-Yih Su (1995). "The New Generation BehaviorTran: Design Philosophy and System Architecture." *Proceedings of the Conference of the Association for Computational Linguistics and Chinese Language Processing* (*ROCLING-VIII*), Yuan-Ze Institute of Technology Chung-Li, Taiwan.

Su, Keh-yih, Chang Jing-shin, Wang Jong-nae, Emma Chang, and Wu Ming-wen (1996). "The Computational Models of the BehaviorTran English-Chinese Machine Translation System." *Journal of Chinese Linguistics*, Vol. 9, pp. 223–245.

Calliope-Aero

Boitet, Christian (1986). "The French National MT-Project: Technical Organization and Translation Results of CALLIOPE-AERO." *Computers and Translation*, Vol. 1, No. 4, pp. 239–267.

Candide

Berger, Adam L., Peter F. Brown, Stephen A. Della Pietra, Vincent J. Della Pietra, John R. Gillet, John D. Lafferty, Robert L. Mercer, Harry Printz, and Lubos Ureš (1994). "The *Candide* System for Machine Translation." *Proceedings of the 1994 ARPA Workshop on Human Language Technology*, Palinsboro, New Jersey, USA.

CULT

Loh, Shiu-chang 樂秀章 (1975). "Computer Translation of Chinese Journals." *American Journal of Computational Linguistics*, Vol. 3, Microfiche 22, p. 43.

Loh, Shiu-chang (1975). "Computer Translation of Chinese Scientific Journals." *ALLC Bulletin*, Vol. 3, No. 3, p. 258.

Loh, Shiu-chang (1976). "CULT: Chinese University Language Translator." *American Journal of Computational Linguistics*, Microfiche, 46, pp. 46–50.

Loh, Shiu-chang (1975). "Machine-aided Translation from Chinese to English." *United College Journal*, Vol. 12, No. 13, pp. 143–155.

Loh, Shiu-chang (1976). "Translation of Three Chinese Scientific Texts into English by Computer." *ALLC Bulletin*, Vol. 4, No. 2, pp. 104–105.

Loh, Shiu-chang and Kong Luan 江鑾 (1979). "An Interactive On-line Machine Translation System (Chinese into English)." In Barbara M. Snell, ed., *Translating and the Computer*. Amsterdam: North-Holland Publishing Company, pp. 135–148.

Loh, Shiu-chang, Kong Luan and Hung Hing-sum 孔慶琛 (1978). "Machine Translation of Chinese Mathematical Articles." *ALLC Bulletin*, Vol. 6, No. 2, pp. 111–120.

Nancarrow, P. H. (1978). "The Chinese University Language Translator (CULT)—A Report." *ALLC Bulletin*, Vol. 6, No. 2, p. 121.

Desktop Translator

Nesbitt, Kiri (2000). "Review of Transparent Language's Desktop Translator 1 Machine Translation Software." *Multilingual Computing and Technology*, Vol. 11, No. 1.

DLT

Hutchins, W. John and Harold L. Somers (1992). "DLT." *An*

Introduction to Machine Translation. London: Academic Press, pp. 297–311.
Sadler, Victor (1989). "Working with Analogical Semantics: Disambiguation Techniques in DLT." *Foris Publications*, Dodrecht, Netherlands.
Schubert, Klaus (1988). "The Architecture of DLT—Interlingual or Double Direct." In Dan Maxwell, Klaus Schubert, and Toon Witkam, eds., *New Directions in Machine Translation*. Dordrecht-Holland: Foris Publications, pp. 131–144.
Witkam, Toon (1988). "DLT—An Industrial R&D Project for Multilingual MT." *Proceedings of the 12th International Conference on Computational Linguistics* (*COLING-88*), Budapest, Hungary, pp. 756–759.

Easy Translator

Salahub, Eric (1998). "Review of *Easy Translator* for Windows." *APA Newsletters*, Vol. 97, No. 2.

Eurotra

Allegranza, Valerio and Annelise Bech (1991). "A Treatment of Unbounded Dependencies in Eurotra with an Experimental Coindexation Tool." *Machine Translation*, Vol. 6, No. 3, pp. 171–182.
Allegranza, Valerio, Steven Krauwer, and Erich H. Steiner (1991). "Introduction." *Machine Translation*, Vol. 6, No. 2, pp. 61–71.
Arnold, Doug J. and Louis des Tombe (1987). "Basic Theory and Methodology in EUROTRA." In Sergei Nirenburg, ed., *Machine Translation: Theoretical and Methodological Issues*. Cambridge: Cambridge University Press, pp. 114–135.
Bech, Annelise, Bente Maegaard, and Anders Nygaard (1991). "The Eurotra MT Formalism." *Machine Translation*, Vol. 6, No. 2, pp. 83–101.
Durand, Jacques, Paul A. Bennett, Valerio Allegranza, Frank van Eynde, Lee Humphreys, Paul Schmidt, and Erich H. Steiner (1991). "The Eurotra Linguistic Specifications: An Overview." *Machine Translation*, Vol. 6, No. 2, pp. 103–147.
Eckert, Ursula and Ulrich Heid (1988). "Semantical Relations in EUROTRA-D and Syntactic Functions in LFG: A Comparison in the

Context of Lexical Transfer in Machine Translation." In Erich H. Steiner, Paul Schmidt, and Comelia Zelinsky-Wibbelt, eds., *From Syntax to Semantics: Insights from Machine Translation*. London: Pinter Publishers Limited, pp. 178–184.

Geens, D. (1981). "Machine Translation: Evaluation of the Eurotra Interface Mechanism." *Universite Libre de Bruxelles Rapport d'Activites de l'Institut de Phonetique*, Vol. 15, pp. 67–108.

Hutchins, W. John and Harold L. Somers (1992). "Eurotra." *An Introduction to Machine Translation*. London: Academic Press, pp. 239–258.

Johnson, Roderick L., Steven Krauwer, Michael A. Rosner, and Giovanni B. Varile (1984). "The Design of the Kernel Architecture for the Eurotra Software." *Proceedings of the 10th International Conference on Computational Linguistics* (*COLING-84*), Stanford University, Stanford, CA, USA, pp. 226–235.

Johnson, Roderick L., Margaret King, and Louis des Tombe (1985). "Eurotra: A Multilingual System under Development." *Computational Linguistics*, Vol. 11, Nos. 2–3, pp. 155–169.

Kenny, Dorothy (1994). "The Introduction of Irish as a Target Language to the Eurotra Machine Translation System." *Teanga*, Vol. 14, pp. 85–95.

King, Margaret (1981). "Design Characteristics of a Machine Translation System" *Proceedings of the 7th International Joint Conference on Artificial Intelligence*, Vancouver, BC, Canada, pp. 43–46.

King, Margaret (1981). "EUROTRA—A European System for Machine Translation." *Lebende Sprachen*, Vol. 26, pp. 12–14.

King, Margaret and Sergei Perschke (1982). "EUROTRA and Its Objectives." *Multilingua*, Vol. 1, No. 1, pp. 27–32.

King, Margaret (1982). "EUROTRA: An Attempt to Achieve Multilingual MT." In Veronica Lawson, ed., *Practical Experience of Machine Translation*. Amsterdam: North-Holland Publishing Company, pp. 139–147.

King, Margaret and Sergei Perschke (1984). "EUROTRA." The Institute for thc Study of Scmantics and Cognition Tutorial on Machinc Translation, Lugano, Switzerland.

King, Margaret and Sergei Perschke (1987). "EUROTRA." In Margaret King, ed., *Machine Translation Today: The State of the Art*. Edinburgh: Edinburgh University Press, pp. 373–391.

Kirchmeier-Andersen, Sabine (1991). "Implementing Monolingual

Grammars and Transfer Components in the Eurotra Formalism." *Machine Translation*, Vol. 6, No. 3, pp. 149–170.

Lau, Peter Behrendt (1988). "Eurotra: Past, Present and Future." In Catriona Picken, ed., *Translating and the Computer 9: Potential and Practice*. London: The Association for Information Management, pp. 186–191.

Maegaard, Bente and Heinz-Dieter Maas (1985). *Definition of the Eurotra User Language*. Final Report (ETS-7DK/D), submitted to the Commission of the European Communities.

Maegaard, Bente (1988). "EUROTRA: The Machine Translation Project of the European Communities." *Literary and Linguistic Computing*, Vol. 3, No. 2, pp. 61–65.

Maegaard, Bente and Sergei Perschke (1991). "Eurotra: General Systems Design." *Machine Translation*, Vol. 6, No. 2, pp. 73–82.

Maegaard, Bente (1995). "Eurotra: History and Results." *Proceedings of MT Summit V: Machine Translation Conference, Exhibition and Tutorial*, Luxembourg.

Michiels, Archibald (1994). "The Frame-for-term Approach to Terminology in EUROTRA." *Meta*, Vol. 39, No. 1, pp. 184–193.

Oakley, Brian (1995). "To Do the Right Thing for the Wrong Reason: The EUROTRA Experience." *Proceedings of MT Summit V: Machine Translation Conference, Exhibition and Tutorial*, Luxembourg.

Perschke, Sergei (1989). "EUROTRA." In Christian Rohrer, ed., *Proceedings of MT Summit II*, Munich, Germany, pp. 113–119.

Schuurman, Ineke (1994). "EUROTRA: The Philosophy behind It." *Meta*, Vol. 39, No. 1, pp. 176–183.

Schütz, Jörg, Gregor Thurmair, and Roberto Cencioni (1991). "An Architecture Sketch of Eurotra-II." *Proceedings of MT Summit III*, Seattle, Washington, DC, USA, pp. 3–10.

Schütz, Jörg, Gregor Thurmair, and Roberto Cencioni (1993). "Architecture Sketch of Eurotra-II." In Sergei Nirenburg, ed., *Progress in Machine Translation*. Amsterdam: IOS and Tokyo: Ohmsha, pp. 15–28.

Sharp, Randall (1991). "CAT2: An Experimental Eurotra Alternative." *Machine Translation*, Vol. 6, No. 3, pp. 215–228.

Somers, Harold L. (1986). "Eurotra Special Issue." *Multilingua*, Vol. 5, No. 3, pp. 129–177.

Steiner, Erich H. (1986). "Generating Semantic Structures in Eurotra-D."

Proceedings of the 11th International Conference on Computational Linguistics (COLING-86), Bonn, Germany, pp. 304–306.
Steiner, Erich H. and Jutta Winter-Thielen (1988). "On the Semantics of Focus Phenomena in Eurotra." *Proceedings of the 11th International Conference on Computational Linguistics (COLING-86)*, Bonn, Germany, pp. 630–635.
van Eynde, Frank (1988). "The Analysis of Tense and Aspect in Eurotra." *Proceedings of the 12th International Conference on Computational Linguistics (COLING-88)*, Budapest, Hungary, pp. 699–704.
Way, Andrew, Ian Crookston, and Jane Shelton (1997). "A Typology of Translation Problems for Eurotra Translation Machines." *Machine Translation*, Vol. 12, No. 4, pp. 323–374.

GETA

Boitet, Christian (1977). *Nouveau systéme: étude de féfinition.* Rapports de recherche nos. NS-PQ-1 et NS-PQ-2, GETA, Grenoble.
Boitet, Christian (1978). *Bases pour l'élaboration d'un logiciel de traduction automatisée multilingue.* Rapport de recherche, GETA, Grenoble.
Boitet, Christian, Pierre Guillaume, and Maurice Quézel-Ambrunaz (1978). "Manipulations d'arborescences et parallélisme: le systéme ROBRA." *Proceedings of the 7th International Conference on Computational Linguistics (COLING-78)*, Bergen, Norway.
Guilbaud, Jean-Philippe (1987). "Principles and Results of a German to French MT System at Grenoble University (GETA)." In Margaret King, ed., *Machine Translation Today: The State of the Art.* Edinburgh: Edinburgh University Press, pp. 278–318.
Whitelock, Peter J. and Kieran Kilby (1995). "GETA Ariane-78." In *Linguistic and Computational Techniques in Machine Translation System Design.* London: UCL Press, pp. 110–146.

Globalink

Allen, Jeffrey (1995). *Review of the Globalink MT Software.* Internal Technical Report, Peoria, Illinois: Technical Information Department, Caterpillar Inc.
Alwang, Greg (1998). "Better Translation: Need to Communicate across

Borders? Blobalin's New Program Helps You Remove Language Barriers." *PC Magazine*, 14 December.

Burnford, Nigel (1992). "The Globalink Translation System—GTS." In *Translating and the Computer 13: The Theory and Practice of Machine Translation—A Marriage of Convenience.* London: The Association for Information Management, pp. 107–111.

Hinman, Lawrence M. (1998). "Review of Globalink Power Translator for Windows, Version 6.02." *APA Newsletters*, Vol. 97, No. 2.

Lozano, M. Carmen (1989). "Globalink Translation System." In Deanna Lindberg Hammond, ed., *Coming of Age: Proceedings of the 30th Annual Conference of the American Translators Association.* Medford, New Jersey: Learned Information, Inc., pp. 489–490.

HICATS/JE

Kaji, Hiroyuki (1989). "HICATS/JE: A Japanese-to-English Machine Translation System Based on Semantics." In Makoto Nagao, ed., *Machine Translation Summit.* Tokyo: Omsha, pp. 101–106.

Kaji, Hiroyuki (1989). "Language Control for Effective Utilization of HICATS/JE." In Christian Rohrer, ed., *Proceedings of MT Summit II*, Munich, Germany, pp. 72–77.

JFY

Liu, Zhuo 劉倬 (1984). 〈JFY-II型英漢機器翻譯系統概述〉 (Introducing the JFY-II English-Chinese Machine Translation System). In Liu Yongquan 劉湧泉 *et al.*, 《中國的機器翻譯》 (*Machine Translation in China*). Shanghai: Knowledge Press 知識出版社, pp. 58–80.

Liu, Zhuo, Fu Aiping, and Li Wei (1989). "JFY-IV Machine Translation System." In Christian Rohrer, ed., *Proceedings of MT Summit II*, Munich, Germany, pp. 88–93.

Liu, Zhuo 劉倬, Fu Aiping 傅愛平, and Li Wei 李維 (1994). 〈JFY-V機器翻譯系統〉 (JFY-V Machine Translation System). In Yang Zijian 楊自儉 and Liu Xueyun 劉學雲, eds., 《翻譯新論》 (*New Essays on Translation*). Wuhan: Hubei Education Press 湖北教育出版社, pp. 256–264.

LMT

Gdaniec, Claudia (1998). "Lexical Choice and Syntactic Generation in a

Translation System: Transformations in the New LMT English-German System." In David L. Farwell, Laurie Gerber, and Eduard Hovy, eds., *Machine Translation and the Information Soup*. Berlin: Springer Verlag, pp. 408–420.

McCord, Michael C. (1985). "LMT: Prolog-based Machine Translation System." *Proceedings of the 1st Conference on Theoretical and Methodological Issues in Machine Translation (TMI-85)*, Colgate University, Hamilton, New York, USA.

McCord, Michael C. (1989). "A New Version of the Machine Translation System LMT." *Literary and Linguistic Computing*, Vol. 4, No. 3, pp. 218–229.

McCord, Michael C. (1989). "Design of LMT: A Prolog-based Machine Translation System." *Computational Linguistics*, Vol. 15, No. 1, pp. 33–52.

McCord, Michael C. (1989). "LMT." In Christian Rohrer, ed., *Proceedings of MT Summit II*, Munich, Germany, pp. 94–99.

McCord, Michael C. and Arendse Bernth (1998). "The LMT Transformational System." In David L. Farwell, Laurie Gerber, and Eduard Hovy, eds., *Machine Translation and the Information Soup*. Berlin: Springer Verlag, pp. 344–355.

LogoMedia TRANSLATE

Akers, Glenn A. (2002). "LogoMedia TRANSLATE, Version 2.0." *International Journal of Translation*, Vol. 14, No. 2, pp. 151–154.

Akers, Glenn A. (2002). "LogoMedia TRANSLATE, Version 2.0." In Stephen D. Richardson, ed., *Machine Translation: From Research to Real Users*. Berlin and New York: Springer Verlag, pp. 220–223.

Bugel-Shunra, Dena (2001). "Review of LogoMedia Translate Machine Translation Software." *Multilingual Computing and Technology*, Vol. 12, No. 8.

LOGOS

Bennett, Winfield S. and Katie Kearns (1994). "Logos Intelligent Translation System." *Proceedings of the 1st Conference of the Association for Machine Translation in the Americas: Technology*

Partnerships for Crossing the Language Barrier (*AMTA-1*), Columbia, Maryland, USA, p. 237.

Bennett, Winfield S. (1996). "Logos Intelligent Translation System." *Proceedings of the 2nd Conference of the Association for Machine Translation in the Americas: Expanding MT Horizons* (*AMTA-2*), Montreal, Quebec, Canada, pp. 264–267.

Bruckert, Friederike (1997). "Logos as an Internet and Intranet Application." In *Translating and the Computer 19*. London: The Association for Information Management.

Cave, Jon R. (1988). "New Developments in Logos Machine Translation." In Deanna Lindberg Hammond, ed., *Languages at Crossroads: Proceedings of the 29th Annual Conference of the American Translators Association*. Medford, New Jersey: Learned Information, Inc., pp. 55–59.

Clark, Robert (1996). "The Logos Living Dictionary—An Unprecedented Internet Resource." In *Translating and the Computer 18*. London: The Association for Information Management.

Gdaniec, Claudia (1994). "The Logos Translatability Index." *Proceedings of the 1st Conference of the Association for Machine Translation in the Americas: Technology Partnerships for Crossing the Language Barrier* (*AMTA-1*), Columbia, Maryland, USA, pp. 97–105.

Gdaniec, Claudia and Patricia Schmid (1995). "Constituent Shifts in the Logos English-German System." *Proceedings of the 6th International Conference on Theoretical and Methodological Issues in Machine Translation* (*TMI-95*), Leuven, Belgium, pp. 311–318.

Hatley, John (1997). "Logos as an Internet and Intranet Application." In *Translating and the Computer 19*. London: The Association for Information Management.

Hatley, John (1997). "Using the Logos Server via the Logos Windows Client." *Proceedings of the 2nd Workshop of the European Association for Machine Translation: Language Technology in Your Organization?* University of Copenhagen, Copenhagen, Denmark, pp. 53–54.

Hawes, R. E. (1985). "Logos: The Intelligent Translation System." In Veronica Lawson, ed., *Tools for the Trade*. London: The Association of Information Management, pp. 131–139.

Heitmann, Wolfang (1986). "A User's Experience of the LOGOS Machine Translation System: A Manager's Viewpoint." In Catriona Picken, ed., *Translating and the Computer 7*. London: The Association for Information Management, pp. 128–140.

Meyer, Joachim (1996). "'Translation and the Internet:' A Sample Application Based on the Logos MT System." *Proceedings of the 1st Workshop of the European Association for Machine Translation: Language Resources, Terminology, Economics, and User Needs* (*TKE-96*), Vienna, Austria, pp. 139–146.

Orliac, Brigitte (1998). "Logos System Description." In David L. Farwell, Laurie Gerber, and Eduard Hovy, eds., *Machine Translation and the Information Soup*. Berlin: Springer Verlag, pp. 526–530.

Orliac, Brigitte and Kutz Arrieta (1999). "Term Builder: A Lexical Knowledge Acquisition Tool for the Logos Machine Translation System." *Proceedings of MT Summit VII: MT in the Great Translation Era*, Singapore.

Schmid, Patricia and Claudia Gdaniec (1996). "Evolution of the Logos Grammar: System Design and Development Methodology." *Proceedings of the 2nd Conference of the Association for Machine Translation in the Americas: Expanding MT Horizons* (*AMTA-2*), Montreal, Quebec, Canada, pp. 86–95.

Scott, Bernard E. (1989). "The Logos System." In Christian Rohrer, ed., *Proceedings of MT Summit II*, Munich, Germany, pp. 137–142.

Scott, Bernard E. (2003). "The Logos Model: An Historical Perspective." *Machine Translation*, Vol. 18, No. 1, pp. 1–72.

Staples, C. O. (1983). "The Logos Intelligent Translation System." *Proceedings of the Joint Conference on Artificial Intelligence*, Karlsruhe, Germany.

Tschira, Klaus E. (1985). "Looking Back at a Year of German-English MT with Logos." In Veronica Lawson, ed., *Tools for the Trade: Translating and the Computer 5*. London: The Association for Information Management, pp. 215–235.

Wheeler, Peter J. (1986). "LOGOS: Single-software and Multi-target System." In Karl Kummer, ed., *Building Bridges: Proceedings of the 27th Annual Conference of the American Translators Association*. Medford, New Jersey: Learned Information Inc., pp. 135–144.

LogoVista

Decker, Nan (2000). "The LogoVista ES Translation System." In John S. White, ed., *Envisioning Machine Translation in the Information Future*. Berlin: Springer Verlag, pp. 209–212.

Richards, John (1994). "LOGOVISTA E to J." *Proceedings of the 1st Conference of the Association for Machine Translation in the Americas: Technology Partnerships for Crossing the Language Barrier (AMTA-1)*, Columbia, Maryland, USA, pp. 238–239.

LRC

Bennett, Winfield S. and Jonathan Slocum (1985). "The LRC Machine Translation System." *Computational Linguistics*, Vol. 11, Nos. 2–3, pp. 111–121.

Bennett, Winfield S. (1988). "The LRC Machine Translation System." In Jonathan Slocum, ed., *Machine Translation Systems.* Cambridge: Cambridge University Press, pp. 111–140.

Slocum, Jonathan (1983). "A Status Report on the LRC Machine Translation System." *Proceedings of the ACL-NRL Conference on Applied Natural Language Processing*, Santa Monica, California, USA, pp. 166–173.

Slocum, Jonathan (1984). "METAL: The LRC Machine Translation System." *The Institute for the Study of Semantics and Cognition Tutorial on Machine Translation*, Lugano, Switzerland.

METAL

Bennett, Winfield S. (1982). *The Linguistic Component of METAL.* Working Paper LRC-82-2. Austin: Linguistic Research Center, The University of Texas, Austin.

Bennett, Winfield S. (1988). "Methodological Considerations in the METAL Project." *Proceedings of the 2nd International Conference on Theoretical and Methodological Issues in Machine Translation of Natural Languages (TMI-88)*, Carnegie Mellon University, Center for Machine Translation, Pittsburgh, Pennsylvania, USA.

Bennett, Winfield S. (1991). "METAL: Past, Present, and Future." *Proceedings of the Machine Translation Workshop*, Hsin-Chu, Taiwan, pp. 25–26.

Gebruers, Rudi (1988). "Valency and MT: Recent Developments in the METAL System." *Proceedings of the 2nd Conference on Applied Natural Language Processing*, Austin, Texas, USA, pp. 168–175.

Höser, Iris and Barbara Rüdiger (1994). "Russian—A Challenge to

METAL? Some Difficulties of Russian-German Machine Translation." *Machine Translation—Ten Years On: Proceedings of the 2nd International Conference Organised by Cranfield University*, Cranfield, England.

Höser, Iris, Gerda Klimonow, Andreas Küstner, and Barbara Rüdiger (1995). "Metal Russian-German on the Way to a Product." In *Translating and the Computer 17*. London: The Association for Information Management.

Hutchins, W. John and Harold L. Somers (1992). "METAL." *An Introduction to Machine Translation*. London: Academic Press, pp. 259–278.

Little, Patrick (1990). "METAL—Machine Translation in Practice." In Catriona Picken, ed., *Translating and the Computer 11: Preparing for the Next Decade*. London: The Association for Information Management, pp. 94–107.

Liu, Jocelyn and Joseph Liro (1987). "The METAL English-to-German System: First Progress Report." *Computers and Translation*, Vol. 2, No. 4, pp. 205–218.

Roberts, Keith (1995). "Practical Aspects of the Use of METAL at Siemens Nixdorf." *Machine Translation Review*, No. 1, pp. 20–22.

Schneider, Thomas (1989). "The METAL System: Status 1987." In Makoto Nagao, ed., *Machine Translation Summit*. Tokyo: Omsha, pp. 122–127.

Schneider, Thomas (1989). "The METAL System, Status 1989." In Christian Rohrer, ed., *Proceedings of MT Summit II*, Munich, Germany, pp. 128–136.

Schneider, Thomas (1989). "Translation of Engineering Documentation with METAL." In Makoto Nagao, ed., *Machine Translation Summit*. Tokyo: Ohmsha, pp. 152–159.

Schneider, Thomas (1991). "The METAL System, Status 1991." *Proceedings of Machine Translation Summit III*, Seattle, Washington, DC, USA, pp. 41–44.

Schneider, Thomas (1992). "User Driven Development: METAL as an Integrated Multilingual System." *Meta*, Vol. 37, pp. 583–594.

Schneider, Thomas (1993). "The METAL System, Status 1991." In Sergei Nirenburg, ed., *Progress in Machine Translation*. Amsterdam: IOS and Tokyo: Ohmsha, pp. 99–103.

Schneider, Thomas (1995). "The METAL System, Status 1995."

Proceedings of MT Summit V: Machine Translation Conference, Exhibition and Tutorial, Luxembourg.

Schwall, Ulrike (1997). "From METAL to T1 Systems and Components for Machine Translation Applications." *Proceedings of MT Summit VI*, San Diego, California, USA.

Shah, R. (1987). "Translation of Engineering Documentation with METAL." In Makoto Nagao, ed., *Machine Translation Summit*. Tokyo: Ohmsha, pp. 152–159.

Slocum, Jonathan, Winfield S. Bennett, Lesley Whiffin, and Edda Norcross (1985). "An Evaluation of METAL: The LRC Machine Translation System." *Proceedings of the 2nd Conference of the European Chapter of the Association for Computational Linguistics*, Geneva, Switzerland, pp. 62–69.

Slocum, Jonathan (1987). "METAL: The LRC Machine Translation System." Margaret King, ed., *Machine Translation Today: The State of the Art*. Edinburgh: Edinburgh University Press, pp. 319–350.

Thurmair, Gregor (1990). "Complex Lexical Transfer in METAL." *Proceedings of the 3rd International Conference on Theoretical and Methodological Issues in Machine Translation of Natural Languages* (*TMI-90*), Linguistics Research Center, University of Texas, Austin, Texas, USA, pp. 91–107.

Thurmair, Gregor (1990). "METAL: Computer Integrated Translation." In John McNaught, ed., *Proceedings of a Workshop on Machine Translation*. Manchester: DTI/Speech and Language Technology Club.

Thurmair, Gregor (1995). "Currently Available Systems: METAL." In Marianne Kugler, Khurshid Ahmad, and Gregor Thurmair, eds., *Translator's Workbench*. Berlin: Springer Verlag, pp. 75–82.

White, John S. (1985). "Characteristics of the METAL Machine Translation System at Production Stage." In Sergei Nirenburg, ed., *Proceedings of the 1st International Conference on Theoretical and Methodological Issues in Machine Translation of Natural Languages* (*TMI-85*). Hamilton, New York: Colgate University, pp. 359–369.

White, John S. (1987). "The Research Environment in the METAL Project." In Sergei Nirenburg, ed., *Machine Translation: Theoretical and Methodological Issues*. Cambridge: Cambridge University Press, pp. 225–246.

Whitelock, Peter J. and Kieran Kilby (1995). "METAL." *Linguistic and*

Computational Techniques in Machine Translation System Design. London: UCL Press, pp. 171–200.
Wiesner, M. (1994). *Metal System Documentation. En-De V 2.0.* Siemens Nixdorf Information Systems Inc., Austin Development Center.

MetaTexis

Lynch, Clove (2002). "Review of MetaTexis .0999g." *Multilingual Computing and Technology*, Vol. 13, No. 3.

Meteo

Chandioux, John (1976). "Meteo: An Operational System for the Translation of Public Weather Forecasts." *American Journal of Computational Linguistics*, No. 46, pp. 27–36.
Chandioux, John (1988). "Meteo: An Operational Translation System." *Proceedings of the 2nd Conference on Recherche d'Informations Assistee par Ordinateur (RIAO)*, Cambridge, MA, USA, pp. 829–839.
Chandioux, John (1989). "Meteo: 100 Million Words Later." In Deanna Lindberg Hammond, ed., *American Translators Association Conference 1989: Coming of Age.* Medford, New Jersey: Learned Information, Inc., pp. 449–453.
Coch, Jose (1998). "Interactive Generation and Knowledge Administration in MultiMeteo." *Proceedings of the 9th International Workshop on Natural Language Generation*, Niagara-on-the-lake, Ontario, Canada, pp. 300–303.
Langlais, Philippe, Thomas Leplus, Simona Gandrabur, and Guy Lapalme (2005). "From the Real World to Real Words: The METEO Case." *Proceedings of the 10th Workshop of the European Association for Machine Translation: Practical Applications of Machine Translation*, Budapest, Hungary, pp. 166–175.
Thouin, Benoit (1982). "The Meteo System." In Veronica Lawson, ed., *Practical Experience of Machine Translation.* Amsterdam: North-Holland Publishing Company, pp. 39–44.
Hutchins, W. John and Harold L. Somers (1992). "Meteo." *An Introduction to Machine Translation.* London: Academic Press, p. 207.

MiMo

Arnold, Doug J. and Louisa Sadler (1990). "The Theoretical Basis of MiMo." *Machine Translation*, Vol. 5, No. 3, pp. 195–222.

van Noord, Gertjan, Joke Dorrepal, Pim van der Eijk, Maria Florenza, and Louis des Tombe (1990). "The MiMo2 Research System." *Proceedings of the 3rd International Conference on Theoretical and Methodological Issues in Machine Translation of Natural Languages* (*TMI-90*), Linguistics Research Center, University of Texas at Austin, Austin, Texas, USA, pp. 213–233.

van Noord, Gertjan, Joke Dorrepaal, Pim van der Eijk, Maria Florenza, Herbert Ruessink, and Louis des Tombes (1991). "An Overview of MiMo2." *Machine Translation*, Vol. 6, No. 3, pp. 201–214.

Mu

Ashizaki, Tatsuo (1989). "Outline of the JICST Machine Translation System." In Christian Rohrer, ed., *Proceedings of MT Summit II*, Munich, Germany, pp. 44–49.

Nagao, Makoto, Toyoaki Nishida, and Jun-ichi Tsujii (1984). "Dealing with Incompleteness of Linguistic Knowledge in Language Translation: Transfer and Generation Stage of Mu Machine Translation Project." *Proceedings of the 10th International Conference on Computational Linguistics* (*COLING-84*), Stanford University, Stanford, CA, USA, pp. 420–427.

Nagao, Makoto (1985). "Structural Transformation in the Generation Stage of Mu Japanese to English Machine Translation System." In Sergei Nirenburg, ed., *Proceedings of the Conference on Theoretical and Methodological Issues in Machine Translation of Natural Languages* (*TMI-85*). Hamilton, New York: Colgate University, pp. 200–223.

Nagao, Makoto and Jun-ichi Tsujii (1986). "The Transfer Phase of the Mu Machine Translation System." *Proceedings of the 11th International Conference on Computational Linguistics* (*COLING-86*), Bonn, Germany, pp. 97–103.

Nakamura, Jun-ichi, Jun-ichi Tsujii, and Makoto Nagao (1984). "Grammar Writing System (GRADE) of Mu-Machine Translation Project and Its Characteristics." *Proceedings of the 10th International Conference on*

Computational Linguistics (*COLING-84*), Stanford University, Stanford, CA, USA, pp. 338–343.

Sakamoto, Yoshiyuki, Masayuki Satoh, and Tetsuya Ishikawa (1984). "Lexicon Features for Japanese Syntactic Analysis in Mu-Project-JE." *Proceedings of the 10th International Conference on Computational Linguistics* (*COLING-84*), Stanford University, Stanford, CA, USA, pp. 42–46.

Sakamoto, Yoshiyuki, Tetsuya Ishikawa, and Masayuki Satoh (1986). "Concept and Structure of Semantic Markers for Machine Translation in Mu-project." *Proceedings of the 11th International Conference on Computational Linguistics* (*COLING-86*), Bonn, Germany, pp. 13–19.

Tsujii, Jun-ichi, Jun-ichi Nakamura, and Makoto Nagao (1984). "Analysis Grammar of Japanese in the MU-Project: A Procedural Approach to Analysis Grammar." *Proceedings of the 10th International Conference on Computational Linguistics* (*COLING-84*), Stanford University, Stanford, CA, USA, pp. 267–274.

Tsujii, Jun-ichi (1987). "The Current Stage of the Mu-project." *Proceedings of Machine Translation Summit*, Hakone, Japan.

Oriental Express

Liu Bin 劉彬 and Tan Waiyuan 譚外元 (2002).〈雅信CAT和東方快車機器翻譯軟件的分析及建議〉(Analysis and Suggestions for Yaxin CAT and Oriental Express).《第一屆學生計算語言學研討會論文集》(*SWCL2002: First Students' Workshop on Computational Linguistics: Proceedings*), Institute of Computational Linguistics, Peking University, Beijing, China, pp. 215–221.

PAHO

León, Marjorie and Julia Aymerich (1994). "SPANAM™ and ENGSPAN™." *Proceedings of the 1st Conference of the Association for Machine Translation in the Americas: Technology Partnerships for Crossing the Language Barrier* (*AMTA-1*), Columbia, Maryland, USA, pp. 244–245.

León, Marjorie and Julia Aymerich (1997). "PAHO Systems: SPANAM and ENGSPAN." *Proceedings of MT Summit VI*, San Diego, California, USA, pp. 259–260.

León, Marjorie (2000). "A New Look for the PAHO MT System." In John S. White, ed., *Envisioning Machine Translation in the Information Future*. Berlin: Springer Verlag, pp. 219–222.

León, Marjorie (2001). "SPANAM and ENGSPAN for Windows 2000: An MT Pioneer Keeps up with Technology." In Bente Maegaard, ed., *Proceedings of MT Summit VIII: Machine Translation in the Information Age*, Santiago de Compostela, Spain.

Tucker, Allen B., Muriel Vasconcellos, and Marjorie León (1980). "PAHO Machine Translation System: Introduction and Users' Manual." Washington, DC: Pan American Health Organization.

Vasconcellos, Muriel (1983). "Management of the Machine Translation Environment." *Proceedings of the ASLIB Conference on Translating and the Computer*, London, England.

Vasconcellos, Muriel (1984). "Machine Translation at the Pan American Health Organization: A Review of Highlights and Insights." *British Computer Society, Natural Language Translation Specialist Group Newsletter,* Vol. 14, pp. 17–34.

Vasconcellos, Muriel (1985). "Management of the Machine Translation Environment: Interaction of Functions at the Pan American Health Organization." In Veronica Lawson, ed., *Tools for the Trade: Translating and the Computer 5*. London: The Association for Information Management, pp. 115–129.

Vasconcellos, Muriel and Marjorie Leon (1985). "SPANAM and ENGSPAN: Machine Translation at the Pan American Health Organization." *Computational Linguistics*, Vol. 11, Nos. 2–3, pp. 122–126.

Vasconcellos, Muriel (1986). "Application of MT in an Integrated Environment: Update on the Pan American Health Organization." In Karl Kummer, ed., *Building Bridges: Proceedings of the 27th Annual Conference of the American Translators Association*. Medford, New Jersey: Learned Information Inc., pp. 129–133.

Vasconcellos, Muriel and Marjorie Leon (1988). "SPANAM and ENGSPAN: Machine Translation at the Pan American Health Organization." Jonathan Slocum, ed., *Machine Translation Systems*. Cambridge: Cambridge University Press, pp. 187–235.

Pangloss

Brown, Ralf D. (1996). "Example-based Machine Translation in the

Pangloss System." *Proceedings from the 16th International Conference on Computational Linguistics* (*COLING-96*), Copenhagen, Denmark, pp. 169–174.

Carbonell, Jaime G., David L. Farwell, Robert Frederking, Steven Helmreich, Eduard Hovy, Kevin Knight, Lori S. Levin, and Sergei Nirenburg (1994). "Pangloss." *Proceedings of the 1st Conference of the Association for Machine Translation in the Americas: Technology Partnerships for Crossing the Language Barrier* (*AMTA-1*), Columbia, Maryland, USA, pp. 240–241.

Frederking, Robert E., Sergei Nirenburg, David L. Farwell, Steven Helmreich, Eduard Hovy, Kevin Knight, Stephen Beale, Constantino Domashnev, Donalee Attardo, Dean Grannes, and Ralf D. Brown (1994). "Integrating Translations from Multiple Sources within the Pangloss Mark III Machine Translation." *Proceedings of the 1st Conference of the Association for Machine Translation in the Americas: Technology Partnerships for Crossing the Language Barrier* (*AMTA-1*), Columbia, Maryland, USA, pp. 73–80.

Frederking, Robert E. and Ralf D. Brown (1996). "The Pangloss-Lite Machine Translation System." *Proceedings of the 2nd Conference of the Association for Machine Translation in the Americas: Expanding MT Horizons* (*AMTA-2*), Montreal, Quebec, Canada, pp. 268–272.

PARS

Blekman, Michael S. (1994). "Through the Looking Glass to the PARS Land." *Machine Translation—Ten Years On: Proceedings of the Second International Conference Organised by Cranfield University*, Cranfield, England.

Blekhman, Michael S. (1995). "News from Lingvistica '93 Co." *MT News International*, No. 12.

Blekhman, Michael S. (1996). "PARS and PARS/U Machine Translation Systems: English-Russian-English and English-Ukrainian-English." *Proceedings of the 2nd Conference of the Association for Machine Translation in the Americas: Expanding MT Horizons* (*AMTA-2*), Montreal, Quebec, Canada, pp. 273–276.

Blekhman, Michael S. (1997). "PARS/U for Windows." *Proceedings of MT Summit VI*, San Diego, California, USA.

Blekhman, Michael S. *et al.* (1997). "PARS/U: The World's First

Commercial Ukrainian-English Machine Translation System." *Proceedings of MT Summi VI*, San Diego, California, USA.
Blekhman, Michael S. (1998). "The PARS MT Family: Practical Usage." *Proceedings of the 3rd Workshop of the European Association for Machine Translation: Translation Technology: Integration in the Workflow Environment*, Geneva, Switzerland, pp. 45–54.
Blekhman, Michael S., Olga Bezhanova, Andrei Kursin, and Alla Rakova (1999). "The PARS Family of MT Systems: A 15-year Love Story." *Proceedings of MT Summit VII: MT in the Great Translation Era*, Singapore.
Blekhman, Michael S., Olga Bezhanova, Andrei Kursin, and Alla Rakova (2000). "Translation Software by Lingvitics '98: The PARS Family of Machine Translation System." *International Journal of Translation*, Vol. 12, Nos. 1–2, pp. 39–59.
Blekhman, Michael S., Andrei Kursin, and Alla Rakova (2002). "A New Family of the PARS Translation Systems." *International Journal of Translation*, Vol. 14, No. 2, pp. 7–15.
Blekhman, Michael S., Andrei Kursin, and Alla Rakova (2002). "A New Family of the PARS Translation Systems." In Stephen D. Richardson, ed., *Machine Translation: From Research to Real Users*. Berlin and New York: Springer Verlag, pp. 232–236.
Kool, Edward A., Michael S. Blekhman, Andrei Kursin, and Alla Rakova (2004). "The PARS Family of Machine Translation Systems for Dutch System Description/Demonstration." In Robert E. Frederking and Kathryn B. Taylors, eds., *Machine Translation: From Real Users to Research*. Berlin: Springer Verlag, pp. 125–129.

PaTrans

Hansen, Viggo (1994). "PaTrans—A MT-system Development and Implementation of and Experiences from a MT-system." *Proceedings of the 1st Conference of the Association for Machine Translation in the Americas: Technology Partnerships for Crossing the Language Barrier (AMTA-1)*, Columbia, Maryland, USA, pp. 114–121.
Ørsnes, B., B. Music, and Bente Maegaard (1996). "PaTrans—A Patent Translation System." *Proceedings from the 16th International Conference on Computational Linguistics (COLING-96)*. Copenhagen, Denmark, pp. 1115–1118.

PENSEE

Sakamoto, Yoshiyuki and T. Shino (1987). "Japanese-English Machine Translation System 'PENSEE'." *Oki Technical Review*, Vol. 126, pp. 9–14.

Shimohata, Sayori, Toshiki Murata, Atsushi Ikeno, Tsuyoshi Fukui, and Hideki Yamamoto (1999). "Machine Translation System PENSEE: System Design and Implementation." *Proceedings of MT Summit VII: MT in the Great Translation Era*, Singapore.

Personal Translator

Bugel-Shunra, G. Daniel (2003). "Review of Personal Translator 2002 Office Plus Machine Translation Software." *Multilingual Computing and Technology*, Vol. 14, No. 1, pp. 19–20.

PIVOT

Muraki, Kazunori (1987). "PIVOT: Two-phrase Machine Translation System." *Proceedings of the MT Summit Manuscripts and Program*, Hakone, Japan, pp. 81–83.

Muraki, Kazunori (1989). "PIVOT: Two-phrase Machine Translation System." In Makoto Nagao, ed., *Proceedings of Machine Translation Summit*. Tokyo: Ohmsha, pp. 113–115.

Okumura, Akitoshi, Kazunori Muraki, and Susume Akamine (1991). "Multi-lingual Sentence Generation from the PIVOT Interlingua." *Proceedings of MT Summit III*, Seattle, Washington, DC, USA, pp. 67–71.

Okumura, Akitoshi, Kazunori Muraki, and Susumu Akamine (1993). "Multi-lingual Sentence Generation from the PIVOT Interlingua." In Sergei Nirenburg, ed., *Progress in Machine Translation*. Amsterdam: IOS and Tokyo: Ohmsha, pp. 119–125.

Power Translator

Gimènez, Mario J. Mirai and Mikel L. Forcada (1998). "Understanding Commercial Machine Translation Systems for Evaluation, Teaching and Reverse Engineering: The Treatment of Noun Phrases in Power Translator Deluxe." *Machine Translation Review*, No. 7, pp. 20–27.

Knupp, Tom (1994). "Power Translator." *Proceedings of the 1st Conference of the Association for Machine Translation in the Americas: Technology Partnerships for Crossing the Language Barrier (AMTA-1)*, Columbia, Maryland, USA, pp. 229–231.

Lewis, Derek (1996). "The Power Translator: An Evaluation of a PC-based MT System." *Machine Translation Review*, No. 4, pp. 22–32.

Nesbitt, Scott (1999). "Review of L&H Power Translator Pro 6.43 Machine Translation Software." *Multilingual Computing and Technology*, Vol. 10, No. 6.

PROMT

Allen, Jeffrey and Thomas Wassmer (2004). "Software Review of Promt Professional 2003, Expert 2003." *MultiLingual Computing and Technology*, Vol. 15, No. 2.

Boehme, Ulrich and Svetlana Svetova (2001). "An Integrated Solution: Applying PROMT Machine Translation Technology, Terminology Mining, And TRADOS's TWB Translation Memory to SAP Content Translation." In Bente Maegaard, ed., *Proceedings of MT Summit VIII: Machine Translation in the Information Age*, Santiago de Composetela, Spain.

Guerra, Lorena (2003). "Review of @Promt Professional Machine Translation Software." *Irish Translators' and Interpreters' Association (ITIA) Bulletin*, September, pp. 5–6.

Martinez, Lorena Guerra (2004). "PROMT Professional and the Importance of Building and Updating Machine Translation Dictionaries." *International Journal of Translation*, Vol. 16, No. 1, pp. 121–139.

Sokolova, Svetlana (1994). "STYLUS—The MT Product Line for Russian: The Current State." *Machine Translation—Ten Years On: Proceedings of the 2nd International Conference Organised by Cranfield University*, Cranfield, England.

Sokolova, Svetlana (1995). "The Tools for Adapting a Machine Translation System to Individual Needs." In *Translating and the Computer 17*. London: The Association for Information Management.

Sokolova, Svetlana (1998). "ProMT98—The Current State." In *Translating and the Computer 20*. London: The Association for Information Management.

Sokolova, Svetlana (1999). "The PROMT Translation Technology for Russian and Other Languages." *Proceedings of the 4th Workshop of the European Association for Machine Translation: EU and the New Languages: Translation—Possibilities, Policies and Practicalities*, Prague, the Czech Republic.

Sokolova, Svetlana (2001). "The PROMT MT Technology Embodied in PROMT-REVERSO Translation System." In Bente Maegaard, ed., *Proceedings of MT Summit VIII: Machine Translation in the Information Age*, Santiago de Compostela, Spain.

Sokolova, Svetlana (2002). "An Overview of PROMT Translation Software." *Multilingual Computing and Technology*, Vol. 13, No. 3, pp. 43–46.

Reverso

Allen, Jeffrey (2001). "Postediting: An Integrated Part of a Translation Software Program (Reverso Pro 4)." *Language International*, Vol. 13, No. 2, pp. 26–29.

Allen, Jeffrey (2002). "Review of Reverso Pro 5 and Reverso Expert Machine Translation Software." *Multilingual Computing and Technology*, Vol. 13, No. 6, pp. 18–21.

Hoffenberg, Théo (1999). "Reverso: A New Generation of Machine Translation Software for English-French-English, German-French-German." *Proceedings of the 4th Workshop of the European Association for Machine Translation: EU and the New Languages: Translation—Possibilities, Policies and Practicalities*, Prague, the Czech Republic.

Rosetta

Appelo, Lisette and André Schenk (1985). "Linguistic Problems in the Machine Translation Project Rosetta." In Germen de Haan and Wim Zonneveld, eds., *Formal Parameters of Generative Grammar I: Yearbook 1985*. Dordrecht: ICG Printing, pp. 11–16.

Appelo, Lisette (1986). "A Compositional Approach to the Translation of Temporal Expressions in the Rosetta System." *Proceedings of the 11th International Conference on Computational Linguistics* (*COLING-86*), Bonn, Germany, pp. 313–318.

Appelo, Lisette and Jan Landsbergen (1986). *The Machine Translation Project Rosetta*. Eindhoven: Philips Research Laboratories.

Appelo, Lisette, C. Fellinger, and Jan Landsbergen (1987). "Subgrammers, Rule Classes and Control in the Rosetta Translation System." In Bente Maegaard, ed., *Proceedings of the 3rd Conference of the European Chapter of the Association for Computational Linguistics*. Copenhagen, Denmark, pp. 118–133.

Appelo, Lisette (1994). "The Rosetta Characteristics." M. T. Rosetta, *Compositional Translation*. Dordrecht: Kluwer Academic Publishers, pp. 85–102.

Dorr, Bonnie J. (1995). "A Review of Rosetta, M. T. (1994)." *Computational Linguistics*, Vol. 21, No. 4, pp. 582–589.

Hutchins, W. John and Harold L. Somers (1992). "Rosetta." *An Introduction to Machine Translation*. London: Academic Press, pp. 279–296.

Landsbergen, Jan (1984). "Isomorphic Grammars and Their Use in the Rosetta Translation System." *The Institute for the Study of Semantics and Cognition Tutorial on Machine Translation*, Lugano, Switzerland.

Landsbergen, Jan (1987). "Isomorphic Grammars and Their Use in the ROSETTA Translation System." In Margaret King, ed., *Machine Translation Today: The State of the Art*. Edinburgh: Edinburgh University Press, pp. 351–372.

Landsbergen, Jan (1989). "The Rosetta Project." In Christian Rohrer, ed., *Proceedings of MT Summit II*, Munich, Germany, pp. 82–87.

Leemakers, Rene and Joep Rous (1986). "The Translation Method of Rosetta." *Computers and Translation*, Vol. 1, No. 3, pp. 169–183.

McTait, K. (2001). "Linguistic Knowledge and Complexity in an EBMT System Based on Translation Patterns." In Bente Maegaard, ed., *Proceedings of the Workshop on Example-based Machine Translation*. Santiago de Compostela, Spain.

Rosetta, M. T. (1994). *Compositional Translation*. Dordrecht: Kluwer Academic Publishers.

Sanders, M. (1988). *The Rosetta Translation System*. Technical Report (15.103). Eindhoven: Philips Research Laboratories.

Schenk, André (1986). "Idioms in the Rosetta Machine Translation System." *Proceedings of the 11th International Conference on Computational Linguistics* (*COLING-86*), Bonn, Germany, pp. 319–324.

van Munster, Elly (1988). "The Treatment of Scope and Negation in Rosetta." *Proceedings of the 12th International Conference on Computational Linguistics (COLING-88)*, Budapest, Hungary, pp. 442–447.

Smart

Mann, Jeffrey S. (1987). "Get Smart! Industrial Strength Language Processing from Smart Communications." *Language Technology*, Vol. 3, pp. 12–15.

SUSY

Hutchins, W. John and Harold L. Somers (1992). "SUSY." *An Introduction to Machine Translation*. London: Academic Press, pp. 191–205.

Luckhardt, Heinz-Dirk (1982). "SUSY: Capabilities and Range of Application." *Multilingua*, Vol. 1, No. 4, pp. 213–220.

Maas, Heinz-Dieter (1977). "The Saarbruecken Automatic Translation System (SUSY)." In *Overcoming the Language Barrier: 3rd European Congress on Information Systems and Networks*. Munchen: Verlag Dokumentation, pp. 585–592.

Maas, Heinz-Dieter (1984). "Control and Data Structures in the MT System SUSY-E." *Proceedings of the International Conference on the Methodology and Techniques of Machine Translation*, Cranfield Institute of Technology, Cranfield, England.

Maas, Heinz-Dieter (1984). "The MT System SUSY." *The Institute for the Study of Semantics and Cognition Tutorial on Machine Translation*, Lugano, Switzerland.

Maas, Heinz-Dieter (1987). "The MT System of SUSY." In Margaret King, ed., *Machine Translation Today: The State of the Art*. Edinburgh: Edinburgh University Press, pp. 209–246.

SWETRA

Sigurd, Bengt (1988). "Translating to and from Swedish by SWETRA—A Multilanguage Translation System." In Dan Maxwell, Klaus Schubert, and Toon Witkam, eds., *New Directions in Machine Translation*. Dordrecht-Holland: Foris Publications, pp. 205–218.

Sigurd, Bengt and Barbara Gawronska-Werngren (1988–1989). "The Potential of Swetra—A Multilanguage MT System." *Computers and Translation*, Vol. 3, Nos. 3–4, pp. 237–250.

SYGMART

Rolf, P. C. and J. Chauche (1986). "Machine Translation and the SYGMART System." *Computers and the Humanities*, Vol. 20, pp. 283–288.

Systran

Akazawa, E. (1986). "Systran Japanese Systems." *Terminologie et Traduction*, Vol. 1, pp. 78–79.

Allen, Jeffrey and Christopher Hogan (2000). "Toward the Development of a Post-editing Module for Machine Translation Raw Output (An Evaluation and Proposal for Improvement of the European Commission SYSTRAN Machine Translation System). *Proceedings of the 3rd International Controlled Language Applications Workshop (CLAW-2000)*, Seattle, Washington, DC, USA.

Allen, Jeffrey and Thomas Wassmer (2003). "Feature Matrix of SYSTRAN 4.0 Personal, Standard, and Premium Machine Translation Software." *Multilingual Computing and Technology*, Vol. 14, No. 6.

Allen, Jeffrey (2003). "Review of SYSTRAN 4.0 Premium Machine Translation Software." *Multilingual Computing and Technology*, Vol. 14, No. 6, pp. 19–22.

Attnäs, Mats, Pierre Senellart, and Jean Senellart (2005). "Integration of SYSTRAN MT Systems in an Open Workflow." *Proceedings of MT Summit X*, Phuket, Thailand.

Bevan, Nigel (1980). *Human Factors in the Use of EURODICAUTOM and SYSTRAN*. Second Report to the Commission of the European Communities (CETIL-80). Luxembourg.

Burden, D. (1981). "Natural Human Languages Automatically Translated by Computer: The SYSTRAN II System." *Computers and People*, Vol. 30, Nos. 5–6, pp. 12–15, 24.

Bus, Annette and Anja Simon (2002). "Working with Machine Translation: How the Euroscript Group Uses Systran for Fast News Translation." *Multilingual Computing and Technology*, No. 50, Vol. 13, Issue 6, pp. 37–41.

Costa, Jean-Cedric and Christiane Panissod (2003). "SYSTRAN Review Manager." *Proceedings of MT Summit IX*, New Orleans, Louisiana, USA.
Dakis, Stephen (1994). "SYSTRAN: Demonstration and Company Profile." *Proceedings of the 1st Conference of the Association for Machine Translation in the Americas: Technology Partnerships for Crossing the Language Barrier (AMTA-1)*, Columbia, Maryland, USA, p. 246.
Gachot, Denis A. (1989). "The SYSTRAN Renaissance." In Christian Rohrer, ed., *Proceedings of MT Summit II*, Munich, Germany, pp. 60–66.
Gerber, Laurie (1996). "SYSTRAN Chinese-English MT, ECI Chinese OCR—CHIOCR." *Proceedings of the 2nd Conference of the Association for Machine Translation in the Americas: Expanding MT Horizons (AMTA-2)*, Montreal, Quebec, Canada, pp. 277–279.
Habermann, F. W. A. (1984). "Application of SYSTRAN for Translation of Nuclear Centre of Karlsruhe." *Proceedings of the International Seminar on Machine Translation*, Cranfield Institute of Technology, Cranfield, England.
Halliday, T. C. and E. A. Briss (1977). *The Evaluation and Systems Analysis of the SYSTRAN Machine Translation System*. New York: Griffiss Air Force Base.
Hovy, Eduard and Laurie Gerber (1997). "MT at the Paragraph Level: Improving English Synthesis in SYSTRAN." *Proceedings of the 7th International Conference on Theoretical and Methodological Issues in Machine Translation (TMI-97)*, St. John's College, Santa Fe, New Mexico, USA.
Hutchins, W. John and Harold L. Somers (1992). "Systran." *An Introduction to Machine Translation*. London: Academic Press, pp. 175–189.
Joscelyne, Andrew (1988). "Jean Gachot Resurrecting Systran." *Language Technology*, Vol. 6, pp. 26–29.
Knowles, Francis E. (1979). "Error Analysis of Systran Output: A Suggested Criterion for the 'Internal' Evaluation of Translation Quality and a Possible Corrective for System Design." In Barbara M. Snell, ed., *Translating and the Computer*. Amsterdam: North-Holland Publishing Company, pp. 109–134.
Lang, E. and Laurie Gerber (1994). "Internal Evaluation: SYSTRAN." In

Muriel Vasconcellos, ed., *MT Evaluation: Basis for Future Directions. Proceedings of a Workshop Sponsored by the National Science Foundation*, Seattle, Washington, DC, USA.

LATSEC (1975). "Technical Proposal for Further Development of the SYSTRAN English-French Machine Translation System and Initial Development of the SYSTRAN French-English Translation System." La Jolla, California: Latsec Incorporated.

Lewis, Derek (1997). "The Telegraph and Systran Translation Systems for Personal Computer: NLTSG Seminar." *Machine Translation Review*, No. 5, pp. 25–26.

Masterman, Margaret (1979). *On the Development Potential of the SYSTRAN System*. Luxembourg: Commission of the European Communities.

Masterman, Margaret and R. Smith (1980). *On the Automatic Annotation of the SYSTRAN System*. Luxembourg: Commission of the European Communities.

Petrits, Angeliki (1994). "The Current State of the Commission's Systran MT System." *Machine Translation—Ten Years On: Proceedings of the 2nd International Conference Organised by Cranfield University*, Cranfield, England.

Pigott, Ian M. (1981). "How Does Systran Translate?" *British Computer Society, Natural Language Translation Specialist Group Newsletter*, No. 10, pp. 21–42.

Pigott, Ian M. (1983). "Systran: A Key to Overcoming Language Barriers in Europe." *Multilingua*, Vol. 2, No. 3, pp. 149–156.

Pigott, Ian M. (1983). "SYSTRAN Machine Translation at the EC Commission: Present Status and History." *Terminologie Bulletin*, No. 45, pp. 23–29.

Pigott, Ian M. (1988). "MT in Large Organizations: Systran at the Commission of the European Communities." In Muriel Vasconcellos, ed., *Technology as Translation Strategy*. New York: State University of New York at Binghamton, pp. 159–167.

Raby, Christian (1998). "System Demonstration: SYSTRAN Enterprise." In David L. Farwell, Laurie Gerber, and Eduard Hovy, eds., *Machine Translation and the Information Soup*. Berlin: Springer Verlag, pp. 498–505.

Ryan, Joann P. (1987). "SYSTRAN: A Machine Translation System to Meet User Needs." *Proceedings of Machine Translation Summit*, Hakone, Japan.

Senellart, Jean, Jin Yang, and Anabel Rebollo (2003). "SYSTRAN Intuitive Coding Technology." *Proceedings of MT Summit IX*, New Orleans, Louisiana, USA.

Senellart, Jean, Christian Boitet, and Laurent Romary (2003). "SYSTRAN New Generation: The XML Translation Workflow." *Proceedings of MT Summit IX*, New Orleans, Louisiana, USA.

Senez, Dorothy (1995). "Development in Systran." *Aslib Proceedings*, Vol. 47, No. 3, pp. 99–107.

Siebenaler, L. (1986). "Systran for ESPRIT and ECAT Bureau Service." *Terminologie et Traduction*, Vol. 1, pp. 54–60.

Smith, Ross (2003). "Overview of PwC/Systranet On-line MT Facility." In *Translating and the Computer 25*. London: The Association for Information Management.

Toma, Peter (1959). *SERNA System*. Washington, DC: Georgetown University Institute of Languages and Linguistics.

Toma, Peter (1976). "An Operational Machine Translation System." In Richard W. Brislin, ed., *Translation: Applications and Research*. New York: Gardner Press, pp. 247–259.

Toma, Peter (1977). "Systran as a Multilingual Machine Translation System." *Overcoming the Language Barrier: 3rd European Congress on Information Systems and Networks*. Munchen: Verlag Dokumentation, pp. 569–581.

Toma, Peter (1986). "Systran's Contribution to Mankind." *Terminologie et Traduction*, Vol. 1, pp. 4–9.

Toma, Peter (1997). "My First 30 Years with MT." In Virginia Teller and Beth Sundheim, eds., *Proceedings of MT Summit VI*. Washington, DC: The Association for Machine Translation in the Americas, pp. 33–34.

Toma, Peter (2000). "From Serna to Systran." In W. John Hutchins, ed., *Early Years in Machine Translation: Memoirs and Biographies of Pioneers*. Amsterdam and Philadelphia: John Benjamins Publishing Company, pp. 135–146.

van Slype, Georges (1978). *Second Evaluation of the SYSTRAN Automatic Translation System*. Draft Report, Bureau Marcel Van Dijk, Bruxelles and CCE.

van Slype, Georges (1979). "Evaluation by the EEC Commission of the SYSTRAN Automatic Translation System, 1978 Version." *International Forum on Information and Documentation*, Vol. 4, pp. 27–35.

van Slype, Georges (1979). *First Evaluation of the SYSTRAN French-English Automatic Translation System of the Commission of the European Communities*. Draft Report, CCE, Luxembourg.

van Slype, Georges (1979). "Systran: Evaluation of the 1978 Version of the Systran English-French Automatic System of the Commission of the European Communities." *The Incorporated Linguist*, Vol. 18, pp. 86–89.

Wagner, Emma (1985). "Post-editing Systran—A Challenge for Commission Translators." *Terminologie et Traduction*, No. 3.

Wagner, Emma (1985). "Rapid Post-editing of Systran." In Veronica Lawson, ed., *Tools for the Trade: Translating and the Computer 5*. London: The Association for Information Management, pp. 199–213.

Wassmer, Thomas (2003). "Review of SYSTRAN 4.0 Premium Machine Translation Software." *Multilingual Computing and Technology*, Vol. 14, No. 6.

Wheeler, Peter J. (1983). "The Errant Avocado (Approaches to Ambiguity in SYSTRAN Translation)." *The British Computer Society Natural Language Translation Specialist Group Newsletter*, No. 13.

Wheeler, Peter J. (1984). "Changes and Improvements to the European Commission's SYSTRAN MT System, 1976-1983." *Proceedings of the International Conference on the Methodology and Techniques of Machine Translation*, Cranfield Institute of Technology, Cranfield, England.

Wheeler, Peter J. (1984). "Changes and Improvements to the European Commission's SYSTRAN MT System, 1976–1983." *Terminologie Bulletin*, Vol. 45, pp. 25–37.

Wheeler, Peter J. (1984). "SYSTRAN." *The Institute for the Study of Semantics and Cognition Tutorial on Machine Translation*, Lugano, Switzerland.

Wheeler, Peter J. (1987). "SYSTRAN." In Margaret King, ed., *Machine Translation Today: The State of the Art*. Edinburgh: Edinburgh University Press, pp. 192–208.

Whitelock, Peter J. and Kieran Kilby (1995). "Systran." *Linguistic and Computational Techniques in Machine Translation System Design*. London: UCL Press, pp. 40–66.

Wilks, Yorick (1992). "SYSTRAN: It Obviously Works but How Much Can It Be Improved?" In John Newton, ed., *Computers in Translation:*

A Practical Appraisal. London and New York: Routledge, pp. 166–188.
Yang, Jin (1997). "SYSTRAN MT Dictionary Development." *Proceedings of MT Summit VI*, San Diego, California, USA.
Yang, Jin and Elke D. Lange (1998). "SYSTRAN on Alta Vista: A User Study on Real-time Machine Translation on the Internet." In David L. Farwell, Laurie Gerber, and Eduard Hovy, eds., *Machine Translation and the Information Soup*. Berlin: Springer Verlag, pp. 275–285.

Taum

Colmerauer, Alain, Henry Kanoui, Robert Pasero, and Philippe Roussel (1971). *TAUM-71*. Montreal: TAUM Group, University of Montreal.
Isabelle, Pierre (1987). "Machine Translation at the TAUM Group." In Margaret King, ed., *Machine Translation Today: The State of the Art*. Edinburgh: Edinburgh University Press, pp. 247–277.
Isabelle, Pierre and Laurent Bourbeau (1981). *Some Views on the Future of the TAUM Group and the TAUM-AVIATION System*. Montreal: University of Montreal.

Taum-aviation

Bostad, Dale A. (1987). "Machine Translation: The USAF Experience." In Karl Kummer, ed., *Across the Language Gap: Proceedings of the 28th Annual Conference of the American Translators Association*. Medford, NJ: Learned Information, Inc., pp. 435–443.
Bourbeau, Laurent, ed. (1981). *Linguistic Documentation of the TAUM-AVIATION Translation System*. Montreal: TAUM Group, University of Montreal.
Gervais, Antoni (1980). *Evaluation of the TAUM-AVIATION Machine Translation Pilot System*. Ottawa: Translation Bureau, Secretary of State, Ottawa.
Isabelle, Pierre and Laurent Bourbeau (1981). *A Linguistic Description of the Taum-Aviation Computerized Translation System*. Montreal: University of Montreal.
Isabelle, Pierre and Laurent Bourbeau (1981). *Some Views on the Future of the TAUM Group and the TAUM-AVIATION System*. Montreal: University of Montreal.

Isabelle, Pierre and Laurent Bourbeau (1985). "TAUM-AVIATION: Its Technical Features and Some Experimental Results." *Computational Linguistics*, Vol. 11, No. 1, pp. 18–27.
Isabelle, Pierre and Laurent Bourbeau (1988). "TAUM-AVIATION: Its Technical Features and Some Experimental Results." In Jonathan Slocum, ed., *Machine Translation Systems*. Cambridge: Cambridge University Press.
Macklovitch, Elliott and Laurent Bourbeau (1981). "The Principal Characteristics of the TAUM-AVIATION System." In Laurent Bourbeau, ed., *Linguistic Documentation of the Computerized Translation Chain of the TAUM-AVIATION System*. Montreal: TAUM.
Whitelock, Peter J. and Kieran Kilby (1995). "Taum Aviation." *Linguistic and Computational Techniques in Machine Translation System Design*. London: UCL Press, pp. 83–109.

Taum-metro

Whitelock, Peter J. and Kieran Kilby (1995). "Taum-metro." *Linguistic and Computational Techniques in Machine Translation System Design*. London: UCL Press, pp. 67–82.

Taurus

Amano, Shinya (1982). *Machine Translation Project at Toshiba Corporation*. Kawasaki: Toshiba Corporation.
Amano, Shinya, Hideki Hirakawa, and Yuji Tsutsumi (1987). "TAURUS: The Toshiba Machine Translation System." *Proceedings of Machine Translation Summit*, Hakone, Japan.

Tongyi

Chen, Guanghuo 陳光火 (2000).〈通譯的實踐與發展〉(The Application and Development of Tongyi).《電子翻譯》(*Electronic Translation*). Tianjin: Tianjin University Press 天津大學出版社, pp. 148–177.
Chen, Guanghuo (2000).〈通譯電子翻譯系統研發〉(Research and Development of the Tongyi Electronic Translation System).《電子翻譯》(*Electronic Translation*). Tianjin: Tianjin University Press, pp. 84–87.
Chen, Guanghuo (2000).〈通譯科技翻譯軟件系統介紹〉(Introducing the

Tongyi Scientific Translation Software System).《電子翻譯》(*Electronic Translation*). Tianjin: Tianjin University Press, pp. 121–147.

Chen, Guanghuo (2000).〈通譯英譯漢語法體系〉(The Grammatical Structure of the Tongyi English-Chinese Translation System).《電子翻譯》(*Electronic Translation*). Tianjin: Tianjin University Press, pp. 88–120.

Translator

Nirenburg, Sergei, Victor Raskin, and Allen B. Tucker (1985). "Interlingua Design for TRANSLATOR." In Sergei Nirenburg, ed., *Proceedings of the Conference on Theoretical and Methodological Issues in Machine Translation of Natural Languages* (*TMI-85*). Hamilton, New York: Colgate University, pp. 224–244.

Nirenburg, Sergei, Victor Raskin, and Allen B. Tucker (1987). "The Structure of Interlingua in TRANSLATOR." In Sergei Nirenburg, ed., *Machine Translation: Theoretical and Methodological Issues*. Cambridge: Cambridge University Press, pp. 90–113.

TransLinGo

Nesbitt, Scott (1998-1999). "Review of Fujitsu Software Corporation's TransLinGo! 1.0 (Japanese to English Web Page Translation) Machine Translation Software." *Multilingual Computing and Technology*, Vol. 9, No. 5.

Transtar

Dong, Zhendong (1995). "Transtar: An English-Chinese Machine Translation System." In Chan Sin-wai and David E. Pollard, eds., *An Encyclopaedia of Translation: Chinese-English. English-Chinese*. Hong Kong: The Chinese University Press, pp. 628–638.

XTRA

Huang, Xiuming (1988). "Semantic Analysis in XTRA, an English-Chinese Machine Translation System." *Computers and Translation*, Vol. 3, No. 2, pp. 101–120.

Huang, Xiuming (1988). "XTRA: The Design and Implementation of a Fully Automatic Machine Translation System." *Memoranda in Computer and Cognitive Science MCCS-88-121*, Computing Research Laboratory, New Mexico State University, Las Cruces, NM, USA.

Computer Translation System Customization

Climent, Salvador, Joaquim Moré, and Antoni Oliver (2003). "Building an Environment for Unsupervised Automatic Email Translation." *Proceedings of the Joint Conference Combining the 8th International Workshop of the European Association for Machine Translation and the Fourth Controlled Language Applications Workshop: Controlled Language Translation (EAMT-CLAW-2003)*, Dublin City University, Ireland.

Costa, Jean-Cedric and Christiane Panissod (2003). "SYSTRAN Review Manager." *Proceedings of MT Summit IX*, New Orleans, Louisiana, USA.

Hong, Munpyo, Young-Gil Kim, Chang-Hyun Kim, Seong-Il Yang, Young-Ae Seo, Cheol Ryu, and Sang-Kyu Park (2005). "Customizing a Korean-English MT System for Patent Translation." *Proceedings of MT Summit X*, Phuket, Thailand.

McClure, Steve and Mary Flanagan (2003). "Overcoming the MT Quality Impasse." IDC Study #29917.

Richardson, Stephen D., William B. Dolan, Arul Menezes, and Monica Corston-Oliver (2001). "Overcoming the Customization Bottleneck Using Example-based MT." *Proceedings of the Association for Computational Linguistics 39th Annual Meeting and 10th Conference of the European Chapter: Data-driven Machine Translation (ACL-EACL-2001)*, Toulouse, France, pp. 9–16.

Senellart, Jean, Jin Yang, and Anabel Rebollo (2003). "SYSTRAN Intuitive Coding Technology." *Proceedings of MT Summit IX*, New Orleans, Louisiana, USA.

Zajac, Rémi and Jean Senellart (2002). "Challenges in MT Customization on Closed and Open Text Styles." SYSTRAN Software, Inc.

Zajac, Remi, Elke Lange, and Yang Jin (2003). "Customizing Complex Lexical Entries for High-quality MT." *Proceedings of MT Summit IX*, New Orleans, Louisiana, USA.

Computer Translation System Design

Chen, Kuang-hua and Chen Hsin-hsi (1997). "A Hybrid Approach to Machine Translation System Design." *Computational Linguistics and Chinese Language Processing*, Vol. 23, pp. 241–265.

Cote, Nathalie (1998). "System Description/Demo of Alis Translation Solutions: Overview." In David L. Farwell, Laurie Gerber, and Eduard Hovy, eds., *Machine Translation and the Information Soup*. Berlin: Springer Verlag, pp. 494–497.

Hutchins, W. John (1994). "Research Methods and System Designs in Machine Translation: A Ten-year Review, 1984–1994." *Machine Translation—Ten Years On: Proceedings of the 2nd International Conference Organised by Cranfield University*, Cranfield, England.

King, Margaret (1981). "Design Characteristics of a Machine Translation System." *Proceedings of the 7th International Joint Conference of Artificial Intelligence*, University of British Columbia, Vancouver, BC, Canada, pp. 43–46.

Klüter, Andreas, Alassane Ndiaye, and Heinz Kirchmann (2000). "Verbmobil from a Software Engineering Point of View: System Design and Software Integration." In Wolfgang Wahlster, ed., *Verbmobil: Foundations of Speech-to-speech Translation*. Berlin: Springer Verlag, pp. 635–658.

Liu, Yang 劉揚 and Yu Shiwen 俞士汶 (2002).〈CCD構造模型及VACOL輔助軟件的設計與實現〉(The Construction Model of the Chinese Concept Dictionary and Its Auxiliary Tool Visualized Auxiliary Construction of Lexicon).《第一屆學生計算語言學研討會論文集》(*SWCL2002: First Students' Workshop on Computational Linguistics: Proceedings*), Institute of Computational Linguistics, Peking University, Beijing, China, pp. 251–256.

Loomis, Thomas (1987). "Software Design Issues for Natural Language Processing." *Computers and Translation*, Vol. 2, No. 4, pp. 219–230.

Magnúsdóttir, Gudrún (1995). "Building Resources for Machine Translation: What the User Hasn't Got We Have to Provide." *Proceedings of MT Summit V: Machine Translation Conference, Exhibition and Tutorial*, Luxembourg.

Nirenburg, Sergei, Stephen Beale, Stephen Helmreich, Kavi Mahesh, Evelyne Viegas, and Remi Zajac (1996). "Two Principles and Six

Techniques for Rapid MT Development." *Proceedings of the 2nd Conference of the Association for Machine Translation in the Americas: Expanding MT Horizons (AMTA-2)*, Montreal, Quebec, Canada, pp. 96–105.

Su, Keh-Yih and Jing-Shin Chang (1990). "Some Key Issues in Designing MT Systems." *Machine Translation*, Vol. 5, No. 4, pp. 265–300.

Whitelock, Peter J. and Kieran Kilby (1995). "Basic Considerations of System Design." *Linguistic and Computational Techniques in Machine Translation System Design*. London: UCL Press, pp. 5–12.

Whitelock, Peter J. and Kieran Kilby (1995). *Linguistic and Computational Techniques in Machine Translation System Design*. London: UCL Press.

Whitelock, Peter J. and Kieran Kilby (1995). "Wilks's PS System." *Linguistic and Computational Techniques in Machine Translation System Design*. London: UCL Press, pp. 147–170.

Computer Translation System Evaluation

Ahrenberg, Lars (2004). "Codified Close Translation as a Standard for MT." *Proceedings of the 10th Workshop of the European Association for Machine Translation: Practical Applications of Machine Translation*, Budapest, Hungary, pp. 13–22.

Albisser, Doris (1993). "Evaluation of MT Systems at Union Bank of Switzerland." *Machine Translation*, Vol. 8, Nos. 1–2, pp. 25–28.

Bezhanova, Olga, Marina Byezhanova, and Olivia Ryan Landry (2002). "Comparative Analysis of the Translation Quality Produced by Three MT Systems (Part 2)." *International Journal of Translation*, Vol. 14, No. 2, pp. 87–115.

Blekhman, Michael S. (1997). "Language Engineering Systems by Lingvistica '93 and ETS Publishers Ltd: English, Russian, Ukrainian." *Machine Translation Review*, No. 5, pp. 10–18.

Blekhman, Michael S. (2002). "Comparative Analysis of the Translation Quality Produced by Three MT Systems (Part 1)." *International Journal of Translation*, Vol. 14, No. 2, pp. 55–85.

Blekhman, Michael S., Olga Bezhanova, and Mirina Byezhanova (2005). "Comparative Analysis of the Translation Quality Produced by Three MT Systems." *International Journal of Translation*, Vol. 17, Nos. 1–2, pp. 39–85.

Cormier, Monique C. (1991). "Evaluation of Machine Translation Systems." *Language International*, Vol. 3, No. 4, p. 8.

Correa, Nelson (2003). "A Fine-grained Evaluation Framework for Machine Translation System Development." *Proceedings of MT Summit IX*, New Orlean, Louisiana, USA.

Estrella, Paula, Andrei Popescu-Belis, and Nancy Underwood (2005). "Finding the System that Suits You Best: Towards the Normalization of MT Evaluation." In *Translating and the Computer 27*. London: The Association for Information Management.

Fourla, Athanasia, Olga Yannoutsou, Ioanna Tsakou, Sofia Stamou, and Angeliki Pe (2000). "The Contribution of a User Group to the Evaluation and Improvement of an MT System." In *Translating and the Computer 22*. London: The Association for Information Management.

Guessoum, Ahmed and Rached Zantout (2004). "A Methodology for Evaluating Arabic Machine Translation Systems." *Machine Translation*, Vol. 18, No. 4, pp. 299–335.

Höge, Monika, Andrea Hohmann, and Khai Le-Hong (1995). "Software Testing and User Reaction." In Marianne Kugler, Khurshid Ahmad, and Gregor Thurmair, eds., *Translator's Workbench*. Berlin: Springer Verlag, pp. 168–173.

Hutchins, W. John and Harold L. Somers (1992). "Evaluation of MT Systems." *An Introduction to Machine Translation*. London: Academic Press, pp. 161–174.

Isahara, Hitoshi, Hajime Uchino, Shiho Ogino, T. Okunishi, Satoshi Kinoshita, S. Shibata, Toshiyuki Sugio, Y. Takayama, Shinichi Doi, T. Nagano, Masumi Narita, and Hirosato Nomura (1994). "Technical Evaluation of MT Systems from the Developer's Point of View: Exploiting Test-sets for Quality Evaluation." *Proceedings of the 1st Conference of the Association for Machine Translation in the Americas: Technology Partnerships for Crossing the Language Barrier (AMTA-1)*, Columbia, Maryland, USA, pp. 126–133.

Isahara, Hitoshi (1995). "JEIDA's Test-sets for Quality Evaluation of MT Systems: Technical Evaluation from the Developer's Point of View." *Proceedings of MT Summit V: Machine Translation Conference, Exhibition and Tutorial*, Luxembourg.

Jordan, Pamela W., Bonnie J. Dorr, and John W. Benoit (1993). "A First-pass Approach for Evaluating Machine Translation Systems." *Machine Translation*, Vol. 8, Nos. 1–2, pp. 49–58.

King, Margaret and Kirsten Falkedal (1990). "Using Test Suites in Evaluation of Machine Translation Systems." *Proceedings of the 13th International Conference on Computational Linguistics* (*COLING-90*), Helsinki, Finland, Vol. 2, pp. 211–216.

Krauwer, Steven (1993). "Evaluation of MT Systems: A Programmatic View." *Machine Translation*, Vol. 8, Nos. 1–2, pp. 59–66.

Lehrberger, John (1988). "A Synthesis of Evaluations of Machine Translation Systems." In John Lehrberger and Laurent Bourbeau, eds., *Machine Translation: Linguistic Characteristics of MT Systems and General Methodology of Evaluation.* Amsterdam and Philadelphia: John Benjamins Publishing Company, pp. 196–222.

Lehrberger, John and Laurent Bourbeau (1988). *Machine Translation: Linguistic Characteristics of MT Systems and General Methodology of Evaluation.* Amsterdam and Philadelphia: John Benjamins Publishing Company.

Lewis, Derek (1997). "MT Evaluation: Science or Art?" *Machine Translation Review*, No. 6, pp. 25–36.

Maier, Elisabeth and Anthony Clarke (2001). "Evaluation of Machine Translation Systems at CLS Corporate Language Services AG." In Bente Maegaard, ed., *Proceedings of MT Summit VIII: Machine Translation in the Information Age*, Santiago de Compostela, Spain.

Marrafa, Palmira and António Ribeiro (2001). "Quantitative Evaluation of Machine Translation Systems: Sentence Level." In Bente Maegaard, ed., *Proceedings of MT Summit VIII: Machine Translation in the Information Age*, Santiago de Compostela, Spain.

Miyazawa, Shinichiro, Shoichi Yokoyama, Masaki Matsudaira, Akira Kumano, Shuji Kodama, Hideki Kashioka, Yoshiko Shirokizawa, and Yasuo Nakajima (1999). "Study on Evaluation of WWW MT Systems." *Proceedings of MT Summit VII: MT in the Great Translation Era*, Singapore, pp. 290–298.

Nübel, Rita and Jörg Schütz (2000). "Evaluation as a Language Technology Deployment Trigger." *Proceedings of the 5th Workshop of the European Association for Machine Translation: Harvesting Existing Resources*, Lubljana, Slovenia.

Rajman, Martin and Anthony F. Hartley (2001). "Automatically Predicting MT Systems Rankings Compatible with Fluency, Adequacy or Informativeness Scores." In Bente Maegaard, ed., *Proceedings of MT*

Summit VIII: Machine Translation in the Information Age, Santiago de Compostela, Spain.

Rajman, Martin and Anthony F. Hartley (2002). "Automatic Ranking of MT Systems." *LREC 2002: 3rd International Conference on Language Resources and Evaluation*, Las Palmas de Gran Canaria, Spain, pp. 1247–1253.

Reeder, Florence (2001). "In One Hundred Words or Less." In Bente Maegaard, ed., *Proceedings of MT Summit VIII: Machine Translation in the Information Age*, Santiago de Compostela, Spain.

Roudaud, Brigitte, Maria Claudia Puerta, and Otemea Gamrat (1993). "A Procedure for the Evaluation and Improvement of an MT System by the End-user." *Machine Translation*, Vol. 8, Nos. 1–2, pp. 106–116.

Staudinger, Bernhard and Nancy Smith (1998). "Some Problems in the Evaluation of the Russian-German Machine Translation System MIROSLAV." *Proceedings of the 1st International Conference on Language Resources and Evaluation*, Granada, Spain.

Su, Keh-Yih, Ming-Wen Wu, and Jin-Shin Chang (1992). "A New Quantitative Quality Measure for Machine Translation Systems." *Proceedings of the 15th International Conference on Computational Linguistics* (*COLING-92*), Nantes, France, pp. 433–439.

Tomita, Masaru, Masako Shirai, Junya Tsutsumi, Miki Matsumura, and Yuki Yoshikawa (1993). "Evaluation of MT Systems by TOEFL." *Proceedings of the 5th International Conference on Theoretical and Methodological Issues in Machine Translation of Natural Languages: MT in the Next Generation* (*TMI-93*), Kyoto, Japan, pp. 252–265.

Xu, Jian 徐劍 and Liang Maocheng 梁茂成 (1999).〈對幾種英漢機器翻譯系統的測評〉(An Evaluation on Several English-Chinese Machine Translation Systems).《語言文字應用》(*Applied Linguistics*), No. 2, pp. 79–102.

Yuste-Rodrigo, Elia and Francine Braun-Chen (2001). "Comparative Evaluation of the Linguistic Output of MT Systems for Translation and Information Purposes." In Bente Maegaard, ed., *Proceedings of MT Summit VIII: Machine Translation in the Information Age*, Santiago de Compostela, Spain.

E-J QuickTran

Nesbitt, Scott (1999). "Review of Language Engineering Corp (LEC) E-J

QuickTransView 1.0, E-J Pro 5.0, E-J Internet Plus Machine Translation Software." *Multilingual Computing and Technology*, Vol. 10, No. 5.

Computer Translation Teaching

Alves, Fernando Ferreira (2006). "GILTy or Not GILTy: Tailoring Translation Training to the Gospel of Standardization." *Proceedings of the 6th Portsmouth Translation Conference: Translation Technologies and Culture,* School of Languages and Area Studies, University of Portsmouth, England.

Amores, J. Gabriel (2002). "Teaching MT with XEpisteme." *Proceedings of the 6th Workshop of the European Association for Machine Translation: Teaching Machine Translation*, Manchester, England, pp. 63–68.

Aráujo, Luzia A. (2000). "Translation, Terminology, Computers, and Translation Training." *Proceedings of the 7th Conference of the International Society for the Study of European Ideas (ISSEI-2000): Workshop 501—Teaching Translation in the Information Age*, Bergen, Norway.

Balkan, Lorna (2001). "Exploiting the WWW for MT Teaching." In Bente Maegaard, ed., *Proceedings of MT Summit VIII: Machine Translation in the Information Age*, Santiago de Compostela, Spain, pp. 7–11.

Balkan, Lorna, Doug Arnold, and Louisa Sadler (1997). *Tools and Techniques for Machine Translation Teaching: A Survey*. Exeter: University of Exeter.

Bandyopadhyay, Sivaji (2002). "Teaching MT—An Indian Perspective." *Proceedings of the 6th Workshop of the European Association for Machine Translation: Teaching Machine Translation*, Manchester, England, pp. 13–22.

Belam, Judith (2001). "Transferable Skills in an MT Course." In Bente Maegaard, ed., *Proceedings of MT Summit VIII: Machine Translation in the Information Age*, Santiago de Compostela, Spain, pp. 31–34.

Belam, Judith (2002). "Teaching Machine Translation Evaluation by Assessed Project Work." *Proceedings of the 6th Workshop of the European Association for Machine Translation: Teaching Machine Translation*, Manchester, England, pp. 131–136.

Bennett, Paul A. (2002). "Teaching Contrastive Linguistics for MT." *Proceedings of the 6th Workshop of the European Association for Machine Translation: Teaching Machine Translation*, Manchester, England, pp. 43–52.

Blanc, Etienne (2001). "An Interactive Hypertextual Environment for MT Training." In Bente Maegaard, ed., *Proceedings of MT Summit VIII: Machine Translation in the Information Age*, Santiago de Compostela, Spain, pp. 51–55.

Bowker, Lynne (2002). "Why Do Translators Need to Learn about Technology?" *Computer-Aided Translation Technology: A Practical Introduction*. Ottawa: University of Ottawa Press, pp. 11–21.

Bowker, Lynne (2003) "Towards a Collaborative Approach to Corpus Building in the Translation Classroom." In Brian James Baer and Geoffrey S. Koby, eds., *Beyond the Ivory Tower: Rethinking Translation Pedagogy*. Amsterdam and Philadelphia: John Benjamins Publishing Company, pp. 193–210.

Burnage, Gavin (1998). "Teachers and Technicians: Working Together for Effective Use of Information Technology." In Sarah Porter and Stuart Sutherland, eds., *Teaching European Literature and Culture with Communication and Information Technologies: Selected Papers*. Oxford: CTI, Oxford University Computing Laboratory.

Clark, Bob (1995). "Language Technology and the New Translator—Is On-the-job Training the Best Approach?" In *Translating and the Computer 17*. London: The Association for Information Management.

Clavier, Viviane and Céline Poudat (2001). "Teaching Machine Translation in Non-computer Science Subjects: Report of an Educational Experience within the University of Orleans." In Bente Maegaard, ed., *Proceedings of MT Summit VIII: Machine Translation in the Information Age*, Santiago de Compostela, Spain, pp. 19–23.

Corness, Patrick (1985). "The ALPS Computer-assisted Translation System in an Academic Environment." In Catriona Picken, ed., *Translating and the Computer* 7. London: The Association for Information Management, pp. 118–127.

Corness, Patrick (1988). "MT in the University Environment in 1988." *Proceedings of the AURA 1988 Conference*, Brussels, Belgium, pp. 47–61.

DeCesaris, Janet Ann (1995). "Computerized Translation Managers as

Teaching Aids." In Cay Dollerup and Vibeke Appel, eds., *Teaching Translation and Interpreting 3: New Horizons*. Amsterdam and Philadelphia: John Benjamins Publishing Company, pp. 263–269.

Forcada, Mikel L. (2002). "Explaining Real MT to Translators: Compositional Semantics and Word-for-word." *Proceedings of the 6th Workshop of the European Association for Machine Translation: Teaching Machine Translation*, Manchester, England, pp. 137–144.

Forcada, Mikel L. (2003). "A 45-hour Computers in Translation Course." *Proceedings of MT Summit IX Workshop on Teaching Translation Technologies and Tools*, New Orleans, Louisiana, USA, pp. 11–16.

Fulford, Heather (2002). "Freelance Translators and Machine Translation: An Investigation of Perceptions, Uptake, Experience and Training Needs." *Proceedings of the 6th Workshop of the European Association for Machine Translation: Teaching Machine Translation*, Manchester, England, pp. 117–122.

Gaspari, Federico (2001). "Teaching Machine Translation to Trainee Translators: A Survey of Their Knowledge and Opinions." In Bente Maegaard, ed., *Proceedings of MT Summit VIII: Machine Translation in the Information Age*, Santiago de Compostela, Spain, pp. 35–44.

Gaspari, Federico (2002). "Using Free On-line Services in MT Teaching." *Proceedings of the 6th Workshop of the European Association for Machine Translation: Teaching Machine Translation*, Manchester, England, pp. 145–154.

Gimènez, Mario J. Mirai and Mikel L. Forcada (1998). "Understanding Commercial Machine Translation Systems for Evaluation, Teaching and Reverse Engineering: The Treatment of Noun Phrases in Power Translator Deluxe." *Machine Translation Review*, Vol. 7, pp. 20–27.

Gurina, Tatyana M. (1997). "Educational Implications of a Machine Translation System." *Machine Translation Review*, Vol. 6, pp. 6–8.

Hartley, Anthony F. (1987). "Using Machine Translation as a Teaching Aid." In Hugh A. Keith and Ian Mason, eds., *Translation in the Modern Languages Degree*. London: Centre for Information on Language Teaching and Research, pp. 72–78.

Hartley, Tony and Klaus Schubert (1998). "From Testbench to Workflow: Relocating MT in Education and Training." In *Translating and the Computer 20*. London: The Association for Information Management.

Haynes, Colin (1998). "Language Learning." *Breaking Down the*

Language Barriers. London: The Association for Information Management, pp. 126–127.
Haynes, Colin (1998). "Training Sadly Lacking." *Breaking Down the Language Barriers*. London: The Association for Information Management, pp. 135–136.
Jääskeläinen, Riitta and Jaana Parviainen (2004). "'Old School' Faced with New Challenges: Report on the Educational Needs of Practising Translators." *Proceedings of the International Conference on Translating with Computer-assisted Technology: Changes in Research, Teaching, Evaluation and Practice*, Rome, Italy.
Johnson, Roderick L. (1993). "MT Technology and Computer-aided Language Learning." In Sergei Nirenburg, ed., *Progress in Machine Translation*. Amsterdam: IOS and Tokyo: Ohmsha, pp. 286–287.
Kalantzi, Dimitra (2002). "Teaching MT/CAT Tools in Greece: The State of the Art." *Proceedings of the 6th Workshop of the European Association for Machine Translation: Teaching Machine Translation*, Manchester, England, pp. 33–42.
Kenny, Dorothy (1999). "CAT Tools in an Academic Environment: What Are They Good for?" *Target*, Vol. 11, pp. 65–82.
Kenny, Dorothy and Andy Way (2001). "Teaching Machine Translation and Translation Technology: A Contrastive Study." In Bente Maegaard, ed., *Proceedings of MT Summit VIII: Machine Translation in the Information Age*, Santiago de Compostela, Spain, pp. 13–17.
Kingscott, Geoffrey (1996). "The Impact of Technology and the Implications for Teaching." In Cay Dollerup and Vibeke Appel, eds., *Teaching Translation and Interpreting 3: New Horizons*. Amsterdam and Philadelphia: John Benjamins Publishing Company, pp. 295–300.
Knight, Kevin (2003). "Teaching Statistical Machine Translation." *MT Summit IX Workshop on Teaching Translation Technologies and Tools*, New Orleans, Louisiana, USA, pp. 17–19.
Koby, Geoffrey S. and Brian James Baer (2003). "Task-based Instruction and the New Technology: Training Translators for the Modern Language Industry." In Brian James Baer and Geoffrey S. Koby, eds., *Beyond the Ivory Tower: Rethinking Translation Pedagogy*. Amsterdam and Philadelphia: John Benjamins Publishing Company, pp. 211–227.
Kosaka, Takashi and Masaki Itagaki (2003). "Building a Curriculum for Japanese Localization Translators: Revisiting Translation Issues in the

Era of New Technologies." In Brian James Baer and Geoffrey S. Koby, eds., *Beyond the Ivory Tower: Rethinking Translation Pedagogy*. Amsterdam and Philadelphia: John Benjamins Publishing Company, pp. 229–249.

Kübler, Natalie (2002). "Teaching Commercial MT to Translators: Bridging the Gap between Human and Machine." *Proceedings of the 6th Workshop of the European Association for Machine Translation: Teaching Machine Translation*, Manchester, England, pp. 155–162.

Levin, Lori S. (1993). "Translator's Workstations and Language Learner's Workstations." In Sergei Nirenburg, ed., *Progress in Machine Translation*. Amsterdam: IOS and Tokyo: Ohmsha, pp. 287–290.

Lewis, Derek (1997). "Machine Translation in a Modern Languages Curriculum." *Computer Assisted Language Learning*, Vol. 10, pp. 255–271.

Li, Defeng (2002). "Information Technology in Translator Training: Reflections on an Aborted Comprehensibility Test of Machine-translated Texts." In Chan Sin-wai, ed., *Translation and Information Technology*. Hong Kong: The Chinese University Press, pp. 165–176.

Martin, Sigrid B. (1996). "Professional Translation: Can It Be Taught?" In *Translating and the Computer 18*. London: The Association for Information Management.

Masterman, Margaret (1979). "The Essential Skills to Be Acquired for Machine Translation." In Barbara M. Snell, ed., *Translating and the Computer*. Amsterdam: North-Holland Publishing Company.

Merten, Pascaline (1998). "Some Reflections on the Teaching of CAT." In *Translating and the Computer 20*. London: The Association for Information Management.

Mitamura, Teruko, Eric H. Nyberg, and Robert E. Frederking (2003). "Teaching Machine Translation in a Graduate Language Technologies Program." *Proceedings of MT Summit IX Workshop on Teaching Translation Technologies and Tools*, New Orleans, Louisiana, USA, pp. 20–26.

Mitkov, Ruslan, J. Higgins-Cezza, and Orie Fukutomi (1996). "Towards a More-efficient Use of PC-based Machine Translation in Education." In *Translating and the Computer 18*. London: The Association for Information Management.

Miyazawa, Orie (2002). "MT Training for Business People and Translators." *Proceedings of the 6th Workshop of the European*

Association for Machine Translation: Teaching Machine Translation, Manchester, England, pp. 7–12.

Myers, Marie J. (2000) "Voice Recognition Software and a Hand-held Translation Machine for Second-language Learning." *Computer Assisted Language Learning*, Vol. 13, pp. 29–41.

O'Brien, Sharon (2002). "Teaching Post-editing: A Proposal for Course Content." *Proceedings of the 6th Workshop of the European Association for Machine Translation: Teaching Machine Translation*, Manchester, England, pp. 99–106.

Pérez-Ortiz, Juan Antonio, and Mikel L. Forcada (2001). "Discovering Machine Translation Strategies beyond Word-for-word Translation: A Laboratory Assignment." In Bente Maegaard, ed., *Proceedings of MT Summit VIII: Machine Translation in the Information Age*, Santiago de Compostela, Spain, pp. 57–60.

Porozinskaya, Galina (1997). "Aspects of Literary and MT Editing in Teaching Translation." In Kinga Klaudy and János Kohn, eds., *Transferre Necesse Est: Proceedings of the 2nd International Conference on Current Trends in Studies of Translation and Interpreting*, Budapest, Hungary, pp. 553–557.

Robichaud, Benoît and Marie-Claude L'Homme (2003). "Teaching the Automation of the Translation Process to Future Translators." *Proceedings of MT Summit IX Workshop on Teaching Translation Technologies and Tools*, New Orleans, Louisiana, USA, pp. 27–34.

Rodrigo, Elia Yuste (2001). "Making MT Commonplace in Translation Training Curricula—Too Many Misconceptions, So Much Potential." *Proceedings of MT Summit VII*, Santiago de Compostela, Spain.

Rodríguez Inés, Patricia (2004). "Evaluating the Use of Tools and Not Only the Quality of the Student's Output in Translation Teaching." *Proceedings of the International Conference on Translating with Computer-assisted Technology: Changes in Research, Teaching, Evaluation and Practice*, Rome, Italy.

Schäler, Reinhard (1998). "The Problem with Machine Translation." In Lynne Bowker, Michael Cronin, Dorothy Kenny, and Jennifer Pearson, eds., *Unity in Diversity? Current Trends in Translation Studies*. Manchester: St. Jerome Publishing, pp. 151–156.

Scherf, Willi G. (1992). "Training, Talent and Technology." In Cay Dollerup and Anne Loddegaard, eds., *Teaching Translation and*

Interpreting: Training, Talent and Experience. Amsterdam and Philadelphia: John Benjamins Publishing Company, pp. 153–160.

Shei, Chi-Chiang and Helen Pain (2001) "Learning a Foreign Language through Machine Translation: Focusing on Sentence Stems and Collocations." *Proceedings of the 10th International Conference on Artificial Intelligence in Education, Workshop on Computer Assisted Language Learning* (*AI-ED-2001*), San Antonio, Texas, USA.

Shei, Chi-Chiang (2002). "Teaching MT through Pre-editing." *Proceedings of the 6th EAMT Workshop on Teaching Machine Translation*, Manchester, England, pp. 89–98.

Sheremeteyva, Svetlana (2002). "An MT Learning Environment for Computational Linguistics Students." *Proceedings of the 6th Workshop of the European Association for Machine Translation: Teaching Machine Translation*, Manchester, England, pp. 79–88.

Shih, Chung-ling (2002). "Using the MT System as an Aid to Translation Teaching." *Proceedings of 2002 International Conference on the Application of English Teaching*. Taipei: The Crane Publishing Co. Ltd., pp. 494–506.

Shih, Chung-ling (2006). "Modifying Current Translation Teaching with the Assistance of MT and TM Technologies." *Helpful Assistance to Translators: MT & TM*. Taipei: Bookman Books Ltd., pp. 344–360.

Shuttleworth, Mark (2002) "Combining MT and CAT on a Technology-oriented Translation Masters." *Proceedings of the 6th Workshop of the European Association for Machine Translation: Teaching Machine Translation*, Manchester, England, pp. 123–130.

Somers, Harold L. (2001). "Three Perspectives on MT in the Classroom." In Bente Maegaard, ed., *Proceedings of MT Summit VIII: Machine Translation in the Information Age*, Santiago de Compostela, Spain, pp. 25–29.

Somers, Harold L. (2003). "Machine Translation in the Classroom." In Harold Somers, ed., *Computers and Translation: A Translator's Guide*. Amsterdam and Philadelphia: John Benjamins Publishing Company, pp. 319–340.

Torrejón, Enrique and Celia Rico (2002). "Controlled Translation: A New Teaching Scenario Tailor-made for the Translation Industry." *Proceedings of the 6th EAMT Workshop on Teaching Machine Translation*, Manchester, England, pp. 107–116.

van Hahn, Walther and Cristina Vertan (2002). "Architectures of 'Toy' Systems for Teaching Machine Translation." *Proceedings of the 6th Workshop of the European Association for Machine Translation: Teaching Machine Translation*, Manchester, England, pp. 69–77.

Vertan, Cristina and Walther van Hahn (2003). "Specification and Evaluation of Machine Translation Toy Systems—Criteria for Laboratory Experiments." *Proceedings of MT Summit IX Workshop on Teaching Translation Technologies and Tools*, New Orleans, Louisiana, USA, pp. 44–48.

Wältermann, Dieter (1992). "Integrating Machine Translation Systems in a Translation Curriculum." In Edith F. Losa, ed., *New Frontiers: Proceedings of the 33rd Annual Conference of the American Translators Association*. Medford, New Jersey: Learned Information Inc., pp. 167–177.

Wältermann, Dieter (1994). "Machine Translation Systems in a Translation Curriculum." In Cay Dollerup and Annette Lindegaard, eds., *Teaching Translation and Interpreting 2: Insights, Aims, Visions*. Amsterdam and Philadelphia: John Benjamins Publishing Company, pp. 309–317.

Way, Andy (2002) "Testing Students' Understanding of Complex Transfer." *Proceedings of the 6th EAMT Workshop on Teaching Machine Translation*, Manchester, England, pp. 53–62.

Way, Andy and Nano Gough (2003). "Teaching and Assessing Empirical Approaches to Machine Translation." *Proceedings of MT Summit IX Workshop on Teaching Translation Technologies and Tools*, New Orleans, Louisiana, USA, pp. 49–55.

Yuste, Elia (2000). "Translation Instruction in the Y2K—Electronic Corpora, Internet, and Translation Technology." *Proceedings of the 7th Conference of the International Society for the Study of European Ideas: Teaching Translation in the Information Age (ISSEI-2000)*, Bergen, Norway.

Yuste, Elia (2002). "MT and the Swiss Language Service Providers: An Analysis and Training Perspective." *Proceedings of the 6th Workshop of the European Association for Machine Translation: Teaching Machine Translation*, Manchester, England, pp. 23–32.

Yuste-Rodrigo, Elia (2001). "Making MT Commonplace in Translation Training Curricula—Too Many Misconceptions, So Much Potential!" In Bente Maegaard, ed., *Proceedings of MT Summit VIII: Machine*

Translation in the Information Age, Santiago de Compostela, Spain, pp. 45–49.

Computer Translation: Types

Automatic Translation

Alshawi, Hiyan, Srinivas Bangalore, and Shona Douglas (1998). "Automatic Acquisition of Hierarchical Transduction Models for Machine Translation." *Proceedings of the 36th Annual Meeting of the Association for Computational Linguistics and 17th International Conference on Computational Linguistics* (*COLING-ACL-98*), Montreal, Quebec, Canada, pp. 41–47.

Andreyewsky, Alexander (1980). "Whither Automation and the Translator." *ATA Chronicle*, Vol. 9, No. 2, pp. 3–4.

Bar-Hillel, Yehoshua (1960). "The Present Status of Automatic Translation of Languages." *Advances in Computers*, Vol. 1, pp. 91–163.

Basi, Harikumar, ed. (1994). *Automatic Translation*. Thiruvananthapuram: International School of Dravidian Linguistics.

Birnbaum, Henrik (1967). "Some Notes on Russian Predicative Infinitives in Automatic Translation." *Mechanical Translation*, Vol. 10, Nos. 1–2, pp. 11–17.

Boitet, Christian (1976). "Towards an Adaptive and Interactive System in Automatic Translation." In Antonio Zampolli, ed., *Computational and Mathematical Linguistics: Proceedings of the ICCL*, Pisa, France.

Boitet, Christian, P. Chatelin, and P. Daun Fraga (1980). "Present and Future Paradigms in the Automatized Translation of Natural Languages." *Proceedings of the 8th International Conference on Computational Linguistics* (*COLING-80*), Tokyo, Japan, pp. 430–436.

Brace, Colin (2000). "Language Automation at the European Commission." In Robert C. Sprung, ed., *Translating into Success: Cutting-edge Strategies for Going Multilingual in a Global Age*. Amsterdam and Philadelphia: John Benjamins Publishing Company, pp. 219–224.

Brown, Antony F. R. (1964). "Automatic Translation of Languages." *Information Storage and Retrieval*, Vol. 2, No. 1, pp. 1–28.

Brown, Antony F. R. (1964). "Automatic Translation of Languages." In

Aldo Ghizzetti, ed., *Automatic Translation of Languages*. Oxford: Pergamon Press, pp. 27–54.

Bruderer, Herbert E. (1979). "300.000 Words Per Hour: Automatic Translation of Languages—Systems, Functions and Spheres of Its Application." *Journal of the Indian Scientific Translators Association*, Vol. 8, Nos. 3–4, pp. 1–7.

Ceccato, Silvio (1966). "Automatic Translation of Languages." *Proceedings of Automatic Translation of Languages: Papers Presented at NATO Summer School*, Venice, Italy. Oxford: Pergamon Press.

Champollion, Yves (2002). "Automated Translation: The Next Frontier." In *Translating and the Computer 24*. London: The Association for Information Management.

Cordier, Marie-Odile and Chadia Moghrabi (1982). "An Experiment Towards More Efficient Automatic Translation." *Proceedings of the 1st European Conference on Artificial Intelligence* (*ECAI-82*), Orsay, France, pp. 228–231.

Cremers, Lou (1998). "Using Automated Translation in a Corporate Setting." *Proceedings of the 3rd Workshop of the European Association for Machine Translation: Translation Technology: Integration in the Workflow Environment*, Geneva, Switzerland, pp. 27–28.

Delavenay, Emile and K. Delavenay, comps. (1960). *Bibliographie de la traduction automatique* (*Bibliography of Mechanical Translation*). The Hague: Mouton.

Feng, Zhiwei 馮志偉 and Yang Ping 楊平 (1987).《自動翻譯》(*Automatic Translation*). Shanghai: Knowledge Press.

Feng, Zhiwei and Yang Ping (1987).〈自動翻譯概述〉(An Introduction to Automatic Translation).《自動翻譯》(*Automatic Translation*). Shanghai: Knowledge Press, pp. 1–31.

Feng, Zhiwei and Yang Ping (1987).〈自動翻譯系統的應用問題〉(Issues Concerning the Application of Automatic Translation Systems).《自動翻譯》(*Automatic Translation*). Shanghai: Knowledge Press, pp. 324–331.

Feng, Zhiwei and Yang Ping (1987).〈自動翻譯中的數學問題〉(Mathematical Issues in Automatic Translation).《自動翻譯》(*Automatic Translation*). Shanghai: Knowledge Press, pp. 148–213.

Feng, Zhiwei and Yang Ping (1987).〈自動翻譯中的語法問題〉(Grammatical Issues in Automatic Translation).《自動翻譯》(*Automatic Translation*). Shanghai: Knowledge Press, pp. 32–89.

Ghizetti, A., ed. (1966). *Automatic Translation of Languages.* Oxford: Pergamon.
Giuliano, Vincent E. and Anthony G. Oettinger (1960). "Research on Automatic Translation of the Harvard Computation Laboratory." *Proceedings of the International Conference on Information Processing*. Paris: Unesco, pp. 163–183.
Hardt, S. L. (1983). "Automated Text Translation and the Organization of Conceptual and Lexical Information." *Proceedings of the IEEE 1983 Trends and Applications Conference: Automating Intelligent Behavior—Applications and Frontiers*, National Bureau of Standards, Gaithersburg, MA, USA, pp. 261–262.
Heriard, Dubreuil, S. (1979). "Automatic Translation and Computer-assisted Translation." *Information et Gestion*, No. 107, pp. 49–54.
Hoffman, Th. (1976). "Semantics in Aid of Automatic Translation." *Proceedings of the International Conference on Computational Linguistics* (*COLING-76*), Ottawa, Canada.
Hoffman, Th. (1978). "Semantics in Aid of Automatic Translation." *Proceedings of the 7th International Conference on Computational Linguistics* (*COLING-78*), Bergen, Norway.
IBM Research (1960). *Automatic Translation.* Yorktown Heights, New York: IBM Research Center.
Isabelle, Pierre, Marc Dymetman, George Foster, Jean-Marc Jutras, Elliott Macklovitch, Francois Perrault, Xiaobo Ren, and Michel Simard (1993). "Translation Analysis and Translation Automation." *Proceedings of the 5th International Conference on Theoretical and Methodological Issues in Machine Translation* (*TMI-93*), Kyoto, Japan.
Joscelyne, Andrew (1999). "Millennium-ready? Are We Entering the Century Where Language Automation Becomes Reality?" *Language International*, Vol. 11, No. 3, pp. 31–33.
Josselson, Harry H. (1971). "Automatic Translation of Languages since 1960: A Linguist's View." *Advances in Computers*, Vol. 2, pp. 1–58.
Kay, Martin (1973). "Automatic Translation of Natural Languages." *Daedalus*, Vol. 102, No. 3, pp. 217–230.
Krupanandam, N. (1994). "Automatic Translation Trials in Telugu." In Harikumar Basi, ed., *Automatic Translation.* Thiruvananthapuram: International School of Dravidian Linguistics, pp. 169–196.
Kulagina, Olga S. and Igor A. Mel'cuk (1967). "Automatic Translation: Some Theoretical Aspects and the Design of a Translation System." In

Andrew D. Booth, ed., *Machine Translation.* Amsterdam: North-Holland Publishing Company, pp. 137–171.

Lecerf, Yves (1962). "Intrinsic Machine Addressing in Automatic Translation." In National Physical Laboratory, ed., *1961 International Conference on Machine Translation of Languages and Applied Language Analysis: Proceedings of the Conference Held at the National Physical Laboratory, Teddington, Middlesex, on 5th, 6th, 7th and 8th September.* London: Her Majesty's Stationery Office, Vol. 1, pp. 284–312.

Lehrberger, John (1982). "Automatic Translation and the Concept of Sublanguage." In Richard I. Kittredge and John Lehrberger, eds., *Sublanguage: Studies of Language in Restricted Semantic Domains.* Berlin: De Gruyter, pp. 81–106.

Lewis, Terence (2001). "Combining Tools to Improve Automatic Translation." In Bente Maegaard, ed., *Proceedings of MT Summit VIII: Machine Translation in the Information Age*, Santiago de Compostela, Spain.

Magnenat-Thalmann, Nadia (1982). "Choosing an Implementation Language for Automatic Translation." *Computational Linguistics*, Vol. 7, Nos. 3–4, pp. 161–170.

Mel'cuk, Igor A. (1967). "Linguistics and Automatic Translation." *International Social Science Journal*, Vol. 19, No. 1, pp. 64–78.

Neary, Orlagh (1996). "Automate, Emigrate or Evaporate! Corel and Translation Automation." In *Translating and the Computer 18.* London: The Association for Information Management.

Oettinger, Anthony G. (1958). "A Survey of Soviet Work on Automatic Translation." *Mechanical Translation*, Vol. 5, No. 3, pp. 101–110.

Oettinger, Anthony G. (1959). "Automatic (Transference, Translation, Remittance, Shunting)." In Reuben A. Brower, ed., *On Translation.* Cambridge, MA: Harvard University Press, pp. 240–267.

Oettinger, Anthony G. (1960). *Automatic Language Translation: Lexical and Technical Aspects with Particular Reference to Russian.* Cambridge, MA: Harvard University Press.

Oettinger, Anthony G. and Murray E. Sherry (1961). "Current Research on Automatic Translation at Harvard University and Predictive Syntactic Analysis." In Harold P. Edmundson, ed., *Proceedings of the National Symposium on Machine Translation.* London: Prentice-Hall, pp. 173–182.

Oettinger, Anthony G. (1963). "The State of the Art of Automatic Language Translation: An Appraisal." *Beiträge zur Sprachkunde und Informationsverarbeitung*, Vol. 2, pp. 17–32.

Panov, D. Yu. (1960). *Automatic Translation.* Oxford: Pergamon Press.

Perschke, Sergei (1970). "Possibilities of Further Development of Automatic Language Translation." *Pensiero e Linguaggio in Operazioni*, Vol. 1, pp. 83–93.

Plath, Warren J. (1967). "Multiple-path Analysis and Automatic Translation." In Andrew D. Booth, ed., *Machine Translation.* Amsterdam: North-Holland Publishing Company, pp. 267–315.

Rajapurohit, B. B. (1994). "Automatic Translation: Then and Now." In Harikumar Basi, ed., *Automatic Translation.* Thiruvananthapuram: International School of Dravidian Linguistics, pp. 11–34.

Rao, G. Uma Maheshwar (1994). "Automatic Translating Systems for Convergent Linguistic Structures." In Harikumar Basi, ed., *Automatic Translation.* Thiruvananthapuram: International School of Dravidian Linguistics, pp. 115–142.

Rolling, Loll (1978). "The Facts about Automatic Translation." *Proceedings of the 6th Annual Conference on Information Science of the Canadian Association for Information Science*, Montreal, Quebec, Canada, pp. 267–269.

Rolling, Loll (1980). "Automatic Translation Today and Tomorrow: The Computer Is Cheaper Than Human Translation." *Umsch Wiss. und Tech.,* Vol. 80, No. 11, pp. 333–338.

Shalyapina, Zoya M. (1980). "Automatic Translation as a Model of the Human Translation Activity." *International Forum on Information and Documentation*, Vol. 5, No. 2, pp. 18–23.

Shalyapina, Zoya M. (1980). "Problems of Formal Representation of Text Structure from the Point of View of Automatic Translation." *The 8th International Conference on Computational Linguistics* (*COLING-80*), Tokyo, Japan, pp. 174–182.

Sigurd, Bengt (1986). "Automatic Translation—Past, Present, Future." In Lars Wollin and Hans Lindquist, eds., *Translation Studies in Scandinavia:. Proceedings from the Scandinavian Symposium on Translation Theory* (*SSOTT*) *II*. Lund: CWK Gleerup.

Tosh, L. W. (1970). "Stratificational Grammar and Interlingual Mapping for Automatic Translation." *Actes du Xe Congres International des Linguistes*, Bucharest, Romania, Vol. 4, pp. 1049–1060.

van der Meer, Jaap (2006). "Fully Automatic Useful Translation." *Proceedings of the 11th Annual Conference of the European Association for Machine Translation* (*EAMT-2006*), Oslo, Norway.

van Zaanen, Menno and Harold L. Somers (2005). "DEMOCRAT: Deciding between Multiple Outputs Created by Automatic Translation." *Proceedings of MT Summit X*, Phuket, Thailand.

Vauquois, Bernard (1976). "Automatic Translation: A Survey of Different Approaches." In Hans Karlgren, ed., *Statistical Methods in Linguistics*. Stockholm, Sweden, pp. 127–135.

Vauquois, Bernard (1984). "The Organization of an Automated Translation System for Multilingual Translations at GETA." *Proceedings of the IBM Seminar on Natural Language Processing*, Davos, Switzerland.

Vauquois, Bernard (1985). "The Approach of GETA to Automatic Translation: Comparison with Some Other Systems." In A. Wahab, A. Razzak, and Mahmoud Esmail Sieny, eds., *Proceedings of the International Workshop on Computer Aided Translation*. Riyadh: King Abdulaziz City for Science and Technology, pp. 27–96.

Vauquois, Bernard and Christian Boitet (1985). "Automated Translation at Grenoble University." *Computational Linguistics*, Vol. 11, No. 1, pp. 28–36.

Vega, Jose (1995). "A Methodological Approach within the Framework of Large-scale Automatic Translation." In *Translating and the Computer 17*. London: The Association for Information Management.

Wilks, Yorick (1996). "Panel Position on the Limits of Automation." *Proceedings of the 2nd Conference of the Association for Machine Translation in the Americas: Expanding MT Horizons* (*AMTA-2*), Montreal, Quebec, Canada, pp. 227–228.

Yngve, Victor H. (1964). "Implications of Mechanical Translation Research." *Proceedings of the American Philosophical Society*, Vol. 108, pp. 275–281.

Commercial Computer Translation System

Ananiadou, Sophie (1987). "A Brief Survey of Some Current Operational Systems." In Margaret King, ed., *Machine Translation Today: The State of the Art*. Edinburgh: Edinburgh University Press, pp. 171–191.

Benjamin, Bryce, Laurie Gerber, Kevin Knight, and Daniel Marcu (2003).

"Language Weaver: The Next Generation of Machine Translation." *Proceedings of MT Summit IX*, New Orleans, Louisiana, USA.
Bennett, Winfield S. (2001). "Creating Enterprise Machine Translation Systems." *International Journal of Translation*, Vol. 13, Nos. 1–2, pp. 209–215.
Blekhman, Michael S. (1997). "Language Engineering Systems by Lingvistica '93 and ETS Publishers Ltd.: English, Russian, Ukrainian." *Machine Translation Review*, No. 5.
Callison-Burch, Chris (2001). "Upping the Ante for 'Best of Breed' Machine Translation Providers." In *Translating and the Computer 23*. London: The Association for Information Management.
Feng, Zhiwei 馮志偉 (1997).〈機器翻譯──從實驗室走向市場〉(Machine Translation—From the Laboratory to the Market).《語言文字應用》(*Applied Linguistics*), No. 3, pp. 73–78.
Forcada, Mikel L. (2000). "Learning Machine Translation Strategies Using Commercial Systems: Discovering Word-reordering Rules." *Proceedings of MT 2000: Machine Translation and Multilingual Applications in the New Millennium*, Exeter, England, pp. 7–18.
Forcada, Mikel L. (2001). "Learning Machine Translation Strategies Using Commercial Systems: Discovering Word-reordering Rules." *Machine Translation Review*, No. 12, pp. 5–7.
Gimènez, Mario J. Mirai and Mikel L. Forcada (1998). "Understanding Commercial Machine Translation Systems for Evaluation, Teaching and Reverse Engineering: The Treatment of Noun Phrases in Power Translator Deluxe." *Machine Translation Review*, Vol. 7, pp. 20–27.
Hutchins, W. John (2003). "Commercial Systems." In Harold L. Somers, ed., *Computers and Translation: A Translator's Guide*. Amsterdam and Philadelphia: John Benjamins Publishing Company, pp. 161–174.
Hutchins, W. John and Walter K. Hartmann (2002). "Compendium of Translation Software: Commercial Machine Translation Systems and Computer-aided Translation Support Tools, Version 1.5." European Association for Machine Translation (http://www.eamt.org/compendium.html).
Hutchins, W. John, Walter K. Hartmann, and Etsuo Ito (2004). "Compendium of Translation Software: Commercial Machine Translation Systems and Computer-aided Translation Support Tools, Eighth Edition (January 2004)." European Association for Machine Translation (http://www.eamt.org /compendium.html).

Hutchins, W. John (2005). "Current Commercial Machine Translation Systems and Computer-based Translation Tools: System Types and Their Uses." *International Journal of Translation*, Vol. 17, Nos. 1–2, pp. 5–38.
Lück, T., Denis A. Gachot, H. Hagerty, B. Garr, and J. O'Hara (1997). "The Shape of Commercial MT Systems." *Proceedings of MT Summit VI*, San Diego, California, USA.
Medhurst, Marianne (1989). "Machine Translation in the Commercial Environment." In Jeremy Peckham, ed., *Recent Developments and Application of Natural Language Processing*. London: Kogan Page, pp. 65–76.
Rosner, Michael A. (1983). "Production Systems." In Margaret King, ed., *Parsing Natural Language*. London: Academic Press, pp. 35–58.
Roturier, Johann (2004). "Assessing Controlled Language Rules: Can They Improve Performance of Commercial Machine Translation Systems?" In *Translating and the Computer 26*. London: The Association for Information Management.
Thurmair, Gregor and Laurie Gerber (1997). "R&D for Commercial MT." *Proceedings of MT Summit VI*, San Diego, California, USA.
Walker, Daniel E. and Jaap van der Meer (2004). "Perspectives from Commercial Translation." *Proceedings of the 6th Conference of the Association for Machine Translation in the Americas* (*AMTA-2004*), Georgetown University, Seattle, Washington, DC, USA.
Weisgerber, John, Yang Jin, and Pete Fisher (2000). "Pacific Rim Portable Translator." In John S. White, ed., *Envisioning Machine Translation in the Information Future*. Berlin: Springer Verlag, pp. 196–201.

Direct Computer Translation

Forcada, Mikel L. (2002). "Using Multilingual Content on the Web to Build Fast Finite-state Direct Translation Systems." *Proceedings of the 9th International Conference on Theoretical and Methodological Issues in Machine Translation* (*TMI-2002*), Keihanna, Japan.
Hutchins, W. John (1986). "Direct Translation Systems since 1965." *Machine Translation: Past, Present and Future*. Chichester: Ellis Horwood, pp. 209–223.
Papineni, Kishore A., Salim Roukos, and Todd Ward (1998). "Maximum

Likelihood and Discriminative Training of Direct Translation Models." *Proceedings of the International Conference on Acoustics, Speech, and Signal processing*, Seattle, Washington, DC, USA, pp. 189–192.

Electronic Translation

Chen, Guanghuo 陳光火 (2000).《電子翻譯》(*Electronic Translation*). Tianjin: Tianjin University Press.

Chen, Guanghuo (2000).〈電子翻譯的歷史和現狀〉(Electronic Translation: Past and Present).《電子翻譯》(*Electronic Translation*). Tianjin: Tianjin University Press, pp. 6–22.

Chen, Guanghuo (2000).〈電子翻譯的應用及展望〉(The Application and Prospect of Electronic Translation).《電子翻譯》(*Electronic Translation*). Tianjin: Tianjin University Press, pp. 22–40.

Chen, Guanghuo (2000).〈電子翻譯過程〉(The Process of Electronic Translation).《電子翻譯》(*Electronic Translation*). Tianjin: Tianjin University Press, pp. 74–83.

Chen, Guanghuo (2000).〈電子翻譯概念〉(Concepts of Electronic Translation).《電子翻譯》(*Electronic Translation*). Tianjin: Tianjin University Press, pp. 1–6.

Chen, Guanghuo (2000).〈電子翻譯的基本原理〉(Fundamental Principles of Electronic Translation).《電子翻譯》(*Electronic Translation*). Tianjin: Tianjin University Press, pp. 41–57.

Ekhtiar, Mansur (1967). "Electronic Translation." *Journal of the Franklin Institute*, pp. 257–260.

Pigott, Ian M. (1984). "Electronic Translation Grows Cheaper and Better." *Intermedia*, Vol. 7, No. 9, p. 12.

Snell, Barbara M. (1980). "Electronic Translation?" *Aslib Proceedings*, Vol. 32, No. 4, pp. 179–186.

Teague, Ben (1989). "A Functioning Electronic Network for Translators." In Deanna Lindberg Hammond, ed., *Coming of Age: Proceedings of the 30th Annual Conference of the American Translators Association*. Medford, New Jersey: Learned Information, Inc., pp. 13–18.

Embedded Computer Translation

Bangalore, Srinivas and Giuseppe Riccardi (2000). "Stochastic Finite-state

Models for Spoken Language Machine Translation." *Proceedings of the Workshop on Embedded Machine Translation Systems (ANLP/NAACL-2000)*, Seattle, Washington, DC, USA, pp. 52–59.

Gaspari, Federico (2005). "Embedding Free Online Machine Translation into Monolingual Websites for Multilingual Dissemination: A Case Study of Implementation." In *Translating and the Computer 27*. London: The Association for Information Management.

Hansen, Inge Gorm, and Henrik Selsøe Sørensen (2002). "LinguaNet: Embedded MT in a Cross-border Messaging System for European Law Enforcement." *Machine Translation*, Vol. 17, No. 2, pp. 139–163.

Holland, Melissa, C. Schlesiger, and Calandra Tate (2000). "Evaluating Embedded Machine Translation in Military Field Exercises." In John S. White, ed., *Envisioning Machine Translation in the Information Future*. Berlin: Springer Verlag, pp. 239–247.

Johnson, Edward (1996). "LinguaNet ... Setting a Linguist to Catch a Thief." In *Translating and the Computer 18*. London: The Association for Information Management.

Laoudi, Jamal, Calandra Tate, and Clare R. Voss (2004). "Towards an Automated Evaluation of an Embedded MT System." *Proceedings of the 9th Workshop of the European Association for Machine Translation: Broadening Horizons of Machine Translation and Its Applications*, Foundation for International Studies, Malta, pp. 106–115.

Pym, Anthony (2004). "Belonging as Resistance." *The Moving Text: Localization, Translation, and Distribution*. Amsterdam and Philadelphia: John Benjamins Publishing Company, pp. 111–132.

Reeder, Florence M. (2000). "At Your Service: Embedded MT as a Service." *Proceedings of the Workshop on Embedded Machine Translation Systems (ANLP/NAACL-2000)—Volume 5*, Seattle, Washington, DC, USA, pp. 17–22.

Voss, Clare R. and Carl J. van Ess-Dykema (2002). "Special Issue on Embedded MT Systems: Overview." *Machine Translation*, Vol. 17, No. 4, pp. 307–319.

Experimental Computer Translation System

Baker, Janet and Patri Pugliese (2006). "From Pipedreams to Products and Promise!" *Proceedings of the Human Language Technology Conference—Annual Meeting of the North American Chapter of the Association for Computational Linguistics* (*HLT-NAACL-2006*), New York, USA.

Bouillon, Pierrette and Katharina Boesefeldt (1993). "Applying an Experimental MT System to a Realistic Problem." In Sergei Nirenburg, ed., *Progress in Machine Translation.* Amsterdam: IOS and Tokyo: Ohmsha, pp. 79–86.

Crawford, T. D. (1974). "Project BABEL: Machine Translation with English as the Target Language." In Antonio Zampolli, ed., *Proceedings of the 3rd Symposium on the Use of JPRS Computers in Literary and Linguistic Research*, Cardiff, England.

Crawford, T. D. (1974). "Machine Translation: The Development of BABEL Program." *Letters*, No. 8, pp. 54–60.

Hybrid Computer Translation

Carl, Michael, Catherine Pease, and Oliver Streiter (1999). "Examples of Hybrid Machine Translation." *Proceedings of the ISMT and CLIP Conference,* Beijing, China.

Groves, Declan and Andy Way (2006). "Hybridity in MT: Experiments on the Europarl Corpus." *Proceedings of the 11th Workshop of the European Association for Machine Translation: Machine Translation/ Translation Aids—Tools to Increase Quality and to Save Money*, the University of Oslo, Oslo, Norway.

Habash, Nizar (2002). "Generation Heavy Hybrid Machine Translation." *Proceedings of the International Workshop on Natural Language Generation* (*INLG-2002*), New York, USA.

Streiter, Oliver, Michael Carl, and Leonid L. Iomdin (2000). "A Virtual Translation Machine for Hybrid Machine Translation."*Proceedings of the Dialogue '2000 International Seminar in Computational Linguistics and Applications*, Tarusa, Russia.

Interactive Computer Translation

Bender, Oliver, Sasa Hasan, David Vilar, Richard Zens, and Hermann Ney (2005). "Comparison of Generation Strategies for Interactive Machine Translation." *Proceedings of the 10th Workshop of the European*

Association for Machine Translation: Practical Applications of Machine Translation, Budapest, Hungary, pp. 33–40.
Coch, José and Karine Chevreau (2001). "Interactive Multilingual Generation." *Proceedings of the 2nd International Conference on Intelligent Text Processing and Computational Linguistics (CICLing-2001)*, Mexico City, Mexico.
Foster, George, Pierre Isabelle, and Pierre Plamondon (1997). "Target-text Mediated Interactive Machine Translation." *Machine Translation*, Vol. 12, Nos. 1–2, pp. 175–194.
Hutchins, W. John (1986). "Interactive and Human-aided Systems." *Machine Translation: Past, Present and Future*. Chichester: Ellis Horwood, pp. 292–306.
Lonsdale, Deryle (1984). "Notes on Interactive Translation." *Proceedings of the International Seminar on Machine Translation*, Cranfield Institute of Technology, Cranfield, England.
Schachtl, Stefani and A. Fraser-Tillmann (2001). "TopTrans: Interactive Machine Translation." In *Translating and the Computer 23*. London: The Association for Information Management.
Sheremetyeva, Svetlana and Sergei Nirenburg (1999). "Interactive MT as Support for Non-native Language Authoring." *Proceedings of MT Summit VII: MT in the Great Translation Era*, Singapore.
Weaver, Alan (1988). "Two Aspects of Interactive Machine Translation." In Muriel Vasconcellos, ed., *Technology as Translation Strategy*. New York: State University of New York at Binghamton, pp. 116–123.
Whitelock, Peter J., Mary McGee Wood, Brian J. Chandler, Natsuko Holden, and Heather J. Horsfall (1986). "Strategies for Interactive Machine Translation: The Experience and Implications of the UMIST Japanese Project." *Proceedings of the 11th International Conference on Computational Linguistics*, Bonn, Germany.

Interlingual Computer Translation

Açıkgöz, Fırat and Olcay Sert (2006). "Interlingual Machine Translation: Prospects and Setbacks." *Translation Journal*, Vol. 10, No. 3.
Arnold, Douglas (1996). "Parameterizing Lexical Conceptual Structure for Interlingual Machine Translation." *Machine Translation*, Vol. 11, No. 4, pp. 217–241.
de Rojas, Ivan Guzman (1988). "ATAMIRI—Interlingual MT Using the

Aymara Language." In Dan Maxwell, Klaus Schubert, and Toon Witkam, eds. *New Directions in Machine Translation*. Dordrecht-Holland: Foris Publications, pp. 123–129.

Dorr, Bonnie J. (1992). "The Use of Lexical Semantics in Interlingual Machine Translation." *Machine Translation*, Vol. 7, No. 3, pp. 135–193.

Dorr, Bonnie J. (1993). "The Interlingual Representation." *Machine Translation: A View from the Lexicon*. Cambridge, MA: MIT Press, pp. 95–162.

Dorr, Bonnie J., Joseph Garman, and Amy Weinberg (1995). "From Syntactic Encodings to Thematic Roles: Building Lexical Entries for Interlingual MT." *Machine Translation*, Vol. 9, No. 3, pp. 71–100.

Dorr, Bonnie J. (1997). "Large-scale Dictionary Construction for Foreign Language Tutoring and Interlingual Machine Translation." *Machine Translation*, Vol. 12, No. 4, pp. 271–322.

Hakkani, Dilek Zeynep, Gökhan Tür, Kemal Oflazer, Teruko Mitamura, and Eric H. Nyberg (1998). "An English-to-Turkish Interlingual MT System." In David L. Farwell, Laurie Gerber, and Eduard Hovy, eds., *Machine Translation and the Information Soup*. Berlin: Springer Verlag, pp. 83–94.

Hutchins, W. John (1986). "Interlingual Systems, 1965–1975." *Machine Translation: Past, Present and Future*. Chichester: Ellis Horwood, pp. 190–200.

Hutchins, W. John (1986). "Other Interlingual Projects since 1975." *Machine Translation: Past, Present and Future*. Chichester: Ellis Horwood, pp. 285–291.

Nirenburg, Sergei, David L. Farwell, and Boyan Onyshkevych (1994). "Interlingual MT." *Technology Partnerships for Crossing the Language Barrier: 1st Conference of the Association for Machine Translation in the Americas*, Columbia, Maryland, USA.

Reeder, Florence, Bonnie J. Dorr, David L. Farwell, Nizar Habash, Stephen Helmreich, Eduard Hovy, Lori S. Levin, Teruko Mitamura, Keith Miller, Owen Rambow, and Advaith Siddharthan (2004). "Interlingual Annotation for MT Development." In Robert E. Frederking and Kathryn B. Taylors, eds., *Machine Translation: From Real Users to Research*. Berlin: Springer Verlag, pp. 236–245.

Richens, Richard H. (1958). "Interlingual Machine Translation." *The Computer Journal*, Vol. 1, No. 3, pp. 144–147.

Schubert, Klaus (1988). "The Architecture of DLT—Interlingual or Double Direct." In Dan Maxwell, Klaus Schubert, and Toon Witkam, eds., *New Directions in Machine Translation*. Dordrecht-Holland: Foris Publications, pp. 131–144.

Slocum, Jonathan (1987). "Concept-lexeme-syntax Triangles: A Gateway to Interlingual Translation." *Computers and Translation*, Vol. 2, No. 4, pp. 243–261.

Wakao, Takahiro and Stephen Helmreich (1993). "Translation of Metonymy in an Interlingual MT System." *Proceedings of the Pacific Association for Computational Linguistics* (*PACLING-93*), Vancouver, BC, Canada.

Witkam, Toon (1987). "Interlingual Machine Translation—An Industrial Initiative." In Makoto Nagao, ed., *Machine Translation Summit*. Tokyo: Ohmsha, pp. 128–132.

Witkam, Toon (1988). "DLT—An Industrial R&D Project for Multilingual MT." *Proceedings of the 12th International Conference on Computational Linguistics* (*COLING-88*), Budapest, Hungary, pp. 756–759.

Lexical Translation

Gopestake, Ann, Ted Briscoe, Piek Vossen, Alicia Ageno, Irene Castellon, Francesc Ribas, German Rigau, Horacio Rodríguez, and Anna Samiotou (1994). "Acquisition of Lexical Translation Relations from MRDS." *Machine Translation*, Vol. 9, Nos. 3–4, pp. 183–219.

Laffling, John (1991). "Review of Various Approaches to Lexical Disambiguation/Translation." *Towards High-precision Machine Translation: Based on Contrastive Textology*. Berlin and New York: Foris Publications, pp. 35–56.

Talbot, David and Miles Osborne (2006). "Modelling Lexical Redundancy for Machine Translation." *Proceedings of the Joint Conference of the International Committee on Computational Linguistics and the Association for Computational Linguistics* (*COLING/ACL-2006*), Sydney, Australia.

Mechanical Translation

Albani, Enrico, Silvio Ceccato, and Enrico Maretti (1961). "Classification, Rules, and Code of an Operational Grammar for Mechanical

Translation." In Allen Kent, ed., *Information Retrieval and Machine Translation*. New York: Interscience, pp. 693–753.
Alt, Franz L. (1965). "Mechanical Translation: U.S.-Japan Joint Conference." *Science*, Vol. 147, pp. 1599–1600.
Bar-Hillel, Yehoshua (1951). "The Present State of Research on Mechanical Translation." *American Documentation*, Vol. 2, No. 4, pp. 229–237.
Bar-Hillel, Yehoshua (1954). "Can Translation Be Mechanized?" *American Scientist*, Vol. 42, pp. 248–260.
Bar-Hillel, Yehoshua (1955). "Can Translation Be Mechanized?" *Journal of Symbolic Logic*, Vol. 20, pp. 192–194.
Bastin, E. W. (1956). "General Mathematical Problems Involved in Mechanical Translation." *Mechanical Translation*, Vol. 3, No. 1, pp. 6–7.
Boitet, Christian (1977). "Mechanical Translation and the Problem of Understanding Natural Languages." *Proceedings of Table-Ronde IFIP*, Toronto, Canada.
Booth, Andrew D. (1953). "Mechanical Translation." *Computers and Automation*, Vol. 2, No. 4, pp. 6–8.
Booth, Andrew D. (1954). "Calculating Machines and Mechanical Translation." *Discovery*, Vol. 15, No. 7, pp. 280–285.
Booth, Andrew, D. (1957). "Mechanical Translations." *Aslib Proceedings*, Vol. 9, No. 6, pp. 177–181.
Booth, Andrew D., Leonard Brandwood, and John P. Cleave (1958). *Mechanical Resolution of Linguistic Problems*. London: Butterworths.
Brandwood, Leonard (1956). "Previous Experiments in Mechanical Translation." *Babel*, Vol. 2, No. 3, pp. 125–127.
Ceccato, Silvio and Enrico Maretti (1956). "Suggestions for Mechanical Translation." In Colin Cherry, ed., *Information Theory: Papers Read at a Symposium on Information Theory*. London: Butterworths.
Ceccato, Silvio (1960). *Thoughts as the Basis of Mechanical Translation and Summarising*. Milano: Centro di Cibernetica e di Attivita Linguistiche.
Ceccato, Silvio (1961). *Linguistic Analysis and Programming for Mechanical Translation*. Milan: Feltrinelli.
Ceccato, Silvio, ed. (1963). *Mechanical Translation: The Correlational Solution*. Milano: Centro di Cibernetica e di Attivita Linguistiche.
Ceccato, Silvio (1965). "Correlational Analysis and Mechanical

Translation." In Andrew D. Booth, ed., *Machine Translation*. Amsterdam: North-Holland Publishing Company, pp. 77–135.
Cleave, John P. (1957). "A Model for Mechanical Translation." *Mechanical Translation*, Vol. 4, Nos. 1–2, pp. 2–4.
Dostert, Leon E. (1956). "Organization and Method in Mechanical Translation Work." *Mechanical Translation*, Vol. 3, No. 2, p. 35.
Glasersfield, Ernest von (1962). "First Draft of an English Input Procedure for Mechanical Translation." *Methodos*, Vol. 14, No. 54, pp. 47–79.
Gode, Alexander (1955). "The Signal System in Interlingua—A Factor in Mechanical Translation." *Mechanical Translation*, Vol. 2, No. 3, pp. 55–60.
Gross, Maurice (1964). "On the Equivalence of Models of Language Used in the Fields of Mechanical Translation and Information Retrieval." *Information Storage and Retrieval*, Vol. 2, No. 1, pp. 43–57.
Hutchins, W. John (1997). "First Steps in Mechanical Translation." *Proceedings of MT Summit VI*, San Diego, California, USA, pp. 14–23.
King, Gilbert W. (1956). "Stochastic Methods of Mechanical Translation." *Mechanical Translation*, Vol. 3, No. 2, pp. 38–39.
Kirk, Robert (1956). "Languages as Codes: A Report on Mechanical Translation." *Chicago Review*, Vol. 9, pp. 39–52.
Korvasová, K. (1962). "A Note on an Experiment in Mechanical Translation on the Computer SAPO." In *Information Processing Machines 8*. Prague: CSAV.
Koutsoudas, Andreas and Robert R. Korfhage (1956). "Mechanical Translation and the Problem of Multiple Meaning." *Mechanical Translation*, Vol. 3, No. 2, pp. 46–51.
Masterman, Margaret, R. M. Needham, and Karen Sparck Jones (1959). "The Analogy between Mechanical Translation and Library Retrieval." *Proceedings of the International Conference on Scientific Information*. Washington, DC: National Academy of Sciences, Vol. 2, pp. 917–935.
Masterman, Margaret (1967). "Mechanical Pidgin Translation: An Estimate of the Research Value of 'Word-for-word' Translation into a Pidgin Language, Rather Than into the Full Normal Form of an Output Language." In Andrew D. Booth, ed., *Machine Translation*. Amsterdam: North-Holland Publishing Company, pp. 195–227.
McDonald, David D. (1985). "Recovering the Speaker's Decisions during Mechanical Translation." In Sergei Nirenburg, ed., *Proceedings of the*

Conference on Theoretical and Methodological Issues in Machine Translation of Natural Languages (*TMI-85*). Hamilton, New York: Colgate University, pp. 183–199.

Micklesen, Lew R. (1956). "Form Classes: Structural Linguistics and Mechanical Translation." In J. R. Firth, ed., *For Roman Jakobson*. The Hague: Mouton, pp. 344–352.

Mukhin, I. S. (1963). *On Some Problems of Mechanical Translation*. Moscow: Institute of Exact Mechanics and Computing Technique.

Ornstein, Jacob (1955). "Mechanical Translation: New Challenge to Communication." *Science*, No. 122, pp. 745–748.

Oswald, Victor A. and Richard H. Lawson (1953). "An Idioglossary for Mechanical Translation." *Modern Language Forum*, Vol. 38, Nos. 3–4, pp. 1–11.

Pacak, Milos (1961). "Morphology in Terms of Mechanical Translation." In Allen Kent, ed., *Information Retrieval and Machine Translation*. New York: Interscience, Vol. 2, pp. 881–885.

Panov, D. Yu. (1956). "On the Problem of Mechanical Translation." *Mechanical Translation*, Vol. 3, No. 2, pp. 42–43.

Parker-Rhodes, Arthur Frederick (1956). "Computer Operations Required for Mechanical Translation." *Proceedings of the Institute of Electrical Engineers*, pp. 453–455.

Reitwiesner, George W. and Martin H. Weik (1958). *Survey of the Field of Mechanical Translation of Languages*. Maryland: Aberdeen Proving Ground.

Richens, Richard H. and Andrew D. Booth (1955). "Some Methods of Mechanized Translation." In William N. Locke and Andrew D. Booth, eds., *Machine Translation of Languages: Fourteen Essays*. Cambridge, MA: Technology Press of the Massachusetts Institute of Technology, pp. 24–46.

Richens, Richard H. (1956). "A General Programme for Mechanical Translation between Two Languages via an Algebraic Interlingua." *Mechanical Translation*, Vol. 3, No. 2, p. 37.

Richens, Richard H. (1956). "Preprogramming for Mechanical Translation." *Mechanical Translation*, Vol. 3, No. 1, pp. 20–27.

Roberts, A. Hood and Michael Zarechnak (1974). "Mechanical Translation." *Current Trends in Linguistics*, Vol. 12, pp. 2825–2870.

Roberts, A. Hood and Michael Zarechnak (1978). "Mechanical

Translation." In Thomas A. Sebeok, ed., *Encyclopedic Dictionary of Semiotics*. Berlin: Mouton de Gruyter, pp. 2825–2868.

Vauquois, Bernard (1968). "A Survey of Formal Grammars and Algorithms for Recognition and Transformation in Mechanical Translation." *Information Processing 68: Proceedings of IFIP Congress 68*. Amsterdam: North-Holland, pp. 1114–1123.

Yngve, Victor H. (1953). *Mechanical Translation*. Quarterly Progress Report of the Research Laboratory of Electronics, MIT, pp. 35–36.

Yngve, Victor H. (1954). *Mechanical Translation*. Quarterly Progress Report of the Research Laboratory of Electronics, MIT, p. 74.

Yngve, Victor H. (1956). "Terminology in the Light of Research on Mechanical Translation." *Babel*, Vol. 2, No. 3, pp. 128–132.

Yngve, Victor H. and George Hubert Matthews (1958). *A Compiler-interpreter for Mechanical Translation*. Quarterly Progress Report of the Research Laboratory of Electronics, MIT, p. 176.

Yngve, Victor H. (1964). "Implications of Mechanical Translation Research." *Journal of the American Philosophical Society*, Vol. 108, No. 4, pp. 275–281.

Multilingual Computer Translation

Boitet, Christian (1988). "Pros and Cons of the Pivot and Transfer Approaches in Multilingual Machine Translation." In Toon Witkam, ed., *New Directions in Machine Translation*. Dordrecht: Foris, pp. 93–106.

Brougham, Martyn (1997). "Publishing Product Information in a Global Market Place." In *Translating and the Computer 19*. London: The Association for Information Management.

Chen, Zhaoxiong 陳肇雄 and Huang Heyan 黃河燕 (2001).〈多語機器翻譯及其系列應用系統研究進展〉(Studies on Advances in Multilingual Machine Translation and Its Series of Application Systems).《輝煌二十年——中國中文信息學會二十周年學術會議》(*Proceedings of Conference of the 20th Anniversary of CIPSC*). Beijing: Tsinghua University Press, pp. 66–73.

Diaz-Labrador, JosuKa, Joseba Abaitua, Ines Jacob, Fernando Quintana, and Garikoitz Araolaza (2003). "Metadata for Multilingual Content Management: A Practical Experience with the SARE-Bi System." In

Translating and the Computer 25. London: The Association for Information Management.

Everaert, Guy and Thierry van Steenberghe (1994). "The Realization of Individual Instances in a Multilingual Generation System." *Meta*, Vol. 39, No. 1, pp. 194–205.

Farwell, David L. and Yorick Wilks (1993). "ULTRA: A Multilingual Machine Translator." In Sergei Nirenburg, ed., *Progress in Machine Translation*. Amsterdam: IOS and Tokyo: Ohmsha, pp. 45–51.

Farwell, David L., Louise Guthrie, and Yorick Wilks (1993). "Automatically Creating Lexical Entries for ULTRA, a Multilingual MT System." *Machine Translation*, Vol. 8, No. 3, pp. 127–145.

Feng, Zhiwei 馮志偉 (1984).〈漢—法/英/日/俄/德多語言自動翻譯試驗〉(Testing on the Automatic Multilingual Translation among Chinese and French, English, Japanese, Russian, and German). In Liu Yongquan 劉湧泉 *et al*.,《中國的機器翻譯》(*Machine Translation in China*). Shanghai: Knowledge Press, pp. 103–184.

Funaki, Susumu (1993). "Multi-lingual Machine Translation (MMT) Project." *Proceedings of MT Summit IV: International Cooperation for Global Communication*, Kobe, Japan, pp. 73–78.

Hajič, Jan, Petr Homola, and Vladislav Kuboň (2003). "A Simple Multilingual Machine Translation System." *Proceedings of MT Summit IX*, New Orleans, Louisiana, USA.

Hartley, Anthony F. and Cécile Paris (1997). "Multilingual Document Production from Support for Translating to Support for Authoring." *Machine Translation*, Vol. 12, Nos. 1–2, pp. 109–129.

Hofmann, Cornelia and Thorsten Mehnert (2000). "Multilingual Information Management at Schneider Automation." In Robert C. Sprung, ed., *Translating into Success: Cutting-edge Strategies for Going Multilingual in a Global Age*. Amsterdam and Philadelphia: John Benjamins Publishing Company, pp. 59–79.

Ichiyama, S. (1989). "Multi-lingual Machine Translation System." *Office Equipment and Products*, Vol. 18, No. 131, pp. 46–48.

Joscelyne, Andrew (2000). "The Role of Translation in an International Organization." In Robert C. Sprung, ed., *Translating into Success: Cutting-edge Strategies for Going Multilingual in a Global Age*. Amsterdam and Philadelphia: John Benjamins Publishing Company, pp. 81–95.

Kamei, Shin-ichiro and Takahiro Wakao (1992). "Metonymy: How to Treat It Properly in a Multilingual Machine Translation System." *Proceedings of the 1st Singapore International Conference on Intelligent Systems* (*SPICIS-92*), Singapore.

Kanayama, Hiroshi and Hideo Watanabe (2003). "Multilingual Translation via Annotated Hub Language." *Proceedings of MT Summit IX*, New Orleans, Louisiana, USA.

Kohlmeier, Bernhard (2000). "Microsoft Encarta Goes Multilingual." In Robert C. Sprung, ed., *Translating into Success: Cutting-edge Strategies for Going Multilingual in a Global Age*. Amsterdam and Philadelphia: John Benjamins Publishing Company, pp. 1–11.

Korovina, T. I. (1978). "Multilingual Word-for-word Translation Using a Display." *Cybernetics*, Vol. 14, No. 2, pp. 282–283.

Krauwer, Steven and Louis des Tombe (1984). "Transfer in a Multilingual MT System." *Proceedings of the 10th International Conference on Computational Linguistics* (*COLING-84*), Stanford University, Stanford, CA, USA, pp. 464–467.

Lu, Jimmy C.M., Lars Åkerman, and Karin Spalink (2000). "LabelTool: A Localization Application for Devices with Restricted Display Areas." In John S. White, ed., *Envisioning Machine Translation in the Information Future*. Berlin: Springer Verlag, pp. 202–208.

Max, Aurélien (2003). "Multi-language Machine Translation through Interactive Document Normalization." *Proceedings of the 7th Workshop of the European Association for Machine Translation: Improving Machine Translation through Other Language Technology Tools: Resources and Tools for Building MT*, Budapest, Hungary, pp. 25–32.

McCallum, Bob (2003). "Streamlining Multilingual Content Delivery for Large Organisations: Case Studies in Enterprise Linguistic Asset Management." In *Translating and the Computer 25*. London: The Association for Information Management.

Moore, Isabella (2004). "Establishing the Foundations for a Multilingual Nation." *Programme of the Annual Conference of the Association of Translation Companies: Getting in Shape for the Future—Working towards a New Environment for the Translation Profession*, School of Oriental and African Studies, University of London, England.

Plitt, Mirko (2004). "Connecting Writers and Translators—XML Based

Content Management of Product Documentation at Autodesk." In *Translating and the Computer 26*. London: The Association for Information Management.

Sharp, Randall (1988). "CAT2—Implementing a Formalism for Multi-lingual MT." *Proceedings of the 2nd International Conference on Theoretical and Methodological Issues in Machine Translation of Natural Languages* (*TMI-88*), Carnegie Mellon University, Center for Machine Translation, Pittsburgh, Pennsylvania, USA.

Sharp, Randall and Oliver Streiter (1995). "Applications in Multilingual Machine Translation." *Proceedings of the 3rd International Conference and Exhibition on Practical Applications of Prolog*, Paris, France, pp. 561–579.

Sigurd, Bengt and Barbara Gawronska-Werngren (1988). "The Potential of Swetra—A Multilanguage MT System." *Machine Translation*, Vol. 3, Nos. 3–4, pp. 237–250.

Sprung, Robert C. and Alberto Vourvoulias-Bush (2000). "Adapting Time Magazine for Latin America." In Robert C. Sprung, ed., *Translating into Success: Cutting-edge Strategies for Going Multilingual in a Global Age*. Amsterdam and Philadelphia: John Benjamins Publishing Company, pp. 13–27.

Sprung, Robert C. (2000). "Mission-critical: Translating for Regulated Industries." In Robert C. Sprung, ed., *Translating into Success: Cutting-edge Strategies for Going Multilingual in a Global Age*. Amsterdam and Philadelphia: John Benjamins Publishing Company, pp. 173–186.

Streiter, Oliver (1996). *Linguistic Modeling for Multilingual Machine Translation*. Aachen: Shaker Verlag.

Tanaka, Hozumi (1993). "Multi-lingual Machine Translation Systems in the Future." In Sergei Nirenburg, ed., *Progress in Machine Translation*. Amsterdam: IOS and Tokyo: Ohmsha, pp. 29–32.

Zarechnak, Michael (1986). "The Intermediary Language for Multilanguage Translation." *Computers and Translation*, Vol. 1, No. 2, pp. 83–91.

Zhang, Guiping 張桂平, Yin Baosheng 尹寶生, Cai Dongfeng 蔡東風, Xu Lijun 徐立軍, Liu Weisong 劉偉松, and Chen Jianjun 陳建軍 (2002). 〈環球使者系列多文種處理軟件〉 (Global Envoy Families Multilingual Processing Software). In Yu Shiwen, ed., *Proceedings of the Second China-Japan Natural Language Processing Joint Research Promotion*

Conference (*CJNLP-2002*). Beijing: Institute of Computational Linguistics, Peking University, pp. 353–362.

Multimedia Computer Translation

Lespinasse, Karine and Bruno Bachimont (2001). "Is Peritext a Key for Audiovisual Documents? The Use of Texts Describing Television Programs to Assist Indexing." *Proceedings of the 2nd International Conference on Intelligent Text Processing and Computational Linguistics* (*CICLing-2001*), Mexico City, Mexico.

Li, Wei and Maosong Sun (2006). "Automatic Image Annotation Based on WordNet and Hierarchical Ensembles." *Proceedings of the 7th International Conference on Intelligent Text Processing and Computational Linguistics* (*CICLing-2006*), Mexico City, Mexico.

Mihalcea, Rada F. and Ben Leong (2006). "Towards Communicating Simple Sentences Using Pictorial Representations." *Proceedings of the 7th Biennial Conference of the Association for Machine Translation in the Americas* (*AMTA-2006*)*: Visions for the Future of Machine Translation*, Boston Marriott, Cambridge, MA, USA.

Wurm, Svenja (2006). "The Technologising of the Sign: An Investigation of Translations from Written into Signed Languages." *Proceedings of the 6th Portsmouth Translation Conference: Translation Technologies and Culture*, School of Languages and Area Studies, University of Portsmouth, England.

Computer Translation User

Ahmad, Khurshed, Andrea Davies, Heather Fulford, Paul Holmes-Higgin, Margaret Rogers, and Monika Höge (1995). "User Participation in Software Development." In Marianne Kugler, Khurshid Ahmad, and Gregor Thurmair, eds., *Translator's Workbench: Tools and Terminology for Translation and Text Processing*. Berlin: Springer Verlag, pp. 8–15.

Bennett, Winfield S. (1987). "The Proper Place of End-users in MT Research." In Karl Kummer, ed., *Across the Language Gap: Proceedings of the 28th Annual Conference of the American Translators Association*. Medford, New Jersey: Learned Information, Inc., pp. 425–427.

Bennett, Winfield S. (1996). "Learning from Users." *Proceedings of the 2nd Conference of the Association for Machine Translation in the Americas: Expanding MT Horizons* (*AMTA-2*), Montreal, Quebec, Canada, pp. 229–231.

Bernhard, Ursula (1994). "Machine Translation: Ten Years On: Where Are the Users?" *Machine Translation—Ten Years On: Proceedings of the 2nd International Conference Organised by Cranfield University*, Cranfield, England.

Brace, Colin (1995). "MT and Its Users." *Proceedings of MT Summit V: Machine Translation Conference, Exhibition and Tutorial*, Luxembourg.

Brace, Colin, Muriel Vasconcellos, and L. Chris Miller (1995). "MT Users and Usage: Europe and the Americas." *Proceedings of MT Summit V: Machine Translation Conference, Exhibition and Tutorial*, Luxembourg.

Church, Kenneth W. (1996). "Optimists and Skeptics." *Proceedings of the 2nd Conference of the Association for Machine Translation in the Americas: Expanding MT Horizons* (*AMTA-2*), Montreal, Quebec, Canada, pp. 224–226.

Fuji, Masaru, Nobutoshi Hatanaka, Etsuo Ito, Shin-ichiro Kamei, Hiroyuki Kumai, Tatsuya Sukehiro, and Hitoshi Isahara (2001). "Evaluation Method for Determining Groups of Users Who Find MT 'Useful'." In Bente Maegaard, ed., *Proceedings of MT Summit VIII: Machine Translation in the Information Age*, Santiago de Compostela, Spain, pp. 103–108.

Gerber, Laurie (2001). "Machine Translation—User's Perspective." *International Journal of Translation*, Vol. 13, Nos. 1–2, pp. 55–64.

Hernandez, Luis, J. Turner, and Melissa Holland (2004). "Feedback from the Field: The Challenge of Users in Motion." In Robert E. Frederking and Kathryn B. Taylors, eds., *Machine Translation: From Real Users to Research*. Berlin: Springer Verlag, pp. 94–101.

Lehmann, Hubert (1995). "Machine Translation for Home and Business Users." *Proceedings of MT Summit V: Machine Translation Conference, Exhibition and Tutorial*, Luxembourg.

Low, Hwee-Boon (1993). "Some Lessons Learnt by a New Comer." *Proceedings of MT Summit IV: International Cooperation for Global Communication*, Kobe, Japan, pp. 181–187.

Macklovitch, Elliott (2004). "The Contribution of End-users to the TransType2 Project." In Robert E. Frederking and Kathryn B. Taylors, eds., *Machine Translation: From Real Users to Research.* Berlin: Springer Verlag, pp. 197–207.

McNaught, John and Harold L. Somers (1980). "The Translator as a Computer User." *Quinquereme*, Vol. 3, No. 2, pp. 149–163.

Morland, Verne (2002). "Nutzlos, Bien Pratique, or Muy Util? Business Users Speak out on the Value of Pure Machine Translation." In *Translating and the Computer 24.* London: The Association for Information Management.

Mowatt, David and Harold L. Somers (2000). "Is MT Software Documentation Appropriate for MT Users?" In John S. White, ed., *Envisioning Machine Translation in the Information Future.* Berlin: Springer Verlag, pp. 223–238.

Scanlan, Phil (2001). "Seamless Translation—Delivering for the User." *Machine Translation Review*, No. 12, pp. 67–74.

Somers, Harold L. and John McNaught (1980). "The Translator as a Computer User." *The Incorporated Linguist*, Vol. 19, No. 2, pp. 49–53.

Teicher, Howard R., Michael Gainet, Edith Losa, Maria Pilar Martinez-Perez, Muriel Jerome O'Keeffe, Sue Walker Toledo, and Michael Zarenchak (1993). "Building the Customer Base." In Sergei Nirenburg, ed., *Progress in Machine Translation.* Amsterdam: IOS and Tokyo: Ohmsha, pp. 213–216.

Vilalta, Elena (2006). "A Pragmatic Approach to User Feedback: How Do Users Perceive the Translated Software? It Would Be Nice to Know." *Proceedings of the Localization World Conference*, Barcelona, Spain.

Westfall, Edith and M. Marubio (1997). "What Do Users Need from MT Systems?"*Proceedings of MT Summit VI*, San Diego, California, USA.

Yamabana, Kiyoshi, Kazunori Muraki, Shin-ichiro Kamei, Kenji Satoh, Shinichi Doi, and Shinko Tamura (1997). "An Interactive Translation Support Facility for Non-professional Users." *Proceedings of the 5th Conference on Applied Natural Language Processing*, Seattle, Washington, DC, USA.

Computer Translator

Cancel, Cruz A. (1984). "Over Oyte of the Translator." In Patricia E. Newman, ed., *American Translators Association Conference—1984.* Medford, New Jersey: Learned Information, Inc., pp. 121–125.

Champollion, Yves (2004). "The Status of the Free-lance Translator in the 21st Century: Greatness or Misery, Prestige or Mediocrity, Globalization Hero or Victim?" In *Translating and the Computer 26*. London: The Association for Information Management.
Rommel, B. (1984). "Language or Information: A New Role for the Translator?" *Proceedings of the International Conference on the Methodology and Techniques of Machine Translation*, Cranfield Institute of Technology, England.
Sinclair, D. A. (1962). "The Machine Translator and the Translating Profession." *Babel*, Vol. 8, No. 2, pp. 76–78.

❖ PART 8 ❖

Concordancing

Concordance

Bonhomme, Patrice and Laurent Romary (1995). "The Lingua Parallel Concordancing Project: Managing Multilingual Texts for Educational Purpose." *Proceedings of the 5th International Conference* (*IA-95*), Montpellier, France.

Church, Kenneth W. and William A. Gale (1991). "Concordances for Parallel Texts." *Using Corpora: Proceedings of the 7th Annual Conference of the UW for the New OED and Text Research*. Oxford: Oxford University Press, pp. 40–62.

Langlois, Lucie (1996). "Bilingual Concordancers: A New Tool for Bilingual Lexicographers." *Proceedings of the 2nd Conference of the Association for Machine Translation in the Americas* (*AMTA-2*), Montreal, Quebec, Canada.

Melby, Alan K. (1981). "A Bilingual Concordance System and Its Use in Linguistic Studies." In Waldemar Gutwinski and Grace Jolly, eds., *Proceedings of the 8th LACUS* (*Linguistic Association of Canada and the United States*) *Forum*. Columbia, South Carolina: Hornbeam Press, pp. 541–549.

Pearson, Jennifer (1996). "Electronic Text and Concordances in the Translation Classroom." *Teanga*, Vol. 16, pp. 85–95.

Sinclair, John (1991). *Corpus, Concordance, Collocation*. Oxford: Oxford University Press.

Ulrych, Margherita (1997). "The Impact of Multilingual Parallel Concordancing on Translation." In Barbara Lewandowska-Tomaszczyk and Patrick James Melia, eds., *Proceedings of the Conference on Practical Applications in Language Corpora* (*PALC-97*), Łódź, Poland, pp. 421–435.

Concordancer

Barlow, Michael (1992). "Using Concordance Software in Language Teaching and Research." *Proceedings of the 2nd International Conference on Foreign Language Education and Technology*, Nagoya, Japan.

King, Philip and David Woolls (1996). "Creating and Using a Multilingual Parallel Concordancer." In Marcel Thelen and Barbara Lewandowska-Tomasczyk, eds., *Proceedings of the Conference on "Translation and Meaning: Part 4*." Maastricht: Euroterm, pp. 459–466.

Simard, Michel, George Foster, and François Perrault (1993). *TransSearch: A Bilingual Concordance Tool*. Laval, Montreal: Centre for Information Technology Innovation Technical Report.

Multiconcord

Corness, Patrick (2002). "Multiconcord: A Computer Tool for Cross-linguistic Research." In Bengt Altenberg and Sylvian Granger, eds., *Lexis in Contrast: Corpus-based Approaches*. Amsterdam and Philadelphia: John Benjamins Publishing Company, pp. 307–326.
Woolls, David (1997). *Multiconcord: Software for Multilingual Parallel Concordancing*. Birmingham: CFL Software Development.

ParaConc

Barlow, Michael (1995). *A Guide to ParaConc*. Houston: Athelstan.
Barlow, Michael (1995). "ParaConc: A Concordancer for Parallel Text." *Computers and Texts*, Vol. 10.
Barlow, Michael (1996). "Analysing Parallel Texts with ParaConc." *Proceedings of the Joint International Conference of the Association for Literary and Linguistic Computing and the Association for Computing and the Humanities* (*ALLC-ACH-96*), University of Bergen, Bergen, Norway.

WordSmith

Scott, Mike (1996). *WordSmith Tools: Software Language Tools for Windows*. Oxford: Oxford University Press.
Scott, Mike (1997). *WordSmith Tools Version 2.0*. Oxford: Oxford University Press.

Concordancer: Types

Bilingual Concordancer

Langlois, Lucie (1996). "Bilingual Concordancers: A New Tool for Bilingual Lexicographers." *Proceedings of the 2nd Conference of the Association for Machine Translation in the Americas: Expanding MT Horizons* (*AMTA-2*), Montreal, Quebec, Canada, pp. 34–42.

Multilingual Concordancer

Woolls, David (2000). "From Purity to Pragmatism: User-driven Development of a Multilingual Parallel Concordancer." In Simon Philip Botley, Anthony Mark McEnery, and Andrew Wilson, eds., *Multilingual Corpora in Teaching and Research*. Amsterdam: Rodopi, pp. 116–133.

Parallel Concordancer

Barlow, Michael (2000). "Designing a Parallel Concordancer." CULT2K.

Barlow, Michael (2004). "Parallel Concordancing and Translation." In *Translating and the Computer 26*. London: The Association for Information Management.

Church, Kenneth W. and William A. Gale (1991). "Concordances for Parallel Text." *Proceedings of the 7th Annual Conference of the UW Centre for the New OED and Text Research: Using Corpora*. Oxford: Oxford University Press, pp. 40–62.

Langlois, Lucie (1996). "Bilingual Concordancers: A New Tool for Bilingual Lexicographers." *Proceedings of the Conference of the Association for Machine Translation in the Americas*, Montreal, Quebec, Canada.

Melby, Alan K. (1981). "A Bilingual Concordance System and Its Use in Linguistic Studies." *Proceedings of the 8th LACUS (Linguistic Association of Canada and the United States) Forum*. Columbia, South Carolina: Hornbeam Press, pp. 541–549.

❖ PART 9 ❖

Controlled Language

Controlled Authoring

Allen, Jeffrey (1999). "Adapting the Concept of TM to Authoring Memory for Controlled Language Writing Environment." In *Translating and the Computer 21*. London: The Association for Information Management.

Allman, Tod and Stephen Beale (2004). "An Environment for Quick Ramp-up Multi-lingual Authoring." *International Journal of Translation*, Vol. 16, No. 1, pp. 73–85.

Bernth, Arendse (1999). "Controlling Input and Output of MT for Greater User Acceptance." In *Translating and the Computer 21*. London: The Association for Information Management.

Ellman, Jeremy (1999). "MABLe: A Multilingual Authoring Tool for Business Letters." In *Translating and the Computer 21*. London: The Association for Information Management.

Hartley, Anthony F. and Cécile Paris (1997). "Multilingual Document Production from Support for Translating to Support for Authoring." *Machine Translation*, Vol. 12, Nos. 1–2, pp. 109–129.

Lieske, Christian, Christine Thielen, Melanie Wells, and Andrew Bredenkamp (2002). "Controlled Authoring at SAP." In *Translating and the Computer 24*. London: The Association for Information Management.

Lockwood, Rose (2000). "Machine Translation and Controlled Authoring at Caterpillar." In Robert C. Sprung, ed., *Translating into Success: Cutting-edge Strategies for Going Multilingual in a Global Age*. Amsterdam and Philadelphia: John Benjamins Publishing Company, pp. 187–202.

Loong, Cheong Tong (1989). "A Data-driven Control Strategy for Grammar Writing Systems." *Machine Translation*, Vol. 4, No. 4, pp. 281–297.

Max, Aurélien (2006). "Writing for Language-impaired Readers." *Proceedings of the 7th International Conference on Intelligent Text Processing and Computational Linguistics (CICLing-2006)*, Mexico City, Mexico.

Netzer, Yael and Michael Elhadad (2006). "Using Semantic Authoring for Blissymbols Communication Boards." *Proceedings of the Human Language Technology Conference—Annual Meeting of the North American Chapter of the Association for Computational Linguistics (HLT-NAACL-2006)*, New York, USA.

Nyberg, Eric H., Teruko Mitamura, and Willem-Olaf Huijsen (2003). "Controlled Language for Authoring and Translation." In Harold L. Somers, ed., *Computers and Translation: A Translator's Guide*. Amsterdam and Philadelphia: John Benjamins Publishing Company, pp. 245–281.

Sakson, Donna and Karen Johnson (2003). "The Uneasy Marriage between Authoring and Localization." *Proceedings of the Localization World Conference 2003*, Seattle, Washington, DC, USA.

Scott, Donia R. (1996). "Computer Support for Authoring Multilingual Software Documentation." In *Translating and the Computer 18*. London: The Association for Information Management.

van der Eijk, Pim and Jacqueline van Wees (1998). "Supporting Controlled Language Authoring." *Proceedings of the 3rd Workshop of the European Association for Machine Translation: Translation Technology: Integration in the Workflow Environment*, Geneva, Switzerland, pp. 65–70.

Zhang, Wei 張偉 (1998).〈受限漢語輔助寫作系統的構想〉(Thoughts on Restrictive Chinese Assisted Authoring System). In Yu Shiwen 俞士汶 and Zhu Xuefeng 朱學鋒, eds.,《計算語言學文集》(*Papers on Computational Linguistics*), Vol. 3. Beijing: Department of Computer Science and Technology and Institute of Computational Linguistics, Peking University, pp. 129–138.

Zydron, Andrzeg (2003). "Xml: tm—Using XML Technology to Reduce the Cost of Authoring and Translation." In *Translating and the Computer 25*. London: The Association for Information Management.

Controlled Language

Adriaens, Geert and Dirk Schreurs (1992). "From Cogram and Alcogram: Toward a Controlled English Grammar Checker." *Proceedings of the 14th International Conference of Computational Linguistics* (*COLING-92*), Nantes, France, pp. 595–601.

Adriaens, Geert (1994). "Simplified English Grammar and Style Correction in an MT Framework: The LRE SECC Project." In *Translating and the Computer 16*. London: The Association for Information Management, pp. 78–88.

Adriaens, Geert and Lieve Macken (1995). "Technological Evaluation of a Controlled Language Application: Precision, Recall and Convergence

Tests for SECC." *Proceedings of the 6th International Conference on Theoretical and Methodological Issues in Machine Translation* (*TMI-95*), Leuven, Belgium, pp. 123–141.

AECMA (1995). *A Guide for the Preparation of Aircraft Maintenance Documentation in the International Aerospace Maintenance Language*—Issue 1. Brussels, Belgium.

Allen, Jeffrey (1999). "Adapting the Concept of 'Translation Memory' to 'Authoring Memory' for a Controlled Language Writing Environment." In *Translating and the Computer 20*. London: The Association for Information Management.

Almqvist, Ingrid and Anna Sågvall Hein (1996). "Defining ScaniaSwedish—A Controlled Language for Truck Maintenance." *Proceedings of the 1st International Workshop on Controlled Language Applications* (*CLAW-96*), Leuven, Belgium, pp. 159–164.

Baker, Kathryn L., Alexander M. Franz, Pamela W. Jordan, Teruko Mitamura, and Eric H. Hyberg (1994). "Coping with Ambiguity in a Large-scale Machine Translation System." *Proceedings of the 15th International Conference on Computational Linguistics* (*COLING-94*), Kyoto, Japan, pp. 90–94.

Barthe, Kathy (1998). "GIFAS Rationalised French: Designing One Controlled Language to Match Another." *Proceedings of the 2nd International Workshop on Controlled Language Applications* (*CLAW-98*), Pittsburgh, PA, USA, pp. 87–102.

Bernth, Arendse (1997). "EasyEnglish: A Tool for Improving Document Quality." *Proceedings of the 5th Conference on Applied Natural Language Processing*, Seattle, Washington, DC, USA.

Betts, Robert G. (2003). "Wycliffe Associates EasyEnglish: Challenges in Cross-cultural Communication." *Proceedings of the Joint Conference Combining the 8th International Workshop of the European Association for Machine Translation and the 4th Controlled Language Applications Workshop: Controlled Language Translation* (*EAMT-CLAW-2003*), Dublin City University, Ireland.

Boitet, Christian (1994). "Dialogue-based MT and Self-explaining Documents as an Alternative to MAHT and MT of Controlled Languages." *Machine Translation—Ten Years On: Proceedings of the 2nd International Conference Organised by Cranfield University*, Cranfield, England.

Boitet, Christian (1999). "Dialogue-based MT and Self-explaining

Documents as an Alternative to MAHT and MT of Controlled Languages." *Machine Translation Review*, No. 10, pp. 6–15.
Brockmann, Daniel (1997). "TR06: Controlled Language and Translation Memory: A Perfect Match to Save Translation Cost." *TC-Forum Translation Issues*, No. 4.
Caeyers, Herman (1997). "Machine Translation and Controlled English." *Proceedings of the 2nd Workshop of the European Association for Machine Translation: Language Technology in Your Organization?* University of Copenhagen, Copenhagen, Denmark, pp. 91–103.
Carbonell, Jaime G., Teruko Mitamura, and Eric H. Nyberg (1992). "The KANT Perspective: A Critique of Pure Transfer (and Pure Interlingua, Pure Statistics ...)." *Proceedings of the 4th International Conference on Theoretical and Methodological Issues in Machine Translation (TMI-92)*, Montreal, Quebec, Canada, pp. 225–235.
Cardey, Sylviane, Peter Greenfield, and Wu Xiaohong (2004). "Designing a Controlled Language for the Machine Translation of Medical Protocols: The Case of English to Chinese." In Stephen D. Richardson, ed., *Machine Translation: From Research to Real Users*. Berlin and New York: Springer Verlag, pp. 37–47.
Cascales, Remedios Ruiz and Richard F. E. Sutcliffe (2003). "A Specification and Validating Parser for Simplified Technical Spanish." *Proceedings of the Joint Conference Combining the 8th International Workshop of the European Association for Machine Translation and the 4th Controlled Language Applications Workshop: Controlled Language Translation (EAMT-CLAW-2003)*, Dublin City University, Ireland.
Chervak, Steven, Colin Drury, and J. P. Ouellette (1996). "Field Evaluation of Simplified English for Aircraft Workcards." *Proceedings of the 10th Federal Aviation Administration/Association for Aerospace Medicine Meeting on Human Factors in Aviation Maintenance and Inspection*, Alexandria, Northern Virginia, USA.
de Koning, Michiel (1996). "Bringing Controlled Language Support to the Desktop." *Proceedings of the 1st Workshop of the European Association for Machine Translation (TKE-96): Language Resources, Terminology, Economics, and User Needs*, Vienna, Austria, pp. 11–19.
de Preux, Nathalie (2005). "Does Using Controlled Language Improve Machine Translation Results?" In *Translating and the Computer 27*. London: The Association for Information Management.

Dodd, Stuart C. (1955). "Model English." In William N. Locke and Andrew D. Booth, eds., *Machine Translation of Languages: Fourteen Essays.* Cambridge, MA: Technology Press of the Massachusetts Institute of Technology, pp. 165–173.

Fields, Glenn (1998). "Proposal for a National Consortium on Controlled Languages and Computer-aided Translation." *Proceedings of the National Consortium to Advance Controlled Language and Computer-Aided Translation Tools (NCCAT-98)* Kick-Off Meeting, Chicago, USA.

Fouvry, Frederik and Lorna Balkan (1996). "Test Suites for Controlled Language Checkers." *Proceedings of the 1st International Workshop on Controlled Language Applications.* Katholieke Universiteit, Leuven, Belgium, pp. 179–192.

Fuchs, Norbert E. and Rolf Schwitter (1996). "Attempto Controlled English (ACE)." *Proceedings of the 1st International Workshop on Controlled Language Applications.* Katholieke Universiteit, Leuven, Belgium, pp. 124–136.

Gaspari, Federico (2004). "Controlled Language, Web Usability and Machine Translation Services on the Internet." *International Journal of Translation*, Vol. 16, No. 1, pp. 41–54.

Glover, Alan, Edward Johnson, Peter Strevens, and Fred Weeks (1983). *Seaspeak Training Manual.* New York: Pergamon Press.

Godden, Kurt (1998). "Controlling the Business Environment for Controlled Language." *Proceedings of the 2nd International Workshop on Controlled Language,* Pittsburgh, Pennsylvania, USA, pp. 185–191.

Goyvaerts, Patrick (1996). "Controlled English, Curse or Blessing? A User's Perspective." *Proceedings of the 1st International Workshop on Controlled Language Applications.* Katholieke Universiteit, Leuven, Belgium, pp. 137–142.

Hartley, Anthony F. and Cecile Paris (2001). "Translation, Controlled Languages, Generation." In Erich H. Steiner and Colin Yallop, eds., *Exploring Translation and Multilingual Text Production: Beyond Content.* Berlin and New York: Mouton de Gruyter, pp. 307–325.

Hu, Qingping 胡清平 (2005).〈受控語言及其在漢英機器翻譯裏的應用前景〉(Controlled Language and Its Prospective Application in Chinese-English Machine Translation). In Luo Xuanmin 羅選民, ed.,《語言認識與翻譯研究》(*Language, Cognition and Translation Studies*). Beijing: Foreign Language Press, pp. 364–372.

Huijsen, Willem-Olaf (1998). "Controlled Language—An Introduction." *Proceedings of the 2nd International Workshop on Controlled Language Applications* (*CLAW-98*), Pittsburgh, Pennsylvania, USA, pp. 1–15.

Hurst, Matthew F. (1997). "Parsing for Targeted Errors in Controlled Languages." In Ruslan Mitkov and Nicolas Nicolov, eds., *Recent Advances in Natural Language Processing*. Amsterdam and Philadelphia: John Benjamins Publishing Company, pp. 59–70.

Janowski, Wladyslaw (1998). "CL 14: Controlled Language—Risks and Side Effects." *TC-Forum Translation Issues,* No. 2.

Johnson, Edward (1995). "Control Languages: MT for Operational Communication." *Proceedings of the 6th International Conference on Theoretical and Methodological Issues in Machine Translation* (*TMI-95*), the University of Leuven, Leuven, Belgium.

Kamprath, Christine, Eric Adolphson, Teruko Mitamura, and Eric H. Nyberg (1998). "Controlled Language Multilingual Document Production: Experience with Caterpillar Technical English." *Proceedings of the 2nd International Workshop on Controlled Language Applications* (*CLAW-98*). Language Technologies Institute, Carnegie Mellon University, Pittsburgh, Pennsylvania, USA, pp. 51–61.

Lee, Arthur (1993). "Controlled English with and without Machine Translation." In *Translating and the Computer 15*. London: The Association for Information Management.

Lehrndorfer, Anne and Stefani Schachtl (1998). "Controlled Siemens Documentary German and TopTrans." *TC-FORUM*, Stuttgart, Germany.

Lehtola, Aarno, Jarno Tenni, and Catherine Bounsaythip (1998). "Controlled Language—An Introduction." *Proceedings of the 2nd International Workshop on Controlled Language Applications*, Carnegie Mellon University, Pittsburgh, USA, pp. 16–29.

Lux, Veronika and Eva Dauphin (1996). "Corpus Studies: A Contribution to the Definition of a Controlled Language." *Proceedings of the 1st International Workshop on Controlled Language Applications* (*CLAW-96*), Leuven, Belgium, pp. 193–204.

Means, Linda and Kurt Godden (1996). "The Controlled Automotive Service Language (CASL) Project." *Proceedings of the 1st International Workshop on Controlled Language Applications*, Katholieke Universiteit, Leuven, Belgium, pp. 106–114.

Milićević, Jasmina (2000). "Communicative Structure of Sentences as a Means of Controlling the Generation of Paraphrases." *Proceedings of the 1st International Conference on Intelligent Text Processing and Computational Linguistics* (*CICLing-2000*), Mexico City, Mexico.

Mitamura, Teruko and Eric H. Nyberg (1995). "Controlled English for Knowledge Based MT: Experience with the KANT System." *Proceedings of the 6th International Conference on Theoretical and Methodological Issues in Machine Translation* (*TMI-95*), Leuven, Belgium, pp. 158–172.

Mitamura, Teruko (1999). "Controlled Language for Multilingual Machine Translation." *Proceedings of MT Summit VII: MT in the Great Translation Era*, Singapore, pp. 46–52.

Mitamura, Teruko, Kathryn Baker, Eric H. Nyberg, and David Svoboda (2003). "Diagnostics for Interactive Controlled Language Checking." *Proceedings of the Joint Conference Combining the 8th International Workshop of the European Association for Machine Translation and the 4th Controlled Language Applications Workshop: Controlled Language Translation* (*EAMT-CLAW-2003*), Dublin City University, Ireland.

Møller, Margrethe H. (2003). "Grammar Metaphor, Controlled Language and Machine Translation." *Proceedings of the Joint Conference Combining the 8th International Workshop of the European Association for Machine Translation and the 4th Controlled Language Applications Workshop: Controlled Language Translation*, Dublin City University, Dublin, Ireland, pp. 95–103.

Murphy, Dawn, Jane Mason, and Stuart Sklair (1998). "Improving Translation at the Source." In *Translating and the Computer 20*. London: The Association for Information Management.

Nagao, Makoto (1983). "A Trial of Controlled Language." *Proceedings of the IPSJ Natural Language Processing Symposium*, Tokyo, Japan, pp. 91–99.

Nagao, Makato (1985). "Evaluation of the Quality of Machine-translated Sentences and the Control of Language." *Journal of the Information Processing Society of Japan*, Vol. 26, No. 10, pp. 1197–1202.

Nyberg, Eric H., Christine Kamprath, and Teruko Mitamura (1998). "The KANT Translation System: From R&D to Large-scale Deployment." *LISA Newsletter*, Vol. 2, No. 1, pp. 1–7.

O'Brien, Sharon (2003). "Controlling Controlled English: An Analysis of Several Controlled English Rule Sets." *Proceedings of the Joint*

Conference Combining the 8th International Workshop of the European Association for Machine Translation and the 4th Controlled Language Applications Workshop: Controlled Language Translation (*EAMT-CLAW-2003*), Dublin City University, Ireland, pp. 105–114.

Polo, Laura Ramirez (2005). "Controlled Language and the Implementation of Machine Translation for Technical Documentation." In *Translating and the Computer 27*. London: The Association for Information Management.

Power, Richard, Donia R. Scott, and Anthony F. Hartley (2003). "Multilingual Generation of Controlled Languages." *Proceedings of the Joint Conference Combining the 8th International Workshop of the European Association for Machine Translation and the 4th Controlled Language Applications Workshop: Controlled Language Translation* (*EAMT-CLAW-2003*), Dublin City University, Ireland, pp. 115–123.

Pym, P. John (1991). "Simplified English and Machine Translation." *Professional Translator and Interpreter*, Vol. 2, pp. 5–9.

Reuther, Ursula (2003). "Two in One—Can It Work? Readability and Translatability by Means of Controlled Language." *Proceedings of the Joint Conference Combining the 8th International Workshop of the European Association for Machine Translation and the 4th Controlled Language Applications Workshop: Controlled Language Translation* (*EAMT-CLAW-2003*), Dublin City University, Ireland, pp. 124–132.

Ruffino, J. Richard (1985). "The Impact of Controlled English on Machine Translation." In Patricia E. Newman, ed., *American Translators Association Conference—1985*. Medford, New Jersey: Learned Information, Inc., pp. 157–162.

Sågvall-Hein, Anna (1997). "Language Control and Machine Translation." *Proceedings of the 7th International Conference on Theoretical and Methodological Issues in Machine Translation* (*TMI-97*), St. John's College, Santa Fe, New Mexico, USA.

Schachtl, Stefanie (1996). "Requirements for Controlled German in Industrial Applications." *Proceedings of the 1st International Workshop on Controlled Language Applications* (*CLAW-96*), Leuven, Belgium, pp. 143–149.

Schwitter, Ralf, Anna Ljungberg, and David Hood (2003). "ECOLE: A Look-ahead Editor of Controlled Language." *Proceedings of the Joint Conference Combining the 8th International Workshop of the European Association for Machine Translation and the 4th Controlled*

Language Applications Workshop: Controlled Language Translation (*EAMT-CLAW-2003*), Dublin City University, Ireland.

Spaggiari, Laurent, Florence Beaujard, and Emmanuelle Cannesson (2003). "A Controlled Language at Airbus." *Proceedings of the Joint Conference Combining the 8th International Workshop of the European Association for Machine Translation and the 4th Controlled Language Applications Workshop: Controlled Language Translation* (*EAMT-CLAW-2003*), Dublin City University, Ireland.

Starlander, Marianne, Pierrette Bouillon, Nikos Chatzichrisafis, Marianne Santaholma, Manny Rayner, Beth Ann Hockey, Hitoshi Isahara, Kyoko Kanzaki, and Yukie Nakao (2005). "Practicing Controlled Language through a Help System Integrated into the Medical Speech Translation System (MedSLT)." *Proceedings of MT Summit X*, Phuket, Thailand.

Sukkarieh, Jana (2003). "Mind Your Language! Controlled Language for Inference Purposes." *Proceedings of the Joint Conference Combining the 8th International Workshop of the European Association for Machine Translation and the 4th Controlled Language Applications Workshop: Controlled Language Translation* (*EAMT-CLAW-2003*), Dublin City University, Ireland.

Torrejon, Enrique and Celia Rico (2004). "Controlled Languages in the Localisation Industry." *Localisation Reader* 2004–2005.

van der Eijk, Pim, Michiel de Koning, and Gert van der Steen (1996). "Controlled Language Correction and Translation." *Proceedings of the 1st International Workshop on Controlled Language Applications* (*CLAW-96*), Katholieke Universiteit Leuven, Belgium, pp. 64–73.

van der Eijk, Pim (1998). *Controlled Languages and Technical Documentation*. Report of Cap Gemeni ATS, Utrecht.

Wojcik, Richard H. and Heather Holmback (1996). "Getting a Controlled Language off the Ground at Boeing." *Proceedings of the 1st International Workshop on Controlled Language Applications* (*CLAW-96*), Katholieke Universiteit Leuven, Belgium, pp. 22–31.

Wojcik, Richard H. and James E. Hoard (1997). "Controlled Languages in Industry." In Giovanni B. Varile and Antonio Zampolli, eds., *Survey of the State of the Art in Human Language Technology*. Cambridge: Cambridge University Press, pp. 238–243.

Yu, Shiwen 俞士汶 and Zhu Xuefeng 朱學鋒 (1998).〈受限漢語研究的必要性〉(The Necessity of Studying Restricted Chinese). In Yu Shiwen and Zhu Xuefeng, eds.,《計算語言學文集》(*Papers on Computational*

Linguistics), Vol. 3. Beijing: Department of Computer Science and Technology and Institute of Computational Linguistics, Peking University, pp. 122–128.

Controlled Language System

Andersen, Peggy (1994). "ClearCheck Demonstration." *Proceedings of the 1st Conference of the Association for Machine Translation in the Americas: Technology Partnerships for Crossing the Language Barrier (AMTA-1)*, Columbia, Maryland, USA, p. 227.

KANT

Allen, Jeffrey (1995). *Review of the Caterpillar KANT English-French MT System*. Internal Technical Report, Peoria, Illinois: Technical Information Department, Caterpillar Inc.

Carbonell, Jaime G., Teruko Mitamura, and Eric H. Nyberg (1992). "The KANT Perspective: A Critique of Pure Transfer (and Pure Interlingua, Pure Statistics, ...)." *Proceedings of the 4th International Conference on Theoretical and Methodological Issues in Machine Translation of Natural Languages: Empiricist vs. Rationalist Methods in MT (TMI-92)*, Montreal, Quebec, Canada, pp. 225–235.

Mitamura, Teruko, Eric H. Nyberg, and Jaime G. Carbonell (1994). "KANT: Knowledge-based, Accurate Natural Language Translation." *Proceedings of the 1st Conference of the Association for Machine Translation in the Americas: Technology Partnerships for Crossing the Language Barrier (AMTA-1)*, Columbia, Maryland, USA, pp. 232–233.

Mitamura, Teruko and Eric H. Nyberg (1995). "Controlled English for Knowledge Based MT: Experience with the KANT System." *Proceedings of the 6th International Conference on Theoretical and Methodological Issues in Machine Translation (TMI-95)*, Leuven, Belgium, pp. 158–172.

Mitamura, Teruko, Eric H. Nyberg, Kathy Baker, David Svoboda, Enrique Torrejon, and Michael Duggan (2001). "The KANTOO MT System: Controlled Language Checker and Knowledge Maintenance Tool." *Proceedings of the 2nd Meeting of the North American Chapter of the Association for Computational Linguistics: Language Technologies 2001 (NAACL-2001)*, Pittsburgh, PA, USA.

Mitamura, Teruko, Eric H. Nyberg, Kathy Baker, Peter Cramer, Jeongwoo Ko, David Svoboda, and Michael Duggan (2002). "The KANTOO MT System: Controlled Language Checker and Lexical Maintenance Tool." In Stephen D. Richardson, ed., *Machine Translation: From Research to Real Users*. Berlin and New York: Springer Verlag, pp. 244–247.

Nyberg, Eric H. and Teruko Mitamura (1992). "The KANT System: Fast, Accurate, High-quality Translation in Practical Domains." *Proceedings of the 14th International Conference of Computational Linguistics (COLING-92)*, Nantes, France, pp. 1069–1073.

Nyberg, Eric H., Teruko Mitamura, and Jaime G. Carbonell (1997). "The KANT Machine System: From R&D to Initial Deployment." *LISA Workshop on Integrating Advanced Translation Technology*, Seattle, Washington, DC, USA.

Nyberg, Eric H. and Teruko Mitamura (2000). "The KANTOO Machine Translation Environment." In John S. White, ed., *Envisioning Machine Translation in the Information Future*. Berlin: Springer Verlag, pp. 192–195.

ScaniaSwedish

Almqvist, Ingrid and Anna Sågvall Hein (1996). "Defining ScaniaSwedish—Controlled Language for Truck Maintenance." *Proceedings of the 1st International Workshop on Controlled Language Applications (CLAW-96)*, Leuven, Belgium, pp. 159–164.

Hein, Anna Sågvall (1997). "ScaniaSwedish—A Basis for Multilingual Translation." In *Translating and the Computer 19*. London: The Association for Information Management.

Controlled Translation

Carl, Michael (2003). "Data-assisted Controlled Translation." *Proceedings of the Joint Conference Combining the 8th International Workshop of the European Association for Machine Translation and the 4th Controlled Language Applications Workshop: Controlled Language Translation (EAMT-CLAW-2003)*, Dublin City University, Ireland, pp. 16–24.

Gough, Nano and Andy Way (2004). "Example-based Controlled

Translation." *Proceedings of the 9th Workshop of the European Association for Machine Translation: Broadening Horizons of Machine Translation and Its Applications*, Foundation for International Studies, Malta, pp. 73–81.

Rico, Celia and Enrique Torrejon (2004). "Controlled Translation as a New Translation Scenario—Training the Future User." In *Translating and the Computer 26*. London: The Association for Information Management.

Roturier, Johann (2004). "Assessing Controlled Language Rules: Can They Improve Performance of Commercial Machine Translation Systems?" In *Translating and the Computer 26*. London: The Association for Information Management.

Torrejón, Enrique (2002). "Controlled Translation: A New Teaching Scenario Tailor-made for the Translation Industry." *Proceedings of the 6th Workshop of the European Association for Machine Translation: Teaching Machine Translation*, Manchester, England, pp. 107–116.

Controlled Vocabulary

Bjarnestam, Anna (2003). "Internationalizing a Controlled Vocabulary Based Search Engine for Japanese." *Proceedings of the Localization World Conference 2003*, Seattle, Washington, DC, USA.

Chen, Kuang-Hua and Chien-Tin Wu (1999). "Automatically Controlled-vocabulary Indexing for Text Retrieval." *Proceedings of the International Conference on Research in Computational Linguistics (ROCLING-XII)*, Taipei, Taiwan.

Probst, Katharina and Lori S. Levin (2002). "Challenges in Automated Elicitation of a Controlled Bilingual Corpus." *Proceedings of the 9th International Conference on Theoretical and Methodological Issues in Machine Translation (TMI-2002)*, Keihanna, Japan, pp. 157–167.

Wasson, Mark (2000). "Large-scale Controlled Vocabulary Indexing for Named Entities." *Proceedings of the 6th Applied Natural Language Processing Conference*, Seattle, Washington, DC, USA, pp. 276–281.

❖ PART 10 ❖

Corpus

Corpus

Aligned Corpus

Ozdowska, Sylwia (2006). "Projecting POS Tags and Syntactic Dependencies from English and French to Polish in Aligned Corpora." *Proceedings of the 11th Conference of the European Chapter of the Association for Computational Linguistics* (*EACL-2006*), Trento, Italy.

Yarowsky, David, Grace Ngai, and Richard Wicentowski (2001). "Introducing Multilingual Text Analysis Tools via Robust Projection across Aligned Corpora." *Proceedings of the Human Language Technology Conference* (*HLT-2001*), San Diego, CA, USA, pp. 109–116.

Annotated Corpus

Colominas, Carme (2005). "BancTrad: A Web Interface for Integrated Access to Annotated Corpora." In Walther van Hahn, W. John Hutchins, and Cristina Vertan, eds., *Proceedings of the International Workshop on Modern Approaches in Translation Technologies*, Borovets, Bulgaria.

Eckart, Richard (2006). "Towards A Modular Data Model for Multi-layer Annotated Corpora." *Proceedings of the Joint Conference of the International Committee on Computational Linguistics and the Association for Computational Linguistics* (*COLING/ACL-2006*), Sydney, Australia.

Feldman, Anna, Jirka Hana, and Chris Brew (2006). "Experiments in Cross-language Morphological Annotation Transfer." *Proceedings of the 7th International Conference on Intelligent Text Processing and Computational Linguistics* (*CICLing-2006*), Mexico City, Mexico.

Ide, Nancy and Laurent Romary (2006). "Representing Linguistic Corpora and Their Annotations." *Proceedings of the 5th International Conference on Language Resources and Evaluation* (*LREC-2006*), Genoa, Italy.

Kallmeyer, Laura (2000). "A Query Tool for Syntactically Annotated Corpora." *Proceedings of the Joint Sigdat Conference on Empirical Methods in Natural Language Processing and Very Large Corpora* (*EMNLP/VLC-2000*), Hong Kong University of Science and Technology, Hong Kong.

Marcus, Beatrice Santorini and Mary Ann Arcinkiewicz (1993). "Building a Large Annotated Corpus of English: The Penn Treebank." *Computational Linguistics*, Vol. 19, pp. 313–330.

Saquete, Estela, Patricio Martínez-Barco, R. Muñoz, Matteo Negri, M. Speranza, and R. Sprugnoli (2006). "Multilingual Extension of a Temporal Expression Normalizer Using Annotated Corpora." *Proceedings of the 11th Conference of the European Chapter of the Association for Computational Linguistics* (*EACL-2006*), Trento, Italy.

Sun, Maosong, Zhang Zhengcao, Benjamin K. Y. T'sou, and Lu Huaming (2006). "Word Frequency Approximation for Chinese without Using Manually Annotated Corpus." *Proceedings of the 7th International Conference on Intelligent Text Processing and Computational Linguistics* (*CICLing-2006*), Mexico City, Mexico.

Vela, Mihaela and Silvia Hansen-Schirra (2006). "The Use of Multi-level Annotation and Alignment for the Translator." In *Translating and the Computer 28*. London: The Association for Information Management.

Bilingual Corpus

Al-Onaizan, Yaser, Ulrich Germann, Ulf Hermjakob, Kevin Knight, Philipp Koehn, Daniel Marcu, and Kenji Yamada (2002). "Translation with Scarce Bilingual Resources." *Machine Translation*, Vol. 17, No. 1, pp. 1–17.

Bai, Xiaojing 柏曉靜, Chang Baobao 常寶寶, and Zhan Weidong 詹衛東 (2002).〈構建大規模的漢英雙語平行語料庫〉(Constructing a Large Chinese-English Bilingual Parallel Corpus). In Huang Heyan 黄河燕 ed.,《2002全國機器翻譯研討會文集》(*Proceedings of the 2000 National Conference on Machine Translation*). Beijing: Electronic Industry Press 電子工業出版社, pp. 124–131.

Chen, Kuang-Hua and Hsin-Hsi Chen (1995). "Aligning Bilingual Corpus: Especially for Language Pairs from Different Families." *Information Sciences*, Vol. 4, pp. 57–81.

Chen, Stanley F. (1993). "Aligning Sentences in Bilingual Corpora Using Lexical Information." *Proceedings of the 31st Annual Meeting of the Association for Computational Linguistics* (*ACL-93*), Columbus, Ohio, USA, pp. 9–16.

Gale, William A. and Kenneth W. Church (1991). "A Program for Aligning Sentences in Bilingual Corpora." *Proceedings of the 29th*

Annual Meeting of the Association for Computational Linguistics (*ACL-91*), Berkeley, CA, USA, pp. 177–184.

Gale, William A. and Kenneth W. Church (1991). "A Program for Aligning Sentences in Bilingual Corpora." *Computational Linguistics*, Vol. 19, pp. 75–102.

Garside, Roger (1995). "Matching Words in a Bilingual Corpus." *Machine Translation Review*, No. 2, pp. 7–18.

Grishman, Ralph (1994). "Iterative Alignment of Syntactic Structures for a Bilingual Corpus." *Proceedings of the 2nd Annual Workshop on Very Large Corpora*, Kyoto, Japan, pp. 57–68.

Gustavii, Ebba (2005). "Target Language Preposition Selection—An Experiment with Transformation-based Learning and Aligned Bilingual Data." *Proceedings of the 10th Workshop of the European Association for Machine Translation: Practical Applications of Machine Translation*, Budapest, Hungary, pp. 112–118.

Huang, Chung-Chi and Jason S. Chang (2006). "Learning to Parse Bilingual Sentences Using Bilingual Corpus and Monolingual CFG." *Proceedings of the Conference of the Association for Computational Linguistics and Chinese Language Processing* (*ROCLING-XVIII*), Taipei, Taiwan.

Kaji, Hiroyuki and Toshiko Aizono (1996). "Extracting Word Correspondences from Bilingual Corpora Based on Word Co-occurrence Information." *Proceedings from the 16th International Conference on Computational Linguistics* (*COLING-96*), Copenhagen, Denmark, pp. 23–28.

Kupiec, Julian (1993). "An Algorithm for Finding Noun Phrase Correspondences in Bilingual Corpora." *Proceedings of the 31st Annual Meeting of the Association of Computational Linguistics* (*ACL-93*), Columbus, Ohio, USA, pp. 17–22.

Langlais, Philippe (1997). *A System to Align Complex Bilingual Corpora*. Technical report TMH-QPSR 4, Kungliska Tekniska Hogskolan, Stockholm, Sweden.

Langlais, Philippe, George Foster, and Guy Lapalme (2001). "Integrating Bilingual Lexicons in a Probabilistic Translation Assistant." In Bente Maegaard, ed., *Proceedings of MT Summit VIII: Machine Translation in the Information Age*, Santiago de Compostela, Spain.

Liu, Xiaoyue 劉曉月, Yang Muyun 楊沐昀, and Zhao Tiejun 趙鐵軍 (2002). 〈迭代策略和詞典相結合的機器翻譯詞典獲取〉 (Bilingual Corpus Based on Chinese-English Translation Dictionary Acquisition). 《第一屆學生計算語言學研討會論文集》(*SWCL2002: First Students' Workshop on Computational Linguistics: Proceedings*), Institute of Computational Linguistics, Peking University, Beijing, China, pp. 257–262.

Meyers, Adam, Roman Yangarber, and Ralph Grishman (1996). "Alignment of Shared Forests for Bilingual Corpora." *Proceedings from the 16th International Conference on Computational Linguistics (COLING-96)*, Copenhagen, Denmark, pp. 459–465.

Moore, Robert C. (2002). "Fast and Accurate Sentence Alignment of Bilingual Corpora." In Stephen D. Richardson, ed., *Machine Translation: From Research to Real Users*. Berlin and New York: Springer Verlag, pp. 135–144.

Peters, Carol and Eugenio Picchi (1998). "Bilingual Reference Corpora for Translators and Translation Studies." In Lynne Bowker, Michael Cronin, Dorothy Kenny, and Jennifer Pearson, eds., *Unity in Diversity: Current Trends in Translation Studies*. Manchester: St. Jerome Publishing, pp. 91–100.

Peters, Carol, Eugenio Picchi, and Lisa Biagini (2000). "Parallel and Comparable Bilingual Corpora in Language Teaching and Learning." In Simon Philip Botley, Anthony Mark McEnery, and Andrew Wilson, eds., *Multilingual Corpora in Teaching and Research*. Amsterdam: Rodopi, pp. 73–85.

Probst, Katharina and Lori S. Levin (2002). "Challenges in Automated Elicitation of a Controlled Bilingual Corpus." *Proceedings of the 9th International Conference on Theoretical and Methodological Issues in Machine Translation (TMI-2002)*, Keihanna, Japan, pp. 157–167.

Simard, Michel, George Foster, and Pierre Isabelle (1992). "Using Cognates to Align Sentences in Bilingual Corpora." *Proceedings of the 4th International Conference on Theoretical and Methodological Issues in Machine Translation (TMI-92)*, Montréal, Quebec, Canada, pp. 67–81.

Tsujii, Keita (2002). "Automatic Extraction of Translational Japanese-KATAKANA and English Word Pairs from Bilingual Corpora." *International Journal of Computer Processing of Oriental Languages*, Vol. 15, No. 3, pp. 261–279.

Utsuro, Takehito, Yuji Matsumoto, and Makoto Nagao (1992). "Lexical Knowledge Acquisition from Bilingual Corpora." *Proceedings of the*

14th International Conference of Computational Linguistics (*COLING-92*), Nantes, France, pp. 581–587.
Wang, Kefei 王克非 (2004). 〈新型雙語語料庫的設計與構建〉 (The Design and Construction of Modern Bilingual Corpora). 《中國翻譯》 (*Chinese Translators' Journal*), No. 6, p. 9.
Wang, Kefei (2005). 〈雙語語料庫及其應用研究〉 (A Study on Bilingual Corpora and Its Application). 《中國英語教育》 (*English Language Education in China*), No. 2.
Zanettin, Federico (1998). "Bilingual Comparable Corpora and the Training of Translators." *Meta*, Vol. 43, No. 4, pp. 616–630.

Comparative Corpus

Alegria, Iñaki, Nerea Ezeiza, and Izaskun Fernandez (2006). "Named Entities Translation Based on Comparable Corpora." *Proceedings of the 11th Conference of the European Chapter of the Association for Computational Linguistics* (*EACL-2006*), Trento, Italy.
Bennison, Peter and Lynne Bowker (2000). "Designing a Tool for Exploiting Bilingual Comparable Corpora." In Maria Gavrilidou, George Carayannis, Stella Markantonatou, Stelios Piperidas, and Gregory Stainbaouer, eds., *Proceedings of the 2nd International Conference on Language Resources and Evaluation*, Paris: ELRA, Vol. 1, pp. 513–516.
Diab, Mona and Steve Finch (2000). "A Statistical Word-level Translation Model for Comparable Corpora." *Proceedings of the Conference on Content-based Multimedia Information Access* (*RIAO*), Paris, France, pp. 1500–1508.
Gaussier, Eric, Jean-Michel Renders, Irina Matveeva, Cyril Goutte, and Herve Dejean (2004). "A Geometric View on Bilingual Lexicon Extraction from Comparable Corpora." *Proceedings of the 42nd Annual Meeting of the Association for Computational Linguistics* (*ACL-2004*), Barcelona, Spain, pp. 526–533.
Gavioli, Laura and Federico Zanettin (1997). "Comparable Corpora and Translation: A Pedagogic Perspective." *Proceedings of the 1st International Conference on Corpus Use and Learning to Translate*, Bertinoro, Italy.
Gliozzo, Alfio and Carlo Strapparava (2006). "Exploiting Comparable Corpora and Bilingual Dictionaries for Cross-language Text

Categorization." *Proceedings of the Joint Conference of the International Committee on Computational Linguistics and the Association for Computational Linguistics* (*COLING/ACL-2006*), Sydney, Australia.
Hansen, Silvia (2000). "A Comparative Analysis of Parallel and Comparable Corpora." *Proceedings of the UMIST/UCL Research Models in Translation Studies Conference*, Manchester, England.
Jantunen, Jarmo (2000). "What Can Corpora Tell Us about Translated Language: A Comparable Corpus of Finnish in Use for Making Hypotheses." *Proceedings of the UMIST/UCL Research Models in Translation Studies Conference*, Manchester, England.
Jantunen, Jarmo (2002). "Comparable Corpora in Translation Studies: Strengths and Limitations." *SKY Journal of Linguistics*, Vol. 15, pp. 105–117.
Kaji, Hiroyuki (2003). "Word Sense Acquisition from Bilingual Comparable Corpora." *Proceedings of the Human Language Technology and North American Chapter of Association of Computational Linguistics 2003* (*HLT/NAACL-2003*), Edmonton, Alberta, Canada.
Laviosa, Sara (1997). "How Comparable Can 'Comparable Corpora' Be?" *Target*, Vol. 9, No. 2, pp. 289–319.
Laviosa, Sara (1998). "The English Comparable Corpus: A Resource and a Methodology." In Lynne Bowker, Michael Cronin, Dorothy Kenny, and Jennifer Pearson, eds., *Unity in Diversity? Current Trends in Translation Studies*. Manchester: St. Jerome Publishing, pp. 101–112.
Laviosa, Sara (1998). "Core Patterns of Lexical Use in a Comparable Corpus of English Narrative Prose." *Meta*, Vol. 43, No. 4, pp. 557–570.
Maia, Belinda (2003). "'Some Languages Are More Equal Than Others': Training Translators in Terminology and Information Retrieval Using Comparable and Parallel Corpora." In Federico Zanettin, Silvia Bernardini, and Dominic Stewart, eds., *Corpora in Translator Education*. Manchester: St. Jerome Publishing, pp. 43–53.
Munteanu, Dragos Stefan and Daniel Marcu (2002). "Processing Comparable Corpora with Bilingual Suffix Trees." *Proceedings of the 2002 Conference on Empirical Methods in Natural Language Processing* (*EMNLP-2002*), University of Pennsylvania, Philadelphia, PA, USA.
Munteanu, Dragos Stefan, Alexander Fraser, and Daniel Marcu (2004). "Improved Machine Translation Performance via Parallel Sentence

Extraction from Comparable Corpora." *Proceedings of the Human Language Technology Conference/North American Chapter of the Association for Computational Linguistics Annual Meeting (HLT/NAACL-2004)*, Boston, MA, USA.

Olohan, Maeve (2004). "Comparable Corpora." *Introducing Corpora in Translation Studies*. London and New York: Routledge, pp. 35–44.

Peters, Carol, Eugenio Picchi, and Lisa Biagini (2000). "Parallel and Comparable Bilingual Corpora in Language Teaching and Learning." In Simon Philip Botley, Anthony Mark McEnery, and Andrew Wilson, eds., *Multilingual Corpora in Teaching and Research*. Amsterdam: Rodopi, pp. 73–85.

Teubert, Wolfgang (1996). "Comparable or Parallel Corpora?" *International Journal of Lexicography*, Vol. 9, No. 3, pp. 238–264.

Zanettin, Federico (1998). "Bilingual Comparable Corpora and the Training of Translators." *Meta*, Vol. 43, No. 4, pp. 616–630.

Corpus

Alvarez, Alison, Lori S. Levin, Robert Frederking, Jeff Good, and Erik Peterson (2005). "Semi-automated Elicitation Corpus Generation." *Proceedings of MT Summit X*, Phuket, Thailand.

Alvarez, Alison, Lori S. Levin, Robert Frederking, Simon Fung, Donna Gates and Jeff Good (2006). "The MILE Corpus for Less Commonly Taught Languages." *Proceedings of the Human Language Technology Conference—Annual Meeting of the North American Chapter of the Association for Computational Linguistics (HLT-NAACL-2006)*, New York, USA.

Arguello, Jamie and Carolyn P. Rose (2006). "InfoMagnets: Making Sense of Corpus Data." *Proceedings of the Human Language Technology Conference—Annual Meeting of the North American Chapter of the Association for Computational Linguistics (HLT-NAACL-2006)*, New York, USA.

Aston, Guy (1999). "Corpus Use and Learning to Translate." In Susan Bassnett, Rosa Maria Bollettieri Bosinelli, and Margherita Ulrych, eds., *Translation Studies Revisited*. Genova: Tilgher, pp. 289–314.

Atkins, Sue, Jeremy Clear, and Nicholas Ostler (1992). "Corpus Design Criteria." *Literary and Linguistic Computing*, Vol. 7, pp. 1–16.

Austermühl, Frank (2001). "Corpora as Translation Tools." *Electronic*

Tools for Translators. Manchester: St. Jerome Publishing Company, pp. 124–133.

Baker, Mona (1995). "Corpora in Translation Studies: An Overview and Some Suggestions for Future Research." *Target*, Vol. 7, No. 2, pp. 223–243.

Baker, Mona (1996). "Corpus-based Translation Studies: The Challenges That Lie Ahead." In Harold L. Somers, ed., *Terminology, LSP and Translation: Studies in Language Engineering in Honour of Juan C. Sager*. Amsterdam and Philadelphia: John Benjamins Publishing Company, pp. 175–186.

Baker, Mona (1999). "The Role of Corpora in Investigating the Linguistic Behaviour of Professional Translators." *International Journal of Corpus Linguistics*, Vol. 4, No. 2, pp. 1–18.

Barlow, Michael (1996). "Corpora for Theory and Practice." *International Journal of Corpus Linguistics*, Vol. 1, No. 1.

Barlow, Michael (1996). "Language and Culture: The Role of Corpus Studies." *Proceedings of Linguisticulture: Where Do We Go from Here*, University of Osaka, Osaka, Japan.

Baroni, Marco, Adam Kilgarriff, Jan Pomikálek, and Pavel Rychlý (2006). "WebBootCaT: Instant Domain-specific Corpora to Support Human Translators." *Proceedings of the 11th Workshop of the European Association for Machine Translation: Machine Translation/Translation Aids—Tools to Increase Quality and to Save Money*, the University of Oslo, Oslo, Norway.

Barriere, Caroline (2006). "Semi-automatic Corpus Construction from Informative Texts." In Lynne Bowker, ed., *Lexicography, Terminology, and Translation: Text-based Studies in Honour of Ingrid Meyer*. Ottawa: University of Ottawa Press, pp. 81–92.

Bowker, Lynne (1998). "Using Specialized Monolingual Native Language Corpora as a Translation Resource: A Pilot Study." *Meta*, Vol. 43, No. 4, pp. 631–651.

Bowker, Lynne (1999). "Exploring the Potential of Corpora for Raising Language Awareness in Student Translators." *Language Awareness*, Vol. 8, Nos. 3–4, pp. 160–173.

Bowker, Lynne (2000). "Towards a Methodology for Exploiting Specialized Target Language Corpora as Translation Resources." *International Journal of Corpus Linguistics*, Vol. 5, No. 1, pp. 17–52.

Bowker, Lynne (2002). "Corpora and Corpus-analysis Tools." *Computer-*

aided Translation Technology: A Practical Introduction. Ottawa: University of Ottawa Press, pp. 43–76.

Bowker, Lynne and Jennifer Pearson (2002). *Working with Specialized Language: A Practical Guide to Using Corpora*. London: Routledge.

Bowker, Lynne and Peter Bennison (2003). "Student Translation Archive: Design, Development and Application." In Federico Zanettin, Silvia Bernardini, and Dominic Stewart, eds., *Corpora in Translator Education*. Manchester: St. Jerome Publishing, pp. 103–117.

Brisaboa, Nieves R., Juan-Ramón López, Miguel R. Penabad, and Ángeles S. Places (2003). "Diachronic Stemmed Corpus and Dictionary of Galician Language." *Proceedings of the 4th International Conference on Intelligent Text Processing and Computational Linguistics* (*CICLing-2003*), Mexico City, Mexico, pp. 412–416.

Calzolari, Nicoletta (1995). "European Efforts towards Standardizing Language Resources." In Petra Steffens, ed., *Machine Translation and the Lexicon*. Berlin: Springer Verlag, pp. 121–130.

Casillas, Arantza, Joseba Abaitua, and Raquel Martinez (2000). "Recycling Annotated Parallel Corpora for Bilingual Document Composition." In John S. White, ed., *Envisioning Machine Translation in the Information Future*. Berlin: Springer Verlag, pp. 117–126.

Chen, Chun-liang 陳俊良, Lee Min-Jer 李明哲, Huang Chien-Kang 黃乾綱, and Chien Lee-Feng 簡立峰 (1999). "Chinese Corpus Storage and Classification from Online Resources." In Huang Changning 黃昌寧 and Dong Zhendong 董振東, eds.,《計算機語言學文集》(*Essays on Computational Linguistics*). Beijing: Tsinghua University Press, pp. 376–381.

Chung, Siaw-Fong, Kathleen Ahrens, and Chu-Ren Huang (2003). "Economy Is a Person: A Chinese-English Corpora and Ontological-based Comparison Using the Conceptual Mapping Model." *Proceedings of the International Conference on Research in Computational Linguistics* (*ROCLING-XV*), Hsin-Chu, Taiwan.

Cicekli, Ilyas and H. Altay Güvenir (1996). "Learning Translation Rules from a Bilingual Corpus." *Proceedings of the 2nd International Conference on New Methods in Language Processing*, Anaka, Turkey, pp. 90–97.

Danielsson, Pernilla and Daniel Ridings (2000). "Corpus and Terminology: Software for the Translation Program at Göteborgs Universitet or Getting Students to Do the Work." In Simon Philip

Botley, Anthony Mark McEnery, and Andrew Wilson, eds., *Multilingual Corpora in Teaching and Research*. Amsterdam: Rodopi, pp. 65–72.

Duan, Huiming 段慧明, Song Jing 松井久仁於, Xu Guowei 徐國偉, Hu Guoxin 胡國昕, and Yu Shiwen 俞士汶 (2000).〈大規模漢語標注語料庫的製作與使用〉(The Development of a Large-scale Tagged Chinese Corpus and Its Applications). In Yu Shiwen 俞士汶 and Zhu Xuefeng 朱學鋒, eds.,《計算語言學文集》(*Papers on Computational Linguistics*), Vol. 4. Beijing: Department of Computer Science and Technology and Institute of Computational Linguistics, Peking University, pp. 116–124.

Ebeling, Jarle (1998). "Contrastive Linguistics, Translation, and Parallel Corpora." *Meta*, Vol. 43, No. 4, pp. 602–615.

Engwall, Gunnel (1994). "Not Chance but Choice: Criteria in Corpus Creation." In Sue Atkins and Antonio Zampolli, eds., *Computational Approaches to the Lexicon*. Oxford: Oxford University Press, pp. 49–82.

Eskin, Eleazar (2000). "Detecting Errors with a Corpus Using Anomaly Detection." *Proceedings of the 1st Meeting of the North American Chapter of the Association for Computational Linguistics*, Seattle, Washington, DC, USA, pp. 148–153.

Feng, Zhiwei 馮志偉 (2002).〈中國語料庫研究的歷史與現狀〉(A Study on Corpora in China: Past and Present). *Journal of Chinese Language and Computing*, Vol. 12, No. 1, pp. 43–62.

Flickinger, Dan (2006). "Identifying Complex Phenomena in a Corpus via a Treebank Lens." *Proceedings of the 11th Workshop of the European Association for Machine Translation: Machine Translation/ Translation Aids—Tools to Increase Quality and to Save Money*, the University of Oslo, Oslo, Norway.

Fukumoto, Fumiyo and Yoshimi Suzuki (2002). "Manipulating Large Corpora for Text Classification." *Proceedings of the 2002 Conference on Empirical Methods in Natural Language Processing (EMNLP-2002)*, University of Pennsylvania, Philadelphia, PA, USA.

Fung, Pascale (1995). "A Pattern Matching Method for Finding Noun and Proper Noun Translations from Noisy Parallel Corpora." *Proceedings of the 33rd Annual Conference of the Association for Computational Linguistics*, Boston, MA, USA, pp. 226–233.

Fung, Pascale (1995). "Compiling Bilingual Lexicon Entries from a Non-parallel English-Chinese Corpus." *Proceedings of the 3rd Annual Workshop on Very Large Corpora*, Boston, MA, USA, pp. 173–183.

Fung, Pascale (1998). "A Statistical View on Bilingual Lexicon Extraction: From Parallel Corpora to Non-parallel Corpora." In David L. Farwell, Laurie Gerber, and Eduard Hovy, eds., *Machine Translation and the Information Soup*. Berlin: Springer Verlag, pp. 1–17.

Gooi, Chung Heong and James Allan (2004). "Cross-document Coreference on a Large Scale Corpus." *Proceedings of the Human Language Technology Conference/North American Chapter of the Association for Computational Linguistics Annual Meeting* (*HLT/NAACL-2004*), Boston, MA, USA.

Huang, Yu 黃玉, Li Sheng 李生, Meng Yao 孟遙, and Ding Fuhua 丁福華 (2002).〈基於大規模語料庫的英語從句識別〉(A Large Scale Corpus-based Approach to English Subordinate Clause Identification).《第一屆學生計算語言學研討會論文集》(*SWCL2002: First Students' Workshop on Computational Linguistics: Proceedings*), Institute of Computational Linguistics, Peking University, Beijing, China, pp. 77–82.

Jiménez-Salazar, Héctor (2003). "A Method of Automatic Detection of Lexical Relationships Using a Raw Corpus." *Proceedings of the 4th International Conference on Intelligent Text Processing and Computational Linguistics* (*CICLing-2003*), Mexico City, Mexico, pp. 327–330.

Johansson, Stig (2003). "Reflections on Corpora and Their Uses in Cross-linguistic Research." In Federico Zanettin, Silvia Bernardini, and Dominic Stewart, eds., *Corpora in Translator Education*. Manchester: St. Jerome Publishing, pp. 135–144.

Jones, Daniel B. and Harold Somers (1997). "Bilingual Vocabulary Estimation from Noisy Parallel Corpora Using Variable Bag Estimation." In Ruslan Mitkov and Nicolas Nicolov, eds., *Recent Advances in Natural Language Processing*. Amsterdam and Philadelphia: John Benjamins Publishing Company, pp. 427–437.

Kaji, Hiroyuki, Yuuko Kida, and Yasututsugo Morimoto (1992). "Learning Translation Templates from Bilingual Text." *Proceedings of the 14th International Conference of Computational Linguistics* (*COLING-92*), Nantes, France, pp. 672–678.

Kallmeyer, Laura (2000). "A Query Tool for Syntactically Annotated Corpora." *Proceedings of the Joint Sigdat Conference on Empirical Methods in Natural Language Processing and Very Large Corpora*

(*EMNLP/VLC-2000*), Hong Kong University of Science and Technology, Hong Kong.

Kemppanen, Hannu (2000). "Looking for Evaluative Keywords in Authentic and Translated Finnish: Corpus Research on Finnish History Texts." *Proceedings of the UMIST/UCL Research Models in Translation Studies Conference*, Manchester, England.

Kenny, Dorothy (1998). "Corpora in Translation Studies." In Mona Baker, ed., *Routledge Encyclopedia of Translation Studies*. London and New York: Routledge, pp. 50–53.

Kilgarriff, Adam and Tony Rose (1998). "Metrics for Corpus Similarity and Homogeneity." *Proceedings of the 3rd Conference on Empirical Methods in Natural Language Processing*, Granada, Spain.

Klavans, Judith and Evelyne Tzoukermann (1995). "Combining Corpus and Machine-readable Dictionary Data for Building Bilingual Lexicons." *Machine Translation*, Vol. 10, No. 3, pp. 185–218.

Kohn, János (1996). "What Can (Corpus) Linguistics Do for Translation?" In Kinga Klaudy, José Lambert, and Anikó Sohár, eds., *Translation Studies in Hungary*. Budapest: Scholastica, pp. 39–52.

Kübler, Natalie (2003). "Corpora and LSP Translation." In Federico Zanettin, Silvia Bernardini, and Dominic Stewart, eds., *Corpora in Translator Education*. Manchester: St. Jerome Publishing, pp. 25–42.

Laviosa, Sara (2003). "Corpora and the Translator." In Harold Somers, ed., *Computers and Translation: A Translator's Guide*. Amsterdam and Philadelphia: John Benjamins Publishing Company, pp. 105–117.

Lindquist, Hans (1999). "Electronic Corpora as Tools for Translation." In Gunilla Anderman and Margaret Rogers, eds., *Words, Text, Translation: Liber Amicorum for Peter Newmark*. Clevedon: Multilingual Matters, pp. 179–189.

Lux, Veronika and Eva Dauphin (1996). "Corpus Studies: A Contribution to the Definition of a Controlled Language." *Proceedings of the 1st International Workshop on Controlled Language Applications* (*EAMT-CLAW-96*), Leuven, Belgium, pp. 193–204.

Ma, Xiaoyi and Christopher Cieri (2006). "Corpus Support for Machine Translation at LDC." *Proceedings of the 5th International Conference on Language Resources and Evaluation* (*LREC-2006*), Genoa, Italy.

Maia, Belinda (2000). "Making Corpora: A Learning Process." In Silvia Bernardini and Federico Zanettin, eds., *Corpus Use and Learning to Translate*. Bologna: CLUEB, pp. 47–60.

Malmkjær, Kirsten (2003). "On a Pseudo-subversive Use of Corpora in Translator Training." In Federico Zanettin, Silvia Bernardini, and Dominic Stewart, eds., *Corpora in Translator Education*. Manchester: St. Jerome Publishing, pp. 119–134.

Marcus, Beatrice Santorini and Mary Ann Arcinkiewicz (1993). "Building a Large Annotated Corpus of English: The Penn Treebank." *Computational Linguistics*, Vol. 19, pp. 313–330.

Maruyama, Hiroshi, Shiho Ogino, and Masaru Hidano (1993). "The Mega-word Tagged-corpus Project." *Proceedings of the 5th International Conference on Theoretical and Methodological Issues in Machine Translation of Natural Languages: MT in the Next Generation* (*TMI-93*), Kyoto, Japan, pp. 15–23.

Matsumoto, Yuji and Mihoko Kitamura (1997). "Acquisition of Translation Rules from Parallel Corpora." In Ruslan Mitkov and Nicolas Nicolov, eds., *Recent Advances in Natural Language Processing*. Amsterdam and Philadelphia: John Benjamins Publishing Company, pp. 405–416.

Mauranen, Anna (2000). "Strange Strings in Translated Language: A Study on Corpora." In Maeve Olohan, ed., *Intercultural Faultlines: Research Models in Translation Studies I: Textual and Cognitive Aspects*. Manchester: St. Jerome Publishing, pp. 119–141.

McEnery, Anthony Mark (1997). "Corpus Resources for Machine Translation." In *Translating and the Computer 19*. London: The Association for Information Management.

McEnery, Tony (1997). "Multilingual Corpora—Current Practice and Future Trends." In *Translating and the Computer 19*. London: The Association for Information Management.

McEnery, Tony and Paul Baker (2003). "Corpora, Translation and Multilingual Computing." In Federico Zanettin, Silvia Bernardini, and Dominic Stewart, eds., *Corpora in Translator Education*. Manchester: St. Jerome Publishing, pp. 89–102.

Meyer, Renee, Mary Ellen Okurowski, and Therese Hand (2000). "Using Authentic Corpora and Language Tools for Adult-centred Learning." In Simon Philip Botley, Anthony Mark McEnery, and Andrew Wilson, eds., *Multilingual Corpora in Teaching and Research*. Amsterdam: Rodopi, pp. 86–91.

Mouček, Roman and Kamil Ekštein (2003). "Corpus Construction within Linguistic Module of City Information Dialogue System." *Proceedings of the 4th International Conference on Intelligent Text Processing and Computational Linguistics* (*CICLing-2003*), Mexico City, Mexico, pp. 408–411.

Murata, Toshiki, Mihoko Kitamura, Tsuyoshi Fukui, and Tatsuya Sukehiro (2003). "Implementation of Collaborative Translation Environment: YakushiteNet." *Proceedings of MT Summit IX*, New Orleans, Louisiana, USA.

Olohan, Maeve (2004). "Corpora in Translation Practice." *Introducing Corpora in Translation Studies*. London and New York: Routledge, pp. 176–189.

Olohan, Maeve (2004). "Corpora in Translator Training." *Introducing Corpora in Translation Studies*. London and New York: Routledge, pp. 168–175.

Olohan, Maeve (2004). "Corpus Design." *Introducing Corpora in Translation Studies*. London and New York: Routledge, pp. 45–61.

Olohan, Maeve (2004). "Corpus Tools and Data Analysis." *Introducing Corpora in Translation Studies*. London and New York: Routledge, pp. 62–89.

Olohan, Maeve (2004). *Introducing Corpora in Translation Studies*. London and New York: Routledge.

Pantel, Patrick and Lin Dekang (2000). "Word-for-word Glossing with Contextually Similar Words." *Proceedings of the 1st Meeting of the North American Chapter of the Association for Computational Linguistics*, Seattle, Washington, DC, USA, pp. 78–85.

Paul, Michael and Eiichiro Sumita (2006). "Exploiting Variant Corpora for Machine Translation." *Proceedings of the Human Language Technology Conference—Annual Meeting of the North American Chapter of the Association for Computational Linguistics* (*HLT-NAACL-2006*), New York, USA.

Poutsma, Arjen (1998). "Data-oriented Translation." *Proceedings of the 9th Conference on Computational Linguistics in the Netherlands*, Leuven, Belgium.

Probst, Katharina and Alon Lavie (2004). "A Structurally Diverse Minimal Corpus for Eliciting Structural Mappings between Languages." In Robert E. Frederking and Kathryn B. Taylors, eds., *Machine Translation: From Real Users to Research*. Berlin: Springer Verlag, pp. 217–226.

Roberts, Roda P. and Jacqueline Bosse-Andrieu (2006). "Corpora and Translation." In Lynne Bowker, ed., *Lexicography, Terminology, and*

Translation: Text-based Studies in Honour of Ingrid Meyer. Ottawa: University of Ottawa Press, pp. 201–214.

Salkie, Raphael (2000). "Unlocking the Power of SMEMUC." In Simon Philip Botley, Anthony Mark McEnery, and Andrew Wilson, eds., *Multilingual Corpora in Teaching and Research*. Amsterdam: Rodopi, pp. 148–156.

Sebba, Mark (1991). "The Adequacy of Corpora in Machine Translation." *Applied Computer Translation*, Vol. 1, No. 1, pp. 15–27.

Smith, Noah A. (2002). "From Words to Corpora: Recognizing Translation." *Proceedings of the 2002 Conference on Empirical Methods in Natural Language Processing* (*EMNLP-2002*), University of Pennsylvania, Philadelphia, PA, USA.

Stewart, Dominic (2000). "Conventionality, Creativity and Translated Text: The Implications of Electronic Corpora in Translation." In Maeve Olohan, ed., *Intercultural Faultlines: Research Models in Translation Studies I: Textual and Cognitive Aspects*. Manchester: St. Jerome Publishing, pp. 73–91.

Tymoczko, Maria (1998). "Computerized Corpora and the Future of Translation Studies." *Meta*, Vol. 43, No. 4, pp. 652–659.

Ushioda, Akira (2005). "Utilization of Corpora for the Full-fledged Practical Application of Machine Translation Technologies." *AAMT Journal*, Vol. 37.

Varantola, Krista (2003). "Translators and Disposable Corpora." In Federico Zanettin, Silvia Bernardini, and Dominic Stewart, eds., *Corpora in Translator Education*. Manchester: St. Jerome Publishing, pp. 55–70.

Wang, Kefei 王克非 (2002).〈語料庫：翻譯教研新途徑〉(Corpus: A New Path for Translation Teaching and Research).《外語與外語教學》(*Foreign Languages and Foreign Language Teaching*), No. 9.

Wang, Kefei (2003).〈以語料觀察翻譯〉(Studying Translation through Linguistic Corpus).《外語與翻譯》(*Foreign Languages and Translation*), No. 4.

Wang, Kefei (2003).〈英漢、漢英語句對應的語料庫考察〉(A Corpus-based Examination of Sentence Correspondence between English and Chinese).《外語教學與研究》(*Foreign Language Teaching and Research*), No. 6.

Wilkinson, Michael (2005). "Using a Specialized Corpus to Improve Translation Quality." *Translation Journal*, Vol. 9, No. 3.

Wilkinson, Michael (2006). "Compiling Corpora for Use as Translation Resources." *Translation Journal*, Vol. 10, No. 1.
Wilks, Yorick (1993). "Corpora and Machine Translation." *Proceedings of MT Summit IV: International Cooperation for Global Communication*, Kobe, Japan, pp. 137–145.
Yu, Shiwen 俞士汶, Zhu Xuefeng 朱學鋒, and Duan Huiming 段慧明 (2000).〈大規模現代漢語標注語料庫的加工規範〉(Guidelines for Segmentation and Part-of-speech Tagging on Very Large Scale Corpus of Contemporary Chinese). In Yu Shiwen 俞士汶 and Zhu Xuefeng 朱學鋒, eds.,《計算語言學文集》(*Papers on Computational Linguistics*), Vol. 4. Beijing: Department of Computer Science and Technology and Institute of Computational Linguistics, Peking University, pp. 125–132.
Zanettin, Federico (2001). "Swimming in Words: Corpora, Translation and Language Learning." In G. Aston, ed., *Learning with Corpora*. Bologna, Houston: Athelstan, pp. 177–197.
Zanettin, Frederico (2002). "DIY Corpora: The WWW and the Translator." In Belinda Maia, Jonathan Haller, and Margherita Urlrych, eds., *Training the Language Services Provider for the New Millennium*. Porto: Faculdade de Letras, Universidade do Porto, pp. 239–248.
Zanettin, Federico, Silvia Bernardini, and Dominic Stewart, eds. (2003). *Corpora in Translator Education*. Manchester: St. Jerome Publishing.
Zanettin, Federico, Silvia Bernardini, and Dominic Stewart (2003). "Corpora in Translator Education: An Introduction." *Corpora in Translator Education*. Manchester: St. Jerome Publishing, pp. 1–13.
Zhou, Qiang 周強 and Yu Shiwen 俞士汶 (1996).〈一個人機互助的漢語語料庫多級加工處理系統CCMP〉(A Man-machine Mutually-dependent Multistage Processing System of Chinese Language Corpus). In Yu Shiwen 俞士汶 and Zhu Xuefeng 朱學鋒, eds.,《計算語言學文集》(*Papers on Computational Linguistics*). Beijing: Department of Computer Science and Technology and Institute of Computational Linguistics, Peking University, pp. 148–154.

Corpus Annotation

Al-Adhaileh, Mosleh H., Tang Enya Kong, and Yusoff Zaharin (2002). "A Synchronization Structure of SSTC and Its Applications in Machine Translation." *Proceedings of the Workshop on Machine Translation in Asia* (*COLING-2002*), Taipei, Taiwan.

Brill, Eric (1997). "Creating and Using Automatic Linguistic Annotation Software." *Proceedings of the 5th Conference on Applied Natural Language Processing*, Seattle, Washington, DC, USA.

Casillas, Arantza, Joseba Abaitua, and Raquel Martinez (2000). "Recycling Annotated Parallel Corpora for Bilingual Document Composition." In John S. White, ed., *Envisioning Machine Translation in the Information Future*. Berlin: Springer Verlag, pp. 117–126.

Eckart, Richard (2006). "Towards a Modular Data Model for Multi-layer Annotated Corpora." *Proceedings of the Joint Conference of the International Committee on Computational Linguistics and the Association for Computational Linguistics* (*COLING/ACL-2006*), Sydney, Australia.

Goyal, Shailly and Niladri Chatterjee (2006). "Parsing Aligned Parallel Corpus by Projecting Syntactic Relations from Annotated Source Corpus." *Proceedings of the Joint Conference of the International Committee on Computational Linguistics and the Association for Computational Linguistics* (*COLING/ACL-2006*), Sydney, Australia.

Hajičová, Eva and Petr Sgall (2006). "Corpus Annotation as a Test of a Linguistic Theory." *Proceedings of the 5th International Conference on Language Resources and Evaluation* (*LREC-2006*), Genoa, Italy.

Kallmeyer, Laura (2000). "A Query Tool for Syntactically Annotated Corpora." *Proceedings of the Joint Sigdat Conference on Empirical Methods in Natural Language Processing and Very Large Corpora* (*EMNLP/VLC-2000*), Hong Kong University of Science and Technology, Hong Kong.

Lai, Tom B. Y. and Huang Changning (2000). "Dependency-based Syntactic Analysis of Chinese and Annotation of Parsed Corpus." *Proceedings of the 38th Annual Meeting of the Association for Computational Linguistics* (*ACL-2000*), Hong Kong.

Marcus, Beatrice Santorini and Mary Ann Arcinkiewicz (1993). "Building a Large Annotated Corpus of English: The Penn Treebank." *Computational Linguistics*, Vol. 19, pp. 313–330.

Ngai, Grace and David Yarowsky (2000). "Rule Writing or Annotation: Cost-efficient Resource Usage for Base Noun Phrase Chunking." *Proceedings of the 38th Annual Meeting of the Association for Computational Linguistics* (*ACL-2000*), Hong Kong.

Ogren, Philip V. (2006). "Knowtator: A Protege Plug-in for Annotated Corpus Construction." *Proceedings of the Human Language*

Technology Conference—Annual Meeting of the North American Chapter of the Association for Computational Linguistics (HLT-NAACL-2006), New York, USA.
Orăsan, Constantin (2005). "Automatic Annotation of Corpora for Text Summarisation: A Comparative Study." *Proceedings of the 6th International Conference on Intelligent Text Processing and Computational Linguistics (CICLing-2005)*, Mexico City, Mexico, pp. 657–668.
Vlachos, Andreas (2006). "Active Annotation." *Proceedings of the 11th Conference of the European Chapter of the Association for Computational Linguistics (EACL-2006)*, Trento, Italy.
Zhang, Yujie, Kiyotaka Uchimoto, Ma Qing, and Hitoshi Isahara (2005). "Building an Annotated Japanese-Chinese Parallel Corpus—A Part of NICT Multilingual Corpora." *Proceedings of MT Summit X*, Phuket, Thailand.

Monolingual Corpus

Biemann, Christian, Stefan Bordag, Gerhard Heyer, Uwe Quasthoff, and Christian Wolff (2004). "Language-independent Methods for Compiling Monolingual Lexical Data." *Proceedings of the 5th International Conference on Intelligent Text Processing and Computational Linguistics (CICLing-2004)*, Chung-Ang University, Seoul, Korea, pp. 214–225.
Bowker, Lynne (1998). "Using Specialized Monolingual Native-language Corpora as a Translation Resource: A Pilot Study." *Meta*, Vol. 43, No. 4, pp. 631–651.
Dagan, Ido and Alon Itai (1994). "Word Sense Disambiguation Using a Second Language Monolingual Corpus." *Computational Linguistics*, Vol. 20, pp. 564–596.
Dologlou, Yannis, Stella Markantonatou, George Tambouratzis, Olga Yannoutsou, Athanassia Fourla, and Nikos Ioannou (2003). "Using Monolingual Corpora for Statistical Machine Translation: The METIS System." *Proceedings of the Joint Conference Combining the 8th International Workshop of the European Association for Machine Translation and the 4th Controlled Language Applications Workshop: Controlled Language Translation (EAMT-CLAW-2003)*, Dublin City University, Ireland.

Koehn, Philipp and Kevin Knight (2000). "Estimating Word Translation Probabilities from Unrelated Monolingual Corpora Using the EM Algorithm." *Proceedings of the 17th National Conference on Artificial Intelligence of the American Association for Artificial Intelligence (AAAI-2000)*, Austin, Texas, USA, pp. 711–715.

Lin, Tracy, Wu Jian-Cheng, and Jason S. Chang (2004). "Extraction of Name and Transliteration in Monolingual and Parallel Corpora." In Robert E. Frederking and Kathryn B. Taylors, eds., *Machine Translation: From Real Users to Research*. Berlin: Springer Verlag, pp. 177–186.

Soricut, Radu, Kevin Knight, and Daniel Marcu (2002). "Using a Large Monolingual Corpus to Improve Translation Accuracy." In Stephen D. Richardson, ed., *Machine Translation: From Research to Real Users*. Berlin and New York: Springer Verlag, pp. 155–164.

Suzuki, Hirokazu and Akira Kumano (2005). "Learning Translations from Monolingual Corpora." *Proceedings of MT Summit X*, Phuket, Thailand.

Multilingual Corpus

Botley, Simon Philip, Anthony Mark McEnery, and Andrew Wilson, eds. (2000). *Multilingual Corpora in Teaching and Research*. Amsterdam: Rodopi.

Ludovik, Yevgeny and Ron Zacharski (1999). "Multilingual Document Language Recognition for Creating Corpora." *Proceedings of MT Summit VII: MT in the Great Translation Era*, Singapore.

McEnery, Tony (1997). "Multilingual Corpora—Current Practice and Future Trends." In *Translating and the Computer 19*. London: The Association for Information Management.

Parallel Corpus

Altenberg, Bengt and Karin Aijmer (2000). "The English-Swedish Parallel Corpus: A Resource for Contrastive Research and Translation Studies." In Christian Mair and Marianne Hundt, eds., *Corpus Linguistics and Linguistics Theory*. Amsterdam and Atlanta, GA: Rodopi, pp. 15–33.

Boutsis, Sotiris and Stelios Piperidis (1996). "Automatic Extraction of

Lexical Equivalences from Parallel Corpora." *Proceedings of the Workshop on Multilinguality in the Software Industry: The AI Contribution (MULSAIC-96) and the 12th European Conference on Artificial Intelligence (ECAI-96)*, Budapest, Hungary, pp. 27–31.

Brown, Peter F., Jennifer C. Lai, and Robert L. Mercer (1991). "Aligning Sentences in Parallel Corpora." *Proceedings of the 29th Annual Meeting of the Association for Computational Linguistics (ACL-91)*, University of California, Berkeley, California, USA, pp. 169–176.

Callison-Burch, Chris and Miles Osborne (2003). "Bootstrapping Parallel Corpora." *Proceedings of the Human Language Technology and North American Chapter of Association of Computational Linguistics 2003 (HLT/NAACL-2003)*, Edmonton, Alberta, Canada.

Chen, Boxing 陳博興 and Du Limin 杜利民 (2002).〈基於雙語語料的單個源語詞匯和目標語多詞單元的對齊〉(Alignment of Single Source Words and Target Multi-word Units from Parallel Corpus).《第一屆學生計算語言學研討會論文集》(*SWCL-2002: First Students' Workshop on Computational Linguistics: Proceedings*), Institute of Computational Linguistics, Peking University, Beijing, China, pp. 318–327.

Diab, Mona and Philip Resnik (2002). "An Unsupervised Method for Word Sense Tagging Using Parallel Corpora." *Proceedings of the 40th Annual Meeting of the Association for Computational Linguistics (ACL-2002)*, Philadelphia, Pennsylvania, USA, pp. 255–262.

Ebeling, Jarle (1998). "Contrastive Linguistics, Translation, and Parallel Corpora." *Meta*, Vol. 43, No. 4, pp. 602–615.

Echizen-ya, Hiroshi, Kenji Araki, Yoshio Momouchi, and Koji Tochinai (2004). "Acquisition of Word Translations Using Local Focus-based Learning in Ainu-Japanese Parallel Corpora." *Proceedings of the 5th International Conference on Intelligent Text Processing and Computational Linguistics (CICLing-2004)*, Chung-Ang University, Seoul, Korea, pp. 297–301.

Frankenberg-Garcia, Ana and Diana Santos (2003). "Introducing *Compara*, the Portuguese-English Parallel Corpus." In Federico Zanettin, Silvia Bernardini, and Dominic Stewart, eds., *Corpora in Translator Education*. Manchester: St. Jerome Publishing, pp. 71–87.

Fung, Pascale and Kathleen R. McKeown (1994). "Aligning Noisy Parallel Corpora across Language Groups: Word Pair Feature Matching by Dynamic Time Warping." *Proceedings of the 1st Conference of the Association for Machine Translation in the Americas: Technology*

Partnerships for Crossing the Language Barrier (*AMTA-1*), Columbia, Maryland, USA, pp. 81–88.

Fung, Pascale (1995). "A Pattern Matching Method for Finding Noun and Proper Noun Translations from Noisy Parallel Corpora." *Proceedings of the 33rd Annual Meeting of the Association of Computational Linguistics* (*ACL-95*), Cambridge, MA, USA, pp. 236–243.

Fung, Pascale and Kathleen R. McKeown (1997). "A Technical Word- and Term-translation Aid Using Noisy Parallel Corpora across Language Groups." *Machine Translation*, Vol. 12, Nos. 1–2, pp. 53–87.

Fung, Pascale (1998). "A Statistical View on Bilingual Lexicon Extraction: From Parallel Corpora to Non-parallel Corpora." In David L. Farwell, Laurie Gerber, and Eduard Hovy, eds., *Machine Translation and the Information Soup*. Berlin. Springer Verlag, pp. 1–17.

Gale, William A. and Kenneth W. Church (1991). "Identifying Word Correspondences in Parallel Texts." *Proceedings of the 4th DARPA Speech and Natural Language Workshop*, Pacific Grove, CA, USA, pp. 152–157.

Gaspari, Federico (2003). "Relevance of Parallel Corpora to the Latest Developments of Machine Translation and Computer-assisted Translation." *International Journal of Translation*, Vol. 15, No. 1, pp. 27–41.

Gliozzo, Alfio Massimiliano, Marcello Ranieri, and Carlo Strapparava (2005). "Crossing Parallel Corpora and Multilingual Lexical Databases for WSD." *Proceedings of the 6th International Conference on Intelligent Text Processing and Computational Linguistics* (*CICLing-2005*), Mexico City, Mexico, pp. 236–239.

Hajlaoui, Najeh and Christian Boitet (2004). "PolyphraZ: A Tool for the Quantitative and Subjective Evaluation of Parallel Corpora." *Proceedings of the International Workshop on Spoken Language Translation* (*IWSLT-2004*), Kyoto, Japan.

Hansen, Silvia (2000). "A Comparative Analysis of Parallel and Comparable Corpora." *Proceedings of the UMIST/UCL Research Models in Translation Studies Conference*, Manchester, England.

Iomdin, Leonid L. and Oliver Streiter (1999). "Learning from Parallel Corpora: Experiments in Machine Translation." *Proceedings of the Dialogue '99: Computational Linguistics and Its Applications International Workshop*, Tarusa, Russia, Vol. 2, pp. 79–88.

Jantunen, Jarmo (2000). "What Can Corpora Tell Us about Translated Language: A Comparable Corpus of Finnish in Use for Making

Hypotheses." *Proceedings of the UMIST/UCL Research Models in Translation Studies Conference*, Manchester, England.

Johansson, Stig and Knut Hofland (1994). "Towards an English-Norwegian Parallel Corpus." In Udo Fries, Gunnel Tottie, and Peter Schneider, eds., *Creating and Using English Language Corpora*. Amsterdam: Rodopi, pp. 25–37.

Johansson, Stig, Jarle Ebeling, and Knut Hofland (1996). "Coding and Aligning the English-Norwegian Parallel Corpus." In Karin Aijmer, Bengt Altenberg, and Mats Johansson, eds., *Languages in Contrast*. Lund: Lund University Press, pp. 87–112.

Johansson, Stig and Knut Hofland (2000). "The English-Norwegian Parallel Corpus: Current Work and New Directions." In Simon Philip Botley, Anthony Mark McEnery, and Andrew Wilson, eds., *Multilingual Corpora in Teaching and Research*. Amsterdam: Rodopi, pp. 134–147.

Kashioka, Hideki, Takehiko Maruyama, and Hideki Tananka (2003). "Building a Parallel Corpus for Monologue with Clause Alignment." *Proceedings of MT Summit IX*, New Orleans, Louisiana, USA.

Kenny, Dorothy (1999). "The German-English Parallel Corpus of Literary Texts (GEPCOLT): A Resource for Translation Scholars." *Teanga*, Vol. 18, pp. 25–42.

Kenny, Dorothy (2000). "Lexical Hide-and-seek: Looking for Creativity in a Parallel Corpus." In Maeve Olohan, ed., *Intercultural Faultlines: Research Models in Translation Studies I: Textual and Cognitive Aspects*. Manchester: St. Jerome Publishing, pp. 93–104.

Kenny, Dorothy (2001). "The How of It: Creating and Using a Parallel Corpus." *Lexis and Creativity in Translation: A Corpus-based Study*. Manchester: St. Jerome Publishing, pp. 105–141.

Kenny, Dorothy (2003). "Parallel Corpora and Translation Studies: Old Questions, New Perspectives? Reporting That in Gepcolt—A Case Study." In Geoff Barnbrook, Pernilla Danielsson, and Michaela Mahlberg, eds., *Meaningful Texts: The Extraction of Semantic Information from Monolingual and Multilingual Corpora*. London: Continuum International Publishing Group, pp. 141–151.

King, Philip (1997). "Parallel Corpora for Translator Training." *Proceedings of "Translation and Meaning,"* Lodz, Poland, pp. 393–402.

Koehn, Philipp (2005). "Europarl: A Parallel Corpus for Statistical Machine Translation." *Proceedings of MT Summit X*, Phuket, Thailand.

Lee, Chun-Jen, Jason S. Chang, and Thomas C. Chuang (2004). "Alignment of Bilingual Named Entities in Parallel Corpora Using Statistical Model." In Robert E. Frederking and Kathryn B. Taylors, eds., *Machine Translation: From Real Users to Research*. Berlin: Springer Verlag, pp. 144–153.

Lin, Tracy, Wu Jian-Cheng, and Jason S. Chang (2004). "Extraction of Name and Transliteration in Monolingual and Parallel Corpora." In Robert E. Frederking and Kathryn B. Taylors, eds., *Machine Translation: From Real Users to Research*. Berlin: Springer Verlag, pp. 177–186.

Maia, Belinda (2003). "'Some Languages Are More Equal Than Others': Training Translators in Terminology and Information Retrieval Using Comparable and Parallel Corpora." In Federico Zanettin, Silvia Bernardini, and Dominic Stewart, eds., *Corpora in Translator Education*. Manchester: St. Jerome Publishing, pp. 43–53.

Malmkjær, Kirsten (1998). "Love Thy Neighbour: Will Parallel Corpora Endear Linguists to Translators?" *Meta*, Vol. 43, No. 4, pp. 532–541.

Martin, Joel, Howard Johnson, Benoit Farley, and Anna Maclachlan (2003). "Aligning and Using an English-Inuktitut Parallel Corpus." *Proceedings of the Human Language Technology and North American Chapter of Association of Computational Linguistics 2003* (*HLT/NAACL-2003*), Edmonton, Alberta, Canada.

Matsumoto, Yuji and Mihoko Kitamura (1995). "Acquisition of Translation Rules from Parallel Corpora." In Nicolas Nicolov and Ruslan Mitkov, eds., *Recent Advances in Natural Language Processing: Selected Papers from the Conference*. Amsterdam and Philadelphia: John Benjamins Publishing Company, pp. 405–416.

Meyers, Adam, Roman Yangarber, and Ralph Grishman (1996). "Alignment of Shared Forests for Bilingual Corpora." *Proceedings from the 16th International Conference on Computational Linguistics* (*COLING-96*), Copenhagen, Denmark, pp. 460–465.

Nevado, Francisco, Francisco Casacuberta, and Enrique Vidal (2003). "Parallel Corpora Segmentation Using Anchor Words." *Proceedings of the 7th Workshop of the European Association for Machine Translation: Improving Machine Translation through Other Language Technology Tools: Resources and Tools for Building MT*, Budapest, Hungary, pp. 33–40.

Nightingale, Stephen and Hideki Tanaka (2003). "The Word is Mightier Than the Count: Accumulating Translation Resources from Parsed Parallel Corpora." *Proceedings of the 4th International Conference on Intelligent Text Processing and Computational Linguistics* (*CICLing-2003*), Mexico City, Mexico, pp. 422–433.

Olohan, Maeve (2004). "Parallel Corpora." *Introducing Corpora in Translation Studies*. London and New York: Routledge, pp. 24–34.

Papageorgiou, Harris, Lambros Cranias, and Stelios Piperidis (1994). "Automatic Alignment in Parallel Corpora." *Proceedings of the 32nd Annual Meeting of the Association for Computational Linguistics* (*ACL-94*), Las Cruces, New Mexico, USA, pp. 334–336.

Peters, Carol, Eugenio Picchi, and Lisa Biagini (2000). "Parallel and Comparable Bilingual Corpora in Language Teaching and Learning." In Simon Philip Botley, Anthony Mark McEnery, and Andrew Wilson, eds., *Multilingual Corpora in Teaching and Research*. Amsterdam: Rodopi, pp. 73–85.

Resnik, Philip, Mari B. Olsen, and Mona Diab (1997). "Creating a Parallel Corpus from the Book of 2000 Tongues." *Proceedings of the TEI* (*Text Encoding Initiative*) *10th Anniversary User Conference*, Brown University Providence, Rhode Island, USA.

Resnik, Philip (1998). "Parallel Strands: A Preliminary Investigation into Mining the Web for Bilingual Text." In David L. Farwell, Laurie Gerber, and Eduard Hovy, eds., *Machine Translation and the Information Soup*. Berlin: Springer Verlag, pp. 72–82.

Resnik, Philip and Noah A. Smith (2003). "The Web as a Parallel Corpus." *Computational Linguistics*, Vol. 29, No. 3, pp. 349–380.

Teubert, Wolfgang (1996). "Comparable or Parallel Corpora?" *International Journal of Lexicography*, Vol. 9, No. 3, pp. 238–264.

Teubert, Wolfgang (2002). "The Role of Parallel Corpora in Translation and Multilingual Lexicography." In Bengt Altenberg and Sylvian Granger, eds., *Lexis in Contrast: Corpus-based Approaches*. Amsterdam and Philadelphia: John Benjamins Publishing Company, pp. 189–214.

Váradi, Tamás (2005). "NP Modification Structures in Parallel Corpora." In Krisztina Károly and Ágota Fóris, eds., *New Trends in Translation Studies: In Honour of Kinga Klaudy*. Budapest: Akadémiai Kiadó, pp. 191–206.

Vintar, Spela (2001). "Using Parallel Corpora for Translation-oriented Term Extraction." *Babel*, Vol. 47, No. 2, pp. 121–132.

Wu, Dekai (1994). "Aligning a Parallel English-Chinese Corpus Statistically with Lexical Criteria." *Proceedings of the 32nd Annual Meeting of the Association for Computational Linguistics* (*ACL-94*), Las Cruces, New Mexico, USA.

Wu, Dekai and Xuanyin Xia (1994). "Learning an English-Chinese Lexicon from a Parallel Corpus." *Proceedings of the 1st Conference of the Association for Machine Translation in the Americas: Technology Partnerships for Crossing the Language Barrier* (*AMTA-1*), Columbia, Maryland, USA, pp. 206–213.

Yamamoto, Kaoru and Yuji Matsumoto (2003). "Extracting Translation Knowledge from Parallel Corpora." In Michael Carl and Andy Way, eds., *Recent Advances in Example-based Machine Translation*. Dordrecht: Kluwer Academic Publishers, pp. 365–395.

Yamamoto, Kaoru, Taku Kudo, Yuta Tsuboi, and Yuji Matsumoto (2003). "Learning Sequence-to-sequence Correspondences from Parallel Corpora via Sequential Pattern Mining." *Proceedings of the Human Language Technology and North American Chapter of Association of Computational Linguistics 2003* (*HLT/NAACL-2003*), Edmonton, Alberta, Canada.

Zanettin, Federico (2000). "Parallel Corpora in Translation Studies: Issues in Corpus Design and Analysis." In Maeve Olohan, ed., *Intercultural Faultlines: Research Models in Translation Studies I: Textual and Cognitive Aspects*. Manchester: St. Jerome Publishing, pp. 105–118.

Semantic Corpus

Hovy, Eduard (2006). "Toward Semantic Corpora: Creating Concepts from Words via Senses, and Storing them in an Ontology." *Proceedings of the 7th International Conference on Intelligent Text Processing and Computational Linguistics* (*CICLing-2006*), Mexico City, Mexico.

Speech Corpus

Alabau, Vicente and Carlos D. Martínez (2006). "Bilingual Speech Corpus in Two Phonetically Similar Languages." *Proceedings of the 5th International Conference on Language Resources and Evaluation* (*LREC-2006*), Genoa, Italy.

Asanoma, Naoki, Setsuo Yamada, Osamu Furuse, and Masahiro Oku (2005). "Building a Conversation Corpus by Text Derivation from 'Germ Dialogs'." *Proceedings of the 10th Workshop of the European Association for Machine Translation: Practical Applications of Machine Translation*, Budapest, Hungary, pp. 27–32.
Chiari, Isabella (2006). "Slips and Errors in Spoken Data Transcription." *Proceedings of the 5th International Conference on Language Resources and Evaluation* (*LREC-2006*), Genoa, Italy.
Cho, She-Yeong, Sang-Hun Kim, Jun Park, and Young-Jik Lee (2004). "Overcoming the Sparseness Problem of Spoken Language Corpora Using Other Large Corpora of Distinct Characteristics." *Proceedings of the 5th International Conference on Intelligent Text Processing and Computational Linguistics* (*CICLing-2004*), Chung-Ang University, Seoul, Korea, pp. 402–405.
Grønnum, Nina (2006). "DanPASS—A Danish Phonetically Annotated Spontaneous Speech Corpus." *Proceedings of the 5th International Conference on Language Resources and Evaluation* (*LREC-2006*), Genoa, Italy.
Itahashi, Shuichi, Hisao Kuwabara, Yong-Ju Lee, Dawa Idomuso, and Hsiao-Chuan Wang (2002). "Recent Activities on Speech Corpora and Assessment in East Asia." In Yu Shiwen, ed., *Proceedings of the 2nd China-Japan Natural Language Processing Joint Research Promotion Conference* (*CJNLP-2002*). Beijing: Institute of Computational Linguistics, Peking University, pp. 17–22.
Kogure, Kiyoshi, Hitoshi Iida, Kei Yoshimoto, Hiroyuki Maeda, Masako Kume, and Susumu Kato (1988). "A Method of Analyzing Japanese Speech Act Types." *Proceedings of the 2nd International Conference on Theoretical and Methodological Issues in Machine Translation of Natural Languages* (*TMI-88*), Carnegie Mellon University, Center for Machine Translation, Pittsburgh, Pennsylvania, USA.
Kuwabara, Hisao, Koichi Takeda, Y. Sagisaka, S. Katagiri, S. Morikawa, and Taro Watanabe (1989). "Construction of a Large-scale Japanese Speech Database and Its Management System." *Proceedings of IEEE International Conference on Acoustics, Speech and Signal Processing* (*ICASSP-89*), Glasgow, Scotland, pp. 560–563.
Lo, Wai Kit, Pak Chung Ching, Tan Lee, and Helen Meng (2001). "Design, Compilation and Processing of CUCall: A Set of Cantonese Spoken Language Corpora Collected over Telephone Networks."

Proceedings of the International Conference on Research in Computational Linguistics (*ROCLING-XIV*), National Chengkung University, Tainan, Taiwan.

Ozaku, Hiromi Itoh, Akinori Abe, Kaoru Sagara, Noriaki Kuwahara, and Kiyoshi Kogure (2006). "A Task Analysis of Nursing Activities Using Spoken Corpora." In Alexander F. Gelbukh, ed., *Advances in Natural Language Processing*, Special Issue of *Research in Computing Science*, No. 18, pp. 125–138.

Patil, Hemant A. and T. K. Basu (2004). "Designing Speech Corpus for Twin Identification Experiments in Marathi." *Proceedings of the International Conference on Natural Language Processing* (*ICON-2004*), International Institute of Information Technology, Hyderabad, India.

Stöber, Karlheinz, Petra Wagner, Jörg Helbig, Stefanie Köster, David Stall, Matthias Thomae, Jen Blauert, Wolfgang Hess, Rüdiger Hoffmann, and Helmut Mangold (2000). "Speech Synthesis Using Multilevel Selection and Concatenation of Units from Large Speech Corpora." In Wolfgang Wahlster, ed., *Verbmobil: Foundations of Speech-to-speech Translation*. Berlin: Springer Verlag, pp. 519–534.

Tomokiyo, Mutsuko and Gérard Chollet (2005). "VoiceUNL: A Semantic Representation of Emotions within Universal Networking Language Formalism Based on a Dialogue Corpus Analysis." *Proceedings of the 6th International Conference on Intelligent Text Processing and Computational Linguistics* (*CICLing-2005*), Mexico City, Mexico, pp. 430–440.

Tsuge, Satoru, Masami Shishibori, Fuji Ren, Kenji Kita, and Shingo Kuroiwa (2006). "Specific Speaker's Japanese Speech Corpus over Long and Short Time Periods." In Alexander F. Gelbukh, ed., *Advances in Natural Language Processing*, Special Issue of *Research in Computing Science*, No. 18, pp. 115–124.

Villaseñor-Pineda, Luis, Manuel Montes-y-Gómez, Dominique Vaufreydaz, Jean-François Serignat (2004). "Experiments on the Construction of a Phonetically Balanced Corpus from the Web." *Proceedings of the 5th International Conference on Intelligent Text Processing and Computational Linguistics* (*CICLing-2004*), Chung-Ang University, Seoul, Korea, pp. 410–413.

Xia, Yunqing, Kam-Fai Wong, and Wenjie Li (2006). "Constructing a Chinese Chat Language Corpus with a Two-stage Incremental

Annotation Approach." *Proceedings of the 5th International Conference on Language Resources and Evaluation* (*LREC-2006*), Genoa, Italy.

Text Corpus

Cachey, Theodore Jr. and Mark Olsen (1987). "Textbase and Translation: The Repertorium Columbianum." *Computers and Translation*, Vol. 2, No. 3, pp. 159–161.

Translation Corpus

Ahrenberg, Lars and Magnus Merkel (1996). "On Translation Corpora and Translation Support Tools: A Project Report." In Karin Aijmer, Bengt Alterberg, and Mats Johansson, eds., *Languages in Contrast*. Lund: Lund University Press, pp. 183–200.
Ebeling, Jarle and Signe Oksefjell (1998). "On the Translation of English There-sentences into Norwegian and Portuguese: What Does a Translation Corpus Tell Us?" In Jo Terje Ydstie and Anne C. Wollebaek, eds., *Working Papers in Applied Linguistics, 4/98*. Oslo: Department of Linguistics, Faculty of Arts, University of Oslo, pp. 188–206.
Ebeling, Jarle (1998). "The Translation Corpus Explorer: A Browser for Parallel Texts." In Stig Johansson and Signe Oksefjell, eds., *Corpora and Cross-linguistic Research*. Amsterdam and Altanta, GA: Rodopi, pp. 101–112.
Ebeling, Jarle (1998). "Using the Translations to Explore Construction Meaning in English and Norwegian." In Stig Johansson and Signe Oksefjell, eds., *Corpora and Cross-linguistic Research*. Amsterdam and Altanta, GA: Rodopi, pp. 169–195.
Halverson, Sandra (1998). "Translations Studies and Representative Corpora: Establishing Links between Translation Corpora, Theoretical/Descriptive Categories and a Conception of the Object of Study." *Meta*, Vol. 43, No. 4, pp. 494–514.
Hansen, Silvia and Elke Teich (2002). "The Creation and Exploitation of a Translation Reference Corpus." *Proceedings of LREC 2002 Workshop: Language Resources and Translation Work and Research*, Las Palmas, Canary Islands, Spain, pp. 1–4.

Hansen-Schirra, Silvia, Stella Neumann, and Mihaela Vela (2006). "Multidimensional Annotation and Alignment in an English-German Translation Corpus." *Proceedings of the 11th Conference of the European Chapter of the Association for Computational Linguistics* (*EACL-2006*), Trento, Italy.

Hofland, Knut and Stig Johansson (1998). "The Translation Corpus Aligner: A Program for Automatic Alignment of Parallel Texts." In Stig Johansson and Signe Oksefjell, eds., *Corpora and Cross-linguistic Research: Theory, Method, and Case Studies*. Amsterdam and Atlanta: Rodopi, pp. 87–100.

Hwa, Rebecca, Carol Nichols, and Khalil Sima'an (2006). "Corpus Variations for Translation Lexicon Induction." *Proceedings of the 7th Biennial Conference of the Association for Machine Translation in the Americas (AMTA-2006): Visions for the Future of Machine Translation*, Boston Marriott, Cambridge, MA, USA.

Saridakis, Ioannis E. and Georgia Kostopoulou (2004). "Exploitation of Computer Text Corpora in the Teaching of Technical Translation." *Proceedings of the International Conference on Translating with Computer-assisted Technology: Changes in Research, Teaching, Evaluation and Practice*, Rome, Italy.

Schmied, Josef (2002). "A Translation Corpus as a Resource for Translators: The Case of English and German Prepositions." In Belinda Maia, ed., *Translators as Service Providers*. Porto: Universidad de Porto, pp. 251–269.

Véronis, Jean (2000). *Parallel Text Processing: Alignment and Use of Translation Corpora*. Dordrecht: Kluwer Academic Publishers.

Web Corpus

Baroni, Marco and Adam Kilgarriff (2006). "Large linguistically-processed Web Corpora for Multiple Languages." *Proceedings of the 11th Conference of the European Chapter of the Association for Computational Linguistics* (*EACL-2006*), Trento, Italy.

Boleda, Gemma, Stefan Bott, Rodrigo Meza, Carlos Castillo, Toni Badia, and Vicente López (2006). "CUC Web: A Catalan Corpus Built from the Web." *Proceedings of the 11th Conference of the European Chapter of the Association for Computational Linguistics* (*EACL-2006*), Trento, Italy.

Cheng, Pu-Jen, Lu Wen-Hsiang, Teng Jei-Wen, and Chien Lee-Feng (2004). "Creating Multilingual Translation Lexicons with Regional Variations Using Web Corpora." *Proceedings of the 42nd Annual Meeting of the Association for Computational Linguistics* (*ACL-2004*), Barcelona, Spain, pp. 534–541.

Ciaramita, Massimiliano and Marco Baroni (2006). "A Figure of Merit for the Evaluation of Web-corpus Randomness." *Proceedings of the 11th Conference of the European Chapter of the Association for Computational Linguistics* (*EACL-2006*), Trento, Italy.

Gleim, Rüdiger, Alexander Mehler, and Matthias Dehmer (2006). "Web Corpus Mining by Instance of Wikipedia." *Proceedings of the 11th Conference of the European Chapter of the Association for Computational Linguistics* (*EACL-2006*), Trento, Italy.

Kornai, András, Péter Halácsy, Viktor Nagy, Csaba Oravecz, Viktor Trón, and Dániel Varga (2006). "Web-based Frequency Dictionaries for Medium Density Languages." *Proceedings of the 11th Conference of the European Chapter of the Association for Computational Linguistics* (*EACL-2006*), Trento, Italy.

Liu, Vinci and James R. Curran (2006). "Web Text Corpus for Natural Language Processing." *Proceedings of the 11th Conference of the European Chapter of the Association for Computational Linguistics* (*EACL-2006*), Trento, Italy.

Rayson, Paul, James Walkerdine, William H. Fletcher, and Adam Kilgarriff (2006). "Annotated Web as Corpus." *Proceedings of the 11th Conference of the European Chapter of the Association for Computational Linguistics* (*EACL-2006*), Trento, Italy.

Ringlstetter, Christoph, Klaus U. Schulz, and Stoyan Mihov (2006). "Orthographic Errors in Web Pages: Toward Cleaner Web Corpora." *Computational Linguistics*, Vol. 32, No. 3, pp. 295–340.

Sethy, Abhinav, Panayiotis Georgiou, and Shrikanth Narayanan (2006). "Selecting Relevant Text Subsets from Web-data for Building Topic Specific Language Models." *Proceedings of the Human Language Technology Conference—Annual Meeting of the North American Chapter of the Association for Computational Linguistics* (*HLT-NAACL-2006*), New York, USA.

Tonoike, Masatsugu, Mitsuhiro Kida, Toshihiro Takagi, Yasuhiro Sasaki, Takehito Utsuro, and Satoshi Sato (2006). "A Comparative Study on Compositional Translation Estimation Using a Domain/Topic-specific

Corpus Collected from the Web." *Proceedings of the 11th Conference of the European Chapter of the Association for Computational Linguistics* (*EACL-2006*), Trento, Italy.

Villaseñor-Pineda, Luis, Manuel Montes-y-Gómez, Dominique Vaufreydaz, and Jean-François Serignat (2004). "Experiments on the Construction of a Phonetically Balanced Corpus from the Web." *Proceedings of the 5th International Conference on Intelligent Text Processing and Computational Linguistics* (*CICLing-2004*), Chung-Ang University, Seoul, Korea, pp. 410–413.

Zuraw, Kie (2006). "Using the Web as a Phonological Corpus: A Case Study from Tagalog." *Proceedings of the 11th Conference of the European Chapter of the Association for Computational Linguistics* (*EACL-2006*), Trento, Italy.

Data

Data Bank

Bowker, Lynne (2002). "Capturing Data in Electronic Form." *Computer-aided Translation Technology: A Practical Introduction*. Ottawa: University of Ottawa Press, pp. 22–42.

Kasper, Walter (2000). "Multilingual Semantic Databases." In Wolfgang Wahlster, ed., *Verbmobil: Foundations of Speech-to-speech Translation*. Berlin: Springer Verlag, pp. 348–356.

Su, Keh-Yih 蘇克毅, Mei-Hui Su 蘇美惠, and Li-Mei Kuan 關麗美 (1989). "Smoothing Statistic Databases in a Machine Translation System." *Proceedings of the Conference of the Association for Computational Linguistics and Chinese Language Processing* (*ROCLING-II*), Taipei, Taiwan.

Vaumoron, Jean A. (1987). "Two-level Data Banks for Translators." *Computers and Translation*, Vol. 2, No. 4, pp. 275–280.

Data Collection

Jekat, Susanne J. and Walther van Hahn (2000). "Multilingual Verbmobil-Dialogs: Experiments, Data Collection and Data Analysis." In Wolfgang Wahlster, ed., *Verbmobil: Foundations of Speech-to-speech Translation*. Berlin: Springer Verlag, pp. 575–582.

Data Management

He, Tingting 何婷婷 (2002). 〈語料庫的數據管理方式的研究〉 (A Study on Data Management of Corpus). 《第一屆學生計算語言學研討會論文集》 (*SWCL2002: First Students' Workshop on Computational Linguistics: Proceedings*), Institute of Computational Linguistics, Peking University, Beijing, China, pp. 306–311.

Keller, Frank, Maria Lapata, and Olga Ourioupina (2002). "Using the Web to Overcome Data Sparseness." *Proceedings of the 2002 Conference on Empirical Methods in Natural Language Processing* (*EMNLP-2002*), University of Pennsylvania, Philadelphia, PA, USA.

Data Processing

Dorstert, Leon E. (1963). "Machine Translation and Automatic Language Data Processing." In Paul William Howerton and David C. Weeks, eds., *Vistas in Information Handling: The Augmentation of Man's Intellect by Machine*, Vol. 1. Washington, DC: Spartan Books, pp. 92–110.

Feng, Zhiwei (1988). *Analysis of Formation of Chinese Terms in Data Processing*. Research Report in Fraunhofer Institute, Stuttgart.

Garvin, Paul L. (1985). "The Current State of Language Data Processing." *Advances in Computers*, Vol. 24, pp. 217–275.

Krollmann, Friedrich (1974). "Data Processing at the Translator's Service." *Babel*, Vol. 20, No. 3, pp. 121–129.

Kwan, Peter (1995). "Unicode—Implications for the Translator." In *Translating and the Computer 17*. London: The Association for Information Management.

Tanke, Eberhard (1975). "Electronic Data Processing in the Service of Translators, Terminologists, and Lexicographers." *Philips Terminology Bulletin*, Vol. 4, Nos. 2–3, pp. 3–19.

Dictionary

Bilingual Dictionary

Chan, Sin-wai (2004). *Translation and Bilingual Dictionaries*. Tubingen: Max Niemeyer Verlag.

Corréard, Marie Hélène (1995). "A Corpus-based Bilingual Dictionary: Why and How?" *Machine Translation Review*, No. 2, pp. 25–26.

Derouin, Marie-Jeanne and André Le Meur (2006). "Integrated Bilingual

Specialist Dictionaries—LexTerm Initiative." In *Translating and the Computer 28*. London: The Association for Information Management.

Gliozzo, Alfio and Carlo Strapparava (2006). "Exploiting Comparable Corpora and Bilingual Dictionaries for Cross-language Text Categorization." *Proceedings of the Joint Conference of the International Committee on Computational Linguistics and the Association for Computational Linguistics (COLING/ACL-2006)*, Sydney, Australia.

Kutsumi, Takeshi, Takehiko Yoshimi, Katsunori Kotani, Ichiko Sata, and Hitoshi Isahara (2005). "Selection of Entries for a Bilingual Dictionary from Aligned Translation Equivalents Using Support Vector Machines." *Proceedings of MT Summit X*, Phuket, Thailand.

Nagata, Masaaki, Teruka Saito, and Kenji Suzuki (2001). "Using the Web as a Bilingual Dictionary." *Proceedings of the Association for Computational Linguistics 39th Annual Meeting and 10th Conference of the European Chapter: Data-driven Machine Translation (ACL-EACL-2001)*, Toulouse, France, pp. 95–102.

Nygård, Lars, Jan Tore Lønning, Torbjørn Nordgård, and Stephan Oepen (2006). "Using a Bi-lingual Dictionary in Lexical Transfer." *Proceedings of the 11th Workshop of the European Association for Machine Translation: Machine Translation/Translation Aids—Tools to Increase Quality and to Save Money*, the University of Oslo, Oslo, Norway.

Okumura, Akitoshi and Eduard Hovy (1994). "Lexicon-to-ontology Concept Association Using a Bilingual Dictionary." *Proceedings of the 1st Conference of the Association for Machine Translation in the Americas: Technology Partnerships for Crossing the Language Barrier (AMTA-1)*, Columbia, Maryland, USA, pp. 177–184.

Pinkham, Jesse and Martine Smets (2002). "Machine Translation without a Bilingual Dictionary." *Proceedings of the 9th International Conference on Theoretical and Methodological Issues in Machine Translation (TMI-2002)*, Keihanna, Japan, pp. 146–156.

Dictionary

Agirre, Eneko, Xabier Arregi, Xabier Artola, Arantza Díaz de Ilarraza, Kepa Sarasola, and Aitor Soroa (2000). "A Methodology for Building Translator-oriented Dictionary Systems." *Machine Translation*, Vol. 15, No. 3, pp. 295–310.

Andrezen, Vladimir, Leonid Kogan, Wladimir Kwiatkowski, Rinat Minvaleev, Rajmund Piotrowski, Vladislav Shumovsky, Elena Tioun, and Yurij Tovmach (1992). "Automatic Dictionary Organization in NLP Systems for Oriental Languages." *Proceedings of the 14th International Conference of Computational Linguistics* (*COLING-92*), Nantes, France, pp. 505–509.

Arnold, Doug J., Lorna Balkan, R. Lee Humphreys, Seity Meijer, and Louisa Sadler (1994). "Dictionaries." *Machine Translation: An Introductory Guide*. Manchester and Oxford: NCC Blackwell, pp. 87–110.

Booth, Andrew D. (1955). "Use of a Computing Machine as a Mechanical Dictionary." *Nature*, No. 176, p. 565.

Chang, Jason S., Sue J. Ker, and Mathis H. Chen (1998). "Taxonomy and Lexical Semantics—From the Perspective of Machine Readable Dictionary." In David L. Farwell, Laurie Gerber, and Eduard Hovy, eds., *Machine Translation and the Information Soup*. Berlin: Springer Verlag, pp. 199–212.

Dillinger, Mike (2001). "Dictionary Development Workflow for MT: Design and Management." In Bente Maegaard, ed., *Proceedings of MT Summit VIII: Machine Translation in the Information Age*, Santiago de Compostela, Spain.

Dorr, Bonnie J. (1997). "Large-scale Dictionary Construction for Foreign Language Tutoring and Interlingual Machine Translation." *Machine Translation*, Vol. 12, No. 4, pp. 271–322.

Dorr, Bonnie J., Joseph Garman, and Amy Weinberg (1995). "From Syntactic Encodings to Thematic Roles: Building Lexical Entries for Interlingual MT." *Machine Translation*, Vol. 9, Nos. 3–4, pp. 221–250.

Feng, Zhiwei 馮志偉 (2004).〈機器翻譯的詞典〉(Dictionaries in Machine Translation).《機器翻譯研究》(*Studies on Machine Translation*). Beijing: China Translation and Publishing Corporation, pp. 702–749.

Fung, Pascale and Wu Dekai (1994). "Statistical Augmentation of a Chinese Machine-readable Dictionary." *Proceedings of the 2nd Annual Workshop on Very Large Corpora* (*WVLC-2*), Kyoto, Japan, pp. 69–85.

Fung, Pascale and Wu Dekai (1999). "Statistical Augmentation of a Chinese Machine-readable Dictionary." In Susan Armstrong, Kenneth W. Church, Pierre Isabelle, Sandra Manzi, Evelyne Tzoukermann, and David Yarowsky, eds., *Natural Language Processing Using Very Large Corpora*. Dordrecht: Kluwer Academic Publishers, pp. 137–155.

Gelbukh, Alexander F. and Grigori Sidorov (2002). "Automatic Selection of Defining Vocabulary in an Explanatory Dictionary." *Proceedings of the 3rd International Conference on Intelligent Text Processing and Computational Linguistics* (*CICLing-2002*), Mexico City, Mexico.

Gelbukh, Alexander F., Grigori Sidorov, and Yoel Ledo-Mezquita (2003). "On Similarity of Word Senses in Explanatory Dictionaries." *International Journal of Translation*, Vol. 15, No. 2, pp. 51–60.

Guralink, Benjamin (2002). "The Multi-purpose Dictionary Experiment." *International Journal of Translation*, Vol. 14, No. 2, pp. 121–125.

Harper, Kenneth E. (1963). "Dictionary Problems in Machine Translation." In Paul L. Garvin, ed., *Natural Language and the Computer*. New York: McGraw-Hill, pp. 215–222.

Heid, Ulrich (1995). "Relating Parallel Monolingual Lexicon Fragments for Translation Purposes." In Petra Steffens, ed., *Machine Translation and the Lexicon*. Berlin: Springer Verlag, pp. 231–251.

Ide, Nancy and Jean Véronis (1995). "Knowledge Extraction from Machine-readable Dictionaries: An Evaluation." In Petra Steffens, ed., *Machine Translation and the Lexicon*. Berlin: Springer Verlag, pp. 19–34.

Jelinek, J. and J. Hawgood (1984). "Automatic Integrated Dictionary Systems." *Proceedings of the International Conference on the Methodology and Techniques of Machine Translation*, Cranfield Institute of Technology, Cranfield, England.

Kamei, Shin-ichiro, Etsuo Itoh, Mikiko Fujii, Tokuyuki Hirai, Yukari Saitoh, Masahito Takahashi, Tsutomu Hiyama, and Kazunori Muraki (1997). "Sharable Formats and Their Supporting Environments for Exchanging User Dictionaries among Different MT Systems as a Part of AAMT Activities." *Proceedings of MT Summit VI*, San Diego, California, USA.

Kim, Yuseop, Byoung-Tak Zhang, and Yung Taek Kim (2001). "Collocation Dictionary Optimization Using WordNet and K-Nearest Neighbor Learning." *Machine Translation*, Vol. 16, No. 2, pp. 89–108.

Kirschner, Zdeněk (1982). "On a Device in Dictionary Operations in Machine Translation." In Jan Horecky, ed., *Proceedings of the 9th International Conference on Computational Linguistics* (*COLING-82*), Prague, the Czech Republic. Amsterdam: North-Holland Publishing Company, pp. 157–160.

Klavans, Judith and Evelyne Tzoukermann (1995). "Combining Corpus and Machine-readable Dictionary Data for Building Bilingual Lexicons." *Machine Translation*, Vol. 10, No. 3, pp. 185–218.

Knowles, Francis E. (1982). "The Pivotal Role of the Various Dictionaries in an MT System." In Veronica Lawson, ed., *Practical Experience of Machine Translation*. Amsterdam: North-Holland Publishing Company, pp. 149–162.

Kukulska-Hulme, Agnes (1990). "Subject Knowledge in Computerised Dictionaries." In Marcel Thelen and Barbara Leeandowska-Tomaszczyk, eds., *Translation and Meaning, Part 1*. Maastricht: Euroterm, pp. 48–56.

Kumano, Akira and Hideki Hirakawa (1994). "Building an MT Dictionary from Parallel Texts Based on Linguistic and Statistical Information." *Proceedings of the 15th International Conference on Computational Linguistics (COLING-94)*, Kyoto, Japan, pp. 76–81.

Kursin, Andrei and Ivan Trufanov (2002). "Web Mining for MT Dictionary Acquisition." *International Journal of Translation*, Vol. 14, No. 2, pp. 117–120.

Lamb, Sydney M. and William C. Jacobsen (1961). "A High-speed Large-capacity Dictionary System." *Mechanical Translation*, Vol. 6, pp. 76–107.

Livbjerg, Inge and I. M. Mees (2003). "Patterns of Dictionary Use in Non-domain-specific Translation." In F. Alves, ed., *Triangulating Translation*. Amsterdam and Philadelphia: John Benjamins Publishing Company, pp. 123–136.

Liu, Zhijie 劉志傑 and Liu Zhuo 劉倬 (1997).〈英漢機器翻譯系統中基本詞典與專業詞典的關係〉(The Relationship between the General Dictionary and Special Dictionary in English-Chinese Machine Translation Systems).《語言文字應用》(*Applied Linguistics*), No. 3, pp. 105–108.

Loh, Siu-chang, Kong Luen, and H. S. Hung (1984). "A New Dictionary Structure for Bi-directional MT System." *Proceedings of the International Seminar on Machine Translation*, Cranfield Institute of Technology, Cranfield, England.

Mackintosh, Kristen (1998). "An Empirical Study of Dictionary Use in L2-L1 Translation." In B. T. Sue Atkins, ed., *Using Dictionaries*. Tübingen: Max Niemeyer Verlag, pp. 123–149.

Maes, Jean-Marie (1990). "The Intelligent Dictionary Project." In Marcel Thelen and Barbara Leeandowska-Tomaszczyk, eds., *Translation and Meaning, Part 1*. Maastricht: Euroterm, pp. 57–69.

Marcuk, Jurij N. (1979). "The Contextological Dictionary: Use in Programmed Language Teaching." *Computers and the Humanities*, Vol. 13, pp. 277–281.

Meyer, Ingrid (1990). "Interlingual Meaning-text Lexicography: Towards a New Type of Dictionary for Translation." In James Steele, ed., *The Meaning-text Theory of Language: Linguistics, Lexicography, and Practical Implications*. Ottawa: University of Ottawa Press, pp. 175–190.

Michklesen, Lew R. (1962). "Source-language Specification with Table Lookup and High-capacity Dictionary." In National Physical Laboratory, ed., *1961 International Conference on Machine Translation of Languages and Applied Language Analysis: Proceedings of the Conference Held at the National Physical Laboratory, Teddington, Middlesex, on 5th, 6th, 7th and 8th September*. London: Her Majesty's Stationery Office, Vol. 1, pp. 318–340.

Nakayama, Keisuke and Akira Kumano (1999). "Collection of Dictionary Data through Internet Translation Service." *Proceedings of MT Summit VII: MT in the Great Translation Era*, Singapore.

Nastase, Vivi and Stan Szpakowicz (2003). "Augmenting WordNet's Structure Using LDOCE." *Proceedings of the 4th International Conference on Intelligent Text Processing and Computational Linguistics* (*CICLing-2003*), Mexico City, Mexico, pp. 283–296.

Neff, Mary S. and Michael C. McCord (1990). "Acquiring Lexical Data from Machine-readable Dictionary Resources for Machine Translation." *Proceedings of the 3rd International Conference on Theoretical and Methodological Issues in Machine Translation* (*TMI-90*), Linguistics Research Center, University of Texas, Austin, Texas, USA, pp. 85–90.

Odijk, Jan, Harm Smit, and Petra de Wit (1994). "Dictionaries." In M. T. Rosetta, *Compositional Translation*. Dordrecht: Kluwer Academic Publishers, pp. 119–132.

Oettinger, Anthony G. (1955). "The Design of an Automatic Russian-English Technical Dictionary." In William N. Locke and Andrew D. Booth, eds., *Machine Translation of Languages: Fourteen Essays*. Cambridge, MA: Technology Press of the Massachusetts Institute of Technology, pp. 47–65.

Oettinger, Anthony G. (1958). "An Input Device for the Harvard Automatic Dictionary." *Mechanical Translation*, Vol. 5, No. 1, pp. 2–7.

Oettinger, Anthony G., William D. Foust, Vincent E. Giuliano, K. Magassy, and L. Matejka (1959). "Linguistic and Machine Methods for Compiling and Updating the Harvard Automatic Dictionary." *Proceedings of the International Conference on Scientific Information*. Washington, DC: National Academy of Sciences, pp. 951–973.

Ostler, Nicholas (1995). "Perception Vocabulary in Five Languages—Towards an Analysis Using Frame Elements." In Petra Steffens, ed., *Machine Translation and the Lexicon*. Berlin: Springer Verlag, pp. 219–230.

Pala, Karel and Eva Mráková (2003). "Building Consistent Dictionary Definitions." *Proceedings of the 4th International Conference on Intelligent Text Processing and Computational Linguistics* (*CICLing-2003*), Mexico City, Mexico, pp. 297–305.

Phillips, Jeremy (1990). "Copyright, Computers, Dictionaries, and Translations." In Catriona Picken, ed., *Translating and the Computer 11: Preparing for the Next Decade*. London: The Association for Information Management, pp. 59–62.

Piotrowski, Rajmund, Yuri Romanov, Yuri Tavomach, Natalia Zaitseva, and Michael S. Blekhman (2001). "Dictionary Organization in Linguistic Automation for Oriental Languages." *International Journal of Translation*, Vol. 13, Nos. 1–2, pp. 105–118.

Probst, Katharina (2003). "Using 'Smart' Bilingual Projection to Feature-tag a Monolingual Dictionary." *Proceedings of the 7th Conference on Natural Language Learning*, Edmonton, Canada, pp. 103–110.

Procter, Paul (1995). "The Cambridge Language Survey." In Petra Steffens, ed., *Machine Translation and the Lexicon*. Berlin: Springer Verlag, pp. 77–84.

Roberts, Roda P. (1992). "Translation Pedagogy: Strategies for Improving Dictionary Use." *TTR*, Vol. 5, No. 1, pp. 49–76.

Roberts, Roda P. (1997). "Using Dictionaries Efficiently." *Proceedings of the 38th Annual Meeting of the American Translators Association (ACL-97)*, San Francisco, California, USA.

Sánchez Ramos, María del Mar (2005). "Research on Dictionary Use by Trainee Translators." *Translation Journal*, Vol. 9, No. 2.

Storrer, Angelika and Ulrike Schwall (1995). "Description and Acquisition of Multiword Lexemes." In Petra Steffens, ed., *Machine Translation and the Lexicon*. Berlin: Springer Verlag, pp. 35–50.

Tronevych, Olena, Eugene Korshykov, and Andrei Kursin (2001).

"Developing an English-Chinese Dictionary of Proper Names." *International Journal of Translation*, Vol. 13, Nos. 1–2, pp. 205–208.

Varantola, Krista (1998). "Translators and Their Use of Dictionaries." In B. T. Sue Atkins, ed., *Using Dictionaries*. Tübingen: Max Niemeyer Verlag, pp. 179–192.

Wachowicz, Krystyna (1986). "On Intelligent Dictionaries." *Computers and Translation*, Vol. 1, No. 4, pp. 225–233.

Wang, Shufeng 王樹峰 and Zhang Yongkui 張永奎 (2002).〈基於英漢詞典和翻譯軟件的跨語言信息檢索實踐〉(An Experiment on English-Chinese Cross-language Information Retrieval Using Bilingual Dictionaries and Machine Translation Software).《第一屆學生計算語言學研討會論文集》(*SWCL2002: First Students' Workshop on Computational Linguistics: Proceedings*), Institute of Computational Linguistics, Peking University, Beijing, China, p. 151.

Wilks, Yorick, Dan Fass, Guo Cheng-ming, James E. McDonard, Tony Plate, and Brian M. Slator (1988). "Machine Tractable Dictionaries as Tools and Resources for Natural Language Processing." *Proceedings of the 12th International Conference on Computational Linguistics* (*COLING-88*), Budapest, Hungary, pp. 750–755.

Wilks, Yorick, Dan Fass, Guo Cheng-ming, James E. McDonald, Tony Plate, and Brian M. Slator (1990). "Providing Machine Tractable Dictionary Tools." *Machine Translation*, Vol. 5, No.2, pp. 99–154.

Wood, R. and L. Wright (1985). "More May Not Be Better—A Discussion Note on CAT Dictionaries." *Language Monthly*, Vol. 19, p. 6.

Yao, Zhaowei 姚兆煒 (1987).〈機器翻譯中英語詞典數值化初探〉(A Preliminary Exploration of the Ways of Digitization of English Vocabulary for MT).《中國翻譯》(*Chinese Translators Journal*), No. 5, pp. 27–32.

Electronic Dictionary

Breidt, Elisabeth and Helmut Feldweg (1997). "Accessing Foreign Languages with Compass." *Machine Translation*, Vol. 12, Nos. 1–2, pp. 153–174.

Calvo, Hiram and Alexander F. Gelbukh (2005). "Extracting WordNet-like Top Concepts from Machine Readable Explanatory Dictionaries." *International Journal of Translation*, pp. 87–95.

Canelli, Maria, Daniele Grasso, and Margaret King (2000). "Methods and

Metrics for the Evaluation of Dictation Systems: A Case Study." *Proceedings of the 2nd International Conference on Language Resources and Evaluation* (*LREC-2000*), Athens, Greece, pp. 1325–1331.
Chiba, Seibi (1993). "The Electronic Dictionary Project—Current Status and Future Plans." *Proceedings of MT Summit IV: International Cooperation for Global Communication*, Kobe, Japan, pp. 65–71.
Ferret, Olivier and Michael Zock (2006). "Enhancing Electronic Dictionaries with an Index Based on Associations." *Proceedings of the Joint Conference of the International Committee on Computational Linguistics and the Association for Computational Linguistics* (*COLING/ACL-2006*), Sydney, Australia.
Isabelle, Pierre (1988). "Electronic Dictionaries and Machine Translation Systems." *Proceedings of the International Symposium on Electronic Dictionaries* (*ISED-88*), Tokyo, Japan.
Ngan, Yuen Wan and Kong Wai Ping (1997). "The Effectiveness of Electronic Dictionaries as a Tool for Translators." *Babel*, Vol. 43, No. 2, pp. 151–165.
Takebayashi, Yoichi (1993). "EDR Electronic Dictionary." *Proceedings of MT Summit IV: International Cooperation for Global Communication*, Kobe, Japan, pp. 117–126.
Tanaka, Yasuhito (1995). "Maintenance of Machine-readable Dictionary." *Proceedings of the Conference of the Association for Computational Linguistics and Chinese Language Processing* (*ROCLING-VIII*), Yuan-Ze Institute of Technology, Chung-Li, Taiwan.
Uchida, Hiroshi (1990). "Electronic Dictionary." *Proceedings of International Workshop on Electronic Dictionaries*, Oiso, Kanagawa, Japan, pp. 23–42.
Yokoi, Toshio (1993). "From Electronic Dictionaries to Very Large-scale Knowledge Bases." *Proceedings of MT Summit IV: International Cooperation for Global Communication*, Kobe, Japan, pp. 47–62.

Translation Dictionary

Ahn, Kisuh and Matthew Frampton (2006). "Automatic Generation of Translation Dictionaries Using Intermediary Languages." *Proceedings of the 11th Conference of the European Chapter of the Association for Computational Linguistics* (*EACL-2006*), Trento, Italy.

❖ PART 11 ❖

Domains of Translation

Advertisement

Blench, Michael (2006). "Services Canada—Use of MT to Translate Online Job Listings." *Proceedings of the 7th Biennial Conference of the Association for Machine Translation in the Americas (AMTA-2006): Visions for the Future of Machine Translation*, Boston Marriott, Cambridge, MA, USA.

Somers, Harold L., Alex Rogers, Joakim Nivre, Annarosa Multari, Torbjorn Lager, Luca Gilardoni, Jeremy Ellman, and Bill Black (1997). "Multilingual Generation and Summarization of Job Adverts: The TREE Project." *Proceedings of the 5th Conference on Applied Natural Language Processing*, Seattle, Washington, DC, USA.

Appointment Scheduling

Busemann, Stephen, Thierry Declerck, Luca Dini, Judith Klein, and Sven Schmeier (1997). "Natural Language Dialog Service for Appointment Scheduling Agents." *Proceedings of the 5th Conference on Applied Natural Language Processing (ANLP-97)*, Seattle, Washington, DC, USA.

Bible, The

Allen, Jeff (2002). "The Bible as a Resource for Translation Software: A Proposal for Machine Translation (MT) Development Using an Untapped Language Resource Database." *Multilingual Computing and Technology*, Vol. 13, No. 7, pp. 40–45.

Beale, Stephen, Sergei Nirenburg, Marjorie McShane, and Tod Allman (2005). "Document Authoring the Bible for Minority Language Translation." *Proceedings of MT Summit X*, Phuket, Thailand.

Braille

Cleave, John P. (1955). "Braille Transcription and Mechanical Translation." *Mechanical Translation*, Vol. 2, No. 3, pp. 50–53.

Cleave, John P. (1956). "A Program for Braille Transcription." In Colin Cherry, ed., *Information Theory: Papers Read at a Symposium on Information Theory*. London: Butterworths, pp. 184–194.

Huang Heyan 黃河燕 and Chen Zhaoxiong 陳肇雄 (2002). 〈集成化盲文信息處理平台的總體設計及關鍵技術研究〉 (The Overall Design and Researches of Key Approaches for Integrated Chinese Braille Information Processing Platform). In Yu Shiwen, ed., *Proceedings of the 2nd China-Japan Natural Language Processing Joint Research Promotion Conference* (*CJNLP-2002*). Beijing: Institute of Computational Linguistics, Peking University, pp. 73–77.

Zhu, Xiaoyan 朱小燕 and Bao Ta 包塔 (2001). "EasyBraille: A Translation System for Mandarin and Braille." In Huang Changning 黃昌寧 and Zhang Pu 張普, eds., 《自然語言理解與機器翻譯》 (*Natural Language Understanding and Machine Translation*). Beijing: Tsinghua University Press, pp. 326–331.

Broadcasting

Ehara, Terumasa (2002). "Speech and Language Processing Technologies for Broadcasting Services." In Yu Shiwen, ed., *Proceedings of the 2nd China-Japan Natural Language Processing Joint Research Promotion Conference* (*CJNLP-2002*). Beijing: Institute of Computational Linguistics, Peking University, pp. 266–270.

Federico, Marcello, Nicola Bertoldi, and Vanessa Sandrini (2002). "Bootstrapping Named Entity Recognition for Italian Broadcast News." *Proceedings of the 2002 Conference on Empirical Methods in Natural Language Processing* (*EMNLP-2002*), University of Pennsylvania, Philadelphia, PA, USA.

Liu, Yang (2006). "Initial Study on Automatic Identification of Speaker Role in Broadcast News Speech." *Proceedings of the Human Language Technology Conference—Annual Meeting of the North American Chapter of the Association for Computational Linguistics* (*HLT-NAACL-2006*), New York, USA.

Nyberg, Eric H. and Teruko Mitamura (1997). "A Real-time MT System for Translating Broadcast Captions." *Proceedings of MT Summit VI*, San Diego, California, USA.

Rosenberg, Andrew and Julia Hirschberg (2006). "Story Segmentation of Broadcast News in English, Mandarin and Arabic." *Proceedings of the Human Language Technology Conference—Annual Meeting of the North American Chapter of the Association for Computational Linguistics* (*HLT-NAACL-2006*), New York, USA.

Business

Meer, Jaap van der (2003). "The Business Case for Machine Translation." In *Translating and the Computer 25*. London: The Association for Information Management.

O'Hagan, Minako (1996). "The Translation Business and the Impact of MT." *The Coming Industry of Teletranslation: Overcoming Communication Barriers through Telecommunication*. Clevedon: Multilingual Matters Ltd., pp. 14–39.

Schuh, Sarah (2006). "Technology in Translation Businesses: An Industry Opinion." *Proceedings of the 6th Portsmouth Translation Conference: Translation Technologies and Culture*, School of Languages and Area Studies, University of Portsmouth, England.

Caption

Czuba, Krzysztof (2000). "Efficient Parsing Strategies for Syntactic Analysis of Closed Captions." *Proceedings of the ANLP-NAACL-2000 Student Research Workshop*, Seattle, Washington, DC, USA, pp. 7–12.

Flanagan, Mary (2006). "Real-time Closed Caption Translation." *Proceedings of the 7th Biennial Conference of the Association for Machine Translation in the Americas (AMTA-2006): Visions for the Future of Machine Translation*, Boston Marriott, Cambridge, MA, USA.

Nybery, Eric H. and Teruko Mitamura (1997). "A Real-time MT System for Translating Broadcast Captions." *Proceedings of MT Summit VI*, San Diego, California, USA, pp. 51–57.

Popowich, Fred, Paul McFetridge, Davide Turcato, and Janine Toole (2000). "Machine Translation of Closed Captions." *Machine Translation*, Vol. 15, No. 4, pp. 311–341.

Seo, Young-Ae, Yoon-Hyung Roh, Ki-Young Lee, and Sung-Kwon Choi (2001). "Caption Eye/EK: A English-to-Korean Caption Translation System Using the Sentence Pattern." In Bente Maegaard, ed., *Proceedings of MT Summit VIII: Machine Translation in the Information Age*, Santiago de Compostella, Spain.

Toole, Janine, Davide Turcato, Fred Popowich, Dan Fass, and Paul McFetridge (1998). "Time-constrained Machine Translation." In David L. Farwell, Laurie Gerber, and Eduard Hovy, eds., *Machine*

Translation and the Information Soup. Berlin: Springer, pp. 103–112.
Turcato, Davide, Fred Popowich, Paul McFetridge, Devlan Nicholson, and Janine Toole (2000). "Pre-processing Closed Captions for Machine Translation." *Proceedings of the ANLP/NAACL-2000 Workshop on Embedded Machine Translation Systems—Volume 5*, Seattle, Washington, DC, USA, pp. 38–45.

Culture

Gerzymisch-Arbogast, Heidrun (1997). "Translating Cultural Specifics: Macro- and Microstructural Decisions." In Christa Hauenschild and Susanne Heizmann, eds., *Machine Translation and Translation Theory*. Berlin and New York: Mouton de Gruyter, pp. 51–67.
Khoutyz, Irina (2006). "Erasing Cultural Boundaries through Technology." *Proceedings of the 6th Portsmouth Translation Conference: Translation Technologies and Culture,* School of Languages and Area Studies, University of Portsmouth, England.

Domains

Alshawi, Hiyan, A. L. Buchbaum, and Fei Xia (1997). "A Comparison of Head Transducers and Transfer for a Limited Domain Translation Application." *Proceedings of the 35th Annual Meeting of the Association for Computational Linguistics and 8th Conference of the European Chapter of the Association for Computational Linguistics*, Madrid, Spain, pp. 360–365.
Bagga, Amit and Alan W. Biermann (1997). "Analyzing the Complexity of a Domain with Respect to an Information Extraction Task." *Proceedings of the International Conference on Research in Computational Linguistics* (*ROCLING-X*), Academia Sinica, Taipei, Taiwan.
Chandioux, John and Annette Grimaila (1996). "'Specialized' Machine Translation." *Proceedings of the 2nd Conference of the Association for Machine Translation in the Americas: Expanding MT Horizons* (*AMTA-2*), Montreal, Quebec, Canada, pp. 206–211.
Filatova, Elena, Vasileios Hatzivassiloglou, and Kathleen R. McKeown (2006). "Automatic Creation of Domain Templates." *Proceedings of*

the Joint Conference of the International Committee on Computational Linguistics and the Association for Computational Linguistics (COLING/ACL-2006), Sydney, Australia.

Hatanaka, Nobutoshi (1999). "Development of an Intranet MT System Adapting to Usage Domain." *Proceedings of MT Summit VII: MT in the Great Translation Era*, Singapore.

Jiménez, Victor M., Enrique Vidal, J. Oncina, Antonio Castellanos, H. Rulot, and J. A. Sánchez (1994). "Spoken-language Machine Translation in Limited-domain Tasks." In Heinrich Niemann, Renato de Mori, and Gerhard Hanrieder, eds., *Progress and Prospects of Speech Research and Technology*. Sankt Augustin: Infix, pp. 262–265.

Jung, Han-Min, Sanhwa Yuh, Chul-Min Sim, Taewan Kim, and Dong-I Park (1998). "A Domain Identifier Using Domain Keywords from Balanced Web Documents." *Proceedings of the 1st International Conference on Language Resources and Evaluation*, Granada, Spain.

Lange, Elke D. and Yang Jin (1999). "Automatic Domain Recognition for Machine Translation." *Proceedings of MT Summit VII: MT in the Great Translation Era*, Singapore.

Lehtola, Aarno, Jarno Tenni, and Tuula Käpylä (2003). "Multilingual Cataloguing of Product Information of Specific Domains: Case Mkbeem System." *Proceedings of the Joint Conference Combining the 8th International Workshop of the European Association for Machine Translation and the 4th Controlled Language Applications Workshop: Controlled Language Translation (EAMT-CLAW-2003)*, Dublin City University, Ireland.

Palmer, Martha, Owen Rambow, and Alexis Nasr (1998). "Rapid Prototyping of Domain-specific Machine Translation Systems." In David L. Farwell, Laurie Gerber, and Eduard Hovy, eds., *Machine Translation and the Information Soup*. Berlin: Springer, pp. 95–102.

Pinkham, Jessie and Monica Corston-Oliver (2001). "Adding Domain Specificity to an MT System." *Proceedings of the Association for Computational Linguistics 39th Annual Meeting and 10th Conference of the European Chapter: Data-driven Machine Translation (ACL-EACL-2001)*, Toulouse, France, pp. 103–110.

Quantz, J. Joachim, Uwe Küssner, and Manfred Gehrke (1995). "Domain Modeling for Machine Translation." *Proceedings of the 6th International Conference on Theoretical and Methodological Issues in Machine Translation (TMI-95)*, Leuven, Belgium, pp. 115–122.

Resnik, Philip and I. Dan Melamed (1997). "Semi-automatic Acquisition of Domain-specific Translation Lexicons." *Proceedings of the 5th Conference on Applied Natural Language Processing* (*ANLP-97*), Seattle, Washington, DC, USA.
Senellart, Jean (1999). "Semi-automatic Acquisition of Lexical Resources for New Languages or New Domains." *Proceedings of the 4th Workshop of the European Association for Machine Translation: EU and the New Languages: Translation—Possibilities, Policies and Practicalities*, Prague, the Czech Republic.
Siddharthan, Advaith and Ann Copestake (2004). "Generating Referring Expressions in Open Domains." *Proceedings of the 42nd Annual Meeting of the Association for Computational Linguistics* (*ACL-2004*), Barcelona, Spain, pp. 407–414.
Yamada, Setsuo, Hiromi Nakaiwa, Kentaro Ogura, and Satoru Ikehara (1995). "A Method for Automatically Adapting an MT System to Different Domains." *Proceedings of the 6th International Conference on Theoretical and Methodological Issues in Machine Translation* (*TMI-95*), Leuven, Belgium, pp. 303–310.

Flight Information

Axelrod, Scott (2000). "Natural Language Generation in the IBM Flight Information System." *Proceedings of the ANLP/NAACL-2000 Workshop on Conversational Systems—Volume 3*, Seattle, Washington, DC, USA, pp. 21–26.
Seneff, Stephanie and Joseph Polifroni (2000). "Dialogue Management in the Mercury Flight Reservation System." *Proceedings of the ANLP/NAACL-2000 Workshop on Conversational Systems—Volume 3*, Seattle, Washington, DC, USA, pp. 11–16.
Seneff, Stephanie, Chao Wang, and John Lee (2006). "Combining Linguistic and Statistical Methods for Bi-directional English Chinese Translation in the Flight Domain." *Proceedings of the 7th Biennial Conference of the Association for Machine Translation in the Americas (AMTA-2006): Visions for the Future of Machine Translation*, Boston Marriott, Cambridge, MA, USA.
Spaggiari, Laurent, Florence Beaujard, and Emmanuelle Cannesson (2003). "A Controlled Language at Airbus." *Proceedings of the Joint Conference Combining the 8th International Workshop of the*

European Association for Machine Translation and the 4th Controlled Language Applications Workshop: Controlled Language Translation (EAMT-CLAW-2003), Dublin City University, Ireland.

Food

Chan, Sin-wai (2002). "The Making of *TransRecipe*: A Translational Approach to the Machine Translation of Chinese Cookbooks." In Chan Sin-wai, ed., *Translation and Information Technology*. Hong Kong: The Chinese University Press, pp. 3–22.

Shirai, Kiyoaki and Hiroshi Ookawa (2006). "Compiling a Lexicon of Cooking Actions for Animation Generation." *Proceedings of the Joint Conference of the International Committee on Computational Linguistics and the Association for Computational Linguistics (COLING/ACL-2006)*, Sydney, Australia.

Vertan, Cristina and Walter van Hahn (2003). "Menu Choice Translation: A Flexible Menu-based Controlled Natural Language System." *Proceedings of the Joint Conference Combining the 8th International Workshop of the European Association for Machine Translation and the 4th Controlled Language Applications Workshop: Controlled Language Translation (EAMT-CLAW-2003)*, Dublin City University, Ireland.

Wang, Hsien-Chang, Jhing-Fa Wang, and Yi-Nan Liu (1997). "A Conversational Agent for Food-ordering Dialog Based on VenusDictate." *Proceedings of the International Conference on Research in Computational Linguistics (ROCLING-X)*, Academia Sinica, Taipei, Taiwan.

Industry

Fukutomi, Orie (1999). "Experiment Report of a Commercial Machine Translation in a Manufacturing Industry Domain." *Proceedings of MT Summit VII: MT in the Great Translation Era*, Singapore.

Fukutomi, Orie (1999). "Report on Commercial Machine Translation in a Manufacturing Industry Domain." *Machine Translation Review*, No. 10, pp. 16–25.

Law

Hansen, Inge Gorm and Henrik Selsøe Sørensen (2002). "LinguaNet:

Embedded MT in a Cross-border Messaging System for European Law Enforcement." *Machine Translation*, Vol. 17, No. 2, pp. 139–163.
Koutsoudas, Andreas (1957). "Mechanical Translation and Zipf's Law." *Language*, Vol. 33, No. 4, pp. 545–552.
Porro, Brian, Jean Acheroy, and Florent Thouvenin (2003). "Generic Text Interface (Canevas/GTi): Producing and Publishing Structured Legal Documents at the Court of Justice of the European Communities." In *Translating and the Computer 25*. London: The Association for Information Management.
Sin, King Kui and D. Roebuck (1996). "Language Engineering for Legal Transplantation: Conceptual Problems in Creating Common Law Chinese." *Language and Communication*, Vol. 16, pp. 235–254.
Wilkinson, Michael (2006). "Legal Aspects of Compiling Corpora to Be Used as Translation Resources: Questions of Copyright." *Translation Journal*, Vol. 10, No. 2.

Literature

Opas, L. L. and T. Rommel (1995). "New Approaches to Computer Applications in Literary Studies." *Literary and Linguistic Computing*, Vol. 10, No. 4, pp. 261–262.
Widmann, R. L. (1975). "Trends in Computer Applications to Literature." *Computers and the Humanities*, Vol. 9, No. 5, pp. 231–235.

Manual

Mori, Tatsunori, Mamoru Matsuo, and Hiroshi Nakawaga (1999). "Zero-subject Resolution Using Linguistic Constraints and Defaults: The Case of Japanese Instruction Manuals." *Machine Translation*, Vol. 19, Nos. 3–4, pp. 231–245.
Tsutsumi, Taijiro (1986). "A Prototype English-Japanese Machine Translation System for Translating IBM Computer Manuals." *Proceedings of the 11th International Conference on Computational Linguistics* (*COLING-86*), Bonn, Germany, pp. 646–648.

Mathematics

Loh, Shiu-chang 樂秀章, Kong Luan 江鑾, and Hung Hing-sum 孔慶琛

(1978). "Machine Translation of Chinese Mathematical Articles." *Bulletin of the Association for Literary and Linguistic Computing*, Vol. 6, No. 2, pp. 111–120.

Medicine

Bagga, Amit, Tomek Strzalkowski, and G. Bowden Wise (2000). "PartsID: A Dialogue-based System for Identifying Parts for Medical Systems." *6th Applied Natural Language Processing Conference and 1st Meeting of the North American Chapter of the Association for Computational Linguistics: Proceedings of the Conferences, and Proceedings of the ANLP-NAACL-2000 Student Research Workshop*, Seattle, Washington, DC, USA, pp. 29–36.

Barkman, Bruce, Lise Bernier, Leo Cousineau, and et Gabrielle Tanguay (1974). "The Translation of S.N.O.P.: A First Step toward the Construction of an Automated Medical Lexicon." *Meta*, Vol. 19, No. 1, pp. 28–42.

Blench, Michael (2006). "GPHIN Use of MT in Disease Outbreak Detection." *Proceedings of the 7th Biennial Conference of the Association for Machine Translation in the Americas (AMTA-2006): Visions for the Future of Machine Translation*, Boston Marriott, Cambridge, MA, USA.

Bouillon, Pierrette, Manny Rayner, Nikolaos Chatzichrisafis, Beth Ann Hockey, Marianne Santaholma, Marianne Starlander, Hitoshi Isahara, Kyoko Kanzaki, and Yukie Nakao (2005). "A Generic Multi-lingual Open Source Platform for Limited-domain Medical Speech Translation." *Proceedings of the 10th Workshop of the European Association for Machine Translation: Practical Applications of Machine Translation*, Budapest, Hungary, pp. 50–58.

Cardey, Sylviane, Peter Greenfield, and Wu Xiaohong (2004). "Designing a Controlled Language for the Machine Translation of Medical Protocols: The Case of English to Chinese." In Robert E. Frederking and Kathryn B. Taylors, eds., *Machine Translation: From Real Users to Research*. Berlin: Springer, pp. 37–47.

Castilla, Andre, Alice Bacic, and Sergio Furuie (2005). "Machine Translation on the Medical Domain: The Role of BLEU/NIST and METEOR in a Controlled Vocabulary Setting." *Proceedings of MT Summit X*, Phuket, Thailand.

Currie, Anne-Marie, Jocelyn Cohan, and Larisa Zlatic (2001). "Information Retrieval of Electronic Medical Records." *Proceedings of the 2nd International Conference on Intelligent Text Processing and Computational Linguistics* (*CICLing-2001*), Mexico City, Mexico.

Deville, Guy, Emmanuel Herbigniaux, P. Mousel, and G. Thienpont (1994). "Reengineering Linguistic Resources for Machine Translation in Medical Applications." *Proceedings of the 1st Conference of the Association for Machine Translation in the Americas: Technology Partnerships for Crossing the Language Barrier* (*AMTA-1*), Columbia, Maryland, USA, pp. 24–31.

Deville, Guy and Emmanuel Herbignaux (1995). "Natural Language Modeling in a Machine Translation Prototype for Healthcare Applications: A Sublanguage Approach." *Proceedings of the 6th International Conference on Theoretical and Methodological Issues in Machine Translation* (*TMI-95*), Leuven, Belgium, pp. 142–157.

Deville, Guy, Emmanuel Herbigniaux, P. Mousel, G. Thienpont, and M. Wéry (1996). "ANTHEM: Advanced Natural Language Interface for Multilingual Text Generation in Healthcare." *Proceedings of the 2nd Conference of the Association for Machine Translation in the Americas: Expanding MT Horizons* (*AMTA-2*), Montreal, Quebec, Canada, pp. 240–243.

Khoo, Christopher S. G., Chan Syin, and Niu Yun (2000). "Extracting Causal Knowledge from a Medical Database Using Graphical Patterns." *Proceedings of the 38th Annual Meeting of the Association for Computational Linguistics* (*ACL-2000*), Hong Kong.

Lee, Young-Suk, Daniel J. Sinder, and Clifford J. Weinstein (2002). "Interlingua-based English–Korean Two-way Speech Translation of Doctor–patient Dialogues with CCLINC." *Machine Translation*, Vol. 17, No. 3, pp. 213–243.

McKeown, Kathleen R., Shimei Pan, James Shaw, Desmond Jordan, and Barry A. Allen (1997). "Language Generation for Multimedia Healthcare Briefings." *Proceedings of the 5th Conference on Applied Natural Language Processing*, Seattle, Washington, DC, USA.

Pratt, Arnold W. and Milos G. Pacak (1969). "Automated Processing of Medical English." *Proceedings of the International Conference of Computational Linguistics* (*COLING-69*), Stockholm, Sweden.

Rindflesch, Thomas C., Jayant V. Rajan, and Lawrence Hunter (2000). "Extracting Molecular Binding Relationships from Biomedical Text."

Proceedings of the 6th Applied Natural Language Processing Conference, Seattle, Washington, D.C., USA, pp. 188–195.
Somers, Harold L. and Hermione Lovel (2003). "Computer-based Support for Patients with Limited English." *Proceedings of the 7th Workshop of the European Association for Machine Translation: Improving Machine Translation through Other Language Technology Tools: Resources and Tools for Building MT*, Budapest, Hungary, pp. 41–49.
Žižka, Jan and Aleš Bourek (2002). "Automated Selection of Interesting Medical Text Documents by the TEA Text Analyzer." *Proceedings of the 3rd International Conference on Intelligent Text Processing and Computational Linguistics (CICLing-2002)*, Mexico City, Mexico.

Navigation

Stoia, Laura, Donna K. Byron, Darla Shockley, and Eric Fosler-Lussier (2006). "Sentence Planning for Realtime Navigational Instruction." *Proceedings of the Human Language Technology Conference—Annual Meeting of the North American Chapter of the Association for Computational Linguistics (HLT-NAACL-2006)*, New York, USA.

News

Aizawa, Temaki, Terumasa Ehara, Nodyoshi Uratani, Hideki Tanaka, Naoto Kato, Sumio Nakase, Norikazu Amga, and Takeo Matsuda (1990). "A Machine Translation System for Foreign News in Satellite Broadcasting." *Proceedings of the 13th International Conference on Computational Linguistics (COLING-90)*, Helsinki, Finland, pp. 308–310.
Bandyopadhyay, Sivaji (2001). "An Example Based MT System in News Items Domain from English to Indian Languages." *Machine Translation Review*, No. 12, pp. 7–10.
Banko, Michele, Vibhu O. Mittal, and Michael J. Witbrock (2000). "Headline Generation Based on Statistical Translation." *Proceedings of the 38th Annual Meeting of the Association for Computational Linguistics (ACL-2000)*, Hong Kong.
Bemish, Nick (2006). "Document and Media Exploitation Evaluation." *Proceedings of the 7th Biennial Conference of the Association for Machine Translation in the Americas (AMTA-2006): Visions for the*

Future of Machine Translation, Boston Marriott, Cambridge, MA, USA.

Bus, Annette and Anja Simon (2002). "Working with Machine Translation: How the Euroscript Group Uses Systran for Fast News Translation." *Multilingual Computing and Technology*, Vol. 13, No. 6, pp. 37–41.

Chin, Chi-on Andy and Benjamin K. Y. T'sou (2000). "Subject Ellipsis in Chinese News Headlines." In Nicolas Nicolov and Ruslan Mitkov, eds., *Recent Advances in Natural Language Processing II*. Amsterdam and Philadelphia: John Benjamins Publishing Company, pp. 167–176.

Collier, Nigel, Hideki Hirakawa, and Akira Kumano (1998). "Machine Translation vs. Dictionary Term Translation—A Comparison for English-Japanese News Article Alignment." *Proceedings of the 36th Annual Meeting of the Association for Computational Linguistics and 17th International Conference on Computational Linguistics* (*COLING-ACL-98*), Montreal, Quebec, Canada.

Cotton, Scott and Yi Szu-ting (2004). "Relation Detection and Characterization in Chinese Newswire and Broadcast News." *Proceedings of the International Conference on Natural Language Processing* (*ICON-2004*), International Institute of Information Technology, Hyderabad, India.

Garbin, Eric and Inderjeet Mani (2005). "Disambiguating Toponyms in News." *Proceedings of Human Language Technology Conference and Conference on Empirical Methods in Natural Language Processing* (*HLT/EMNLP-2005*), Vancouver, BC, Canada.

Hu, Jinghe 胡景賀 (2002). 〈《人民日報》1998年語料庫中若干基本語言數據的統計與分析〉 (Statistics and Analyses of Some Fundamental Linguistic Data in a 1998 *People's Daily* Corpus).《第一屆學生計算語言學研討會論文集》 (*SWCL2002: First Students' Workshop on Computational Linguistics: Proceedings*), Institute of Computational Linguistics, Peking University, Beijing, China, pp. 299–305.

Katoh, Naoto, Noriyoshi Uratani, and Teruaki Aizawa (1991). "Processing Proper Nouns in Machine Translation for English News." *Proceedings of the Conference on Current Issues in Computational Linguistics*, Penang, Malaysia, pp. 431–439.

Mani, Inderjeet, Barry Schiffman, and Jianping Zhang (2003). "Inferring Temporal Ordering of Events in News." *Proceedings of the Human Language Technology and North American Chapter of Association of*

Computational Linguistics 2003 (*HLT/NAACL-2003*), Edmonton, Alberta, Canada.

McKeown, Kathleen R., Regina Barzilay, John Chen, David Elson, David Evans, Judith Klavans, Ani Nenkova, Barry Schiffman, and Sergey Sigelman (2003). "Columbia's Newsblaster: New Features and Future Directions." *Proceedings of the Human Language Technology and North American Chapter of Association of Computational Linguistics 2003* (*HLT/NAACL-2003*), Edmonton, Alberta, Canada.

Montes-y-Gómez, Manuel, Aurelio López-López, and Alexander F. Gelbukh (2001). "Finding Correlative Associations among News Topics." *Proceedings of the 2nd International Conference on Intelligent Text Processing and Computational Linguistics* (*CICLing-2001*), Mexico City, Mexico.

Nightingale, Stephen and Hideki Tanaka (2003). "Comparing the Sentence Alignment Yield from Two News Corpora Using a Dictionary-based Alignment System." *Proceedings of the Human Language Technology and North American Chapter of Association of Computational Linguistics 2003* (*HLT/NAACL-2003*), Edmonton, Alberta, Canada.

Ono, Kenji (2003). "Translation of News Headlines." *Proceedings of MT Summit IX*, New Orleans, Louisiana, USA.

Scheytt, Peter, Michael Finke, and Petra Geutner (1997). *Speech Recognition on Serbo-Croatian Dictation and Broadcast News Data.* Pittsburgh: Language Technologies Institute, Carnegie Mellon University.

Tang, Rong, Kwong Bor Ng, Tomek Strzalkowski, and Paul B. Kantor (2003). "Automatically Predicting Information Quality in News Documents." *Proceedings of the Human Language Technology and North American Chapter of Association of Computational Linguistics 2003* (*HLT/NAACL-2003*), Edmonton, Alberta, Canada.

Utsuro, Takehito, Takashi Horiuchi, Yasunobu Chiba, and Takeshi Hamamoto (2002). "Semi-automatic Compilation of Bilingual Lexicon Entries from Cross-lingually Relevant News Articles on WWW News Sites." In Stephen D. Richardson, ed., *Machine Translation: From Research to Real Users.* Berlin and New York: Springer, pp. 165–176.

Utsuro, Takehito (2002). "Translation Knowledge Acquisition from Cross-lingually Relevant News Articles." In Yu Shiwen, ed., *Proceedings of the 2nd China-Japan Natural Language Processing Joint Research*

Promotion Conference (*CJNLP-2002*). Beijing: Institute of Computational Linguistics, Peking University, pp. 123–134.
Wang, Houfeng, Li Sujian, Yu Shiwen, and Kang Byeong Kwu (2004). "A Combining Approach to Automatic Keyphrases Indexing for Chinese News Documents." *Proceedings of the 5th International Conference on Intelligent Text Processing and Computational Linguistics* (*CICLing-2004*), Chung-Ang University, Seoul, Korca, pp. 435–438.
Wu, Shih-Hung, Pey-Ching Yang, and Von-Wun Soo (1997). "An Assessment on Character-based Chinese News Filtering Using Latent Semantic Indexing." *Proceedings of the International Conference on Research in Computational Linguistics* (*ROCLING-X*), Academia Sinica, Taipei, Taiwan.
Xu, Donghua and Chew Lim Tan (1999). "Alignment and Matching of Bilingual English–Chinese News Texts." *Machine Translation*, Vol. 14, No. 1, pp. 1–33.
Yoshimi, Takehiko and Ichiko Sata (1999). "Improvement of Translation Quality of English Newspaper Headlines by Automatic Pre-editing." *Proceedings of MT Summit VII: MT in the Great Translation Era*, Singapore.
Yoshimi, Takehiko (2001). "Improvement of Translation Quality of English Newspaper Headlines by Automatic Pre-editing." *Machine Translation*, Vol. 16, No. 4, pp. 233–250.

Patent

Higuchi, Shigeto, Masatoshi Fukui, Atsushi Fujii, and Tetsuya Ishikawa (2001). "PRIME: A System for Multi-lingual Patent Retrieval." In Bente Maegaard, ed., *Proceedings of MT Summit VIII: Machine Translation in the Information Age*, Santiago de Compostela, Spain.
Hong, Munpyo, Young-Gil Kim, Chang-Hyun Kim, Seong-Il Yang, Young-Ae Seo, Cheol Ryu, and Sang-Kyu Park (2005). "Customizing a Korean-English MT System for Patent Translation." *Proceedings of MT Summit X*, Phuket, Thailand.
Makita, Mitsuharu, Shigeto Higuchi, Atsushi Fujii, and Tetsuya Ishikawa (2003). "A System for Japanese/English/Korean Multilingual Patent Retrieval." *Proceedings of MT Summit IX*, New Orleans, Louisiana, USA.

Safety

Takala, J., J. Pesonen, L. Kulikov, and H. Jäppinen (1991). "Machine Translation for Chemical Safety Information." *Journal of Hazardous Materials*, Vol. 27, pp. 213–230.

Science

Bezhanova, Olga (1997). "Translating Scientific Texts Using MT and MAT Systems: Practical Experience of a Professional Translator." *Proceedings of MT Summit VI*, San Diego, California, USA.

Chang, Baobao, Yu Shiwen, and Kang Byeong-Kwu (2006). "Developing CAT Tools for Translating Chinese Scientific Monographs." *Programme of an International Conference on Computer-aided Translation: Theory and Practice*, Department of Translation, The Chinese University of Hong Kong, Hong Kong.

Kashioka, Hideki, Hiroko Ohta, Yoshiko Shirokizawa, and Kazutaka Takao (1999). "Applying TDMT to Abstracts on Science and Technology." *Proceedings of MT Summit VII: MT in the Great Translation Era*, Singapore.

Loh, Shiu-chang (1976). "Translation of Three Chinese Scientific Texts into English by Computer." *ALLC Bulletin*, Vol. 4, No. 2, pp. 104–105.

Loh, Shiu-chang (1977). "Computer Translation of Chinese Scientific Journals." *Overcoming the Language Barrier: 3rd European Congress on Information Systems and Networks*, Luxembourg. Muchen: Verlag Dokumentation, pp. 631–645.

Nagao, Makoto and Jun-ichi Tsujii (1979). "A Machine Translation System from English into Japanese for Titles of Scientific Papers." *Proceedings of the 2nd International Seminar on Machine Translation*, Moscow, Russia, p. 11.

Teufel, Simone and Marc Moens (2000). "What's Yours and What's Mine: Determining Intellectual Attribution in Scientific Text." *Proceedings of the Joint Sigdat Conference on Empirical Methods in Natural Language Processing and Very Large Corpora (EMNLP/VLC-2000)*, Hong Kong University of Science and Technology, Hong Kong.

Speech

Vilar, David Evgeny Matusov, Sasa Hasan, Richard Zens, and Hermann

Ney (2005). "Statistical Machine Translation of European Parliamentary Speeches." *Proceedings of MT Summit X*, Phuket, Thailand.

Subtitle

Armstrong, Stephen (2006). "Improving the Quality of Automated DVD Subtitles via Example-based Machine Translation (EBMT)." In *Translating and the Computer 28*. London: The Association for Information Management.

Bouayad-Agha, Nadjet, Angel Gil, Oriol Valentin, and Victor Pascual (2006). "A Sentence Compression Module for Machine-assisted Subtitling." *Proceedings of the 7th International Conference on Intelligent Text Processing and Computational Linguistics* (*CICLing-2006*), Mexico City, Mexico.

Gonzalez, Antoni Oliver (2006). "Automatic Multilingual Subtitling in the eTitle Project." In *Translating and the Computer 28*. London: The Association for Information Management.

O'Hagan, Minako (2003). "Can Language Technology Respond to the Subtitler's Dilemma?—A Preliminary Study." In *Translating and the Computer 25*. London: The Association for Information Management.

Spalink, Karin (2002). "Small-screen Devices and Translation." In *Translating and the Computer 24*. London: The Association for Information Management.

Tsai, Ming-Hong (2006). "Subtitle Translation Strategies as a Reflection of Technical Limitations: A Case Study of Ang Lee's Films." *Proceedings of the 6th Portsmouth Translation Conference: Translation Technologies and Culture*, School of Languages and Area Studies, University of Portsmouth, England.

Technology

de Ilarraza, Arantxa Diaz, Aingeru Mayor, and Kepa Sarasola (2000). "Reusability of Wide-coverage Linguistic Resources in the Construction of Multilingual Technical Documentation." *Proceedings of the International Conference on Machine Translation and Multilingual Applications in the New Millenium* (*MT-2000*), University of Exeter, England.

Telephone

Benedí, José-Miguel, Eduardo Lleida, Amparo Varona, María-José Castro, Isabel Galiano, Raquel Justo, Iñigo López de Letona, and Antonio Miguel (2006). "Design and Acquisition of a Telephone Spontaneous Speech Dialogue Corpus in Spanish: DIHANA." *Proceedings of the 5th International Conference on Language Resources and Evaluation* (*LREC-2006*), Genoa, Italy.

Davies, K., R. Donovan, M. Epstein, Martin Franz, Abraham Ittycheriah, E. E. Jan, J. M. LeRoux, David Lubensky, Chalapathy Neti, Mukund Padmanabhan, K. Papineni, Salim Roukos, A. Sakrajda, Jeffrey S. Sorensen, B. Tydlitat, and T. Ward (1999). "The IBM Conversational Telephony System for Financial Applications." *Proceedings of the 6th European Conference on Speech Communication and Technology* (*EuroSpeech-99*), Budapest, Hungary, pp. 275–278.

Fosler-Lussier, Eric and C. Anton Rytting (2005). "A Cost-benefit Analysis of Hybrid Phone-manner Representations for ASR." *Proceedings of Human Language Technology Conference and Conference on Empirical Methods in Natural Language Processing* (*HLT/EMNLP-2005*), Vancouver, BC, Canada.

Frederking, Robert, Christopher Hogan, and Alexander Rudnicky (1999). "A New Approach to the Translating Telephone." *Proceedings of MT Summit VII: MT in the Great Translation Era*, Singapore.

Hu, Hai-Hsu 胡海旭, Jen-i Li 李臻儀, Tzu-Ying Hu 胡祖櫻, and Ren-Rong Hsu 許仁榮 (1990). 〈電話轉接對話模式與表達轉接要求句型的分析〉 (Analyses of Dialogue Patterns and Sentence Patterns of Telephone Switching). *Proceedings of the Conference of the Association for Computational Linguistics and Chinese Language Processing* (*ROCLING-III*), Taipei, Taiwan.

Kirchmann, Heinz, Alassane Ndiaye, and Andreas Klüter (2000). "From a Stationary Prototype to Telephone Translation Services." In Wolfgang Wahlster, ed., *Verbmobil: Foundations of Speech-to-speech Translation*. Berlin: Springer, pp. 659–669.

Kurematsu, Akira (1989). "Research on Automatic Telephone Interpretation." In Christian Rohrer, ed., *Proceedings of MT Summit II,* Munich, Germany, pp. 80–81.

Morimoto, Tsuyoshi, Hitoshi Iida, Akira Kurematsu, Kiyohiro Shikano, and Temaki Aizawa (1990). "Spoken Language Translation: Towards

Realizing an Automatic Telephone Interpretation." *Proceedings of the International Conference of the Information Processing Society of Japan* (*INFO JAPAN-90*), pp. 553–559.
Shen, Jia-Lin, Ying-Chieh Tu, Po-Yu Liang, and Lin-Shan Lee (1998). "Speaker-independent Continuous Mandarin Speech Recognition under Telephone Environments." *Proceedings of the International Conference on Research in Computational Linguistics* (*ROCLING-XI*), Hsin-Chu, Taiwan.
Zhu, Xuefeng 朱學鋒 and Yu Shiwen 俞士汶 (1996).〈自動翻譯電話與口語信息處理研究〉(A Study on Automatic Translation Telephones and Speech Information Processing). In Yu Shiwen and Zhu Xuefeng, eds., 《計算語言學文集》(*Papers on Computational Linguistics*). Beijing: Department of Computer Science and Technology and Institute of Computational Linguistics, Peking University, pp. 99–103.

Title

Hubert, Jérôme, J. Ibuki, Masako Kume, and Makoto Nagao (1983). "A System of Japanese–French Automatic Translation for Paper Titles." *Proceedings of the 26th Annual Convention of the Information Processing Society of Japan*, Kyoto, Japan.
Jin, Rong and Alexander G. Hauptmann (2001). "Title Generation Using a Training Corpus." *Proceedings of the 2nd International Conference on Intelligent Text Processing and Computational Linguistics* (*CICLing-2001*), Mexico City, Mexico.
Nagao, Makoto, Jun-ichi Tsujii, Koji Yada, and Toshihiro Kakimoto (1982). "An English–Japanese Machine Translation System for the Titles of Scientific and Engineering Papers." In Jan Horecky, ed., *Proceedings of the 9th International Conference on Computational Linguistics* (*COLING-82*), Prague, the Czech Republic. Amsterdam: North-Holland Publishing Company, pp. 245–252.

Travel

Blanchon, Herve, Christian Boitet, Francis Brunet-Manquat, Mutsuko Tomokiyo, Agnes Hamon, Vo Trung Hung, and Youcef Bey (2004). "Towards Fairer Evaluations of Commercial MT Systems on Basic Travel Expressions Corpora." *Proceedings of the International*

Workshop on Spoken Language Translation (*IWSLT-2004*), Kyoto, Japan.

Kageura, Kyo and Genichiro Kikui (2006). "A Self-referring Quantitative Evaluation of the ATR Basic Travel Expression Corpus (BTEC)." *Proceedings of the 5th International Conference on Language Resources and Evaluation* (*LREC-2006*), Genoa, Italy.

Stallard, David (2000). "Talk'N'Travel: A Conversational System for Air Travel Planning." *6th Applied Natural Language Processing Conference and 1st Meeting of the North American Chapter of the Association for Computational Linguistics: Proceedings of the Conferences, and Proceedings of the ANLP-NAACL-2000 Student Research Workshop*, Seattle, Washington, DC, USA, pp. 68–75.

Takezawa, Toshiyuki, Eiichiro Sumita, Fumiaki Sugaya, Hirofumi Yamamoto, and Seiichi Yamamoto (2002). "Toward a Broad-coverage Bilingual Corpus for Speech Translation of Travel Conversations in the Real World." *Proceedings of the 3rd International Conference on Language Resources and Evaluation* (*LREC-2002*), Las Palmas, Canary Islands, Spain, Vol. 1, pp. 147–152.

Wilkinson, Michael (2005). "Discovering Translation Equivalents in a Tourism Corpus by Means of Fuzzy Searching." *Translation Journal*, Vol. 9, No. 4.

War

Holland, Melissa and C. Schlesigner (1998). "High-mobility Machine Translation for a Battlefield Environment." *Proceedings of NATO/RTO Systems Concepts and Integration Symposium*, Monterary, California, USA, pp. 1–3.

Moore, Robert, John Dowding, Harry Bratt, J. Mark Gawron, and Adam Cheyer (1997). "CommandTalk: A Spoken-language Interface for Battlefield Simulations." *Proceedings of the 5th Conference on Applied Natural Language Processing*, Seattle, Washington, DC, USA.

Weather

Goldberg, Eli, Norbert Driedger, and Richard I. Kittredge (1994). "Using Natural Language Processing to Produce Weather Forecasts." *IEEE Expert*, Vol. 9, No. 2, pp. 45–53.

Kittredge, Richard I., Alain Polguère, and Eli Goldberg (1986). "Synthesizing Weather Reports from Formatted Data." *Proceedings of the 11th International Conference on Computational Linguistics (COLING-86)*, Bonn, Germany, pp. 563–565.

Langlais, Philippe, Simona Gandrabur, Thomas Leplus, and Guy Lapalme (2005). "The Long-term Forecast for Weather Bulletin Translation." *Machine Translation*, Vol. 19, No. 1, pp. 83–112.

Leplus, Thomas, Philippe Langlais, and Guy Lapalme (2004). "A Corpus-based Approach to Weather Report Translation." *Technical Report*, University of Montreal, Quebec, Canada.

Leplus, Thomas, Philippe Langlais, and Guy Lapalme (2004). "Weather Report Translation Using a Translation Memory." In Robert E. Frederking and Kathryn B. Taylors, eds., *Machine Translation: From Real Users to Research*. Berlin: Springer, pp. 154–163.

Pérez, Alicia, Inés Torres, Francisco Casacuberta, and Víctor Guijarrubia (2006). "A Spanish-Basque Weather Forecast Corpus for Probabilistic Speech Translation." *Proceedings of the 5th SALTMIL Workshop on Minority Languages and the 5th International Conference on Language Resources and Evaluation (LREC-2006): Strategies for Developing Machine Translation for Minority Languages*, Genoa, Italy, pp. 99–102.

❖ PART 12 ❖

Editing

Editing

Akiba, Yasuhiro, Kenji Imamura, and Eiichiro Sumita (2001). "Using Multiple Edit Distances to Automatically Rank Machine Translation Output." In Bente Maegaard, ed., *Proceedings of MT Summit VIII: Machine Translation in the Information Age*, Santiago de Compostela, Spain, pp. 15–20.

Bangalore, Srinivas and Michael Johnston (2006). "Edit Machines for Robust Multimodal Language Processing." *Proceedings of the 11th Conference of the European Chapter of the Association for Computational Linguistics (EACL-2006)*, Trento, Italy.

Boitet, Christian and Wang-Ju Tsai (2002). "Coedition to Share Text Revision across Languages and Improve MT a Posteriori." *Proceedings of the Workshop on Machine Translation in Asia (COLING-2002)*, Taipei, Taiwan.

Boualem, Abdel-Malek (1996). "MtScript—A Multilingual Text Editor." In *Translating and the Computer 18*. London: The Association for Information Management.

Callison-Burch, Chris, Colin Bannard, and Josh Schroeder (2004). "Improving Statistical Translation through Editing." *Proceedings of the 9th Workshop of the European Association for Machine Translation: Broadening Horizons of Machine Translation and Its Applications*, Foundation for International Studies, Malta, pp. 26–32.

Cunningham, Dale S. (1971). "Translation and Editing." *Meta*, Vol. 16, pp. 135–152.

Dale, Robert (1989). "Computer-based Editorial Aids." In Jeremy Peckham, ed., *Recent Developments and Applications of Natural Language Understanding*. London: Kogan, pp. 12–20.

Karlgren, Hans (1987). "Good Use of Poor Translations." *Forum Information and Docum*, Vol. 12, No. 4, pp. 23–29.

Kukich, Karen (1992). "Techniques for Automatically Correcting Words in Text." *ACM Computing Surveys*, Vol. 24, No. 4, pp. 377–438.

Kuo, June-Jei (1999). "An Automated Mandarin Document Revision System Using Both Phonetic and Radical Approaches." *Proceedings of MT Summit VII: MT in the Great Translation Era*, Singapore.

Merkel, Magnus (1996). "Checking Translations for Inconsistency—A Tool for the Editor." *Proceedings of the 2nd Conference of the*

Association for Machine Translation in the Americas: Expanding MT Horizons (*AMTA-2*), Montreal, Quebec, Canada, pp. 157–167.

Mossop, Brian (2001). *Revising and Editing for Translators*. Manchester: St. Jerome Publishing.

Pigott, Ian M. (1982). "The Importance of Feedback from Translators in the Development of High-quality Machine Translation." In Veronica Lawson, ed., *Practical Experience of Machine Translation*. Amsterdam: North-Holland Publishing Company, pp. 61–73.

Porozinskaya, Galina (1997). "Aspects of Literary and MT Editing in Teaching Translation." In Kinga Klaudy and János Kohn, eds., *Transferre Necesse Est: Proceedings of the 2nd International Conference on Current Trends in Studies of Translation and Interpreting*, Budapest, Hungary, pp. 553–557.

Przybocki, Mark, Gregory Sanders, and Audrey Le (2006). "Edit Distance: A Metric for Machine Translation Evaluation." *Proceedings of the 5th International Conference on Language Resources and Evaluation* (*LREC-2006*), Genoa, Italy.

Ray, Jayanta (1995). "Machine-aided Translation (MAT)—Aspects of Editing." *International Journal of Translation*, Vol. 7, Nos. 1–2, pp. 47–57.

Ruffino, J. Richard (1982). "Coping with Machine Translation." In Veronica Lawson, ed., *Practical Experience of Machine Translation*. Amsterdam: North-Holland Publishing Company, pp. 57–60.

Shih, Chung-ling (2006). "Tailoring MT Editing to Diverse Audiences and Purposes." *Helpful Assistance to Translators: MT & TM*. Taipei: Bookman Books Ltd., pp. 195–226.

Snover, Matthew, Bonnie J. Dorr, Rich Schwartz, Linnea Micciulla, and John Makhoul (2006). "A Study of Translation Edit Rate with Targeted Human Annotation." *Proceedings of the 7th Biennial Conference of the Association for Machine Translation in the Americas* (*AMTA-2006*): *Visions for the Future of Machine Translation*, Boston Marriott, Cambridge, MA, USA.

Tribble, Alicia, Benjamin Lambert, and Scott E. Fahlman (2006). "SconeEdit: a Text-guided Domain Knowledge Editor." *Proceedings of the Human Language Technology Conference—Annual Meeting of the North American Chapter of the Association for Computational Linguistics* (*HLT-NAACL-2006*), New York, USA.

Uchimoto, Kiyotaka, Naoko Hayashida, Toru Ishida, and Hitoshi Isahara

(2006). "Automatic Detection and Semi-automatic Revision of Non-machine-translatable Parts of a Sentence." *Proceedings of the 5th International Conference on Language Resources and Evaluation* (*LREC-2006*), Genoa, Italy.

Post-editing

Akiba, Yasuhiro, Kenji Imamura, and Eiichiro Sumita (2001). "Using Multiple Edit Distances to Automatically Rank Machine Translation Output." In Bente Maegaard, ed., *Proceedings of MT Summit VIII: Machine Translation in the Information Age*, Santiago de Compostela, Spain, pp. 15–20.

Allen, Jeffrey and Christopher Hogan (2000). "Toward the Development of a Post-editing Module for Raw Machine Translation Output: A Controlled Language Perspective." *Proceedings of the 3rd International Workshop on Controlled Language Applications*, Seattle, Washington, DC, USA, pp. 62–71.

Allen, Jeffrey (2001). "Postediting: An Integrated Part of a Translation Software Program (Reverso Pro 4)." *Language International*, Vol. 13, No. 2, pp. 26–29.

Allen, Jeffrey (2002). "Review of Repairing Texts: Empirical Investigations of Machine Translation Post-editing Processes." *Multilingual Computing and Technology*, Vol. 13, No. 2, pp. 27–29.

Allen, Jeffrey (2003). "Post-editing." In Harold L. Somers, ed., *Computers and Translation*. Amsterdam and Philadelphia: John Benjamins Publishing Company, pp. 297–317.

Bar-Hillel, Yehoshua (1952). "MT with Post-editor." *Proceedings of the M.I.T. Conference on Mechanical Translation,* Massachusetts Institute of Technology, Cambridge, MA, USA.

Belam, Judith (2003) "Buying up to Falling Down: A Deductive Approach to Teaching Post-editing." *Proceedings of the MT Summit IX Workshop on Teaching Translation Technologies and Tools*, New Orleans, Louisiana, USA, pp. 1–10.

Booth, Kathleen H. V. (1967). "Machine Aided Translation with a Post-editor." In Andrew D. Booth, ed., *Machine Translation*. Amsterdam: North-Holland Publishing Company, pp. 51–76.

Brown, Corinne (1972). "Post-editing English-French Machine

Translation: An Experiment." *Thought and Language in Operation: A Quarterly Review*, Vol. 3, pp. 98–107.

Donomae, Susumu (1995). "Pre- and Post-editing MT Text for Better Communication and Documentation." *Proceedings of MT Summit V: Machine Translation Conference, Exhibition and Tutorial*, Luxembourg.

Gomez, Antonio Sayáns and Elena Villar Conde (2003). "The Functionality of a Tool Bar for Post-edition in Machine Translation between Languages with Linguistic Interference: The Spanish-Galician Case." *Proceedings of MT Summit IX*, New Orleans, Louisiana, USA.

Green, Roy (1982). "The MT Errors Which Cause Most Trouble to Posteditors." In Veronica Lawson, ed., *Practical Experience of Machine Translation.* Amsterdam: North-Holland Publishing Company, pp. 101–104.

Habermann, F. W. A. (1986). "Provision and Use of Raw Machine Translation." *Terminologie et Traduction*, No. 1, pp. 29–42.

Hyland, Catherine (2003). "Testing 'Prompt': The Development of a Rapid Post-editing Service at CLS Corporate Language Services." *Proceedings of MT Summit IX*, New Orleans, Louisiana, USA.

Kliffer, Michael D. (2005). "An Experiment in MT Post-editing by a Class of Intermediate/Advanced French Majors." *Proceedings of the 10th Workshop of the European Association for Machine Translation: Practical Applications of Machine Translation*, Budapest, Hungary, pp. 160–165.

Knight, Kevin and Ishwar Chander (1994). "Automated Post-editing of Documents." *Proceedings of the 12th National Conference on Artificial Intelligence*, Seattle, Washington, DC, USA, pp. 779–784.

Kostrewski, Barbara and Peter Taylor (1982). "Discussion on Session 3: The Posteditors' Experience." In Veronica Lawson, ed., *Practical Experience of Machine Translation.* Amsterdam: North-Holland Publishing Company, pp. 111–112.

Krings, Hans (2001). *Repairing Texts. Empirical Investigations of Machine Translation Post-editing Processes*, edited by Geoffrey Koby and translated from German to English by Geoffrey Koby, Gregory Shreve, Katjz Mischerikow, and Sarah Litzer. Ohio: Kent State University Press.

Lavorel, Bernhard (1982). "Experience in English-French Post-editing." In

Veronica Lawson, ed., *Practical Experience of Machine Translation*. Amsterdam: North-Holland Publishing Company, pp. 105–109.
Loffler-Laurian and Anne-Marie (1984). "Machine Translation: What Type of Post-editing on What Type of Documents for What Type of Users." *Proceedings of the 10th International Conference on Computational Linguistics (COLING-84)*, Stanford University, Stanford, California, USA, pp. 236–238.
Martinez, Lorena Guerra (2004). "Human Translation versus Machine Translation and Full Post-editing of Raw Machine Translation Output." *International Journal of Translation*, Vol. 16, No. 2, pp. 81–113.
McElhaney, Terrence and Muriel Vasconcellos (1988). "The Translator and the Post-editing Experience." In Muriel Vasconcellos, ed., *Technology as Translation Strategy*. New York: State University of New York, pp. 140–148.
Melby, Alan K. (1984). "Machine Translation with Post-editing vs. a Tri-level Integrated Translator Aid System." *Proceedings of the International Conference on the Methodology and Techniques of Machine Translation*, Cranfield Institute of Technology, Cranfield, England.
Mossop, Brian (2001). *Revising and Editing for Translators*. Manchester: St. Jerome Publishing.
Nishida, Fujio and Shinobu Takamatsu (1990). "Automated Procedures for the Improvement of a Machine Translation System by Feedback from Postediting." *Machine Translation*, Vol. 5, No. 3, pp. 223–246.
O'Brien, Sharon (2002). "Teaching Post-editing: A Proposal for Course Content." *Proceedings of the 6th Workshop of the European Association for Machine Translation: Teaching Machine Translation*, Manchester, England, pp. 99–106.
Povlsen, Claus and Annelise Bech (2001). "Ape: Reducing the Monkey Business in Post-editing by Automating the Task Intelligently." In Bente Maegaard, ed., *Proceedings of MT Summit VIII: Machine Translation in the Information Age*, Santiago de Compostela, Spain.
Rossi, Francesco (1982). "The Impact of Posteditors' Feedback on the Quality of MT." In Veronica Lawson, ed., *Practical Experience of Machine Translation*. Amsterdam: North-Holland Publishing Company, pp. 113–117.
Schäfer, Falko (2003). "MT Post-editing: How to Shed Light on the

'Unknown Task': Experiences Made at SAP." *Proceedings of the Joint Conference Combining the 8th International Workshop of the European Association for Machine Translation and the 4th Controlled Language Applications Workshop: Controlled Language Translation* (*EAMT-CLAW-2003*), Dublin City University, Ireland, pp. 133–140.

Senez, Dorothy (1998). "Post-editing Service for Machine Translation Users at the European Commission." In *Translating and the Computer 20*. London: The Association for Information Management.

Senez, Dorothy (1998). "The Machine Translation Help Desk and the Postediting Service." *Terminologie et Traduction*, No. 1, pp. 289–295.

Shih, Chung-ling 史宗玲 (2004).〈語篇相關之後機器翻譯編輯訓練〉(Discourse-related Post-editing Training).《電腦輔助翻譯》(*MT and TM*). Taipei: The Bookman Press, pp. 95–138.

Shih, Chung-ling (2004).〈語域相關之後機器翻譯編輯訓練〉(Register-related Post-editing Training).《電腦輔助翻譯》(*MT and TM*). Taipei: The Bookman Press, pp. 25–94.

Shih Chung-ling (2006). "Mapping Students' Translation Process Based on Post-MT Editing." *Proceedings of the 10th Taiwan Symposium on Translator and Interpreter Training: Modelling the Processes of Translation and Interpretation*〈第十屆台灣國際口筆譯教學研討會：如何將口筆譯過程模型化〉, Fu Jen University, Taipei, Taiwan.

Shih, Chung-ling (2006). "Training in Post-MT Editing." *Helpful Assistance to Translators: MT & TM*. Taipei: Bookman Books Ltd., pp. 97–127.

Somers, Harold L. (1997). "A Practical Approach to Using Machine Translation Software: 'Post-editing' the Source Text." *The Translator*, Vol. 3, pp. 193–212.

Spalink, Karin (1997). "Post-editing MT." *Proceedings of MT Summit VI*, San Diego, California, USA.

Vasconcellos, Muriel (1986). "Functional Considerations in the Postediting of Machine-translated Output." *Computers and Translation*, Vol. 1, No. 1, pp. 21–38.

Vasconcellos, Muriel (1987). "A Comparison of MT Postediting and Traditional Revision." In Karl Kummer, ed., *Across the Language Gap: Proceedings of the 28th Annual Conference of the American Translators Association*. Medford, New Jersey: Learned Information, Inc., pp. 409–416.

Vasconcellos, Muriel (1987). "Post-editing On-screen: Machine Translation from Spanish into English." In Catriona Picken, ed., *Translating and the Computer 8: A Profession on the Move*. London: The Association for Information Management, pp. 133–146.

Vasconcellos, Muriel (1990). "Practical and Linguistic Strategies for Post-editing Machine Translation." In A. Leslie Willson, ed., *Looking Ahead: Proceedings of the 31st Annual Conference of American Translators Association*. Medford, New Jersey: Learned Information Inc., pp. 339–351.

Wagner, Emma (1985). "Post-editing Systran—A Challenge for Commission Translators." *Terminologie et Traduction*, No. 3.

Wagner, Emma (1985). "Rapid Post-editing of Systran." In Veronica Lawson, ed., *Tools for the Trade: Translating and the Computer 5*. London: The Association for Information Management, pp. 199–213.

Wagner, Emma (1987). "Post-editing—Practical Considerations." In Catriona Picken, ed., *The Business of Translation and Interpreting*. London: The Association for Information Management, pp. 71–78.

Pre-editing

Donomae, Susumu (1995). "Pre- and Post-editing MT Text for Better Communication and Documentation." *Proceedings of MT Summit V: Machine Translation Conference, Exhibition and Tutorial*, Luxembourg.

Ikehara, Satoru, Satoshi Shirai, Akio Yokoo, and Hiromi Nakaiwa (1991). "Toward an MT System without Pre-editing—Effects of New Methods in ALT-J/E." *Machine Translation Summit III*, Seattle, Washington, DC, USA, pp. 101–106.

Ikehara, Satoru, Satoshi Shirai, Akio Yokoo, and Hiromi Nakaiwa (1993). "Toward an MT System without Pre-editing—Effects of New Methods in ALT-J/E." In Sergei Nirenburg, ed., *Progress in Machine Translation*. Amsterdam: IOS and Tokyo: Ohmsha, pp. 161–169.

Pym, P. John (1990). "Pre-editing and the Use of Simplified Writing for MT: An Engineer's Experience of Operating an MT System." In Pamela Mayorcas, ed., *Translating and the Computer: The Translation Environment 10 Years On*. London: The Association for Information Management, pp. 80–95.

Reifler, Erwin (1952). "MT with Pre-editor and Writing for MT."

Proceedings of the M.I.T. Conference on Mechanical Translation, Massachusetts Institute of Technology, Cambridge, MA, USA.
Shei, Chi-Chiang (2002). "Teaching MT through Pre-editing: Three Case Studies." *Proceedings of the 6th Workshop of the European Association for Machine Translation: Teaching Machine Translation*, Manchester, England, pp. 89–98.
Shih, Chung-ling 史宗鈴 (2004).〈前機器翻譯編輯訓練〉(Pre-MT Editing Training).《電腦輔助翻譯》(*MT and TM*). Taipei: The Bookman Press, pp. 139–177.
Shih, Chung-ling (2006). "Controlled Translation and Pre-MT Editing." *Helpful Assistance to Translators: MT & TM*. Taipei: Bookman Books Ltd., pp. 128–151.
Shirai, Satoshi, Satoru Ikehara, and Tsukasa Kawaoka (1993). "Effects of Automatic Rewriting of Source Language within a Japanese to English MT System." *Proceedings of the 5th International Conference on Theoretical and Methodological Issues in Machine Translation (TMI-93): MT in the Next Generation*, Kyoto, Japan, pp. 226–239.
Smart, J. M. (1988). "Getting Smart in Many Languages: MT with an Option of Preprocessing." In Muriel Vasconcellos, ed., *Technology as Translation Strategy*. New York: State University of New York at Binghamton, pp. 124–126.
Yoshimi, Takehiko (2001). "Improvement of Translation Quality of English Newspaper Headlines by Automatic Pre-editing." *Machine Translation*, Vol. 16, No. 4, pp. 233–250.

❖ PART 13 ❖

Grammar

Context-free Grammar

Chen, Tai-Hung, Chun-Han Tseng, and Chia-Ping Chen (2006). "Automatic Learning of Context-free Grammar." *Proceedings of the Conference of the Association for Computational Linguistics and Chinese Language Processing* (*ROCLING-XVIII*), Taipei, Taiwan.

Corazza, Anna and Giorgio Satta (2006). "Cross-entropy and Estimation of Probabilistic Context-free Grammars." *Proceedings of the Human Language Technology Conference—Annual Meeting of the North American Chapter of the Association for Computational Linguistics* (*HLT-NAACL-2006*), New York, USA.

Feng, Zhiwei 馮志偉 (2004). 〈基於上下文無關語法的自動句法分析〉 (Automatic Parsing Based on Context-free Grammar). 《機器翻譯研究》 (*Studies on Machine Translation*). Beijing: China Translation and Publishing Corporation, pp. 208–342.

Kita, Kenji and Tatsuya Iwasa (1995). "Probabilistic Language Modeling Based on Mixture Probabilistic Context-free Grammar." *Proceedings of the Conference of the Association for Computational Linguistics and Chinese Language Processing* (*ROCLING-VIII*), Yuan-Ze Institute of Technology, Chung-Li, Taiwan.

Lavie, Alon and Masaru Tomita (1996). "GLR*—An Efficient Noise-skipping Parsing Algorithm for Context-free Grammars." In Harry Bunt and Masaru Tomita, eds., *Recent Advances in Parsing Technology*. Dordrecht: Kluwer Academic Publishers, pp. 183–200.

Minnen, Guido, William Thompson, Harry Bliss, and Dale Russell (2001). "Direct Bottom-up Chart Parsing Using Abbreviated Context-free Grammars." *Proceedings of the 7th International Workshop on Parsing Technologies* (*IWPT-2001*), Peking University, Beijing, China. Beijing: Tsinghua University Press, pp. 233–236.

Mohri, Mehryar and Brian Roark (2006). "Probabilistic Context-free Grammar Induction Based on Structural Zeros." *Proceedings of the Human Language Technology Conference—Annual Meeting of the North American Chapter of the Association for Computational Linguistics* (*HLT-NAACL-2006*), New York, USA.

Moore, Robert C. (2000). "Removing Left Recursion from Context-free Grammars." *Proceedings of the 1st Meeting of the North American Chapter of the Association for Computational Linguistics*, Seattle, Washington, DC, USA, pp. 249–255.

Nederhof, Mark-Jan and Giorgio Satta (2000). "Left-to-right Parsing and Bilexical Context-free Grammars." *Proceedings of the 1st Meeting of the North American Chapter of the Association for Computational Linguistics*, Seattle, Washington, DC, USA, pp. 272–279.

Nederhof, Mark-Jan and Giorgio Satta (2006). "Estimation of Consistent Probabilistic Context-free Grammars." *Proceedings of the Human Language Technology Conference—Annual Meeting of the North American Chapter of the Association for Computational Linguistics* (*HLT-NAACL-2006*), New York, USA.

Sampson, Geoffrey R. (1983). "Context Free Parsing and the Adequacy of Context-free Grammars." In Margaret King, ed., *Parsing Natural Language*. London: Academic Press, pp. 151–170.

Satta, Giorgio and Enoch Peserico (2005). "Some Computational Complexity Results for Synchronous Context-free Grammars." *Proceedings of Human Language Technology Conference and Conference on Empirical Methods in Natural Language Processing* (*HLT/EMNLP-2005*), Vancouver, BC, Canada.

Scha, Remko and Livia Polanyi (1988). "An Augmented Context-free Grammar for Discourse." *Proceedings of 12th International Conference on Computational Linguistics* (*COLING-88*), Budapest, Hungary, pp. 573–577.

Takeda, Koichi (1996). "Pattern-based Context-free Grammars for Machine Translation." *Proceedings of the 34th Annual Meeting of the Association for Computational Linguistics* (*ACL-96*), Santa Cruz, CA, USA, pp. 144–151.

Xia, Xuanyin and Wu Dekai (1996). "Parsing Chinese with an Almost-context-free Grammar." *Proceedings of the Conference on Empirical Methods in Natural Language Processing*, University of Pennsylvania, PA, USA.

Dependency Grammar

Allegranza, Valerio (1993). "Translation Fills the Gaps: A New Approach to Unbounded Dependencies." In Frank van Eynde, ed., *Linguistics Issues in Machine Translation*. London and New York: Pinter Publishers, pp. 160–234.

Badia, Toni (1993). "Dependency and Machine Translation." In Frank van

Eynde, ed., *Linguistics Issues in Machine Translation*. London and New York: Pinter Publishers, pp. 105–137.

Cahill, Aoife, Michael Burke, Ruth O'Donovan, Josef van Genabith, and Andy Way (2004). "Long-distance Dependency Resolution in Automatically Acquired Wide-coverage PCFG-based LFG Approximations." *Proceedings of the 42nd Annual Meeting of the Association for Computational Linguistics* (*ACL-2004*), Barcelona, Spain, pp. 319–326.

Che, Wanxiang 車萬翔, Liu Ting 劉挺, Qin Bing 秦兵, and Li Sheng 李生 (2001).〈面向依存文法分析的搭配抽取方法研究〉(A Method to Fetch Collocations Orienting Dependency Grammar). In Huang Changning 黃昌寧 and Zhang Pu 張普, eds.,《自然語言理解與機器翻譯》(*Natural Language Understanding and Machine Translation*). Beijing: Tsinghua University Press, pp. 153–159.

Debusmann, Ralph, Oana Postolache, and Maarika Traat (2005). "A Modular Account of Information Structure in Extensible Dependency Grammar." *Proceedings of the 6th International Conference on Intelligent Text Processing and Computational Linguistics* (*CICLing-2005*), Mexico City, Mexico, pp. 26–37.

Harper, Mary P., Christopher M. White, Wen Wang, Michael T. Johnson, and Randall A. Helzerman (2000). "The Effectiveness of Corpus-induced Dependency Grammars for Post-processing Speech." *Proceedings of the 1st Meeting of the North American Chapter of the Association for Computational Linguistics*, Seattle, Washington, DC, USA, pp. 102–109.

Hays, David G. (1961). "On the Value of Dependency Connection." In National Physical Laboratory, ed., *1961 International Conference on Machine Translation of Languages and Applied Language Analysis: Proceedings of the Conference Held at the National Physical Laboratory, Teddington, Middlesex, on 5th, 6th, 7th and 8th September*. London: Her Majesty's Stationery Office, Vol. 1, pp. 579–590.

Hays, David G. (1961). "Dependency Theory: A Formalism and Some Observations." *Language*, Vol. 40, No. 4, pp. 511–525.

Kirschner, Zdeněk (1982). "A Dependency-based Analysis of English for the Purpose of Machine Translation." *Explizite Beschreibung der Sprache und Automatische Textbearbeitung*, Vol. 1. Faculty of Mathematics and Physics, Charles University.

Kirschner, Zdeněk (1984). "On a Dependency Analysis of English for

Automatic Translation." In Petr Sgall, ed., *Contributions to Functional Syntax, Semantics, and Language Comprehension*. Amsterdam and Philadelphia: John Benjamins Publishing Company, pp. 335–358.

Klein, Dan and Christopher Manning (2004). "Corpus-based Induction of Syntactic Structure: Models of Dependency and Constituency." *Proceedings of the 42nd Annual Meeting of the Association for Computational Linguistics* (*ACL-2004*), Barcelona, Spain, pp. 478–485.

Lesmo, Leonardo and Livio Robaldo (2004). "Dependency Tree Semantics and Underspecification." *Proceedings of the International Conference on Natural Language Processing* (*ICON-2004*), International Institute of Information Technology, Hyderabad, India.

Liu, Haitao 劉海濤 (1997).〈依存語法和機器翻譯〉(Dependency Grammar and Machine Translation).《語言文字應用》(*Applied Linguistics*), No. 3, pp. 89–93.

Masakazu, Fujio and Matsumoto Yuji (1998). "Japanese Dependency Structure Analysis Based on Lexicalized Statistics."*Proceedings of the 3rd Conference on Empirical Methods in Natural Language Processing*, Granada, Spain.

Maxwell, Dan (1989). "English-Esperanto Metataxis." In Dan Maxwell and Klaus Schubert, eds., *Metataxis in Practice: Dependency Syntax for Multilingual Machine Translation*. Dordrecht: Foris Publications, pp. 267–297.

Maxwell, Dan and Klaus Schubert, eds. (1989). *Metataxis in Practice: Dependency Syntax for Multilingual Machine Translation*. Dordrecht: Foris Publications.

Plátek, Martin, Tomáš Holan, Vladislav Kuboň, and Karel Oliva (2001). "Word-order Relaxations and Restrictions within a Dependency Grammar." *Proceedings of the 7th International Workshop on Parsing Technologies* (*IWPT-2001*), Peking University, Beijing, China. Beijing: Tsinghua University Press, pp. 237–240.

Rambow, Owen, Ravi Bhimavarapu, and Srinivas Bangalore (2004). "Supertagging Nodes of a Dependency Tree." *Proceedings of the International Conference on Natural Language Processing* (*ICON-2004*), International Institute of Information Technology, Hyderabad, India.

Schubert, Klaus (1987). *Metataxis: Contrastive Dependency Syntax for Machine Translation*. Dordrecht-Holland: Foris Publications.

Schubert, Klaus (1989). "The Theory and Practice of Metataxis." In Dan Maxwell and Klaus Schubert, eds., *Metataxis in Practice: Dependency Syntax for Multilingual Machine Translation*. Dordrecht: Foris Publications, pp. 233–245.

Tamis, Dorine (1989). "Esperanto-French Metataxis." In Dan Maxwell and Klaus Schubert, eds., *Metataxis in Practice: Dependency Syntax for Multilingual Machine Translation*. Dordrecht: Foris Publications, pp. 247–266.

van Zuijlen, Job M. (1989). "Aspects of Metataxis Formalization." In Dan Maxwell and Klaus Schubert, eds., *Metataxis in Practice: Dependency Syntax for Multilingual Machine Translation*. Dordrecht: Foris Publications, pp. 299–320.

Weidmann, Dietrich M. (1988). "Universal Applicability of Dependency Grammar." In Dan Maxwell, Klaus Schubert, and Toon Witkam, eds., *New Directions in Machine Translation*. Dordrecht-Holland: Foris Publications, pp. 195–204.

Functional Grammar

Arnold, Doug J. and Louisa Sadler (1992). "Unification and Machine Translation." *Meta*, Vol. 37, No. 4, pp. 657–680.

Elhadad, Michael and Jacques Robin (1992). "Controlling Content Realization with Functional Unification Grammars." In Robert Dale, Eduard Hovy, Dieter Rosner, and Oliviero Stock, eds., *Aspects of Automated Natural Language Generation*. Berlin: Springer, pp. 89–104.

Kay, Martin (1984). "Functional Unification Grammar: A Formalism for Machine Translation." *Proceedings of the 10th International Conference on Computational Linguistics* (*COLING-84*), Stanford University, Stanford, CA, USA, pp. 75–78.

Sadler, Louisa and Doug J. Arnold (1992). "Unification and Machine Translation." *Meta*, Vol. 37, No. 4, pp. 681–692.

Steiner, Erich H. (1990). "Aspects of a Functional Grammar for Machine Translation." *Proceedings of the 3rd International Conference on Theoretical and Methodological Issues in Machine Translation of Natural Languages* (*TMI-90*), Linguistics Research Center, University of Texas at Austin, Austin, Texas, USA, pp. 159–169.

Grammar

Abeillé, Anne, Yves Schabes, and Aravind K. Joshi (1990). "Using Lexicalized Tree Adjoining Grammars for Machine Translation." *Proceedings of the 13th International Conference on Computational Linguistics* (*COLING-90*), Helsinki, Finland.

Alono, Miguel A. and Victor J. Díaz (2001). "Bidirectional Automata for Three Adjoining Grammars." *Proceedings of the 7th International Workshop on Parsing Technologies* (*IWPT-2001*), Peking University, Beijing, China. Beijing: Tsinghua University Press, pp. 42–53.

Alt, Franz L. and Ida Rhodes (1962). "Recognition of Clauses and Phrases in Machine Translation of Languages." In National Physical Laboratory, ed., *1961 International Conference on Machine Translation of Languages and Applied Language Analysis: Proceedings of the Conference Held at the National Physical Laboratory, Teddington, Middlesex, on 5th, 6th, 7th and 8th September*. London: Her Majesty's Stationery Office, Vol. 1, pp. 126–142.

Andrei, Ştefan (2001). "Bidirectional Ascendant Parsing for Natural Language Processing." *Proceedings of the 7th International Workshop on Parsing Technologies* (*IWPT-2001*), Peking University, Beijing, China. Beijing: Tsinghua University Press, pp. 54–65.

Appelo, Lisette (1994). "Categorical Divergences." In M. T. Rosetta, *Compositional Translation*. Dordrecht: Kluwer Academic Publishers, pp. 247–276.

Appelo, Lisette (1994). "Modular and Controlled M-grammars." In M. T. Rosetta, *Compositional Translation*. Dordrecht: Kluwer Academic Publishers, pp. 149–183.

Biskri, Ismail and Jean-Pierre Desclès (1997). "Applicative and Combinatory Categorical Grammar (From Syntax to Functional Semantics)." In Ruslan Mitkov and Nicolas Nicolov, eds., *Recent Advances in Natural Language Processing*. Amsterdam and Philadelphia: John Benjamins Publishing Company, pp. 71–84.

Carroll, John and Ted Briscoe (2001). "High Precision Extraction of Grammatical Relations." *Proceedings of the 7th International Workshop on Parsing Technologies* (*IWPT-2001*), Peking University, Beijing, China. Beijing: Tsinghua University Press, pp. 78–89.

Chen, Keh-jiann and Huang Chu-ren (1996). "Information-based Case

Grammar: A Unification-based Formalism for Parsing Chinese." *Journal of Chinese Linguistics*, Vol. 9, pp. 23–45.

Chitoran, D. and Alexander Petrovanu (1971). "Some Aspects of Translation in the Light of Generative Grammar." *Revue Roumaine de Linguistique*, Vol. 16, No. 5, pp. 379–399.

Ciortuz, Liviu (2001). "On Specialised Compilation of Rules in Unification Grammars." *Proceedings of the 7th International Workshop on Parsing Technologies* (*IWPT-2001*), Peking University, Beijing, China. Beijing: Tsinghua University Press, pp. 209–212.

Cucerzan, Silviu and David Yarowsky (2003). "Minimally Supervised Induction of Grammatical Gender." *Proceedings of the Human Language Technology and North American Chapter of Association of Computational Linguistics 2003* (*HLT/NAACL-2003*), Edmonton, Alberta, Canada.

DiMarco, Chrysanne and Graeme Hirst (1988). "Stylistic Grammars in Language Translation." *Proceedings of 12th International Conference on Computational Linguistics* (*COLING-88*), Budapest, Hungary, pp. 148–153.

Ding, Yuan and Martha Palmer (2005). "Machine Translation Using Probabilistic Synchronous Dependency Insertion Grammars." *Proceedings of the 43rd Annual Meeting of the Association of Computational Linguistics* (*ACL-2005*), Ann Arbor, Michigan, USA.

Dymetman, Marc and Pierre Isabelle (1988). "Reversible Logic Grammars for Machine Translation." *Proceedings of the 2nd International Conference on Theoretical and Methodological Issues in Machine Translation of Natural Languages* (*TMI-88*), Carnegie Mellon University, Center for Machine Translation, Pittsburgh, Pennsylvania, USA.

Eisner, Jason (2002). "Transformational Priors over Grammars." *Proceedings of the 2002 Conference on Empirical Methods in Natural Language Processing* (*EMNLP-2002*), University of Pennsylvania, Philadelphia, PA, USA.

Emele, Martin C. and Rémi Zajac (1990). "Typed Unification Grammars." *Proceedings of the 13th International Conference on Computational Linguistics* (*COLING-90*), Helsinki, Finland, pp. 293–298.

Feng, Zhiwei 馮志偉 and Yang Ping 楊平 (1987). 〈自動翻譯中的語法問題〉 (Grammatical Issues in Automatic Translation). 《自動翻譯》 (*Automatic Translation*). Shanghai: Knowledge Press, pp. 32–89.

Ferro, M. Vilares, D. Cabrero Souto, and M. A. Alonso Pardo (2000). "On Non-termination in DCGs." *Proceedings of the 1st International Conference on Intelligent Text Processing and Computational Linguistics (CICLing-2000)*, Mexico City, Mexico.

Flickinger, Dan, Jan Tore Lønning, Helge Dyvik, Stephan Oepen, and Francis Bond (2005). "SEM-I Rational MT: Enriching Deep Grammars with a Semantic Interface for Scalable Machine Translation." *Proceedings of MT Summit X*, Phuket, Thailand.

Green, Thomas R. G. (1975). "Computer Translation with Paired Grammars." *Behavior Research Methods and Instrumentation*, Vol. 7, No. 6, pp. 557–562.

Guo, Yikun, Weng Fuliang, and Wu Lide (2001). "Grammar Induction by MDL-based Distributional Classification." *Proceedings of the 7th International Workshop on Parsing Technologies (IWPT-2001)*, Peking University, Beijing, China. Beijing: Tsinghua University Press, pp. 112–122.

Harman, Gilbert H. and Victor H. Yngve (1963). "Generative Grammars without Transformation Rules." *Quarterly Progress Report of the Research Laboratory of Electronics, MIT*, pp. 171–173.

Hausser, Roland (1988). "Computational Complexity of Left-associative Grammar." *Proceedings of the 2nd International Conference on Theoretical and Methodological Issues in Machine Translation of Natural Languages (TMI-88)*, Carnegie Mellon University, Center for Machine Translation, Pittsburgh, Pennsylvania, USA.

Hausser, Roland (1988). "Left-associative Grammar: An Informal Outline." *Machine Translation*, Vol. 3, No. 1, pp. 23–67.

Hausser, Roland (1988). "Left-associative Grammar: The Algebraic Definitions." *Machine Translation*, Vol. 3, No. 2, pp. 121–155.

Heberden, Mary V. (1956). "Teaching the Machine Grammar." *Babel*, Vol. 2, No. 3, pp. 119–124.

Hwa, Rebecca (2000). "Sample Selection for Statistical Grammar Induction." *Proceedings of the Joint Sigdat Conference on Empirical Methods in Natural Language Processing and Very Large Corpora (EMNLP/VLC-2000)*, Hong Kong University of Science and Technology, Hong Kong.

Infante-Lopez, Gabriel and Maarten de Rijke (2004). "Alternative Approaches for Generating Bodies of Grammar Rules." *Proceedings of the 42nd Annual Meeting of the Association for Computational Linguistics* (*ACL-2004*), Barcelona, Spain, pp. 454–461.

Jones, Douglas and Rick Havrilla (1998). "Twisted Pair Grammar: Support for Rapid Development of Machine Translation for Low Density Languages." In David L. Farwell, Laurie Gerber, and Eduard Hovy, eds., *Machine Translation and the Information Soup*. Berlin: Springer Verlag, pp. 318–332.

Joshi, Aravind K. (1997). "Some Linguistic, Computational and Statistical Implications of Lexicalised Grammars." In Ruslan Mitkov and Nicolas Nicolov, eds., *Recent Advances in Natural Language Processing*. Amsterdam and Philadelphia: John Benjamins Publishing Company, pp. 3–14.

Kang, Shiyong 亢世勇 (2000).〈計算機時代漢語語法研究的特點〉(Features of the Study of Chinese Grammar in the Age of Computers). In Yu Shiwen 俞士汶 and Zhu Xuefeng 朱學鋒, eds.,《計算語言學文集》(*Papers on Computational Linguistics*), Vol. 4. Beijing: Department of Computer Science and Technology and Institute of Computational Linguistics, Peking University, pp. 54–58.

Klima, Edward S. (1962). "Structure at the Lexical Level and Its Implications for Transfer Grammar." In National Physical Laboratory, ed., *1961 International Conference on Machine Translation of Languages and Applied Language Analysis: Proceedings of the Conference Held at the National Physical Laboratory, Teddington, Middlesex, on 5th, 6th, 7th and 8th September*. London: Her Majesty's Stationery Office, Vol. 1, pp. 98–108.

Kuhn, Jonas (2004). "Experiments in Parallel-text Based Grammar Induction." *Proceedings of the 42nd Annual Meeting of the Association for Computational Linguistics* (*ACL-2004*), Barcelona, Spain, pp. 470–477.

Leermakers, René and Joep Rous (1994). "An Attribute Grammar View." In M. T. Rosetta, *Compositional Translation*. Dordrecht: Kluwer Academic Publishers, pp. 379–388.

Leermakers, René and Jan Landsbergen (1994). "The Formal Definition of M-grammars." In M. T. Rosetta, *Compositional Translation*. Dordrecht: Kluwer Academic Publishers, pp. 353–377.

Liou, Hsien-Chin, Hui-Li Hsu, Yong-Chang Huang, and Von-Wun Soo (1991). "Development of an Automatic English Grammar Debugger for Chinese Students: A Progress Report." *Proceedings of the Conference of the Association for Computational Linguistics and Chinese Language Processing* (*ROCLING-IV*), National Chiao-Tung University, Hsin-Chu, Taiwan.

Llitjós, Ariadna Font, Katharina Probst, and Jaime G. Carbonell (2004). "Error Analysis of Two Types of Grammar for the Purpose of Automatic Rule Refinement." In Robert E. Frederking and Kathryn B. Taylors, eds., *Machine Translation: From Real Users to Research*. Berlin: Springer Verlag, pp. 187–196.

Matthews, George Hubert (1961). "The Use of Grammars within the Mechanical Translation Routine." In Harold P. Edmundson, ed., *Proceedings of the National Symposium on Machine Translation*. Englewood Cliffs: Prentice-Hall.

Melamed, I. Dan (2003). "Multitext Grammars and Synchronous Parsers." *Proceedings of the Human Language Technology and North American Chapter of Association of Computational Linguistics 2003* (*HLT/NAACL-2003*), Edmonton, Alberta, Canada.

Melamed, I. Dan, Giorgio Satta, and Benjamin Wellington (2004). "Generalized Multitext Grammars." *Proceedings of the 42nd Annual Meeting of the Association for Computational Linguistics* (*ACL-2004*), Barcelona, Spain, pp. 661–668.

Mel'cuk, Igor A. (1974). "Grammatical Meanings in Interlinguas for Automatic Translation and the Concept of Grammatical Meaning." *Machine Translation and Applied Linguistics*, Vol. I, pp. 95–113.

Mitchell, R. P. (1962). "A Note on Categorical Grammars." In National Physical Laboratory, ed., *1961 International Conference on Machine Translation of Languages and Applied Language Analysis: Proceedings of the Conference Held at the National Physical Laboratory, Teddington, Middlesex, on 5th, 6th, 7th and 8th September*. London: Her Majesty's Stationery Office, Vol. 1, pp. 212–219.

Nagao, Makoto (1992). "Are the Grammars So Far Developed Appropriate to Recognize the Real Structure of a Sentence?" *Proceedings of the 4th International Conference on Theoretical and Methodological Issues in Machine Translation of Natural Languages: Empiricist vs. Rationalist Methods in MT* (*TMI-92*), Montreal, Quebec, Canada, pp. 127–137.

Nariyama, Shigeko (2002). "Grammar for Ellipsis Resolution in Japanese." *Proceedings of the 9th International Conference on Theoretical and Methodological Issues in Machine Translation* (*TMI-2002*), Keihanna, Japan, pp. 135–145.

Nesson, Rebecca, Stuart M. Shieber, and Alexander Rush (2006). "Induction of Probabilistic Synchronous Tree-insertion Grammars for Machine Translation." *Proceedings of the 7th Biennial Conference of the Association for Machine Translation in the Americas (AMTA-2006): Visions for the Future of Machine Translation*, Boston Marriott, Cambridge, MA, USA.

Newman, Paula (1990). "Symmetric Slot Grammar (SSG): A Bi-directional Design for MT." *Proceedings of the 3rd International Conference on Theoretical and Methodological Issues in Machine Translation of Natural Languages (TMI-90)*, Linguistics Research Center, University of Texas at Austin, Austin, Texas, USA, pp. 145–157.

Niyogi, Sourabh (2001). "A Minimalist Implementation of Verb Subcategorization." *Proceedings of the 7th International Workshop on Parsing Technologies (IWPT-2001)*, Peking University, Beijing, China. Beijing: Tsinghua University Press, pp. 142–153.

Nomoto, Tadashi (1997). "Effects of Grammatical Annotation on a Topic Identification Task." In Ruslan Mitkov and Nicolas Nicolov, eds., *Recent Advances in Natural Language Processing*. Amsterdam and Philadelphia: John Benjamins Publishing Company, pp. 235–246.

Odjik, Jan (1994). "Compositionality and Syntactic Generalisations." In M. T. Rosetta, *Compositional Translation*. Dordrecht: Kluwer Academic Publishers, pp. 185–201.

Odjik, Jan (1994). "M-grammars." In M. T. Rosetta, *Compositional Translation*. Dordrecht: Kluwer Academic Publishers, pp. 35–56.

Peng, Ping (1991). "A Trace & Unification Grammar for Chinese Hans Ulrich Block." *Proceedings of the Conference of the Association for Computational Linguistics and Chinese Language Processing (ROCLING-IV)*, National Chiao-Tung University, Hsin-Chu, Taiwan.

Prolo, Carlos A. (2002). "Fast LR Parsing Using Rich (Tree Adjoining) Grammars." *Proceedings of the 2002 Conference on Empirical Methods in Natural Language Processing (EMNLP-2002)*, University of Pennsylvania, Philadelphia, PA, USA.

Qian, Feng (1991). "A Synopsis of CPSG—Chinese Phrase Structure Grammar." In Victor H. Mair and Liu Yongquan, eds., *Characters and Computers*. Amsterdam: IOS Press, pp. 37–57.

Sgall, Petr (1999). "On Intermediate Structures and Tectogrammatics." *Proceedings of the 4th Workshop of the European Association for*

Machine Translation: EU and the New Languages: Translation—Possibilities, Policies and Practicalities, Prague, the Czech Republic.
Shih, Hsue-Hueh and Steve Young (1997). "A Study on the Portability of a Grammatical Inference System." *Proceedings of the International Conference on Research in Computational Linguistics* (*ROCLING-X*), Academia Sinica, Taipei, Taiwan.
Shih, Hsue-Hueh (1998). "The Design of Sem-syn Initial Grammar in Chinese Grammatical Inference." *Proceedings of the International Conference on Research in Computational Linguistics* (*ROCLING-XI*), Hsin-Chu, Taiwan.
Steels, Luc (2004). "Constructivist Development of Grounded Construction Grammar." *Proceedings of the 42nd Annual Meeting of the Association for Computational Linguistics* (*ACL-2004*), Barcelona, Spain, pp. 9–16.
Stymne, Sara and Lars Ahrenberg (2006). "A Bilingual Grammar for Translation of English-Swedish Verb Frame Divergences." *Proceedings of the 11th Workshop of the European Association for Machine Translation: Machine Translation/Translation Aids—Tools to Increase Quality and to Save Money*, the University of Oslo, Oslo, Norway.
Voss, Clare R. and Bonnie J. Dorr (1995). "Toward a Lexicalized Grammar for Interlinguas." *Machine Translation*, Vol. 10, Nos. 1–2, pp. 143–184.
Weng, Fuliang, Jin Naiyong, Meng Jie, and Zhu Yujia (2001). "A Novel Probabilistic Model for Link Unification Grammar." *Proceedings of the 7th International Workshop on Parsing Technologies* (*IWPT-2001*), Peking University, Beijing, China. Beijing: Tsinghua University Press, pp. 189–198.
Wilks, Yorick (1972). *Grammar, Meaning and the Machine Analysis of Language*. London: Routledge and Kegan Paul.
Wong, Andy Man Hon and Suen Caesar Lun (1993). "Fawrmt: With Special Emphasis on Grammar Designs and Partitioned Parsing." *Proceedings of the Conference of the Association for Computational Linguistics and Chinese Language Processing* (*ROCLING-VI*), Nantou, Taiwan.
Xia, Fei, Martha Palmer, and Aravind Joshi (2000). "A Uniform Method of Grammar Extraction and Its Applications." *Proceedings of the Joint Sigdat Conference on Empirical Methods in Natural Language*

Processing and Very Large Corpora (*EMNLP/VLC-2000*), Hong Kong University of Science and Technology, Hong Kong.
Yang, Y. and Shuji Doshita (1988). "The Construction of a Semantic Grammar for Chinese Language Processing and Its Implementation." *Transactions of the Information Processing Society of Japan*, Vol. 27, No. 2, pp. 155–164.
Yeh, Alexander (2000). "Using Existing Systems to Supplement Small Amounts of Annotated Grammatical Relations Training Data." *Proceedings of the 38th Annual Meeting of the Association for Computational Linguistics* (*ACL-2000*), Hong Kong.
Yu, Shiwen 俞士汶 (1998).〈語法知識在語言信息處理研究中的作用〉(The Role of Linguistic Knowledge in Research on Language Information Processing). In Yu Shiwen 俞士汶 and Zhu Xuefeng 朱學鋒, eds.,《計算語言學文集》(*Papers on Computational Linguistics*), Vol. 3. Beijing: Department of Computer Science and Technology and Institute of Computational Linguistics, Peking University, pp. 8–16.
Zhan, Weidong 詹衛東, Chang Baobao 常寶寶, and Yu Shiwen 俞士汶 (1998).〈現代漢語短語本位語法體系在機器翻譯中的應用及其問題〉(Applications and Problems of Chinese Phrase-based Grammar in Machine Translation). In Yu Shiwen and Zhu Xuefeng, eds.,《計算語言學文集》(*Papers on Computational Linguistics*), Vol. 3. Beijing: Department of Computer Science and Technology and Institute of Computational Linguistics, Peking University, pp. 87–93.

Head-driven Phrase Structure Grammar

Badia, Toni and Roser Saurí (2000). "Enlarging HPSG with Lexical Semantics." *Proceedings of the 1st International Conference on Intelligent Text Processing and Computational Linguistics* (*CICLing-2000*), Mexico City, Mexico.
Becker, Tilman and Patrice Lopez (2000). "The Application of HPSG-to-TAG Compilation Techniques." In Wolfgang Wahlster, ed., *Verbmobil: Foundations of Speech-to-speech Translation*. Berlin: Springer Verlag, pp. 497–506.
Flickinger, Dan, Ann Copestake, and Ivan A. Sag (2000). "HPSG Analysis of English." In Wolfgang Wahlster, ed., *Verbmobil: Foundations of Speech-to-speech Translation*. Berlin: Springer Verlag, pp. 254–263.

Müller, Stefan and Walter Kasper (2000). "HPSG Analysis of German." In Wolfgang Wahlster, ed., *Verbmobil: Foundations of Speech-to-speech Translation*. Berlin: Springer Verlag, pp. 238–253.

Siegel, Melanie (2000). "HPSG Analysis of Japanese." In Wolfgang Wahlster, ed., *Verbmobil: Foundations of Speech-to-speech Translation*. Berlin: Springer Verlag, pp. 264–279.

Uszkoreit, Hans, Dan Flickinger, Walter Kasper, and Ivan A. Sag (2000). "Deep Linguistic Analysis with HPSG." In Wolfgang Wahlster, ed., *Verbmobil: Foundations of Speech-to-speech Translation*. Berlin: Springer Verlag, pp. 216–237.

Lexical-functional Grammar

Alam, Yukiko Sasaki (1986). "A Lexical-functional Approach to Japanese for the Purpose of Machine Translation." *Machine Translation*, Vol. 1, No. 4, pp. 199–214.

Amores, J. Gabriel and Gloria Alvarez (1994). "Resultative and Depictive Constructions in English: An LFG-based Approach for Machine Translation." In Carlos Martin Vide, ed., *Lenguajes Naturales y Lenguajes Naturales X*. Barcelona: PPU.

Berwick, Robert C. (1982). "Computational Complexity and Lexical Functional Grammar." *American Journal of Computational Linguistics*, Vol. 8, Nos. 3–4, pp. 97–109.

Cancedda, Nicola and Christer Samuelsson (2000). "Experiments with Corpus-based LFG Specialization." *Proceedings of the 6th Applied Natural Language Processing Conference*, Seattle, Washington, DC, USA, pp. 204–209.

Clark, Stephen and James R. Curran (2006). "Partial Training for a Lexicalized-grammar Parser." *Proceedings of the Human Language Technology Conference—Annual Meeting of the North American Chapter of the Association for Computational Linguistics* (*HLT-NAACL-2006*), New York, USA.

Frank, Anette and Katrin Erk (2004). "Towards an LFG Syntax-semantics Interface for Frame Semantics Annotation." *Proceedings of the 5th International Conference on Intelligent Text Processing and Computational Linguistics* (*CICLing-2004*), Chung-Ang University, Seoul, Korea, pp. 1–12.

Güngördü, Zealal and Kemal Oflazer (1995). "Parsing Turkish Using the

Lexical Functional Grammar Formalism." *Machine Translation*, Vol. 10, No. 4, pp. 293–319.

Kahane, Sylvain (2001). "A Fully Lexicalized Grammar for French Based on Meaning-text Theory." *Proceedings of the 2nd International Conference on Intelligent Text Processing and Computational Linguistics* (*CICLing-2001*), Mexico City, Mexico.

Kaplan, Ronald M. and Joan Bresnan (1982). "Lexical-functional Grammar: A Formal System for Grammatical Representation." In Joan Bresnan, ed., *The Mental Representation of Grammatical Relations*. Cambridge, MA: MIT Press, pp. 173–281.

Kudo, Ikuo and Hirosato Nomura (1986). "Lexical-functional Transfer: A Transfer Framework in a Machine Translation Based in LFG." *Proceedings of the 11th International Conference on Computational Linguistics* (*COLING-86*), Bonn, Germany, pp. 112–114.

Riezler, Stefan, Tracy H. King, Richard Crouch, and Annie Zaenen (2003). "Statistical Sentence Condensation Using Ambiguity Packing and Stochastic Disambiguation Methods for Lexical-functional Grammar." *Proceedings of the Human Language Technology and North American Chapter of Association of Computational Linguistics 2003* (*HLT/NAACL-2003*), Edmonton, Alberta, Canada.

Sadler, Louisa, Ian Crookston, Doug J. Arnold, and Andy Way (1990). "LFG and Translation." *Proceedings of the 3rd International Conference on Theoretical and Methodological Issues in Machine Translation of Natural Languages* (*TMI-90*), Linguistics Research Center, University of Texas, Austin, Texas, USA, pp. 121–130.

Montague Grammar

Godden, Kurt (1981). "Montague Grammar and Machine Translation between Thai and English." PhD dissertation, University of Kansas.

Landsbergen, Jan (1981). "Adaptation of Montague Grammar to the Requirements of Parsing." In Jeroen Groenendijk, Theo Janssen, and Martin Stokhof, eds., *Formal Methods in the Study of Language*. Amsterdam: Mathematical Centre, pp. 399–419.

Landsbergen, Jan (1982). "Machine Translation Based on Logically Isomorphic Montague Grammars." In Jan Horecky, ed., *Proceedings of the 9th International Conference on Computational Linguistics*

(*COLING-82*), Prague, the Czech Republic. Amsterdam: North-Holland Publishing Company, pp. 175–181.
Landsbergen, Jan (1987). "Montague Grammar and Machine Translation." In Peter J. Whitelock, Mary McGee Wood, Harold L. Somers, Roderick L. Johnson, and Paul A. Bennett, eds., *Linguistic Theory and Computer Applications*. London: Academic Press, pp. 113–147.

Phrase Structure Grammar

Gazdar, Gerald, Ewan Klein, Geoffrey Pullum, and Ivan Sag (1985). *Generalized Phrase Structure Grammar*. Oxford: Blackwell.
Qian, Feng (1991). "A Synopsis of CPSG—Chinese Phrase Structure Grammar." In Victor H. Mair and Liu Yongquan, eds., *Characters and Computers*. Amsterdam: IOS Press, pp. 37–57.

Stochastic Grammar

Bangalore, Srinivas and Giuseppe Riccardi (2000). "Stochastic Finite-state Models for Spoken Language Machine Translation." *Proceedings of the ANLP/NAACL-2000 Workshop on Embedded Machine Translation Systems—Volume 5*, Seattle, Washington, DC, USA, pp. 52–59.
Bangalore, Srinivas and Giuseppe Riccardi (2001). "A Finite-state Approach to Machine Translation." *Proceedings of the 2nd Meeting of the North American Chapter of the Association for Computational Linguistics*, Pittsburgh, Pennsylvania, USA, pp. 135–142.
Dermatas, Evangelos and George Kokkinakis (1995). "Automatic Stochastic Tagging of Natural Language Texts." *Computational Linguistics*, Vol. 21, No. 2, pp. 137–163.
Johnson, Mark and Stefan Riezler (2000). "Exploiting Auxiliary Distributions in Stochastic Unification-based Grammars." *Proceedings of the 1st Meeting of the North American Chapter of the Association for Computational Linguistics*, Seattle, Washington, DC, USA, pp. 154–161.
King, Gilbert W. (1956). "Stochastic Methods of Mechanical Translation." *Mechanical Translation*, Vol. 3, No. 2, pp. 38–39.
Minker, Wolfgang (1997). "Stochastically-based Natural Language

Understanding across Tasks and Languages." *Proceedings of the 5th European Conference on Speech Communication and Technology* (*EuroSpeech-97*), Rhodes, Greece, pp. 1423–1426.

Minker, Wolfgang, Samir K. Bennacef, and Jean-Luc Gauvain (1996). "Stochastic Case Frame Approach for Natural Language Understanding." *Proceedings of the 3rd European Conference on Speech, Communication, and Technology* (*EuroSpeech-96*), Berlin, Germany, pp. 1013–1016.

Minker, Wolfgang, Marsal Gavaldá, and Alex H. Waibel (1999). "Stochastically-based Semantic Analysis for Machine Translation." *Computer Speech and Language*, Vol. 13, pp. 177–194.

Ney, Hermann (2001). "Stochastic Modelling: From Pattern Classification to Language Translation." *Proceedings of the Association for Computational Linguistics 39th Annual Meeting and 10th Conference of the European Chapter: Data-driven Machine Translation* (*ACL-EACL-2001*), Toulouse, France, pp. 33–37.

Riccardi, Giuseppe, E. Bocchieri, and R. Pieraccini (1995). "Non-deterministic Stochastic Language Models for Speech Recognition." *Proceedings of the IEEE International Conference on Acoustics, Speech and Signal Processing* (*ICASSP-95*), Detroit, MI, USA, pp. 247–250.

Riccardi, Giuseppe, R. Pieraccini, and E. Bocchieri (1996). "Stochastic Automata for Language Modeling." *Computer Speech and Language*, Vol. 10, pp. 265–293.

Riccardi, Giuseppe and Srinivas Bangalore (1998). "Automatic Acquisition of Phrase Grammars for Stochastic Language Modeling." *Proceedings of the 6th Workshop on Very Large Corpora*, Montreal, Quebec, Canada, pp. 188–196.

Riccardi, Giuseppe and Allen Gorin (2000). "Stochastic Language Adaptation over Time and State in Natural Spoken Dialogue Systems." *IEEE Transactions on Speech and Audio Processing*, Vol. 8, pp. 3–10.

Riezler, Stefan, Detlef Prescher, Jonas Kuhn, and Mark Johnson (2000). "Lexicalized Stochastic Modeling of Constraint-based Grammars Using Log-linear Measures and EM Training." *Proceedings of the 38th Annual Meeting of the Association for Computational Linguistics* (*ACL-2000*), Hong Kong.

Soricut, Radu and Daniel Marcu (2006). "Stochastic Language Generation

Using WIDL-expressions and Its Application in Machine Translation and Summarization." *Proceedings of the Joint Conference of the International Committee on Computational Linguistics and the Association for Computational Linguistics (COLING/ACL-2006)*, Sydney, Australia.

Sproat, Richard, Chilin Shih, William A. Gale, and Nancy Chang (1996). "A Stochastic Finite-state Word-segmentation Algorithm for Chinese." *Computational Linguistics*, Vol. 22, No. 3, pp. 377–404.

Wu, Dekai (1995). "Stochastic Inversion Transduction Grammars, with Application to Segmentation, Bracketing, and Alignment of Parallel Corpora." *Proceedings of the 14th International Joint Conference on Artificial Intelligence*, Montreal, Quebec, Canada, pp. 1328–1335.

Wu, Dekai (1997). "Stochastic Inversion Transduction Grammars and Bilingual Parsing of Parallel Corpora." *Computational Linguistics*, Vol. 23, pp. 377–404.

Wu, Dekai and Hongsing Wong (1998). "Machine Translation with a Stochastic Grammatical Channel." *Proceedings of the 36th Annual Meeting of the Association for Computational Linguistics and 17th International Conference on Computational Linguistics (COLING-ACL-98)*, Montreal, Quebec, Canada, pp. 1408–1414.

Translation Grammar

Carl, Michael (2001). "Inducing Translation Grammars from Aligned Texts." In Bente Maegaard, ed., *Proceedings of MT Summit VIII: Machine Translation in the Information Age*, Santiago de Compostela, Spain.

Carl, Michael (2003). "Inducing Translation Grammars from Bracketed Alignments." In Michael Carl and Andy Way, eds., *Recent Advances in Example-based Machine Translation*. Dordrecht: Kluwer Academic Publishers, pp. 339–361.

Sánchez, J. A. and José-Miguel Benedí (2006). "Obtaining Word Phrases with Stochastic Inversion Translation Grammars for Phrase-based Statistical Machine Translation." *Proceedings of the 11th Workshop of the European Association for Machine Translation: Machine Translation/Translation Aids—Tools to Increase Quality and to Save Money*, the University of Oslo, Oslo, Norway.

Universal Grammar

Reifler, Erwin (1952). "General MT and Universal Grammar." *Proceedings of the M.I.T. Conference on Mechanical Translation,* Massachusetts Institute of Technology, Cambridge, MA, USA.

❖ PART 14 ❖

Human Translation

Human-aided Computer Translation

Boitet, Christian (1998). "(Human-aided) Machine Translation: A Better Future?" In Ronald Cole, Joseph Mariani, Hans Uszkoreit, Annie Zaenen, and V. Zue, eds., *Survey of the State of the Art in Human Language Technology*. Pisa: Giardini, pp. 251–256.

Franco Sabarís, Marcos, J. Luis Rojas, Carlos Dafonte, and Bernardino Arcay (2001). "Universal Translation Language: A New Approach to Multilingual Human Assisted Machine Translation." In Bente Maegaard, ed., *Proceedings of MT Summit VIII: Machine Translation in the Information Age*, Santiago de Compostela, Spain.

Hutchins, W. John (1986). "Interactive and Human-aided Systems." *Machine Translation: Past, Present and Future.* Chichester: Ellis Horwood, pp. 292–306.

Masterman, Margaret (1967). "Man-aided Computer Translation from English into French Using an Online System to Manipulate a Bi-lingual Conceptual Dictionary, or Thesaurus." *Deuxieme Conference Internationale sur le Traitement Automatique des Langues*, Grenoble, France.

Human-computer Interaction

Bennett, Paul A. (1998). "Machine Translation as a Model of Human Translation." In Lynne Bowker, Michael Cronin, Dorothy Kenny, and Jennifer Pearson, eds., *Unity in Diversity? Current Trends in Translation Studies*. Manchester: St. Jerome Publishing, pp. 157–166.

Brown, Ralf D. and Sergei Nirenburg (1990). "Human-computer Interaction for Semantic Disambiguation." *Proceedings of the 13th International Conference on Computational Linguistics* (*COLING-90*), Helsinki, Finland, Vol. 3, pp. 42–47.

Foster, George, Pierre Isabelle, and Pierre Plamondon (1997). "Target-text Mediated Interactive Machine Translation." *Machine Translation*, Vol. 12, Nos. 1–2, pp. 175–194.

Hays, David G. (1979). "Communication and Control in Man and Machine." *International Forum on Information and Documentation*, Vol. 5, No. 2, pp. 6–8.

Heizmann, Susanne (1994). "Human Strategies in Translation and

Interpretation—What MT Can Learn from Translators." *Machine Translation—Ten Years On: Proceedings of the 2nd International Conference Organised by Cranfield University*, Cranfield, England.

Kay, Martin (1997). "It's Still the Proper Place." *Machine Translation*, Vol. 12, Nos. 1–2, pp. 35–38.

Kay, Martin (1997). "The Proper Place of Men and Machines in Language Translation." *Machine Translation*, Vol. 12, Nos. 1–2, pp. 3–23.

Langlais, Philippe and George Foster (2000). "Using Context-dependent Interpolation to Combine Statistical Language and Translation Models for Interactive Machine Translation." *Proceedings of the 6th International Conference on Computer-assisted Information Retrieval* (*RIAO*), Paris, France, pp. 507–519.

Melby, Alan K. (1981). "Translators and Machines—Can They Cooperate?" *Meta*, Vol. 26, No. 1, pp. 23–34.

Melby, Alan K. (1987). "On Human-machine Interaction in Translation." In Sergei Nirenburg, ed., *Machine Translation: Theoretical and Methodological Issue*. New York: Cambridge University Press, pp. 145–154.

Melby, Alan K. (1997). "Some Notes on the Proper Place of Men and Machines in Language Translation." *Machine Translation*, Vol. 12, Nos. 1–2, pp. 29–34.

Moser-Mercer, Barbara (1987). "Man/Machine Interface in Translation and Terminology." *Meta*, Vol. 32, No. 2, pp. 156–163.

Pan, Youbo 潘幼博 (1994).〈人工翻譯是否將被機器替代？〉(Will Human Translation Be Replaced by Machine?). In Li Yashu 李亞舒, Yan Yutang 嚴毓棠, Zhang Ming 張明, and Zhao Lanhui 趙蘭慧, eds.,《科技翻譯論著集萃》(*Collected Essays on Scientific and Technical Translation*). Beijing: Chinese Scientific Technology Press 中國科學技術出版社, pp. 501–508.

Panov, D. Yu. (1960). "Machine Translation and the Human Being." *Impact of Science on Society*, Vol. 10, pp. 16–25.

Porzel, Robert and Manja Baudis (2004). "The Tao of CHI: Towards Effective Human-computer Interaction." *Proceedings of the Human Language Technology Conference/North American Chapter of the Association for Computational Linguistics Annual Meeting* (*HLT/NAACL-2004*), Boston, MA, USA.

Reeder, Florence (2006). "Human Factors Introducing MT." *Proceedings of the 7th Biennial Conference of the Association for Machine*

Translation in the Americas (AMTA-2006): Visions for the Future of Machine Translation, Boston Marriott, Cambridge, MA, USA.

Richens, Richard H. (1958). "Tigris and Euphrates—A Comparison between Human and Machine Translation." *Mechanisation of Thought Processes: Proceedings of a Symposium Held at the National Physical Laboratory on 24th–27th November 1958*. London: Her Majesty's Stationery Office, pp. 281–302.

Svanholm, Flemming (1992). "The Happy Triad—The Human, the MAT, and the MT." In *Translating and the Computer 14: Quality Standards and the Implementation of Technology in Translation*. London: The Association for Information Management.

Villaseñor-Pineda, Luis, Manuel Montes-y-Gómez, and Jean Caelen (2004). "A Modal Logic Framework for Human-computer Spoken Interaction." *Proceedings of the 5th International Conference on Intelligent Text Processing and Computational Linguistics (CICLing-2004)*, Chung-Ang University, Seoul, Korea, pp. 45–53.

Vitek, Steve Vlasta (2000). "Reflections of a Human Translator on Machine Translation, Or Will MT Become the 'Deus Ex Machina' Rendering Humans Obsolete in an Age When 'Deus Est Machina'?" *Translation Journal*, Vol. 4, No. 3.

Ward, Karen and Peter A. Heeman (2000). "Acknowledgments in Human-computer Interaction." *Proceedings of the 1st Meeting of the North American Chapter of the Association for Computational Linguistics*, Seattle, Washington, DC, USA, pp. 280–287.

Weaver, Alan (1988). "Two Aspects of Interactive Machine Translation." In Muriel Vasconcellos, ed., *Technology as Translation Strategy*. Binghamton, New York: State University of New York at Binghamton, pp. 116–123.

Whitelock, Peter J., Mary McGee Wood, Brian J. Chandler, Natsuko Holden, and Heather J. Horsfall (1986). "Strategies for Interactive Machine Translation: The Experience and Implications of the UMIST Japanese Project." *Proceedings of the 11th International Conference on Computational Linguistics (COLING-86)*, Bonn, Germany, pp. 329–334.

Wilks, Yorick (2002). "Human-computer Dialogue: Where Are We Now? Or Computer Measures of Text Reuse." *Proceedings of the 3rd International Conference on Intelligent Text Processing and Computational Linguistics (CICLing-2002)*, Mexico City, Mexico.

Yamabana, Kiyoshi, Shin-ichiro Kamei, Kazunori Muraki, Shinichi Doi, Shinko Tamura, and Kenji Satoh (1997). "A Hybrid Approach to Interactive Machine Translation—Integrating Rule-based, Corpus-based, and Example-based Method." *Proceedings of the 15th International Joint Conference on Artificial Intelligence* (*IJCAI-97*), Nagoya, Japan, pp. 977–982.

Yngve, Victor H. (1954). "The Machine and the Man." *Mechanical Translation*, Vol. 1, No. 2, pp. 20–22.

Human Translation

Bennett, Paul A. (1994). "The Translation Unit in Human and Machine." *Babel*, Vol. 40, No. 1, pp. 12–20.

Bédard, Claude (1996). "Juggling with Words: Some Insights from the Human Translation Process." *Proceedings of the 2nd Conference of the Association for Machine Translation in the Americas: Expanding MT Horizons* (*AMTA-2*), Montreal, Quebec, Canada, pp. 24–33.

Ceccato, Silvio and Bruna Zonta (1962). "Human Translation and Translation by Machine." In National Physical Laboratory, ed., *1961 International Conference on Machine Translation of Languages and Applied Language Analysis: Proceedings of the Conference Held at the National Physical Laboratory, Teddington, Middlesex, on 5th, 6th, 7th and 8th September.* London: Her Majesty's Stationery Office, Vol. 1, pp. 221–246.

Glasersfeld, von Ernst, Sergei Perschke, and Elsa Samet (1962). "Human Translation and Translation by Machine." In National Physical Laboratory, ed., *1961 International Conference on Machine Translation of Languages and Applied Language Analysis: Proceedings of the Conference Held at the National Physical Laboratory, Teddington, Middlesex, on 5th, 6th, 7th and 8th September.* London: Her Majesty's Stationery Office, Vol. 2, pp. 508–528.

Hutchins, W. John (2001). "Machine Translation and Human Translation: In Competition or in Complementation?" *International Journal of Translation*, Vol. 13, Nos. 1–2, pp. 5–20.

Lufkin, J. M. (1966). "Human versus Machine Translation of Foreign Languages." *The Incorporated Linguist*, Vol. 5, pp. 9–15.

Martinez, Lorena Guerra (2004). "Human Translation versus Machine Translation and Full Post-editing of Raw Machine Translation

Output." *International Journal of Translation*, Vol. 16, No. 2, pp. 81–113.

Melby, Alan K. (1987). "On Human-machine Interaction in Translation." In Sergei Nirenburg, ed., *Machine Translation: Theoretical and Methodological Issues*. Cambridge: Cambridge University Press, pp. 145–154.

Melby, Alan K. (1995). *The Possibility of Language: A Discussion of the Nature of Language, with Implications for Human and Machine Translation*. Amsterdam: John Benjamins Publishing Company.

Nord, Christiane (1997). "The Importance of Functional Markers in (Human) Translation." In Christa Hauenschild and Susanne Heizmann, eds., *Machine Translation and Translation Theory*. Berlin and New York: Mouton de Gruyter, pp. 35–50.

Sharoff, Serge, Bogdan Babych, and Tony Hartley (2006). "Using Comparable Corpora to Solve Problems Difficult for Human Translators." *Proceedings of the Joint Conference of the International Committee on Computational Linguistics and the Association for Computational Linguistics* (*COLING/ACL-2006*), Sydney, Australia.

❖ PART 15 ❖

Information

Information

Amigo, Enrique, Julio Gonzalo, Victor Peinado, Anselmo Peñas, and Felisa Verdejo (2004). "An Empirical Study of Information Synthesis Task." *Proceedings of the 42nd Annual Meeting of the Association for Computational Linguistics (ACL-2004)*, Barcelona, Spain, pp. 207–214.

Horiguchi, Keiko (2001). "Information-based Machine Translation." *Proceedings of the 2nd Meeting of the North American Chapter of the Association for Computational Linguistics: Language Technologies 2001 (NAACL-2001)*, Pittsburgh, PA, USA.

Perschke, Sergei (1970). "Machine Translation: A Necessary Component of an International Information System." *Handling of Nuclear Information: Proceedings of the Symposium.* Vienna: International Atomic Energy Agency, pp. 291–304.

Yao, Jianmin, Hao Yu, Tiejun Zhao, and Xiaohong Li (2002). "Automatic Information Transfer between English and Chinese." *Proceedings of the Workshop on Machine Translation in Asia (COLING-2002)*, Taipei, Taiwan.

Information Extraction

Abney, Steven, Michael Collins, and Amit Singhal (2000). "Answer Extraction." *Proceedings of the 6th Applied Natural Language Processing Conference*, Seattle, Washington, DC, USA, pp. 296–301.

Alfonseca, Castells, Manabu Okumura, and Maria Ruiz-Casado (2006). "A Rote Extractor with Edit Distance-based Generalisation and Multi-corpora Precision Calculation." *Proceedings of the Joint Conference of the International Committee on Computational Linguistics and the Association for Computational Linguistics (COLING/ACL-2006)*, Sydney, Australia.

Aone, Chinatsu, Nicholas Charocopos, and James Gorlinsky (1997). "An Intelligent Multilingual Information Browsing and Retrieval System Using Information Extraction." *Proceedings of the 5th Conference on Applied Natural Language Processing*, Seattle, Washington, DC, USA.

Aone, Chinatsu and Mila Ramos-Santacruz (2000). "REES: a Large-scale Relation and Event Extraction System." *Proceedings of the 6th Applied*

Natural Language Processing Conference, Seattle, Washington, DC, USA, pp. 76–83.

Appelt, Douglas E. and David Israel (1997). "Building Information Extraction Systems." *Proceedings of the 5th Conference on Applied Natural Language Processing*, Seattle, Washington, DC, USA.

Bunescu, Razvan and Raymond J. Mooney (2004). "Collective Information Extraction with Relational Markov Networks." *Proceedings of the 42nd Annual Meeting of the Association for Computational Linguistics* (*ACL-2004*), Barcelona, Spain, pp. 438–445.

Chelba, Ciprian and Milind Mahajan (2001). "Information Extraction Using the Structured Language Model." *Proceedings of the 2001 Conference on Empirical Methods in Natural Language Processing* (*EMNLP-2001*), Carnegie Mellon University, Pittsburgh, PA, USA.

Chen, Jinxiu, Donghong Ji, Chew Lim Tan, and Zhengyu Niu (2006). "Semi-supervised Relation Extraction with Label Propagation." *Proceedings of the Human Language Technology Conference—Annual Meeting of the North American Chapter of the Association for Computational Linguistics* (*HLT-NAACL-2006*), New York, USA.

Cheng, Xueqi 程學旗, Yu Zhihua 余智華, Bai Shuo 白碩, and Xia Wei 夏威 (1999). 〈WWW站點的自動信息提取與分類〉 (Automatic Information Extraction and Classification to the Web Sites). In Huang Changning 黃昌寧 and Dong Zhendong 董振東, eds., 《計算機語言學文集》 (*Essays on Computational Linguistics*). Beijing: Tsinghua University Press, pp. 388–396.

Chun, Hong-Woo, Young-Sook Hwang, and Hae-Chang Rim (2004). "Unsupervised Event Extraction from Biomedical Text Based on Event and Pattern Information." *Proceedings of the 5th International Conference on Intelligent Text Processing and Computational Linguistics* (*CICLing-2004*), Chung-Ang University, Seoul, Korea, pp. 527–530.

Cohen, William W. (2001). "Issues in Extracting Information from the Web." *Proceedings of the 7th International Workshop on Parsing Technologies* (*IWPT-2001*), Peking University, Beijing, China. Beijing: Tsinghua University Press, p. 3.

Creswell, Cassandre, Matthew Beal, John Chen, Tom Cornell, Lars Nilsson, and Rohini Srihari (2006). "Automatically Extracting Nominal Mentions of Events with a Bootstrapped Probabilistic Classifier." *Proceedings of the Joint Conference of the International Committee on*

Computational Linguistics and the Association for Computational Linguistics (*COLING/ACL-2006*), Sydney, Australia.
Crystal, Michael, Alex Baron, Katherine Godfrey, Linnea Micciulla, Yvette Tenney, and Ralph Weischedel (2005). "A Methodology for Extrinsically Evaluating Information Extraction Performance." *Proceedings of Human Language Technology Conference and Conference on Empirical Methods in Natural Language Processing* (*HLT/EMNLP-2005*), Vancouver, BC, Canada.
Duan, Jianyong, Ruzhan Lu, Weilin Wu, Yi Hu, and Yan Tian (2006). "A Bio-inspired Approach for Multi-word Expression Extraction." *Proceedings of the Joint Conference of the International Committee on Computational Linguistics and the Association for Computational Linguistics* (*COLING/ACL-2006*), Sydney, Australia.
Fang, Yifei 房一飛 and Zhang Dongmo 張冬茉 (2001). 〈基於Boosting的文本分類在股市領域信息抽取系統中的應用〉 (A Boosting-based Text Categorization System and Its Application in Information Extraction). 《輝煌二十年——中國中文信息學會二十周年學術會議》 (*Proceedings of Conference of the 20th Anniversary of CIPSC*). Beijing: Tsinghua University Press, pp. 205–214.
Feldman, Ronen, Yonatan Aumann, Michal Finkelstein-Landau, Eyal Hurvitz, Yizhar Regev, and Ariel Yaroshevich (2002). "A Comparative Study of Information Extraction Strategies." *Proceedings of the 3rd International Conference on Intelligent Text Processing and Computational Linguistics* (*CICLing-2002*), Mexico City, Mexico.
Gaizauskas, Robert and Yorick Wilks (1998). "Information Extraction: Beyond Document Retrieval." *Proceedings of the International Conference on Research in Computational Linguistics* (*ROCLING-XI*), Hsin-Chu, Taiwan.
Geleijnse, Gijs and Jan Korst (2006). "Learning Effective Surface Text Patterns for Information Extraction." *Proceedings of the 11th Conference of the European Chapter of the Association for Computational Linguistics* (*EACL-2006*), Trento, Italy.
Giuliano, Claudio, Alberto Lavelli, and Lorenza Romano (2006). "Simple Information Extraction (SIE): A Portable and Effective IE System." *Proceedings of the 11th Conference of the European Chapter of the Association for Computational Linguistics* (*EACL-2006*), Trento, Italy.
Gliozzo, Alfio Massimiliano, Claudio Giuliano, and Raffaella Rinaldi (2005). "Instance Pruning by Filtering Uninformative Words: An

Information Extraction Case Study." *Proceedings of the 6th International Conference on Intelligent Text Processing and Computational Linguistics* (*CICLing-2005*), Mexico City, Mexico, pp. 487–498.

Guo, Wenhong 郭文宏, Zhang Yongkui 張永奎, and Long Yifei 龍一飛 (1999).〈基於義類搭配的漢語文本特徵信息抽取研究〉(Research of Extraction of Chinese Text Information Based on Semantic Category Collocation). In Huang Changning 黃昌寧 and Dong Zhendong 董振東, eds.,《計算機語言學文集》(*Essays on Computational Linguistics*). Beijing: Tsinghua University Press, pp. 199–203.

Huang, Xiaohong 黃曉宏, Lian Li 連理, Xia Yingju 夏迎炬, and Xu Guowei 徐國偉 (2001).〈關於規則和非規則方法的WEB信息提取〉(Web Information Extraction Based on Rule and Non-rule Methods). In Huang Changning 黃昌寧 and Zhang Pu 張普, eds.,《自然語言理解與機器翻譯》(*Natural Language Understanding and Machine Translation*). Beijing: Tsinghua University Press, pp. 386–392.

Hulth, Anette, Jussi Karlgren, Anna Jonsson, Henrik Boström, and Lars Asker (2001). "Automatic Keyword Extraction Using Domain Knowledge." *Proceedings of the 2nd International Conference on Intelligent Text Processing and Computational Linguistics* (*CICLing-2001*), Mexico City, Mexico.

Iria, Jose, Neil Ireson, and Fabio Ciravegna (2006). "An Experimental Study on Boundary Classification Algorithms for Information Extraction Using SVM." *Proceedings of the 11th Conference of the European Chapter of the Association for Computational Linguistics* (*EACL-2006*), Trento, Italy.

Jansche, Martin and Steven Abney (2002). "Information Extraction from Voicemail Transcripts." *Proceedings of the 2002 Conference on Empirical Methods in Natural Language Processing* (*EMNLP-2002*), University of Pennsylvania, Philadelphia, PA, USA.

Kim, Jee-Hyub and Melanie Hilario (2005). "Learning Information Extraction Rules for Protein Annotation from Unannotated Corpora." *Proceedings of the 6th International Conference on Intelligent Text Processing and Computational Linguistics* (*CICLing-2005*), Mexico City, Mexico, pp. 511–522.

Kim, Sanghee, Paul Lewis, and Kirk Martinez (2004). "The Impact of Enriched Linguistic Annotation on the Performance of Extracting Relation Triples." *Proceedings of the 5th International Conference on*

Intelligent Text Processing and Computational Linguistics (*CICLing-2004*), Chung-Ang University, Seoul, Korea, pp. 541–552.

Lee, Jae-Woo and Doo-Kwon Baik (2004). "A Model for Extracting Keywords of Document Using Term Frequency and Distribution." *Proceedings of the 5th International Conference on Intelligent Text Processing and Computational Linguistics* (*CICLing-2004*), Chung-Ang University, Seoul, Korea, pp. 431–434.

Lin, Hongfei 林鴻飛, Zhan Xuegang 戰學剛, Zhang Yue 張躍, and Yao Tianshun 姚天順 (1999). 〈中文文本挖掘中特徵抽取和表示〉(Features Extraction and Representation for Chinese Text Mining). In Huang Changning 黃昌寧 and Dong Zhendong 董振東, eds.,《計算機語言學文集》(*Essays on Computational Linguistics*). Beijing: Tsinghua University Press, pp. 204–209.

Maslennikov, Mstislav, Hai-Kiat Goh, and Tat-Seng Chua (2006). "ARE: Instance Splitting Strategies for Dependency Relation-based Information Extraction." *Proceedings of the Joint Conference of the International Committee on Computational Linguistics and the Association for Computational Linguistics* (*COLING/ACL-2006*), Sydney, Australia.

McLernon, Brian and Nicholas Kushmerick (2006). "Transductive Pattern Learning for Information Extraction." *Proceedings of the 11th Conference of the European Chapter of the Association for Computational Linguistics* (*EACL-2006*), Trento, Italy.

Miller, Scott, Jethran Guinness, and Alex Zamanian (2004). "Name Tagging with Word Clusters and Discriminative Training." *Proceedings of the Human Language Technology Conference/North American Chapter of the Association for Computational Linguistics Annual Meeting* (*HLT/NAACL-2004*), Boston, MA, USA.

Nahm, Un Yong (2005). "Transformation-based Information Extraction Using Learned Meta-rules." *Proceedings of the 6th International Conference on Intelligent Text Processing and Computational Linguistics* (*CICLing-2005*), Mexico City, Mexico, pp. 523–526.

Narupiyakul, Lalita, Calvin Thomas, Nick Cercone, and Booncharoen Sirinaovakul (2004). "Thai Syllable-based Information Extraction Using Hidden Markov Models." *Proceedings of the 5th International Conference on Intelligent Text Processing and Computational Linguistics* (*CICLing-2004*), Chung-Ang University, Seoul, Korea, pp. 531–540.

Niu, Cheng, Rohini Srihari, and Wei Li (2004). "Corpus Level Information Extraction." *Proceedings of the International Conference on Natural Language Processing* (*ICON-2004*), International Institute of Information Technology, Hyderabad, India.

Penagos, Carlos Rodriguez (2004). "Mining Metalinguistic Activity in Corpora to Create Lexical Resources Using Information Extraction Techniques: The MOP System." *Proceedings of the 42nd Annual Meeting of the Association for Computational Linguistics* (*ACL-2004*), Barcelona, Spain, pp. 215–222.

Peng, Fuchun and Andrew McCallum (2004). "Accurate Information Extraction from Research Papers Using Conditional Random Fields." *Proceedings of the Human Language Technology Conference/North American Chapter of the Association for Computational Linguistics Annual Meeting* (*HLT/NAACL-2004*), Boston, MA, USA.

Qian, Yueliang 錢躍良 and Liu Kaiying 劉開瑛 (2001).〈農作物模板自動生成的技術研究〉(Research on the Automatic Generation of Agricultural Products Templates). In Huang Changning 黃昌寧 and Zhang Pu 張普, eds.,《自然語言理解與機器翻譯》(*Natural Language Understanding and Machine Translation*). Beijing: Tsinghua University Press, pp. 198–203.

Rinaldi, Fabio, Michael Hess, Diego Mollá, Rolf Schwitter, James Dowdall, Gerold Schneider, and Rachel Fournier (2002). "Answer Extraction in Technical Domains." *Proceedings of the 3rd International Conference on Intelligent Text Processing and Computational Linguistics* (*CICLing-2002*), Mexico City, Mexico.

Rodríguez, Carlos (2002). "Automatic Extraction of Non-standard Lexical Data for a Metalinguistic Information Database." *Proceedings of the 3rd International Conference on Intelligent Text Processing and Computational Linguistics* (*CICLing-2002*), Mexico City, Mexico.

Rosenfeld, Benjamin and Ronen Feldman (2006). "URES: An Unsupervised Web Relation Extraction System." *Proceedings of the Joint Conference of the International Committee on Computational Linguistics and the Association for Computational Linguistics* (*COLING/ACL-2006*), Sydney, Australia.

Schneider, Karl-Michael (2004). "Using Information Extraction to Build a Directory of Conference Announcements." *Proceedings of the 5th International Conference on Intelligent Text Processing and Computational Linguistics* (*CICLing-2004*), Chung-Ang University, Seoul, Korea, pp. 515–526.

Sekine, Satoshi (2006). "On-demand Information Extraction." *Proceedings of the Joint Conference of the International Committee on Computational Linguistics and the Association for Computational Linguistics* (*COLING/ACL-2006*), Sydney, Australia.

Shinyama, Yusuke and Satoshi Sekine (2006). "Preemptive Information Extraction Using Unrestricted Relation Discovery." *Proceedings of the Human Language Technology Conference—Annual Meeting of the North American Chapter of the Association for Computational Linguistics* (*HLT-NAACL-2006*), New York, USA.

Siefkes, Christian (2005). "Incremental Information Extraction Using Tree-based Context Representations." *Proceedings of the 6th International Conference on Intelligent Text Processing and Computational Linguistics* (*CICLing-2005*), Mexico City, Mexico, pp. 499–510.

Srihari, Rohini and Li Wei (2000). "Multilingual Coreference Resolution." *Proceedings of the 6th Applied Natural Language Processing Conference*, Seattle, Washington, DC, USA, pp. 166–172.

Su, Guiyang 蘇貴洋, Wang Yongcheng 王永成, and Ma Yinghua 馬穎華 (2002).〈信息自動獲取的結構模型〉(Automatic Information Access Structure Model).《第一屆學生計算語言學研討會論文集》(*SWCL2002: First Students' Workshop on Computational Linguistics: Proceedings*), Institute of Computational Linguistics, Peking University, Beijing, China, p. 152.

Sudo, Kiyoshi, Satoshi Sekine, and Ralph Grishman (2003). "Pre-CODIE-crosslingual On-demand Information Extraction." *Proceedings of the Human Language Technology and North American Chapter of Association of Computational Linguistics 2003* (*HLT/NAACL-2003*), Edmonton, Alberta, Canada.

Surdeanu, Mihai, Jordi Turmo, and Alicia Ageno (2006). "A Hybrid Approach for the Acquisition of Information Extraction Patterns." *Proceedings of the 11th Conference of the European Chapter of the Association for Computational Linguistics* (*EACL-2006*), Trento, Italy.

Téllez-Valero, Alberto, Manuel Montes-y-Gómez, and Luis Villaseñor-Pineda (2005). "A Machine Learning Approach to Information Extraction." *Proceedings of the 6th International Conference on Intelligent Text Processing and Computational Linguistics* (*CICLing-2005*), Mexico City, Mexico, pp. 527–535.

White, Michael, Claire Cardie, Chung-hye Han, Nari Kim, Benoit Lavoie,

Martha Palmer, Owen Rambow, and Juntae Yoon (2000). "Towards Translingual Information Access Using Portable Information Extraction." *Proceedings of the ANLP/NAACL-2000 Workshop on Embedded Machine Translation Systems—Volume 5*, Seattle, Washington, DC, USA, pp. 31–37.

Yangarber, Roman, Ralph Grishman, Pasi Tapanainen, and Silja Huttunen (2000). "Unsupervised Discovery of Scenario-level Patterns for Information Extraction." *Proceedings of the 6th Applied Natural Language Processing Conference*, Seattle, Washington, DC, USA, pp. 282–289.

Yeh, Ching-Long and Yu-Chih Su (2005). "Web Information Extraction for the Creation of Metadata in Semantic Web." *Proceedings of the International Conference on Computational Linguistics and Speech Processing (ROCLING-XVII)*, National Cheng Kung University, Tainan, Taiwan.

Information Management

Hofmann, Cornelia and Thorston Mehnert (2000). "Multilingual Information Management at Schneider Automation." In Robert C. Spring, ed., *Translating into Success: Cutting-edge Strategies for Going Multilingual in a Global Age*. Amsterdam and Philadelphia: John Benjamins Publishing Company, pp. 59–79.

Lapata, Mirella (2006). "Automatic Evaluation of Information Ordering: Kendall's Tau." *Computational Linguistics*, Vol. 32, No. 4, pp. 457–469.

Rico Pérez, Celia (2002). "Translation and Project Management." *Translation Journal*, Vol. 6, No. 4.

Rueten, Anja (2003). "Computer-based Information Management for Conference Interpreters or How Will I Make My Computer Act Like an Infallible Information Butler?" In *Translating and the Computer 25*. London: The Association for Information Management.

Information Processing

Al-Onaizan, Yaser, Radu Florian, Martin Franz, Hany Hassan, Young-Suk Lee, J. Scott McCarley, Kishore Papineni, Salim Roukos, Jeffrey Sorensen, Christoph Tillmann, Todd Ward, and Fei Xia (2003). "TIPS:

A Translingual Information Processing System." *Proceedings of the Human Language Technology and North American Chapter of Association of Computational Linguistics 2003* (*HLT/NAACL-2003*), Edmonton, Alberta, Canada.

Austermühl, Frank (2001). "Translator-client Communication and Information Transfer." *Electronic Tools for Translators*. Manchester: St. Jerome Publishing Company, pp. 18–37.

Budzikowska, Margo (2000). "Information Structure Transfer: Bridging the Information Gap in Structurally Different Languages." In John S. White, ed., *Envisioning Machine Translation in the Information Future*. Berlin: Springer Verlag, pp. 80–88.

Carthy, Joe (2004). "Lexical Chains versus Keywords for Topic Tracking." *Proceedings of the 5th International Conference on Intelligent Text Processing and Computational Linguistics* (*CICLing-2004*), Chung-Ang University, Seoul, Korea, pp. 500–503.

Chen, Liwei (1987). "Some Key Issues in Chinese Information Processing and Their Prospective Development." *Proceedings of the Conference on Translation Today*, Hong Kong.

Chen, Mingyuan (1982).《語言文字的信息處理》(*Information Processing of Spoken and Written Languages*). Shanghai: Knowledge Press.

Chen, Qunxiu 陳群秀, Li Jian 李堅, and Wang Jian 王健 (2001).〈信息處理用現代漢語語義分類詞典的設計與實現〉(The Design and Implementation of the Thesaurus Dictionary of Contemporary Chinese for Information Processing).《輝煌二十年——中文信息學會二十周年學術會議》(*Proceedings of Conference of the 20th Anniversary of CIPSC*). Beijing: Tsinghua University Press, pp. 148–155.

Feng, Zhiwei 馮志偉 (1992).《中文信息處理與漢語研究》(*Chinese Information Processing and Chinese Language Studies*). Beijing: The Commercial Press.

Feng, Zhiwei (1992).〈中文信息MMT模型〉(The MMT Model for Chinese Information).《語言文字應用》(*Applied Linguistics*), No. 4, pp. 21–30.

Fujii, Atsushi and Tetsuya Ishikawa (2000). "Applying Machine Translation to Two-stage Cross-language Information Retrieval." In John S. White, ed., *Envisioning Machine Translation in the Information Future*. Berlin: Springer Verlag, pp. 13–24.

Hroza, Jiří, Jan Žižka, and Aleš Bourek (2004). "Filtering Very Similar Text Documents: A Case Study." *Proceedings of the 5th International Conference on Intelligent Text Processing and Computational*

Linguistics (*CICLing-2004*), Chung-Ang University, Seoul, Korea, pp. 504–514.
Li, Ronglu 李榮陸, Zhang Yongkui 張永奎, and Niu Weixia 牛偉霞 (2001). 〈基於概念的信息過濾技術探討〉(A Survey of Conceptual Information Filtering). In Huang Changning and Zhang Pu, eds.,《自然語言理解與機器翻譯》(*Natural Language Understanding and Machine Translation*). Beijing: Tsinghua University Press, pp. 353–358.
Li, Zhu 李竹 (1999).〈信息處理用現代漢語詞類劃分研究〉(Research on Parts-of-speech in Chinese Information Processing." In Huang Changning 黃昌寧 and Dong Zhendong 董振東, eds.,《計算機語言學文集》(*Essays on Computational Linguistics*). Beijing: Tsinghua University Press, pp. 141–146.
Liu, Yongquan (1982). "Aspects of Chinese Information Processing." *Proceedings of the Conference on International Cooperation in Chinese Bibliographical Automation*, Canberra, Australia.
Liu, Yongquan (1989). "Aspects of Chinese Information Processing." *Selected Papers of Applied Linguistics*. Beijing: The Commercial Press, pp. 104–121.
Liu, Yongquan (1989). "Language Use and Modernization—The Study of Chinese Information Processing." *Selected Papers of Applied Linguistics*. Beijing: The Commercial Press, pp. 88–103.
Liu, Yongquan (1991). "Difficulties in Chinese Information Processing and Ways to Their Solution." In Victor H. Mair and Liu Yongquan, eds., *Characters and Computers*. Amsterdam: IOS Press, pp. 9–19.
Mair, Victor H. (1991). "Preface: Building the Future of Information Processing in East Asia Demands Facing Linguistic and Technological Reality." In Victor H. Mair and Liu Yongquan, eds., *Characters and Computers*. Amsterdam: IOS Press, pp. 1–8.
Mao, Ying 毛穎, Zhou Yuanyuan 周源遠, and Wang Jicheng 王繼成 (2002). 〈信息過濾技術研究〉(A Study on Information Filtering Techniques). 《第一屆學生計算語言學研討會論文集》(*SWCL2002: First Students' Workshop on Computational Linguistics: Proceedings*), Institute of Computational Linguistics, Peking University, Beijing, China, pp. 137–142.
McCarley, J. Scott and Salim Roukos (1998). "Fast Document Translation for Cross-language Information Retrieval." In David L. Farwell, Laurie Gerber, and Eduard Hovy, eds., *Machine Translation and the Information Soup*. Berlin: Springer Verlag, pp. 150–157.

O'Donovan, John and John Dunnion (2004). "A Framework for Evaluation of Information Filtering Techniques in an Adaptive Recommender System." *Proceedings of the 5th International Conference on Intelligent Text Processing and Computational Linguistics* (*CICLing-2004*), Chung-Ang University, Seoul, Korea, pp. 496–499.

Paggio, Patrizia (2000). "Information Structure and Machine Translation: Generating Danish Existential Sentences." In Nicolas Nicolov and Ruslan Mitkov, eds., *Recent Advances in Natural Language Processing II*. Amsterdam and Philadelphia: John Benjamins Publishing Company, pp. 271–282.

Shi, Dingxu 石定栩 (1999). 〈漢語理解的基本單位〉 (The Smallest Unit in Processing Chinese). In Huang Changning and Dong Zhendong, eds., 《計算機語言學文集》 (*Essays on Computational Linguistics*). Beijing: Tsinghua University Press, pp. 256–260.

Sun, Maosong 孫茂松 (1999). 〈《信息處理用現代漢語分詞詞表》的設計原則〉 (Principles in Designing *Contemporary Chinese Wordlist for Information Processing*). In Huang Changning 黃昌寧 and Dong Zhendong 董振東, eds., 《計算機語言學文集》 (*Essays on Computational Linguistics*). Beijing: Tsinghua University Press, pp. 193–198.

Thurmair, Gregor (1995). "Multilingual Information Processing." *Proceedings of MT Summit V: Machine Translation Conference, Exhibition and Tutorial*, Luxembourg.

Xu, Jialu 許嘉璐 (1996). 〈語言學研究與中文信息處理〉 (The Study of Linguistics and the Information Processing of Chinese). In Luo Zhensheng 羅振聲 and Yuan Yulin 袁毓林, eds., 《計算機時代的漢語和漢字研究》 (*The Studies of Chinese Language and Characters in the Epoch of Computer*). Beijing: Tsinghua University Press, pp. 3–5.

Yang, Quan and Feng Zhiwei (2005). 〈面向中文信息處理的現代漢語"V + v"結構歧義問題研究〉 ("V + v" Structure Ambiguity Study in Contemporary Chinese for Chinese Information Processing). 《語言文字應用》 (*Applied Linguistics*), No. 1, pp. 123–129.

Yu, Shiwen 俞士汶 (1998). 〈關於語言信息處理技術的展望〉 (Prospects of Language Information Processing Technology). In Yu Shiwen 俞士汶 and Zhu Xuefeng 朱學鋒, eds., 《計算語言學文集》 (*Papers on Computational Linguistics*), Vol. 3. Beijing: Department of Computer Science and Technology and Institute of Computational Linguistics, Peking University, pp. 4–7.

Zhang, Xiaobing 張小斌, Cheng Xueqi 程學旗, Bai Shuo 白碩, and Zhu

Jianmin 朱建民 (1999).〈「天羅」個人信息代理系統的設計與實現〉(The Design and Implementation of TechRoute Personal Information Agent). In Huang Changning 黄昌寧 and Dong Zhendong 董振東, eds.,《計算機語言學文集》(*Essays on Computational Linguistics*). Beijing: Tsinghua University Press, pp. 397–402.

Zimmermann, Harald H. (1995). "Machine Translation as a Practical Tool in Information Processing." *Proceedings of MT Summit V: Machine Translation Conference, Exhibition and Tutorial*, Luxembourg.

Information Retrieval

Baeza-Yates, Ricardo (2004). "Challenges in the Interaction of Information Retrieval and Natural Language Processing." *Proceedings of the 5th International Conference on Intelligent Text Processing and Computational Linguistics* (*CICLing-2004*), Chung-Ang University, Seoul, Korea, pp. 439–450.

Berger, Adam L. and John D. Lafferty (1999). "Information Retrieval as Statistical Translation." *Proceedings of the 22nd Annual International ACM SIGIR Conference on Research and Development in Information Retrieval* (*SIGIR-1999*), Berkeley, CA, USA, pp. 222–229.

Bookstein, Abraham (1983). "Explanation and Generalization of Vector Models in Information Retrieval." In Jennifer J. Kuehn, ed., *Proceedings of the 6th Annual International ACM SIGIR Conference on Research and Development in Information Retrieval* (*SIGIR-1983*), Washington, DC, USA, pp. 118–132.

Booth, Andrew D. (1959). "Information Retrieval and Machine Translation." *Automatic Data Processing*, Vol. 1, pp. 35–36.

Burton, Paul F. (1987). "Principles of Information Retrieval for Personal Information Systems." In Catriona Picken, ed., *Translating and the computer 8: A Profession on the Move*. London: The Association for Information Management, pp. 40–52.

Cafarella, Michael J., Doug Downey, Stephen Soderland, and Oren Etzioni (2005). "KnowItNow: Fast, Scalable Information Extraction from the Web." *Proceedings of Human Language Technology Conference and Conference on Empirical Methods in Natural Language Processing* (*HLT/EMNLP-2005*), Vancouver, BC, Canada.

Carthy, Joe, David C. Wilson, Ruichao Wang, John Dunnion, and Anne Drummond (2004). "Using T-Ret System to Improve Incident Report

Retrieval." *Proceedings of the 5th International Conference on Intelligent Text Processing and Computational Linguistics* (*CICLing-2004*), Chung-Ang University, Seoul, Korea, pp. 463–466.

Chen, Jen Nan and Jason S. Chang (1998). "Topical Clustering of MRD Senses Based on Information Retrieval Techniques." *Computational Linguistics*, Vol. 24, No. 1, pp. 61–95.

Csomai, Andras and Rada F. Mihalcea (2006). "Creating a Testbed for the Evaluation of Automatically Generated Back-of-the-book Indexes." *Proceedings of the 7th International Conference on Intelligent Text Processing and Computational Linguistics* (*CICLing-2006*), Mexico City, Mexico.

Culicover, Peter W. (1968). "Paraphrase Generation and Information Retrieval from Stored Text." *Mechanical Translation*, Vol. 11, Nos. 3–4, pp. 78–88.

Currie, Anne-Marie, Jocelyn Cohan, and Larisa Zlatic (2001). "Information Retrieval of Electronic Medical Records." *Proceedings of the 2nd International Conference on Intelligent Text Processing and Computational Linguistics* (*CICLing-2001*), Mexico City, Mexico.

Drexel, Guido (2001). "Knowledge Engineering for Intelligent Information Retrieval." *Proceedings of the 2nd International Conference on Intelligent Text Processing and Computational Linguistics* (*CICLing-2001*), Mexico City, Mexico.

Dura, Elżbieta (2003). "Natural Language in Information Retrieval." *Proceedings of the 4th International Conference on Intelligent Text Processing and Computational Linguistics* (*CICLing-2003*), Mexico City, Mexico, pp. 539–542.

Escorial, David (2001). "An Information Space Using Topic Identification for Retrieved Documents." *Proceedings of the 2nd International Conference on Intelligent Text Processing and Computational Linguistics* (*CICLing-2001*), Mexico City, Mexico.

Fapšo, Michal, Pavel Smrž, Petr Schwarz, Igor Szöke, Milan Schwarz, Jan Ĉernocký, Martin Karafiát, and Lukáš Burget (2006). "Information Retrieval from Spoken Documents." *Proceedings of the 7th International Conference on Intelligent Text Processing and Computational Linguistics* (*CICLing-2006*), Mexico City, Mexico.

Flank, Sharon (2000). "Sentences vs. Phrases: Syntactic Complexity in Multimedia Information Retrieval." In Carol J. van Ess-Dykema, Clare R. Voss, and Florence Reeder, eds., *Proceedings of the 2nd Workshop on Embedded MT Systems: Language Technology Joint Conference of the North American Association for Computational Linguistics and Applied Natural Language Processing* (*NAACL-ANLP-2000*), Seattle, Washington, DC, USA, pp. 1–5.

Fujii, Atsushi, Katunobu Itou, and Tetsuya Ishikawa (2002). "A Method for Open-vocabulary Speech-driven Text Retrieval." *Proceedings of the 2002 Conference on Empirical Methods in Natural Language Processing* (*EMNLP-2002*), University of Pennsylvania, Philadelphia, PA, USA.

Gelbukh, Alexander F., Nam-O Kang, and Sang-Yong Han (2005). "Experiment on Combining Sources of Evidence for Passage Retrieval." *Proceedings of the 6th International Conference on Intelligent Text Processing and Computational Linguistics* (*CICLing-2005*), Mexico City, Mexico, pp. 616–619.

Hahn, Udo, Kornel Marko, and Stefan Schulz (2005). "Subword Clusters as Light-weight Interlingua for Multilingual Document Retrieval." *Proceedings of MT Summit X*, Phuket, Thailand.

Hull, David A. and Gregory Grefenstette (1996). "A Dictionary-based Approach to Multilingual Information Retrieval." *Proceedings of the 19th Annual International ACM SIGIR Conference on Research and Development in Information Retrieval* (*SIGIR-96*), Zurich, Switzerland, pp. 49–57.

Hyusein, Byurhan and Ahmed Patel (2003). "Web Document Indexing and Retrieval." *Proceedings of the 4th International Conference on Intelligent Text Processing and Computational Linguistics* (*CICLing-2003*), Mexico City, Mexico, pp. 575–581.

Kang, Bo-Yeong, Hae-Jung Kim, and Sang-Jo Lee (2004). "Performance Analysis of Semantic Indexing in Text Retrieval." *Proceedings of the 5th International Conference on Intelligent Text Processing and Computational Linguistics* (*CICLing-2004*), Chung-Ang University, Seoul, Korea, pp. 427–430.

Kent, Allen, ed. (1961). *Information Retrieval and Machine Translation.* New York: Interscience, 2 vols.

Koster, Cornelis H. A. (2004). "Head/Modifier Frames for Information Retrieval." *Proceedings of the 5th International Conference on Intelligent Text Processing and Computational Linguistics* (*CICLing-2004*), Chung-Ang University, Seoul, Korea, pp. 414–426.

Králiková, K. and J. Panevová (1990). "ASIMUT—A Method for

Automatic Information Retrieval from Full Texts." *Explizite Beschreibung der Sprache und Automatische Textbearbeitung*, Vol. 17. Faculty of Mathematics and Physics, Charles University.

Lee, Hsi-chieh 李錫捷, Chang Ru-ying 張如瑩, and Cihan H. Dagli (2002). "The Design and Development of the KeyPAgent." In Yu Shiwen, ed., *Proceedings of the Second China-Japan Natural Language Processing Joint Research Promotion Conference* (*CJNLP-2002*). Beijing: Institute of Computational Linguistics, Peking University, pp. 370–382.

Li, Zhenxing 李振星 and Xu Zeping 徐澤平 (2002).〈基於興趣模型的WEB信息預測採集過濾方法〉(Forecast and Filter Method for Web Page Information Gathering Based on Interested Model).《第一屆學生計算語言學研討會論文集》(*SWCL2002: First Students' Workshop on Computational Linguistics: Proceedings*), Institute of Computational Linguistics, Peking University, Beijing, China, pp. 143–149.

Llopis, Fernando, Antonio Ferrández, and José Luis Vicedo (2002). "Text Segmentation for Efficient Information Retrieval." *Proceedings of the 3rd International Conference on Intelligent Text Processing and Computational Linguistics* (*CICLing-2002*), Mexico City, Mexico.

Masuda, Katsuya, Takashi Ninomiya, Yusuke Miyao, Tomoko Ohta, and Jun-ichi Tsujii (2003). "A Robust Retrieval Engine for Proximal and Structural Search." *Proceedings of the Human Language Technology and North American Chapter of Association of Computational Linguistics 2003* (*HLT/NAACL-2003*), Edmonton, Alberta, Canada.

Matsumoto, Naoko and Akifumi Tokosum (2004). "Intention Retrieval with a Socially-supported Belief System." *Proceedings of the 5th International Conference on Intelligent Text Processing and Computational Linguistics* (*CICLing-2004*), Chung-Ang University, Seoul, Korea, pp. 66–69.

Meng, Helen, Sanjeev Khudanpur, Gina Levow, Douglas W. Oard, and Hsin-Min Wang (2000). "Mandarin-English Information (MEI): Investigating Translingual Speech Retrieval." *Proceedings of the ANLP/NAACL-2000 Workshop on Embedded Machine Translation Systems—Volume 5*, Seattle, Washington, DC, USA, pp. 23–30.

Miller, D. H., T. Leek, and R. Schwartz (1999). "A Hidden Markov Model Information Retrieval System." *Proceedings of the 22nd Annual International ACM SIGIR Conference on Research and Development in Information Retrieval* (*SIGIR-1999*), Berkeley, CA, USA, pp. 214–221.

Murata, Masaki, Masao Utiyama, Toshiyuki Kanamaru, and Hitoshi Isahara (2006). "Fast Search Algorithm for Sequences of Hierarchically Structured Data." In Alexander F. Gelbukh, ed., *Advances in Natural Language Processing*, Special Issue of *Research in Computing Science*, No. 18, pp. 163–176.

Murdock, Vanessa and W. Bruce Croft (2005). "A Translation Model for Sentence Retrieval." *Proceedings of Human Language Technology Conference and Conference on Empirical Methods in Natural Language Processing* (*HLT/EMNLP-2005*), Vancouver, BC, Canada.

Oard, Douglas W. (2003). "Information Retrieval Systems as Integration Platforms for Language Technologies." *Proceedings of the Human Language Technology and North American Chapter of Association of Computational Linguistics 2003* (*HLT/NAACL-2003*), Edmonton, Alberta, Canada.

Oettinger, Anthony G. (1965). "An Essay in Information Retrieval or the Birth of a Myth." *Information and Control*, Vol. 8, pp. 64–79.

Pevzner, Boris (2003). "Intermediary Agent Simulator—A Search Assistant." *International Journal of Translation*, Vol. 15, No. 1, pp. 143–147.

Ravin, Yael (1991). "Extracting Semantic Information from On-line Sources." *Proceedings of the Conference of the Association for Computational Linguistics and Chinese Language Processing* (*ROCLING-IV*), National Chiao-Tung University, Hsin-Chu, Taiwan.

Ritchie, Anna, Simone Teufel, and Stephen Robertson (2006). "Creating a Text Collection for Citation-based IR Experiments." *Proceedings of the Human Language Technology Conference—Annual Meeting of the North American Chapter of the Association for Computational Linguistics* (*HLT-NAACL-2006*), New York, USA.

Rosso, Paolo, Antonio Molina, Ferran Pla, Daniel Jiménez, and Vicent Vidal (2004). "Information Retrieval and Text Categorization with Semantic Indexing." *Proceedings of the 5th International Conference on Intelligent Text Processing and Computational Linguistics* (*CICLing-2004*), Chung-Ang University, Seoul, Korea, pp. 591–595.

Roussinov, Dmitri and Weiguo Fan (2005). "Discretization Based Learning for Information Retrieval." *Proceedings of Human Language Technology Conference and Conference on Empirical Methods in Natural Language Processing* (*HLT/EMNLP-2005*), Vancouver, BC, Canada.

Sierra, Gerardo and John McNaught (2003). "Natural Language System for Terminological Information Retrieval." *Proceedings of the 4th International Conference on Intelligent Text Processing and Computational Linguistics* (*CICLing-2003*), Mexico City, Mexico, pp. 543–554.

Stamou, Sofia and Dimitris Christodoulakis (2005). "Retrieval Efficiency of Normalized Query Expansion." *Proceedings of the 6th International Conference on Intelligent Text Processing and Computational Linguistics* (*CICLing-2005*), Mexico City, Mexico, pp. 592–595.

Stokoe, Christopher (2005). "Differentiating Homonymy and Polysemy in Information Retrieval." *Proceedings of Human Language Technology Conference and Conference on Empirical Methods in Natural Language Processing* (*HLT/EMNLP-2005*), Vancouver, BC, Canada.

Strzalkowski, Tomek, Fang Lin, Jose Perez-Carballo, and Jin Wang (1997). "Building Effective Queries in Natural Language Information Retrieval." *Proceedings of the 5th Conference on Applied Natural Language Processing*, Seattle, Washington, DC, USA.

Tao, Tao, Xuanhui Wang, Qiaozhu Mei, and Chengxiang Zhai (2006). "Language Model Information Retrieval with Document Expansion." *Proceedings of the Human Language Technology Conference—Annual Meeting of the North American Chapter of the Association for Computational Linguistics* (*HLT-NAACL-2006*), New York, USA.

Ulicny, Brian (2006). "Lycos Retriever: An Information Fusion Engine." *Proceedings of the Human Language Technology Conference—Annual Meeting of the North American Chapter of the Association for Computational Linguistics* (*HLT-NAACL-2006*), New York, USA.

Veale, Tony (2004). "The Challenge of Creative Information Retrieval." *Proceedings of the 5th International Conference on Intelligent Text Processing and Computational Linguistics* (*CICLing-2004*), Chung-Ang University, Seoul, Korea, pp. 451–462.

Vechtomova, Olga and Murat Karamuftuoglu (2004). "Comparison of Two Interactive Search Refinement Techniques." *Proceedings of the Human Language Technology Conference/North American Chapter of the Association for Computational Linguistics Annual Meeting* (*HLT/NAACL-2004*), Boston, MA, USA.

Vilares, Jesús, Francisco-Mario Barcala, and Miguel A. Alonso (2002). "Using Syntactic Dependency-pairs Conflation to Improve Retrieval Performance in Spanish." *Proceedings of the 3rd International*

Conference on Intelligent Text Processing and Computational Linguistics (*CICLing-2002*), Mexico City, Mexico.

Vu, Huyen-Trang and Patrick Gallinari (2006). "A Machine Learning-based Approach to Evaluating Retrieval Systems." *Proceedings of the Human Language Technology Conference—Annual Meeting of the North American Chapter of the Association for Computational Linguistics* (*HLT-NAACL-2006*), New York, USA.

Wang, Hongtao, Sun Maosong, and Liu Shaoming (2005). "Merging Case Relations into VSM to Improve Information Retrieval Precision." *Proceedings of the 6th International Conference on Intelligent Text Processing and Computational Linguistics* (*CICLing-2005*), Mexico City, Mexico, pp. 572–580.

Wang, Hsin-min (1999). "A New Syllable-based Approach for Retrieving Mandarin Spoken Documents Using Short Speech Queries." *Proceedings of the International Conference on Research in Computational Linguistics* (*ROCLING-XII*), Taipei, Taiwan.

Woods, William A., Lawrence A. Bookman, Ann Houston, Robert J. Kuhns, Paul Martin, and Stephen Green (2000). "Linguistic Knowledge Can Improve Information Retrieval." *Proceedings of the 6th Applied Natural Language Processing Conference*, Seattle, Washington, DC, USA, pp. 262–267.

Wu, Mei-Mei (1994). "Interaction in Information Retrieval: Discourse Analysis and the Identification of an Elicitation." *Proceedings of the Conference of the Association for Computational Linguistics and Chinese Language Processing* (*ROCLING-VII*), National Tsing Hua University, Hsin-Chu, Taiwan.

Xu, Huanqing 許歡慶, Wang Yongcheng 王永成, and Sun Qiang 孫強 (2002). 〈基於遺傳算法的定題信息搜索策略〉 (Focused Crawling Based on Genetic Algorithm). 《第一屆學生計算語言學研討會論文集》 (*SWCL2002: First Students' Workshop on Computational Linguistics: Proceedings*), Institute of Computational Linguistics, Peking University, Beijing, China, pp. 125–136.

Yang, Lingpeng, Ji Donghong, Nie Yu, and Zhou Guodong (2005). "Document Re-ordering Based on Key Terms in Top Retrieved Documents." *Proceedings of the 6th International Conference on Intelligent Text Processing and Computational Linguistics* (*CICLing-2005*), Mexico City, Mexico, pp. 560–571.

Ye, Yunming, Yan Li, Joshua Huang, and Xiaofei Xu (2006). "Improved

Focused Web Crawling Based on Incremental Q-learning." In Alexander F. Gelbukh, ed., *Advances in Natural Language Processing*, Special Issue of *Research in Computing Science*, No. 18, pp. 139–150.

Zhang, Min, Ma Shaoping, and Gao Jianfeng (2002). "Study on Link-based Approaches for Web IR in TREC Experiments." 《第一屆學生計算語言學研討會論文集》 (*SWCL2002: First Students' Workshop on Computational Linguistics: Proceedings*), Institute of Computational Linguistics, Peking University, Beijing, China, pp. 119–124.

Zhou, Zheng-Yu, Peng Yu, Ciprian Chelba, and Frank Seide (2006). "Towards Spoken-document Retrieval for the Internet: Lattice Indexing for Large-scale Web-search Architectures." *Proceedings of the Human Language Technology Conference—Annual Meeting of the North American Chapter of the Association for Computational Linguistics* (*HLT-NAACL-2006*), New York, USA.

Cross-language Information Retrieval

Bali, Kalika, Partha Pratim Talukdar, A. G. Ramakrishnan, Sameer Badaskar, and S. Sriram (2004). "Phonetic Distance Based Cross-lingual Search." *Proceedings of the International Conference on Natural Language Processing* (*ICON-2004*), International Institute of Information Technology, Hyderabad, India.

Ballesteros, Lisa and W. Bruce Croft (1997). "Phrasal Translation and Query Expansion Techniques for Cross-language Information Retrieval." *Proceedings of the 20th Annual International ACM SIGIR Conference on Research and Development in Information Retrieval* (*SIGIR-1997*), Philadelphia, PA, USA, pp. 84–91.

Ballesteros, Lisa and W. Bruce Croft (1998). "Resolving Ambiguity for Cross-language Retrieval." *Proceedings of the 21st Annual International ACM SIGIR Conference on Research and Development in Information Retrieval* (*SIGIR-1998*), Melbourne, Australia, pp. 64–71.

Ballesteros, Lisa and W. Bruce Croft (1998). "Statistical Methods for Cross-language Information Retrieval." In Gregory Grefenstette, ed., *Cross-language Information Retrieval*. Boston: Kluwer Academic Publishers, pp. 23–40.

Bian, Guo-Wei and Chen Hsin-Hsi (1998). "Integrating Query Translation and Document Translation in a Cross-language Information Retrieval System." In David L. Farwell, Laurie Gerber, and Eduard Hovy, eds.,

Machine Translation and the Information Soup. Berlin: Springer Verlag, pp. 250–265.

Brown, Ralf D. (1998). "Automatically-extracted Thesauri for Cross-language IR: When Better Is Worse." *Proceedings of the 1st Workshop on Computational Terminology (CompuTerm-98)*, Montreal, Quebec, Canada, pp. 15–21.

Calzolari, Nicoletta and Alessandro Lenci (2002). "Computational Lexicons for Cross-language Information Retrieval." *Proceedings of Cross-language Information Retrieval: A Research Roadmap Workshop*, Tampere, Finland.

Carbonell Jaime G., Yiming Yang, Robert E. Frederking, Ralf D. Brown, Yibing Geng, and Danny Lee (1997). "Translingual Information Retrieval: A Comparative Evaluation." *Proceedings of the 15th International Joint Conference on Artificial Intelligence (IJCAI-97)*, Nagoya, Japan, Vol. I, pp. 708–715.

Chen, Aitao, Hailing Jiang, and Fredric Gey (2000). "Combining Multiple Sources for Short Query Translation in Chinese–English Cross-language Information Retrieval." *Proceedings of the 5th International Workshop on Information Retrieval with Asian Languages*, Hong Kong, pp. 17–23.

Chen, Hsin-Hsi, Guo-Wei Bian, and Wen-Cheng Lin (1999). "Resolving Translation Ambiguity and Target Polysemy in Cross-language Information Retrieval." *Proceedings of 37th Annual Meeting of the Association for Computational Linguistics (ACL-99)*, University of Maryland, College Park, MD, USA, pp. 215–222.

Chen, Jiang and Nie Jian-Yun (2000). "Automatic Construction of Parallel English-Chinese Corpus for Cross-language Information Retrieval." *Proceedings of the Conference on Applied Natural Language Processing (ANLP-2000)*, Paris, France.

Chen, Jiang and Nie Jian-Yun (2000). "Machine Translation of Very Close Languages." *Proceedings of the 6th Applied Natural Language Processing Conference*, Seattle, Washington, DC, USA, pp. 21–28.

Davis, Mark W. and William C. Ogden (1998). "Free Resources and Advanced Alignment for Cross-language Text Retrieval." In Ellen M. Voorhees and Donna K. Harman, eds., *Proceedings of the 6th Text Retrieval Conference (TREC-6)*, Gaithersburg, MD: NIST Special Publication, pp. 385–394.

Flank, Sharon (2000). "Cross-language Multimedia Information

Retrieval." *Proceedings of the 6th Applied Natural Language Processing Conference*, Seattle, Washington, DC, USA, pp. 13–20.

Fujii, Atsushi and Tetsuya Ishikawa (1999). "Cross-language Information Retrieval for Technical Documents." *Proceedings of the Joint SIGDAT Conference on Empirical Methods in NLP and Very Large Corpora* (*EMNLP/VLC-99*), University of Maryland, College Park, MD, USA.

Gao, Jianfeng, Nie Jian-yun, Endong Xun, Jian Zhang, Ming Zhou, and Changning Huang (2001). "Improving Query Translation for Cross-language Information Retrieval Using Statistical Models." In W. Bruce Croft, David J. Harper, Donald H. Kraft, and Justin Zobel, eds., *Proceedings of the 24th Annual International ACM SIGIR Conference on Research and Development in Information Retrieval* (*SIGIR-2001*), New Orleans, Louisiana, USA, pp. 96–104.

Grefenstette, Gregory (1998). *Cross-language Information Retrieval.* Boston: Kluwer Academic Publishers.

Inkpen, Diana Zaiu, Muath Alzghool, Gareth Jones, and Douglas W. Oard (2006). "Investigating Cross-language Speech Retrieval for a Spontaneous Conversational Speech Collection." *Proceedings of the Human Language Technology Conference—Annual Meeting of the North American Chapter of the Association for Computational Linguistics* (*HLT-NAACL-2006*), New York, USA.

Jones, Gareth (2000). "Applying Machine Translation Resources for Cross-language Information Access from Spoken Documents." *Proceedings of the International Conference on Machine Translation and Multilingual Applications in the New Millenium* (*MT-2000*), University of Exeter, England.

Klavans, Judith, Eduard Hovy, Christian Fluhr, Robert E. Frederking, Douglas W. Oard, Akitoshi Okumura, Kai Ishikawa, and Kenji Satoh (1999). "Multilingual (or Cross-lingual) Information Retrieval." In Eduard Hovy, Nancy Ide, Robert E. Frederking, Joseph Mariani, and Antonio Zampolli, eds., *Multilingual Information Management: Current Levels and Future Abilities*. Report for National Science Foundation.

Lin, Chin-Yew (1999). "Machine Translation for Information Access across the Language Barrier: The MuST System." *Proceedings of MT Summit VII: MT in the Great Translation Era*, Singapore.

Liu, Xiaoyong Mary, Ted Diamond, and Anne R. Diekema (2000). "Word Sense Disambiguation for Cross-language Information Retrieval."

Proceedings of the ANLP-NAACL 2000, Student Research Workshop, Seattle, Washington, DC, USA, pp. 35–40.
McCarley, J. Scott and Salim Roukos (1998). "Fast Document Translation for Cross-language Information Retrieval." In David L. Farwell, Laurie Gerber, and Eduard H. Hovy, eds., *Machine Translation and the Information Soup*, Berlin: Springer Verlag, pp. 150–157.
McCarley, J. Scott (1999). "Should We Translate the Documents or the Queries in Cross-language Information Retrieval?" *Proceedings of the 37th Annual Meeting of the Association for Computational Linguistics (ACL-99)*, University of Maryland, College Park, MD, USA.
Muraki, Kazunori (1995). "Cross Language Service Technology of Digital Text Information." *Proceedings of MT Summit V: Machine Translation Conference, Exhibition and Tutorial*, Luxembourg.
Oard, Douglas W. (1998). "A Comparative Study of Query and Document Translation for Cross-language Information Retrieval." In David L. Farwell, Laurie Gerber, and Eduard Hovy, eds., *Machine Translation and the Information Soup*. Berlin: Springer Verlag, pp. 472–483.
Seo, Hee-Cheol, Sang-Bum Kim, B. I. Kim, Hae-Chang Rim, and S. Z. Lee (2003). "KUNLP System for NTCIR-3 English-Korean Cross-language Information Retrieval." In Keizo Oyama, Emi Ishida, and Noriko Kando, eds., *Proceedings of the 3rd NTCIR Workshop on Research in Information Retrieval, Automatic Text Summarization and Question Answering*, Tokyo, Japan.
Wang, Shufeng 王樹峰 and Zhang Yongkui 張永奎 (2002).〈基於英漢詞典和翻譯軟件的跨語言信息檢索實踐〉(An Experiment on English-Chinese Cross-language Information Retrieval Using Bilingual Dictionaries and Machine Translation Software).《第一屆學生計算語言學研討會論文集》(*SWCL2002: First Students' Workshop on Computational Linguistics: Proceedings*), Institute of Computational Linguistics, Peking University, Beijing, China, p. 151.
Xu, Jinxi and Ralph Weischedel (2000). "Cross-lingual Information Retrieval Using Hidden Markov Models." *Proceedings of the Joint Sigdat Conference on Empirical Methods in Natural Language Processing and Very Large Corpora (EMNLP/VLC-2000)*, Hong Kong University of Science and Technology, Hong Kong.
Yang, Yiming and Nianli Ma (2003). "CMU in Cross-language Information Retrieval at NTCIR-3." In Keizo Oyama, Emi Ishida, and

Noriko Kando, eds., *Proceedings of the 3rd NTCIR Workshop on Research in Information Retrieval, Automatic Text Summarization and Question Answering*, Tokyo, Japan.
Zhang, Yibo, Le Sun, Lin Du, and Yufang Sun (2000). "Query Translation in Chinese-English Cross-language Information Retrieval." *Proceedings of the Joint Sigdat Conference on Empirical Methods in Natural Language Processing and Very Large Corpora* (*EMNLP/VLC-2000*), Hong Kong University of Science and Technology, Hong Kong.
Zhu, Jiang and Haifeng Wang (2006). "The Effect of Translation Quality in MT-based Cross-language Information Retrieval." *Proceedings of the Joint Conference of the International Committee on Computational Linguistics and the Association for Computational Linguistics* (*COLING/ACL-2006*), Sydney, Australia.

Query Translation

Aceves-Pérez, Rita M., Luis Villaseñor-Pineda, and Manuel Montes-y-Gómez (2006). "Using N-gram Models to Combine Query Translations in Cross-language Question Answering." *Proceedings of the 7th International Conference on Intelligent Text Processing and Computational Linguistics* (*CICLing-2006*), Mexico City, Mexico.
Bian, Guo-Wei and Chen Hsin-Hsi (1998). "Integrating Query Translation and Document Translation in a Cross-language Information Retrieval System." In David L. Farwell, Laurie Gerber, and Eduard Hovy, eds., *Machine Translation and the Information Soup*. Berlin: Springer Verlag, pp. 250–265.
Davis, Mark and Ted Dunning (1995). "A TREC Evaluation of Query Translation Methods for Multi-lingual Text Retrieval." In Donna Hartman, ed., *Proceedings of the 4th Text REtrieval Conference* (*TREC-4*), Gaithersburg, Maryland, USA.
Davis, Mark and Ted Dunning (1995). "Query Translation Using Evolutionary Programming for Multilingual Information Retrieval." In John R. McDonnell, Robert G. Reynolds, and David B. Fogel, eds., *Evolutionary Programming IV: Proceedings of the 4th Annual Conference on Evolutionary Programming* (*EP-95*), San Diego, CA, USA.
Dunlavy, Daniel M., John Conroy, and Dianne P. O'Leary (2003). "QCS: A Tool for Querying, Clustering, and Summarizing Documents."

Proceedings of the Human Language Technology and North American Chapter of Association of Computational Linguistics 2003 (*HLT/NAACL-2003*), Edmonton, Alberta, Canada.

Gao, Jianfeng, Nie Jian-yun, Endong Xun, Jian Zhang, Ming Zhou, and Changning Huang (2001). "Improving Query Translation for Cross-language Information Retrieval Using Statistical Models." In W. Bruce Croft, David J. Harper, Donald H. Kraft, and Justin Zobel, eds., *Proceedings of the 24th Annual International ACM SIGIR Conference on Research and Development in Information Retrieval* (*SIGIR-2001*), New Orleans, Louisiana, USA.

Gao, Jianfeng, Nie Jian-yun, He Hongzhao, Chen Weijun, and Zhou Ming (2002). "Resolving Query Translation Ambiguity Using a Decaying Co-occurrence Model and Syntactic Dependency Relations." *Proceedings of the 25th Annual International Conference on Research and Development in Information Retrieval* (*SIGIR-2002*), Tampere, Finland, pp. 183–190.

Huang, Chien-Kang, Lee-Feng Chien, and Yen-Jen Oyang (2000). "Clustering Similar Query Sessions Toward Interactive Web Search." *Proceedings of the International Conference on Research in Computational Linguistics* (*ROCLING-XIII*), Taipei, Taiwan.

Jang, Gil Myung, Pyung Kim, Yun Jin, Suk-Hyun Cho, and Sung Hyon Myaeng (2002). "Simple Query Translation Methods for Korean-English and Korean-Chinese CLIR in NTCIR Experiments." *Proceedings of the NTCIR Workshop 3 Meeting: Evaluation of Information Retrieval, Automatic Text Summarization and Question Answering*, National Center of Sciences, Tokyo, Japan.

Lin, Shan-Mu and Chuen-Min Huang (2006). "Personalized Optimal Search in Local Query Expansion." *Proceedings of the Conference of the Association for Computational Linguistics and Chinese Language Processing* (*ROCLING-XVIII*), Taipei, Taiwan.

Pizzato, Luiz Augusto Sangoi and Vera Lúcia Strube de Lima (2003). "Query Expansion Based on Thesaurus Relations: Evaluation over Internet." *Proceedings of the 4th International Conference on Intelligent Text Processing and Computational Linguistics* (*CICLing-2003*), Mexico City, Mexico, pp. 555–558.

Prager, John, Jennifer Chu-Carroll, and Krzysztof Czuba (2004). "Question Answering Using Constraint Satisfaction: QA-by-dossier-with-constraints." *Proceedings of the 42nd Annual Meeting of the*

Association for Computational Linguistics (*ACL-2004*), Barcelona, Spain, pp. 574–581.
Saquete, Estela, Patricio Martinez-Barco, Rafael Munoz, and Jose Luis Vicedo Gonzalez (2004). "Splitting Complex Temporal Questions for Question Answering Systems." *Proceedings of the 42nd Annual Meeting of the Association for Computational Linguistics* (*ACL-2004*), Barcelona, Spain, pp. 566–573.
Skowron, Marcin and Kenji Araki (2005). "Learning the Query Generation Patterns." *Proceedings of the 6th International Conference on Intelligent Text Processing and Computational Linguistics* (*CICLing-2005*), Mexico City, Mexico, pp. 608–611.
Zhang, Yibo, Le Sun, Lin Du, and Yufang Sun (2000). "Query Translation in Chinese-English Cross-language Information Retrieval." *Proceedings of the Joint Sigdat Conference on Empirical Methods in Natural Language Processing and Very Large Corpora* (*EMNLP/VLC-2000*), Hong Kong University of Science and Technology, Hong Kong.

Information Technology

Ahmad, Khurshid and Margaret Rogers (1992). "Translation and Information Technology: The Translator's Workbench." *ReCALL*, No. 6, pp. 3–9.
Bennett, Paul A., Rod L. Johnson, John McNaught, Jeanette Pugh, Juan C. Sager, and Harold L. Somers (1986). *Multilingual Aspects of Information Technology*. Aldershot: Gower Press.
Chan, Sin-wai, ed. (2002). *Translation and Information Technology*. Hong Kong: The Chinese University Press.
Chan Sin-wai (2002). "Translation and Information Technology: Machine and Machine-aided Translation in the New Century." In Chan Sin-wai, ed., *Translation and Information Technology*. Hong Kong: The Chinese University Press, pp. vii–xii.
Huang, Chu-Ren 黃居仁 (2006). "Towards Global Wordnet Grid: Infrastructure for Language Technology in the Age of Multi-lingualism." *Proceedings of the Conference of the Association for Computational Linguistics and Chinese Language Processing* (*ROCLING-XVIII*), Taipei, Taiwan.
Li, Yun 李芸 and Wang Qiangjun 王強軍 (2002).〈信息技術領域術語字頻、詞頻及術語長度統計〉(Character Frequency, Word Frequency and

Length of Terms in the Field of Information Technology). 《第一屆學生計算語言學研討會論文集》 (*SWCL2002: First Students' Workshop on Computational Linguistics: Proceedings*), Institute of Computational Linguistics, Peking University, Beijing, China, pp. 263–274.

Sager, Juan C. (1981). "New Developments in Information Technology for Interlingual Communication." *Aslib Proceedings*, Vol. 33, Nos. 7–8, pp. 320–323.

Smith, Ross (2001). "Using Information Technology to Optimise Translation Processes at Pricewaterhouse Coopers Madrid." In Bente Maegaard, ed., *Proceedings of MT Summit VIII: Machine Translation in the Information Age*, Santiago de Compostela, Spain.

❖ PART 16 ❖

Inputting

Dictation Machine

Brousseau, Julie, Caroline Drouin, George Foster, Pierre Isabelle, Ronald Kuhn, Yves Normandin, and Pierre Plamondon (1995). "French Speech Recognition in an Automatic Dictation System for Translators: The TransTalk Project." *Proceedings of the 4th European Conference on Speech Communication and Technology* (*EuroSpeech-95*), Madrid, Spain, pp. 193–196.

Chien, Lee-feng, Keh-Jiann Chen, and Lee Lin-shan (1996). "A Mandarin Dictation Machine with Improved Chinese Language Modeling." *Journal of Chinese Linguistics*, Vol. 9, pp. 175–198.

Dymetman, Marc, Julie Brousseau, George Foster, Pierre Isabelle, Yves Normandin, and Pierre Plamondon (1994). "Towards an Automatic Dictation System for Translators: The TransTalk Project." *Proceedings of the International Conference on Spoken Language Processing*. Yokohama, Japan, pp. 691–694.

Inputting

Arnold, Doug J., Lorna Balkan, R. Lee Humphreys, Seity Meijer, and Louisa Sadler (1994). "Input." *Machine Translation: An Introductory Guide*. Manchester and Oxford: NCC Blackwell, pp. 147–164.

Bokor, Gabe (1997). "Electronic File Transfer and Conversion." *Translation Journal*, Vol. 1, No. 1.

Brasser, Michael (2000). "Enhancing Traditional Input Methods through Part-of-speech Tagging." *Proceedings of the 38th Annual Meeting of the Association for Computational Linguistics* (*ACL-2000*), Hong Kong.

Chen, Zheng and Lee Kai-Fu (2000). "A New Statistical Approach to Chinese Pinyin Input." *Proceedings of the 38th Annual Meeting of the Association for Computational Linguistics* (*ACL-2000*), Hong Kong.

Delgado, Jaime and Montserrat Meya (1995). "Document Access—Networks and Converters." In Marianne Kugler, Khurshid Ahmad, and Gregor Thurmair, eds., *Translator's Workbench*. Berlin: Springer Verlag, pp. 29–39.

Fan, Chang-Kang 范長康 and Wen-Hsiang Tsai 蔡文祥 (1988). "Disambiguation of Phonetic Chinese Input by Relaxation-based Word Identification." *Proceedings of the Conference of the Association for*

Computational Linguistics and Chinese Language Processing (ROCLING-I), Nantou, Taiwan.

Glasersfield, von Ernest (1962). "First Draft of an English Input Procedure for Mechanical Translation." *Methodos*, Vol. 14, No. 54, pp. 47–79.

Gu, Hung-yan 古鴻炎 and Jr-yiau Chen 陳志耀 (1994).〈使用新式注音鍵盤及複合馬可夫語言模型之中文輸入系統〉(A Chinese-character Inputting System Using a New Type of Phonetic Keyboard and a Compound Markov Language Model). *Proceedings of the Conference of the Association for Computational Linguistics and Chinese Language Processing (ROCLING-VII)*, National Tsing Hua University, Hsin-Chu, Taiwan.

Gu, Hung-yan and Chung-Chieh Yang 楊仲捷 (1998).〈應用動態、靜待辭典以加速鍵盤輸入中文之方法〉(A Dynamic-and-static-dictionaries Based Method for Accelerating Chinese-character Inputting with Keyboard). *Proceedings of the International Conference on Research in Computational Linguistics (ROCLING-XI)*, Hsin-Chu, Taiwan.

Heasly, Clyde C. (1957). "Character Sensing as an Input to Machine Translation." In Leon E. Dostert, ed., *Research in Machine Translation*. Washington, DC: Georgetown University Press, pp. 53–59.

Miller, David, Sean Boisen, Richard Schwartz, Rebecca Stone, and Ralph Weischedel (2000). "Named Entity Extraction from Noisy Input: Speech and OCR." *Proceedings of the 6th Applied Natural Language Processing Conference*, Seattle, Washington, DC, USA, pp. 316–324.

Oettinger, Anthony G. (1958). "An Input Device for the Harvard Automatic Dictionary." *Mechanical Translation*, Vol. 5, No. 1, pp. 2–7.

Tsai, Jia-Lin (2006). "Using Word Support Model to Improve Chinese Input System." *Proceedings of the Joint Conference of the International Committee on Computational Linguistics and the Association for Computational Linguistics (COLING/ACL-2006)*, Sydney, Australia.

Weischedel, Ralph M. (1987). "A Personal View of Ill-formed Input Processing." *Proceedings of the Northeast Artificial Intelligence Consortium's Natural Language Planning Workshop*, Blue Mountain Lake, New York, pp. 23–44.

TransType

Cubel, Elsa, Jorge González, Antonio Lagarda, Francisco Casuberta, Alfons Juan, and Enrique Vidal (2003). "Adapting Finite-state Translation to the TransType2 Project." *Proceedings of the Joint Conference Combining the 8th International Workshop of the European Association for Machine Translation and the 4th Controlled Language Applications Workshop: Controlled Language Translation* (*EAMT-CLAW-2003*), Dublin City University, Ireland.

Langlais, Philippe, George Foster, and Guy Lapalme (2000). "TransType: A Computer-aided Translation Typing System." *Proceedings of the ANLP/NAACL-2000 Workshop on Embedded Machine Translation Systems—Volume 5*, Seattle, Washington, DC, USA, pp. 46–51.

Langlais, Philippe, George Foster, and Guy Lapalme (2000). "Unit Completion for a Computer-aided Translation Typing System." *Proceedings of the 6th Applied Natural Language Processing Conference*, Seattle, Washington, DC, USA, pp. 135–141.

Langlais, Philippe, George Foster, and Guy Lapalme (2001). "TransType: A User Oriented Interactive Machine Translation System." *Proceedings of the 2nd Meeting of the North American Chapter of the Association for Computational Linguistics: Language Technologies 2001* (*NAACL-2001*), Pittsburgh, PA, USA.

Langlais, Philippe and Guy Lapalme (2002). "TransType: Development-Evaluation Cycles to Boost Translator's Productivity." *Machine Translation*, Vol. 17, No. 2, pp. 77–98.

Macklovitch, Elliott (2006). "TransType2: The Last Word." *Proceedings of the 5th International Conference on Language Resources and Evaluation* (*LREC-2006*), Genoa, Italy.

Valderrábanos, Antonio S., José Esteban, and Luis Iraola (2003). "TransType2—A New Paradigm for Translation Automation." *Proceedings of MT Summit IX*, New Orleans, Louisiana, USA.

Optical Character Recognition

Belaïd, Abdel (1998). "OCR: Print." In Giovanni B. Varile and Antonio Zampolli, eds., *Survey of the State of the Art in Human Language Technology*. Cambridge: Cambridge University Press, pp. 71–74.

Kolak, Okan and Philip Resnik (2005). "OCR Post-processing for Low

Density Languages." *Proceedings of Human Language Technology Conference and Conference on Empirical Methods in Natural Language Processing* (*HLT/EMNLP-2005*), Vancouver, BC, Canada.

Lee, Chun-Jen 李俊仁, Keh-Hwa Shyu 徐克華, Eng-Fong Huang 黃英峰, and Bor-Shenn Jeng 鄭伯順 (1994). "A Text Conversion System between Simplified and Complex Chinese Characters Based on OCR Approaches." *Proceedings of the Conference of the Association for Computational Linguistics and Chinese Language Processing* (*ROCLING-VII*), National Tsing Hua University, Hsin-Chu, Taiwan.

Miller, David, Sean Boisen, Richard Schwartz, Rebecca Stone, and Ralph Weischedel (2000). "Named Entity Extraction from Noisy Input: Speech and OCR." *Proceedings of the 6th Applied Natural Language Processing Conference*, Seattle, Washington, DC, USA, pp. 316–324.

Nagata, Masaaki (2000). "Synchronous Morphological Analysis of Grapheme and Phoneme for Japanese OCR." *Proceedings of the 38th Annual Meeting of the Association for Computational Linguistics* (*ACL-2000*), Hong Kong.

Proof-reading

Kugler, Marianne (1995). "Proof-reading Documentation—Introduction." In Marianne Kugler, Khurshid Ahmad, and Gregor Thurmair, eds., *Translator's Workbench*. Berlin: Springer Verlag, p. 109.

Masterman, Margaret and B. Williams (1984). "The Nature of Proof in Machine Translation." *Proceedings of the International Conference on the Methodology and Techniques of Machine Translation*, Cranfield Institute of Technology, Cranfield, England.

van Dyke, Parunak H. (1981). "Quality-controlled Proofreading of Machine-readable Texts." *Literary and Linguistic Computing*, Vol. 2, No. 2, pp. 51–54.

Punctuation

Gregory, Michelle, Mark Johnson, and Eugene Charniak (2004). "Sentence-internal Prosody Does not Help Parsing the Way Punctuation Does." *Proceedings of the Human Language Technology Conference/North American Chapter of the Association for Computational Linguistics Annual Meeting* (*HLT/NAACL-2004*), Boston, MA, USA.

Salton, Gerard (1958). "The Use of Punctuation Patterns in Machine Translation." *Mechanical Translation*, Vol. 5, No. 1, pp. 16–24.
Santos, Diana (1998). "Punctuation and Multilinguality: Reflections from a Language Engineering Perspective." In Jo Terje Ydstie and Anne C. Wollebak, eds., *Working Papers in Applied Linguistics*, Department of Linguistics, University of Oslo, Vol. 4, pp. 138–160.
Shieber, Stuart M. and Xiaopeng Tao (2003). "Comma Restoration Using Constituency Information." *Proceedings of the Human Language Technology and North American Chapter of Association of Computational Linguistics 2003* (*HLT/NAACL-2003*), Edmonton, Alberta, Canada.

Writing System

Liu, Ting, Ming Zhou, Jianfeng Gao, Endong Xun, and Changning Huang (2000). "PENS: A Machine-aided English Writing System for Chinese Users." *Proceedings of the 38th Annual Meeting of the Association for Computational Linguistics* (*ACL-2000*), Hong Kong.
Loong, Cheong Tong (1989). "A Data-driven Control Strategy for Grammar Writing Systems." *Machine Translation*, Vol. 4, No. 4, pp. 281–297.
Nakamura, Jun-ichi, Jun-ichi Tsujii, and Makoto Nagao (1984). "Grammar Writing System (GRADE) of Mu-Machine Translation Project and Its Characteristics." *Proceedings of the 10th International Conference on Computational Linguistics* (*COLING-84*), Stanford University, Stanford, CA, USA, pp. 338–343.
Penn, Gerald and Travis Choma (2006). "Quantitative Methods for Classifying Writing Systems." *Proceedings of the Human Language Technology Conference—Annual Meeting of the North American Chapter of the Association for Computational Linguistics* (*HLT-NAACL-2006*), New York, USA.

❖ PART 17 ❖

Interpreting

Conference Interpreting

Mouzourakis, Takis (2006). "Machine Conference Interpreting: Is It Feasible?" In Dominic W. Massaro and Barbara Moser-Mercer, eds., *Proceedings of ASCONA III: Interactive Media: The Enhancement of Multilingual Communication and Learning through Technology*, Zurich, Switzerland.

Ruetten, Anja (2006). "Termprofile.com—Supporting a Conference Interpreter's Workflow." In *Translating and the Computer 28*. London: The Association for Information Management.

Interpreting

Block, Hans Ulrich (2000). "Example-based Incremental Synchronous Interpretation." In Wolfgang Wahlster, ed., *Verbmobil: Foundations of Speech-to-speech Translation*. Berlin: Springer Verlag, pp. 411–417.

Gomez, Laura Parrilla (2006). "Teleinterpreting: The Future of Community Interpreting?" *Proceedings of the 6th Portsmouth Translation Conference: Translation Technologies and Culture*, School of Languages and Area Studies, University of Portsmouth, England.

Hönig, Hans G. (1997). "Using Text Mappings in Teaching Consecutive Interpreting." In Christa Hauenschild and Susanne Heizmann, eds., *Machine Translation and Translation Theory*. Berlin and New York: Mouton de Gruyter, pp. 19–34.

Huber, Dieter (1994). "From Machine Translation to Automatic Spoken Language Interpretation." *Proceedings of the 1st Conference of the Association for Machine Translation in the Americas: Technology Partnerships for Crossing the Language Barrier* (*AMTA-1*), Columbia, Maryland, USA, pp. 122–125.

Jekat, Susanne (1997). "Automatic Interpreting of Dialogue Acts." In Christa Hauenschild and Susanne Heizmann, eds., *Machine Translation and Translation Theory*. Berlin and New York: Mouton de Gruyter, pp. 145–155.

Schmitz, Birte (1997). "Eliminating Traces of Spoken Language Production in Automatic Dialogue Interpreting." *Proceedings of the 7th International Conference on Theoretical and Methodological Issues in*

Machine Translation (*TMI-97*), St. John's College, Santa Fe, New Mexico, USA.
Schmitz, Birte (1997). "The Translation Objective in Automatic Dialogue Interpreting." In Christa Hauenschild and Susanne Heizmann, eds., *Machine Translation and Translation Theory*. Berlin and New York: Mouton de Gruyter, pp. 193–210.

Simultaneous Interpreting

Loehr, Dan (1998). "Can Simultaneous Interpretation Help Machine Translation?" In David L. Farwell, Laurie Gerber, and Eduard Hovy, eds., *Machine Translation and the Information Soup*. Berlin: Springer Verlag, pp. 213–224.
Mima, Hideki, Hitoshi Iida, and Osamu Furuse (1998). "Simultaneous Interpretation Utilizing Example-based Incremental Transfer." *Proceedings of the 36th Annual Meeting of the Association for Computational Linguistics and 17th International Conference on Computational Linguistics* (*COLING-ACL-98*), Montreal, Quebec, Canada, pp. 855–861.
Moser-Mercer, Barbara (1997). "Process Models in Simultaneous Interpretation." In Christa Hauenschild and Susanne Heizmann, eds., *Machine Translation and Translation Theory*. Berlin and New York: Mouton de Gruyter, pp. 3–17.
Barbara Moser-Mercer (2006). "Simultaneous Interpreting: How a Complex Cognitive Task Can Be Constrained by Technology While Benefiting from It." In Dominic W. Massaro and Barbara Moser-Mercer, eds., *Proceedings of ASCONA III: Interactive Media: The Enhancement of Multilingual Communication and Learning through Technology*, Zurich, Switzerland.
Tomabechi, Hideto, Hiroaki Kitano, Teruko Mitamura, Lori S. Levin, and Masaru Tomita (1989). *Direct Memory Access Speech-to-speech Translation: A Theory of Simultaneous Interpretation*. Pittsburgh: Centre for Machine Translation, Carnegie Mellon University.

❖ PART 18 ❖

Knowledge

Knowledge

Amores, J. Gabriel and Jose F. Quesada (2000). "Machine Translation with Episteme: Linguistic Knowledge Representation, Computational Efficiency and Formal Properties." In Nicolas Nicolov and Ruslan Mitkov, eds., *Recent Advances in Natural Language Processing II*. Amsterdam and Philadelphia: John Benjamins Publishing Company, pp. 315–326.

Bean, David and Ellen Riloff (2004). "Unsupervised Learning of Contextual Role Knowledge for Coreference Resolution." *Proceedings of the Human Language Technology Conference/North American Chapter of the Association for Computational Linguistics Annual Meeting* (*HLT/NAACL-2004*), Boston, MA, USA.

Cardie, Claire, Vincent Ng, David Pierce, and Chris Buckley (2000). "Examining the Role of Statistical and Linguistic Knowledge Sources in a General-knowledge Question-answering System." *Proceedings of the 6th Applied Natural Language Processing Conference*, Seattle, Washington, DC, USA, pp. 180–187.

Dong, Zhendong 董振東 (1998). 〈語義關係的表達和知識系統的建造〉 (The Representation of Semantic Relationships and the Construction of Knowledge Systems). 《語言文字應用》 (*Applied Linguistics*), No. 3, pp. 76–82.

Drexel, Guido (2001). "Knowledge Engineering for Intelligent Information Retrieval." *Proceedings of the 2nd International Conference on Intelligent Text Processing and Computational Linguistics* (*CICLing-2001*), Mexico City, Mexico.

Gaines, Brian R. and Mildred L. G. Shaw (1993). "Eliciting Knowledge and Transferring It Effectively to a Knowledge-based System." *IEEE Transactions on Knowledge and Data Engineering*, Vol. 5, pp. 4–14.

Gillam, Lee, Khurshid Ahmad, David Dalby, and Christopher Coz (2002). "Knowledge Exchange and Terminology Interchange: The Role of Standards." In *Translating and the Computer 24*. London: The Association for Information Management.

Gupta, Rakesh and Ken Hennacy (2006). "Finite State Grammar Transduction from Distributed Collected Knowledge." *Proceedings of the 7th International Conference on Intelligent Text Processing and Computational Linguistics* (*CICLing-2006*), Mexico City, Mexico.

Hildebrandt, Wesley, Boris Katz, and Jimmy Lin (2004). "Answering

Definition Questions with Multiple Knowledge Sources." *Proceedings of the Human Language Technology Conference/North American Chapter of the Association for Computational Linguistics Annual Meeting* (*HLT/NAACL-2004*), Boston, MA, USA.

Khoo, Christopher S. G., Chan Syin, and Niu Yun (2000). "Extracting Causal Knowledge from a Medical Database Using Graphical Patterns." *Proceedings of the 38th Annual Meeting of the Association for Computational Linguistics* (*ACL-2000*), Hong Kong.

McShane, Marjorie, Sergei Nirenburg, James Cowie, and Ron Zacharski (2002). "Embedding Knowledge Elicitation and MT Systems within a Single Architecture." *Machine Translation*, Vol. 17, No. 4, pp. 271–305.

Nirenburg, Sergei (1987). "Knowledge and Choices in Machine Translation." In Sergei Nirenburg, ed., *Machine Translation—Theoretical and Methodological Issues.* Cambridge: Cambridge University Press, pp. 1–21.

Nirenburg, Sergei and Lori S. Levin (1989). "Knowledge Representation Support." *Machine Translation*, Vol. 4, No. 1, pp. 25–52.

Nirenburg, Sergei, Ira Monarch, and Todd Kaufmann (1991). "World Knowledge and Text Meaning." In Kenneth Goodman and Sergei Nirenburg, eds., *The KBMT Project: A Case Study in Knowledge-based Machine Translation.* San Meteo, California: Morgan Kaufmann, pp. 17–48.

Paul, Michael (2001). "Translation Knowledge Recycling for Related Languages." In Bente Maegaard, ed., *Proceedings of MT Summit VIII: Machine Translation in the Information Age*, Santiago de Compostela, Spain.

Otani, Miyo and Nathalie Simonin (1988). "Functional Descriptions as a Formalism for Linguistic Knowledge Representation in a Generation Oriented Approach." *Proceedings of the 2nd International Conference on Theoretical and Methodological Issues in Machine Translation of Natural Languages* (*TMI-88*), Carnegie Mellon University, Center for Machine Translation, Pittsburgh, Pennsylvania, USA.

Sawai, Susumu, Hiromichi Fukushima, Masakatsu Sugimoto, and Naoya Ukai (1982). "Knowledge Representation and Machine Translation." *Fujitsu Science and Technology Journal*, Vol. 18, No. 1, pp. 117–134.

Sawai, Susumu, Hiromichi Fukushima, Masakatsu Sugimoto, and Naoya Ukai (1982). "Knowledge Representation and Machine Translation." In Jan Horecky, ed., *Proceedings of the 9th International Conference on*

Computational Linguistics (*COLING-82*), Prague, the Czech Republic. Amsterdam: North-Holland Publishing Company, pp. 351–356.
Schubert, Klaus (1986). "Linguistic and Extra-linguistic Knowledge: A Catalogue of Language-related Rules and Their Computational Application in Machine Translation." *Machine Translation*, Vol. 1, pp. 125–152.
Shah, Mohak, Marina Sokolova, and Stan Szpakowicz (2004). "The Role of Domain-specific Knowledge in Classifying the Language of E-negotiations." *Proceedings of the International Conference on Natural Language Processing* (*ICON-2004*), International Institute of Information Technology, Hyderabad, India.
Stutzman, Walter J. (1976). "Organizing Knowledge for English-Chinese Translation." *American Journal of Computational Linguistics*, Microfiche, 48, p. 28.
Walker, Donald E. (1987). "Knowledge Resource Tools for Accessing Large Text Files." In Sergei Nirenburg, ed., *Machine Translation: Theoretical and Methodological Issues*. Cambridge: Cambridge University Press, pp. 247–261.
Wieschedel, Ralph M. and Lance A. Ramshaw (1987). "Reflections on the Knowledge Needed to Process Ill-formed Language." In Sergei Nirenburg, ed., *Machine Translation: Theoretical and Methodological Issues*. Cambridge: Cambridge University Press, pp. 155–167.
Woods, William A., Lawrence A. Bookman, Ann Houston, Robert J. Kuhns, Paul Martin, and Stephen Green (2000). "Linguistic Knowledge Can Improve Information Retrieval." *Proceedings of the 6th Applied Natural Language Processing Conference*, Seattle, Washington, DC, USA, pp. 262–267.
Yamada, Setsuo, Kenji Imamura, and Kazuhide Yamamoto (2002). "Corpus-assisted Expansion of Manual MT Knowledge." *Proceedings of the 9th International Conference on Theoretical and Methodological Issues in Machine Translation* (*TMI-2002*), Keihanna, Japan, pp. 199–208.
Yu, Shiwen 俞士汶 (1997).〈語法知識在語言信息處理研究中的作用〉(The Role of Linguistic Knowledge in Research on Language Information Processing).《語言文字應用》(*Applied Linguistics*), No. 4, pp. 81–87.
Zhou, Guodong (2005). "Combining Various Knowledge in Relation Extraction." *Proceedings of the 43rd Annual Meeting of the Association of Computational Linguistics* (*ACL-2005*), Ann Arbor, Michigan, USA.

Lexical Knowledge

Hitoshi, Isahara, Inui Hiroko, and Uchida Yuriko (1996). "Lexical Knowledge from Large Corpora and Its Application to Text Generation." *Proceedings of the 2nd Conference of the Association for Machine Translation in the Americas: Expanding MT Horizons* (*AMTA-2*), Montreal, Quebec, Canada, pp. 66–75.

Inkpen, Diana Zaiu and Graeme Hirst (2006). "Building and Using a Lexical Knowledge Base of Near-Synonyms." *Computational Linguistics*, Vol. 32, No. 2, pp. 223–262.

Ji, Hyungsuk, Sabine Ploux, and Eric Wehrli (2003). "Lexical Knowledge Representation with Contextonyms." *Proceedings of MT Summit IX*, New Orleans, Louisiana, USA.

Li, Hang 李航 (2001). "A Statistical Learning Approach to Lexical Knowledge Acquisition and Structural Disambiguation." In Huang Changning 黃昌寧 and Zhang Pu 張普, eds.,《自然語言理解與機器翻譯》(*Natural Language Understanding and Machine Translation*). Beijing: Tsinghua University Press, pp. 173–179.

Marrafa, Palmira (2005). "Modelling Grammatical and Lexical Knowledge: A Declarative Approach." *Proceedings of the 6th International Conference on Intelligent Text Processing and Computational Linguistics* (*CICLing-2005*), Mexico City, Mexico, pp. 38–48.

Pustejovsky, James (1990). "On the Nature of Lexical Knowledge." *Machine Translation*, Vol. 5, No. 1, pp. 1–4.

Utsuro, Takehito, Yuji Matsumoto, and Makoto Nagao (1992). "Lexical Knowledge Acquisition from Bilingual Corpora." *Proceedings of the 14th International Conference of Computational Linguistics* (*COLING-92*), Nantes, France, pp. 581–587.

Linguistic Knowledge

Amores, J. Gabriel and Jose F. Quesada (2000). "Machine Translation with Episteme: Linguistic Knowledge Representation, Computational Efficiency and Formal Properties." In Nicolas Nicolov and Ruslan Mitkov, eds., *Recent Advances in Natural Language Processing II*. Amsterdam and Philadelphia: John Benjamins Publishing Company, pp. 315–326.

Bouma, Gosse (2006). "Linguistic Knowledge and Question Answering."

Proceedings of the 11th Conference of the European Chapter of the Association for Computational Linguistics (*EACL-2006*), Trento, Italy.

Brown, Ralf D. (1999). "Adding Linguistic Knowledge to a Lexical Example-based Translation System." *Proceedings of the 8th International Conference on Theoretical and Methodological Issues in Machine Translation* (*TMI-99*), Chester, England, pp. 22–32.

Cardie, Claire (1996). "Automating Feature Set Selection for Case-based Learning of Linguistic Knowledge." *Proceedings of the Conference on Empirical Methods in Natural Language Processing*, University of Pennsylvania, PA, USA.

Cardie, Claire, Vincent Ng, David Pierce, and Chris Buckley (2000). "Examining the Role of Statistical and Linguistic Knowledge Sources in a General-knowledge Question-answering System." *Proceedings of the 6th Applied Natural Language Processing Conference*, Seattle, Washington, DC, USA, pp. 180–187.

McTait, Kevin (2001). "Linguistic Knowledge and Complexity in an EBMT System Based on Translation Patterns." *Proceedings of the Workshop on Example-based Machine Translation*, Santiago de Compostela, Spain, pp. 23–34.

McTait, Kevin (2003). "Translation Patterns, Linguistic Knowledge and Complexity in EBMT." In Michael Carl and Andy Way, eds., *Recent Advances in Example-based Machine Translation*. Dordrecht: Kluwer Academic Publishers, pp. 307–338.

Ng, Vincent, Sajib Dasgupta, and S. M. Niaz Arifin (2006). "Examining the Role of Linguistic Knowledge Sources in the Automatic Identification and Classification of Reviews." *Proceedings of the Joint Conference of the International Committee on Computational Linguistics and the Association for Computational Linguistics* (*COLING/ACL-2006*), Sydney, Australia.

Otani, Miyo and Nathalie Simonin (1988). "Functional Descriptions as a Formalism for Linguistic Knowledge Representation in a Generation Oriented Approach." *Proceedings of the 2nd International Conference on Theoretical and Methodological Issues in Machine Translation of Natural Languages* (*TMI-88*), Carnegie Mellon University, Center for Machine Translation, Pittsburgh, Pennsylvania, USA.

Schubert, Klaus (1986). "Linguistic and Extra-linguistic Knowledge: A Catalogue of Language-related Rules and Their Computational

Application in Machine Translation." *Computers and Translation*, Vol. 1, No. 3, pp. 125–152.
Somers, Harold L. (1999). "Sources of Linguistic Knowledge for Minority Languages." *Proceedings of MT Summit VII: MT in the Great Translation Era*, Singapore.
Su, Keh-Yih, Yu-Ling Hsu, and Claire Saillard (1991). "Constructing A Phrase Structure Grammar by Incorporating Linguistic Knowledge and Statistical Log-likelihood Ratio." *Proceedings of the Conference of the Association for Computational Linguistics and Chinese Language Processing (ROCLING-IV)*, National Chiao-Tung University, Hsin-Chu, Taiwan.
Woods, William A., Lawrence A. Bookman, Ann Houston, Robert J. Kuhns, Paul Martin, and Stephen Green (2000). "Linguistic Knowledge Can Improve Information Retrieval." *Proceedings of the 6th Applied Natural Language Processing Conference*, Seattle, Washington, DC, USA, pp. 262–267.
Zhu, Xuefeng and Yu Shiwen (1996).〈自然語言處理與語言知識庫〉(Natural Language Processing and Linguistic Knowledge Database). In Yu Shiwen and Zhu Xuefeng, eds.,《計算語言學文集》(*Papers on Computational Linguistics*). Beijing: Department of Computer Science and Technology and Institute of Computational Linguistics, Peking University, pp. 92–98.

Semantic Knowledge

Chen, Qunxiu 陳群秀 (2002).〈現代漢語語義知識表示的研究〉(Research on the Representation of Semantic Knowledge of Chinese). In Yu Shiwen, ed., *Proceedings of the Second China-Japan Natural Language Processing Joint Research Promotion Conference (CJNLP-2002)*. Beijing: Institute of Computational Linguistics, Peking University, pp. 198–210.
Gasperin, Caroline Varaschin and Vera Lúcia Strube de Lima (2003). "Experiments on Extracting Semantic Relations from Syntactic Relations." *Proceedings of the 4th International Conference on Intelligent Text Processing and Computational Linguistics (CICLing-2003)*, Mexico City, Mexico, pp. 316–326.
Nyberg, Eric H., Teruko Mitamura, Kathryn Baker, David Svoboda, Brian Peterson, and Jennifer Williams (2002). "Deriving Semantic

Knowledge from Descriptive Texts Using an MT System." In Stephen D. Richardson, ed., *Machine Translation: From Research to Real Users*. Berlin and New York: Springer Verlag, pp. 145–154.

Syntactic Knowledge

Basili, Roberto, Alessandro Marziali, Maria Teresa Pazienza, and Paola Velardi (1996). "Unsupervised Learning of Syntactic Knowledge: Methods and Measures." *Proceedings of the Conference on Empirical Methods in Natural Language Processing*, University of Pennsylvania, PA, USA.

Gasperin, Caroline Varaschin and Vera Lúcia Strube de Lima (2003). "Experiments on Extracting Semantic Relations from Syntactic Relations." *Proceedings of the 4th International Conference on Intelligent Text Processing and Computational Linguistics* (*CICLing-2003*), Mexico City, Mexico, pp. 316–326.

Yang, Xiaofeng, Jian Su, and Chew Lim Tan (2006). "Kernel-based Pronoun Resolution with Structured Syntactic Knowledge." *Proceedings of the Joint Conference of the International Committee on Computational Linguistics and the Association for Computational Linguistics* (*COLING/ACL-2006*), Sydney, Australia.

Terminological Knowledge

Karkaletsis, Evangelos A. (1995). "The Use of Terminological Knowledge Bases in Software Localisation." In Petra Steffens, ed., *Machine Translation and the Lexicon*. Berlin: Springer Verlag, pp. 175–188.

Schütz, Jörg (1994). "Terminological Knowledge in Multilingual Language Processing." *Machine Translation—Ten Years On: Proceedings of the 2nd International Conference Organised by Cranfield University*, Cranfield, England.

Translation Knowledge

Carl, Michael and Philippe Langlais (2003). "Turning General Translation Knowledge to a Sublanguage." *Proceedings of the Joint Conference Combining the 8th International Workshop of the European Association for Machine Translation and the 4th Controlled Language*

Applications Workshop: Controlled Language Translation (*EAMT-CLAW-2003*), Dublin City University, Ireland.

Imamura, Kenji (2002). "Application of Translation Knowledge Acquired by Hierarchical Phrase Alignment for Pattern-based MT." *Proceedings of the 9th International Conference on Theoretical and Methodological Issues in Machine Translation* (*TMI-2002*), Keihanna, Japan, pp. 74–84.

Yamamoto, Kaoru and Yuji Matsumoto (2003). "Extracting Translation Knowledge from Parallel Corpora." In Michael Carl and Andy Way, eds., *Recent Advances in Example-based Machine Translation*. Dordrecht: Kluwer Academic Publishers, pp. 365–395.

Knowledge Acquisition

Abrett, Glenn (1987). *The BBN Knowledge Acquisition Project Phase I—Final Report: Functional Description; Test Plan*. Technical Report (6543). Cambridge, MA: Bolt, Beranek, and Newman.

Blythe, Jim, Jihie Kim, Surya Ramachandran, and Yolanda Gil (2001). "An Integrated Environment for Knowledge Acquisition." *Proceedings of the International Conference on Intelligent User Interfaces*, Santa Fe, New Mexico, USA, pp. 13–20.

Boose, John H. and Jeffrey M. Bradshaw (1987). "Expertise Transfer and Complex Problems: Using AQUINAS as a Knowledge Acquisition Workbench for Knowledge-based Systems." *International Journal of Man-Machine Studies*, Vol. 26, pp. 3–28.

Burstein, Mark H. (1990). *The BBN Knowledge Acquisition Project: Phase Two*. Technical Report (7190). Cambridge, MA: Bolt, Beranek, and Newman.

Chen, Guanghuo 陳光火 (2000). 〈知識及知識學習〉 (Knowledge and Knowledge Acquisition). 《電子翻譯》 (*Electronic Translation*). Tianjin: Tianjin University Press, pp. 72–74.

Eshelman, Larry, Damien Ehret, John McDermott, and Ming Tan (1987). "MOLE: A Tenacious Knowledge Acquisition Tool." *International Journal of Man-Machine Studies*, Vol. 26, pp. 41–54.

Knight, Kevin, Elaine Rich, and David Wroblewski (1989). "Integrating Language Acquisition and Knowledge Acquisition." *Proceedings of the 11th International Joint Conference on Artificial Intelligence* (*IJCAI-89*), Detroit, Michigan, USA.

Knight, Kevin (1997). "Automating Knowledge Acquisition for Machine Translation." *The AI Magazine*, Vol. 18, No. 4.

Lenat, Douglas B., Mayank Prakash, and Mary Shepheard (1986). "CYC: Using Common Sense Knowledge to Overcome Brittleness and Knowledge Acquisition Bottlenecks." *The AI Magazine*, Vol. 6, No. 4, pp. 65–85.

Li, Sheng 李盛 and Yang Erhong 楊爾弘 (2002).〈一種基於聚類的漢語詞語知識的獲取方法〉(A Method of Knowledge Acquisition from Chinese Words Based on Clustering).《第一屆學生計算語言學研討會論文集》(*SWCL2002: First Students' Workshop on Computational Linguistics: Proceedings*), Institute of Computational Linguistics, Peking University, Beijing, China, pp. 275–280.

Moldovan, Dan, Roxana Girju, and Vasile Rus (2000). "Domain-specific Knowledge Acquisition from Text." *Proceedings of the 6th Applied Natural Language Processing Conference*, Seattle, Washington, DC, USA, pp. 268–275.

Nirenburg, Sergei, Jaime G. Carbonell, Masaru Tomita, and Kenneth Goodman (1992). "Lexicography and Knowledge Acquisition." *Machine Translation: A Knowledge-based Approach*. San Matero, California: Morgan Kaufmann, pp. 95–116.

Sgall, Petr and Eva Hajicova (1987). "On One Aspect of Natural-language Based Knowledge Acquisition." In Ivan Plander, ed., *Artificial Intelligence and Information-control Systems of Robots*. Amsterdam: Elsevier, pp. 49–54.

Shin, Jung H., Young S. Han, and Key-Sun Choi (1996). "Bilingual Knowledge Acquisition from Korean-English Parallel Corpus Using Alignment Method (Korean-English Alignment at Word and Phrase Level)." *Proceedings of the 16th International Conference on Computational Linguistics* (*COLING-96*), Copenhagen, Denmark.

Utsuro, Takehito (2002). "Translation Knowledge Acquisition from Cross-lingually Relevant News Articles." In Yu Shiwen, ed., *Proceedings of the Second China-Japan Natural Language Processing Joint Research Promotion Conference* (*CJNLP-2002*). Beijing: Institute of Computational Linguistics, Peking University, pp. 123–134.

Xu, Yong 許勇 and Song Rou 宋柔 (2002).〈基於百科詞典的知識獲取系統的研究與實踐〉(An Experimental Encyclopedia-based Text Knowledge Acquisition System).《第一屆學生計算語言學研討會論文集》

(*SWCL2002: First Students' Workshop on Computational Linguistics: Proceedings*), Institute of Computational Linguistics, Peking University, Beijing, China, pp. 154–160.

Knowledge Bank

Bedard, Claude (1989). "The BKB (Bilingual Knowledge Bank): A Promising New Approach to Machine Translation." In Deanna Lindberg Hammond, ed., *Coming of Age: Proceedings of the 30th Annual Conference of the American Translators Association*. Medford, New Jersey: Learned Information, Inc., pp. 437–442.

Cabré Castellvi, M. Teresa (2006). "From Terminological Data Banks to Knowledge Databases: The Text as the Starting Point." In Lynne Bowker, ed., *Lexicography, Terminology, and Translation: Text-based Studies in Honour of Ingrid Meyer*. Ottawa: University of Ottawa Press, pp. 93–106.

Kawasaki, Zenshiro, Fumiyuki Yamano, and Noriyuki Yamasaki (1991). "Translator Knowledge Base for Machine Translation Systems." *Machine Translation*, Vol. 6, No. 4, pp. 265–278.

Knight, Kevin, Ishwar Chander, Matthew Haines, Vasileios Hatzivassiloglou, Eduard Hovy, Masayo lida, Steve K. Luk, Akitoshi Okumura, Richard Whitney, and Kenji Yamada (1994). "Integrating Knowledge Bases and Statistics in MT." *Proceedings of the 1st Conference of the Association for Machine Translation in the Americas: Technology Partnerships for Crossing the Language Barrier (AMTA-1)*, Columbia, Maryland, USA, pp. 134–141.

Mitamura, Teruko, Eric H. Nyberg, and Jaime G. Carbonell (1993). "Automated Corpus Analysis and the Acquisition of Large, Multilingual Knowledge Bases for MT." *Proceedings of the 5th International Conference on Theoretical and Methodological Issues in Machine Translation of Natural Languages: MT in the Next Generation (TMI-93)*, Kyoto, Japan, pp. 312–328.

Nirenburg, Sergei, Ira Monarch, Todd Kaufmann, Irene Nirenburg, and Jaime G. Carbonell (1988). *Acquisition of Very Large Knowledge Bases*. Technical Report (CMU-CMT 88-108). Pittsburgh: Centre for Machine Translation, Carnegie Mellon University.

Sadler, Victor and Ronald Vendelmans (1990). "Pilot Implementation of a Bilingual Knowledge Bank." *Proceedings of the 13th International*

Conference on Computational Linguistics (*COLING-90*), Helsinki, Finland, Vol. 3, pp. 449–451.
Sadler, Victor (1991). "The Textual Knowledge Bank: Design, Construction, Applications." *International Workshop on Fundamental Research for the Future Generation of Natural Language Processing* (*FGNLP*), Kyoto, Japan, pp. 17–32.
Tanaka, Yasuhito (1994). "The Acquisition and Expansion of Knowledge Data by Analyzing Natural Language Using Five-character Kanji (Chinese Character) Strings." *Proceedings of the Conference of the Association for Computational Linguistics and Chinese Language Processing* (*ROCLING-VII*), National Tsing Hua University, Hsin-Chu, Taiwan.
Tang, Enya Kong and Mosleh H. Al-Adhaileh (2001). "Converting a Bilingual Dictionary into a Bilingual Knowledge Bank Based on the Synchronous SSTC." In Bente Maegaard, ed., *Proceedings of MT Summit VIII: Machine Translation in the Information Age*, Santiago de Compostela, Spain.
Turcato, Davide, Fred Popowich, Paul McFetridge, and Janine Toole (2000). "Creating High-quality, Large-scale Bilingual Knowledge Bases Using Minimal Resources." *Proceedings of the LREC-2000 Workshop on Developing Language Resources for Minority Languages: Reusability and Strategic Priorities.* Athens, Greece, pp. 92–99.
Viegas, Evelyne (1999). "Developing Knowledge Bases for MT with Linguistically Motivated Quality-based Learning." *Proceedings of MT Summit VII: MT in the Great Translation Era*, Singapore.
Walker, Donald E. (1987). "Knowledge Resource Tools for Accessing Large Text Files." In Sergei Nirenburg, ed., *Machine Translation: Theoretical and Methodological Issues*. Cambridge: Cambridge University Press, pp. 247–277.
Yu, Shiwen 俞士汶, Duan Huiming 段慧明, and Zhu Xuefeng 朱學鋒 (2000). 〈綜合型漢語知識庫及其在漢語教學中的應用〉 (A Comprehensive Chinese Language Knowledge Base and Its Applications in the Teaching of Chinese Language). In Yu Shiwen 俞士汶 and Zhu Xuefeng 朱學鋒, eds., 《計算語言學文集》 (*Papers on Computational Linguistics*), Vol. 4. Beijing: Department of Computer Science and Technology and Institute of Computational Linguistics, Peking University, pp. 59–67.
Zhou, Qiang and Zushun Chen (2005). "Building a Situation-based

Language Knowledge Base." *Proceedings of the 6th International Conference on Intelligent Text Processing and Computational Linguistics* (*CICLing-2005*), Mexico City, Mexico, pp. 327–327.

Zhu, Xuefeng and Yu Shiwen (1996). 〈自然語言處理與語言知識庫〉 (Natural Language Processing and Linguistic Knowledge Database). In Yu Shiwen and Zhu Xuefeng, eds., 《計算語言學文集》 (*Papers on Computational Linguistics*). Beijing: Department of Computer Science and Technology and Institute of Computational Linguistics, Peking University, pp. 92–98.

Knowledge Extraction

Ide, Nancy and Jean Véronis (1995). "Knowledge Extraction from Machine-readable Dictionaries: An Evaluation." In Petra Steffens, ed., *Machine Translation and the Lexicon*. Berlin: Springer Verlag, pp. 19–34.

Inkpen, Diana Zaiu and Graeme Hirst (2001). "Experiments on Extracting Knowledge from a Machine-readable Dictionary of Synonym Differences." *Proceedings of the 2nd International Conference on Intelligent Text Processing and Computational Linguistics* (*CICLing-2001*), Mexico City, Mexico.

Kinoshita, Satoshi, Miwako Shimazu, and Hideki Hirakawa (1993). "Better Translation with Knowledge Extracted from Source Text." *Proceedings of the 5th International Conference on Theoretical and Methodological Issues in Machine Translation of Natural Languages: MT in the Next Generation* (*TMI-93*), Kyoto, Japan, pp. 240–251.

Li, Hui-Feng, Namwon Heo, Kyonghi Moon, and Lee Jong-Hyeok (1999). "The Use of Abstracted Knowledge from Automatically Sense-tagged Corpus for Lexical Transfer Ambiguity Resolution." *Proceedings of MT Summit VII: MT in the Great Translation Era*, Singapore.

Lin, Kuei-Kuang and Hsin-Hsi Chen (2004). "Extracting Domain Knowledge for Dialogue Model Adaptation." *Proceedings of the 5th International Conference on Intelligent Text Processing and Computational Linguistics* (*CICLing-2004*), Chung-Ang University, Seoul, Korea, pp. 70–78.

Penagos, Carlos Rodríguez (2000). "Extraction of Knowledge about Terms from Indications of Metalinguistic Activity in Texts." *Proceedings of the 1st International Conference on Intelligent Text Processing and Computational Linguistics* (*CICLing-2000*), Mexico City, Mexico.

❖ PART 19 ❖

Language and Translation

Languages

ALPAC (1966). *Language and Machines: Computers in Translation and Linguistics.* Washington, DC: Publication 1416, National Academy of Sciences.

Andreev, Nikolaj Dmitrievic (1967). "The Intermediary Language as the Focal Point of Machine Translation." In Andrew D. Booth, ed., *Machine Translation.* Amsterdam: North-Holland Publishing Company.

Appelo, Lisette (1994). "Divergences between Languages." In M. T. Rosetta, *Compositional Translation.* Dordrecht: Kluwer Academic Publishers, pp. 229–245.

Barnbrook, Geoff (1996). *Language and Computers.* Edinburgh: Edinburgh University Press.

Barnett, James, Inderjeet Mani, and Elaine Rich (1994). "Reversible Machine Translation: What to Do When the Languages Don't Match Up." In Tomek Strzalkowski, ed., *Reversible Grammar in Natural Language Processing.* Amsterdam: Kluwer Academic Publishers, pp. 321–364.

Baron, Naomi S. (1986). "Language, Sublanguage, and the Promise of Machine Translation." *Computers and Translation*, Vol. 1, No. 1, pp. 3–19.

Bolshakov, Igor A. and Sofia N. Galicia-Haro (2003). "Can We Correctly Estimate the Total Number of Pages in Google for a Specific Language?" *Proceedings of the 4th International Conference on Intelligent Text Processing and Computational Linguistics* (*CICLing-2003*), Mexico City, Mexico, pp. 417–421.

Booth, Kathleen H. V. and Andrew D. Booth (1976). "Language Translation." In Anthony Ralston and Chester L. Meek, eds., *Encyclopedia of Computer Science.* New York: Petroceli/Charter, pp. 764–768.

Bronowski, Jacob (1956). "The Theory and Philosophy of Language." *Mechanical Translation*, Vol. 3, No. 1, pp. 12–13.

Falkehahn, W. von (1960). "Machine Translation versus Scientific Language Studies." *Scientific World*, Vol. 4, No. 2, pp. 24–25.

Feng, Zhiwei 馮志偉 and Yang Ping 楊平 (1987). 〈媒介語〉 (Intermediary Language). 《自動翻譯》 (*Automatic Translation*). Shanghai: Knowledge Press, pp. 117–147.

Gelbukh, Alexander F. and Grigori Sidorov (2001). "Zipf and Heaps Laws' Coefficients Depend on Language." *Proceedings of the 2nd International Conference on Intelligent Text Processing and Computational Linguistics* (*CICLing-2001*), Mexico City, Mexico.

Hajic, Jan, Jan Hric, and Vladislav Kubon (2000). "Machine Translation of Very Close Languages." *Proceedings of the 6th Applied Natural Language Processing Conference*, Seattle, Washington, DC, USA, pp. 7–12.

Holmes, Glyn and Marilyn Kidd (1980). "The Evolving Case for Computers in the Study of Modern Languages." *ALLC*, Vol. 1, No. 1, pp. 7–10.

Kumar, G. Bharadwaja and Kavi Narayana Murthy (2004). "Language Identification from Small Text Samples." *Proceedings of the International Conference on Natural Language Processing* (*ICON-2004*), International Institute of Information Technology, Hyderabad, India.

Lamb, Sydney M. (2000). "Translation and the Structure of Language." In W. John Hutchins, ed., *Early Years in Machine Translation: Memoirs and Biographies of Pioneers*. Amsterdam and Philadelphia: John Benjamins Publishing Company, pp. 177–196.

Lehmann, Winfred P. and Winfield S. Bennett (1985). "Human Language and Computers." *Computers and the Humanities*, Vol. 19, No. 2, pp. 77–83.

Melby, Alan K. (1994). "Machine Translation and Philosophy of Language." *Machine Translation—Ten Years On: Proceedings of the 2nd International Conference Organised by Cranfield University*, Cranfield, England.

Pendergraft, Eugene D. (1967). "Translating Languages." In Harold Borko, ed., *Automated Language Processing: The State of the Art*. New York: Wiley.

Rouvray, D. and G. Wilkinson (1984). "Machines Break the Language Barrier." *New Scientist*, 22 March.

Schank, Roger C. and Kenneth Mark Colby, eds. (1973). *Computer Models of Thought and Languages*. San Francisco, California: W. H. Freeman and Company.

Schubert, Klaus (1992). "Esperanto as an Intermediate Language for Machine Translation." In John Newton, ed., *Computers in Translation: A Practical Appraisal*. London and New York: Routledge, pp. 78–95.

Shann, Patrick (1987). "Machine Translation: A Problem of Linguistic Engineering or of Cognitive Modelling?" In Margaret King, ed., *Machine Translation Today: The State of the Art*. Edinburgh: Edinburgh University Press, pp. 71–90.

Sokolova, Marina, Stan Szpakowicz, and Vivi Nastase (2004). "Language in Electronic Negotiations: Patterns in Completed and Uncompleted Negotiations." *Proceedings of the International Conference on Natural Language Processing (ICON-2004)*, International Institute of Information Technology, Hyderabad, India.

Stevens, Dave (1999). "The Language of Change." In *Translating and the Computer 21*. London: The Association for Information Management.

Stout, Thomas M. (1954). "Computering Machines for Language Translation." *Mechanical Translation*, Vol. 1, No. 3, pp. 41–46.

Tsujii, Jun-ichi (1997). "Machine Translation: Productivity and Conventionality of Language." In Ruslan Mitkov and Nicolas Nicolov, eds., *Recent Advances in Natural Language Processing*. Amsterdam and Philadelphia: John Benjamins Publishing Company, pp. 377–392.

Vamos, Tibor (1988). "Language and the Computer Society." In Dan Maxwell, Klaus Schubert and Toon Witkam, eds., *New Directions in Machine Translation*. Dordrecht-Holland: Foris Publications, pp. 65–74.

Amharic

Adafre, Sisay Fissaha (2004). *Adding Amharic to a Unification-based Machine Translation System*. Berlin: Peter Lang.

Adafre, Sisay Fissaha (2004). "Formal Analysis of Some Aspects of Amharic Noun Phrases." *Proceedings of the 9th Workshop of the European Association for Machine Translation: Broadening Horizons of Machine Translation and Its Applications*, Foundation for International Studies, Malta, pp. 43–52.

Amsalu, Saba and Sisay Fissaha Adafre (2006). "Machine Translation for Amharic: Where We Are." *Proceedings of the 5th SALTMIL Workshop on Minority Languages and the 5th International Conference on Language Resources and Evaluation (LREC-2006): Strategies for Developing Machine Translation for Minority Languages*, Genoa, Italy, pp. 47–50.

Arabic

Alsharaf, Haytham, Sylviane Cardey, Peter Greenfield, and Yihui Shen (2004). "Problems and Solutions in Machine Translation, Involving Arabic, Chinese and French." *Actes de l'International Conference on Information Technology, ITCC 2004*, Las Vegas, Nevada, USA, Vol. 2, pp. 293–297.

Aristar, Anthony (1987). "Unification and the Computational Analysis of Arabic." *Computers and Translation*, Vol. 2, No. 2, pp. 67–75.

Chalabi, Achraf (2000). "MT-based Transparent Arabization of the Internet, TARJIM.COM." In John S. White, ed., *Envisioning Machine Translation in the Information Future*. Berlin: Springer Verlag, pp. 189–191.

Darke, Diana (1984). "Arabic Translation by Computer." *Middle East Computing*, Vol. 13, pp. 16–18.

Darke, Diana (1986). "Machine Translation for Arabic." *Language Monthly*, Vol. 28, pp. 10–11.

de Roeck, Anne and Waleed Al-Fares (2000). "A Morphologically Sensitive Clustering Algorithm for Identifying Arabic Roots." *Proceedings of the 38th Annual Meeting of the Association for Computational Linguistics (ACL-2000)*, Hong Kong.

Diab, Mona and Nizar Habash (2006). "Arabic Dialect Processing." *Proceedings of the 7th Biennial Conference of the Association for Machine Translation in the Americas (AMTA-2006): Visions for the Future of Machine Translation*, Boston Marriott, Cambridge, MA, USA.

Eades, Domenyk, Lakshmi Prakash, Mark Pedersen, and Samir Amin (2004). "A Paninian Approach to Parsing Relative Clauses in Hindi and Arabic." *Proceedings of the International Conference on Natural Language Processing (ICON-2004)*, International Institute of Information Technology, Hyderabad, India.

Freeman, Andrew, Sherri Condon, and Christopher Ackerman (2006). "Cross Linguistic Name Matching in English and Arabic." *Proceedings of the Human Language Technology Conference—Annual Meeting of the North American Chapter of the Association for Computational Linguistics (HLT-NAACL-2006)*, New York, USA.

Habash, Nizar and Owen Rambow (2005). "Tokenization, Morphological Analysis, and Part-of-speech Tagging for Arabic in One Fell Swoop."

Proceedings of the 43rd Annual Meeting of the Association of Computational Linguistics (*ACL-2005*), Ann Arbor, Michigan, USA.

Lamia, Belguith Hadrich, Ben Hamadou Abdelmajid, and Aloulou Chafik (1997). "An Agreement Error Correction Method Based on a Multicriteria Approach: An Application to Arabic Language." *Proceedings of the International Conference on Research in Computational Linguistics* (*ROCLING-X*), Academia Sinica, Taipei, Taiwan.

Maegaard, Bente (2004). "The NEMLAR Project on Arabic Language Resources." *Proceedings of the 9th Workshop of the European Association for Machine Translation: Broadening Horizons of Machine Translation and Its Applications*, Foundation for International Studies, Malta, pp. 124–128.

Miller, Keith J. and Michelle Vanni (2006). "Formal vs. Informal: Register-differentiated Arabic MT Evaluation in the PLATO Paradigm." *Proceedings of the 5th International Conference on Language Resources and Evaluation* (*LREC-2006*), Genoa, Italy.

Nezda, Luke, Andrew Hickl, John Lehmann, and Sarmand Fayyaz (2006). "What in the World Is a Shahab? Wide Coverage Named Entity Recognition for Arabic." *Proceedings of the 5th International Conference on Language Resources and Evaluation* (*LREC-2006*), Genoa, Italy.

Rosenberg, Andrew and Julia Hirschberg (2006). "Story Segmentation of Broadcast News in English, Mandarin and Arabic." *Proceedings of the Human Language Technology Conference—Annual Meeting of the North American Chapter of the Association for Computational Linguistics* (*HLT-NAACL-2006*), New York, USA.

Shaalan, Khaled F. and Habib E. Talhami (2006). "Arabic Error Feedback in an Online Arabic Learning System." In Alexander F. Gelbukh, ed., *Advances in Natural Language Processing*, Special Issue of *Research in Computing Science*, No. 18, pp. 203–212.

Snider, Neal and Mona Diab (2006). "Unsupervised Induction of Modern Standard Arabic Verb Classes." *Proceedings of the Human Language Technology Conference—Annual Meeting of the North American Chapter of the Association for Computational Linguistics* (*HLT-NAACL-2006*), New York, USA.

Vauquois, Bernard (1983). "Automatic Computer Aided Translation and the Arabic Languages." *First Arab School on Science and Technology:*

Applied Arabic Linguistics and Signal and Information Processing, Rabat, Morocco.

Zollmann, Andreas, Venugopal Ashish, and Vogel Stephan (2006). "Bridging the Inflection Morphology Gap for Arabic Statistical Machine Translation." *Proceedings of the Human Language Technology Conference—Annual Meeting of the North American Chapter of the Association for Computational Linguistics* (*HLT-NAACL-2006*), New York, USA.

Asian Languages

McEnery, Anthony, Paul Baker, Rob Gaizauskas, and Hamish Cunningham (2000). "EMILLE: Building a Corpus of South Asian Languages." *Proceedings of the International Conference on Machine Translation and Multilingual Applications in the New Millenium* (*MT-2000*), University of Exeter, England.

Tokunaga, Takenobu, Virach Sornlertlamvanich, Thatsanee Charoenporn, Nicoletta Calzolari, Monica Monachini, Claudia Soria, Chu-Ren Huang, Laurent Prevot, Xia YingJu, Yu Hao, and Kiyoaki Shirai (2006). "Infrastructure for Standardization of Asian Language Resources." *Proceedings of the Joint Conference of the International Committee on Computational Linguistics and the Association for Computational Linguistics* (*COLING/ACL-2006*), Sydney, Australia.

Basque

Aduriz, Itziar, Maxux J. Aranzabe, Jose Mari Arriola, Arantza Díaz de Ilarraza, Koldo Gojenola, Maite Oronoz, and Larraitz Uria (2004). "A Cascaded Syntactic Analyser for Basque." *Proceedings of the 5th International Conference on Intelligent Text Processing and Computational Linguistics* (*CICLing-2004*), Chung-Ang University, Seoul, Korea, pp. 121–131.

Alegria, Iñaki, Bertol Arrieta, Arantza Diaz de Ilarraza, Elisabete Izagirre, and Montse Maritxalar (2006). "Using Machine Learning Techniques to Build a Comma Checker for Basque." *Proceedings of the Joint Conference of the International Committee on Computational Linguistics and the Association for Computational Linguistics* (*COLING/ACL-2006*), Sydney, Australia.

de Ilarraza, Arantza Díaz, Koldo Gojenola, and Maite Oronoz (2005). "Design and Development of a System for the Detection of Agreement Errors in Basque." *Proceedings of the 6th International Conference on Intelligent Text Processing and Computational Linguistics* (*CICLing-2005*), Mexico City, Mexico, pp. 781–790.

Stroppa, Nicolas, Declan Groves, Andy Way, and Kepa Separasola (2006). "Example-based Machine Translation of the Basque Language." *Proceedings of the 7th Biennial Conference of the Association for Machine Translation in the Americas* (*AMTA-2006*)*: Visions for the Future of Machine Translation*, Boston Marriott, Cambridge, MA, USA.

Bengali

Basu, Anupam, Ashwini Agarwal, Biswajit Ray, Monojit Choudhury, and Sudeshna Sarkar (2004). "Automatic Extraction of Multiword Expressions in Bengali: An Approach for Miserly Resource Scenarios." *Proceedings of the International Conference on Natural Language Processing* (*ICON-2004*), International Institute of Information Technology, Hyderabad, India.

Chorkrabarti, Ajit (1977). *A Syntactic Comparison of a Fragment of the Grammar of Hindi and Bengali Which May Be Used as a Base for Machine Translation*. Bombay: University of Bombay.

Dasgupta, Probal (1989). "A Dependency Syntax for Bangla." In Dan Maxwell and Klaus Schubert, eds., *Metataxis in Practice: Dependency Syntax for Multilingual Machine Translation*. Dordrecht: Foris Publications, pp. 89–113.

Bulgarian

Koeva, Svetla, Svetlozara Lesseva, and Maria Todorova (2006). "Bulgarian Sense Tagged Corpus." *Proceedings of the 5th SALTMIL Workshop on Minority Languages and the 5th International Conference on Language Resources and Evaluation* (*LREC-2006*)*: Strategies for Developing Machine Translation for Minority Languages*, Genoa, Italy, pp. 79–86.

Tanev, Hristo and Ruslan Mitkov (2000). "LINGUA: A Robust Architecture for Text Processing and Anaphora Resolution in

Bulgarian." *Proceedings of the International Conference on Machine Translation and Multilingual Applications in the New Millenium* (*MT-2000*), University of Exeter, England.

Catalan

Armentano-Oller, Carme and Mikel L. Forcada (2006). "Open-source Machine Translation between Small Languages: Catalan and Aranese Occitan." *Proceedings of the 5th SALTMIL Workshop on Minority Languages and the 5th International Conference on Language Resources and Evaluation* (*LREC-2006*): *Strategies for Developing Machine Translation for Minority Languages*, Genoa, Italy, pp. 51–54.
Arranz, Victoria, Elisabet Comelles, and David L. Farwell (2005). "The FAME Speech-to-Speech Translation System for Catalan, English and Spanish." *Proceedings of MT Summit X*, Phuket, Thailand.
Boleda, Gemma, Stefan Bott, Rodrigo Meza, Carlos Castillo, Toni Badia, and Vicente López (2006). "CUC Web: A Catalan Corpus Built from the Web." *Proceedings of the 11th Conference of the European Chapter of the Association for Computational Linguistics* (*EACL-2006*), Trento, Italy.
Moreno, Asunción, Albert Febrer, and Lluis Márquez (2006). "Generation of Language Resources for the Development of Speech Technologies in Catalan." *Proceedings of the 5th International Conference on Language Resources and Evaluation* (*LREC-2006*), Genoa, Italy.

Chinese

Alsharaf, Haytham, Sylviane Cardey, Peter Greenfield, and Yihui Shen (2004). "Problems and Solutions in Machine Translation, Involving Arabic, Chinese and French." *Actes de l'International Conference on Information Technology, ITCC 2004*, Las Vegas, Nevada, Vol. 2, pp. 293–297.
Boitet, Christian and F. X. Tcheou (1990). "On a Phonetic and Structural Encoding of Chinese Characters in Chinese Texts." *Proceedings of the Conference of the Association for Computational Linguistics and Chinese Language Processing* (*ROCLING-III*), Taipei, Taiwan.
Chang, Chao-Huang 張照煌 and Cheng-Der Chen 陳正德 (1993). "Automatic Clustering of Chinese Characters and Words." *Proceedings*

of the Conference of the Association for Computational Linguistics and Chinese Language Processing (*ROCLING-VI*), Nantou, Taiwan.

Chang, Jyun-sheng and Yuh-Juh Lin (1994). "An Estimation of the Entropy of Chinese—A New Approach to Constructing Class-based N-gram Models." *Proceedings of the Conference of the Association for Computational Linguistics and Chinese Language Processing* (*ROCLING-VII*), National Tsing Hua University, Hsin-Chu, Taiwan.

Chang, Yuan-Sheng 張元昇 and Hsi-Jian Lee 李錫堅 (1990). "Parsing Chinese Nominalizations Based On Hpsg." *Proceedings of the Conference of the Association for Computational Linguistics and Chinese Language Processing (ROCLING-III)*, Taipei, Taiwan.

Chen, Feng-yi, Ruo-ping Jean Mo, Chu-Ren Huang, and Keh-Jiann Chen (1992). "Reduplication in Mandarin Chinese: Their Formation Rules, Syntactic Behavior and Icg Representation." *Proceedings of the Conference of the Association for Computational Linguistics and Chinese Language Processing* (*ROCLING-V*), National Taiwan University, Taipei, Taiwan.

Chen, Keh-jiann and Huang Chu-ren (1996). "Information-based Case Grammar: A Unification-based Formalism for Parsing Chinese." *Journal of Chinese Linguistics*, Vol. 9, pp. 23–45.

Dorr, Bonnie J., Gina-Anne Levow, and Lin Dekang (2000). "Building a Chinese-English Mapping between Verb Concepts for Multilingual Applications." In John S. White, ed., *Envisioning Machine Translation in the Information Future*. Berlin: Springer Verlag, pp. 1–12.

Feng, Zhiwei (1984). "Automatic Generation and Analysis of Chinese Language in Machine Translation." *Proceedings of South East Asia Regional Computer Confederation* (*SEARCC-84*) *Conference*, Hong Kong.

Feng, Zhiwei 馮志偉 (1989).《現代漢字和計算機》(*Modern Chinese Characters and Computers*). Beijing: Peking University Press.

Hacioglu, Kadri, Ying Chen, and Benjamin Douglas (2005). "Automatic Time Expression Labeling for English and Chinese Text." *Proceedings of the 6th International Conference on Intelligent Text Processing and Computational Linguistics* (*CICLing-2005*), Mexico City, Mexico, pp. 536–547.

Halpern, Jack and Jouni Kerman (1999). "The Pitfalls and Complexities of Chinese to Chinese Conversion." *Proceedings of MT Summit VII: MT in the Great Translation Era*, Singapore.

Hsieh, Shu-Kai and Huang Chu-Ren (2006). "When Conset Meets Synset: A Preliminary Survey of an Ontological Lexical Resource Based on Chinese Characters." *Proceedings of the Joint Conference of the International Committee on Computational Linguistics and the Association for Computational Linguistics* (*COLING/ACL-2006*), Sydney, Australia.

Huang, Liang, Yinan Peng, Zhenyu Wu, Zhihao Yuan, Huan Wang, and Hui Liu (2003). "Pseudo Context-sensitive Models for Parsing Isolating Languages: Classical Chinese—A Case Study." *Proceedings of the 4th International Conference on Intelligent Text Processing and Computational Linguistics* (*CICLing-2003*), Mexico City, Mexico, pp. 49–52.

Jin, Wanying and Robert F. Simmons (1986). "Symmetric Rules for Translation of English and Chinese." *Computers and Translation*, Vol. 1, No. 3, pp. 153–167.

Jin, Wanying (1993). "Translation Techniques in Chinese." In Sergei Nirenburg, ed., *Progress in Machine Translation*. Amsterdam: IOS and Tokyo: Ohmsha, pp. 53–66.

King, Gilbert W. and H. W. Chang (1963). "Machine Translation of Chinese." *Scientific America*, Vol. 208, pp. 124–135.

Lee, Hsi-Jian and Chun-Hsiao Lee (1989). "Computer Interpretation of Chinese Declarative Sentences Based on Situation Semantics." *Journal of Information Science and Engineering*, Vol. 5, No. 4, pp. 379–394.

Lee, Hsi-Jian 李錫堅 and Ren-Rong Hsu 許仁榮 (1990). "An ERS Model for Tense and Aspect Information in Chinese Sentences." *Proceedings of the Conference of the Association for Computational Linguistics and Chinese Language Processing* (*ROCLING-III*), Taipei, Taiwan.

Lee, Hsiu-Hui 李秀惠, I-Peng Lin 林一鵬, and Chien-Ping Wu 吳建平 (1990). "A Logic-based Temporal Knowledge Representation in Mandarin Chinese." *Proceedings of the Conference of the Association for Computational Linguistics and Chinese Language Processing* (*ROCLING-III*), Taipei, Taiwan.

Lee, Shu-hang 李叔航 and Hsi-Jian Lee 李錫堅 (1990). "A Unification-Based Approach for Chinese Inquiry Sentences Processing." *Proceedings of the Conference of the Association for Computational Linguistics and Chinese Language Processing* (*ROCLING-III*), Taipei, Taiwan.

Li, Tangqiu, Yang Xiaofeng, Hong Qingyang, and Li Shaozi (2002). "A Hybrid Method for Syntactic and Semantic Structure Disambiguation of Chinese." In Chan Sin-wai, ed., *Translation and Information Technology*. Hong Kong: The Chinese University Press, pp. 43–55.

Liao, Jen-Wen 廖甄文 and Jyun-Sheng Chang 張俊盛 (1990). "Computer Generation of Chinese Commentary on Othello Games." *Proceedings of the Conference of the Association for Computational Linguistics and Chinese Language Processing* (*ROCLING-III*), Taipei, Taiwan.

Liao, Yuan-Fu, Wern-Jun Wang, Shu-Ling Lee, and Sin-Hong Chen (1997). "A First Study on Mandarin Prosodic State Detection." *Proceedings of the International Conference on Research in Computational Linguistics* (*ROCLING-X*), Academia Sinica, Taipei, Taiwan.

Lin, Koong H. C. and Von-Wun Soo (1993). "Toward Discourse-guided Theta-grid Chart Parsing for Mandarin Chinese—A Preliminary Report." *Proceedings of the Conference of the Association for Computational Linguistics and Chinese Language Processing* (*ROCLING-VI*), Nantou, Taiwan.

Luo, Zhensheng 羅振聲 and Yuan Yulin 袁毓林, eds. (1996).《計算機時代的漢語和漢字研究》(*The Studies of Chinese Language and Characters in the Epoch of Computer*). Beijing: Tsinghua University Press.

Mao, Jia-ju, Qiu-lin Chen, and Ru-zhan Lu (2003). "Formal Representation and Semantics of Modern Chinese Interrogative Sentences." *Proceedings of the 4th International Conference on Intelligent Text Processing and Computational Linguistics* (*CICLing-2003*), Mexico City, Mexico, pp. 66–75.

Mo, Ruo-ping Jean, Yao-Jung Yang, Keh-Jiann Chen, and Chu-Ren Huang (1991). "Determinative-measure Compounds in Mandarin Chinese Formation Rules and Parser Implementation." *Proceedings of the Conference of the Association for Computational Linguistics and Chinese Language Processing* (*ROCLING-IV*), National Chiao-Tung University, Hsin-Chu, Taiwan.

Rosenberg, Andrew and Julia Hirschberg (2006). "Story Segmentation of Broadcast News in English, Mandarin and Arabic." *Proceedings of the Human Language Technology Conference—Annual Meeting of the North American Chapter of the Association for Computational Linguistics* (*HLT-NAACL-2006*), New York, USA.

Sproat, Richard (1990). "An Application of Statistical Optimization with

Dynamic Programming to Phonemic-input-to-character Conversion for Chinese." *Proceedings of the Conference of the Association for Computational Linguistics and Chinese Language Processing* (*ROCLING-III*), Taipei, Taiwan.

Sun, Maosong, Shengfen Luo, and Benjamin K. Y. T'sou (2005). "Word Extraction Based on Semantic Constraints in Chinese Word-formation." *Proceedings of the 6th International Conference on Intelligent Text Processing and Computational Linguistics* (*CICLing-2005*), Mexico City, Mexico, pp. 196–208.

Sun, Maosong, Zhang Zhengcao, Benjamin K. Y. T'sou, and Lu Huaming (2006). "Word Frequency Approximation for Chinese without Using Manually Annotated Corpus." *Proceedings of the 7th International Conference on Intelligent Text Processing and Computational Linguistics* (*CICLing-2006*), Mexico City, Mexico.

T'sou, Benjamin K. Y., H. C. Ho, Lin Hing-lung, Godfrey K. F. Liu, Caesar S. Lun, and Alan Y. L. Heung (1990). "Automated Chinese Text Abstraction: A Human-machine Co-operative Approach." *Computer Processing of Chinese and Oriental Languages*, Vol. 5, No. 1, pp. 33–41.

T'sou, Benjamin K. Y., H. L. Lin, H. C. Ho, and Tom B. Y. Lai (1996). "From Argumentative Discourse to Inference Trees: Using Syntactic Markers as Cues in Chinese Text Abstraction." *Journal of Chinese Linguistics,* Vol. 9, pp. 199–222.

Wang, Houfeng and Mei Zheng (2004). "An Empirical Study on Pronoun Resolution in Chinese." *Proceedings of the 5th International Conference on Intelligent Text Processing and Computational Linguistics* (*CICLing-2004*), Chung-Ang University, Seoul, Korea, pp. 210–213.

Wang, Houfeng and Shi Wuguang (2005). "A Simple Rule-based Approach to Organization Name Recognition in Chinese Text." *Proceedings of the 6th International Conference on Intelligent Text Processing and Computational Linguistics* (*CICLing-2005*), Mexico City, Mexico, pp. 757–760.

Xia, Yunqing, Kam-Fai Wong, and Wenjie Li (2006). "A Phonetic-based Approach to Chinese Chat Text Normalization." *Proceedings of the Joint Conference of the International Committee on Computational Linguistics and the Association for Computational Linguistics* (*COLING/ACL-2006*), Sydney, Australia.

Xue, Nianwen (2006). "Semantic Role Labeling of Nominalized Predicates in Chinese." *Proceedings of the Human Language Technology Conference—Annual Meeting of the North American Chapter of the Association for Computational Linguistics* (*HLT-NAACL-2006*), New York, USA.

Yeh, Ching-long and Chris Mellish (1997). "An Empirical Study on the Generation of Descriptions for Nominal Anaphors in Chinese." In Ruslan Mitkov and Nicolas Nicolov, eds., *Recent Advances in Natural Language Processing*. Amsterdam and Philadelphia: John Benjamins Publishing Company, pp. 353–364.

Zhang, Guiping and Yao Tianshun (1990). "The Chinese Analyzer for Multilingua Machine Translation." *Computer Processing of Chinese and Oriental Languages*, Vol. 5, No. 1, pp. 1–8.

Zhou, Joe and Liu Weiqian (2000). "A Real-time Integration of Concept-based Search and Summarization of Chinese Websites." *Proceedings of the Joint Sigdat Conference on Empirical Methods in Natural Language Processing and Very Large Corpora* (*EMNLP/VLC-2000*), Hong Kong University of Science and Technology, Hong Kong.

Zhou, Shuigeng and Jihong Guan (2002). "Chinese Document Classification Based on N-grams." *Proceedings of the 3rd International Conference on Intelligent Text Processing and Computational Linguistics* (*CICLing-2002*), Mexico City, Mexico.

Zhou, Xiaokang and Francis Y. Lin (1997). "Attributive Clauses in Chinese: Theory and Implementation." *Proceedings of the International Conference on Research in Computational Linguistics* (*ROCLING-X*), Academia Sinica, Taipei, Taiwan.

Zou, Feng, Fu Lee Wang, Xiaotie Deng, and Song Han (2006). "Automatic Identification of Chinese Stop Words." In Alexander F. Gelbukh, ed., *Advances in Natural Language Processing*, Special Issue of *Research in Computing Science*, No. 18, pp. 151–162.

Czech

Holan, Tomas, Vladimir Kubon, and Martin Platek (1997). "A Prototype of Grammar Checker for Czech." *Proceedings of the 5th Conference on Applied Natural Language Processing*, Seattle, Washington, DC, USA.

Horák, Aleš and Pavel Smrž (2001). "Efficient Sentence Parsing with Language Specific Features: A Case Study of Czech." *Proceedings of the 7th International Workshop on Parsing Technologies (IWPT-2001)*, Peking University, Beijing, China. Beijing: Tsinghua University Press, pp. 221–224.

Mráková, Eva and Radek Sedláček (2003). "From Czech Morphology through Partial Parsing to Disambiguation." *Proceedings of the 4th International Conference on Intelligent Text Processing and Computational Linguistics (CICLing-2003)*, Mexico City, Mexico, pp. 129–138.

Obrová, Pavlina (1999). "Government Language Policy: Translation of EC Legislation into the Czech Language." *Proceedings of the 4th Workshop of the European Association for Machine Translation: EU and the New Languages: Translation—Possibilities, Policies and Practicalities*, Prague, the Czech Republic.

Oliva, Karel (1989). "A Parser for Czech Implemented in Systems-Q." *Explizite Beschreibung der Sprache und Automatische Textbearbeitung*, Vol. 16, Faculty of Mathematics and Physics, Charles University.

Sgall, Petr, Eva Hajicova, and Jarmila Panevova (1986). "Experiments with Automatic Comprehension of Czech Sentences." *International Forum on Information and Documentation*, Vol. 11, No. 1, pp. 34–36.

Urrea, Alfonso Medina and Jaroslava Hlaváèová (2005). "Automatic Recognition of Czech Derivational Prefixes." *Proceedings of the 6th International Conference on Intelligent Text Processing and Computational Linguistics (CICLing-2005)*, Mexico City, Mexico, pp. 183–191.

Danish

Paggio, Patrizia (2000). "Spelling and Grammar Correction for Danish in SCARRIE." *Proceedings of the 6th Applied Natural Language Processing Conference*, Seattle, Washington, DC, USA, pp. 255–261.

Paggio, Patrizia (2006). "Annotating Information Structure in a Corpus of Spoken Danish." *Proceedings of the 5th International Conference on Language Resources and Evaluation (LREC-2006)*, Genoa, Italy.

Pedersen, Bolette Sandford (1999). "Systematic Verb Polysemy in MT: A Study of Danish Motion Verbs with Comparisons with Spanish." *Machine Translation*, Vol. 14, No. 1, pp. 35–82.

Schubert, Ingrid (1989). "A Dependency Syntax for Danish." In Dan

Maxwell and Klaus Schubert, eds., *Metataxis in Practice: Dependency Syntax for Multilingual Machine Translation*. Dordrecht: Foris Publications, pp. 39–67.

Dutch

Hoste, Véronique and Guy De Pauw (2006). "KNACK-2002: A Richly Annotated Corpus of Dutch Written Text." *Proceedings of the 5th International Conference on Language Resources and Evaluation* (*LREC-2006*), Genoa, Italy.

Kool, Edward A. (2004). "Representing Dutch Morphology in a Machine Translation System." *International Journal of Translation*, Vol. 16, No. 1, pp. 109–120.

English

Almeida, Ashish Francis, Pushpak Bhattacharyya, Rajat Kumar Mohanty, and Srinivas Samala (2004). "The Complexity of OF in English." *Proceedings of the International Conference on Natural Language Processing* (*ICON-2004*), International Institute of Information Technology, Hyderabad, India.

Arranz, Victoria, Elisabet Comelles, and David L. Farwell (2005). "The FAME Speech-to-Speech Translation System for Catalan, English and Spanish." *Proceedings of MT Summit X*, Phuket, Thailand.

Barrett, Leslie and Anthony R. Davis (2003). "Diagnostics for Determining Compatibility in English Support-verb-nominalization Pairs." *Proceedings of the 4th International Conference on Intelligent Text Processing and Computational Linguistics* (*CICLing-2003*), Mexico City, Mexico, pp. 87–93.

Blekhman, Michael S., Maryna Byezhanova, Andrei Kursin, Igor Backlam, Alexander Kazakov, and Vladimir Petrov (1999). "Computer-aided Translation Tools for Russian, Ukrainian, and English." *Proceedings of MT Summit VII: MT in the Great Translation Era*, Singapore.

Darlington, Jared L. (1965). "Machine Methods for Providing Logical Arguments Expressed in English." *Mechanical Translation*, Vol. 8, Nos. 3–4, pp. 41–67.

Dodd, Charles S. (1952). "Model English for MT." *Proceedings of the*

M.I.T. Conference on Mechanical Translation, Massachusetts Institute of Technology, Cambridge, MA, USA.

Flickinger, Dan, Ann Copestake, and Ivan A. Sag (2000). "HPSG Analysis of English." In Wolfgang Wahlster, ed., *Verbmobil: Foundations of Speech-to-speech Translation*. Berlin: Springer Verlag, pp. 254–263.

Habash, Nizar and Bonnie J. Dorr (2003). "A Categorical Variation Database for English." *Proceedings of the Human Language Technology and North American Chapter of Association of Computational Linguistics 2003* (*HLT/NAACL-2003*), Edmonton, Alberta, Canada, pp. 96–102.

Habash, Nizar and Bonnie J. Dorr (2003). "CatVar: A Database of Categorical Variations for English." *Proceedings of MT Summit IX*, New Orleans, Louisiana, USA.

Hacioglu, Kadri, Ying Chen, and Benjamin Douglas (2005). "Automatic Time Expression Labeling for English and Chinese Text." *Proceedings of the 6th International Conference on Intelligent Text Processing and Computational Linguistics* (*CICLing-2005*), Mexico City, Mexico, pp. 536–547.

Harris, Brian (1967). "Towards Recognizing English Phrasal Verbs for Machine Translation." *Recherches sur la traduction automatique*, Vol. 6, pp. 48–74.

Murata, Masaki, Kiyotaka Uchimoto, Qing Ma, and Hitoshi Isahara (2001). "Magical Number Seven Plus or Minus Two: Syntactic Structure Recognition in Japanese and English Sentences." *Proceedings of the 2nd International Conference on Intelligent Text Processing and Computational Linguistics* (*CICLing-2001*), Mexico City, Mexico.

Pym, P. John (1991). "Simplified English and Machine Translation." *Professional Translator and Interpreter*, Vol. 2, pp. 5–9.

Ramsay, Allan and Reinhard Schäler (1997). "Case and Word Order in English and German." In Ruslan Mitkov and Nicolas Nicolov, eds., *Recent Advances in Natural Language Processing*. Amsterdam and Philadelphia: John Benjamins Publishing Company, pp. 15–33.

Rosenberg, Andrew and Julia Hirschberg (2006). "Story Segmentation of Broadcast News in English, Mandarin and Arabic." *Proceedings of the Human Language Technology Conference—Annual Meeting of the North American Chapter of the Association for Computational Linguistics* (*HLT-NAACL-2006*), New York, USA.

Schwartz, Lee Ann (1988). "Coordination: Some Problems and Solutions for the Analysis of English with an ATN." *Proceedings of the 2nd International Conference on Theoretical and Methodological Issues in Machine Translation of Natural Languages* (*TMI-88*), Carnegie Mellon University, Center for Machine Translation, Pittsburgh, Pennsylvania, USA.

Silla Jr., Carlos N. and Celso A. A. Kaestner (2004). "An Analysis of Sentence Boundary Detection Systems for English and Portuguese Documents." *Proceedings of the 5th International Conference on Intelligent Text Processing and Computational Linguistics* (*CICLing-2004*), Chung-Ang University, Seoul, Korea, pp. 132–138.

Somers, Harold, Hideki Hirakawa, Seiji Miike, and Shinya Amano (1988). "The Treatment of Complex English Nominalizations in Machine Translation." *Computers and Translation*, Vol. 3, No. 1, pp. 3–21.

Xun, Endong, Huang Changning, and Zhou Ming (2000). "A Unified Statistical Model for the Identification of English BaseNP." *Proceedings of the 38th Annual Meeting of the Association for Computational Linguistics* (*ACL-2000*), Hong Kong.

Esperanto

Minnaja, Carlo and Laura Paccagnella (2000). "A Part-of-speech Tagger for Esperanto Oriented to MT." *Proceedings of the International Conference on Machine Translation and Multilingual Applications in the New Millenium* (*MT-2000*), University of Exeter, England.

Schubert, Klaus (1989). "A Dependency Syntax of Esperanto." In Dan Maxwell and Klaus Schubert, eds., *Metataxis in Practice: Dependency Syntax for Multilingual Machine Translation*. Dordrecht: Foris Publications.

Estonian

Kaalep, Heiki-Jaan and Kadri Muischnek (2006). "Multi-word Verbs in a Flective Language: The Case of Estonian." *Proceedings of the 11th Conference of the European Chapter of the Association for Computational Linguistics* (*EACL-2006*), Trento, Italy.

Farsi

Abolhassani Chime, Zahra (2006). "An Account for Compound Prepositions in Farsi." *Proceedings of the Joint Conference of the International Committee on Computational Linguistics and the Association for Computational Linguistics (COLING/ACL-2006)*, Sydney, Australia.

Finnish

Santaholma, Marianne (2005). "Linguistic Representation of Finnish in a Limited-domain Speech-to-speech Language Translation System." *Proceedings of the 10th Workshop of the European Association for Machine Translation: Practical Applications of Machine Translation*, Budapest, Hungary, pp. 226–234.

Tarvainen, Kalevi (1989). "A Dependency Syntax for Finnish." In Dan Maxwell and Klaus Schubert, eds., *Metataxis in Practice: Dependency Syntax for Multilingual Machine Translation*. Dordrecht: Foris Publications, pp. 115–150.

Foreign Languages

Brandwood, Leonard (1956). "The Translation of a Foreign Language by Machine." *Babel*, Vol. 2, No. 3, pp. 111–118.

Bull, William E. (1952). "Teaching of Foreign Languages." *Proceedings of the M.I.T. Conference on Mechanical Translation,* Massachusetts Institute of Technology, Cambridge, MA, USA.

Kertesz, Francois (1974). "How to Cope with the Foreign-language Problems: Experience Gained at a Multidisciplinary Laboratory." *Journal of the American Society for Information Science*, Vol. 25, No. 2, pp. 86–104.

Liu, Yongquan 劉涌泉 (1984).〈外漢機器翻譯中的中介成分體系〉(The Intermediary Componential System in Machine Translation Systems for Foreign Languages and Chinese). In Liu Yongquan *et al.*,《中國的機器翻譯》(*Machine Translation in China*). Shanghai: Knowledge Press, pp. 46–57.

Lufkin, J. M. (1966). "Human versus Machine Translation of Foreign Languages." *The Incorporated Linguist*, Vol. 5, pp. 9–15.

Zagar, Galvão Elena (2005). "Translating into the Foreign Language: Using Website 'Internationalization' as a Pedagogic Tool." *International Journal of Translation*, No. 4, pp. 37–40.

French

Alsharaf, Haytham, Sylviane Cardey, Peter Greenfield, and Yihui Shen (2004). "Problems and Solutions in Machine Translation, Involving Arabic, Chinese and French." *Actes de l'International Conference on Information Technology* (*ITCC-2004*), Las Vegas, Nevada, USA, Vol. 2, pp. 293–297.

Brandwood, Leonard (1956). "Mechanical Translation of French." *Mechanical Translation*, Vol. 3, No. 2, pp. 52–61.

Eynde, Karel van den, Erik Broeders, Carmen Eggermont, and Ludo Vangilbergen (1988). "The Pronominal Approach in NLP: A Pronominal Feature Analysis of Coordination in French." *Machine Translation*, Vol. 3, Nos. 3–4, pp. 177–213.

Maegaard, Bente (1976). "The Recognition of Finite Verbs in French Texts." *ALLC Bulletin*, Vol. 4, No. 1, pp. 49–52.

Meile, P. (1962). "On Problems of Address in an Automatic Dictionary of French." In National Physical Laboratory, ed., *1961 International Conference on Machine Translation of Languages and Applied Language Analysis: Proceedings of the Conference Held at the National Physical Laboratory, Teddington, Middlesex, on 5th, 6th, 7th and 8th September*. London: Her Majesty's Stationery Office, Vol. 1, pp. 380–399.

Simard, Michel (1998). "Automatic Insertion of Accents in French Text." *Proceedings of the 3rd Conference on Empirical Methods in Natural Language Processing*, Granada, Spain.

German

Brandwood, Leonard (1958). "Some Problems in the Mechanical Translation of German." *Mechanical Translation*, Vol. 5, No. 2, pp. 60–66.

Brew, Chris and Sabine Schulte im Walde (2002). "Spectral Clustering for German Verbs." *Proceedings of the 2002 Conference on Empirical Methods in Natural Language Processing* (*EMNLP-2002*), University of Pennsylvania, Philadelphia, PA, USA.

Feng, Zhiwei 馮志偉 (2001).〈基於集合運算的德語冠詞歧義消解〉(German Article Disambiguation Based on Set Operation). In Huang Changning 黃昌寧 and Zhang Pu 張普, eds.,《自然語言理解與機器翻譯》(*Natural Language Understanding and Machine Translation*). Beijing: Tsinghua University Press, pp. 272–277.

Gamon, Michael, Eric K. Ringger, Simon Corston-Oliver, and Robert C. Moore (2002). "Machine-learned Contexts for Linguistic Operations in German Sentence Realization." *Proceedings of the 40th Annual Meeting of the Association for Computational Linguistics* (*ACL-2002*), Philadelphia, PA, USA, pp. 25–32.

im Walde, Sabine Schulte (2006). "Experiments on the Automatic Induction of German Semantic Verb Class." *Computational Linguistics*, Vol. 32, No. 2, pp. 159–194.

Kempen, Gerard and Karin Harbusch (2004). "Generating Natural Word Orders in a Semi-free Word Order Language: Treebank-based Linearization Preferences for German." *Proceedings of the 5th International Conference on Intelligent Text Processing and Computational Linguistics* (*CICLing-2004*), Chung-Ang University, Seoul, Korea, pp. 346–350.

Lobin, Henning (1989). "A Dependency Syntax for German." In Dan Maxwell and Klaus Schubert, eds., *Metataxis in Practice: Dependency Syntax for Multilingual Machine Translation*. Dordrecht: Foris Publications, pp. 17–38.

Matthews, George H. and S. Rogovin (1958). "German Sentence Recognition." *Mechanical Translation*, Vol. 5, No. 3, pp. 114–120.

Mueller, Hugo J. (1957). "German Pre-nominal Modifiers as Clues in Machine Translation." In Leon E. Dostert, ed., *Research in Machine Translation*. Washington, DC: Georgetown University Press, pp. 89–102.

Müller, Stefan and Walter Kasper (2000). "HPSG Analysis of German." In Wolfgang Wahlster, ed., *Verbmobil: Foundations of Speech-to-speech Translation*. Berlin: Springer Verlag, pp. 238–253.

Nerbonne, John, Klaus Netter, Abdel Kader Diagne, Judith Klein, and Ludwig Dickmann (1993). "A Diagnostic Tool for German Syntax." *Machine Translation*, Vol. 8, Nos. 1–2, pp. 85–107.

Oswald, Victor A. and Stuart L. Fletcher (1951). "Proposals for the Mechanical Resolution of German Syntax Patterns." *Modern Language Forum*, Vol. 36, Nos. 3–4, pp. 1–24.

Ramsay, Allan and Reinhard Schäler (1997). "Case and Word Order in English and German." In Ruslan Mitkov and Nicolas Nicolov, eds., *Recent Advances in Natural Language Processing*. Amsterdam and Philadelphia: John Benjamins Publishing Company, pp. 15–33.

Reifler, Erwin (1955). "Mechanical Determination of the Constituents of German Substantive Compounds." *Mechanical Translation*, Vol. 2, No. 1, pp. 3–14.

Greek

Karamanlakis, Stratis and Alexios Zavras (1995). "Greek Language Tools." In Marianne Kugler, Khurshid Ahmad, and Gregor Thurmair, eds., *Translator's Workbench*. Berlin: Springer Verlag, pp. 145–154.

Michailidis, Ionas, Konstantinos Diamantaras, Spiros Vasileiadis, and Yannick Frère (2006). "Greek Named Entity Recognition Using Support Vector Machines, Maximum Entropy and Onetime." *Proceedings of the 5th International Conference on Language Resources and Evaluation* (*LREC-2006*), Genoa, Italy.

Vassiliou, Marina, Stella Markantonatou, Yanis Maistros, and Vangelis Karkaletsis (2003). "Evaluating Specifications for Controlled Greek." *Proceedings of the Joint Conference Combining the 8th International Workshop of the European Association for Machine Translation and the 4th Controlled Language Applications Workshop: Controlled Language Translation* (*EAMT-CLAW-2003*), Dublin City University, Ireland.

Hebrew

Ephratt, Michal (1988). "Semantic Properties of the Root-pattern Array." *Machine Translation*, Vol. 3, Nos. 3–4, pp. 215–236.

Goldberg, Yoav, Menachem Adler, and Michael Elhadad (2006). "Noun Phrase Chunking in Hebrew—Influence of Lexical and Morphological Features." *Proceedings of the Joint Conference of the International Committee on Computational Linguistics and the Association for Computational Linguistics* (*COLING/ACL-2006*), Sydney, Australia.

Hindi

Chorkrabarti, Ajit (1977). *A Syntactic Comparison of a Fragment of the*

Grammar of Hindi and Bengali Which May Be Used as a Base for Machine Translation. Bombay: University of Bombay.

Eades, Domenyk, Lakshmi Prakash, Mark Pedersen, and Samir Amin (2004). "A Paninian Approach to Parsing Relative Clauses in Hindi and Arabic." *Proceedings of the International Conference on Natural Language Processing (ICON-2004)*, International Institute of Information Technology, Hyderabad, India.

Hungarian

Proszeky, Gabor (1988). "Hungarian—A Special Challenge to Machine Translation?" In Dan Maxwell, Klaus Schubert, and Toon Witkam, eds., *New Directions in Machine Translation*. Dordrecht-Holland: Foris Publications, pp. 219–223.

Proszeky, Gabor (1989). "A Dependency Syntax for Hungarian." In Dan Maxwell and Klaus Schubert, eds., *Metataxis in Practice: Dependency Syntax for Multilingual Machine Translation*. Dordrecht: Foris Publications, pp. 151–181.

Indian

Bandyopadhyay, Sivaji (2002). "Teaching MT—An Indian Perspective." *Proceedings of the 6th Workshop of the European Association for Machine Translation: Teaching Machine Translation*, Manchester, England, pp. 13–22.

Pinto, Joel, Kalika Bali, Sandeep Manocha, Satinder Pal Singh, and R. N. V. Sitaram (2004). "Building Large Vocabulary Speech Recognition Systems for Indian Languages." *Proceedings of the International Conference on Natural Language Processing (ICON-2004)*, International Institute of Information Technology, Hyderabad, India.

Raman, S. and N. Rama Krishna Reddy (1995). "A Parallel Machine Translation System for Indian Languages." *International Journal of Translation*, Vol. 7, Nos. 1–2, pp. 31–45.

Rao, K. Sreenivasa and B. Yegnanarayana (2004). "Impact of Constraints on Prosody Modeling for Indian Languages." *Proceedings of the International Conference on Natural Language Processing (ICON-2004)*, International Institute of Information Technology, Hyderabad, India.

Sobha, L. and B. Patnaik (2000). "VASISTH: An Ellipsis Resolution Algorithm for Indian Languages." *Proceedings of the International Conference on Machine Translation and Multilingual Applications in the New Millenium* (*MT-2000*), University of Exeter, England.

Interlingua

Amano, Shinya (1989). "On Interlingua Approaches—From the Point of View of *Traduttori Traditori*." *Proceedings of the "MT into the '90s" Workshop*, Manchester, England.

Dorr, Bonnie J. (1993). "Generation from the Interlingua." *Machine Translation: A View from the Lexicon*. Cambridge, MA: MIT Press, pp. 193–231.

Dorr, Bonnie J. (1993). "Parameterization of the Interlingua." *Machine Translation: A View from the Lexicon*. Cambridge, MA: MIT Press, pp. 163–192.

Dorr, Bonnie J. and Clare R. Voss (1994). "The Case for a MT Developers' Tool with a Two-component View of the Interlingua." *Proceedings of the 1st Conference of the Association for Machine Translation in the Americas: Technology Partnerships for Crossing the Language Barrier* (*AMTA-1*), Columbia, Maryland, USA, pp. 40–47.

Mesli, Nadia (1994). "Interlingua vs. Transfer: Knowledge Sharing across Projects." *Proceedings of the 1st Conference of the Association for Machine Translation in the Americas: Technology Partnerships for Crossing the Language Barrier* (*AMTA-1*), Columbia, Maryland, USA, pp. 169–176.

Nirenburg, Sergei, Jaime G. Carbonell, Masaru Tomita, and Kenneth Goodman (1992). "The Concept of Interlingua." *Machine Translation: A Knowledge-based Approach*. San Matero, California: Morgan Kaufmann, pp. 65–93.

Richens, Richard H. (1959). "Logical Looseness of Interlinguas." *Essays on and in Machine Translation*. Cambridge: Cambridge Language Research Unit.

Sgall, Petr and Jarmila Panevova (1987). "On the Notion of an Interlingua." *KAM Series: Discrete Mathematics and Combinatorics: Operations Research, Mathematical Linguistics*. Prague: Charles University.

Uchida, Hiroshi and Zhu Meiying (1993). "Interlingua for Multilingual

Machine Translation." *Proceedings of MT Summit IV: International Cooperation for Global Communication*, Kobe, Japan, pp. 157–169.
Xiong, Wenxin 熊文新 (1998).〈中間語言機器翻譯的有關問題〉(Issues Relating to Interlingua in Machine Translation).《語言文字應用》(*Applied Linguistics*), No. 3, pp. 69–75.

Irish

Wogan, John, Brian Ó Raghallaigh, Áine Ní Bhriain, Eric Zoerner, Harald Berthelsen, Ailbhe Ní Chasaide, and Christer Gobl (2006). "Developing a Spoken Corpus and a Synthesiser for Irish." *Proceedings of the 5th SALTMIL Workshop on Minority Languages and the 5th International Conference on Language Resources and Evaluation (LREC-2006): Strategies for Developing Machine Translation for Minority Languages*, Genoa, Italy, pp. 113–116.

Italian

Calzolari, Nicoletta, Ornella Corazzari, and Antonio Zampolli (2001). "Lexical-semantic Tagging of an Italian Corpus." *Proceedings of the 2nd International Conference on Intelligent Text Processing and Computational Linguistics (CICLing-2001)*, Mexico City, Mexico.

Japanese

Alam, Yukiko S. (1986). "A Lexical-functional Approach to Japanese for the Purpose of Machine Translation." *Computers and Translation*, Vol. 1, No. 4, pp. 199–214.
Bjarnestam, Anna (2003). "Internationalizing a Controlled Vocabulary Based Search Engine for Japanese." *Proceedings of the Localization World Conference 2003*, Seattle, Washington, USA.
Echizen-ya, Hiroshi, Kenji Araki, Yoshio Momouchi, and Koji Tochinai (2004). "Acquisition of Word Translations Using Local Focus-based Learning in Ainu-Japanese Parallel Corpora." *Proceedings of the 5th International Conference on Intelligent Text Processing and Computational Linguistics (CICLing-2004)*, Chung-Ang University, Seoul, Korea, pp. 297–301.
Fais, Laurel and Kentaro Ogura (2001). "Discourse Issues in the

Translation of Japanese Email." *The 5th Pacific Association for Computational Linguistics Conference* (*PACLING-2001*), Fukuoka, Japan.

Harada, Yasunari, Takao Gunji, Hideo Miyoshi, Hidetosi Sirai, and Koiti Hasida (1988). "JPSG—A Phrase Structure Grammar for Japanese." *Proceedings of the Conference of the Association for Computational Linguistics and Chinese Language Processing* (*ROCLING-I*), Nantou, Taiwan.

Hashimoto, Taiichi, Kosuke Nishidate, Kiyoaki Shirai, Takenobu Tokunaga, and Hozumi Tanaka (2001). "Decision Lists for Determining Adjective Dependency in Japanese." In Bente Maegaard, ed., *Proceedings of MT Summit VIII: Machine Translation in the Information Age*, Santiago de Compostela, Spain.

Ichikawa, Akira, Masahiro Araki, Y. Horiuchi, Masato Ishizaki, Shuichi Itabashi, Toshihiko Itoh, Hideki Kashioka, Keiji Kato, Hideki Kikuchi, Hanae Koiso, Tomoko Kumagai, Akira Kurematsu, Kikuo Maekawa, Shu Nakazato, Masafumi Tamoto, Syun Tutiya, Yoichi Yamashita, and Takashi Yoshimura (1999). "Evaluation of Annotation Schemes for Japanese Discourse." In Marilyn Walker, ed., *Proceedings of the ACL-99 Workshop: Towards Standards and Tools for Discourse Tagging*, University of Maryland, College Park, MD, USA, pp. 26–34.

Ikeda, Nobuko (2004). "Machine Translation from Japanese to Various Languages." *AAMT Journal*, No. 36.

Ishioka, Tsunenori and Masayuki Kameda (2000). "Automated Japanese Essay Scoring System Based on Articles Written by Experts." *Proceedings of the Joint Conference of the International Committee on Computational Linguistics and the Association for Computational Linguistics* (*COLING/ACL-2006*), Sydney, Australia.

Ito, Noriko, Toru Sugimoto, and Michio Sugeno (2004). "A Systemic-functional Approach to Japanese Text Understanding." *Proceedings of the 5th International Conference on Intelligent Text Processing and Computational Linguistics* (*CICLing-2004*), Chung-Ang University, Seoul, Korea, pp. 25–36.

Kakegawa, Jun-ichi, Hisayuki Kanda, Eitaro Fujioka, Makoto Itami, and Kohji Itoh (2000). "Diagnostic Processing of Japanese for Computer-assisted Second Language Learning." *Proceedings of the 38th Annual Meeting of the Association for Computational Linguistics* (*ACL-2000*), Hong Kong.

Kawada, Tsutomu, Shinya Amano, and Kunio Sakai (1980). "Linguistic Error Correction of Japanese Sentences." *Proceedings of the 8th International Conference on Computational Linguistics* (*COLING-80*), Tokyo, Japan, pp. 257–261.

Kawahara, Daisuke and Sadao Kurohashi (2006). "A Fully-lexicalized Probabilistic Model for Japanese Syntactic and Case Structure Analysis." *Proceedings of the Human Language Technology Conference—Annual Meeting of the North American Chapter of the Association for Computational Linguistics* (*HLT-NAACL-2006*), New York, USA.

Kay, Carl and David Fine (2002). "Japanese Language: An Introduction for Language Technology Professionals and Researchers." In *Translating and the Computer 24*. London: The Association for Information Management.

Kimura, Yasutomo, Kenji Araki, and Koji Tochinai (2004). "Evaluation of Japanese Dialogue Processing Method Based on Similarity Measure Using tf · AoI." *Proceedings of the 5th International Conference on Intelligent Text Processing and Computational Linguistics* (*CICLing-2004*), Chung-Ang University, Seoul, Korea, pp. 366–377.

Kogure, Kiyoshi, Hitoshi Iida, Kei Yoshimoto, Hiroyuki Maeda, Masako Kume, and Susumu Kato (1988). "A Method of Analyzing Japanese Speech Act Types." *Proceedings of the 2nd International Conference on Theoretical and Methodological Issues in Machine Translation of Natural Languages* (*TMI-88*), Carnegie Mellon University, Center for Machine Translation, Pittsburgh, Pennsylvania, USA.

Maruyama, Hiroshi, Hideo Watanabe, and Shiho Ogino (1990). "An Interactive Japanese Parser for Machine Translation." *Proceedings of the 13th International Conference on Computational Linguistics* (*COLING-90*), Helsinki, Finland, Vol. 2, pp. 257–262.

Masakazu, Fujio and Yuji Matsumoto (1998). "Japanese Dependency Structure Analysis Based on Lexicalized Statistics."*Proceedings of the 3rd Conference on Empirical Methods in Natural Language Processing*, Granada, Spain.

Mori, Tatsunori, Mamoru Matsuo, and Hiroshi Nakawaga (1999). "Zero-subject Resolution Using Linguistic Constraints and Defaults: The Case of Japanese Instruction Manuals." *Machine Translation*, Vol. 19, Nos. 3–4, pp. 231–245.

Muraki, Kazunori, Shin-ichiro Kamei, and Shinichi Doi (1997). "A

Virtually Parallel Algorithm for Subcategorization Frame Selection of Japanese Verbs." *Proceedings of the 7th International Conference on Theoretical and Methodological Issues in Machine Translation* (*TMI-97*), St. John's College, Santa Fe, New Mexico, USA.

Murata, Masaki, Kiyotaka Uchimoto, Qing Ma, and Hitoshi Isahara (2001). "A Machine-learning Approach to Estimating the Referential Properties of Japanese Noun Phrases." *Proceedings of the 2nd International Conference on Intelligent Text Processing and Computational Linguistics* (*CICLing-2001*), Mexico City, Mexico.

Murata, Masaki, Kiyotaka Uchimoto, Qing Ma, and Hitoshi Isahara (2001). "Magical Number Seven Plus or Minus Two: Syntactic Structure Recognition in Japanese and English Sentences." *Proceedings of the 2nd International Conference on Intelligent Text Processing and Computational Linguistics* (*CICLing-2001*), Mexico City, Mexico.

Murata, Masaki and Hitoshi Isahara (2003). "Conversion of Japanese Passive/Causative Sentences into Active Sentences Using Machine Learning." *Proceedings of the 4th International Conference on Intelligent Text Processing and Computational Linguistics* (*CICLing-2003*), Mexico City, Mexico, pp. 118–128.

Murata, Masaki, Toshiyuki Kanamaru, Tamotsu Shirado, and Hitoshi Isahara (2006). "Machine-learning-based Transformation of Passive Japanese Sentences into Active by Separating Training Data into Each Input Particle." *Proceedings of the Joint Conference of the International Committee on Computational Linguistics and the Association for Computational Linguistics* (*COLING/ACL-2006*), Sydney, Australia.

Nagata, Masaaki (2000). "Synchronous Morphological Analysis of Grapheme and Phoneme for Japanese OCR." *Proceedings of the 38th Annual Meeting of the Association for Computational Linguistics* (*ACL-2000*), Hong Kong, China.

Nakaiwa, Hiromi and Satoru Ikehara (1995). "Intrasentential Resolution of Japanese Zero Pronouns in a Machine Translation System Using Semantic and Pragmatic Constraints." *Proceedings of the 6th International Conference on Theoretical and Methodological Issues in Machine Translation* (*TMI-95*), Leuven, Belgium, pp. 96–105.

Nariyama, Shigeko (2001). "Multiple Argument Ellipses Resolution in Japanese." In Bente Maegaard, ed., *Proceedings of MT Summit VIII:*

Machine Translation in the Information Age, Santiago de Compostela, Spain.

Nariyama, Shigeko (2002). "Grammar for Ellipsis Resolution in Japanese." *Proceedings of the 9th International Conference on Theoretical and Methodological Issues in Machine Translation (TMI-2002)*, Keihanna, Japan, pp. 135–145.

Nobata, Chikashi, Satoshi Sekine, and Jun-ichi Tsujii (2000). "Difficulty Indices for the Named Entity Task in Japanese." *Proceedings of the 38th Annual Meeting of the Association for Computational Linguistics (ACL-2000)*, Hong Kong.

Ohno, Tomohiro, Shigeki Matsubara, Hideki Kashioka, Naoto Kato, and Yasuyoshi Inagaki (2006). "A Syntactically Annotated Corpus of Japanese Spoken Monologue." *Proceedings of the 5th International Conference on Language Resources and Evaluation (LREC-2006)*, Genoa, Italy.

Sakaki, Alam Yukiko (1986). "A Lexical-functional Approach to Japanese for the Purposes of Machine Translation." *Computers and Translation*, Vol. 1, No. 4, pp. 199–214.

Sakao, Yohsuke, Takahiro Ikeda, Kenji Satoh, and Susumu Akamine (2005). "Japanese Language Analysis for Syntactic Tree Mining to Extract Characteristic Contents." *Proceedings of MT Summit X*, Phuket, Thailand.

Seligman, Mark, Junko Hosaka, and Harald Singer (1997). "'Pause Units' and Analysis of Spontaneous Japanese Dialogues: Preliminary Studies." In Elisabeth Maier, Marion Mast, and Susann LuperFoy, eds., *Dialogue Processing in Spoken Language Systems*. Berlin: Springer Verlag, pp. 110–112.

Shirado, Tamotsu and Hitoshi Isahara (2001). "Numerical Model of the Strategy for Choosing Polite Expressions." *Proceedings of the 2nd International Conference on Intelligent Text Processing and Computational Linguistics (CICLing-2001)*, Mexico City, Mexico.

Shirado, Tamotsu and Hitoshi Isahara (2002). "A Computational Model of Change in Politeness with the Addition of Word Endings." *Proceedings of the 3rd International Conference on Intelligent Text Processing and Computational Linguistics (CICLing-2002)*, Mexico City, Mexico.

Siegel, Melanie (2000). "HPSG Analysis of Japanese." In Wolfgang Wahlster, ed., *Verbmobil: Foundations of Speech-to-speech Translation*. Berlin: Springer Verlag, pp. 264–279.

Sigurdson, Jon and Roger Greatrex (1987). *Machine Translation of On-line Searches in Japanese Databases*. Lund: Research Policy Institute, Lund University.

Torisawa, Kentaro (2006). "Acquiring Inference Rules with Temporal Constraints by Using Japanese Coordinated Sentences and Noun-verb Co-occurrences." *Proceedings of the Human Language Technology Conference—Annual Meeting of the North American Chapter of the Association for Computational Linguistics* (*HLT-NAACL-2006*), New York, USA.

Tsuchiya, Masatoshi, Takao Shime, Toshihiro Takagi, Takehito Utsuro, Kiyotaka Uchimoto, Suguru Matsuyoshi, Satoshi Sato, and Seiichi Nakagawa (2006). "Chunking Japanese Compound Functional Expressions by Machine Learning." *Proceedings of the 11th Conference of the European Chapter of the Association for Computational Linguistics* (*EACL-2006*), Trento, Italy.

Utsuro, Takehito, Shigeyuki Nishiokayama, Masakazu Fujio, and Yuji Matsumoto (2000). "Analyzing Dependencies of Japanese Subordinate Clauses Based on Statistics of Scope Embedding Preference." *Proceedings of the 1st Meeting of the North American Chapter of the Association for Computational Linguistics*, Seattle, Washington, DC, USA, pp. 110–117.

Whitelock, Peter J., Mary McGee Wood, Brian J. Chandler, Natsuko Holden, and Heather J. Horsfall (1986). "Strategies for Interactive Machine Translation: The Experience and Implications of the UMIST Japanese Project." *Proceedings of the 11th International Conference on Computational Linguistics* (*COLING-86*), Bonn, Germany, pp. 329–334.

Whitelock, Peter J., Mary McGee Wood, Brian J. Chandler, Natsuko Holden, and Heather J. Horsfall (1987). "Strategies for Interactive Machine Translation: The Experience and Implication of the UMIST Japanese Project." In Peter J. Whitelock, Mary McGee Wood, Harold L. Somers, Roderick L. Johnson, and Paul A. Bennett, eds., *Linguistic Theory and Computer Applications*. London: Academic Press, pp. 147–159.

Korean

Cho, Franklin S. (1995). "Implementing Scrambling in Korean: A

Principles and Parameters Approach." *Proceedings of the Conference of the Association for Computational Linguistics and Chinese Language Processing* (*ROCLING-VIII*), Yuan-Ze Institute of Technology, Chung-Li, Taiwan.

Cho, Jung-Won, Seung-Do Jeong, and Byung-Uk Choi (2004). "Automatic Classification and Skimming of Articles in a News Video Using Korean Closed-caption." *Proceedings of the 5th International Conference on Intelligent Text Processing and Computational Linguistics* (*CICLing-2004*), Chung-Ang University, Seoul, Korea, pp. 492–495.

Choi, Ho-cheol and Sang-yong Han (2005). "Korma 2003: Newly Improved Korean Morpheme Analysis Module for Reducing Terminological and Spacing Errors in Document Analysis." *Proceedings of the 6th International Conference on Intelligent Text Processing and Computational Linguistics* (*CICLing-2005*), Mexico City, Mexico, pp. 192–195.

Jung, Youngim, Aesun Yoon, and Hyuk-Chul Kwon (2006). "Disambiguation Based on Wordnet for Transliteration of Arabic Numerals for Korean TTS." *Proceedings of the 7th International Conference on Intelligent Text Processing and Computational Linguistics* (*CICLing-2006*), Mexico City, Mexico.

Kim, Jong-Bok and Jaehyung Yang (2004). "Projections from Morphology to Syntax in the Korean Resource Grammar: Implementing Typed Feature Structures." *Proceedings of the 5th International Conference on Intelligent Text Processing and Computational Linguistics* (*CICLing-2004*), Chung-Ang University, Seoul, Korea, pp. 13–24.

Kim, Jong-Bok and Jaehyung Yang (2006). "Parsing Korean Case Phenomena in a Type-feature Structure Grammar." *Proceedings of the 6th International Conference on Intelligent Text Processing and Computational Linguistics* (*CICLing-2005*), Mexico City, Mexico, pp. 61–72.

Kim, Nari (1998). "Statistical Approach for Korean Analysis: A Method Based on Structural Patterns." In David L. Farwell, Laurie Gerber, and Eduard Hovy, eds., *Machine Translation and the Information Soup*. Berlin: Springer Verlag, pp. 308–317.

Kim, Seonho, Zooil Yang, Mansuk Song, and Jung-Ho Ahn (1999). "Retrieving Collocations from Korean Text." *Proceedings of the Joint SIGDAT Conference on Empirical Methods in NLP and Very Large*

Corpora (*EMNLP/VLC-99*), University of Maryland, College Park, MD, USA.

Lee, Sang-Zoo, Jun-ichi Tsujii, and Rim Hae-Chang (2000). "Hidden Markov Model-based Korean Part-of-speech Tagging Considering High Agglutinativity, Word-spacing, and Lexical Correlativity." *Proceedings of the 38th Annual Meeting of the Association for Computational Linguistics* (*ACL-2000*), Hong Kong.

Lim, Joon-Ho, So-Young Park, Yong-Jae Kwak, and Hae-Chang Rim (2004). "A Semi-automatic Tree Annotating Workbench for Building a Korean Treebank." *Proceedings of the 5th International Conference on Intelligent Text Processing and Computational Linguistics* (*CICLing-2004*), Chung-Ang University, Seoul, Korea, pp. 250–253.

Paik, Kyong-Hee, Kiyonori Ohtake, Francis Bond, and Kazuhide Yamamoto (2004). "Source Language Effect on Translating Korean Honorifics." *Proceedings of the 5th International Conference on Intelligent Text Processing and Computational Linguistics* (*CICLing-2004*), Chung-Ang University, Seoul, Korea, pp. 330–334.

Park, Seong-Bae, Jeong-Ho Chang, and Byoung-Tak Zhang (2004). "Korean Compound Noun Decomposition Using Syllabic Information Only." *Proceedings of the 5th International Conference on Intelligent Text Processing and Computational Linguistics* (*CICLing-2004*), Chung-Ang University, Seoul, Korea, pp. 143–154.

Seo, S. O. (1977). "An Analysis of Korean by Junction Theory—With Reference to Machine Translation." *Dhak Yonku*, Vol. 13, pp. 139–163.

Yun, Bo-Hyun, Tae-Hyun Kim, Yi-Gyu Hwang, Pal-Jin Lee, and Seung-Shik Kang (2003). "Event Sentence Extraction in Korean Newspapers." *Proceedings of the 4th International Conference on Intelligent Text Processing and Computational Linguistics* (*CICLing-2003*), Mexico City, Mexico, pp. 582–585.

Latin

Bowden, Paul R. (2003). "A Latin Morphological Processor." *Machine Translation Review*, No. 14, pp. 6–16.

Koster, Cornelis H. A. (2005). "Constructing a Parser for Latin." *Proceedings of the 6th International Conference on Intelligent Text Processing and Computational Linguistics* (*CICLing-2005*), Mexico City, Mexico, pp. 49–60.

Malay

Varghese, Anila, Miriam Butt, and Tracy Holloway King (2004). "A Computational Treatment of Differential Case Marking in Malayalam." *Proceedings of the International Conference on Natural Language Processing (ICON-2004)*, International Institute of Information Technology, Hyderabad, India.

Zaharin, Yusoff (1995). "Towards a Language Information Centre for Malay." *Proceedings of MT Summit V: Machine Translation Conference, Exhibition and Tutorial*, Luxembourg.

Minority Languages

Allman, Tod and Stephen Beale (2006). "A Natural Language Generator for Minority Languages." *Proceedings of the 5th SALTMIL Workshop on Minority Languages and the 5th International Conference on Language Resources and Evaluation (LREC-2006): Strategies for Developing Machine Translation for Minority Languages*, Genoa, Italy, pp. 39–46.

Barnes, Janet (1987). "A User Perspective on Computer-assisted Translation for Minority Languages." *Computers and Translation*, Vol. 2, No. 3, pp. 131–134.

Beale, Stephen, Sergei Nirenburg, Marjorie McShane, and Tod Allman (2005). "Document Authoring the Bible for Minority Language Translation." *Proceedings of MT Summit X*, Phuket, Thailand.

Diz Gamallo, Inés (2001). "The Importance of MT for the Survival of Minority Languages: Spanish-Galician MT System." In Bente Maegaard, ed., *Proceedings of MT Summit VIII: Machine Translation in the Information Age*, Santiago de Compostela, Spain.

Dvoøák, Boštjan, Petr Homola, and Vladislav Kubo (2006). "Exploiting Similarity in the MT into a Minority Language." *Proceedings of the 5th SALTMIL Workshop on Minority Languages and the 5th International Conference on Language Resources and Evaluation (LREC-2006): Strategies for Developing Machine Translation for Minority Languages*, Genoa, Italy, pp. 59–64.

Forcada, Mikel L. (2006). "Open Source Machine Translation: An Opportunity for Minor Languages." *Proceedings of the 5th SALTMIL Workshop on Minority Languages and the 5th International*

Conference on Language Resources and Evaluation (LREC-2006): Strategies for Developing Machine Translation for Minority Languages, Genoa, Italy, pp. 1–6.

Hein, Anna Sågvall and Per Weijnitz (2006). "Approaching a New Language in Machine Translation." *Proceedings of the 5th SALTMIL Workshop on Minority Languages and the 5th International Conference on Language Resources and Evaluation (LREC-2006): Strategies for Developing Machine Translation for Minority Languages*, Genoa, Italy.

Homola, Petr and Vladislav Kuboň (2005). "A Machine Translation System into a Minority Language." In Walther van Hahn, W. John Hutchins, and Cristina Vertan, eds., *Proceedings of the International Workshop on Modern Approaches in Translation Technologies*, Borovets, Bulgaria.

Jones, Douglas and Rick Havrilla (1998). "Twisted Pair Grammar: Support for Rapid Development of Machine Translation for Low Density Languages." In David L. Farwell, Laurie Gerber, and Eduard Hovy, eds., *Machine Translation and the Information Soup*. Berlin: Springer Verlag, pp. 318–332.

Jones, Rosie and Rayid Ghani (2000). "Automatically Building a Corpus for a Minority Language from the Web." *Proceedings of the 38th Annual Meeting of the Association for Computational Linguistics (ACL-2000)*, Hong Kong.

Probst, Katharina, Ralf D. Brown, Jaime G. Carbonell, Alon Lavie, Lori S. Levin, and Erik Peterson (2001). "Design and Implementation of Controlled Elicitation for Machine Translation of Low-density Languages." In Bente Maegaard, ed., *Proceedings of MT Summit VIII: Machine Translation in the Information Age*, Santiago de Compostela, Spain, pp. 44–49.

Probst, Katharina, Lori S. Levin, Erik Peterson, Alon Lavie, and Jaime G. Carbonell (2002). "MT for Minority Languages Using Elicitation-based Learning of Syntactic Transfer Rules." *Machine Translation*, Vol. 17, No. 4, pp. 245–270.

Somers, Harold L. (1997). "Machine Translation and Minority Languages." In *Translating and the Computer 19*. London: The Association for Information Management.

Somers, Harold L. (1998). "Machine Translation and Minority Languages." In *Translating and the Computer 20*. London: The Association for Information Management.

Somers, Harold L. (1999). "Sources of Linguistic Knowledge for Minority Languages." *Proceedings of MT Summit VII: MT in the Great Translation Era*, Singapore.
Vandeghinste, Vincent, Ineke Schuurman, Michael Carl, Stella Markantonatou, and Toni Badia (2006). "METIS-II: Machine Translation for Low Resource Languages." *Proceedings of the 5th International Conference on Language Resources and Evaluation (LREC-2006)*, Genoa, Italy.

Mongolian

Huashabao 華沙寶 (1999).〈蒙古語詞類標注系統—AYIMAG〉(The Mongolian Part-of-speech Tagging System—AYIMAG). In Huang Changning 黃昌寧 and Dong Zhendong 董振東, eds.,《計算機語言學文集》(*Essays on Computational Linguistics*). Beijing: Tsinghua University Press, pp. 210–214.
Nasun-urtu 那順烏日圖, Liu Qun 劉群, and Badmaodsar 巴達瑪敖德斯爾 (2001).〈面向機器翻譯的蒙古語生成〉(Mongolian Generation in Machine Translation). In Huang Changning and Zhang Pu, eds.,《自然語言理解與機器翻譯》(*Natural Language Understanding and Machine Translation*). Beijing: Tsinghua University Press, pp. 285–291.

Norwegian

Maegaard, Bente, Jens-Erik Fenstad, Lars Ahrenberg, Knut Kvale, Katarina Mühlenbock, and Bernt-Erik Heid (2006). "KUNSTI—Knowledge Generation for Norwegian Language Technology." *Proceedings of the 5th International Conference on Language Resources and Evaluation (LREC-2006)*, Genoa, Italy.

Persian

Megerdoomian, Karine (2000). "Unification-based Persian Morphology." *Proceedings of the 1st International Conference on Intelligent Text Processing and Computational Linguistics (CICLing-2000)*, Mexico City, Mexico.
Sanamrad, Mohammad Ali and Haruya Matsumoto (1986). "PERSIS: A Natural Language Analyzer for Persian." *Journal of Information Processing*, Vol. 8, No. 4, pp. 271–279.

Polish

Gawronska, Barbara (2001). "PolVerbNet: An Experimental Database for Polish Verbs." In Bente Maegaard, ed., *Proceedings of MT Summit VIII: Machine Translation in the Information Age*, Santiago de Compostela, Spain.

Gulak, Eugene, Nadiya Byezhanova, Michael S. Blekhman, Alla Rakova, and Andrei Kursin (2003). "Polish Translation Software by Lingvistica '98 Inc." *International Journal of Translation*, Vol. 15, No. 1, pp. 115–124.

Knas, Iwona (2006). "Polish Equivalents of Spatial 'at'." *Proceedings of the 11th Conference of the European Chapter of the Association for Computational Linguistics* (*EACL-2006*), Trento, Italy.

Styś, Malgorzata E. and Stefan S. Zemke (1997). "Incorporating Discourse Aspects in English-Polish MT." In Ruslan Mitkov and Nicolas Nicolov, eds., *Recent Advances in Natural Language Processing*. Amsterdam and Philadelphia: John Benjamins Publishing Company, pp. 213–223.

Swidzinski, Marek (1989). "A Dependency Syntax for Polish." In Dan Maxwell and Klaus Schubert, eds., *Metataxis in Practice: Dependency Syntax for Multilingual Machine Translation*. Dordrecht: Foris Publications, pp. 69–87.

Trawinski, Beata (2006). "A Quantitative Approach to Preposition-pronoun Contraction in Polish." *Proceedings of the 11th Conference of the European Chapter of the Association for Computational Linguistics* (*EACL-2006*), Trento, Italy.

Portuguese

Hana, Jirka, Anna Feldman, Luiz Amaral, and Chris Brew (2006). "Tagging Portuguese with a Spanish Tagger." *Proceedings of the 11th Conference of the European Chapter of the Association for Computational Linguistics* (*EACL-2006*), Trento, Italy.

Landry, Olivia Ryan (2002). "A Linguistic Approach to Improving the Quality of Machine Translated Portuguese." *International Journal of Translation*, Vol. 14, No. 2, pp. 27–31.

Silla Jr., Carlos N. and Celso A. A. Kaestner (2004). "An Analysis of Sentence Boundary Detection Systems for English and Portuguese Documents." *Proceedings of the 5th International Conference on*

Intelligent Text Processing and Computational Linguistics (*CICLing-2004*), Chung-Ang University, Seoul, Korea, pp. 132–138.

Solorio, Thamar, Manuel Pérez-Coutiño, Manuel Montes-y-Gómez, Luis Villaseñor-Pineda, and Aurelio López López (2005). "Question Classification in Spanish and Portuguese." *Proceedings of the 6th International Conference on Intelligent Text Processing and Computational Linguistics* (*CICLing-2005*), Mexico City, Mexico, pp. 600–607.

Romanian

Şerban, Gabriela and Doina Tătar (2003). "Word Sense Disambiguation for Untagged Corpus: Application to Romanian Language." *Proceedings of the 4th International Conference on Intelligent Text Processing and Computational Linguistics* (*CICLing-2003*), Mexico City, Mexico, pp. 270–274.

Russian

Blekhman, Michael S., Maryna Byezhanova, Andrei Kursin, Igor Backlam, Alexander Kazakov, and Vladimir Petrov (1999). "Computer-aided Translation Tools for Russian, Ukrainian, and English." *Proceedings of MT Summit VII: MT in the Great Translation Era*, Singapore.

Blekhman, Michael and Boris Pevzner (2000). "First Steps of Language Engineering in the USSR: The 50s through 70s." *Machine Translation Review*, No. 11, pp. 4–6.

Boguslavsky, Igor (1999). "Translation to and from Russian: The ETAP System." *Proceedings of the 4th Workshop of the European Association for Machine Translation: EU and the New Languages: Translation—Possibilities, Policies and Practicalities*, Prague, the Czech Republic.

Curtin, Constance (1972). "Teaching the Translation of Russian by Computer." *The Modern Language*, Vol. 56, No. 6, pp. 354–360.

Davis, Donald W. and A. M. Day (1962). "A Technique for Consistent Splitting of Russian Words." In National Physical Laboratory, ed., *1961 International Conference on Machine Translation of Languages and Applied Language Analysis: Proceedings of the Conference Held at the National Physical Laboratory, Teddington, Middlesex, on 5th,*

6th, 7th and 8th September. London: Her Majesty's Stationery Office, Vol. 1, pp. 344–362.

Garvin, Paul L. (1967). "The Fulcrum Syntactic Analyzer for Russian." *2ieme Conference Internationale sur la Traitement Automatique des Langues*, Grenbole, France.

Gerrard, M. (1976). "Regular Use of Machine Translation of Russian at Oak Ridge National Laboratory." *American Journal of Computational Linguistics* (2, microfiche 46), pp. 53–56.

Harper, Kenneth E. (1953). "The Mechanical Translation of Russian: A Preliminary Report." *Modern Language Forum*, Vol. 38, Nos. 3–4, pp. 12–29.

Harper, Kenneth E. (1955). "A Preliminary Study of Russian." In William N. Locke and Andrew D. Booth, eds., *Machine Translation of Languages: Fourteen Essays*. Cambridge, MA: Technology Press of the Massachusetts Institute of Technology, pp. 66–85.

Harper, Kenneth E. (1964). "The Position of Prepositional Phrases in Russian." *Mechanical Translation*, Vol. 8, No. 1, pp. 5–10.

Hays, David G. (1958). "Order of Subject and Object in Scientific Russian When Other Differentia Are Lacking." *Mechanical Translation*, Vol. 5, No. 3, pp. 111–113.

Hays, David G. (1964). "Connectibility Calculations, Syntactic Functions, and Russian Syntax." *Mechanical Translation*, Vol. 8, No. 1, pp. 32–51.

Jordan, S. R., Antony F. R. Brown, and F. C. Hutton (1977). *SLC Primer for Russian Translation Users*. Oak Ridge, Tennessee: Computer Sciences Division, Oak Ridge National Laboratory.

Jordan, S. R., Antony F. R. Brown, and F. C. Hutton (1977). "Computerized Russian Translation at ORNL." *Journal of the American Society for Information Science*, Vol. 28, pp. 26–33.

Khegai, Janna and Aarne Ranta (2004). "Building and Using a Russian Resource Grammar in GF." *Proceedings of the 5th International Conference on Intelligent Text Processing and Computational Linguistics (CICLing-2004)*, Chung-Ang University, Seoul, Korea, pp. 37–40.

Knisbacher, Jeffrey Mark (1970). "Methods for Reducing Multiple Analyses in a Machine Translation Grammar of Russian." *Actes du Xe congres International des Linguistes*, Vol. 10, No. 4, pp. 979–982.

Lehiste, Ilse (1957). "Order of Subject and Predicate in Scientific

Russian." *Mechanical Translation*, Vol. 4, No. 3, pp. 66–67.
Luther, David A., Christine A. Montgomery, and Ronald M. Case (1977). "An Interactive Text-editing System in Support of Russian Translation by Machine." *IFIPS National Computer Conference Proceedings.* Montvale, New Jersey: AFIPS Press, Vol. 46, pp. 789–790.
Lynch, Irina (1962). "Russian-СЯ Verbs, Impersonally Used Verbs and Subject/Object Ambiguities." In National Physical Laboratory, ed., *1961 International Conference on Machine Translation of Languages and Applied Language Analysis: Proceedings of the Conference Held at the National Physical Laboratory, Teddington, Middlesex, on 5th, 6th, 7th and 8th September.* London: Her Majesty's Stationery Office, Vol. 2, pp. 478–502.
Lyons, John (1963). "Coding the Russian Alphabet for the Purpose of Mechanical Translation." *Mechanical Translation*, Vol. 7, No. 2, pp. 43–46.
McDaniel, J. and S. Whelan (1962). "The Grammatical Interpretation of Russian Inflected Forms Using a Stem Dictionary." In National Physical Laboratory, ed., *1961 International Conference on Machine Translation of Languages and Applied Language Analysis: Proceedings of the Conference Held at the National Physical Laboratory, Teddington, Middlesex, on 5th, 6th, 7th and 8th September.* London: Her Majesty's Stationery Office, Vol. 1, pp. 364–377.
Oettinger, Anthony G. (1954). "The Distribution of Word Length in Technical Russian." *Mechanical Translation*, Vol. 1, No. 3, pp. 38–40.
Oettinger, Anthony G. (1960). *Automatic Language Translation: Lexical and Technical Aspects with Particular Reference to Russian.* Cambridge, MA: Harvard University Press.
Perry, James W. (1955). "A Practical Development Problem." In William N. Locke and Andrew D. Booth, eds., *Machine Translation of Languages: Fourteen Essays.* Cambridge, MA: Technology Press of the Massachusetts Institute of Technology, pp. 174–182.
Perry, James W. (1955). "Translation of Russian Technical Literature by Machine: Notes on Preliminary Experiments." *Mechanical Translation*, Vol. 2, No. 1, pp. 15–24.
Reddiar, K. Murugesan (1997). "Lexical and Semantic Features of Scientific and Technical Russian—Compilation of a Dictionary for MT." *International Journal of Translation*, Vol. 9, Nos. 1–2, pp. 85–91.

Rhodes, Ida (1959). *A New Approach to the Mechanical Syntactic Analysis of Russian*. Washington, DC: National Bureau of Standards.

Rhodes, Ida (1961). "A New Approach to the Mechanical Syntactic Analysis of Russian." *Mechanical Translation*, Vol. 6, pp. 33–50.

Wahlgren, John H. (1962). "Linguistic Analysis of Russian Chemical Terminology." In National Physical Laboratory, ed., *1961 International Conference on Machine Translation of Languages and Applied Language Analysis: Proceedings of the Conference Held at the National Physical Laboratory, Teddington, Middlesex, on 5th, 6th, 7th and 8th September*. London: Her Majesty's Stationery Office, Vol. 1, pp. 250–263.

Worth, Dean S. (1962). "Transformation Criteria for the Classification of Predicative Genitive Constructions in Russian." In National Physical Laboratory, ed., *1961 International Conference on Machine Translation of Languages and Applied Language Analysis: Proceedings of the Conference Held at the National Physical Laboratory, Teddington, Middlesex, on 5th, 6th, 7th and 8th September*. London: Her Majesty's Stationery Office, Vol. 1, pp. 726–735.

Zacharov, B. (1957). "A Refinement in Coding the Russian Cyrillic Alphabet." *Mechanical Translation*, Vol. 4, No. 3, pp. 76–78.

Zarechnak, Michael (1957). "Types of Russian Sentences." In Leon Dostert, ed., *Research in Machine Translation*. Washington, DC: Georgetown University Press, pp. 135–141.

Zarechnak, Michael (1987). "Russian SJA Verbs as a Source of Translation Problems." In Karl Kummer, ed., *Across the Language Gap: Proceedings of the 28th Annual Conference of the American Translators Association*. Medford, New Jersey: Learned Information Inc., pp. 145–160.

Sign Language

Hausser, Roland (2002). "A Hypothesis on the Origin of the Sign Types." *Proceedings of the 3rd International Conference on Intelligent Text Processing and Computational Linguistics* (*CICLing-2002*), Mexico City, Mexico.

Holden, Eun-Jung and Geoffrey G. Roy (1992). "The Graphical Translation of English Text into Signed English in the Hand Sign Translator System." *Computer Graphics Forum*, Vol. 113, pp. 357–366.

Huenerfauth, Matt (2005). "American Sign Language Generation: Multimodal NLG with Multiple Linguistic Channels." *Proceedings of the 43rd Annual Meeting of the Association of Computational Linguistics* (*ACL-2005*), Ann Arbor, Michigan, USA.

Lee, Jintae and Tosiyasu L. Kunii (1992). "Visual Translation from Native Language to Sign Language." *Proceedings of the IEEE Workshop on Visual Languages*, Seattle, WA, USA, pp. 45–53.

Marshall, Ian and Eva Safar (2002). "Sign Language Generation Using HPSG." *Proceedings of the 9th International Conference on Theoretical and Methodological Issues in Machine Translation* (*TMI-2002*), Keihanna, Japan, pp. 105–114.

Morrissey, Sara and Andy Way (2006). "Lost in Translation: The Problems of Using Mainstream MT Evaluation Metrics for Sign Language Translation." *Proceedings of the 5th SALTMIL Workshop on Minority Languages and the 5th International Conference on Language Resources and Evaluation* (*LREC-2006*): *Strategies for Developing Machine Translation for Minority Languages*, Genoa, Italy, pp. 91–98.

Patten, T. and J. Hartigan (1993). "Automatic Translation of English to American Sign Language." *Proceedings of the 1993 National Conference on Deafness*, Columbus, Ohio, USA, pp. 55–65.

Sáfár, Éva and Ian Marshall (2002). "Sign Language Translation via DRT and HPSG." *Proceedings of the 3rd International Conference on Intelligent Text Processing and Computational Linguistics* (*CICLing-2002*), Mexico City, Mexico.

Stein, Daniel, Jan Bungeroth, and Hermann Ney (2006). "Morpho-syntax Based Statistical Methods for Automatic Sign Language Translation." *Proceedings of the 11th Workshop of the European Association for Machine Translation: Machine Translation/Translation Aids– Tools to Increase Quality and to Save Money*, the University of Oslo, Oslo, Norway.

Veale, Tony and Alan Conway (1994). "Cross-modal Comprehension in Zardoz, An English to Sign-language Translation System." *Proceedings of the 4th International Workshop on Natural Language Generation*, Kennebunkport, ME, USA, pp. 67–72.

Veale, Tony and Bróna Collins (1996). "Space, Schematization and Metaphor in Sign: Sign Language Translation in the Zardoz System." *Proceedings of the 2nd Conference of the Association for Machine*

Translation in the Americas: Expanding MT Horizons (*AMTA-2*), Montreal, Quebec, Canada, pp. 150–158.
Veale, Tony, Alan Conway, and Bróna Collins (1998). "The Challenges of Cross-modal Translation: English-to-Sign-Language Translation in the Zardoz System." *Machine Translation*, Vol. 13, No. 1, pp. 81–106.
Zhao, Liwei, Karin Kipper, William Schuler, Christian Vogler, Norman Badler, and Martha Palmer (2000). "A Machine Translation System from English to American Sign Language." In John S. White, ed., *Envisioning Machine Translation in the Information Future*. Berlin: Springer Verlag, pp. 54–67.

Slavonic Languages

Blekhman, Michael S., Arndrei Kursin, and Igor Fagradiants (1998). "Machine-aided Translation Tools for Slavonic Languages." *Machine Translation Review*, No. 7, pp. 20–27.

Slovenian

Žgank, Andrej, Darinka Verdonik, Aleksandra Zögling Markuš, and Zdravko Kačič (2006). "SINOD—Slovenian Non-native Speech Database." *Proceedings of the 5th International Conference on Language Resources and Evaluation* (*LREC-2006*), Genoa, Italy.

Somali

Abdillahi, Nimaan, Nocera Pascal, and Bonastre Jean-François (2006). "Towards Automatic Transcription of Somali Language." *Proceedings of the 5th International Conference on Language Resources and Evaluation* (*LREC-2006*), Genoa, Italy.
Lecarme, Jacqueline and Carole Maury (1987). "A Software Tool for Research in Linguistics and Lexicography: Application to Somali." *Computers and Translation*, Vol. 2, No. 1, pp. 21–36.

Spanish

Arranz, Victoria, Elisabet Comelles, and David L. Farwell (2005). "The FAME Speech-to-speech Translation System for Catalan, English and Spanish." *Proceedings of MT Summit X*, Phuket, Thailand.

Bezhanova, Olga (2001). "Software for Processing Spanish: Products by Word Magic Software." *International Journal of Translation*, Vol. 13, Nos. 1–2, pp. 159–166.

Bolshakov, Igor A., Alexander F. Gelbukh, and Grigori Sidorov (2000). "On Subject-predicate Agreement in Spanish." *Proceedings of the 1st International Conference on Intelligent Text Processing and Computational Linguistics* (*CICLing-2000*), Mexico City, Mexico.

Bolshakov, Igor A., Sofia N. Galicia-Haro, and Alexander F. Gelbukh (2002). "Quantitative Comparison of Homonymy in Spanish EuroWordNet and Traditional Dictionaries." *Proceedings of the 3rd International Conference on Intelligent Text Processing and Computational Linguistics* (*CICLing-2002*), Mexico City, Mexico.

Bolshakov, Igor A. (2002). "Surface Syntactic Relations in Spanish." *Proceedings of the 3rd International Conference on Intelligent Text Processing and Computational Linguistics* (*CICLing-2002*), Mexico City, Mexico.

Bolshakov, Igor A. and Sabino Miranda-Jiménez (2004). "A Small System Storing Spanish Collocations." *Proceedings of the 5th International Conference on Intelligent Text Processing and Computational Linguistics* (*CICLing-2004*), Chung-Ang University, Seoul, Korea, pp. 245–249.

Brines, Natalia (2000). "The Spanish Impersonal Construction: A Lexical Rule-free Analysis of the Cliticalization Process." *Proceedings of the 1st International Conference on Intelligent Text Processing and Computational Linguistics* (*CICLing-2000*), Mexico City, Mexico.

Bustamante, Flora Ramírez, Alfredo Arnaiz, and Mar Ginés (2006). "A Spell Checker for a World Language: The New Microsoft's Spanish Spell Checker." *Proceedings of the 5th International Conference on Language Resources and Evaluation* (*LREC-2006*), Genoa, Italy.

Cascales, Remedios Ruiz and Richard F. E. Sutcliffe (2003). "A Specification and Validating Parser for Simplified Technical Spanish." *Proceedings of the Joint Conference Combining the 8th International Workshop of the European Association for Machine Translation and the 4th Controlled Language Applications Workshop: Controlled Language Translation* (*EAMT-CLAW-2003*), Dublin City University, Ireland.

Chrupa, Grzegorz and Josef van Genabith (2006). "Using Machine-learning to Assign Function Labels to Parser Output for Spanish."

Proceedings of the Joint Conference of the International Committee on Computational Linguistics and the Association for Computational Linguistics (*COLING/ACL-2006*), Sydney, Australia.

Cowan, Brooke and Michael Collins (2005). "Morphology and Reranking for the Statistical Parsing of Spanish." *Proceedings of Human Language Technology Conference and Conference on Empirical Methods in Natural Language Processing* (*HLT/EMNLP-2005*), Vancouver, BC, Canada.

Cuayáhuitl, Heriberto (2004). "A Syllabification Algorithm for Spanish." *Proceedings of the 5th International Conference on Intelligent Text Processing and Computational Linguistics* (*CICLing-2004*), Chung-Ang University, Seoul, Korea, pp. 406–409.

Farwell, David L., Steven Helmreich, Wanying Jin, Mark Casper, Jim Hargrave, Hugo Molina-Salgado, and Weng Fuliang (1994). "Panglyzer: Spanish Language Analysis System." *Proceedings of the 1st Conference of the Association for Machine Translation in the Americas: Technology Partnerships for Crossing the Language Barrier* (*AMTA-1*), Columbia, Maryland, USA, pp. 56–64.

Ferrández, Antonio, Manuel Palomar, and Lidia Moreno (1999). "An Empirical Approach to Spanish Anaphora Resolution." *Machine Translation*, Vol. 19, Nos. 3–4, pp. 191–216.

Ferrández, Antonio and Jesús Peral (2000). "A Computational Approach to Zero-pronouns in Spanish." *Proceedings of the 38th Annual Meeting of the Association for Computational Linguistics* (*ACL-2000*), Hong Kong.

Gelbukh, Alexander F., Grigori Sidorov, and Liliana Chanona-Hernández (2002). "Compilation of a Spanish Representative Corpus." *Proceedings of the 3rd International Conference on Intelligent Text Processing and Computational Linguistics* (*CICLing-2002*), Mexico City, Mexico.

Giménez, Jesús and Lluís Màrquez (2006). "Low-cost Enrichment of Spanish WordNet with Automatically Translated Glosses: Combining General and Specialized Models." *Proceedings of the Joint Conference of the International Committee on Computational Linguistics and the Association for Computational Linguistics* (*COLING/ACL-2006*), Sydney, Australia.

Jiménez, Héctor and Guillermo Morales (2002). "Sepe: A POS Tagger for Spanish." *Proceedings of the 3rd International Conference on*

Intelligent Text Processing and Computational Linguistics (*CICLing-2002*), Mexico City, Mexico.
Leon, Marjorie and Lee Ann Schwartz (1986). *Integrated Development of English-Spanish Machine Translation: From Pilot to Full Operational Capability*. Washington, DC: Pan American Health Organization.
Medina-Urrea, Alfonso (2006). "Towards the Automatic Lemmatization of 16th Century Mexican Spanish: A Stemming Scheme for the CHEM." *Proceedings of the 7th International Conference on Intelligent Text Processing and Computational Linguistics* (*CICLing-2006*), Mexico City, Mexico.
Meza, Ivan V. and Luis A. Pineda (2002). "The Spanish Auxiliary Verb System in HPSG." *Proceedings of the 3rd International Conference on Intelligent Text Processing and Computational Linguistics* (*CICLing-2002*), Mexico City, Mexico.
Mezquita, Yoel Ledo, Grigori Sidorov, and Alexander F. Gelbukh (2003). "Tool for Computer-aided Spanish Word Sense Disambiguation." *Proceedings of the 4th International Conference on Intelligent Text Processing and Computational Linguistics* (*CICLing-2003*), Mexico City, Mexico, pp. 279–282.
Palomar, Manual, Maximiliano Saiz Noeda, Rafael Muñoz, Armando Suárez, Patricio Martínez-Barco, and Andrés Montoyo (2001). "PHORA: A NLP System for Spanish." *Proceedings of the 2nd International Conference on Intelligent Text Processing and Computational Linguistics* (*CICLing-2001*), Mexico City, Mexico.
Peñas, Anselmo, Felisa Verdejo, and Jesús Herrera (2004). "Spanish Question Answering Evaluation." *Proceedings of the 5th International Conference on Intelligent Text Processing and Computational Linguistics* (*CICLing-2004*), Chung-Ang University, Seoul, Korea, pp. 467–478.
Peñas, Anselmo, Álvaro Rodrigo, and Felisa Verdejo (2006). "SPARTE, a Test Suite for Recognising Textual Entailment in Spanish." *Proceedings of the 7th International Conference on Intelligent Text Processing and Computational Linguistics* (*CICLing-2006*), Mexico City, Mexico.
Pineda, Luis A. and Ivan V. Meza (2005). "A Computational Model of the Spanish Clitic System." *Proceedings of the 6th International Conference on Intelligent Text Processing and Computational Linguistics* (*CICLing-2005*), Mexico City, Mexico, pp. 73–82.

Sepulveda, Julio Sergio Santana, Nora La Serna, and Luis Alberto Pineda Cortés (2000). "Towards a Computational Grammar of Spanish." *Proceedings of the 1st International Conference on Intelligent Text Processing and Computational Linguistics (CICLing-2000)*, Mexico City, Mexico.

Solorio, Thamar, Manuel Pérez-Coutiño, Manuel Montes-y-Gómez, Luis Villaseñor-Pineda, and Aurelio López-López (2005). "Question Classification in Spanish and Portuguese." *Proceedings of the 6th International Conference on Intelligent Text Processing and Computational Linguistics (CICLing-2005)*, Mexico City, Mexico, pp. 600–607.

Uraga, Esmeralda and Luis Alberto Pineda Cortés (2000). "A Set of Phonological Rules for Mexican Spanish." *Proceedings of the 1st International Conference on Intelligent Text Processing and Computational Linguistics (CICLing-2000)*, Mexico City, Mexico.

Uraga, Esmeralda and Luis A. Pineda (2002). "Automatic Generation of Pronunciation Lexicons for Spanish." *Proceedings of the 3rd International Conference on Intelligent Text Processing and Computational Linguistics (CICLing-2002)*, Mexico City, Mexico.

Vilares, Jesús, David Cabrero, and Miguel A. Alonso (2001). "Applying Productive Derivational Morphology to Term Indexing of Spanish Texts." *Proceedings of the 2nd International Conference on Intelligent Text Processing and Computational Linguistics (CICLing-2001)*, Mexico City, Mexico.

Sublanguage

Arranz, M. Victoria, Ian Radford, Sofia Anaiadou, and Jun-ichi Tsuiji (1997). "Towards a Sublanguage-based Semantic Clustering Algorithm." In Ruslan Mitkov and Nicolas Nicolov, eds., *Recent Advances in Natural Language Processing*. Amsterdam: John Benjamins Publishing Company, pp. 125–136.

Baron, Naomi S. (1986). "Language, Sublanguage, and the Promise of Machine Translation." *Machine Translation*, Vol. 1, No. 1, pp. 3–19.

Basili, Roberto, Maria Teresa Pazienza, and Paola Velardi (1993). "Acquisition of Selectional Patterns in Sublanguages." *Machine Translation*, Vol. 8, No. 3, pp. 175–201.

Basili, Roberto, Michelangelo Della Rocca, Maria Teresa Pazienza, and

Paola Velardi (1997). "Customising a Verb Classification to a Sublanguage." In Ruslan Mitkov and Nicolas Nicolov, eds., *Recent Advances in Natural Language Processing*. Amsterdam: John Benjamins Publishing Company, pp. 137–148.

Bastin, E. W. (1956). "General Mathematical Problems Involved in Mechanical Translation." *Mechanical Translation*, Vol. 3, No. 1, pp. 5–6.

Buchmann, Beat, Susan Warwick, and Patrick Shann (1984). "Design of a Machine Translation System for a Sublanguage." *Proceedings of the 10th International Conference on Computational Linguistics (COLING-84)*, Stanford University, Stanford, CA, USA, pp. 334–337.

Grishman, Ralph and Richard I. Kittredge, eds. (1986). *Analyzing Language in Restricted Domains: Sublanguage Description and Processing*. Hillsdale, New Jersey: Lawrence Erlbaum Associates.

Khegai, Janna (2006). "Grammatical Framework (GF) for MT in Sublanguage Domains." *Proceedings of the 11th Workshop of the European Association for Machine Translation: Machine Translation/ Translation Aids—Tools to Increase Quality and to Save Money*, the University of Oslo, Oslo, Norway.

Kittredge, Richard I. (1987). "The Significance of Sublanguage for Automatic Translation." In Sergei Nirenburg, ed., *Machine Translation: Theoretical and Methodological Issues*. Cambridge: Cambridge University Press, pp. 59–67.

Kittredge, Richard I. and John Lehrberger, eds. (1982). *Sublanguage: Studies of Language in Restricted Semantic Domains*. Berlin and New York: De Gruyter.

Kittredge, Richard I. (1982). "Sublanguages." *American Journal of Computational Linguistics*, Vol. 8, No. 2, pp. 79–84.

Kittredge, Richard I. (1983). *Sublanguage: Specific Computer Aids to Translation—A Survey of the Most Promising Areas*. Montreal: Universite de Montreal and Bureau des Traductions.

Kittredge, Richard I. and Igor A. Mel'cuk (1983). "Towards a Computable Model of Meaning—Text Relations within a Natural Sublanguage." *Proceedings of the 8th Annual Meeting of the International Joint Conference for Artificial Intelligence (IJCAI-83)*, Karlsruhe, Germany, pp. 657–659.

Kittredge, Richard I. (1987). "The Significance of Sublanguage for Automatic Translation." In Sergei Nirenburg, ed., *Machine*

Translation: Theoretical and Methodological Issues. Cambridge: Cambridge University Press, pp. 59–66.

Lehrberger, John (1982). "Automatic Translation and the Concept of Sub-language." In Richard I. Kittredge and John Lehrberger, eds., *Sublanguage: Studies of Language in Restricted Semantic Domains*. Berlin: De Gruyter, pp. 81–106.

Lehrberger, John (1986). "Sublanguage Analysis." In Ralph Grishman and Richard I. Kittredge, eds., *Analyzing Language in Restricted Domains: Sublanguage Description and Processing*. Hillsdale, New Jersey: Lawrence Erlbaum Associates, pp. 19–38.

Somers, Harold L. (2003). "Sublanguage." In Harold Somers, ed., *Computers and Translation: A Translator's Guide*. Amsterdam and Philadelphia: John Benjamins Publishing Company, pp. 283–295.

Symonenko, Svetlana, Steven Rowe, and Elizabeth D. Liddy (2006). "Illuminating Trouble Tickets with Sublanguage Theory." *Proceedings of the Human Language Technology Conference—Annual Meeting of the North American Chapter of the Association for Computational Linguistics* (*HLT-NAACL-2006*), New York, USA.

Swedish

Berglund, Anders, Richard Johansson, and Pierre Nugues (2006). "A Machine Learning Approach to Extract Temporal Information from Texts in Swedish and Generate Animated 3D Scenes." *Proceedings of the 11th Conference of the European Chapter of the Association for Computational Linguistics* (*EACL-2006*), Trento, Italy.

Danielsson, Pernilla and Katarina Muhlenbock (2000). "Small But Efficient: The Misconception of High-frequency Words in Scandinavian Translation." In John S. White, ed., *Envisioning Machine Translation in the Information Future*. Berlin: Springer Verlag, pp. 158–168.

Hein, Anna Sågvall, Ingrid Almqvist, and Per Starbäck (1997). "Scania Swedish—A Basis for Multilingual Machine Translation." In *Translating and the Computer 19*. London: The Association for Information Management.

Johansson, Richard and Pierre Nugues (2006). "A FrameNet-based Semantic Role Labeler for Swedish." *Proceedings of the Joint*

Conference of the International Committee on Computational Linguistics and the Association for Computational Linguistics (COLING/ACL-2006), Sydney, Australia.

Sigurd, Bengt (1988). "Translating to and from Swedish by SWETRA—A Multilanguage Translation System." In Dan Maxwell, Klaus Schubert, and Toon Witkam, eds. *New Directions in Machine Translation*. Dordrecht-Holland: Foris Publications, pp. 205–218.

Thai

Charoenpornsawat, Paisarn, Sanjika Hewavitharana, and Tanja Schultz (2006). "Thai Grapheme-based Speech Recognition." *Proceedings of the Human Language Technology Conference—Annual Meeting of the North American Chapter of the Association for Computational Linguistics (HLT-NAACL-2006)*, New York, USA.

Chotthan, Anirut, Chumsak Siboonr, Jantima Polpini, Rapeeporn Chamc, and Somnuk Puangpro (2004). "Automated Thai Text Summarization Using a Similarity Measure." *Proceedings of the International Conference on Natural Language Processing (ICON-2004)*, International Institute of Information Technology, Hyderabad, India.

Haruechaiyasak, Choochart, Chatchawal Sangkeettrakarn, Pornpimon Palingoon, Sarawoot Kongyoung, and Chaianun Damrongrat (2006). "A Collaborative Framework for Collecting Thai Unknown Words from the Web." *Proceedings of the Joint Conference of the International Committee on Computational Linguistics and the Association for Computational Linguistics (COLING/ACL-2006)*, Sydney, Australia.

Narupiyakul, Lalita, Calvin Thomas, Nick Cercone, and Booncharoen Sirinaovakul (2004). "Thai Syllable-based Information Extraction Using Hidden Markov Models." *Proceedings of the 5th International Conference on Intelligent Text Processing and Computational Linguistics (CICLing-2004)*, Chung-Ang University, Seoul, Korea, pp. 531–540.

Sathapornrungkij, Patanakul and Charnyote Pluempitiwiriyawej (2005). "Construction of Thai WordNet Lexical Database from Machine Readable Dictionaries." *Proceedings of MT Summit X*, Phuket, Thailand.

Turkish

Güngördü, Zealal and Kemal Oflazer (1995). "Parsing Turkish Using the Lexical Functional Grammar Formalism." *Machine Translation*, Vol. 10, No. 4, pp. 293–319.

Karagol-Ayan, Burcu (2000). "Morphosyntactic Generation of Turkish from Predicate-argument Structure." *Proceedings of the 38th Annual Meeting of the Association for Computational Linguistics* (*ACL-2000*), Hong Kong.

Stoop, Albert (1990). "TRANSIT: TRANslation System Into Turkish." In Marcel Thelen and Barbara Leeandowska-Tomaszczyk, eds., *Translation and Meaning, Part 1*. Maastricht: Euroterm, pp. 98–108.

Yuret, Deniz and Ferhan Ture (2006). "Learning Morphological Disambiguation Rules for Turkish." *Proceedings of the Human Language Technology Conference—Annual Meeting of the North American Chapter of the Association for Computational Linguistics* (*HLT-NAACL-2006*), New York, USA.

Ukrainian

Blekhman, Michael S., Maryna Byezhanova, Andrei Kursin, Igor Backlam, Alexander Kazakov, and Vladimir Petrov (1999). "Computer-aided Translation Tools for Russian, Ukrainian, and English." *Proceedings of MT Summit VII: MT in the Great Translation Era*, Singapore.

Uyhur

Wushour, Islam 吾守爾・斯拉木 and Maojuda Zunun 毛居德・祖農 (1999). 〈維語自然語言理解及處理研究的應用成果〉 (Achievements on Applications of the Research in Comprehending and Processing Uyhur Natural Language). In Huang Changning 黃昌寧 and Dong Zhendong 董振東, eds., 《計算機語言學文集》 (*Essays on Computational Linguistics*). Beijing: Tsinghua University Press, pp. 453–457.

Language Features

Ellipsis

Chin, Chi-on Andy and Benjamin K. Y. T'sou (2000). "Subject Ellipsis in

Chinese News Headlines." In Nicolas Nicolov and Ruslan Mitkov, eds., *Recent Advances in Natural Language Processing II*. Amsterdam and Philadelphia: John Benjamins Publishing Company, pp. 167–176.

Hahn, Udo and Michael Strube (1997). "Parsetalk about Textual Ellipsis." In Ruslan Mitkov and Nicolas Nicolov, eds., *Recent Advances in Natural Language Processing*. Amsterdam and Philadelphia: John Benjamins Publishing Company, pp. 85–96.

Lee, Hsi-Jian and Shin-Jiang Hwang (1988). "Functional Representation of Query Sentences and Meaning Determination of Elliptical Sentences." *Proceedings of the Conference of the Association for Computational Linguistics and Chinese Language Processing* (*ROCLING-I*), Nantou, Taiwan.

Nariyama, Shigeko (2002). "Grammar for Ellipsis Resolution in Japanese." *Proceedings of the 9th International Conference on Theoretical and Methodological Issues in Machine Translation* (*TMI-2002*), Keihanna, Japan, pp. 135–145.

Sobha, L. and B. Patnaik (2000). "VASISTH: An Ellipsis Resolution Algorithm for Indian Languages." *Proceedings of the International Conference on Machine Translation and Multilingual Applications in the New Millenium* (*MT-2000*), University of Exeter, England.

Idiom

Bar-Hillel, Yehoshua (1955). "Idioms." In William N. Locke and Andrew Donald Booth, eds., *Machine Translation of Languages: Fourteen Essays*. Cambridge, MA: Technology Press of the Massachusetts Institute of Technology, pp. 183–193.

Hashimoto, Chikara, Satoshi Sato, and Takehito Utsuro (2006). "Japanese Idiom Recognition: Drawing a Line between Literal and Idiomatic Meanings." *Proceedings of the Joint Conference of the International Committee on Computational Linguistics and the Association for Computational Linguistics* (*COLING/ACL-2006*), Sydney, Australia.

Lee, Hagyu and Yung Taek Kim (1993). "An Idiom-based Approach to Machine Translation." *Proceedings of the 5th International Conference on Theoretical and Methodological Issues in Machine Translation of Natural Languages: MT in the Next Generation* (*TMI-93*), Kyoto, Japan, pp. 168–182.

Moirón, Begoña Villada and Jörg Tiedemann (2006). "Identifying Idiomatic Expressions Using Automatic Word-alignment." *Proceedings of the 11th Conference of the European Chapter of the Association for Computational Linguistics* (*EACL-2006*), Trento, Italy.

Santos, Diana (1990). "Lexical Gaps and Idioms in Machine Translation." *Proceedings of the 13th International Conference on Computational Linguistics*, Helsinki, Finland, Vol. 2, pp. 220–235.

Schenk, André (1994). "Idioms and Complex Predicates." In M. T. Rosetta, *Compositional Translation*. Dordrecht: Kluwer Academic Publishers, pp. 307–327.

Wehrli, Eric (1998). "Translating Idioms." *Proceedings of the 36th Annual Meeting of the Association for Computational Linguistics and 17th International Conference on Computational Linguistics* (*COLING-ACL-98*), Montreal, Quebec, Canada.

Metaphor

Alonge, Antonietta (2006). "The Italian Metaphor Database." *Proceedings of the 5th International Conference on Language Resources and Evaluation* (*LREC-2006*), Genoa, Italy.

Carbonell, Jaime G. (1982). "Metaphor: An Inescapable Phenomenon in Natural Language Comprehension." In Wendy G. Lehnert and Martin H. Ringle eds., *Strategies for Natural Language Processing*. Hillsdale, New Jersey: Lawrence Erlbaum Associates, pp. 415–434.

Fass, Dan and Yorick Wilks (1983). "Preference Semantics, Ill-formedness, and Metaphor." *Computational Linguistics*, Vol. 9, pp. 178–187.

Veale, Tony and Mark T. Keane (1992). "Conceptual Scaffolding: A Spatially Founded Meaning Representation for Metaphor Comprehension." *Computational Intelligence*, Vol. 83, pp. 494–519.

Veale, Tony and Mark T. Keane (1992). "Conceptual Scaffolding: Using Metaphors to Build Knowledge Structures." *Proceedings of the 10th European Conference on Artificial Intelligence*, Vienna, Austria, pp. 93–100.

Metonymy

Kamei, Shin-ichiro and Takahiro Wakao (1992). "Metonymy: How to

Treat It Properly in a Multilingual Machine Translation System." *Proceedings of the 1st Singapore International Conference on Intelligent Systems* (*SPICIS-92*), Singapore.
Wakao, Takahiro and Stephen Helmreich (1993). "Translation of Metonymy in an Interlingual MT System." *Proceedings of the Pacific Association for Computational Linguistics* (*PACLING-93*), Vancouver, BC, Canada.

Style

DiMarco, Chrysanne and Graeme Hirst (1990). "Accounting for Style in Machine Translation." *Proceedings of the 3rd International Conference on Theoretical and Methodological Issues in Machine Translation of Natural Language* (*TMI-90*), Linguistics Research Center, University of Texas, Austin, Texas, USA, pp. 65–73.
DiMarco, Chrysanne and Keith Mah (1994). "A Model of Comparative Stylistics for Machine Translation." *Machine Translation*, Vol. 9, No. 1, pp. 21–59.
DiMarco, Chrysanne (1994). "Stylistic Choice in Machine Translation." *Proceedings of the 1st Conference of the Association for Machine Translation in the Americas: Technology Partnerships for Crossing the Language Barrier* (*AMTA-1*), Columbia, Maryland, USA, pp. 32–39.
Laurian, Anne-Marie (1986). "Stylistics and Computing: Machine Translation as a Tool for a New Approach to Stylistics." *Machine Translation*, Vol. 1, No. 4, pp. 215–221.
McDonald, David and James Pustejovsky (1985). "A Computational Theory of Prose Style for Natural Language Generation." *Proceedings of the 2nd Meeting of the European Chapter of the Association for Computational Linguistics* (*EACL-85*), Geneva, Switzerland, pp. 187–193.
Morgan, Richard, Mark Smith, and Sengan Short (1994). "Translation by Meaning and Style in LOLITA." *Machine Translation—Ten Years On: Proceedings of the 2nd International Conference Organised by Cranfield University*, Cranfield, England.
Paiva, Daniel (2000). "Investigating Style in a Corpus of Pharmaceutical Leaflets: Results of a Factor Analysis." *Proceedings of the 38th Annual Meeting of the Association for Computational Linguistics* (*ACL-2000*), Hong Kong.

Power, Richard, Donia R. Scott, and Nadjet Bouayad-Agha (2003). "Generating Texts with Style." *Proceedings of the 4th International Conference on Intelligent Text Processing and Computational Linguistics (CICLing-2003)*, Mexico City, Mexico, pp. 446–454.

Language Functions

Communication

Gachot, Denis (1996). "Assimilation or Dissemination? That Is the Question." *Proceedings of the 2nd Conference of the Association for Machine Translation in the Americas: Expanding MT Horizons (AMTA-2)*, Montreal, Quebec, Canada, pp. 226–227.

Grimes, William J. (1984). "Communications and the Translator." In Patricia E. Newman, ed., *American Translators Association Conference—1984.* Medford, New Jersey: Learned Information Inc., pp. 149–154.

Morimoto, Tsuyoshi (1995). "Issues in Multimodal Telecommunications." *Proceedings of MT Summit V: Machine Translation Conference, Exhibition and Tutorial*, Luxembourg.

Nozay, Philippe and Adriane Rinsche (2003). "LTC Communicator." In *Translating and the Computer 25.* London: The Association for Information Management.

O'Hagan, Minako (1996). "Communications Technology and the Language Problem." *The Coming Industry of Teletranslation: Overcoming Communication Barriers through Telecommunication.* Clevedon: Multilingual Matters Ltd., pp. 1–13.

O'Hagan, Minako (1996). "Global Network of Communications." *The Coming Industry of Teletranslation: Overcoming Communication Barriers through Telecommunication.* Clevedon: Multilingual Matters Ltd., pp. 40–68.

O'Hagan, Minako (1996). "Marrying Language Services to Telecommunications: The Coming Industry of Teletranslation." *The Coming Industry of Teletranslation: Overcoming Communication Barriers through Telecommunication.* Clevedon: Multilingual Matters Ltd., pp. 69–90.

Picken, Catriona, ed. (1985). *Translation and Communication: Translating and the Computer 6.* London: The Association for Information Management.

Rinsche, Adriane (2005). "Computer-assisted Multilingual E-communication in a Variety of Application Area." *Proceedings of MT Summit X*, Phuket, Thailand.

Sager, Juan C. (1979). "Multilingual Communication: Chairman's Introductory Review of Translation and the Computer." In Barbara M. Snell, ed., *Translating and the Computer*. Amsterdam: North-Holland Publishing Company, pp. 1–25.

Salam, Muhammad Abdus (2000). "Machine Translation and Multilingual Communication on the Internet." *Proceedings of the International Conference on Machine Translation and Multilingual Applications in the New Millenium* (*MT-2000*), University of Exeter, England.

Stecconi, Ubaldo (2002). "Not a Melting Pot: The Challenges of Multilingual Communication in the European Commission." *Proceedings of the Translation Industry Today*, Rimini, Italy.

Email

Busemann, Stephan, Sven Schmeier, and Roman G. Arens (2000). "Multilingual Coreference Resolution." *Proceedings of the 6th Applied Natural Language Processing Conference*, Seattle, Washington, DC, USA, pp. 158–165.

Fais, Laurel and Kentaro Ogura (2001). "Discourse Issues in the Translation of Japanese Email." *Proceedings of the 5th Pacific Association for Computational Linguistics Conference* (*PACLING-2001*), Fukuoka, Japan.

Goodman, Joshua (2006). "Email and Spam and Spim and Spat." *Proceedings of the Human Language Technology Conference—Annual Meeting of the North American Chapter of the Association for Computational Linguistics* (*HLT-NAACL-2006*), New York, USA.

Han, Benjamin, Donna Gates, and Lori S. Levin (2006). "Understanding Temporal Expressions in Emails." *Proceedings of the Human Language Technology Conference—Annual Meeting of the North American Chapter of the Association for Computational Linguistics* (*HLT-NAACL-2006*), New York, USA.

Jokinen, Kristina and Karl Kanto (2004). "User Expertise Modeling and Adaptivity in a Speech-based E-mail System." *Proceedings of the 42nd Annual Meeting of the Association for Computational Linguistics* (*ACL-2004*), Barcelona, Spain, pp. 87–94.

Matsuda, Junichi and Hiroyuki Kumai (1999). "Transfer-based Japanese-Chinese Translation Implemented on an E-mail System." *Proceedings of MT Summit VII: MT in the Great Translation Era*, Singapore.

Rooke, Robert (1985). "Electronic Mail." In Catriona Picken, ed., *Translation and Communication: Translating and the Computer 6*. London: The Association for Information Management, pp. 105–115.

Xia, Yunqing, Angelo Dalli, Yorick Wilks, and Louise Guthrie (2005). "FASiL Adaptive Email Categorization System." *Proceedings of the 6th International Conference on Intelligent Text Processing and Computational Linguistics* (*CICLing-2005*), Mexico City, Mexico, pp. 710–721.

Language Identification

Beesley, Kenneth R. (1988). "Language Identifier: A Computer Program for Automatic Natural Language Identification of On-line Text." In Deanna Lindberg Hammond, ed., *Languages at Crossroads: Proceedings of the 29th Annual Conference of the American Translators Association*. Medford, New Jersey: Learned Information Inc., pp. 47–54.

Biemann, Chris and Sven Teresniak (2005). "Disentangling from Babylonian Confusion—Unsupervised Language Identification." *Proceedings of the 6th International Conference on Intelligent Text Processing and Computational Linguistics* (*CICLing-2005*), Mexico City, Mexico, pp. 761–772.

Dinu, Anca and Liviu P. Dinu (2005). "On the Syllabic Similarities of Romance Languages." *Proceedings of the 6th International Conference on Intelligent Text Processing and Computational Linguistics* (*CICLing-2005*), Mexico City, Mexico, pp. 773–776.

James J., Vinosh Babu and Baskaran Sankaran (2005). "Automatic Language Identification Using Multivariate Analysis." *Proceedings of the 6th International Conference on Intelligent Text Processing and Computational Linguistics* (*CICLing-2005*), Mexico City, Mexico, pp. 777–780.

Kumar, G. Bharadwaja and Kavi Narayana Murthy (2004). "Language Identification from Small Text Samples." *Proceedings of the International Conference on Natural Language Processing* (*ICON-2004*), International Institute of Information Technology, Hyderabad, India.

Lazzari, Gianni, Robert E. Frederking, and Walter Minker (1999). "Speaker-language Identification and Speech Translation." In Eduard Hovy, Nancy Ide, Robert E. Frederking, J. Mariani, and Antonio Zampolli, eds., *Multilingual Information Management: Current Levels and Future Abilities*. Report for National Science Foundation.

Liu, Jia, Liu Runsheng, and Wang Shizhen (2004). "Confidence Measure Based Language Models Used in Language Identification." *Proceedings of the International Conference on Natural Language Processing* (*ICON-2004*), International Institute of Information Technology, Hyderabad, India.

Qu, Yan and Gregory Grefenstette (2004). "Finding Ideographic Representations of Japanese Names Written in Latin Script via Language Identification and Corpus Validation." *Proceedings of the 42nd Annual Meeting of the Association for Computational Linguistics* (*ACL-2004*), Barcelona, Spain, pp. 183–190.

Takcı, Hidayet and İbrahim Soğukpınar (2004). "Centroid-based Language Identification Using Letter Feature Set." *Proceedings of the 5th International Conference on Intelligent Text Processing and Computational Linguistics* (*CICLing-2004*), Chung-Ang University, Seoul, Korea, pp. 635–644.

Language Learning

Anderson, Don D. (1995) "Machine Translation as a Tool in Second Language Learning." *CALICO Journal*, Vol. 13, No. 1, pp. 68–97.

Ball, R. V. (1989). "Computer-assisted Translation and the Modern Languages Curriculum." *The CTISS File*, Vol. 8, pp. 52–55.

Johnson, Roderick L. (1993). "MT Technology and Computer-aided Language Learning." In Sergei Nirenburg, ed., *Progress in Machine Translation*. Amsterdam: IOS and Tokyo: Ohmsha, pp. 286–287.

Moschitti, Alessandro (2006). "Making Tree Kernels Practical for Natural Language Learning." *Proceedings of the 11th Conference of the European Chapter of the Association for Computational Linguistics* (*EACL-2006*), Trento, Italy.

Newport, Elissa (2003). "Statistical Language Learning: Mechanisms for Language Acquisition in Human Learners." *Proceedings of the Human Language Technology and North American Chapter of Association of*

Computational Linguistics 2003 (*HLT/NAACL-2003*), Edmonton, Alberta, Canada.

Ng, Vincent and Claire Cardie (2003). "Weakly Supervised Natural Language Learning without Redundant Views." *Proceedings of the Human Language Technology and North American Chapter of Association of Computational Linguistics 2003* (*HLT/NAACL-2003*), Edmonton, Alberta, Canada.

Pierce, David and Claire Cardie (2001). "Limitations of Co-training for Natural Language Learning from Large Datasets." *Proceedings of the 2001 Conference on Empirical Methods in Natural Language Processing* (*EMNLP-2001*), Carnegie Mellon University, Pittsburgh, PA, USA.

Smith, Noah A. and Jason Eisner (2004). "Annealing Techniques for Unsupervised Statistical Language Learning." *Proceedings of the 42nd Annual Meeting of the Association for Computational Linguistics* (*ACL-2004*), Barcelona, Spain, pp. 486–493.

Language Modeling

Alexandrescu, Andrei and Katrin Kirchhoff (2006). "Factored Neural Language Models." *Proceedings of the Human Language Technology Conference—Annual Meeting of the North American Chapter of the Association for Computational Linguistics* (*HLT-NAACL-2006*), New York, USA.

Bilmes, Jeff A. and Katrin Kirchhoff (2003). "Factored Language Models and Generalized Parallel Backoff." *Proceedings of the Human Language Technology and North American Chapter of Association of Computational Linguistics 2003* (*HLT/NAACL-2003*), Edmonton, Alberta, Canada.

Brants, Thorsten (1996). "Better Language Models with Model Merging." *Proceedings of the Conference on Empirical Methods in Natural Language Processing*, University of Pennsylvania, PA, USA.

Brown, Ralf D. and Robert Frederking (1995). "Applying Statistical English Language Modelling to Symbolic Machine Translation." *Proceedings of the 6th International Conference on Theoretical and Methodological Issues in Machine Translation* (*TMI-95*), Leuven, Belgium, pp. 221–239.

Bruce, Rebecca W., Janyce Wiebe, and Ted Pedersen (1996). "The

Measure of a Model." *Proceedings of the Conference on Empirical Methods in Natural Language Processing*, University of Pennsylvania, PA, USA.

Casillas, Arantza, Amparo Varona, and Ines Torres (2003). "Experiments with Linguistic Categories for Language Model Optimization." *Proceedings of the 4th International Conference on Intelligent Text Processing and Computational Linguistics* (*CICLing-2003*), Mexico City, Mexico, pp. 513–517.

Chen, Chun-Liang, Bo-Ren Bai, Lee-Feng Chien, and Lin-Shan Lee (1998). "CPT-tree-based Language Models with an Application for Text Verification in Chinese." *Proceedings of the International Conference on Research in Computational Linguistics* (*ROCLING-XI*), Hsin-Chu, Taiwan.

Deng, Yonggang and Sanjeev Khudanpur (2003). "Latent Semantic Information in Maximum Entropy Language Models for Conversational Speech Recognition." *Proceedings of the Human Language Technology and North American Chapter of Association of Computational Linguistics 2003* (*HLT/NAACL-2003*), Edmonton, Alberta, Canada.

Deville, Guy and Emmanuel Herbignaux (1995). "Natural Language Modeling in a Machine Translation Prototype for Healthcare Applications: A Sublanguage Approach." *Proceedings of the 6th International Conference on Theoretical and Methodological Issues in Machine Translation* (*TMI-95*), the University of Leuven, Leuven, Belgium.

Erkan, Gunes (2006). "Language Model-based Document Clustering Using Random Walks." *Proceedings of the Human Language Technology Conference—Annual Meeting of the North American Chapter of the Association for Computational Linguistics* (*HLT-NAACL-2006*), New York, USA.

Gamon, Michael, Anthony Aue, and Martine Smets (2005). "Sentence-level MT Evaluation without Reference Translations: Beyond Language Modeling." *Proceedings of the 10th Annual Conference of the European Association for Machine Translation* (*EAMT-2005*), Budapest, Hungary.

Gao, Jianfeng, Hisami Suzuki, and Yang Wen (2002). "Exploiting Headword Dependency and Predictive Clustering for Language Modeling." *Proceedings of the 2002 Conference on Empirical Methods in Natural Language Processing* (*EMNLP-2002*), University of Pennsylvania, Philadelphia, PA, USA.

Gao, Jianfeng, Hao Yu, Wei Yuan, and Peng Xu (2005). "Minimum Sample Risk Methods for Language Modeling." *Proceedings of Human Language Technology Conference and Conference on Empirical Methods in Natural Language Processing* (*HLT/EMNLP-2005*), Vancouver, BC, Canada.

Gao, Jianfeng, Hisami Suzuki, and Bin Yu (2006). "Approximation Lasso Methods for Language Modeling." *Proceedings of the Joint Conference of the International Committee on Computational Linguistics and the Association for Computational Linguistics* (*COLING/ACL-2006*), Sydney, Australia.

Goodman, Joshua (2003). "Language Modeling." *Proceedings of the Human Language Technology and North American Chapter of Association of Computational Linguistics 2003* (*HLT/NAACL-2003*), Edmonton, Alberta, Canada.

Hasan, Sasa and Hermann Ney (2005). "Clustered Language Models Based on Regular Expressions for SMT." *Proceedings of the 10th Workshop of the European Association for Machine Translation: Practical Applications of Machine Translation*, Budapest, Hungary, pp. 119–125.

Heeman, Peter A. (1999). "POS Tags and Decision Trees for Language Modeling." *Proceedings of the Joint SIGDAT Conference on Empirical Methods in NLP and Very Large Corpora* (*EMNLP/VLC-99*), University of Maryland, College Park, MD, USA.

Ho, Tai-Hsuan, Kae-Chemg Yang, Juei-Sung Lin, and Lin-Shan Lee (1997). "Integrating Long-distance Language Modeling to Phoneme-to-text Conversion." *Proceedings of the International Conference on Research in Computational Linguistics* (*ROCLING-X*), Academia Sinica, Taipei, Taiwan.

Hung, K. Y., R. W. P. Luk, D. Yeung, K. F. L. Chung, and W. Shu (2000). "Detection of Language (Model) Errors." *Proceedings of the Joint Sigdat Conference on Empirical Methods in Natural Language Processing and Very Large Corpora* (*EMNLP/VLC-2000*), Hong Kong University of Science and Technology, Hong Kong.

Kita, Kenji and Tatsuya Iwasa (1995). "Probabilistic Language Modeling Based on Mixture Probabilistic Context-free Grammar." *Proceedings of the Conference of the Association for Computational Linguistics and*

Chinese Language Processing (*ROCLING-VIII*), Yuan-Ze Institute of Technology, Chung-Li, Taiwan.
Kittredge, Richard I. (2000). "Interlingual Modelling: An Applications Perspective." *Proceedings of the 1st International Conference on Intelligent Text Processing and Computational Linguistics* (*CICLing-2000*), Mexico City, Mexico.
Kurohashi, Sadao and Manabu Ori (2000). "Nonlocal Language Modeling Based on Context Co-occurrence Vectors." *Proceedings of the Joint Sigdat Conference on Empirical Methods in Natural Language Processing and Very Large Corpora* (*EMNLP/VLC-2000*), Hong Kong University of Science and Technology, Hong Kong.
Liu, Jia, Liu Runsheng, and Wang Shizhen (2004). "Confidence Measure Based Language Models Used in Language Identification." *Proceedings of the International Conference on Natural Language Processing* (*ICON-2004*), International Institute of Information Technology, Hyderabad, India.
Peters, Jochen (2003). "LM Studies on Filled Pauses in Spontaneous Medical Dictation." *Proceedings of the Human Language Technology and North American Chapter of Association of Computational Linguistics 2003* (*HLT/NAACL-2003*), Edmonton, Alberta, Canada.
Schwenk, Holger and Jean-Luc Gauvain (2005). "Training Neural Network Language Models on Very Large Corpora." *Proceedings of Human Language Technology Conference and Conference on Empirical Methods in Natural Language Processing* (*HLT/EMNLP-2005*), Vancouver, BC, Canada.
Sharoff, Serge (2000). "Application of Object-oriented Approach to Linguistic Modeling." *Proceedings of the 1st International Conference on Intelligent Text Processing and Computational Linguistics* (*CICLing-2000*), Mexico City, Mexico.
Suzuki, Hisami and Gao Jianfeng (2005). "A Comparative Study on Language Model Adaptation Techniques Using New Evaluation Metrics." *Proceedings of Human Language Technology Conference and Conference on Empirical Methods in Natural Language Processing* (*HLT/EMNLP-2005*), Vancouver, BC, Canada.
Villaseñor-Pineda, Luis, Manuel Montes-y-Gómez, Manuel Alberto Pérez-Coutiño, and Dominique Vaufreydaz (2003). "A Corpus Balancing Method for Language Model Construction." *Proceedings of the 4th International Conference on Intelligent Text Processing and*

Computational Linguistics (*CICLing-2003*), Mexico City, Mexico, pp. 395–403.

Wang, Wen and Mary P. Harper (2002). "The SuperARV Language Model: Investigating the Effectiveness of Tightly Integrating Multiple Knowledge Sources." *Proceedings of the 2002 Conference on Empirical Methods in Natural Language Processing* (*EMNLP-2002*), University of Pennsylvania, Philadelphia, PA, USA.

Yang, Kae-Chemg, Tai-Hsuan Ho, Juei-Sung Lin, and Lin-Shan Le (1997). "Truncation on Combined Word-based and Class-based Language Model Using Kullback-Leibler Distance Criterion." *Proceedings of the International Conference on Research in Computational Linguistics* (*ROCLING-X*), Academia Sinica, Taipei, Taiwan.

Yu, Ge, Xiaoguang Li, Yubin Bao, and Daling Wang (2005). "Evaluating Document-to-document Relevance Based on Document Language Model: Modeling, Implementation and Performance Evaluation." *Proceedings of the 6th International Conference on Intelligent Text Processing and Computational Linguistics* (*CICLing-2005*), Mexico City, Mexico, pp. 581–591.

Language Translation

Booth, Andrew D. (1961). "Progress in Automatic Language Translation." *Control*, Vol. 4, No. 40, pp. 103–105.

Brown, Antony F. R. (1957). "Conclusions on Language Translation." *Computers and Automation*, Vol. 6, No. 3, pp. 13, 21.

Brown, Antony F. R. (1958). "Language Translation." *Journal of the Association for Computing Machinery*, Vol. 5, No. 1, pp. 1–8.

Brown, Peter, John Cocke, Stephen A. Della Pietra, Vincent J. Della Pietra, Fredrick Jelinek, Robert L. Mercer, and Paul S. Roossin (1988). "A Statistical Approach to Language Translation." *Proceedings of the 12th International Conference on Computational Linguistics* (*COLING-88*), Budapest, Hungary, pp. 71–76.

Cleave, John P. and B. Zacharow (1955). "Language Translations by Electronics." *Wireless World*, Vol. 61, No. 9, pp. 433–435.

Estival, Dominique (2005). "The Language Translation Interface." *Proceedings of the 10th Annual Conference of the European Association for Machine Translation* (*EAMT-2005*), Budapest, Hungary.

Hajič, Jan, Jan Hric, and Vladislav Kuboň (1999). "Machine Translation of Very Closely Related Languages." *Proceedings of the 4th Workshop of the European Association for Machine Translation: EU and the New Languages: Translation—Possibilities, Policies and Practicalities*, Prague, the Czech Republic.

Homola, Petr and Vladislav Kuboò (2004). "A Translation Model for Languages of Acceding Countries." *Proceedings of the 9th Workshop of the European Association for Machine Translation: Broadening Horizons of Machine Translation and Its Applications*, Foundation for International Studies, Malta, pp. 90–97.

Huang, Xiuming (1990). "Machine Translation in a Monolingual Environment." *Proceedings of the 3rd International Conference on Theoretical and Methodological Issues in Machine Translation of Natural Languages (TMI-90)*, Linguistics Research Center, University of Texas at Austin, Austin, Texas, USA.

Lehmann, Winfred P. (1965). "Towards Experimentation with Language." *Foundations of Language*, Vol. 1, pp. 237–248.

Lippmann, Edward O. (1975). "On-line Generation of Terminological Digests in Language Translation: An Aid in Terminology Processing." *IEEE Transactions on Professional Communications*, Vol. 18, No. 4, pp. 309–319.

Locke, William N. and Andrew D. Booth, eds. (1955). *Machine Translation of Languages*. Cambridge, MA: The Technology Press of the Massachusetts Institute of Technology.

Macdonald, Neil (1954). "Language Translation by Machine—A Report of the First Successful Trial." *Computers and Automation*, Vol. 3, No. 2, pp. 6–10.

Macdonald, Neil (1960). "The Photoscopic Language Translator." *Computers and Automation*, Vol. 9, No. 8, pp. 6–8.

Monson, Christian, Ariadna Font Llitjós, Roberto Aranovich, Lori S. Levin, Ralf D. Brown, Eric Peterson, Jaime G. Carbonell, and Alon Lavie (2006). "Building NLP Systems for Two Resource-scarce Indigenous Languages: Mapudungun and Quechua." *Proceedings of the 5th SALTMIL Workshop on Minority Languages and the 5th International Conference on Language Resources and Evaluation (LREC-2006): Strategies for Developing Machine Translation for Minority Languages*, Genoa, Italy, pp. 15–24.

Oard, Douglas W. and Franz Josef Och (2003). "Rapid Response Machine

Translation for Unexpected Languages." *Proceedings of MT Summit IX*, New Orleans, Louisiana, USA.

Pendergraft, Eugene D. (1967). "Translating Languages." In Harold Borko, ed., *Automated Language Processing*. New York: Wiley, pp. 291–323.

Prys, Delyth (2006). "The BLARK Matrix and Its Relation to the Language Resources Situation for the Celtic Languages." *Proceedings of the 5th SALTMIL Workshop on Minority Languages and the 5th International Conference on Language Resources and Evaluation (LREC-2006): Strategies for Developing Machine Translation for Minority Languages*, Genoa, Italy, pp. 31–32.

Reifler, Erwin (1962). "Machine Language Translation." *Digitale Informationswandler*. Braunschweig: Friedrich Vieweg, pp. 444–507.

Salton, Gerard and R. W. Thorpe (1962). "An Approach to the Segmentation Problem in Speech Analysis and Language Translation." In National Physical Laboratory, ed., *1961 International Conference on Machine Translation of Languages and Applied Language Analysis: Proceedings of the Conference Held at the National Physical Laboratory, Teddington, Middlesex, on 5th, 6th, 7th and 8th September*. London: Her Majesty's Stationery Office, Vol. 1, pp. 704–724.

Scannell, Kevin (2006). "Machine Translation for Closely Related Language Pairs." *Proceedings of the 5th SALTMIL Workshop on Minority Languages and the 5th International Conference on Language Resources and Evaluation (LREC-2006): Strategies for Developing Machine Translation for Minority Languages*, Genoa, Italy, pp. 103–108.

Sheridan, Peter (1955). "Research in Language Translation on the IBM Type 701." *IBM Technical Newsletter*, No. 9, pp. 5–24.

Sinaiko, H. Wallace and George R. Klare (1972). "Further Experiments in Language Translation: Readability of Computer Translations." *ITL* (*Review of Institute of Applied Linguistics, Louvain*), Vol. 15, pp. 1–29.

Sinaiko, H. Wallace and George R. Klare (1973). "Further Experiments in Language Translation: A Second Evaluation of the Readability of Computer Translation." *ITL* (*Review of Institute of Applied Linguistics, Louvain*), Vol. 19, pp. 29–52.

Sinaiko, H. Wallace and Richard W. Brislin (1973). "Evaluating Language Translations: Experiments of Three Assessment Methods." *Journal of Applied Psychology*, Vol. 57, No. 3, pp. 328–334.

Speck, J. (1958). "Four Language Translation by Automatic Computer." *Computers and Automation*, Vol. 7, No. 3, p. 11.

Stout, Thomas M. (1954). "Computing Machines for Language Translation." *Mechanical Translation*, Vol. 1, No. 3, pp. 41–46.

Stout, Thomas M. (1954). "Computing Machines for Language Translation." *The Trend in Engineering at the University of Washington*, Vol. 6, No. 3, pp. 11–29.

Thurmair, Gregor and Johannes Ritzke (1999). "The L&H Approach to Development of Tools for New Languages." *Proceedings of the 4th Workshop of the European Association for Machine Translation: EU and the New Languages: Translation—Possibilities, Policies and Practicalities*, Prague, the Czech Republic.

Yacob, Daniel (2006). "Unicode Development for Under-resourced Languages." *Proceedings of the 5th SALTMIL Workshop on Minority Languages and the 5th International Conference on Language Resources and Evaluation (LREC-2006): Strategies for Developing Machine Translation for Minority Languages*, Genoa, Italy, pp. 33–38.

Yngve, Victor H. (1956). "The Translation of Languages by Machine." In Colin Cherry, ed., *Information Theory*. London: Butterworths, pp. 196–205.

Arabic-English

Chalabi, Achraf (1998). "Sakhr Arabic-English Computer-aided Translation System." In David L. Farwell, Laurie Gerber, and Eduard Hovy, eds., *Machine Translation and the Information Soup*. Berlin: Springer Verlag, pp. 518–521.

Habash, Nizar, Bonnie J. Dorr, and Christof Monz (2006). "Challenges in Building an Arabic-English GHMT System with SMT Components." *Proceedings of the 7th Biennial Conference of the Association for Machine Translation in the Americas (AMTA-2006): Visions for the Future of Machine Translation*, Boston Marriott, Cambridge, MA, USA.

Arabic-French

Hasan, Saša, Anas El Isbihani, and Hermann Ney (2006). "Creating a Large-scale Arabic to French Statistical Machine Translation System."

Proceedings of the 5th International Conference on Language Resources and Evaluation (*LREC-2006*), Genoa, Italy.

Bangla-English

Asaduzzaman, Mohammad M. and Masroor M. Ali (2003). "A Knowledge Based Approach to Bangla-English Machine Translation for Simple Assertive Sentences." *International Journal of Translation*, Vol. 15, No. 2, pp. 77–97.

Cantonese-English

Wu, Yan and James Liu (1999). "A Cantonese-English Machine Translation System Poly U-MT-99." *Proceedings of MT Summit VII: MT in the Great Translation Era*, Singapore.

Catalan-English

de Gispert, Adrià and José B. Mariño (2006). "Catalan-English Statistical Machine Translation without Parallel Corpus: Bridging through Spanish." *Proceedings of the 5th SALTMIL Workshop on Minority Languages and the 5th International Conference on Language Resources and Evaluation* (*LREC-2006*): *Strategies for Developing Machine Translation for Minority Languages*, Genoa, Italy, pp. 65–68.

Catalan-Spanish

Alonso, Juan Alberto (2005). "Machine Translation for Catalan↔Spanish: The Real Case for Productive MT." *Proceedings of the 10th Workshop of the European Association for Machine Translation: Practical Applications of Machine Translation*, Budapest, Hungary, pp. 23–26.

Chinese-Arabic

Malky, Hesham El 希夏姆・馬利克 (2001).〈漢阿機譯研究（一）：從漢語單句若干結構談論漢阿機譯〉(Chinese-Arabic Machine Translation (1): A Discussion on Chinese-Arabic Machine Translation from the Perspective of Some Simple Chinese Sentences).《輝煌二十年──中國

中文信息學會二十周年學術會議》(*Proceedings of Conference of the 20th Anniversary of CIPSC*). Beijing: Tsinghua University Press, pp. 226–240.

Chinese-English

Byrne, William, Sanjeev Khudanpur, Woosung Kim, Shankar Kumar, Pavel Pecina, Paola Virga, Peng Xu, and David Yarowsky (2003). "The John Hopkins University 2003 Chinese-English Machine Translation System." *Proceedings of MT Summit IX*, New Orleans, Louisiana, USA.

Chai, D. T. (1967). "Chinese-English Machine Translation." *Law and Computer Technology*, Vol. 1, No. 8, pp. 10–16.

Chang, Baobao 常寶寶, Zhan Weidong 詹衛東, Bai Xiaojing 柏曉靜, Wu Yunfang 吳雲芳, and Zhang Huarui 張化瑞 (2002).〈服務於漢英機器翻譯的雙語對齊語料庫和短語庫建設〉(Building Aligned Parallel Corpus and Bilingual Phrase Information Bank for Chinese-English Machine Translation). In Yu Shiwen, ed., *Proceedings of the Second China-Japan Natural Language Processing Joint Research Promotion Conference* (*CJNLP-2002*). Beijing: Institute of Computational Linguistics, Peking University, pp. 147–154.

Chang, Baobao, Zhang Huarui, and Yu Shiwen (2002). "Bilingual Corpus Construction and Its Management for Chinese-English Machine Translation." In Chan Sin-wai, ed., *Translation and Information Technology*. Hong Kong: The Chinese University Press, pp. 31–41.

Chen, Conrad and Hsin-Hsi Chen (2006). "A High-accurate Chinese-English Backward NE Translation System Combining Both Lexical Information and Web Statistics." *Proceedings of the Joint Conference of the International Committee on Computational Linguistics and the Association for Computational Linguistics* (*COLING/ACL-2006*), Sydney, Australia.

Gerber, Laurie (1996). "SYSTRAN Chinese-English MT, ECI Chinese OCR—CHIOCR." *Proceedings of the 2nd Conference of the Association for Machine Translation in the Americas: Expanding MT Horizons* (*AMTA-2*), Montreal, Quebec, Canada, pp. 277–279.

Guo, Honglei 郭宏蕾, Jiang Jianmin 蔣建民, and Hu Gang 胡崗 (2001).〈漢日韓英多語機譯系統的通用英語生成器〉(Universal English Generator in Chinese-Japanese-Korean-English Multilingual MT System). In

Huang Changning 黃昌寧 and Zhang Pu 張普, eds.,《自然語言理解與機器翻譯》(*Natural Language Understanding and Machine Translation*). Beijing: Tsinghua University Press, pp. 332–337.

Jin, Wanying (1986). "Machine Translation between Chinese and English." *Proceedings of the 6th Canadian Conference on Artificial Intelligence*. Canada: Press de l'Universite du Quebec, pp. 129–133.

Jin, Wanying and Robert F. Simmons (1986). "Symmetric Rules for Translation English and Chinese." *Computers and Translation*, Vol. 1, No. 3, pp. 153–176.

Langlais, Philippe, Michael Carl, and Oliver Streiter (2004). "Experimenting with Phrase-based Statistical Translation within the IWSLT 2004 Chinese-to-English Shared Translation Task." *Proceedings of the International Workshop on Spoken Language Translation* (*IWSLT-2004*), Kyoto, Japan.

Lee, Theresa, H. T. Wang, Shou-Chuan Yang, and E. L. Farmer (1966). *Linguistic Studies for Chinese to English Machine Translation*. New York: Rome Air Development Center, Research and Technology Division, Air Force Systems Command, Griffiss Air Force Base.

Li, Ying 李穎 (2002).〈漢英機器翻譯中要素句蛻處理初探〉(Constituent Degraded Sentence Processing in Chinese-English Machine Translation).《第一屆學生計算語言學研討會論文集》(*SWCL2002: First Students' Workshop on Computational Linguistics: Proceedings*), Institute of Computational Linguistics, Peking University, Beijing, China p. 232.

Liu, Qun and Yu Shiwen (1998). "TransEasy: A Chinese-English Machine Translation System Based on Hybrid Approach." In David L. Farwell, Laurie Gerber, and Eduard Hovy, eds., *Machine Translation and the Information Soup*. Berlin: Springer Verlag, pp. 514–517.

Liu, Qun and Yu Shiwen (2000).〈漢英機器翻譯的難點分析〉(An Analysis of the Difficulties of Chinese-English Machine Translation). In Yu Shiwen 俞士汶 and Zhu Xuefeng 朱學鋒, eds.,《計算語言學文集》(*Papers on Computational Linguistics*), Vol. 4. Beijing: Department of Computer Science and Technology and Institute of Computational Linguistics, Peking University, pp. 198–205.

Liu, Qun, Zhan Weidong, Chang Baobao, and Liu Ying (2000).〈一個漢英機器翻譯系統的計算模型與語言模型〉(The Computing and Language Model of a Chinese-English Machine Translation System). In Yu Shiwen and Zhu Xuefeng, eds.,《計算語言學文集》(*Papers on

Computational Linguistics), Vol. 4. Beijing: Department of Computer Science and Technology and Institute of Computational Linguistics, Peking University, pp. 192–197.

Liu, Qun (2002). "A Chinese-English Machine Translation System Based on Micro-engine Architecture." In Chan Sin-wai, ed., *Translation and Information Technology*. Hong Kong: The Chinese University Press, pp. 23–30.

Loh, Shiu-chang (1975). "Machine-aided Translation from Chinese to English." *United College Journal*, Vol. 12, No. 13, pp. 143–155.

Loh, Shiu-chang and Kong Luen (1979). "An Interactive On-line Machine Translation System (Chinese into English)." In Barbara M. Snell, ed., *Translating and the Computer*. Amsterdam: North-Holland Publishing Company, pp. 135–148.

Luo, Ziqing 羅自清 and Zhang Yanhong 張艷紅 (2002).〈漢英翻譯中主輔變換的類型〉(Varieties of the Transformation between PSC and SSC in Chinese-English MT).《第一屆學生計算語言學研討會論文集》(*SWCL2002: First Students' Workshop on Computational Linguistics: Proceedings*), Institute of Computational Linguistics, Peking University, Beijing, China, pp. 209–214.

Ma, Hongmei 馬紅妹, Wang Ting 王挺, and Chen Huowang 陳火旺 (2001).〈漢英機器翻譯中語境知識的表示與應用〉(Representation and Application of the Linguistic Context Knowledge in Chinese-English Machine Translation). In Huang Changning 黃昌寧 and Zhang Pu 張普, eds.,《自然語言理解與機器翻譯》(*Natural Language Understanding and Machine Translation*). Beijing: Tsinghua University Press, pp. 278–284.

Ma, Hongmei, Qi Xuan, Wang Ting, and Chen Huowang (2002).〈漢英機譯系統ICENT中主語省略句的處理〉(The Processing of Zero Anaphoric Subject of Chinese Sentences in the Chinese-English Machine Translation System ICENT).《第一屆學生計算語言學研討會論文集》(*SWCL2002: First Students' Workshop on Computational Linguistics: Proceedings*), Institute of Computational Linguistics, Peking University, Beijing, China, pp. 203–208.

Mathias, J. (1973). "The Chinese-English Translation Assistance Group and Its Computerized Glossary Project." *Federal Linguist*, Vol. 5, Nos. 3–4, pp. 7–13.

Olsen, Mari, David Traum, Carol J. van Ess-Dykema, Amy Weinberg, and Ron Dolan (2000). "Telicity as a Cue to Temporal and Discourse

Structure in Chinese-English Machine Translation." *Proceedings of the NAACL-ANLP 2000 Workshop on Applied Interlinguas: Practical Applications of Interlingual Approaches to NLP—Volume 2*, Seattle, Washington, DC, USA, pp. 34–41.

Olsen, Mari, David Traum, Carol J. van Ess-Dykema, and Amy Weinberg (2001). "Implicit Cues for Explicit Generation: Using Telicity as a Cue for Tense Structure in a Chinese to English MT System." In Bente Maegaard, ed., *Proceedings of MT Summit VIII: Machine Translation in the Information Age*, Santiago de Compostela, Spain.

Parker-Rhodes, Arthur Frederick (1956). "An Electronic Computer Program for Translating Chinese into English." *Mechanical Translation*, Vol. 3, No. 1, pp. 14–19.

Qian, Feng 錢鋒 (1987). "Introducing Chemats—ECNU Chinese to English Machine Aided Translation System." *Proceedings of the Conference on Translation Today*, Hong Kong.

Reifler, Erwin (1967). "Chinese-English Machine Translation: Its Lexicographic and Linguistic Problems." In Andrew D. Booth, ed., *Machine Translation*. Amsterdam: North-Holland Publishing Company, pp. 317–328.

Seneff, Stephanie, Chao Wang, and John Lee (2006). "Combining Linguistic and Statistical Methods for Bi-directional English Chinese Translation in the Flight Domain." *Proceedings of the 7th Biennial Conference of the Association for Machine Translation in the Americas (AMTA-2006): Visions for the Future of Machine Translation*, Boston Marriott, Cambridge, MA, USA.

Shi, Xiaodong Mandel 史曉東 (2002).〈漢語象聲詞的漢英機器翻譯研究〉(Treatment of Onomatopoeia in Chinese-English Machine Translation). In Yu Shiwen, ed., *Proceedings of the Second China-Japan Natural Language Processing Joint Research Promotion Conference (CJNLP-2002)*. Beijing: Institute of Computational Linguistics, Peking University, pp. 142–146.

T'sou, Benjamin K. Y. and Kwong Oi Yee (2001). "Evaluating Chinese-English Translation Systems for Personal Name Coverage." In Bente Maegaard, ed., *Proceedings of MT Summit VIII: Machine Translation in the Information Age*, Santiago de Compostela, Spain.

Wang, William S. Y. and S. W. Chan (1974). *Development of Chinese-English Machine Translation System*. Berkeley: University of California.

Wang, William S. Y. (1976). "Chinese-English Machine Translation."

American Journal of Computational Linguistics, Vol. 2, Microfiche, p. 24.
Wu, Yunfang 吳雲芳 (2001).〈疑問句中的「怎麼」在漢英機器翻譯中的詞匯歧義化解〉(Lexical Disambiguation of "Zen Me" in Questions in Chinese-English Machine Translation).《輝煌二十年 — 中國中文信息學會二十周年學術會議》(*Proceedings of Conference of the 20th Anniversary of CIPSC*). Beijing: Tsinghua University Press, pp. 263–271.
Yang, Jin and Laurie Gerber (1996). "Chinese-English Machine Translation System." *International Conference on Chinese Computing '96—The Latest Technological Advancement and Application* (*ICCC-96*), Chinese and Oriental Languages Information Processing Society, Singapore.
Yang, Muyun, Zhao Tiejun, Liu Haijie, Shi Xiasheng, and Jiang Hongfei (2004). "Auto Word Alignment Based Chinese-English EBMT." *Proceedings of the International Workshop on Spoken Language Translation* (*IWSLT-2004*), Kyoto, Japan.
Yang, Xiaofeng 楊曉峰, Li Tangqiu 李堂秋, and Hong Qingyang 洪青陽 (2001).〈漢英機器翻譯系中的一種詞義排歧方法〉(Word Sense Disambiguation Method in Chinese-English Machine Translation System). In Huang Changning 黃昌寧 and Zhang Pu 張普, eds.,《自然語言理解與機器翻譯》(*Natural Language Understanding and Machine Translation*). Beijing: Tsinghua University Press, pp. 300–305.
Yang, Ye and Zhu Zhang (2005). "Building a Temporal Reference Distinction Resolution Module in Chinese-to-English Machine Translation." *Proceedings of MT Summit X*, Phuket, Thailand.
Yao, Tianshun 姚天順, Yang Erbao 楊二寶, Zhang Le 張樂, and Lü Xueqiang 呂學強 (2002). "The Method of Similar Template for Spoken Language Chinese-English MT System." In Yu Shiwen, ed., *Proceedings of the 2nd China-Japan Natural Language Processing Joint Research Promotion Conference* (*CJNLP-2002*), Institute of Computational Linguistics, Peking University, China, pp. 96–103.
Yu, Shiwen, Duan Huiming, and Sui Zhifang (2000).〈關於漢英機器翻譯測試大綱的思考〉(Thoughts on an Outline of Chinese-English Machine Translation Testing). In Yu Shiwen 俞士汶 and Zhu Xuefeng 朱學鋒, eds.,《計算語言學文集》(*Papers on Computational Linguistics*), Vol. 4. Beijing: Department of Computer Science and Technology and Institute of Computational Linguistics, Peking University, pp. 206–208.

Zhang, Keliang 張克亮 (2002).〈基於HNC理論的漢英機器翻譯策略研究〉(A Strategic Study of HNC-based Chinese-English Machine Translation).《第一屆學生計算語言學研討會論文集》(*SWCL2002: First Students' Workshop on Computational Linguistics: Proceedings*), Institute of Computational Linguistics, Peking University, Beijing, China, p. 231.

Zhang, Yanhong (2001).〈英漢互譯中的過渡處理〉(The Transition of MT between English and Chinese). In Huang Changning 黃昌寧 and Zhang Pu 張普, eds.,《自然語言理解與機器翻譯》(*Natural Language Understanding and Machine Translation*). Beijing: Tsinghua University Press, pp. 312–318.

Zuo, Yuncun, Zhou Yu, and Zong Chengqing (2004). "Multi-engine Based Chinese-to-English Translation System." *Proceedings of the International Workshop on Spoken Language Translation* (*IWSLT-2004*), Kyoto, Japan.

Chinese-Foreign Language

Wu, Huitian 吳蔚天 (1997).〈漢外機器翻譯與漢語分析器〉(Machine Translation from Chinese into Foreign Languages and Chinese Analyzer).《語言文字應用》(*Applied Linguistics*), No. 3, pp. 83–88.

Chinese-Japanese

Zhou, Ming 周明 (1999).〈中-日機器翻譯系統J-北京〉(J-Beijing: Chinese-Japanese Machine Translation System). In Huang Changning 黃昌寧 and Dong Zhendong 董振東, eds.,《計算機語言學文集》(*Essays on Computational Linguistics*). Beijing: Tsinghua University Press, pp. 312–319.

Chinese-Korean

Huang, Jin-Xia and Key-Sun Choi (2000). "Chinese-Korean Word Alignment Based on Linguistic Comparison." *Proceedings of the 38th Annual Meeting of the Association for Computational Linguistics* (*ACL-2000*), Hong Kong.

Li, Junjie and Key-Sun Choi (1997). "Corpus-based Chinese-Korean Abstracting Translation System." *Proceedings of the 15th International Joint Conference on Artificial Intelligence* (*IJCAI-97*), Nagoya, Japan.

Zhang, Min and Choi Key-Sun (1999). "A Pipelined Multi-engine Approach to Chinese-to-Korean Machine Translation: MATES/CK." *Proceedings of MT Summit VII: MT in the Great Translation Era*, Singapore.

Chinese-Tibetan

Kanzhuo, Caidan Hu 看卓才旦, Jin Weixun 金為勛, Luo Zhihua 洛智華, and Pengmao Zhaxi 朋毛扎西 (2002). 〈漢藏翻譯系統中的動詞處理研究〉 (A Study of the Treatment of Verbs in a Chinese-Tibetan Translation System). 《第一屆學生計算語言學研討會論文集》 (*SWCL2002: First Students' Workshop on Computational Linguistics: Proceedings*), Institute of Computational Linguistics, Peking University, Beijing, China, pp. 222–230.

Czech-English

Bojar, Ondřej and Magdalena Prokopová (2006). "Czech-English Word Alignment." *Proceedings of the 5th International Conference on Language Resources and Evaluation* (*LREC-2006*), Genoa, Italy.

Havelka, Jiri, Martin Cmejrek, Jan Curin, and Jan Hajic (2005). "Prague Czech-English Dependency Treebank—Resource for Structure-based MT." *Proceedings of the 10th Workshop of the European Association for Machine Translation: Practical Applications of Machine Translation*, Budapest, Hungary, pp. 73–78.

Kruijff-Korbayová, Ivana, Klára Chvátalová, and Oana Postolache (2006). "Annotation Guidelines for Czech-English Word Alignment." *Proceedings of the 5th International Conference on Language Resources and Evaluation* (*LREC-2006*), Genoa, Italy.

English-Arabic

Fattah, Mohamed Abdel, Fuji Ren, and Shingo Kuroiwa (2006). "Probabilistic Neural Network Based English-Arabic Sentence Alignment." *Proceedings of the 7th International Conference on Intelligent Text Processing and Computational Linguistics* (*CICLing-2006*), Mexico City, Mexico.

Ibrahim, M. (1984). "A Generalized Computer-assisted Language

Translation Model: English to Arabic—Problems and Solutions." *Proceedings of the International Conference on the Methodology and Techniques of Machine Translation*, Cranfield Institute of Technology, Cranfield, England.

Mokhtar, Hoda M. O., Nevin M. Darwish, and Ahmed A. Rafea (2000). "An Automated System for English-Arabic Translation of Scientific Texts (SEATS)." *Proceedings of the International Conference on Machine Translation and Multilingual Applications in the New Millenium* (*MT-2000*), University of Exeter, England.

English-Basque

de Ilarraza, Arantxa Diaz, Aingeru Mayor, and Kepa Sarasola (2000). "Building a Lexicon for an English-Basque MT System from Heterogeneous Wide-coverage Dictionaries." *Proceedings of the International Conference on Machine Translation and Multilingual Applications in the New Millenium* (*MT-2000*), University of Exeter, England.

English-Bengali

Naskar, Sudip Kumar and Sivaji Bandyopadhyay (2005). "A Phrasal EBMT System for Translating English to Bangla." *Proceedings of MT Summit X*, Phuket, Thailand.

Naskar, Sudip Kumar and Sivaji Bandyopadhyay (2006). "Handling of Prepositions in English to Bengali Machine Translation." *Proceedings of the 11th Conference of the European Chapter of the Association for Computational Linguistics* (*EACL-2006*), Trento, Italy.

English-Chinese

Alshawi, Hiyan and Fei Xiang (1997). "English-to-Mandarin Speech Translation with Head Transducers." *Spoken Language Translation: Proceedings of a Workshop Sponsored by the Association for Computational Linguistics and by the European Network in Language and Speech* (*ELSNET-97*), Madrid, Spain, pp. 54–60.

Cardey, Sylviane, Peter Greenfield, and Wu Xiaohong (2004). "Designing a Controlled Language for the Machine Translation of Medical

Protocols: The Case of English to Chinese." In Stephen D. Richardson, ed., *Machine Translation: From Research to Real Users*. Berlin and New York: Springer Verlag, pp. 37–47.
Chen, Shu-Chuan and Keh-Yih Su (1988). "The Processing of English Compound and Complex Words in an English-Chinese Machine Translation System." *Proceedings of the Conference of the Association for Computational Linguistics and Chinese Language Processing* (*ROCLING-I*), Nantou, Taiwan.
Chen, Shu-chuan, Chang Jing-shin, Wang Jong-nae, and Su Keh-yih (1993). "ArchTran: A Corpus-based Statistics-oriented English-Chinese Machine Translation System." In Sergei Nirenburg, ed., *Progress in Machine Translation*. Amsterdam: IOS and Tokyo: Ohmsha, pp. 87–98.
Dong, Zhendong 董振東 and Zhang Deling 張德琴 (1987).〈語言、翻譯、機器翻譯，兼談「科譯1號」英漢機譯系統〉(On Language, Translation, Machine Translation and a Discussion of the KY-1 English-Chinese Machine Translation System). *Proceedings of the Conference on Translation Today*, Hong Kong.
Fu, Aiping 傅愛平 (1999).〈英漢機器翻譯的轉換生成策略〉(A Transfer-generation Strategy in English-Chinese Machine Translation). In Huang Changning and Dong Zhendong, eds.,《計算機語言學文集》(*Essays on Computational Linguistics*). Beijing: Tsinghua University Press, pp. 341–346.
Fu, Aiping (2001). "Linguistic and Computational Aspects of English-Chinese Machine Translation).《輝煌二十年——中國中文信息學會二十周年學術會議》(*Proceedings of Conference of the 20th Anniversary of CIPSC*). Beijing: Tsinghua University Press, pp. 241–248.
Jin, Wanying and Robert F. Simmons (1986). "Symmetric Rules for Translation of English and Chinese." *Machine Translation*, Vol. 1, No. 3, pp. 153–167.
Lee, Chun-Jen and Jason S. Chang (2003). "Acquisition of English-Chinese Transliterated Word Pairs from Parallel-aligned Texts Using a Statistical Machine Transliteration Model." *Proceedings of the Human Language Technology and North American Chapter of Association of Computational Linguistics 2003* (*HLT/NAACL-2003*), Edmonton, Alberta, Canada.
Li, Yaoyong 李耀勇 (2001).〈利用HNC理論進行基於實例的英漢機器翻譯〉(Example-based English-Chinese Machine Translation by Using HNC

Theory). In Huang Changning 黃昌寧 and Zhang Pu 張普, eds.,《自然語言理解與機器翻譯》(*Natural Language Understanding and Machine Translation*). Beijing: Tsinghua University Press, pp. 319–325.

Lin, Frank and Teruko Mitamura (2004). "Keyword Translation from English to Chinese for Multilingual QA." In Robert E. Frederking and Kathryn B. Taylors, eds., *Machine Translation: From Real Users to Research*. Berlin: Springer Verlag, pp. 164–176.

Liu, S. S. (1984). "Translation of English into Chinese on a Microcomputer." *Proceedings of the International Conference on the Methodology and Techniques of Machine Translation*, Cranfield Institute of Technology, Cranfield, England.

Liu, Yongquan 劉湧泉, Wu Sun 吳遜, Wang Guangyi 王廣義, and Fu Aiping 傅愛平 (1984).〈ECMT-78英漢機器翻譯系統簡介〉(A Brief Introduction of the ECMT-78 English-Chinese Machine Translation System). In Liu Yongquan *et al.*,《中國的機器翻譯》(*Machine Translation in China*). Shanghai: Knowledge Press, pp. 81–101.

Liu, Zhijie 劉志傑 (1999).〈英漢機器翻譯軟件長句分析芻議〉(Some Views on the Analysis of Long Sentences for English-Chinese Translation Software). In Huang Changning 黃昌寧 and Dong Zhendong 董振東, eds.,《計算機語言學文集》(*Essays on Computational Linguistics*). Beijing: Tsinghua University Press, pp. 305–311.

Palmer, Martha and Zhibiao Wu (1995). "Verb Semantics for English-Chinese Translation." *Machine Translation*, Vol. 10, Nos. 1–2, pp. 59–92.

Pan, Haihua (1986). "A Machine Translation System for Scientific Titles of English." *Proceedings of 1986 International Conference on Chinese Computing*, Singapore.

Seneff, Stephanie, Chao Wang, and John Lee (2006). "Combining Linguistic and Statistical Methods for Bi-directional English Chinese Translation in the Flight Domain." *Proceedings of the 7th Biennial Conference of the Association for Machine Translation in the Americas (AMTA-2006): Visions for the Future of Machine Translation*, Boston Marriott, Cambridge, MA, USA.

Shi, Xiaodong 史曉東 (2001).〈英漢機器翻譯：現狀和未來〉(English-Chinese Machine Translation: Past and Future).《輝煌二十年——中國中文信息學會二十周年學術會議》(*Proceedings of Conference of the 20th Anniversary of CIPSC*). Beijing: Tsinghua University Press, pp. 74–78.

Stutzman, Walter J. (1976). "Organizing Knowledge for English-Chinese

Translation." *American Journal of Computational Linguistics*, Microfiche, 48, p. 28.
Su, Keh-yih, Jason S. Chang, and H.-H. Hsu (1987). "A Powerful Language Processing System for English-Chinese Machine Translation." *Proceedings of the 1987 International Conference on Chinese and Oriental Language Computing*, Chicago, Illinois, USA, pp. 95–104.
Su, Keh-yih, Chang Chia-lan, and Chen Shu-chuan (1987). "Hands-on Experiences in the Development of an English-Chinese Machine Translation System." *Proceedings of the Conference on Translation Today*, Hong Kong.
Su, Keh-yih, Chang Jing-shin, Wang Jong-nae, Emma Chang, and Wu Ming-wen (1996). "The Computational Models of the BehaviorTran English-Chinese Machine Translation System." *Journal of Chinese Linguistics*, Vol. 9, pp. 223–245.
Sun, Chung-Teng and Jyun-Sheng Chang (1991). "Lexicon-driven Transfer in English-Chinese Machine Translation." *Proceedings of the Conference of the Association for Computational Linguistics and Chinese Language Processing* (*ROCLING-IV*), National Chiao-Tung University, Hsin-Chu, Taiwan.
Wang, Xuexing 王學興 (1982).〈英漢機器翻譯簡介〉(Introducing English-Chinese Machine Translation).《翻譯通訊》(*Translators' Notes*), No. 6, pp. 49–55.
Wei, Mo 未末, Zheng Jie 鄭傑, and Mao Yuhang 茅于杭 (1999).〈外掛式英漢網絡翻譯瀏覽器的研究與實現〉(The Design and Implementation of Attached English-Chinese Translation Browser). In Huang Changning 黃昌寧 and Dong Zhendong 董振東, eds.,《計算機語言學文集》(*Essays on Computational Linguistics*). Beijing: Tsinghua University Press, pp. 327–334.
Wu, Dekai (1994). "Aligning Parallel English-Chinese Text Statistically with Lexical Criteria." *Proceedings of the 32nd Annual Meeting of the Association for Computational Linguistics* (*ACL-94*), Las Cruces, New Mexico, USA, pp. 80–87.
Zhang, Liangping 張良平 (1987). "Practical Considerations on English-Chinese Machine Translation System." *Proceedings of the Conference on Translation Today*, Hong Kong.
Zhang, Wen 張文 (1993).〈機器翻譯研究最新進展——介紹「863」智能型英漢機譯系統〉(Introducing the English-Chinese Translation Model

IMT/863).《中國翻譯》(*Chinese Translators Journal*), No. 5, pp. 56–57.

Zhang, Yanhong (2001).〈英漢互譯中的過渡處理〉(The Transition of MT between English and Chinese). In Huang Changning 黃昌寧 and Zhang Pu 張普, eds.,《自然語言理解與機器翻譯》(*Natural Language Understanding and Machine Translation*). Beijing: Tsinghua University Press, pp. 312–318.

Zheng, Baoshan 鄭保山, Liu Qun 劉群, and Zhang Xiang 張祥 (1999).〈機器翻譯模板的建立原則和方法〉(Establishing Principles and Methods of the Templates for Machine Translation). In Huang Changning 黃昌寧 and Dong Zhendong 董振東, eds.,《計算機語言學文集》(*Essays on Computational Linguistics*). Beijing: Tsinghua University Press, pp. 299–304.

Zheng, Jie, Mao Yuhang, and Wei Mo (1999).〈英漢機譯系統中的難點分析〉(An Analysis of the Difficulties of English-Chinese Machine Translation). In Huang Changning 黃昌寧 and Dong Zhendong 董振東, eds.,《計算機語言學文集》(*Essays on Computational Linguistics*). Beijing: Tsinghua University Press, pp. 320–326.

English-Czech

Čmejrek, Martin and Jan Cuřin (1999). "Automatic Translation Lexicon Extraction from English-Czech Parallel Texts." *Proceedings of the 4th Workshop of the European Association for Machine Translation: EU and the New Languages: Translation—Possibilities, Policies and Practicalities*, Prague, the Czech Republic.

Hajicova, Eva and Zdenek Kirschner (1981). "Automatic Translation from English to Czech." *The Prague Bulletin of Mathematical Linguistics*, Vol. 35, pp. 55–65.

Kirschner, Zdeněk (1987). "APAC3-2: An English-to-Czech Machine Translation System." *Explizite Beschreibung der Sprache und Automatische Textbearbeitung*, Vol. 13, Faculty of Mathematics and Physics, Charles University.

Kirschner, Zdeněk and Alexandr Rosen (1989). "APAC—An Experiment in Machine Translation." *Machine Translation*, Vol. 4, No. 3, pp. 177–193.

Strossa, Petr (1987). "SPSS—An Algorithm and Data Structures Design for a Machine-aided English to Czech Translation System." *Prague Bulletin of Mathematical Linguistics*, Vol. 47, pp. 25–36.

Strossa, Petr (1994). "Machine Assisted Translation from English to a Slavic Language: What Linguistics and Programming Methodologies Can Do for It." *Machine Translation*, Vol. 9, No. 1, pp. 61–80.

English-French

Booth, Kathleen H. V., C. A. Brown, and C. Stock (1971). "English-French Translation on a Computer." In Anthony Ralston and Chester L. Meek, eds., *Encyclopedia of Computer Science*. New York: Van Nostrand, pp. 764–769.

Farrington, B. (1984). "A Microcomputer Program for Checking English/French Translation at Sentence Level." *Proceedings of the International Conference on the Methodology and Techniques of Machine Translation*, Cranfield Institute of Technology, Cranfield, England.

LATSEC (1975). *Technical Proposal for Further Development of the SYSTRAN English-French Machine Translation System and Initial Development of the SYSTRAN French-English Translation System*. La Jolla, California: Latsec Incorporated.

Lavorel, Bernhard (1982). "Experience in English-French Post-editing." In Veronica Lawson, ed., *Practical Experience of Machine Translation*. Amsterdam: North-Holland Publishing Company, pp. 103–111.

Masterman, Margaret (1967). "Man-aided Computer Translation from English into French Using an Online System to Manipulate a Bi-lingual Conceptual Dictionary, or Thesaurus." *Deuxieme Conference Internationale sur le Traitement Automatique des Langues*, Grenoble, France.

English-German

Bernth, Arendse (1997). "EasyEnglish: A Tool for Improving Document Quality." *Proceedings of the 5th Conference on Applied Natural Language Processing (ANLP-97)*, Washington, DC, USA, pp. 159–165.

Bernth, Arendse (1998). "EasyEnglish: Preprocessing for MT." *Proceedings of the 2nd International Workshop on Controlled Language Applications*, Carnegie-Mellon University, Pittsburgh, USA, pp. 30–41.

Bernth, Arendse (1999). *Tools for Improving E-G MT Quality*. Yorktown Heights: IBM T. J. Watson Research Center.

Gdaniec, Claudia and Patricia Schmid (1995). "Constituent Shifts in the Logos English-German System." *Proceedings of the 6th International Conference on Theoretical and Methodological Issues in Machine Translation* (*TMI-95*), Leuven, Belgium, pp. 311–318.

Gdaniec, Claudia (1998). "Lexical Choice and Syntactic Generation in a Translation System: Transformations in the New LMT English-German System." In David L. Farwell, Laurie Gerber, and Eduard Hovy, eds., *Machine Translation and the Information Soup*. Berlin: Springer Verlag, pp. 408–420.

Liu, Jocelyn and Joseph Liro (1987). "The METAL English-to-German System: First Progress Report." *Computers and Translation*, Vol. 2, No. 4, pp. 205–218.

Samuelsdorf, P. O. (1977). "Relation of Machine Translation to Linguistics Exemplified by an English-German Translation Project." *Proceedings of the 3rd International Conference on Computers in the Humanities*, Waterloo, Ontario, Canada.

English-Hindi

Chatterjee, Niladri, Shailly Goyal, and Anjali Naithani (2005). "Resolving Pattern Ambiguity for English to Hindi Machine Translation Using WordNet." In Walther van Hahn, W. John Hutchins, and Cristina Vertan, eds., *Proceedings of the International Workshop on Modern Approaches in Translation Technologies*, Borovets, Bulgaria.

Ganeshsundaram, P. C. (1978). "Automatic Translation from English into Hindi Using the PCG-Theory and a Scheme of Pre-editing." *Proceedings of the Conference of the International Association of Applied Linguistics* (*AILA-78*), Montreal, Canada.

Gupta, Deepa and Niladri Chatterjee (2003). "Divergence in English to Hindi Translation: Some Studies." *International Journal of Translation*, Vol. 15, No. 2, pp. 5–24.

Rao, Durgesh, Kavita Mohanraj, Jayprakash Hegde, Vivek Mehta, and Parag Mahadane (2000). "A Practical Framework for Syntactic Transfer of Compound-complex Sentences for English-Hindi Machine Translation." *Proceedings of the International Conference on Knowledge Based Computer Systems* (*KBCS-2000*), Mumbai, India, pp. 343–354.

Sinha, R. Mahesh K. and Ajai Jain (2003). "AnglaHindi: An English to

Hindi Machine-aided Translation System." *Proceedings of MT Summit IX*, New Orleans, Louisiana, USA.
Sinha, R. Mahesh K. and Anil Thakur (2005). "Divergence Patterns in Machine Translation between Hindi and English." *Proceedings of MT Summit X*, Phuket, Thailand.
Sinha, R. Mahesh K. and Anil Thakur (2005). "Translation Divergence in English-Hindi MT." *Proceedings of the 10th Workshop of the European Association for Machine Translation: Practical Applications of Machine Translation*, Budapest, Hungary, pp. 245–254.

English-Indian

Bandyopadhyay, Sivaji (2001). "An Example Based MT System in News Items Domain from English to Indian Languages." *Machine Translation Review*, No. 12, pp. 7–10.

English-Italian

Bressan, Dino (1987). "Emphatic Devices in English-Italian Translation." *Multilingua*, Vol. 6, pp. 69–75.
Cavalli-Sforza, Violetta, Krzysztof Czuba, Teruko Mitamura, and Eric H. Nyberg (2000). "Challenges in Adapting an Interlingua for Bidirectional English-Italian Translation." In John S. White, ed., *Envisioning Machine Translation in the Information Future*. Berlin: Springer Verlag, pp. 169–178.

English-Japanese

Brockett, Chris, Takako Aikawa, Anthony Aue, Arul Menezes, Chris Quirk, and Hisami Suzuki (2002). "English-Japanese Example-based Machine Translation Using Abstract Linguistic Representation." *Proceedings of the Workshop on Machine Translation in Asia (COLING-2002),* Taipei, Taiwan.
Darwin, Maki (2001). "Trial and Error: An Evaluation Project on Japanese↔English MT Output Quality." In Bente Maegaard, ed., *Proceedings of MT Summit VIII: Machine Translation in the Information Age*, Santiago de Compostela, Spain.
Matsubara, Shigeki and Yasuyoshi Inagaki (1997). "Utilizing Extra-

grammatical Phenomena in Incremental English-Japanese Machine Translation." *Proceedings of the 7th International Conference on Theoretical and Methodological Issues in Machine Translation* (*TMI-97*), St. John's College, Santa Fe, New Mexico, USA.

Nagao, Makoto, Jun-ichi Tsujii, Koyi Yada, and Toshihiro Kakimoto (1982). "An English-Japanese Machine Translation System for the Titles of Scientific and Engineering Papers." In Jan Horecky, ed., *Proceedings of the 9th International Conference on Computational Linguistics* (*COLING-82*), Prague, the Czech Republic. Amsterdam: North-Holland Publishing Company, pp. 245–252.

Narita, Masumi (2000). "A Corpus-based English Language Assistant to Japanese Software Engineers." *Proceedings of the International Conference on Machine Translation and Multilingual Applications in the New Millenium* (*MT-2000*), University of Exeter, England.

Nishida, Fujio, Shinobu Takamatsu, and Hiroaki Kuroki (1980). "English-Japanese Translation through Case-structure Conversion." *Proceedings of the 8th International Conference on Computational Linguistics* (*COLING-80*), Tokyo, Japan, pp. 447–454.

Nishida, Toyoaki and Shuji Doshita (1982). "An English-Japanese Machine Translation System Based on Formal Semantics of Natural Language." In Jan Horecky, ed., *Proceedings of the 9th International Conference on Computational Linguistics* (*COLING-82*), Prague, the Czech Republic. Amsterdam: North-Holland Publishing Company, pp. 277–282.

Nishida, Toyoaki and Shuji Doshita (1983). "An Application of Montague Grammar to English-Japanese Machine Translation." *Proceedings of the ACL-NRL Conference on Applied Natural Language Processing*, Santa Monica, California, USA, pp. 156–165.

Nitta, Yoshihiko, Atsushi Okajima, Fumiyuki Yamano, and Koichiro Ishihara (1982). "A Heuristic Approach to English-into-Japanese Machine Translation." In Jan Horecky, ed., *Proceedings of the 9th International Conference on Computational Linguistics* (*COLING-82*), Prague, the Czech Republic. Amsterdam: North-Holland Publishing Company, pp. 283–288.

Richards, John (1994). "LOGOVISTA E to J." *Proceedings of the 1st Conference of the Association for Machine Translation in the Americas: Technology Partnerships for Crossing the Language Barrier* (*AMTA-1*), Columbia, Maryland, USA, pp. 238–239.

Ryu, Koichiro, Shigeki Matsubara, and Yasuyoshi Inagaki (2006). "Simultaneous English-Japanese Spoken Language Translation Based on Incremental Dependency Parsing and Transfer." *Proceedings of the Joint Conference of the International Committee on Computational Linguistics and the Association for Computational Linguistics* (*COLING/ACL-2006*), Sydney, Australia.

Sugita, Shigeharu (1973). "Mechanical Translation between English and Japanese." In S. Gould, ed., *Proceedings of the 1st International Symposium on Computers and the Chinese Input/Output Systems*. Taipei: Academia Sinica, pp. 555–572.

Takahashi, Shigeru, Hiroshi Wada, Ryouchi Tadenuma, and S. Watanabe (1959). "English-Japanese Machine Translation." In *Information Processing 1959: Proceedings of the International Conference on Information Processing*, Paris. London: Butterworths, pp. 194–199.

Tsujii, Jun-ichi (1982). "The Transfer Phase in an English-Japanese Translation System." In Jan Horecky, ed., *Proceedings of the 9th International Conference on Computational Linguistics* (*COLING-82*), Prague, the Czech Republic. Amsterdam: North-Holland Publishing Company, pp. 383–390.

English-Korean

Choi, Sung-Kwon, Han-Min Jung, Chul-Min Sim, Taewan Kim, Dong-In Park, Jun-Sik Park, and Key-Sun Choi (1998). "Hybrid Approaches to Improvement of Translation Quality in Web-based English-Korean Machine Translation." *Proceedings of the 36th Annual Meeting of the Association for Computational Linguistics and 17th International Conference on Computational Linguistics* (*COLING-ACL-98*), Montreal, Quebec, Canada, pp. 251–255.

Choi, Sung-Kwon, Taewan Kim, Sanghwa Yuh, Han-Min Jung, Chul-Min Sim, and Sang-Kyu Park (1999). "English-to Korean Web Translator: 'From To/Web-EK'." *Proceedings of MT Summit VII: MT in the Great Translation Era*, Singapore.

Jung, Han-Min, Hee-Kwan Koo, Won-Kyung Sung, and Dong-In Park (2006). "Clustering of English-Korean Translation Word Pairs Using Bi-grams." In Alexander F. Gelbukh, ed., *Advances in Natural Language Processing*, Special Issue of *Research in Computing Science*, No. 18, pp. 15–26.

Kim, Seonho, Juntae Yoon, and Mansuk Song (2001). "Improving Lexical Mapping Model of English-Korean Bitext Using Structural Features." *Proceedings of the 2001 Conference on Empirical Methods in Natural Language Processing* (*EMNLP-2001*), Carnegie Mellon University, Pittsburgh, PA, USA.

Kim, Yuseop and Yung Taek Kim (1998). "Semantic Implementation Based on Extended Idiom for English to Korean Machine Translation." *The Asia-Pacific Association for Machine Translation Journal*, Vol. 21, pp. 23–39.

Kim, Yu Seop, Sung Dong Kim, Seong Bae Park, Jong Woo Lee, Jeong Ho Chang, Kyu Baek Hwang, Jang Min O, and Yung Taek Kim (2000). "Machine Translation Systems: E-K, K-E, J-K, K-J." In John S. White, ed., *Envisioning Machine Translation in the Information Future*. Berlin: Springer Verlag, pp. 248–251.

Koh, Sungryong, Jinee Maeng, Lee Ji-Young, Chae Young-Sook, and Choi Key-Sun (2001). "A Test Suite for Evaluation of English-to-Korean Machine Translation Systems." In Bente Maegaard, ed., *Proceedings of MT Summit VIII: Machine Translation in the Information Age*, Santiago de Compostela, Spain.

Lee, C. (1987). "Machine Translation: English-Korean." In Ilah Fleming, ed., *Proceedings of the 13th LACUS Forum 1986*. Lake Bluff, Illinois: Linguistic Association of Canada and the United States, pp. 410–416.

Lee, Hyun-Ah, Jun-Tae Yoon, and Gil-Chang Kim (2004). "Exploiting a Mono-bilingual Dictionary for English-Korean Translation Selection and Sense Disambiguation." *Proceedings of the 5th International Conference on Intelligent Text Processing and Computational Linguistics* (*CICLing-2004*), Chung-Ang University, Seoul, Korea, pp. 318–329.

Lin, Dekang, Bonnie J. Dorr, Jye-Hoon Lee, and Sungki Suh (1994). "A Parameter-based Message-passing Parser for MT of Korean and English." *Proceedings of the 1st Conference of the Association for Machine Translation in the Americas: Technology Partnerships for Crossing the Language Barrier* (*AMTA-1*), Columbia, Maryland, USA, pp. 149–156.

Roh, Yoon-Hyung, Munpyo Hong, Sung-Kwon Choi, Ki-Young Lee, and Sang-Kyu Park (2003). "For the Proper Treatment of Long Sentences in a Sentence Pattern-based English-Korean MT System." *Proceedings of MT Summit IX*, New Orleans, Louisiana, USA.

Seo, Young-Ae, Yoon-Hyung Roh, Ki-Young Lee, and Sung-Kwon Choi (2001). "Caption Eye/EK: An English-to-Korean Caption Translation System Using the Sentence Pattern." In Bente Maegaard, ed., *Proceedings of MT Summit VIII: Machine Translation in the Information Age*, Santiago de Compostella, Spain.

Weinstein, Clifford, Young-Suk Lee, Stephanie Seneff, Dinesh Tummala, Beth Carlson, John T. Lynch, Jung-Taik Hwang, and Linda Kukolich (1997). "Automated English-Korean Translation for Enhanced Coalition Communications." *The Lincoln Laboratory Journal*, Vol. 10, pp. 35–60.

English-Malay

Tong, Loong-Cheong (1986). "English-Malay Translation System: A Laboratory Prototype." *Proceedings of the 11th International Conference on Computational Linguistics (COLING-86)*, Bonn, Germany, pp. 638–642.

English-Persian

Eman, H. and D. Clarke (1984). "Machine Translation of English into Persian." *Proceedings of the International Conference on the Methodology and Techniques of Machine Translation*, Cranfield Institute of Technology, Cranfield, England.

English-Polish

Gawronska, Barbara, Björn Erlendsson, and Hanna Duczak (2002). "Extracting Semantic Classes and Morphosyntactic Features for English-Polish Machine Translation." *Proceedings of the 9th International Conference on Theoretical and Methodological Issues in Machine Translation (TMI-2002)*, Keihanna, Japan, pp. 63–73.

Krzysztof, Jassem (2004). "Applying Oxford-PWN English-Polish Dictionary to Machine Translation." *Proceedings of the 9th Workshop of the European Association for Machine Translation: Broadening Horizons of Machine Translation and Its Applications*, Foundation for International Studies, Malta, pp. 98–105.

Kupść, Anna (2003). "Two Approaches to Aspect Assignment in an

English-Polish Machine Translation System." *Proceedings of the 7th Workshop of the European Association for Machine Translation: Improving Machine Translation through Other Language Technology Tools: Resources and Tools for Building MT*, Budapest, Hungary, pp. 17–24.

Styś, Malgorzata E. and Stefan S. Zemke (1997). "Incorporating Discourse Aspects in English-Polish MT." In Ruslan Mitkov and Nicolas Nicolov, eds., *Recent Advances in Natural Language Processing*. Amsterdam: John Benjamins Publishing Company, pp. 213–223.

English-Russian

Blekhman, Michael S., Andrei Jursin, and Marina Bezhanova (2000). "Computer-assisted Russian↔English Dictionary." *International Journal of Translation*, Vol. 12, Nos. 1–2, pp. 61–70.

English-Spanish

Bezhanova, Olga (2003). "Analysis of the Translation Quality of the WordMagic English↔Spanish Interpreter Professional." *International Journal of Translation*, Vol. 15, No. 1, pp. 71–79.

Cressey, William W. (1987). "Review Article: Project for Integrated Development of English-Spanish Machine Translation." *Computers and Translation*, Vol. 2, No. 1, pp. 45–53.

Decker, Nan (2000). "The LogoVista ES Translation System." In John S. White, ed., *Envisioning Machine Translation in the Information Future*. Berlin: Springer Verlag, pp. 209–212.

de Gregorio-Godeo, Eduardo and Silvia Molina-Plaza (2006). "Exploring the Culture-technology Interface in the Design of Translation Tools: Creating an English-Spanish/Spanish-English Dictionary of Phaseological Units." *Proceedings of the 6th Portsmouth Translation Conference: Translation Technologies and Culture,* School of Languages and Area Studies, University of Portsmouth, England.

Leon, Marjorie (1984). "Development of English-Spanish Machine Translation." *Proceedings of the International Seminar on Machine Translation*, Cranfield Institute of Technology, Cranfield, England.

Leon, Marjorie and Lee Ann Schwartz (1986). *Integrated Development of English-Spanish Machine Translation: From Pilot to Full*

Operational Capability. Washington, DC: Pan American Health Organization.
Mantica, Ricardo Arguello (2003). "Inside a High Quality English-Spanish MT Engine." *International Journal of Translation*, Vol. 15, No. 1, pp. 43–70.
Mitamura, Teruko, Eric H. Nyberg, Enrique Torrejón, David Svoboda, and Kathryn Baker (2001). "Pronominal Anaphora Resolution in KANTOO English-to-Spanish Machine Translation System." In Bente Maegaard, ed., *Proceedings of MT Summit VIII: Machine Translation in the Information Age*, Santiago de Compostela, Spain.
Toole, Janine, Davide Turcato, Fred Popowich, Dan Fass, and Paul McFetridge (1998). "Time-constrained Machine Translation." In David L. Farwell, Laurie Gerber, and Eduard Hovy, eds., *Machine Translation and the Information Soup*. Berlin: Springer Verlag, pp. 103–112.

English-Swedish

Gambäck, Björn and Ivan Bretan (1994). "Complex Verb Transfer Phenomena in the SLT System." *Proceedings of the 1st Conference of the Association for Machine Translation in the Americas: Technology Partnerships for Crossing the Language Barrier* (*AMTA-1*), Columbia, Maryland, USA, pp. 89–96.

English-Thai

Boonkwan, Prachya and Asanee Kawtrakul (2002). "Plaesarn: Machine-aided Translation Tool for English-to-Thai." *Proceedings of the Workshop on Machine Translation in Asia* (*COLING-2002*), Taipei, Taiwan.
Kanchanawan, N. (1983). "Automatic Translation of English to Thai." *Proceedings of the 31st International Congress of Human Sciences in Asia and North Africa*, Tokyo-Kyoto, Japan.

English-Turkish

Hakkani, Dilek Zeynep, Gökhan Tür, Kemal Oflazer, Teruko Mitamura, and Eric H. Nyberg (1998). "An English-to-Turkish Interlingual MT

System." In David L. Farwell, Laurie Gerber, and Eduard Hovy, eds., *Machine Translation and the Information Soup*. Berlin: Springer Verlag, pp. 83–94.

Turhan, Cigdem K. (1997). "An English to Turkish Machine Translation System Using Structural Mapping." *Proceedings of the 5th Conference on Applied Natural Language Processing*, Washington, DC, USA, pp. 320–323.

English-Uyghur

Kadir, Polat, Koichi Yamada, and Hiroshi Kinukawa (2005). "Comparative Study on Japanese and Uyghur Grammars for an English-Uyghur Machine Translation System." *Proceedings of MT Summit X*, Phuket, Thailand.

English-Vietnamese

Dinh, Dien (2002). "Building a Training Corpus for Word Sense Disambiguation in English-to-Vietnamese Machine Translation." *Proceedings of the Workshop on Machine Translation in Asia (COLING-2002),* Taipei, Taiwan.

Dinh, Dien, Hoang Kiem, and Eduard Hovy (2003). "BTL: A Hybrid Model for English-Vietnamese Machine Translation." *Proceedings of MT Summit IX*, New Orleans, Louisiana, USA.

Dinh, Dien, Nguyen Luu Thuy Ngan, Do Xuan Quang, and Van Chi Nam (2003). "A Hybrid Approach to Word Order Transfer in English-to-Vietnamese Machine Translation." *Proceedings of MT Summit IX*, New Orleans, Louisiana, USA.

Dinh, Dien and Hoang Kiem (2003). "POS-Tagger for English Vietnamese Bilingual Corpus." *Proceedings of the Human Language Technology and North American Chapter of Association of Computational Linguistics 2003* (*HLT/NAACL-2003*), Edmonton, Alberta, Canada.

Finnish-English

Harri, Arnola, Kaarina Hyvönen, Jukka-Pekka Juntunen, Tim Linnanvirta, and Petteri Suoranta (1996). "KIELIKONE Finnish-English MT System *TRANSMART* in Practical Use." In *Translating and*

the Computer 18. London: The Association for Information Management.
Nuutila, Pertti (1996). "Roughlate Service for In-house Customers." In *Translating and the Computer 18*. London: The Association for Information Management.

Foreign Language-Chinese

Liu, Yunquan (1981). "The System of Intermediate Constituents in Machine Translation from Foreign Languages into Chinese." *Proceedings of the Conference on Chinese Language Use*, The Australian National University, Canberra, Australia.

French-Arabic

Alsharaf, Haytham, Sylviane Cardey, and Peter Greenfield (2004). "French to Arabic Machine Translation: The Specificity of Language Couples." *Proceedings of the 9th Workshop of the European Association for Machine Translation: Broadening Horizons of Machine Translation and Its Applications*, Foundation for International Studies, Malta, pp. 11–17.

French-English

Brown, Peter F., John Cocke, Stephen A. Della Pietra, Vincent J. Della Pietra, Fredrick Jelinek, Robert L. Mercer, and Paul S. Roossin (1988). "A Statistical Approach to French/English Translation." *Proceedings of the 2nd International Conference on Theoretical and Methodological Issues in Machine Translation of Natural Languages* (*TMI-88*), Carnegie Mellon University, Center for Machine Translation, Pittsburgh, Pennsylvania, USA.
LATSEC (1975). *Technical Proposal for Further Development of the SYSTRAN English-French Machine Translation System and Initial Development of the SYSTRAN French-English Translation System*. La Jolla, California: Latsec Incorporated.
Pinkham, Jessie, Monica Corston-Oliver, Martine Smets, and Mertine Pettenaro (2001). "Rapid Assembly of a Large-scale French-English MT System." In Bente Maegaard, ed., *Proceedings of MT Summit VIII:*

Machine Translation in the Information Age, Santiago de Compostela, Spain.

French-German

Biewer, Axel, Christian Feneyrol, Johannes Ritzke, and Ervin Stegentritt (1985) "ASCOF: A Modular Multilevel System for French-German Translation." *Computational Linguistics*, Vol. 11, Nos. 2–3, pp. 137–155.

French-Japanese

Robitaille, Xavier, Yasuhiro Sasaki, Masatsugu Tonoike, Satoshi Sato, and Takehito Utsuro (2006). "Compiling French-Japanese Terminologies from the Web." *Proceedings of the 11th Conference of the European Chapter of the Association for Computational Linguistics (EACL-2006)*, Trento, Italy.

French-Polish

Gajer, Mirosław (2002). "The Pattern-based French-to-Polish Machine Translation System." *Machine Translation Review*, No. 13, pp. 6–34.

German-English

Grasmick, Daniel and Chris Pyne(1997). "... To Boldly Go...." In *Translating and the Computer 19*. London: The Association for Information Management.

Lehmann, Winfred P., Rolf A. Stachowitz, and L. W. Tosh (1970). *Research in German-English Machine Translation on Syntactic Level*, 2 vols. Austin: Texas: Linguistics Research Center.

Lehmann, Winfred P. and Rolf A. Stachowitz (1973). *Development of German-English Machine Translation System.* Austin: Linguistics Research Centre, University of Texas.

Moore, G. W., U. N. Riede, R. A. Polacsek, R. E. Miller, and G. M. Hutchins (1986). "Automated Translation of German to English Medical Text." *American Journal of Medicine*, Vol. 81, pp. 103–111.

Tschira, Klaus E. (1985). "Looking Back at a Year of German-English MT with Logos." In Veronica Lawson, ed., *Tools for the Trade: Translating and the Computer 5*. London: The Association for Information Management, pp. 215–235.

German-French

Guilbaud, Jean-Phillippe (1984). "Principles and Results of a German to French MT System at Grenoble University (GETA)." *The Institute for the Study of Semantics and Cognition Tutorial on Machine Translation*, Lugano, Switzerland.

German-Russian

Melčuk, Igor A. and Leo Wanner (2001). "Towards a Lexicographic Approach to Lexical Transfer in Machine Translation (Illustrated by the German–Russian Language Pair)." *Machine Translation*, Vol. 16, No. 1, pp. 21–87.

Hebrew-English

Arad, Iris (1991). "BITS, A Hebrew-English Bibliographic Translation System." *Machine Translation*, Vol. 6, No. 4, pp. 247–263.

Hindi-Bengali

Chakraborty, Asit R., S. R. Kundu, and A. S. Raizada (1978). "An Experiment on Machine Translation from Hindi to Bengali (A Step towards a Translation Interlingua for Indian Languages)." *Journal of the Indian Scientific Translators Association*, Vol. 7, Nos. 3–4, pp. 38–52.

Chakraborty, Asit R., A. M. Arora, and Deepa Bhardwaj (1980). "The Post-positional Definite Article in Bengali and Its Semantic Interpretation for Hindi-Bengali Machine Translation." *Proceedings of the 10th Delhi Linguistic Association Conference*, University of Delhi, India.

Chakraborty, Asit R. and A. M. Arora (1982). "The Post-positional Definite Article in Bengali and Its Semantic Interpretation for Hindi-Bengali Machine Translation." *Journal of the Indian Scientific Translators Association*, Vol. 11, Nos. 1–2, pp. 15–34.

Hindi-English

Lavie, Alon, Stephen Vogel, Lori S. Levin, Eric Peterson, Katharina Probst, Ariadna Font Llitjós, Rachel Reynolds, Jaime G. Carbonell, and Richard Cohen (2003). "Experiments with a Hindi-to-English Transfer-based MT System under a Miserly Data Scenario." *ACM Transactions on Asian Language Information Processing* (*TALIP*), Vol. 2, No. 2.

Raina, Achla M., Amitabha Mukherjee, Pankaj Goyal, and Pushpraj Shukla (2004). "A Unified Computational Lexicon for Hindi-English Code-switching." *Proceedings of the International Conference on Natural Language Processing* (*ICON-2004*), International Institute of Information Technology, Hyderabad, India.

Sinha, R. Mahesh K. and Anil Thakur (2005). "Dealing with Replicative Words in Hindi for Machine Translation to English." *Proceedings of MT Summit X*, Phuket, Thailand.

Sinha, R. Mahesh K. and Anil Thakur (2005). "Divergence Patterns in Machine Translation between Hindi and English." *Proceedings of MT Summit X*, Phuket, Thailand.

Sinha, R. Mahesh K. and Anil Thakur (2005). "Handling *Ki* in Hindi for Hindi-English MT." *Proceedings of MT Summit X*, Phuket, Thailand.

Sinha, R. Mahesh K. and Anil Thakur (2005). "Machine Translation of Bilingual Hindi-English (Hinglish) Text." *Proceedings of MT Summit X*, Phuket, Thailand.

Italian-English

Gaspari, Federico (2006). "The Added Value of Free Online MT Services: Confidence Boosters for Linguistically-challenged Internet Users, a Case Study for the Language Pair Italian-English." *Proceedings of the 7th Biennial Conference of the Association for Machine Translation in the Americas* (*AMTA-2006*)*: Visions for the Future of Machine Translation*, Boston Marriott, Cambridge, MA, USA.

Italian-Greek

Antona, Margherita and Jun-ichi Tsujii (1993). "Treatment of Tense and Aspect in Translation from Italian to Greek—An Example of Treatment of Implicit Information in Knowledge-based Transfer MT."

Proceedings of the 5th International Conference on Theoretical and Methodological Issues in Machine Translation of Natural Languages: MT in the Next Generation (*TMI-93*), Kyoto, Japan, pp. 131–153.

Japanese-Chinese

Feng, Zhiwei (2002). "PAR-based Japanese-Chinese MT." In Yu Shiwen, ed., *Proceedings of the Second China-Japan Natural Language Processing Joint Research Promotion Conference* (*CJNLP-2002*). Beijing: Institute of Computational Linguistics, Peking University, pp. 104–117.

Hayashi, Minoru, Setsuo Yamada, Akira Kataoka, and Akio Yokoo (2001). "ALT-J/C A Prototype Japanese-to-Chinese Automatic Language Translation System." In Bente Maegaard, ed., *Proceedings of MT Summit VIII: Machine Translation in the Information Age*, Santiago de Compostela, Spain.

Hsieh, Miao-Ling 許妙玲 and June-Jei Kuo 郭俊桔 (1990). "A Cognitive Treatment of Aspect in Japanese to Chinese Machine Translation." *Proceedings of the Conference of the Association for Computational Linguistics and Chinese Language Processing* (*ROCLING-III*), Taipei, Taiwan.

Kuo, June-jei, Hsieh Mao-ling, and Wu Jia-kwang (1990). "Transfer Processing and Chinese Generation in Japanese-Chinese Machine Translation System." *Computer Processing of Chinese and Oriental Languages*, Vol. 5, No. 1, pp. 9–23.

Matsuda, Junichi and Hiroyuki Kumai (1999). "Transfer-based Japanese-Chinese Translation Implemented on an E-mail System." *Proceedings of MT Summit VII: MT in the Great Translation Era*, Singapore.

Tan, Chew Lim and Makoto Nagao (1995). "Automatic Alignment of Japanese-Chinese Bilingual Texts." *IEICE Transactions on Information and Systems*, E78-D.1, pp. 68–76.

Zhang, Jie and Chen Qunxiu (2002).〈日漢機器翻譯系統中的多Agent研究〉(Research on Multi-agent in MTS from Japanese to Chinese).《第一屆學生計算語言學研討會論文集》(*SWCL-2002: First Students' Workshop on Computational Linguistics: Proceedings*), Institute of Computational Linguistics, Peking University, Beijing, China, pp. 197–202.

Zhang, Ying (2006). "Chinese Adverb Processing in Japanese-to-Chinese Machine Translation." *Proceedings of the 6th Portsmouth Translation*

Conference: Translation Technologies and Culture, School of Languages and Area Studies, University of Portsmouth, England.

Zhang, Yujie and Ma Qing (2002). "Aiming at Developing a Japanese-Chinese Machine Translation System Capable of Self-learning and Self-organizing." In Yu Shiwen, ed., *Proceedings of the 2nd China-Japan Natural Language Processing Joint Research Promotion Conference* (*CJNLP-2002*). Beijing: Institute of Computational Linguistics, Peking University, pp. 118–122.

Zhang, Yujie, Ma Qing, and Hitoshi Isahara (2005). "A Multi-aligner for Japanese-Chinese Parallel Corpora." *Proceedings of MT Summit X*, Phuket, Thailand.

Zhang, Yujie, Kiyotaka Uchimoto, Ma Qing, and Hitoshi Isahara (2005). "Building an Annotated Japanese-Chinese Parallel Corpus—A Part of NICT Multilingual Corpora." *Proceedings of MT Summit X*, Phuket, Thailand.

Zhao, Xin, Ren Fuji, and Stefan Voß (2004). "A Super-function Based Japanese-Chinese Machine Translation System for Business Users." In Robert E. Frederking and Kathryn B. Taylors, eds., *Machine Translation: From Real Users to Research*. Berlin: Springer Verlag, pp. 272–281.

Japanese-English

Baldwin, Timothy and Takaaki Tanaka (2003). "Translation Selection for Japanese-English Noun-noun Compounds." *Proceedings of MT Summit IX*, New Orleans, Louisiana, USA.

Bond, Francis, Kentaro Ogura, and Satoru Ikehara (1994). "Countability and Number in Japanese to English Machine Translation." *Proceedings of the 15th International Conference on Computational Linguistics* (*COLING-94*), Kyoto, Japan, pp. 32–38.

Bond, Francis, Kentaro Ogura, and Tsukasa Kawaoka (1995). "Noun Phrase Reference in Japanese-to-English Machine Translation." *Proceedings of the 6th International Conference on Theoretical and Methodological Issues in Machine Translation* (*TMI-95*), Leuven, Belgium, pp. 1–14.

Bond, Francis, Kentaro Ogura, and Hajime Uchino (1997). "Temporal Expressions in Japanese-to-English Machine Translation." *Proceedings of the 7th International Conference on Theoretical and*

Methodological Issues in Machine Translation (*TMI-97*), St. John's College, Santa Fe, New Mexico, USA.

Bond, Francis and Kentaro Ogura (1998). "Reference in Japanese–English Machine Translation." *Machine Translation*, Vol. 13, Nos. 2–3, pp. 107–134.

Chen, Liang and Naoyuki Tokuda (1999). "A New Diagnostic System for J-E Translation ILTS By Global Matching Algorithm and POST Parser." *Proceedings of MT Summit VII: MT in the Great Translation Era*, Singapore.

Darwin, Maki (2001). "Trial and Error: An Evaluation Project on Japanese↔English MT Output Quality." In Bente Maegaard, ed., *Proceedings of MT Summit VIII: Machine Translation in the Information Age*, Santiago de Compostela, Spain.

Guo, Honglei, Jiang Jianmin, and Hu Gang (2001). 〈漢日韓英多語機譯系統的通用英語生成器〉 (Universal English Generator in Chinese-Japanese-Korean-English Multilingual MT System). In Huang Changning 黃昌寧 and Zhang Pu 張普, eds.,《自然語言理解與機器翻譯》 (*Natural Language Understanding and Machine Translation*). Beijing: Tsinghua University Press, pp. 332–337.

Hirakawa, Hideki, Hiroyasu Nogami, and Shinya Amano (1993). "EJ/JE Machine Translation System ASTRANSAC—Extensions toward Personalization." In Sergei Nirenburg, ed., *Progress in Machine Translation*. Amsterdam: IOS and Tokyo: Ohmsha, pp. 127–138.

Johnson, David E. and Hideo Watanabe (1991). "Relational-grammar-based Generation in the JETS Japanese-English Machine Translation System." *Machine Translation*, Vol. 6, No. 1, pp. 1–20.

Knight, Kevin, Yaser Al-Onaizan, Ishwar Chander, Eduard Hovy, Irene Langkilde, Richard Whitney, and Kenji Yamada (1996). "Japangloss: Using Statistics to Fill Knowledge Gaps in MT." *Proceedings of the 2nd Conference of the Association for Machine Translation in the Americas: Expanding MT Horizons* (*AMTA-2*), Montreal, Quebec, Canada, p. 256.

Kosaka, Michiko, Virginia Teller, and Ralph Grishman (1988). "A Sublanguage Approach to Japanese-English Machine Translation." In Dan Maxwell, Klaus Schubert, and Toon Witkam, eds., *New Directions in Machine Translation*. Dordrecht-Holland: Foris Publications, pp. 109–121.

Kuno, Susumu (1962). "A Preliminary Approach to Japanese-English

Automatic Translation." In National Physical Laboratory, ed., *1961 International Conference on Machine Translation of Languages and Applied Language Analysis: Proceedings of the Conference Held at the National Physical Laboratory, Teddington, Middlesex, on 5th, 6th, 7th and 8th September*. London: Her Majesty's Stationery Office, Vol. 1, pp. 8–23.

Murata, Masaki and Makoto Nagao (1993). "Determination of Referential Property and Number of Nouns in Japanese Sentences for Machine Translation into English." *Proceedings of the 5th International Conference on Theoretical and Methodological Issues in Machine Translation of Natural Languages: MT in the Next Generation* (*TMI-93*), Kyoto, Japan, pp. 218–225.

Murata, Masaki, Qing Ma, Kiyotaka Uchimoto, and Hitoshi Isahara (1999). "An Example-based Approach to Japanese-to-English Translation of Tense, Aspect, and Modality." *Proceedings of the 8th International Conference on Theoretical and Methodological Issues in Machine Translation* (*TMI-99*), Chester, England, pp. 66–76.

Murata, Masaki, Kiyotaka Uchimoto, Qing Ma, and Hitoshi Isahara (2001). "Using a Support-vector Machine for Japanese-to-English Translation of Tense, Aspect, and Modality." *Proceedings of the Association for Computational Linguistics 39th Annual Meeting and 10th Conference of the European Chapter: Data-driven Machine Translation* (*ACL-EACL-2001*), Toulouse, France, pp. 111–119.

Nagao, Makoto (1984). "A Framework of a Mechanical Translation between Japanese and English by Analogy Principle." In Alick Elithorn and Ranan Banerji, eds., *Artificial and Human Intelligence*. Amsterdam: North-Holland Publishing Company, pp. 173–180.

Nagao, Makoto, Jun-ichi Tsujii, K. Mitamura, Hideki Hirakawa, and Masako Kume (1980). "A Machine Translation System from Japanese into English: Another Perspective of MT Systems." *The 8th International Conference on Computational Linguistics* (*COLING-80*), Tokyo, Japan, pp. 414–423.

Nakaiwa, Hiromi (1999). "Automatic Extraction of Rules for Anaphora Resolution of Japanese Zero Pronouns in Japanese-English Machine Translation from Aligned Sentence Pairs." *Machine Translation*, Vol. 19, Nos. 3–4, pp. 247–279.

Nirenburg, Sergei, Constantino Domashnev, and Dean J. Grannes (1993). "Two Approaches to Matching in Example-based Machine

Translation." *Proceedings of the 5th International Conference on Theoretical and Methodological Issues in Machine Translation of Natural Languages: MT in the Next Generation* (*TMI-93*), Kyoto, Japan, pp. 47–57.

Nishida, Fujio and Shinobu Takamatsu (1982). "Japanese-English Translation through Internal Expressions." In Jan Horecky, ed., *Proceedings of the 9th International Conference on Computational Linguistics* (*COLING-82*), Prague, the Czech Republic. Amsterdam: North-Holland Publishing Company, pp. 271–276.

Ogura, Kentaro, Satoshi Shirai, and Francis Bond (2003). "English Adverb Processing in Japanese-to-English Machine Translation." *Proceedings of the 7th International Conference on Theoretical and Methodological Issues in Machine Translation* (*TMI-97*), St. John's College, Santa Fe, New Mexico, USA.

O'Neill-Brown, Patricia (1996). "JICST Japanese-English Machine Translation System." *Proceedings of the 2nd Conference of the Association for Machine Translation in the Americas: Expanding MT Horizons* (*AMTA-2*), Montreal, Quebec, Canada, pp. 257–260.

Sakai, T., Shigeharu Sugita, and A. Watanabe (1970). "Mechanical Translation from Japanese into English." *Information Processing in Japan*, Vol. 10, pp. 32–39.

Sakamoto, Yoshiyuki and T. Shino (1987). "Japanese-English Machine Translation System 'PENSEE'." *Oki Technical Review*, Vol. 126, pp. 9–14.

Shirai, Satoshi, Satoru Ikehara, and Tsukasa Kawaoka (1993). "Effects of Automatic Rewriting of Source Language within a Japanese to English MT System." *Proceedings of the 5th International Conference on Theoretical and Methodological Issues in Machine Translation of Natural Languages: MT in the Next Generation* (*TMI-93*), Kyoto, Japan, pp. 226–239.

Shirai, Satoshi, Yamamoto Kazuhide, and Francis Bond (2001). "Japanese-English Paraphrase Corpus." *Proceedings of the 6th Natural Language Processing Pacific Rim Symposium*, National Center of Sciences, Tokyo, Japan, pp. 23–30.

Shudo, Kosho (1973). "On Machine Translation from Japanese into English for a Technical Field." *Journal of Information Processing Society of Japan*, Vol. 14, No. 9, pp. 44–50.

Sugita, Shigeharu (1973). "Mechanical Translation between English and

Japanese." In S. Gould, ed., *Proceedings of the 1st International Symposium on Computers and the Chinese Input/Output Systems*. Taipei: Academia Sinica, pp. 555–572.

Teller, Virginia, Michiko Kosaka, and Ralph Grishman (1988). "A Comparative Study of Japanese and English Sublanguage Patterns." *Proceedings of the 2nd International Conference on Theoretical and Methodological Issues in Machine Translation of Natural Languages* (*TMI-88*), Carnegie Mellon University, Center for Machine Translation, Pittsburgh, Pennsylvania, USA.

Uchida, Hiroshi and Kenji Sugiyama (1980). "A Machine Translation System from Japanese into English Based on Conceptual Structure." *The 8th International Conference on Computational Linguistics* (*COLING-80*), Tokyo, Japan, pp. 455–462.

Uchino, Hajime, Yoshifumi Ooyama, and Osamu Furuse (1999). "ALTFLASH: A Japanese-to-English Machine Translation System for Market Flash Reports." *Proceedings of MT Summit VII: MT in the Great Translation Era*, Singapore.

Japanese-French

Hubert, Jérôme, J. Ibuki, Masako Kume, and Makoto Nagao (1983). "A System of Japanese-French Automatic Translation for Paper Titles." *Proceedings of the 26th Annual Convention of the Information Processing Society of Japan*, Tokyo, Japan.

Japanese-German

Hanakata, Kenji, A. Lesniewski, and Shoichi Yokoyama (1986). "Semantic-based Generation of Japanese-German Translation System." *Proceedings of the 11th International Conference on Computational Linguistics* (*COLING-86*), Bonn, Germany, pp. 560–562.

Laubsch, Joachim, Dietmar F. Roesner, Kenji Hanakata, and A. Lesniewski (1984). "Language Generation from Conceptual Structure: Synthesis of German in a Japanese/German MT Project." *Proceedings of the 10th International Conference on Computational Linguistics* (*COLING-84*), Stanford University, Stanford, CA, USA, pp. 491–494.

Seligman, Mark, Masami Suzuki, and Tsuyoshi Morimoto (1993). *Semantic-level Transfer in Japanese-German Speech Translation: Some Experiences*. Technical Report NLC93-13, Institute of Electronics, Information, and Communication Engineers (IEICE), Japan.

Japanese-Korean

Kim, EunJa and Jong-Hyeok Lee (1993). "A Collocation-based Transfer Model for Japanese-to-Korean Machine Translation." *Proceedings of the Natural Language Processing Pacific Rim Symposium* (*NLPRS-93*), Fukuoka, Japan, pp. 223–231.

Kim, Yu Seop, Sung Dong Kim, Seong Bae Park, Jong Woo Lee, Jeong Ho Chang, Kyu Baek Hwang, Jang Min O, and Yung Taek Kim (2000). "Machine Translation Systems: E-K, K-E, J-K, K-J." In John S. White, ed., *Envisioning Machine Translation in the Information Future*. Berlin: Springer Verlag, pp. 248–251.

Japanese-Malay

Bond, Francis, Ruhaida Binti Sulong, Takefumi Yamazaki, and Kentaro Ogura (2001). "Design and Construction of a Machine-tractable Japanese-Malay Dictionary." *Proceedings of TM Summit VIII*, Santiago de Compostela, Spain, pp. 53–58.

Ogura, Kentaro, Francis Bond, and Yoshifumi Ooyama (1999). "ALT-J/M A Prototype Japanese-to-Malay Translation System." *Proceedings of MT Summit VII: MT in the Great Translation Era*, Singapore, pp. 444–448.

Japanese-Uighur

Mahsut, Muhtar, Yasuhiro Ogawa, Kazue Sugino, and Yasuyoshi Inagaki (2001). "Utilizing Agglutinative Features Japanese-Uighur Machine Translation." In Bente Maegaard, ed., *Proceedings of MT Summit VIII: Machine Translation in the Information Age*, Santiago de Compostela, Spain.

Mahsut, Muhtar, Yasuhiro Ogawa, Kazue Sugino, Katsuhiko Toyama, and Yasuyoshi Inagaki (2004). "An Experiment on Japanese-Uighur

Machine Translation and Its Evaluation." In Robert E. Frederking and Kathryn B. Taylors, eds., *Machine Translation: From Real Users to Research*. Berlin: Springer Verlag, pp. 208–216.

Korean-Chinese

Kim, Changhyun, Munpyo Hong, Yinxia Huang, Young Kil Kim, Sung Il Yang, Young Ae Seo, and Sung-Kwon Choi (2002). "Korean-Chinese Machine Translation Based on Verb Patterns." In Stephen D. Richardson, ed., *Machine Translation: From Research to Real Users*. Berlin and New York: Springer Verlag, pp. 94–103.

Korean-English

Egedi, Dania, Martha Palmer, Hyun S. Park, and Aravind K. Joshi (1994). "Korean to English Translation Using Synchronous TAGs." *Proceedings of the 1st Conference of the Association for Machine Translation in the Americas: Technology Partnerships for Crossing the Language Barrier* (*AMTA-1*), Columbia, Maryland, USA, pp. 48–55.

Guo, Honglei, Jiang Jianmin, and Hu Gang (2001). 〈漢日韓英多語機譯系統的通用英語生成器〉 (Universal English Generator in Chinese-Japanese-Korean-English Multilingual MT System). In Huang Changning 黃昌寧 and Zhang Pu 張普, eds., 《自然語言理解與機器翻譯》 (*Natural Language Understanding and Machine Translation*). Beijing: Tsinghua University Press, pp. 332–337.

Han, Chung-hye, Benoit Lavoie, Martha Palmer, Owen Rambow, Richard I. Kittredge, Tanya Korelsky, Nari Kim, and Myunghee Kim (2000). "Handling Structural Divergences and Recovering Dropped Arguments in a Korean/English Machine Translation System." In John S. White, ed., *Envisioning Machine Translation in the Information Future*. Berlin: Springer Verlag, pp. 40–53.

Hong, Munpyo (1998). "Multiple-subject Constructions in the Multilingual MT-System CAT2." In David L. Farwell, Laurie Gerber, and Eduard Hovy, eds., *Machine Translation and the Information Soup*. Berlin: Springer Verlag, pp. 174–186.

Hong, Munpyo, Young-Gil Kim, Chang-Hyun Kim, Seong-Il Yang, Young-Ae Seo, Cheol Ryu, and Sang-Kyu Park (2005). "Customizing

a Korean-English MT System for Patent Translation." *Proceedings of MT Summit X*, Phuket, Thailand.
Kim, Jung-jae, Key-Sun Choi, and Young-Soog Chae (2000). "Phrase-pattern-based Korean to English Machine Translation Using Two Level Translation Pattern Selection." *Proceedings of the 38th Annual Meeting of the Association for Computational Linguistics (ACL-2000)*, Hong Kong.
Kim, Nari and Yung Taek Kim (1994). "Determining Target Expression Using Parameterized Collocations from Corpus in Korean-English Machine Translation." *Proceedings of the Pacific Rim International Conference on Artificial Intelligence*, Beijing, China, pp. 732–736.
Kim, Yu Seop, Sung Dong Kim, Seong Bae Park, Jong Woo Lee, Jeong Ho Chang, Kyu Baek Hwang, Jang Min O, and Yung Taek Kim (2000). "Machine Translation Systems: E-K, K-E, J-K, K-J." In John S. White, ed., *Envisioning Machine Translation in the Information Future*. Berlin: Springer Verlag, pp. 248–251.
Lavoie, Benoit, Michael White, and Tanya Korelsky (2002). "Learning Domain-specific Transfer Rules: An Experiment with Korean to English Translation." *Proceedings of the Workshop on Machine Translation in Asia (COLING-2002),* Taipei, Taiwan.
Lee, Young-Suk, Wu Sok Yi, Stephanie Seneff, and Clifford Weinstein (2001). "Interlingua-based Broad-coverage Korean-to-English Translation in CCLINC." *Proceedings of Human Language Technology 2001 Conference*, San Diego, CA, USA.
Lee, Young-Suk (2001). "Interlingua-based Open Domain Machine Translation: A Case Study from Korean-to-English Translation." MS-15178, MIT Lincoln Laboratory.
Lin, Dekang, Bonnie J. Dorr, Jye-hoon Lee, and Sungki Suh (1994). "A Parameter-based Message-passing Parser for MT of Korean and English." *Proceedings of the 1st Conference of the Association for Machine Translation in the Americas: Technology Partnerships for Crossing the Language Barrier (AMTA-1)*, Columbia, Maryland, USA, pp. 149–156.
Park, Seong-Bae and Jeong-Woo Son (2005). "Augmentation of Modality Translation Rules in Korean-to-English Machine Translation by Rule Learning." *Proceedings of MT Summit X*, Phuket, Thailand.
Ryu, Byong-Rae, Kim Youngkil, Yuh Sanghwa, and Park Sangkyu (1999). "From To K/E: A Korean-English Machine Translation System Based

on Idiom Recognition and Fail Softening." *Proceedings of MT Summit VII: MT in the Great Translation Era*, Singapore.

Korean-French

Cardey, Sylviane, Peter Greenfield, and M. S. Hong (2003). "The TACT Machine Translation System: Problems and Solutions for the Pair Korean-French." *Translation Quarterly*, No. 27, pp. 22–44.

Korean-German

Hong, Munpyo (1998). "Multiple-subject Constructions in the Multilingual MT-System CAT2." In David L. Farwell, Laurie Gerber, and Eduard Hovy, eds., *Machine Translation and the Information Soup*. Berlin: Springer Verlag, pp. 174–186.

Korean-Japanese

Chung, Hee Sung (1988). "A Principle-based Korean/Japanese Machine Translation System: NARA." *Proceedings of the 2nd International Conference on Theoretical and Methodological Issues in Machine Translation of Natural Languages* (*TMI-88*), Carnegie Mellon University, Center for Machine Translation, Pittsburgh, Pennsylvania, USA.

Chung, You-Jin, Sin-Jae Kang, Kyong-Hi Moon, and Jong-Hyeok Lee (2002). "Word Sense Disambiguation in a Korean-to-Japanese MT System Using Neural Networks." *Proceedings of the Workshop on Machine Translation in Asia* (*COLING-2002*), Taipei, Taiwan.

Kim, Yu Seop, Sung Dong Kim, Seong Bae Park, Jong Woo Lee, Jeong Ho Chang, Kyu Baek Hwang, Jang Min O, and Yung Taek Kim (2000). "Machine Translation Systems: E-K, K-E, J-K, K-J." In John S. White, ed., *Envisioning Machine Translation in the Information Future*. Berlin: Springer Verlag, pp. 248–251.

Latin-English

Bowden, Paul R. (2001). "Latin to English Machine Translation—A Direct Approach." *Machine Translation Review*, No. 12, pp. 6–12.

Whitaker, William A. and John F. White (2003). "Blitz Latin—A Machine Translator for Latin to English." *Machine Translation Review*, No. 14, pp. 17–28.

Polish-English

Jassem, Krzysztof, Maciej Lison, Filip Graliński, and Boguslaw Rutkowski (1998). "A Polish-to-English Electronic Dictionary Designed for the Purposes of MT." *Proceedings of the 10th European Summer School on Logic, Linguistics and Information: Workshop on Machine Translation*, Saarbrücken, Germany.

Jassem, Krzysztof, Filip Graliński, and Grzegorz Krynicki (2000). "POLENG—Adjusting a Rule-based Polish-English Machine Translation System by Means of Corpus Analysis." *Proceedings of the 5th Workshop of the European Association for Machine Translation: Harvesting Existing Resources*, Lubljana, Slovenia.

Portuguese-Chinese

Li, Yiping, Pun Chiman, and Wu Fei (1999). "Portuguese-Chinese Machine Translation in Macao." *Proceedings of MT Summit VII: MT in the Great Translation Era*, Singapore, pp. 236–243.

Portuguese-English

Maia, Belinda (1998). "Word Order and the First Person Singular in Portuguese and English." *Meta*, Vol. 43, No. 4, pp. 589–601.

Russian-Chinese

Gao, Zushun (1959). "Successful Accomplishment of the First Experiment in MT from Russian into Chinese." 《中國語文》 (*The Chinese Language*), Vol. 11, p. 550.

Liu, Yongquan (1959). "Problems of Word Order and Its Resolution in Machine Translation from Russian into Chinese." 《語文研究》 (*Language Studies*), No. 4, pp. 105–114.

Liu, Yongquan (1989). "Problems of Word Order in Russian-Chinese Machine Translation and Methods to Their Solution." *Selected Papers of Applied Linguistics*. Beijing: The Commercial Press, pp. 40–54.

Zhang, Guiping 張桂平, Fan Yongming 范永明, Xu Lijun 徐立軍, and Lu Jianfeng 呂建峰 (1999).〈俄語輔助閱讀系統的詞法規則設計〉(The Design of a Russian Computer-aided Reading System's Lexical Rules). In Huang Changning 黃昌寧 and Dong Zhendong 董振東, eds.,《計算機語言學文集》(*Essays on Computational Linguistics*). Beijing: Tsinghua University Press, pp. 347–352.

Zhang, Xinhong 張心紅, Li Xiangdong 李向東, Zhang Lei 張蕾, and Shang Sho 閃爍 (1999).〈俄漢機器翻譯系統中基於多知識交叉分析的俄語詞法分析〉(Russian Morphological Analysis Based on Multiknowledge Alternate Processing [Map] in Russian-Chinese Machine Translation System). In Huang Changning and Dong Zhendong, eds.,《計算機語言學文集》(*Essays on Computational Linguistics*). Beijing: Tsinghua University Press, pp. 293–298.

Russian-English

Blekhman, Michael S., Andrei Jursin, and Marina Bezhanova (2000). "Computer-assisted Russian↔English Dictionary." *International Journal of Translation*, Vol. 12, Nos. 1–2, pp. 61–70.

Boguslavsky, Igor (1995). "A Bi-directional Russian-to-English Machine Translation System (ETAP-3)." *Proceedings of MT Summit V: Machine Translation Conference, Exhibition and Tutorial*, Luxembourg.

Bostad, Dale (1982). "Quality Control Procedures in Modification of the Air Force Russian-English MT System." In Veronica Lawson, ed., *Practical Experience of Machine Translation*. Amsterdam: North-Holland Publishing Company, pp. 129–133.

Garvin, Paul L. (1958). *Research in Machine Translation from Russian to English: Fulcrum Approach*. Seminar Work Paper MT-73. Group II, Georgetown University.

Janiotis, Amelia and Harry H. Josselson (1962). "Multiple Meaning in Machine Translation." In National Physical Laboratory, ed., *1961 International Conference on Machine Translation of Languages and Applied Language Analysis: Proceedings of the Conference Held at the National Physical Laboratory, Teddington, Middlesex, on 5th, 6th, 7th and 8th September*. London: Her Majesty's Stationery Office, Vol. 2, pp. 406–114.

Martins, Gary R. (1964). "Preliminary Report on the Insertion of English

Articles in Russian-English MT Output." *Mechanical Translation*, Vol. 8, No. 1, pp. 2–4.
Micklesen, Lew R. (1958). "Russian-English MT." *American Contributions to the 4th International Congress of Slavicists*, Moscow, Russia.
Oettinger, Anthony G. (1955). "The Design of an Automatic Russian-English Technical Dictionary." In William N. Locke and Andrew D. Booth, eds., *Machine Translation of Languages: Fourteen Essays*. Cambridge, MA: Technology Press of the Massachusetts Institute of Technology, pp. 47–65.
Summers, Lawrence (1962). "Machine Translation of Russian Organic Chemical Names into English by Analysis and Resynthesis of the Component Fragments." In National Physical Laboratory, ed., *1961 International Conference on Machine Translation of Languages and Applied Language Analysis: Proceedings of the Conference Held at the National Physical Laboratory, Teddington, Middlesex, on 5th, 6th, 7th and 8th September*. London: Her Majesty's Stationery Office, Vol. 1, pp. 266–277.
Zarechnak, Michael (1962). "A Fourth Level of Linguistic Analysis." In National Physical Laboratory, ed., 1961 *International Conference on Machine Translation of Languages and Applied Language Analysis: Proceedings of the Conference Held at the National Physical Laboratory, Teddington, Middlesex, on 5th, 6th, 7th and 8th September*. London: Her Majesty's Stationery Office, Vol. 1, pp. 160–171.

Russian-French

Boitet, Christian and Nedobejkine Nikolai (1980). "Russian-French at GETA: Outline of the Method and Detailed Example." *Proceedings of the 8th International Conference on Computational Linguistics (COLING-80)*, Tokyo, Japan.
Boitet, Christian and Nedobejkine Nikolai (1981). "Recent Developments in Russian-French Machine Translation at Grenoble." *Linguistics*, Vol. 19, pp. 199–271.

Russian-German

Geldbach, Stefanie (1999). "Anaphora and Translation Discrepancies

in Russian–German MT." *Machine Translation*, Vol. 19, Nos. 3–4, pp. 217–230.
Höser, Iris and Barbara Rüdiger (1994). "Russian—A Challenge to METAL? Some Difficulties of Russian-German Machine Translation." *Machine Translation—Ten Years On: Proceedings of the 2nd International Conference Organised by Cranfield University*, Cranfield, England.
Höser, Iris, Gerda Klimonow, Andreas Küstner, and Barbara Rüdiger (1995). "Metal Russian-German on the Way to a Product." In *Translating and the Computer 17*. London: The Association for Information Management.

Russian-Hungarian

Sipöczy, György (1964). "Some Semantic Aspects of the Machine Translation from Russian into Hungarian." *Computational Linguistics*, Vol. 2, pp. 159–177.

Russian-Tamil

Chellamuthu, K. C., K. Rangan, and K. C. Murugesan (1986). *Tamil University Machine Translation System (TUMTS), Russian-Tamil.* Thanjavur: Tamil University.

Slovenian-English

Erjavec, Tomaž (2000). "Slovene-English Datasets for MT." *Proceedings of the 5th Workshop of the European Association for Machine Translation: Harvesting Existing Resources*, Lubljana, Slovenia.
Gros, J. Zganec, A. Mihelic, M. Zganec, F. Mihelic, S. Dobrisek, J. Zibert, S. Vintar, T. Korosec, T. Erjavec, and M. Romih (2005). "Initial Considerations in Building a Speech-to-speech Translation System for the Slovenian-English Language Pair." *Proceedings of the 10th Annual Conference of the European Association for Machine Translation (EAMT-2005)*, Budapest, Hungary.
Vintar, Špela (2000). "Extracting Terms and Terminological Collocations from the ELAN Slovene-English Parallel Corpus." *Proceedings of the*

5th Workshop of the European Association for Machine Translation: Harvesting Existing Resources, Lubljana, Slovenia.

Spanish-Basque

Casillas, Arantza, Arantza Díaz de Illarraza, Jon Igartua, Raquel Martínez and Kepa Sarasola (2006). "Compilation and Structuring of a Spanish-Basque Parallel Corpus." *Proceedings of the 5th SALTMIL Workshop on Minority Languages and the 5th International Conference on Language Resources and Evaluation (LREC-2006): Strategies for Developing Machine Translation for Minority Languages*, Genoa, Italy, pp. 55–58.

Pérez, Alicia, Inés Torres, Francisco Casacuberta, and Víctor Guijarrubia (2006). "A Spanish-Basque Weather Forecast Corpus for Probabilistic Speech Translation." *Proceedings of the 5th SALTMIL Workshop on Minority Languages and the 5th International Conference on Language Resources and Evaluation (LREC-2006): Strategies for Developing Machine Translation for Minority Languages*, Genoa, Italy, pp. 99–102.

Spanish-Catalan

Alonso, Juan Alberto (2005). "Machine Translation for Catalan↔Spanish: The Real Case for Productive MT." *Proceedings of the 10th Workshop of the European Association for Machine Translation: Practical Applications of Machine Translation*, Budapest, Hungary, pp. 23–26.

Canals-Marote, Raül, Anna Esteve-Guillén, Alicia Garrido-Alenda, M. Isabel Guardiola-Savall, Amaia Iturraspe-Bellver, Sandra Montserrat-Buendía, Sergio Ortiz-Rojas, Herminia Pastor-Pina, Pedro M. Pérez-Antón, and Mikel L. Forcada (2001). "The Spanish-Catalan Machine Translation System InterNOSTRUM." In Bente Maegaard, ed., *Proceedings of MT Summit VIII: Machine Translation in the Information Age*, Santiago de Compostela, Spain.

González, Jorge, Antonio L. Lagarda, José R. Navarro, Laura Eliodoro, Adrià Giménez, Francisco Casacuberta, Joan M. de Val, and Ferran Fabregat (2006). "SisHiTra: A Spanish-to-Catalan Hybrid Machine Translation System." *Proceedings of the 5th SALTMIL Workshop on Minority Languages and the 5th International Conference on Language*

Resources and Evaluation (LREC-2006): Strategies for Developing Machine Translation for Minority Languages, Genoa, Italy, pp. 69–74.

Spanish-English

Aymerich, Julia (2001). "Generation of Noun-noun Compounds in the Spanish-English Machine Translation System SPANAM." In Bente Maegaard, ed., *Proceedings of MT Summit VIII: Machine Translation in the Information Age*, Santiago de Compostela, Spain.

Bezhanova, Olga (2003). "Analysis of the Translation Quality of the WordMagic English↔Spanish Interpreter Professional." *International Journal of Translation*, Vol. 15, No. 1, pp. 71–79.

de Gregorio-Godeo, Eduardo and Silvia Molina-Plaza (2006). "Exploring the Culture-technology Interface in the Design of Translation Tools: Creating an English-Spanish/Spanish-English Dictionary of Phaseological Units." *Proceedings of the 6th Portsmouth Translation Conference: Translation Technologies and Culture,* School of Languages and Area Studies, University of Portsmouth, England.

Gupta, Deepa and Marcello Federico (2006). "Exploiting Word Transformation in Statistical Machine Translation from Spanish to English." *Proceedings of the 11th Workshop of the European Association for Machine Translation: Machine Translation/Translation Aids—Tools to Increase Quality and to Save Money*, the University of Oslo, Oslo, Norway.

Habash, Nizar (2003). "Matador: A Large-scale Spanish-English GHMT System." *Proceedings of MT Summit IX*, New Orleans, Louisiana, USA.

Vasconcellos, Muriel (1987). "Post-editing On-screen: Machine Translation from Spanish into English." In Catriona Picken, ed., *Translating and the Computer 8: A Profession on the Move*. London: The Association for Information Management, pp. 133–146.

Spanish-Galician

Diz Gamallo, Inés (2001). "The Importance of MT for the Survival of Minority Languages: Spanish-Galician MT System." In Bente Maegaard, ed., *Proceedings of MT Summit VIII: Machine Translation in the Information Age*, Santiago de Compostela, Spain.

Swahili-English

Woodhouse, David (1968). "A Note on the Translation of Swahili into English." *Mechanical Translation*, Vol. 11, Nos. 3–4, pp. 75–77.

Thai-English

Modhiran, Teerapong, Krit Kosawat, Supon Klaithin, Monthika Boriboon, and Thepchai Supnithi (2005). "PARSIT-TE: Online Thai-English Machine Translation." *Proceedings of MT Summit X*, Phuket, Thailand.

Welsh-English

Jones, Dafydd and Andreas Eisele (2006). "Phrase-based Statistical Machine Translation between Welsh and English." *Proceedings of the 5th SALTMIL Workshop on Minority Languages and the 5th International Conference on Language Resources and Evaluation (LREC-2006): Strategies for Developing Machine Translation for Minority Languages*, Genoa, Italy, pp. 75–78.

❖ PART 20 ❖

Lexicography

Lexicography

Chen, Shu-Chuan 陳淑娟, Mei-Hui Wang 王美會, and Keh-Yih Su 蘇克毅 (1989). "A Unification-based Approach to Lexicography for Machine Translation System." *Proceedings of the Conference of the Association for Computational Linguistics and Chinese Language Processing (ROCLING-II)*, Taipei, Taiwan.

Kenny, Dorothy (2001). *Lexis and Creativity in Translation: A Corpus-based Study*. Manchester: St. Jerome Publishing.

Lecarme, Jacqueline and Carole Maury (1987). "A Software Tool for Research in Linguistics and Lexicography: Application to Somali." *Machine Translation*, Vol. 2, No. 1, pp. 21–36.

Nirenburg, Sergei, Jaime G. Carbonell, Masaru Tomita, and Kenneth Goodman (1992). "Lexicography and Knowledge Acquisition." *Machine Translation: A Knowledge-based Approach*. San Matero, California: Morgan Kaufmann, pp. 95–116.

Reifler, Erwin (1961). "The Solution of MT Linguistic Problems through Lexicography." In Harold P. Edmundson, ed., *Proceedings of the National Symposium on Machine Translation*. London: Prentice-Hall, pp. 312–316.

Schmied, Josef and Barbara Fink (2000). "Corpus-based Contrastive Lexicology: The Case of English *with* and Its German Translation Equivalents." In Simon Philip Botley, Anthony Mark McEnery, and Andrew Wilson, eds., *Multilingual Corpora in Teaching and Research*. Amsterdam: Rodopi, pp. 157–176.

Computational Lexicography

Al-Hafez, Mohammed Y., Alfred D. Vella, and Douglas Clarke (1994). "A Semantic Knowledge-based Computational Dictionary." *Machine Translation—Ten Years On: Proceedings of the 2nd International Conference Organised by Cranfield University*, Cranfield, England.

Bachut, Daniel, Isabella Duquennoy, Lee Humphreys, Tita Kyriakopoulou, Anne Monceaux, Fiammetta Namer, Jean-Michel Ombrouck, Claire Perrey, Anne Poncet-Montange, Maria-Claudia Puerta, Caroline Raffy, Brigitte Roudaud, and Simon Sabbagh (1995). "A Generic Lexical Model." In Petra Steffens, ed., *Machine Translation and the Lexicon*. Berlin: Springer Verlag, pp. 141–158.

Boguraev, Branimir K. and T. Briscoe, eds. (1989). *Computational Lexicography for Natural Language Processing*. London: Longman.

Daelemans, Walter (1995). "Memory-based Lexical Acquisition and Processing." In Petra Steffens, ed., *Machine Translation and the Lexicon*. Berlin: Springer Verlag, pp. 85–98.

Grishman, Ralph, Catherine Macleod, and Adam Meyers (1994). "COMLEX Syntax: Building a Computational Lexicon." *Proceedings of the 15th International Conference on Computational Linguistics (COLING-94)*, Kyoto, Japan, pp. 268–272.

Guillén, Rocio (1998). "Reusing Translated Terms to Expand a Multilingual Thesaurus." In David L. Farwell, Laurie Gerber, and Eduard Hovy, eds., *Machine Translation and the Information Soup*. Berlin: Springer Verlag, pp. 374–383.

Huang, Chu-Ren, Zhoa-ming Gao, Claude C. C. Shen, and Keh-jian Chen (1998). "Quantitative Criteria for Computational Chinese Lexicography." *Proceedings of the International Conference on Research in Computational Linguistics (ROCLING-XI)*, Hsin-Chu, Taiwan.

Lippmann, Edward O. (1974). "On Computational Linguistics and Computer-aided Translation." *ATA Chronicle*, Vol. 3, No. 5, pp. 7–8.

Meekhof, Timothy and David Clements (2000). "L&H Lexicography Toolkit for Machine Translation." In John S. White, ed., *Envisioning Machine Translation in the Information Future*. Berlin: Springer Verlag, pp. 213–218.

Melamed, I. Dan (1998). "Empirical Methods for MT Lexicon Development." In David L. Farwell, Laurie Gerber, and Eduard Hovy, eds., *Machine Translation and the Information Soup*. Berlin: Springer Verlag, pp. 18–30.

Sheremeteyva, Svetlana (2002). "An MT Learning Environment for Computational Linguistics Students." *Proceedings of the 6th EAMT Workshop Teaching Machine Translation*, Manchester, England, pp. 79–88.

Zhang, Yihua (2006). "Computational Lexicography and Computer-Aided Dictionary-making." *Programme of an International Conference on Computer-aided Translation: Theory and Practice*, Department of Translation, The Chinese University of Hong Kong, Hong Kong.

Corpus Lexicography

Atkins, B. T. Sue and Charles J. Fillmore (1994). "Starting Where the Dictionaries Stop: The Challenge of Corpus Lexicography." In B. T. Sue Atkins and Antonio Zampolli, eds., *Conceptual Approaches to the Lexicon*. Oxford: Oxford University Press, pp. 350–393.

Lexicon

Alam, Yukiko Sasaki (1998). "Machine Translation among Languages with Transitivity Divergences Using the Causal Relation in the Interlingual Lexicon." In David L. Farwell, Laurie Gerber, and Eduard Hovy, eds., *Machine Translation and the Information Soup*. Berlin: Springer Verlag, pp. 461–471.

Baldwin, Timothy and Francis Bond (2002). "Alternation-based Lexicon Reconstruction." *Proceedings of the 9th International Conference on Theoretical and Methodological Issues in Machine Translation (TMI-2002)*, Keihanna, Japan, pp. 1–11.

Bellynck, Valérie, Christian Boitet, and John Kenwright (2005). "ITOLDU, a Web Service to Pool Technical Lexical Terms in a Learning Environment and Contribute to Multilingual Lexical Databases." *Proceedings of the 6th International Conference on Intelligent Text Processing and Computational Linguistics (CICLing-2005)*, Mexico City, Mexico, pp. 315–323.

Bergler, Sabine (1994). "Generative Lexicon Principles for Machine Translation: A Case for Meta-lexical Structure." *Machine Translation*, Vol. 9, Nos. 3–4, pp. 155–182.

Cahill, Lynne (2000). "Semi-automatic Construction of Multilingual Lexicons." *Proceedings of the International Conference on Machine Translation and Multilingual Applications in the New Millenium (MT-2000)*, University of Exeter, England.

Cahill, Lynne (2001). "Semi-automatic Construction of Multilingual Lexicons." *Machine Translation Review*, No. 12, pp. 58–66.

Calzolari, Nicoletta, Alessandro Lenci, Antonio Zampolli, Nuria Bel, Marta Villegas, and Gregor Thurmair (2001). "The ISLE in the Ocean: Transatlantic Standards for Multilingual Lexicons (with an Eye to Machine Translation)." In Bente Maegaard, ed., *Proceedings of MT Summit VIII: Machine Translation in the Information Age*, Santiago de Compostela, Spain.

Cercone, Nick and Robert Mercer (1980). "Design of Lexicons in Some Natural Language Systems." *Literary and Linguistic Computing*, Vol. 1, No. 2, pp. 37–50.

Cullingford, Richard E. and Boyan A. Onyshkevych (1987). "An Experiment in Lexicon-driven Machine Translation." In Sergei Nirenburg, ed., *Machine Translation: Theoretical and Methodological Issues*. Cambridge: Cambridge University Press, pp. 278–301.

Dorr, Bonnie J. (1993). *Machine Translation: A View from the Lexicon*. Cambridge, MA: MIT Press.

Dorr, Bonnie J. and Judith Klavans (1994). "Introduction: Special Issue: Building Lexicons for Machine Translation." *Machine Translation*, Vol. 9, Nos. 3–4, pp. 151–153.

Dorr, Bonnie J. and Judith Klavans (1995). "Special Issue: Building Lexicons for Machine Translation." *Machine Translation*, Vol. 10, Nos. 1–2, pp. 1–3.

Dorr, Bonnie J. (1997). "Large-scale Acquisition of LCS-based Lexicons for Foreign Language Tutoring." *Proceedings of the ACL 5th Conference on Applied Natural Language Processing*, Seattle, Washington, DC, USA, pp. 139–146.

Dorr, Bonnie J., Gina-Anne Levow, and Dekang Lin (2002). "Construction of a Chinese-English Verb Lexicon for Machine Translation and Embedded Multilingual Applications." *Machine Translation*, Vol. 17, No. 2, pp. 99–137.

Fung, Pascale (1995). "Compiling Bilingual Lexicon Entries from a Non-parallel English-Chinese Corpus." *Proceedings of the 3rd Annual Workshop on Very Large Corpora*, Boston, MA, USA, pp. 173–183.

Gates, Donna, Dawn Haberlach, Todd Kaufmann, Marion Kee, Rita McCardell, Teruko Mitamura, Ira Monarch, Stephen Morrisson, Sergei Nirenburg, Eric H. Nyberg, Koichi Takeda, and Margalit Zabludowski (1989). "Lexicons." *Machine Translation*, Vol. 4, No. 1, pp. 67–112.

Gdaniec, Claudia and Esmé Manandise (2002). "Using Word Formation Rules to Extend MT Lexicons." In Stephen D. Richardson, ed., *Machine Translation: From Research to Real Users*. Berlin and New York: Springer Verlag, pp. 64–73.

Guo, Jin (1996). "Context-centered Template Matching for Chinese Lexicon Construction." *Proceedings of the Conference of the Association for Computational Linguistics and Chinese Language*

Processing (*ROCLING-IX*), Tseng-Wen Reservoir Youth Activity Center, Tainan County, Taiwan.

Guessoum, Ahmed and Rached Zantout (2001). "A Methodology for a Semi-automatic Evaluation of the Lexicons of Machine Translation Systems." *Machine Translation*, Vol. 16, No. 2, pp. 127–149.

Han, Xiwu, Tiejun Zhao, and Xingshang Fu (2006). "Improving English Subcategorization Acquisition with Diathesis Alternations as Heuristic Information." *Proceedings of the Joint Conference of the International Committee on Computational Linguistics and the Association for Computational Linguistics* (*COLING/ACL-2006*), Sydney, Australia.

Heyer, Gerhard and Klemens Waldhör (1995). "General Language Resources: Lexica." Marianne Kugler, Khurshid Ahmad, and Gregor Thurmair, eds., *Translator's Workbench*. Berlin: Springer Verlag, pp. 40–48.

Koeling, Rob, Adam Kilgarriff, David Tugwell, and Roger Evans (2003). "An Evaluation of a Lexicographer's Workbench: Building Lexicons for Machine Translation." *Proceedings of the 7th Workshop of the European Association for Machine Translation*: *Improving Machine Translation through Other Language Technology Tools: Resources and Tools for Building MT*, Budapest, Hungary.

Levin, Lori S. and Sergei Nirenburg (1994). "Construction-based MT Lexicons." In Antonio Zampolli, Nicoletta Calzolari, and Martha Palmer, eds., *Current Issues in Computational Linguistics: In Honour of Don Walker*. Dordrecht: Kluwer Academic Publishers.

Lieske, Christian, Susan McCormick, and Gregor Thurmair (2001). "The Open Lexicon Interchange Format (OLIF) Comes of Age." In Bente Maegaard, ed., *Proceedings of MT Summit VIII: Machine Translation in the Information Age*, Santiago de Compostela, Spain.

Melamed, I. Dan (1996). "Automatic Construction of Clean Broad-coverage Translation Lexicons." *Expanding MT Horizons: Proceedings of the 2nd Conference of the Association for Machine Translation in the Americas*, Montreal, Quebec, Canada, pp. 125–134.

Mel'čuk, Igor A. (2000). "Semantics and the Lexicon in Modern Linguistics." *Proceedings of the 1st International Conference on Intelligent Text Processing and Computational Linguistics* (*CICLing-2000*), Mexico City, Mexico.

Mel'čuk, Igor A. and Leo Wanner (2001). "Towards a Lexicographic Approach to Lexical Transfer in Machine Translation (Illustrated by the

German-Russian Language Pair)." *Machine Translation*, Vol. 16, No. 1, pp. 21–87.
Miller, George A., Richard Beckwith, Christiane Fellbaum, Derek Gross, and Katherine Miller (1990). "Introduction to WordNet: An On-Line Lexical Database." *International Journal of Lexicography*, Vol. 3, pp. 235–244.
Miller, Keith J. and David M. Zajic (1998). "Lexicons as Gold: Mining, Embellishment, and Reuse." In David L. Farwell, Laurie Gerber, and Eduard Hovy, eds., *Machine Translation and the Information Soup*. Berlin: Springer Verlag, pp. 484–493.
Nirenburg, Sergei and Victor Raskin (1987). "The Analysis Lexicon and the Lexicon Management System." *Computers and Translation*, Vol. 2, No. 3, pp. 177–188.
Nirenburg, Sergei and Victor Raskin (1987). "The Subworld Concept Lexicon and the Lexicon Management System." *Computational Linguistics*, Vol. 13, Nos. 3–4, pp. 276–289.
Onyshkevich, Boyan and Sergei Nirenburg (1995). "A Lexicon for Knowledge-based MT." *Machine Translation*, Vol. 10, Nos. 1–2, pp. 5–57.
Oswald, Victor A. (1957). "Lexical Problems in Machine Translation: The Rationale of the Idioglossary Technique." In Leon E. Dostert, ed., *Report of the 8th Annual Round Table Meeting on Linguistics and Language Studies: Research on Machine Translation*. Washington, DC: Georgetown University Press, pp. 63–69.
Phillips, William and Ellen Riloff (2002). "Exploiting Strong Syntactic Heuristics and Co-training to Learn Semantic Lexicons." *Proceedings of the 2002 Conference on Empirical Methods in Natural Language Processing (EMNLP-2002)*, University of Pennsylvania, Philadelphia, PA, USA.
Raina, Achla M., Amitabha Mukerjee, Himanshu Gupta, and Kumar Gaurav (2004). "Incorporating Pragmatic-semantic Domain Lexicons for Converting Arithmetic Word Problems into Symbolic Equations." *Proceedings of the International Conference on Natural Language Processing (ICON-2004)*, International Institute of Information Technology, Hyderabad, India.
Sedelow, Sally Yeates and Walter A. Sedelow (1986). "The Lexicon in the Background." *Computers and Translation*, Vol. 1, No. 2, pp. 73–81.
Trujillo, Arturo and David A. Plowman (1993). "Automation of Bilingual

Lexicon Compilation." In Sergei Nirenburg, ed., *Progress in Machine Translation*. Amsterdam: IOS and Tokyo: Ohmsha, pp. 191–196.

Utsuro, Takehito, Takashi Horiuchi, Yasunobu Chiba, and Takeshi Hamamoto (2002). "Semi-automatic Compilation of Bilingual Lexicon Entries from Cross-lingually Relevant News Articles on WWW News Sites." In Stephen D. Richardson, ed., *Machine Translation: From Research to Real Users*. Berlin and New York: Springer Verlag, pp. 165–176.

Váradi, Tamás (2006). "Multiword Units in an MT Lexicon." *Proceedings of the 11th Conference of the European Chapter of the Association for Computational Linguistics* (*EACL-2006*), Trento, Italy.

Weerasinghe, Ruvan (2002). "Bootstrapping the Lexicon Building Process for Machine Translation between 'New' Languages." In Stephen D. Richardson, ed., *Machine Translation: From Research to Real Users*. Berlin and New York: Springer Verlag, pp. 177–186.

Wilks, Yorick and Roberta Catizone (2002). "Lexical Tuning." *Proceedings of the 3rd International Conference on Intelligent Text Processing and Computational Linguistics* (*CICLing-2002*), Mexico City, Mexico.

Wu, Dekai and Xuanyin Xia (1994). "Large-scale Automatic Extraction of an English-Chinese Translation Lexicon." *Machine Translation*, Vol. 9, Nos. 3–4, pp. 285–313.

Lexical Acquisition

Daelemans, Walter (1995). "Memory-based Lexical Acquisition and Processing." In Petra Steffens, ed., *Machine Translation and the Lexicon*. Berlin: Springer Verlag, pp. 85–98.

Dorr, Bonnie J. (1993). "Current and Future Research: Tense, Aspect, and Lexical Acquisition." *Machine Translation: A View from the Lexicon*. Cambridge, MA: MIT Press, pp. 319–350.

Karagol-Ayan, Burcu, David Doermann, and Bonnie J. Dorr (2003). "Acquisition of Bilingual MT Lexicons from OC Read Dictionaries." *Proceedings of MT Summit IX*, New Orleans, Louisiana, USA.

Liu, Rey-Long 劉瑞瓏 and Von-wun Soo 蘇豐文 (1990). "Parsing-driven Generalization for Natural Language Acquisition." *Proceedings of the Conference of the Association for Computational Linguistics and Chinese Language Processing* (*ROCLING-III*), Taipei, Taiwan.

McCormick, Susan (1998). "A Centralized Approach to Managing Multiple Lexical Resources." *Proceedings of the 3rd Workshop of the European Association for Machine Translation: Translation Technology: Integration in the Workflow Environment*, Geneva, Switzerland, pp. 19–26.
Zernik, Uri (1990). "Lexical Acquisition: Where Is the Semantics?" *Machine Translation*, Vol. 5, No. 2, pp. 155–174.

Phrasal Lexicon

Schäler, Reinhard (1996). "Machine Translation, Translation Memories and the Phrasal Lexicon: The Localisation Perspective." *Proceedings of the 1st Workshop of the European Association for Machine Translation (TKE-96): Language Resources, Terminology, Economics, and User Needs*, Vienna, Austria, pp. 21–33.

Translation Lexicon

Mann, Gideon S. and David Yarowsky (2001). "Multipath Translation Lexicon Induction via Bridge Languages." *Proceedings of the 2nd Meeting of the North American Chapter of the Association for Computational Linguistics: Language Technologies 2001 (NAACL-2001)*, Pittsburgh, PA, USA.
Melamed, I. Dan (1996). "Automatic Construction of Clean Broad-coverage Translation." *Proceedings of the 2nd Conference of the Association for Machine Translation in the Americas: Expanding MT Horizons (AMTA-2)*, Montreal, Quebec, Canada, pp. 125–134.
Resnik, Philip and I. Dan Melamed (1997). "Semi-automatic Acquisition of Domain-specific Translation Lexicons." *Proceedings of the 5th Conference on Applied Natural Language Processing*, Seattle, Washington, DC, USA.

❖ PART 21 ❖

Linguistics

Chinese Linguistics

Gao, Jianzhong 高建忠 (2001).〈漢語動賓搭配的自動識別研究〉(Automatic Identification of Verb-object Phrase for Chinese Language). In Huang Changning 黃昌寧 and Zhang Pu 張普, eds.,《自然語言理解與機器翻譯》(*Natural Language Understanding and Machine Translation*). Beijing: Tsinghua University Press, pp. 135–140.

Wang, William S. Y., S. W. Chan, and Benjamin K. Y. T'sou (1973). "Chinese Linguistics and the Computer." *Linguistics*, Vol. 118, pp. 89–117.

Zhang, Weiguo 張衛國 (2001).〈名詞短語：定語、中心語的語義類別及定中搭配〉(Noun Phrase: Semantic Classification of Modifiers and Head in Modifier-head Constructions). In Huang Changning and Zhang Pu, eds.,《自然語言理解與機器翻譯》(*Natural Language Understanding and Machine Translation*). Beijing: Tsinghua University Press, pp. 1–7.

Computational Linguistics

Abramson, Harvey (1991). "Logic Grammar Tools Computational Linguistics." *Proceedings of the Conference of the Association for Computational Linguistics and Chinese Language Processing (ROCLING-IV)*, National Chiao-Tung University, Hsin-Chu, Taiwan.

Dong, Zhendong 董振東 and Huang Changning 黃昌寧, eds. (1999).《計算語言學文集》(*Essays on Computational Linguistics*). Beijing: Tsinghua University Press.

Feng, Zhiwei 馮志偉 (1992).〈計算語言學對理論語言學的挑戰〉(The Challenge of Computational Linguistics to Theoretical Linguistics).《語言文字應用》(*Applied Linguistics*), No. 1, pp. 84–97.

Feng, Zhiwei (2001).《計算語言學基礎》(*Foundation of Computational Linguistics*). Beijing: The Commercial Press.

Feng, Zhiwei (2002).《計算語言學探索》(*Explorations into Computational Linguistics*). Harbin: Heilongjiang Education Press.

Hutchins, W. John and Harold L. Somers (1992). "Computational Aspects." *An Introduction to Machine Translation*. London: Academic Press, pp. 47–68.

Isahara, Hitoshi (2002). "Computational Linguistics at Communications Research Laboratory, Japan." In Yu Shiwen, ed., *Proceedings of the*

2nd China-Japan Natural Language Processing Joint Research Promotion Conference (*CJNLP-2002*). Beijing: Institute of Computational Linguistics, Peking University, pp. 40–44.
Joshi, Aravind K. (2003). "Starting with Complex Primitives Pays Off." *Proceedings of the 4th International Conference on Intelligent Text Processing and Computational Linguistics* (*CICLing-2003*), Mexico City, Mexico, pp. 1–11.
Kaplan, Ronald M. and Annie Zaenen (2003). "Things Are Not Always Equal." *Proceedings of the 4th International Conference on Intelligent Text Processing and Computational Linguistics* (*CICLing-2003*), Mexico City, Mexico, pp. 12–22.
Lenders, Winfried (2001). "Past and Future Goals of Computational Linguistics." *Proceedings of the International Conference on Research in Computational Linguistics* (*ROCLING-XIV*), National Chengkung University, Tainan, Taiwan.
Lin, Sung-Chien 林頌堅 (2004). 〈以自組織映射圖進行計算語言學領域術語視覺化之研究〉 (Visualizing the Terms of Computational Linguistics). *Proceedings of the International Conference on Research in Computational Linguistics* (*ROCLING-XVI*), Taipei, Taiwan.
Mostow, Jack (2004). "If I Have a Hammer: Computational Linguistics in a Reading Tutor That Listens." *Proceedings of the 42nd Annual Meeting of the Association for Computational Linguistics* (*ACL-2004*), Barcelona, Spain.
Paris, Cecile, William R. Swartout, and William C. Mann, eds. (1991). *Natural Language Generation in Artificial Intelligence and Computational Linguistics*. Boston: Kulwer Academic.
Pevzner, Boris (2002). "Computational Linguistics and E-commerce." *International Journal of Translation*, Vol. 14, No. 2, pp. 17–25.
Sadler, Louisa (1993). "Co-description and Translation." In Frank van Eynde, ed., *Linguistics Issues in Machine Translation*. London and New York: Pinter Publishers, pp. 44–71.
Sheremeteyva, Svetlana (2002). "An MT Learning Environment for Computational Linguistics Students." *Proceedings of the 6th Workshop of the European Association for Machine Translation: Teaching Machine Translation*, Manchester, England, pp. 79–88.
Trujillo, Arturo (1999). "Computational Linguistics Techniques." *Translation Engines: Techniques for Machine Translation*. Berlin and New York: Springer Verlag, pp. 85–119.

van Eynde, Frank, ed. (1993). *Linguistics Issues in Machine Translation*. London and New York: Pinter Publishers.

van Eynde, Frank (1993). "Machine Translation and Linguistic Motivation." In Frank van Eynde, ed., *Linguistics Issues in Machine Translation*. London and New York: Pinter Publishers, pp. 1–43.

Xu, Huanqing 許歡慶, Wang Yongcheng 王永成, and Sun Qiang 孫強 (2002).〈基於加權概念網絡的用戶興趣建模〉(User Modeling Based on Weighted Concept Network).《第一屆學生計算語言學研討會論文集》(*SWCL2002: First Students' Workshop on Computational Linguistics: Proceedings*), Institute of Computational Linguistics, Peking University, Beijing, China, pp. 35–43.

Yu, Shiwen 俞士汶 (2001).〈計算語言學的應用研究與基礎研究〉(Applied Research and Foundational Research in Computational Linguistics).《輝煌二十年——中國中文信息學會二十周年學術會議》(*Proceedings of Conference of the 20th Anniversary of CIPSC*). Beijing: Tsinghua University Press, pp. 54–65.

Yu, Shiwen 俞士汶 and Zhu Xuefeng 朱學鋒, eds. (2000).《計算語言學文集(第四集)》(*Collected Essays on Computational Linguistics*, Vol. 4). Beijing: Institute of Computational Linguistics, Peking University.

Zhao, Yan 趙岩, Wang Xilong 王曉龍, and Guan Yi 關毅 (2002).〈計算語言學領域程序編制的工程問題探討〉(Technical Problems in Computational Linguistics Software Construction).《第一屆學生計算語言學研討會論文集》(*SWCL2002: First Students' Workshop on Computational Linguistics: Proceedings*), Institute of Computational Linguistics, Peking University, Beijing, China, p. 352.

Contrastive Linguistics

Bennett, Paul A. (2002). "Teaching Contrastive Linguistics for MT." *Proceedings of the 6th EAMT Workshop: Teaching Machine Translation*, Manchester, England, pp. 43–52.

Corpus Linguistics

Ahmad, Khurshid and Margaret Rogers (2001). "Corpus Linguistics and Terminology Extraction." In Sue Ellen Wright and Gerhard Budin, eds., *Handbook of Terminology Management*. Amsterdam and Philadelphia: John Benjamins Publishing Company, Vol. 2, pp. 725–760.

Baker, Mona (1993). "Corpus Linguistics and Translation Studies: Implications and Applications." In Mona Baker, Gill Francis, and Elena Tognini-Bonelli, eds., *Text and Technology: In Honour of John Sinclair*. Amsterdam and Philadelphia: John Benjamins Publishing Company, pp. 233–250.

Huang, Chu-ren, K. Ahrens, and Chen Keh-jiann (1993). "A Data-driven Approach to Psychological Reality of the Mental Lexicon: Two Studies in Chinese Corpus Linguistics." *Proceedings of the International Conference on the Biological Basis of Language*. Chiayi: Center of Cognitive Science, National Chung Cheng University, pp. 53–68.

Kenny, Dorothy (2001). "The Soft Option: Corpus Linguistics." *Lexis and Creativity in Translation: A Corpus-based Study*. Manchester: St. Jerome Publishing, pp. 22–47.

Kenny, Dorothy (2001). "Turning Corpus Linguistics on Its Head: Corpus-based Translation Studies." *Lexis and Creativity in Translation: A Corpus-based Study*. Manchester: St. Jerome Publishing, pp. 48–72.

Kohn, János (1996). "What Can (Corpus) Linguistics Do for Translation?" Kinga Klaudy, José Lambert, and Anikó Sohár, eds., *Translation Studies in Hungary*. Budapest: Scholastica, pp. 39–52.

Olohan, Maeve (2004). "Corpus Linguistics and Translation." *Introducing Corpora in Translation Studies*. London and New York: Routledge, pp. 2–23.

Discourse

Althaus, Ernst, Nikiforos Karamanis, and Alexander Koller (2004). "Computing Locally Coherent Discourses." *Proceedings of the 42nd Annual Meeting of the Association for Computational Linguistics (ACL-2004)*, Barcelona, Spain, pp. 399–406.

Bos, Johan and Julia Heine (2000). "Discourse and Dialog Semantics for Translation." In Wolfgang Wahlster, ed., *Verbmobil: Foundations of Speech-to-speech Translation*. Berlin: Springer Verlag, pp. 336–347.

Delmonte, Rodolfo, Dario Bianchi, and Emanuele Pianta (2000). "Generating from a Discourse Model." *Proceedings of the International Conference on Machine Translation and Multilingual Applications in the New Millenium (MT-2000)*, University of Exeter, England.

Grosz, Barbara J., Aravind K. Joshi, and Scott Weinstein (1983).

"Providing a Unified Account of Definite Noun Phrases in Discourse." *Proceedings of the 21st Annual Meeting of the Association for Computational Linguistics* (*ACL-83*), Cambridge, MA, USA, pp. 44–50.

Haenelt, Karin (1992). "Towards a Quality Improvement in Machine Translation: Modelling Discourse Structure and Including Discourse Development in the Determination of Translation Equivalents." *Proceedings of the 4th International Conference on Theoretical and Methodological Issues in Machine Translation of Natural Languages: Empiricist vs. Rationalist Methods in MT* (*TMI-92*), Montreal, Quebec, Canada, pp. 205–212.

Hauenschild, Christa (1988). "Discourse Structure—Some Implications for Machine Translation." In Dan Maxwell, Klaus Schubert, and Toon Witkam, eds., *New Directions in Machine Translation*. Dordrecht-Holland: Foris Publications, pp. 145–156.

Hutchinson, Ben (2004). "Acquiring the Meaning of Discourse Markers." *Proceedings of the 42nd Annual Meeting of the Association for Computational Linguistics* (*ACL-2004*), Barcelona, Spain, pp. 684–691.

Joshi, Aravind K. and Scott Weinstein (1981). "Control of Inference: Role of Some Aspects of Discourse Structure—Centering." *Proceedings of the 7th International Joint Conference on Artificial Intelligence* (*IJCAI-81*), Vancouver, BC, Canada, pp. 385–387.

Kim, Soo-Min and Eduard H. Hovy (2006). "Identifying and Analyzing Judgment Opinions." *Proceedings of the Human Language Technology Conference—Annual Meeting of the North American Chapter of the Association for Computational Linguistics* (*HLT-NAACL-2006*), New York, USA.

Koch, Gregers (2000). "Some Perspectives on Induction in Discourse Representation." *Proceedings of the 1st International Conference on Intelligent Text Processing and Computational Linguistics* (*CICLing-2000*), Mexico City, Mexico.

Kruijff, Geert-Jan M. and Jan Schaake (1997). "Discerning Relevant Information in Discourses Using TFA." In Ruslan Mitkov and Nicolas Nicolov, eds., *Recent Advances in Natural Language Processing*. Amsterdam and Philadelphia: John Benjamins Publishing Company, pp. 259–270.

Le, Huong T. and Geetha Abeysinghe (2003). "A Study to Improve the

Efficiency of a Discourse Parsing System." *Proceedings of the 4th International Conference on Intelligent Text Processing and Computational Linguistics* (*CICLing-2003*), Mexico City, Mexico, pp. 104–117.

Marcu, Daniel, Lynn Carlson, and Maki Watanabe (2000). "The Automatic Translation of Discourse Structures." *Proceedings of the 1st Meeting of the North American Chapter of the Association for Computational Linguistics*, Seattle, Washington, DC, USA, pp. 9–17.

Nasukawa, Tetsuya (1993). "Discourse Constraint in Computer Manuals." *Proceedings of the 5th International Conference on Theoretical and Methodological Issues in Machine Translation of Natural Languages: MT in the Next Generation* (*TMI-93*), Kyoto, Japan, pp. 183–194.

Nomoto, Tadashi and Yoshihiko Nitta (1994). "A Grammatico-statistical Approach to Discourse Partitioning." *Proceedings of the 15th International Conference on Computational Linguistics* (*COLING-94*), Kyoto, Japan, pp. 1145–1150.

Nomoto, Tadashi and Yuji Matsumoto (1999). "Learning Discourse Relations with Active Data Selection." *Proceedings of the Joint SIGDAT Conference on Empirical Methods in NLP and Very Large Corpora* (*EMNLP/VLC-99*), University of Maryland, College Park, MD, USA.

Pérez-Ramírez, Miguel and Chris Fox (2003). "Imperatives as Obligatory and Permitted Actions." *Proceedings of the 4th International Conference on Intelligent Text Processing and Computational Linguistics* (*CICLing-2003*), Mexico City, Mexico, pp. 53–65.

Pustejovsky, James (1987). "An Integrated Theory of Discourse Analysis." In Sergei Nirenburg, ed., *Machine Translation: Theoretical and Methodological Issues*. Cambridge: Cambridge University Press, pp. 168–191.

Pym, Anthony (2004). "Humanizing Discourse." *The Moving Text: Localization, Translation, and Distribution*. Amsterdam and Philadelphia: John Benjamins Publishing Company, pp. 181–198.

Ramm, Wiebke (1997). "Discourse Constraints on Theme Selection." In Ruslan Mitkov and Nicolas Nicolov, eds., *Recent Advances in Natural Language Processing*. Amsterdam and Philadelphia: John Benjamins Publishing Company, pp. 247–258.

Stede, Manfred and Birte Schmitz (2000). "Discourse Particles and

Discourse Functions." *Machine Translation*, Vol. 15, Nos. 1–2, pp. 125–147.
Styś, Malgorzata E. and Stefan S. Zemke (1997). "Incorporating Discourse Aspects in English-Polish MT." In Ruslan Mitkov and Nicolas Nicolov, eds., *Recent Advances in Natural Language Processing*. Amsterdam and Philadelphia: John Benjamins Publishing Company, pp. 213–223.
Tseng, Shu-Chuan and Dafydd Gibbon (2006). "Discourse Functions of Duration in Mandarin: Resource Design and Implementation." *Proceedings of the 5th International Conference on Language Resources and Evaluation* (*LREC-2006*), Genoa, Italy.
Tsujii, Jun-ichi (1988). "What Is a Cross-linguistically Valid Interpretation of Discourse." In Dan Maxwell, Klaus Schubert, and Toon Witkam, eds., *New Directions in Machine Translation*. Dordrecht-Holland: Foris Publications, pp. 157–166.
Zacharski, Ron (2003). "A Discourse System for Conversational Characters." *Proceedings of the 4th International Conference on Intelligent Text Processing and Computational Linguistics* (*CICLing-2003*), Mexico City, Mexico, pp. 492–495.

Linguistics

Apresjan, Jury D., Igor M. Boguslavskij, Leonid L. Iomdin, Alexander V. Lazurskij, Vladimir Z. Sannikov, and Leonid L. Tsinman (1992). "The Linguistics of a Machine Translation System." *Meta*, Vol. 37, No. 1, pp. 97–112.
Bar-Hillel, Yehoshua (1953). "Some Linguistic Problems Connected with Machine Translation." *Philosophy of Science*, Vol. 20, pp. 217–225.
Bar-Hillel, Yehoshua (1958). "Some Linguistic Obstacles to Machine Translation." *Proceedings of the 2nd International Congress on Cybernetics*, Namur, Belgium, pp. 197–207.
Bar-Hillel, Yehoshua (1966). "Four Lectures on Algebraic Linguistics and Machine Translation." In Aldo Ghizzetti, ed., *Automatic Translation of Languages*. Oxford: Pergamon, pp. 1–26.
Bennett, Paul A. (2002). "Teaching Contrastive Linguistics for MT." *Proceedings of the 6th EAMT Workshop: Teaching Machine Translation*, Manchester, England, pp. 43–52.
Bennett, Paul A. (2003). "The Relevance of Linguistics for Machine Translation." In Harold L. Somers, ed., *Computers and Translation: A*

Translator's Guide. Amsterdam and Philadelphia: John Benjamins Publishing Company, pp. 143–160.

Block, Hans Ulrich and Tobias Ruland (2000). "Integrated Shallow Linguistic Processing." In Wolfgang Wahlster, ed., *Verbmobil: Foundations of Speech-to-speech Translation*. Berlin: Springer Verlag, pp. 143–146.

Booth, Andrew D. (1962). "Machine Translation—A Challenge to the Linguist." *The Incorporated Linguist*, Vol. 1, No. 2, pp. 34–41.

Caroli, Folker (1995). "Types of Lexical Co-occurrences: Descriptive Parameters." In Petra Steffens, ed., *Machine Translation and the Lexicon*. Berlin: Springer Verlag, pp. 203–218.

Crossland, R.A. (1956). "Graphic Linguistics and Its Terminology." *Mechanical Translation*, Vol. 3, No. 1, pp. 8–11.

de Roeck, Anne (1987). "Linguistic Theory and Early Machine Translation." In Margaret King, ed., *Machine Translation Today: The State of the Art*. Edinburgh: Edinburgh University Press, pp. 38–57.

Dorr, Bonnie J. (1990). "A Cross-linguistic Approach to Machine Translation." *Proceedings of the 3rd International Conference on Theoretical and Methodological Issues in Machine Translation of Natural Languages* (*TMI-90*), Linguistics Research Center, University of Texas, Austin, Texas, USA, pp. 13–32.

Dorr, Bonnie J. and Maria Katsova (1998). "Lexical Selection for Cross-language Applications: Combining LCS with WordNet." In David L. Farwell, Laurie Gerber, and Eduard Hovy, eds., *Machine Translation and the Information Soup*. Berlin: Springer Verlag, pp. 438–447.

Emele, Martin, Ulrich Heid, Stefan Momma, and Rémi Zajac (1992). "Interactions between Linguistic Constraints: Procedural vs. Declarative Approaches." *Machine Translation*, Vol. 7, Nos. 1–2, pp. 61–98.

Feng, Zhiwei 馮志偉 (1986).〈現代信息科學對語言學的影響〉(The Impact of Modern Information Science on Linguistics).《黑龍江大學學報》(*Journal of Heilongjiang University*), No. 1.

Feng, Zhiwei (1994).〈機器翻譯與現代語言學理論〉(Machine Translation and Modern Theories of Linguistics).《自然語言機器翻譯新論》(*New Essays on Machine Translation of Natural Languages*). Beijing: Language Press, pp. 42–60.

Garvin, Paul L. (1956). "Some Linguistic Problems in Machine

Translation." In M. Halle *et al.*, eds., *For Roman Jakobson*. The Hague: Mouton, pp. 180–186.

Gawronska, Barbara and Hanna Duczak (2000). "Understanding Politics by Studying Weather: A Cognitive Approach to Representation of Polish Verbs of Motion, Appearance, and Existence." In John S. White, ed., *Envisioning Machine Translation in the Information Future*. Berlin: Springer Verlag, pp. 147–157.

Halliday, M. A. K. (1956). "The Linguistic Basis of a Mechanical Thesaurus." *Mechanical Translation*, Vol. 3, No. 3, pp. 81–88.

Halliday, M. A. K. (1962). "Linguistics and Machine Translation." *Zeitschrift fur Phonetik, Sprachwissenschaft und Kommunikations Forschung*, Vol. 15, Nos. 1–2, pp. 145–158.

Hays, David G. (1962). "An Introduction to Computational Procedures in Linguistic Research." In A. Ghizzetti, ed., *Automatic Translation of Languages*. Oxford: Pergamon Press, pp. 139–165.

Hutchins, W. John (1979). "Linguistic Models in Machine Translation." *University of East Anglia Papers in Linguistics*, Vol. 9, pp. 29–52.

Hutchins, W. John and Harold L. Somers (1992). "Linguistic Background." *An Introduction to Machine Translation*. London: Academic Press, pp. 11–45.

Joynes, M. L. and Winfred P. Lehmann (1964). "Linguistic Theories Underlying the Work of Various MT Groups." *Linguistics*, Vol. 8, pp. 62–71.

Kenny, Dorothy (2001). "Is 'Linguistics' Singular or Plural?" *Lexis and Creativity in Translation: A Corpus-based Study*. Manchester: St. Jerome Publishing, pp. 1–21.

Koutsoudas, Andreas and A. Humecky (1959). "Linguistics and Machine Translation." *Word*, Vol. 15, pp. 489–491.

Krieger, Hans-Ulrich (1995). "Typed Feature Formalisms as a Common Basis for Linguistic Specification." In Petra Steffens, ed., *Machine Translation and the Lexicon*. Berlin: Springer Verlag, pp. 101–119.

Lamb, Sydney M. (1973). "Stratificational Linguistics as a Basis for Machine Translation." In A. Makkai and D. G. Lockwood, eds., *Readings in Stratificational Linguistics*. Alabama: University of Alabama Press, pp. 34–59.

Liu, Yongquan 劉湧泉 (1997).〈機器翻譯歸根到底是個語言學問題〉(Machine Translation Is Ultimately a Matter of Linguistics).《語言文字應用》(*Applied Linguistics*), No. 3, pp. 79–82.

Melby, Alan K. (1981). "Linguistics and Machine Translation." In J. Copeland and P. Davis, eds., *The Seventh LACUS Forum 1980*. Columbia, South Carolina: Hornbeam Press.
Mel'cuk, Igor A. (1963). "Machine Translation and Linguistics." In O. S. Akhmanova, I. A. Mel'cuk, R. M. Frumkina, and E. V. Paducheva, eds., *Exact Methods in Linguistic Research*. Berkeley: University of California Press, pp. 44–79.
Mel'cuk, Igor A. (1967). "Linguistics and Automatic Translation." *International Social Science Journal*, Vol. 19, No. 1, pp. 64–78.
Micklesen, Lew R. (1956). "From Classes, Structural Linguistics and Mechanical Translation." *Essays for Roman Jakobson*. The Hague: Mouton, pp. 344–352.
Odjik, Jan and Elena Pinillos Bartolomé (1994). "Incorporating Theoretical Linguistic Insights." In M. T. Rosetta, *Compositional Translation*. Dordrecht: Kluwer Academic Publishers, pp. 203–228.
Raskin, Victor (1987). "Linguistics and Natural Language Processing." In Sergei Nirenburg, ed., *Machine Translation: Theoretical and Methodological Issues*. Cambridge: Cambridge University Press, pp. 42–58.
Rohrer, Christian (1986). "Linguistic Bases for Machine Translation." *Proceedings of the 11th International Conference on Computational Linguistics* (*COLING-86*), Bonn, Germany, pp. 353–355.
Rossi, Francesco (1974). *Machine Translation and Applied Linguistics*. Frankfurt: Athenaeum.
Rozencvejg, V. Ju., ed. (1974). *Machine Translation and Applied Linguistics*, 2 Vols. Frankfurt am Main: Athenaion Verlag.
Samuelsdorf, P. O. (1977). "Relation of Machine Translation to Linguistics Exemplified by an English-German Translation Project." *Proceedings of the 3rd International Conference on Computers in the Humanities*, Waterloo, Ontario, Canada.
Shann, Patrick (1987). "Machine Translation: A Problem of Linguistic Engineering or of Cognitive Modelling?" In Margaret King, ed., *Machine Translation Today: The State of the Art*. Edinburgh: Edinburgh University Press, pp. 71–90.
Wang, William S. Y. 王士元 (1988).〈電腦在語言學裡的運用〉(The Use of Linguistics in Computers). *Proceedings of the Conference of the Association for Computational Linguistics and Chinese Language Processing* (*ROCLING-I*), Nantou, Taiwan.

Wang, William S. Y. (1996). "The Use of Computers in Chinese Linguistics." *Journal of Chinese Linguistics*, Vol. 9, pp. iii–viii.

Wehrli, Eric (1987). "Recent Developments in Theoretical Linguistics and Implications for Machine Translation." In Margaret King, ed., *Machine Translation Today: The State of the Art*. Edinburgh: Edinburgh University Press, pp. 58–70.

Whitelock, Peter J. and Kieran Kilby (1995). "Linguistic Representation of Texts." *Linguistic and Computational Techniques in Machine Translation System Design*. London: UCL Press, pp. 20–29.

Whitelock, Peter J. and Kieran Kilby (1995). "Linguistic Problems in Translation." *Linguistic and Computational Techniques in Machine Translation System Design*. London: UCL Press, pp. 13–19.

Whitelock, Peter J., Mary McGee Wood, Harold L. Somers, Roderick L. Johnson, and Peter Bennett, eds. (1987). *Linguistic Theory and Computer Applications*. London: Academic Press.

Wehrli, Eric (1987). "Recent Developments in Theoretical Linguistics and Implications for Machine Translation." In Margaret King, ed., *Machine Translation Today: The State of the Art*. Edinburgh: Edinburgh University Press, pp. 58–70.

Yngve, Victor (1997). "MT and the New Foundations for General Linguistics." *Proceedings of the 7th International Conference on Theoretical and Methodological Issues in Machine Translation (TMI-97)*, St. John's College, Santa Fe, New Mexico, USA.

Zhan, Weidong 詹衛東, Chang Baobao 常寶寶, and Yu Shiwen 俞士汶 (2002).〈機器翻譯與語言研究〉(Machine Translation and Linguistic Studies).《語言科學》(*Linguistic Science*), Vol. 1, No. 1, pp. 47–61.

Morphology

Alegria, Ińaki, Xabier Artola, and Kepa Sarasola (1997). "Improving a Robust Morphological Analyser Using Lexical Transducers." In Ruslan Mitkov and Nicolas Nicolov, eds., *Recent Advances in Natural Language Processing*. Amsterdam and Philadelphia: John Benjamins Publishing Company, pp. 97–108.

Amtrup, Jan W. (2003). "Morphology in Machine Translation Systems: Efficient Integration of Finite State Transducers and Feature Structure Descriptions." *Machine Translation*, Vol. 18, No. 3, pp. 217–238.

Alonso, Juan A., Ramón Fanlo, and Albert Llorens (2001). "Collapsing

Morphological Information in Lexical Databases for NLP Applications." In Bente Maegaard, ed., *Proceedings of MT Summit VIII: Machine Translation in the Information Age*, Santiago de Compostela, Spain.

Bennett, Paul A. (1993). "The Interaction of Syntax and Morphology in Machine Translation." In Frank van Eynde, ed., *Linguistics Issues in Machine Translation*. London and New York: Pinter Publishers, pp. 72–104.

Beesley, Kenneth R. and Lauri Karttunen (2000). "Finite-state Non-concatenative Morphotactics." *Proceedings of the 38th Annual Meeting of the Association for Computational Linguistics (ACL-2000)*, Hong Kong.

Byrd, Roy J., Judith L. Klavans, Mark Aronoff, and Frank Anshen (1986). "Computer Methods for Morphological Analysis." *Proceedings of the 24th Annual Meeting of the Association for Computational Linguistics (ACL-86)*, New York, USA, pp. 120–127.

Cavalli-Sforza, Violetta, Soudi Abdelhadi, and Teruko Mitamura (2000). "Arabic Morphology Generation Using a Concatenative Strategy." *Proceedings of the 1st Meeting of the North American Chapter of the Association for Computational Linguistics*, Seattle, Washington, DC, USA, pp. 86–93.

Chan, Stanley K. (1997). "The Application of the Similarities between the Morphemes of the English and Chinese Languages to Represent Chinese Characters Phonetically with English Letters to Facilitate Computer Applications Manually and by Voice with the Character-based Languages Chinese, Japanese and Korean." *Proceedings of the International Conference on Research in Computational Linguistics (ROCLING-X)*, Academia Sinica, Taipei, Taiwan.

Cohen-Sygal, Yael and Shuly Wintner (2006). "Finite-state Registered Automata for Non-concatenative Morphology." *Computational Linguistics*, Vol. 32, No. 1, pp. 49–82.

Dhonnchadha, Uí, Caoilfhionn Nic Pháidín, and Josef Van Genabith (2003). "Design, Implementation and Evaluation of an Inflectional Morphology Finite State Transducer for Irish." *Machine Translation*, Vol. 18, No. 3, pp. 173–193.

Dorr, Bonnie J. (1993). "Morphological Processing." *Machine Translation: A View from the Lexicon*. Cambridge, MA: MIT Press, pp. 79–92.

Feng, Zhiwei 馮志偉 (1994). 〈形態分析器和結構分析生成器〉(Morphological Analyser and Structural Analysis Generator).《自然語言機器翻譯新論》(*New Essays on Machine Translation of Natural Languages*). Beijing: Language Press, pp. 144–196.

Feng, Zhiwei (2004). 〈形態自動分析〉 (Automatic Morphological Analysis).《機器翻譯研究》(*Studies on Machine Translation*). Beijing: China Translation and Publishing Corporation, pp. 103–180.

Gambäck, Björn (2001). "Unification-based Lexicon and Morphology with Speculative Feature Signalling." *Proceedings of the 2nd International Conference on Intelligent Text Processing and Computational Linguistics* (*CICLing-2001*), Mexico City, Mexico.

Ganeshan, M. (1994). "Functioning of the Morphological Analyser Developed at CIIL, Mysore." In Harikumar Basi, ed., *Automatic Translation*. Thiruvananthapuram: International School of Dravidian Linguistics, pp. 79–114.

Gdaniec, Claudia, Esmé Manandise, and Michael C. McCord (2001). "Derivational Morphology to the Rescue: How It Can Help Resolve Unfound Words in MT." In Bente Maegaard, ed., *Proceedings of MT Summit VIII: Machine Translation in the Information Age*, Santiago de Compostela, Spain.

Gurevich, Olga (2006). "A Finite-state Model of Georgian Verbal Morphology." *Proceedings of the Human Language Technology Conference—Annual Meeting of the North American Chapter of the Association for Computational Linguistics* (*HLT-NAACL-2006*), New York, USA.

Johnson, Howard and Joel Martin (2003). "Unsupervised Learning of Morphology for English and Inuktitut." *Proceedings of the Human Language Technology and North American Chapter of Association of Computational Linguistics 2003* (*HLT/NAACL-2003*), Edmonton, Alberta, Canada.

Karttunen, Lauri (2003). "Computing with Realizational Morphology." *Proceedings of the 4th International Conference on Intelligent Text Processing and Computational Linguistics* (*CICLing-2003*), Mexico City, Mexico, pp. 205–216.

Kool, Edward A. (2004). "Representing Dutch Morphology in a Machine Translation System." *International Journal of Translation*, Vol. 16, No. 1, pp. 109–120.

Matthews, Peter H. (1966). "A Procedure for Morphological Encoding." *Mechanical Translation*, Vol. 9, pp. 15–21.

Megerdoomian, Karine (2000). "Unification-based Persian Morphology." *Proceedings of the 1st International Conference on Intelligent Text Processing and Computational Linguistics* (*CICLing-2000*), Mexico City, Mexico.

Mráková, Eva and Radek Sedláček (2003). "From Czech Morphology through Partial Parsing to Disambiguation." *Proceedings of the 4th International Conference on Intelligent Text Processing and Computational Linguistics* (*CICLing-2003*), Mexico City, Mexico, pp. 129–138.

Pacak, Milos G. (1961). "Morphology in Terms of Mechanical Translation." In Allen Kent, ed., *Information Retrieval and Machine Translation*. New York: Interscience, Vol. 2, pp. 881–885.

Pacak, Milos G. (1966). "Computational Morphology." *T. A. Informations 1966*, Part 1, pp. 25–36.

Pretorius, Laurette and Sonja E. Bosch (2003). "Finite-state Computational Morphology: An Analyzer Prototype For Zulu." *Machine Translation*, Vol. 18, No. 3, pp. 195–216.

Rous, Joep and Harm Smit (1994). "Morphology." In M. T. Rosetta, *Compositional Translation*. Dordrecht: Kluwer Academic Publishers, pp. 103–118.

Schmid, Helmut (2005). "Disambiguation of Morphological Structure Using a PCFG." *Proceedings of Human Language Technology Conference and Conference on Empirical Methods in Natural Language Processing* (*HLT/EMNLP-2005*), Vancouver, BC, Canada.

Sheremetyeva, Svetlana, Wanying Jin, and Sergei Nirenburg (1998). "Rapid Deployment Morphology." *Machine Translation*, Vol. 13, No. 4, pp. 239–268.

Shimohata, Mitsuo and Eiichiro Sumita (2001). "Converting Morphological Information Using Lexicalized and General Conversion." *Proceedings of the 2nd International Conference on Intelligent Text Processing and Computational Linguistics* (*CICLing-2001*), Mexico City, Mexico.

Shinnou, Hiroyuki (1998). "Revision of Morphological Analysis Errors through the Person Name Construction Model." In David L. Farwell, Laurie Gerber, and Eduard Hovy, eds., *Machine Translation and the Information Soup*. Berlin: Springer Verlag, pp. 398–407.

Smith, Noah A., David A. Smith, and Roy W. Tromble (2005). "Context-based Morphological Disambiguation with Random Fields." *Proceedings of Human Language Technology Conference and Conference on Empirical Methods in Natural Language Processing (HLT/EMNLP-2005)*, Vancouver, BC, Canada.

Suleymanov, Dj. Sh. (2002). "Tatar Morphological Implementation." *Proceedings of the 3rd International Conference on Intelligent Text Processing and Computational Linguistics (CICLing-2002)*, Mexico City, Mexico.

Varma, Vasudev (1993). "Issues Involved in Developing Morphological Analyser and Machine Readable Dictionary for a Machine Translation System." *International Journal of Translation*, Vol. 5, Nos. 1–2, pp. 1–18.

Vilares, Jesús, David Cabrero, and Miguel A. Alonso (2001). "Applying Productive Derivational Morphology to Term Indexing of Spanish Texts." *Proceedings of the 2nd International Conference on Intelligent Text Processing and Computational Linguistics (CICLing-2001)*, Mexico City, Mexico.

Woods, William A. (2000). "Aggressive Morphology for Robust Lexical Coverage." *Proceedings of the 6th Applied Natural Language Processing Conference*, Seattle, Washington, DC, USA, pp. 218–223.

Zollmann, Andreas, Venugopal Ashish, and Vogel Stephan (2006). "Bridging the Inflection Morphology Gap for Arabic Statistical Machine Translation." *Proceedings of the Human Language Technology Conference—Annual Meeting of the North American Chapter of the Association for Computational Linguistics (HLT-NAACL-2006)*, New York, USA.

Pragmatics

Farwell, David L. and Stephen Helmreich (1999). "Pragmatics and Translation." *Procesamiento de Languaje Natural*, Vol. 24, pp. 19–36.

Feng, Zhiwei 馮志偉 (2004).〈語用的自動分析〉(Automatic Analysis of Pragmatics).《機器翻譯研究》(*Studies on Machine Translation*). Beijing: China Translation and Publishing Corporation, pp. 596–636.

Galley, Michel, Kathleen R. McKeown, Julia Hirschberg, and Elizabeth Shriberg (2004). "Identifying Agreement and Disagreement in

Conversational Speech: Use of Bayesian Networks to Model Pragmatic Dependencies." *Proceedings of the 42nd Annual Meeting of the Association for Computational Linguistics* (*ACL-2004*), Barcelona, Spain, pp. 669–676.
Komiya, Kanako, Yasuhiro Tajima, Nobuo Inui, and Yoshiyuki Kotani (2006). "Generating a Sct of Rules to Determine Honorific Expression Using Decision Tree Learning." *Proceedings of the 7th International Conference on Intelligent Text Processing and Computational Linguistics* (*CICLing-2006*), Mexico City, Mexico.

Semantics

Alberti, Gábor, Katalin Balogh, Judit Kleiber, and Anita Viszket (2003). "Total Lexicalism and GASGrammars: A Direct Way to Semantics." *Proceedings of the 4th International Conference on Intelligent Text Processing and Computational Linguistics* (*CICLing-2003*), Mexico City, Mexico, pp. 37–48.
Arranz, M. Victoria, Ian Radford, Sofia Anaiadou, and Jun-ichi Tsuiji (1997). "Towards a Sublanguage-based Semantic Clustering Algorithm." In Ruslan Mitkov and Nicolas Nicolov, eds., *Recent Advances in Natural Language Processing*. Amsterdam and Philadelphia: John Benjamins Publishing Company, pp. 125–136.
Bennett, Winfield S. (1989). "The Place of Semantics in MT Systems." *Literary and Linguistic Computing*, Vol. 4, No. 3, pp. 200–202.
Bennett, Winfield S. (1990). "How Much Semantics Is Necessary for MT Systems?" *Proceedings of the 3rd International Conference on Theoretical and Methodological Issues in Machine Translation of Natural Languages* (*TMI-90*), Linguistics Research Center, University of Texas, Austin, Texas, USA, pp. 261–270.
Cassidy, Patrick J. (2000). "An Investigation of the Semantic Relations in the Roget's Thesaurus: Preliminary Results." *Proceedings of the 1st International Conference on Intelligent Text Processing and Computational Linguistics* (*CICLing-2000*), Mexico City, Mexico.
Chang, Baobao 常寶寶 and Zhan Weidong 詹衛東 (1998).〈一個漢英機器翻譯系統中的語義處理框架及其作用〉(A Framework of Semantic Processing in a Chinese-English Machine Translation System). In Yu Shiwen 俞士汶 and Zhu Xuefeng 朱學鋒, eds.,《計算語言學文集》(*Papers on Computational Linguistics*), Vol. 3. Beijing: Department of

Computer Science and Technology and Institute of Computational Linguistics, Peking University, pp. 94–100.

Charney, Elinor K. (1962). "On the Semantical Interpretation of Linguistic Entities That Function Structurally." In National Physical Laboratory, ed., *1961 International Conference on Machine Translation of Languages and Applied Language Analysis: Proceedings of the Conference Held at the National Physical Laboratory, Teddington, Middlesex, on 5th, 6th, 7th and 8th September*. London: Her Majesty's Stationery Office, Vol. 2, pp. 544–556.

Cooper, Robin (1995). "Making Semantics Useful for Translation." *Proceedings of the 6th International Conference on Theoretical and Methodological Issues in Machine Translation* (*TMI-95*), the University of Leuven, Belgium.

Copestake, Ann, Dan Flickinger, Rob Malouf, Susanne Riehemann, and Ivan Sag (1995). "Translation Using Minimal Recursion Semantics." *Proceedings of the 6th International Conference on Theoretical and Methodological Issues in Machine Translation* (*TMI-95*), Leuven, Belgium, pp. 15–32.

Culhane, P. T. (1977). "Semantics via Machine Translation." *Russian Language Journal*, Vol. 31, No. 108, pp. 35–42.

Dahlgren K. (1988). *Naïve Semantics for Natural Language Understanding*. Dordrecht: Kluwer Academic Publishers.

Daudé, Jordi, Lluis Padró, and German Rigau (2000). "Mapping WordNets Using Structural Information." *Proceedings of the 38th Annual Meeting of the Association for Computational Linguistics* (*ACL-2000*), Hong Kong.

Dong, Zhendong 董振東 (1984).〈邏輯語義及其在機譯中的應用〉(Logic Semantics and Its Application in Machine Translation). In Liu Yongquan 劉湧泉 *et al.*,《中國的機器翻譯》(*Machine Translation in China*). Shanghai: Knowledge Press, pp. 25–45.

Dorna, Michael and Martin C. Emele (1996). "Efficient Implementation of a Semantic-based Transfer Approach." *Proceedings of the 12th European Conference on Artificial Intelligence*, Budapest, Hungary, pp. 567–571.

Dorna, Michael and Martin C. Emele (1996). "Semantic-based Transfer." *Proceedings from the 16th International Conference on Computational Linguistics* (*COLING-96*). Copenhagen, Denmark, pp. 316–321.

Feng, Zhiwei 馮志偉 and Yang Ping 楊平 (1987).〈語義的形式描述〉(A

Formal Description of Semantic Meaning). 《自動翻譯》(*Automatic Translation*). Shanghai: Knowledge Press, pp. 90–116.

Fuchss, Ruth, Alexander Koller, Joachim Niehren, and Stefan Thater (2004). "Minimal Recursion Semantics as Dominance Constraints: Translation, Evaluation, and Analysis." *Proceedings of the 42nd Annual Meeting of the Association for Computational Linguistics (ACL-2004)*, Barcelona, Spain, pp. 247–254.

Germann, Ulrich (1998). "Making Semantic Interpretation Parser-independent." In David L. Farwell, Laurie Gerber, and Eduard Hovy, eds., *Machine Translation and the Information Soup*. Berlin: Springer Verlag, pp. 286–299.

Gildea, Daniel and Daniel Jurafsky (2000). "Automatic Labeling of Semantic Roles." *Proceedings of the 38th Annual Meeting of the Association for Computational Linguistics (ACL-2000)*, Hong Kong.

Girju, Roxana, Adriana Badulescu, and Dan I. Moldovan (2006). "Automatic Discovery of Part-whole Relations." *Computational Linguistics*, Vol. 32, No. 1, pp. 83–135.

Harper, Kenneth E. (1962). "Procedures for the Determination of Distributional Classes." In National Physical Laboratory, ed., *1961 International Conference on Machine Translation of Languages and Applied Language Analysis: Proceedings of the Conference Held at the National Physical Laboratory, Teddington, Middlesex, on 5th, 6th, 7th and 8th September*. London: Her Majesty's Stationery Office, Vol. 1, pp. 688–698.

Hausser, Roland (2001). "Spatio-temporal Indexing in Database Semantics." *Proceedings of the 2nd International Conference on Intelligent Text Processing and Computational Linguistics (CICLing-2001)*, Mexico City, Mexico.

Hoffman, Th. (1976). "Semantics in Aid of Automatic Translation." *Proceedings of the 6th International Conference on Computational Linguistics (COLING-76)*, Ottawa, Canada.

Hoffman, Th. (1978). "Semantics in Aid of Automatic Translation." *Proceedings of the 7th International Conference on Computational Linguistics (COLING-78)*, Bergen, Norway.

Ikehara, Satoru (2002). "Toward the Realization of Typological Semantic Pattern Dictionaries for MT." *Proceedings of the 9th International Conference on Theoretical and Methodological Issues in Machine Translation (TMI-2002)*, Keihanna, Japan.

Jones, K. Sparck (1962). "Mechanised Semantic Classification." In National Physical Laboratory, ed., *1961 International Conference on Machine Translation of Languages and Applied Language Analysis: Proceedings of the Conference Held at the National Physical Laboratory, Teddington, Middlesex, on 5th, 6th, 7th and 8th September*. London: Her Majesty's Stationery Office, Vol. 1, pp. 418–433.

Koch, Gregers (2000). "A Method for Making Computational Sense of Situation Semantics." *Proceedings of the 1st International Conference on Intelligent Text Processing and Computational Linguistics* (*CICLing-2000*), Mexico City, Mexico.

Kozima, Hideki and Akira Ito (1997). "Context-sensitive Word Distance by Adaptive Scaling of a Semantic Space." In Ruslan Mitkov and Nicolas Nicolov, eds., *Recent Advances in Natural Language Processing*. Amsterdam and Philadelphia: John Benjamins Publishing Company, pp. 111–124.

Kumar, R. Sathish and R. S. D. Wahida Banu (2004). "Selectional Preferences Acquisition Using Tree Cut Model and Semantic Similarity." *Proceedings of the International Conference on Natural Language Processing* (*ICON-2004*), International Institute of Information Technology, Hyderabad, India.

Loukanova, Roussanka (2000). "Nominal Scope in Situation Semantics." *Proceedings of the 1st International Conference on Intelligent Text Processing and Computational Linguistics* (*CICLing-2000*), Mexico City, Mexico.

Loukanova, Roussanka (2001). "Russellian and Strawsonian Definite Description in Situation Semantics." *Proceedings of the 2nd International Conference on Intelligent Text Processing and Computational Linguistics* (*CICLing-2001*), Mexico City, Mexico.

Lytinen, Steven L. (1987). "Integrating Syntax and Semantics." In Sergei Nirenburg, ed., *Machine Translation: Theoretical and Methodological Issues*. Cambridge: Cambridge University Press, pp. 302–316.

Mao, Jia-ju, Qiu-lin Chen, and Ru-zhan Lu (2003). "Analyzing V + Adj in Situation Semantics." *Proceedings of the 4th International Conference on Intelligent Text Processing and Computational Linguistics* (*CICLing-2003*), Mexico City, Mexico, pp. 76–86.

Masterman, Margaret (1957). "The Thesaurus in Syntax and Semantics." *Mechanical Translation*, Vol. 4, No. 2, pp. 35–43.

Masterman, Margaret (1962). "Semantic Message Detection for Machine Translation, Using an Interlingua." In National Physical Laboratory, ed., *1961 International Conference on Machine Translation of Languages and Applied Language Analysis: Proceedings of the Conference Held at the National Physical Laboratory, Teddington, Middlesex, on 5th, 6th, 7th and 8th September*. London: Her Majesty's Stationery Office, Vol. 2, pp. 438–474.

McCarthy, Diana (2000). "Using Semantic Preferences to Identify Verbal Participation in Role Switching Alternations." *Proceedings of the 1st Meeting of the North American Chapter of the Association for Computational Linguistics*, Seattle, Washington, DC, USA, pp. 256–263.

McGlashan, Scott (1994). "The Role of Semantics in Spoken Dialogue Translation Systems." *Machine Translation—Ten Years On: Proceedings of the 2nd International Conference Organised by Cranfield University*, Cranfield, England.

Mel'čuk, Igor A. (2000). "Semantics and the Lexicon in Modern Linguistics." *Proceedings of the 1st International Conference on Intelligent Text Processing and Computational Linguistics* (*CICLing-2000*), Mexico City, Mexico.

Mohanty, Rajat Kumar, Anupama Dutta, and Pushpak Bhattacharyya (2005). "Semantically Relatable Sets: Building Blocks for Representing Semantics." *Proceedings of MT Summit X*, Phuket, Thailand.

Nerbonne, John (1993). "Constraint-based Semantics." *Proceedings of the Conference of the Association for Computational Linguistics and Chinese Language Processing* (*ROCLING-VI*), Nantou, Taiwan.

Nitta, Yoshihiko *et al.* (1984). "A Proper Treatment of Syntax and Semantics in Machine Translation." *Proceedings of the 10th International Conference on Computational Linguistics* (*COLING-84*), Stanford University, Stanford, CA, USA, pp. 159–166.

Ornan, Uzzi and Israel Gutter (2000). "Machine Translation by Semantic Features." *Proceedings of the International Conference on Machine Translation and Multilingual Applications in the New Millenium* (*MT-2000*), University of Exeter, England.

Oswald, Victor A. (1952). "Microsemantical Investigations." *Proceedings of the M.I.T. Conference on Mechanical Translation*, Massachusetts Institute of Technology, Cambridge, MA, USA.

Palmer, Martha and Yi Szu-ting (2004). "Pushing the Boundaries of Semantic Role Labeling with SVM." *Proceedings of the International Conference on Natural Language Processing (ICON-2004)*, International Institute of Information Technology, Hyderabad, India.

Papegaaij, Bart C. (1986). *Word Expert Semantics: An Interlingual Knowledge-based Approach*. Dordrecht: Foris Publication.

Pedersen, Bolette Sandford (1999). "Systematic Verb Polysemy in MT: A Study of Danish Motion Verbs with Comparisons with Spanish." *Machine Translation*, Vol. 14, No. 1, pp. 35–82.

Pigott, Ian M. (1979). "Theoretical Options and Practical Limitations of Using Semantics to Solve Problems of Natural Language Analysis and Machine Translation." In Maxine MacCafferty and Kathleen Gray, eds., *Informatics 5: The Analysis of Meaning*. London: The Association for Information Management, pp. 239–268.

Pimsleur, Paul (1957). "Semantic Frequency Counts." *Mechanical Translation*, Vol. 4, Nos. 1–2, pp. 11–13.

Pogodalla, Sylvain (2000). "Generation in the Lambek Calculus Framework: An Approach with Semantic Proof Nets." *Proceedings of the 1st Meeting of the North American Chapter of the Association for Computational Linguistics*, Seattle, Washington, DC, USA, pp. 70–77.

Raskin, Victor (1987). "What Is There in Linguistic Semantics for Natural Language Processing?" *Proceedings of the Northeast Artificial Intelligence Consortium's Natural Language Planning Workshop*, Blue Mountain Lake, New York, USA, pp. 78–96.

Reifler, Erwin (1955). "The Mechanical Determination of Meaning." In William N. Locke and Andrew Donald Booth, eds., *Machine Translation of Languages: Fourteen Essays*. Cambridge, MA: Technology Press of the Massachusetts Institute of Technology, pp. 136–164.

Romacker, Martin and Udo Hahn (2000). "An Empirical Assessment of Semantic Interpretation." *Proceedings of the 1st Meeting of the North American Chapter of the Association for Computational Linguistics*, Seattle, Washington, DC, USA, pp. 327–334.

Root, Rebecca (1986). "Semantics, Translation, and Anaphora." *Computers and Translation*, Vol. 1, No. 2, pp. 93–108.

Rosé, Carolyn (2000). "A Framework for Robust Semantic Interpretation." *Proceedings of the 1st Meeting of the North American Chapter of the Association for Computational Linguistics*, Seattle, Washington, DC, USA, pp. 311–318.

Saba, Walid S. (2006). "On Types, Intension and Compositionality." In Alexander F. Gelbukh, ed., *Advances in Natural Language Processing*, Special Issue of *Research in Computing Science*, No. 18, pp. 93–104.

Sadler, Victor (1990). "A Corpus-based Measure of Semantic Proximity." In Marcel Thelen and Barbara Leeandowska-Tomaszczyk, eds., *Translation and Meaning, Part 1*. Maastricht: Euroterm, pp. 70–78.

Schiehlen, Michael (2000). "Semantic Construction." In Wolfgang Wahlster, ed., *Verbmobil: Foundations of Speech-to-speech Translation*. Berlin: Springer Verlag, pp. 200–215.

Sedelow, Walter A. and Sally Yeates Sedelow (1987). "Semantic Space." *Computers and Translation*, Vol. 2, No. 4, pp. 231–242.

Sgall, Petr (1989). "The Tasks of Semantics and the Perspectives of Computers." *Computers and Artificial Intelligence*, Vol. 8, pp. 403–421.

Terra, Egidio L. and Charles L. A. Clarke (2003). "Frequency Estimates for Statistical Word Similarity Measures." *Proceedings of the Human Language Technology and North American Chapter of Association of Computational Linguistics 2003* (*HLT/NAACL-2003*), Edmonton, Alberta, Canada.

Tosh, Wayne Leo (1969). "Translation Model with Semantic Capability." *Linguistics*, Vol. 55, pp. 56–69.

Tsai, Mei-chih, Chu-Ren Huang, Keh-jiann Chen, and Kathleen Ahrens (1997). "Towards a Representation of Verbal Semantics—An Approach Based on Near Synonyms." *Proceedings of the International Conference on Research in Computational Linguistics* (*ROCLING-X*), Academia Sinica, Taipei, Taiwan.

Turney, Peter D. (2006). "Expressing Implicit Semantic Relations without Supervision." *Proceedings of the Joint Conference of the International Committee on Computational Linguistics and the Association for Computational Linguistics* (*COLING/ACL-2006*), Sydney, Australia.

Zarechnak, Michael (1965). "An Applied Radical Semantics." *Mechanical Translation and Computational Linguistics*, Vol. 8, Nos. 3–4, pp. 90–96.

Zarechnak, Michael (1980). "Outline of Semantic Research for Future MT Development." *International Forum on Information and Documentation*, Vol. 5, No. 2, pp. 12–14.

Zernik, Uri (1990). "Lexical Acquisition: Where Is the Semantics?" *Machine Translation*, Vol. 5, No. 2, pp. 155–174.
Zhan, Weidong 詹衛東 and Chang Baobao 常寶寶 (1998).〈詞的語義分類在漢英機器翻譯中所起的作用以及難以處理的問題〉(Using Word Semantic Knowledge in a Chinese-English Machine Translation System). In Yu Shiwen 俞士汶 and Zhu Xuefeng 朱學鋒, eds.,《計算語言學文集》(*Papers on Computational Linguistics*), Vol. 3. Beijing: Department of Computer Science and Technology and Institute of Computational Linguistics, Peking University, pp. 101–107.
Zheng, Fengbin 鄭逢斌, Jiang Baoqing 姜保慶, Guo Zhengwei 郭拯危, Qiu Xiaoping 邱小平, and Qiao Baojun 喬保軍 (2002).〈特定領域中的語義校對系統 (YYJDS) 的設計與實現〉(The Design and Execution of the Semantic Collation System in a Special Field).《第一屆學生計算語言學研討會論文集》(*SWCL2002: First Students' Workshop on Computational Linguistics: Proceedings*), Institute of Computational Linguistics, Peking University, Beijing, China, p. 351.

Compositional Semantics

Forcada, Mikel L. (2002) "Explaining Real MT to Translators: Compositional Semantics and Word-for-word Translation." *Proceedings of the 6th EAMT Workshop: Teaching Machine Translation*, Manchester, England, pp. 137–144.
Landsbergen, Jan (1998). "Compositional Translation Revisited." *Proceedings of the 10th European Summer School on Logic, Linguistics and Information: Workshop on Machine Translation*, Saarbrücken, Germany.

Computational Semantics

Creary, Lewis G. and Carl J. Pollard (1985). "A Computational Semantics for Natural Language." *Proceedings of the 23rd Annual Meeting of the Association for Computational Linguistics* (*ACL-85*), Chicago, USA, pp. 172–179.
Palmer, Martha and Szu-ting Yi (2000). "Computational Lexical Semantics and Its Constraints." *Proceedings of the International Conference on Research in Computational Linguistics* (*ROCLING-XIII*), Taipei, Taiwan.

Viegas, Evelyne, Jin Wanying, and Stephen Beale (1999). "Using Computational Semantics for Chinese Translations." *Proceedings of MT Summit VII: MT in the Great Translation Era*, Singapore.

Meaning

Ahrens, Kathleen, Li-li Chang, Keh-Jiann Chen, and Chu-Ren Huang (1997). "Meaning Representation and Meaning Instantiation for Chinese Nominals." *Proceedings of the International Conference on Research in Computational Linguistics* (*ROCLING-X*), Academia Sinica, Taipei, Taiwan.

Arnold, Doug J., Lorna Balkan, R. Lee Humphreys, Seity Meijer, and Louisa Sadler (1994). "Representation and Processing Revisited: Meaning." *Machine Translation: An Introductory Guide*. Manchester and Oxford: NCC Blackwell, pp. 129–145.

Bateman, John A. (1992). "Towards Meaning-based Machine Translation: Using Abstractions from Text Generation for Preserving Meaning." *Machine Translation*, Vol. 7, Nos. 1–2, pp. 5–40.

Carl, Michael (1998). "Meaning Preservation in Machine Translation." *Proceedings of the 10th European Summer School on Logic, Linguistics and Information: Workshop on Machine Translation*, Saarbrücken, Germany.

Danielsson, Pernilla (2003). "Unit of Meaning in Translation—How to Make Real Use of Corpus Evidence." In *Translating and the Computer 25*. London: The Association for Information Management.

Helbig, Hermann and Carsten Gnörlich (2002). "Multilayered Extended Semantic Networks as a Language for Meaning Representation in NLP Systems." *Proceedings of the 3rd International Conference on Intelligent Text Processing and Computational Linguistics* (*CICLing-2002*), Mexico City, Mexico.

Janiotis, A. and Harry H. Josselson (1962). "Multiple Meaning in Machine Translation." In National Physical Laboratory, ed., *1961 International Conference on Machine Translation of Languages and Applied Language Analysis: Proceedings of the Conference Held at the National Physical Laboratory, Teddington, Middlesex, on 5th, 6th, 7th and 8th September*. London: Her Majesty's Stationery Office, Vol. 1, pp. 406–414.

Joos, Marlin (1956). "Systems of Logic in Machine Translation: Meaning in Relation to MT." In Leon E. Dostert, ed., *Research in Machine Translation*. Washington, DC: Georgetown University Press, pp. 13–38.

Koutsoudas, Andreas and R. Korfhage (1956). "Mechanical Translation and the Problem of Multiple Meaning." *Mechanical Translation*, Vol. 3, No. 2, pp. 46–51.

Kozarinsky, Meir (2002). "Calculus of Meanings." *International Journal of Translation*, Vol. 14, No. 2, pp. 47–50.

Morgan, Richard, Mark Smith, and Sengan Short (1994). "Translation by Meaning and Style in LOLITA." *Machine Translation—Ten Years On: Proceedings of the 2nd International Conference Organised by Cranfield University*, Cranfield, England.

Murata, Masaki, Kyoko Kanzaki, Kiyotaka Uchimoto, Qing Ma, and Hitoshi Isahara (2001). "Meaning Sort—Three Examples: Dictionary Construction, Tagged Corpus Construction, and Information Presentation System." *Proceedings of the 2nd International Conference on Intelligent Text Processing and Computational Linguistics (CICLing-2001)*, Mexico City, Mexico.

Nirenburg, Sergei and Kenneth Goodman (1990). "Treatment of Meaning in MT Systems." *Proceedings of the Conference of the Association for Computational Linguistics and Chinese Language Processing (ROCLING-III)*, Taipei, Taiwan.

Nirenburg, Sergei and Kenneth Goodman (1990). "Treatment of Meaning in MT Systems." *Proceedings of the 3rd International Conference on Theoretical and Methodological Issues in Machine Translation of Natural Languages (TMI-90)*, Linguistics Research Center, University of Texas, Austin, Texas, USA, pp. 171–188.

Nirenburg, Sergei, Jaime G. Carbonell, Masaru Tomita, and Kenneth Goodman (1992). "Treatment of Meaning in MT Systems." *Machine Translation: A Knowledge-based Approach*. San Matero, California: Morgan Kaufmann, pp. 41–63.

Nomura, Hirosato (1988). "Meaning Understanding in Machine Translation." *Proceedings of the 2nd International Conference on Theoretical and Methodological Issues in Machine Translation of Natural Languages (TMI-88)*, Carnegie Mellon University, Center for Machine Translation, Pittsburgh, Pennsylvania, USA.

Pinkal, Manfred and Michael Kohlhase (2000). "Feature Logic for Dotted Types: A Formalism for Complex Word Meanings." *Proceedings of the*

38th Annual Meeting of the Association for Computational Linguistics (ACL-2000), Hong Kong.

Reifler, Erwin (1955). "The Mechanical Determination of Meaning." In William N. Locke and Andrew D. Booth, eds., *Machine Translation of Languages*. Cambridge, MA: The Technology Press of the Massachusetts Institute of Technology, pp. 136–164.

Resnik, Philip (2004). "Exploiting Hidden Meanings: Using Bilingual Text for Monolingual Annotation." *Proceedings of the 5th International Conference on Intelligent Text Processing and Computational Linguistics (CICLing-2004)*, Chung-Ang University, Seoul, Korea, pp. 280–296.

Solovyev, Valery D. (2000). "Improving Semantic Component of the Meaning ⇔ Text Model." *Proceedings of the 1st International Conference on Intelligent Text Processing and Computational Linguistics (CICLing-2000)*, Mexico City, Mexico.

Wang, Xiaojie and Zhong Yixin (1999). "A New Way to Conceptual Meaning Representation." *Proceedings of MT Summit VII: MT in the Great Translation Era*, Singapore.

Semantic Network

Budanitsky, Alexander and Graeme Hirst (2006). "Evaluating WordNet-based Measures of Lexical Semantic Relatedness." *Computational Linguistics*, Vol. 32, No. 1, pp. 13–47.

Higinbotham, Dan W. (1990). "Semantic Cooccurrence Networks." *Proceedings of the 3rd International Conference on Theoretical and Methodological Issues in Machine Translation of Natural Languages (TMI-90)*, Linguistics Research Center, University of Texas at Austin, Austin, Texas, USA, pp. 75–84.

Klebanov, Beata Beigman (2006). "Measuring Semantic Relatedness Using People and WordNet." *Proceedings of the Human Language Technology Conference—Annual Meeting of the North American Chapter of the Association for Computational Linguistics (HLT-NAACL-2006)*, New York, USA.

Smith, Andrew E. (2003). "Automatic Extraction of Semantic Networks from Text Using Leximancer." *Proceedings of the Human Language Technology and North American Chapter of Association of Computational Linguistics 2003 (HLT/NAACL-2003)*, Edmonton, Alberta, Canada.

Turney, Peter D. (2006). "Similarity of Semantic Relations." *Computational Linguistics*, Vol. 32, No. 3, pp. 379–416.

Semantic Processing

Pinkal, Manfred, C. J. Rupp, and Karsten Worm (2000). "Robust Semantic Processing of Spoken Language." In Wolfgang Wahlster, ed., *Verbmobil: Foundations of Speech-to-speech Translation*. Berlin: Springer Verlag, pp. 321–335.

Semantic Web

Lenci, Alessandro, Nicoletta Calzolari, and Antonio Zampolli (2002). "From Text to Content: Computational Lexicons and the Semantic Web." *Proceedings of the 18th National Conference on Artificial Intelligence*, Edmonton, Canada.

Matsui, Kunio (2002). "The Semantic Web and Its Meta-data." In Yu Shiwen, ed., *Proceedings of the 2nd China-Japan Natural Language Processing Joint Research Promotion Conference* (*CJNLP-2002*). Beijing: Institute of Computational Linguistics, Peking University, pp. 178–182.

Stylistics

Laurian, Anne-Marie (1986). "Stylistics and Computing: Machine Translation as a Tool for a New Approach to Stylistics." *Computers and Translation*, Vol. 1, No. 4, pp. 215–223.

Syntax

Bar-Hillel, Yehoshua (1952). "Operational Syntax." *Proceedings of the M.I.T. Conference on Mechanical Translation,* Massachusetts Institute of Technology, Cambridge, MA, USA.

Bar-Hillel, Yehoshua (1953). "A Quasi Arithmetical Notation for Syntactic Representation." *Language*, Vol. 29.

Bennett, Paul A. (1993). "The Interaction of Syntax and Morphology in Machine Translation." In Frank van Eynde, ed., *Linguistics Issues in Machine Translation*. London and New York: Pinter Publishers, pp. 72–104.

Booth, Andrew D. (1961). "Syntactic Processing in Machine Translation and Its Implications for Cost and Speed." In Allen Kent, ed., *Information Retrieval and Machine Translation*. New York: Interscience, Vol. 2, pp. 759–763.

Corbe, M. and R. Tabory (1962). "Introduction to an Automatic English Syntax." In National Physical Laboratory, ed., *1961 International Conference on Machine Translation of Languages and Applied Language Analysis: Proceedings of the Conference Held at the National Physical Laboratory, Teddington, Middlesex, on 5th, 6th, 7th and 8th September*. London: Her Majesty's Stationery Office, Vol. 1, pp. 617–652.

Dorna, Michael, Anette Frank, Josef van Genabith, and Martin C. Emele (1998). "Syntactic and Semantic Transfer with F-structures." *Proceedings of the 36th Annual Meeting of the Association for Computational Linguistics and 17th International Conference on Computational Linguistics* (*COLING-ACL-98*), Montreal, Quebec, Canada, pp. 341–347.

Dorr, Bonnie J. (1993). "Syntactic Component." *Machine Translation: A View from the Lexicon*. Cambridge, MA: MIT Press, pp. 43–77.

Ferres-Trahtenbroit, Leo (2000). "Thematic Proto-roles and Argument-predicate Interaction." *Proceedings of the 1st International Conference on Intelligent Text Processing and Computational Linguistics* (*CICLing-2000*), Mexico City, Mexico.

Garvin, Paul L. (1963). "Syntax in Machine Translation." In Paul L. Garvin, ed., *Natural Language and the Computer*. New York: McGraw-Hill, pp. 223–232.

Green, T. R. G. (1979). "The Necessity of Syntax Markers: Two Experiments with Artificial Languages." *Journal of Verbal Learning and Behavior*, Vol. 18, pp. 481–496.

Hays, David G. (1962). "On the Value of Dependency Connection." In National Physical Laboratory, ed., *1961 International Conference on Machine Translation of Languages and Applied Language Analysis: Proceedings of the Conference Held at the National Physical Laboratory, Teddington, Middlesex, on 5th, 6th, 7th and 8th September*. London: Her Majesty's Stationery Office, Vol. 2, pp. 579–590.

Hays, David G. (1964). "Connectibility Calculations, Syntactic Functions, and Russian Syntax." *Mechanical Translation*, Vol. 8, No. 1, pp. 32–51.

Hsieh, Hsin-I (1994). "A Computational Syntax and Its Application to Parsing." *Proceedings of the Conference of the Association for Computational Linguistics and Chinese Language Processing (ROCLING-VII)*, National Tsing Hua University, Hsin-Chu, Taiwan.

Khegai, Janna, Bengt Nordström, and Aarne Ranta (2003). "Multilingual Syntax Editing in GF." *Proceedings of the 4th International Conference on Intelligent Text Processing and Computational Linguistics (CICLing-2003)*, Mexico City, Mexico, pp. 455–466.

Kuhn, Jonas (2000). "Processing Optimality-theoretic Syntax by Interleaved Chart Parsing and Generation." *Proceedings of the 38th Annual Meeting of the Association for Computational Linguistics (ACL-2000)*, Hong Kong.

Kuhn, Jonas (2002). "OT Syntax—Decidability of Generation-based Optimization." *Proceedings of the 40th Annual Meeting of the Association for Computational Linguistics (ACL-2002)*, Philadelphia, PA, USA, pp. 48–55.

Lamb, Sydney M. (1962). "On the Mechanization of Syntactic Analysis." In National Physical Laboratory, ed., *1961 International Conference on Machine Translation of Languages and Applied Language Analysis: Proceedings of the Conference Held at the National Physical Laboratory, Teddington, Middlesex, on 5th, 6th, 7th and 8th September.* London: Her Majesty's Stationery Office, Vol. 1, pp. 674–684.

Levin, Lori S. (1990). "Syntactic Theory and Grammar Design for Machine Translation." *Proceedings of the 3rd International Conference on Theoretical and Methodological Issues in Machine Translation of Natural Languages (TMI-90)*, Linguistics Research Center, University of Texas at Austin, Austin, Texas, USA, pp. 109–120.

Lytinen, Steven L. (1987). "Integrating Syntax and Semantics." In Sergei Nirenburg, ed., *Machine Translation: Theoretical and Methodological Issues*. Cambridge: Cambridge University Press, pp. 302–316.

Marcus, Mitchell P. (1980). *A Theory of Syntactic Recognition for Natural Language*. Cambridge, MA: MIT Press.

Masterman, Margaret (1957). "The Thesaurus in Syntax and Semantics." *Mechanical Translation*, Vol. 4, No. 2, pp. 35–43.

Nitta, Yoshihiko, Atsushi Okajima, Hiroyuki Kaji, Youichi Hidano, and Koichiro Ishihara (1984). "A Proper Treatment of Syntax and Semantics in Machine Translation." *Proceedings of the 10th*

International Conference on Computational Linguistics (*COLING-84*), Stanford University, Stanford, CA, USA, pp. 159–166.

Odjik, Jan (1994). "Compositionality and Syntactic Generalisations." In M. T. Rosetta, *Compositional Translation*. Dordrecht: Kluwer Academic Publishers, pp. 185–201.

Odijk, Jan (1994). "Syntactic Rules." In M. T. Rosetta, *Compositional Translation*. Dordrecht: Kluwer Academic Publishers, pp. 133–148.

Parker-Rhodes, Arthur Frederick (1962). "A New Model of Syntactic Description." In National Physical Laboratory, ed., *1961 International Conference on Machine Translation of Languages and Applied Language Analysis: Proceedings of the Conference Held at the National Physical Laboratory, Teddington, Middlesex, on 5th, 6th, 7th and 8th September*. London: Her Majesty's Stationery Office, Vol. 1, pp. 26–60.

Pyne, Jane A. (1957). "Some Ideas on Inter-structural Syntax." In Leon E. Dostert, ed., *Report of the 8th Annual Round Table Meeting on Linguistics and Language Studies: Research on Machine Translation*. Washington, DC: Georgetown University Press, pp. 143–149.

Sakai, Itiroo (1962). "Syntax in Universal Translation." In National Physical Laboratory, ed., *1961 International Conference on Machine Translation of Languages and Applied Language Analysis: Proceedings of the Conference Held at the National Physical Laboratory, Teddington, Middlesex, on 5th, 6th, 7th and 8th September*. London: Her Majesty's Stationery Office, Vol. 1, pp. 594–608.

Sherry, Murray E. (1962). "The Identification of Nested Structures in Predictive Syntactic Analysis." In National Physical Laboratory, ed., *1961 International Conference on Machine Translation of Languages and Applied Language Analysis: Proceedings of the Conference Held at the National Physical Laboratory, Teddington, Middlesex, on 5th, 6th, 7th and 8th September*. London: Her Majesty's Stationery Office, Vol. 1, pp. 144–155.

Snow, Rion, Lucy Vanderwende, and Arul Menezes (2006). "Effectively Using Syntax for Recognizing False Entailment." *Proceedings of the Human Language Technology Conference—Annual Meeting of the North American Chapter of the Association for Computational Linguistics* (*HLT-NAACL-2006*), New York, USA.

Tosh, Wayne L. (1965). *Syntactic Translation*. London: Mouton.

Ueki, Masahiro, Takenobu Tokunaga, and Hozumi Tanaka (1999).

"Sharing Syntactic Structures." *Proceedings of MT Summit VII: MT in the Great Translation Era*, Singapore.

Wundheiler, Luitgard and Alex Wundheiler (1955). "Some Logical Concepts for Syntax." In William N. Locke and Andrew D. Booth, eds., *Machine Translation of Languages: Fourteen Essays.* Cambridge, MA: Technology Press of the Massachusetts Institute of Technology, pp. 194–207.

Yang, Muyun 楊沐昀, Zhao Tiejun 趙鐵軍, and Yu Hao 于浩 (2001).〈自底向上的漢語句法標注體系設計與實踐〉(Bottom-up Design of Chinese Syntax Annotation Scheme). In Huang Changning 黃昌寧 and Zhang Pu 張普, eds.,《自然語言理解與機器翻譯》(*Natural Language Understanding and Machine Translation*). Beijing: Tsinghua University Press, pp. 160–166.

Yngve, Victor H. (1955). "Syntax and the Problem of Multiple Meaning." In William N. Locke and Andrew D. Booth, eds., *Machine Translation of Languages: Fourteen Essays.* Cambridge, MA: Technology Press of the Massachusetts Institute of Technology, pp. 208–226.

Yngve, Victor H. (1957). "A Framework for Syntactic Translation." *Mechanical Translation*, Vol. 43, pp. 59–65.

Zhang, Min, Jie Zhang, and Jian Su (2006). "Exploring Syntactic Features for Relation Extraction Using a Convolution Tree Kernel." *Proceedings of the Human Language Technology Conference—Annual Meeting of the North American Chapter of the Association for Computational Linguistics* (*HLT-NAACL-2006*), New York, USA.

Zhou, Qiang 周強 (2001).〈漢語句法知識的自動獲取研究〉(Automatic Syntactic Knowledge Acquisition for the Chinese Language).《輝煌二十年——中國中文信息學會二十周年學術會議》(*Proceedings of Conference of the 20th Anniversary of CIPSC*). Beijing: Tsinghua University Press, pp. 156–165.

Noun Phrase

Bond, Francis, Kentaro Ogura, and Tsukasa Kawaoka (1995). "Noun Phrase Reference in Japanese-to-English Machine Translation." *Proceedings of the 6th International Conference on Theoretical and Methodological Issues in Machine Translation* (*TMI-95*), the University of Leuven, Belgium.

Cardie, Claire and Kiri Wagstaff (1999). "Noun Phrase Coreference as Clustering." *Proceedings of the Joint SIGDAT Conference on Empirical Methods in NLP and Very Large Corpora* (*EMNLP/VLC-99*), University of Maryland, College Park, MD, USA.

Kupiec, Julian (1993). "An Algorithm for Finding Noun Phrase Correspondences in Bilingual Corpora." *Proceedings of the 31st Annual Meeting of the Association of Computational Linguistics* (*ACL-93*), Ohio State University, Columbus, Ohio, USA, pp. 17–22.

Lee, Jonwoo, Zhang Byoung-Tak, and Yung Taek Kim (1999). "Compound Noun Decomposition Using a Markov Model." *Proceedings of MT Summit VII: MT in the Great Translation Era*, Singapore.

Lehmann, Winfred P. (1957). "Structure of Noun Phrases in German." In Leon E. Dostert, ed., *Research in Machine Translation*. Washington, DC: Georgetown University Press, pp. 125–133.

Murata, Masaki, Kiyotaka Uchimoto, Qing Ma, and Hitoshi Isahara (2001). "A Machine-learning Approach to Estimating the Referential Properties of Japanese Noun Phrases." *Proceedings of the 2nd International Conference on Intelligent Text Processing and Computational Linguistics* (*CICLing-2001*), Mexico City, Mexico.

Ngai, Grace and David Yarowsky (2000). "Rule Writing or Annotation: Cost-efficient Resource Usage for Base Noun Phrase Chunking." *Proceedings of the 38th Annual Meeting of the Association for Computational Linguistics* (*ACL-2000*), Hong Kong, China.

Nogaito, Izuru and Hitoshi Iida (1988). "Noun Phrase Identification in Dialogue and Its Application." *Proceedings of the 2nd International Conference on Theoretical and Methodological Issues in Machine Translation of Natural Languages* (*TMI-88*), Carnegie Mellon University, Center for Machine Translation, Pittsburgh, Pennsylvania, USA.

Sang, Erik F. Tjong Kim (2000). "Noun Phrase Recognition by System Combination." *Proceedings of the 1st Meeting of the North American Chapter of the Association for Computational Linguistics*, Seattle, Washington, DC, USA, pp. 50–55.

Wacholder, Nina and Peng Song (2003). "Toward a Task-based Gold Standard for Evaluation of NP Chunks and Technical Terms." *Proceedings of the Human Language Technology and North American Chapter of Association of Computational Linguistics 2003* (*HLT/NAACL-2003*), Edmonton, Alberta, Canada.

Wang, Zhimin, Houfeng Wang, Huiming Duan, Shuang Han, and Shiwen Yu (2006). "Chinese Noun Phrase Metaphor Recognition with Maximum Entropy Approach." *Proceedings of the 7th International Conference on Intelligent Text Processing and Computational Linguistics* (*CICLing-2006*), Mexico City, Mexico.

Xun, Endong, Huang Changning, and Zhou Ming (2000). "A Unified Statistical Model for the Identification of English BaseNP." *Proceedings of the 38th Annual Meeting of the Association for Computational Linguistics* (*ACL-2000*), Hong Kong.

Yang, Xiaofeng, Jian Su, and Lingpeng Yang (2005). "Entity-based Noun Phrase Coreference Resolution." *Proceedings of the 6th International Conference on Intelligent Text Processing and Computational Linguistics* (*CICLing-2005*), Mexico City, Mexico, pp. 212–215.

Phrase

Chang, Jason S., David Yu, and Lee Chun-Jen (2001). "Statistical Translation Model for Phrases." *Computational Linguistics and Chinese Language Processing*, Vol. 6, No. 2, pp. 43–64.

Culik, Karel (1967). "Machine Translation and Connectedness between Phrases." *Prague Studies in Mathematical Linguistics*, No. 2, pp. 245–259.

Merkel, Magnus, Bernt Nilsson, and Lars Ahrenberg (1994). "A Phrase-retrieval System Based on Recurrence." *Proceedings of the 2nd Annual Workshop on Very Large Corpora* (*WVLC-2*). Kyoto, Japan, pp. 99–108.

Murray, G. Craig, Bonnie J. Dorr, Jimmy Lin, Jan Hajic, and Pavel Pecina (2006). "Leveraging Recurrent Phrase Structure in Large-scale Ontology Translation." *Proceedings of the 11th Workshop of the European Association for Machine Translation: Machine Translation/Translation Aids—Tools to Increase Quality and to Save Money*, the University of Oslo, Oslo, Norway.

Nadeau, David, Caroline Barrière, and George Foster (2005). "Bike: Bilingual Keyphrase Experiments." In Walther van Hahn, W. John Hutchins, and Cristina Vertan, eds., *Proceedings of the International Workshop on Modern Approaches in Translation Technologies*, Borovets, Bulgaria.

Saito, Manami, Kazuhide Yamamoto, and Satoshi Sekine (2006). "Using

Phrasal Patterns to Identify Discourse Relations." *Proceedings of the Human Language Technology Conference—Annual Meeting of the North American Chapter of the Association for Computational Linguistics* (*HLT-NAACL-2006*), New York, USA.

Sarich, Ace J. (2004). "Development and Fielding of the Phraselator® Phrase Translation System." In *Translating and the Computer 26*. London: The Association for Information Management.

Setiawan, Hendra, Li Haizhou, Zhang Min, and Ooi Beng Chin (2005). "Learning Phrase Translation Using Level of Detail Approach." *Proceedings of MT Summit X*, Phuket, Thailand.

Simard, Michel, Nicola Cancedda, Bruno Cavestro, Marc Dymetman, Eric Gaussier, Cyril Goutte, Kenji Yamada, Philippe Langlais, and Arne Mauser (2005). "Translating with Non-contiguous Phrases." *Proceedings of Human Language Technology Conference and Conference on Empirical Methods in Natural Language Processing* (*HLT/EMNLP-2005*), Vancouver, BC, Canada.

Sun, Honglin 孫宏林 and Duan Huiming 段慧明 (1998).〈面向自然語言處理的現代漢語短語信息庫〉(Contemporary Chinese Phrasal Database Oriented for Natural Language Processing). In Yu Shiwen 俞士汶 and Zhu Xuefeng 朱學鋒, eds.,《計算語言學文集》(*Papers on Computational Linguistics*), Vol. 3. Beijing: Department of Computer Science and Technology and Institute of Computational Linguistics, Peking University, pp. 41–48.

Wang, Guangyi (1982). "Fixed Phrases and Constructions in Machine Translation." *Language and Computer*, Vol. 1, pp. 23–28.

Wu, Yu-Chieh, Chia-Hui Chang, and Yue-Shi Lee (2006). "A General and Multi-lingual Phrase Chunking Model Based on Masking Method." *Proceedings of the 7th International Conference on Intelligent Text Processing and Computational Linguistics* (*CICLing-2006*), Mexico City, Mexico.

Wu, Yunfang, Chang Baobao, and Zhan Weidong (2002).〈漢英雙語短語信息數據庫的構建〉(Building Chinese-English Bilingual Phrase Database).《第一屆學生計算語言學研討會論文集》(*SWCL2002: First Students' Workshop on Computational Linguistics: Proceedings*), Institute of Computational Linguistics, Peking University, Beijing, China, pp. 240–245.

Zhan, Weidong, Chang Baobao, and Yu Shiwen (2000).〈漢語短語結構定界歧義類型分析及分佈統計〉(An Analysis of the Types of Phrase

Boundary Ambiguity in Contemporary Chinese). In Yu Shiwen and Zhu Xuefeng, eds.,《計算語言學文集》(*Papers on Computational Linguistics*), Vol. 4. Beijing: Department of Computer Science and Technology and Institute of Computational Linguistics, Peking University, pp. 158–167.

Zhan, Weidong, Chang Baobao, and Yu Shiwen (2000).〈基於詞組本位語法的語義模型〉(A Semantic Model Based on Phrase-standard Grammar of Contemporary Chinese). In Yu Shiwen and Zhu Xuefeng, eds.,《計算語言學文集》(*Papers on Computational Linguistics*), Vol. 4. Beijing: Department of Computer Science and Technology and Institute of Computational Linguistics, Peking University, pp. 168–176.

Phrase Translation

Carl, Michael and Ecaterina Rascu (2006). "A Dictionary Lookup Strategy for Translating of Discontinuous Phrases." *Proceedings of the 11th Workshop of the European Association for Machine Translation: Machine Translation/Translation Aids—Tools to Increase Quality and to Save Money*, the University of Oslo, Oslo, Norway.

Huang, Fei, Zhang Ying, and Stephan Vogel (2005). "Mining Key Phrase Translations from Web Corpora." *Proceedings of Human Language Technology Conference and Conference on Empirical Methods in Natural Language Processing* (*HLT/EMNLP-2005*), Vancouver, BC, Canada.

❖ PART 22 ❖

Localization

Globalization

Arnold, David (2005). "'Global Power Brands'" and Marketing Economies of Scale: Fact or Fiction?" *Proceedings of the Localization World Conference*, Bonn, Germany.

Ashworth, David and Minako O'Hagan (2002). *Translation-mediated Communication in a Digital World: Facing the Challenges of Globalization and Localization*. Clevedon: Multilingual Matters.

Bradley, Stephen P., Richard L. Nolan, and Jerry A. Hausman, eds. (1993). *Globalization, Technology, and Competition: The Fusion of Computers and Telecommunications in the 1990s*. Boston, MA: Harvard Business School Press.

Brooks, David (2000). "What Price Globalization? Managing Costs at Microsoft." In Robert C. Sprung, ed., *Translating into Success: Cutting-edge Strategies for Going Multilingual in a Global Age*. Amsterdam and Philadelphia: John Benjamins Publishing Company, pp. 43–57.

Cheng, Susan (2000). "Globalizing an e-Commerce Web Site." In Robert C. Sprung, ed., *Translating into Success: Cutting-edge Strategies for Going Multilingual in a Global Age*. Amsterdam and Philadelphia: John Benjamins Publishing Company, pp. 29–42.

DePalma, Donald A. and Hans Fenstermacher (2003). "Global Product Development Simulation." *Proceedings of the Localization World Conference 2003*, Seattle, Washington, DC, USA.

Elrich, Manya (2006). "Virtual Hermes or Globalisation by Localisation." *Proceedings of the 6th Portsmouth Translation Conference: Translation Technologies and Culture*, School of Languages and Area Studies, University of Portsmouth, England.

Esselink, Bert (2003). "The Changing Face of Content Changes the Face of Translation." *Proceedings of Translation and Globalization*, Canadian Association of Translation Studies, Halifax, Canada.

Federman, Mark (2003). "The Cultural Paradox of the Global Village." *Proceedings of the Localization World Conference 2003*, Seattle, Washington, DC, USA.

Hall, Stuart (1997). "The Local and the Global: Globalization and Ethnicity." In Anthony D. King, ed., *Culture, Globalization and the World-system: Contemporary Conditions for the Representation of Identity*. Minneapolis: University of Minnesota Press, pp. 19–39.

Kay, Carl and Anthony Wong (2003). "Japan and China: Are You Missing out on 25% of the World's ICT Spending?" *Proceedings of the Localization World Conference 2003*, Seattle, Washington, DC, USA.

Kostner, Jaclyn (2003). "WOW eTeamwork." *Proceedings of the Localization World Conference 2003*, Seattle, Washington, DC, USA.

Lau, Chi-chuen Paris (2002). "Globalisation on Language: Death of the Translator in the Technological Age." In Chan Sin-wai, ed., *Translation and Information Technology*. Hong Kong: The Chinese University Press, pp. 177–183.

Lockwood, Rose, Jean Leston, and Laurent Lachal (1995). *Globalisation: Creating New Markets with Translation Technology*. London: Ovum Limited.

McKethan, Kenneth A. and Graciela White (2005). "Demystifying Software Globalization." *Translation Journal*, Vol. 9, No. 2.

Moreira, Marcio M. (2003). "The Borderless Brand." *Proceedings of the Localization World Conference 2003*, Seattle, Washington, DC, USA.

Pym, Anthony (1999). "Globalization and Segmented Language Services." *Facköversättaren*, Vol. 10, No. 6, p. 10.

Rockley, Ann (2003). "Managing Enterprise Content: A Unified Content Strategy." *Proceedings of the Localization World Conference 2003*, Seattle, Washington, DC, USA.

Wang, Ning (2000). "Globalisation, Cultural Studies and Translation Studies." *Translation Quarterly*, No. 15, pp. 37–50.

Warbourton, Kara (2001). "Globalization and Terminology Management." In Sue Ellen Wright and Gerhard Budin, eds., *Handbook of Terminology Management*. Amsterdam and Philadelphia: John Benjamins Publishing Company, Vol. 2, pp. 677–696.

Zervaki, Thei (2002). *Globalize, Localize, Translate: Tips and Resources for Success*. Bloomington: First Book Library.

Internationalization

Kumhyr, David, Carla Merrill, and Karin Spalink (1994). "Internationalization and Translatability." *Proceedings of the 1st Conference of the Association for Machine Translation in the Americas: Technology Partnerships for Crossing the Language Barrier* (AMTA-*1*), Columbia, Maryland, USA, pp. 142–148.

Lieske, Christian (2006). "W3C Internationalization Tag Set: A Gentle

Introduction." In *Translating and the Computer 28*. London: The Association for Information Management.
Luong, Tuoc V., James S. H. Lok, David J. Taylor, and Kevin Driscoll (1995). *Internationalization: Developing Software for Global Markets*. New York: John Wiley.
O'Donnell, Sandra Martin (1994). *Programming for the World: A Guide to Internationalization*. Engelwood Cliffs: Prentice Hall Inc.
Poliak, Dan (2003). "Selecting the Right Product Name: International Trademark Concerns." *Proceedings of the Localization World Conference 2003*, Seattle, Washington, DC, USA.
Stevens, Debbie (2006). "Teaching and Learning through Internationalisation, Culture and Translation." *Proceedings of the 6th Portsmouth Translation Conference: Translation Technologies and Culture*, School of Languages and Area Studies, University of Portsmouth, England.
Uren, Emmanuel, Robert Howard, and Tiziana Perinotti (1993). *Software International and Localization*. New York: Van Nostrand Reinhold.

Localization

Allied Business Intelligence (2002). *Language Translation, Localization, and Globalization: World Market Forecasts, Industry Drivers, and eSolutions*. New Jersey: Allied Business Intelligence.
Altanero, Tim (1999). "Building a Curriculum for Localization: Austin Community College Takes the First Steps toward a Training Program in Partnership with Industry." *Multilingual Computing and Technology*, Vol. 11, No. 8, pp. 35–36.
Ashworth, David and Minako O'Hagan (2002). *Translation-mediated Communication in a Digital World: Facing the Challenges of Globalization and Localization*. Clevedon: Multilingual Matters.
Bass, Scott (2006). "Quality in the Real World." In Keiran Dunne, ed., *Perspectives on Localization*. Amsterdam and Philadelphia: John Benjamins Publishing Company.
Bengtsson, Teddy, Henri Broekmate, and Leonid Glazytchev (2003). "'Offshore': A Valid Localization Concept?" *Proceedings of the Localization World Conference 2003*, Seattle, Washington, DC, USA.
Bernal, Miguel (2006). "Video Games: Translation, Localisation, or Transcreation?" *Proceedings of the 6th Portsmouth Translation*

Conference: Translation Technologies and Culture, School of Languages and Area Studies, University of Portsmouth, England.
Bruns, David (2003). "Customer Loyalty One Country at a Time." *Proceedings of the Localization World Conference 2003*, Seattle, Washington, DC, USA.
Burgett, Will (2006). "Developing and Using a Holistic Localization ROI Model: Lessons on How to Prove the Value of Localization." *Proceedings of the Localization World Conference*, Barcelona, Spain.
Campbell, Charles (2006). "Training Initiatives in Localisation—The Vendor's View." In *Translating and the Computer 28*. London: The Association for Information Management.
Camrass, Roger (2006). "Atomization of the Localization Industry." *Proceedings of the Localization World Conference*, Barcelona, Spain.
Cañestro, Andrés Pérez (2005). "Localisation: Searching for the Origins of the Terms and Its Meaning: An Introduction to the Localisation Process as Opposed to Traditional Translation." *Translating Today*, No. 2.
Combe, Karen (2000). "Localization at Hewlett-Packard's LaserJet Solutions Group." In Robert C. Sprung, ed., *Translating into Success: Cutting-edge Strategies for Going Multilingual in a Global Age*. Amsterdam and Philadelphia: John Benjamins Publishing Company, pp. 97–109.
Combe, Karen (2003). "The Localization Metrics Initiative." *Proceedings of the Localization World Conference 2003*, Seattle, Washington, DC, USA.
Corbolante, Licia and Ulrike Irmler (2001). "Software Terminology and Localization." In Sue Ellen Wright and Gerhard Budin, eds., *Handbook of Terminology Management*. Amsterdam and Philadelphia: John Benjamins Publishing Company, Vol. 2, pp. 516–535.
Cronin, Liam (2006). "Training Needs in Localisation—The Client's View." In *Translating and the Computer 28*. London: The Association for Information Management.
Dain, Len, Lisa Frumkes, and Ivo Sanchez (2003). "In Lieu of Content Management Systems: Internal Management of Medium-sized Web Site Localization." *Proceedings of the Localization World Conference 2003*, Seattle, Washington, DC, USA.
de Biasi, Romona and Stuart Brown (2006). "Lost in Localization—How to Find a Happy Ending: How an Internal Translation Department Fights the Same Battles as Many External Localization Agencies Do

Every Day—A Practical Story." *Proceedings of the Localization World Conference*, Barcelona, Spain.
DePalma, Donald A. (2006). "Quantifying the Return on Localization Investment." In Keiran Dunne, ed., *Perspectives on Localization.* Amsterdam and Philadelphia: John Benjamins Publishing Company.
der Meer, Vand (1997). "On Localization." *Language International*, Vol. 5, No. 5, p. 43.
Dietz, Frank (2006). "Issues in Localizing Computer Games." Keiran Dunne, ed., *Perspectives on Localization.* Amsterdam and Philadelphia: John Benjamins Publishing Company.
DiFranco, Carla and Ulrike Irmler (2003). "Localization Process Standardization in the Windows Localization Group." *Proceedings of the Localization World Conference 2003*, Seattle, Washington, DC, USA.
DiFranco, Carla (2006). "Localization Cost." In Keiran Dunne, ed., *Perspectives on Localization.* Amsterdam and Philadelphia: John Benjamins Publishing Company.
Dohler, Per N. (1997). "Facets of Software Localization: A Translator's View." *Translation Journal*, Vol. 1, No. 1.
Dray, Susan M. and David A. Siegel (2006). "Melding Paradigms: Meeting the Needs of International Customers through Localization and User-centered Design." In Keiran Dunne, ed., *Perspectives on Localization.* Amsterdam and Philadelphia: John Benjamins Publishing Company.
Dube, Daniel W. (1999). "Case Study: Document Management and Localization." In *Translating and the Computer 21.* London: The Association for Information Management.
Dube, Daniel W. and John D. Rice (2000). "XML and the Localisation Process." In *Translating and the Computer 22.* London: The Association for Information Management.
Dube, Daniel W. (2002). "Reducing Localisation Costs with XML-based Technology." In *Translating and the Computer 24.* London: The Association for Information Management.
Dunne, Keiran (2006). "Introduction: A Copernican Revolution, Focusing on the Big Picture of Localization." In Keiran Dunne, ed., *Perspectives on Localization.* Amsterdam and Philadelphia: John Benjamins Publishing Company.
Dunne, Keiran, ed. (2006). *Perspectives on Localization.* Amsterdam and Philadelphia: John Benjamins Publishing Company.

Dunne, Keiran (2006). "Putting the Cart behind the Horse: Rethinking Localization Quality Management." In Keiran Dunne, ed., *Perspectives on Localization*. Amsterdam and Philadelphia: John Benjamins Publishing Company.

Elrich, Manya (2006). "Virtual Hermes or Globalisation by Localisation." *Proceedings of the 6th Portsmouth Translation Conference: Translation Technologies and Culture*, School of Languages and Area Studies, University of Portsmouth, England.

Esselink, Bert (1998, 2000). *A Practical Guide to Localization*, rev. ed. Amsterdam and Philadelphia: John Benjamins Publishing Company.

Esselink, Bert (2003). "Localisation and Translation." In Harold L. Somers, ed., *Computers and Translation: A Translator's Guide*. Amsterdam and Philadelphia: John Benjamins Publishing Company, pp. 67–86.

Fluixà, Noemi (2004). "Software Localisation: Outsourcing or In-house?" *Localisation Reader 2004–2005*.

Folaron, Debbie (2006). "A Discipline Coming of Age in the Digital Age." In Keiran Dunne, ed., *Perspectives on Localization*. Amsterdam and Philadelphia: John Benjamins Publishing Company.

Forssell, Dag (2001). "One Translator's Thoughts on Software Localization." *Translation Journal*, Vol. 5, No. 3.

Francois, Monica (2003). "Training Localization: Success for Global Audiences." *Proceedings of the Localization World Conference 2003*, Seattle, Washington, DC, USA.

Freivalds, John (2001). "Calculating Return on Localization." *Multilingual Computing and Technology*, Vol. 12, p. 4.

Freivalds, John (2004). "Pricing Translation and Localization Services." *Localisation Reader 2004–2005*.

Fry, Deborah (2000). *The Localization Industry Primer*. Féchy, Switzerland: Localization Industry Standards Association (LISA).

Gagny, Todd (2003). "Localizing the Enterprise: Corporate Expense Management." *Proceedings of the Localization World Conference 2003*, Seattle, Washington, DC, USA.

Gannon, Tom (2006). "Localization at AOL: An Example of Tight Client-vendor Integration." *Proceedings of the Localization World Conference*, Barcelona, Spain.

Groethuysen, C. (2001). "Real-life Training for Translators: Software Localization and Technical Documentation at the Sprachen-und

Dolmetscher Institut Munchen." *Language International*, Vol. 13, No. 4, pp. 16–19.
Guzmán, Rafael (2005). "Learning for Localisation Tools Training: Importance of E-learning for Translators." *Translating Today*, No. 2.
Hall, Bill and John O'Conner (2003). "Dueling Platforms: .NET Versus J2SE Localization." *Proceedings of the Localization World Conference 2003*, Seattle, Washington, DC, USA.
Hall, Pat (2004). "Localising Nations, Saving Languages: Moving from Unicode to Language Engineering." In *Translating and the Computer 26*. London: The Association for Information Management.
Heimburg, Eric (2006). "Localizing MMORPGs." In Keiran Dunne, ed., *Perspectives on Localization*. Amsterdam and Philadelphia: John Benjamins Publishing Company.
Karsch, Barbara Inge (2006). "Terminology Workflow in the Localization Process." In Keiran Dunne, ed., *Perspectives on Localization*. Amsterdam and Philadelphia: John Benjamins Publishing Company.
Kosaka, Takashi and Masaki Itagaki (2003). "Building a Curriculum for Japanese Localization Translators: Revisiting Translation Issues in the Era of New Technologies." In Brian James Baer and Geoffrey S. Koby, eds., *Beyond the Ivory Tower: Rethinking Translation Pedagogy*. Amsterdam and Philadelphia: John Benjamins Publishing Company, pp. 229–249.
Larsen, Inger (2004). "Training Tomorrow's Localisers." *The Linguist*, Vol. 43, No. 5.
Lommel, Arle (2006). "Localization Standards, Knowledge- and Information-centric Business Models, and the Commoditization of Linguistic Information." In Keiran Dunne, ed., *Perspectives on Localization*. Amsterdam and Philadelphia: John Benjamins Publishing Company.
Lynch, Clove (2006). "GMS Technology Making the Localization Business Case." In Keiran Dunne, ed., *Perspectives on Localization*. Amsterdam and Philadelphia: John Benjamins Publishing Company.
MacDermott, Lynda (2004). "Localising the Web." *The Linguist*, Vol. 43, No. 1.
Macias, Jordi and Eric van Thorre (2006). "A Microsoft Big Project Experience: Localizing Microsoft's Visual Studio 2005 and .NET Framework 2.0: A Case Study in Client-vendor Partnership." *Proceedings of the Localization World Conference*, Barcelona, Spain.

Macondray, Alison (2003). "WIRED for a Global Audience: The Localization of Wired.com.." *Proceedings of the Localization World Conference 2003*, Seattle, Washington, DC, USA.

Maroto, Jesus (2004). "Localisation Is Not for the Faint-hearted." *The Linguist*, Vol. 43, No. 4.

Moral, Rafa (2006). "Lionbridge—Two Case Studies Using MT in Localization." *Proceedings of the 7th Biennial Conference of the Association for Machine Translation in the Americas (AMTA-2006): Visions for the Future of Machine Translation*, Boston Marriott, Cambridge, MA, USA.

Neary, Orlagh (1996). "Automate, Emigrate or Evaporate! Automating the Localisation Process." In *Translating and the Computer 18*. London: The Association for Information Management.

O'Brien, Sharon (1998). "Practical Experience of Computer-aided Translation Tools in the Localization Industry." In Lynne Bowker, Michael Cronin, Dorothy Kenny, and Jennifer Pearson, eds., *Unity in Diversity? Current Trends in Translation Studies*. Manchester: St. Jerome Publishing, pp. 115–122.

O'Donoghue, Tim (1997). "Localizing Canon's User Documentation in Europe." *Proceedings of the 2nd Workshop of the European Association for Machine Translation: Language Technology in Your Organization?* University of Copenhagen, Copenhagen, Denmark.

O'Hagan, Minako (2003). "Conceptualising the Future of Translation with Localization." *International Journal of Localisation*.

Papaioannou, John (2003). "The Localization Outsourcing Decision: How to." *International Journal of Localisation*.

Pehkonen, Mika (2006). "Making Localization Lean and Agile: How More Emphasis on the Role of the Translator in Software Localization Leads to a Better Process." *Proceedings of the Localization World Conference*, Barcelona, Spain.

Pluke, Michael (2006). "Personal Localization: Localize for the Individual." *Proceedings of the Localization World Conference*, Barcelona, Spain.

Pym, Anthony (2001). "To Localize and Humanize: On Academics and Translation." *Language International*, Vol. 13, No. 4, pp. 26–28.

Pym, Anthony (2004). "Asymmetries of Distribution." *The Moving Text: Localization, Translation, and Distribution*. Amsterdam and Philadelphia: John Benjamins Publishing Company, pp. 29–50.

Pym, Anthony (2004). "Distribution." *The Moving Text: Localization, Translation, and Distribution*. Amsterdam and Philadelphia: John Benjamins Publishing Company, pp. 1–28.

Pym, Anthony (2004). *The Moving Text: Localization, Translation, and Distribution*. Amsterdam and Philadelphia: John Benjamins Publishing Company.

Rinsche, Adriane (2001). "Managing Translation and Localisation Projects with LTC Organiser." In Bente Maegaard, ed., *Proceedings of MT Summit VIII: Machine Translation in the Information Age*, Santiago de Compostela, Spain.

Sakson, Donna and Karen Johnson (2003). "The Uneasy Marriage between Authoring and Localization." *Proceedings of the Localization World Conference 2003*, Seattle, Washington, DC, USA.

Schäler, Reinhard (1996). "Machine Translation, Translation Memories and the Phrasal Lexicon: The Localisation Perspective." *Proceedings of the 1st European Association for Machine Translation Workshop (TKE-96)*, Vienna, Austria, pp. 21–34.

Schäler, Reinhard (2003). "Making a Business Case for Localisation." In *Translating and the Computer 25*. London: The Association for Information Management.

Schäler, Reinhard (2004). "The Certified Localisation Professional." In *Translating and the Computer 26*. London: The Association for Information Management.

Schäler, Reinhard (2005). "Reverse Localisation." In *Translating and the Computer 27*. London: The Association for Information Management.

Schildhauer, Erich (2004). "Integrating Localization Process with Software Development." *Localisation Reader 2004–2005*.

Seron-Ordonez, Inmaculada C. (2006). "Local History? Localising Digital Games with Historical and Cultural Content." *Proceedings of the 6th Portsmouth Translation Conference: Translation Technologies and Culture*, School of Languages and Area Studies, University of Portsmouth, England.

Shreve, Gregory M. (2006). "Corpus Enhancement and Computer-assisted Localization and Translation." In Keiran Dunne, ed., *Perspectives on Localization*. Amsterdam and Philadelphia: John Benjamins Publishing Company.

Stoeller, Willem (2003). "Risky Business: Risk Management for

Localization Project Managers." *Proceedings of the Localization World Conference 2003*, Seattle, Washington, DC, USA.
Thibodeau, Ricky P. (2000). "Making a Global Product at MapInfo Corporation." In Robert C. Sprung, ed., *Translating into Success: Cutting-edge Strategies for Going Multilingual in a Global Age*. Amsterdam and Philadelphia: John Benjamins Publishing Company, pp. 127–146.
Thibodeau, Ricky P. (2000). "Translating for Success: How MapInfo Created a Localization Process That Cut Cost and Time." *Language International*, Vol. 12, No. 2, pp. 30–33, 44.
Topping, Suzanne (2000). "Shortening the Translation Cycle at Eastman Kodak." In Robert C. Sprung, ed., *Translating into Success: Cutting-edge Strategies for Going Multilingual in a Global Age*. Amsterdam and Philadelphia: John Benjamins Publishing Company, pp. 111–125.
Walmer, Daphne (1999). "One Company's Efforts to Improve Translation and Localization." *Technical Communication*, Vol. 46, No. 2, pp. 230–237.
Wright, Sue Ellen (2006). "Localization-related Standards and Standards Bodies." In Keiran Dunne, ed., *Perspectives on Localization*. Amsterdam and Philadelphia: John Benjamins Publishing Company.
Wright, Sue Ellen (2006). "The Creation and Application of Language Industry Standards." In Keiran Dunne, ed., *Perspectives on Localization*. Amsterdam and Philadelphia: John Benjamins Publishing Company.
Zervaki, Thei (2002). *Globalize, Localize, Translate: Tips and Resources for Success*. Bloomington: First Book Library.
Zetzsche, Jost (2003). *Translation Databases for Web Site Localization*. London: Multilingual Press.

Localization System

Bolen, Kevin and Dmitry Grenader (2006). "Lionbridge: Localization 2.0." *Proceedings of the Localization World Conference*, Barcelona, Spain.
Cruz-Lara, Samuel, Nadia Bellalem, Julien Ducret, and Isabelle Kramer (2006). "Interoperability between Translation Memories and Localization Tools by Using the MultiLingual Information Framework." *Proceedings of the 11th Workshop of the European Association*

for Machine Translation: Machine Translation/Translation Aids—Tools to Increase Quality and to Save Money, the University of Oslo, Norway.

Fenstermacher, Hans and Martha Geller (2006). "Translations.com and ArchiText." *Proceedings of the Localization World Conference*, Barcelona, Spain.

Martin, Robert, Beverley White, and Tim Swales (2006). "Developing Effective Localisation Tools Strategies." In *Translating and the Computer 28*. London: The Association for Information Management.

Alchemy Catalyst

Martin, Robert and Tony O'Dowd (2006). "Alchemy Software Development Ltd.: Alchemy CATALYST 6.0 & Alchemy Layout Manager 2.0—The New Generation of Localization Intelligence." *Proceedings of the Localization World Conference*, Barcelona, Spain.

LTC-Communicator

Goffe, Nigel (2004). "LTC-Communicator: A Web-based Multilingual Help Desk." *International Journal of Translation*, Vol. 16, No. 1, pp. 33–39.

Rinsche, Adriane (2004). "LTC-Communicator—A Web-based E-communication Tool." *Proceedings of the 9th Workshop of the European Association for Machine Translation: Broadening Horizons of Machine Translation and Its Applications*, Foundation for International Studies, Malta.

Multilizer

Wassmer, Thomas (2003). "Review of Comparative Review of Four Localization Tools: Déjà Vu, MULTILIZER, MultiTrans and TRANS Suite 2000." *Multilingual Computing and Technology*, No. 55, Vol. 14, Issue 3.

MultiTrans

Gervais, Dan (2003). "MultiTrans System Presentation Translation

Support and Language Management Solutions." *Proceedings of MT Summit IX*, New Orleans, Louisiana, USA.
Locke, Nancy and Marc-Olivier Giguere (2002). "Review of MultiCorpora MultiTrans 3.0 (Corpus-based Translation Support Tool)." *Multilingual Computing and Technology*, Vol. 13, No. 7.
Wassmer, Thomas (2003). "Review of Comparative Review of Four Localization Tools: Déjà Vu, MULTILIZER, MultiTrans and TRANS Suite 2000." *Multilingual Computing and Technology*, Vol. 14, No. 3.

Passolo

Guzman, Rafael (2005). "Passolo 5." *Translation Today*, No. 3, pp. 42–44.
Sachse, Florian (2006). "PASS Engineering." *Proceedings of the Localization World Conference*, Barcelona, Spain.

Trans Suite

Wassmer, Thomas (2003). "Review of Comparative Review of Four Localization Tools: Déjà Vu, MULTILIZER, MultiTrans and TRANS Suite 2000." *Multilingual Computing and Technology*, Vol. 14, No. 3.

❖ PART 23 ❖

National/Regional Developments

America

Hovy, Eduard and Elliott Macklovitch (1997). "MT R&D in America." *Proceedings of MT Summit VI*, San Diego, California, USA.

Asia

Tanaka, Hozumi and Su Keh-Yih (1997). "MT R&D in Asia." *Proceedings of MT Summit VI*, San Diego, California, USA.

Austria

Wormwood, M. J. (1992). "MT Project at University of Innsbruck." *Meta*, Vol. 37, No. 2, pp. 302–315.

Canada

Adshead, Mariam (1986). "TERMIUM—The Canadian Government Linguistic Data Bank." *Computers and Translation*, Vol. 1, No. 4, pp. 235–238.

Gotlieb, C. C. and L. d'Haenens (1991). "Machine Translation of Non-literary Texts: Some Canadian Experiences." *Machine Translation*, Vol. 6, No. 1, pp. 21–33.

Isabelle, Pierre (1981). "Some Views on the Future of the TAUM Group and the TAUM-AVIATION System." Montreal: TAUM Group, University of Montreal.

Isabelle, Pierre (1984). "Machine Translation at the TAUM Group." *The Institute for the Study of Semantics and Cognition Tutorial on Machine Translation*, Lugano, Switzerland.

Kittredge, Robert I. (1972). "The Montreal MT Prototype." *Cahiers Linguistiques d'ottawa*, Vol. 2, No. 2, pp. 69–81.

Kittredge, Robert I. (1981). "The Development of Automated Translation Systems in Canada." *Lebende Sprachen*, Vol. 26, No. 3, pp. 100–103.

Macklovitch, Elliott (1984). "Recent Canadian Experience in MT." *Proceedings of the International Conference on the Methodology and Techniques of Machine Translation*, Cranfield Institute of Technology, Cranfield, England.

Pertsov, N. V. (1973). "Automatic Translation Research at Montreal University." *Nauchno-Tekh. Information*, Vol. 2, No. 1, pp. 36–44.

China

Dong, Zhendong (1988). "MT Research in China." In Dan Maxwell, Klaus Schubert, and Toon Witkam, eds., *New Directions in Machine Translation*. Dordrecht-Holland: Foris Publications, pp. 85–91.

Du, C. Z. and R. Li (1987). *An Overview of MT Research in China*. Xi'an: Xi'an University.

Duan, Huiming 段慧明 and Yu Shiwen 俞士汶 (1996). 〈關於1995年度機器翻譯評測的總結報告〉 (Final Report on Machine Translation Evaluation in 1995). In Yu Shiwen 俞士汶 and Zhu Xuefeng 朱學鋒, eds.,《計算語言學文集》(*Papers on Computational Linguistics*). Beijing: Department of Computer Science and Technology and Institute of Computational Linguistics, Peking University, pp. 127–131.

Feng, Zhiwei 馮志偉 (1985). 〈我國機器翻譯研究工作的發展〉 (The Progress of Research Work on Machine Translation in China). 《情報學報》 (*Journal of the China Society for Scientific and Technical Information*), Vol. 3, No. 3.

Feng, Zhiwei (1999). 〈中國的翻譯技術：過去，現在和將來〉 (Translation Technology in China: Past, Present and Future). In Huang Changning 黃昌寧 and Dong Zhendong 董振東, eds.,《計算機語言學文集》(*Essays on Computational Linguistics*). Beijing: Tsinghua University Press, pp. 335–340.

Hutchins, W. John (1986). "Projects and Groups in Japan, China, and Mexico (1956–1966)." *Machine Translation: Past, Present and Future*. Chichester: Ellis Horwood, pp. 146–149.

Kit-yee, P. C. (1988). "The Future of Chinese Translation." *Language Monthly*, Vol. 53, pp. 6–10.

Liu, Yongquan 劉湧泉 (1980). "Machine Translation in China—A Report." *Journal of the Association for Literary and Linguistic Computing*, Vol. 1, No. 2, pp. 60–66.

Liu, Yongquan (1990). "Current Natural Language Computing in China." *Literary and Linguistic Computing*, Vol. 5, No. 2, pp. 145–150.

Liu, Yongquan (1989). *Selected Papers of Applied Linguistics*. Beijing: The Commercial Press.

Liu, Zhuo 劉倬 (1983). 〈我國機器翻譯研究的歷史和現狀〉 (The Study of Machine Translation in China: Past and Present). 《翻譯通訊》 (*Translators' Notes*), No. 11, pp. 36–37.

Liu, Yongquan *et al*. (1984).《中國的機器翻譯》(*Machine Translation in China*). Shanghai: Knowledge Press.

Liu, Yongquan (1984).〈中國的機器翻譯〉(Machine Translation in China).《中國的機器翻譯》(*Machine Translation in China*). Shanghai: Knowledge Press, pp. 1–14.

Qian, Duoxiu (2005). "Prospects of Machine Translation in the Chinese Context." *Meta*, Vol. 50, No. 4.

Song, Rou 宋柔 (2002).〈北京語言大學計算機系語言信息處理研究所當前研究工作介紹〉(Introducing Current Research Work of the Institute of Language Information Processing at Beijing Languages and Culture University." In Yu Shiwen, ed., *Proceedings of the 2nd China-Japan Natural Language Processing Joint Research Promotion Conference* (*CJNLP-2002*). Beijing: Institute of Computational Linguistics, Peking University, pp. 65–72.

Yang, Tianxing (1993). "The R&D Activities of MT in China." *Proceedings of MT Summit IV: International Cooperation for Global Communication*, Kobe, Japan, pp. 223–224.

Czechoslovakia

Hajik, Jan, Eva Hajicova, and Alexander Rosen (1992). "Machine Translation Research in Czechoslovakia." *Meta*, Vol. 37, No. 4, pp. 802–816.

Hajik, Jan (1995). "Machine Translation in the Czech Republic: History, Methods, Systems." *Proceedings of MT Summit V: Machine Translation Conference, Exhibition and Tutorial*, Luxembourg.

Kirschner, Zdeněk (2000). "Pioneer Work in Machine Translation in Czechoslovakia." In W. John Hutchins, ed., *Early Years in Machine Translation: Memoirs and Biographies of Pioneers*. Amsterdam and Philadelphia: John Benjamins Publishing Company, pp. 349–360.

Konečná, D., P. Novák, and Petr Sgall (1966). "Machine Translation in Prague." *Prague Studies in Mathematical Linguistics*, Vol. 1, pp. 185–194.

Sgall, Petr, Eva Hajicova, and Jarmila Panevova (1990). "Recent Results of Automation Projects in Prague." *Revue Informatique et Statistique*, Vol. 25, pp. 35–42.

Europe

Ananiadou, Sophia (1998). "Machine Translation Trends in Europe and Japan." In *Translating and the Computer 20*. London: The Association for Information Management.

Blatt, Achim (1998). "Workflow Using Linguistic Technology at the Translation Service of the European Commission." *Proceedings of the 3rd Workshop of the European Association for Machine Translation: Translation Technology: Integration in the Workflow Environment*, Geneva, Switzerland, pp. 7–18.

Brace, Colin (2000). "Language Automation at the European Commission." In Robert C. Sprung, ed., *Translating into Success: Cutting-edge Strategies for Going Multilingual in a Global Age*. Amsterdam and Philadelphia: John Benjamins Publishing Company, pp. 219–224.

Calzolari, Nicoletta and Antonio Zampolli (1999). "Harmonised Large-scale Syntactic/Semantic Lexicons: A European Multilingual Infrastructure." *Proceedings of MT Summit VII: MT in the Great Translation Era*, Singapore.

Cencioni, Roberto (1995). "Language Engineering and the Commission." *Proceedings of MT Summit V: Machine Translation Conference, Exhibition and Tutorial*, Luxembourg.

Drugan, Joanna (2004). "Multilingual Document Management and Workflow in the European Institutions." In *Translating and the Computer 26*. London: The Association for Information Management.

Hutchins, W. John (1986). "Groups and Projects in the Soviet Union and Eastern Europe (1955–1967)." *Machine Translation: Past, Present and Future*. Chichester: Ellis Horwood, pp. 132–145.

Hutchins, W. John (1986). "Groups and Projects in the United Kingdom and Western Europe (1954–66)." *Machine Translation: Past, Present and Future*. Chichester: Ellis Horwood, pp. 112–131.

Hutchins, W. John (1986). "Projects and Systems at the Commission of the European Communities (1976–)." *Machine Translation: Past, Present and Future*. Chichester: Ellis Horwood, pp. 258–271.

Hutchins, W. John (1996). "The State of Machine Translation in Europe." *Proceedings of the 2nd Conference of the Association for Machine Translation in the Americas: Expanding MT Horizons (AMTA-2)*, Montreal, Quebec, Canada, pp. 198–205.

Ke, Ping 柯平 (1995). 〈歐美的機器翻譯〉 (Machine Translation in Europe and America). 《中國翻譯》 (*Chinese Translators Journal*), No. 2, pp. 47–54.

King, Maghi (1994). "The Current Status of Machine Translation in Europe." *Technology Partnerships for Crossing the Language Barrier: The 1st Conference of the Association for Machine Translation in the Americas*, Columbia, Maryland, USA.

Kingscott, Geoffrey (1996). "The European Translation Platform." In *Translating and the Computer 18*. London: The Association for Information Management.

Krstič, Adriana (2000). "Translation of EU Legislation in Slovenia." *Proceedings of the 5th Workshop of the European Association for Machine Translation: Harvesting Existing Resources*, Lubljana, Slovenia.

Lehmann, Winfred P. and Rolf A. Stachowitz (1972). "Machine Translation in Western Europe: A Survey." In Einar Haugen and Werner Winter, eds., *Current Trends in Linguistics, Vol. 9: Linguistics in Western Europe*. The Hague: Mouton, Vol. 9, pp. 688–701.

Leick, Jean-Marie (1995). "EURAMIS: Integrated Multilingual Services for a Large Multilingual Community." *Proceedings of MT Summit V: Machine Translation Conference, Exhibition and Tutorial*, Luxembourg.

Leick, Jean-Marie (1996). "Generalised Language Resources: EURODICAUTOM, SYSTRAN and EURAMIS—A Case Study." *Proceedings of the 1st Workshop of the European Association for Machine Translation (TKE-96): Language Resources, Terminology, Economics, and User Needs*, Vienna, Austria, pp. 53–62.

Maegaard, Bente (1999). "Human Language Technologies—Possibilities in the EU 5th Framework Programme for Research and Technological Development." *Proceedings of the 4th Workshop of the European Association for Machine Translation: EU and the New Languages: Translation—Possibilities, Policies and Practicalities*, Prague, the Czech Republic.

Martínez, Jesús Manuel (2001). "MT in the European Commission: A View from the Translator's Desk." In Bente Maegaard, ed., *Proceedings of MT Summit VIII: Machine Translation in the Information Age*, Santiago de Compostela, Spain.

Nedoma, Andrew and Jurek Nedoma (2004). "Problems with CAT Tools in Translations into Central and Eastern European Languages." In

Translating and the Computer 26. London: The Association for Information Management.
Obrová, Pavlina (1999). "Government Language Policy: Translation of EC Legislation into the Czech Language." *Proceedings of the 4th Workshop of the European Association for Machine Translation: EU and the New Languages: Translation—Possibilities, Policies and Practicalities*, Prague, the Czech Republic.
Paskaleva, Elena (1999). "Aligning and Extracting Translation Equivalents from EU Documents—A Possible Look on EU Integration." *Proceedings of the 4th Workshop of the European Association for Machine Translation: EU and the New Languages: Translation—Possibilities, Policies and Practicalities*, Prague, the Czech Republic.
Petrits, Angeliki (1994). "The Current State of the Commission's Systran MT System." *Machine Translation—Ten Years On: Proceedings of the 2nd International Conference Organised by Cranfield University*, Cranfield, England.
Petrits, Angeliki, Francine Braun-Chen, Cameron Ross, Rosemarie Sauer, Angelo Torquati, and Alain Reichling (2001). "The Commission's MT System: Today and Tomorrow." In Bente Maegaard, ed., *Proceedings of MT Summit VIII: Machine Translation in the Information Age*, Santiago de Compostela, Spain.
Prószéky, Gábor (1999). "Experience from Translation of EU Documents." *Proceedings of the 4th Workshop of the European Association for Machine Translation: EU and the New Languages: Translation—Possibilities, Policies and Practicalities*, Prague, the Czech Republic.
Pugh, Jeanette and Juan C. Sager (1994). "Machine Translation in Europe." In R. E. Asher, ed., *The Encyclopedia of Language and Linguistics*. Oxford: Pergamon Press Ltd., pp. 2314–2322.
Quartier, P. and R. Havenith (1997). "MT R&D in Europe." *Proceedings of MT Summit VI*, San Diego, California, USA.
Quintero, Arturo (2003). "The New Europe: New Members, More Languages." *Proceedings of the Localization World Conference 2003*, Seattle, Washington, DC, USA.
Rolling, Loll (1993). "E.C. Language Projects." *Proceedings of MT Summit IV: International Cooperation for Global Communication*, Kobe, Japan, pp. 97–115.

Sandrelli, Annalisa and Claudio Bendazzoli (2006). "Tagging a Corpus of Interpreted Speeches: The European Parliament Interpreting Corpus (EPIC)." *Proceedings of the 5th International Conference on Language Resources and Evaluation* (*LREC-2006*), Genoa, Italy.

Schütz, Joerg (1996). "European Research and Development in Machine Translation." *MT News International*, Vol. 15, pp. 8–11.

Senez, Dorothy (1995). "The Use of Machine Translation in the Commission." *Proceedings of MT Summit V: Machine Translation Conference, Exhibition and Tutorial*, Luxembourg.

Senez, Dorothy (1996). "Machine Translation Feasibility Study at the European Commission." *Proceedings of the 1st Workshop of the European Association for Machine Translation* (*TKE-96*)*: Language Resources, Terminology, Economics, and User Needs*, Vienna, Austria, pp. 63–70.

Smith, David J. (1987). "Translation Practice in Europe." In Catriona Picken, ed., *Translating and the Computer 8: A Profession on the Move*. London: The Association for Information Management, pp. 74–82.

Theologitis, Dimitri (1997). "EURAMIS, the Platform of the EC Translator." *Proceedings of the 2nd Workshop of the European Association for Machine Translation*: *Language Technology in Your Organization?* University of Copenhagen, Copenhagen, Denmark, pp. 17–32.

Theologitis, Dimitri (1999). "EU: Preparing for New Languages." *Proceedings of the 4th Workshop of the European Association for Machine Translation: EU and the New Languages: Translation—Possibilities, Policies and Practicalities*, Prague, the Czech Republic.

Theologitis, Dimitri (2000). "Language Technology in EU Institutions." *Proceedings of the 5th Workshop of the European Association for Machine Translation: Harvesting Existing Resources*, Lubljana, Slovenia.

France

Blanc, Etienne (2000). "From the UNL Hypergraph to GETA's Multilevel Tree." *Proceedings of the International Conference on Machine Translation and Multilingual Applications in the New Millenium* (*MT-2000*), University of Exeter, England.

Boitet, Christian (1977). "Where Does GETA Stand at the Beginning of 1977?" In *Overcoming the Language Barrier: Third European Congress on Information Systems and Networks*, Luxembourg. Munchen: Verlag Dokumentation, pp. 88–120.

Boitet, Christian and N. Nedobejkine (1981). "Recent Developments in Russian-French Machine Translation at Grenoble." *Linguistics*, Vol. 19, Nos. 3–4, pp. 199–271.

Boitet, Christian (1987). "Current Machine Translation Systems Developed with GETA's Methodology and Software Tools." In Catriona Picken, ed., *Translating and the Computer 8: A Profession on the Move*. London: The Association for Information Management, pp. 114–132.

Boitet, Christian (1987). "Current State and Future Outlook of the Research at GETA." *Proceedings of Machine Translation Summit*, Hakone, Japan.

Boitet, Christian (1987). "Research and Development on MT and Related Techniques at Grenoble University (GETA)." In Margaret King, ed., *Machine Translation Today: The State of the Art*. Edinburgh: Edinburgh University Press, pp. 133–153.

Boitet, Christian (1988). "Pros and Cons of the Pivot and Transfer Approaches in Multilingual Machine Translation." In Dan Maxwell, Klaus Schubert, and Toon Witkam, eds., *New Directions in Machine Translation*. Dordrecht-Holland: Foris Publications, pp. 93–107.

Boitet, Christian (1989). "Motivations, Aims and Architecture of the LIDIA Project." In Christian Rohrer, ed., *Proceedings of MT Summit II*, Munich, Germany, pp. 52–54.

Gross, Maurice (2000). "Early MT in France." In W. John Hutchins, ed., *Early Years in Machine Translation: Memoirs and Biographies of Pioneers*. Amsterdam and Philadelphia: John Benjamins Publishing Company, pp. 325–330.

Guilbaud, Jean-Philippe (1987). "Principles and Results of a German to French MT System at Grenoble University (GETA)." In Margaret King, ed., *Machine Translation Today: The State of the Art*. Edinburgh: Edinburgh University Press, pp. 278–318.

Isabelle, Pierre (2003). "Multilingual Document Processing at XRCE." *Proceedings of MT Summit IX*, New Orleans, Louisiana, USA.

Vauquois, Bernard (1984). "The Organization of an Automated

Translation System for Multilingual Translations at GETA." *IBM Europe Institute on Natural Language Processing*, Davos, Switzerland.

Vauquois, Bernard (1985). "The Approach of GETA to Automatic Translation: Comparison with Some Other Systems." In A. R. A. Wahab and Mahmoud Esmail Sieny, eds., *Proceedings of the International Workshop on Computer Aided Translation*. Riyadh: King Abdulaziz City for Science and Technology, pp. 27–96.

Vauquois, Bernard and Christian Boitet (1985). "Automated Translation at Grenoble University." *Computational Linguistics*, Vol. 11, No. 1, pp. 28–36.

Vaquois, Bernard and Christian Boitet (1988). "Automated Translation at Grenoble University." In Jonathan Slocum, ed., *Machine Translation Systems*. Cambridge: Cambridge University Press, pp. 85–110.

Germany

Bernardi, Ulrike, András Bocsák, and Jörg Porsiel (2005). "Are We Making Ourselves Clear? Terminology Management and Machine Translation at Volkswagen." *Proceedings of the 10th Workshop of the European Association for Machine Translation: Practical Applications of Machine Translation*, Budapest, Hungary, pp. 41–49.

Czermak, Jan-Michael (1993). "Government Support for MT in Germany." In Sergei Nirenburg, ed., *Progress in Machine Translation*. Amsterdam: IOS and Tokyo: Ohmsha, pp. 199–201.

Daley, Denitra H. and Rinaldo F. Vachino (1973). "The West German Federal Bureau of Languages and Machine-aided Translation in Germany." *Federal Linguist*, Vol. 5, Nos. 3–4, pp. 14–18.

Freigang, Karl-Heinz (1987). "Research on Machine Translation at the University of Saarbrucken." In Catriona Picken, ed., *Translating and the Computer 8: A Profession on the Move*. London: The Association for Information Management, pp. 83–97.

Weissenborn, J. (1977). "The Role and Form of Analysis in Machine Translation: The Automatic Analysis of French at Saarbrücken." In *Overcoming the Language Barrier: Third European Congress on Information Systems and Networks*. Munchen: Verlag Dokumentation, pp. 593–611.

Greece

Fourla, Athanassia, and Olga Yannoutsou (1998). "Implementing MT in the Greek Public Sector: A Users' Survey." In David L. Farwell, Laurie Gerber, and Eduard Hovy, eds., *Machine Translation and the Information Soup*. Berlin: Springer Verlag, pp. 300–307.

Kalantzi, Dimitra (2002). "Teaching MT/CAT Tools in Greece: The State of the Art." *Proceedings of the 6th Workshop of the European Association for Machine Translation: Teaching Machine Translation*, Manchester, England, pp. 33–42.

Hong Kong

Chan, Sin-wai (2001). "Machine Translation in Hong Kong." In Chan Sin-wai, ed., *Translation in Hong Kong: Past, Present and Future*. Hong Kong: The Chinese University Press, pp. 205–217.

Chiu, Aman and Björn Jernudd (2002). "Chinese IT Terminology Management in Hong Kong." In Chan Sin-wai, ed., *Translation and Information Technology*. Hong Kong: The Chinese University Press, pp. 95–114.

Loh, Shiu-chang (1972). "Machine Translation at The Chinese University of Hong Kong." In J. Mathias, ed., *Proceedings of the CETA Workshop on Chinese Language and Chinese Research Materials*, Washington, DC, USA.

To, Charlotte and Björn Jernudd (2002). "Terminological Problems and Language Management for Internet Language Professionals in Hong Kong." In Chan Sin-wai, ed., *Translation and Information Technology*. Hong Kong: The Chinese University Press, pp. 115–129.

T'sou, Benjamin K. Y., Tom B. Y. Lai, K. K. Sin, and Lawrence Y. L. Cheung (2006). "Court Stenography-to-text ("STT") in Hong Kong: A Jurilinguistic Engineering Effort." *Proceedings of the 5th International Conference on Language Resources and Evaluation (LREC-2006)*, Genoa, Italy.

Wu, Dekai (2003). "The HKUST Leading Question Translation System." *Proceedings of MT Summit IX*, New Orleans, Louisiana, USA.

Hungary

Kiefer, Ferenc (1964). "Mathematical Linguistics and Machine

Translation in the Computing Centre of the Hungarian Academy of Sciences." *Computational Linguistics*, Vol. 2, pp. 203–211.
Papp, Ferenc (1964). "Mathematical and Applied Linguistics at the University of Debrecen." *Computational Linguistics*, Vol. 2, pp. 213–218.

India

Bandyopadhyay, Sivaji (2000). "The State and Role of Machine Translation in India." *Machine Translation Review*, No. 11, pp. 25–26.
Bandyopadhyay, Sivaji (2004). "Use of Machine Translation in India." *AAMT Journal*, No. 36.
Bandyopadhyay, Sivaji (2005). "NLP Activities at Computer Science and Engineering Department, Jadavpur University, India." *AAMT Journal*, No. 38.
Choudhury, Monojit, Sudeshna Sarkar, and Anupam Basu (2005). "NLP Research Activities at IIT Kharagpur." *AAMT Journal*, No. 38.
Naskar, Sudip and Sivaji Bandyopadhyay (2005). "Use of Machine Translation in India: Current Status." *Proceedings of MT Summit X*, Phuket, Thailand.
Sharma, R. K. (2005). "NLP Activities at TIET, Patiala, India." *AAMT Journal*, No. 38.
Sinha, R. Mahesh K. (2005). "Machine Translation R&D Activities at IIT Kanpur." *AAMT Journal*, No. 38.
Sobha, L. (2005). "NLP Activities at AU-KBU Research Centre." *AAMT Journal*, No. 38.
Vikas, Om (2005). "Machine Translation Activities in India." *AAMT Journal*, No. 38.

Japan

Amano, Shinya (1982). *Machine Translation Project at Toshiba Corporation*. Kawasaki: Toshiba Corporation.
Ananiadou, Sophia (1998). "Machine Translation Trends in Europe and Japan." In *Translating and the Computer 20*. London: The Association for Information Management.
Ananiadou, Sophia (1998). "Machine Translation Trends in Japan." *Lisa Newsletter*, Vol. 7, No. 2, pp. 10–14.

Dong, Wen 董文 (1987).〈日本機器翻譯研究近況〉(Recent Developments in Japan's MT R&D).《中國翻譯》(*Chinese Translators Journal*), No. 5, pp. 35–36.

Fine, David (2003). "Software Development for Japan." *Proceedings of the Localization World Conference 2003*, Seattle, Washington, DC, USA.

Hutchins, W. John (1986). "Projects and Groups in Japan, China, and Mexico (1956–1966)." *Machine Translation: Past, Present and Future.* Chichester: Ellis Horwood, pp. 146–149.

Hutchins, W. John (1986). "Projects and Systems in the Soviet Union and Japan (1974–)." *Machine Translation: Past, Present and Future.* Chichester: Ellis Horwood, pp. 307–321.

Ikeda, Takashi (2002). "Machine Translation System *j-aw* and Other NLP Activities of Our Laboratory." In Yu Shiwen, ed., *Proceedings of the 2nd China-Japan Natural Language Processing Joint Research Promotion Conference* (*CJNLP-2002*). Beijing: Institute of Computational Linguistics, Peking University, pp. 135–141.

Isahara, Hitoshi (1997). "JEIDA's Bilingual Corpus and Other Corpora for NLP Research in Japan." *Proceedings of MT Summit VI*, San Diego, California, USA.

Isahara, Hitoshi (2002). "Computational Linguistics at Communications Research Laboratory, Japan." In Yu Shiwen, ed., *Proceedings of the 2nd China-Japan Natural Language Processing Joint Research Promotion Conference* (*CJNLP-2002*). Beijing: Institute of Computational Linguistics, Peking University, pp. 40–44.

Ishihara, K. *et al.* (1986). "Hitachi's Research and Development in Knowledge Engineering." *Proceedings of the Annual Congress of the Italian Computing Society* (*AICA-86*). Palermo, Italy.

Kinoshita, Satoshi (2002). "Language Technology in Toshiba." In Yu Shiwen, ed., *Proceedings of the 2nd China-Japan Natural Language Processing Joint Research Promotion Conference* (*CJNLP-2002*). Beijing: Institute of Computational Linguistics, Peking University, p. 275.

Morimoto, Tsuyoshi (1993). "Automatic Speech Translation at ATR." *Proceedings of MT Summit IV: International Cooperation for Global Communication*, Kobe, Japan, pp. 83–96.

Nagao, Makoto (1982). "A Survey of Natural Language Processing and Machine Translation in Japan, 1980–1982." In T. Kitagawa, ed., *Computer Science and Technologies*. Tokyo: OHM, pp. 64–70.

Nagao, Makoto (1983). "Natural Language Processing and Machine Translation in Japan." *Digest of Papers: Spring COMPCON 83, Intellectual Leverage for the Information Society*, Institute of Electronics and Electrical Engineers, New York, pp. 306–307.

Nagao, Makoto, Jun-ichi Tsujii, and Jun-ichi Nakamura (1985). "The Japanese Government Project for Machine Translation System." *Computational Linguistics*, Vol. 11, Nos. 2–3, pp. 91–110.

Nagao, Makoto (1992). "Current Practical Machine Translation Systems in Japan and Future Directions." In *Translating and the Computer 13: The Theory and Practice of Machine Translation—A Marriage of Convenience?* London: The Association for Information Management, pp. 129–136.

Nagao, Makoto (1993). "Machine Translation: The Japanese Experience." In Sergei Nirenburg, ed., *Progress in Machine Translation*. Amsterdam: IOS and Tokyo: Ohmsha, pp. 203–208.

Nishida, Toyoaki and Shuji Doshita (1986). "Machine Translation: Japanese Perspectives." In Catriona Picken, ed., *Translating and the Computer 7*. London: The Association for Information Management, pp. 152–174.

Sato, Shigeru (1989). "A Dependency Syntax of Japanese." In Dan Maxwell and Klaus Schubert, eds., *Metataxis in Practice: Dependency Syntax for Multilingual Machine Translation*. Dordrecht: Foris Publications, pp. 183–206.

Tanaka, Hozumi, Shun Ishizaki, Akira Uehara, and Hiroshi Uchida (1989). "Research and Development of Cooperation Project on a Machine Translation System for Japan and Its Neighboring Countries." In Christian Rohrer, ed., *Proceedings of MT Summit II*, Munich, Germany, pp. 146–151.

Tsujii, Jun-ichi (2002). "Research Topics of the NLP Laboratory of the University of Tokyo." In Yu Shiwen, ed., *Proceedings of the 2nd China-Japan Natural Language Processing Joint Research Promotion Conference* (*CJNLP-2002*). Beijing: Institute of Computational Linguistics, Peking University, p. 9.

Tsuji, Y. (1987). "Research and Development Project of Machine Translation System with Japan's Neighboring Countries." *Proceedings of Machine Translation Summit*, Hakone, Japan.

Whitelock, Peter J. (1987). "Machine Translation in Japan and the Rest of the World." In Catriona Picken, ed., *Translating and the Computer 8:*

A Profession on the Move. London: The Association for Information Management, pp. 147–159.

Yamada, Setsuo, Syuuji Kodama, Taeko Matsuoka, Hiroshi Araki, Yoshiaki Murakami, Osamu Takano, and Yoshiyuki Sakamoto (2005). "A Report on the Machine Translation Market in Japan." *Proceedings of MT Summit X*, Phuket, Thailand.

Korea

Kuo, June-jie and Hsieh Miao-ling (1996). "A Cognitive Treatment of Aspect in Japanese to Chinese Machine Translation." *Journal of Chinese Linguistics*, Vol. 9, pp. 77–101.

Macau

Li, Yiping 李怡平 (1995).〈機器翻譯及澳門的研究〉(Machine Translation and the Study of Macau). In Huang Hanqiang 黃漢強 and Feng Shaorong 馮少榮, eds.,《澳門研究》(*Journal of Macau Studies*), No. 3.

Li, Yiping, Pun Chiman, and Wu Fei (1999). "Portuguese-Chinese Machine Translation in Macao." *Proceedings of MT Summit VII: MT in the Great Translation Era*, Singapore, pp. 236–243.

Malaysia

Aziz, Normaziah Abdul (2006). "Machine Translation R&D in Malaysia—A Brief Update." *AAMT Journal*, Vol. 38.

Bakar, Ahmad Zaki Abu (1993). "Utilization of Machine Translation in Malaysia." *Proceedings of MT Summit IV: International Cooperation for Global Communication*, Kobe, Japan, pp. 79–81.

Hussain, Haji Khalid M. (1989). "Governmental Views of MT." In Christian Rohrer, ed., *Proceedings of MT Summit II*, Munich, Germany, p. 66.

Warotamasikkhadit, Udom (1986). "Computer Aided Translation Project, University Sains Malaysia, Penang, Malaysia." *Computers and Translation*, Vol. 1, No. 2, p. 113.

Mexico

Hutchins, W. John (1986). "Projects and Groups in Japan, China, and

Mexico (1956–1966)." *Machine Translation: Past, Present and Future.* Chichester: Ellis Horwood, pp. 146–149.

Russia

Harper, Kenneth E. (1961). "Soviet Research in Machine Translation." In Harold P. Edmundson, ed., *Proceedings of the National Symposium on Machine Translation Held at the University of California Los Angeles.* London: Englewood Cliffs, pp. 2–12.

Harper, Kenneth E. (1963). "Machine Translation." *Current Trends in Linguistics, Vol. 1: Soviet and East European Linguistics.* The Hague: Mouton, pp. 133–142.

Hutchins, W. John (1986). "Groups and Projects in the Soviet Union and Eastern Europe (1955–1967)." *Machine Translation: Past, Present and Future.* Chichester: Ellis Horwood, pp. 132–145.

Hutchins, W. John (1986). "Projects and Systems in the Soviet Union and Japan (1974–)." *Machine Translation: Past, Present and Future.* Chichester: Ellis Horwood, pp. 307–321.

Knowles, Francis E. (1979). "Recent Soviet Work on Computer Techniques for Representing Natural Language Meaning." *Informatics*, Vol. 5.

Kulagina, Olga S., A. I. Martynova, and T. M. Nicolaeva (1961). "Mechanical Translation at the Academy of Sciences of the USSR." In Allen Kent, ed., *Information Retrieval and Machine Translation.* New York: Interscience, pp. 867–879.

Kulagina, Olga S. (2000). "Pioneering MT in the Soviet Union." In W. John Hutchins, ed., *Early Years in Machine Translation: Memoirs and Biographies of Pioneers.* Amsterdam and Philadelphia: John Benjamins Publishing Company, pp. 197–204.

Marčuk, Jurij N. (1977). "Machine Translation in the All-Union Translation Centre." In *Overcoming the Language Barrier: Third European Congress on Information Systems and Networks.* Munchen: Verlag Dokumentation, pp. 623–624.

Marčuk, Jurij N. (1984). "Machine Translation in the USSR." *International Forum on Information and Documentation*, Vol. 9, No. 2, pp. 3–8.

Marčuk, Jurij N. (1989). "Machine Translation in the USSR." In Allen Kent, ed., *Encyclopedia of Library and Information Science*, Vol. 44, pp. 184–195.

Marčuk, Jurij N. (2000). "Machine Translation: Early Years in the USSR." In W. John Hutchins, ed., *Early Years in Machine Translation: Memoirs and Biographies of Pioneers*. Amsterdam and Philadelphia: John Benjamins Publishing Company, pp. 243–252.

Mel'cuk, Igor A. (2000). "Machine Translation and Formal Linguistics in the USSR." In W. John Hutchins, ed., *Early Years in Machine Translation: Memoirs and Biographies of Pioneers*. Amsterdam and Philadelphia: John Benjamins Publishing Company, pp. 205–226.

Mološnaja, Tat'jan N. (2000). "My Memoirs of MT in the Soviet Union." In W. John Hutchins, ed., *Early Years in Machine Translation: Memoirs and Biographies of Pioneers*. Amsterdam and Philadelphia: John Benjamins Publishing Company, pp. 227–232.

Neljubin, L. L. (1997). "A Survey of Machine Translation in the Former USSR." *Perspectives: Studies in Translatology*, Vol. 5, No. 1, pp. 125–138.

Nikolaeva, Tat'jana Mixajlovna (1958). "Soviet Developments in Machine Translation: Russian Sentence Analysis." *Mechanical Translation*, Vol. 5, No. 2, pp. 51–59.

Oettinger, Anthony G. (1954). "The Distribution of Word Length in Technical Russian." *Mechanical Translation*, Vol. 1, No. 3, pp. 38–40.

Oettinger, Anthony G. (1958). "A Survey of Soviet Work on Automatic Translation." *Mechanical Translation*, Vol. 5, No. 3, pp. 101–110.

Oubine, Ivan I. and Boris D. Tikhomirov (1988). "The State of the Art in Machine Translation in the U.S.S.R." In Dan Maxwell, Klaus Schubert, and Toon Witkam, eds., *New Directions in Machine Translation*. Dordrecht-Holland: Foris Publications, pp. 75–84.

Papp, Ferenc (1966). *Mathematical Linguistics in the Soviet Union*. The Hague: Mouton.

Pevzner, Boris (2001). "First Steps of Language Engineering in the USSR: The 50s through 70s." *International Journal of Translation*, Vol. 13, Nos. 1–2, pp. 81–86.

Piotrovskij, Raimund G. (1980). "Machine Translation in the Research Group on Speech Statistics: Theory, Results and Outlook." *International Forum on Information and Documentation*, Vol. 5, No. 2, pp. 9–11.

Piotrovskij, Raimund G. (1996). "Machine Translation in New Russia." In

D. Tufis, ed., *Limbaj si Technologie*. Bucuresti: Editura Academiei Romane.

Piotrovskij, Raimund G. (2000). "MT in the Former USSR and in the Newly Independent States (NIS): Prehistory, Romantic Era, Prosaic Time." In W. John Hutchins, ed., *Early Years in Machine Translation: Memoirs and Biographies of Pioneers*. Amsterdam and Philadelphia: John Benjamins Publishing Company, pp. 233–242.

Piotrowska, Xenia, Rajmund Piotrowski, Yuri Romanov, Natalia Zaitseva, and Michael S. Blekhman (2001). "Former Soviet Union and in the New Russia." *International Journal of Translation*, Vol. 13, Nos. 1–2, pp. 87–104.

Reddiar, Murugesan K. (1996). "On Machine Translation: The Tamil University Experiment." *International Journal of Translation*, Vol. 8, Nos. 1–2, pp. 17–31.

Rozentsveig, V. Yu (1958). "The Work on Machine Translation in the Soviet Union: 4th International Congress of Slavicists Reports, Sept. 1958." *Mechanical Translation*, Vol. 5, No. 3, pp. 95–100.

Saudi Arabia

Sieny, Mahmoud Esma'il (1989). "Machine Translation in Saudi Arabia." In Christian Rohrer, ed., *Proceedings of MT Summit II*, Munich, Germany, pp. 143–145.

Slovenia

Krstič, Adriana (2000). "Translation of EU Legislation in Slovenia." *Proceedings of the 5th Workshop of the European Association for Machine Translation: Harvesting Existing Resources*, Lubljana, Slovenia.

South Africa

Jordaan-Weiss, Milde (1996). "Machine Translation, Terminology and the African Languages in South Africa: An Overview." *Proceedings of the 1st Workshop of the European Association for Machine Translation (TKE-96): Language Resources, Terminology, Economics, and User Needs*, Vienna, Austria, pp. 95–98.

Spain

Corbi-Bellot, Antonio M., Mikel L. Forcada, Sergio Ortíz-Rojas, Juan Antonio Pérez-Ortiz, Gema Ramírez-Sánchez, Felipe Sánchez-Martínez, Iñaki Alegria, Aingeru Mayor, and Kepa Sarasola (2005). "An Open-source Shallow-transfer Machine Translation Engine for the Romance Languages of Spain." *Proceedings of the 10th Workshop of the European Association for Machine Translation: Practical Applications of Machine Translation*, Budapest, Hungary, pp. 79–86.

Sweden

Danielsson, Pernilla and Daniel Ridings (2000). "Corpus and Terminology: Software for the Translation Program at Göteborgs Universitet or Getting Students to Do the Work." In Simon Philip Botley, Anthony Mark McEnery, and Andrew Wilson, eds., *Multilingual Corpora in Teaching and Research*. Amsterdam: Rodopi, pp. 65–72.

Switzerland

Bruderer, Herbert E. (1975). "Control of an Automatic Translation System in the Computer Centre of Zurich University." *ALLC Bulletin*, Vol. 3, No. 3, pp. 197–200.

Bruderer, Herbert E. and David G. Hays (1975). "LATSEC Shows MT in Zuerich." *American Journal of Computational Linguistics* (4, microfiche 29), p. 9.

Bruderer, Herbert E. (1977). "Automatic Language Processing in Switzerland: A State of the Art Report." *Spracheund Datenverarbeitung*, Vol. 1, No. 1, pp. 76–77.

Coray, Giovanni (1989). "Needs, Research and Perspectives in Switzerland." In Christian Rohrer, ed., *Proceedings of MT Summit II*, Munich, Germany, pp. 55–57.

Devas, H. (1982). "Developing an Automatic Translation System at the Computing Centre for the University of Zurich." *A Motivation for Literary and Linguistic Computing Bulletin*, Vol. 3, No. 3, pp. 197–200.

Ebermann, Basle Martha (1996). "Use and Value of Computer-assisted Translation in the Central Translation Service of Coop Switzerland,

Basle." *Proceedings of the 1st Workshop of the European Association for Machine Translation (TKE-96): Language Resources, Terminology, Economics, and User Needs*, Vienna, Austria, pp. 89–94.
Marty-Albisser, Doris (1997). "Economics of Translation Tools—Experience Gained at Swiss Bank Corporation." *Proceedings of the 2nd Workshop of the European Association for Machine Translation: Language Technology in Your Organization?* University of Copenhagen, Copenhagen, Denmark, pp. 8–16.

Thailand

Sornlertlamvanich, Virach and Canasai Kruengkrai (2005). "NLP R&D in Thai Computational Linguistics Laboratory (TCL)." *AAMT Journal*, Vol. 38.

The United Kingdom

Bar-Hillel, Yehoshua (1959). *Report on the State of Machine Translation in the United States and Great Britain*. Technical Report. Jerusalem: Hebrew University.
Booth, Andrew D. (1956). "Present Objectives of MT Research in the United Kingdom." *Babel*, Vol. 2, No. 3, pp. 108–110.
Booth, Andrew D. (1980). "Computers in the University of London, 1945–1962," In N. Metropolis, J. Howlett, and G.-C. Rota, eds., *A History of Computing in the Twentieth Century: A Collection of Essays*. New York: Academic Press, pp. 551–561.
Candeland, Richard (1987). "The British Term Bank Project: A Prototype Software." *Computers and Translation*, Vol. 2, No. 1, pp. 3–20.
Crawford, T. D. (1974). "A Review of the Cardiff Machine Translation Project." In Antonio Zampolli, ed., *Proceedings of the 3rd Symposium on the Use of JPRS Computers in Literary and Linguistic Research*, Cardiff, England.
Hutchins, W. John (1986). "Groups and Projects in the United Kingdom and Western Europe (1954–66)." *Machine Translation: Past, Present and Future*. Chichester: Ellis Horwood, pp. 112–131.
Mason, Adrienne (2006). "Bridging the Gap—From HE to Professional Practice within the UK." *Proceedings of the 6th Portsmouth Translation Conference: Translation Technologies and Culture*,

School of Languages and Area Studies, University of Portsmouth, England.
Masterman, Margaret (1956). "Report on Research at the Cambridge Language Research Unit." *Mechanical Translation*, Vol. 3, No. 2, pp. 36–37.
Masterman, Margaret (1970). "Cambridge Language Research Unit (CLRU)." In Allen Kent and Harold Lancour, eds., *Encyclopedia of Library and Information Science*. New York: Dekker, Vol. 4, pp. 33–50.
McDaniel J., A. M. Day, W. L. Price, A. J. Szanser, S. Whelan, and D. M. Yates (1967). "Machine Translation at the National Physical Laboratory, Teddington, Middlesex, England." In Andrew D. Booth, ed., *Machine Translation*. Amsterdam: North-Holland Publishing Company, pp. 229–266.
Szanser, A. J. (1966). "Machine Translation Research at the National Physical Laboratory, Teddington." *The Incorporated Linguist*, Vol. 5, No. 4, pp. 102–109.

The United Nations

McCallum, Bob (2004). "Translation Technology at the United Nations." *Localisation Reader 2004–2005*.

The United States of America

Bar-Hillel, Yehoshua (1959). *Report on the State of Machine Translation in the United States and Great Britain*. Technical Report. Jerusalem: Hebrew University.
Bennett, Winfield S. (1994). "Machine Translation in North America." In R. E. Asher, ed., *The Encyclopedia of Language and Linguistics*. Oxford: Pergamon Press Ltd., pp. 2332–2338.
Bennett, Winfield S. (1995). "Machine Translation in North America." E. F. K. Koerner and R. E. Asher, eds., *Concise History of the Language Sciences: From the Sumerians to the Cognitivists*. Oxford: Pergamon, pp. 445–451.
Bostad, Dale A. (1986). "Machine Translation in the USAF." *Terminologie et Traduction*, No. 1, pp. 68–72.
Bostad, Dale A. (1995). "Machine Translation at NAIC—A Perspective."

Proceedings of MT Summit V: Machine Translation Conference, Exhibition and Tutorial, Luxembourg.

Dostert, Bozena (1973). *User's Evaluation of Machine Translation, Georgetown MT System, 1963–1973*. Rome Air Development Center Report AD-768-451. Texas A&M University.

Dostert, Leon E. (1955). "The Georgetown-I.B.M. Experiment." In William N. Locke and Andrew D. Booth, eds., *Machine Translation of Languages: Fourteen Essays*. Cambridge, MA: Technology Press of the Massachusetts Institute of Technology, pp. 124–135.

Douthwaite, Geoff (1956). "The University of Washington Automatic Language Translator." *Washington Engineer*, Vol. 8, No. 4, pp. 12–13, 24.

Garvin, Paul L. (1967). "The Georgetown-IBM Experiment of 1954: An Evaluation in Retrospect." In William M. Austin, ed., *Paper in Linguistics in Honor of Leon Dostert*. The Hague: Mouton, pp. 46–56.

Giuliano, Vincent E. and Anthony G. Oettinger (1960). "Research on Automatic Translation of the Harvard Computation Laboratory." *Information Process: Proceedings of the International Conference on Information Processing*. Paris: Unesco, pp. 163–183.

Hammond, Deanna (1993). "MT, the Federal Government, and the Role of Translator Associations." In Sergei Nirenburg, ed., *Progress in Machine Translation*. Amsterdam: IOS and Tokyo: Ohmsha, pp. 209–210.

Hays, David G. (1961). "Linguistic Research at the RAND Corporation." In Harold P. Edmundson, ed., *Proceedings of the National Symposium on Machine Translation*. Englewood Cliffs, New Jersey: Prentice-Hall, pp. 13–25.

Hutchins, W. John (1986). "Groups and Projects in the United States, 1950–66." *Machine Translation: Past, Present and Future*. Chichester: Ellis Horwood, pp. 61–111.

Hutchins, W. John (1994). "The Georgetown-IBM Demonstration, 7th January 1954." *MT News International*, Vol. 8, pp. 15–18.

Hutchins, W. John (2004). "The Georgetown-IBM Experiment Demonstrated in January 1954." In Robert E. Frederking and Kathryn B. Taylors, eds., *Machine Translation: From Real Users to Research*. Berlin: Springer Verlag, pp. 102–114.

Hutton, F. C. (1976). "Georgetown University MT System Usage."

American Journal of Computational Linguistics (2, microfiche 46), p. 57.
Josselson, Harry H. (1972). "Fourteen Year Summary of the Work of the Wayne State University Machine Translation Project." *The 14th Annual Report on Research in Computer-aided Translation Russian-English,* Wayne State University, USA, pp. 124–400.
Koutsoudas, Andreas and R. Machol (1956). "Mechanical Translation Work at the University of Michigan." *Mechanical Translation*, Vol. 3, No. 2, pp. 34, 41.
Lamb, Sydney M. (1961). "MT at the University of California, Berkeley." In Harold P. Edmundson, ed., *Proceedings of the National Symposium on Machine Translation*. Englewood Cliffs: Prentice-Hall, pp. 140–145.
Ke, Ping 柯平 (1995). 〈歐美的機器翻譯〉 (Machine Translation in Europe and America). 《中國翻譯》 (*Chinese Translators Journal*), No. 2, pp. 47–54.
Koutsoudas, Andreas and Robert Engel Machol (1956). "Mechanical Translation Work at the University of Michigan." *Mechanical Translation*, Vol. 3, No. 2, pp. 34, 41.
Locke, William N. and Victor H. Yngve (1958). "Research in Translation by Machine at M.I.T.." *Proceedings of the 8th International Congress of Linguists*, University of Solo, Oslo, Norway, pp. 510–514.
Mersel, Jules (1961). "Research in Machine Translation at Ramo-Wooldridge." In Harold P. Edmundson, ed., *Proceedings of the National Symposium on Machine Translation*. London: Prentice-Hall, pp. 26–38.
Micklesen, Lew R. and Robert E. Wall (1961). "Logical Programming Research in the University of Washington Machine Translation Project." In Allen Kent, ed., *Information Retrieval and Machine Translation*. New York: Interscience, pp. 853–866.
Morton, S. E. (1978). "Designing a Multilingual Terminology Bank for United States Translators." *Journal of the American Society for Information Science*, Vol. 29, pp. 297–303.
Moyne, John A. (1962). *Georgetown Automatic Translation: General Information and Operation Manual.* Washington, DC: Georgetown University Machine Translation Research.
Nirenburg, Sergei (2001). "CRL: A Center of Research Excellence in

Machine Translation." *International Journal of Translation*, Vol. 13, Nos. 1–2, pp. 41–53.
Oettinger, Anthony G. and Murray E. Sherry (1961). "Current Research on Automatic Translation at Harvard University and Predictive Syntactic Analysis." In Harold P. Edmundson, ed., *Proceedings of the National Symposium on Machine Translation*. London: Prentice-Hall, pp. 173–182.
Oettinger, Anthony G. (2000). "Machine Translation at Harvard." In W. John Hutchins, ed., *Early Years in Machine Translation: Memoirs and Biographies of Pioneers*. Amsterdam and Philadelphia: John Benjamins Publishing Company, pp. 73–86.
Pedtke, T. R. (1997). "U.S. Government Support and Use of Machine Translation: Current Status." *Proceedings of MT Summit VI*, San Diego, California, USA, pp. 3–13.
Reifler, Erwin (1956). "Machine Translation Development at the University of Washington." *Mechanical Translation*, Vol. 3, No. 2, pp. 33, 41.
Reifler, Erwin (1957). "The Machine Translation Project at the University of Washington, Seattle, Washington, USA." *Proceedings of the VIII International Congress of Linguists*. Oslo: University Press, pp. 514–518.
Reifler, Erwin (1961). "Current Research at the University of Washington." In Harold P. Edmundson, ed., *Proceedings of the National Symposium on Machine Translation*. London: Prentice-Hall, pp. 155–159.
Reifler, Erwin (1961). "MT Linguistics and MT Lexicography at the University of Washington." *Advances in Documentation and Library Science*, Vol. 3, No. 2, pp. 841–852.
Reifler, Erwin (1961). "Outline of the Machine Translation Project at the University of Washington." *Mechanical Translation*, Vol. 6, pp. 25–32.
Rhodes, Ida (1961). "The National Bureau of Standards Method of Syntactic Integration." In Harold P. Edmundson, ed., *Proceedings of the National Symposium on Machine Translation*. London: Prentice-Hall, pp. 39–44.
Rimon, Mori, Michael McCord, Ulrike Schwall, and Pilar Martínez (1993). "Advances in Machine Translation in IBM." In Sergei Nirenburg, ed., *Progress in Machine Translation*. Amsterdam: IOS and Tokyo: Ohmsha, pp. 3–13.

Sheridan, Peter (1955). "Research in Language Translation on the IBM Type 701." *IBM Technical Newsletter*, Vol. 9, pp. 5–24.

Tosh, L. W. (1968). "Initial Results of Syntactic Translation at the Linguistics Research Center." *Lingua*, Vol. 42, pp. 96–116.

Vasconcellos, Muriel (2000). "The Georgetown Project and Leon Dostert: Recollections of a Young Assistant." In W. John Hutchins, ed., *Early Years in Machine Translation: Memoirs and Biographies of Pioneers*. Amsterdam and Philadelphia: John Benjamins Publishing Company, pp. 87–96.

Werbow, S. N. (1961). "Research on the Texas Project." In Harold P. Edmundson, ed., *Proceedings of the National Symposium on Machine Translation*. Englewood Cliffs, New Jersey: Prentice-Hall, pp. 121–125.

Wilks, Yorick (1973). "The Stanford Machine Translation and Understanding Project." In Randall Rustin, ed., *Natural Language Processing*. New York: Algorithmics Press, pp. 243–290.

Yang, Yiming and Nianli Ma (2003). "CMU in Cross-language Information Retrieval at NTCIR-3." *Proceedings of the 3rd NTCIR Workshop on Research in Information Retrieval, Automatic Text Summarization and Question Answering*, Tokyo, Japan.

Yngve, Victor H. (1956). "Mechanical Translation Research at MIT." *Mechanical Translation*, Vol. 3, No. 2, pp. 44–45.

Yngve, Victor H. (1961). "MT at the Massachusetts Institute of Technology." In Harold P. Edmundson, ed., *Proceedings of the National Symposium on Machine Translation*. London: Prentice-Hall, pp. 126–132.

Yngve, Victor H. (1967). "MT at M.I.T. 1965." In Andrew D. Booth, ed., *Machine Translation*. Amsterdam: North-Holland Publishing Company, pp. 451–523.

Yngve, Victor H. (2000). "Early MT Research at M.I.T.: The Search for Context." In David G. Lockwood, Peter H. Fries, and James E. Copeland, eds., *Functional Approaches to Language, Culture and Cognition*. Amsterdam and Philadelphia: John Benjamins Publishing Company, pp. 593–628.

Yngve, Victor H. (2000). "Early Research at M.I.T.: In Search of Adequate Theory." In W. John Hutchins, ed., *Early Years in Machine Translation: Memoirs and Biographies of Pioneers*. Amsterdam and Philadelphia: John Benjamins Publishing Company, pp. 39–72.

Zarechnack, Michael (1958). "Report on the Work in MT at Georgetown University." *Proceedings of the 8th International Congress of Linguists*. Oslo: Oslo University Press, pp. 518–521.

Zarechnack, Michael and Antony F. R. Brown (1961). "Current Research at Georgetown University." In Harold P. Edmundson, ed., *Proceedings of the National Symposium on Machine Translation*. London: Prentice-Hall, pp. 67–87.

Zarechnack, Michael (2000). "The Early Days of GAT-SLC." In W. John Hutchins, ed., *Early Years in Machine Translation: Memoirs and Biographies of Pioneers*. Amsterdam and Philadelphia: John Benjamins Publishing Company, pp. 111–128.

Vietnam

Dien, Dinh and Hoang Kiem (2005). "State of the Art of Machine Translation in Vietnam." *AAMT Journal*, Vol. 38.

❖ PART 24 ❖

Natural Language

Natural Language

Alonso-Lavernia, María de los Ángeles, Argelio Víctor De-la-Cruz-Rivera, and Grigori Sidorov (2006). "Generation of Natural Language Explanations of Rules in an Expert System." *Proceedings of the 7th International Conference on Intelligent Text Processing and Computational Linguistics* (*CICLing-2006*), Mexico City, Mexico.

Chu-Carroll, Jennifer, John Prager, Yael Ravin, and Christian Cesar (2002). "A Hybrid Approach to Natural Language Web Search." *Proceedings of the 2002 Conference on Empirical Methods in Natural Language Processing* (*EMNLP-2002*), University of Pennsylvania, Philadelphia, PA, USA.

Díaz, Isabel, Lidia Moreno, Inmaculada Fuentes, and Oscar Pastor (2005). "Integrating Natural Language Techniques in OO-method." *Proceedings of the 6th International Conference on Intelligent Text Processing and Computational Linguistics* (*CICLing-2005*), Mexico City, Mexico, pp. 548–559.

Dura, Elżbieta (2003). "Natural Language in Information Retrieval." *Proceedings of the 4th International Conference on Intelligent Text Processing and Computational Linguistics* (*CICLing-2003*), Mexico City, Mexico, pp. 539–542.

Earp, R. and J. Cherinka (1978). "Getting Started in a Natural Language Translating Project." *Journal of Educational Data Processing*, Vol. 15, No. 2, pp. 25–34.

Feng, Zhiwei 馮志偉 (1994). 〈自然語言的複雜特徵描述與運算〉 (A Description of the Complicated Features of the Natural Language and Its Calculation). 《自然語言機器翻譯新論》 (*New Essays on Machine Translation of Natural Languages*). Beijing: Language Press, pp. 122–143.

Feng, Zhiwei (1994). 《自然語言機器翻譯新論》 (*New Essays on Machine Translation of Natural Languages*). Beijing: Language Press.

Garvin, Paul L., ed. (1963). *Natural Language and the Computer*. New York: McGraw-Hill.

Goshawke, Walter, Ian D. K. Keily, and J. David Wigg (1987). *Computer Translation of Natural Language*. Winslow: Sigma.

Hofmann, T. R. (1971). "Utilization of Computer Networks in Translation of Natural Language." *Universite de Montreal Publications internes*, pp. 23–28.

Hovy, Eduard (1988). *Generating Natural Language under Pragmatic Constraints*. Hillsdale, New Jersey: Lawrence Erlbaum Associates.

Kahane, Sylvain (2001). "What Is a Natural Language and How to Describe It? Meaning-text Approaches in Contrast with Generative Approaches." *Proceedings of the 2nd International Conference on Intelligent Text Processing and Computational Linguistics* (*CICLing-2001*), Mexico City, Mexico.

Kamei, Shin-ichiro and Kazunori Muraki (1997). "Logical Operators and Quantifiers in Natural Language." *Proceedings of the International Conference on Research in Computational Linguistics* (*ROCLING-X*), Academia Sinica, Taipei, Taiwan.

Kay, Martin (1973). "Automatic Translation of Natural Languages." *Daedalus*, Vol. 102, pp. 217–230.

Knapp, Melanie and Jens Woch (2002). "Towards a Natural Language Driven Automated Help Desk." *Proceedings of the 3rd International Conference on Intelligent Text Processing and Computational Linguistics* (*CICLing-2002*), Mexico City, Mexico.

Matthews, G. H. (1962). "Analysis by Synthesis of Sentences of Natural Languages." In National Physical Laboratory, ed., *1961 International Conference on Machine Translation of Languages and Applied Language Analysis: Proceedings of the Conference Held at the National Physical Laboratory, Teddington, Middlesex, on 5th, 6th, 7th and 8th September*. London: Her Majesty's Stationery Office, pp. 532–540.

Moschitti, Alessandro (2006). "Syntactic Kernels for Natural Language Learning: The Semantic Role Labeling Case." *Proceedings of the Human Language Technology Conference—Annual Meeting of the North American Chapter of the Association for Computational Linguistics* (*HLT-NAACL-2006*), New York, USA.

Ren, Fuji, Shunji Mitsuyoshi, Kang Yen, Chengqing Zong, and Hongbing Zhu (2003). "An Estimate Method of the Minimum Entropy of Natural Languages." *Proceedings of the 4th International Conference on Intelligent Text Processing and Computational Linguistics* (*CICLing-2003*), Mexico City, Mexico, pp. 384–394.

Roth, Dan (2002). "Learning and Inference in Natural Language." *Proceedings of the 2002 Conference on Empirical Methods in Natural Language Processing* (*EMNLP-2002*), University of Pennsylvania, Philadelphia, PA, USA.

Schank, Roger C. (1973). "Identification of Conceptualizations Underlying Natural Language." In Roger C. Schank and Kenneth Mark Colby, eds., *Computer Models of Thought and Language*. San Francisco: W. H. Freeman, pp. 187–247.

Schwartz, Richard (1999). "Why Doesn't Natural Language Come Naturally?" *Proceedings of the Joint SIGDAT Conference on Empirical Methods in NLP and Very Large Corpora* (*EMNLP/VLC-99*), University of Maryland, College Park, MD, USA.

Sheremetyeva, Svetlana (2003). "Towards Designing Natural Language Interfaces." *Proceedings of the 4th International Conference on Intelligent Text Processing and Computational Linguistics* (*CICLing-2003*), Mexico City, Mexico, pp. 479–491.

Sherry, Murray E. and Anthony G. Oettinger (1961). "A New Model of Natural Language for Predictive Syntactic Analysis." In Colin Cherry, ed., *Information Theory*. London: Butterworths, pp. 458–468.

Sierra, Gerardo and John McNaught (2003). "Natural Language System for Terminological Information Retrieval." *Proceedings of the 4th International Conference on Intelligent Text Processing and Computational Linguistics* (*CICLing-2003*), Mexico City, Mexico, pp. 543–554.

Zaharin, Yusoff (1986). "Strategies and Heuristics in the Analysis of a Natural Language in Machine Translation." *Proceedings of the 11th International Conference on Computational Linguistics* (*COLING-86*), Bonn, Germany, pp. 136–139.

Zárate M., J. Antonio, Rodolfo A. Pazos R., Alexander F. Gelbukh, and J. Isabel Padrón C. (2003). "A Portable Natural Language Interface for Diverse Databases Using Ontologies." *Proceedings of the 4th International Conference on Intelligent Text Processing and Computational Linguistics* (*CICLing-2003*), Mexico City, Mexico, pp. 496–507.

Natural Language Generation

ACM (1973). "Natural Language Translation by Computer Emerges from Government Research Stage." *CACM*, Vol. 16, No. 3, p. 196.

Aikawa, Takako, Maite Melero, Lee Schwartz, and Andi Wu (2001). "Multilingual Natural Language Generation." In Bente Maegaard,

ed., *Proceedings of MT Summit VIII: Machine Translation in the Information Age*, Santiago de Compostella, Spain.
Allman, Tod and Stephen Beale (2006). "A Natural Language Generator for Minority Languages." *Proceedings of the 5th SALTMIL Workshop on Minority Languages and the 5th International Conference on Language Resources and Evaluation (LREC-2006): Strategies for Developing Machine Translation for Minority Languages*, Genoa, Italy, pp. 39–46.
Axelrod, S. (2000). "Natural Language Generation in the IBM Flight Information System." *Proceedings of the ANLP/NAACL 2000 Workshop, Conversational Systems*, Seattle, Washington, DC, USA, pp. 21–26.
Bangalore, Srinivas and Owen Rambow (2000). "Corpus-based Lexical Choice in Natural Language Generation." *Proceedings of the 38th Annual Meeting of the Association for Computational Linguistics (ACL-2000)*, Hong Kong.
Barzilay, Regina and Mirella Lapata (2006). "Aggregation via Set Partitioning for Natural Language Generation." *Proceedings of the Human Language Technology Conference—Annual Meeting of the North American Chapter of the Association for Computational Linguistics (HLT-NAACL-2006)*, New York, USA.
Belz, Anja and Ehud Reiter (2006). "Comparing Automatic and Human Evaluation of NLG Systems." *Proceedings of the 11th Conference of the European Chapter of the Association for Computational Linguistics (EACL-2006)*, Trento, Italy.
Bernardos, Ma del Socorro (2004). "Guideline for Developing a Software Life Cycle Process in Natural Language Generation Projects." *Proceedings of the 5th International Conference on Intelligent Text Processing and Computational Linguistics (CICLing-2004)*, Chung-Ang University, Seoul, Korea, pp. 351–354.
Bontcheva, Kalina (1997). "Generation of Multilingual Explanations from Conceptual Graphs." In Ruslan Mitkov and Nicolas Nicolov, eds., *Recent Advances in Natural Language Processing*. Amsterdam and Philadelphia: John Benjamins Publishing Company, pp. 365–374.
D'Souza, Rayner, G. V. Shivakumar, D. Swathi, and Pushpak Bhattacharyya (2001). "Natural Language Generation from Semantic Net Like Structures with Application to Hindi." *Proceedings of the*

Symposium on Translation Support Systems (*STRANS-2001*). Kanpur, India.
Dai, Jiong 戴炯 and Wang Qian 王纖 (1999).〈自然語言宏觀規劃器知識庫的擬人化實現〉(The Implementation of the Knowledge-base of the Macro-planner of the Natural Language Generation System). In Huang Changning 黃昌寧 and Dong Zhendong 董振東, eds.,《計算機語言學文集》(*Essays on Computational Linguistics*). Beijing: Tsinghua University Press, pp. 267–273.
Earp, R. and J. Cherinka (1978). "Getting Started in a Natural Language Translation Project." *Journal of Educational Data Processing*, Vol. 15, No. 2, pp. 25–34.
Feng, Zhiwei (2004).〈目標語言生成〉(Target Language Generation).《機器翻譯研究》(*Studies on Machine Translation*). Beijing: China Translation and Publishing Corporation, pp. 679–701.
Guo, Zhongwei 郭忠偉, Xu Yanyong 徐延勇, Zhou Xianzhong 周獻中, and Huang Zhitong 黃志同 (2001).〈自然語言生成系統中的優化聚合〉(The Aggregation in Natural Language Generating System). In Huang Changning 黃昌寧 and Zhang Pu 張普, eds.,《自然語言理解與機器翻譯》(*Natural Language Understanding and Machine Translation*). Beijing: Tsinghua University Press, pp. 193–197.
Habash, Nizar and Bonnie J. Dorr (2001). "Large Scale Language Independent Generation Using Thematic Hierarchies." In Bente Maegaard, ed., *Proceedings of MT Summit VIII: Machine Translation in the Information Age*, Santiago de Compostela, Spain.
Habash, Nizar, Bonnie J. Dorr, and David Traum (2003). "Hybrid Natural Language Generation from Lexical Conceptual Structures." *Machine Translation*, Vol. 18, No. 2, pp. 81–128.
Harbusch, Karin and Jens Woch (2002). "Integrated Natural Language Generation with Schema—Tree Adjoining Grammars." *Proceedings of the 3rd International Conference on Intelligent Text Processing and Computational Linguistics* (*CICLing-2002*), Mexico City, Mexico.
Hartley, Anthony F. and Cecile Paris (2001). "Translation, Controlled Languages, Generation." In Erich H. Steiner and Colin Yallop, eds., *Exploring Translation and Multilingual Text Production: Beyond Content*. Berlin and New York: Mouton de Gruyter, pp. 307–325.
Jones, Daniel (1996). *Analogical Natural Language Processing*. London: UCL Press.
Kempen, Gerard and Karin Harbusch (2004). "Generating Natural Word

Orders in a Semi-free Word Order Language: Treebank-based Linearization Preferences for German." *Proceedings of the 5th International Conference on Intelligent Text Processing and Computational Linguistics* (*CICLing-2004*), Chung-Ang University, Seoul, Korea, pp. 346–350.

Lavoie, Benoit, Richard I. Kittredge, Tanya Korelsky, and Own Rambow (2000). "A Framework for MT and Multilingual NLG Systems Based on Uniform Lexico-structural Processing." *Proceedings of the 6th Applied Natural Language Processing Conference*, Seattle, Washington, DC, USA, pp. 60–67.

McDonald, David D. (1983). "Natural Language Generation as Computational Problem." In Michael Brady and Robert Berwick, eds., *Computational Models of Discourse*. Cambridge, MA: MIT Press, pp. 209–266.

McDonald, David D. (1987). "Natural Language Generation: Complexities and Techniques." In Sergei Nirenburg, ed., *Machine Translation: Theoretical and Methodological Issues*. Cambridge: Cambridge University Press, pp. 192–224.

McDonald, David D., M. Vaughan, and James Pustejovsky (1987). "Factors Contributing to Efficiency in Natural Language Generation." In Gerard Kempen, ed., *Natural Language Generation*. Dordrecht: Kluwer Academic Publishers.

Mellish, Chris, Roger Evans, Lynne Cahill, Christy Doran, Daniel Paiva, Mike Reape, Donia R. Scott, and Neil Tipper (2000). "A Representation for Complex and Evolving Data Dependencies in Generation." *Proceedings of the 6th Applied Natural Language Processing Conference*, Seattle, Washington, DC, USA, pp. 119–126.

Nicolov, Nicolas, Chris Mellish, and Graeme Ritchie (1997). "Approximate Chart Generation from Non-hierarchical Representations." In Ruslan Mitkov and Nicolas Nicolov, eds., *Recent Advances in Natural Language Processing*. Amsterdam and Philadelphia: John Benjamins Publishing Company, pp. 273–294.

Nirenburg, Sergei (1987). "A System for Natural Language Generation That Emphasizes Lexical Selection." *Proceedings of the Northeast Artificial Intelligence Consortium's Natural Language Planning Workshop*, Blue Mountain Lake, New York, USA, pp. 124–152.

Nirenburg, Sergei and Irene Nirenburg (1988). "A Framework for Lexical Selection in Natural Language Generation." *Proceedings of the 12th*

International Conference on Computational Linguistics (*COLING-88*), Budapest, Hungary, pp. 471–475.

Nirenburg, Sergei, Rita McCardell, Eric H. Nyberg, Scott Huffman, Edward Kernschaft, and Irene Nirenburg (1988). "Lexical Realization in Natural Language Generation." *Proceedings of the 2nd International Conference on Theoretical and Methodological Issues in Machine Translation of Natural Languages* (*TMI-88*), Carnegie Mellon University, Center for Machine Translation, Pittsburgh, Pennsylvania, USA.

Nirenburg, Sergei, Victor Lesser, and Eric H. Nyberg (1989). "Controlling a Language Generation Planner." *Proceedings of 11th Annual Meeting of the International Joint Conference for Artificial Intelligence* (*IJCAI-89*), Detroit, USA, pp. 1524–1530.

Oates, Sarah Louise (2000). "Multiple Discourse Marker Occurrence: Creating Hierarchies for Natural Language Generation." *Proceedings of the ANLP-NAACL-2000 Student Research Workshop*, Seattle, Washington, DC, USA, pp. 41–45.

Och, Franz Joseph and Hans Weber (1998). "Improving Statistical Natural Language Translation with Categories and Rules." *Proceedings of the 36th Annual Meeting of the Association for Computational Linguistics and 17th International Conference on Computational Linguistics* (*COLING-ACL-98*), Montreal, Quebec, Canada, pp. 985–989.

Ogino, Shiho and Tetsuya Nasukawa (1997). "Generating Natural Sentences by Using Shallow Discourse Information." *Proceedings of the 7th International Conference on Theoretical and Methodological Issues in Machine Translation* (*TMI-97*), St. John's College, Santa Fe, New Mexico, USA.

Paiva, Daniel and Roger Evans (2005). "Empirically-based Control of Natural Language Generation." *Proceedings of the 43rd Annual Meeting of the Association of Computational Linguistics* (*ACL-2005*), Ann Arbor, Michigan, USA.

Pelizzoni, Jorge Marques and Maria das Graças Volpe Nunes (2005). "Reconciling Parameterization, Configurability and Optimality in Natural Language Generation via Multiparadigm Programming." *Proceedings of the 6th International Conference on Intelligent Text Processing and Computational Linguistics* (*CICLing-2005*), Mexico City, Mexico, pp. 343–347.

Ratnaparkhi, Adwait (2000). "Trainable Methods for Surface Natural

Language Generation." *Proceedings of the 1st Meeting of the North American Chapter of the Association for Computational Linguistics*, Seattle, Washington, DC, USA, pp. 194–201.

Reiter, Ehud and Robert Dale (1997). "Building Applied Natural Language Generation Systems." *Proceedings of the 5th Conference on Applied Natural Language Processing*, Seattle, Washington, DC, USA.

Reiter, Ehud and Robert Dale (2000). *Building Natural Language Generation Systems*. Cambridge: Cambridge University Press.

Samuelsson, Christer (1997). "Example-based Optimisation of Surface-generation Tables." In Ruslan Mitkov and Nicolas Nicolov, eds., *Recent Advances in Natural Language Processing*. Amsterdam and Philadelphia: John Benjamins Publishing Company, pp. 295–315.

Stent, Amanda, Matthew Marge, and Mohit Singhai (2005). "Evaluating Evaluation Methods for Generation in the Presence of Variation." *Proceedings of the 6th International Conference on Intelligent Text Processing and Computational Linguistics* (*CICLing-2005*), Mexico City, Mexico, pp. 332–342.

Varges, Sebastian and Chris Mellish (2001). "Instance-based Natural Language Generation." *Proceedings of the Second Meeting of the North American Chapter of the Association for Computational Linguistics: Language Technologies 2001* (*NAACL-2001*), Pittsburgh, PA, USA.

Zhou, Lina 周莉娜, Shen Gang 沈鋼, and Yu Shiwen 俞士汶 (1996).〈面向圖像碼的自然語言語句生成技術〉(Technology for Image Code Oriented Natural Language Sentence Generation). In Yu Shiwen and Zhu Xuefeng, eds.,《計算語言學文集》(*Papers on Computational Linguistics*). Beijing: Department of Computer Science and Technology and Institute of Computational Linguistics, Peking University, pp. 104–112.

Zock, Michael (1997). "Sentence Generation by Pattern Matching: The Problem of Syntactic Choice." In Ruslan Mitkov and Nicolas Nicolov, eds., *Recent Advances in Natural Language Processing*. Amsterdam and Philadelphia: John Benjamins Publishing Company, pp. 317–352.

Natural Language Processing

Armstrong-Warwick, Susan (1994). "Acquisition and Exploitation of Textual Resources for NLP." In Antonio Zampolli, Nicoletta Calzolari, and Martha Palmer, eds., *Current Issues in Computational Linguistics:*

In Honour of Don Walker. Special Edition of *Linguistica Computazionale*, Vols. 9–10, pp. 451–465.

Arnold, Doug J. and Roderick L. Johnson (1984). "Robust Processing in Machine Translation." *Proceedings of the International Conference on the Methodology and Techniques of Machine Translation*, Cranfield Institute of Technology, Cranfield, England.

Arnold, Doug J. and Roderick L. Johnson (1984). "Robust Processing in Machine Translation." *Proceedings of the 10th International Conference on Computational Linguistics* (*COLING-84*), Stanford University, Stanford, CA, USA, pp. 472–475.

Arnold, Doug J., Lorna Balkan, R. Lee Humphreys, Seity Meijer, and Louisa Sadler (1994). "Representation and Processing." *Machine Translation: An Introductory Guide*. Manchester and Oxford: NCC Blackwell, pp. 37–62.

Arranz, M. Victoria (1997). "Lexical Bottleneck in Machine Translation and Natural Language Processing: A Case Study." In *Translating and the Computer 19*. London: The Association for Information Management.

Baeza-Yates, Ricardo (2004). "Challenges in the Interaction of Information Retrieval and Natural Language Processing." *Proceedings of the 5th International Conference on Intelligent Text Processing and Computational Linguistics* (*CICLing-2004*), Chung-Ang University, Seoul, Korea, pp. 439–450.

Balkan, Lorna, Klaus Netter, Doug J. Arnold, and Seity Meijer (1994). "TSNLP—Test Suites for Natural Language Processing." *Proceedings of the Language Engineering Convention of the European Network of Excellence in Human Language Technologies* (*ELSNET-94*), Paris, France, pp. 17–22.

Barnett, Jim, Kevin Knight, Inderjeet Mani, and Elaine Rich (1990). "Knowledge and Natural Language Processing." *Communications of the ACM*, Vol. 33, No. 8, pp. 50–71.

Berger, Adam L., Stephen A. Della Pietra, and Vincent J. Della Pietra (1996). "A Maximum Entropy Approach to Natural Language Processing." *Computational Linguistics*, Vol. 22, No. 1, pp. 39–71.

Bharati, Akshar, Vineet Chaitanya, and Rajeev Sangal (1995). *Natural Language Processing: A Pāainian Perspective*. New Delhi: Prentice Hall of India.

Blanchon, Hervé (1996). "A Customizable Interactive Disambiguation

Methodology and Two Implementations to Disambiguate French and English Input." In Christian Boitet, ed., *Proceedings of MIDDIM-96 Post-COLING Seminar on Interactive Disambiguation*, Le Col de Porte, France, pp. 190–200.

Boguraev, Branimir K. and Ted Briscoe, eds. (1989). *Computational Lexicography for Natural Language Processing*. London: Longman.

Borko, Harold, ed. (1967). *Automated Language Processing: The State of the Art*. New York: Wiley.

Brill, Eric (1995). "Transformation-based Error-driven Learning and Natural Language Processing: A Case-study in Part of Speech Tagging," *Computational Linguistics*, Vol. 21, No. 4, pp. 543–565.

Brill, Eric (2000). "Pattern-based Disambiguation for Natural Language Processing." *Proceedings of the Joint Sigdat Conference on Empirical Methods in Natural Language Processing and Very Large Corpora (EMNLP/VLC-2000)*, Hong Kong University of Science and Technology, Hong Kong.

Brill, Eric (2003). "Processing Natural Language without Natural Language Processing." *Proceedings of the 4th International Conference on Intelligent Text Processing and Computational Linguistics (CICLing-2003)*, Mexico City, Mexico, pp. 362–371.

Chang, Chao-Huang (1998). "Corpus-based Evaluation of Language Processing Systems Using Information Restoration Model." *Proceedings of the International Conference on Research in Computational Linguistics (ROCLING-XI)*, Hsin-Chu, Taiwan.

Chien, Lee-Feng 簡立峰 (2006). "Natural Language Processing versus Web Search Engine." *Proceedings of the Conference of the Association for Computational Linguistics and Chinese Language Processing (ROCLING-XVIII)*, Taipei, Taiwan.

Church, Kenneth W., John Lowe, Drago Radev, and Joe Zhou (2000). "NLP for the Web: Critical Technology or Luxury?" *Proceedings of the Joint Sigdat Conference on Empirical Methods in Natural Language Processing and Very Large Corpora (EMNLP/VLC-2000)*, Hong Kong University of Science and Technology, Hong Kong.

Church, Kenneth W. (2001). "Empirical Methods in Natural Language Processing: What's Happened Since the First SIGDAT Meeting?" *Proceedings of the 2nd Meeting of the North American Chapter of the Association for Computational Linguistics: Language Technologies 2001 (NAACL-2001)*, Pittsburgh, PA, USA.

Copeland, Charles, Jacques Durand, Steven Krauwer, and Bente Maergaard (1991). *Studies in Machine Translation and Natural Language Processing*, Vols. 1–2. Luxembourg: Office for Official Publications of the European Community.

Costa, Fabrizio, Sauro Menchetti, Alessio Ceroni, Andrea Passerini, and Paolo Frasconi (2006). "Decomposition Kernels for Natural Language Processing." *Proceedings of the 11th Conference of the European Chapter of the Association for Computational Linguistics (EACL-2006)*, Trento, Italy.

Dale, Robert, Hermann Moisl, and Harold L. Somers, eds. (2003). *A Handbook of Natural Language Processing*. New York: Marcel Dekker.

Day, David, John Aberdeen, Lynette Hirschman, Robyn Kozierok, Patricia Robinson, and Marc Vilain (1997). "Mixed-initiative Development of Language Processing Systems." *Proceedings of the 5th Conference on Applied Natural Language Processing*, Seattle, Washington, DC, USA.

Eynde, Karel van den, Erik Broeders, Carmen Eggermont, and Ludo Vangilbergen (1988). "The Pronominal Approach in NLP: A Pronominal Feature Analysis of Coordination in French." *Machine Translation*, Vol. 3, Nos. 3–4, pp. 177–213.

Feng, Zhiwei 馮志偉 (1994).《自然語言機器翻譯新論》(*New Essays on Machine Translation of Natural Languages*). Beijing: Language Press.

Feng, Zhiwei 馮志偉 (1996).《自然語言的計算機處理》(*Computer Processing of Natural Language*). Shanghai: Foreign Language Education Press.

Ferret, Olivier and Brigitte Grau (1997). "An Episodic Memory for Understanding and Learning." In Ruslan Mitkov and Nicolas Nicolov, eds., *Recent Advances in Natural Language Processing*. Amsterdam and Philadelphia: John Benjamins Publishing Company, pp. 173–184.

Gazdar, Gerald (1996). "Paradigm Merger in Natural Language Processing." In Ian Wand and Robin Milner, eds., *Computing Tomorrow: Future Research Directions in Computer Science*. Cambridge: Cambridge University Press, pp. 88–109.

Gazdar, Gerald and Chris Mellish (1989). *Natural Language Processing in Prolog*. England: Addison Wesley.

Grefenstette, Gregory (1997). "Daniel Jones, Analogical Natural Language Processing." *Machine Translation*, Vol. 12, No. 3, pp. 253–259.

Habash, Nizar (2005). "Arabic Natural Language Processing." *Proceedings of the 43rd Annual Meeting of the Association of Computational Linguistics* (*ACL-2005*), Ann Arbor, Michigan, USA.

Hays, David G., ed. (1966). *Readings in Automatic Language Processing*. New York: American Elsevier.

Henderson, John and Eric Brill (1999). "Exploiting Diversity in Natural Language Processing: Combining Parsers." *Proceedings of the Joint SIGDAT Conference on Empirical Methods in NLP and Very Large Corpora* (*EMNLP/VLC-99*), University of Maryland, College Park, MD, USA.

Hirst, Graeme (2003). "Introduction to Non-statistical Natural Language Processing." *Proceedings of the Human Language Technology and North American Chapter of Association of Computational Linguistics 2003* (*HLT/NAACL-2003*), Edmonton, Alberta, Canada.

Huang, Chu-Ren and Chen Keh-jiann (1996). "Issues and Topics in Chinese Natural Language Processing." *Journal of Chinese Linguistics*, Vol. 9, pp. 1–22.

Jones, Daniel B. (1996). *Analogical Natural Language Processing*. London: UCL Press.

Jones, Daniel B. and Harold L. Somers, eds. (1997). *New Methods in Language Processing*. London: UCL Press.

Joshi, Aravind K. (2001). "The XTAG Project at Penn." *Proceedings of the 7th International Workshop on Parsing Technologies* (*IWPT-2001*), Peking University, Beijing, China. Beijing: Tsinghua University Press, pp. 16–27.

Klein, Dan and Christopher D. Manning (2002). "Conditional Structure versus Conditional Estimation in NLP Models." *Proceedings of the 2002 Conference on Empirical Methods in Natural Language Processing* (*EMNLP-2002*), University of Pennsylvania, Philadelphia, PA, USA.

Knight, Kevin and Jonathan Graehl (2005). "An Overview of Probabilistic Tree Transducers for Natural Language Processing." *Proceedings of the 6th International Conference on Intelligent Text Processing and Computational Linguistics* (*CICLing-2005*), Mexico City, Mexico, pp. 1–25.

Kolak, Okan, William Byrne, and Philip Resnik (2003). "A Generative Probabilistic OCR Model for NLP Applications." *Proceedings of the Human Language Technology and North American Chapter of*

Association of Computational Linguistics 2003 (*HLT/NAACL-2003*), Edmonton, Alberta, Canada.

Lehmann, Sabine, Stephan Oepen, Sylvie Regnier-Prost, Klaus Netter, Veronika Lux, Judith Klein, Kirsten Falkedal, Frederik Fouvry, Dominique Estival, Eva Dauphin, Herv Compagnion, Judith Baur, Lorna Balkan, and Doug Arnold (1996). "TSNLP—Test Suites for Natural Language Processing." *Proceedings from the 16th International Conference on Computational Linguistics* (*COLING-96*), Copenhagen, Denmark, pp. 711–716.

Lewis, Terence (1994). "Aspects of an Empirical Approach to Language Processing." *Machine Translation—Ten Years On: Proceedings of the 2nd International Conference Organised by Cranfield University,* Cranfield, England.

Li, Wenjie, Haihua Pan, Ming Zhou, Kam-Fai Wong, and Vincent Lum (1995). "Are Statistics-based Approaches Good Enough for NLP? A Case Study of Maximal-length NP Extraction in Mandarin Chinese." *Proceedings of the Conference of the Association for Computational Linguistics and Chinese Language Processing* (*ROCLING-VIII*), Yuan-Ze Institute of Technology, Chung-Li, Taiwan.

Lin, Sung-Chen 林頌堅 (2003).〈基於自然語言處理技術的研究主題抽取與分析〉(Extraction and Analysis of Research Topics Based on NLP Technologies). *Proceedings of the International Conference on Research in Computational Linguistics* (*ROCLING-XV*), Hsin-Chu, Taiwan.

Liu, Qun 劉群, Hang Hao 張浩, and Bai Shuo 白碩 (2002).〈中文信息處理開放平台的設計〉(An Open Source Platform for Chinese NLP).《第一屆學生計算語言學研討會論文集》(*SWCL2002: First Students' Workshop on Computational Linguistics: Proceedings*), Institute of Computational Linguistics, Peking University, Beijing, pp. 339–345.

Liu, Qun, Hang Hao, and Bai Shuo (2002).〈自然語言處理開放資源平台〉(An Open Source Platform for Chinese NLP). In Yu Shiwen, ed., *Proceedings of the Second China-Japan Natural Language Processing Joint Research Promotion Conference* (*CJNLP-2002*). Beijing: Institute of Computational Linguistics, Peking University, pp. 363–369.

Loomis, Thomas (1987). "Software Design Issues for Natural Language Processing." *Machine Translation*, Vol. 2, No. 4, pp. 219–230.

Lytle, Eldon G., D. Packard, D. Gibb, Alan K. Melby, and F. H. Billings

(1975). "Junction Grammar as a Base for Natural Language Processing." *American Journal of Computational Linguistics*, Vol. 3, pp. 1–73.

Ma, Yinghua 馬穎華 and Su Guiyang 蘇貴祥 (2002). 〈基於概念的自然語言處理〉 (Natural Language Processing Based on Concepts). 《第一屆學生計算語言學研討會論文集》(*SWCL2002: First Students' Workshop on Computational Linguistics: Proceedings*), Institute of Computational Linguistics, Peking University, Beijing, China, p. 44.

Marusenko, Michael A., Rajmund H. Piotrowski, and Yulia P. Vyshenskaya (2004). "Natural Language Processing and Attribution of Anonymous and Pseudonymic Texts: A Pattern Recognition Approach." *International Journal of Translation*, Vol. 16, No. 2, pp. 35–55.

McShane, Marjorie and Sergei Nirenburg (2003). "Parameterizing and Eliciting Text Elements across Languages for Use in Natural Language Processing Systems." *Machine Translation*, Vol. 18, No. 2, pp. 129–165.

Mitkov, Ruslan (1997). "Two Engines Are Better Than One: Generating More Power and Confidence in the Search for the Antecedent." In Ruslan Mitkov and Nicolas Nicolov, eds., *Recent Advances in Natural Language Processing*. Amsterdam and Philadelphia: John Benjamins Publishing Company, pp. 225–234.

Mitkov, Ruslan and Nicolas Nicolov, eds. (1997). *Recent Advances in Natural Language Processing*. Amsterdam and Philadelphia: John Benjamins Publishing Company.

Morin, Jean-Yves (1995). "Theoretical and Effective Complexity in Natural Language Processing." *Proceedings of the Conference of the Association for Computational Linguistics and Chinese Language Processing* (*ROCLING-VIII*), Yuan-Ze Institute of Technology, Chung-Li, Taiwan.

Munson, Art, Claire Cardie, and Rich Caruana (2005). "Optimizing to Arbitrary NLP Metrics Using Ensemble Selection." *Proceedings of Human Language Technology Conference and Conference on Empirical Methods in Natural Language Processing* (*HLT/EMNLP-2005*), Vancouver, BC, Canada.

Nagao, Makoto and Jun-ichi Tsujii (1980). "Some Topics of Language Processing for Machine Translation." *International Forum on Information and Documentation*, Vol. 5, No. 2, pp. 32–37.

Nirenburg, Sergei and Jaime G. Carbonell (1987). "Integrating Discourse Pragmatics and Prepositional Knowledge for Multilingual Natural Language Processing." *Computers and Translation*, Vol. 2, No. 2, pp. 105–116.

Oettinger, Anthony G. (1965). "Automatic Processing of Natural and Formal Languages." *Information Processing 65: Proceedings of the IFIP Congress 65*. Washington, DC: Spartan Books, Vol. 1, pp. 9–16.

Pardelli, Gabriella, Manuela Sassi, Sara Goggi, and Paola Orsolini (2006). "Natural Language Processing: A Terminological and Statistical Approach." *Proceedings of the 5th International Conference on Language Resources and Evaluation* (*LREC-2006*), Genoa, Italy.

Radev, Dragomir, John Prager, and Valerie Samn (2000). "Ranking Suspected Answers to Natural Language Questions Using Predictive Annotation." *Proceedings of the 6th Applied Natural Language Processing Conference*, Seattle, Washington, DC, USA, pp. 150–157.

Raskin, Victor (1987). "Linguistics and Natural Language Processing." In Sergei Nirenburg, ed., *Machine Translation: Theoretical and Methodological Issues*. Cambridge: Cambridge University Press, pp. 42–58.

Raskin, Victor (1987). "What Is There in Linguistic Semantics for Natural Language Processing?" *Proceedings of the Northeast Artificial Intelligence Consortium's Natural Language Planning Workshop*, Blue Mountain Lake, New York, USA, pp. 78–96.

Raskin, Victor, Salvatore Attardo, and Donalee H. Attardo (1994). "Augmenting Formal Semantic Representation for NLP: The Story of SMEARR." *Machine Translation*, Vol. 9, No. 2, pp. 81–98.

Raskin, Victor and Sergei Nirenburg (1998). "An Applied Ontological Semantic Microtheory of Adjective Meaning for Natural Language Processing." *Machine Translation*, Vol. 13, Nos. 2–3, pp. 135–227.

Rayner, Manny (1988). "Applying Explanation-based Generalization to Natural Language Processing." *Proceedings of the International Conference on 5th Generation Computer Systems*, Kyoto, Japan, pp. 1267–1274.

Read, Tim (1997). "Java and Its Role in Natural Language Processing and Machine Translation." *Proceedings of MT Summit VI*, San Diego, California, USA.

Ren, Fuji (2001). "A Hybrid Approach of Text Segmentation Based on

Sensitive Word Concept for NLP." *Proceedings of the 2nd International Conference on Intelligent Text Processing and Computational Linguistics* (*CICLing-2001*), Mexico City, Mexico.

Sable, Carl, Kathleen R. McKeown, and Kenneth W. Church (2002). "NLP Found Helpful (at Least for One Text Categorization Task)." *Proceedings of the 2002 Conference on Empirical Methods in Natural Language Processing* (*EMNLP-2002*), University of Pennsylvania, Philadelphia, PA, USA.

Sag, Ivan A., Timothy Baldwin, Francis Bond, Ann Copestake, and Dan Flickinger (2002). "Multi-word Expressions: A Pain in the Neck for NLP." *Proceedings of the 3rd International Conference on Intelligent Text Processing and Computational Linguistics* (*CICLing-2002*), Mexico City, Mexico.

Saggion, Horacio, Katerina Pastra, and Yorick Wilks (2003). "Using Natural Language Processing for Semantic Indexing of Scene-of-crime Photographs." *Proceedings of the 4th International Conference on Intelligent Text Processing and Computational Linguistics* (*CICLing-2003*), Mexico City, Mexico, pp. 528–538.

Sakamoto, Yoshiyuki (1970). "Automatic Language Processing System in Natural Language Dictionary for Machine Translation." *Research of the Electro-technical Laboratory*, No. 707.

Santos, Diana (1999). "Toward Language-dependent Applications." *Machine Translation*, Vol. 14, No. 2, pp. 83–112.

Sgall, Petr (1989). "What Linguistics Can and Should Offer for Natural Language Processing." *Prague Bulletin of Mathematical Linguistics*, Vol. 51, pp. 9–13.

Streiter, Oliver (1996). *Linguistic Modeling for Multilingual Machine Translation*. Aachen: Shaker Verlag.

Streiter, Oliver, Mathias Stuflesser, and Qiu Lan Weng (2006). "Models of Cooperation for the Development of NLP Resources: A Comparison of BLARK and XNLRDF." *Proceedings of the 5th SALTMIL Workshop on Minority Languages and the 5th International Conference on Language Resources and Evaluation* (*LREC-2006*): *Strategies for Developing Machine Translation for Minority Languages*, Genoa, Italy, pp. 109–112.

Suzuki, Jun, Hideki Isozaki, and Eisaku Maeda (2004). "Convolution Kernels with Feature Selection for Natural Language Processing Tasks." *Proceedings of the 42nd Annual Meeting of the Association for*

Computational Linguistics (*ACL-2004*), Barcelona, Spain, pp. 119–126.

Tennant, Harry (1981). *Natural Language Processing*. Princeton: Petrocelli.

Tomita, Masaru (1986). *Efficient Parsing for Natural Language*. Dordrecht: Kluwer Academic Publishers.

Troussov, Alexander, Brian O'Donovan, Seppo Koskenniemi, and Nikolay Glushnev (2003). "Per-node Optimization of Finite-state Mechanisms for Natural Language Processing." *Proceedings of the 4th International Conference on Intelligent Text Processing and Computational Linguistics* (*CICLing-2003*), Mexico City, Mexico, pp. 223–226.

Wasson, Mark (2003). "NLP R&D and Commercial Deployment." *Proceedings of the Human Language Technology and North American Chapter of Association of Computational Linguistics 2003* (*HLT/NAACL-2003*), Edmonton, Alberta, Canada.

Wigg, David (1995). "Multilingual Natural Language Processing (MNLP) Project." *Machine Translation Review*, No. 1, pp. 8–9.

Wilks, Yorick (1990). "Where Am I Coming From: The Reversibility of Analysis and Generation in Natural Language Processing." *Memoranda in Computer and Cognitive Science*, MCCS-90-195. Las Cruces, NM: Computer Research Laboratory, New Mexico State University.

Yu, Shiwen 俞士汶 (1998).〈關於語言信息處理技術的展望〉(Prospects of Language Information Processing Technology). In Yu Shiwen 俞士汶 and Zhu Xuefeng 朱學鋒, eds.,《計算語言學文集》(*Papers on Computational Linguistics*), Vol. 3. Beijing: Department of Computer Science and Technology and Institute of Computational Linguistics, Peking University, pp. 4–7.

Zhou, Qiang 周強 (1996).〈基於語料庫和面向統計學的自然語言處理技術介紹〉(Introducing a Natural Language Processing Technology Based on Corpora and Oriented to Statistics). In Yu Shiwen and Zhu Xuefeng, eds.,《計算語言學文集》(*Papers on Computational Linguistics*). Beijing: Department of Computer Science and Technology and Institute of Computational Linguistics, Peking University, pp. 135–147.

Finite State Transducer

Abney, Steven (1996). "Partial Parsing via Finite-state Cascades." *The*

European Summer School in Logic, Language and Information Workshop on Robust Parsing (*ESSLLI-96*). Prague, the Czech Republic.

Alshawi, Hiyan, Shona Douglas, and Srinivas Bangalore (2000). "Learning Dependency Translation Models as Collections of Finite-state Head Transducers." *Computational Linguistics*, Vol. 26, No. 1, pp. 45–60.

Amengual, Juan Carlos, José Miguel Benedí, K. Beulen, Francisco Casacuberta, Asunción Castaño, Antonio Castellanos, Victor M. Jiménez, David Liorens, Andrés Marzal, Hermann Ney, Federico Prat, Enrique Vidal, and Juan Miguel Vilar (1997). "Speech Translation Based on Automatically Trainable Finite-state Models." *Proceedings of the 5th European Conference on Speech Communication and Technology* (*EuroSpeech-97*), Rhodes, Greece, pp. 1439–1442.

Amtrup, Jan W. (2003). "Morphology in Machine Translation Systems: Efficient Integration of Finite State Transducers and Feature Structure Descriptions." *Machine Translation*, Vol. 18, No. 3, pp. 217–238.

Bangalore, Srinivas and Giuseppe Riccardi (2000). "Stochastic Finite-state Models for Spoken Language Machine Translation." *Proceedings of the ANLP/NAACL-2000 Workshop on Embedded Machine Translation Systems*, Seattle, Washington, DC, USA, pp. 52–59.

Bangalore, Srinivas and Giuseppe Riccardi (2001). "A Finite-state Approach to Machine Translation." *Proceedings of the 2nd Meeting of the North American Chapter of the Association for Computational Linguistics*, Pittsburgh, Pennsylvania, USA, pp. 135–142.

Bouma, Gosse (2000). "A Finite State and Data-oriented Method for Grapheme to Phoneme Conversion." *Proceedings of the 1st Meeting of the North American Chapter of the Association for Computational Linguistics*, Seattle, Washington, DC, USA, pp. 303–310.

Casacuberta, Francisco, Enrique Vidal, and Juan Miguel Vilar (2002). "Architectures for Speech-to-speech Translation Using Finite-state Models." *Proceedings of the Workshop on Speech-to-Speech Translation: Algorithms and Systems*, Philadelphia, USA, pp. 39–44.

Dhonnchadha, Uí, Caoilfhionn Nic Pháidín, and Josef van Genabith (2003). "Design, Implementation and Evaluation of an Inflectional Morphology Finite State Transducer for Irish." *Machine Translation*, Vol. 18, No. 3, pp. 173–193.

Eisner, Jason (2002). "Parameter Estimation for Probabilistic Finite-state

Transducers." *Proceedings of the 40th Annual Meeting of the Association for Computational Linguistics* (*ACL-2002*), Philadelphia, PA, USA, pp. 1–8.

Eisner, Jason (2003). "Simpler and More General Minimization for Weighted Finite-state Automata." *Proceedings of the Human Language Technology and North American Chapter of Association of Computational Linguistics 2003* (*HLT/NAACL-2003*), Edmonton, Alberta, Canada.

Gurevich, Olga (2006). "A Finite-state Model of Georgian Verbal Morphology." *Proceedings of the Human Language Technology Conference—Annual Meeting of the North American Chapter of the Association for Computational Linguistics* (*HLT-NAACL-2006*), New York, USA.

Knight, Kevin and Yaser Al-Onaizan (1998). "Translation with Finite-state Devices." In David L. Farwell, Laurie Gerber, and Eduard Hovy, eds., *Machine Translation and the Information Soup*. Berlin: Springer Verlag, pp. 421–437.

Mohri, Mehryar (1997). "Finite-state Transducers in Language and Speech Processing." *Computational Linguistics*, Vol. 23, pp. 269–311.

Park, Jihyun and Chris Brew (2006). "A Finite-state Model of Human Sentence Processing." *Proceedings of the Joint Conference of the International Committee on Computational Linguistics and the Association for Computational Linguistics* (*COLING/ACL-2006*), Sydney, Australia.

Poibeau, Thierry (2001). "Parsing Natural Language Idioms with Bidirectional Finite-state Machines." *Theoretical Computer Science*, Vol. 267, pp. 131–140.

Pretorius, Laurette and Sonja E. Bosch (2003). "Finite-state Computational Morphology: An Analyzer Prototype For Zulu." *Machine Translation*, Vol. 18, No. 3, pp. 195–216.

Roche, Emmanuel and Yves Schabes (1995). "Deterministic Part-of-speech Tagging with Finite-state Transducers." *Computational Linguistics*, Vol. 21, pp. 227–253.

Sanchís, Alberto, David Picó, Joan Miquel del Val, Ferran Fabregat, Jesús Tomás, Moisés Pastor, and Francisco Casacuberta (2001). "A Morphological Analyzer for Machine Translation Based on Finite-state Transducers." In Bente Maegaard, ed., *Proceedings of MT Summit VIII:*

Machine Translation in the Information Age, Santiago de Compostela, Spain.
Schafer, Charles (2006). "Novel Probabilistic Finite-state Transducers for Cognate and Transliteration Modeling." *Proceedings of the 7th Biennial Conference of the Association for Machine Translation in the Americas (AMTA-2006): Visions for the Future of Machine Translation*, Boston Marriott, Cambridge, MA, USA.
Skut, Wojciech, Stefan Ulrich, and Kathrine Hammervold (2003). "A Generic Finite State Compiler for Tagging Rules." *Machine Translation*, Vol. 18, No. 3, pp. 239–250.
Tromble, Roy W. and Jason Eisner (2006). "A Fast Finite-state Relaxation Method for Enforcing Global Constraints on Sequence Decoding." *Proceedings of the Human Language Technology Conference—Annual Meeting of the North American Chapter of the Association for Computational Linguistics* (*HLT-NAACL-2006*), New York, USA.
Vilar, Juan Miguel, Victor M. Jiménez, Juan Carlos Amengual, Antonio Castellanos, David Llorens, and Enrique Vidal (1999). "Text and Speech Translation by Means of Subsequential Transducers." In András Kornai, ed., *Extended Finite State Models of Language*. Cambridge: Cambridge University Press, pp. 121–139.
Vilares, Manuel, Juan Otero, and Jorge Graña (2005). "Regional vs. Global Finite-state Error Repair." *Proceedings of the 6th International Conference on Intelligent Text Processing and Computational Linguistics* (*CICLing-2005*), Mexico City, Mexico, pp. 119–130.
Vogel, Stephan and Hermann Ney (2000). "Translation with Cascaded Finite State Transducers." *Proceedings of the 38th Annual Meeting of the Association for Computational Linguistics* (*ACL-2000*), Hong Kong.
Walther, Markus (2000). "Finite-state Reduplication in One-level Prosodic Morphology." *Proceedings of the 1st Meeting of the North American Chapter of the Association for Computational Linguistics*, Seattle, Washington, DC, USA, pp. 296–302.
Wellington, Benjamin, Joseph P. Turian, Chris Pike, and I. Dan Melamed (2006). "Scalable Discriminative Training for Word and Tree Transducers." *Proceedings of the 7th Biennial Conference of the Association for Machine Translation in the Americas* (*AMTA-2006*)*: Visions for the Future of Machine Translation*, Boston Marriott, Cambridge, MA, USA.

Head-transducer Model

Alshawi, Hiyan, Adam L. Buchbaum, and Fei Xia (1997). "A Comparison of Head Transducers and Transfer for a Limited Domain Translation Application." *Proceedings of the 35th Annual Meeting of the Association for Computational Linguistics and 8th Conference of the European Chapter of the Association for Computational Linguistics*, Madrid, Spain, pp. 360–365.

Alshawi, Hiyan and Fei Xia (1997). "English-to-Mandarin Speech Translation with Head Transducers." *Spoken Language Translation: Proceedings of a Workshop Sponsored by the Association for Computational Linguistics and by the European Network in Language and Speech* (*ELSNET-97*), Madrid, Spain, pp. 54–60.

Alshawi, Hiyan, Srinivas Bangalore, and Shona Douglas (1998). "Learning Phrase-based Head Transduction Models for Translation of Spoken Utterances." *Proceedings of the 5th International Conference on Spoken Language Processing* (*ICSLP-98*), Sydney, Australia, pp. 2767–2770.

Alshawi, Hiyan, Srinivas Bangalore, and Shona Douglas (2000). "Head-transducer Models for Speech Translation and Their Automatic Acquisition from Bilingual Data." *Machine Translation*, Vol. 15, Nos. 1–2, pp. 105–124.

Maximum Entropy

Ayan, Necip Fazil and Bonnie J. Dorr (2006). "A Maximum Entropy Approach to Combining Word Alignments." *Proceedings of the Human Language Technology Conference—Annual Meeting of the North American Chapter of the Association for Computational Linguistics* (*HLT-NAACL-2006*), New York, USA.

Bender, Oliver, Klaus Macherey, Franz Josef Och, and Hermann Ney (2003). "Comparison of Alignment Templates and Maximum Entropy Models for Natural Language Understanding." *Proceedings of the 10th Conference of the European Chapter of the Association of Computational Linguistics* (*EACL-2003*), Budapest, Hungary.

Berger, Adam L., Stephen Della Pietra, and Vincent Della Pietra (1996). "A Maximum Entropy Approach to Natural Language Processing." *Computational Linguistics*, Vol. 22, No. 1, pp. 39–72.

Berger, Adam L. and Harry Printz (1998). "A Natural Criterion for Maximum Entropy/Minimum Divergence Feature Selection." *Proceedings of the 3rd Conference on Empirical Methods in Natural Language Processing*, Granada, Spain.

Charniak, Eugene (2000). "A Maximum-entropy-inspired Parser." *Proceedings of the 1st Meeting of the North American Chapter of the Association for Computational Linguistics*, Seattle, Washington, DC, USA, pp. 132–139.

Fleischman, Michael and Eduard Hovy (2003). "A Maximum Entropy Approach to FrameNet Tagging." *Proceedings of the Human Language Technology and North American Chapter of Association of Computational Linguistics 2003* (*HLT/NAACL-2003*), Edmonton, Alberta, Canada.

Foster, George (2000). "A Maximum Entropy/Minimum Divergence Translation Model." *Proceedings of the 38th Annual Meeting of the Association for Computational Linguistics* (*ACL-2000*), Hong Kong.

Foster, George (2000). "Incorporating Position Information into a Maximum Entropy/Minimum Divergence Translation Model." *Proceedings of the 4th Conference on Computational Language Learning* (*CoNLL-2000*) *and the 2nd Learning Language in Logic Workshop* (*LLL-2000*), Lisbon, Portugal, pp. 37–42.

Goodman, Joshua (2004). "Exponential Priors for Maximum Entropy Models." *Proceedings of the Human Language Technology Conference/North American Chapter of the Association for Computational Linguistics Annual Meeting* (*HLT/NAACL-2004*), Boston, MA, USA.

Goto, Isao, Naoto Kato, Noriyoshi Uratani, and Terumasa Ehara (2003). "Transliteration Considering Context Information Based on the Maximum Entropy Method." *Proceedings of MT Summit IX*, New Orleans, Louisiana, USA.

Gu, Liang and Gao Yuqing (2004). "On Feature Selection in Maximum Entropy Approach to Statistical Concept-based Speech-to-speech Translation." *Proceedings of the International Workshop on Spoken Language Translation* (*IWSLT-2004*), Kyoto, Japan.

Ittycheriah, Abraham, Lucian Lita, Nanda Kambhatla, Nicolas Nicolov, Salim Roukos, and Margo Stys (2003). "Identifying and Tracking Entity Mentions in a Maximum Entropy Framework." *Proceedings of the Human Language Technology and North American Chapter of*

Association of Computational Linguistics 2003 (*HLT/NAACL-2003*), Edmonton, Alberta, Canada.

Kim, Sung Dong and Byoung-Tak Zhang (2000). "Reducing Parsing Complexity by Intra-sentence Segmentation Based on Maximum Entropy Model." *Proceedings of the Joint Sigdat Conference on Empirical Methods in Natural Language Processing and Very Large Corpora* (*EMNLP/VLC-2000*), Hong Kong University of Science and Technology, Hong Kong.

Kit, Chunyu, Xiaoyue Liu, and Jonathan J. Webster (2006). "Abbreviation Recognition with MaxEnt Model." *Proceedings of the 7th International Conference on Intelligent Text Processing and Computational Linguistics* (*CICLing-2006*), Mexico City, Mexico.

Li, Sujian and Liu Qun (2002). "Maximum Entropy Model for Chinese Chunking." In Yu Shiwen, ed., *Proceedings of the 2nd China-Japan Natural Language Processing Joint Research Promotion Conference* (*CJNLP-2002*). Beijing: Institute of Computational Linguistics, Peking University, pp. 247–252.

Malouf, Robert (2002). "A Comparison of Algorithms for Maximum Entropy Parameter Estimation." *Proceedings of the 6th Conference on Natural Language Learning* (*CoNLL-2002*), Taipei, Taiwan, pp. 49–55.

Och, Franz Josef and Hermann Ney (2002). "Discriminative Training and Maximum Entropy Models for Statistical Machine Translation." *Proceedings of the Annual Meeting of the Association for Computational Linguistics* (*ACL-2002*), Philadelphia, PA, USA, pp. 295–302.

Ratnaparkhi, Adwait (1996). "A Maximum Entropy Model for POS Tagging." *Proceedings of the Conference on Empirical Methods in Natural Language Processing*, University of Pennsylvania, PA, USA.

Sandrini, Vanessa, Marcello Federico, and Mauro Cettolo (2006). "Maximum Entropy Tagging with Binary and Real-valued Features." *Proceedings of the 11th Conference of the European Chapter of the Association for Computational Linguistics* (*EACL-2006*), Trento, Italy.

Varea, Ismael García, Franz Josef Och, Hermann Ney, and Francisco Casacuberta (2002). "Improving Alignment Quality in Statistical Machine Translation Using Context-dependent Maximum Entropy Models." *Proceedings of the 19th International Conference on Computational Linguistics* (*COLING-2002*), Taipei, Taiwan, pp. 1051–1054.

Velldal, Erik and Stephan Oepen (2005). "Maximum Entropy Models for Realization Ranking." *Proceedings of MT Summit X*, Phuket, Thailand.

Wu, Dekai (1992). "Approximate Maximum-entropy Integration of Syntactic and Semantic Constraints." *Proceedings of the Conference of the Association for Computational Linguistics and Chinese Language Processing (ROCLING-V)*, National Taiwan University, Taipei, Taiwan.

Xie, Guodong, Chengqing Zong, and Bo Xu (2003). "A Maximum Entropy Approach for Spoken Chinese Understanding." *Proceedings of the 4th International Conference on Intelligent Text Processing and Computational Linguistics (CICLing-2003)*, Mexico City, Mexico, pp. 94–103.

Xu, Kui, Helen Meng, and Fuliang Weng (2006). "A Maximum Entropy Framework That Integrates Word Dependencies and Grammatical Relations for Reading Comprehension." *Proceedings of the Human Language Technology Conference—Annual Meeting of the North American Chapter of the Association for Computational Linguistics (HLT-NAACL-2006)*, New York, USA.

N-gram

Aceves-Pérez, Rita M., Luis Villaseñor-Pineda, and Manuel Montes-y-Gómez (2006). "Using N-gram Models to Combine Query Translations in Cross-language Question Answering." *Proceedings of the 7th International Conference on Intelligent Text Processing and Computational Linguistics (CICLing-2006)*, Mexico City, Mexico.

Babych, Bogdan, Anthony F. Hartley, and Debbie Elliott (2005). "Estimating the Predictive Power of N-gram MT Evaluation Metrics across Languages and Text Types." *Proceedings of MT Summit X*, Phuket, Thailand.

Banerjeet, Satanjeev and Ted Pedersen (2003). "The Design, Implementation and Use of the Ngram Statistics Package." *Proceedings of the 4th International Conference on Intelligent Text Processing and Computational Linguistics (CICLing-2003)*, Mexico City, Mexico, pp. 372–383.

Banko, Michele and Lucy Vanderwende (2004). "Using N-grams to Understand the Nature of Summaries." *Proceedings of the Human Language Technology Conference/North American Chapter of the*

Association for Computational Linguistics Annual Meeting (*HLT/NAACL-2004*), Boston, MA, USA.

Bickel, Steffen, Peter Haider, and Tobias Scheffer (2005). "Predicting Sentences Using N-Gram Language Models." *Proceedings of Human Language Technology Conference and Conference on Empirical Methods in Natural Language Processing* (*HLT/EMNLP-2005*), Vancouver, BC, Canada.

Brown, Peter F., Vincent J. Della Pietra, Peter V. deSouza, Jenifer C. Lai, and Robert L. Mercer (1992). "Class-based N-gram Models of Natural Language." *Computational Linguistics*, Vol. 18, No. 4, pp. 467–479.

Chen, Cheng-Der 陳正德 and Chao-Huang Chang 張照煌 (1994). "Some Issues on Applying SA-class Bigram Language Models." *Proceedings of the Conference of the Association for Computational Linguistics and Chinese Language Processing* (*ROCLING-VII*), National Tsing Hua University, Hsin-Chu, Taiwan.

Crego, Josep Maria, José B. Mariño, and Adrià de Gispert (2005). "Reordered Search and Tuple Unfolding for Ngram-based SMT." *Proceedings of MT Summit X*, Phuket, Thailand.

Doddington, George (2002). "Automatic Evaluation of Machine Translation Quality Using N-gram Co-occurrence Statistics." *Proceedings of the 2nd Conference on Human Language Technology* (*HLT-2002*), San Diego, CA, USA, pp. 128–132.

Eck, Matthias, Stephan Vogel, and Alex H. Waibel (2005). "Low Cost Portability for Statistical Machine Translation Based on N-gram Coverage." *Proceedings of MT Summit X*, Phuket, Thailand.

Ha, Le Q., Philip Hanna, Darryl W Stewart, and Francis J. Smith (2006). "Reduced N-gram Models for English and Chinese Corpora." *Proceedings of the Joint Conference of the International Committee on Computational Linguistics and the Association for Computational Linguistics* (*COLING/ACL-2006*), Sydney, Australia.

Imai, Hiroki, Hui Li, and Hozumi Tanaka (1997). "Incorporating Bigram Constraints into an LR Table." *Proceedings of the International Conference on Research in Computational Linguistics* (*ROCLING-X*), Academia Sinica, Taipei, Taiwan.

Jung, Hanmin, Hee-Kwan Koo, Won-Kyung Sung, and Dong-In Park (2006). "Clustering of English-Korean Translation Word Pairs Using Bi-grams." In Alexander F. Gelbukh, ed., *Advances in Natural*

Language Processing, Special Issue of *Research in Computing Science*, No. 18, pp. 15–26.
Lin, Chin-Yew and Eduard Hovy (2003). "Automatic Evaluation of Summaries Using N-gram Co-occurrence Statistics." *Proceedings of the Human Language Technology and North American Chapter of Association of Computational Linguistics 2003* (*HLT/NAACL-2003*), Edmonton, Alberta, Canada, pp. 71–78.
Mariño, José B., Rafael E. Banchs, Josep Maria Crego, Adrià de Gispert, Patrik Lambert, José A. R. Fonollosa, and Marta Ruiz (2005). "Bilingual N-gram Statistical Machine Translation." *Proceedings of MT Summit X*, Phuket, Thailand.
Nagao, Makoto and Shinsuke Mori (1994). "A New Method of N-gram Statistics for Large Number of N and Automatic Extraction of Words and Phrases from Large Text Data of Japanese." *Proceedings of the 15th International Conference on Computational Linguistics* (*COLING-94*), Kyoto, Japan, pp. 611–615.
Pereira, Fernando C., Yoram Singer, and Naftali Tishby (1995). "Beyond Word N-Grams." *Proceedings of the 3rd Workshop on Very Large Corpora*, Cambridge, pp. 95–106.
Pereira, Fernando C., Yoram Singer, and Naftali Tishby (1999). "Beyond Word N-grams." In Susan Armstrong, Kenneth W. Church, Pierre Isabelle, Sandra Manzi, Evelyne Tzoukermann, and David Yarowsky, eds., *Natural Language Processing Using Very Large Corpora.* Dordrecht: Kluwer Academic Publishers, pp. 121–136.
Tsay, Jyh-Jong and Jing-Doo Wang (1999). "Term Selection with Distributional Clustering for Chinese Text Categorization Using N-grams." *Proceedings of the International Conference on Research in Computational Linguistics* (*ROCLING-XII*), Taipei, Taiwan.
Zhou, Shuigeng and Jihong Guan (2002). "Chinese Document Classification Based on N-grams." *Proceedings of the 3rd International Conference on Intelligent Text Processing and Computational Linguistics* (*CICLing-2002*), Mexico City, Mexico.

Ontology

Cassidy, Patrick J. (2003). "Dimensional Analysis to Clarify Relations among the Top-level Concepts of an Upper Ontology: Process, Event, Substance, Object." *Proceedings of the 4th International Conference on Intelligent Text Processing and Computational Linguistics* (*CICLing-2003*), Mexico City, Mexico, pp. 335–348.

García, Rafael Valencia, Dagoberto Castellanos Nieves, Jesualdo Tomás Fernández Breis, and Pedro José Vivancos Vicente (2006). "A Methodology for Extracting Ontological Knowledge from Spanish Documents." *Proceedings of the 7th International Conference on Intelligent Text Processing and Computational Linguistics* (*CICLing-2006*), Mexico City, Mexico.

Hovy, Eduard H. (2006). "A Gentle Introduction to Ontologies." *Proceedings of the 7th Biennial Conference of the Association for Machine Translation in the Americas* (*AMTA-2006*)*: Visions for the Future of Machine Translation*, Boston Marriott, Cambridge, MA, USA.

Makagonov, Pavel P. and Alejandro Ruiz Figueroa (2005). "A Method of Rapid Prototyping of Evolving Ontologies." *Proceedings of the 6th International Conference on Intelligent Text Processing and Computational Linguistics* (*CICLing-2005*), Mexico City, Mexico, pp. 734–737.

Pérez, Guillermo, Gabriel J. Amores, Pilar Manchón, and David González (2006). "Generating Multilingual Grammars from OWL Ontologies." In Alexander F. Gelbukh, ed., *Advances in Natural Language Processing*, Special Issue of *Research in Computing Science*, No. 18, pp. 3–14.

Tiun, Sabrina, Rosni Abdullah, and Tang Enya Kong (2001). "Automatic Topic Identification Using Ontology Hierarchy." *Proceedings of the 2nd International Conference on Intelligent Text Processing and Computational Linguistics* (*CICLing-2001*), Mexico City, Mexico.

Xu, Wei, Wenjie Li, Mingli Wu, Wei Li, and Chunfa Yuan (2006). "Deriving Event Relevance from the Ontology Constructed with Formal Concept Analysis." *Proceedings of the 7th International Conference on Intelligent Text Processing and Computational Linguistics* (*CICLing-2006*), Mexico City, Mexico.

Tokenization

Graña, Jorge, Francisco-Mario Barcala, and Jesús Vilares (2002). "Formal Methods of Tokenization for Part-of-speech Tagging." *Proceedings of the 3rd International Conference on Intelligent Text Processing and Computational Linguistics* (*CICLing-2002*), Mexico City, Mexico.

Grover, Claire, Michael Matthews, and Richard Tobin (2006). "Tools to Address the Interdependence between Tokenization and Standoff Annotation." *Proceedings of the 11th Conference of the European Chapter of the Association for Computational Linguistics* (*EACL-2006*), Trento, Italy.

Habash, Nizar and Owen Rambow (2005). "Tokenization, Morphological Analysis, and Part-of-speech Tagging for Arabic in One Fell Swoop." *Proceedings of the 43rd Annual Meeting of the Association of Computational Linguistics* (*ACL-2005*), Ann Arbor, Michigan, USA.

Habert, B. G. Adda, M. Adda-Decker, P. Boula de Mareuil, S. Ferrari, O. Ferret, G. Illouz, and P. Paroubek (1998). "Towards Tokenization Evaluation." In Antonio Rubio *et al.*, eds., *Proceedings of the 1st International Conference on Language Resources and Evaluation* (*LREC-98*), Granada, Spain, Vol. I, pp. 427–431.

Luo, Xiaoqiang and Martin Franz (2000). "Semantic Tokenization of Verbalized Numbers in Language Modeling." *Proceedings of the International Conference on Spoken Language Processing* (*ICSLP-2000*), Beijing, China, Vol. 1, pp. 158–161.

Melamed, I. Dan (2001). "Models of Co-occurrence." *Empirical Methods for Exploiting Parallel Texts*. Cambridge, MA: MIT Press, pp. 57–63.

Webster, Jonathan J. and Kit Chunyu (1992). "Tokenization for Machine Translation: What Can Be Learned from Chinese Word Identification." *Proceedings of the 3rd International Conference on Chinese Information Processing*, Beijing, China.

Wu, Dekai and Pascale Fung (1994). "Improving Chinese Tokenization with Linguistic Filters on Statistical Lexical Acquisition." *Proceedings of the 4th Conference on Applied Natural Language Processing* (*ANLP-94*), Stuttgart, Germany, pp. 180–181.

Natural Language Processing System

Galindo, Ma del Socorro Bernardos and Guadalupe Aguado de Cea (2001). "A New Approach in Building a Corpus for Natural Language Generation Systems." *Proceedings of the 2nd International Conference on Intelligent Text Processing and Computational Linguistics* (*CICLing-2001*), Mexico City, Mexico.

Palomar, Manual, Maximiliano Saiz Noeda, Rafael Muñoz, Armando Suárez, Patricio Martínez-Barco, and Andrés Montoyo (2001).

"PHORA: A NLP System for Spanish." *Proceedings of the 2nd International Conference on Intelligent Text Processing and Computational Linguistics* (*CICLing-2001*), Mexico City, Mexico.

Natural Language Understanding

Addis, Robert T. (1977). "Machine Understanding of Natural Language." *International Journal for Man-Machine Studies*, Vol. 9, No. 2, pp. 207–222.

Anikin, Natalie, Leonid Vainer, and Bernard Zagatsky (2004). "Ambiguity and Conflict Resolution in the Situator Natural Language Understanding System." *International Journal of Translation*, Vol. 16, No. 1, pp. 55–72.

Anikin, Natalie and Bernard Zagatsky (2005). "Equivalent Transformations in a Natural Language Understanding System." *International Journal of Translation*, Vol. 17, No. 2, pp. 109–120.

Bender, Oliver, Klaus Macherey, Franz Josef Och, and Hermann Ney (2003). "Comparison of Alignment Templates and Maximum Entropy Models for Natural Language Understanding." *Proceedings of the 10th Conference of the European Chapter of the Association for Computational Linguistics* (*EACL-2003*), Budapest, Hungary.

Carbonell, Jaime G. and Philip J. Hayes (1987). "Natural Language Understanding." In Stuart C. Shapiro, ed., *Encyclopedia of Artificial Intelligence*. New York: Wiley and Sons, pp. 660–677.

Chen, Guanghuo 陳光火 (2000). 〈自然語言理解〉 (Natural Language Understanding). 《電子翻譯》 (*Electronic Translation*). Tianjin: Tianjin University Press, pp. 57–63.

Dahlgren, Kathleen (1988). *Naïve Semantics for Natural Language Understanding*. Dordrecht: Kluwer Academic Publishers.

Flank, Sharon, Aaron Temin, Hatte Blejer, Andrew Kehler, and Sherman Greenstein (1993). "Module-level Testing for Natural Language Understanding." *Machine Translation*, Vol. 8, Nos. 1–2, pp. 39–48.

Gardent, Claire and Karsten Konrad (2000). "Understanding 'Each Other'." *Proceedings of the 1st Meeting of the North American Chapter of the Association for Computational Linguistics*, Seattle, Washington, DC, USA, pp. 319–326.

Helmreich, Stephen and David L. Farwell (2000). "Text Meaning Representation as a Basis for Representation of Text Interpretation." In

John S. White, ed., *Envisioning Machine Translation in the Information Future*. Berlin: Springer Verlag, pp. 179–188.

Huang, Changning 黃昌寧 and Zhang Pu 張普, eds. (2001).《自然語言理解與機器翻譯》(*Natural Language Understanding and Machine Translation*). Beijing: Tsinghua University Press.

Lu, Ruzhang 陸汝占 and Jin Guangjin 靳光瑾 (1999).〈基於計算機理解的存現句的結構分類特徵及語義特徵〉(Computer-understanding Based Construction Classifying Feature and Semantic Feature of Locative Existential Construction in Modern Chinese). In Huang Changning 黃昌寧 and Dong Zhendong 董振東, eds.,《計算機語言學文集》(*Essays on Computational Linguistics*). Beijing: Tsinghua University Press, pp. 40–44.

Macherey, Klaus, Franz Josef Och, and Hermann Ney (2001). "Natural Language Understanding Using Statistical Machine Translation." *Proceedings of the 7th European Conference on Speech Communication and Technology* (*EuroSpeech-2001*), Aalborg, Denmark, pp. 2205–2208.

Magnusson, Martin (2006). "Natural Language Understanding Using Temporal Action Logic." *Proceedings of the 11th Conference of the European Chapter of the Association for Computational Linguistics* (*EACL-2006*), Trento, Italy.

Minker, Wolfgang (1997). "Stochastically-based Natural Language Understanding across Tasks and Languages." *Proceedings of the 5th European Conference on Speech Communication and Technology* (*EuroSpeech-97*), Rhodes, Greece, pp. 1423–1426.

Minker, Wolfgang, Samir K. Bennacef, and Jean-Luc Gauvain (1996). "Stochastic Case Frame Approach for Natural Language Understanding." *Proceedings of the 3rd European Conference on Speech, Communication, and Technology* (*EuroSpeech-96*), Berlin, Germany, pp. 1013–1016.

Minker, Wolfgang, Marsal Gavaldá, and Alex H. Waibel (1999). "Stochastically-based Semantic Analysis for Machine Translation." *Computer Speech and Language*, Vol. 13, pp. 177–194.

Nagao, Makato (1997). "Machine Translation through Language Understanding." *Proceedings of MT Summit VI*, San Diego, California, USA.

Pan, Haihua (1987). "Towards Understanding-based MT." *Proceedings of the International Conference on Chinese Information Processing*, Beijing, China.

Schank, Roger C. (1972). "Conceptual Dependency: A Theory of Natural Language Understanding." *Cognitive Psychology*, Vol. 3, pp. 552–631.

Sgall, Petr, Eva Hajicova, and Petr Pit'ha (1990). "On the Notion of Language Understanding." *Prague Studies in Mathematical Linguistics*, Vol. 10, pp. 177–185.

Stalls, Bonnie Glover, Robert Belvin, Alfredo Arnaiz, Christine Montgomery, and Robert Stumberger (1994). "An Adaptation of Lexical Conceptual Structure to Multilingual Processing in an Existing Text Understanding System." *Proceedings of the 1st Conference of the Association for Machine Translation in the Americas: Technology Partnerships for Crossing the Language Barrier* (*AMTA-1*), Columbia, Maryland, USA, pp. 106–113.

Tanaka, Hozumi, Takenobu Tokunaga, and Shinyama Yusuke (2002). "Animated Agents That Understand Natural Language and Perform Actions." In Yu Shiwen, ed., *Proceedings of the 2nd China-Japan Natural Language Processing Joint Research Promotion Conference* (*CJNLP-2002*). Beijing: Institute of Computational Linguistics, Peking University, pp. 10–16.

Tsujii, Jun-ichi (1989). "Machine Translation in Natural Language Understanding." *Literary and Linguistic Computing*, Vol. 4, No. 3, pp. 214–217.

Waltz, David L. (1982). "The State of Art in Natural Language Understanding." In Wendy G. Lehnert and Martin H. Ringle, eds., *Strategies for Natural Language Processing*. Hillsdale, New Jersey: Lawrence Erlbaum Associates, pp. 3–32.

Wang, Yongcheng 王永成 (2002).〈漢語理解初探〉(On Chinese Understanding). In Yu Shiwen, ed., *Proceedings of the 2nd China-Japan Natural Language Processing Joint Research Promotion Conference* (*CJNLP-2002*). Beijing: Institute of Computational Linguistics, Peking University, pp. 306–313.

Winograd, Terry (1972). *Understanding Natural Language*. Edinburgh: Edinburgh University Press.

Yao, Tianshun 姚天順 (1995).《自然語言理解 —— 一種讓機器懂得人類語言的研究》(*Natural Language Understanding—Studies on a Kind of Machine Tractable Human Language*). Beijing: Tsinghua University Press.

Yu, Shiwen 俞士汶 (1996).〈自然語言理解與語法研究〉(Natural Language Understanding and Grammatical Studies). In Yu Shiwen 俞士汶 and

Zhu Xuefeng 朱學鋒, eds.,《計算語言學文集》(*Papers on Computational Linguistics*). Beijing: Department of Computer Science and Technology and Institute of Computational Linguistics, Peking University, pp. 1–7.

Zagatsky, Bernard, Natalie Anikin, and Leonid Vainer (2003). "Situator: Artificial Intelligence System Understanding Natural Language." *International Journal of Translation*, Vol. 15, No. 1, pp. 125–130.

Zhong, Yixin 鍾義信 (2002).〈全信息自然語言理解的方法論〉(A Methodology of Natural Language Understanding Based on Comprehensive Information). In Yu Shiwen, ed., *Proceedings of the 2nd China-Japan Natural Language Processing Joint Research Promotion Conference (CJNLP-2002)*. Beijing: Institute of Computational Linguistics, Peking University, pp. 23–31.

Zhou, Xiling 周錫令 (1997).〈關於自然語言理解的理解〉(On Natural Language Understanding).《語言文字應用》(*Applied Linguistics*), No. 4, pp. 95–99.

Zhu, Xuefeng 朱學鋒 and Yu Shiwen 俞士汶 (1996).〈自然語言處理與語言知識庫〉(Natural Language Processing and Linguistic Knowledge Database). In Yu Shiwen 俞士汶 and Zhu Xuefeng 朱學鋒, eds.,《計算語言學文集》(*Papers on Computational Linguistics*). Beijing: Department of Computer Science and Technology and Institute of Computational Linguistics, Peking University, pp. 92–98.

Artificial Intelligence

Coughlin, Josette M. (1987). "Artificial Intelligence and Machine Translation: Present Developments and Future Prospects." In Karl Kummer, ed., *Across the Language Gap: Proceedings of the 28th Annual Conference of the American Translators Association*. Medford, New Jersey: Learned Information Inc., pp. 429–433.

Coughlin, Josette M. (1988). "Artificial Intelligence and Machine Translation: Present Developments and Future Prospects." *Babel*, Vol. 34, No. 1, pp. 3–9.

Haller, Johann (1996). "Multilint—A Technical Documentation System with Multilingual Intelligence." In *Translating and the Computer 18*. London: The Association for Information Management.

Haynes, Colin (1998). "Fuzzy Logic, Artificial Intelligence, Neural

Networks and Parallel Processing." *Breaking Down the Language Barriers*. London: The Association for Information Management, pp. 85–89.

Huang, Long 黃龍 (1989).〈翻譯的人工智能觀〉(Artificial Intelligence in Translation). In《翻譯藝術教程》(*A Course in Translative Art*). Nanjing: Nanjing University Press, pp. 209–294.

Hutchins, W. John (1986). "Artificial Intelligence Systems." *Machine Translation: Past, Present and Future*. Chichester: Ellis Horwood, pp. 272–284.

Lippmann, Edward O. (1986). "Artificial Intelligence in Linguistics: Text and Style Critiquing by Computer Program." In Karl Kummer, ed., *Building Bridges: Proceedings of the 27th Annual Conference of the American Translators Association*. Medford, New Jersey: Learned Information Inc., pp. 157–159.

Liu, Yang 劉洋 (2002).〈一種基於Web Intelligence的智能信息代理系統初探〉(An Intelligent Information Agent System Based on Web Intelligence).《第一屆學生計算語言學研討會論文集》(*SWCL-2002: First Students' Workshop on Computational Linguistics: Proceedings*), Institute of Computational Linguistics, Peking University, Beijing, China, p. 150.

McCorduck, Pamela (1979). *Machines Who Think*. San Francisco: Freeman.

Piotrowski, Rajmund and Yuri Romanov (2002). "Behavior-based Artificial Intelligence and 21st Century: MT Conception." *International Journal of Translation*, Vol. 14, No. 2, pp. 127–150.

Sgall, Petr and Eva Hajicova (1990). "Linguistic Aspects of Artificial Intelligence." In Vladimír Marík, Olga Stepánková, Zdenek Zdráhal, eds., *Artificial Intelligence in Higher Education*. Berlin: Springer Verlag, pp. 54–59.

Shann, Patrick (1984). "AI Approaches to MT." *The Institute for the Study of Semantics and Cognition Tutorial on Machine Translation*, Lugano, Switzerland.

Turing, Alan M. (1948). "Intelligent Machinery." In Bernard Meltzer and Donald Michie, eds., *Machine Intelligence*. Edinburgh: Edinburgh University Press, pp. 3–23.

Turing, Alan M. (1950). "Computing Machinery and Intelligence." *Mind*, Vol. 59, pp. 433–460.

Wilks, Yorick (1973). "An Artificial Intelligence Approach to Machine

Translation." In Roger C. Schank and Kenneth Mark Colby, eds., *Computer Models of Thought and Language*. San Francisco: W. H. Freeman, pp. 114–151.

Wilks, Yorick (1979). "Machine Translation and Artificial Intelligence." In Barbara M. Snell, ed., *Translating and the Computer*. Amsterdam: North-Holland Publishing Company, pp. 27–43.

Wilks, Yorick (1983). "Machine Translation and the Artificial Intelligence Paradigm of Language Processes." In Walter A. Sedelow and Sally Yeates Sedelow, eds., *Trends in Linguistics, Studies and Monographs, 19: Computers in Language Research.* Berlin: Mouton Publishers, Vol. 2, pp. 61–111.

Wilks, Yorick (1985). "Machine Translation and Artificial Intelligence: Issues and Their Histories." *Memorada in Computer and Cognitive Science*, MCCS-85-29. Las Cruces, NM: Computer Research Laboratory, New Mexico State University.

Yang, Xianze 楊憲澤 (2006).《人工智能與機器翻譯》(*Artificial Intelligence and Machine Translation*). Chengdu: Southwest Jiaotong University.

Yao, Tianshun (1988). "A Word-based Chinese Language Understanding System." *International Journal of Pattern Recognition and Artificial Intelligence*, Vol. 2, No. 1.

Zagatsky, Bernard, Natalie Anikin, and Leonid Vainer (2003). "Situator: Artificial Intelligence System Understanding Natural Language." *International Journal of Translation*, Vol. 15, No. 1, pp. 125–130.

Zaitseva, Natalia (2002). "Thesaurus and Frame as Modern Instruments for Improving the 'Intelligence' of Information Systems." *International Journal of Translation*, Vol. 14, No. 2, pp. 33–46.

Hierarchical Networks of Concepts (HNC)

Chen, Li 陳磊 (1999).〈基於HNC語義分析的中文標題分類方法〉(A Chinese Document Title's Classification Method Based on HNC Semantic Analysis). In Huang Changning 黃昌寧 and Dong Zhendong 董振東, eds.,《計算機語言學文集》(*Essays on Computational Linguistics*). Beijing: Tsinghua University Press, pp. 371–375.

Chi, Yuhuan 池毓煥 (2002).〈黃曾陽先生語料庫思想概述〉(Introducing Huang Zengyang's Thoughts on Corpus Linguistics).《第一屆學生計算語言學研討會論文集》(*SWCL2002: First Students' Workshop on

Computational Linguistics: Proceedings), Institute of Computational Linguistics, Peking University, Beijing, China, pp. 312–317.

Huang, Zengyang 黃曾陽 (1998).《HNC (概念層次網絡) 理論 —— 計算機理解語言研究的新思路》(*HNC Theory—New Thoughts on the Study of Natural Language Understanding*). Beijing: Tsinghua University Press.

Huang, Zengyang (1997).〈HNC理論概要〉(A Gist of the HNC Theory).《中文信息學報》(*Journal of Chinese Information Processing*), No. 4.

Ke, Hang 柯航 (2002).〈現代漢語「被」字句的HNC分析〉(An Analysis of "Bei" Sentence by the Theory of HNC).《第一屆學生計算語言學研討會論文集》(*SWCL-2002: First Students' Workshop on Computational Linguistics: Proceedings*), Institute of Computational Linguistics, Peking University, Beijing, China, p. 45.

Li, Yaoyong 李耀勇 (2001).〈利用HNC理論進行基於實例的英漢機器翻譯〉(Example-based English-Chinese Machine Translation by Using HNC Theory). In Huang Changning 黃昌寧 and Zhang Pu 張普, eds.,《自然語言理解與機器翻譯》(*Natural Language Understanding and Machine Translation*). Beijing: Tsinghua University Press, pp. 319–325.

Lin, Xingguang 林杏光 (2001).〈為NLP創立模式，用HNC研究漢語〉(Application of HNC Theory to Chinese Study—A Paradigm of NLP). In Huang Changning 黃昌寧 and Zhang Pu 張普, eds.,《自然語言理解與機器翻譯》(*Natural Language Understanding and Machine Translation*). Beijing: Tsinghua University Press, pp. 265–271.

Liu, Zhiwen 劉志文, Zhuang Yongmiao 莊詠璆, Hao Huining 郝惠寧, Xiao Youfu 蕭友芙, and Huang Zengyang 黃曾陽 (1998).〈自然語言語句的HNC表示〉(The Indication of HNC in Natural Language Sentences).《語言文字應用》(*Applied Linguistics*), No. 2, pp. 89–92.

Tang, Xingquan 唐興全 (2001).〈HNC理論的五元組與詞性〉(The Quintuple of HNC Theory and Parts of Speech). In Huang Changning and Zhang Pu, eds.,《自然語言理解與機器翻譯》(*Natural Language Understanding and Machine Translation*). Beijing: Tsinghua University Press, pp. 253–258.

Wei, Xiangfeng 韋向峰 (2002).〈動態記憶結構與HNC的語境研究〉(The Structures of Dynamic Memory and the Research of the Context Based on HNC Theory).《第一屆學生計算語言學研討會論文集》(*SWCL-2002: First Students' Workshop on Computational Linguistics: Proceedings*), Institute of Computational Linguistics, Peking University, Beijing, China, pp. 29–34.

Xiong, Liang 熊亮 (2002).〈HNC理論下對「得」的理解和處理〉(The Understanding and Processing of "*De*" Based on the Theory of HNC).《第一屆學生計算語言學研討會論文集》(*SWCL-2002: First Students' Workshop on Computational Linguistics: Proceedings*), Institute of Computational Linguistics, Peking University, Beijing, China, pp. 23–28.

❖ PART 25 ❖

Online Translation

Internet

Austermühl, Frank (2001). "Translation and the Internet." *Electronic Tools for Translators*. Manchester: St. Jerome Publishing Company, pp. 38–51.

Bergeron, Manon and Susan Larsson (1999). "Internet Search Strategies for Translators." *ATA Chronicle*, Vol. 28, No. 7, pp. 22–25.

Brander, Maria and Verena Jung (2006). "Free as in Free Beer vs. Free as in Free Speech: Volunteer Translation on the Internet." *Proceedings of the 6th Portsmouth Translation Conference: Translation Technologies and Culture,* School of Languages and Area Studies, University of Portsmouth, England.

Byrne, Jody (2006). "Translation and the Internet: Changing the Face of an Industry." *Proceedings of the 6th Portsmouth Translation Conference: Translation Technologies and Culture,* School of Languages and Area Studies, University of Portsmouth, England.

Carter-Sigglow, Janet (1999). "The Internet and the Single Translator." In *Translating and the Computer 21*. London: The Association for Information Management.

Cordon, Anna (1995). "The Translator in the Communications Web." In *Translating and the Computer 17*. London: The Association for Information Management.

Fujii, Atsushi and Tetsuya Ishikawa (2000). "Utilizing the World Wide Web as an Encyclopedia: Extracting Term Descriptions from Semi-structured Texts." *Proceedings of the 38th Annual Meeting of the Association for Computational Linguistics* (*ACL-2000*), Hong Kong.

Gelbukh, Alexander F. and Igor A. Bolshakov (2003). "Internet, a True Friend of the Translator." *International Journal of Translation*, Vol. 15, No. 2, pp. 31–50.

Harris, Roger (1995). "Linguistic Resources on the Internet." *Machine Translation Review*, No. 1, pp. 23–30.

Harris, Roger (1995). "Translators, the Internet and Standing Still." In *Translating and the Computer 17*. London: The Association for Information Management.

Haynes, Colin (1998). "Warning." *Breaking Down the Language Barriers*. London: The Association for Information Management, pp. 1–24.

Hu, Yi 胡熠, Zheng Dequan 鄭德權, Zhao Tiejun 趙鐵軍, Yu Hao 于浩, and

Wang Qingsong 王青松 (2002).〈WWW頁面信息中特定內容的過濾研究〉(Research on Machine Learning Method for Specific Information Recognition on the Internet).《第一屆學生計算語言學研討會論文集》(*SWCL-2002: First Students' Workshop on Computational Linguistics: Proceedings*), Institute of Computational Linguistics, Peking University, Beijing, China, p. 152.

Jin, Yang and Elke Lange (2003). "Going Live on the Internet." In Harold L. Somers, ed., *Computers and Translation: A Translator's Guide*. Amsterdam and Philadelphia: John Benjamins Publishing Company, pp. 191–210.

McLaughlin, Steve and Ulrike Schwall (1998). "Spicing Up the Information Soup: Machine Translation and the Internet." In David L. Farwell, Laurie Gerber, and Eduard Hovy, eds., *Machine Translation and the Information Soup*. Berlin: Springer Verlag, pp. 384–397.

Pearson, Jennifer (2000). "Surfing the Internet: Teaching Students to Choose Their Texts Wisely." In Lou Burnard and Tony McEnery, eds., *Rethinking Language Pedagogy from a Corpus Perspective*. Frankfurt: Peter Lang, pp. 235–239.

Radev, Dragomir, Hong Qi, Adam Winkel, and Daniel Tam (2004). "Computational Linguistics: Word Triggers across Hyperlinks." *Proceedings of the Human Language Technology Conference/North American Chapter of the Association for Computational Linguistics Annual Meeting* (*HLT/NAACL-2004*), Boston, MA, USA.

Robinson, Lyn (1996). "The Internet—Myth and Reality." In *Translating and the Computer 18*. London: The Association for Information Management.

Salam, Muhammad Abdus (2000). "Machine Translation and Multilingual Communication on the Internet." *Proceedings of the International Conference on Machine Translation and Multilingual Applications in the New Millenium* (*MT-2000*), University of Exeter, England.

Schneider, Thomas (2000). "Stop the Presses—Why the Web Has Not Changed Machine Translation." *Language International*, Vol. 12, No. 4, pp. 22–24.

Shi, Xiaodong (2006). "Weaving the Net and CAT Together." *Programme of an International Conference on Computer-aided Translation: Theory and Practice*, Department of Translation, The Chinese University of Hong Kong, Hong Kong.

Zhang, Baoyan 張寶艷 and Wang Qinghui 王慶輝 (2002).〈中文文本聚類的

研究與實踐〉(Research and Realization of Chinese Document Clustering).《第一屆學生計算語言學研討會論文集》(*SWCL-2002: First Students' Workshop on Computational Linguistics: Proceedings*), Institute of Computational Linguistics, Peking University, Beijing, China, pp. 125–129.

Online Translation

Clements, David (1996). "The Value of Online MT in the Age of the 'Cyber Society'." *Proceedings of the 2nd Conference of the Association for Machine Translation in the Americas: Expanding MT Horizons* (*AMTA-2*), Montreal, Quebec, Canada, pp. 220–221.

Duckitt, Pauline (1981). "Translating and Online." *Aslib Proceedings*, Vol. 33, Nos. 7–8, pp. 290–296.

Flanagan, Mary A. (1995). "MT in the Online Environment: Challenges and Opportunities." *Proceedings of MT Summit V: Machine Translation Conference, Exhibition and Tutorial*, Luxembourg.

Flanagan, Mary A. (1996). "Online MT at CompuServe." *Proceedings of the 2nd Conference of the Association for Machine Translation in the Americas: Expanding MT Horizons* (*AMTA-2*), Montreal, Quebec, Canada, pp. 244–246.

Flanagan, Mary A. (1996). "Two Years Online: Experiences, Challenges, and Trends." *Proceedings of the 2nd Conference of the Association for Machine Translation in the Americas: Expanding MT Horizons* (*AMTA-2*), Montreal, Quebec, Canada, pp. 192–197.

Flanagan, Mary A. (1997). "Online Translation: MT's New Frontier." In *Translating and the Computer 19*. London: The Association for Information Management.

Gaspari, Federico (2004). "Enhancing Free On-line Machine Translation Services." In M. Lee, ed., *Proceedings of the 7th Annual CLUK Research Colloquium*, University of Birmingham, Birmingham, England, pp. 68–74.

Gaspari, Federico (2004). "Integrating On-line MT Services into Monolingual Web-sites for Dissemination Purposes: An Evaluation Perspective." *Proceedings of the 9th Workshop of the European Association for Machine Translation: Broadening Horizons of Machine Translation and Its Applications*, Foundation for International Studies, Malta, pp. 62–72.

Gaspari, Federico (2004). "Online MT Services and Real Users' Needs: An Empirical Usability Evaluation." In Robert E. Frederking and Kathryn B. Taylors, eds., *Machine Translation: From Real Users to Research*. Berlin: Springer Verlag, pp. 74–85.

Gaspari, Federico (2006). "The Added Value of Free Online MT Services: Confidence Boosters for Linguistically-challenged Internet Users, a Case Study for the Language Pair Italian-English." *Proceedings of the 7th Biennial Conference of the Association for Machine Translation in the Americas (AMTA-2006): Visions for the Future of Machine Translation*, Boston Marriott, Cambridge, MA, USA.

Loh, Shiu-chang and Kong Luen (1979). "An Interactive On-line Machine Translation System (Chinese into English)." In Barbara M. Snell, ed., *Translating and the Computer*. Amsterdam: North-Holland Publishing Company, pp. 135–148.

McCarthy, Brian (2004). "Does Online Machine Translation Spell the End of Take-home Translation Assignments?" *CALL-EJ Online*, Vol. 6, No. 1.

Mellebeek, Bart, Anna Khasin, Josef Van Genabith, and Andy Way (2005). "Improving Online Machine Translation Systems." *Proceedings of MT Summit X*, Phuket, Thailand.

Miyazawa, Shinichiro, Shoichi Yokoyama, Masaki Matsudaira, Akira Kumano, Shuji Kodama, Hideki Kashioka, Yoshiko Shirokizawa, and Yasuo Nakajima (1999). "Study on Evaluation of WWW MT Systems." *Proceedings of MT Summit VII: MT in the Great Translation Era*, Singapore.

O'Neill-Brown, Patricia (1996). "Online Machine Translation." *Proceedings of the 2nd Conference of the Association for Machine Translation in the Americas: Expanding MT Horizons (AMTA-2)*, Montreal, Quebec, Canada, pp. 222–223.

Smith, Ross (2003). "Overview of PwC/Systranet On-line MT Facility." In *Translating and the Computer 25*. London: The Association for Information Management.

Somers, Harold L. (2006). "Detecting Inappropriate Use of Free Online Machine Translation by Language Students: A Special Case of Plagiarism Detection." *Proceedings of the 11th Workshop of the European Association for Machine Translation: Machine Translation/ Translation Aids—Tools to Increase Quality and to Save Money*, the University of Oslo, Oslo, Norway.

Sullivan, Fergus (2003). "Real-time Translation, the Yahoo!/FIFAWorldCup.com Experience." *Proceedings of the Localization World Conference 2003*, Seattle, Washington, DC, USA.
Westfall, Edith (1996). "Legal Implications of MT On-line." *Proceedings of the 2nd Conference of the Association for Machine Translation in the Americas: Expanding MT Horizons* (*AMTA-2*), Montreal, Quebec, Canada, pp. 231–232.
Zervaki, Thei (2002). "Online Free Translation Services." In *Translating and the Computer 24*. London: The Association of Information Management.

Web Translation

Austermühl, Frank (2001). "Searching the Web." *Electronic Tools for Translators*. Manchester: St. Jerome Publishing Company, pp. 52–67.
Austermühl, Frank (2001). "Translation Resources on the Worldwide Web." *Electronic Tools for Translators*. Manchester: St. Jerome Publishing Company, pp. 68–89.
Balkan, Lorna (2001). "Exploiting the WWW for MT Teaching." In Bente Maegaard, ed., *Proceedings of MT Summit VIII: Machine Translation in the Information Age*, Santiago de Compostela, Spain, pp. 7–11.
Cordon, Anna (1995). "The Translator in the Communications Web." In *Translating and the Computer 17*. London: The Association for Information Management.
Fleming, Michael and Robin Cohen (2000). "Mixed-initiative Translation of Web Pages." In John S. White, ed., *Envisioning Machine Translation in the Information Future*. Berlin: Springer Verlag, pp. 25–29.
Gaspari, Federico (2006). "Look Who's Translating: Impersonations, Chinese Whispers and Fun with Machine Translation on the Internet." *Proceedings of the 11th Workshop of the European Association for Machine Translation: Machine Translation/Translation Aids—Tools to Increase Quality and to Save Money*, the University of Oslo, Oslo, Norway.
Harris, Ian (2003). "Translation Web Services—A Reality." In *Translating and the Computer 25*. London: The Association for Information Management.
Kit, Chunyu (2006). "Lexical Resources from the Web for MT." *Programme of an International Conference on Computer-aided*

Translation: Theory and Practice, Department of Translation, The Chinese University of Hong Kong, Hong Kong.

Lehtola, Aarno, Jarno Tenni, Catherine Bounsaythip, and Kristiina Jaaranen (1999). "WEBTRAN: A Controlled Language Machine Translation System for Building Multilingual Services on Internet." *Proceedings of MT Summit VII: MT in the Great Translation Era*, Singapore.

Lu, Wen-Hsiang, Lee-Feng Chien, and Hsi-Jian Lee (2003). "LiveTrans: Translation Suggestion for Cross-language Web Search from Web Anchor Texts and Search Results." *Proceedings of the International Conference on Research in Computational Linguistics* (*ROCLING-XV*), Hsin-Chu, Taiwan.

Melby, Alan K. (2000). "XML and the Translator." *Translation Journal*, Vol. 4, No. 2.

Miyazawa, Shinichiro, Shoichi Yokoyama, Masaki Matsudaira, Akira Kumano, Shuji Kodama, Hideki Kashioka, Yoshiko Shirokizawa, and Yasuo Nakajima (1999). "Study on Evaluation of WWW MT Systems." *Proceedings of MT Summit VII: MT in the Great Translation Era*, Singapore, pp. 290–298.

Nesbitt, Scott (1997). "Web Translation Made Easy." *MultiLingual Communications and Technology*, Vol. 8, No. 14, Issue 3, pp. 20–21.

Shih, Chung-ling (2006). "Using Trados TagEditor in the Teaching of Web Translation." *Helpful Assistance to Translators: MT & TM*. Taipei: Bookman Books Ltd., pp. 321–343.

Shimohata, Sayori, Mihoko Kitamura, Tatsuya Sukehiro, and Toshiki Murata (2001). "Collaborative Translation Environment on the Web." In Bente Maegaard, ed., *Proceedings of MT Summit VIII: Machine Translation in the Information Age*, Santiago de Compostela, Spain.

Sklair, Stuart (1999). "Multilingual Component Management: Trends and Implications." In *Translating and the Computer 21*. London: The Association for Information Management.

Yoshimura, Yumiko, Satoshi Kinoshita, and Miwako Shimazu (1997). "Processing of Proper Nouns and Use of Estimated Subject Area for Web Page Translation." *Proceedings of the 7th International Conference on Theoretical and Methodological Issues in Machine Translation* (*TMI-97*), St. John's College, Santa Fe, New Mexico, USA.

Zhu, Kai 朱凱, Zhou Jie 周杰, and He Tingting 何婷婷 (2002).〈因特網語料

自動下載分析軟件的設計〉(The Design of Software for Downloading and Analysing Web-pages Automatically).《第一屆學生計算語言學研討會論文集》(*SWCL-2002: First Students' Workshop on Computational Linguistics: Proceedings*), Institute of Computational Linguistics, Peking University, Beijing, China, pp. 293–298.

❖ PART 26 ❖

Parsing

Parser

Aha, David W. and Kalyan Moy Gupta (2004). "RuMoP: A Rule-based Morphotactic Parser." *Proceedings of the International Conference on Natural Language Processing* (*ICON-2004*), International Institute of Information Technology, Hyderabad, India.

Araujo, Lourdes (2004). "A Probabilistic Chart Parser Implemented with an Evolutionary Algorithm." *Proceedings of the 5th International Conference on Intelligent Text Processing and Computational Linguistics* (*CICLing-2004*), Chung-Ang University, Seoul, Korea, pp. 79–90.

Bigert, Johnny, Jonas Sjöbergh, Ola Knutsson, and Magnus Sahlgren (2005). "Unsupervised Evaluation of Parser Robustness." *Proceedings of the 6th International Conference on Intelligent Text Processing and Computational Linguistics* (*CICLing-2005*), Mexico City, Mexico, pp. 141–152.

Bod, Rens (2000). "An Improved Parser for Data-oriented Lexical-functional Analysis." *Proceedings of the 38th Annual Meeting of the Association for Computational Linguistics* (*ACL-2000*), Hong Kong.

Charniak, Eugene (2000). "A Maximum-entropy-inspired Parser." *Proceedings of the 1st Meeting of the North American Chapter of the Association for Computational Linguistics*, Seattle, Washington, DC, USA, pp. 132–139.

Chung, Hoo-Jung and Hae-Chang Rim (2004). "Unlexicalized Dependency Parser for Variable Word Order Languages Based on Local Contextual Pattern." *Proceedings of the 5th International Conference on Intelligent Text Processing and Computational Linguistics* (*CICLing-2004*), Chung-Ang University, Seoul, Korea, pp. 109–120.

Clark, Stephen and James Curran (2006). "Partial Training for a Lexicalized-grammar Parser." *Proceedings of the Human Language Technology Conference—Annual Meeting of the North American Chapter of the Association for Computational Linguistics* (*HLT-NAACL-2006*), New York, USA.

Collins, Michael J. (1996). "A New Statistical Parser Based on Bigram Lexical Dependencies." *Proceedings of the 34th Annual Meeting of the Association for Computational Linguistics* (*ACL-96*), Santa Cruz, CA, USA, pp. 184–191.

Dorr, Bonnie J. (1988). "UNITRAN: A Principle-based Parser for Machine Translation." In Steven Abney, ed., *The MIT Parsing Volume, 1987–88*, Parsing Project Work Papers No. 1. Cambridge, MA: Center for Cognitive Science, MIT.

Evans, J. Gareth (1996). "Implementing an Efficient Compact Parser for a Machine Translation System." *Machine Translation Review*, No. 3, pp. 7–20.

Fang, Alex Chengyu (2006). "Evaluating the Performance of the Survey Parser with the NIST Scheme." *Proceedings of the 7th International Conference on Intelligent Text Processing and Computational Linguistics* (*CICLing-2006*), Mexico City, Mexico.

Germann, Ulrich (1999). "A Deterministic Dependency Parser for Japanese." *Proceedings of MT Summit VII: MT in the Great Translation Era*, Singapore.

Harbusch, Karin (2003). "An Efficient Online Parser for Contextual Grammars with at Most Context-free Selectors." *Proceedings of the 4th International Conference on Intelligent Text Processing and Computational Linguistics* (*CICLing-2003*), Mexico City, Mexico, pp. 171–182.

Henderson, John C. and Eric Brill (2000). "Bagging and Boosting a Treebank Parser." *Proceedings of the 1st Meeting of the North American Chapter of the Association for Computational Linguistics*, Seattle, Washington, DC, USA, pp. 34–41.

Hermjakob, Ulf (2000). "Rapid Parser Development: A Machine Learning Approach for Korean." *Proceedings of the 1st Meeting of the North American Chapter of the Association for Computational Linguistics*, Seattle, Washington, DC, USA, pp. 118–123.

Hollingshead, Kristy, Seeger Fisher, and Brian Roark (2005). "Comparing and Combining Finite-state and Context-free Parsers." *Proceedings of Human Language Technology Conference and Conference on Empirical Methods in Natural Language Processing* (*HLT/EMNLP-2005*), Vancouver, BC, Canada.

Jijkoun, Valentin and Maarten de Rijke (2004). "Enriching the Output of a Parser Using Memory-based Learning." *Proceedings of the 42nd Annual Meeting of the Association for Computational Linguistics* (*ACL-2004*), Barcelona, Spain, pp. 311–318.

Koster, Cornelis H. A. (2005). "Constructing a Parser for Latin." *Proceedings of the 6th International Conference on Intelligent Text*

Processing and Computational Linguistics (CICLing-2005), Mexico City, Mexico, pp. 49–60.
Levy, Roger and Christopher Manning (2004). "Deep Dependencies from Context-free Statistical Parsers: Correcting the Surface Dependency Approximation." *Proceedings of the 42nd Annual Meeting of the Association for Computational Linguistics* (*ACL-2004*), Barcelona, Spain, pp. 327–334.
Liu, Chao-Lin 劉昭麟 and Keh-Yih Su 蘇克毅 (1989). "A Quantitative Comparison between an LR Parser and an ATN Interpreter." *Proceedings of the Conference of the Association for Computational Linguistics and Chinese Language Processing* (*ROCLING-II*), Taipei, Taiwan.
Morris, J. L. (1997). "The Ergo Parser Challenge." *Machine Translation Review*, No. 5, pp. 19–24.
Nederhof, Mark-Jan and Giorgio Satta (2004). "An Alternative Method of Training Probabilistic LR Parsers." *Proceedings of the 42nd Annual Meeting of the Association for Computational Linguistics* (*ACL-2004*), Barcelona, Spain, pp. 550–557.
Prószéky, Gábor, László Tihanyi, and Gábor L. Ugray (2004). "Moose: A Robust High-performance Parser and Generator." *Proceedings of the 9th Workshop of the European Association for Machine Translation: Broadening Horizons of Machine Translation and Its Applications*, Foundation for International Studies, Malta, pp. 138–142.
Rupp, C. J., Jörg Spiler, Martin Klarner, and Karsten L. Worm (2000). "Combining Analyses from Various Parsers." In Wolfgang Wahlster, ed., *Verbmobil: Foundations of Speech-to-speech Translation*. Berlin: Springer Verlag, pp. 311–320.
Sagae, Kenji and Alon Lavie (2006). "Parser Combination by Reparsing." *Proceedings of the Human Language Technology Conference—Annual Meeting of the North American Chapter of the Association for Computational Linguistics* (*HLT-NAACL-2006*), New York, USA.
Seagull, Amon and Lenhart Schubert (1999). "Guiding a Well-founded Parser with Corpus Statistics." *Proceedings of the Joint SIGDAT Conference on Empirical Methods in NLP and Very Large Corpora* (*EMNLP/VLC-99*), University of Maryland, College Park, MD, USA.
Tanaka, Hozumi and K. G. Suresh (1991). "YAGLR: Yet Another Generalized LR Parser." *Proceedings of the Conference of the Association for Computational Linguistics and Chinese Language*

Processing (*ROCLING-IV*), National Chiao-Tung University, Hsin-Chu, Taiwan.

Vilares, Manuel, Miguel A. Alonso, and Victor M. Darriba (2003). "Generation of Incremental Parsers." *Proceedings of the 4th International Conference on Intelligent Text Processing and Computational Linguistics* (*CICLing-2003*), Mexico City, Mexico, pp. 193–204.

Yamada, Kenji (1996). "A Controlled Skip Parser." *Proceedings of the 2nd Conference of the Association for Machine Translation in the Americas: Expanding MT Horizons* (*AMTA-2*), Montreal, Quebec, Canada, pp. 14–23.

Yamada, Kenji (1998). "A Controlled Skip Parser." *Machine Translation*, Vol. 13, No. 1, pp. 1–15.

Parsing

Abney, Steven (1991). "Parsing by Chunks." In Robert Berwick, Steven Abney, and Carol Tenny, eds., *Principle-based Parsing: Computation and Psycholinguistics*. Dordrecht: Kluwer Academic Publishers, pp. 257–278.

Abney, Steven (1996). "Partial Parsing via Finite-state Cascades." *The European Summer School in Logic, Language and Information Workshop on Robust Parsing* (*ESSLLI-96*), Prague, the Czech Republic.

Abney, Steven (1997). "Part-of-speech Tagging and Partial Parsing." In Steve Young and Gerrit Bloothooft, eds., *Corpus-based Methods in Language and Speech Processing*. Dordrecht: Kluwer Academic Publishers, pp. 118–136.

Ageno, Alicia and Horacio Rodriguez (2001). "Probabilistic Modelling of Island-driven Parsing." *Proceedings of the 7th International Workshop on Parsing Technologies* (*IWPT-2001*), Peking University, Beijing, China. Beijing: Tsinghua University Press, pp. 31–41.

Ahlswede, Thomas E. and Martha Evens (1988). "Parsing vs. Text Processing in the Analysis of Dictionary Definitions." *Proceedings of the 26th Annual Meeting of the Association for Computational Linguistics*, Buffalo, USA, pp. 217–224.

Aho, Alfred V. and Jeffrey D. Ullman (1972). *The Theory of Parsing, Translation, and Compiling. Vol. 1. Parsing*. Englewood Cliffs, New Jersey: Prentice-Hall.

Aït-Mokhtar, Salah, Jean-Pierre Chanod, and Claude Roux (2001). "A Multi-input Dependency Parser." *Proceedings of the 7th International Workshop on Parsing Technologies (IWPT-2001)*, Peking University, Beijing, China. Beijing: Tsinghua University Press, pp. 201–204.

Al-Adhaileh, Mosleh Hmoud and Enya Kong Tang (1998). "A Flexible Example-based Parser Based on the SSTC." *Proceedings of the 36th Annual Meeting of the Association for Computational Linguistics and 17th International Conference on Computational Linguistics (COLING-ACL-98)*, Montreal, Quebec, Canada, pp. 687–693.

Bangalore, Srinivas and Aravind K. Joshi (1999). "Supertagging: An Approach to Almost Parsing." *Computational Linguistics*, Vol. 25, pp. 237–265.

Barcala, Francisco-Mario, Oscar Sacristán, and Jorge Graña (2001). "Stochastic Parsing and Parallelism." *Proceedings of the 2nd International Conference on Intelligent Text Processing and Computational Linguistics (CICLing-2001)*, Mexico City, Mexico.

Bertsch, Eberhard and Mark-Jan Nederhof (2001). "On the Complexity of Some Extensions of RCG Parsing." *Proceedings of the 7th International Workshop on Parsing Technologies (IWPT-2001)*, Peking University, Beijing, China. Beijing: Tsinghua University Press, pp. 66–77.

Bickel, Daniel M. (2000). "A Statistical Model for Parsing and Word-sense Disambiguation." *Proceedings of the 38th Annual Meeting of the Association for Computational Linguistics (ACL-2000)*, Hong Kong.

Bickel, Daniel M. (2000). "A Statistical Model for Parsing and Word-sense Disambiguation." *Proceedings of the Joint Sigdat Conference on Empirical Methods in Natural Language Processing and Very Large Corpora (EMNLP/VLC-2000)*, Hong Kong University of Science and Technology, Hong Kong.

Blache, Philippe and Jean-Marie Balfourier (2001). "Property Grammars: A Flexible Constraint-based Approach to Parsing." *Proceedings of the 7th International Workshop on Parsing Technologies (IWPT-2001)*, Peking University, Beijing, China. Beijing: Tsinghua University Press, pp. 205–208.

Blache, Philippe and David-Olivier Azulay (2002). "Parsing Ill-formed Inputs with Constraint Graphs." *Proceedings of the 3rd International Conference on Intelligent Text Processing and Computational Linguistics (CICLing-2002)*, Mexico City, Mexico.

Bod, Rens (1992). "A Computational Model of Language Performance: Data Oriented Parsing." *Proceedings of the 14th International Conference of Computational Linguistics* (*COLING-92*), Nantes, France, pp. 855–859.

Bod, Rens (1996). "Monte Carlo Parsing." In Harry Bunt and Masaru Tomita, eds., *Recent Advances in Parsing Technology*. Dordrecht: Kluwer Academic Publishers, pp. 255–280.

Bonfante, Andréia Gentil and Maria das Graças Volpe Nunes (2001). "The Implementation Process of a Statistical Parser for Brazilian Portuguese." *Proceedings of the 7th International Workshop on Parsing Technologies* (*IWPT-2001*), Peking University, Beijing, China. Beijing: Tsinghua University Press, pp. 217–220.

Bonnema, Remko, Paul Buying, and Remko Scha (2000). "Parse Tree Probability in Data Oriented Parsing." *Proceedings of the 1st International Conference on Intelligent Text Processing and Computational Linguistics* (*CICLing-2000*), Mexico City, Mexico.

Brill, Eric (1996). "Learning to Parse with Transformations." In Harry Bunt and Masaru Tomita, eds., *Recent Advances in Parsing Technology*. Dordrecht: Kluwer Academic Publishers, pp. 221–240.

Bunt, Harry and Ko van der Sloot (1996). "Parsing as Dynamic Interpretation of Feature Structures." In Harry Bunt and Masaru Tomita, eds., *Recent Advances in Parsing Technology*. Dordrecht: Kluwer Academic Publishers, pp. 91–114.

Bunt, Harry (1996). "Parsing Technologies, and Why We Need Them." In Harry Bunt and Masaru Tomita, eds., *Recent Advances in Parsing Technology*. Dordrecht: Kluwer Academic Publishers, pp. 1–10.

Bunt, Harry and Masaru Tomita, eds. (1996). *Recent Advances in Parsing Technology*. Dordrecht: Kluwer Academic Publishers.

Caeyers, Herman and Geert Adriaens (1990). "Efficient Parsing Using Preferences." *Proceedings of the 3rd International Conference on Theoretical and Methodological Issues in Machine Translation of Natural Languages* (*TMI-90*), Linguistics Research Center, University of Texas, Austin, Texas, USA, pp. 168–175.

Caraballo, Sharon A. and Eugene Charniak (1996). "Figures of Merit for Best-first Probabilistic Chart Parsing." *Proceedings of the Conference on Empirical Methods in Natural Language Processing*, University of Pennsylvania, PA, USA.

Carpenter, Bob and Gerald Penn (1996). "Efficient Parsing of Compiled Typed Attribute Value Logic Grammars." In Harry Bunt and Masaru Tomita, eds., *Recent Advances in Parsing Technology*. Dordrecht: Kluwer Academic Publishers, pp. 145–168.

Carroll, John and Ted Briscoe (1996). "Apportioning Development Effort in a Probabilistic LR Parsing System through Evaluation." *Proceedings of the Conference on Empirical Methods in Natural Language Processing*, University of Pennsylvania, PA, USA.

Chang, Ming-Wei, Quang Do, and Dan Roth (2006). "A Pipeline Framework for Dependency Parsing." *Proceedings of the Joint Conference of the International Committee on Computational Linguistics and the Association for Computational Linguistics* (*COLING/ACL-2006*), Sydney, Australia.

Charniak, Eugene (1983). "A Parser with Something for Everyone." In Margaret King, ed., *Parsing Natural Language*. London: Academic Press, pp. 117–149.

Charniak, Eugene (1983). "Parsing, How to." In K. Sparch Jones and Yorick Wilks, eds., *Automatic Natural Language Parsing*. Chichester: Ellis Horwood, pp. 156–181.

Charniak, Eugene, Mark Johnson, Micha Elsner, Joseph Austerweil, David Ellis, Isaac Haxton, Catherine Hill, R. Shrivaths, Jeremy Moore, Michael Pozar, and Theresa Vu (2006). "Multilevel Coarse-to-fine PCFG Parsing." *Proceedings of the Human Language Technology Conference—Annual Meeting of the North American Chapter of the Association for Computational Linguistics* (*HLT-NAACL-2006*), New York, USA.

Chen, C.-G., Chen Keh-Jiann, and Lee Lin-shan (1986). "A Model for Lexical Analysis and Parsing of Chinese Sentences." *Proceedings of 1986 International Conference on Chinese Computing,* Singapore, pp. 33–40.

Chen, Hsin-hsi (1990). "A Logic-based Government-binding Parser for Mandarin Chinese." *Proceedings of the 13th International Conference on Computational Linguistics* (*COLING-90*), Helsinki, Finland, pp. 48–53.

Chen, Hsin-hsi (1996). "Logic-based Parsing of Chinese." *Journal of Chinese Linguistics*, Vol. 9, pp. 47–76.

Chen, Hsin-hsi, Lin I-peng, and Wu Chien-ping (1988). "A New Design of Prolog-based Bottom-up Parsing System with Government-binding."

Proceedings of the 12th International Conference on Computational Linguistics (*COLING-88*), Budapest, Hungary, pp. 112–116.

Chen, Keh-Jiann and Huang Chu-ren (1996). "Information-based Case Grammar: A Unification-based Formalism for Parsing Chinese." *Journal of Chinese Linguistics*, Vol. 9, pp. 23–45.

Ciortzu, Liviu (2001). "On Compilation of the Quick-check Filter for Feature Structure Unification." *Proceedings of the 7th International Workshop on Parsing Technologies* (*IWPT-2001*), Peking University, Beijing, China. Beijing: Tsinghua University Press, pp. 90–100.

Clark, Stephen and James R. Curran (2004). "Parsing the WSJ Using CCG and Log-linear Models." *Proceedings of the 42nd Annual Meeting of the Association for Computational Linguistics* (*ACL-2004*), Barcelona, Spain, pp. 103–110.

Collins, Christopher, Bob Carpenter, and Gerald Penn (2004). "Head-driven Parsing for Word Lattices." *Proceedings of the 42nd Annual Meeting of the Association for Computational Linguistics* (*ACL-2004*), Barcelona, Spain, pp. 231–238.

Collins, Michael J. (1996). "A New Statistical Parser Based on Bigram Lexical Dependencies." *Proceedings of the 34th Annual Meeting of the Association for Computational Linguistics*, Santa Cruz, California, USA, pp. 184–191.

Collins, Michael J. (1997). "Three Generative, Lexicalised Models for Statistical Parsing." *Proceedings of the 35th Annual Meeting of the Association for Computational Linguistics* (*ACL-97*), Madrid, Spain, pp. 16–23.

Collins, Michael J. (2001). "Parameter Estimation for Statistical Parsing Models: Theory and Practice of Distribution-free Methods." *Proceedings of the 7th International Workshop on Parsing Technologies* (*IWPT-2001*), Peking University, Beijing, China. Beijing: Tsinghua University Press, pp. 4–15.

Collins, Michael J. and Brian Roark (2004). "Incremental Parsing with the Perceptron Algorithm." *Proceedings of the 42nd Annual Meeting of the Association for Computational Linguistics* (*ACL-2004*), Barcelona, Spain, pp. 111–118.

Cori, Marcel, Michel de Fornel, and Jean-Marie Marandin (1997). "Parsing Repairs." In Ruslan Mitkov and Nicolas Nicolov, eds., *Recent Advances in Natural Language Processing*. Amsterdam and Philadelphia: John Benjamins Publishing Company, pp. 47–58.

Corston-Oliver, Simon, Anthony Aue, Kevin Duh, and Eric Ringger (2006). "Multilingual Dependency Parsing Using Bayes Point Machines." *Proceedings of the Human Language Technology Conference—Annual Meeting of the North American Chapter of the Association for Computational Linguistics* (*HLT-NAACL-2006*), New York, USA.

Czuba, Krzysztof (2000). "Efficient Parsing Strategies for Syntactic Analysis of Closed Captions." *Proceedings of the ANLP-NAACL-2000 Student Research Workshop*, Seattle, Washington, DC, USA, pp. 7–12.

De Roeck, An (1983). "An Underview of Parsing." In Margaret King, ed., *Parsing Natural Language*. London: Academic Press, pp. 3–17.

Dinh, Dien and Kiem Hoang (2001). "An Approach to Parsing Vietnamese Noun Compounds." *Proceedings of the 7th International Workshop on Parsing Technologies* (*IWPT-2001*), Peking University, Beijing, China. Beijing: Tsinghua University Press, pp. 213–216.

Engel, Donald, Eugene Charniak, and Mark Johnson (2002). "Parsing and Disfluency Placement." *Proceedings of the 2002 Conference on Empirical Methods in Natural Language Processing* (*EMNLP-2002*), University of Pennsylvania, Philadelphia, PA, USA.

Feng, Zhiwei 馮志偉 (2004).〈基於概率的自動句法分析〉(Automatic Parsing Based on Probability).《機器翻譯研究》(*Studies on Machine Translation*). Beijing: China Translation and Publishing Corporation, pp. 444–466.

Feng, Zhiwei (2004).〈基於上下文無關語法的自動句法分析〉(Automatic Parsing Based on Context-free Grammar).《機器翻譯研究》(*Studies on Machine Translation*). Beijing: China Translation and Publishing Corporation, pp. 208–342.

Feng, Zhiwei (2004).〈基於特徵結構的自動句法分析〉(Automatic Parsing Based on Feature Structures).《機器翻譯研究》(*Studies on Machine Translation*). Beijing: China Translation and Publishing Corporation, pp. 343–411.

Feng, Zhiwei (2004).〈基於依存語法的自動句法分析〉(Automatic Parsing Based on Dependency Grammar).《機器翻譯研究》(*Studies on Machine Translation*). Beijing: China Translation and Publishing Corporation 中國對外翻譯出版公司, pp. 412–443.

Feng, Zhiwei (2004).〈基於轉移網絡的自動句法分析〉(Automatic Parsing Based on Transition Network).《機器翻譯研究》(*Studies on Machine Translation*). Beijing: China Translation and Publishing Corporation 中國對外翻譯出版公司, pp. 181–207.

Ferro, M. Vilares, D. Cabrero Souto, and Francisco J. Ribadas Pena (2000). "On Integration of Parsing and Tree Matching Schemes." *Proceedings of the 1st International Conference on Intelligent Text Processing and Computational Linguistics* (*CICLing-2000*), Mexico City, Mexico.

Franz, Alexander (1992). *Ambiguity Resolution in Natural Language Parsing*. Pittsburgh: Language Technologies Institute, Carnegie Mellon University.

Fu, Aiping 傅愛平 (2001).〈廣義依存關係和漢語自動分析〉(Generalized Dependency and Chinese Parsing). In Huang Changning 黃昌寧 and Zhang Pu 張普, eds.,《自然語言理解與機器翻譯》(*Natural Language Understanding and Machine Translation*). Beijing: Tsinghua University Press, pp. 240–245.

Furuse, Osamu and Hitoshi Iida (1994). "Constituent Boundary Parsing for Example-based Machine Translation." *Proceedings of the 15th International Conference on Computational Linguistics* (*COLING-94*), Kyoto, Japan, pp. 105–111.

Gabbard, Ryan, Seth Kulick, and Mitchell P. Marcus (2006). "Fully Parsing the Penn Treebank." *Proceedings of the Human Language Technology Conference—Annual Meeting of the North American Chapter of the Association for Computational Linguistics* (*HLT-NAACL-2006*), New York, USA.

Gálvez, Jose Fortes and Jacques Farré (2001). "Generalized ∈-skip Discriminating-reverse Parsing on Graph-structured Stack." *Proceedings of the 7th International Workshop on Parsing Technologies* (*IWPT-2001*), Peking University, Beijing, China. Beijing: Tsinghua University Press, pp. 101–111.

Gálvez, José Fortes, Jacques Farré, and Miguel Angel Pérez Aguiar (2001). "Practical Nondeterministic DR(*k*) Parsing on Graph-structured Stack." *Proceedings of the 2nd International Conference on Intelligent Text Processing and Computational Linguistics* (*CICLing-2001*), Mexico City, Mexico.

Germann, Ulrich (1998). "Making Semantic Interpretation Parser-independent." In David L. Farwell, Laurie Gerber, and Eduard Hovy, eds., *Machine Translation and the Information Soup*. Berlin: Springer Verlag, pp. 286–299.

Ghorbel, Hatem and Vincenzo Pallotta (2000). "A Weighted Robust Parsing Approach to Semantic Annotation." *Proceedings of the ANLP-*

NAACL-2000 Student Research Workshop, Seattle, Washington, DC, USA, pp. 19–23.

Glaysher, Elliot and Dan Moldovan (2006). "Speeding up Full Syntactic Parsing by Leveraging Partial Parsing Decisions." *Proceedings of the Joint Conference of the International Committee on Computational Linguistics and the Association for Computational Linguistics (COLING/ACL-2006)*, Sydney, Australia.

Goodman, Joshua (1996). "Efficient Algorithms for Parsing the DOP Model." *Proceedings of the Conference on Empirical Methods in Natural Language Processing*, University of Pennsylvania, PA, USA.

Gregory, Michelle, Mark Johnson, and Eugene Charniak (2004). "Sentence-internal Prosody Does Not Help Parsing the Way Punctuation Does." *Proceedings of the Human Language Technology Conference/North American Chapter of the Association for Computational Linguistics Annual Meeting (HLT/NAACL-2004)*, Boston, MA, USA.

Güngördü, Zealal and Kemal Oflazer (1995). "Parsing Turkish Using the Lexical Functional Grammar Formalism." *Machine Translation*, Vol. 10, No. 4, pp. 293–319.

Hahn, Udo and Michael Strube (1997). "Parsetalk about Textual Ellipsis." In Ruslan Mitkov and Nicolas Nicolov, eds., *Recent Advances in Natural Language Processing*. Amsterdam and Philadelphia: John Benjamins Publishing Company, pp. 85–96.

Hanneforth, Thomas, Silvan Heintze, and Manfred Stede (2003). "Rhetorical Parsing with Underspecification and Forests." *Proceedings of the Human Language Technology and North American Chapter of Association of Computational Linguistics 2003 (HLT/NAACL-2003)*, Edmonton, Alberta, Canada.

Hayes, Philip J., Alexander G. Hauptmann, Jaime G. Carbonell, and Masaru Tomita (1987). *Parsing Spoken Language: A Semantic Caseframe Approach*. Pittsburgh: Center for Machine Translation, Carnegie Mellon University.

Hinrichs, Erhard W., Sandra Kübler, Valia Kordoni, and Frank H. Müller (2000). "Robust Chunk Parsing for Spontaneous Speech." In Wolfgang Wahlster, ed., *Verbmobil: Foundations of Speech-to-speech Translation*. Berlin: Springer Verlag, pp. 163–182.

Hopkins, Mark and Jonas Kuhn (2006). "A Framework for Incorporating Alignment Information in Parsing." *Proceedings of the 11th*

Conference of the European Chapter of the Association for Computational Linguistics (*EACL-2006*), Trento, Italy.

Horák, Aleš and Pavel Smrž (2001). "Efficient Sentence Parsing with Language Specific Features: A Case Study of Czech." *Proceedings of the 7th International Workshop on Parsing Technologies* (*IWPT-2001*), Peking University, Beijing, China. Beijing: Tsinghua University Press, pp. 221–224.

Hsieh, Hsin-I (1994). "A Computational Syntax and Its Application to Parsing." *Proceedings of the Conference of the Association for Computational Linguistics and Chinese Language Processing* (*ROCLING-VII*), National Tsing Hua University, Hsin-Chu, Taiwan.

Hsieh, Yu-Ming, Duen-Chi Yang, and Keh-Jiann Chen (2006). "Improve Parsing Performance by Self-learning." *Proceedings of the Conference of the Association for Computational Linguistics and Chinese Language Processing* (*ROCLING-XVIII*), Taipei, Taiwan.

Huang, Chu-ren, Chen Keh-jiann, Chen Wan-pei, and Hu Tzu-ying (1990). "Resolution of Long-distance Dependencies in Mandarin Chinese with an Algorithm Based on Functional Uncertainty." *Computer Processing of Chinese and Oriental Languages*, Vol. 5, No. 1, pp. 25–32.

Hurst, Matthew F. (1997). "Parsing for Targeted Errors in Controlled Languages." In Ruslan Mitkov and Nicolas Nicolov, eds., *Recent Advances in Natural Language Processing*. Amsterdam and Philadelphia: John Benjamins Publishing Company, pp. 59–70.

Johnson, Roderick L. (1983). "Parsing—An MT Perspective." In K. Sparck Jones and Yorick Wilks, eds., *Automatic Natural Language Parsing*. Chichester: Ellis Horwood, Ltd.

Johnson, Roderick L. (1983). "Parsing with Transition Networks." In Margaret King, ed., *Parsing Natural Language*. London: Academic Press, pp. 59–72.

Kahn, Jeremy G., Mari Ostendorf, and Ciprian Chelba (2004). "Parsing Conversational Speech Using Enhanced Segmentation." *Proceedings of the Human Language Technology Conference/North American Chapter of the Association for Computational Linguistics Annual Meeting* (*HLT/NAACL-2004*), Boston, MA, USA.

Kato, Yoshihide, Shigeki Matsubara, Katsuhiko Toyama, and Yasuyoshi Inagaki (2001). "Efficient Incremental Dependency Parsing." *Proceedings of the 7th International Workshop on Parsing*

Technologies (*IWPT-2001*), Peking University, Beijing, China. Beijing: Tsinghua University Press, pp. 225–228.

Kim, Sung Dong and Byoung-Tak Zhang (2000). "Reducing Parsing Complexity by Intra-sentence Segmentation Based on Maximum Entropy Model." *Proceedings of the Joint Sigdat Conference on Empirical Methods in Natural Language Processing and Very Large Corpora* (*EMNLP/VLC-2000*), Hong Kong University of Science and Technology, Hong Kong.

King, Margaret, ed. (1983). *Parsing Natural Language*. London: Academic Press.

King, Margaret (1983). "Transformational Parsing." In Margaret King, ed., *Parsing Natural Language*. London: Academic Press, pp. 19–34.

Klein, Dan and Christopher D. Manning (2001). "Parsing and Hypergraphs." *Proceedings of the 7th International Workshop on Parsing Technologies* (*IWPT-2001*), Peking University, Beijing, China. Beijing: Tsinghua University Press, pp. 123–134.

Klein, Dan and Christopher D. Manning (2003). "A* Parsing: Fast Exact Viterbi Parse Selection." *Proceedings of the Human Language Technology and North American Chapter of Association of Computational Linguistics 2003* (*HLT/NAACL-2003*), Edmonton, Alberta, Canada.

Koller, Alexander and Kristina Striegnitz (2002). "Generation as Dependency Parsing." *Proceedings of the 40th Annual Meeting of the Association for Computational Linguistics* (*ACL-2002*), Philadelphia, PA, USA, pp. 17–24.

Koo, Terry and Michael Collins (2005). "Hidden-variable Models for Discriminative Reranking." *Proceedings of Human Language Technology Conference and Conference on Empirical Methods in Natural Language Processing* (*HLT/EMNLP-2005*), Vancouver, BC, Canada.

Krymolowski, Yuval and Ido Dagan (2000). "Incorporating Compositional Evidence in Memory-based Partial Parsing." *Proceedings of the 38th Annual Meeting of the Association for Computational Linguistics* (*ACL-2000*), Hong Kong.

Kurohashi, Sadao and Makoto Nagao (1996). "Structural Disambiguation in Japanese by Case Structure Evaluation Based on Examples in a Case Frame Dictionary." In Harry Bunt and Masaru Tomita, eds., *Recent Advances in Parsing Technology*. Dordrecht: Kluwer Academic Publishers, pp. 343–358.

Kwak, Yong-Jae, So-Young Park, Joon-Ho Lim, and Hae-Chang Rim (2004). "Probabilistic Shift-reduce Parsing Model Using Rich Contextual Information." *Proceedings of the 5th International Conference on Intelligent Text Processing and Computational Linguistics* (*CICLing-2004*), Chung-Ang University, Seoul, Korea, pp. 91–94.

Lavie, Alon (1994). "An Integrated Heuristic Scheme for Partial Parse Evaluation." *Proceedings of the 32nd Annual Meeting of the Association for Computational Linguistics* (*ACL-94*), Las Cruces, New Mexico, USA, pp. 316–318.

Lavie, Alon, Lori S. Levin, Alex H. Waibel, Donna Gates, Marsal Gavalda, and Laura Mayfield (1996). "System Description JANUS, Multilingual Translation of Spontaneous Speech in a Limited Domain." *Expanding MT Horizons: Proceedings of the 2nd Conference of the Association for Machine Translation in the Americas*, Montreal, Quebec, Canada, pp. 252–255.

Lavie, Alon and Masaru Tomita (1996). "GLR*—An Efficient Noise-skipping Parsing Algorithm for Context-free Grammars." In Harry Bunt and Masaru Tomita, eds., *Recent Advances in Parsing Technology*. Dordrecht: Kluwer Academic Publishers, pp. 183–200.

Lin, I-Peng and Shuan-fan Huang (1988). "The Parsing Environment for Mandarin Syntax." *Proceedings of the Conference of the Association for Computational Linguistics and Chinese Language Processing* (*ROCLING-I*), Nantou, Taiwan.

Ling, Yi-Chung and Keh-Yih Su (1998). "Error Recovery in Natural Language Parsing with a Level-synchronous Approach." *Proceedings of the International Conference on Research in Computational Linguistics* (*ROCLING-XI*), Hsin-Chu, Taiwan.

Lozinskii, Eliezer L. and Sergei Nirenburg (1986). "Parsing in Parallel." *Journal of Computer Languages*, Vol. 11, pp. 39–51.

Luk, Po Chui, Weng Fuliang, and Helen Meng (2001). "Automatic Grammar Partitioning for Syntactic Parsing." *Proceedings of the 7th International Workshop on Parsing Technologies* (*IWPT-2001*), Peking University, Beijing, China. Beijing: Tsinghua University Press, pp. 229–232.

Lutz, Rudi (1996). "Flowgraph Parsing." In Harry Bunt and Masaru Tomita, eds., *Recent Advances in Parsing Technology*. Dordrecht: Kluwer Academic Publishers, pp. 359–383.

McClosky, David, Eugene Charniak, and Mark Johnson (2006). "Effective Self-training for Parsing." *Proceedings of the Human Language Technology Conference—Annual Meeting of the North American Chapter of the Association for Computational Linguistics* (*HLT-NAACL-2006*), New York, USA.

McDonald, David D. (1992). "An Efficient Chart-based Algorithm for Partial-parsing of Unrestricted Texts." *Third Conference on Applied Natural Language Processing*, Trento, Italy, pp. 193–200.

McDonald, David D. (1996). "The Interplay of Syntactic and Semantic Node Labels in Parsing." In Harry Bunt and Masaru Tomita, eds., *Recent Advances in Parsing Technology*. Dordrecht: Kluwer Academic Publishers, pp. 295–323.

McDonald, Ryan, Fernando Pereira, Kiril Ribarov, and Jan Hajic (2005). "Non-projective Dependency Parsing Using Spanning Tree Algorithms." *Proceedings of Human Language Technology Conference and Conference on Empirical Methods in Natural Language Processing* (*HLT/EMNLP-2005*), Vancouver, BC, Canada.

Mellish, Chris S. (1989). "Some Chart-based Techniques for Parsing Ill-formed Input." *Proceedings of the 27th Annual Meeting of the Association for Computational Linguistics* (*ACL-89*), Vancouver, BC, Canada, pp. 102–109.

Meng, Yao 孟遙, Huang Yu 黃玉, Shao Tiejun 趙鐵軍, and Li Sheng 李生 (2001). 〈一個包含複雜特徵的統計英語句法分析模型〉 (A Complex-feature-oriented Statistic English Parsing Model). In Huang Changning 黃昌寧 and Zhang Pu 張普, eds.,《自然語言理解與機器翻譯》(*Natural Language Understanding and Machine Translation*). Beijing: Tsinghua University Press, pp. 167–172.

Merlo, Paola and Gabriele Musillo (2005). "Accurate Function Parsing." *Proceedings of Human Language Technology Conference and Conference on Empirical Methods in Natural Language Processing* (*HLT/EMNLP-2005*), Vancouver, BC, Canada.

Miller, Scott, Heidi Fox, Lance Ramshaw, and Ralph Weischedel (2000). "A Novel Use of Statistical Parsing to Extract Information from Text." *Proceedings of the 1st Meeting of the North American Chapter of the Association for Computational Linguistics*, Seattle, Washington, DC, USA, pp. 226–233.

Minnen, Guido, William Thompson, Harry Bliss, and Dale Russell (2001). "Direct Bottom-up Chart Parsing Using Abbreviated Context-free

Grammars." *Proceedings of the 7th International Workshop on Parsing Technologies (IWPT-2001)*, Peking University, Beijing, China. Beijing: Tsinghua University Press, pp. 233–236.

Mo, Ruo-ping, Yang Yao-jung, Chen Keh-jiann, and Huang Chu-ren (1996). "Determinative-measure Compounds in Mandarin Chinese Formation Rules and Parser Implementation." *Journal of Chinese Linguistics*, Vol. 9, pp. 123–146.

Mráková, Eva and Radek Sedláček (2003). "From Czech Morphology through Partial Parsing to Disambiguation." *Proceedings of the 4th International Conference on Intelligent Text Processing and Computational Linguistics (CICLing-2003)*, Mexico City, Mexico, pp. 129–138.

Mullen, Tony (2000). "Overfitting Reduction through Feature Merging for Maximum Entropy-based Parse Selection." *Proceedings of the 38th Annual Meeting of the Association for Computational Linguistics (ACL-2000)*, Hong Kong.

Munteanu, Cosmin and Gerald Penn (2004). "Optimizing Typed Feature Structure Grammar Parsing through Non-statistical Indexing." *Proceedings of the 42nd Annual Meeting of the Association for Computational Linguistics (ACL-2004)*, Barcelona, Spain, pp. 223–230.

Musillo, Gabriele and Paola Merlo (2006). "Accurate Parsing of the Proposition Bank." *Proceedings of the Human Language Technology Conference—Annual Meeting of the North American Chapter of the Association for Computational Linguistics (HLT-NAACL-2006)*, New York, USA.

Nagao, Makoto (1996). "Varieties of Heuristics in Sentence Parsing." In Harry Bunt and Masaru Tomita, eds., *Recent Advances in Parsing Technology*. Dordrecht: Kluwer Academic Publishers, pp. 79–90.

Nederhof, Mark-Jan and Janos J. Sarbo (1996). "Increasing the Applicability of LR Parsing." In Harry Bunt and Masaru Tomita, eds., *Recent Advances in Parsing Technology*. Dordrecht: Kluwer Academic Publishers, pp. 35–57.

Nederhof, Mark-Jan and Giorgio Satta (2000). "Left-to-right Parsing and Bilexical Context-free Grammars." *Proceedings of the 1st Meeting of the North American Chapter of the Association for Computational Linguistics*, Seattle, Washington, DC, USA, pp. 272–279.

Nederhof, Mark-Jan and Giorgio Satta (2004). "Probabilistic Parsing

Strategies." *Proceedings of the 42nd Annual Meeting of the Association for Computational Linguistics* (*ACL-2004*), Barcelona, Spain, pp. 542–549.

Osborne, Miles and Jason Baldridge (2004). "Ensemble-based Active Learning for Parse Selection." *Proceedings of the Human Language Technology Conference/North American Chapter of the Association for Computational Linguistics Annual Meeting* (*HLT/NAACL-2004*), Boston, MA, USA.

Poibeau, Thierry (2001). "Parsing Natural Language Idioms with Bidirectional Finite-state Machines." *Theoretical Computer Science*, Vol. 267, pp. 131–140.

Pradhan, Sameer S., Honglin Sun, Wayne Ward, James H. Martin, and Dan Jurafsky (2004). "Parsing Arguments of Nominalizations in English and Chinese." *Proceedings of the Human Language Technology Conference/North American Chapter of the Association for Computational Linguistics Annual Meeting* (*HLT/NAACL-2004*), Boston, MA, USA.

Prins, Robbert and Gertjan van Noord (2001). "Unsupervised Pos-tagging Improves Parsing Accuracy and Parsing Efficiency." *Proceedings of the 7th International Workshop on Parsing Technologies* (*IWPT-2001*), Peking University, Beijing, China. Beijing: Tsinghua University Press, pp. 154–165.

Pulman, Stephen G. (1983). "Trace Theory Parsing and Constraints." In Margaret King, ed., *Parsing Natural Language*. London: Academic Press, pp. 171–196.

Raaijmakers, Stephan (1996). "Proof Theory for HPSG Parsing." In Harry Bunt and Masaru Tomita, eds., *Recent Advances in Parsing Technology*. Dordrecht: Kluwer Academic Publishers, pp. 115–144.

Ramsay, Allan and Reinhard Schäler (1997). "Case and Word Order in English and German." In Ruslan Mitkov and Nicolas Nicolov, eds., *Recent Advances in Natural Language Processing*. Amsterdam and Philadelphia: John Benjamins Publishing Company, pp. 15–33.

Ritchie, Graeme D. (1983). "Semantics in Parsing." In Margaret King, ed., *Parsing Natural Language*. London: Academic Press, pp. 199–217.

Rogers, James and K. Vijay-Shanker (1996). "Towards a Formal Understanding of the Determinism Hypothesis in D-Theory." In Harry Bunt and Masaru Tomita, eds., *Recent Advances in Parsing Technology*. Dordrecht: Kluwer Academic Publishers, pp. 59–78.

Rosner, Michael A. (1983). "Production Systems." In Margaret King, ed., *Parsing Natural Language*. London: Academic Press, pp. 35–58.

Ruland, Tobias (2000). "Probabilistic LR-parsing with Symbolic Postprocessing." In Wolfgang Wahlster, ed., *Verbmobil: Foundations of Speech-to-speech Translation*. Berlin: Springer Verlag, pp. 147–162.

Sagae, Kenji, Alon Lavie, and Brian MacWhinney (2001). "Parsing the Childes Database: Methodology and Lessons Learned." *Proceedings of the 7th International Workshop on Parsing Technologies* (*IWPT-2001*), Peking University, Beijing, China. Beijing: Tsinghua University Press, pp. 166–176.

Sampson, Geoffrey R. (1983). "Context Free Parsing and the Adequacy of Context-free Grammars." In Margaret King, ed., *Parsing Natural Language*. London: Academic Press, pp. 151–170.

Sampson, Geoffrey R. (1983). "Deterministic Parsing." In Margaret King, ed., *Parsing Natural Language*. London: Academic Press, pp. 91–116.

Schabes, Yves and Richard C. Waters (1996). "Stochastic Lexicalized Tree-insertion Grammar." In Harry Bunt and Masaru Tomita, eds., *Recent Advances in Parsing Technology*. Dordrecht: Kluwer Academic Publishers, pp. 281–294.

Schubert, Klaus (1989). "Dependency Syntax for Parsing and Generation." In Dan Maxwell and Klaus Schubert, eds., *Metataxis in Practice: Dependency Syntax for Multilingual Machine Translation*. Dordrecht: Foris Publications, pp. 7–15.

Shen, Libin 沈李斌, Chen Xuan 陳宣, Chen Yuquan 陳玉泉, Dong Tiansi 董天石, and Lu Ruzhan 陸汝占 (1999).〈一個漢語句法分析器的設計與實現〉(The Design and Implementation of a Chinese Parser). In Huang Changning 黃昌寧 and Dong Zhendong 董振東, eds.,《計算機語言學文集》(*Essays on Computational Linguistics*). Beijing: Tsinghua University Press, pp. 274–279.

Shen, Libin and Lu Ruzhan (1999).〈雙向圖分析器的改進〉(Improvement of Bidirectional Chart Parser). Huang Changning and Dong Zhendong, eds.,《計算機語言學文集》(*Essays on Computational Linguistics*). Beijing: Tsinghua University Press, pp. 438–444.

Shen, Libin and Aravind Joshi (2005). "Incremental LTAG Parsing." *Proceedings of Human Language Technology Conference and Conference on Empirical Methods in Natural Language Processing* (*HLT/EMNLP-2005*), Vancouver, BC, Canada.

Sikkel, Klaas and Rieks op den Akker (1996). "Predictive Head-corner

Chart Parsing." In Harry Bunt and Masaru Tomita, eds., *Recent Advances in Parsing Technology*. Dordrecht: Kluwer Academic Publishers, pp. 169–182.

Sima'an, Khalil (1997). "An Optimised Algorithm for Data Oriented Parsing." In Ruslan Mitkov and Nicolas Nicolov, eds., *Recent Advances in Natural Language Processing*. Amsterdam and Philadelphia: John Benjamins Publishing Company, pp. 35–46.

Sima'an, Khalil (1997). "Tree-gram Parsing: Lexical Dependencies and Structural Relations." *Proceedings of the 38th Annual Meeting of the Association for Computational Linguistics* (*ACL-2000*), Hong Kong.

Slocum, Jonathan (1981). *A Practical Comparison of Parsing Strategies for Machine Translation and Other Natural Language Processing Purposes*. Ann Arbor, Michigan: University of Michigan Press.

Small, Steven L. (1983). "Parsing as Cooperative Distributed Inference: Understanding through Memory Interactions." In Margaret King, ed., *Parsing Natural Language*. London: Academic Press, pp. 247–276.

Sobashima, Yauhiro and Hitoshi Iida (1995). "A Multi-dimensional Analogy-based, Context-dependent, Bottom-up Parsing Method for Spoken Dialogues." *Proceedings of the 3rd Natural Language Processing Pacific Rim Symposium* (*NLPRS-95*), Seoul, Korea, pp. 586–591.

Streiter Oliver (2000). "Parsing Chinese by Examples." *Proceedings of the International Conference on Research in Computational Linguistics* (*ROCLING-XIII*), Taipei, Taiwan.

Streiter, Oliver (2001). "Memory-based Parsing: Enhancing Recursive Top-down Fuzzy Match with Bottom-up Chunking." *Proceedings of the 19th International Conference on Computer Processing of Oriental Languages* (*ICCPOL-2001*), Seoul, Korea, pp. 219–224.

Strzalkowski, Tomek and Peter G. N. Scheyen (1996). "Evaluation of the Tagged Text Parser." In Harry Bunt and Masaru Tomita, eds., *Recent Advances in Parsing Technology*. Dordrecht: Kluwer Academic Publishers, pp. 201–220.

Su, Keh-Yih (1988). "Principles and Techniques of Natural Language Parsing: A Tutorial." *Proceedings of the Conference of the Association for Computational Linguistics and Chinese Language Processing* (*ROCLING-I*), Nantou, Taiwan.

Sun, Bin (2001). "Buffered Shift-reduce Parsing." *Proceedings of the 7th International Workshop on Parsing Technologies* (*IWPT-2001*),

Peking University, Beijing, China. Beijing: Tsinghua University Press, pp. 249–252.

Tanaka, Hozumi, Takenobu Tokunaga, and Michio Aizawa (1996). "Integration of Morphological and Syntactic Analysis Based on GLR Parsing." In Harry Bunt and Masaru Tomita, eds., *Recent Advances in Parsing Technology*. Dordrecht: Kluwer Academic Publishers, pp. 325–342.

Temizsoy, Murat and Ilyas Cicekli (1998). "An Ontology-based Approach to Parsing Turkish Sentences." In David L. Farwell, Laurie Gerber, and Eduard Hovy, eds., *Machine Translation and the Information Soup*. Berlin: Springer Verlag, pp. 124–135.

Tomita, Masaru (1986). *Efficient Parsing for Natural Language: A Fast Algorithm for Practical Systems*. Dordrecht: Kluwer Academic Publishers.

Tomita, Masaru (1987). "An Efficient Augmented-context-free Parsing Algorithm." *Computational Linguistics*, Vol. 13, pp. 31–46.

Tomita, Masaru, ed. (1991). *Current Trends in Parsing Technology*. Boston: Kluwer Academic Publishers.

Tomita, Masaru, ed. (1991). *Generalized LR-Parsing*. Boston: Kluwer Academic Publishers.

Tomita, Masaru and Jaime G. Carbonell (1987). *The Universal Parser Architecture for Knowledge-based Machine Translation*. Pittsburgh: Language Technologies Institute, Carnegie Mellon University.

Tuells, Toni, German Rigau, and Horacio Rodríguez (2003). "Off-line Compilation of Chains for Head-driven Generation with Constraint-based Grammars." *Proceedings of the 4th International Conference on Intelligent Text Processing and Computational Linguistics* (*CICLing-2003*), Mexico City, Mexico, pp. 183–192.

Ushioda, Akira, David A. Evans, Ted Gibson, and Alex H. Waibel (1996). "Estimation of Verb Subcategorization Frame Frequencies Based on Syntactic and Multimensional Statistical Analysis." In Harry Bunt and Masaru Tomita, eds., *Recent Advances in Parsing Technology*. Dordrecht: Kluwer Academic Publishers, pp. 241–253.

Varile, Giovanni B. (1983). "Charts: A Data Structure for Parsing." In Margaret King, ed., *Parsing Natural Language*. London: Academic Press, pp. 73–87.

Vilares, Manuel, Victor M. Darriba, and Jesús Vilares (2004). "Parsing Incomplete Sentences Revisited." *Proceedings of the 5th International*

Conference on Intelligent Text Processing and Computational Linguistics (*CICLing-2004*), Chung-Ang University, Seoul, Korea, pp. 99–108.
Wilks, Yorick (1983). "Deep and Superficial Parsing." In Margaret King, ed., *Parsing Natural Language*. London: Academic Press, pp. 119–246.
Wintner, Shuly (1998). "Parsing Schemata Berlin and Heidelberg." *Machine Translation*, Vol. 13, Nos. 2–3, pp. 233–237.
Wirén, Mats and Ralph Rönnquist (1996). "Fully Incremental Parsing." In Harry Bunt and Masaru Tomita, eds., *Recent Advances in Parsing Technology*. Dordrecht: Kluwer Academic Publishers, pp. 11–34.
Wittenburg, Kent (1996). "Predictive Parsing for Unordered Relational Languages." In Harry Bunt and Masaru Tomita, eds., *Recent Advances in Parsing Technology*. Dordrecht: Kluwer Academic Publishers, pp. 385–407.
Woods, William A. (1973). "An Experimental Parsing System for Transition Network Grammars." In Randall Rustin, ed., *Natural Language Processing*. New York: Algorithmic Press, pp. 111–154.
Xia, Xuanyin and Wu Dekai (1996). "Parsing Chinese with an Almost-context-free Grammar." *Proceedings of the Conference on Empirical Methods in Natural Language Processing*, University of Pennsylvania, PA, USA.
Xiong, Deyi, Qun Liu, and Shouxun Lin (2005). "Lexicalized Beam Thresholding Parsing with Prior and Boundary Estimates." *Proceedings of the 6th International Conference on Intelligent Text Processing and Computational Linguistics* (*CICLing-2005*), Mexico City, Mexico, pp. 131–140.
Yamada, Kenji (1998). "A Controlled Skip Parser." *Machine Translation*, Vol. 13, No. 1, pp. 1–15.
Yao, Jianmin 姚建民, Zhang Jing 張晶, Zhao Tiejun 趙鐵軍, Yu Hao 于浩, and Li Sheng 李生 (2001).〈英語句法分析樹向漢語分析樹的轉換〉(English Chinese Transfer of a Syntactic Parsing Tree). In Huang Changning 黃昌寧 and Zhang Pu 張普, eds.,《自然語言理解與機器翻譯》(*Natural Language Understanding and Machine Translation*). Beijing: Tsinghua University Press, pp. 306–311.
Zeman, Daniel (2001). "How Much Will a Rebased Preprocessor Help a Statistical Parser." *Proceedings of the 7th International Workshop on Parsing Technologies* (*IWPT-2001*), Peking University, Beijing, China. Beijing: Tsinghua University Press, pp. 253–256.

Zhao, Tiejun 趙鐵軍, Li Shen 李生, Meng Yao 孟遙, Huang Yu 黄玉, and Yang Muyun 楊沐昀 (2001).〈機器翻譯系統中句法分析技術的研究實踐〉(Research on Parsing Technology in Machine Translation System).《輝煌二十年——中國中文信息學會二十周年學術會議》(*Proceedings of Conference of the 20th Anniversary of CIPSC*). Beijing: Tsinghua University Press, pp. 249–257.

Dependency Parsing

Yang, Mei and Katrin Kirchhoff (2006). "Phrase-based Backoff Models for Machine Translation of Highly Inflected Languages." *Proceedings of the 11th Conference of the European Chapter of the Association for Computational Linguistics* (*EACL-2006*), Trento, Italy.

Robust Parsing

Blache, Philippe (2006). "A Robust and Efficient Parser for Non-canonical Inputs." *Proceedings of the 11th Conference of the European Chapter of the Association for Computational Linguistics* (*EACL-2006*), Trento, Italy.

Foth, Kilian and Wolfgang Menzel (2006). "Robust Parsing: More with Less." *Proceedings of the 11th Conference of the European Chapter of the Association for Computational Linguistics* (*EACL-2006*), Trento, Italy.

Ghorbel, Hatem and Vincenzo Pallotta (2000). "A Weighted Robust Parsing Approach to Semantic Annotation." *Proceedings of the ANLP-NAACL-2000 Student Research Workshop*, Seattle, Washington, DC, USA, pp. 19–23.

Kiefer, Bernd, Hans-Ulrich Krieger, and Mark-Jan Nederhof (2000). "Efficient and Robust Parsing of Word Hypotheses Graphs." In Wolfgang Wahlster, ed., *Verbmobil: Foundations of Speech-to-speech Translation*. Berlin: Springer Verlag, pp. 280–295.

Musillo, Gabriele and Paola Merlo (2006). "Robust Parsing of the Proposition Bank." *Proceedings of the 11th Conference of the European Chapter of the Association for Computational Linguistics* (*EACL-2006*), Trento, Italy.

van Noord, Gertjan (2006). "Robust Parsing, Error Mining, Automated Lexical Acquisition, and Evaluation." *Proceedings of the 11th*

Conference of the European Chapter of the Association for Computational Linguistics (*EACL-2006*), Trento, Italy.

Semantic Parsing

Gao, Yuqing, Bowen Zhou, Zijian Diao, Jeffrey Sorensen, and Michael Picheny (2002). "MARS: A Statistical Semantic Parsing and Generation-based Multilingual Automatic Translation System." *Machine Translation*, Vol. 17, No. 3, pp. 185–212.

Pradhan, Sameer S., Wayne H. Ward, Kadri Hacioglu, James H. Martin, and Dan Jurafsky (2004). "Shallow Semantic Parsing Using Support Vector Machines." *Proceedings of the Human Language Technology Conference/North American Chapter of the Association for Computational Linguistics Annual Meeting* (*HLT/NAACL-2004*), Boston, MA, USA.

Shi, Lei and Rada F. Mihalcea (2005). "Putting Pieces Together: Combining FrameNet, VerbNet and WordNet for Robust Semantic Parsing." *Proceedings of the 6th International Conference on Intelligent Text Processing and Computational Linguistics* (*CICLing-2005*), Mexico City, Mexico, pp. 99–110.

Tang, Lappoon R. and Raymond J. Mooney (2000). "Automated Construction of Database Interfaces: Integrating Statistical and Relational Learning for Semantic Parsing." *Proceedings of the Joint Sigdat Conference on Empirical Methods in Natural Language Processing and Very Large Corpora* (*EMNLP/VLC-2000*), Hong Kong University of Science and Technology, Hong Kong.

Wong, Yuk Wah and Raymond J. Mooney (2006). "Learning for Semantic Parsing with Statistical Machine Translation." *Proceedings of the Human Language Technology Conference—Annual Meeting of the North American Chapter of the Association for Computational Linguistics* (*HLT-NAACL-2006*), New York, USA.

Sentence Parsing

Lin, Yi-Chung and Keh-Yih Su (1997). "A Level-synchronous Approach to Ill-formed Sentence Parsing." *Proceedings of the International Conference on Research in Computational Linguistics* (*ROCLING-X*), Academia Sinica, Taipei, Taiwan.

Shiu, Yu-Ling Una 許玉玲 and Keh-Yih Su 蘇克毅 (1988). "Criteria for the Classification of Lexical Categories in a Syntax-oriented Parsing System." *Proceedings of the Conference of the Association for Computational Linguistics and Chinese Language Processing (ROCLING-I)*, Nantou, Taiwan.

Soricut, Radu and Daniel Marcu (2003). "Sentence Level Discourse Parsing Using Syntactic and Lexical Information." *Proceedings of the Human Language Technology and North American Chapter of Association of Computational Linguistics 2003 (HLT/NAACL-2003)*, Edmonton, Alberta, Canada.

Shallow Parsing

Kaplan, Ron, Stefan Riezler, Tracy H. King, John T. Maxwell III, Alex Vasserman, and Richard Crouch (2004). "Speed and Accuracy in Shallow and Deep Stochastic Parsing." *Proceedings of the Human Language Technology Conference/North American Chapter of the Association for Computational Linguistics Annual Meeting (HLT/NAACL-2004)*, Boston, MA, USA.

Li, Baoli, Lu Qin, and Li Yin (2003). "Building a Chinese Shallow Parsed TreeBank for Collocation Extraction." *Proceedings of the 4th International Conference on Intelligent Text Processing and Computational Linguistics (CICLing-2003)*, Mexico City, Mexico, pp. 404–407.

Moschitti, Alessandro (2004). "A Study on Convolution Kernels for Shallow Statistic Parsing." *Proceedings of the 42nd Annual Meeting of the Association for Computational Linguistics (ACL-2004)*, Barcelona, Spain, pp. 335–342.

Munoz, Marcia, Vasin Punyakanok, Dan Roth, and Dav Zimak (1999). "A Learning Approach to Shallow Parsing." *Proceedings of the Joint SIGDAT Conference on Empirical Methods in NLP and Very Large Corpora (EMNLP/VLC-99)*, University of Maryland, College Park, MD, USA.

Neumann, Günter, Christian Braun, and Jakub Piskorski (2000). "A Divide-and-conquer Strategy for Shallow Parsing of German." *Proceedings of the 6th Applied Natural Language Processing Conference*, Seattle, Washington, DC, USA, pp. 239–246.

Reinberger, Marie-Laure and Walter Daelemans (2003). "Is Shallow

Parsing Useful for Unsupervised Learning of Semantic Clusters?" *Proceedings of the 4th International Conference on Intelligent Text Processing and Computational Linguistics* (*CICLing-2003*), Mexico City, Mexico, pp. 306–315.

Sha, Fei and Fernando Pereira (2003). "Shallow Parsing with Conditional Random Fields." *Proceedings of the Human Language Technology and North American Chapter of Association of Computational Linguistics 2003* (*HLT/NAACL-2003*), Edmonton, Alberta, Canada.

Sun, Honglin, Lu Qin, and Yu Shiwen (1999). "Two-level Shallow Parser for Unrestricted Chinese Text." In Huang Changning 黃昌寧 and Dong Zhendong 董振東, eds.,《計算機語言學文集》(*Essays on Computational Linguistics*). Beijing: Tsinghua University Press, pp. 280–286.

Sun, Honglin 孫宏林 and Yu Shiwen 俞士汶 (2000).〈淺層句法分析方法概述〉(A Description of the Shallow Parsing Method). In Yu Shiwen 俞士汶 and Zhu Xuefeng 朱學鋒, eds.,《計算語言學文集》(*Papers on Computational Linguistics*), Vol. 4. Beijing: Department of Computer Science and Technology and Institute of Computational Linguistics, Peking University, pp. 209–219.

Sun, Honglin and Daniel Jurafsky (2004). "Shallow Semantic Parsing of Chinese." *Proceedings of the Human Language Technology Conference/North American Chapter of the Association for Computational Linguistics Annual Meeting* (*HLT/NAACL-2004*), Boston, MA, USA.

Tan, Yongmei, Tianshun Yao, Qing Chen, and Jingbo Zhu (2005). "Applying Conditional Random Fields to Chinese Shallow Parsing." *Proceedings of the 6th International Conference on Intelligent Text Processing and Computational Linguistics* (*CICLing-2005*), Mexico City, Mexico, pp. 165–171.

Wu, Shih-Hung, Cheng-Wei Shih, Chia-Wei Wu, and Tzong-Han Tsai (2005). "Applying Maximum Entropy to Robust Chinese Shallow Parsing." *Proceedings of the International Conference on Computational Linguistics and Speech Processing* (*ROCLING-XVII*), National Cheng Kung University, Tainan, Taiwan.

Statistical Parsing

Booth, Kathleen H. V. (1970). "Statistical Parsing by Computer." *Pensiero e Linguaggio*, Vol. 1, pp. 107–110.

Chiang, David (2000). "Statistical Parsing with an Automatically-extracted Tree Adjoining Grammar." *Proceedings of the 38th Annual Meeting of the Association for Computational Linguistics* (*ACL-2000*), Hong Kong.

Collins, Michael J. (1997). "Three Generative, Lexicalised Models for Statistical Parsing." *Proceedings of the 35th Annual Meeting of the Association for Computational Linguistics* (*ACL-97*), Madrid, Spain, pp. 16–23.

Collins, Michael J. (2001). "Parameter Estimation for Statistical Parsing Models: Theory and Practice of Distribution-free Methods." *Proceedings of the 7th International Workshop on Parsing Technologies* (*IWPT-2001*), Peking University, Beijing, China. Beijing: Tsinghua University Press, pp. 4–15.

Diab, Mona and Philip Resnik (2002). "An Unsupervised Method for Word Sense Tagging Using Parallel Corpora." *Proceedings of the 40th Anniversary Meeting of the Association for Computational Linguistics* (*ACL-2002*), Philadelphia, PA, USA.

Henderson, James (2003). "Inducing History Representations for Broad Coverage Statistical Parsing." *Proceedings of the Human Language Technology and North American Chapter of Association of Computational Linguistics 2003* (*HLT/NAACL-2003*), Edmonton, Alberta, Canada.

Henderson, James (2004). "Discriminative Training of a Neural Network Statistical Parser." *Proceedings of the 42nd Annual Meeting of the Association for Computational Linguistics* (*ACL-2004*), Barcelona, Spain, pp. 95–102.

Kiyoaki, Shirai, Inui Kentaro, Tokunaga Takenobu, and Tanaka Hozumi (1998). "An Empirical Evaluation on Statistical Parsing of Japanese Sentences Using Lexical Association Statistics." *Proceedings of the 3rd Conference on Empirical Methods in Natural Language Processing*, Granada, Spain.

Miller, Scott, Heidi Fox, Lance Ramshaw, and Ralph Weischedel (2000). "A Novel Use of Statistical Parsing to Extract Information from Text." *Proceedings of the 1st Meeting of the North American Chapter of the Association for Computational Linguistics*, Seattle, Washington, DC, USA, pp. 226–233.

Steedman, Mark, Rebecca Hwa, Stephen Clark, Miles Osborne, Anoop Sarkar, Julia Hockenmaier, Paul Ruhlen, Steven Baker, and Jeremiah

Crim (2003). "Example Selection for Bootstrapping Statistical Parsers." *Proceedings of the Human Language Technology and North American Chapter of Association of Computational Linguistics 2003* (*HLT/NAACL-2003*), Edmonton, Alberta, Canada.

Sui, Zhifang, Jun Zhao, and Dekai Wu (2000). "An Information-theory-based Feature Type Analysis for the Modeling of Statistical Parsing." *Proceedings of the 38th Annual Meeting of the Association for Computational Linguistics* (*ACL-2000*), Hong Kong.

❖ PART 27 ❖

Parts of Speech

Adjective

Alonge, Antonietta, Francesca Bertagna, Nicoletta Calzolari, Adriana Roventini, and Antonio Zampolli (2000). "Encoding Information on Adjectives in a Lexical-semantic Net for Computational Applications." *Proceedings of the 1st Meeting of the North American Chapter of the Association for Computational Linguistics*, Seattle, Washington, DC, USA, pp. 42–49.

Amoia, Marilisa and Claire Gardent (2006). "Adjective Based Inference." *Proceedings of the 11th Conference of the European Chapter of the Association for Computational Linguistics* (*EACL-2006*), Trento, Italy.

Arkhelyuk, Valentyna (2001). "Statistical Methods in Studying the Semantics of Size Adjectives." *Proceedings of the 2nd International Conference on Intelligent Text Processing and Computational Linguistics* (*CICLing-2001*), Mexico City, Mexico.

Lapata, Maria (2001). "A Corpus-based Account of Regular Polysemy: The Case of Context-sensitive Adjectives." *Proceedings of the 2nd Meeting of the North American Chapter of the Association for Computational Linguistics: Language Technologies 2001* (*NAACL-2001*), Pittsburgh, PA, USA.

Marrafa, Palmira and Sara Mendes (2006). "Modeling Adjectives in Computational Relational Lexica." *Proceedings of the Joint Conference of the International Committee on Computational Linguistics and the Association for Computational Linguistics* (*COLING/ACL-2006*), Sydney, Australia.

Adverb

Appelo, Lisette (1994). "Translation of Temporal Expressions." In M. T. Rosetta, *Compositional Translation*. Dordrecht: Kluwer Academic Publishers, pp. 277–305.

Bresnan, Joan (1989). "The Syntactic Projection Problem and the Comparative Syntax of Locative." *Proceedings of the Conference of the Association for Computational Linguistics and Chinese Language Processing* (*ROCLING-II*), Taipei, Taiwan.

Chang, Li-ping 張莉萍 (1988). 〈漢語的時間詞組和語言剖析〉 (Chinese Temporal Phrases and Their Linguistic Analysis). *Proceedings of the*

Conference of the Association for Computational Linguistics and Chinese Language Processing (*ROCLING-I*), Nantou, Taiwan.

Defrise, Christine (1989). "Lexical Description for NLP: The Case of the French Adverb *presque*." *Machine Translation*, Vol. 4, No. 3, pp. 195–232.

Han, Benjamin, Donna Gates, and Lori Levin (2006). "Understanding Temporal Expressions in Emails." *Proceedings of the Human Language Technology Conference—Annual Meeting of the North American Chapter of the Association for Computational Linguistics* (*HLT-NAACL-2006*), New York, USA.

Li, Wenjie and Wong Kam-Fai (2002). "Temporal Information Processing and Inference." In Yu Shiwen, ed., *Proceedings of the 2nd China-Japan Natural Language Processing Joint Research Promotion Conference* (*CJNLP-2002*). Beijing: Institute of Computational Linguistics, Peking University, pp. 303–305.

Pustejovsky, James and Inderjeet Mani (2003). "Annotation of Temporal and Event Expressions." *Proceedings of the Human Language Technology and North American Chapter of Association of Computational Linguistics 2003* (*HLT/NAACL-2003*), Edmonton, Alberta, Canada.

Saquete, Estela and Patricio Martínez-Barco (2000). "Grammar Specification for the Recognition of Temporal Expressions." *Proceedings of the International Conference on Machine Translation and Multilingual Applications in the New Millenium* (*MT-2000*), University of Exeter, England.

van Eynde, Frank (1995). "A Sign-based Approach to the Translation of Temporal Expressions." *Proceedings of the 6th International Conference on Theoretical and Methodological Issues in Machine Translation* (*TMI-95*), Leuven, Belgium, pp. 67–86.

Article

Barton, J. (1962). "The Application of the Article in English." In National Physical Laboratory, ed., *1961 International Conference on Machine Translation of Languages and Applied Language Analysis: Proceedings of the Conference Held at the National Physical Laboratory, Teddington, Middlesex, on 5th, 6th, 7th and 8th September*. London: Her Majesty's Stationery Office, Vol. 1, pp. 112–118.

Brewer, Jocelyn (1966). "English Article Insertion." *Mechanical Translation*, Vol. 9, Nos. 3–4.

Chang, Baobao, Liu Ying, and Liu Qun (1998).〈漢英機器翻譯中的冠詞處理研究〉(A Study on the Treatment of Articles in Chinese-English Machine Translation). In Yu Shiwen 俞士汶 and Zhu Xuefeng 朱學鋒, eds.,《計算語言學文集》(*Papers on Computational Linguistics*), Vol. 3. Beijing: Department of Computer Science and Technology and Institute of Computational Linguistics, Peking University, pp. 108–114.

Martins, Gary R. (1964). "Preliminary Report on the Insertion of English Articles in Russian-English MT Output." *Mechanical Translation*, Vol. 8, No. 1, pp. 2–4.

Minnen, Guido, Francis Bond, and Ann Copestake (2000). "Automated Article Selection Using Corpus Data." *Proceedings of the 18th International Conference on Computational Linguistics* (*COLING-2000*), Saarbrucken, Germany.

Minnen, Guido, Francis Bond, and Ann Copestake (2000). "Memory-based Learning for Article Generation." *Proceedings of the 4th Conference on Computational Natural Language Learning and of the 2nd Learning Language in Logic Workshop* (*CoNLL-2000*), Lisbon, Portugal.

Classifier

Aone, Chinatsu (1991). "Classifiers and an Interlingua for Multilingual Machine Translation." *Proceedings of the International Conference on Current Issues in Computational Linguistics*, Penang, Malaysia.

Bond, Francis and Kyonghee Paik (2000). "Re-using an Ontology to Generate Numeral Classifiers." *Proceedings of the 18th International Conference on Computational Linguistics* (*COLING-2000*), Saarbrucken, Germany, Vol. 1, pp. 90–96.

Hahn, Sangyun, Richard Ladner, and Mari Ostendorf (2006). "Agreement/Disagreement Classification: Exploiting Unlabeled Data Using Contrast Classifiers." *Proceedings of the Human Language Technology Conference—Annual Meeting of the North American Chapter of the Association for Computational Linguistics* (*HLT-NAACL-2006*), New York, USA.

Paik, Kyonghee and Francis Bond (2001). "Multilingual Generation of

Numeral Classifiers Using a Shared Ontology." *Proceedings of the 19th International Conference on Computer Processing of Oriental Languages (ICCPOL-2001)*, Korea University, Seoul, Korea, pp. 141–147.

Paik, Kyonghee and Francis Bond (2002). "Generation of Chinese Numeral Classifiers Using Semantic Classes." *Proceedings of the 8th Annual Meeting of the Association for Natural Language Processing*, Keihanna, Japan, pp. 635–638.

Pancardo-Rodríguez, Aarón, Manuel Montes-y-Gómez, Luis Villaseñor-Pineda, and Paolo Rosso (2005). "A Mapping between Classifiers and Training Conditions for WSD." *Proceedings of the 6th International Conference on Intelligent Text Processing and Computational Linguistics (CICLing-2005)*, Mexico City, Mexico, pp. 240–243.

Sakkis, Georgios, Ion Androutsopoulos, Georgios Paliouras, Vangelis Karkaletsis, Constantine D. Spyropoulos, and Panagiotis Stamatopoulos (2001). "Stacking Classifiers for Anti-spam Filtering of E-mail." *Proceedings of the 2001 Conference on Empirical Methods in Natural Language Processing (EMNLP-2001)*, Carnegie Mellon University, Pittsburgh, PA, USA.

Wiebe, Janyce and Ellen Riloff (2005). "Creating Subjective and Objective Sentence Classifiers from Unannotated Texts." *Proceedings of the 6th International Conference on Intelligent Text Processing and Computational Linguistics (CICLing-2005)*, Mexico City, Mexico, pp. 475–486.

Wu, Weilin, Ruzhan Lu, Feng Gao, and Yan Yuan (2005). "Combining Multiple Statistical Classifiers to Improve the Accuracy of Task Classification." *Proceedings of the 6th International Conference on Intelligent Text Processing and Computational Linguistics (CICLing-2005)*, Mexico City, Mexico, pp. 441–451.

Conjunction

Huang, Xiuming (1983). "Dealing with Conjunctions in a Machine Translation Environment." *Proceedings of the 1st Conference on European Chapter of the Association for Computational Linguistics*, Pisa, Italy, pp. 81–85.

Huang, Xiuming (1984). "Dealing with Conjunctions in a Machine Translation Environment." *Proceedings of the 10th International*

Conference on Computational Linguistics (*COLING-84*), Stanford University, Stanford, CA, USA, pp. 243–246.
Liu, Rey-Long 劉瑞瓏 and Von-Wun Soo 蘇豐文 (1989). "Parsing English Conjunctions and Comparatives Using the Wait-and-see Strategy." *Proceedings of the Conference of the Association for Computational Linguistics and Chinese Language Processing* (*ROCLING-II*), Taipei, Taiwan.

Measure Word

Zhu, Xuefeng 朱學鋒 and Wang Hui 王惠 (1996). 〈現代漢語量詞與名詞的子類劃分〉 (Sub-categorization of Contemporary Chinese Measure-words and Nouns). In Yu Shiwen 俞士汶 and Zhu Xuefeng 朱學鋒, eds., 《計算語言學文集》 (*Papers on Computational Linguistics*). Beijing: Department of Computer Science and Technology and Institute of Computational Linguistics, Peking University, pp. 61–69.

Noun

Calvo, Hiram and Alexander F. Gelbukh (2004). "Extracting Semantic Categories of Nouns for Syntactic Disambiguation from Human-oriented Explanatory Dictionaries." *Proceedings of the 5th International Conference on Intelligent Text Processing and Computational Linguistics* (*CICLing-2004*), Chung-Ang University, Seoul, Korea, pp. 254–257.
Caraballo, Sharon A. and Eugene Charniak (1999). "Determining the Specificity of Nouns from Text." *Proceedings of the Joint SIGDAT Conference on Empirical Methods in NLP and Very Large Corpora* (*EMNLP/VLC-99*), University of Maryland, College Park, MD, USA.
Miller, George A. and Florentina Hristea (2006). "WordNet Nouns: Classes and Instances." *Computational Linguistics*, Vol. 32, No. 1, pp. 1–3.
Rosario, Barbara and Marti Hearst (2001). "Classifying the Semantic Relations in Noun Compounds via a Domain-specific Lexical Hierarchy." *Proceedings of the 2001 Conference on Empirical Methods in Natural Language Processing* (*EMNLP-2001*), Carnegie Mellon University, Pittsburgh, PA, USA.
Somers, Harold, Hideki Hirakawa, Seiji Miike, and Shinya Amano (1988).

"The Treatment of Complex English Nominalizations in Machine Translation." *Computers and Translation*, No. 3, pp. 3–21.

Abbreviation

Kit, Chunyu, Xiaoyue Liu, and Jonathan J. Webster (2006). "Abbreviation Recognition with MaxEnt Model." *Proceedings of the 7th International Conference on Intelligent Text Processing and Computational Linguistics* (*CICLing-2006*), Mexico City, Mexico.

Park, Youngja and Roy J. Byrd (2001). "Hybrid Text Mining for Finding Abbreviations and Their Definitions." *Proceedings of the 2001 Conference on Empirical Methods in Natural Language Processing* (*EMNLP-2001*), Carnegie Mellon University, Pittsburgh, PA, USA.

Sumita, Eiichiro and Fumiaki Sugaya (2006). "Using the Web to Disambiguate Acronyms." *Proceedings of the Human Language Technology Conference—Annual Meeting of the North American Chapter of the Association for Computational Linguistics* (*HLT-NAACL-2006*), New York, USA.

Proper Noun

Chen, Hsin-Hsi and Guo-Wei Bian (1997). "Proper Name Extraction from Web Pages for Finding People in Internet." *Proceedings of the International Conference on Research in Computational Linguistics* (*ROCLING-X*), Academia Sinica, Taipei, Taiwan.

Park, Bong-Rae, Young-Sook Hwang, and Hae-Chang Rim (1997). "Recognizing Korean Unknown Proper Nouns by Using Automatically Extracted Lexical Clues." *Proceedings of the International Conference on Research in Computational Linguistics* (*ROCLING-X*), Academia Sinica, Taipei, Taiwan.

Shia, Min-Shiang, Jiun-Hung Lin, Scott Yu, and Wen-Hsiang Lu (2005). "Improving Translation of Unknown Proper Names Using a Hybrid Web-based Translation Extraction Method." *Proceedings of the International Conference on Computational Linguistics and Speech Processing* (*ROCLING-XVII*), National Cheng Kung University, Tainan, Taiwan.

Wacholder, Nina and Yael Ravin (1997). "Disambiguation of Proper

Names in Text." *Proceedings of the 5th Conference on Applied Natural Language Processing*, Seattle, Washington, DC, USA.
Yoshimura, Yumiko, Satoshi Kinoshita, and Miwako Shimazu (1997). "Processing of Proper Nouns and Use of Estimated Subject Area for Web Page Translation." *Proceedings of the 7th International Conference on Theoretical and Methodological Issues in Machine Translation (TMI-97)*, St. John's College, Santa Fe, New Mexico, USA.

Preposition

Chui, Ka-Wai, Yia-ping Lin, Shuanfan Huang, and I-Peng Lin (1989). "NTUMT Strategy for Prepositional Phrase Attachment." *Proceedings of the Conference of the Association for Computational Linguistics and Chinese Language Processing (ROCLING-II)*, Taipei, Taiwan.
Costello, Fintan J. and John D. Kelleher (2006). "Spatial Prepositions in Context: The Semantics of 'Near' in the Presence of Distractor Objects." *Proceedings of the 11th Conference of the European Chapter of the Association for Computational Linguistics (EACL-2006)*, Trento, Italy.
Durand, Jacques (1993). "On the Translation of Prepositions in Multilingual MT." In Frank van Eynde, ed., *Linguistics Issues in Machine Translation*. London and New York: Pinter Publishers, pp. 138–159.
Harper, Kenneth E. (1964). "The Position of Prepositional Phrases in Russian." *Mechanical Translation*, Vol. 8, No. 1, pp. 5–10.
Hartrumpf, Sven (1999). "Hybrid Disambiguation of Prepositional Phrase Attachment and Interpretation." *Proceedings of the Joint SIGDAT Conference on Empirical Methods in NLP and Very Large Corpora (EMNLP/VLC-99)*, University of Maryland, College Park, MD, USA.
Hartrumpf, Sven, Hermann Helbig, and Rainer Osswald (2006). "Semantic Interpretation of Prepositions for NLP Applications." *Proceedings of the 11th Conference of the European Chapter of the Association for Computational Linguistics (EACL-2006)*, Trento, Italy.
Lassen, Tine (2006). "An Ontology Based View on Prepositional Senses." *Proceedings of the 11th Conference of the European Chapter of the Association for Computational Linguistics (EACL-2006)*, Trento, Italy.

Litkowski, Kenneth C. and Orin Hargraves (2006). "Coverage and Inheritance in the Preposition Project." *Proceedings of the 11th Conference of the European Chapter of the Association for Computational Linguistics* (*EACL-2006*), Trento, Italy.

Liu, Yongquan 劉湧泉 and Jiang Yiping 姜一平 (1984).〈機器翻譯與介詞研究〉(Machine Translation and the Study of Prepositions). In Liu Yongquan *et al.*《中國的機器翻譯》(*Machine Translation in China*). Shanghai: Knowledge Press, pp. 15–24.

Merio, Paola and Eva Esteve Ferrer (2006). "The Notion of Argument in Prepositional Phrase Attachment." *Computational Linguistics*, Vol. 32, No. 3, pp. 341–378.

Pantel, Patrick and Dekang Lin (2000). "An Unsupervised Approach to Prepositional Phrase Attachment Using Contextually Similar Words." *Proceedings of the 38th Annual Meeting of the Association for Computational Linguistics* (*ACL-2000*), Hong Kong.

Schwartz, Lee, Takako Aikawa, and Chris Quirk (2003). "Disambiguation of English PP-Attachment Using Multilingual Aligned Data." *Proceedings of MT Summit IX*, New Orleans, Louisiana, USA.

Trujillo, Arturo (1992). "Locations in the Machine Translation of Prepositional Phrases." *Proceedings of the 4th International Conference on Theoretical and Methodological Issues in Machine Translation of Natural Languages: Empiricist vs. Rationalist Methods in MT* (*TMI-92*), Montreal, Quebec, Canada, pp. 13–20.

Trujillo, Arturo (1995). "Towards a Cross-linguistically Valid Classification of Spatial Prepositions." *Machine Translation*, Vol. 10, Nos. 1–2, pp. 93–141.

White, James H. (1964). "The Methodology of Sememic Analysis with Special Application to the English Preposition." *Mechanical Translation*, Vol. 8, No. 1, pp. 15–31.

Wu, Shih-Hung and Su Chen-Yu (2006). "An Evaluation of Adopting Language Model as the Checker of Preposition Usage." *Proceedings of the Conference of the Association for Computational Linguistics and Chinese Language Processing* (*ROCLING XVIII*), Taipei, Taiwan.

Zarechnak, Michael (1961). "Nesting within the Prepositional Structure." In Harold P. Edmundson, ed., *Proceedings of the National Symposium on Machine Translation*. London: Prentice-Hall, pp. 267–279.

Pronoun

Bergsma, Shane and Dekang Lin (2006). "Bootstrapping Path-based Pronoun Resolution." *Proceedings of the Joint Conference of the International Committee on Computational Linguistics and the Association for Computational Linguistics* (*COLING/ACL-2006*), Sydney, Australia.

Bolshakov, Igor A. (2001). "Treatment of Personal Pronouns Based on Their Parameterization." *Proceedings of the 2nd International Conference on Intelligent Text Processing and Computational Linguistics* (*CICLing-2001*), Mexico City, Mexico.

Gegg-Harrison, Whitney and Donna K. Byron (2006). "PYCOT: An Optimality Theory-based Pronoun Resolution Toolkit." *Proceedings of the 5th International Conference on Language Resources and Evaluation* (*LREC-2006*), Genoa, Italy.

Jordan, Pamela W. and Marilyn Walker (2000). "Learning Attribute Selections for Non-pronominal Expressions." *Proceedings of the 38th Annual Meeting of the Association for Computational Linguistics* (*ACL-2000*), Hong Kong.

Kehler, Andrew, Douglas Appelt, Lara Taylor, and Aleksandr Simma (2004). "Competitive Self-trained Pronoun Interpretation." *Proceedings of the Human Language Technology Conference/North American Chapter of the Association for Computational Linguistics Annual Meeting* (*HLT/NAACL-2004*), Boston, MA, USA.

Kehler, Andrew, Douglas Appelt, Lara Taylor, and Aleksandr Simma (2004). "The (Non)Utility of Predicate-argument Frequencies for Pronoun Interpretation." *Proceedings of the Human Language Technology Conference/North American Chapter of the Association for Computational Linguistics Annual Meeting* (*HLT/NAACL-2004*), Boston, MA, USA.

Nakaiwa, Hiromi and Satoru Ikehara (1995). "Intrasentential Resolution of Japanese Zero Pronouns in a Machine Translation System Using Semantic and Pragmatic Constraints." *Proceedings of the 6th International Conference on Theoretical and Methodological Issues in Machine Translation* (*TMI-95*), the University of Leuven, Belgium.

Nariyama, Shigeko, Eric Nichols, Francis Bond, Takaaki Tanaka, and Hiromi Nakaiwa (2005). " Extracting Representative Arguments from Dictionaries for Resolving Zero Pronouns." *Proceedings of MT Summit X*, Phuket, Thailand.

van den Eynde, Karel, Erik Broeders, Carmen Eggermont, and Ludo Vangilbergen (1988–1989). "The Pronominal Approach in NLP: A Pronominal Feature Analysis of Coordination in French." *Computers and Translation*, Vol. 3, Nos. 3–4, pp. 177–213.

Wang, Houfeng and Mei Zheng (2004). "An Empirical Study on Pronoun Resolution in Chinese." *Proceedings of the 5th International Conference on Intelligent Text Processing and Computational Linguistics* (*CICLing-2004*), Chung-Ang University, Seoul, Korea, pp. 210–213.

Yang, Xiaofeng, Su Jian, Zhou Guodong, and Chew-lim Tan (2004). "Improving Pronoun Resolution by Incorporating Coreferential Information of Candidates." *Proceedings of the 42nd Annual Meeting of the Association for Computational Linguistics* (*ACL-2004*), Barcelona, Spain, pp. 127–134.

Yang, Xiaofeng, Su Jian, and Chew Lim Tan (2005). "Improving Pronoun Resolution Using Statistics-based Semantic Compatibility Information." *Proceedings of the 43rd Annual Meeting of the Association of Computational Linguistics* (*ACL-2005*), Ann Arbor, Michigan, USA.

Yang, Xiaofeng, Jian Su, and Chew Lim Tan (2006). "Kernel-based Pronoun Resolution with Structured Syntactic Knowledge." *Proceedings of the Joint Conference of the International Committee on Computational Linguistics and the Association for Computational Linguistics* (*COLING/ACL-2006*), Sydney, Australia.

Anaphora

Azzam, Saliha (1995). "An Algorithm to Coordinate Anaphora Resolution and PPS Disambiguation Process." *Proceedings of the 7th Conference of the European Chapter of the Association for Computational Linguistics*, Dublin, Ireland, pp. 284–285.

Barbu, Catalina and Ruslan Mitkov (2000). "Evaluation Environment for Anaphora Resolution." *Proceedings of the International Conference on Machine Translation and Multilingual Applications in the New Millenium* (*MT-2000*), University of Exeter, England.

Chan, Samuel W. K. and Benjamin K. Y. T'sou (1999). "Semantic Inference for Anaphora Resolution: Toward a Framework in Machine Translation." *Machine Translation*, Vol. 14, Nos. 3–4, pp. 163–190.

Connolly, Dennis, John D. Burger, and David S. Day (1994). "A Machine Learning Approach to Anaphoric Reference." *Proceedings of the International Conference on New Methods in Language Processing, (NeMLaP-94)*, Manchester, England, pp. 255–261.

Cui, Yuzhen, Qinan Hu, Haihua Pan, and Jianhua Hu (2006). "Zero Anaphora Resolution in Chinese Discourse." *Proceedings of the 7th International Conference on Intelligent Text Processing and Computational Linguistics (CICLing-2006)*, Mexico City, Mexico.

Delmonte, Rodolfo, Antonella Bristot, Marco Aldo Piccolino Boniforti, and Sara Tonelli (2006). "Another Evaluation of Anaphora Resolution Algorithms and a Comparison with GETARUNS' Knowledge Rich Approach." *Proceedings of the 11th Conference of the European Chapter of the Association for Computational Linguistics (EACL-2006)*, Trento, Italy.

Ferrández, Antonio, Manuel Palomar, and Lidia Moreno (1999). "An Empirical Approach to Spanish Anaphora Resolution." *Machine Translation*, Vol. 19, Nos. 3–4, pp. 191–216.

Geldbach, Stefanie (1999). "Anaphora and Translation Discrepancies in Russian-German MT." *Machine Translation*, Vol. 19, Nos. 3–4, pp. 217–230.

Iida, Ryu, Kentaro Inui, and Yuji Matsumoto (2006). "Exploiting Syntactic Patterns as Clues in Zero-anaphora Resolution." *Proceedings of the Joint Conference of the International Committee on Computational Linguistics and the Association for Computational Linguistics (COLING/ACL-2006)*, Sydney, Australia.

Lappin, Shalom and Michael C. McCord (1990). "Anaphora Resolution in Slot Grammar." *Computational Linguistics*, Vol. 16, pp. 197–212.

Liang, Tyne and Dian-Song Wu (2003). "Automatic Pronominal Anaphora Resolution in English Texts." *Proceedings of the International Conference on Research in Computational Linguistics (ROCLING-XV)*, Hsin-Chu, Taiwan.

Lin, Yu-Hsiang and Tyne Liang (2004). "Pronominal and Sortal Anaphora Resolution for Biomedical Literature." *Proceedings of the International Conference on Research in Computational Linguistics (ROCLING-XVI)*, Taipei, Taiwan.

Matulevich, Tamara (2001). "The Referring Expressions in the Other's Comment." *Proceedings of the 2nd International Conference on*

Intelligent Text Processing and Computational Linguistics (*CICLing-2001*), Mexico City, Mexico.

Mitamura, Teruko, Eric H. Nyberg, Enrique Torrejon, Dave Svoboda, Annelen Brunner, and Kathryn Baker (2002). "Pronominal Anaphora Resolution in the KANTOO Multilingual Machine Translation System." *Proceedings of the 9th International Conference on Theoretical and Methodological Issues in Machine Translation* (*TMI-2002*), Keihanna, Japan, pp. 115–124.

Mitkov, Ruslan, Choi Sung-Kwon, and Randall Sharp (1995). "Anaphora Resolution in Machine Translation." *Proceedings of the 6th International Conference on Theoretical and Methodological Issues in Machine Translation* (*TMI-95*), Leuven, Belgium, pp. 87–95.

Mitkov, Ruslan (1996). "Anaphora and Machine Translation." *Machine Translation Review*, No. 4, pp. 6–16.

Mitkov, Ruslan and Lamia Belguith (1998). "Multilingual Robust Anaphora Resolution." *Proceedings of the 3rd Conference on Empirical Methods in Natural Language Processing*, Granada, Spain.

Mitkov, Ruslan (1999). "Introduction: Special Issue on Anaphora Resolution in Machine Translation and Multilingual NLP." *Machine Translation*, Vol. 14, Nos. 3–4, pp. 159–161.

Mitkov, Ruslan (1999). "Multilingual Anaphora Resolution." *Machine Translation*, Vol. 19, Nos. 3–4, pp. 281–299.

Mitkov, Ruslan (2001). "Outstanding Issues in Anaphora Resolution." *Proceedings of the 2nd International Conference on Intelligent Text Processing and Computational Linguistics* (*CICLing-2001*), Mexico City, Mexico.

Mitkov, Ruslan (2002). "Evaluation Issue in Anaphora Resolution and Beyond." *Proceedings of the 3rd International Conference on Intelligent Text Processing and Computational Linguistics* (*CICLing-2002*), Mexico City, Mexico.

Mitkov, Ruslan, Richard Evans, and Constantin Orasan (2002). "MARS and the Limits of Anaphora Resolution: Which Are the Ways Forward?" *Proceedings of the 3rd International Conference on Intelligent Text Processing and Computational Linguistics* (*CICLing-2002*), Mexico City, Mexico.

Ng, Vicent (2004). "Learning Noun Phrase Anaphoricity to Improve Coreference Resolution: Issues in Representation and Optimization." *Proceedings of the 42nd Annual Meeting of the Association for*

Computational Linguistics (*ACL-2004*), Barcelona, Spain, pp. 151–158.

Noeda, Saiz Maximiliano, Manual Palomar, and David L. Farwell (2000). "NLP System Oriented to Anaphora Resolution." *Proceedings of the International Conference on Machine Translation and Multilingual Applications in the New Millenium* (*MT-2000*), University of Exeter, England.

Nøklestad, Anders, Øystein Reigem, and Christer Johansson (2006). "Developing a Re-usable Web-demonstrator for Automatic Anaphora Resolution with Support for Manual Editing of Coreference Chains." *Proceedings of the 5th International Conference on Language Resources and Evaluation* (*LREC-2006*), Genoa, Italy.

Peral, Jesús and Antonio Ferrández (2002). "Pronominal Anaphora Generation in an English-Spanish MT Approach." *Proceedings of the 3rd International Conference on Intelligent Text Processing and Computational Linguistics* (*CICLing-2002*), Mexico City, Mexico.

Rich, Elaine and Susann Luperfoy (1988). "An Architecture for Anaphora Resolution." *Proceedings of the 2nd Conference on Applied Natural Language Processing*, Austin, Texas, USA.

Roger, Sandra (2001). "Belief Revision on Anaphora Resolution." *Proceedings of the 2nd International Conference on Intelligent Text Processing and Computational Linguistics* (*CICLing-2001*), Mexico City, Mexico.

Root, Rebecca (1986). "Semantics, Translation, and Anaphora." *Machine Translation*, Vol. 1, No. 2, pp. 93–108.

Saggion, Horacio and Ariadne Carvalho (1994). "Anaphora Resolution in a Machine Translation System." *Machine Translation—Ten Years On: Proceedings of the 2nd International Conference Organised by Cranfield University*, Cranfield, England.

Steinberger, Josef, Mijail Kabadjov, Massimo Poesio, and Olivia Sanchez-Graillet (2005). "Improving LSA-based Summarization with Anaphora Resolution." *Proceedings of Human Language Technology Conference and Conference on Empirical Methods in Natural Language Processing* (*HLT/EMNLP-2005*), Vancouver, BC, Canada.

Tanev, Hristo and Ruslan Mitkov (2000). "LINGUA: A Robust Architecture for Text Processing and Anaphora Resolution in Bulgarian." *Proceedings of the International Conference on Machine*

Translation and Multilingual Applications in the New Millenium (MT-2000), University of Exeter, England.
Werner, P. and Sergei Nirenburg (1988). "A Specification Language That Supports the Realization of Intersentential Anaphora." *Proceedings of the AAAI Workshop on Natural Language Generation*, Saint Paul, Minnesota, USA.
Yeh, Ching-Long and Yi-Jun Chen (2001). "An Empirical Study of Zero Anaphora Resolution in Chinese Based on Centering Model." *Proceedings of the International Conference on Research in Computational Linguistics (ROCLING-XIV)*, National Chengkung University, Tainan, Taiwan.

Reference

Arnold, Doug and Louisa Sadler (1992). "Rationalism and the Treatment of Referential Dependencies." *Proceedings of the 4th International Conference on Theoretical and Methodological Issues in Machine Translation of Natural Languages: Empiricist vs. Rationalist Methods in MT (TMI-92)*, Montreal, Quebec, Canada, pp. 195–204.
Byron, Donna K. (2002). "Resolving Pronominal Reference to Abstract Entities." *Proceedings of the 42nd Annual Meeting of the Association for Computational Linguistics (ACL-2004)*, Barcelona, Spain, pp. 80–87.
Chai, Joyce Y., Zahar Prasov, and Hong Pengyu (2004). "Performance Evaluation and Error Analysis for Multimodal Reference Resolution in a Conversation System." *Proceedings of the Human Language Technology Conference/North American Chapter of the Association for Computational Linguistics Annual Meeting (HLT/NAACL-2004)*, Boston, MA, USA.
Harabagiu, Sanda M. and Steven J. Maiorano (2000). "Multilingual Coreference Resolution." *Proceedings of the 6th Applied Natural Language Processing Conference*, Seattle, Washington, DC, USA, pp. 142–149.
Heng, Ji, David Westbrook, and Ralph Grishman (2005). "Using Semantic Relations to Refine Coreference Decisions." *Proceedings of Human Language Technology Conference and Conference on Empirical Methods in Natural Language Processing (HLT/EMNLP-2005)*, Vancouver, BC, Canada.

Eisenstein, Jacob and Randall Davis (2006). "Gesture Improves Coreference Resolution." *Proceedings of the Human Language Technology Conference—Annual Meeting of the North American Chapter of the Association for Computational Linguistics* (*HLT-NAACL-2006*), New York, USA.

Luo, Xiaoqiang, Abe Ittycheriah, Jing Hongyan, Nanda Kambhatla, and Salim Roukos (2004). "A Mention-synchronous Coreference Resolution Algorithm Based on the Bell Tree." *Proceedings of the 42nd Annual Meeting of the Association for Computational Linguistics* (*ACL-2004*), Barcelona, Spain, pp. 135–142.

Luo, Xiaoqiang and Imed Zitouni (2005). "Multi-lingual Coreference Resolution with Syntactic Features." *Proceedings of Human Language Technology Conference and Conference on Empirical Methods in Natural Language Processing* (*HLT/EMNLP-2005*), Vancouver, BC, Canada.

Luo, Xiaoqiang (2005). "On Coreference Resolution Performance Metrics." *Proceedings of Human Language Technology Conference and Conference on Empirical Methods in Natural Language Processing* (*HLT/EMNLP-2005*), Vancouver, BC, Canada.

Morton, Thomas S. (2000). "Coreference for NLP Applications." *Proceedings of the 38th Annual Meeting of the Association for Computational Linguistics* (*ACL-2000*), Hong Kong.

Muñoz, Rafael, Maximiliano Saiz-Noeda, Armando Suárez, and Manual Palomar (2000). "Semantic Approach to Bridging Reference Resolution." *Proceedings of the International Conference on Machine Translation and Multilingual Applications in the New Millenium* (*MT-2000*), University of Exeter, England.

Ng, Vincent and Claire Cardie (2002). "Combining Sample Selection and Error-driven Pruning for Machine Learning of Coreference Rules." *Proceedings of the 2002 Conference on Empirical Methods in Natural Language Processing* (*EMNLP-2002*), University of Pennsylvania, Philadelphia, PA, USA.

Poesio, Massimo, Rahul Mehta, Axel Maroudas, and Janet Hitzeman (2004). "Learning to Resolve Bridging References." *Proceedings of the 42nd Annual Meeting of the Association for Computational Linguistics* (*ACL-2004*), Barcelona, Spain, pp. 143–150.

Ponzetto, Simone Paolo and Michael Strube (2006). "Exploiting Semantic Role Labeling, WordNet and Wikipedia for Coreference Resolution."

Proceedings of the Human Language Technology Conference—Annual Meeting of the North American Chapter of the Association for Computational Linguistics (*HLT-NAACL-2006*), New York, USA.

Postolache, Oana, Ivana Kruijff-Korbayova, and Geert-Jan Kruijff (2005). "Data-driven Approaches for Information Structure Identification." *Proceedings of Human Language Technology Conference and Conference on Empirical Methods in Natural Language Processing* (*HLT/EMNLP-2005*), Vancouver, BC, Canada.

Schauer, Holger (2000). "Using Coreferences for Coherence Relations." *Proceedings of the 38th Annual Meeting of the Association for Computational Linguistics* (*ACL-2000*), Hong Kong.

Strube, Michael, Stefan Rapp, and Christoph Müller (2002). "The Influence of Minimum Edit Distance on Reference Resolution." *Proceedings of the 2002 Conference on Empirical Methods in Natural Language Processing* (*EMNLP-2002*), University of Pennsylvania, Philadelphia, PA, USA.

van Deemter, Kees (2006). "Generating Referring Expressions That Involve Gradable Properties." *Computational Linguistics*, Vol. 32, No. 2, pp. 195–222.

Zelinsky-Wibbelt, Cornelia (1991). "Token Reference vs. Type Reference: Implications for Machine Translation." *Machine Translation*, Vol. 6, No. 3, pp. 183–192.

Verb

Akiba, Yasuhiro, Megumi Ishii, Hussein Almuallim, and Shigeo Kaneda (1995). "Learning English Verb Selection Rules from Hand-made Rules and Translation Examples." *Proceedings of the 6th International Conference on Theoretical and Methodological Issues in Machine Translation* (*TMI-95*), the University of Leuven, Belgium.

Batori, Istvan S. (1969). "Disambiguating Verbs with Multiple Meaning in the MT-system of IBM Germany." *ITL*, No. 5, pp. 5–16.

Bennett, Winfield S., Tanya Herlick, Katherine Hoyt, Joseph Liro, and Ana Santisteban (1989). "Toward a Computational Model of Aspect and Verb Semantics." *Machine Translation*, Vol. 4, No. 4, pp. 247–280.

Bojar, Ondřej and Jan Hajič (2005). "Extracting Translation Verb Frames." In Walther van Hahn, W. John Hutchins, and Cristina

Vertan, eds., *Proceedings of the International Workshop on Modern Approaches in Translation Technologies*, Borovets, Bulgaria.

Chakrabarti, Debasri and Pushpak Bhattacharya (2004). "An Investigation in Verb Knowledge Base Creation." *Proceedings of the International Conference on Natural Language Processing (ICON-2004)*, International Institute of Information Technology, Hyderabad, India.

Chatman, Seymour (1962). "The Classification of English Verbs by Object Types." In National Physical Laboratory, ed., *1961 International Conference on Machine Translation of Languages and Applied Language Analysis: Proceedings of the Conference Held at the National Physical Laboratory, Teddington, Middlesex, on 5th, 6th, 7th and 8th September*. London: Her Majesty's Stationery Office, Vol. 1, pp. 84–94.

Chen, Jinying and Martha Palmer (2004). "Chinese Verb Sense Discrimination Using an EM Clustering Model with Rich Linguistic Features." *Proceedings of the 42nd Annual Meeting of the Association for Computational Linguistics (ACL-2004)*, Barcelona, Spain, pp. 295–302.

Ferres, Leo (2001). "Modeling the Level of Involvement of Verbal Arguments." *Proceedings of the 2nd International Conference on Intelligent Text Processing and Computational Linguistics (CICLing-2001)*, Mexico City, Mexico.

Gomez, Fernando (2004). "Building Verb Predicates: A Computational View." *Proceedings of the 42nd Annual Meeting of the Association for Computational Linguistics (ACL-2004)*, Barcelona, Spain, pp. 359–366.

Lin, Fu-Wen 林甫雯 (1989). "The Verb-Complement (V-R) Compounds in Mandarin Chinese." *Proceedings of the Conference of the Association for Computational Linguistics and Chinese Language Processing (ROCLING-II)*, Taipei, Taiwan.

Liu, Mei-Chun, Chu-Ren Huang, and Jia-Ying Lee (1999). "Semantic Representation of Verbal Information—A Case from Mandarin Verbs of Judging." *Proceedings of the International Conference on Research in Computational Linguistics (ROCLING-XII)*, Taipei, Taiwan.

Meza, Ivan V. and Luis A. Pineda (2002). "The Spanish Auxiliary Verb System in HPSG." *Proceedings of the 3rd International Conference on Intelligent Text Processing and Computational Linguistics (CICLing-2002)*, Mexico City, Mexico.

Mukerjee, Amitabha, Pradeepsinh B Vaghela, and V. Shreeniwas (2004). "Pre-linguistic Verb Acquisition from Repeated Language Exposure for Visual Events." *Proceedings of the International Conference on Natural Language Processing* (*ICON-2004*), International Institute of Information Technology, Hyderabad, India.

Neumann, Christoph (1999). "Towards an Interlingual Treatment of Modality." *Proceedings of MT Summit VII: MT in the Great Translation Era*, Singapore.

Palmer, Martha (1990). "Customizing Verb Definitions for Specific Semantic Domains." *Machine Translation*, Vol. 5, No. 1, pp. 5–30.

Palmer, Martha and Joseph Rosenzweig (1996). "Capturing Motion Verb Generalizations in Synchronous Tree Adjoining Grammars." *Proceedings of the 2nd Conference of the Association for Machine Translation in the Americas: Expanding MT Horizons* (*AMTA-2*), Montreal, Quebec, Canada, pp. 76–85.

Pardo, Thiago Alexandre Salgueiro, Daniel Marcu, and Maria das Graças Volpe Nunes (2006). "Unsupervised Learning of Verb Argument Structures." *Proceedings of the 7th International Conference on Intelligent Text Processing and Computational Linguistics* (*CICLing-2006*), Mexico City, Mexico.

Pedersen, Bolette Sandford (1999). "Systematic Verb Polysemy in MT: A Study of Danish Motion Verbs with Comparisons with Spanish." *Machine Translation*, Vol. 14, No. 1, pp. 35–82.

Pekar, Viktor (2006). "Acquisition of Verb Entailment from Text." *Proceedings of the Human Language Technology Conference—Annual Meeting of the North American Chapter of the Association for Computational Linguistics* (*HLT-NAACL-2006*), New York, USA.

Rapoport, T. R. (1990). "Secondary Predication and the Lexical Representation of Verbs." *Machine Translation*, Vol. 5, No. 1, pp. 31–56.

Schulte, Sabine, I. Walde, and Alissa Melinger (2005). "Identifying Semantic Relations and Functional Properties of Human Verb Associations." *Proceedings of Human Language Technology Conference and Conference on Empirical Methods in Natural Language Processing* (*HLT/EMNLP-2005*), Vancouver, BC, Canada.

Tan, Yee Fan, Min-Yen Kan, and Hang Cui (2006). "Extending Corpus-based Identification of Light Verb Constructions Using a Supervised Learning Framework." *Proceedings of the 11th Conference of the*

European Chapter of the Association for Computational Linguistics (*EACL-2006*), Trento, Italy.

Wadensjö, Birgit Apfelbaum-Cecilia (1997). "How Does a Verbmobil Affect Conversation? Discourse Analysis and Machine-supported Translatory Interaction." In Christa Hauenschild and Susanne Heizmann, eds., *Machine Translation and Translation Theory*. Berlin-New York: Mouton de Gruyter, pp. 93–122.

Yan, Wei 顏偉 and Kang Shiyong 亢世勇 (2002).〈基於語料庫的現代漢語新詞語動詞語法特徵的研究〉(A Study of the New Verbs of Contemporary Chinese Based on Corpora).《第一屆學生計算語言學研討會論文集》(*SWCL-2002: First Students' Workshop on Computational Linguistics: Proceedings*), Institute of Computational Linguistics, Peking University, Beijing, China, pp. 281–285.

Yeh, Ching-Long and Hsi-Jian Lee (1992). "A Lexicon-driven Analysis of Chinese Serial Verb Constructions." *Proceedings of the Conference of the Association for Computational Linguistics and Chinese Language Processing* (*ROCLING-V*), National Taiwan University, Taipei, Taiwan.

Valency

Bond, Francis and Timothy Baldwin (1999). "A Valency Dictionary Architecture for Machine Translation." *Proceedings of the 8th International Conference on Theoretical and Methodological Issues in Machine Translation* (*TMI-99*), Chester, England, pp. 207–217.

Bond, Francis and Timothy Baldwin (1999). "Construction of an Alternation-based English Valency Dictionary." *Proceedings of the 5th Annual Meeting of the Association for Natural Language Processing* (*NLP-99*), pp. 197–200.

Bond, Francis, Timothy Baldwin, and Sanae Fujita (2002). "Detecting Alternation Instances in a Valency Dictionary." *Proceedings of the 8th Annual Meeting of the Ássociation for Natural Language Processing* (*NLP-2002*), pp. 519–22.

Bond, Francis and Sanae Fujita (2003). "Evaluation of a Method of Creating New Valency Entries Alternations." *Proceedings of MT Summit IX*, New Orleans, Louisiana, USA.

Carroll, Glenn and Mats Rooth (1998). "Valence Induction with a Head-lexicalized PCFG." *Proceedings of the 3rd Conference on Empirical Methods in Natural Language Processing*, Granada, Spain.

Fu, Aiping 傅愛平 (1997).〈英漢機器翻譯中的源語配價分析〉(Source Language Valency Analysis in English-Chinese Machine Translation).《語言文字應用》(*Applied Linguistics*), No. 3, pp. 94–100.

Fujita, Sanae and Francis Bond (2002). "A Method of Adding New Entries to a Valency Dictionary by Exploiting Existing Lexical Resources." *Proceedings of the 9th International Conference on Theoretical and Methodological Issues in Machine Translation* (*TMI-2002*), Keihanna, Japan, pp. 42–52.

Fujita, Sanae and Francis Bond (2002). "Extending the Coverage of a Valency Dictionary." *Proceedings of the Workshop on Machine Translation in Asia* (*COLING-2002*), Taipei, Taiwan.

Gebruers, Rudi (1988). "Valency and MT: Recent Developments in the METAL System." *Proceedings of the 2nd Conference on Applied Natural Language Processing*, Austin, Texas, USA, pp. 168–175.

Somers, Harold L. (1987). *Valency and Case in Computational Linguistics*. Edinburgh: Edinburgh University Press.

Zhan, Weidong 詹衛東 (2000).〈一個漢語語義知識表達框架：廣義配價模式〉(A Framework of Chinese Semantic Representation: Generalized Valence Mode). In Yu Shiwen 俞士汶 and Zhu Xuefeng 朱學鋒, eds.,《計算語言學文集》(*Papers on Computational Linguistics*), Vol. 4. Beijing: Department of Computer Science and Technology and Institute of Computational Linguistics, Peking University, pp. 177–183.

❖ PART 28 ❖

Profiles

Artsrouni, Georges

Hutchins, W. John (2004). "Two Precursors of Machine Translation: Artsrouni and Trojanskij." *International Journal of Translation*, Vol. 16, No. 1, pp. 11–31.

Bar-Hillel, Yehoshua

Hutchins, W. John (2000). "Yehoshua Bar-Hillel: A Philosopher's Contribution to Machine Translation." In W. John Hutchins, ed., *Early Years in Machine Translation: Memoirs and Biographies of Pioneers*. Amsterdam and Philadelphia: John Benjamins Publishing Company, pp. 299–312.

Kasher, Asa, ed. (1976). *Language in Focus: Foundations, Methods and Systems: Essays in Memory of Yehoshua Bar-Hillel*. Dordrecht: Reidel.

Koppel, Moshe and Eli Shamir, eds. (1996). *Proceedings of the 4th Bar-Ilan Symposium on the Foundations of Artificial Intelligence*, Ramat Gan, Israel. Menlo Park: American Association for Artificial Intelligence.

Macklovitch, Elliott (1996). "The Future of MT Is Now and Bar-Hillel Was (Almost Entirely) Right." In Moshe Koppel and Eli Shamir, eds., *Proceedings of the 4th Bar-Ilan Symposium on the Foundations of Artificial Intelligence*, Ramat Gan, Israel. Menlo Park: American Association for Artificial Intelligence, pp. 137–148.

Nirenburg, Sergei (1996). "Bar-Hillel and Machine Translation: Then and Now." In Moshe Koppel and Eli Shamir, eds., *Proceedings of the 4th Bar-Ilan Symposium on the Foundations of Artificial Intelligence*, Ramat Gan, Israel. Menlo Park: American Association for Artificial Intelligence, pp. 300–305.

Ceccato, Silvio

von Glasersfeld, Ernst (2000). "Silvio Ceccato and the Correlational Grammar." In W. John Hutchins, ed., *Early Years in Machine Translation: Memoirs and Biographies of Pioneers*. Amsterdam and Philadelphia: John Benjamins Publishing Company, pp. 313–324.

Dostert, Leon

Austin, William M., ed. (1967). *Papers in Linguistics in Honor of Leon Dostert*. The Hague: Mouton Publishers.

Garvin, Paul L.

Montgomery, Christine A. (1994). "Obituary: Paul Lucian Garvin (1919–1994)." *MT News International*, Vol. 9, pp. 17–18.

Montgomery, Christine A. (2000). "Is FAHQ(M)T Impossible? Memories of Paul Garvin and Other MT Colleagues." In W. John Hutchins, ed., *Early Years in Machine Translation: Memoirs and Biographies of Pioneers*. Amsterdam and Philadelphia: John Benjamins Publishing Company, pp. 97–110.

Hays, David G.

Kay, Martin (2000). "David G. Hays." In W. John Hutchins, ed., *Early Years in Machine Translation: Memoirs and Biographies of Pioneers*. Amsterdam and Philadelphia: John Benjamins Publishing Company, pp. 165–170.

King, Gilbert W.

Hutchins, W. John (2000). "Gilbert W. King and the IBM-USAF Translator." In W. John Hutchins, ed., *Early Years in Machine Translation: Memoirs and Biographies of Pioneers*. Amsterdam and Philadelphia: John Benjamins Publishing Company, pp. 171–176.

Lehmann, Winfred P.

Lehmann, Winfred P. (2000). "My Early Years in Machine Translation." In W. John Hutchins, ed., *Early Years in Machine Translation: Memoirs and Biographies of Pioneers*. Amsterdam and Philadelphia: John Benjamins Publishing Company, pp. 147–164.

Liu, Zhongde 劉重德 (1984).〈美國勒曼談機器翻譯〉(Lehmann of the United States on Machine Translation).《翻譯漫談》(*Remarks on Translation*). Xi'an: Shaanxi People's Publishing House, pp. 163–174.

Ljudskanov, Alexander

Paskaleva, Elena (2000). "Alexander Ljudskanov." In W. John Hutchins, ed., *Early Years in Machine Translation: Memoirs and Biographies of Pioneers*. Amsterdam and Philadelphia: John Benjamins Publishing Company, pp. 361–376.

Masterman, Margaret

Wilks, Yorick (2000). "Margaret Masterman." In W. John Hutchins, ed., *Early Years in Machine Translation: Memoirs and Biographies of Pioneers*. Amsterdam and Philadelphia: John Benjamins Publishing Company, pp. 279–298.

Williams, William and Frank Knowles (1987). "Margaret Masterman: In Memoriam." *Computers and Translation*, Vol. 2, No. 4, pp. 197–203.

Pankowicz, Zbigniew L.

Scott, Bernard E. (1986). "Zbigniew L. Pankowicz: An Appreciation." *Machine Translation*, Vol. 1, No. 4, p. 273.

Reifler, Erwin

Micklesen, Lew R. (2000). "Erwin Reifler and Machine Translation at the University of Washington." In W. John Hutchins, ed., *Early Years in Machine Translation: Memoirs and Biographies of Pioneers*. Amsterdam and Philadelphia: John Benjamins Publishing Company, pp. 21–38.

Richens, R. H.

Jones, Karen Sparck (2000). "R. H. Richens: Translation in the Nude." In W. John Hutchins, ed., *Early Years in Machine Translation: Memoirs and Biographies of Pioneers*. Amsterdam and Philadelphia: John Benjamins Publishing Company, pp. 263–278.

Troyanskii, Petr Petrovich

Hutchins, John and Evgenii Lovtskii (2000). "Petr Petrovich Troyanskii

(1894–1950): A Forgotten Pioneer of Mechanical Translation." *Machine Translation*, Vol. 15, No. 3, pp. 187–221.
Hutchins, W. John (2004). "Two Precursors of Machine Translation: Artsrouni and Trojanskij." *International Journal of Translation*, Vol. 16, No. 1, pp. 11–31.

Vauqois, Bernard

Boitet, Christian (1988). "Bernard Vauqois' Contribution to the Theory and Practice of Building MT Systems: A Historical Perspective." *Proceedings of the 2nd International Conference on Theoretical and Methodological Issues in Machine Translation of Natural Languages (TMI-88)*, Carnegie Mellon University, Center for Machine Translation, Pittsburgh, Pennsylvania, USA.
Boitet, Christian (1990). "The Evolution of Ideas in Classical MT: B. Vauquois' Contribution to the Theory and Practice of MT (1960–1985)." *Proceedings of the Conference of the Association for Computational Linguistics and Chinese Language Processing (ROCLING-III)*, Taipei, Taiwan.

Wada, Hiroshi

Wada, Hiroshi (2000). "Memoirs of a Survivor." In W. John Hutchins, ed., *Early Years in Machine Translation: Memoirs and Biographies of Pioneers*. Amsterdam and Philadelphia: John Benjamins Publishing Company, pp. 377–386.

Weaver, Warren

Hutchins, W. John (2000). "Warren Weaver and the Launching of MT: Brief Biographical Note." In W. John Hutchins, ed., *Early Years in Machine Translation: Memoirs and Biographies of Pioneers*. Amsterdam and Philadelphia: John Benjamins Publishing Company, pp. 17–20.

❖ PART 29 ❖

Segmentation

Automatic Segmentation

Hou, Min 侯敏 and Sun Jianjun 孫建軍 (1996).〈漢語自動分詞中的歧義問題〉(Disambiguation in the Automatic Segmentation of the Chinese Language).《語言文字應用》(*Applied Linguistics*), No. 1, pp. 68–72.

Li, Xiaoming 李小明, Yi Lifu 易立夫, Yang Jing 楊靜, and Sun Jincheng 孫金城 (2002).〈一種新的針對漢語TTS的韻律詞自動切分方法〉(A New Automatic Segmentation Method of Prosodic Word for Chinese TTS).《第一屆學生計算語言學研討會論文集》(*SWCL-2002: First Students' Workshop on Computational Linguistics: Proceedings*), Institute of Computational Linguistics, Peking University, Beijing, China, pp. 329–333.

Nagao, Makoto, Jun-ichi Tsujii, A. Yamagami, and S. Tatebe (1978). "Japanese Dictionary in Computer, and an Automatic Segmentation of Japanese Sentences." *Journal of the Information Processing Society of Japan*, Vol. 19, No. 6.

Qu, Weiguang 曲維光 (2002).〈解決漢語自動分詞的方法選擇〉(The Selection of Methodology on Automatic Word Segmentation of Chinese).《第一屆學生計算語言學研討會論文集》(*SWCL-2002: First Students' Workshop on Computational Linguistics: Proceedings*), Institute of Computational Linguistics, Peking University, Beijing, China, p. 118.

Sun, Maosong 孫茂松 and Benjamin K. Y. T'sou 鄒嘉彥 (1995).〈漢語自動分詞研究中的若干理論問題〉(Several Theoretical Issues Relating to Automatic Segmentation of the Chinese Language).《語言文字應用》(*Applied Linguistics*), No. 4, pp. 40–46.

Sun, Maosong (2001).〈漢語自動分詞研究的若干最新進展〉(New Advances in the Study of Automatic Segmentation of the Chinese Language).《輝煌二十年──中國中文信息學會二十周年學術會議》(*Proceedings of Conference of the 20th Anniversary of CIPSC*). Beijing: Tsinghua University Press 清華大學出版社, pp. 20–40.

Morphological Segmentation

Riesa, Jason and David Yarowsky (2006). "Minimally Supervised Morphological Segmentation with Applications to Machine Translation." *Proceedings of the 7th Biennial Conference of the Association for Machine Translation in the Americas* (*AMTA-2006*):

Visions for the Future of Machine Translation, Boston Marriott, Cambridge, MA, USA.

Segmentation

Chen, Yuzhong 陳玉忠, Li Baoli 李保利, Yu Shiwen 俞士汶, and Lan Cuoji 蘭措吉 (2002).〈基於格助詞和接續特徵的藏文自動分詞方案〉(A Tibetan Segmentation Scheme Based on Case-auxiliary Word and Continuous Features).《第一屆學生計算語言學研討會論文集》(*SWCL-2002: First Students' Workshop on Computational Linguistics: Proceedings*), Institute of Computational Linguistics, Peking University, Beijing, China, pp. 98–105.

Dragsted, Barbara (2005). "Segmentation in Translation: Differences across Levels of Expertise and Difficulty." *Target*, Vol. 17, No. 1, pp. 49–70.

He, Yan 何燕 (2001).〈基於單字詞轉移概率的未登錄詞識別〉(Identification of Unlisted Words on Transitive Probability of Monosyllabic Words). In Huang Changning 黃昌寧 and Zhang Pu 張普, eds.,《自然語言理解與機器翻譯》(*Natural Language Understanding and Machine Translation*). Beijing: Tsinghua University Press, pp. 141–146.

Hearst, Marti A. (1994). "Multi-paragraph Segmentation of Expository Text." *Proceedings of the 32nd Annual Meeting of the Association for Computational Linguistics* (*ACL-94*), Las Cruces, New Mexico, USA, pp. 9–16.

Huang, Changning (1997).〈中文信息處理中的分詞問題〉(The Issue of Segmentation in Chinese Information Processing).《語言文字應用》(*Applied Linguistics*), No. 1, pp. 72–78.

Huang, Chu-ren, Chen Keh-jiann, and Chang Li-ping (1995). "Segmentation Standard for Chinese Natural Language Processing." *Proceedings of the 16th International Conference on Computational Linguistics*, Copenhagen, Denmark.

Kim, Sung-Dong, Byoung-Tak Zhang, and Yung Taek Kim (2001). "Learning-based Intrasentence Segmentation for Efficient Translation of Long Sentences." *Machine Translation*, Vol. 16, No. 3, pp. 151–174.

Lamb, Sydney M. (1961). "Segmentation." In Harold P. Edmundson, ed., *Proceedings of the National Symposium on Machine Translation*. Englewood Cliffs: Prentice-Hall, pp. 335–342.

Liu, Xiaoqin 劉小勤, Guo Bingyan 郭炳炎, and Liu Kaiying 劉開瑛 (1999).

〈基於規則剔除和統計的分詞詞表選詞方法〉(An Approach to Word Extraction for Segmentation Vocabulary Using Rule Elimination and Statistics). In Huang Changning 黃昌寧 and Dong Zhendong 董振東, eds.,《計算機語言學文集》(*Essays on Computational Linguistics*). Beijing: Tsinghua University Press, pp. 135–140.

Melamed, I. Dan (2001). "Automatic Discovery of Non-compositional Compounds." *Empirical Methods for Exploiting Parallel Texts*. Cambridge, MA: MIT Press, pp. 123–145.

Nie, Jian-Yun, Xiaobo Ren, and Martin Brisebois (1995). "A Unifying Approach to Segmentation of Chinese and Its Application to Text Retrieval." *Proceedings of the Conference of the Association for Computational Linguistics and Chinese Language Processing* (*ROCLING-VIII*), Yuan-Ze Institute of Technology, Chung-Li, Taiwan.

Rosenberg, Andrew and Julia Hirschberg (2006). "Story Segmentation of Broadcast News in English, Mandarin and Arabic." *Proceedings of the Human Language Technology Conference—Annual Meeting of the North American Chapter of the Association for Computational Linguistics* (*HLT-NAACL-2006*), New York, USA.

Salvetti, Franco and Nicolas Nicolov (2006). "Weblog Classification for Fast Splog Filtering: A URL Language Model Segmentation Approach." *Proceedings of the Human Language Technology Conference—Annual Meeting of the North American Chapter of the Association for Computational Linguistics* (*HLT-NAACL-2006*), New York, USA.

Shillan, David (1967). "Segmenting Natural Language by Articulatory Features." *Deuxieme Conference Internationale sur le Traitement Automatique des Langues*, Grenoble, France.

Stevenson, Mark and Robert Gaizauskas (2000). "Experiments on Sentence Boundary Detection." *Proceedings of the 6th Applied Natural Language Processing Conference*, Seattle, Washington, DC, USA, pp. 84–89.

Swen, Bing (2002). "A General Output Model of Hidden Markov Models and Its Applications to Chinese Segmentation and Tagging." In Yu Shiwen, ed., *Proceedings of the Second China-Japan Natural Language Processing Joint Research Promotion Conference* (*CJNLP-2002*). Beijing: Institute of Computational Linguistics, Peking University, pp. 236–246.

Wang, Fu Lee, Xiaotie Deng, and Feng Zou (2006). "Towards Unified Chinese Segmentation Algorithm." *Proceedings of the 5th*

International Conference on Language Resources and Evaluation (*LREC-2006*), Genoa, Italy.
Yoon, Juntae (2000). "Compound Noun Segmentation Based on Lexical Data Extracted from Corpus." *Proceedings of the 6th Applied Natural Language Processing Conference*, Seattle, Washington, DC, USA, pp. 196–203.
Yu, Shiwen, Zhu Xuefeng, and Duan Huiming (2000). 〈大規模現代漢語標注語料庫的加工規範〉 (Guidelines for Segmentation and Part-of-speech Tagging on Very Large Scale Corpus of Contemporary Chinese). In Yu Shiwen 俞士汶 and Zhu Xuefeng 朱學鋒, eds., 《計算語言學文集》 (*Papers on Computational Linguistics*), Vol. 4. Beijing: Department of Computer Science and Technology and Institute of Computational Linguistics, Peking University, pp. 125–132.
Zheng, Jiaheng 鄭家恒 and Wu Fangfang 吳芳芳 (1999). 〈多義型歧義字段切分研究〉 (Study on Segmentation of Ambiguous Phrase of Combination Type). In Huang Changning 黃昌寧 and Dong Zhendong 董振東, eds., 《計算機語言學文集》 (*Essays on Computational Linguistics*). Beijing: Tsinghua University Press, pp. 129–134.
Zhou, Guodong, Yang Lingpeng, Su Jian, and Ji Donghong (2005). "Mutual Information Independence Model Using Kernel Density Estimation for Segmenting and Labeling Sequential Data." *Proceedings of the 6th International Conference on Intelligent Text Processing and Computational Linguistics* (*CICLing-2005*), Mexico City, Mexico, pp. 153–164.
Zhou, Yun 周雲 and Huang Taiyi 黃泰翼 (2001). 〈基於決策樹方法的口語句子邊界切分〉 (Utterance Segmentation Based on Decision Tree Method). In Huang Changning 黃昌寧 and Zhang Pu 張普, eds., 《自然語言理解與機器翻譯》 (*Natural Language Understanding and Machine Translation*). Beijing: Tsinghua University Press, pp. 246–252.

Sentence Segmentation

Kim, Sung Dong and Byoung-Tak Zhang (2000). "Reducing Parsing Complexity by Intra-sentence Segmentation Based on Maximum Entropy Model." *Proceedings of the Joint Sigdat Conference on Empirical Methods in Natural Language Processing and Very Large Corpora* (*EMNLP/VLC-2000*), Hong Kong University of Science and Technology, Hong Kong.

Matusov, Evgeny, Gregor Leusch, Oliver Bender, and Hermann Ney (2005). "Evaluating Machine Translation Output with Automatic Sentence Segmentation." *Proceedings of the International Workshop on Spoken Language Translation* (*IWSLT-2005*), Pittsburgh, PA, USA.

Xu, Jia, Richard Zens, and Hermann Ney (2005). "Sentence Segmentation Using IBM Word Alignment Model 1." *Proceedings of the 10th Workshop of the European Association for Machine Translation: Practical Applications of Machine Translation*, Budapest, Hungary, pp. 280–287.

Statistical Segmentation

Ando, Rie Kubota and Lillian Lee (2000). "Mostly-unsupervised Statistical Segmentation of Japanese: Applications to Kanji." *Proceedings of the 1st Meeting of the North American Chapter of the Association for Computational Linguistics*, Seattle, Washington, DC, USA, pp. 241–248.

Text Segmentation

Beeferman, D., Adam L. Berger, and John D. Lafferty (1999). "Statistical Models for Text Segmentation." *Machine Learning*, Vol. 4, pp. 177–210.

Bestgen, Yves (2006). "Improving Text Segmentation Using Latent Semantic Analysis." *Computational Linguistics*, Vol. 32, No. 1, pp. 5–12.

Choi, Freddy Y. Y. (2000). "Advances in Domain Independent Linear Text Segmentation." *Proceedings of the 1st Meeting of the North American Chapter of the Association for Computational Linguistics*, Seattle, Washington, DC, USA, pp. 26–33.

Choi, Freddy Y. Y., Peter Wiemer-Hastings, and Johanna D. Moore (2001). "Latent Semantic Analysis for Text Segmentation." *Proceedings of the 2001 Conference on Empirical Methods in Natural Language Processing* (*EMNLP-2001*), Carnegie Mellon University, Pittsburgh, PA, USA.

Llopis, Fernando, Antonio Ferrández, and José Luis Vicedo (2002). "Text Segmentation for Efficient Information Retrieval." *Proceedings of the 3rd International Conference on Intelligent Text Processing and Computational Linguistics* (*CICLing-2002*), Mexico City, Mexico.

Marx, Zvika, Ido Dagan, and Eli Shamir (2005). "A Generalized Framework for Revealing Analogous Themes across Related Topics." *Proceedings of Human Language Technology Conference and Conference on Empirical Methods in Natural Language Processing* (*HLT/EMNLP-2005*), Vancouver, BC, Canada.

McDonald, Ryan, Koby Crammer, and Fernando Pereira (2005). "Flexible Text Segmentation with Structured Multilabel Classification." *Proceedings of Human Language Technology Conference and Conference on Empirical Methods in Natural Language Processing* (*HLT/EMNLP-2005*), Vancouver, BC, Canada.

Olney, Andrew and Cai Zhiqiang (2005). "An Orthonormal Basis for Topic Segmentation in Tutorial Dialogue." *Proceedings of Human Language Technology Conference and Conference on Empirical Methods in Natural Language Processing* (*HLT/EMNLP-2005*), Vancouver, BC, Canada.

Ren, Fuji (2001). "A Hybrid Approach of Text Segmentation Based on Sensitive Word Concept for NLP." *Proceedings of the 2nd International Conference on Intelligent Text Processing and Computational Linguistics* (*CICLing-2001*), Mexico City, Mexico.

Word Segmentation

Bikel, Daniel M. (2000). "A Statistical Model for Parsing and Word-sense Disambiguation." *Proceedings of the Joint Sigdat Conference on Empirical Methods in Natural Language Processing and Very Large Corpora* (*EMNLP/VLC-2000*), Hong Kong University of Science and Technology, Hong Kong.

Chen, Yaodong, Ting Wang, and Huowang Chen (2005). "Using Directed Graph Based BDMM Algorithm for Chinese Word Segmentation." *Proceedings of the 6th International Conference on Intelligent Text Processing and Computational Linguistics* (*CICLing-2005*), Mexico City, Mexico, pp. 212–215.

Chiang, Tung-Hui, Jing-Shin Chang, Ming-Yu Lin, and Keh-Yih Su (1992). "Statistical Models for Word Segmentation and Unknown Word Resolution." *Proceedings of the Conference of the Association*

for Computational Linguistics and Chinese Language Processing (*ROCLING-V*), National Taiwan University, Taipei, Taiwan.
Chiang, Tung-Hui, Chang Jing-shin, Lin Ming-yu, and Su Keh-yih (1996). "Statistical Word Segmentation." *Journal of Chinese Linguistics*, Vol. 9, pp. 147–173.
Escudero, Gerard, Lluis Marquez, and German Rigau (2000). "An Empirical Study of the Domain Dependence of Supervised Word Sense Disambiguation Systems." *Proceedings of the Joint Sigdat Conference on Empirical Methods in Natural Language Processing and Very Large Corpora* (*EMNLP/VLC-2000*), Hong Kong University of Science and Technology, Hong Kong.
Gao, Jianfeng, Wu Andi, Huang Cheng-Ning, Li Hongqiao, Xia Xinsong, and Qin Hauwei (2004). "Adaptive Chinese Word Segmentation." *Proceedings of the 42nd Annual Meeting of the Association for Computational Linguistics* (*ACL-2004*), Barcelona, Spain, pp. 462–469.
Gao, Shan 高山, Zhang Yan 張艷, Xu Bo 徐波, Zong Chengqing 宗成慶, and Han Zhaobing 韓兆兵 (2001).〈基於三元統計模型的漢語分詞及標注一體化研究〉(Research on Integrated Chinese Words Segmentation and Labeling Based on Trigram Statistical Model). In Huang Changning 黃昌寧 and Zhang Pu 張普, eds.,《自然語言理解與機器翻譯》(*Natural Language Understanding and Machine Translation*). Beijing: Tsinghua University Press, pp. 116–122.
Hacioglu, Kadri and Wayne Ward (2003). "Target Word Detection and Semantic Role Chunking Using Support Vector Machines." *Proceedings of the Human Language Technology and North American Chapter of Association of Computational Linguistics 2003* (*HLT/NAACL-2003*), Edmonton, Alberta, Canada.
Huang, Jinhu and David Powers (2002). "Experiments on Unsupervised Chinese Word Segmentation and Classification."《第一屆學生計算語言學研討會論文集》(*SWCL2002: First Students' Workshop on Computational Linguistics: Proceedings*), Institute of Computational Linguistics, Peking University, Beijing, China, pp. 83–89.
Jin, Zhihui and Tanaka-Ishii Kumiko (2006). "Unsupervised Segmentation of Chinese Text by Use of Branching Entropy." *Proceedings of the Joint Conference of the International Committee on Computational Linguistics and the Association for Computational Linguistics* (*COLING/ACL-2006*), Sydney, Australia.

Lai, Tom B. Y., Maosong Sun, Benjamin K. Y. T'sou, and S. Caesar Lun (1997). "Chinese Word Segmentation and Part-of-speech Tagging in One Step." *Proceedings of the International Conference on Research in Computational Linguistics* (*ROCLING-X*), Academia Sinica, Taipei, Taiwan.

Li, Jianfeng, Haifeng Wang, Dengjun Ren, and Guohua Li (2006). "Discriminative Pruning of Language Models for Chinese Word Segmentation." *Proceedings of the Joint Conference of the International Committee on Computational Linguistics and the Association for Computational Linguistics* (*COLING/ACL-2006*), Sydney, Australia.

Lian, Zhujun 廉竹鈞 (2002).〈漢語組合型切分歧義字段消歧方法研究〉(A Study on the Disambiguation of Combinatorial Ambiguities in Chinese Word Segmentation).《第一屆學生計算語言學研討會論文集》(*SWCL-2002: First Students' Workshop on Computational Linguistics: Proceedings*), Institute of Computational Linguistics, Peking University, Beijing, China, pp. 65–70.

Lin, Ming-Yu, Tung-Hui Chiang, and Keh-Yih Su (1993). "A Preliminary Study on Unknown Word Problem in Chinese Word Segmentation." *Proceedings of the Conference of the Association for Computational Linguistics and Chinese Language Processing* (*ROCLING-VI*), Nantou, Taiwan.

Luk, Wing-Pong 陸永邦 (1994). "Chinese-word Segmentation Based on Maximal-matching and Bigram Techniques." *Proceedings of the Conference of the Association for Computational Linguistics and Chinese Language Processing* (*ROCLING-VII*), National Tsing Hua University, Hsin-Chu, Taiwan.

Qian, Yili 錢揖麗 and Zhang Hu 張虎 (2002).〈漢語分詞及詞性標注自動校驗方法研究〉(Research on the Verification Methods of Chinese Word Segmentation and Part-of-speech Tagging).《第一屆學生計算語言學研討會論文集》(*SWCL-2002: First Students' Workshop on Computational Linguistics: Proceedings*), Institute of Computational Linguistics, Peking University, Beijing, China, pp. 59–64.

Sproat, Richard, Shih Chilin, William A. Gale, and Nancy A. Chang (1996). "Stochastic Finite-state Word-segmentation Algorithm for Chinese." *Computational Linguistics*, Vol. 22, No. 3, pp. 377–404.

Sun, Maosong, Shen Dayang, and Huang Changning (1997). "Cseg & Tag1.0: A Practical Word Segmenter and POS Tagger for Chinese

Texts." *Proceedings of the 5th Conference on Applied Natural Language Processing*, Seattle, Washington, DC, USA.

Wong, Wing-Kwong, Chenming Hsu, Jien-Jao Chen, and Jien-Chi Yu (1997). "A Simple Heuristic Approach for Word Segmentation." *Proceedings of the International Conference on Research in Computational Linguistics* (*ROCLING-X*), Academia Sinica, Taipei, Taiwan.

Xu, Jia, Evgeny Matusov, Richard Zens, and Hermann Ney (2005). "Integrated Chinese Word Segmentation in Statistical Machine Translation." *Proceedings of the International Workshop on Spoken Language Translation* (*IWSLT-2005*), Pittsburgh, PA, USA.

Zhang, Ruiqiang, Kikui Genichiro, and Sumita Eiichiro (2006). "Subword-based Tagging by Conditional Random Fields for Chinese Word Segmentation." *Proceedings of the Human Language Technology Conference—Annual Meeting of the North American Chapter of the Association for Computational Linguistics* (*HLT-NAACL-2006*), New York, USA.

❖ PART 30 ❖

Sentence

Sentence

Derr, Marcia A. and Kathleen R. McKeown (1984). "Using Focus to Generate Complex and Simple Sentences." *Proceedings of the 10th International Conference on Computational Linguistics* (*COLING-84*), Stanford University, Stanford, California, USA, pp. 319–326.

Hillard, Dustin, Mari Ostendorf, Andreas Stolcke, Yang Liu, and Elizabeth Shriberg (2004). "Improving Automatic Sentence Boundary Detection with Confusion Networks." *Proceedings of the Human Language Technology Conference/North American Chapter of the Association for Computational Linguistics Annual Meeting* (*HLT/NAACL-2004*), Boston, MA, USA.

Karamanis, Nikiforos (2006). "Evaluating Centering for Sentence Ordering in Two New Domains." *Proceedings of the Human Language Technology Conference—Annual Meeting of the North American Chapter of the Association for Computational Linguistics* (*HLT-NAACL-2006*), New York, USA.

Kim, Sung-Dong, Byoung-Tak Zhang, and Yung Taek Kim (2001). "Learning-based Intrasentence Segmentation for Efficient Translation of Long Sentences." *Machine Translation*, Vol. 16, No. 3, pp. 151–174.

Kim, Yeun-bae and Terumasa Ehara (1994). "A Method for Partitioning of Long Japanese Sentences with Subject Resolution in J/E Machine Translation." *Proceedings of the International Conference on Computer Processing of Oriental Languages* (*ICCPOL-94*), Taejon, Korea, pp. 467–473.

Kiss, Tibor and Jan Strunk (2006). "Unsupervised Multilingual Sentence Boundary Detection." *Computational Linguistics*, Vol. 32, No. 4, pp. 485–525.

Kurohashi, Sadao and Makoto Nagao (1994). "A Syntactic Analysis Method of Long Japanese Sentences Based on the Detection of Conjunctive Structures." *Computational Linguistics*, Vol. 20, No. 4, pp. 507–534.

Lee, Do-Gil and Hae-Chang Rim (2004). "Towards Language-independent Sentence Boundary Detection." *Proceedings of the 5th International Conference on Intelligent Text Processing and Computational Linguistics* (*CICLing-2004*), Chung-Ang University, Seoul, Korea, pp. 139–142.

Lesmo, Leonardo and Pietro Torasso (1984). "Interpreting Syntactically

Ill-formed Sentences." *Proceedings of the 10th International Conference on Computational Linguistics* (*COLING-84*), Stanford University, Stanford, California, USA, pp. 534–539.

Li, Wei-chuan, Pei Tzusheng, Lee Bing-huang, and Chiou Chuei-feng (1990). "Parsing Long English Sentences with Pattern Rules." *Proceedings of the 13th International Conference on Computational Linguistics* (*COLING-90*), Helsinki, Finland, Vol. 3, pp. 410–412.

Murata, Masaki, Toshiyuki Kanamaru, and Hitoshi Isahara (2005). "Automatic Synonym Acquisition Based on Matching of Definition Sentences in Multiple Dictionaries." *Proceedings of the 6th International Conference on Intelligent Text Processing and Computational Linguistics* (*CICLing-2005*), Mexico City, Mexico, pp. 284–295.

Pérez-Ramírez, Miguel and Chris Fox (2004). "Agents Interpreting Imperative Sentences." *Proceedings of the 5th International Conference on Intelligent Text Processing and Computational Linguistics* (*CICLing-2004*), Chung-Ang University, Seoul, Korea, pp. 54–65.

Wilson, Theresa, David R. Pierce, and Janyce Wiebe (2003). "Identifying Opinionated Sentences." *Proceedings of the Human Language Technology and North American Chapter of Association of Computational Linguistics 2003* (*HLT/NAACL-2003*), Edmonton, Alberta, Canada.

Zhang, Min 張民 and Li Sheng 李生 (1995).〈一種漢語句子間相似度的度量演算法及其實現〉(Calculation of Measuring the Syntactical Similarity in Chinese Sentences).《計算語言學進展與應用》(*Developments and Applications in Computational Linguistics*). Beijing: Tsinghua University Press.

Sentence Boundary

Liu, Yang, Elizabeth Shriberg, Andreas Stolcke, and Mary Harper (2005). "Using Conditional Random Fields for Sentence Boundary Detection in Speech." *Proceedings of the 43rd Annual Meeting of the Association of Computational Linguistics* (*ACL-2005*), Ann Arbor, Michigan, USA.

Pan, Shimei and James C. Shaw (2005). "Instance-based Sentence Boundary Determination by Optimization." *Proceedings of the 43rd*

Annual Meeting of the Association of Computational Linguistics (*ACL-2005*), Ann Arbor, Michigan, USA.

Sentence Generation

Adorni, Giovanni and Lina Massone (1984). "Production of Sentences: A General Algorithm and Case Studies." *Proceedings of the International Conference on the Methodology and Techniques of Machine Translation*, Cranfield Institute of Technology, Cranfield, England.

Chen, Chung-Cherng 陳忠誠 and Jyun-Sheng Chang 張俊盛 (1990). "Bilingual Sentence Generation." *Proceedings of the Conference of the Association for Computational Linguistics and Chinese Language Processing* (*ROCLING-III*), Taipei, Taiwan.

Huang, Xiuming (1984). "The Generation of Chinese Sentences from the Semantic Representation of the Input English Text." *Proceedings of the International Conference on the Methodology and Techniques of Machine Translation*, Cranfield Institute of Technology, Cranfield, England.

Kuo, Hwei-Ming 郭惠民 and Jyun-Sheng Chang 張俊盛 (1989). "Systemic Generation of Chinese Sentences." *Proceedings of the Conference of the Association for Computational Linguistics and Chinese Language Processing* (*ROCLING-II*), Taipei, Taiwan.

Langkilde, Irene (2000). "Forest-based Statistical Sentence Generation." *Proceedings of the 1st Meeting of the North American Chapter of the Association for Computational Linguistics*, Seattle, Washington, DC, USA, pp. 170–177.

Nagao, Makoto (1965). "Sentence Generation by Semantic Concordance." *Proceedings of the International Conference on Computational Linguistics*, New York, USA.

Nagao, Makoto (1989). "The Selection of Words for Translation and Sentence Generation." In Norman D. Cook, trans., *Machine Translation: How Far Can It Go?* Oxford: Oxford University Press, pp. 105–122.

Takeda, Koichi (2002). "Sentence Generation for Pattern-based Machine Translation." *Proceedings of the 9th International Conference on Theoretical and Methodological Issues in Machine Translation* (*TMI-2002*), Keihanna, Japan, pp. 168–177.

Yngve, Victor H. (1962). "Random Generation of English Sentences." In National Physical Laboratory, ed., *1961 International Conference on*

Machine Translation of Languages and Applied Language Analysis: Proceedings of the Conference Held at the National Physical Laboratory, Teddington, Middlesex, on 5th, 6th, 7th and 8th September. London: Her Majesty's Stationery Office, Vol. 1, pp. 65–80.

Sentence Length

Gerber, Laurie and Eduard Hovy (1998). "Improving Translation Quality by Manipulating Sentence Length." In David L. Farwell, Laurie Gerber, and Eduard Hovy, eds., *Machine Translation and the Information Soup*. Berlin: Springer Verlag, pp. 448–460.

Jing, Hongyan (2000). "Sentence Reduction for Automatic Text Summarization." *Proceedings of the 6th Applied Natural Language Processing Conference*, Seattle, Washington, DC, USA, pp. 310–315.

Liu, Xin, Zhou Ming, and Huang Changning (1995). "Experiment on an Alignment Algorithm for Chinese-English Parallel Texts Based on Sentence Lengths." In Chen Liwei, ed., *Progress and Application in Computational Linguistics*, Beijing: Tsinghua University Press, pp. 62–76.

Sentence Pattern

Mastermann, Margaret (1956). "New Techniques for Analyzing Sentence Patterns." *Mechanical Translation*, Vol. 3, No. 1, pp. 4–6.

Zheng, Keliang 張克亮 (2002).〈一個特殊句法結構的英漢句類轉換〉(On the English-Chinese SC Transfer of a Special Syntactic Structure).《第一屆學生計算語言學研討會論文集》(*SWCL-2002: First Students' Workshop on Computational Linguistics: Proceedings*), Institute of Computational Linguistics, Peking University, Beijing, China, pp. 189–196.

Sentence Splitting

Doi, Takao and Eiichiro Sumita (2003). "Input Sentence Splitting and Translating." *Proceedings of the Human Language Technology and North American Chapter of Association of Computational Linguistics 2003* (*HLT/NAACL-2003*), Edmonton, Alberta, Canada.

Vogel, Stephan (2005). "PESA: Phrase Pair Extraction as Sentence Splitting." *Proceedings of MT Summit X*, Phuket, Thailand.

Sentence Structure

Nagao, Makoto (1989). "Methods of Analysis of Sentence Structure." In Norman D. Cook, trans., *Machine Translation: How Far Can It Go?* Oxford: Oxford University Press, pp. 83–104.

Nagao, Makoto (1992). "Are the Grammars So Far Developed Appropriate to Recognize the Real Structure of a Sentence?" *Proceedings of the 4th International Conference on Theoretical and Methodological Issues in Machine Translation of Natural Languages: Empiricist vs. Rationalist Methods in MT* (*TMI-92*), Montreal, Quebec, Canada, pp. 127–137.

Sentence Translation

Asakura, S. and S. Nakano (1974). "An Experimental System of Machine Translation by the Programmed Sentence Scan Method." *Mem Chubu Institute of Technology*, 10A, pp. 73–84.

Danlos, Laurence and Pollet Samvelian (1992). "Translation of the Predicative Element of a Sentence: Category Switching, Aspect and Diathesis." *Proceedings of the 4th International Conference on Theoretical and Methodological Issues in Machine Translation of Natural Languages*: *Empiricist vs. Rationalist Methods in MT* (*TMI-92*), Montreal, Quebec, Canada, pp. 21–34.

Gerber, Laurie and Eduard Hovy (1998). "Improving Translation Quality by Manipulating Sentence Length." In David L. Farwell, Laurie Gerber, and Eduard Hovy, eds., *Machine Translation and the Information Soup*. Berlin: Springer Verlag, pp. 448–460.

Katoh, Naoto and Teruaki Aizawa (1994). "Machine Translation of Sentences with Fixed Expressions." *Proceedings of the 4th Conference on Applied Natural Language Processing*, Stuttgart, Germany, pp. 28–33.

Lewis, Derek (2001). "PC-based Machine Translation: An Illustration of Capabilities in Response to Submitted Test Sentences." *Machine Translation Review*, No. 12, pp. 21–25.

Mihalcea, Rada F. and Ben Leong (2006). "Towards Communicating Simple Sentences Using Pictorial Representations." *Proceedings of the 7th Biennial Conference of the Association for Machine Translation in the Americas* (*AMTA-2006*)*: Visions for the Future of Machine Translation*, Boston Marriott, Cambridge, MA, USA.

Nagao, Makato (1985). "Evaluation of the Quality of Machine-translated

Sentences and the Control of Language." *Journal of the Information Processing Society of Japan*, Vol. 26, pp. 1197–1202.
Nagao, Makoto (1987). "Role of Structural Transformation in a Machine Translation System." In Sergei Nirenburg, ed., *Machine Translation: Theoretical and Methodological Issues*. Cambridge: Cambridge University Press, pp. 262–277.
Roh, Yoon-Hyung, Munpyo Hong, Sung-Kwon Choi, Ki Young Lee, and Sang-Kyu Park (2003). "For the Proper Treatment of Long Sentences in a Sentence Pattern-based English-Korean MT System." *Proceedings of MT Summit IX*, New Orleans, Louisiana, USA.
Satterthwait, Arnold C. (1965). "Sentence-for-sentence Translation: An Example." *Mechanical Translation*, Vol. 8, No. 2, pp. 14–38.
Sheremetyeva, Svetlana (2006). "Handling Low Translatability in Machine Translation of Long Sentences." *Proceedings of the 11th Workshop of the European Association for Machine Translation: Machine Translation/Translation Aids—Tools to Increase Quality and to Save Money*, the University of Oslo, Oslo, Norway.
Smets, Martine, Michael Gamon, Jessie Pinkham, Tom Reutter, and Martine Pettenaro (2003). "High Quality Machine Translation Using Automatic Sentence Realization." *Proceedings of MT Summit IX*, New Orleans, Louisiana, USA.
Stoia, Laura, Donna Byron, Darla Shockley, and Eric Fosler-Lussier (2006). "Sentence Planning for Realtime Navigational Instruction." *Proceedings of the Human Language Technology Conference—Annual Meeting of the North American Chapter of the Association for Computational Linguistics* (*HLT-NAACL-2006*), New York, USA.
Yngve, Victor H. (1955). "Sentence-for-sentence Translation." *Mechanicial Translation*, Vol. 2, No. 2, pp. 29–37.
Yngve, Victor H. (1957). "A Framework for Syntactic Translation." *Mechanical Translation*, Vol. 4, No. 3, pp. 59–65.
Zhang, Keliang (2005).〈面向機器翻譯的漢英語句格式轉換研究〉(An MT-oriented Study of Chinese-English Sentence Format Transfer).《語言文字應用》(*Applied Linguistics*), No. 3, pp. 135–142.

❖ PART 31 ❖

Speech

DIALOGUE

Dialogue

Abella, Alicia, Allen Gorin, Guiseppe Riccardi, Tirso Alonso, and Jerry Wright (2001). "'How May I Help You?': Automated Customer Service via Natural Spoken Dialog." *Proceedings of the 2nd Meeting of the North American Chapter of the Association for Computational Linguistics: Language Technologies 2001* (*NAACL-2001*), Pittsburgh, PA, USA.

Arguello, Jaime and Carolyn P. Rose (2006). "Museli: A Multi-source Evidence Integration Approach to Topic Segmentation of Spontaneous Dialogue." *Proceedings of the Human Language Technology Conference—Annual Meeting of the North American Chapter of the Association for Computational Linguistics* (*HLT-NAACL-2006*), New York, USA.

Bohus, Dan and Alexander Rudnicky (2005). "Error Handling in the Raven Claw Dialog Management Architecture." *Proceedings of Human Language Technology Conference and Conference on Empirical Methods in Natural Language Processing* (*HLT/EMNLP-2005*), Vancouver, BC, Canada.

Callaway, Charles (2001). "A Computational Feature Analysis for Multilingual Character-to-character Dialogue." *Proceedings of the 2nd International Conference on Intelligent Text Processing and Computational Linguistics* (*CICLing-2001*), Mexico City, Mexico.

Coria, Sergio and Luis A. Pineda (2006). "Predicting Dialogue Acts from Prosodic Information." *Proceedings of the 7th International Conference on Intelligent Text Processing and Computational Linguistics* (*CICLing-2006*), Mexico City, Mexico.

English, Michael and Peter Heeman (2005). "Learning Mixed Initiative Dialog Strategies by Using Reinforcement Learning on Both Conversants." *Proceedings of Human Language Technology Conference and Conference on Empirical Methods in Natural Language Processing* (*HLT/EMNLP-2005*), Vancouver, BC, Canada.

Feng, Donghui, Erin Shaw, Jihie Kim, and Eduard H. Hovy (2006). "Learning to Detect Conversation Focus of Threaded Discussions." *Proceedings of the Human Language Technology Conference—Annual Meeting of the North American Chapter of the Association for Computational Linguistics* (*HLT-NAACL-2006*), New York, USA.

Forbes-Riley, Kate and Diane J. Litman (2004). "Predicting Emotion in Spoken Dialogue from Multiple Knowledge Sources." *Proceedings of the Human Language Technology Conference/North American Chapter of the Association for Computational Linguistics Annual Meeting* (*HLT/NAACL-2004*), Boston, MA, USA.

Freedman, Reva (2000). "Plan-based Dialogue Management in a Physics Tutor." *Proceedings of the 6th Applied Natural Language Processing Conference*, Seattle, Washington, DC, USA, pp. 52–59.

Ginzburg, Jonathan and Raquel Fernandez (2005). "Scaling up from Dialogue to Multilogue: Some Principles and Benchmarks." *Proceedings of the 43rd Annual Meeting of the Association of Computational Linguistics* (*ACL-2005*), Ann Arbor, Michigan, USA.

Ji, Gang and Jeff A. Bilmes (2006). "Backoff Model Training Using Partially Observed Data: Application to Dialog Act Tagging." *Proceedings of the Human Language Technology Conference—Annual Meeting of the North American Chapter of the Association for Computational Linguistics* (*HLT-NAACL-2006*), New York, USA.

Kahn, Jeremy G., Matthew Lease, Eugene Charniak, Mark Johnson, and Mari Ostendorf (2005). "Effective Use of Prosody in Parsing Conversational Speech." *Proceedings of Human Language Technology Conference and Conference on Empirical Methods in Natural Language Processing* (*HLT/EMNLP-2005*), Vancouver, BC, Canada.

Kogure, Kiyoshi (1990). "Illocutionary Act Based Translation of Dialogues." *Proceedings of the 3rd International Conference on Theoretical and Methodological Issues in Machine Translation of Natural Languages* (*TMI-90*), Linguistics Research Center, University of Texas at Austin, Austin, Texas, USA, pp. 47–55.

Kozima, Hideki and Akira Ito (1997). "The Role of Shared Attention in Human-computer Conversation." *Proceedings of the International Conference on Research in Computational Linguistics* (*ROCLING-X*), Academia Sinica, Taipei, Taiwan.

Mairesse, Françis and Marilyn Walker (2006). "Automatic Recognition of Personality in Conversation." *Proceedings of the Human Language Technology Conference—Annual Meeting of the North American Chapter of the Association for Computational Linguistics* (*HLT-NAACL-2006*), New York, USA.

Milward, David (2000). "Distributing Representation for Robust Interpretation of Dialogue Utterances." *Proceedings of the 38th Annual*

Meeting of the Association for Computational Linguistics (*ACL-2000*), Hong Kong.

Moore, Johanna D. and Cécile Paris (1989). "Planning Text for Advisory Dialogues." *Proceedings of the 21st Annual Meeting of the Association for Computational Linguistics* (*ACL-89*), Vancouver, BC, Canada, pp. 203–211.

Rayner, Manny, Beth Ann Hockey, and Frankie James (2000). "A Compact Architecture for Dialogue Management Based on Scripts and Meta-outputs." *Proceedings of the 6th Applied Natural Language Processing Conference*, Seattle, Washington, DC, USA, pp. 112–118.

Reitter, David, Frank Keller, and Johanna D. Moore (2006). "Computational Modelling of Structural Priming in Dialogue." *Proceedings of the Human Language Technology Conference—Annual Meeting of the North American Chapter of the Association for Computational Linguistics* (*HLT-NAACL-2006*), New York, USA.

Teruhisa, Misu and Kawahara Tatsuya (2005). "Speech-based Information Retrieval System with Clarification Dialogue Strategy." *Proceedings of Human Language Technology Conference and Conference on Empirical Methods in Natural Language Processing* (*HLT/EMNLP-2005*), Vancouver, BC, Canada.

Tetreault, Joel and Diane J. Litman (2006). "Comparing the Utility of State Features in Spoken Dialogue Using Reinforcement Learning." *Proceedings of the Human Language Technology Conference—Annual Meeting of the North American Chapter of the Association for Computational Linguistics* (*HLT-NAACL-2006*), New York, USA.

Villaseñor-Pineda, Luis, José Antonio Massé Márquez, and Luis Alberto Pineda Cortés (2000). "Towards a Multimodal Dialogue Coding Scheme." *Proceedings of the 1st International Conference on Intelligent Text Processing and Computational Linguistics* (*CICLing-2000*), Mexico City, Mexico.

Wu, Chung-Hsien and Jau-Hung Chen (1997). "Prosody Generation in a Chinese TTS System Based on a Hierarchical Word Prosody Template Tree." *Proceedings of the International Conference on Research in Computational Linguistics* (*ROCLING-X*), Academia Sinica, Taipei, Taiwan.

Yamada, Setsuo, Eiichiro Sumita, and Hideki Kashioka (2000). "Translation Using Information on Dialogue Participants."

Proceedings of the 6th Applied Natural Language Processing Conference, Seattle, Washington, DC, USA, pp. 37–43.

Dialogue-based Computer Translation

Bagga, Amit, Tomek Strzalkowski, and G. Bowden Wise (2000). "PartsID: A Dialogue-based System for Identifying Parts for Medical Systems." *Proceedings of the 6th Applied Natural Language Processing Conference*, Seattle, Washington, DC, USA, pp. 29–36.

Boitet, Christian (1994). "Dialogue-based MT and Self-explaining Documents as an Alternative to MAHT and MT of Controlled Languages." *Machine Translation—Ten Years On: Proceedings of the 2nd International Conference Organised by Cranfield University*, Cranfield, England.

Boitet, Christian and Hervé Blanchon (1994). "Multilingual Dialogue-based MT for Monolingual Authors: The LIDIA Project and a First Mockup." *Machine Translation*, Vol. 9, No. 2, pp. 99–132.

Boitet, Christian (1996). "Dialogue-based Machine Translation for Monolinguals and Future Self-explaining Documents." In Christian Boitet, ed., *Proceedings of MIDDIM-96 Post-COLING Seminar on Interactive Disambiguation*, Le Col de Porte, France, pp. 75–85.

Boitet, Christian (1999). "Dialogue-based MT and Self-explaining Documents as an Alternative to MAHT and MT of Controlled Languages." *Machine Translation Review*, No. 10, pp. 6–15.

Jones, Daniel B. and Jun-ichi Tsujii (1990). "High Quality Machine-driven Text Translation." *Proceedings of the 3rd International Conference on Theoretical and Methodological Issues in Machine Translation of Natural Languages (TMI-90)*, Linguistics Research Center, University of Texas, Austin, Texas, USA, pp. 43–46.

Jönsson, Arne and Nils Dahlbäck (2000). "Distilling Dialogues—A Method Using Natural Dialogue Corpora for Dialogue Systems Development." *Proceedings of the 6th Applied Natural Language Processing Conference*, Seattle, Washington, DC, USA, pp. 44–51.

Saito, Hiroaki and Masaru Tomita (1986). *On Automatic Composition of Stereotypic Documents in Foreign Languages*. Department of Computer Science, Carnegie Mellon University, CMU-Cs-86-107.

Somers, Harold L., Jun-ichi Tsujii, and Daniel B. Jones (1990). "Machine Translation without a Source Text." *Proceedings of the 13th*

International Conference on Computational Linguistics (*COLING-90*), Helsinki, Finland, pp. 271–276.
Somers, Harold L. (1992). "Interactive Multilingual Text Generation for a Monolingual User." *Proceedings of the 4th International Conference on Theoretical and Methodological Issues in Machine Translation of Natural Languages* (*TMI-92*), Montreal, Quebec, Canada, pp. 151–161.

Dialogue Processing

Alexandersson, Jan, Peter Poller, and Michael Kipp (2000). "Generating Multilingual Dialog Summaries and Minutes." In Wolfgang Wahlster, ed., *Verbmobil: Foundations of Speech-to-speech Translation*. Berlin: Springer Verlag, pp. 507–518.
Alexandersson, Jan, Ralf Engel, Michael Kipp, Stephan Koch, Uwe Küssner, Norbert Reithinger, and Manfred Stede (2000). "Modeling Negotiation Dialogs." In Wolfgang Wahlster, ed., *Verbmobil: Foundations of Speech-to-speech Translation*. Berlin: Springer Verlag, pp. 441–451.
Kimura, Yasutomo, Kenji Araki, and Koji Tochinai (2004). "Evaluation of Japanese Dialogue Processing Method Based on Similarity Measure Using tf · AoI." *Proceedings of the 5th International Conference on Intelligent Text Processing and Computational Linguistics* (*CICLing-2004*), Chung-Ang University, Seoul, Korea, pp. 366–377.
Kipp, Michael, Jan Alexandersson, Ralf Engel, and Norbert Reithinger (2000). "Dialog Processing." In Wolfgang Wahlster, ed., *Verbmobil: Foundations of Speech-to-speech Translation*. Berlin: Springer Verlag, pp. 452–465.
Matheson, Colin, Massimo Poesio, and David Traum (2000). "Modelling Grounding and Discourse Obligations Using Update Rules." *Proceedings of the 1st Meeting of the North American Chapter of the Association for Computational Linguistics*, Seattle, Washington, DC, USA, pp. 1–8.
Reithinger, Norbert and Ralf Engel (2000). "Robust Content Extraction for Translation and Dialog Processing." In Wolfgang Wahlster, ed., *Verbmobil: Foundations of Speech-to-speech Translation*. Berlin: Springer Verlag, pp. 428–437.
Wang, Ye-Yi and Alex H. Waibel (1991). "A Connectionist Model for Dialog Processing." *Proceedings of the IEEE International Conference*

on Acoustics, Speech and Signal Processing (*ICASSP-91*), Toronto, Canada.

Dialogue Translation

Batliner, Anton, Richard Huber, Heinrich Niemann, Elmar Nöth, Jörg Spilker, and Kerstin Fischer (2000). "The Recognition of Emotion." In Wolfgang Wahlster, ed., *Verbmobil: Foundations of Speech-to-speech Translation*. Berlin: Springer Verlag, pp. 122–130.
Becker, Tilman, Wolfgang Finkler, Anne Kilger, and Peter Poller (1998). "An Efficient Kernel for Multilingual Generation in Speech-to-Speech Dialogue Translation." *Proceedings of the 36th Annual Meeting of the Association for Computational Linguistics and 17th International Conference on Computational Linguistics* (*COLING-ACL-98*), Montreal, Quebec, Canada, pp. 110–116.
Jekat, Susanne (1997). "Automatic Interpreting of Dialogue Acts." In Christa Hauenschild and Susanne Heizmann, eds., *Machine Translation and Translation Theory*. Berlin-New York: Mouton de Gruyter, pp. 145–155.
Jokinen, Kristiina, Hideki Tanaka, and Akio Yokoo (1998). "Context Management with Topics for Spoken Dialogue Systems." *Proceedings of the 36th Annual Meeting of the Association for Computational Linguistics and 17th International Conference on Computational Linguistics* (*COLING-ACL-98*), Montreal, Quebec, Canada, pp. 631–637.
Kitano, Hiroaki (1990). "ΦdmDialog: A Speech-to-speech Dialogue Translation System." *Machine Translation*, Vol. 5, No. 4, pp. 301–338.
Kitano, Hiroaki (1991). *Massively Parallel Model of Speech-to-speech Dialogue Translation: The ΦdmDialog System*. Pittsburgh: Center for Machine Translation, Carnegie Mellon University.
Lee, Jae-Won, Jungyun Seo, and Gil Chang Kim (1998). "A Statistical Dialogue Analysis Model Based on Speech Acts for Dialogue Machine Translation." *Machine Translation*, Vol. 13, No. 4, pp. 269–286.
Miike, Seiji, Koichi Hasebe, Harold L. Somers, and Shinya Amano (1988). "Experiences with an On-line Translating Dialogue System." *Proceedings of the 26th Annual Meeting of the Association for Computational Linguistics* (*ACL-88*), Buffalo, New York, USA, pp. 155–162.

Mima, Hideki, Osamu Furuse, and Hitoshi Iida (1997). "A Situation-based Approach to Spoken Dialog Translation between Different Social Roles." *Proceedings of the 7th International Conference on Theoretical and Methodological Issues in Machine Translation* (*TMI-97*), St. John's College, Santa Fe, New Mexico, USA.

Nagata, Masaaki and Tsuyoshi Morimoto (1993). "An Experimental Statistical Dialogue Model to Predict the Speech Act Type of the Next Utterance." *Proceedings of the International Symposium on Spoken Dialogue—New Directions in Human and Man-machine Communication* (*ISSD-93*), Tokyo, Japan, pp. 83–86.

Reithinger, Norbert and Martin Klesen (1997). "Dialogue Act Classification Using Language Models." *Proceedings of the 5th European Conference on Speech Communication and Technology* (*EuroSpeech-97*), Rhodes, Greece, pp. 2235–2238.

Schmitz, Birte and J. Joachim Quantz (1995). "Speech-event Types in Automatic Dialogue Interpreting." *Proceedings of the 6th International Conference on Theoretical and Methodological Issues in Machine Translation* (*TMI-95*), Leuven, Belgium, pp. 33–47.

Schmitz, Birte (1997). "The Translation Objective in Automatic Dialogue Interpreting." In Christa Hauenschild and Susanne Heizmann, eds., *Machine Translation and Translation Theory*. Berlin-New York: Mouton de Gruyter, pp. 193–210.

Seligman, Mark, Laurel Fais, and Mutsuko Tomokiyo (1995). *A Bilingual Set of Communicative Act Labels for Spontaneous Dialogues*. Technical Report TR-IT-0081, ATR Interpreting Telecommunications Laboratories, Kyoto, Japan.

Sobashima, Yasuhiro, Osamu Furuse, Susumu Akamine, Jun Kawai, and Hitoshi Iida (1994). "A Bidirectional, Transfer-driven Machine Translation System for Spoken Dialogues." *Proceedings of the 15th International Conference on Computational Linguistics* (*COLING-94*), Kyoto, Japan, pp. 64–68.

Dialogue Translation System

Aist, Gregory (2005). "Empirical Methods for Dialogue System Research." *Proceedings of the 43rd Annual Meeting of the Association of Computational Linguistics* (*ACL-2005*), Ann Arbor, Michigan, USA.

Allen, James, Donna Byron, Dave Costello, Myroslava Dzikovska, George

Ferguson, Lucian Galescu, and Amanda Stent (2000). "TRIPS-911 System Demonstration." *Proceedings of the ANLP/NAACL-2000 Workshop on Conversational Systems—Volume 3*, Seattle, Washington, DC, USA, pp. 33–35.

Bangalore, Srinivas and Michael Johnston (2004). "Balancing Data-driven and Rule-based Approaches in the Context of a Multimodal Conversational System." *Proceedings of the Human Language Technology Conference/North American Chapter of the Association for Computational Linguistics Annual Meeting* (*HLT/NAACL-2004*), Boston, MA, USA.

Chai, Joyce Y. and Shaolin Qu (2005). "A Salience Driven Approach to Robust Input Interpretation in Multimodal Conversational Systems." *Proceedings of Human Language Technology Conference and Conference on Empirical Methods in Natural Language Processing* (*HLT/EMNLP-2005*), Vancouver, BC, Canada.

Chai, Joyce Y., Chen Zhang, and Tyler Baldwin (2006). "Towards Conversational QA: Automatic Identification of Problematic Situations and User Intent." *Proceedings of the Joint Conference of the International Committee on Computational Linguistics and the Association for Computational Linguistics* (*COLING/ACL-2006*), Sydney, Australia.

Channarukul, Songsak, Susan W. McRoy, and Syed S. Ali (2003). "DOGHED: A Template-based Generator for Multimodal Dialog Systems Targeting Heterogeneous Devices." *Proceedings of the Human Language Technology and North American Chapter of Association of Computational Linguistics 2003* (*HLT/NAACL-2003*), Edmonton, Alberta, Canada.

Chu-Carroll, Jennifer and Jill Suzanne Nickerson (2000). "Evaluating Automatic Dialogue Strategy Adaptation for a Spoken Dialogue System." *Proceedings of the 1st Meeting of the North American Chapter of the Association for Computational Linguistics*, Seattle, Washington, DC, USA, pp. 202–209.

Chung, Grace (2004). "Developing a Flexible Spoken Dialog System Using Simulation." *Proceedings of the 42nd Annual Meeting of the Association for Computational Linguistics* (*ACL-2004*), Barcelona, Spain, pp. 63–70.

Demberg, Vera and Johanna D. Moore (2006). "Information Presentation in Spoken Dialogue Systems." *Proceedings of the 11th Conference of the European Chapter of the Association for Computational Linguistics (EACL-2006)*, Trento, Italy.

Gabsdil, Malte and Oliver Lemon (2004). "Combining Acoustic and Pragmatic Features to Predict Recognition Performance in Spoken Dialogue Systems." *Proceedings of the 42nd Annual Meeting of the Association for Computational Linguistics (ACL-2004)*, Barcelona, Spain, pp. 343–350.

Goldwater, Sharon J., Elizabeth Owen Bratt, Jean Mark Gawron, and John Dowding (2000). "Building a Robust Dialogue System with Limited Data." *Proceedings of the ANLP/NAACL-2000 Workshop on Conversational Systems—Volume 3*, Seattle, Washington, DC, USA, pp. 61–65.

Gupta, Narendra and Srinivas Bangalore (2002). "Extracting Clauses for Spoken Language Understanding in Conversational Systems." *Proceedings of the 2002 Conference on Empirical Methods in Natural Language Processing (EMNLP-2002)*, University of Pennsylvania, Philadelphia, PA, USA.

Hardy, Hilda, Tomek Strzalkowski, Min Wu, Cristian Ursu, Nick Webb, Alan Biermann, R. Bryce Inouye, and Ashley McKenzie (2004). "Data-driven Strategies for an Automated Dialogue System." *Proceedings of the 42nd Annual Meeting of the Association for Computational Linguistics (ACL-2004)*, Barcelona, Spain, pp. 71–78.

Hirschberg, Julia, Diane J. Litman, and Marc Swerts (2001). "Identifying User Corrections Automatically in Spoken Dialogue Systems." *Proceedings of the 2nd Meeting of the North American Chapter of the Association for Computational Linguistics: Language Technologies 2001 (NAACL-2001)*, Pittsburgh, PA, USA.

Larsson, Staffan, Peter Ljunglöf, Robin Cooper, Elisabet Engdahl, and Stina Ericsson (2000). "GoDiS: An Accommodating Dialogue System." *Proceedings of the ANLP/NAACL-2000 Workshop on Conversational Systems—Volume 3*, Seattle, Washington, DC, USA, pp. 7–10.

Lemon, Oliver, Kallirroi Georgila, James Henderson, and Matthew Stuttle (2006). "An ISU Dialogue System Exhibiting Reinforcement Learning of Dialogue Policies: Generic Slot-filling in the TALK In-car System." *Proceedings of the 11th Conference of the European Chapter of the Association for Computational Linguistics (EACL-2006)*, Trento, Italy.

Litman, Diane J., Satinder Singh, Michael Kearns, and Marilyn Walker (2000). "NJFun: A Reinforcement Learning Spoken Dialogue System." *Proceedings of the ANLP/NAACL 2000 Workshop on Conversational Systems—Volume 3*, Seattle, Washington, DC, USA, pp. 17–20.

Litman, Diane J., Julia Hirschberg, and Marc Swerts (2006). "Characterizing and Predicting Corrections in Spoken Dialogue Systems." *Computational Linguistics*, Vol. 32, No. 3, pp. 417–438.

Martínez-Hinarejos, Carlos, Ramón Granell, and José Miguel Benedí (2006). "Segmented and Unsegmented Dialogue-act Annotation with Statistical Dialogue Models." *Proceedings of the Joint Conference of the International Committee on Computational Linguistics and the Association for Computational Linguistics (COLING/ACL-2006)*, Sydney, Australia.

McGlashan, Scott (1994). "The Role of Semantics in Spoken Dialogue Translation Systems." *Machine Translation—Ten Years On: Proceedings of the 2nd International Conference Organised by Cranfield University*, Cranfield, England.

Mima, Hideki, Osamu Furuse, and Hitoshi Iida (1997). "Multi-lingual Spoken Dialog Translation System." *Proceedings of MT Summit VI*, San Diego, California, USA.

Oh, Alice H. and Alexander I. Rudnicky (2000). "Stochastic Language Generation for Spoken Dialogue Systems." *Proceedings of the ANLP/NAACL-2000 Workshop on Conversational Systems—Volume 3*, Seattle, Washington, DC, USA, pp. 27–32.

Paek, Tim and Eric Horvitz (2004). "Optimizing Automated Call Routing by Integrating Spoken Dialog Models with Queuing Models." *Proceedings of the Human Language Technology Conference/North American Chapter of the Association for Computational Linguistics Annual Meeting (HLT/NAACL-2004)*, Boston, MA, USA.

Raux, Antoine and Maxine Eskenazi (2004). "Non-native Users in the Let's Go!! Spoken Dialogue System: Dealing with Linguistic Mismatch." *Proceedings of the Human Language Technology Conference/North American Chapter of the Association for Computational Linguistics Annual Meeting (HLT/NAACL-2004)*, Boston, MA, USA.

Sagawa, Hirohiko, Teruko Mitamura, and Eric H. Nyberg (2004). "Correction Grammars for Error Handling in a Speech Dialog

System." *Proceedings of the Human Language Technology Conference/North American Chapter of the Association for Computational Linguistics Annual Meeting* (*HLT/NAACL-2004*), Boston, MA, USA.

Stent, Amanda, Rashmi Prassad, and Marilyn Walker (2004). "Trainable Sentence Planning for Complex Information Presentations in Spoken Dialog Systems." *Proceedings of the 42nd Annual Meeting of the Association for Computational Linguistics* (*ACL-2004*), Barcelona, Spain, pp. 79–86.

Toney, Dave, Johanna D. Moore, and Oliver Lemon (2006). "Evolving Optimal Inspectable Strategies for Spoken Dialogue Systems." *Proceedings of the Human Language Technology Conference—Annual Meeting of the North American Chapter of the Association for Computational Linguistics* (*HLT-NAACL-2006*), New York, USA.

Walker, Marilyn, Irene Langkilde, Jerry Wright, Allen Gorin, and Diane J. Litman (2000). "Learning to Predict Problematic Situations in a Spoken Dialogue System: Experiments with How May I Help You?" *Proceedings of the 1st Meeting of the North American Chapter of the Association for Computational Linguistics*, Seattle, Washington, DC, USA, pp. 210–217.

Yeh, Jui-Feng, Chung-Hsien Wu, and Mao-Zhu Yang (2006). "Stochastic Discourse Modeling in Spoken Dialogue Systems Using Semantic Dependency Graphs." *Proceedings of the Joint Conference of the International Committee on Computational Linguistics and the Association for Computational Linguistics* (*COLING/ACL-2006*), Sydney, Australia.

SPEECH

Speech Generation

Bilange, Eric, Jean-Marie Lancel, and Miyo Otani (1992). "Utterance Generation Using Conceptual Representations." *Machine Translation*, Vol. 7, Nos. 1–2, pp. 41–60.

Speech Processing

Black, Alan W. and Kevin A. Lenzo (2001). "Building Synthetic Voices."

Proceedings of the 2nd Meeting of the North American Chapter of the Association for Computational Linguistics: Language Technologies 2001 (*NAACL-2001*), Pittsburgh, PA, USA.

Ekštein, Kamil and Roman Mouček (2003). "Time-domain Structural Analysis of Speech." *Proceedings of the 4th International Conference on Intelligent Text Processing and Computational Linguistics* (*CICLing-2003*), Mexico City, Mexico, pp. 508–512.

Gibbon, Dafydd and Harald Lüngen (2000). "Speech Lexica and Consistent Multilingual Vocabularies." In Wolfgang Wahlster, ed., *Verbmobil: Foundations of Speech-to-speech Translation*. Berlin: Springer Verlag, pp. 296–307.

Hall, Keith B. and Mark Johnson (2004). "Attention Shifting for Parsing Speech." *Proceedings of the 42nd Annual Meeting of the Association for Computational Linguistics* (*ACL-2004*), Barcelona, Spain, pp. 40–46.

Johnson, Mark and Eugene Charniak (2004). "A TAG-based Noisy-channel Model of Speech Repairs." *Proceedings of the 42nd Annual Meeting of the Association for Computational Linguistics* (*ACL-2004*), Barcelona, Spain, pp. 33–39.

Jurafsky, Daniel and James H. Martin (2000). *Speech Processing and Language Processing*. New Jersey: Prentice Hall.

Kosarev, Yu. and R. Piotrowski (1997). "Synergetics and 'Insight' Strategy for Speech Processing." *Literary and Linguistic Computing*, Vol. 12, No. 2.

Kuroiwa, Shingo, Satoru Tsuge, Koji Tanaka, Kazuma Hara, and Fuji Ren (2006). "Acoustic Model Adaptation for Codec Speech Based on Learning-by-doing Concept." In Alexander F. Gelbukh, ed., *Advances in Natural Language Processing*, Special Issue of *Research in Computing Science*, No. 18, pp. 105–114.

Lease, Matthew and Mark Johnson (2006). "Early Deletion of Fillers in Processing Conversational Speech." *Proceedings of the Human Language Technology Conference—Annual Meeting of the North American Chapter of the Association for Computational Linguistics* (*HLT-NAACL-2006*), New York, USA.

Lee, Chin-Hui (1996). "An Overview on Spoken Language Processing." *Proceedings of the Conference of the Association for Computational Linguistics and Chinese Language Processing* (*ROCLING-IX*), Tseng-Wen Reservoir Youth Activity Center, Tainan County, Taiwan.

Lee, Yue-Shi and Hsin-Hsi Chen (1996). "Correcting Chinese Repetition Repairs in Spontaneous Speech." *Proceedings of the Conference of the Association for Computational Linguistics and Chinese Language Processing* (*ROCLING-IX*), Tseng-Wen Reservoir Youth Activity Center, Tainan County, Taiwan.

Mohri, Mehryar (1997). "Finite-state Transducers in Language and Speech Processing." *Computational Linguistics*, Vol. 23, pp. 269–311.

Morimoto, Tsuyoshi, Kentaro Ogura, Kenji Kita, K. Kogure, and Koji Kakigahara (1989). "Spoken Language Processing in SL-TRANS." *Proceedings of the ATR Symposium on Basic Research for Telephone Interpretation*, Tokyo, Japan.

Thompson, H. S. (1984). "Artificial Intelligence and Speech Processing: The Good News and the Bad News." In J. N. Holmes, ed., *Proceedings of the 1st International Conference on Speech Technology*. Institute of Acoustics, Hertfordshire, England.

Wang, Li 王麗, Lü Xin 呂馨, Zhao Tiejun 趙鐵軍, and Liu Zhanyi 劉占一 (2002).〈一種新的基於特殊點的基音提取方法〉(A New Pitch Detection Algorithm Based on Special Points).《第一屆學生計算語言學研討會論文集》(*SWCL-2002: First Students' Workshop on Computational Linguistics: Proceedings*), Institute of Computational Linguistics, Peking University, Beijing, China, p. 334.

Ward, Wayne (1994). "Extracting Information in Spontaneous Speech." *Proceedings of the International Conference on Spoken Language Processing* (*ICSLP-94*), Yokohama, Japan, pp. 83–86.

Wu, Bing-Fei, Kun-Ching Wang, and Lung-Yi Kuo (2004). "A Noise Estimator with Rapid Adaptation in Variable-level Noisy Environments." *Proceedings of the International Conference on Research in Computational Linguistics* (*ROCLING-XVI*), Taipei, Taiwan.

Zhu, Xuefeng and Yu Shiwen (1996).〈自動翻譯電話與口語信息處理研究〉(A Study on Automatic Translation Telephones and Speech Information Processing). In Yu Shiwen and Zhu Xuefeng, eds.,《計算語言學文集》(*Papers on Computational Linguistics*). Beijing: Department of Computer Science and Technology and Institute of Computational Linguistics, Peking University, pp. 99–103.

Speech Recognition

Applebaum, Ted H. and Brian A. Hanson (1991). "Regression Features for

Recognition of Speech in Quiet and in Noise." *Proceedings of the IEEE International Conference on Acoustics, Speech, and Signal Processing 1991* (*ICASSP-91*), Toronto, Canada, pp. 985–988.

Barnett, Jim, A. Corrada, G. Gao, Larry Gillik, Yoshiko Ito, S. Lowe, L. Manganaro, and Barbara Peskin (1996). "Multilingual Speech Recognition at Dragon System." *Proceedings of the 4th International Conference on Spoken Language Processing* (*ICSLP-96*), Philadelphia, PA, USA, pp. 2191–2194.

Boulard, Herve and Stephane Dupont (1997). "Subband-based Speech Recognition." *Proceedings of the IEEE International Conference on Acoustics, Speech, and Signal Processing* (*ICASSP-97*), Munich, Germany, pp. 545–548.

Brousseau, Julie, Caroline Drouin, George Foster, Pierre Isabelle, Roland Kuhn, Yves Normandin, and Pierre Plamondon (1995). "French Speech Recognition in an Automatic Dictation System for Translators: The TransTalk Project." *Proceedings of the 4th European Conference on Speech Communication and Technology* (*EuroSpeech-95*), Madrid, Spain, pp. 193–196.

Charoenpornsawat, Paisarn, Sanjika Hewavitharana, and Tanja Schultz (2006). "Thai Grapheme-based Speech Recognition." *Proceedings of the Human Language Technology Conference—Annual Meeting of the North American Chapter of the Association for Computational Linguistics* (*HLT-NAACL-2006*), New York, USA.

Chen, C. Julian, Ramesh A. Gopinath, Michael D. Monkowski, Michael A. Picheny, and Katherine Shen (1997). "New Methods in Continuous Mandarin Speech Recognition." *Proceedings of the 5th European Conference on Speech Communication and Technology* (*EuroSpeech-97*), Rhodes, Greece, pp. 1543–1546.

Chien, Chung-Hung and Hsiao-Chuan Wang (1997). "A Robust Keyword Spotting System for Mandarin Speech." *Proceedings of the International Conference on Research in Computational Linguistics* (*ROCLING-X*), Academia Sinica, Taipei, Taiwan.

Cole, Ronald A., Richard M. Stern, Michael S. Phillips, Scott M. Brill, Phillipe Specker, and Andrew P. Pilant (1983). "Feature-based Speaker Independent Recognition of English Letters." *Proceedings of the IEEE International Conference on Acoustics, Speech and Signal Processing* (*ICASSP-83*), Boston, MA, USA, pp. 731–783.

Collins, Michael, Brian Roark, and Murat Saraclar (2005). "Discriminative

Syntactic Language Modeling for Speech Recognition." *Proceedings of the 43rd Annual Meeting of the Association of Computational Linguistics* (*ACL-2005*), Ann Arbor, Michigan, USA.

Compernolle, D. Van (1987). "Improve Noise Immunity in Large Vocabulary Speech Recognition with the Aid of Spectral Subtraction." *Proceedings of the International Conference on Acoustics, Speech, and Signal Processing* (*ICASSP-87*), Dallas, Texas, USA, pp. 1143–1146.

Cutter, Anne (2004). "The Flexibility of Human Speech Recognition and the Seeds of Language Change." *Proceedings of the 42nd Annual Meeting of the Association for Computational Linguistics* (*ACL-2004*), Barcelona, Spain.

Fatechand, R. (1960). "Machine Recognition of Spoken Words." *Advances in Computers*, Vol. 1, p. 193.

Franzini, Michael A., M. Witbrock, and Kai-Fu Lee (1989). "A Connectionist Approach to Continuous Speech Recognition." *Proceedings of IEEE International Conference on Acoustics, Speech and Signal Processing* (*ICASSP-89*), Glasgow, Scotland, pp. 425–428.

Franzini, Michael A., Kai-Fu Lee, and Alex H. Waibel (1990). "Connectionist Viterbi Training: A New Hybrid Method for Continuous Speech Recognition." *Proceedings of IEEE International Conference on Acoustics, Speech and Signal Processing* (*ICASSP-90*), Albuquerque, North Mexico, USA, pp. 425–428.

Furui, Sadaoki (1986). "Cepstral Analysis Technique for Automatic Speaker Verification." *Proceedings of IEEE International Conference on Acoustics, Speech and Signal Processing* (*ICASSP-86*), Tokyo, Japan, pp. 52–59.

Furui, Sadaoki (1986). "Speaker Independent Isolated Word Recognition Using Dynamic Features of Speech Spectrum." *Proceedings of IEEE International Conference on Acoustics, Speech and Signal Processing* (*ICASSP-86*), Tokyo, Japan.

Furui, Sadaoki, Chiori Hori, and Takahiro Shinozaki (2001). "Toward the Realization of Spontaneous Speech Recognition and Summarization." *Proceedings of the International Conference on Research in Computational Linguistics* (*ROCLING-XIV*), National Chengkung University, Tainan, Taiwan.

Gao, Sheng, Xu Bo, and Huang Taiyi (2000). "A New Framework for Mandarin LVCSR Based on One-pass Decoder." *International Symposium Conference on Spoken Language Processing*, Beijing, China.

Gao, Yuqing, Bhuvana Ramabhadran, and Michael Picheny (2000). "New Adaptation Techniques for Large Vocabulary Continuous Speech Recognition." *Proceedings of the Conference on Automatic Speech Recognition: Challenges for the New Millenium* (*ASR-2000*), Paris, France, pp. 107–111.

Gao, Yuqing, Hakan Erdogan, Yongxin Li, Vaibhava Goel, and Michael Picheny (2001). "Recent Advances in Speech Recognition System for IBM DARPA Communicator." *Proceedings of the 7th European Conference on Speech Communication and Technology* (*EuroSpeech-2001*), Aalborg, Denmark, pp. 503–506.

García-Varea, Ismael, Alberto Sanchis, and Francisco Casacuberta (2000). "A New Approach to Speech-input Statistical Translation." *Proceedings of the 15th International Conference on Pattern Recognition* (*ICPR-2000*), Barcelona, Spain, Vol. 3, pp. 907–910.

Ghitza, Oded (1987). "Auditory Nerve Representation as a Front-end for Speech Recognition in a Noisy Environment." *Computer Speech and Language*, Vol. 1, No. 2, pp. 109–131.

Gunawardana, Raj (1985). "Automatic Speech Recognition: Fact or Fantasy?" In Catriona Picken, ed., *Translating and the Computer 7*. London: The Association for Information Management, pp. 167–177.

Hermansky, Hynek, Nelson Morgan, and H.-G. Hirsh (1993). "Recognition of Speech in Additive and Convolutional Noise Based on RASTA Spectral Processing." *Proceedings of the International Conference on Acoustics, Speech, and Signal Processing* (*ICASSP-93*), Vol. 2, pp. 83–86.

Hsieh, Ching-Tang, Eugene Lai, and You-Chuang Wang (1997). "Automatic Speaker Identification Based on Fuzzy Theory and Neural Network Using Genetic Algorithm." *Proceedings of the International Conference on Research in Computational Linguistics* (*ROCLING-X*), Academia Sinica, Taipei, Taiwan.

Inkpen, Diana Zaiu and Alain D'esilets (2005). "Semantic Similarity for Detecting Recognition Errors in Automatic Speech Transcripts." *Proceedings of Human Language Technology Conference and Conference on Empirical Methods in Natural Language Processing* (*HLT/EMNLP-2005*), Vancouver, BC, Canada.

Iwasa, Tatsuya and Kenji Kita (1995). "Error Correction of Speech Recognition Outputs Using Generalized LR Parsing and Confusion Matrix." *Proceedings of the Conference of the Association for*

Computational Linguistics and Chinese Language Processing (*ROCLING-VIII*), Yuan-Ze Institute of Technology, Chung-Li, Taiwan.

Jelinek, Frederick (1990). "Self-organized Language Modeling for Speech Recognition." In Alex H. Waibel and Kai-Fu Lee, eds., *Readings in Speech Recognition*. San Francisco: Morgan Kaufmann, pp. 450–506.

Jelinek, Frederick (1997). *Statistical Methods for Speech Recognition*. Cambridge, MA: The MIT Press.

Kanthak, Stephan, Achim Sixtus, Sirko Molau, Ralf Schlüter, and Hermann Ney (2000). "Fast Search for Large Vocabulary Speech Recognition." In Wolfgang Wahlster, ed., *Verbmobil: Foundations of Speech-to-speech Translation*. Berlin: Springer Verlag, pp. 63–78.

Khan, A. Nayeemulla (2004). "Syllable as a Unit for Speech Recognition: An Information Theoretic Perspective." *Proceedings of the International Conference on Natural Language Processing* (*ICON-2004*), International Institute of Information Technology, Hyderabad, India.

Kita, Kenji, Takeshi Kawabata, and Hiroaki Saito (1989). "HMM Continuous Speech Recognition Using Predictive LR Parsing." *Proceedings of the IEEE International Conference on Acoustics, Speech and Signal Processing* (*ICASSP-89*), Gloasgow, North Mexico, USA, pp. 703–706.

Kurimo, Mikko, Antti Puurula, Ebru Arisoy, Vesa Siivola, Teemu Hirsimki, Janne Pylkknen, Tanel Alume, and Murat Saraclar (2006). "Unlimited Vocabulary Speech Recognition for Agglutinative Languages." *Proceedings of the Human Language Technology Conference—Annual Meeting of the North American Chapter of the Association for Computational Linguistics* (*HLT-NAACL-2006*), New York, USA.

Kusher, W. M., G. Vladimir, C. Wu, V. Nguyen, and J. N. Damoulakis (1989). "The Effect of Substractive-type Speech Enhancement/Noise Reduction Algorithm on Parameter Estimation for Improved Recognition and Coding in High Noise Environments." *Proceedings of the IEEE International Conference on Acoustics, Speech and Signal Processing* (*ICASSP-89*), Glasgow, North Mexico, USA, pp. 211–214.

Lee, Chun-Jen, Eng-Fong Huang, and Jung-Kuei Chen (1998). "Using Keyword Spotting and Utterance Verification to a Prank Call Rejection

System." *Proceedings of the International Conference on Research in Computational Linguistics* (*ROCLING-XI*), Hsin-Chu, Taiwan.

Levinson, Stephen E., Lawrence R. Rabiner, and Man Mohan Sondhi (1983). "An Introduction to the Application of the Theory of Probabilistic Functions of a Markov Process to Automatic Speech Recognition." *Bell Systems Technical Journal*, Vol. 62, No. 4, pp. 1035–1074.

Levow, Gina-Anne (2006). "Unsupervised and Semi-supervised Learning of Tone and Pitch Accent." *Proceedings of the Human Language Technology Conference—Annual Meeting of the North American Chapter of the Association for Computational Linguistics* (*HLT-NAACL-2006*), New York, USA.

Litman, Diane J., Julia B. Hirschberg, and Marc Swerts (2000). "Predicting Automatic Speech Recognition Performance Using Prosodic Cues." *Proceedings of the 1st Meeting of the North American Chapter of the Association for Computational Linguistics*, Seattle, Washington, DC, USA, pp. 218–225.

Liu, Fu-Hua, Richard M. Stern, Alejandro Acero, and Pedro J. Moreno (1994). "Environment Normalization for Robust Speech Recognition Using Direct Cepstral Comparison." *Proceedings of the IEEE International Conference on Acoustics, Speech and Signal Processing* (*ICASSP-94*), Adelaide, Australia, Vol. 2, pp. 61–64.

Livescu, Karen and James Glass (2004). "Feature-based Pronunciation Modeling for Speech Recognition." *Proceedings of the Human Language Technology Conference/North American Chapter of the Association for Computational Linguistics Annual Meeting* (*HLT/NAACL-2004*), Boston, MA, USA.

Locke, William N. (1955). "Speech Input." In William N. Locke and Andrew D. Booth, eds., *Machine Translation of Languages: Fourteen Essays*. Cambridge, MA: Technology Press of the Massachusetts Institute of Technology, pp. 104–118.

LuperFoy, Susann (1997). "Discourse Processing for Voice-to-voice Machine Translation." In Christa Hauenschild and Susanne Heizmann, eds., *Machine Translation and Translation Theory*. Berlin-New York: Mouton de Gruyter, pp. 223–250.

Lyu, Ren-Yuan, Yuang-Jin Chiang, Ren-Jou Fang, and Wen-Ping Hsieh (1998). "A Large-vocabulary Taiwanese (Min-nan) Speech Recognition System Based on Inter-syllabic Initial-final Modeling and

Lexicon Tree Search." *Proceedings of the International Conference on Research in Computational Linguistics* (*ROCLING-XI*), Hsin-Chu, Taiwan.

Malenke, Michael, Marcus Bäumler, and Erwin Paulus (2000). "Speech Recognition Performance Assessment." In Wolfgang Wahlster, ed., *Verbmobil: Foundations of Speech-to-speech Translation*. Berlin: Springer Verlag, pp. 583–591.

Markowitz, Judith (1997). "Using Speech Recognition." *Proceedings of the 5th Conference on Applied Natural Language Processing*, Seattle, Washington, DC, USA.

McCourt, Paul M., Saeed V. Vaseghi, and B. Doherty (2000). "Multi-resolution Subband Features and Models for HMM-based Phonetic Modelling." *Computer Speech and Language*, Vol. 14, pp. 241–259.

Meteer, Marie and Rukmini Iyer (1996). "Modeling Conversational Speech for Speech Recognition." *Proceedings of the Conference on Empirical Methods in Natural Language Processing*, University of Pennsylvania, PA, USA.

Mihalcea, Rada F. and Carlo Strapparava (2005). "Making Computers Laugh: Investigations in Automatic Humor Recognition." *Proceedings of Human Language Technology Conference and Conference on Empirical Methods in Natural Language Processing* (*HLT/EMNLP-2005*), Vancouver, BC, Canada.

Minami, Yasuhiro, Kiyohiro Shikano, Satoshi Takahashi, Tomokazu Yamada, Osamu Yoshioka, and Sadaoki Furui (1995). "Large-vocabulary Continuous Speech Recognition Algorithm Applied to a Multi-modal Telephone Directory Assistance System." *Speech Communication*, Vol. 15, pp. 301–310.

Myers, Marie J. (2000). "Voice Recognition Software and a Hand-held Translation Machine for Second-language Learning." *Computer Assisted Language Learning*, Vol. 13, pp. 29–41.

Nagai, Akito, Yasushi Ishikawa, and Kunio Nakajima (1997). "Concept-driven Search Algorithm Incorporating Semantic Interpretation and Speech Recognition." In Ruslan Mitkov and Nicolas Nicolov, eds., *Recent Advances in Natural Language Processing*. Amsterdam and Philadelphia: John Benjamins Publishing Company, pp. 149–160.

Ney, Hermann, D. Mergel, A. Noll, and A. Paeseler (1992). "Data Driven Search Organization for Continuous Speech Recognition in the

SPICOS System." *IEEE Transactions on Signal Processing*, Vol. 40, No. 2, pp. 272–281.

Och, Franz Josef and Hermann Ney (2001). "What Can Machine Translation Learn from Speech Recognition?" In Bente Maegaard, ed., *Proceedings of MT Summit VIII: Machine Translation in the Information Age*, Santiago de Compostela, Spain, pp. 26–31.

Gong, Yifan (1995). "Speech Recognition in Noisy Environments: A Survey." *Speech Communication*, Vol. 16, pp. 261–291.

Pereira, Fernando C. and Michael D. Riley (1997). "Speech Recognition by Composition of Weighted Finite Automata." In Emmanuel Roche and S. Yves Schabes, eds., *Finite State Language Processing*. Cambridge, MA: MIT Press, pp. 431–453.

Peters, Jochen and Dietrich Klakow (2000). "Capturing Long Range Correlations Using Log-linear Language Models." In Wolfgang Wahlster, ed., *Verbmobil: Foundations of Speech-to-speech Translation*. Berlin: Springer Verlag, pp. 79–94.

Pinto, Joel, Kalika Bali, Sandeep Manocha, Satinder Pal Singh, and R. N. V. Sitaram (2004). "Building Large Vocabulary Speech Recognition Systems for Indian Languages." *Proceedings of the International Conference on Natural Language Processing (ICON-2004)*, International Institute of Information Technology, Hyderabad, India.

Rabiner, Lawrence and Biing-Hwang Juang (1993). *Fundamentals of Speech Recognition*. New Jersey: Prentice Hall.

Rayner, Manny and Pierrette Bouillon (1995). "Hybrid Transfer in an English-French Spoken Language Translator." *Proceedings of the 5th International Conference (IA-95)*, Montpellier, France, pp. 153–162.

Reithinger, Nobert, Elisabeth Maier, and Jan Alexandersson (1995). "Treatment of Incomplete Dialogues in a Speech-to-speech Translation System." *Proceedings of the ESCA Workshop on Spoken Dialogue Systems*, Aalborg University, Vigs, Denmark, pp. 33–36.

Samudravijaya, K. (2004). "Variable Frame Size Analysis for Speech Recognition." *Proceedings of the International Conference on Natural Language Processing (ICON-2004)*, International Institute of Information Technology, Hyderabad, India.

Scheytt, Peter, Michael Finke, and Petra Geutner (1997). *Speech Recognition on Serbo-Croatian Dictation and Broadcast News Data*. Pittsburgh: Language Technologies Institute, Carnegie Mellon University.

Schultz, T. and Alex H. Waibel (1998). "Language Independent and Language Adaptive LVSCR." *Proceedings of the 5th International Conference on Spoken Language Processing* (*ICSLP-98*), Sydney, Australia, pp. 1819–1822.
Selouani, Sid-Ahmed, Hesham Tolba, and Douglas O'Shaughnessy (2003). "Auditory-based Acoustic Distinctive Features and Spectral Cues for Robust Automatic Speech Recognition in Low-SNR Car Environments." *Proceedings of the Human Language Technology and North American Chapter of Association of Computational Linguistics 2003* (*HLT/NAACL-2003*), Edmonton, Alberta, Canada.
Shen, Jia-Lin, Ying-Chieh Tu, Po-Yu Liang, and Lin-Shan Lee (1998). "Speaker-independent Continuous Mandarin Speech Recognition under Telephone Environments." *Proceedings of the International Conference on Research in Computational Linguistics* (*ROCLING-XI*), Hsin-Chu, Taiwan.
Stallard, David and Robert Bobrow (1993). "The Semantic Linker's New Fragment Combining Method." *Proceedings of the ARPA Human Language Technology Workshop*, Princeton, New Jersey, USA, pp. 37–42.
Sumita, Eiichiro and Fumiaki Sugaya (2006). "Word Pronunciation Disambiguation Using the Web." *Proceedings of the Human Language Technology Conference—Annual Meeting of the North American Chapter of the Association for Computational Linguistics* (*HLT-NAACL-2006*), New York, USA.
Tan, Tien-Ping and Laurent Besacier (2006). "A French Non-native Corpus for Automatic Speech Recognition." *Proceedings of the 5th International Conference on Language Resources and Evaluation* (*LREC-2006*), Genoa, Italy.
Tebelskis, Joe, Alex H. Waibel, B. Petek, and O. Schmidbauer (1991). "Continuous Speech Recognition Using Linked Predictive Neural Networks." *Proceedings of the 1991 IEEE International Conference on Acoustics, Speech, and Signal Processing* (*ICASSP-91*), Toronto, Canada, pp. 61–64.
Thompson, Henry (1990). "Speech Recognition, Artificial Intelligence and Translation: How Rosy a Future?" In Catriona Picken, ed., *Translating and the Computer 11: Preparing for the Next Decade*. London: The Association for Information Management, pp. 113–117.
Tomita, Masaru (1986). "An Efficient Word Lattice Parsing Algorithm for

Continuous Speech Recognition." *Proceedings of IEEE International Conference on Acoustics, Speech and Signal Processing* (*ICASSP-86*), Tokyo, Japan, pp. 1569–1572.

Waibel, Alex H., Hidelumi Sawai, and Kiyohiro Shikano (1989). "Consonant and Phoneme Recognition by Modular Construction of Large Phonemic Time-delay Neural Networks." *Proceedings of IEEE International Conference on Acoustics, Speech and Signal Processing* (*ICASSP-89*), Glasgow, Scotland, pp. 112–115.

Waibel, Alex H., Toshiyuki Hanazawa, Geoffrey E. Hinton, Kiyohiro Shikano, and Kevin J. Lang (1989). "Phoneme Recognition Using Time-delay Neural Networks." *Proceedings of IEEE International Conference on Acoustics, Speech and Signal Processing* (*ICASSP-89*), Glasgow, Scotland, pp. 328–339.

Waibel, Alex H., Hagen Soltau, Tanja Schultz, Thomas Schaaf, and Florian Metze (2000). "Multilingual Speech Recognition." In Wolfgang Wahlster, ed., *Verbmobil: Foundations of Speech-to-speech Translation*. Berlin: Springer Verlag, pp. 33–45.

Wang, Hsin-Min, Tai-Hsuan Ho, Rung-Chiung Yang, Jia-Lin Shen, Bo-Ren Bai, Jenn-Chau Hong, Wei-Peng Chen, Tong-Lo Yu, and Lin-Shan Lee (1997). "Complete Recognition of Continuous Mandarin Speech for Chinese Language with Very Large Vocabulary Using Limited Training Data." *IEEE Transactions on Speech and Audio Processing*, Vol. 5, No. 2, pp. 195–200.

Wang, Jinjia 王金甲, Wang Chengru 王成儒, and Li Jing 李靜 (2002).〈自組織混合神經網絡在說話人識別中的應用〉(Self-organizing Mixture Network for Speaker Identification).《第一屆學生計算語言學研討會論文集》(*SWCL2002: First Students' Workshop on Computational Linguistics: Proceedings*), Institute of Computational Linguistics, Peking University, Beijing, China, p. 335.

Wang, Zuoying and Gao Hongge (1996). "An Inhomogeneous HMM Recognition Algorithm." *Proceedings of the 4th National Conference on Man-machine Speech Communications* (*NCMMSC-96*), Beijing, China, pp. 105–109.

Wright, J. H. and E. N. Wrigley (1988). "Linguistic Control in Speech Recognition." *Proceedings of the 7th FASE Symposium*, Edinburgh, Scotland, pp. 545–552.

Xu, Mingxing, Fang Zheng, and Wenhu Wu (1997). "Rejection in Speech Recognition Based on CDCPMs." *Proceedings of the International*

Conference on Research in Computational Linguistics (*ROCLING-X*), Academia Sinica, Taipei, Taiwan.

Xu, Bo, Gao Sheng, Cao Yang, Wu Hua, and Huang Taiyi (1999). "Integrating Tone Information in Continuous Mandarin Recognition." *Proceedings of the International Symposium on Signal Processing and Intelligent System* (*ISSPIS-99*), Guangzhou, China.

Young, Sheryl R., Alexander G. Hauptmann, and Wayne H. Ward (1988). *An Integrated Speech and Natural Language Dialog System: Using Dialog Knowledge in Speech Recognition*. Technical Report (CMU-CS 88-128). Pittsburgh: Computer Science Department, Carnegie Mellon University.

Yu, Hua and Tanja Schultz (2003). "Implicit Trajectory Modeling through Gaussian Transition Models for Speech Recognition." *Proceedings of the Human Language Technology and North American Chapter of Association of Computational Linguistics 2003* (*HLT/NAACL-2003*), Edmonton, Alberta, Canada.

Zechner, Klaus and Isaac Bejar (2006). "Towards Automatic Scoring of Non-native Spontaneous Speech." *Proceedings of the Human Language Technology Conference—Annual Meeting of the North American Chapter of the Association for Computational Linguistics* (*HLT-NAACL-2006*), New York, USA.

Zhan, Puming and Alex H. Waibel (1997). *Vocal Tract Length Normalization for Large Vocabulary Continuous Speech Recognition*. CMU-CS-97-148, Carnegie Mellon University, Pittsburgh, PA, USA.

Zhang, Quan 張全, Zhang Ni 張倪, and Wei Xiangfeng 韋向峰 (2001).〈漢語語音識別的糾錯處理〉(Correction in Chinese Speech Recognition). In Huang Changning 黃昌寧 and Zhang Pu 張普, eds.,《自然語言理解與機器翻譯》(*Natural Language Understanding and Machine Translation*). Beijing: Tsinghua University Press, pp. 448–453.

Zheng, Fang, Mingxing Xu, and Wenhu Wu (1997). "The Description of the Intra-state Feature Space in Speech Recognition." *Proceedings of the International Conference on Research in Computational Linguistics* (*ROCLING-X*), Academia Sinica, Taipei, Taiwan.

Hidden Markov Model

Baum, Leonard E., Ted Petrie, George Soules, and Norman Weiss (1970). "A Maximization Technique Occurring in the Statistical Analysis of

Probabilistic Functions of Markov Chains." *The Annals of Mathematical Statistics*, Vol. 41, No. 1, pp. 164–171.
Boite, R., H. Leich, and G. Zanellato (1986). "Isolated Word Recognition by Hidden Markov Models." *Proceedings of the European Signal Processing Conference* (*EUSIPCO-86*), Hague, the Netherlands, Vol. 1, pp. 541–544.
Collins, Michael (2002). "Discriminative Training Methods for Hidden Markov Models: Theory and Experiments with Perceptron Algorithms." *Proceedings of the 2002 Conference on Empirical Methods in Natural Language Processing* (*EMNLP-2002*), University of Pennsylvania, Philadelphia, PA, USA.
Fung, Pascale and Wu Dekai (1995). "Coerced Markov Models for Cross-lingual Lexical-tag Relations." *Proceedings of the 6th International Conference on Theoretical and Methodological Issues in Machine Translation* (*TMI-95*), Leuven, Belgium, pp. 240–255.
Gu, Zhenmei and Nick Cercone (2006). "Segment-based Hidden Markov Models for Information Extraction." *Proceedings of the Joint Conference of the International Committee on Computational Linguistics and the Association for Computational Linguistics* (*COLING/ACL-2006*), Sydney, Australia.
Jung, Jaeyoung, Maki Miyake, and Hiroyuki Akama (2006). "Markov Cluster Shortest Path Founded upon the Alibi-breaking Algorithm." *Proceedings of the 7th International Conference on Intelligent Text Processing and Computational Linguistics* (*CICLing-2006*), Mexico City, Mexico.
Kim, Jae-Hoon (1997). "Combining Multiword Units into a Hidden Markov Model for Part-of-speech Tagging." *Proceedings of the International Conference on Research in Computational Linguistics* (*ROCLING-X*), Academia Sinica, Taipei, Taiwan.
Kim, Jin-Dong, Sang-Zoo Lee, and Hae-Chang Rim (1999). "HMM Specialization with Selective Lexicalization." *Proceedings of the Joint SIGDAT Conference on Empirical Methods in NLP and Very Large Corpora* (*EMNLP/VLC-99*), University of Maryland, College Park, MD, USA.
Kita, Kenji and Takeshi Kawabata (1989). "HMM Continuous Speech Recognition Using Predictive LR Parsing." *Proceedings of IEEE International Conference on Acoustics, Speech and Signal Processing* (*ICASSP-89*), Glasgow, Scotland, pp. 703–706.

Lafferty, John (1996). "Gibbs-markov Models." *Computing Science and Statistics*, Vol. 27, pp. 370–377.

Lee, Sang-Zoo, Jun-ichi Tsujii, and Rim Hae-Chang (2000). "Hidden Markov Model-based Korean Part-of-speech Tagging Considering High Agglutinativity, Word-spacing, and Lexical Correlativity." *Proceedings of the 38th Annual Meeting of the Association for Computational Linguistics* (*ACL-2000*), Hong Kong.

Lee, Sang-Zoo, Jun-ichi Tsujii, and Rim Hae-Chang (2000). "Lexicalized Hidden Markov Models for Part-of-speech Tagging." *Proceedings of the 18th International Conference on Computational Linguistics* (*COLING-2000*), Saarbrücken, Germany, pp. 481–487.

Lin, Weiyong 林文永, Shi Zhiguo 石志國, Xue Weimin 薛為民, and Chen Fengjun 陳鋒軍 (2002).〈隱馬爾可夫模型實現語音和視頻識別〉(Hidden Markov Model Based on Audio and Video Recognition).《第一屆學生計算語言學研討會論文集》(*SWCL-2002: First Students' Workshop on Computational Linguistics: Proceedings*), Institute of Computational Linguistics, Peking University, Beijing, China, p. 338.

Maskey, Sameer and Julia Hirschberg (2006). "Summarizing Speech Without Text Using Hidden Markov Models." *Proceedings of the Human Language Technology Conference—Annual Meeting of the North American Chapter of the Association for Computational Linguistics* (*HLT-NAACL-2006*), New York, USA.

Mei, Xiao-dan, Sheng-he Sun, Jeng-shuang Pan, and Tsong-yi Chen (2001). "Optimization of HMM by the Tabu Search Algorithm." *Proceedings of the International Conference on Research in Computational Linguistics* (*ROCLING-XIV*), National Chengkung University, Tainan, Taiwan.

Miller, David H., Tim Leek, and Richard M. Schwartz (1999). "A Hidden Markov Model Information Retrieval System." *Proceedings of the 1999 ACM SIGIR Conference on Research and Development in Information Retrieval*, pp. 214–221.

Narupiyakul, Lalita, Calvin Thomas, Nick Cercone, and Booncharoen Sirinaovakul (2004). "Thai Syllable-based Information Extraction Using Hidden Markov Models." *Proceedings of the 5th International Conference on Intelligent Text Processing and Computational Linguistics* (*CICLing-2004*), Chung-Ang University, Seoul, Korea, pp. 531–540.

Palanisamy, Arulmozhi and Sobha Lalitha Devi (2006). "HMM Based

POS Tagger for a Relatively Free Word Order Language." In Alexander F. Gelbukh, ed., *Advances in Natural Language Processing*, Special Issue of *Research in Computing Science*, No. 18, pp. 37–48.
Poritz, Alan (1988). "Hidden Markov Models: A Guided Tour." *Proceedings of IEEE International Conference on Acoustics, Speech and Singal Processing* (*ICASSP-88*), New York, USA, pp. 7–13.
Rabiner, Lawrence R., Jay G. Wilpon, and Frank K. Soong (1988). "High Performance Connected Digit Recognition Using Hidden Markov Models." *Proceedings of the IEEE International Conference on Acoustics, Speech and Signal Processing* (*ICASSP-88*), New York, USA, pp. 1214–1225.
Shibata, Tomohide and Sadao Kurohashi (2006). "Unsupervised Topic Identification by Integrating Linguistic and Visual Information Based on Hidden Markov Models." *Proceedings of the Joint Conference of the International Committee on Computational Linguistics and the Association for Computational Linguistics* (*COLING/ACL-2006*), Sydney, Australia.
Swen, Bing (2002). "A General Output Model of Hidden Markov Models and Its Applications to Chinese Segmentation and Tagging." In Yu Shiwen, ed., *Proceedings of the 2nd China-Japan Natural Language Processing Joint Research Promotion Conference* (*CJNLP-2002*). Beijing: Institute of Computational Linguistics, Peking University, pp. 236–246.
Vogel, Stephan, Hermann Ney, and Christoph Tillmann (1996). "HMM-based Word Alignment in Statistical Translation." *Proceedings from the 16th International Conference on Computational Linguistics* (*COLING-96*), Copenhagen, Denmark, pp. 836–841.
Waibel, Alex H., Toshiyuki Hanazawa, Geoffrey E. Hinton, Kiyohiro Shikano, and Kevin J. Lang (1988). "Phoneme Recognition: Neural Networks vs. Hidden Markov Models." *Proceedings of the IEEE International Conference on Acoustics, Speech and Signal Processing* (*ICASSP-88*), New York, USA, pp. 107–110.
Xu, Jinxi and Ralph Weischedel (2000). "Cross-lingual Information Retrieval Using Hidden Markov Models." *Proceedings of the Joint Sigdat Conference on Empirical Methods in Natural Language Processing and Very Large Corpora* (*EMNLP/VLC-2000*), Hong Kong University of Science and Technology, Hong Kong.

Zhu, Jing and Jian-Hua Li (2006). "An HMM-based Approach to Automatic Phrasing for Mandarin Text-to-speech Synthesis." *Proceedings of the Joint Conference of the International Committee on Computational Linguistics and the Association for Computational Linguistics* (*COLING/ACL-2006*), Sydney, Australia.

Pitch Detection

Jo, Wang Rae, Jong Kuk Kim, and Myung Jin Bae (2005). "A Study on Pitch Detection in Time-frequency Hybrid Domain." *Proceedings of the 6th International Conference on Intelligent Text Processing and Computational Linguistics* (*CICLing-2005*), Mexico City, Mexico, pp. 426–429.

Kim, Jong Kuk, Ki Young Lee, and Myung Jin Bae (2005). "On a Pitch Detection Method Using Noise Reduction." *Proceedings of the 6th International Conference on Intelligent Text Processing and Computational Linguistics* (*CICLing-2005*), Mexico City, Mexico, pp. 418–421.

Robustness

Furuse, Osamu, Setsuo Yamada, Kazuhide Yamamoto (1998). "Splitting Long or Ill-formed Input for Robust Spoken-language Translation." *Proceedings of the 36th Annual Meeting of the Association for Computational Linguistics and 17th International Conference on Computational Linguistics* (*COLING-ACL-98*), Montreal, Quebec, Canada, pp. 421–427.

Haiber, Udo, Helmut Mangold, Thilo Pfau, Peter Regel-Brietzmann, Günther Ruske, and Volker Schleß (2000). "Robust Recognition of Spontaneous Speech." In Wolfgang Wahlster, ed., *Verbmobil: Foundations of Speech-to-speech Translation*. Berlin: Springer Verlag, pp. 46–62.

Hobbs, Jerry R., Douglas E. Appelt, John Bear, and Mabry Tyson (1992). "Robust Processing of Real-world Natural Language Texts." *Proceedings of the 3rd Conference on Applied Natural Language Processing*, Trento, Italy, pp. 186–192.

Jackson, Eric, Doug Appelt, John Bear, Robert Moore and Ann Podlozny (1991). "A Template Matcher for Robust NL Interpretation."

Proceedings of the Workshop on Speech and Natural Language Processing, Asilomar, California, USA, pp. 190–194.

Minker, Wolfgang (2001). "Robustness and Portability Issues in Multilingual Speech Processing." *Machine Translation*, Vol. 16, No. 2, pp. 109–126.

Piotrowska, Xenia, Rajmund Piotrowski, and Yuri Romanov (2003). "Robustness in the Linguistic Automation." *International Journal of Translation*, Vol. 15, No. 1, pp. 82–86.

Romanov, Yuri (2004). "Robustness in Speech and Text Processing Systems." *International Journal of Translation*, Vol. 16, No. 2, pp. 131–136.

Sima'an, Khalil (2001). "Robust Data Oriented Parsing of Speech Utterances." *Proceedings of the 7th International Workshop on Parsing Technologies (IWPT-2001)*, Peking University, Beijing, China. Beijing: Tsinghua University Press, pp. 177–188.

Simard, Michel and Pierre Plamondon (1996). "Bilingual Sentence Alignment: Balancing Robustness and Accuracy." *Proceedings of the 2nd Conference of the Association for Machine Translation in the Americas: Expanding MT Horizons (AMTA-2)*, Montreal, Quebec, Canada, pp. 135–144.

Simard, Michel and Pierre Plamondon (1998). "Bilingual Sentence Alignment: Balancing Robustness and Accuracy." *Machine Translation*, Vol. 13, No. 1, pp. 59–80.

Su, Keh-Yih and Lee Chin-Hui (1991). "Robustness and Discrimination Oriented Speech Recognition Using Weighted HMM and Subspace Projection Approach." *Proceedings of the IEEE International Conference on Acoustics, Speech and Signal Processing (ICASSP-91)*, Toronto, Canada, pp. 541–544.

Way, Andy (1999). "A Hybrid Architecture for Robust MT Using LFG-DOP." *Journal of Experimental and Theoretical Artificial Intelligence*, Vol. 11, pp. 441–471.

Worm, Karsten L. (1998). "A Model for Robust Processing of Spontaneous Speech by Integrating Viable Fragments." *Proceedings of the 36th Annual Meeting of the Association for Computational Linguistics and 17th International Conference on Computational Linguistics (COLING-ACL-98)*, Montreal, Quebec, Canada, pp. 1403–1407.

Speech Recognition System

Chow, Yen-Lu, M. Dunham, Owen Kimball, M. Krasner, Francis G. Kubala, John Makhoul, S. Roucos, and Richard Schwartz (1987). "BYBLOS: The BBN Continuous Speech Recognition System." *Proceedings of the IEEE International Conference on Acoustics, Speech and Signal Processing* (*ICASSP-87*), Dallas, USA, pp. 89–92.

Gao, Yuqing, Hakan Erdogan, Yongxin Li, Vaibhava Goel, and Michael Picheny (2001). "Recent Advances in Speech Recognition System for IBM DARPA Communicator." *Proceedings of the 7th European Conference on Speech Communication and Technology* (*EuroSpeech 2001—Scandinavia*), Aalborg, Denmark, pp. 503–506.

IBM Speech Recognition Group (1985). "A Real-time, Isolated-word, Speech-recognition System for Dictation Transcription." *Proceedings of IEEE International Conference on Acoustics, Speech and Signal Processing* (*ICASSP-85*), Tampa, Florida, USA.

Lee, Kai-Fu, Hsiao-Wuen Hon, and Raj D. Reddy (1990). "An Overview of the SPHINX Speech Recognition System." *IEEE Transactions on Acoustics, Speech, and Signal Processing*, Vol. 38, pp. 35–45.

Lowerre, Bruce T. and Raj D. Reddy (1980). "The HARPY Speech Recognition System." In Wayne A. Lea, ed., *Trends in Speech Recognition*. Englewood Cliffs, New Jersey: Prentice-Hall, pp. 340–360.

Morii, Shuji, Katsuyuki Niyada, Satoru Fujii, and Masakatsu Hoshimi (1985). "Large Vocabulary Speaker-independent Japanese Speech Recognition System." *Proceedings of the IEEE International Conference on Acoustics, Speech and Signal Processing* (*ICASSP-85*), Tampa, Florida, USA, pp. 866–869.

Nakamura, Satoshi, Konstantin Markov, Takatoshi Jitsuhiro, Zhang Jin-Song, Hirofumi Yamamoto, and Genichiro Kikui (2004). "Multilingual Speech Recognition System for Speech-to-speech Translation." *Proceedings of the International Workshop on Spoken Language Translation* (*IWSLT-2004*), Kyoto, Japan.

NaturallySpeaking

Grimes, William J. (1997). "Voice Recognition Software: NaturallySpeaking from Dragon Systems." *Translation Journal*, Vol. 1, No. 2.

ViaVoice

Fletcher, Roger (1997). "First Impressions of ViaVoice: Continuous Dictation Software from IBM." *Translation Journal*, Vol. 1, No. 2.

Speech Summarization

Chatain, Pierre, Edward Whittaker, Joanna Mrozinski, and Sadaoki Furui (2006). "Class Model Adaptation for Speech Summarisation." *Proceedings of the Human Language Technology Conference—Annual Meeting of the North American Chapter of the Association for Computational Linguistics* (*HLT-NAACL-2006*), New York, USA.

Maskey, Sameer and Julia Hirschberg (2006). "Summarizing Speech without Text Using Hidden Markov Models." *Proceedings of the Human Language Technology Conference—Annual Meeting of the North American Chapter of the Association for Computational Linguistics* (*HLT-NAACL-2006*), New York, USA.

Murray, Gabriel, Steve Renals, Jean Carletta, and Johanna D. Moore (2006). "Incorporating Speaker and Discourse Features into Speech Summarization." *Proceedings of the Human Language Technology Conference—Annual Meeting of the North American Chapter of the Association for Computational Linguistics* (*HLT-NAACL-2006*), New York, USA.

Park, Youngja and Ying Li (2006). "Extracting Salient Keywords from Instructional Videos Using Joint Text, Audio and Visual Cues." *Proceedings of the Human Language Technology Conference—Annual Meeting of the North American Chapter of the Association for Computational Linguistics* (*HLT-NAACL-2006*), New York, USA.

Speech Synthesis

Campbell, Nick (2004). "Specifying Affect and Emotion for Expressive Speech Synthesis." *Proceedings of the 5th International Conference on Intelligent Text Processing and Computational Linguistics* (*CICLing-2004*), Chung-Ang University, Seoul, Korea, pp. 390–401.

Donovan, Robert E., Martin Franz, Jeffrey S. Sorensen, and Salim Roukos (1999). "Phrase Splicing and Variable Substitution Using the IBM Trainable Speech Synthesis System." *Proceedings of the IEEE*

International Conference on Acoustics, Speech, and Signal Processing (*ICASSP-99*), Phoenix, Arizona, USA, pp. 373–376.
Guyomard, Marc, Jacques Siroux, Dominique Pernici, and Christophe Royer (1997). "A General Public Application of Pedagogic and Linguistic Vocations of Speech Synthesis: Ordictee." *Proceedings of the International Conference on Research in Computational Linguistics* (*ROCLING-X*), Academia Sinica, Taipei, Taiwan.
Hanazawa, Toshiyuki, Kenji Kita, Satoshi Nakamura, Takeshi Kawabata, and Kiyohiro Shikano (1990). "ATR HMM-LR Continuous Speech Recognition System." *Proceedings of IEEE International Conference on Acoustics, Speech and Signal Processing* (*ICASSP-90*), Albuquerque, North Mexico, USA.
Mohri, Mehryar, Cyril Allauzen, and Michael Riley (2004). "Statistical Modeling for Unit Selection in Speech Synthesis." *Proceedings of the 42nd Annual Meeting of the Association for Computational Linguistics* (*ACL-2004*), Barcelona, Spain, pp. 55–62.
Shen, Jinyuan 沈晉苑 (2002).〈語音合成技術的現狀及發展前景〉(The Present and Future Prospects of Speech Synthesis Technology).《第一屆學生計算語言學研討會論文集》(*SWCL-2002: First Students' Workshop on Computational Linguistics: Proceedings*), Institute of Computational Linguistics, Peking University, Beijing, China, p. 336.
Steffens, Jochen and Erwin Paulus (2000). "Speech Synthesis Quality Assessment." In Wolfgang Wahlster, ed., *Verbmobil: Foundations of Speech-to-speech Translation*. Berlin: Springer Verlag, pp. 592–596.
Stöber, Karlheinz, Petra Wagner, Jörg Helbig, Stefanie Köster, David Stall, Matthias Thomae, Jen Blauert, Wolfgang Hess, Rüdiger Hoffmann, and Helmut Mangold (2000). "Speech Synthesis Using Multilevel Selection and Concatenation of Units from Large Speech Corpora." In Wolfgang Wahlster, ed., *Verbmobil: Foundations of Speech-to-speech Translation*. Berlin: Springer Verlag, pp. 519–534.
Tao, Jianhua 陶建華, Cai Lianhong 蔡蓮紅, and Zhao Sheng 趙晟 (2001).〈漢語語音合成中的文本分析和韻律處理〉(Text Analysis and Prosody Processing for Chinese Speech Synthesis).《輝煌二十年 —— 中國中文信息學會二十周年學術會議》(*Proceedings of the Conference of the 20th Anniversary of CIPSC*). Beijing: Tsinghua University Press, pp. 272–279.
Wang, Renhua 王仁華 and Hu Guoping 胡國平 (2002).〈面向語音合成的自然語言處理〉(Speech Synthesis Oriented Natural Language

Processing). In Yu Shiwen, ed., *Proceedings of the 2nd China-Japan Natural Language Processing Joint Research Promotion Conference* (*CJNLP-2002*). Beijing: Institute of Computational Linguistics, Peking University, pp. 253–258.

Speech Technology

Guo, Chen 郭晨 (2002).〈漢語語音技術〉(Technology on Chinese Speech).《第一屆學生計算語言學研討會論文集》(*SWCL-2002: First Students' Workshop on Computational Linguistics: Proceedings*), Institute of Computational Linguistics, Peking University, Beijing, China, p. 337.

Speech Translation

Abella, Alicia and Allen L. Gorin (1997). "Generating Semantically Consistent Inputs to a Dialog Manager." *Proceedings of the European Conference on Speech Communication and Technology* (*EuroSpeech-97*), Rhodes, Greece, pp. 1879–1882.

Alexandrovna, Isaeva Anna (2006). "Structure of Thematic Monologues in Spontaneous Speech Translation." *Proceedings of the 6th Portsmouth Translation Conference: Translation Technologies and Culture,* School of Languages and Area Studies, University of Portsmouth, England.

Alshawi, Hiyan and Fei Xia (1997). "English-to-Mandarin Speech Translation with Head Transducers." *Spoken Language Translation: Proceedings of a Workshop Sponsored by the Association for Computational Linguistics and by the European Network in Language and Speech* (*ELSNET-97*), Madrid, Spain, pp. 54–60.

Alshawi, Hiyan, Srinivas Bangalore, and Shona Douglas (1998). "Learning Phrase-based Head Transduction Models for Translation of Spoken Utterances." *Proceedings of the 5th International Conference on Spoken Language Processing* (*ICSLP-98*), Sydney, Australia, pp. 2767–2770.

Alshawi, Hiyan, Srinivas Bangalore, and Shona Douglas (2000). "Head-transducer Models for Speech Translation and Their Automatic Acquisition from Bilingual Data." *Machine Translation*, Vol. 15, Nos. 1–2, pp. 105–124.

Amengual, Juan Carlos, José Miguel Benedí, K. Beulen, Francisco

Casacuberta, Asunción Castaño, Antonio Castellanos, Victor M. Jiménez, David Liorens, Andrés Marzal, Hermann Ney, Federico Prat, Enrique Vidal, and Juan Miguel Vilar (1997). "Speech Translation Based on Automatically Trainable Finite-state Models." *Proceedings of the 5th European Conference on Speech Communication and Technology* (*EuroSpeech-97*), Rhodes, Greece, pp. 1439–1442.

Amtrup, Jan (1997). "Layered Charts for Speech Translation." *Proceedings of the 7th International Conference on Theoretical and Methodological Issues in Machine Translation* (*TMI-97*), St. John's College, Santa Fe, New Mexico, USA.

Bangalore, Srinivas and Giuseppe Riccardi (2000). "Stochastic Finite-state Models for Spoken Language Machine Translation." In Carol J. van Ess-Dykema, Clare R. Voss, and Florence Reeder, eds., *Proceedings of the Workshop of Embedded Machine Translation Systems* (*ANLP/NAACL-2000*), Association for Computational Linguistics, Seattle, Washington, DC, USA, pp. 52–59.

Bernth, Arendse (2003). "Controlled Generation for Speech-to-speech MT Systems." *The Joint Conference of the 8th International Workshop of the European Association for Machine Translation and the 4th Controlled Language Applications Workshop* (*EAMT/CLAW-2003*), Dublin City University, Dublin, Ireland, pp. 1–7.

Block, Hans Ulrich, Stefanie Schachtl, and Manfred Gehrke (2000). "Adapting a Large Scale MT System for Spoken Language." In Wolfgang Wahlster, ed., *Verbmobil: Foundations of Speech-to-speech Translation*. Berlin: Springer Verlag, pp. 394–410.

Casacuberta, Francisco, Enrique Vidal, and Juan Miguel Vilar (2002). "Architectures for Speech-to-speech Translation Using Finite-state Models." *Proceedings of the Workshop on Speech-to-Speech Translation: Algorithms and Systems*, Philadelphia, USA, pp. 39–44.

Forbes-Riley, Kate and Diane J. Litman (2006). "Modelling User Satisfaction and Student Learning in a Spoken Dialogue Tutoring System with Generic, Tutoring, and User Affect Parameters." *Proceedings of the Human Language Technology Conference—Annual Meeting of the North American Chapter of the Association for Computational Linguistics* (*HLT-NAACL-2006*), New York, USA.

Frederking, Robert E., Alexander Rudnicky, Christopher Hogan, and Kevin Lenzo (2000). "Interactive Speech Translation in the Diplomat Project." *Machine Translation*, Vol. 15, Nos. 1–2, pp. 27–42.

Gao, Yuqing, Bowen Zhou, Zijian Diao, Jeffrey Sorensen, and Michael Picheny (2002). "MARS: A Statistical Semantic Parsing and Generation-based Multilingual Automatic Translation System." *Machine Translation*, Vol. 17, No. 3, pp. 185–212.

Gerver, David (1972). "ASPA-Automatic Speech Pause Analyzer." *Behavior Research Methods and Instrumentation*, Vol. 4, pp. 265–270.

Hayes, Philip J., Alexander G. Hauptmann, Jaime G. Carbonell, and Masaru Tomita (1987). *Parsing Spoken Language: A Semantic Caseframe Approach*. Pittsburgh: Center for Machine Translation, Carnegie Mellon University.

Huang, Chao, Xu Peng, Zhang Xin, Zhao Shubin, Huang Taiyi, and Xu Bo (1999). "LODESTAR: A Mandarin Spoken Dialogue System for Travel Information Retrieval." *Proceedings of the 6th European Conference on Speech Communication and Technology* (*EuroSpeech-99*), Budapest, Hungary, Vol. 3, pp. 1159–1162.

Huang, Fei 黃非, Xu Bo 徐波, Huang Taiyi 黃泰翼, and Hu Baogang 胡包鋼 (1999).〈基於領域關鍵詞的詞典及語言模型自適應〉(Domain-keyword Based on Lexicon and Language Model Adaptation). In Huang Changning 黃昌寧 and Dong Zhendong 董振東, eds.,《計算機語言學文集》(*Essays on Computational Linguistics*). Beijing: Tsinghua University Press, pp. 235–241.

Iida, Hiroshi (1995). "Spoken Dialogue Translation Technologies and Speech Translation." *Proceedings of MT Summit V: Machine Translation Conference, Exhibition and Tutorial*, Luxembourg.

Iida, Hiroshi, Eichiro Sumita, and Osamu Furuse (1996). "Spoken Language Translation Method Using Examples." *Proceedings from the 16th International Conference on Computational Linguistics* (*COLING-96*), Copenhagen, Denmark, pp. 1074–1077.

Jiménez, Victor M., Amenguaf Benedf Castellanos, and Enrique Vidal (1995). "Some Results with a Trainable Speech Translation and Understanding System." *Proceedings of the IEEE International Conference on Acoustics, Speech, and Signal Processing* (*ICASSP-95*), Detroit, Michigan, USA, pp. 113–116.

Jiménez, Victor M., Enrique Vidal, J. Oncina, Amenguaf Benedf Castellanos, H. Rulot, and J. A. Sánchez (1994). "Spoken-language Machine Translation in Limited-domain Tasks." In Heinrich Niemann, R. de Mon, and G. Hanrieder, eds., *Progress and Prospects of Speech Research and Technology*. Sankt Augustin: Infix, pp. 262–265.

Jones, Douglas A., Timothy Anderson, Sabine Atwell, Brian Delaney, James Dirgin, Michael Emonts, Neil Granoein, Martha Herzog, Timothy Hunter, Sargon Jabri, Wade Shen, and Jurgen Sottung (2006). "Toward an Interagency Language Roundtable Based Assessment of Speech-to-speech Translation Capabilities." *Proceedings of the 7th Biennial Conference of the Association for Machine Translation in the Americas (AMTA-2006): Visions for the Future of Machine Translation*, Boston Marriott, Cambridge, MA, USA.

Kompe, Ralf, Andreas Kiessling, Heinrich Niemann, E. Noeth, Anton Batliner, Stefani Schachtl, R. Ruland, and H. U. Block (1997). "Improving Parsing of Spontaneous Speech with the Help of Prosodic Boundaries." *Proceedings of the IEEE International Conference on Acoustics, Speech, and Signal Processing (ICASSP-97)*, Munich, Germany, pp. 811–814.

Krauwer, Steven (2000). "Introduction: Special Issue on Spoken Language Translation." *Machine Translation*, Vol. 15, Nos. 1–2, pp. 1–2.

Kurematsu, Akira (1993). "Overview of Speech Translation at ATR." In Sergei Nirenburg, ed., *Progress in Machine Translation*. Amsterdam: IOS and Tokyo: Ohmsha, pp. 33–41.

Kurematsu, Akira and Tsuyoshi Morimoto (1996). *Automatic Speech Translation: Fundamental Technology for Future Cross-language Communication*. Amsterdam: Gaordan and Breach.

Lavie, Alon, Donna Gates, Noah Coccaro, and Lori S. Levin (1996). "Input Segmentation of Spontaneous Speech in Janus: A Speech-to-Speech Translation System." *Proceedings of the 12th European Conference on Artificial Intelligence*, Budapest, Hungary, pp. 54–59.

Lavie, Alon, Lori S. Levin, Tanja Schultz, Chad Langley, Benjamin Han, Alicia Tribble, Donna Gates, Dorcas Wallace, and Kay Peterson (2001). "Domain Portability in Speech-to-speech Translation." *Proceedings of the 1st International Conference on Human Language Technology Conference*, San Diego, California, USA.

Lazzari, Gianni, Robert E. Frederking, and Walter Minker (1999). "Speaker-language Identification and Speech Translation." In Eduard Hovy, Nancy Ide, Robert E. Frederking, J. Mariani, and Antonio Zampolli, eds., *Multilingual Information Management: Current Levels and Future Abilities*. Report for National Science Foundation.

Lazzari, Gianni (2000). "Spoken Translation: Challenges and Opportunities." *Proceedings of the 6th International Conference on Spoken Language Processing* (*ICSLP-2000*), Beijing, China.

Lee, Tan, Wai Kit Lo, and Pak Chung Ching (2002). "Towards Highly Usable and Robust Spoken Language Technologies for Chinese." In Yu Shiwen, ed., *Proceedings of the 2nd China-Japan Natural Language Processing Joint Research Promotion Conference* (*CJNLP-2002*). Beijing: Institute of Computational Linguistics, Peking University, pp. 259–265.

Lee, Young-Suk, Daniel J. Sinder, and Clifford J. Weinstein (2002). "Interlingua-based English–Korean Two-way Speech Translation of Doctor–patient Dialogues with CCLINC." *Machine Translation*, Vol. 17, No. 3, pp. 213–243.

Locke, William N. (1952). "MT of Printed and Spoken Material." *Proceedings of the M.I.T. Conference on Mechanical Translation,* Massachusetts Institute of Technology, Cambridge, MA, USA.

Loehr, Dan (1998). "Can Simultaneous Interpretation Help Machine Translation?" In David L. Farwell, Laurie Gerber, and Eduard Hovy, eds., *Machine Translation and the Information Soup*. Berlin: Springer Verlag, pp. 213–224.

Lu, Xin, Zhao Tiejun, Liu Zhanyi, and Yang Muyun (2001). "Automatic Detection of Prosody Phrase Boundaries for Text-to-speech System." *Proceedings of the 7th International Workshop on Parsing Technologies* (*IWPT-2001*), Peking University, Beijing, China. Beijing: Tsinghua University Press, pp. 135–141.

Mayfield, Laura J., Marsal Gavalda, Y.-H. Seo, Bernhard Suhm, Wayne Ward, and Alex H. Waibel (1995). "Concept-based Parsing for Speech Translation." *Proceedings of the 6th International Conference on Theoretical and Methodological Issues in Machine Translation* (*TMI-95*), Leuven, Belgium, pp. 196–205.

Mayfield, Laura J., Marsal Gavaldá, Wayne Ward, and Alex H. Waibel (1995). "Concept-based Speech Translation." *Proceedings of the IEEE International Conference on Acoustics, Speech, and Signal Processing* (*ICASSP-95*), Detroit, USA, pp. 97–100.

McKenzie, Fred (1990). "The Use of Computer Technology to Store and Redistribute Voice as an Aid to Translation Services." In Catriona Picken, ed., *Translating and the Computer 11: Preparing for the Next*

Decade. London: The Association for Information Management, pp. 79–83.

Montgomery, Christine A. and Naicong Li (2002). "Approaches to Spoken Translation." In Stephen D. Richardson, ed., *Machine Translation: From Research to Real Users*. Berlin and New York: Springer Verlag, pp. 248–252.

Morimoto, Tsuyoshi, Toshiyuki Takezawa, F. Yato, S. Sagayama, T. Tashiro, Masaaki Nagata, and A. Kurematsu (1993). "ATR's Speech Translation System: ASURA." *European Conference on Speech Communication and Technology*, Berlin, Germany, pp. 1295–1298.

Morimoto, Tsuyoshi (1993). "Automatic Speech Translation at ATR." *Proceedings of MT Summit IV: International Cooperation for Global Communication*, Kobe, Japan, pp. 83–96.

Nakaiwa, Hiromi (2002). "Research Activities at ATR Spoken Language Translation Research Laboratories." In Yu Shiwen, ed., *Proceedings of the 2nd China-Japan Natural Language Processing Joint Research Promotion Conference* (*CJNLP-2002*). Beijing: Institute of Computational Linguistics, Peking University, pp. 271–274.

Ney, Hermann, Sonja Niessen, Franz Josef Och, Hassan Sawaf, Christoph Tillmann, and Stephan Vogel (2000). "Algorithms for Statistical Translation of Spoken Language." *IEEE Transactions on Speech and Audio Processing*, Vol. 8, pp. 24–36.

Nirenburg, Sergei, Jaime G. Carbonell, Masaru Tomita, and Kenneth Goodman (1992). "Speech-to-speech Translation." *Machine Translation: A Knowledge-based Approach*. San Matero, California: Morgan Kaufmann, pp. 165–190.

Oi, Kozo, Eiichiro Sumita, Osamu Fruruse, Hitoshi Iida, and Tetsuya Higuchi (1994). "Real-time Spoken Language Translation Using Associative Processors." *Proceedings of the 4th Conference on Applied Natural Language Processing*, Stuttgart, Germany, pp. 101–106.

Okumura, Akitoshi (2003). "Development of Speech Translation for Hand-held Devices." *Proceedings of MT Summit IX*, New Orleans, Louisiana, USA.

Paul, Michael, Takao Doi, Youngsook Hwang, Kenji Imamura, Hideo Okuma, and Eiichiro Sumita (2005). "Nobody Is Perfect: ATR's Hybrid Approach to Spoken Language Translation." *Proceedings of the International Workshop on Spoken Language Translation* (*IWSLT-2005*), Pittsburgh, PA, USA.

Pérez, Alicia, Inés Torres, Francisco Casacuberta, and Víctor Guijarrubia (2006). "A Spanish-Basque Weather Forecast Corpus for Probabilistic Speech Translation." *Proceedings of the 5th SALTMIL Workshop on Minority Languages and the 5th International Conference on Language Resources and Evaluation (LREC-2006): Strategies for Developing Machine Translation for Minority Languages*, Genoa, Italy, pp. 99–102.
Pérez, Javier and Antonio Bonafonte (2006). "GAIA: Common Framework for the Development of Speech Translation Technologies." *Proceedings of the 5th International Conference on Language Resources and Evaluation (LREC-2006)*, Genoa, Italy.
Rayner, Manny (1995). "Speech Translation and Text Translation: Similarities and Differences." *Proceedings of the 6th International Conference on Theoretical and Methodological Issues in Machine Translation (TMI-95)*, the University of Leuven, Belgium.
Salton, Gerard and R. W. Thorpe (1962). "An Approach to the Segmentation Problem in Speech Analysis and Language Translation." In National Physical Laboratory, ed., *1961 International Conference on Machine Translation of Languages and Applied Language Analysis: Proceedings of the Conference Held at the National Physical Laboratory, Teddington, Middlesex, on 5th, 6th, 7th and 8th September*. London: Her Majesty's Stationery Office, Vol. 1, pp. 704–724.
Seligman, Mark and Christian Boitet (1993). "A 'Whiteboard' Architecture for Automatic Speech Translation." *Proceedings of the International Symposium on Spoken Dialogue (ISSD-93)—New Directions in Human and Man-machine Communication*, Tokyo, Japan, pp. 243–246.
Seligman, Mark, Mary A. Flanagan, and Sophie Toole (1998). "Dictated Input for Broad-coverage Speech Translation." *Association for Machine Translation in the Americas (AMTA-98), Workshop on Embedded MT Systems: Design, Construction, and Evaluation of Systems with an MT Component*, Langhorne, PA, USA.
Seligman, Mark (2000). "Nine Issues in Speech Translation." *Machine Translation*, Vol. 15, Nos. 1–2, pp. 149–186.
Seneff, Stephanie (1992). "A Relaxation Method for Understanding Spontaneous Speech Utterances." *Proceedings of the Speech and Natural Language Workshop*, Harriman, NY, USA, pp. 299–304.
Shimohata, Mitsuo, Eiichiro Sumita, and Yuji Matsumoto (2003).

"Example-based Rough Translation for Speech-to-speech Translation." *Proceedings of MT Summit IX*, New Orleans, Louisiana, USA.

Spiler, Jörg, Martin Klarner, and Günther Görz (2000). "Processing Self-corrections in a Speech-to-speech System." In Wolfgang Wahlster, ed., *Verbmobil: Foundations of Speech-to-speech Translation*. Berlin: Springer Verlag, pp. 131–140.

Stentiford, Frederick W. and Martin G. Steer (1988). "Machine Translation of Speech." *British Telecom Technology Journal*, Vol. 6, No. 2.

Sumita, Eiichiro, Setsuo Yamada, Kazuhide Yamamoto, Michael Paul, Hideki Kashioka, Kai Ishikawa, and Satoshi Shirai (1999). "Solutions to Problems Inherent in Spoken-language Translation: The ATR-MATRIX Approach." *Proceedings of MT Summit VII: MT in the Great Translation Era*, Singapore.

Takezawa, Toshiyuki, Keiji Yasuda, Masahide Mizushima, and Genichiro Kikui (2005). "Assessing Degradation of Spoken Language Translation by Measuring Speech Recognizer's Output against Non-native Speakers' Listening Capabilities." *Proceedings of MT Summit X*, Phuket, Thailand.

Tillimann, Christoph, Stephan Vogel, Hermann Ney, and Hassan Sawaf (2000). "Statistical Translation of Text and Speech: First Results with the RWTH System." *Machine Translation*, Vol. 15, Nos. 1–2, pp. 43–73.

Tomabechi, Hideto, Hiroaki Kitano, Teruko Mitamura, Lori S. Levin, and Masaru Tomita (1989). *Direct Memory Access Speech-to-speech Translation: A Theory of Simultaneous Interpretation*. Pittsburgh: Centre for Machine Translation, Carnegie Mellon University.

Villar, Juan Miguel, Juan Carlos Amengual, Jose Miguel Benedi, Antonio Castellanos, Victor M. Jimenez, J. A. Sanchez, E. Vidal, J. Oncina, and H. Rulot (1995). "Spoken-language Machine Translation in Limited Domains: Can It Be Achieved by Finite-state Models?" *Proceedings of the 6th International Conference on Theoretical and Methodological Issues in Machine Translation* (*TMI-95*), Leuven, Belgium, pp. 326–333.

Villar, Juan Miguel, Victor M. Jiménez, Juan Carlos Amengual, José Miguel Benedí, Antonio Castellanos, David Llorens, and Enrique Vidal (1999). "Text and Speech Translation by Means of Subsequential Transducers." In András Kornai, ed., *Extended Finite State Models of Language*. Cambridge: Cambridge University Press, pp. 121–139.

Waibel, Alex H. (1996). "Interactive Translation of Conversational Speech?" *Computer*, Vol. 27, pp. 41–48.
Waibel, Alex H. (1999). "Interactive Translation of Conversational Speech?" In K. Ponting, ed., *Computational Models of Speech Pattern Processing,* Berlin: Springer Verlag.
Wang, Jhing-Fa, Shun-Chieh Lin, and Hsueh-Wei Yang (2004). "A New Two-layer Approach for Spoken Language Translation." *Proceedings of the International Conference on Research in Computational Linguistics* (*ROCLING-XVI*), Taipei, Taiwan.
Woszczyna, Monika, Matthew Broadhead, Donna Gates, Marsal Gavaldà, Alon Lavie, Lori S. Levin, and Alex H. Waibel (1998). "A Modular Approach to Spoken Language Translation for Large Domains." In David L. Farwell, Laurie Gerber, and Eduard Hovy, eds., *Machine Translation and the Information Soup*. Berlin: Springer Verlag, pp. 31–40.
Wu, Hua 吳華 and Huang Taiyi 黃泰翼 (1999).〈基於中間語義框架的系統響應生成〉(Interlingua-based Response Generation). In Huang Changning 黃昌寧 and Dong Zhendong 董振東, eds.,《計算機語言學文集》(*Essays on Computational Linguistics*). Beijing: Tsinghua University Press, pp. 248–255.
Yamamoto, Seiichi (2000). "Toward Speech Communications Beyond Language Barrier—Research of Spoken Language Translation Technologies at ATR." *Proceedings of the International Conference on Spoken Language Processing 2000* (*ICSLP-2000*), Beijing, China.
Zhang, Ruiqiang, Genichiro Kikui, Hirofumi Yamamoto, and Lo Wai-Kit (2005). "A Decoding Algorithm for Word Lattice Translation in Speech Translation." *Proceedings of the International Workshop on Spoken Language Translation* (*IWSLT-2005*), Pittsburgh, PA, USA.
Zhang, Ruiqiang, Genichiro Kikui, and Hirofumi Yamamoto (2005). "Using Multiple Recognition Hypotheses to Improve Speech Translation." *Proceedings of the International Workshop on Spoken Language Translation* (*IWSLT-2005*), Pittsburgh, PA, USA.
Zong, Chengqing 宗成慶 (2002).〈語音翻譯技術研究現狀〉(Current Research Situation in Speech-to-speech Translation). In Yu Shiwen, ed., *Proceedings of the 2nd China-Japan Natural Language Processing Joint Research Promotion Conference* (*CJNLP-2002*). Beijing: Institute of Computational Linguistics, Peking University, pp. 32–39.

Zong, Chengqing and Fuji Ren (2003). "Chinese Utterance Segmentation in Spoken Language Translation." *Proceedings of the 4th International Conference on Intelligent Text Processing and Computational Linguistics* (*CICLing-2003*), Mexico City, Mexico, pp. 518–527.

Speech Translation System

Arranz, Victoria, Elisabet Comelles, David L. Farwell, Climent Nadeu, Jaume Padrell, Albert Febrer, Dorcas Alexander, and Kay Peterson (2004). "A Speech-to-speech Translation System for Catalan, Spanish, and English." In Robert E. Frederking and Kathryn B. Taylors, eds., *Machine Translation: From Real Users to Research*. Berlin: Springer Verlag, pp. 7–16.

Arranz, Victoria, Elisabet Comelles, and David L. Farwell (2005). "The FAME Speech-to-Speech Translation System for Catalan, English and Spanish." *Proceedings of MT Summit X*, Phuket, Thailand.

Bernth, Arendse (2003). "Controlled Generation for Speech-to-speech MT Systems." *Proceedings of the Joint Conference Combining the 8th International Workshop of the European Association for Machine Translation and the 4th Controlled Language Applications Workshop: Controlled Language Translation* (*EAMT-CLAW-2003*), Dublin City University, Dublin, Ireland.

Bilmes, Jeff A., Xiao Li, Jonathan Malkin, Kelley Kilanski, Richard Wright, Katrin Kirchhoff, Amar Subramanya, Susumu Harada, James Landay, Patricia Dowden, and Howard Chizeck (2005). "The Vocal Joystick: A Voice-based Human-computer Interface for Individuals with Motor Impairments." *Proceedings of Human Language Technology Conference and Conference on Empirical Methods in Natural Language Processing* (*HLT/EMNLP-2005*), Vancouver, BC, Canada.

Black, Alan W., Ralf D. Brown, Robert E. Frederking, Rita Singh, John Moody, and Eric Steinbrecher (2002). "TONGUES: Rapid Development of a Speech-to-speech Translation System." *Proceedings of the 2nd International Conference on Human Language Technology Research* (*HLT-2002*), San Diego, CA, USA, pp. 183–189.

Boitet, Christian (1993). "Practical Speech Translation Systems Will Integrate Human Expertise, Multimodal Communication, and Interactive Disambiguation." *Proceedings of MT Summit IV:*

International Cooperation for Global Communication, Kobe, Japan, pp. 173–176.

Burger, Susanne, Erica Costantini, and Fabio Pianesi (2003). "Communicative Strategies and Patterns of Multimodal Integration in a Speech-to-speech Translation System." *Proceedings of MT Summit IX*, New Orleans, Louisiana, USA.

Choi, John, Hsiao-Wuen Hon, Jean-Luc Lebrun, Sun-Pin Lee, Gareth Loudon, Viet-Hoang Phan, and S. Yogananthan (1994). "*Yanhui* (宴會), A Software Based High Performance Mandarin Text-to-speech System." *Proceedings of the Conference of the Association for Computational Linguistics and Chinese Language Processing (ROCLING-VII)*, National Tsing Hua University, Hsin-Chu, Taiwan.

Chu-Carroll, Jennifer (2000). "MIMIC: An Adaptive Mixed Initiative Spoken Dialogue System for Information Queries." *Proceedings of the 6th Applied Natural Language Processing Conference*, Seattle, Washington, DC, USA, pp. 97–104.

Davies, K. (1999). "The IBM Conversational Telephony System for Financial Applications." *Proceedings of the 6th European Conference on Speech Communication and Technology* (*EuroSpeech-99*), Budapest, Hungary, pp. 275–278.

de Castro, Imelda P. (2003). "The Philippine Style Chat—Instant Messenger Translation System" In *Translating and the Computer 25*. London: The Association for Information Management.

de Gispert, Adria and Jose B. Marino (2004). "TALP: Xgram-based Spoken Language Translation System." *Proceedings of the International Workshop on Spoken Language Translation* (*IWSLT-2004*), Kyoto, Japan.

Dillinger, Mike and Mark Seligman (2004). "System Description: A Highly Interactive Speech-to-speech Translation System." In Robert E. Frederking and Kathryn B. Taylors, eds., *Machine Translation: From Real Users to Research*. Berlin: Springer Verlag, pp. 58–63.

Engelbrecht, Herman A. and Tanja Schultz (2005). "Rapid Development of an Afrikaans-English Speech-to-speech Translator." *Proceedings of the International Workshop on Spoken Language Translation* (*IWSLT-2005*), Pittsburgh, PA, USA.

Fulkerson, Michael S. and Alan W. Biermann (2000). "Javox: A Toolkit for Building Speech-enabled Applications." *Proceedings of the 6th*

Applied Natural Language Processing Conference, Seattle, Washington, DC, USA, pp. 105–111.
Gros, J. Zganec, A. Mihelic, M. Zganec, F. Mihelic, S. Dobrisek, J. Zibert, S. Vintar, T. Korosec, T. Erjavec, and M. Romih (2005). "Initial Considerations in Building a Speech-to-speech Translation System for the Slovenian-English Language Pair." *Proceedings of the 10th Workshop of the European Association for Machine Translation: Practical Applications of Machine Translation*, Budapest, Hungary, pp. 288–293.
Hu, Fengguo 胡鳳國 (2002).〈一個簡單人機對話系統的實現方法〉(The Realization of a Simple QA-system).《第一屆學生計算語言學研討會論文集》(*SWCL-2002: First Students' Workshop on Computational Linguistics: Proceedings*), Institute of Computational Linguistics, Peking University, Beijing, China, pp. 182–187.
Kitano, Hiroaki (1990). "IDMDIALOG: A Speech-to-speech Dialogue Translation System." *Machine Translation*, Vol. 5, No. 4, pp. 301–338.
Konuma, Tomohiro, Kenji Matsui, Yumi Wakita, Kenji Mizutani, Mitsuru Endo, and Masashi Murata (2002). "An Experimental Multilingual Bi-directional Speech Translation System." *Proceedings of the 9th International Conference on Theoretical and Methodological Issues in Machine Translation* (*TMI-2002*), Keihanna, Japan, pp. 96–104.
Metze, Florian, John McDonough, Hagen Soltau, Alex Waibel, Alon Lavie, Susanne Burger, Chad Langley, Lori Levin, Tanja Schultz, Fabio Pianesi, Roldano Cattoni, Gianni Lazzari, Nadia Mana, and Emanuele Pianta (2002). "The NESPOLE! Speech-to-speech Translation System." *Proceedings of the Human Language Technology Conference* (*HLT-2002*), San Diego, California, USA.
Montgomery, Christine A., Bonnie Glover Stalls, Robert E. Stumberger, Naicong Li, Robert S. Belvin, Alfredo R. Arnaiz, and Susan Hirsh Litenatsky (1994). "Machine-aided Voice Translation (MAVT) Advanced Development Model." *Proceedings of the 1st Conference of the Association for Machine Translation in the Americas: Technology Partnerships for Crossing the Language Barrier* (*AMTA-1*), Columbia, Maryland, USA, pp. 235–236.
Montgomery, Christine A., Bonnie Glover Stalls, Robert E. Stumberger, Naicong Li, Robert S. Belvin, Alfredo R. Arnaiz, and Susan Hirsh Litenatsky (1995). "The Machine-aided Voice Translation (MAVT) System." *Proceedings of the 14th Annual International Voice*

Technologies Application Conference (*AVIOS-95*), San Jose, California, USA, pp. 101–110.
Moore, Robert, John Dowding, Harry Bratt, J. Mark Gawron, and Adam Cheyer (1997). "CommandTalk: A Spoken-language Interface for Battlefield Simulations." *Proceedings of the 5th Conference on Applied Natural Language Processing*, Seattle, Washington, DC, USA.
Nagata, Masaaki and Kiyoshi Kogure (1990). "HPSG-based Lattice Parser for Spoken Japanese in a Spoken Language Translation System." *Proceedings of the 9th European Conference on Artificial Intelligence* (*ECAI-90*), Stockholm, Sweden, pp. 461–466.
Park, Jun and Jae-Woo Yang (1999). "ETRI Speech Translation System." *Proceedings of CSTAR Workshop*, Schwetzingen, Germany.
Ravichandran, Deepak and Eduard H. Hovy (2002). "Learning Surface Text Patterns for a Question Answering System." *Proceedings of the 40th Annual Meeting of the Association for Computational Linguistics*, Philadelphia, PA, USA, pp. 41–47.
Santaholma, Marianne (2005). "Linguistic Representation of Finnish in a Limited-domain Speech-to-speech Language Translation System." *Proceedings of the 10th Annual Conference of the European Association for Machine Translation* (*EAMT-2005*), Budapest, Hungary.
Seneff, Stephanie (1992). "TINA: A Natural Language System for Spoken Language Applications." *Computational Linguistics*, Vol. 18, pp. 61–92.
Seneff, Stephanie, Ed Hurley, Raymond Lau, Christine Pao, Philipp Schmid, and Victor Zue (1998). "Galaxy-II: A Reference Architecture for Conversational System Development." *Proceedings of the 5th International Conference on Spoken Language Processing* (*ICSLP-98*), Sydney, Australia.
Stallard, David (2000). "Talk'N'Travel: A Conversational System for Air Travel Planning." *Proceedings of the 6th Applied Natural Language Processing Conference*, Seattle, Washington, DC, USA, pp. 68–75.
Starlander, Marianne, Pierrette Bouillon, Nikos Chatzichrisafis, Marianne Santaholma, Manny Rayner, Beth Ann Hockey, Hitoshi Isahara, Kyoko Kanzaki, and Yukie Nakao (2005). "Practicing Controlled Language through a Help System Integrated into the Medical Speech Translation System (MedSLT)." *Proceedings of MT Summit X*, Phuket, Thailand.
Sugaya, Fumiaki, Keiji Yasuda, Toshiyuki Takezawa, and Seiichi

Yamamoto (2001). "Precise Measurement Method of a Speech Translation System's Capability with a Pair Comparison Method between the System and Humans." In Bente Maegaard, ed., *Proceedings of MT Summit VIII: Machine Translation in the Information Age*, Santiago de Compostela, Spain.

Sumita, Eiichiro, Yasuhiro Akiba, Takao Doi, Andrew Finch, Kenji Imamura, Hideo Okuma, Michael Paul, Mitsuo Shimohata, and Taro Watanabe (2004). "EBMT, SMT, Hybrid and More: ATR Spoken Language Translation System." *Proceedings of the International Workshop on Spoken Language Translation* (*IWSLT-2004*), Kyoto, Japan.

Tomita, Masaru, Marion Kee, Hiroaki Saito, Teruko Mitamura, and Hideto Tomabechi (1988). "Towards a Speech-to-speech Translation System." *INTERFACE: Journal of Applied Linguistics*, Vol. 3, pp. 57–77.

Tomita, Masaru, Marion Kee, Hiroaki Saito, Teruko Mitamura, and Hideto Tomabechi (1988). "The Universal Parser Compiler and Its Application to a Speech Translation System." *Proceedings of the 2nd International Conference on Theoretical and Methodological Issues in Machine Translation of Natural Languages* (*TMI-88*), Carnegie Mellon University, Center for Machine Translation, Pittsburgh, Pennsylvania, USA.

Verdonik, Darinka and Matej Rojc (2006). "Are You Ready for a Call?—Spontaneous Conversations in Tourism for Speech-to-speech Translation Systems." *Proceedings of the 5th International Conference on Language Resources and Evaluation* (*LREC-2006*), Genoa, Italy.

Waibel, Alex H., Arthur E. McNair, Hiroaki Saito, and Joe Tebelskis (1991). "A Speech-to-speech Translation System Using Connectionist and Symbolic Processing Strategies." *Proceedings of the IEEE International Conference on Acoustics, Speech and Signal Processing* (*ICASSP-91*), Toronto, Canada, pp. 793–796.

Waibel, Alex H., Ahmed Badran, Alan W. Black, Robert Frederking, Donna Gates, Alon Lavie, Lori S. Levin, Kevin Lenzo, Laura Mayfield Tomokiyo, Juergen Reichert, Tanja Schultz, Dorcas Wallace, Monika Woszczyna, and Jing Zhang (2003). "Speechalator: Two-way Speech-to-speech Translation in Your Hand." *Proceedings of the Human Language Technology and North American Chapter of Association of*

Computational Linguistics 2003 (*HLT/NAACL-2003*), Edmonton, Alberta, Canada.
Ward, Wayne and Sunil Issar (1995). "The CMU ATIS System." *Proceedings of ARPA Workshop on Spoken Language Technology*, San Mateo, CA: Morgan Kaufmann, pp. 249–251.
Yoon, Kyuchul (2005). "A Prosodic Diphone Database for Korean Text-to-Speech Synthesis System." *Proceedings of the 6th International Conference on Intelligent Text Processing and Computational Linguistics* (*CICLing-2005*), Mexico City, Mexico, pp. 414–417.
Zhang, Qiong 張瓊 and Chen Qunxiu 陳群秀 (2002).〈面向網絡的問答系統研究綜述〉(An Overview of Web-oriented QA Systems).《第一屆學生計算語言學研討會論文集》(*SWCL-2002: First Students' Workshop on Computational Linguistics: Proceedings*), Institute of Computational Linguistics, Peking University, Beijing, China, p. 188.
Zue, Victor W. (1994). "Research Challenges for the Development of Interactive Spoken Language System." *Proceedings of the Conference of the Association for Computational Linguistics and Chinese Language Processing* (*ROCLING-VII*), National Tsing Hua University, Hsin-Chu, Taiwan.

C-Star

Ahlén, Sondra, Brian Connelly, Michelle Corkadel, Rob Malkin, Anuj Vaidya, and Rodolfo Vega (1997). *Data Collection Scenarios for C-Star Travel Domain*. Pittsburgh: Center for Machine Translation, Carnegie Mellon University.
Blanchon, Hervé and Christian Boitet (2000). "Speech Translation for French within the C-Star II Consortium and Future Perspectives." *Proceedings of the International Conference on Spoken Language Processing* (*ICSLP-2000*), Beijing, China.
Bonafonte, A., H. Höge, I. Kiss, A. Moreno, U. Ziegenhain, H. van den Heuvel, H.-U. Hain, X. S. Wang, and M. N. Garcia (2006). "TC-STAR: Specifications of Language Resources and Evaluation for Speech Synthesis." *Proceedings of the 5th International Conference on Language Resources and Evaluation* (*LREC-2006*), Genoa, Italy.
Mostefa, Djamel, Olivier Hamon, and Khalid Choukri (2006). "Evaluation of Automatic Speech Recognition and Speech Translation within TC-STAR: Results from the First Evaluation Campaign." *Proceedings of*

the 5th International Conference on Language Resources and Evaluation (*LREC-2006*), Genoa, Italy.

van den Heuvel, Henk, Khalid Choukri, Christian Gollan, Asuncion Moreno, and Djamel Mostefa (2006). "TC-STAR: New Language Resources for ASR and SLT Purposes." *Proceedings of the 5th International Conference on Language Resources and Evaluation* (*LREC-2006*), Genoa, Italy.

Diplomat

Allen, Jeffrey (1998). *Testing and Review of the DIPLOMAT Haitian Creole MT System.* Internal Technical Report, Center for Machine Translation, Carnegie Mellon University.

Frederking, Robert E., Alexander Rudnicky, and Christopher Hogan (1997). "Interactive Speech Translation in the DIPLOMAT Project." *Spoken Language Translation: Proceedings of a Workshop Sponsored by the Association for Computational Linguistics and by the European Network in Language and Speech* (*ELSNET-97*), Madrid, Spain, pp. 61–66.

Frederking, Robert E., Alexander Rudnicky, Christopher Hogan, and Kevin Lenzo (2000). "Interactive Speech Translation in the Diplomat Project." *Machine Translation*, Vol. 15, Nos. 1–2, pp. 27–42.

EuTrans

Amengual, Juan Carlos, Asunción Castaño, Antonio Castellanos, Victor M. Jiménez, David Llorens, Andrés Marzal, Federico Prat, Juan Miguel Vilar, José Miguel Benedi, Francisco Casacuberta, Moisés Pastor, and Enrique Vidal (2000). "The EuTrans Spoken Language Translation System." *Machine Translation*, Vol. 15, Nos. 1–2, pp. 75–103.

Janus

Cumming, Susanna and Robert Albano (1986). *A Guide to Lexical Acquisition in the JANUS System.* Research Report (ISI/RR-85-162), University of Southern California, Marina del Rey.

Gates, Donna, Alon Lavie, Lori S. Levin, Alex H. Waibel, Marsal Gavaldá, Laura Mayfield, Monika Woszczyna, and Puming Zahn (1996). "End-to-end Evaluation in JANUS: A Speech-to-speech Translation

System." *Proceedings of the 12th European Conference on Artificial Intelligence* (*ECAI-96*), Budapest, Hungary, pp. 35–40.
Geutner, Petra, Michael Finke, and Peter Scheytt (1997). *Hypothesis Driven Lexical Adaptation for Transcribing Multilingual Broadcast News*. Pittsburgh: Language Technologies Institute.
Jain, Ajai N., Arthur E. McNair, Alex H. Waibel, Hiroaki Saito, Alexander G. Hauptmann, and Joe Tebelskis (1993). "Connectionist and Symbolic Processing in Speech-to-speech Translation: The JANUS System." In Sergei Nirenburg, ed., *Progress in Machine Translation*. Amsterdam: IOS and Tokyo: Ohmsha, pp. 153–160.
Lavie, Alon, Donna Gates, Noah Coccaro, and Lori S. Levin (1996). "Input Segmentation of Spontaneous Speech in JANUS: A Speech-to-Speech Translation System." *Proceedings of the 12th European Conference on Artificial Intelligence* (*ECAI-96*), Budapest, Hungary, pp. 54–59.
Lavie, Alon, Lori S. Levin, Alex H. Waibel, Donna Gates, Marsal Gavalda, and Laura Mayfield (1996). "JANUS: Multilingual Translation of Spontaneous Speech in a Limited Domain." *Proceedings of the 2nd Conference of the Association for Machine Translation in the Americas: Expanding MT Horizons* (*AMTA-2*), Montreal, Quebec, Canada, pp. 252–255.
Lavie, Alon, Alex H. Waibel, Lori S. Levin, Michael Finke, Donna Gates, Marsal Gavaldá, Torsten Zeppenfeld, and Puming Zhan (1997). "JANUS III: Speech-to-Speech Translation in Multiple Languages." *Proceedings of the IEEE International Conference on Acoustics, Speech, and Signal Processing* (*ICASSP-97*), Munich, Germany, Vol. 1, pp. 99–102.
Lavie, Alon, Lori S. Levin, Monika Woszczyna, Donna Gates, Marsal Gavalda, and Alex H. Waibel (1999). "The Janus-III Translation System: Speech-to-speech Translation in Multiple Domains." *Proceedings of CSTAR Workshop*, Schwetzingen, Germany.
Levin, Lori S., Alon Lavie, Monika Woszczyna, Donna Gates, Marsal Gavaldá, Detlef Koll, and Alex H. Waibel (2000). "The JANUS-III Translation System: Speech-to-speech Translation in Multiple Domains ." *Machine Translation*, Vol. 15, Nos. 1–2, pp. 3–25.
Waibel, Alex H., Ajai N. Jain, Arthur E. McNair, Hiroaki Saito, Alexander G. Hauptmann, and Joe Tebelskis (1991). "JANUS: A Speech-to-speech Translation System Using Connectionist and Symbolic

Processing Strategies." *Proceedings of the IEEE International Conference on Acoustics, Speech, and Signal Processing* (*ICASSP-91*), Toronto, Canada, Vol. 2, pp. 793–796.
Woszczyna, Monika, Noah Coccaro, Andreas Eisele, Alon Lavie, Arthur E. McNair, Thomas Polzin, Ivica Rogina, Carolyn Rose, Tilo Sloboda, Masaru Tomita, Junya Tsutsumi, N. Aoki-Waibel, Alex H. Waibel, and Wayne Ward (1993). "Recent Advances in JANUS: A Speech Translation System." *Proceedings of the 3rd European Conference on Speech Communication and Technology* (*EuroSpeech-93*), Berlin, Germany, pp. 1295–1298.
Woszczyna, Monika, Noah Coccaro, Andreas Eisele, Alon Lavie, Arthur E. McNair, Thomas Polzin, Ivica Rogina, Carolyn Rose, Tilo Sloboda, Masaru Tomita, Junya Tsutsumi, N. Aoki-Waibel, Alex H. Waibel, and Wayne Ward (1993). "Recent Advances in JANUS: A Speech Translation System." *Proceedings of the 5th International Conference on Theoretical and Methodological Issues in Machine Translation of Natural Languages: MT in the Next Generation* (*TMI-93*), Kyoto, Japan, pp. 195–200.

NESPOLE

Lavie, Alon, Lori S. Levin, Robert E. Frederking, and Fabio Pianesi (2002). "The NESPOLE! Speech-to-speech Translation System." In Stephen D. Richardson, ed., *Machine Translation: From Research to Real Users*. Berlin and New York: Springer Verlag, pp. 240–243.

Question Answering System

Aceves-Pérez, Rita M., Luis Villaseñor-Pineda, and Manuel Montes-y-Gómez (2006). "Using N-gram Models to Combine Query Translations in Cross-language Question Answering." *Proceedings of the 7th International Conference on Intelligent Text Processing and Computational Linguistics* (*CICLing-2006*), Mexico City, Mexico.
Alink, Wouter, Valentin Jijkoun, David Ahn, Maarten de Rijke, Peter Boncz, and Arjen de Vries (2006). "Representing and Querying Multi-dimensional Markup for Question Answering." *Proceedings of the 11th Conference of the European Chapter of the Association for Computational Linguistics* (*EACL-2006*), Trento, Italy.

Benamara, Farah (2006). "Language and Reasoning for Question Answering: State of the Art and Future Directions." *Proceedings of the 11th Conference of the European Chapter of the Association for Computational Linguistics* (*EACL-2006*), Trento, Italy.

Brill, Eric, Susan Dumais, and Michele Banko (2002). "An Analysis of the AskMSR Question-answering System." *Proceedings of the 2002 Conference on Empirical Methods in Natural Language Processing* (*EMNLP-2002*), University of Pennsylvania, Philadelphia, PA, USA.

Burger, John and John Henderson (2003). "Exploiting Diversity for Answering Questions." *Proceedings of the Human Language Technology and North American Chapter of Association of Computational Linguistics 2003* (*HLT/NAACL-2003*), Edmonton, Alberta, Canada.

Chu-Carroll, Jennifer, Krzysztof Czuba, John Prager, and Abraham Ittycheriah (2003). "In Question Answering, Two Heads Are Better Than One." *Proceedings of the Human Language Technology and North American Chapter of Association of Computational Linguistics 2003* (*HLT/NAACL-2003*), Edmonton, Alberta, Canada.

Costa, Luís Fernando and Luís Sarmento (2006). "Component Evaluation in a Question Answering System." *Proceedings of the 5th International Conference on Language Resources and Evaluation* (*LREC-2006*), Genoa, Italy.

Czuba, Krzysztof, John Prager, and Jennifer Chu-Carroll (2002). "A Machine-learning Approach to Introspection in a Question Answering System." *Proceedings of the 2002 Conference on Empirical Methods in Natural Language Processing* (*EMNLP-2002*), University of Pennsylvania, Philadelphia, PA, USA.

de Boni, Marco and Suresh Manandhar (2003). "An Analysis of Clarification Dialogue for Question Answering." *Proceedings of the Human Language Technology and North American Chapter of Association of Computational Linguistics 2003* (*HLT/NAACL-2003*), Edmonton, Alberta, Canada.

Demner-Fushman, Dina and Jimmy Lin (2006). "Answer Extraction, Semantic Clustering, and Extractive Summarization for Clinical Question Answering." *Proceedings of the Joint Conference of the International Committee on Computational Linguistics and the Association for Computational Linguistics* (*COLING/ACL-2006*), Sydney, Australia.

Doan-Nguyen, Hai and Leila Kosseim (2006). "Using Terminology and a Concept Hierarchy for Restricted-domain Question-answering." In Alexander F. Gelbukh, ed., *Advances in Natural Language Processing*, Special Issue of *Research in Computing Science*, No. 18, pp. 183–194.

Duboue, Pablo and Jennifer Chu-Carroll (2006). "Answering the Question You Wish They Had Asked: The Impact of Paraphrasing for Question Answering." *Proceedings of the Human Language Technology Conference—Annual Meeting of the North American Chapter of the Association for Computational Linguistics* (*HLT-NAACL-2006*), New York, USA.

Ferrández, Sergio and Antonio Ferrández (2006). "Cross-lingual Question Answering Using InterLingual Index Module of EuroWordNet." In Alexander F. Gelbukh, ed., *Advances in Natural Language Processing*, Special Issue of *Research in Computing Science*, No. 18, pp. 177–182.

Fliedner, Gerhard (2006). "Towards Natural Interactive Question Answering." *Proceedings of the 5th International Conference on Language Resources and Evaluation* (*LREC-2006*), Genoa, Italy.

Garcia, Vanessa Lopez, Enrico Motta, and Victoria Uren (2006). "AquaLog: An Ontology-driven Question Answering System to Interface the Semantic Web." *Proceedings of the Human Language Technology Conference—Annual Meeting of the North American Chapter of the Association for Computational Linguistics* (*HLT-NAACL-2006*), New York, USA.

Hacioglu, Kadri and Wayne Ward (2003). "Question Classification with Support Vector Machines and Error Correcting Codes." *Proceedings of the Human Language Technology and North American Chapter of Association of Computational Linguistics 2003* (*HLT/NAACL-2003*), Edmonton, Alberta, Canada.

Harabagiu, Sanda and Dan Moldovan (2001). "Open-domain Textual Question Answering." *Proceedings of the 2nd Meeting of the North American Chapter of the Association for Computational Linguistics: Language Technologies 2001* (*NAACL-2001*), Pittsburgh, PA, USA.

Harabagiu, Sanda, Andrew Hickl, and John Lehamnn (2005). "Experiments with Interactive Question-answering." *Proceedings of the 43rd Annual Meeting of the Association of Computational Linguistics* (*ACL-2005*), Ann Arbor, Michigan, USA.

Kim, Hae-Jung, Ki-Dong Bu, Jung-Hyun Kim, and Sang-Jo Lee (2005). "Exploiting Question Concepts for Query Expansion." *Proceedings of the 6th International Conference on Intelligent Text Processing and Computational Linguistics* (*CICLing-2005*), Mexico City, Mexico, pp. 612–615.

Laurent, Dominique (2006). "Industrial Concerns of a Question-answering System." *Proceedings of the 11th Conference of the European Chapter of the Association for Computational Linguistics* (*EACL-2006*), Trento, Italy.

Lin, Jimmy and Dina Demner-Fushman (2006). "Will Pyramids Built of Nuggets Topple Over?" *Proceedings of the Human Language Technology Conference—Annual Meeting of the North American Chapter of the Association for Computational Linguistics* (*HLT-NAACL-2006*), New York, USA.

Lowe, John B. (2000). "What's in Store for Question Answering? Prognostications Based on Corpus Analysis of Several Hundred Million Questions." *Proceedings of the Joint Sigdat Conference on Empirical Methods in Natural Language Processing and Very Large Corpora* (*EMNLP/VLC-2000*), Hong Kong University of Science and Technology, Hong Kong.

Marton, Gregory and Alexey Radul (2006). "Nuggeteer: Automatic Nugget-based Evaluation Using Descriptions and Judgements." *Proceedings of the Human Language Technology Conference—Annual Meeting of the North American Chapter of the Association for Computational Linguistics* (*HLT-NAACL-2006*), New York, USA.

Moldovan, Dan, Sanda Harabagiu, Marius Pasca, Rada F. Mihalcea, Roxana Girju, Richard Goodrum, and Vasile Rus (2000). "The Structure and Performance of an Open-domain Question Answering System." *Proceedings of the 38th Annual Meeting of the Association for Computational Linguistics* (*ACL-2000*), Hong Kong.

Moldovan, Dan, Christine Clark, Sanda Harabagiu, and Steve Maiorano (2003). "COGEX: A Logic Prover for Question Answering." *Proceedings of the Human Language Technology and North American Chapter of Association of Computational Linguistics 2003* (*HLT/NAACL-2003*), Edmonton, Alberta, Canada.

Moriceau, Véronique (2006). "Numerical Data Integration for Cooperative Question-answering." *Proceedings of the 11th Conference of the European Chapter of the Association for Computational Linguistics* (*EACL-2006*), Trento, Italy.

Moschitti, Alessandro and Roberto Basili (2006). "A Tree Kernel

Approach to Question and Answer Classification in Question Answering Systems." *Proceedings of the 5th International Conference on Language Resources and Evaluation* (*LREC-2006*), Genoa, Italy.

Ng, Hwee Tou, Jennifer Lai Pheng Kwan, and Xia Yiyuan (2001). "Question Answering Using a Large Text Database: A Machine Learning Approach." *Proceedings of the 2001 Conference on Empirical Methods in Natural Language Processing* (*EMNLP-2001*), Carnegie Mellon University, Pittsburgh, PA, USA.

Nyberg, Eric H. and Robert Frederking (2003). "JAVELIN: A Flexible, Planner-based Architecture for Question Answering." *Proceedings of the Human Language Technology and North American Chapter of Association of Computational Linguistics 2003* (*HLT/NAACL-2003*), Edmonton, Alberta, Canada.

Peñas, Anselmo, Felisa Verdejo, and Jesús Herrera (2004). "Spanish Question Answering Evaluation." *Proceedings of the 5th International Conference on Intelligent Text Processing and Computational Linguistics* (*CICLing-2004*), Chung-Ang University, Seoul, Korea, pp. 467–478.

Quarteroni, Silvia and Suresh Manandhar (2006). "Incorporating User Models in Question Answering to Improve Readability." *Proceedings of the 11th Conference of the European Chapter of the Association for Computational Linguistics* (*EACL-2006*), Trento, Italy.

Ravichandran, Deepak, Abraham Ittycheriah, and Salim Roukos (2003). "Automatic Derivation of Surface Text Patterns for a Maximum Entropy Based Question Answering System." *Proceedings of the Human Language Technology and North American Chapter of Association of Computational Linguistics 2003* (*HLT/NAACL-2003*), Edmonton, Alberta, Canada.

Sasaki, Yutaka (2005). "Question Answering as Question-biased Term Extraction: A New Approach toward Multilingual QA." *Proceedings of the 43rd Annual Meeting of the Association of Computational Linguistics* (*ACL-2005*), Ann Arbor, Michigan, USA.

Solorio, Thamar, Manuel Pérez-Coutiño, Manuel Montes-y-Gómez, Luis Villaseñor-Pineda, and Aurelio López López (2005). "Question Classification in Spanish and Portuguese." *Proceedings of the 6th International Conference on Intelligent Text Processing and Computational Linguistics* (*CICLing-2005*), Mexico City, Mexico, pp. 600–607.

Thompson, Paul (2003). "Dynamic Integration of Distributed Semantic Services: Infrastructure for Process Queries and Question Answering." *Proceedings of the Human Language Technology and North American Chapter of Association of Computational Linguistics 2003* (*HLT/NAACL-2003*), Edmonton, Alberta, Canada.

Vicedo, José Luis and Antonio Ferrández (2000). "Importance of Pronominal Anaphora Resolution in Question Answering Systems." *Proceedings of the 38th Annual Meeting of the Association for Computational Linguistics* (*ACL-2000*), Hong Kong.

Voorhees, Ellen M. (2003). "Evaluating Answers to Definition Questions." *Proceedings of the Human Language Technology and North American Chapter of Association of Computational Linguistics 2003* (*HLT/NAACL-2003*), Edmonton, Alberta, Canada.

Voorhees, Ellen M. (2003). "Evaluating the Evaluation: A Case Study Using the TREC 2002 Question Answering Track." *Proceedings of the Human Language Technology and North American Chapter of Association of Computational Linguistics 2003* (*HLT/NAACL-2003*), Edmonton, Alberta, Canada.

Wu, Min and Tomek Strzalkowski (2006). "Utilizing Co-occurrence of Answers in Question Answering." *Proceedings of the Joint Conference of the International Committee on Computational Linguistics and the Association for Computational Linguistics* (*COLING/ACL-2006*), Sydney, Australia.

Yousefi, Jamileh and Leila Kosseim (2006). "Automatic Acquisition of Semantic-based Question Reformulations for Question Answering." *Proceedings of the 7th International Conference on Intelligent Text Processing and Computational Linguistics* (*CICLing-2006*), Mexico City, Mexico.

Spoken Language Translator

Amengual, Juan Carlos, Asunción Castaño, Antonio Castellanos, Victor M. Jiménez, David Llorens, Andrés Marzal, Federico Prat, Juan Miguel Vilar, José Miguel Benedi, Francisco Casacuberta, Moisés Pastor, and Enrique Vidal (2000). "The EuTrans Spoken Language Translation System." *Machine Translation*, Vol. 15, Nos. 1–2, pp. 75–103.

Carter, David (1995). "The Spoken-language Translator." In *Translating and the Computer 17*. London: The Association for Information Management.

Jiménez, Victor M., Enrique Vidal, J. Oncina, Antonio Castellanos, H. Rulot, and J. A. Sánchez (1994). "Spoken-language Machine Translation in Limited-domain Tasks." In Heinrich Niemann, Renato de Mori, and Gerhard Hanrieder, eds., *Progress and Prospects of Speech Research and Technology*. Sankt Augustin: Infix, pp. 262–265.

Rayner, Manny, Pierrette Bouillon, and David Carter (1995). "Using Corpora to Develop Limited-domain Speech Translation Systems." In *Translating and the Computer 17*. London: The Association for Information Management.

Rayner, Manny and David Carter (1997). "Hybrid Processing in the Spoken Language Translator." *Proceedings of the IEEE International Conference on Acoustics, Speech, and Signal Processing* (*ICASSP-97*), Munich, Germany, pp. 107–110.

Verbmobil

Alexandersson, Jan, Norbert Reithinger, and Elisabeth Maier (1997). "Insights into the Dialog Processing of Verbmobil." *Proceedings of the 5th Conference on Applied Natural Language Processing*, Seattle, Washington, DC, USA.

Batliner, Anton, Jan Buckow, Heinrich Niemann, Elmar Nöth, and Volker Warnke (2000). "The Prosody Module." In Wolfgang Wahlster, ed., *Verbmobil: Foundations of Speech-to-speech Translation*. Berlin: Springer Verlag, pp. 106–121.

Becker, Tilman, Anne Kilger, Patrice Lopez, and Peter Poller (2000). "The Verbmobil Generation Component VM-GECO." In Wolfgang Wahlster, ed., *Verbmobil: Foundations of Speech-to-speech Translation*. Berlin: Springer Verlag, pp. 481–496.

Bos, Johan, Bjirn Gamback, Christian Lieske, Yoshiki Mori, Manfred Pinkal, and Karsten Worm (1996). "Compositional Semantics in Verbmobil." *Proceedings of the 16th International Conference on Computational Linguistics* (*COLING-96*), Copenhagen, Denmark, pp. 131–136.

Bub, Thomas, Wolfgang Wahlster, and Alex H. Waibel (1997). "Verbmobil: The Combination of Deep and Shallow Processing for Speech Translation." *Proceedings of the IEEE International*

Conference on Acoustics, Speech, and Signal Processing (ICASSP-97), Munich, Germany.

Burger, Susanne, Karl Weilhammer, Florian Schiel, and Hans G. Tillmann (2000). "Verbmobil Data Collection and Annotation." In Wolfgang Wahlster, ed., *Verbmobil: Foundations of Speech-to-speech Translation*. Berlin: Springer Verlag, pp. 537–549.

Eichner, Matthias, Matthias Wolff, and Rüdiger Hoffmann (2000). "Facts and Figures about the Verbmobil Project." In Wolfgang Wahlster, ed., *Verbmobil: Foundations of Speech-to-speech Translation*. Berlin: Springer Verlag, pp. 95–105.

Finke, Michael, Petra Geutner, Hermann Hild, Thomas Kemp, Klaus Ries, and Martin Westphal (1997). "The Karlsruhe-Verbmobil Speech Recognition Engine." *Proceedings of the IEEE International Conference on Acoustics, Speech, and Signal Processing (ICASSP-97)*, Munich, Germany, Vol. 1, pp. 83–86.

Görz, Günther, Marcus Kesseler, Jörg Spilker, and Hans Weber (1996). "Research on Architectures for Integrated Speech/Language Systems in Verbmobil." *Proceedings from the 16th International Conference on Computational Linguistics (COLING-96)*, Copenhagen, Denmark, pp. 484–489.

Jekat, Susanne J. and Walther van Hahn (2000). "Multilingual Verbmobil-Dialogs: Experiments, Data Collection and Data Analysis." In Wolfgang Wahlster, ed., *Verbmobil: Foundations of Speech-to-speech Translation*. Berlin: Springer Verlag, pp. 575–582.

Karger, Reinhard and Wolfgang Wahlster (2000). "Facts and Figures about the Verbmobil Project." In Wolfgang Wahlster, ed., *Verbmobil: Foundations of Speech-to-speech Translation*. Berlin: Springer Verlag, pp. 22–30.

Kay, Martin, Jean Mark Gawron, and Peter Norvig (1994). *Verbmobil: A Translation System for Face-to-face Dialog*. Stanford: Center for the Study of Language and Information.

Klüter, Andreas, Alassane Ndiaye, and Heinz Kirchmann (2000). "Verbmobil from a Software Engineering Point of View: System Design and Software Integration." In Wolfgang Wahlster, ed., *Verbmobil: Foundations of Speech-to-speech Translation*. Berlin: Springer Verlag, pp. 635–658.

Nübel, Rita (1997). "End-to-end Evaluation in Verbmobil I." *Proceedings of MT Summit VI*. San Diego, California, USA, pp. 232–239.

Rapoport, Tova R. (1990). "Secondary Predication and the Lexical Representation of Verbs." *Machine Translation*, Vol. 5, No. 1, pp. 31–55.

Schiehlen, Michael, John Bos, and Michael Dorna (2000). "Vermobil Interface Terms (VITs)." In Wolfgang Wahlster, ed., *Verbmobil: Foundations of Speech-to-speech Translation*. Berlin: Springer Verlag, pp. 183–199.

Tessiore, Lorenzo and Walther van Hahn (2000). "Functional Validation of a Machine Interpretation System: Verbmobil." In Wolfgang Wahlster, ed., *Verbmobil: Foundations of Speech-to-speech Translation*. Berlin: Springer Verlag, pp. 611–631.

Wahlster, Wolfgang (1993). "Verbmobil, Translation of Face-to-face Dialogs." *Proceedings of MT Summit IV: International Cooperation for Global Communication*, Kobe, Japan, pp. 127–135.

Wahlster, Wolfgang (1993). "Verbmobil: Translation of Face-to-face Dialogues?" *Proceedings of the 3rd European Conference on Speech Communication and Technology* (*EuroSpeech-93*), Berlin, Germany.

Wahlster, Wolfgang (1995). "Verbmobil: Towards a DRT-based Translation of Spontaneous Negotiation Dialogs." *Proceedings of MT Summit V: Machine Translation Conference, Exhibition and Tutorial*, Luxembourg.

Wahlster, Wolfgang (2000). "Mobile Speech-to-speech Translation of Spontaneous Dialogs: An Overview of the Final Verbmobil System." In Wolfgang Wahlster, ed., *Verbmobil: Foundations of Speech-to-speech Translation*. Berlin: Springer Verlag, pp. 3–21.

Wahlster, Wolfgang, ed. (2000). *Verbmobil: Foundations of Speech-to-speech Translation*. Berlin: Springer Verlag.

Speech Translation System Evaluation

Blanchon, Herve, Christian Boitet, and Laurent Besacier (2004). "Spoken Dialogue Translation Systems Evaluation: Results, New Trends, Problems and Proposals." *Proceedings of the International Workshop on Spoken Language Translation* (*IWSLT-2004*), Kyoto, Japan.

Ćavar, Damir, Uwe Küssner, and Dan Tidhar (2000). "From Off-line Evaluation to On-line Selection." In Wolfgang Wahlster, ed.,

Verbmobil: Foundations of Speech-to-speech Translation. Berlin: Springer Verlag, pp. 597–610.
Koehn, Philipp, Amittai Axelrod, Alexandra Birch Mayne, Chris Callison-Burch, Miles Osborne, and David Talbot (2005). "Edinburgh System Description for the 2005 IWSLT Speech Translation Evaluation." *Proceedings of the International Workshop on Spoken Language Translation* (*IWSLT-2005*), Pittsburgh, PA, USA.
Lee, Young-Suk and Salim Roukos (2004). "IBM Spoken Language Translation System Evaluation." *Proceedings of the International Workshop on Spoken Language Translation* (*IWSLT-2004*), Kyoto, Japan.
Moldovan, Dan I., Marius Pasca, Sanda M. Harabagiu, and Mihai Surdeanu (2002). "Performance Issues and Error Analysis in an Open-domain Question Answering System." *Proceedings of the 40th Annual Meeting of the Association for Computational Linguistics* (*ACL-2002*), Philadelphia, PA, USA, pp. 33–40.
Somers, Harold L. and Yuri Sugita (2003). "Evaluating Commercial Spoken Language Translation Software." *Proceedings of MT Summit IX*, New Orleans, Louisiana, USA.
Takezawa, Toshiyuki, Fumiaki Sugaya, Akio Yokoo, and Seiichi Yamamoto (1999). "A New Evaluation Method for Speech Translation Systems and a Case Study on ATR-MATRIX from Japanese to English." *Proceedings of MT Summit VII: MT in the Great Translation Era*, Singapore.

Speech Understanding

Chai, Joyce Y., Pengyu Hong, Michelle X. Zhou, and Zahar Prasov (2004). "Optimization in Multimodal Interpretation." *Proceedings of the 42nd Annual Meeting of the Association for Computational Linguistics* (*ACL-2004*), Barcelona, Spain, pp. 1–8.
Hirschman, Lynette, Madeleine Bates, Deborah Dahl, William Fisher, John Garofolo, David Pallett, Kate Hunicke-Smith, Patti Price, Alex Rudnicky, and Evelyne Tzoukermann (1993). "Multi-site Data Collection and Evaluation in Spoken Language Understanding." *Proceedings of the Human Language Technology Workshop*, San Francisco, USA, pp. 19–24.
Huewel, Sonja and Britta Wrede (2006). "Spontaneous Speech

Understanding for Robust Multi-modal Human-robot Communication." *Proceedings of the Joint Conference of the International Committee on Computational Linguistics and the Association for Computational Linguistics* (*COLING/ACL-2006*), Sydney, Australia.

Jeong, Minwoo and Gary Geunbae Lee (2006). "Exploiting Non-local Features for Spoken Language Understanding." *Proceedings of the Joint Conference of the International Committee on Computational Linguistics and the Association for Computational Linguistics* (*COLING/ACL-2006*), Sydney, Australia.

Razakov, Alexander (2001). "Computer-assisted Text and Speech Understanding Project." *International Journal of Translation*, Vol. 13, Nos. 1–2, pp. 203–204.

Wang, Ye-Yi, Milind Mahajan, Alex Acero, and John Lee (2006). "Combining Statistical and Knowledge-based Spoken Language Understanding in Conditional Models." *Proceedings of the Joint Conference of the International Committee on Computational Linguistics and the Association for Computational Linguistics* (*COLING/ACL-2006*), Sydney, Australia.

Wolf, Jared J. and William A. Woods (1980). "The HWIM Speech Understanding System." In Wayne A. Lea, ed., *Trends in Speech Recognition*. Englewood Cliffs, New Jersey: Prentice-Hall, pp. 316–339.

Xie, Guodong 解國棟, Zong Chengqing 宗成慶, and Xu Bo 徐波 (2002). 〈面向中間語義表示格式的漢語口語解析方法〉 (Chinese Spoken Language Analysis Facing the Middle Semantic Representation). 《第一屆學生計算語言學研討會論文集》 (*SWCL-2002: First Students' Workshop on Computational Linguistics: Proceedings*), Institute of Computational Linguistics, Peking University, Beijing, China, pp. 71–76.

Xie, Guodong, Chengqing Zong, and Bo Xu (2003). "A Maximum Entropy Approach for Spoken Chinese Understanding." *Proceedings of the 4th International Conference on Intelligent Text Processing and Computational Linguistics* (*CICLing-2003*), Mexico City, Mexico, pp. 94–103.

❖ PART 32 ❖

Tagging

Part-of-speech Tagging

Abney, Steven (1997). "Part-of-speech Tagging and Partial Parsing." In Steve Young and Gerrit Bloothooft, eds., *Corpus-based Methods in Language and Speech Processing*. Dordrecht: Kluwer Academic Publishers, pp. 118–136.

Ando, Kazuaki, Tae-hun Lee, Masami Shishibori, and Jun-ichi Aoe (2001). "A Method of Pre-computing Connectivity Relations for Japanese/Korean POS Tagging." *Proceedings of the 2nd International Conference on Intelligent Text Processing and Computational Linguistics* (*CICLing-2001*), Mexico City, Mexico.

Araujo, Lourdes (2002). "Part-of-speech Tagging with Evolutionary Algorithms." *Proceedings of the 3rd International Conference on Intelligent Text Processing and Computational Linguistics* (*CICLing-2002*), Mexico City, Mexico.

Brants, Thorsten (2000). "TnT—A Statistical Part-of-speech Tagger." *Proceedings of the 1st Meeting of the North American Chapter of the Association for Computational Linguistics* (*NAACL-2000*), Seattle, WA, USA, pp. 224–231.

Brasser, Michael (2000). "Enhancing Traditional Input Methods through Part-of-speech Tagging." *Proceedings of the 38th Annual Meeting of the Association for Computational Linguistics* (*ACL-2000*), Hong Kong.

Brill, Eric (1992). "A Simple Rule-based Part-of-speech Tagger." *Proceedings of the 3rd Conference on Applied Natural Language Processing*, Trento, Italy, pp. 152–155.

Brill, Eric (1995). "Transformation-based Error-driven Learning and Natural Language Processing: A Case Study in Part-of-speech Tagging." *Computational Linguistics*, Vol. 21, No. 4, pp. 543–565.

Chen, Wenliang 陳文亮, Zhu Jingbo 朱靖波, Lü Xueqiang 呂學強, and Yao Tianshun 姚天順 (2002). 〈詞性標注規則的獲取和優化〉 (Acquisition and Optimization of Rules for Part of Speech Tagging). 《第一屆學生計算語言學研討會論文集》 (*SWCL-2002: First Students' Workshop on Computational Linguistics: Proceedings*), Institute of Computational Linguistics, Peking University, Beijing, China, pp. 106–111.

Church, Kenneth W. (1993). "Part of Speech Tagging and Suggestions for the Future." *Proceedings of the Conference of the Association for Computational Linguistics and Chinese Language Processing* (*ROCLING-VI*), Nantou, Taiwan.

Dias, Gaël, Sylvie Guilloré, José Gabriel, and Pereira Lopes (2000). "Extracting Textual Associations in Part-of-speech Tagged Corpora." *Proceedings of the 5th Workshop of the European Association for Machine Translation: Harvesting Existing Resources*, Lubljana, Slovenia.

Dien, Dinh and Hoang Kiem (2003). "POS-Tagger for English Vietnamese Bilingual Corpus." *Proceedings of the Human Language Technology and North American Chapter of Association of Computational Linguistics 2003* (*HLT/NAACL-2003*), Edmonton, Alberta, Canada.

Graña, Jorge, Francisco-Mario Barcala, and Jesús Vilares (2002). "Formal Methods of Tokenization for Part-of-speech Tagging." *Proceedings of the 3rd International Conference on Intelligent Text Processing and Computational Linguistics* (*CICLing-2002*), Mexico City, Mexico.

Habash, Nizar and Owen Rambow (2005). "Tokenization, Morphological Analysis, and Part-of-speech Tagging for Arabic in One Fell Swoop." *Proceedings of the 43rd Annual Meeting of the Association of Computational Linguistics* (*ACL-2005*), Ann Arbor, Michigan, USA.

Han, Chung-hye and Na-Rae Han (2001). *Part of Speech Tagging Guidelines for Penn Korean Treebank*. IRCS Report 01-09, IRCS, University of Pennsylvania.

Harris, Roger (1997). "The AMALGAM Parts-of-speech Tagger." *Machine Translation Review*, No. 5, pp. 6–9.

Heeman, Peter A. (1999). "POS Tags and Decision Trees for Language Modeling." *Proceedings of the Joint SIGDAT Conference on Empirical Methods in NLP and Very Large Corpora* (*EMNLP/VLC-99*), University of Maryland, College Park, MD, USA.

Hepple, Mark (2000). "Independence and Commitment: Assumptions for Rapid Training and Execution of Rule-based POS Taggers." *Proceedings of the 38th Annual Meeting of the Association for Computational Linguistics* (*ACL-2000*), Hong Kong.

Infante-Lopez, Gabriel and Maarten de Rijke (2006). "Sequences of Part of Speech Tags vs. Sequences of Phrase Labels: How Do They Help in Parsing?" *Proceedings of the 7th International Conference on Intelligent Text Processing and Computational Linguistics* (*CICLing-2006*), Mexico City, Mexico.

Kempe, Andre (2000). "Part-of-speech Tagging with Two Sequential Transducers." *Proceedings of the 11th Meeting of Computational Linguistics in the Netherlands* (*CLIN-2000*), Tilburg, Netherlands, pp. 88–96.

Lee, Sang-Zoo, Jun-ichi Tsujii, and Rim Hae-Chang (2000). "Lexicalized Hidden Markov Models for Part-of-speech Tagging." *Proceedings of the 18th International Conference on Computational Linguistics (COLING-2000)*, Saarbrücken, Germany, pp. 481–487.

Lee, Sang-Zoo, Jun-ichi Tsujii, and Rim Hae-Chang (2000). "Part-of-speech Tagging Based on Hidden Markov Model Assuming Joint Independence." *Proceedings of the 38th Annual Meeting of the Association for Computational Linguistics (ACL-2000)*, Hong Kong.

Lim, Hewui Seok, Jin-Dong Kim, and Hae-Chang Rim (1997). "A Korean Part-of-speech Tagger Using Transformation-based Error-driven Learning." *Proceedings of the 1997 International Conference on Computer Processing of Oriental Languages*, Hong Kong, China, pp. 456–459.

Lüdtke, Dirk and Satoshi Sato (2003). "Fast Base NP Chunking with Decision Trees—Experiments on Different POS Tag Settings." *Proceedings of the 4th International Conference on Intelligent Text Processing and Computational Linguistics (CICLing-2003)*, Mexico City, Mexico, pp. 139–150.

Marquez, Lluis, Horacio Rodriguez, Josep Carmona, and Josep Montolio (1999). "Improving POS Tagging Using Machine-learning Techniques." *Proceedings of the Joint SIGDAT Conference on Empirical Methods in NLP and Very Large Corpora (EMNLP/VLC-99)*, University of Maryland, College Park, MD, USA.

Mihalcea, Rada F. (2003). "Performance Analysis of a Part of Speech Tagging Task." *Proceedings of the 4th International Conference on Intelligent Text Processing and Computational Linguistics (CICLing-2003)*, Mexico City, Mexico, pp. 161–170.

Minnaja, Carlo and Laura Paccagnella (2000). "A Part-of-speech Tagger for Esperanto Oriented to MT." *Proceedings of the International Conference on Machine Translation and Multilingual Applications in the New Millenium (MT-2000)*, University of Exeter, England.

Ratnaparkhi, Adwait (1996). "A Maximum Entropy Model for POS Tagging." *Proceedings of the Conference on Empirical Methods in Natural Language Processing*, University of Pennsylvania, PA, USA, pp. 133–142.

Reynolds, Sheila M. and Jeff A. Bilmes (2005). "Part-of-speech Tagging Using Virtual Evidence and Negative Training." *Proceedings of Human Language Technology Conference and Conference on*

Empirical Methods in Natural Language Processing (*HLT/EMNLP-2005*), Vancouver, BC, Canada.

Roche, Emmanuel and Yves Schabes (1995). "Deterministic Part-of-speech Tagging with Finite-state Transducers." *Computational Linguistics*, Vol. 21, pp. 227–253.

Schmid, Helmut (1994). "Probabilistic Part-of-speech Tagging Using Decision Trees." *Proceedings of the International Conference on New Methods in Language Processing* (*NeMLaP-94*), Manchester, England, pp. 44–49.

Song, Honglin 孫宏林, Lu Qin 陸勤, and Yu Shiwen 俞士汶 (2000). 〈利用遺傳算法實現詞類標記集的優化〉 (Using Genetic Algorithms for Optimizing Part-of-speech Tagset). In Yu Shiwen 俞士汶 and Zhu Xuefeng 朱學鋒, eds., 《計算語言學文集》 (*Papers on Computational Linguistics*), Vol. 4. Beijing: Department of Computer Science and Technology and Institute of Computational Linguistics, Peking University, pp. 133–142.

Toutanova, Kristina and Christopher D. Manning (2000). "Enriching the Knowledge Sources Used in a Maximum Entropy Part-of-speech Tagger." *Proceedings of the Joint Sigdat Conference on Empirical Methods in Natural Language Processing and Very Large Corpora* (*EMNLP/VLC-2000*), Hong Kong University of Science and Technology, Hong Kong.

Toutanova, Kristina, Dan Klein, Christopher D. Manning, and Yoram Singer (2003). "Feature-rich Part-of-speech Tagging with a Cyclic Dependency Network." *Proceedings of the Human Language Technology and North American Chapter of Association of Computational Linguistics 2003* (*HLT/NAACL-2003*), Edmonton, Alberta, Canada.

Tsai, Yu-Fang and Keh-Jiann Chen (2003). "Reliable and Cost-effective PoS-tagging." *Proceedings of the International Conference on Research in Computational Linguistics* (*ROCLING-XV*), Hsin-Chu, Taiwan.

Wilks, Yorick and Mark Stevenson (1998). "The Grammar of Sense: Using Part-of-speech Tags as a First Step in Semantic Discrimination." *Natural Language Engineering*, Vol. 4, pp. 135–144.

Yu, Shiwen, Zhu Xuefeng, and Duan Huiming (2000). 〈大規模現代漢語標注語料庫的加工規範〉 (Guidelines for Segmentation and Part-of-speech Tagging on Very Large Scale Corpus of Contemporary Chinese). In Yu

Shiwen and Zhu Xuefeng, eds.,《計算語言學文集》(*Papers on Computational Linguistics*), Vol. 4. Beijing: Department of Computer Science and Technology and Institute of Computational Linguistics, Peking University, pp. 125–132.

Tagger

Brants, Thorsten (2000). "A Statistical Part-of-speech Tagger." *Proceedings of the 6th Applied Natural Language Processing Conference*, Seattle, Washington, DC, USA, pp. 224–231.

Brill, Eric (1992). "A Simple Rule-based Part of Speech Tagger." *Proceedings of the 3rd Conference on Applied Natural Language Processing*, Trento, Italy, pp. 152–155.

Chen, Keh-jiann, Shing-Huan Liu, Li-ping Chang, and Yeh-Hao Chin (1994). "A Practical Tagger for Chinese Corpora." *Proceedings of the Conference of the Association for Computational Linguistics and Chinese Language Processing* (*ROCLING-VII*), National Tsing Hua University, Hsin-Chu, Taiwan.

Cutting, D., J. Jupiec, J. Pedersen, and P. Sibun (1992). "A Practical Part-of-speech Tagger." *Proceedings of the 3rd Conference on Applied Natural Language Processing*, Trento, Italy, pp. 133–140.

Jiménez, Héctor and Guillermo Morales (2002). "Sepe: A POS Tagger for Spanish." *Proceedings of the 3rd International Conference on Intelligent Text Processing and Computational Linguistics* (*CICLing-2002*), Mexico City, Mexico.

Macklovitch, Elliott (1992). "Where the Tagger Falters." *Proceedings of the 4th International Conference on Theoretical and Methodological Issues in Machine Translation of Natural Languages: Empiricist vs. Rationalist Methods in MT* (*TMI-92*), Montreal, Quebec, Canada, pp. 113–126.

Mohammad, Saif and Ted Pedersen (2003). "Guaranteed Pre-tagging for the Brill Tagger." *Proceedings of the 4th International Conference on Intelligent Text Processing and Computational Linguistics* (*CICLing-2003*), Mexico City, Mexico, pp. 151–160.

Palanisamy, Arulmozhi and Sobha Lalitha Devi (2006). "HMM based POS Tagger for a Relatively Free Word Order Language." In Alexander F. Gelbukh, ed., *Advances in Natural Language Processing*, Special Issue of *Research in Computing Science*, No. 18, pp. 37–48.

Zhou, Guodong and Su Jian (2000). "Error-driven HMM-based Chunk Tagger with Context-dependent Lexicon." *Proceedings of the Joint Sigdat Conference on Empirical Methods in Natural Language Processing and Very Large Corpora* (*EMNLP/VLC-2000*), Hong Kong University of Science and Technology, Hong Kong.

Tagging

Abney, Steven (1997). "Part-of-speech Tagging and Partial Parsing." In Steve Young and Gerrit Bloothooft, eds., *Corpus-based Methods in Language and Speech Processing*. Dordrecht: Kluwer Academic Publishers, pp. 118–136.

Abney, Steven, Robet E. Schapire, and Yoram Singer (1999). "Boosting Applied to Tagging and PP Attachment." *Proceedings of the Joint SIGDAT Conference on Empirical Methods in NLP and Very Large Corpora* (*EMNLP/VLC-99*), University of Maryland, College Park, MD, USA.

Allwood, Jens, Grönqvist Leif, and A. P. Hendrikse (2003). "Developing a Tag Set and Tagger for the African Languages of Southern Africa with Special Reference to Xhosa." *Journal of Southern African Linguistics and Applied Language Studies*, Vol. 21, pp. 223–237.

Blaheta, Don and Eugene Charniak (2000). "Assigning Function Tags to Parsed Text." *Proceedings of the 1st Meeting of the North American Chapter of the Association for Computational Linguistics*, Seattle, Washington, DC, USA, pp. 234–240.

Dermatas, Evangelos and George Kokkinakis (1995). "Automatic Stochastic Tagging of Natural Language Texts." *Computational Linguistics*, Vol. 21, No. 2, pp. 137–163.

Diab, Mona and Philip Resnik (2002). "An Unsupervised Method for Word Sense Tagging Using Parallel Corpora." *Proceedings of the 40th Annual Meeting of the Association for Computational Linguistics* (*ACL 2002*), Philadelphia, Pennsylvania, USA, pp. 255–262.

Fliedl, Günther, Christian Kop, Heinrich C. Mayr, Jürgen Vöhringer, Georg Weber, and Christian Winkler (2006). "Extended Tagging in Requirements Engineering." In Alexander F. Gelbukh, ed., *Advances in Natural Language Processing*, Special Issue of *Research in Computing Science*, No. 18, pp. 49–56.

Garside, Roger G. (1984). "The Grammatical Tagging of Unrestricted

English Text." *Proceedings of the International Conference on the Methodology and Techniques of Machine Translation*, Cranfield Institute of Technology, Cranfield, England.

Hajič, Jan and Barbora Hladkà (1998). "Tagging Inflective Languages: Prediction of Morphological Categories for a Rich, Structured Tagset." *Proceedings of the 36th Annual Meeting of the Association for Computational Linguistics and 17th International Conference on Computational Linguistics* (*COLING-ACL-98*), Montreal, Quebec, Canada, pp. 483–490.

Hajič, Jan (2000). "Morphological Tagging: Data vs. Dictionaries." *Proceedings of the 1st Meeting of the North American Chapter of the Association for Computational Linguistics*, Seattle, Washington, DC, USA, pp. 94–101.

Hajič, Jan, Pavel Krbec, Pavel Kvĕtoň, Karel Oliva, and Vladimír Petkevičc (2001). "Serial Combination of Rules and Statistics: A Case Study in Czech Tagging." *Proceedings of the Association for Computational Linguistics 39th Annual Meeting and 10th Conference of the European Chapter*, Toulouse, France, pp. 260–267.

Han, Chung-Hye and Martha Palmer (2004). "A Morphological Tagger for Korean: Statistical Tagging Combined with Corpus-based Morphological Rule Application." *Machine Translation*, Vol. 18, No. 4, pp. 275–297.

Huashabao 華沙寶 (1999).〈蒙古語詞類標注系統 —— AYIMAG〉(The Mongolian Part-of-speech Tagging System—AYIMAG). In Huang Changning 黃昌寧 and Dong Zhendong 董振東, eds.,《計算機語言學文集》(*Essays on Computational Linguistics*). Beijing: Tsinghua University Press, pp. 210–214.

Johnson, Christopher and Charles J. Fillmore (2000). "The FrameNet Tagset for Frame-semantic and Syntactic Coding of Predicate-argument Structure." *Proceedings of the 1st Meeting of the North American Chapter of the Association for Computational Linguistics*, Seattle, Washington, DC, USA, pp. 56–62.

Kang, Shiyong 亢世勇, Chang Baobao 常寶寶, Liu Hairun 劉海潤, Xu Yanhua 徐艷華, and Yu Shiwen 俞士汶 (2001).〈全信息標注語料庫的開發與應用〉(The Development and Application of the All-information-tagged Corpus).《輝煌二十年 —— 中國中文信息學會二十周年學術會議》(*Proceedings of Conference of the 20th Anniversary of CIPSC*). Beijing: Tsinghua University Press, pp. 125–130.

Kang, Shiyong and Liu Hairun (2001).〈基於數據庫的現代漢語詞類優勢語法功能統計研究〉(A Study on the Advantageous Grammatical Functions of Chinese Parts of Speech on Language Database).《輝煌二十年——中國中文信息學會二十周年學術會議》(*Proceedings of Conference of the 20th Anniversary of CIPSC*). Beijing: Tsinghua University Press, pp. 166–170.

Karttunen, Lauri (2003). "Computing with Realizational Morphology." In Alexander F. Gelbukh, ed., *Proceedings of the 4th International Conference on Computational Linguistics and Intelligent Text Processing* (*CICLing-2003*), Mexico City, Mexico. Berlin: Springer Verlag, pp. 205–216.

Kogut, Dariusz J. (2002). "Fuzzy Set Tagging." *Proceedings of the 3rd International Conference on Intelligent Text Processing and Computational Linguistics* (*CICLing-2002*), Mexico City, Mexico.

Leech, Geoffrey (1997). "Grammatical Tagging." In Roger Garside, Geoffrey Leech, and Anthony McEnery, eds., *Corpus Annotation: Linguistic Information from Computer Text Corpora*. London: Longman, pp. 19–33.

Lin, Yi-Chung and Tung-Hui Chiang (1992). "Discrimination Oriented Probabilistic Tagging." *Proceedings of the Conference of the Association for Computational Linguistics and Chinese Language Processing* (*ROCLING-V*), National Taiwan University, Taipei, Taiwan.

Meng, Helen and Chun Wah Ip (1999). "An Analytical Study of Transformational Tagging for Chinese Text." *Proceedings of the International Conference on Research in Computational Linguistics* (*ROCLING-XII*), Taipei, Taiwan.

Merialdo, Bernard (1990). "Tagging Text with a Probabilistic Model." *Proceedings of the IBM Natural Language ITL*, Paris, France, pp. 161–172.

Mikheev, Andrei (2000). "Tagging Sentence Boundaries." *Proceedings of the 1st Meeting of the North American Chapter of the Association for Computational Linguistics*, Seattle, Washington, DC, USA, pp. 264–271.

Pantel, Patrick and Deepak Ravichandran (2004). "Automatically Labeling Semantic Classes." *Proceedings of the Human Language Technology Conference/North American Chapter of the Association for Computational Linguistics Annual Meeting* (*HLT/NAACL-2004*), Boston, MA, USA.

Prins, Robbert and Gertjan van Noord (2001). "Unsupervised Pos-tagging

Improves Parsing Accuracy and Parsing Efficiency." *Proceedings of the 7th International Workshop on Parsing Technologies* (*IWPT-2001*), Peking University, Beijing, China. Beijing: Tsinghua University Press, pp. 154–165.

Samuelsson, Christer (2000). "Extending N-gram Tagging to Word Graphs." In Nicolas Nicolov and Ruslan Mitkov, eds., *Recent Advances in Natural Language Processing II*. Amsterdam and Philadelphia: John Benjamins Publishing Company, pp. 3–19.

Schuler, William, David Chiang, and Mark Dras (2000). "Multi-component TAG and Notions of Formal Power." *Proceedings of the 38th Annual Meeting of the Association for Computational Linguistics* (*ACL-2000*), Hong Kong.

Shin, Jung H., Young S. Han, and Key-sun Choi (1997). "A HMM Part-of-speech Tagger for Korean with Wordphrasal Relations." In Ruslan Mitkov and Nicolas Nicolov, eds., *Recent Advances in Natural Language Processing*. Amsterdam and Philadelphia: John Benjamins Publishing Company, pp. 439–449.

Siefkes, Christian (2006). "A Comparison of Tagging Strategies for Statistical Information Extraction." *Proceedings of the Human Language Technology Conference—Annual Meeting of the North American Chapter of the Association for Computational Linguistics* (*HLT-NAACL-2006*), New York, USA.

Skut, Wojciech, Stefan Ulrich, and Kathrine Hammervold (2003). "A Generic Finite State Compiler for Tagging Rules." *Machine Translation*, Vol. 18, No. 3, pp. 239–250.

Srihari, Rohini, Niu Cheng, and Li Wei (2000). "A Hybrid Approach for Named Entity and Sub-type Tagging." *Proceedings of the 6th Applied Natural Language Processing Conference*, Seattle, Washington, DC, USA, pp. 247–254.

Stolcke, Andreas (2000). "Dialogue Act Modeling for Automatic Tagging and Recognition of Conversational Speech." *Computational Linguistics*, Vol. 26, pp. 339–373.

Swen, Bing (2002). "A General Output Model of Hidden Markov Models and Its Applications to Chinese Segmentation and Tagging." In Yu Shiwen, ed., *Proceedings of the 2nd China-Japan Natural Language Processing Joint Research Promotion Conference* (*CJNLP-2002*). Beijing: Institute of Computational Linguistics, Peking University, pp. 236–246.

Tong, Xiang, Huang Chang-ning, and Guo Cheng-ming (1999). "Example-based Sense Tagging of Running Chinese Text." In Susan Armstrong, Kenneth W. Church, Pierre Isabelle, Sandra Manzi, Evelyne Tzoukermann, and David Yarowsky, eds., *Natural Language Processing Using Very Large Corpora*. Dordrecht: Kluwer Academic Publishers, pp. 67–75.

Tsuruoka, Yoshimasa and Jun-ichi Tsujii (2005). "Bidirectional Inference with the Easiest-first Strategy for Tagging Sequence Data." *Proceedings of Human Language Technology Conference and Conference on Empirical Methods in Natural Language Processing* (*HLT/EMNLP-2005*), Vancouver, BC, Canada.

Wang, Suge 王素格, Zhang Yongkui 張永奎, and Liu Kaiying 劉開瑛 (1999). 〈漢詞詞性注中兼類詞排歧算法探討〉 (A Discussion of Ambiguous Algorithm to the Chinese Part-of-speech Tagging). In Huang Changning 黃昌寧 and Dong Zhendong 董振東, eds.,《計算機語言學文集》(*Essays on Computational Linguistics*). Beijing: Tsinghua University Press, pp. 162–166.

Xing, Hongbing 邢紅兵 (1999). 〈詞性標注中難歸類詞語分析〉 (Analysis on Words Hard to Be Classified in Part-of-speech Tagging). In Huang Changning and Dong Zhendong, eds.,《計算機語言學文集》(*Essays on Computational Linguistics*). Beijing: Tsinghua University Press, pp. 187–192.

Zhang, Ruiqiang, Kikui Genichiro, and Sumita Eiichiro (2006). "Subword-based Tagging by Conditional Random Fields for Chinese Word Segmentation." *Proceedings of the Human Language Technology Conference—Annual Meeting of the North American Chapter of the Association for Computational Linguistics* (*HLT-NAACL-2006*), New York, USA.

Zhang, Yuqi 張昱琪 and Zhou Qiang 周強 (2001). 〈大規模真實文本中漢語動詞語法搭配模版的自動識別〉 (Automatic Acquisition of Chinese Verb Subcategorization Frames from Large Scale Tagged Corpora). In Huang Changning and Zhang Pu, eds.,《自然語言理解與機器翻譯》(*Natural Language Understanding and Machine Translation*). Beijing: Tsinghua University Press, pp. 129–134.

Zhu, Jingbo 朱靖波 and Yao Tianshun 姚天順 (1999). 〈基於NAA的詞性自動標注模型〉 (POS Tagging Model Based on NAA). In Huang Changning and Dong Zhendong, eds.,《計算機語言學文集》(*Essays on Computational Linguistics*). Beijing: Tsinghua University Press, pp. 180–186.

❖ PART 33 ❖

Terminology

Terminology

Ahmad, Khurshid, Andrea Davies, Heather Fulford, Paul Holmes-Higgin, and Margaret Rogers (1995). "Creating Terminology Resources." In Marianne Kugler, Khurshid Ahmad, and Gregor Thurmair, eds., *Translator's Workbench*. Berlin: Springer Verlag, pp. 59–71.

Aráujo, Luzia A. (2000). "Translation, Terminology, Computers, and Translation Training." *Proceedings of the 7th Conference of the International Society for the Study of European Ideas (ISSEI-2000), Workshop 501: Teaching Translation in the Information Age*, Bergen, Norway.

Arthern, Peter J. (1979). "Machine Translation and Computerized Terminology Systems: A Translator's Viewpoint." In Barbara M. Snell, ed., *Translating and the Computer*. Amsterdam: North-Holland Publishing Company, pp. 77–108.

Bläser, Brigitte (1995). "TransLexis: An Integrated Environment for Lexicon and Terminology Management." In Petra Steffens, ed., *Machine Translation and the Lexicon*. Berlin: Springer Verlag, pp. 159–173.

Bokor, Gabe (1999). "Terminology Search on the World-wide Web." *Translation Journal*, Vol. 3, No. 1.

Bowker, Lynne (1996). "Towards a Corpus-based Approach to Terminography." *Terminology*, Vol. 3, No. 1, pp. 27–52.

Bowker, Lynne, ed. (2006). *Lexicography, Terminology, and Translation: Text-based Studies in Honour of Ingrid Meyer*. Ottawa: University of Ottawa Press.

Bowker, Lynne (2006). "Terminography in the Age of Translation Memory Tools: Reflections on Past Developments and Suggestions for the Future." *Programme of an International Conference on Computer-aided Translation: Theory and Practice*, Department of Translation, The Chinese University of Hong Kong, Hong Kong.

Brinkmann, Karl-Heinz (1974). "Terminologists, Lexicographers, and Computers." *Philips Terminology Bulletin*, Vol. 3, Nos. 3–4, pp. 8–9.

Cabré, M. Teresa, Rosa Estopà, and Jordi Vivaldi (2001). "Automatic Term Detection: A Review of Current Systems." In Didier Bourigault, Christian Jacquemin, and Marie-Claude L'Homme, eds., *Recent Advances in Computational Terminology*. Amsterdam and Philadelphia: John Benjamins Publishing Company, pp. 53–87.

Chaffey, Patrick Nigel (1986). "The Translation of Administrative Terminology." In Lars Wollin and Hans Lindquist, eds., *Translation Studies in Scandinavia: Proceedings from the Scandinavian Symposium on Translation Theory (SSOTT) II*, Lund, Sweden, pp. 63–70.

Cole, Wayne D. (1987). "Terminology: Principles and Methods." *Computers and Translation*, Vol. 2, No. 2, pp. 77–87.

Dagan, Ido and Kenneth W. Church (1997). "Termight: Coordinating Humans and Machines in Bilingual Terminology Acquisition." *Machine Translation*, Vol. 12, Nos. 1–2, pp. 89–107.

Danielsson, Pernilla and Daniel Ridings (2000). "Corpus and Terminology: Software for the Translation Program at Göteborgs Universitet or Getting Students to Do the Work." In Simon Philip Botley, Anthony Mark McEnery, and Andrew Wilson, eds., *Multilingual Corpora in Teaching and Research*. Amsterdam: Rodopi, pp. 65–72.

Eckmann, Carol B. (1995). "The Use of Translation-oriented Terminology Methodology in the Translation Process." In *Translating and the Computer 17*. London: The Association for Information Management.

Feng, Zhiwei 馮志偉 (1996).《現代術語學引論》(*Introduction to Modern Terminology*). Beijing: Language Press.

Galinski, Christian (1995). "Terminology and Standardization under a Machine Translation Perspective." *Proceedings of MT Summit V: Machine Translation Conference, Exhibition and Tutorial*, Luxembourg.

Gillam, Lee, Khurshid Ahmad, David Dalby, and Christopher Coz (2002). "Knowledge Exchange and Terminology Interchange: The Role of Standards." In *Translating and the Computer 24*. London: The Association for Information Management.

Goetschalckx, Jacques (1974). "Translation, Terminology and Documentation in International Organizations." *Babel*, Vol. 20, No. 4, pp. 185–187.

Goetschalckx, Jacques (1979). "Eurodicautom." In Barbara M. Snell, ed., *Translating and the Computer*. Amsterdam: North-Holland Publishing Company, pp. 71–75.

Hartley, Anthony F. and Emmanuel J. Yannakoudakis (1987). "An Intelligent Computational Environment for Terminology and Text Handling." *Meta*, Vol. 32, No. 2, pp. 139–148.

Hays, David G. (1977). "Machine Translation and Abstract Terminology." In Paul J. Hopper, ed., *Studies in Descriptive and Historical Linguistics*. Amsterdam and Philadelphia: John Benjamins Publishing Company, pp. 95–108.

Hoffmann, Erika (1988). "The LEXIS Termbank." In Catriona Picken, ed., *Translating and the Computer 9: Potential and Practice*. London: The Association for Information Management, pp. 154–160.

Hoppenbrouwers, Geer (1990). "The Term Bank of the RHOTV-Maastricht." In Marcel Thelen and Barbara Leeandowska-Tomaszczyk, eds., *Translation and Meaning, Part 1*. Maastricht: Euroterm, pp. 39–47.

Jaekel, Gary (2000). "Terminology Management at Ericsson." In Robert C. Sprung, ed., *Translating into Success: Cutting-edge Strategies for Going Multilingual in a Global Age*. Amsterdam and Philadelphia: John Benjamins Publishing Company, pp. 159–171.

Kageura, Kyo and Bin Umino (1996). "Methods of Automatic Term Recognition: A Review." *Terminology*, Vol. 3, No. 2, pp. 259–290.

Karkaletsis, Evangelos A. (1995). "The Use of Terminological Knowledge Bases in Software Localisation." In Petra Steffens, ed., *Machine Translation and the Lexicon*. Berlin: Springer Verlag, pp. 175–188.

Karsch, Barbara Inge (2006). "Terminology Workflow in the Localization Process." In Keiran Dunne, ed., *Perspectives on Localization*. Amsterdam and Philadelphia: John Benjamins Publishing Company.

Koch, Katharina (1995). "Machine Translation and Terminology Database—Uneasy Bedfellows?" In Petra Steffens, ed., *Machine Translation and the Lexicon*. Berlin: Springer Verlag, pp. 131–140.

Lauriston, Andy (1997). "Terminology and the Computer." In Robert Dubuc, ed., *Terminology: A Practical Approach*. Brossard, Quebec: Linguatech, pp. 179–192.

L'Homme, Marie-Claude and Elizabeth Marshman (2006). "Terminological Relationships and Corpus-based Methods for Discovering Them: An Assessment for Terminographers." In Lynne Bowker, ed., *Lexicography, Terminology, and Translation: Text-based Studies in Honour of Ingrid Meyer*. Ottawa: University of Ottawa Press, pp. 67–80.

Lin, Gang 林綱 (2002).〈試析網絡術語及其標準化〉(An Analysis of Computer Network Terms and Its Standardization).《第一屆學生計算語言學研討會論文集》(*SWCL2002: First Students' Workshop on*

Computational Linguistics: Proceedings), Institute of Computational Linguistics, Peking University, Beijing, p. 292.
Lombard, Robin (2006). "A Practical Case for Managing Source Language Terminology." In Keiran Dunne, ed., *Perspectives on Localization*. Amsterdam and Philadelphia: John Benjamins Publishing Company.
Maia, Belinda (2003). "'Some Languages Are More Equal Than Others': Training Translators in Terminology and Information Retrieval Using Comparable and Parallel Corpora." In Federico Zanettin, Silvia Bernardini, and Dominic Stewart, eds., *Corpora in Translator Education*. Manchester: St. Jerome Publishing, pp. 43–53.
Mayer, Renate (1995). "Navigation through Terminological Databases." In Petra Steffens, ed., *Machine Translation and the Lexicon*. Berlin: Springer Verlag, pp. 189–199.
McNaught, John (1981). "Terminological Data Banks: A Model for a British Linguistic Data Bank (LDB)." *Aslib Proceedings*, Vol. 33, Nos. 7–8, pp. 297–308.
Melby, Alan (2006). "Standard Formats for Sharing Terminology and Translation Memories: All You Ever Wanted to Know about the TMX and TBX Standards." *Proceedings of the Localization World Conference*, Barcelona, Spain.
Moser-Mercer, Barbara (1987). "Man/Machine Interface in Translation and Terminology." *Meta*, Vol. 32, No. 2, pp. 156–163.
Pearson, Jennifer (2000). "Teaching Terminology Using Electronic Resources." In Simon Philip Botley, Anthony Mark McEnery, and Andrew Wilson, eds., *Multilingual Corpora in Teaching and Research*. Amsterdam: Rodopi, pp. 92–105.
Quinn, David (1997). "Terminology for Machine Translation: A Study." *Machine Translation Review*, No. 6, pp. 9–21.
Quirion, Jean and Jacynthe Lanthier (2006). "Intrinsic Qualities Favouring Term Implantation: Verifying the Axioms." In Lynne Bowker, ed., *Lexicography, Terminology, and Translation: Text-based Studies in Honour of Ingrid Meyer*. Ottawa: University of Ottawa Press, pp. 107–118.
Reifler, Erwin (1957). "Some New Terminology." *Mechanical Translation*, Vol. 6, No. 3, pp. 52–53.
Rey, Alain, ed. (1995). *Essays on Terminology*. Amsterdam and Philadelphia: John Benjamins Publishing Company.
Rogers, Margaret and Khurshid Ahmad (1994). "Computerised

Terminology for Translators: The Role of Text." In Magnar Brekke, Øivin Andersen, Trine Dahl, and Johan Myking, eds., *Applications and Implications of Current LSP Research: Proceedings of the 9th European Symposium on LSP*, Fagbokforlaget, Norway, Vol. II, pp. 840–851.

Sager, Juan C. (1990). *A Practical Course in Terminology Processing*. Amsterdam and Philadelphia: John Benjamins Publishing Company.

Sager, Juan C. (1994). *Language Engineering and Translation: Consequences of Automation*. Amsterdam and Philadelphia: John Benjamins Publishing Company.

Sager, Juan C. (1998). "Terminology: Standardization." In Mona Baker, ed., *Routledge Encyclopedia of Translation Studies*. London and New York: Routledge, pp. 255–258.

Sager, Juan C. (1998). "Terminology: Theory." In Mona Baker, ed., *Routledge Encyclopedia of Translation Studies*. London and New York: Routledge, pp. 258–262.

Schmitz, Klaus-Dirk (1996). "Terminology Management Systems." In Rachel Owens, ed., *The Translator's Handbook*, 3rd ed. London: The Association for Information Management, pp. 221–239.

Schütz, Jörg and Bärbel Ripplinger (1993). "Machine Translation Supported by Terminological Information." *Proceedings of the 5th International Conference on Theoretical and Methodological Issues in Machine Translation of Natural Languages: MT in the Next Generation* (*TMI-93*), Kyoto, Japan, pp. 102–116.

Sérasset, Gilles, Francis Brunet-Manquat, and Elena Chiocchetti (2006). "Multilingual Legal Terminology on the Jibiki Platform: The LexALP Project." *Proceedings of the Joint Conference of the International Committee on Computational Linguistics and the Association for Computational Linguistics* (*COLING/ACL-2006*), Sydney, Australia.

Shih, Chung-ling (2006). "Term Base Use and Development: Effects on Specialized Translation Learning." *Helpful Assistance to Translators: MT & TM*. Taipei: Bookman Books Ltd., pp. 299–320.

Sonneveld, Helmi (1997). "The European Association for Terminology (EAFT): Objectives and Plans for the Future." In *Translating and the Computer 19*. London: The Association for Information Management.

Stefanov, Olaf-Michael (1998). "Towards a Multi-language Multi Script Web Based Reference and Terminology System." In *Translating and the Computer 20*. London: The Association for Information Management.

Trujillo, Arturo (1999). "Basic Terminology and Background." *Translation Engines: Techniques for Machine Translation*. Berlin and New York: Springer Verlag, pp. 9–36.

Yngve, Victor H. (1956). "Terminology in the Light of Research on Mechanical Translation." *Babel*, Vol. 2, No. 3, pp. 128–132.

Zaitseva, Natalia (2003). "Matrix-and-frame Methods as a Means of Structural and Semantic Systematization of Terminological Vocabulary." *International Journal of Translation*, Vol. 15, No. 1, pp. 87–105.

Zajac, Rémi and Michelle Vanni (1997). "Glossary-based MT Engines in a Multilingual Analyst's Workstation Architecture." *Machine Translation*, Vol. 12, Nos. 1–2, pp. 131–151.

Zauberga, Ieva (2005). "Handling Terminology in Translation." In Krisztina Károly and Ágota Fóris, eds., *New Trends in Translation Studies: In Honour of Kinga Klaudy*. Budapest: Akadémiai Kiadó, pp. 107–116.

Terminology Acquisition

Ahmad, Khurshid (1995). "Pragmatics of Specialist Terms: The Acquisition and Representation of Terminology." In Petra Steffens, ed., *Machine Translation and the Lexicon*. Berlin: Springer Verlag, pp. 51–76.

Kumar, R. Sathish and R. S. D. Wahida Banu (2004). "Selectional Preferences Acquisition Using Tree Cut Model and Semantic Similarity." *Proceedings of the International Conference on Natural Language Processing* (*ICON-2004*), International Institute of Information Technology, Hyderabad, India.

Terminology Bank

Brinkmann, Karl-Heinz (1974). "On the Development and Operation of Terminology Data Banks as a Requirement for Machine-aided Translation." *Nachrichten fuer Dokumentation*, Vol. 25, No. 3, pp. 99–104.

Brinkmann, Karl-Heinz (1980). "Terminology Data Banks as a Basis for

High-quality Translation." *Proceedings of the 8th International Conference on Computational Linguistics (COLING-80)*, Tokyo, Japan.

Cabré Castellvi, M. Teresa (2006). "From Terminological Data Banks to Knowledge Databases: The Text as the Starting Point." In Lynne Bowker, ed., *Lexicography, Terminology, and Translation: Text-based Studies in Honour of Ingrid Meyer*. Ottawa: University of Ottawa Press, pp. 93–106.

Candeland, Richard (1987). "The British Term Bank Project: A Prototype Software." *Machine Translation*, Vol. 2, No. 1, pp. 3–20.

Dong, Zhendong and Dong Qiang (2002). "Questions and Answers about HowNet." In Yu Shiwen, ed., *Proceedings of the 2nd China-Japan Natural Language Processing Joint Research Promotion Conference (CJNLP-2002)*. Beijing: Institute of Computational Linguistics, Peking University, pp. 155–162.

Hilsen, Venlig (2001). "The IATE Project—Towards a Single Terminology Database for the EU." In *Translating and the Computer 23*. London: The Association for Information Management.

Hoppenbrouwers, Geer (1990). "The Term Bank of the RHOTV-Maastricht." In Marcel Thelen and Barbara Leeandowska-Tomaszczyk, eds., *Translation and Meaning, Part 1*. Maastricht: Euroterm, pp. 39–47.

Kohn, Kurt and Michaela Albl (1995). "Extended Termbank Information." In Marianne Kugler, Khurshid Ahmad, and Gregor Thurmair, eds., *Translator's Workbench*. Berlin: Springer Verlag, pp. 100–106.

Mayer, Renate and Antonius van Hoof (1995). "Special Language Resources: Termbank, Cardbox." In Marianne Kugler, Khurshid Ahmad, and Gregor Thurmair, eds., *Translator's Workbench*. Berlin: Springer Verlag, pp. 49–58.

Morton, Sara E. (1978). "Designing a Multilingual Terminology Bank for United States Translators." *Journal of the American Society of Information Science*, Vol. 29, No. 6, pp. 297–303.

Morton, Sara E. (1978). "Multilingual Terminology Banks Here and Abroad: Online Terminology Dissemination as an Aid to Translation." In Everett H. Brenner, ed., *The Information Age in Perspective: Proceedings of the American Society of Information Science Annual Meeting*, Vol. 15, pp. 242–244.

Nkwenti-Azeh, Blaise (1998). "Term Banks." In Mona Baker, ed., *Routledge Encyclopedia of Translation Studies*. London and New York: Routledge, pp. 249–251.
Snell, Barbara M., ed. (1983). *Term Banks for Tomorrow's World: Translating and the Computer 4*. London: The Association for Information Management.
Yu, Jiangsheng, Zan Hongying, Liu Yang, and Wen Zhenshan (2002). "Building WordNet-like Term Bank." In Yu Shiwen, ed., *Proceedings of the 2nd China-Japan Natural Language Processing Joint Research Promotion Conference (CJNLP-2002)*. Beijing: Institute of Computational Linguistics, Peking University, pp. 45–51.

Treebank

Blanc, Etienne (2000). "From the UNL Hypergraph to GETA's Multilevel Tree." *Proceedings of the International Conference on Machine Translation and Multilingual Applications in the New Millenium (MT-2000)*, University of Exeter, Exeter, England.
Chen, Keh-Jiann and Hsieh Yu-Ming (2002). "Chinese Treebanks and Grammar Extraction." In Yu Shiwen, ed., *Proceedings of the 2nd China-Japan Natural Language Processing Joint Research Promotion Conference (CJNLP-2002)*. Beijing: Institute of Computational Linguistics, Peking University, pp. 163–177.
Eisner, Jason (2003). "Learning Non-isomorphic Tree Mappings for Machine Translation." *Proceedings of the 41st Annual Meeting of the Association for Computational Linguistics (ACL-2003)*, Supporo, Japan.
Graehl, Jonathan and Kevin Knight (2004). "Training Tree Transducers." *Proceedings of the Human Language Technology Conference/North American Chapter of the Association for Computational Linguistics Annual Meeting (HLT/NAACL-2004)*, Boston, MA, USA.
Hinrichs, Erhard W., Julia Bartels, Yasuhiro Kawata, Valia Kordoni, and Heike Telljohann (2000). "The Tübingen Treebanks for Spoken German, English, and Japanese." In Wolfgang Wahlster, ed., *Verbmobil: Foundations of Speech-to-speech Translation*. Berlin: Springer Verlag, pp. 550–574.
Kepser, Stephan (2005). "Using MONA for Querying Linguistic Treebanks." *Proceedings of Human Language Technology Conference*

and Conference on Empirical Methods in Natural Language Processing (*HLT/EMNLP-2005*), Vancouver, BC, Canada.

Marcus, Mitchell P., Beatrice Santorini, and Mary Ann Marcinkiewicz (1993). "Building a Large Annotated Corpus of English: The Penn Treebank." *Computational Linguistics*, Vol. 19, No. 2, pp. 313–330.

O'Donovan, Ruth, Michael Burke, Aoife Cahill, Josef van Genabith, and Andy Way (2004). "Large-scale Induction and Evaluation of Lexical Resources from the Penn-II Treebank." *Proceedings of the 42nd Annual Meeting of the Association for Computational Linguistics* (*ACL-2004*), Barcelona, Spain, pp. 367–374.

Rogers, James (2004). "Wrapping of Trees." *Proceedings of the 42nd Annual Meeting of the Association for Computational Linguistics* (*ACL-2004*), Barcelona, Spain, pp. 558–565.

Xue, Nianwen and Seth Kulick (2003). "Automatic Predicate Argument Structure Analysis of the Penn Chinese Treebank." *Proceedings of MT Summit IX*, New Orleans, Louisiana, USA.

Zhou, Qiang 周強, Zhang Wei 張偉, and Yu Shiwen 俞士汶 (1998). 〈漢語樹庫的構建〉 (The Construction of a Chinese Treebank). In Yu Shiwen 俞士汶 and Zhu Xuefeng 朱學鋒, eds., 《計算語言學文集》 (*Papers on Computational Linguistics*), Vol. 3. Beijing: Department of Computer Science and Technology and Institute of Computational Linguistics, Peking University, pp. 68–77.

Zhou, Qiang 周強, Ren Haibo 任海波, and Sun Maosong 孫茂松 (2002). 〈分階段構建漢語樹庫〉 (Building a Large Scale Chinese Treebank by Two Stages). In Yu Shiwen, ed., *Proceedings of the 2nd China-Japan Natural Language Processing Joint Research Promotion Conference* (*CJNLP-2002*). Beijing: Institute of Computational Linguistics, Peking University, pp. 189–197.

Terminology Extraction

Aha, David W. and Kalyan Moy Gupta (2004). "Heuristic Acronym Extraction Using Linguistic Features." *Proceedings of the International Conference on Natural Language Processing* (*ICON-2004*), International Institute of Information Technology, Hyderabad, India.

Ahmad, Khurshid, Andrea Davies, Heather Fulford, and Margaret Rogers (1994). "What Is a Term? The Semi-automatic Extraction of Terms from Text." In Mary Snell-Hornby, Franz Pöchhacker, and Klaus

Kaindl, eds., *Translation Studies: An Interdiscipline*. Amsterdam and Philadelphia: John Benjamins Publishing Company, pp. 267–278.

Bolshakova, Elena I. (2001). "Recognition of Author's Scientific and Technical Terms." *Proceedings of the 2nd International Conference on Intelligent Text Processing and Computational Linguistics* (*CICLing-2001*), Mexico City, Mexico.

Chang, Jing-Shin and Keh-Yih Su (1997). "A Multivariate Gaussian Mixture Model for Automatic Compound Word Extraction." *Proceedings of the International Conference on Research in Computational Linguistics* (*ROCLING-X*), Academia Sinica, Taipei, Taiwan.

Chantrier, Cyril (2005). "EXTER: A Breakthrough Solution for Efficient Terminology Extraction." In *Translating and the Computer 27*. London: The Association for Information Management.

Chien, Lee-Feng, Chung-Liang Chen, Wen-Hsiang Lu, and Yuan-Lu Chang (1999). "Recent Results on Domain-specific Term Extraction from Online Chinese Text Resources." *Proceedings of the International Conference on Research in Computational Linguistics* (*ROCLING-XII*), Taipei, Taiwan.

Čmejrek, Martin and Jan Cuřin (1999). "Automatic Translation Lexicon Extraction from English-Czech Parallel Texts." *Proceedings of the 4th Workshop of the European Association for Machine Translation: EU and the New Languages: Translation—Possibilities, Policies and Practicalities*, Prague, the Czech Republic.

Curran, James (2002). "Ensemble Methods for Automatic Thesaurus Extraction." *Proceedings of the 2002 Conference on Empirical Methods in Natural Language Processing* (*EMNLP-2002*), University of Pennsylvania, Philadelphia, PA, USA.

Daille, Beatrice, Eric Gaussier, and Jean-Marc Langé (1994). "Towards Automatic Extraction of Monolingual and Bilingual Terminology." *Proceedings of the 15th International Conference on Computational Linguistics* (*COLING-94*), Kyoto, Japan, pp. 515–521.

Deane, Paul (2005). "A Nonparametric Method for Extraction of Candidate Phrasal Terms." *Proceedings of the 43rd Annual Meeting of the Association of Computational Linguistics* (*ACL-2005*), Ann Arbor, Michigan, USA.

Fung, Pascale (1998). "A Statistical View on Bilingual Lexicon Extraction: From Parallel Corpora to Non-parallel Corpora."

Proceedings of the Association for Machine Translation in the Americas (*AMTA-98*), Langhorne, PA, USA.

Fung, Pascale (1998). "Extracting Key Terms from Chinese and Japanese Texts." *The International Journal on Computer Processing of Oriental Language, Special Issue on Information Retrieval on Oriental Languages*, Vol. 12, No. 1, pp. 99–121.

Gaussier, Eric and Jean-Marc Langé (1997). "Some Methods for the Extraction of Bilingual Terminology." In Daniel B. Jones and Harold L. Somers, eds., *New Methods in Language Processing*. London: UCL Press, pp. 145–153.

Jacquin, Ch. and M. Liscouet (1996). "Terminology Extraction from Texts Corpora: Application to Document Keeping via Internet." In Ch. Galinski and K.-D. Schmitz, eds., *Proceedings of the 4th International Congress on Terminology and Knowledge Engineering: Terminology and Knowledge Engineering* (*TKE-96*), Vienna, Austria. Frankfurt: INDEKS, pp. 74–83.

Kit, Chunyu (1994). "Automatic Terminology Extraction for Thematic Corpus Based on Subterm Co-occurrence." *Proceedings of the Conference of the Association for Computational Linguistics and Chinese Language Processing* (*ROCLING-VII*), National Tsing Hua University, Hsin-Chu, Taiwan.

Liu, Tongju 劉桐菊, Yu Hao 于浩, and Yang Muyun 楊沐昀 (2002).〈基於TFIDF的專業領域詞匯獲取的研究〉(A Study of Term Extraction in the Professional Field).《第一屆學生計算語言學研討會論文集》(*SWCL-2002: First Students' Workshop on Computational Linguistics: Proceedings*), Institute of Computational Linguistics, Peking University, Beijing, China, pp. 263–267.

Mohit, Behrang and Srini Narayanan (2003). "Semantic Extraction with Wide-coverage Lexical Resources." *Proceedings of the Human Language Technology and North American Chapter of Association of Computational Linguistics 2003* (*HLT/NAACL-2003*), Edmonton, Alberta, Canada.

Nagata, Makato (1996). "Automatic Extraction of New Words from Japanese Texts Using Generalized Forward-backward Search." *Proceedings of the Conference on Empirical Methods in Natural Language Processing*, University of Pennsylvania, PA, USA.

Nakagawa, Hiroshi (2004). "Term Extraction from Small Text." *AAMT Journal*, No. 36.

Piao, Scott S. L., Guangfan Sun, Paul Rayson, and Qi Yuan (2006). "Automatic Extraction of Chinese Multiword Expressions with a Statistical Tool." *Proceedings of the 11th Conference of the European Chapter of the Association for Computational Linguistics* (*EACL-2006*), Trento, Italy.

Sauron, Véronique (2002). "Tearing out the Terms: Evaluating Terms Extractors." In *Translating and the Computer 24*. London: The Association for Information Management.

Smith, Andrew E. (2003). "Automatic Extraction of Semantic Networks from Text Using Leximancer." *Proceedings of the Human Language Technology and North American Chapter of Association of Computational Linguistics 2003* (*HLT/NAACL-2003*), Edmonton, Alberta, Canada.

Thurmair, Gregor (2003). "Making Term Extraction Tools Usable." *Proceedings of the Joint Conference Combining the 8th International Workshop of the European Association for Machine Translation and the 4th Controlled Language Applications Workshop: Controlled Language Translation* (*EAMT-CLAW-2003*), Dublin City University, Ireland.

Vega, José (2005). "MyCaTEx, A Language Independent Term Extractor." In *Translating and the Computer 27*. London: The Association for Information Management.

Vintar, Spela (2001). "Using Parallel Corpora for Translation-oriented Term Extraction." *Babel*, Vol. 47, No. 2, pp. 121–132.

Wang, Qiangjun 王強軍, Li Yun 李芸, and Zhang Pu 張普 (2002). 〈信息技術領域術語提取的初步研究〉(Automatic Term Extraction in the Field of Information Technology). 《第一屆學生計算語言學研討會論文集》(*SWCL2002: First Students' Workshop on Computational Linguistics: Proceedings*), Institute of Computational Linguistics, Peking University, Beijing, China, pp. 246–250.

Yamamoto, Kaoru, Yuji Matsumoto, and Mihoko Kitamura (2001). "A Comparative Study on Translation Units for Bilingual Lexicon Extraction." *Proceedings of the Association for Computational Linguistics 39th Annual Meeting and 10th Conference of the European Chapter: Data-driven Machine Translation* (*ACL-EACL-2001*), Toulouse, France, pp. 87–94.

Zielinski, Daniel (2005). "Research Meets Practice: T-survey 2005: An Online Survey on Terminology Extraction and Terminology

Management." In *Translating and the Computer 27*. London: The Association for Information Management.

Terminology Management

Ahmad, Khurshid and Margaret Rogers (1992). "Terminology Management: A Corpus-based Approach." In *Translating and the Computer 14: Quality Standards and the Implementation of Technology in Translation*. London: The Association for Information Management, pp. 33–44.

Austermühl, Frank (2001). "Computer-assisted Terminology Management." *Electronic Tools for Translators*. Manchester: St. Jerome Publishing Company, pp. 102–123.

Bédard, Claude (1991). "Machine PreTranslation: A Further Step in Terminology Management." *ATA Chronicle*, pp. 19–20.

Bernardi, Ulrike, András Bocsák, and Jörg Porsiel (2005). "Are We Making Ourselves Clear? Terminology Management and Machine Translation at Volkswagen." *Proceedings of the 10th Workshop of the European Association for Machine Translation: Practical Applications of Machine Translation*, Budapest, Hungary, pp. 41–49.

Briscoe, Philip (2004). "Getting to Grips with Global Terminology Management." *Programme of the Annual Conference of the Association of Translation Companies: Getting in Shape for the Future—Working towards a New Environment for the Translation Profession*, School of Oriental and African Studies, University of London, England.

Chiu, Aman and Björn Jernudd (2002). "Chinese IT Terminology Management in Hong Kong." In Chan Sin-wai, ed., *Translation and Information Technology*. Hong Kong: The Chinese University Press, pp. 95–114.

Galinski, Christian and Gerhard Budin (1993). "New Trends in Translation-oriented Terminology Management." In Sue Ellen Wright and Leland D. Wright Jr., eds., *Scientific and Technical Translation*. Amsterdam and Philadelphia: John Benjamins Publishing Company, pp. 209–215.

Jaekel, Gary (2000). "Terminology Management at Ericsson." In Robert C. Sprung, ed., *Translating into Success: Cutting-edge Strategies for*

Going Multilingual in a Global Age. Amsterdam and Philadelphia: John Benjamins Publishing Company, pp. 159–171.
Jones, Ian (1999). "Terminology Management in NATO." In *Translating and the Computer 21*. London: The Association for Information Management.
Melby, Alan K. (1995). "Organization-wide Terminology Management Using MTX/Termex." In Roberta Schwarz, ed., *Proceedings of the 3rd TermNet Symposium on Terminology in Advanced Microcomputer Applications* (*TAMA-94*). Vienna: Die Deutsche Bibliothek, pp. 107–116.
To, Charlotte and Björn Jernudd (2002). "Terminological Problems and Language Management for Internet Language Professionals in Hong Kong." In Chan Sin-wai, ed., *Translation and Information Technology*. Hong Kong: The Chinese University Press, pp. 115–129.
Wright, Sue Ellen and Gerhard Budin (1997). *Handbook of Terminology Management*. Amsterdam and Philadelphia: John Benjamins Publishing Company.
Zielinski, Daniel (2005). "Research Meets Practice: T-survey 2005: An Online Survey on Terminology Extraction and Terminology Management." In *Translating and the Computer 27*. London: The Association for Information Management.

Terminology Management System

Ball, Sylvia (2003). "Joined-up Terminology—The IATE System Enters Production." In *Translating and the Computer 25*. London: The Association for Information Management.
Blanke, Wera (1988). "Terminologia Esperanto-centro." In Dan Maxwell, Klaus Schubert, and Toon Witkam, eds., *New Directions in Machine Translation*. Dordrecht-Holland: Foris Publications, pp. 183–194.
Bowker, Lynne (2002). "Terminology-management Systems." *Computer-aided Translation Technology: A Practical Introduction*. Ottawa: University of Ottawa Press, pp. 77–91.
Brinkmann, Karl-Heinz and Eberhard Tanke (1976). "The TEAM Program System and International Co-operation in Terminology." *Proceedings of the 1st Infoterm Symposium on International Co-operation in Terminology*, Vienna, Austria. Munich: Infoterm Series, Vol. 3, pp. 180–192.

Pux, Simone (2003). "Implementing a Client/Server Based Terminology Management System." *Proceedings of the Localization World Conference 2003*, Seattle, Washington, DC, USA.
Schmitz, Klaus-Dirk (1996). "Terminology Management Systems." In Rachel Owens, ed., *The Translator's Handbook*, 3rd edition. London: The Association for Information Management, pp. 221–246.
Sestier, C. (2001). "eTermino Q&A—Multilingual Terminology Assistant." In *Translating and the Computer 23*. London: The Association for Information Management.

Termight

Dagan, Ido and Kenneth W. Church (1994). "Termight: Identifying and Translating Technical Terminology." *Proceedings of the 15th International Conference on Computational Linguistics* (*COLING-94*), Kyoto, Japan, pp. 34–40.
Dagan, Ido and Kenneth W. Church (1997). "Termight: Coordinating Humans and Machines in Bilingual Terminology Acquisition." *Machine Translation*, Vol. 12, Nos. 1–2, pp. 89–107.

Termium

Adshead, Mariam (1986). "Termium—The Canadian Government Linguistic Data Bank." *Machine Translation*, Vol. 1, No. 4, pp. 235–238.
Dubuc, Robert (1972). "TERMIUM: System Description." *Meta*, Vol. 17, No. 4, pp. 203–219.
Landry, Alain (1988). "The Termium Termbank: Today and Tomorrow." In Catriona Picken, ed., *Translating and the Computer 9: Potential and Practice*. London: The Association for Information Management, pp. 130–144.

Terminology Processing

Gerzymisch-Arbogast, Heidrun (1994). "Identifying Term Variants in Context: The SYSTEXT Approach." In Mary Snell-Hornby, Franz Pöchhacker, and Klaus Kaindl, eds., *Translation Studies: An Interdiscipline*. Amsterdam and Philadelphia: John Benjamins Publishing Company, pp. 279–290.

Lippmann, Edward O. (1975). "On-line Generation of Terminological Digests in Language Translation: An Aid in Terminology Processing." *IEEE Transactions on Professional Communications*, Vol. 18, No. 4, pp. 309–319.

McDonald, Scott and Chris Brew (2004). "A Distributional Model of Semantic Context Effects in Lexical Processing." *Proceedings of the 42nd Annual Meeting of the Association for Computational Linguistics (ACL-2004)*, Barcelona, Spain, pp. 17–24.

Oh, Jong-Hoon, KyungSoon Lee, and Key-Sun Choi (2000). "Term Recognition Using Technical Dictionary Hierarchy." *Proceedings of the 38th Annual Meeting of the Association for Computational Linguistics (ACL-2000)*, Hong Kong.

Wacholder, Nina, Judith L. Klavans, and David K. Evans (2000). "Evaluation of Automatically Identified Index Terms for Browsing Electronic Documents." *Proceedings of the 6th Applied Natural Language Processing Conference*, Seattle, Washington, DC, USA, pp. 302–309.

Terminology Recognition

Okazaki, Naoaki and Sophia Ananiadou (2006). "A Term Recognition Approach to Acronym Recognition." *Proceedings of the Joint Conference of the International Committee on Computational Linguistics and the Association for Computational Linguistics (COLING/ACL-2006)*, Sydney, Australia.

Sui, Zhifang 穗志方 (2002). 〈信息科學技術領域術語自動識別策略〉 (The Strategies on the Automatic Term Recognition in the Domain of Information Science and Technology). In Yu Shiwen, ed., *Proceedings of the 2nd China-Japan Natural Language Processing Joint Research Promotion Conference (CJNLP-2002)*. Beijing: Institute of Computational Linguistics, Peking University, pp. 318–322.

Terminology Tool

Bowker, Lynne (2003). "Terminology Tools for Translators." In Harold Somers, ed., *Computers and Translation: A Translator's Guide*. Amsterdam and Philadelphia: John Benjamins Publishing Company, pp. 49–65.

Childs, Larry G. (1989). "ALPNET Terminology Tools." In Deanna Lindberg Hammond, ed., *Coming of Age: Proceedings of the 30th Annual Conference of the American Translators Association*. Medford, New Jersey: Learned Information Inc., pp. 455–460.

Thurmair, Gregor (2003). "Making Term Extraction Tools Usable." *Proceedings of the Joint Conference Combining the 8th International Workshop of the European Association for Machine Translation and the 4th Controlled Language Applications Workshop: Controlled Language Translation* (*EAMT-CLAW-2003*), Dublin City University, Dublin, Ireland.

Terminology Translation

Fang, Gaolin, Hao Yu, and Fumihito Nishino (2006). "Chinese-English Term Translation Mining Based on Semantic Prediction." *Proceedings of the Joint Conference of the International Committee on Computational Linguistics and the Association for Computational Linguistics* (*COLING/ACL-2006*), Sydney, Australia.

❖ PART 34 ❖

Text

Text

Akhtar, Shazia, Ronan G. Reilly, and John Dunnion (2002). "AutoMarkup: A Tool for Automatically Marking up Text Documents." *Proceedings of the 3rd International Conference on Intelligent Text Processing and Computational Linguistics* (*CICLing-2002*), Mexico City, Mexico.

Akhtar, Shazia, Ronan G. Reilly, and John Dunnion (2003). "Automating XML Markup of Text Documents." *Proceedings of the Human Language Technology and North American Chapter of Association of Computational Linguistics 2003* (*HLT/NAACL-2003*), Edmonton, Alberta, Canada.

Alexandrov, Mikhail A., Alexander F. Gelbukh, and Pavel P. Makagonov (2000). "Some Keyword-based Characteristics for Evaluation of Thematic Structure of Multidisciplinary Documents." *Proceedings of the 1st International Conference on Intelligent Text Processing and Computational Linguistics* (*CICLing-2000*), Mexico City, Mexico.

Arnold, Doug J. (1990). "Text Typology and Machine Translation: An Overview." In Pamela Mayorcas, ed., *Translating and the Computer 10*. London: The Association for Information Management, pp. 73–89.

Basili, Roberto, Maria Teresa Pazienza, and Paola Velardi (1993). "What Can Be Learned from Raw Texts? An Integrated Tool for the Acquisition of Case Roles, Taxonomic Relations and Disambiguation Criteria." *Machine Translation*, Vol. 8, No. 3, pp. 147–173.

Beesley, Kenneth R. (1988). "Language Identifier: A Computer Program for Automatic Natural Language Identification of On-line Text." In Deanna Lindberg Hammond, ed., *Languages at Crossroads: Proceedings of the 29th Annual Conference of the American Translators Association*. Medford, New Jersey: Learned Information Inc., pp. 47–54.

Boitet, Christian (2005). "Message Automata for Messages with Variants, and Methods for Their Translation." *Proceedings of the 6th International Conference on Intelligent Text Processing and Computational Linguistics* (*CICLing-2005*), Mexico City, Mexico, pp. 348–367.

Cachey, Theodore, Jr. and Mark Olsen (1987). "Textbase and Translation: The Repertorium Columbianum." *Computers and Translation*, Vol. 2, No. 3, pp. 159–162.

Cheng, Hua (2000). "Experimenting with the Interaction between Aggregation and Text Structuring." *Proceedings of the ANLP-NAACL-2000 Student Research Workshop*, Seattle, Washington, DC, USA, pp. 1–6.

Culotta, Aron, Andrew McCallum, and Jonathan Betz (2006). "Integrating Probabilistic Extraction Models and Data Mining to Discover Relations and Patterns in Text." *Proceedings of the Human Language Technology Conference—Annual Meeting of the North American Chapter of the Association for Computational Linguistics* (*HLT-NAACL-2006*), New York, USA.

Dalli, Angelo (2006). "Temporal Classification of Text and Automatic Document Dating." *Proceedings of the Human Language Technology Conference—Annual Meeting of the North American Chapter of the Association for Computational Linguistics* (*HLT-NAACL-2006*), New York, USA.

Foster, George, Philippe Langlais, and Guy Lapalme (2002). "User-friendly Text Prediction for Translators." *Proceedings of the 2002 Conference on Empirical Methods in Natural Language Processing* (*EMNLP-2002*), University of Pennsylvania, Philadelphia, PA, USA.

Gajer, Miroslaw (2001). "Towards a Fully-automatic High-quality Machine Translation System for Unrestricted Text." *Machine Translation Review*, No. 12, pp. 10–20.

Hwang, Feng-Long, Ming-shing Yu, Ming-Mer Wu, and Shyh-Yang Hwang (1999). "Semantic Classification for Patterns Containing Non-text Symbols in Mandarin Text." *Proceedings of the International Conference on Research in Computational Linguistics* (*ROCLING-XII*), Taipei, Taiwan.

Joy, Lorna (2002). "Translating Tagged Text—Imperfect Matches and a Good Finished Job." In *Translating and the Computer 24*. London: The Association for Information Management.

Kumar, G. Bharadwaja and Kavi Narayana Murthy (2004). "Language Identification from Small Text Samples." *Proceedings of the International Conference on Natural Language Processing* (*ICON-2004*), International Institute of Information Technology, Hyderabad, India.

MacCartney, Bill, Trond Grenager, Marie-Catherine de Marneffe, Daniel Cer, and Christopher D. Manning (2006). "Learning to Recognize

Features of Valid Textual Entailments." *Proceedings of the Human Language Technology Conference—Annual Meeting of the North American Chapter of the Association for Computational Linguistics (HLT-NAACL-2006)*, New York, USA.

Mihalcea, Rada F. (2006). "Random Walks on Text Structures." *Proceedings of the 7th International Conference on Intelligent Text Processing and Computational Linguistics (CICLing-2006)*, Mexico City, Mexico.

Muegge, Uwe (2006). "Fully Automatic High Quality Machine Translation of Restricted Text—A Case Study." In *Translating and the Computer 28*. London: The Association for Information Management.

Papegaaij, Bart C. and Klaus Schubert (1988). *Text Coherence in Translation.* Dordrecht: Foris Publication.

Sager, Juan C. (1982). "Types of Translation and Text Forms in the Environment of Machine Translation." In Veronica Lawson, ed., *Practical Experience of Machine Translation.* Amsterdam: North-Holland Publishing Company, pp. 11–19.

van Dyke, Parunak H. (1981). "Quality-controlled Proofreading of Machine-readable Texts." *Literary and Linguistic Computing*, Vol. 2, No. 2, pp. 51–54.

Vázquez, Sonia, Ma Carmen Calle, Susana Soler, and Andrés Montoyo (2002). "Specification Marks Method: Design and Implementation." *Proceedings of the 3rd International Conference on Intelligent Text Processing and Computational Linguistics (CICLing-2002)*, Mexico City, Mexico.

Wilks, Yorick (1998). "Senses and Texts." *Proceedings of the International Conference on Research in Computational Linguistics (ROCLING-IX)*, Tseng-Wen Reservoir Youth Activity Center, Tainan County, Taiwan.

Yang, C. J. (1981). "High Level Memory Structures and Text BCS Coherence in Translation." *Proceedings of the 7th Conference of the Association of Computational Linguistics and International Joint Conference on Artificial Intelligence*, Vancouver, BC, Canada, Vol. 1, pp. 47–49.

Zavarsky, Pavol, Yoshiki Mikami, and Shota Wada (2005). "Language and Encoding Scheme Identification of Extremely Large Sets of Multilingual Text Documents." *Proceedings of MT Summit X*, Phuket, Thailand.

Bilingual Text

Catizone, Roberta, Graham Russell, and Susan Warwick (1989). "Deriving Translation Data from Bilingual Texts." *Proceedings of the 1st International Lexical Acquisition Workshop*, Detroit, MI, USA, pp. 1–7.

Ma, Xiaoyi and Mark Y. Liberman (1999). "BITS: A Method for Bilingual Text Search over the Web." *Proceedings of MT Summit VII: MT in the Great Translation Era*, Singapore.

Resnik, Philip (1998). "Parallel Strands: A Preliminary Investigation into Mining the Web for Bilingual Text." In David L. Farwell, Laurie Gerber, and Eduard Hovy, eds., *Machine Translation and the Information Soup*. Berlin: Springer Verlag, pp. 72–78.

Resnik, Philip (1999). "Mining the Web for Bilingual Text." *Proceedings of the 37th Annual Meeting of the Association for Computational Linguistics (ACL-99)*, College Park, MD USA.

Tan, Chew Lim and Makoto Nagao (1995). "Automatic Alignment of Japanese-Chinese Bilingual Texts." *IEICE Transactions on Information and Systems*, E78-D.1, pp. 68–76.

Turcato, Davide (1998). "Automatically Creating Bilingual Lexicons for Machine Translation from Bilingual Text." *Proceedings of the 36th Annual Meeting of the Association for Computational Linguistics and 17th International Conference on Computational Linguistics (COLING-ACL-98)*, Montreal, Quebec, Canada.

Bitext

Casillas, Arantza and Raquel Martinez (2004). "Bitext Generation through Rich Markup." *Computers and the Humanities*, Vol. 38, Issue 4.

Isabelle, Pierre (1992). "Bi-textual Aids for Translators." *Proceedings of the 8th Annual Conference of the UW Centre for the New OED and Text Research*, Waterloo, Canada, pp. 1–15.

Kondrak, Grzegorz (2005). "Cognates and Word Alignment in Bitexts." *Proceedings of MT Summit X*, Phuket, Thailand.

Lavoie, Benoit, Michael White, and Tanya Korelsky (2001). "Inducing Lexico-structural Transfer Rules from Parsed Bi-texts." *Proceedings of ACL-2001 Workshop on Data-Driven Machine Translation*, Toulouse, France, pp. 17–24.

Melamed, I. Dan (1996). "A Geometric Approach to Mapping Bitext Correspondence." *Proceedings of the Conference on Empirical Methods in Natural Language Processing*, University of Pennsylvania, PA, USA, pp. 1–12.

Melamed, I. Dan (1997). "A Portable Algorithm for Mapping Bitext Correspondence." *Proceedings of the 38th Annual Meeting of the American Translators Association* (*ACL-97*), San Francisco, California, USA.

Melamed, I. Dan (2001). "A Geometric Approach to Mapping Bitext Correspondence." *Empirical Methods for Exploiting Parallel Texts*. Cambridge, MA: MIT Press, pp. 7–34.

Pytlik, Brock and David Yarowsky (2006). "Machine Translation for Languages Lacking Bitext via Multilingual Gloss Transduction." *Proceedings of the 7th Biennial Conference of the Association for Machine Translation in the Americas* (*AMTA-2006*)*: Visions for the Future of Machine Translation*, Boston Marriott, Cambridge, MA, USA.

Colloquial Text

Popowich, Fred, Davide Turcato, Olivier Laurens, Paul McFetridge, J. Devlan Nicholson, Patrick McGivern, Maricela Corzo-Pena, Lisa Pidruchney, and Scott McDonald (1997). "A Lexicalist Approach to the Translation of Colloquial Text." *Proceedings of the 7th International Conference on Theoretical and Methodological Issues in Machine Translation* (*TMI-97*), St. John's College, Santa Fe, New Mexico, USA, pp. 76–86.

Takezawa, Toshiyuki, Satoshi Shirai, and Yoshifumi Ooyama (2001). "Characteristics of Colloquial Expressions in a Bilingual Travel Conversation Corpus." *Proceedings of the 19th International Conference on Computer Processing of Oriental Languages* (*ICCPOL-2001*), Korea University, Seoul, Korea.

Comparative Text

Fung, Pascale and Lo Yuen Yee (1998). "An IR Approach for Translating New Words from Nonparallel, Comparable Texts." *Proceedings of the 36th Annual Meeting of the Association for Computational Linguistics and 17th International Conference on Computational Linguistics (COLING-ACL-98)*, Montreal, Quebec, Canada.

Parallel Text

Ahrenberg, Lars, Mikael Andersson, and Magnus Merkel (1998). "A Simple Hybrid Aligner for Generating Lexical Correspondences in Parallel Texts." *Proceedings of the 36th Annual Meeting of the Association for Computational Linguistics and 17th International Conference on Computational Linguistics (COLING-ACL-98)*, Montreal, Quebec, Canada, pp. 29–35.

Barlow, Michael (2000). "Parallel Texts in Language Teaching." In Simon Philip Botley, Anthony Mark McEnery, and Andrew Wilson, eds., *Multilingual Corpora in Teaching and Research*. Amsterdam: Rodopi, pp. 106–115.

Boutis, Sotiris and Stelios Piperidis (1998). "Aligning Clauses in Parallel Text." In Martin Jacobsen, ed., *Proceedings of the 3rd Conference on Empirical Methods in Natural Language Processing (EMNLP-3)*, Granada, Spain.

Clodfelder, Katri A. (2003). "An LSA Implementation against Parallel Texts in French and English." *Proceedings of the Human Language Technology and North American Chapter of Association of Computational Linguistics 2003 (HLT/NAACL-2003)*, Edmonton, Alberta, Canada.

Fung, Pascale and Kenneth W. Church (1994). "K-vec: A New Approach for Aligning Parallel Texts." *Proceedings of the 15th International Conference on Computational Linguistics (COLING-94)*, Kyoto, Japan, pp. 1096–1102.

Fung, Pascale and Lo Yuen Yee (1998). "An IR Approach for Translating New Words from Nonparallel, Comparable Texts." *Proceedings of the 36th Annual Meeting of the Association for Computational Linguistics and 17th International Conference on Computational Linguistics (COLING-ACL-98)*, Montreal, Quebec, Canada, pp. 414–420.

Gale, William A. and Kenneth W. Church (1991). "Identifying Word Correspondences in Parallel Texts." *Proceedings of the 4th DARPA Speech and Natural Language Workshop*, Pacific Grove, CA, USA, pp. 152–157.

Hartmann, Reinhard R. K. (1994). "The Use of Parallel Text Corpora in the

Generation of Translation Equivalents for Bilingual Lexicography." In Willy Martin, Willem Meijs, Margreet Moerland, Elsemiek ten Pas, Piet van Sterkenburg, and Piek Vossen, eds., *Euralex 1994 Proceedings*, Amsterdam, the Netherlands, pp. 291–297.

Izuha, Tatsuya (2001). "Machine Translation Using Bilingual Term Entries Extracted from Parallel Texts." In Bente Maegaard, ed., *Proceedings of MT Summit VIII: Machine Translation in the Information Age*, Santiago de Compostela, Spain.

Kraif, Olivier (2000). "Evaluation of Statistical Tools for Automatic Extraction of Lexical Correspondences between Parallel Texts." *Proceedings of the International Conference on Machine Translation and Multilingual Applications in the New Millenium (MT-2000)*, University of Exeter, England.

Ma, Xiaoyi (1999). "Parallel Text Collections at Linguistic Data Consortium." *Proceedings of MT Summit VII: MT in the Great Translation Era*, Singapore.

Macklovitch, Elliott (2003). "On the Pleasure of Being Bi-textual, or My Life in Parallel Text." *Proceedings of the Human Language Technology and North American Chapter of Association of Computational Linguistics 2003 (HLT/NAACL-2003)*, Edmonton, Alberta, Canada.

Matsumoto, Yuji, Hiroyuki Ishimoto, Takehito Utsuro, and Makato Nagao (1993). "Structural Matching of Parallel Texts." *Proceedings of the 31st Annual Meeting of the Association for Computational Linguistics (ACL-93)*, Columbus, Ohio, USA, pp. 23–30.

Melamed, I. Dan (2001). *Empirical Methods for Exploiting Parallel Texts.* Cambridge, MA: MIT Press.

Mihalcea, Rada F. and Michel Simard (2005). "Parallel Texts." *Natural Language Engineering*, Vol. 11, No. 3, pp. 239–246.

Pearson, Jennifer (2003). "Using Parallel Texts in the Translator Training Environment." In Federico Zanettin, Silvia Bernardini, and Dominic Stewart, eds., *Corpora in Translator Education.* Manchester: St. Jerome Publishing, pp. 15–24.

Piotrowska, Maria (1997). "Criteria for Selecting Parallel Texts in Teaching a Translation Course." In Barbara Lewandowska-Tomaszczyk and Patrick James Melia, eds., *Practical Applications in Language Corpora: PALC 1997 Proceedings.* Łódz: Łódz University Press, pp. 411–420.

Rapp, Reinhard (1995). "Identifying Word Translations in Non-parallel Texts." *Proceedings of the 33rd Annual Meeting of the Association for Computational Linguistics* (*ACL-95*), Cambridge, MA, USA, pp. 320–322.

Schäffner, Christina (1998). "Parallel Texts in Translation." In Lynne Bowker, Michael Cronin, Dorothy Kenny, and Jennifer Pearson, eds., *Unity in Diversity: Current Trends in Translation Studies*. Manchester: St. Jerome Publishing, pp. 83–90.

van der Eijk, Pim (1999). "Comparative Discourse Analysis of Parallel Texts." In Susan Armstrong, Kenneth W. Church, Pierre Isabelle, Sandra Manzi, Evelyne Tzoukermann, and David Yarowsky, eds., *Natural Language Processing Using Very Large Corpora*. Dordrecht: Kluwer Academic Publishers, pp. 253–268.

Wu, Dekai (1995). "An Algorithm for Simultaneously Bracketing Parallel Texts by Aligning Words." *Proceedings of the 33rd Annual Meeting of the Association of Computational Linguistics* (*ACL-95*), Cambridge, MA, USA, pp. 244–251.

Wu, Dekai (1995). "Grammarless Extraction of Phrasal Translation Examples from Parallel Texts." *Proceedings of the 6th International Conference on Theoretical and Methodological Issues in Machine Translation* (*TMI-95*), the University of Leuven, Leuven, Belgium, pp. 354–372.

Wu, Dekai (1999). "Trainable Coarse Bilingual Grammar for Parallel Text Bracketing." In Susan Armstrong, Kenneth W. Church, Pierre Isabelle, Sandra Manzi, Evelyne Tzoukermann, and David Yarowsky, eds., *Natural Language Processing Using Very Large Corpora*. Dordrecht: Kluwer Academic Publishers, pp. 235–252.

Source Text

Somers, Harold L., Jun-ichi Tsujii, and Daniel B. Jones (1990). "Machine Translation without a Source Text." *Proceedings of the 13th International Conference on Computational Linguistics* (*COLING-90*), Helsinki, Finland, Vol. 3, pp. 271–276.

Text Categorization

Alexandrov, Mikhail A., Alexander F. Gelbukh, and Pavel P. Makagonov

(2000). "On Metrics for Keyword-based Document Selection and Classification." *Proceedings of the 1st International Conference on Intelligent Text Processing and Computational Linguistics* (*CICLing-2000*), Mexico City, Mexico.

Alexandrov, Mikhail A., Alexander F. Gelbukh, and George Lozovoi (2001). "Chi-square Classifier for Document Categorization." *Proceedings of the 2nd International Conference on Intelligent Text Processing and Computational Linguistics* (*CICLing-2001*), Mexico City, Mexico.

Chen, Wenliang, Zhu Jingbo, Wu Honglin, and Yao Tianshun (2004). "Automatic Learning Features Using Bootstrapping for Text Categorization." *Proceedings of the 5th International Conference on Intelligent Text Processing and Computational Linguistics* (*CICLing-2004*), Chung-Ang University, Seoul, Korea, pp. 565–574.

Chowdhury, Nirmalya and Diganta Saha (2005). "Unsupervised Text Classification Using Kohonen's Self Organizing Network." *Proceedings of the 6th International Conference on Intelligent Text Processing and Computational Linguistics* (*CICLing-2005*), Mexico City, Mexico, pp. 702–705.

D'Alessio, Stephen, Keitha Murray, Robert Schiaffino, and Aaron Kershenbaum (1998). "Category Levels in Hierarchical Text Categorization." *Proceedings of the 3rd Conference on Empirical Methods in Natural Language Processing*, Granada, Spain.

Fukumoto, Fumiyo and Yoshimi Suzuki (1998). "An Empirical Approach to Text Categorization Based on Term Weight Learning." *Proceedings of the 3rd Conference on Empirical Methods in Natural Language Processing*, Granada, Spain.

Gliozzo, Alfio and Carlo Strapparava (2006). "Exploiting Comparable Corpora and Bilingual Dictionaries for Cross-language Text Categorization." *Proceedings of the Joint Conference of the International Committee on Computational Linguistics and the Association for Computational Linguistics* (*COLING/ACL-2006*), Sydney, Australia.

Guo, Gongde, Hui Wang, David Bell, Yaxin Bi, and Kieran Greer (2004). "An kNN Model-based Approach and Its Application in Text Categorization." *Proceedings of the 5th International Conference on Intelligent Text Processing and Computational Linguistics* (*CICLing-2004*), Chung-Ang University, Seoul, Korea, pp. 553–564.

Hadjarian, Ali, Jerzy Bala, and Peter Pachowicz (2001). "Text Categorization through Multistrategy Learning and Visualization." *Proceedings of the 2nd International Conference on Intelligent Text Processing and Computational Linguistics* (*CICLing-2001*), Mexico City, Mexico.

Hulth, Anette and Beáta B. Megyesi (2006). "A Study on Automatically Extracted Keywords in Text Categorization." *Proceedings of the Joint Conference of the International Committee on Computational Linguistics and the Association for Computational Linguistics* (*COLING/ACL-2006*), Sydney, Australia.

Johnsen, Lars G. and Christer Johansson (2005). "Efficient Modeling of Analogy." *Proceedings of the 6th International Conference on Intelligent Text Processing and Computational Linguistics* (*CICLing-2005*), Mexico City, Mexico, pp. 682–690.

Kim, Sang-Bum and Hae-Chang Rim (2004). "Recomputation of Class Relevance Scores for Improving Text Classification." *Proceedings of the 5th International Conference on Intelligent Text Processing and Computational Linguistics* (*CICLing-2004*), Chung-Ang University, Seoul, Korea, pp. 575–578.

Li, Baoli, Chen Yuzhong, Bai Xiaojing, and Yu Shiwen (2003). "Experimental Study on Representing Units in Chinese Text Categorization." *Proceedings of the 4th International Conference on Intelligent Text Processing and Computational Linguistics* (*CICLing-2003*), Mexico City, Mexico, pp. 604–616.

Li, Jingyang, Maosong Sun, and Xian Zhang (2006). "A Comparison and Semi-quantitative Analysis of Words and Character-bigrams as Features in Chinese Text Categorization." *Proceedings of the Joint Conference of the International Committee on Computational Linguistics and the Association for Computational Linguistics* (*COLING/ACL-2006*), Sydney, Australia.

Li, Xiaoguang, Ge Yu, Daling Wang, and Yubin Bao (2005). "ESPClust: An Effective Skew Prevention Method for Model-based Document Clustering." *Proceedings of the 6th International Conference on Intelligent Text Processing and Computational Linguistics* (*CICLing-2005*), Mexico City, Mexico, pp. 722–733.

Masuyama, Takeshi and Hiroshi Nakagawa (2003). "Cascaded Feature Selection in SVMs Text Categorization." *Proceedings of the 4th International Conference on Intelligent Text Processing and*

Computational Linguistics (*CICLing-2003*), Mexico City, Mexico, pp. 590–593.

Moyotl-Hernández, Edgar and Héctor Jiménez-Salazar (2005). "Enhancement of DTP Feature Selection Method for Text Categorization." *Proceedings of the 6th International Conference on Intelligent Text Processing and Computational Linguistics* (*CICLing-2005*), Mexico City, Mexico, pp. 706–709.

Pappuswamy, Umarani, Dumisizwe Bhembe, Pamela W. Jordan, and Kurt VanLehn (2005). "A Supervised Clustering Method for Text Classification." *Proceedings of the 6th International Conference on Intelligent Text Processing and Computational Linguistics* (*CICLing-2005*), Mexico City, Mexico, pp. 691–701.

Peng, Fuchun, Dale Schuurmans, and Shaojun Wang (2003). "Language and Task Independent Text Categorization with Simple Language Models." *Proceedings of the Human Language Technology and North American Chapter of Association of Computational Linguistics 2003* (*HLT/NAACL-2003*), Edmonton, Alberta, Canada.

Rosso, Paolo, Antonio Molina, Ferran Pla, Daniel Jiménez, and Vicent Vidal (2004). "Information Retrieval and Text Categorization with Semantic Indexing." *Proceedings of the 5th International Conference on Intelligent Text Processing and Computational Linguistics* (*CICLing-2004*), Chung-Ang University, Seoul, Korea, pp. 591–595.

Sable, Carl and Kenneth W. Church (2001). "Using Bins to Empirically Estimate Term Weights for Text Categorization." *Proceedings of the 2001 Conference on Empirical Methods in Natural Language Processing* (*EMNLP-2001*), Carnegie Mellon University, Pittsburgh, PA, USA.

Schneider, Karl-Michael (2005). "Techniques for Improving the Performance of Naive Bayes for Text Classification." *Proceedings of the 6th International Conference on Intelligent Text Processing and Computational Linguistics* (*CICLing-2005*), Mexico City, Mexico, pp. 669–680.

Shin, Kwangcheol, Ajith Abraham, and Sang-Yong Han (2006). "Improving kNN Text Categorization by Removing Outliers from Training Set." *Proceedings of the 7th International Conference on Intelligent Text Processing and Computational Linguistics* (*CICLing-2006*), Mexico City, Mexico.

Takamura, Hiroya and Yuji Matsumoto (2001). "Feature Space Restructuring for SVMs with Application to Text Categorization." *Proceedings of the 2001 Conference on Empirical Methods in Natural Language Processing* (*EMNLP-2001*), Carnegie Mellon University, Pittsburgh, PA, USA.

Tsay, Jyh-Jong and Jing-Doo Wang (1999). "Term Selection with Distributional Clustering for Chinese Text Categorization Using N-grams." *Proceedings of the International Conference on Research in Computational Linguistics* (*ROCLING-XII*), Taipei, Taiwan.

Vert, Jean-Philippe (2001). "Text Categorization Using Adaptive Context Trees." *Proceedings of the 2nd International Conference on Intelligent Text Processing and Computational Linguistics* (*CICLing-2001*), Mexico City, Mexico.

Xia, Yunqing, Angelo Dalli, Yorick Wilks, and Louise Guthrie (2005). "FASiL Adaptive Email Categorization System." *Proceedings of the 6th International Conference on Intelligent Text Processing and Computational Linguistics* (*CICLing-2005*), Mexico City, Mexico, pp. 710–721.

Xue, Dejun and Maosong Sun (2003). "A Study on Feature Weighting in Chinese Text Categorization." *Proceedings of the 4th International Conference on Intelligent Text Processing and Computational Linguistics* (*CICLing-2003*), Mexico City, Mexico, pp. 594–603.

Xue, Dejun and Maosong Sun (2004). "Raising High-degree Overlapped Character Bigrams into Trigrams for Dimensionality Reduction in Chinese Text Categorization." *Proceedings of the 5th International Conference on Intelligent Text Processing and Computational Linguistics* (*CICLing-2004*), Chung-Ang University, Seoul, Korea, pp. 579–590.

Zelaia, Ana, Iñaki Alegria, Olatz Arregi, and Basilio Sierra (2006). "A Multiclassifier Based Document Categorization System: Profiting from the Singular Value Decomposition Dimensionality Reduction Technique." *Proceedings of the 11th Conference of the European Chapter of the Association for Computational Linguistics* (*EACL-2006*), Trento, Italy.

Zhou, Shuigeng and Jihong Guan (2002). "Chinese Document Classification Based on N-grams." *Proceedings of the 3rd International Conference on Intelligent Text Processing and Computational Linguistics* (*CICLing-2002*), Mexico City, Mexico.

Text Chunking

Ando, Rie Kubota and Tong Zhang (2005). "A High-performance Semi-supervised Learning Method for Text Chunking." *Proceedings of the 43rd Annual Meeting of the Association of Computational Linguistics (ACL-2005)*, Ann Arbor, Michigan, USA.

Chen, Kuang-hua and Hsin-Hsi Chen (1993). "A Probabilistic Chunker." *Proceedings of the Conference of the Association for Computational Linguistics and Chinese Language Processing (ROCLING-VI)*, Nantou, Taiwan.

Chen, Wenliang, Yujie Zhang, and Hitoshi Isahara (2006). "An Empirical Study of Chinese Chunking." *Proceedings of the Joint Conference of the International Committee on Computational Linguistics and the Association for Computational Linguistics (COLING/ACL-2006)*, Sydney, Australia.

Goldberg, Yoav, Menachem Adler, and Michael Elhadad (2006). "Noun Phrase Chunking in Hebrew—Influence of Lexical and Morphological Features." *Proceedings of the Joint Conference of the International Committee on Computational Linguistics and the Association for Computational Linguistics (COLING/ACL-2006)*, Sydney, Australia.

Grover, Claire and Richard Tobin (2006). "Rule-based Chunking and Reusability." *Proceedings of the 5th International Conference on Language Resources and Evaluation (LREC-2006)*, Genoa, Italy.

Hacioglu, Kadri and Wayne Ward (2003). "Target Word Detection and Semantic Role Chunking Using Support Vector Machines." *Proceedings of the Human Language Technology and North American Chapter of Association of Computational Linguistics 2003 (HLT/NAACL-2003)*, Edmonton, Alberta, Canada.

Li, Sujian and Liu Qun (2002). "Maximum Entropy Model for Chinese Chunking." In Yu Shiwen, ed., *Proceedings of the 2nd China-Japan Natural Language Processing Joint Research Promotion Conference (CJNLP-2002)*. Beijing: Institute of Computational Linguistics, Peking University, pp. 247–252.

Lüdtke, Dirk and Satoshi Sato (2003). "Fast Base NP Chunking with Decision Trees—Experiments on Different POS Tag Settings." *Proceedings of the 4th International Conference on Intelligent Text Processing and Computational Linguistics (CICLing-2003)*, Mexico City, Mexico, pp. 139–150.

Ngai, Grace and David Yarowsky (2000). "Rule Writing or Annotation: Cost-efficient Resource Usage for Base Noun Phrase Chunking." *Proceedings of the 38th Annual Meeting of the Association for Computational Linguistics (ACL-2000)*, Hong Kong.

Shimizu, Nobuyuki and Andrew Haas (2006). "Exact Decoding for Jointly Labeling and Chunking Sequences." *Proceedings of the Joint Conference of the International Committee on Computational Linguistics and the Association for Computational Linguistics (COLING/ACL-2006)*, Sydney, Australia.

Sporleder, Caroline and Mirella Lapata (2005). "Discourse Chunking and Its Application to Sentence Compression." *Proceedings of Human Language Technology Conference and Conference on Empirical Methods in Natural Language Processing (HLT/EMNLP-2005)*, Vancouver, BC, Canada.

Streiter, Oliver (2001). "Memory-based Parsing: Enhancing Recursive Top-down Fuzzy Match with Bottom-up Chunking." *Proceedings of the 19th International Conference on Computer Processing of Oriental Languages (ICCPOL-2001)*, Seoul, Korea, pp. 219–224.

Text Clustering

Brew, Chris and Sabine Schulte im Walde (2002). "Spectral Clustering for German Verbs." *Proceedings of the 2002 Conference on Empirical Methods in Natural Language Processing (EMNLP-2002)*, University of Pennsylvania, Philadelphia, PA, USA.

Buscaldi, Davide, Paolo Rosso, Mikhail A. Alexandrov, and Alfons Juan Ciscar (2006). "Sense Cluster Based Categorization and Clustering of Abstracts." *Proceedings of the 7th International Conference on Intelligent Text Processing and Computational Linguistics (CICLing-2006)*, Mexico City, Mexico.

Cardie, Claire and Kiri Wagstaff (1999). "Noun Phrase Coreference as Clustering." *Proceedings of the Joint SIGDAT Conference on Empirical Methods in NLP and Very Large Corpora (EMNLP/VLC-99)*, University of Maryland, College Park, MD, USA.

Casillas, Arantza, Mayte González de Lena, and Raquel Martínez (2003). "Partitional Clustering Experiments with News Documents." *Proceedings of the 4th International Conference on Intelligent Text*

Processing and Computational Linguistics (*CICLing-2003*), Mexico City, Mexico, pp. 617–620.

Casillas, Arantza, Mayte T. González de Lena, and Raquel Martínez (2004). "Sampling and Feature Selection in a Genetic Algorithm for Document Clustering." *Proceedings of the 5th International Conference on Intelligent Text Processing and Computational Linguistics* (*CICLing-2004*), Chung-Ang University, Seoul, Korea, pp. 596–607.

Chang, Chao-Huang 張照煌 and Cheng-Der Chen 陳正德 (1993). "Automatic Clustering of Chinese Characters and Words." *Proceedings of the Conference of the Association for Computational Linguistics and Chinese Language Processing* (*ROCLING-VI*), Nantou, Taiwan.

Chen, Jen Nan and Jason S. Chang (1998). "Topical Clustering of MRD Senses Based on Information Retrieval Techniques." *Computational Linguistics*, Vol. 24, No. 1, pp. 61–95.

Chen, Jinxiu, Donghong Ji, Chew Lim Tan, and Zhengyu Niu (2006). "Unsupervised Relation Disambiguation Using Spectral Clustering." *Proceedings of the Joint Conference of the International Committee on Computational Linguistics and the Association for Computational Linguistics* (*COLING/ACL-2006*), Sydney, Australia.

Dunlavy, Daniel M., John Conroy, and Dianne P. O'Leary (2003). "QCS: A Tool for Querying, Clustering, and Summarizing Documents." *Proceedings of the Human Language Technology and North American Chapter of Association of Computational Linguistics 2003* (*HLT/NAACL-2003*), Edmonton, Alberta, Canada.

Erkan, Gunes (2006). "Language Model-based Document Clustering Using Random Walks." *Proceedings of the Human Language Technology Conference—Annual Meeting of the North American Chapter of the Association for Computational Linguistics* (*HLT-NAACL-2006*), New York, USA.

Gangadharaiah, Rashmi, Ralf D. Brown, and Jaime G. Carbonell (2006). "Spectral Clustering for Example Based Machine Translation." *Proceedings of the Human Language Technology Conference—Annual Meeting of the North American Chapter of the Association for Computational Linguistics* (*HLT-NAACL-2006*), New York, USA.

Gao, Jianfeng, Hisami Suzuki, and Yang Wen (2002). "Exploiting Headword Dependency and Predictive Clustering for Language Modeling." *Proceedings of the 2002 Conference on Empirical Methods in Natural Language Processing* (*EMNLP-2002*), University of Pennsylvania, Philadelphia, PA, USA.

Li, Sheng 李盛 and Yang Erhong 楊爾弘 (2002). 〈一種基於聚類的漢語詞語知識的獲取方法〉 (A Method of Knowledge Acquisition from Chinese Words Based on Clustering). 《第一屆學生計算語言學研討會論文集》 (*SWCL2002: First Students' Workshop on Computational Linguistics: Proceedings*), Institute of Computational Linguistics, Peking University, Beijing, China, pp. 275–280.

Li, Xiaoguang, Ge Yu, Daling Wang, and Yubin Bao (2005). "ESPClust: An Effective Skew Prevention Method for Model-based Document Clustering." *Proceedings of the 6th International Conference on Intelligent Text Processing and Computational Linguistics* (*CICLing-2005*), Mexico City, Mexico, pp. 722–733.

Makagonov, Pavel P. and Konstantin Sboychakov (2001). "Software for Creating Domain-oriented Dictionaries and Document Clustering in Full-text Databases." *Proceedings of the 2nd International Conference on Intelligent Text Processing and Computational Linguistics* (*CICLing-2001*), Mexico City, Mexico.

Navigli, Roberto (2006). "Meaningful Clustering of Senses Helps Boost Word Sense Disambiguation Performance." *Proceedings of the Joint Conference of the International Committee on Computational Linguistics and the Association for Computational Linguistics* (*COLING/ACL-2006*), Sydney, Australia.

Niu, Zhengyu, Donghong Ji, and Chew Lim Tan (2005). "A Semi-supervised Feature Clustering Algorithm with Application to Word Sense Disambiguation." *Proceedings of Human Language Technology Conference and Conference on Empirical Methods in Natural Language Processing* (*HLT/EMNLP-2005*), Vancouver, BC, Canada.

Pappuswamy, Umarani, Dumisizwe Bhembe, Pamela W. Jordan, and Kurt VanLehn (2005). "A Supervised Clustering Method for Text Classification." *Proceedings of the 6th International Conference on Intelligent Text Processing and Computational Linguistics* (*CICLing-2005*), Mexico City, Mexico, pp. 691–701.

Pinto, David, Héctor Jiménez-Salazar, and Paolo Rosso (2006). "Clustering Abstracts of Scientific Texts Using the Transition Point Technique." *Proceedings of the 7th International Conference on Intelligent Text Processing and Computational Linguistics* (*CICLing-2006*), Mexico City, Mexico.

Savova, Guergana, Terry Therneau, and Christopher Chute (2006). "Cluster Stopping Rules for Word Sense Discrimination." *Proceedings of the 11th Conference of the European Chapter of the Association for Computational Linguistics* (*EACL-2006*), Trento, Italy.

Shin, Kwangcheol and Sangyong Han (2003). "Fast Clustering Algorithm for Information Organization." *Proceedings of the 4th International Conference on Intelligent Text Processing and Computational Linguistics* (*CICLing-2003*), Mexico City, Mexico, pp. 621–624.

Shin, Kwangcheol and Sangyong Han (2004). "A New Efficient Clustering Algorithm for Organizing Dynamic Data Collection." *Proceedings of the 5th International Conference on Intelligent Text Processing and Computational Linguistics* (*CICLing-2004*), Chung-Ang University, Seoul, Korea, pp. 608–611.

Sierra, Gerardo and John McNaught (2000). "Analogy-based Method for Semantic Clustering." *Proceedings of the 1st International Conference on Intelligent Text Processing and Computational Linguistics* (*CICLing-2000*), Mexico City, Mexico.

Tsay, Jyh-Jong and Jing-Doo Wang (1999). "Term Selection with Distributional Clustering for Chinese Text Categorization Using N-grams." *Proceedings of the International Conference on Research in Computational Linguistics* (*ROCLING-XII*), Taipei, Taiwan.

Zhang, Baoyan 張寶艷 and Wang Qinghui 王慶輝 (2002). 〈中文文本聚類的研究與實踐〉 (Research and Realization of Chinese Document Clustering). 《第一屆學生計算語言學研討會論文集》 (*SWCL-2002: First Students' Workshop on Computational Linguistics: Proceedings*), Institute of Computational Linguistics, Peking University, Beijing, China, pp. 125–129.

Text Generation

Adkins, K. (1988). "Evaluation of Software and Hardware for Multilingual Text Production." In Catriona Picken, ed., *ITI Conference 2: Translators and Interpreters Mean Business*. London: The Association for Information Management, pp. 45–52.

Barrutieta, Guillermo, Joseba Abaitua, and Josuha Díaz (2001). "Gross-grained RST through XML Metadata for Multilingual Document Generation." In Bente Maegaard, ed., *Proceedings of MT Summit VIII:*

Machine Translation in the Information Age, Santiago de Compostela, Spain.

Boldasov, Michael V. and Elena G. Sokolova (2003). "QGen—Generation Module for the Register Restricted InBASE System." *Proceedings of the 4th International Conference on Intelligent Text Processing and Computational Linguistics* (*CICLing-2003*), Mexico City, Mexico, pp. 467–478.

Casillas, Arantza and Raquel Martínez (2002). "Experiments with a Bilingual Document Generation Environment." *Proceedings of the 3rd International Conference on Intelligent Text Processing and Computational Linguistics* (*CICLing-2002*), Mexico City, Mexico.

Chang, Jason S. and Hwei-Ming Kou (1988). "A New Approach to Quality Text Generation." *Proceedings of the Conference of the Association for Computational Linguistics and Chinese Language Processing* (*ROCLING-I*), Nantou, Taiwan.

Danlos, Laurence (1984). "Conceptual and Linguistic Decisions in Generation." *Proceedings of the 10th International Conference on Computational Linguistics* (*COLING-84*), Stanford University, Stanford, California, USA, pp. 501–504.

Doherty, Monika (1997). "Textual Garden Paths—Parametrized Obstacles to Target Language Adequate Translations." In Christa Hauenschild and Susanne Heizmann, eds., *Machine Translation and Translation Theory*. Berlin and New York: Mouton de Gruyter, pp. 69–89.

Dorr, Bonnie J. and Mari B. Olsen (1996). "Multilingual Generation: The Role of Telicity in Lexical Choice and Syntactic Realization." *Machine Translation*, Vol. 11, Nos. 1–3, pp. 37–74.

Dorr, Bonnie J., Nizar Habash, and David Traum (1998). "A Thematic Hierarchy for Efficient Generation from Lexical-conceptual Structure." In David L. Farwell, Laurie Gerber, and Eduard Hovy, eds., *Machine Translation and the Information Soup*. Berlin: Springer Verlag, pp. 333–343.

Foster, George, Philippe Langlais, and Guy Lapalme (2002). "User-friendly Text Prediction for Translators." *Proceedings of the 2002 Conference on Empirical Methods in Natural Language Processing* (*EMNLP-2002*), Philadelphia, USA, pp. 148–155.

Garibay, Ivan I. (2000). "Generating Text with a Theorem Prover." *Proceedings of the ANLP-NAACL-2000 Student Research Workshop*, Seattle, Washington, DC, USA, pp. 13–18.

Habash, Nizar (2000). "Oxygen: A Language Independent Linearization Engine." In John S. White, ed., *Envisioning Machine Translation in the Information Future*. Berlin: Springer Verlag, pp. 68–79.

Harbusch, Karin (1997). "How to Solve the Conflict of Structure-preserving Translation and Fluent Text Production." *Proceedings of the 7th International Conference on Theoretical and Methodological Issues in Machine Translation* (*TMI-97*), St. John's College, Santa Fe, New Mexico, USA.

Hartley, Anthony F. and Cécile Paris (1996). "Automatic Text Generation for Software Development and Use." In Harold L. Somers, ed., *Terminology, LSP and Translation*. Amsterdam and Philadelphia: John Benjamins Publishing Company, pp. 221–242.

Hitoshi, Isahara, Inui Hiroko, and Uchida Yuriko (1996). "Lexical Knowledge from Large Corpora and Its Application to Text Generation." *Proceedings of the 2nd Conference of the Association for Machine Translation in the Americas: Expanding MT Horizons* (*AMTA-2*), Montreal, Quebec, Canada, pp. 66–75.

Hutchins, W. John and Harold L. Somers (1992). "Generation." *An Introduction to Machine Translation*. London: Academic Press, pp. 131–146.

Kittredge, Richard I., Lidija Iordanskaja, and Alain Polguère (1988). "Multi-lingual Text Generation and the Meaning-text Theory." *Proceedings of the 2nd International Conference on Theoretical and Methodological Issues in Machine Translation of Natural Languages* (*TMI-88*), Carnegie Mellon University, Center for Machine Translation, Pittsburgh, Pennsylvania, USA.

Kittredge, Richard I. (1989). "Translation and Computers: Multilingual Text Generation as an Alternative to Machine." In Deanna Lindberg Hammond, ed., *Coming of Age: Proceedings of the 30th Annual Conference of the American Translators Association*. Medford, New Jersey: Learned Information Inc., pp. 465–470.

Kobayashi, Ichiro (2001). "A Study on Text Generation from Non-verbal Information on 2D Charts." *Proceedings of the 2nd International Conference on Intelligent Text Processing and Computational Linguistics* (*CICLing-2001*), Mexico City, Mexico.

Lin, Hing-Lung, Benjamin K. Y. T'sou, Hing-Cheung Ho, Tom B. Y. Lai, Suen Caesar Lun, Chi-yuen Choi, and Chun-yu Kit (1991). "Automatic Chinese Text Generation Based on Inference Trees." *Proceedings of the Conference of the Association for Computational Linguistics and Chinese Language Processing* (*ROCLING-IV*), National Chiao-Tung University, Hsin-Chu, Taiwan.

McKeown, Kathleen R. (1985). *Text Generation*. Cambridge: Cambridge University Press.

Moghrabi, Chadia (1994). "On Parametering the Choice of Words in Text Generation and Its Usefulness in Machine Translation." *Machine Translation—Ten Years On: Proceedings of the 2nd International Conference Organised by Cranfield University*, Cranfield, England.

Nirenburg, Sergei, Jaime G. Carbonell, Masaru Tomita, and Kenneth Goodman (1992). "Target Language Generation." *Machine Translation: A Knowledge-based Approach*. San Matero, California: Morgan Kaufmann, pp. 135–164.

Nirenburg, Sergei (1992). "Text Planning with Opportunistic Control." *Machine Translation*, Vol. 7, Nos. 1–2, pp. 99–124.

Nyberg, Eric H., Rita McCardell, Donna Gates, and Sergei Nirenburg (1989). "Generation." *Machine Translation*, Vol. 4, No. 2, pp. 149–168.

Nyberg, Eric H., Rita McCardell, Donna Gates, and Sergei Nirenburg (1991). "Target Text Generation." In Kenneth Goodman and Sergei Nirenburg, eds., *A Case Study in Knowledge-based Machine Translation*. San Mater, CA: Morgan Kaufmann.

Phillips, John D. (1993). "Generation of Text from Logical Formulae." *Machine Translation*, Vol. 8, No. 4, pp. 209–235.

Power, Richard, Donia R. Scott, and Nadjet Bouayad-Agha (2003). "Generating Texts with Style." *Proceedings of the 4th International Conference on Intelligent Text Processing and Computational Linguistics* (*CICLing-2003*), Mexico City, Mexico, pp. 446–454.

Somers, Harold L. (1992). "Interactive Multilingual Text Generation for a Monolingual User." *Proceedings of the 4th International Conference on Theoretical and Methodological Issues in Machine Translation of Natural Languages: Empiricist vs. Rationalist Methods in MT* (*TMI-92*), Montreal, Quebec, Canada, pp. 151–161.

Somers, Harold L. and Daniel B. Jones (1992). "Machine Translation Seen as Interactive Multilingual Text Generation." In *Translating and the Computer 13: The Theory and Practice of Machine Translation—A Marriage of Convenience?* London: The Association for Information Management, pp. 153–165.

Sondheimer, Norman, Susanna Cumming, and Robert Albano (1990). "How to Realize a Concept: Lexical Selection and the Conceptual Network in Text Generation." *Machine Translation*, Vol. 5, No. 1, pp. 57–78.

Stede, Manfred (1996). "Lexical Paraphrases in Multilingual Sentence Generation." *Machine Translation*, Vol. 11, Nos. 1–3, pp. 75–107.

Steiner, Erich H. and Colin Yallop, eds. (2001). *Exploring Translation and Multilingual Text Production: Beyond Content*. Berlin and New York: Mouton de Gruyter.

Wanner, Leo (1996). "Lexical Choice in Text Generation and Machine Translation." *Machine Translation*, Vol. 11, Nos. 1–3, pp. 3–35.

Wu, Hua 吳華 and Huang Taiyi 黃泰翼 (2001).〈漢語篇章生成系統中的用戶模型和文本規劃〉(User Modeling and Text Planning in a Chinese Text Generation System). In Huang Changning 黃昌寧 and Zhang Pu 張普, eds.,《自然語言理解與機器翻譯》(*Natural Language Understanding and Machine Translation*). Beijing: Tsinghua University Press, pp. 180–186.

Yngve, Victor H. (1962). "Random Generation of English Sentences." In National Physical Laboratory, ed., *1961 International Conference on Machine Translation of Languages and Applied Language Analysis: Proceedings of the Conference Held at the National Physical Laboratory, Teddington, Middlesex, on 5th, 6th, 7th and 8th September*. London: Her Majesty's Stationery Office, Vol. 1, pp. 66–80.

Zhang, Dongmo 張冬茉, Ge Yong 葛永, and Yao Tianfang 姚天昉 (1999).〈多語種文本自動生成系統中的語言知識表示模型〉(A Model of Language Knowledge Representation for Multilingual Text Generation). In Huang Changning 黃昌寧 and Dong Zhendong 董振東, eds.,《計算機語言學文集》(*Essays on Computational Linguistics*). Beijing: Tsinghua University Press, pp. 45–50.

Text Processing

Ahlswede, Thomas E. and Martha Evens (1988). "Parsing vs. Text Processing in the Analysis of Dictionary Definitions." *Proceedings of the 26th Annual Meeting of the Association for Computational Linguistics (ACL-88)*, Buffalo, New York, USA, pp. 217–224.

Andreev, Sergei (2004). "Classification of Language Elements by Means of Discriminant Analysis for Further Use in Automatic Text Processing

Applications." *International Journal of Translation*, Vol. 16, No. 1, pp. 151–153.

Aone, Chinatsu, Hatte Blejer, Mary Ellen Okurowski, and Carol Van Ess-Dykema (1994). "A Hybrid Approach to Multilingual Text Processing: Information Extraction and Machine Translation." *Proceedings of the 1st Conference of the Association for Machine Translation in the Americas: Technology Partnerships for Crossing the Language Barrier (AMTA-1)*, Columbia, Maryland, USA, pp. 1–7.

Garrett, Edward John (2005). "A Finite State Network for Phonetic Text Processing." *Proceedings of the 6th International Conference on Intelligent Text Processing and Computational Linguistics (CICLing-2005)*, Mexico City, Mexico, pp. 452–462.

Heyer, Gerhard (1995). "Market Trends for Text Processing Tools." In Marianne Kugler, Khurshid Ahmad, and Gregor Thurmair, eds., *Translator's Workbench.* Berlin: Springer Verlag, pp. 24–25.

López-Rincón, Carmen and Jaime Sarabia Álvarez-Ude (2000). "Semi-structured Documents Reengineering." *Proceedings of the 1st International Conference on Intelligent Text Processing and Computational Linguistics (CICLing-2000)*, Mexico City, Mexico.

Quinn, David (1996). "Using Icon for Text Processing." *Machine Translation Review*, No. 3, pp. 21–31.

Tanev, Hristo and Ruslan Mitkov (2000). "LINGUA: A Robust Architecture for Text Processing and Anaphora Resolution in Bulgarian." *Proceedings of the International Conference on Machine Translation and Multilingual Applications in the New Millenium (MT-2000)*, University of Exeter, England.

Trujillo, Arturo (1999). "Text Processing." *Translation Engines: Techniques for Machine Translation.* Berlin and New York: Springer Verlag, pp. 39–56.

Tzeng, Ovid J. L., Daisy L. Hung, and Chin Wei Hue (1997). "Opposing Effects of Word and Character Frequency in the Processing of Chinese Text." *Proceedings of the International Conference on Research in Computational Linguistics (ROCLING-X)*, Academia Sinica, Taipei, Taiwan.

Zhao, Jun 趙軍 (2002). 〈多語言文本信息處理的方法和框架〉 (The Approaches and a Framework of Translingual Text Processing). In Yu Shiwen, ed., *Proceedings of the 2nd China-Japan Natural Language Processing Joint Research Promotion Conference (CJNLP-2002)*.

Beijing: Institute of Computational Linguistics, Peking University, pp. 52–64.

Automatic Abstracting

Buscaldi, Davide, Paolo Rosso, Mikhail A. Alexandrov, and Alfons Juan Ciscar (2006). "Sense Cluster Based Categorization and Clustering of Abstracts." *Proceedings of the 7th International Conference on Intelligent Text Processing and Computational Linguistics* (*CICLing-2006*), Mexico City, Mexico.

Haynes, Colin (1998). "Databases, Smart Agents and Abstracts, Teleworking and Other MT Benefits." *Breaking Down the Language Barriers*. London: The Association for Information Management, pp. 153–158.

Kirschner, Zdeněk (1983). "MOSAIC—A Method of Automatic Extraction of Significant Terms from Texts." *Explizite Beschreibung der Sprache und Automatische Textbearbeitung*, Vol. 10. Faculty of Mathematics and Physics, Charles University.

Liu, Gongshen 劉功申, Hu Peihua 胡佩華, Yue Yi 岳奕, and Wang Yongcheng 王永成 (2002).〈偏重摘要及其實現技術〉(A Biased Summary and Its Implementation Technology).《第一屆學生計算語言學研討會論文集》(*SWCL-2002: First Students' Workshop on Computational Linguistics: Proceedings*), Institute of Computational Linguistics, Peking University, Beijing, China, pp. 161–167.

Pinto, David, Héctor Jiménez-Salazar, and Paolo Rosso (2006). "Clustering Abstracts of Scientific Texts Using the Transition Point Technique." *Proceedings of the 7th International Conference on Intelligent Text Processing and Computational Linguistics* (*CICLing-2006*), Mexico City, Mexico.

Shirai, Satoshi, Satoru Ikehara, and Tsukasa Kawaoka (1993). "Effects of Automatic Rewriting of Source Language within a Japanese to English MT System." *Proceedings of the 5th International Conference on Theoretical and Methodological Issues in Machine Translation* (*TMI-93*), Kyoto, Japan, pp. 226–239.

Shirai, Satoshi, Satoru Ikehara, Akio Yokoo, and Yoshifumi Ooyama (1998). "Automatic Rewriting Method for International Expressions in Japanese to English MT and Its Effects." *Proceedings of the Controlled Language Applications Workshop*, Pittsburgh, USA, pp. 62–75.

Wan, Min 萬敏, Luo Zhensheng 羅振聲, and Guo Yuqing 郭玉箐 (2001). 〈自動文摘系統中的意義段劃分問題研究〉 (Study on Semantic Paragraph Partition in Automatic Abstracting System). In Huang Changning 黃昌寧 and Zhang Pu 張普, eds.,《自然語言理解與機器翻譯》(*Natural Language Understanding and Machine Translation*). Beijing: Tsinghua University Press, pp. 338–343.
Yu, Shiwen and Duan Huiming (1996). 〈關於1995年度自動文摘評測的總結報告〉 (Final Report on Automatic Abstracting Evaluation in 1995). In Yu Shiwen 俞士汶 and Zhu Xuefeng 朱學鋒, eds.,《計算語言學文集》 (*Papers on Computational Linguistics*). Beijing: Department of Computer Science and Technology and Institute of Computational Linguistics, Peking University, pp. 132–134.
Yu, Shiwen, Duan Huiming, and Tian Jianqiu 田剪秋 (1998). 〈機械文摘自動評測的原理及實現〉 (The Theory and Implementation of Automatic Evaluation of Mechanical Abstraction). In Yu Shiwen and Zhu Xuefeng, eds., 《計算語言學文集》 (*Papers on Computational Linguistics*), Vol. 3. Beijing: Department of Computer Science and Technology and Institute of Computational Linguistics, Peking University, pp. 149–153.

Text Summarization

Amigo, Enrique and Julio Gonzalo (2005). "A Probabilistic Framework for the Evaluation of Text Summarization Systems." *Proceedings of the 43rd Annual Meeting of the Association of Computational Linguistics* (*ACL-2005*), Ann Arbor, Michigan, USA.
Ando, Rie Kubota, Branimir K. Boguraev, Roy J. Byrd, and Mary S. Neff (2000). "Multi-document Summarization by Visualizing Topical Content." *Proceedings of the NAACL-ANLP 2000 Workshop on Automatic Summarization—Volume 4*, Seattle, Washington, DC, USA, pp. 79–98.
Baldwin, Breck and Thomas S. Morton (1998). "Dynamic Coreference-based Summarization." *Proceedings of the 3rd Conference on Empirical Methods in Natural Language Processing*, Granada, Spain.
Berger, Adam L. and Vibhu O. Mittal (2000). "Query-relevant Summarization Using FAQs." *Proceedings of the 38th Annual Meeting of the Association for Computational Linguistics* (*ACL-2000*), Hong Kong.

Carenini, Giuseppe, Raymond Ng, and Adam Pauls (2006). "Multi-document Summarization of Evaluative Text." *Proceedings of the 11th Conference of the European Chapter of the Association for Computational Linguistics* (*EACL-2006*), Trento, Italy.

Chan, Samuel W. K., Tom B. Y. Lai, W. J. Gao, and Benjamin K. Y. T'sou (2000). "Mining Discourse Markers for Chinese Textual Summarization." *Proceedings of the NAACL-ANLP 2000 Workshop on Automatic Summarization—Volume 4*, Seattle, Washington, DC, USA, pp. 11–20.

Chotthan, Anirut, Chumsak Siboonr, Jantima Polpini, Rapeeporn Chamc, and Somnuk Puangpro (2004). "Automated Thai Text Summarization Using a Similarity Measure." *Proceedings of the International Conference on Natural Language Processing* (*ICON-2004*), International Institute of Information Technology, Hyderabad, India.

Clarke, James and Mirella Lapata (2006). "Constraint-based Sentence Compression: An Integer Programming Approach." *Proceedings of the Joint Conference of the International Committee on Computational Linguistics and the Association for Computational Linguistics* (*COLING/ACL-2006*), Sydney, Australia.

Conroy, John M., Dianne P. O'Leary, and Judith D. Schlesinger (2006). "Topic-focused Multi-document Summarization Using an Approximate Oracle Score." *Proceedings of the Joint Conference of the International Committee on Computational Linguistics and the Association for Computational Linguistics* (*COLING/ACL-2006*), Sydney, Australia.

Cristea, Dan, Oana Postolache, and Ionu Pistol (2005). "Summarisation through Discourse Structure." *Proceedings of the 6th International Conference on Intelligent Text Processing and Computational Linguistics* (*CICLing-2005*), Mexico City, Mexico, pp. 620–631.

Cruz, Carlos Méndez and Alfonso Medina Urrea (2005). "Extractive Summarization Based on Word Information and Sentence Position." *Proceedings of the 6th International Conference on Intelligent Text Processing and Computational Linguistics* (*CICLing-2005*), Mexico City, Mexico, pp. 640–643.

Daume III, Hal and Daniel Marcu (2006). "Bayesian Query-focused Summarization." *Proceedings of the Joint Conference of the International Committee on Computational Linguistics and the Association for Computational Linguistics* (*COLING/ACL-2006*), Sydney, Australia.

Donaway, Robert L., Kevin W. Drummey, and Laura A. Mather (2000). "A Comparison of Rankings Produced by Summarization Evaluation Measures." *Proceedings of the NAACL-ANLP-2000 Workshop on Automatic Summarization—Volume 4*, Seattle, Washington, DC, USA, pp. 69–78.

Doran, William, Nicola Stokes, Joe Carthy, and John Dunnion (2004). "Assessing the Impact of Lexical Chain Scoring Methods and Sentence Extraction Schemes on Summarization." *Proceedings of the 5th International Conference on Intelligent Text Processing and Computational Linguistics* (*CICLing-2004*), Chung-Ang University, Seoul, Korea, pp. 622–630.

Duboue, Pablo and Jennifer Chu-Carroll (2006). "Answering the Question You Wish They Had Asked: The Impact of Paraphrasing for Question Answering." *Proceedings of the Human Language Technology Conference—Annual Meeting of the North American Chapter of the Association for Computational Linguistics* (*HLT-NAACL-2006*), New York, USA.

Fukumoto, Fumiyo and Yoshimi Suzuki (2000). "Extracting Key Paragraph Based on Topic and Event Detection: Towards Multi-document Summarization." *Proceedings of the NAACL-ANLP-2000 Workshop on Automatic Summarization—Volume 4*, Seattle, Washington, DC, USA, pp. 31–39.

Gao, Jun and Xixian Chen (1997). "Chinese Text Compression Using Chinese Language Information Processing." *Proceedings of the International Conference on Research in Computational Linguistics* (*ROCLING-X*), Academia Sinica, Taipei, Taiwan.

Garcia-Menier, Everardo (2000). "On Automatic Text Summarization: Some Ideas and an Illustration." *Proceedings of the 1st International Conference on Intelligent Text Processing and Computational Linguistics* (*CICLing-2000*), Mexico City, Mexico.

Goldstein, Jade, Vibhu Mittal, Jaime G. Carbonell, and Mark Kantrowitz (2000). "Multi-document Summarization by Sentence Extraction." *Proceedings of the NAACL-ANLP-2000 Workshop on Automatic Summarization—Volume 4*, Seattle, Washington, DC, USA, pp. 40–48.

Cohen-Kerner, Yaakov Ha, Zuriel Gross, and Asaf Masa (2005). "Automatic Extraction and Learning of Key Phrases from Scientific Articles." *Proceedings of the 6th International Conference on*

Intelligent Text Processing and Computational Linguistics (*CICLing-2005*), Mexico City, Mexico, pp. 644–656.

Hassel, Martin and Jonas Sjöbergh (2006). "Towards Holistic Summarization—Selecting Summaries, Not Sentences." *Proceedings of the 5th International Conference on Language Resources and Evaluation* (*LREC-2006*), Genoa, Italy.

Hirao, Tsutomu, Manabu Okumura, and Hideki Isozaki (2005). "Kernel-based Approach for Automatic Evaluation of Natural Language Generation Technologies: Application to Automatic Summarization." *Proceedings of Human Language Technology Conference and Conference on Empirical Methods in Natural Language Processing* (*HLT/EMNLP-2005*), Vancouver, BC, Canada.

Hovy, Eduard, Chin-Yew Lin, Liang Zhou, and Junichi Fukumoto (2006). "Automated Summarization Evaluation with Basic Elements." *Proceedings of the 5th International Conference on Language Resources and Evaluation* (*LREC-2006*), Genoa, Italy.

Jaoua, Maher and Abdelmajid Ben Hamadou (2003). "Automatic Text Summarization of Scientific Articles Based on Classification of Extract's Population." *Proceedings of the 4th International Conference on Intelligent Text Processing and Computational Linguistics* (*CICLing-2003*), Mexico City, Mexico, pp. 625–636.

Jing, Hongyan and Kathleen R. McKeown (2000). "Cut and Paste Based Text Summarization." *Proceedings of the 1st Meeting of the North American Chapter of the Association for Computational Linguistics*, Seattle, Washington, DC, USA, pp. 178–185.

Jing, Hongyan (2000). "Sentence Reduction for Automatic Text Summarization." *Proceedings of the 6th Applied Natural Language Processing Conference*, Seattle, Washington, DC, USA, pp. 310–315.

Kuo, June-Jei, Hung-Chia Wung, Chuan-Jie Lin, and Hsin-Hsi Chen (2002). "Multi-document Summarization Using Informative Words and Its Evaluation with a QA System." *Proceedings of the 3rd International Conference on Intelligent Text Processing and Computational Linguistics* (*CICLing-2002*), Mexico City, Mexico.

Leontyeva, Nina N. (2003). "Semantic Dictionary for Text Understanding and Summarization." *International Journal of Translation*, Vol. 15, No. 1, pp. 107–114.

Li, Jun-Jie and Key-Sun Choi (1997). "Corpus-based Chinese Text Summarization System." *Proceedings of the International Conference on Research in Computational Linguistics* (*ROCLING-X*), Academia Sinica, Taipei, Taiwan.

Lin, Chin-Yew, Guihong Cao, Jianfeng Gao, and Jian-Yun Nie (2006). "An Information-theoretic Approach to Automatic Evaluation of Summaries." *Proceedings of the Human Language Technology Conference—Annual Meeting of the North American Chapter of the Association for Computational Linguistics* (*HLT-NAACL-2006*), New York, USA.

Liu, Gongshen, Wang Yongcheng, and Hu Peihua (2002). "The Processing of Article Texture—The Significance and Method of Heading Recognition." In Yu Shiwen, ed., *Proceedings of the 2nd China-Japan Natural Language Processing Joint Research Promotion Conference* (*CJNLP-2002*). Beijing: Institute of Computational Linguistics, Peking University, pp. 323–327.

Liu, Weiquan and Joe Zhou (2000). "Building a Chinese Text Summarizer with Phrasal Chunks and Domain Knowledge." *Proceedings of the International Conference on Research in Computational Linguistics* (*ROCLING-XIII*), Taipei, Taiwan.

Loukachevitch, Natalia V. and Boris V. Dobrov (2000). "Thesaurus-based Structural Thematic Summary in Multilingual Information Systems." *Machine Translation Review*, No. 11, pp. 10–20.

Mani, Inderjeet, Kristian Concepcion, and Linda van Guilder (2000). "Using Summarization for Automatic Briefing Generation." *Proceedings of the NAACL-ANLP 2000 Workshop on Automatic Summarization—Volume 4*, Seattle, Washington, DC, USA, pp. 99–108.

Mani, Inderjeet (2001). *Automatic Summarization*. Amsterdam: John Benjamins Publishing Company.

McDonald, Ryan (2006). "Discriminative Sentence Compression with Soft Syntactic Evidence." *Proceedings of the 11th Conference of the European Chapter of the Association for Computational Linguistics* (*EACL-2006*), Trento, Italy.

Mohamed, Ahmed and Sanguthevar Rajasekaran (2006). "Efficient Randomized Algorithms for Text Summarization." In Alexander F. Gelbukh, ed., *Advances in Natural Language Processing*, Special Issue of *Research in Computing Science*, No. 18, pp. 195–202.

Muraki, Kazunori (1982). "On a Semantic Model for Multi-lingual Paraphrasing." In Jan Horecky, ed., *Proceedings of the 9th*

International Conference on Computational Linguistics (*COLING-82*), Prague, the Czech Republic. Amsterdam: North-Holland Publishing Company, pp. 239–244.

Nakao, Yoshio (2000). "An Algorithm for One-page Summarization of a Long Text Based on Thematic Hierarchy Detection." *Proceedings of the 38th Annual Meeting of the Association for Computational Linguistics* (*ACL-2000*), Hong Kong.

Nanba, Hidetsugu, Manabu Okumura, and Takahiro Fukusima (2002). "Two Work on Automatic Text Summarization: Text Summarization Evaluation and a Survey Support System." In Yu Shiwen, ed., *Proceedings of the 2nd China-Japan Natural Language Processing Joint Research Promotion Conference* (*CJNLP-2002*). Beijing: Institute of Computational Linguistics, Peking University, pp. 290–293.

Nenkova, Ani and Rebecca Passonneau (2004). "Evaluating Content Selection in Summarization: The Pyramid Method." *Proceedings of the Human Language Technology Conference/North American Chapter of the Association for Computational Linguistics Annual Meeting* (*HLT/NAACL-2004*), Boston, MA, USA.

Nenkova, Ani, Advaith Siddharthan, and Kathleen R. McKeown (2005). "Automatically Learning Cognitive Status for Multi-document Summarization of Newswire." *Proceedings of Human Language Technology Conference and Conference on Empirical Methods in Natural Language Processing* (*HLT/EMNLP-2005*), Vancouver, BC, Canada.

Nomoto, Tadashi (2005). "Bayesian Learning in Text Summarization." *Proceedings of Human Language Technology Conference and Conference on Empirical Methods in Natural Language Processing* (*HLT/EMNLP-2005*), Vancouver, BC, Canada.

Oka, Mamiko and Yoshihiro Ueda (2000). "Evaluation of Phrase-representation Summarization Based on Information Retrieval." *Proceedings of the NAACL-ANLP-2000 Workshop on Automatic Summarization—Volume 4*, Seattle, Washington, DC, USA, pp. 59–68.

Okurowski, Mary Ellen, Harold Wilson, Joaquin Urbina, Tony Taylor, Ruth Colvin Clark, and Frank Krapcho (2000). "Text Summarizer in Use: Lessons Learned from Real World Deployment and Evaluation." *Proceedings of the NAACL-ANLP-2000 Workshop on Automatic Summarization—Volume 4*, Seattle, Washington, DC, USA, pp. 49–58.

Orăsan, Constantin and Laura Hasler (2006). "Computer-aided Summarization—What the User Really Wants." *Proceedings of the 5th International Conference on Language Resources and Evaluation* (*LREC-2006*), Genoa, Italy.
Radev, Dragomir R., Hongyan Jing, and Malgorzata Budzikowska (2000). "Centroid-based Summarization of Multiple Documents: Sentence Extraction, Utility-based Evaluation, and User Studies." *Proceedings of the NAACL-ANLP-2000 Workshop on Automatic Summarization—Volume 4*, Seattle, Washington, DC, USA, pp. 21–30.
Reithinger, Norbert, Michael Kipp, Ralf Engel, and Jan Alexandersson (2000). "Summarizing Multilingual Spoken Negotiation Dialogues." *Proceedings of the 38th Annual Meeting of the Association for Computational Linguistics* (*ACL-2000*), Hong Kong.
Saggion, Horacio and Guy Lapalme (2000). "Concept Identification and Presentation in the Context of Technical Text Summarization." *Proceedings of the NAACL-ANLP-2000 Workshop on Automatic Summarization—Volume 4*, Seattle, Washington, DC, USA, pp. 1–10.
Sarkar, Kamal and Sivaji Bandyopadhyay (2005). "Generating Headline Summary from a Document Set." *Proceedings of the 6th International Conference on Intelligent Text Processing and Computational Linguistics* (*CICLing-2005*), Mexico City, Mexico, pp. 636–639.
Siddharthan, Advaith and Kathleen R. McKeown (2005). "Improving Multilingual Summarization: Using Redundancy in the Input to Correct MT Errors." *Proceedings of Human Language Technology Conference and Conference on Empirical Methods in Natural Language Processing* (*HLT/EMNLP-2005*), Vancouver, BC, Canada.
Song, Young-In, Kyoung-Soo Han, and Hae-Chang Rim (2004). "A Term Weighting Method Based on Lexical Chain for Automatic Summarization." *Proceedings of the 5th International Conference on Intelligent Text Processing and Computational Linguistics* (*CICLing-2004*), Chung-Ang University, Seoul, Korea, pp. 631–634.
Sporleder, Caroline and Mirella Lapata (2005). "Discourse Chunking and Its Application to Sentence Compression." *Proceedings of Human Language Technology Conference and Conference on Empirical Methods in Natural Language Processing* (*HLT/EMNLP-2005*), Vancouver, BC, Canada.
Takeuchi, Kazuhiro (2000). "Role of Text Structure for Summary Generation: Clues for Sentence Combination." *Proceedings of the 38th*

Annual Meeting of the Association for Computational Linguistics (*ACL-2000*), Hong Kong.

T'sou, Benjamin K. Y., Hing-Lung Lin, and Tom B. Y. Lai (1997). "Human Judgment as a Basis for Evaluation of Discourse-connective-based Full-text Abstraction in Chinese." *Proceedings of the International Conference on Research in Computational Linguistics* (*ROCLING-X*), Academia Sinica, Taipei, Taiwan.

Unno, Yuya, Takashi Ninomiya, Yusuke Miyao, and Jun-ichi Tsujii (2006). "Trimming CFG Parse Trees for Sentence Compression Using Machine Learning Approaches." *Proceedings of the Joint Conference of the International Committee on Computational Linguistics and the Association for Computational Linguistics* (*COLING/ACL-2006*), Sydney, Australia.

Wan, Xiaojun and Jianwu Yang (2006). "Improved Affinity Graph Based Multi-document Summarization." *Proceedings of the Human Language Technology Conference—Annual Meeting of the North American Chapter of the Association for Computational Linguistics* (*HLT-NAACL-2006*), New York, USA.

Wang, Ruichao, Nicola Stokes, William Doran, Eamonn Newman, John Dunnion, and Joe Carthy (2005). "LexTrim: A Lexical Cohesion Based Approach to Parse-and-trim Style Headline Generation." *Proceedings of the 6th International Conference on Intelligent Text Processing and Computational Linguistics* (*CICLing-2005*), Mexico City, Mexico, pp. 632–635.

Zechner, Klaus and Alex H. Waibel (2000). "Minimizing Word Error Rate in Textual Summaries of Spoken Language." *Proceedings of the 1st Meeting of the North American Chapter of the Association for Computational Linguistics*, Seattle, Washington, DC, USA, pp. 186–193.

Zhou, Liang and Eduard Hovy (2003). "A Web-trained Extraction Summarization System." *Proceedings of the Human Language Technology and North American Chapter of Association of Computational Linguistics 2003* (*HLT/NAACL-2003*), Edmonton, Alberta, Canada.

Zhu, Xiaodan and Gerald Penn (2006). "Comparing the Roles of Textual, Acoustic and Spoken-language Features on Spontaneous Conversation Summarization." *Proceedings of the Human Language Technology Conference—Annual Meeting of the North American Chapter of the*

Association for Computational Linguistics (*HLT-NAACL-2006*), New York, USA.

Text Understanding

Ito, Noriko, Toru Sugimoto, and Michio Sugeno (2004). "A Systemic-functional Approach to Japanese Text Understanding." *Proceedings of the 5th International Conference on Intelligent Text Processing and Computational Linguistics* (*CICLing-2004*), Chung-Ang University, Seoul, Korea, pp. 25–36.

❖ PART 35 ❖

Translation

Translation

Cyrus, Lea (2006). "Building a Resource for Studying Translation Shifts." *Proceedings of the 5th International Conference on Language Resources and Evaluation* (*LREC-2006*), Genoa, Italy.

Davis, Paul C. and Chris Brew (2002). "Stone Soup Translation." *Proceedings of the 9th International Conference on Theoretical and Methodological Issues in Machine Translation* (*TMI-2002*), Keihanna, Japan, pp. 31–41.

Lehmann, Hubert and Nikolaus Ott (1992). "Translation Relations and the Combination of Analytical and Statistical Methods in Machine Translation." *Proceedings of the 4th International Conference on Theoretical and Methodological Issues in Machine Translation of Natural Languages: Empiricist vs. Rationalist Methods in MT* (*TMI-92*), Montreal, Quebec, Canada, pp. 237–248.

Macklovitch, Elliott, Ngoc Tran Nguyen, and Guy Lapalme (2005). "Tracing Translation in the Making." *Proceedings of MT Summit X*, Phuket, Thailand.

Malavazos, Christos, Stelios Piperidis, and George Carayannis (2000). "Towards Memory and Template-based Translation Synthesis." *Proceedings of the International Conference on Machine Translation and Multilingual Applications in the New Millenium* (*MT-2000*), University of Exeter, England.

Translation Aid

Andreyewsky, Alexander (1981). "Translation: Aids, Robots, and Automation." *Meta*, Vol. 26, No. 1, pp. 57–66.

Arthern, P.J. (1981). "Aids Unlimited: The Scope for Machine Aids in a Large Organization." *Aslib Proceedings*, Vol. 3, pp. 7–8.

Aslib, ed. (1981). *Machine Aids for Translators: Translating and the Computer 2*. London: The Association for Information Management.

Boitet, Christian (1999). "A Research Perspective on How to Democratize Machine Translation and Translation Aides Aiming at High Quality Final Output." *Proceedings of MT Summit VII: MT in the Great Translation Era*, Singapore.

Brinkmann, Karl-Heinz (1980). "Present and Future Technical Aids to Easier Communication in Foreign Language." *Babel*, Vol. 26, No. 2, pp. 67–75.

Brinkmann, Karl-Heinz (1981). "Machine Aids to Translation." *Meta*, Vol. 26, No. 1, pp. 67–75.

Clark, R. (1981). "Machine Aids: A Small User's Reaction." *Machine Aids for Translators: ASLIB Proceedings*, Vol. 33, pp. 7–8.

Isabelle, Pierre (1993). *Bi-text Aids for Translators*. Technical Report. Laval, Quebec: Centre for Information Technologies Innovation.

Krollmann, Friedrich (1976). "Translation Aids." *American Journal of Computational Linguistics*, Vol. 13, No. 2, p. 58.

Krollmann, Friedrich (1977). *User Aspects of an Automatic Aid to Translation as Employed in a Large Translation Service*. Brussels: Commission of the European Communities.

Krollmann, Friedrich (1981). "Computer Aids to Translation." *Meta*, Vol. 26, No. 1, pp. 85–94.

Melby, Alan K. (1982). "Multi-level Translation Aids in a Distributed System." In Jan Horecky, ed., *Proceedings of the 9th International Conference on Computational Linguistics* (*COLING-82*), Prague, the Czech Republic. Amsterdam: North-Holland Publishing Company, pp. 215–220.

Melby, Alan K. (1981). "A Suggestion Box Translator Aid." *Proceedings of the DLLS Symposium*, Brigham Young University, Provo, Utah, USA.

Schneider, Thomas (1983). "Some Notes on Machine Aids for Translators." *Meta*, Vol. 28, No. 4, pp. 344–351.

Sugden, Don (1985). "Machine Aids to Translation: Automated Language Processing System (ALPS)." *Meta*, Vol. 30, No. 4, pp. 403–404.

Sumita, Eiichiro and Yutaka Tsutsumi (1988). "A Translation Aid System Using Flexible Text Retrieval Based on Syntax-matching." *Proceedings of the 2nd International Conference on Theoretical and Methodological Issues in Machine Translation of Natural Languages* (*TMI-88*), Carnegie Mellon University, Center for Machine Translation, Pittsburgh, Pennsylvania, USA.

Trujillo, Arturo (1999). "Translator's Workbench and Translation Aids." *Translation Engines: Techniques for Machine Translation*. Berlin and New York: Springer Verlag, pp. 57–82.

Translation Automation

Andreyewsky, Alexander (1980). "Whither Automation and the Translator." *ATA Chronicle*, Vol. 9, No. 2, pp. 3–4.

Isabelle, Pierre, Marc Dymetman, George Foster, Jean-Marc Jutras, Elliott Macklovitch, Francois Perrault, Ren Xiaobo, and Michel Simard (1993). "Translation Analysis and Translation Automation." *Proceedings of the 5th International Conference on Theoretical and Methodological Issues in Machine Translation* (*TMI-93*), Kyoto, Japan, pp. 201–217.

Isabelle, Pierre (1993). "Translation Automation: History, State-of-the-art and Prospects." *Proceedings of the 13th International Conference on Artificial Intelligence Expert Systems and Natural Language*, Avignon, France.

Translation Company

Lewis, Terence and Rudolf M. Meier (2005). "The MT Developer/Provider and the Global Corporation." *Proceedings of the 10th Workshop of the European Association for Machine Translation: Practical Applications of Machine Translation*, Budapest, Hungary, pp. 176–180.

Rinsche, Adriane (2000). "Computer Assisted Business Process Management in Translation and Localisation Companies." *Proceedings of the 5th Workshop of the European Association for Machine Translation: Harvesting Existing Resources*, Lubljana, Slovenia.

Schäler, Reinhard (2002). "Can Translation Companies Survive the Current Economic Climate?" In *Translating and the Computer 24*. London: The Association for Information Management.

Schuh, Sarah (2006). "Growing a Translation Business from Zero to International Play." *Programme of the 30th Anniversary Conference of the Association of Translation Companies 30th Anniversary Conference 2006: Building Strong Markets for Translations—Making Links and Seizing Opportunities*, School of Oriental and African Studies, University of London, England.

Waley-Cohen, Jack (2006). "Exploiting the Internet to Develop a Virtual Translation Company." *Programme of the 30th Anniversary Conference of the Association of Translation Companies 30th Anniversary Conference 2006: Building Strong Markets for Translations—Making Links and Seizing Opportunities*, School of Oriental and African Studies, University of London, England.

Wallace, Alison (2004). "When Is an Employee Not an Employee? Putting the Freelancer and Translation Company Relationship under Legal Microscope." *Programme of the Annual Conference of the Association of Translation Companies: Getting in Shape for the Future—Working towards a New Environment for the Translation Profession*, School of Oriental and African Studies, University of London, England.

Translation Conference

Alt, Franz L. (1965). "Mechanical Translation: U.S.-Japan Joint Conference." *Science*, Vol. 147, pp. 1599–1600.

Belam, Judith and Derek Lewis (2002). "Report on the 6th EAMT Workshop *Teaching Machine Translation* 14–15 November 2002: UMIST, Manchester, England." *Machine Translation Review*, No. 13, pp. 35–39.

Hutchins, W. John (1997). "Looking Back to 1953: The First MT Conference." *Proceedings of the 7th International Conference on Theoretical and Methodological Issues in Machine Translation (TMI-97)*, St. John's College, Santa Fe, New Mexico, USA, pp. 19–30.

Lewis, Derek (1994). "Machine Translation—Ten Years On: An Overview of the Conference." *Machine Translation—Ten Years On: Proceedings of the 2nd International Conference Organised by Cranfield University*, Cranfield, England, pp. 1–8.

Lewis, Derek (1995). "Machine Translation—Ten Years On: Cranfield Conference Report." *Machine Translation Review*, No. 1, pp. 10–17.

Nagao, Makoto (1989). "Two Years after the MT Summit." *Proceedings of MT Summit II*, Munchen, Germany, pp. 100–105.

Reifler, Erwin (1954). "The First Conference on Mechanical Translation." *Machine Translation*, Vol. 1, No. 2, pp. 23–32.

Reynolds, A. Craig (1954). "The Conference on Mechanical Translation." *Mechanical Translation*, Vol. 1, No. 3, pp. 47–55.

Sgall, Petr (1988). "On Some Results of the Conference." In Dan Maxwell, Klaus Schubert, and Toon Witkam, eds. (1988), *New Directions in Machine Translation*. Dordrecht-Holland: Foris Publications, pp. 243–250.

Translation Database

Berry, Mark (1997). "Who Owns Translation Databases?" *MultiLingual Communications and Technology*, Vol. 13, No. 2, pp. 22–23.

Catizone, Roberta, Graham Russell, and Susan Warwick-Armstrong (1992). "Deriving Translation Data from Bilingual Texts." In Uri Zernik, ed., *Lexical Acquisition: Using On-line Resources to Build a Lexicon*. Lawrence Erlbaum.

Fry, Deborah (1997). "Defining a Translation Database Exchange Format." *MultiLingual Communications and Technology*, Vol. 8, No. 15, Issue 4, pp. 31–32.

Zachary, Wayne W. (1980). "Translation Databases: Their Content, Use, and Structure." In Joseph Raben and Gregory Marks, eds., *Data Bases in the Humanities and Social Sciences*. Amsterdam: North-Holland Publishing Company, pp. 217–221.

Translation Divergence

Dorr, Bonnie J. (1993). "Formalization of Machine Translation Divergences." *Machine Translation: A View from the Lexicon*. Cambridge, MA: MIT Press, pp. 233–281.

Dorr, Bonnie J. (1994). "Machine Translation Divergences: A Formal Description and Proposed Solution." *Computational Linguistics*, Vol. 20, pp. 579–634.

Habash, Nizar and Bonnie J. Dorr (2002). "Handling Translation Divergences: Combining Statistical and Symbolic Techniques in Generation-heavy Machine Translation." In Stephen D. Richardson, ed., *Machine Translation: From Research to Real Users*. Berlin and New York: Springer Verlag, pp. 84–93.

Lin, Shun-Chieh, Jia-Ching Wang, and Jhing-Fa Wang (2005). "Translation Divergence Analysis and Processing for Mandarin-English Parallel Text Exploitation." *Proceedings of the International Conference on Computational Linguistics and Speech Processing (ROCLING-XVII)*, National Cheng Kung University, Tainan, Taiwan.

Sinha, R. Mahesh K. and Anil Thakur (2005). "Divergence Patterns in Machine Translation between Hindi and English." *Proceedings of MT Summit X*, Phuket, Thailand.

Sinha, R. Mahesh K. and Anil Thakur (2005). "Translation Divergence in English-Hindi MT." *Proceedings of the 10th Annual Conference of the European Association for Machine Translation* (*EAMT-2005*), Budapest, Hungary.

Viegas, Evelyne (1997). "Mismatches and Divergences: The Continuum

Perspective." *Proceedings of the 7th International Conference on Theoretical and Methodological Issues in Machine Translation* (*TMI-97*), St. John's College, Santa Fe, New Mexico, USA.

Translation Engine

Arnold, Doug J., Lorna Balkan, R. Lee Humphreys, Seity Meijer, and Louisa Sadler (1994). "Machine Translation Engines." *Machine Translation: An Introductory Guide*. Manchester and Oxford: NCC Blackwell, pp. 63–86.

Callison-Burch, Chris and Raymond S. Flournoy (2001). "A Program for Automatically Selecting the Best Output from Multiple Machine Translation Engines." In Bente Maegaard, ed., *Proceedings of MT Summit VIII: Machine Translation in the Information Age*, Santiago de Compostela, Spain.

Corbi-Bellot, Antonio M., Mikel L. Forcada, Sergio Ortiz-Rojas, Juan Antonio Perez-Ortiz, Gema Ramirez-Sanchez, Felipe Sanchez-Martinez, Inaki Alegria, Aingeru Mayor, and Kepa Sarasola (2005). "An Open-source Shallow-transfer Machine Translation Engine for the Romance Languages of Spain." *Proceedings of the 10th Annual Conference of the European Association for Machine Translation* (*EAMT-2005*), Budapest, Hungary.

Jayaraman, Shyamsundar, Alon Lavie, Robert Frederking, and Ralf D. Brown (2005). "Multi-engine Machine Translation Guided by Explicit Word Matching." *Proceedings of the 10th Workshop of the European Association for Machine Translation: Practical Applications of Machine Translation*, Budapest, Hungary, pp. 143–152.

Mellebeek, Bart, Karolina Owczarzak, Josef Van Genabith, and Andy Way (2006). "Multi-engine Machine Translation by Recursive Sentence Decomposition." *Proceedings of the 7th Biennial Conference of the Association for Machine Translation in the Americas* (*AMTA-2006*): *Visions for the Future of Machine Translation*, Boston Marriott, Cambridge, MA, USA.

Nomoto, Tadashi (2003). "Predictive Models of Performance in Multi-engine Machine Translation." *Proceedings of MT Summit IX*, New Orleans, Louisiana, USA.

Nomoto, Tadashi (2004). "Multi-engine Machine Translation with Voted Language Model." *Proceedings of the 42nd Annual Meeting of the*

Association for Computational Linguistics (ACL-2004), Barcelona, Spain, pp. 494–501.
Trujillo, Arturo (1999). *Translation Engines: Techniques for Machine Translation*. Berlin and New York: Springer Verlag.
Voss, Clare R. and Calandra R. Tate (2006). "Task-based Evaluation of Machine Translation (MT) Engines: Measuring How Well People Extract Who, When, Where-type Elements in MT Output." *Proceedings of the 11th Workshop of the European Association for Machine Translation: Machine Translation/Translation Aids—Tools to Increase Quality and to Save Money*, the University of Oslo, Norway.

Translation Equivalent

Gamallo, Pablo (2005). "Extraction of Translation Equivalents from Parallel Corpora Using Sense-sensitive Contexts." *Proceedings of the 10th Workshop of the European Association for Machine Translation: Practical Applications of Machine Translation*, Budapest, Hungary, pp. 97–102.
Haenelt, Karin (1992). "Towards a Quality Improvement in Machine Translation: Modelling Discourse Structure and Including Discourse Development in the Determination of Translation Equivalents." *Proceedings of the 4th International Conference on Theoretical and Methodological Issues in Machine Translation of Natural Languages: Empiricist vs. Rationalist Methods in MT (TMI-92)*, Montreal, Quebec, Canada, pp. 205–212.
Kutsumi, Takeshi, Takehiko Yoshimi, Katsunori Kotani, Ichiko Sata, and Hitoshi Isahara (2005). "Selection of Entries for a Bilingual Dictionary from Aligned Translation Equivalents Using Support Vector Machines." *Proceedings of MT Summit X*, Phuket, Thailand.
Melamed, I. Dan (1997). "A Word-to-word Model of Translational Equivalence." *Proceedings of the 35th Annual Meeting of the Association for Computational Linguistics and 8th Conference of the European Chapter of the Association for Computational Linguistics*, Madrid, Spain, pp. 490–497.
Melamed, I. Dan (2000). "Models of Translational Equivalence among Words." *Computational Linguistics*, Vol. 26, No. 2, pp. 221–249.
Melamed, I. Dan (2001). "Manual Annotation of Translational

Equivalence." *Empirical Methods for Exploiting Parallel Texts*. Cambridge, MA: MIT Press, pp. 65–77.

Melamed, I. Dan (2001). "Sense-to-sense Models of Translation Equivalence." *Empirical Methods for Exploiting Parallel Texts*. Cambridge, MA: MIT Press, pp. 147–163.

Melamed, I. Dan (2001). "Word-to-word Models of Translation Equivalence." *Empirical Methods for Exploiting Parallel Texts*. Cambridge, MA: MIT Press, pp. 81–121.

Paskaleva, Elena (1999). "Aligning and Extracting Translation Equivalents from EU Documents—A Possible Look on EU Integration." *Proceedings of the 4th Workshop of the European Association for Machine Translation: EU and the New Languages: Translation—Possibilities, Policies and Practicalities*, Prague, the Czech Republic.

Pym, Anthony (2004). "Equivalence, *Malgré Tout*." *The Moving Text: Localization, Translation, and Distribution*. Amsterdam and Philadelphia: John Benjamins Publishing Company, pp. 51–65.

Sanfilippo, Antonio, Ted Briscoe, Ann Copestake, Maria Antonia Marti, Mariona Taulé, and Antonietta Alonge (1992). "Translation Equivalence and Lexicalization in the ACQUILEX LKB." *Proceedings of the 4th International Conference on Theoretical and Methodological Issues in Machine Translation of Natural Languages: Empiricist vs. Rationalist Methods in MT* (*TMI-92*), Montreal, Quebec, Canada, pp. 1–11.

Sanfilippo, Antonio and Ralf Steinberger (1997). "Automatic Selection and Ranking of Translation Candidates." *Proceedings of the 7th International Conference on Theoretical and Methodological Issues in Machine Translation* (*TMI-97*), St. John's College, Santa Fe, New Mexico, USA.

Tanaka, Takaaki and Yoshihiro Matsuo (1999). "Extraction of Translation Equivalents from Non-parallel Corpora." *Proceedings of the 8th International Conference on Theoretical and Methodological Issues in Machine Translation* (*TMI-99*), Chester, England, pp. 109–119.

Wellington, Benjamin and Sonjia Waxmonsky (2006). "Empirical Lower Bounds on the Complexity of Translational Equivalence." *Proceedings of the Joint Conference of the International Committee on Computational Linguistics and the Association for Computational Linguistics* (*COLING/ACL-2006*), Sydney, Australia.

Wilkinson, Michael (2005). "Discovering Translation Equivalents in a Tourism Corpus by Means of Fuzzy Searching." *Translation Journal*, Vol. 9, No. 4.

Translation Error

Amengual, Juan C., José Miguel Benedi, Francisco Casacuberta, Asunción Castaño, Antonio Castellanos, David Llorens, Andrés Marzal, Federico Prat, Enrique Vidal, and Juan M. Vilar (1997). "Error Correcting Parsing for Text-to-text Machine Translation Using Finite State Models." *Proceedings of the 7th International Conference on Theoretical and Methodological Issues in Machine Translation* (*TMI-97*), St. John's College, Santa Fe, New Mexico, USA.

Brill, Eric and Robert C. Moore (2000). "An Improved Error Model for Noisy Channel Spelling Correction." *Proceedings of the 38th Annual Meeting of the Association for Computational Linguistics* (*ACL-2000*), Hong Kong.

Cettolo, Mauro and Marcello Federico (2004). "Minimum Error Training of Log-linear Translation Models." *Proceedings of the International Workshop on Spoken Language Translation* (*IWSLT-2004*), Kyoto, Japan.

Higgins, Derrick (2000). "The Use of Error Tags in ARTFL's *Encyclopedie*: Does Good Error Identification Lead to Good Error Correction?" *Proceedings of the ANLP-NAACL-2000 Student Research Workshop*, Seattle, Washington, DC, USA, pp. 30–34.

Murata, Masaki, Masao Utiyama, Kiyotaka Uchimoto, Qing Ma, and Hitoshi Isahara (2002). "Correction of Errors in a Modality Corpus Used for Machine Translation Using Machine-learning." *Proceedings of the 9th International Conference on Theoretical and Methodological Issues in Machine Translation* (*TMI-2002*), Keihanna, Japan, pp. 125–134.

Russell, Graham (2005). "Automatic Detection of Translation Errors: The TransCheck System." In *Translating and the Computer 20*. London: The Association for Information Management.

Shi, Yongmei and Zhou Lina (2005). "Error Detection Using Linguistic Features." *Proceedings of Human Language Technology Conference and Conference on Empirical Methods in Natural Language Processing* (*HLT/EMNLP-2005*), Vancouver, BC, Canada.

Siddharthan, Advaith and Kathleen R. McKeown (2005). "Improving Multilingual Summarization: Using Redundancy in the Input to Correct MT Errors." *Proceedings of Human Language Technology Conference and Conference on Empirical Methods in Natural Language Processing* (*HLT/EMNLP-2005*), Vancouver, BC, Canada.

Sporleder, Caroline, Marieke van Erp, Tijn Porcelijn, and Antal van den Bosch (2006). "Spotting the 'Odd-one-out': Data-driven Error Detection and Correction in Textual Databases." *Proceedings of the 11th Conference of the European Chapter of the Association for Computational Linguistics* (*EACL-2006*), Trento, Italy.

Yangarber, Roman and Lauri Jokipii (2005). "Redundancy-based Correction of Automatically Extracted Facts." *Proceedings of Human Language Technology Conference and Conference on Empirical Methods in Natural Language Processing* (*HLT/EMNLP-2005*), Vancouver, BC, Canada.

Zhang, Lei, Zhou Ming, Huang Changning, and Pan Haihua (2000). "Automatic Detecting/Correcting Errors in Chinese Text by an Approximate Word-matching Algorithm." *Proceedings of the 38th Annual Meeting of the Association for Computational Linguistics* (*ACL-2000*), Hong Kong.

Translation Output

Akiba, Yasuhiro, Kenji Imamura, and Eiichiro Sumita (2001). "Using Multiple Edit Distances to Automatically Rank Machine Translation Output." In Bente Maegaard, ed., *Proceedings of MT Summit VIII: Machine Translation in the Information Age*, Santiago de Compostela, Spain, pp. 15–20.

Almberg, Evangeline S. P. (2002). "Shall We Dance, When the Smart Machines Take Over, Virtually?" In Chan Sin-wai, ed., *Translation and Information Technology*. Hong Kong: The Chinese University Press, pp. 185–193.

Fuji, Masaru (1999). "Evaluation Experiment for Reading Comprehension of Machine Translation Outputs." *Proceedings of MT Summit VII: MT in the Great Translation Era*, Singapore, pp. 285–289.

Habermann, F. W. A. (1986). "Provision and Use of Raw Machine Translation." *Terminologie et Traduction*, Vol. 1, pp. 29–42.

Knowles, Francis E. (1979). "Error Analysis of Systran Output—A

Suggested Criterion for the 'Internal' Evaluation of Translation Quality and a Possible Corrective for System Design." In Barbara M. Snell, ed., *Translating and the Computer*. Amsterdam: North-Holland Publishing Company, pp. 109–134.
Riabtseva, Nadeshda K. (1987). "Machine Translation Output and Translation Theory." *Computers and Translation*, Vol. 2, No. 1, pp. 37–43.
Vasconcellos, Muriel (1986). "Functional Considerations in the Postediting of Machine-translated Output." *Machine Translation*, Vol. 1, No. 1, pp. 21–38.
Voss, Clare R. and Calandra R. Tate (2006). "Task-based Evaluation of Machine Translation (MT) Engines: Measuring How Well People Extract Who, When, Where-type Elements in MT Output." *Proceedings of the 11th Workshop of the European Association for Machine Translation: Machine Translation/Translation Aids—Tools to Increase Quality and to Save Money*, the University of Oslo, Norway.
White, John S., Jennifer B. Doyon, and Susan W. Talbott (2000). "Task Tolerance of MT Output in Integrated Text Processes." *Proceedings of the ANLP/NAACL-2000 Workshop on Embedded Machine Translation Systems—Volume 5*, Seattle, Washington, DC, USA, pp. 9–16.

Translation Pattern

McTait, Kevin and Arturo Trujillo (1999). "A Language-neutral Sparse-data Algorithm for Extracting Translation Patterns." *Proceedings of the 8th International Conference on Theoretical and Methodological Issues in Machine Translation* (*TMI-99*), Chester, England, pp. 98–108.
McTait, Kevin (2001). "Linguistic Knowledge and Complexity in an EBMT System Based on Translation Patterns." *Proceedings of the Workshop on Example-based Machine Translation*, Santiago de Compostela, Spain, pp. 23–34.
McTait, Kevin (2003). "Translation Patterns, Linguistic Knowledge and Complexity in EBMT." In Michael Carl and Andy Way, eds., *Recent Advances in Example-based Machine Translation*. Dordrecht: Kluwer Academic Publishers, pp. 307–338.
Vassiliou, Marina (2006). "Using Patterns for Machine Translation." *Proceedings of the 11th Workshop of the European Association for Machine Translation: Machine Translation/Translation Aids—Tools*

to Increase Quality and to Save Money, the University of Oslo, Norway.
Watanabe, Hideo (1993). "A Method for Extracting Translation Patterns from Translation Examples." *Proceedings of the 5th International Conference on Theoretical and Methodological Issues in Machine Translation of Natural Languages: MT in the Next Generation (TMI-93)*, Kyoto, Japan, pp. 292–301.
Wastanabe, Hideo, Sadao Kurohashi, and Eiji Aramaki (2003). "Finding Translation Patterns from Paired Source and Target Dependency Structures." In Michael Carl and Andy Way, eds., *Recent Advances in Example-based Machine Translation*. Dordrecht: Kluwer Academic Publishers, pp. 397–420.

Translation Problem

Arnold, Doug J., Lorna Balkan, R. Lee Humphreys, Seity Meijer, and Louisa Sadler (1994). "Translation Problems." *Machine Translation: An Introductory Guide*. Manchester and Oxford: NCC Blackwell, pp. 111–128.
Helmreich, Stephen and David L. Farwell (2004). "Counting, Measuring, Ordering: Translation Problems and Solutions." In Robert E. Frederking and Kathryn B. Taylors, eds., *Machine Translation: From Real Users to Research*. Berlin: Springer Verlag, pp. 86–93.

Translation Quality

Babych, Bogdan and Anthony F. Hartley (2003). "Improving Machine Translation Quality with Automatic Named Entity Recognition." *Proceedings of EAMT/EACL Workshop on MT*, Budapest, Hungary.
Balkan, Lorna (1991). "Quality Criteria for MT." *Proceedings of the Evaluators' Forum*, Les Rasses, Vaud, Switzerland.
Bar-Hillel, Yehoshua (1971). "Some Reflections on the Present Outlook for High-quality Machine Translation." In Winfred P. Lehmann and Rolf A. Stachowitz, eds., *Feasibility Study on Fully Automatic High Quality Translation*. New York: Rome Air Development Center, pp. 72–76.
Bevan, Nigel (1997). "Quality in Use; Incorporating Human Factors into the Software Engineering Lifecycle." *Proceedings of the 3rd*

International Symposium and Forum on Software Engineering Standards (*ISESS-97*), Arizona, USA.
Bezhanova, Olga (2003). "Analysis of the Translation Quality of the WordMagic English↔Spanish Interpreter Professional." *International Journal of Translation*, Vol. 15, No. 1, pp. 71–79.
Boitet, Christian (2001). "Four Technical and Organizational Keys to Handle More Languages and Improve Quality (on Demand) in MT." In Bente Maegaard, ed., *Proceedings of MT Summit VIII: Machine Translation in the Information Age*, Santiago de Compostela, Spain.
Brunette, Louise (2000). "A Comparison of Translation Quality Assessment Practices." *The Translator*, Vol. 6, No. 2, pp. 169–182.
Buschbeck-Wolf, Bianka and Michael Dorna (1998). "Quality and Robustness in MT—A Balancing Act." In David L. Farwell, Laurie Gerber, and Eduard Hovy, eds., *Machine Translation and the Information Soup*. Berlin: Springer Verlag, pp. 62–71.
Carroll, John B. (1966). "An Experiment in Evaluating the Quality of Translations." *Mechanical Translation*, Vol. 9, Nos. 3–4, pp. 55–66.
Charoenpornsawat, Paisarn, Virach Sornlertlamvanich, and Thatsanee Charoenporn (2002). "Improving Translation Quality of Rule-based Machine Translation." *Proceedings of the Workshop on Machine Translation in Asia* (*COLING-2002*), Taipei, Taiwan.
Choi, Sung-Kwon, Han-Min Jung, Chul-Min Sim, Taewan Kim, Dong-In Park, Jun-Sik Park, and Key-Sun Choi (1998). "Hybrid Approaches to Improvement of Translation Quality in Web-based English-Korean Machine Translation." *Proceedings of the 36th Annual Meeting of the Association for Computational Linguistics and 17th International Conference on Computational Linguistics* (*COLING-ACL-98*), Montreal, Quebec, Canada, pp. 251–255.
Coughlin, Deborah (2003). "Correlating Automated and Human Assessments of Machine Translation Quality." *Proceedings of MT Summit IX*, New Orleans, Louisiana, USA, pp. 63–70.
Doddington, George (2002). "Automatic Evaluation of Machine Translation Quality Using N-gram Co-occurrence Statistics." *Proceedings of the 2nd International Conference on Human Language Technology Research*, San Diego, CA, USA, pp. 138–145.
Drugan, Joanna (2006). "The Effects of Computer-assisted Translation Tools on Translation Quality." *Proceedings of the 6th Portsmouth Translation Conference: Translation Technologies and Culture*,

School of Languages and Area Studies, University of Portsmouth, England.
Furuse, Osamu and Hitoshi Iida (1992). "An Example-based Method for Transfer-driven Machine Translation." *Proceedings of the 4th International Conference on Theoretical and Methodological Issues in Machine Translation* (*TMI-92*), Montréal, Quebec, Canada, pp. 139–150.
Furuse, Osamu and Hitoshi Iida (1992). "Cooperation between Transfer and Analysis in Example-based Framework." *Proceedings of the 14th International Conference on Computational Linguistics* (*COLING-92*), pp. 645–651.
Gerber, Laurie and Eduard Hovy (1998). "Improving Translation Quality by Manipulating Sentence Length." In David L. Farwell, Laurie Gerber, and Eduard Hovy, eds., *Machine Translation and the Information Soup*. Berlin: Springer Verlag, pp. 448–460.
Gross, Maurice (1973). *Notes on the Feasibility of High Quality Mechanical Translation*. Paris: University of Paris.
Haenelt, Karin (1992). "Towards a Quality Improvement in Machine Translation: Modelling Discourse Structure and Including Discourse Development in the Determination of Translation Equivalents." *Proceedings of the 4th International Conference on Theoretical and Methodological Issues in Machine Translation of Natural Languages: Empiricist vs. Rationalist Methods in MT* (*TMI-92*), Montreal, Quebec, Canada, pp. 205–212.
Jones, Douglas A. and Gregory M. Rusk (2000). "Toward a Scoring Function for Quality-driven Machine Translation." *Proceedings of the 18th International Conference on Computational Linguistics* (*COLING-2000*), Saarbrucken, Germany.
Knowles, Francis E. (1979). "Error Analysis of Systran Output—A Suggested Criterion for the 'Internal' Evaluation of Translation Quality and a Possible Corrective for System Design." In Barbara M. Snell, ed., *Translating and the Computer*. Amsterdam: North-Holland Publishing Company, pp. 109–134.
Koo, Siu Ling and Harold Kinds (2000). "A Quality-assurance Model for Language Projects." In Robert C. Sprung, ed., *Translating into Success: Cutting-edge Strategies for Going Multilingual in a Global Age*. Amsterdam and Philadelphia: John Benjamins Publishing Company, pp. 147–157.

Lange, Elke and Laurie Gerber (1992). "Internal Evaluation: Quality Analysis, an Internal Evaluation Tool at SYSTRAN." *MT Evaluation: Basis for Future Directions. Proceedings of a Workshop Sponsored by the National Science Foundation.* San Diego, California, USA, pp. 55–56.

Lauscher, Susanne (2000). "Translation Quality Assessment: Where Can Theory and Practice Meet?" *The Translator*, Vol. 6, No. 2, pp. 149–168.

Leavitt, A., J. Gates, and S. Shannon (1971). *Machine Translation Quality and Production Process Evaluation.* Report RADC-TR-71-206, Rome Air Development Center, Griffiss Air Force Base, New York.

Lehmann, Winfred P. and Rolf A. Stachowitz, eds. (1971). *Feasibility Study on Fully Automatic High Quality Translation.* New York: Rome Air Development Center.

Lewis, Terence (1995). "Can We Make Do with Near Human Quality?" *Translating and the Computer 17.* London: The Association for Information Management.

Lin, Chin-Yew and Franz Josef Och (2004). "Automatic Evaluation of Machine Translation Quality Using Longest Common Subsequence and Skip-bigram Statistics." *Proceedings of the 42nd Annual Meeting of the Association for Computational Linguistics (ACL-2004)*, Barcelona, Spain, pp. 605–612.

Macklovitch, Elliott and Antonio S. Valderrábanos (2001). "Rethinking Interaction: The Solution for High-quality MT?" In Bente Maegaard, ed., *Proceedings of MT Summit VIII: Machine Translation in the Information Age*, Santiago de Compostela, Spain.

Mehnert, Thorsten (1998). "Quality Policy: Comply or Compete?" *Language International*, Vol. 10, No. 5, pp. 12–15.

Miller, George A. and John Gilbert Beebe-Center (1958). "Some Psychological Methods for Evaluating the Quality of Translations." *Mechanical Translation*, Vol. 3, No. 3, pp. 73–80.

Miller, Keith J. and Michelle Vanni (2001). "Scaling the ISLE Taxonomy: Development of Metrics for the Multi-dimensional Characterisation of MT Quality." In Bente Maegaard, ed., *Proceedings of MT Summit VIII: Machine Translation in the Information Age*, Santiago de Compostela, Spain, pp. 229–234.

Morland, Verne (2002). "Nutzlos, Bien Pratique, or Muy Util? Business Users Speak Out on the Value of Pure Machine Translation." In *Translating and the Computer 24.* London: The Association for Information Management.

Oepen, Stephan, Helge Dyvik, Dan Flickinger, Jan Tore Lonning, Paul Meurer, and Victoria Rosen (2005). "Holistic Regression Testing for High-quality MT—Some Methodological and Technological Reflections." *Proceedings of the 10th Workshop of the European Association for Machine Translation: Practical Applications of Machine Translation*, Budapest, Hungary, pp. 198–204.

Pigott, Ian M. (1982). "The Importance of Feedback from Translators in the Development of High-quality Machine Translation." In Veronica Lawson, ed., *Practical Experience of Machine Translation*. Amsterdam: North-Holland Publishing Company, pp. 61–73.

Robertson, Liz and Monique-Paule Tubb (2005). "Quality Street—Comparing the Contrasting European and American Standards for Translation." *Programme of the Annual Conference of the Association of Translation Companies: Surviving and Prospering in a Changing Translation Market*, School of Oriental and African Studies, University of London, England.

Rojas, David M. and Takako Aikawa (2006). "Predicting MT Quality as a Function of the Source Language." *Proceedings of the 5th International Conference on Language Resources and Evaluation (LREC-2006)*, Genoa, Italy.

Rossi, Francesco (1982). "The Impact of Posteditors' Feedback on the Quality of MT." In Veronica Lawson, ed., *Practical Experience of Machine Translation*. Amsterdam: North-Holland Publishing Company, pp. 113–117.

Schuetz, Joerg (1999). "Applying SAE J2450 Translation Quality Metric in Language Evaluation Projects." In *Translating and the Computer 21*. London: The Association for Information Management.

Schutz, Joerg (1999). "Deploying the SAE J2450 Translation Quality Metric in MT Projects." *Proceedings of MT Summit VII: MT in the Great Translation Era*, Singapore.

Serasset, Gilles and Christian Boitet (1999). "UNL-French Deconversion as Transfer and Generation from an Interlingua with Possible Quality Enhancement through Offline Human Interaction." *Proceedings of MT Summit VII: MT in the Great Translation Era*, Singapore.

Thompson, Henry S. (1991). "Automatic Evaluation of Translation Quality: Outline of Methodology and Report on Pilot Experiment." In Kirsten Falkedal, ed., *Proceedings of the Evaluators' Forum*, Institute for the Study of Semantics and Cognition, Geneva, Switzerland.

van Slype, Georges (1979). *Critical Study of Methods for Evaluating the Quality of Machine Translation*. Final Report. Brussels: Bureau Marcel van Dijk [for] European Commission.

Vanni, Michelle and Keith J. Miller (2001). "Scaling the ISLE Framework: Validating Tests of Machine Translation Quality for Multi-dimensional Measurement." In Bente Maegaard, ed., *Proceedings of MT Summit VIII: Machine Translation in the Information Age*, Santiago de Compostela, Spain.

Vanni, Michelle and Keith J. Miller (2001). "Scoring Methods for Multi-dimensional Measurement of Machine Translation Quality." In Bente Maegaard, ed., *Proceedings of MT Summit VIII: Machine Translation in the Information Age*, Santiago de Compostela, Spain, pp. 21–28.

Vogel, Stephen, Sonja Niessen, and Hermann Ney (2000). "Automatic Extrapolation of Human Assessment of Translation Quality." In Bente Maegaard, ed., *Proceedings of the Workshop on Machine Translation Evaluation at LREC-2000*, Athens, Greece.

Walker, Daniel J., David E. Clements, Maki Darwin, and Jan W. Amtrup (2001). "Sentence Boundary Detection: A Comparison of Paradigms for Improving MT Quality." In Bente Maegaard, ed., *Proceedings of MT Summit VIII: Machine Translation in the Information Age*, Santiago de Compostela, Spain.

Weber, Nico (1998). "Machine Translation, Evaluation, and Translation Quality Assessment." In Nico Weber, ed., *Machine Translation: Theory, Applications, and Evaluation: An Assessment of the State-of-the-art*. St. Augustin: Gardez, pp. 47–84.

Wilkinson, Michael (2005). "Using a Specialized Corpus to Improve Translation Quality." *Translation Journal*, Vol. 9, No. 3.

Wilks, Yorick and LATSEC Inc. (1979). *Comparative Translation Quality Analysis*. Final Report. Contract F33657-77-C-0695, LATSEC Inc. La Jolla, California.

Yamauchi, Satoshi (1999). "A Method of Evaluation of the Quality of Translated Text." *Proceedings of MT Summit VII: MT in the Great Translation Era*, Singapore.

Yoshimi, Takehiko (2001). "Improvement of Translation Quality of English Newspaper Headlines by Automatic Pre-editing." *Machine Translation*, Vol. 16, No. 4, pp. 233–250.

Yu, Shiwen, Jiang Xin, and Zhu Xuefeng (1996).〈機器翻譯譯文質量評價的實踐與分析〉(The Practice and Analysis of Machine Translated Texts

Quality Assessment). In Yu Shiwen 俞士汶 and Zhu Xuefeng 朱學鋒, eds.,《計算語言學文集》(*Papers on Computational Linguistics*). Beijing: Department of Computer Science and Technology and Institute of Computational Linguistics, Peking University, pp. 113–120.

Yu, Shiwen, Duan Huiming, and Tian Jianqiu (1998).〈機械文摘自動評測的原理及實現〉(The Theory and Implementation of Automatic Evaluation of Mechanical Abstraction). In Yu Shiwen and Zhu Xuefeng, eds.,《計算語言學文集》(*Papers on Computational Linguistics*), Vol. 3. Beijing: Department of Computer Science and Technology and Institute of Computational Linguistics, Peking University, pp. 149–153.

Zarechnak, Michael (1988). "Complex Procedures for MT Quality." *Proceedings of the 32nd International Conference on Theoretical and Methodological Issues in Machine Translation of Natural Languages* (*TMI-88*), Carnegie Mellon University, Center for Machine Translation, Pittsburgh, Pennsylvania, USA.

Zhu, Jiang and Haifeng Wang (2006). "The Effect of Translation Quality in MT-based Cross-language Information Retrieval." *Proceedings of the Joint Conference of the International Committee on Computational Linguistics and the Association for Computational Linguistics* (*COLING/ACL-2006*), Sydney, Australia.

Translation Rule

Akiba, Yasuhiro, Megumi Ishii, Hussein Almuallim, and Shigeo Kaneda (1995). "Learning English Verb Selection Rules from Hand-made Rules and Translation Examples." *Proceedings of the 6th International Conference on Theoretical and Methodological Issues in Machine Translation* (*TMI-95*), Leuven, Belgium, pp. 206–220.

Almuallim, Hussein, Yasuhiro Akiba, Takefumi Yamazaki, Akio Yokoo, and Shigeo Kaneda (1994). "Two Methods for Learning ALT-J/E Translation Rules from Examples and a Semantic Hierarchy." *Proceedings of the 15th International Conference on Computational Linguistics* (*COLING-94*), Kyoto, Japan, pp. 57–63.

Cicekli, Ilyas and H. Altay Güvenir (1996). "Learning Translation Rules from a Bilingual Corpus." *Proceedings of the 2nd International Conference on New Methods in Language Processing* (*NeMlaP-2*), Ankara, Turkey, pp. 90–97.

Echizen-ya, Hiroshi, Kenji Araki, Yoshio Momouchi, and Koji Tochinai (2000). "Effectiveness of Layering Translation Rules Based on Transition Networks in Machine Translation Using Inductive Learning with Genetic Algorithms." *Proceedings of the International Conference on Machine Translation and Multilingual Applications in the New Millenium (MT-2000)*, University of Exeter, Exeter, England.

Galley, Michel, Mark Hopkins, Kevin Knight, and Daniel Marcu (2004). "What's in a Translation Rule?" *Proceedings of the Human Language Technology Conference/North American Chapter of the Association for Computational Linguistics Annual Meeting (HLT/NAACL-2004)*, Boston, MA, USA.

Jin, Wanying and Robert F. Simmons (1986). "Symmetric Rules for Translation of English and Chinese." *Computers and Translation*, Vol. 1, No. 3, pp. 153–167.

Matsumoto, Yuji and Mihoko Kitamura (1995). "Acquisition of Translation Rules from Parallel Corpora." In Nicolas Nicolov and Ruslan Mitkov, eds., *Recent Advances in Natural Language Processing: Selected Papers from the Conference*. Amsterdam and Philadelphia: John Benjamins Publishing Company, pp. 405–416.

Meyers, Adam, Roman Yangarber, Ralph Grishman, Catherine Macleod, and Antonio Moreno-Sandeval (1998). "Deriving Transfer Rules from Dominance-preserving Alignments." *Proceedings of the 36th Annual Meeting of the Association for Computational Linguistics and 17th International Conference on Computational Linguistics (COLING-ACL-98)*, Montreal, Quebec, Canada, pp. 843–847.

Sato, Kengo and Masakazu Nakanishi (1998). "Maximum Entropy Model Learning of the Translation Rules." *Proceedings of the 36th Annual Meeting of the Association for Computational Linguistics and 17th International Conference on Computational Linguistics (COLING-ACL-98)*, Montreal, Quebec, Canada.

Turcato, Davide, Paul McFetridge, Fred Popowich, and Janine Toole (1999). "A Bootstrap Approach to Automatically Generating Lexical Transfer Rules." *Proceedings of MT Summit VII: MT in the Great Translation Era*, Singapore.

Yang, Jin (1999). "Towards the Automatic Acquisition of Lexical Selection Rules." *Proceedings of MT Summit VII: MT in the Great Translation Era*, Singapore.

Zhu, Jiang and Wang Haifeng (2005). "The Effect of Adding Rules into the

Rule-based MT System." *Proceedings of MT Summit X*, Phuket, Thailand.

Translation Service

Blumenthal, Dalia (2001). "Computer Translation Service Provided by Babylon.com." *International Journal of Translation*, Vol. 13, Nos. 1–2, pp. 195–201.

Flanagan, Mary A. and Philip Jensen (1994). "Machine Translation on CompuServe Forums." *Proceedings of the 1st Conference of the Association for Machine Translation in the Americas: Technology Partnerships for Crossing the Language Barrier* (*AMTA-1*), Columbia, Maryland, USA, p. 228.

Gaspari, Federico (2004). "Controlled Language, Web Usability and Machine Translation Services on the Internet." *International Journal of Translation*, Vol. 16, No. 1, pp. 41–54.

Gaspari, Federico (2004). "Enhancing Free On-line Machine Translation Services." In M. Lee, ed., *Proceedings of the 7th Annual CLUK Research Colloquium*, University of Birmingham, England, pp. 68–74.

Jaekel, Gary (1995). "In the Balance—Ericsson Language Services." In *Translating and the Computer 17*. London: The Association for Information Management.

Jones, Ian (1998). "Managing a Translation Service to Maximize Quality and Efficiency." In *Translating and the Computer 20*. London: The Association for Information Management.

Kirchmann, Heinz, Alassane Ndiaye, and Andreas Klüter (2000). "From a Stationary Prototype to Telephone Translation Services." In Wolfgang Wahlster, ed., *Verbmobil: Foundations of Speech-to-speech Translation*. Berlin: Springer Verlag, pp. 659–669.

Lewis, Terence (1997). "MT as a Commercial Service: Three Case Studies." *Proceedings of MT Summit VI*, San Diego, California, USA, pp. 219–223.

Lueke, Dirk (1995). "MT at SAP—A Successful Integration." In *Translating and the Computer 17*. London: The Association for Information Management.

Magnusson-Murray, Ulla (1985). "Operational Experience of a Machine Translation Service." In Veronica Lawson, ed., *Tools for the Trade*. London: The Association of Information Management, pp. 171–180.

Masion, B. (1995). "Offering MT as a Service from a Profit Center Point of View." *Proceedings of MT Summit V: Machine Translation Conference, Exhibition and Tutorial*, Luxembourg.
McLaughlin, Steve and A. Schmidt (2001). "DTS: A Delivery System for Translation and Translation-Related Services." In *Translating and the Computer 23*. London: The Association for Information Management.
Mehnert, Thorsten (1998). "LCC—Language Consulting Centre." *Proceedings of the 3rd Workshop of the European Association for Machine Translation: Translation Technology: Integration in the Workflow Environment*, Geneva, Switzerland, pp. 85–88.
Nuutila, Pertti (1996). "Roughlate Service for In-house Customers." In *Translating and the Computer 18*. London: The Association for Information Management.
O'Hagan, Minako (1996). "A Teletranslation Service." *The Coming Industry of Teletranslation: Overcoming Communication Barriers through Telecommunication*. Clevedon: Multilingual Matters Ltd., pp. 91–108.
Pyne, Chris (1996). "Making a Service out of MT." In *Translating and the Computer 18*. London: The Association for Information Management.
Robertson, Liz (2004). "Gearing up for New Quality Dawn in Translation Services." *Programme of the Annual Conference of the Association of Translation Companies: Getting in Shape for the Future—Working towards a New Environment for the Translation Profession*, School of Oriental and African Studies, University of London, England.
Roche, Mike (2002). "Web Services for Translation." In *Translating and the Computer 24*. London: The Association for Information Management.
Schubert, Klaus (1996). "Accessing Internet-based Business Communication Services in Your Own Language: Outline of an R&D Effort for Small Enterprises." In *Translating and the Computer 18*. London: The Association for Information Management.
Schubert, Klaus (1997). "Remote Access Translation Services: Software Design with the User in Focus." In *Translating and the Computer 19*. London: The Association for Information Management.
Schütz, Jörg (1996). "Combining Language Technology and Web Technology to Streamline an Automative Hotline Support Service." *Proceedings of the 2nd Conference of the Association for Machine*

Translation in the Americas: Expanding MT Horizons (*AMTA-2*), Montreal, Quebec, Canada, pp. 180–189.
Schütz, Jörg (1996). "Network-based Machine Translation Services." *Proceedings of the 1st Workshop of the European Association for Machine Translation* (*TKE-96*)*: Language Resources, Terminology, Economics, and User Needs*, Vienna, Austria, pp. 147–160.
Tihanyi, László (2005). "MetaMorpho, a New Machine Translation Service." *Proceedings of 10th Annual Conference of the European Association for Machine Translation* (*EAMT-2005*), Budapest, Hungary.
Vasconcellos, Muriel (1989). "The Place of MT in an In-house Translation Service." In Christian Rohrer, ed., *Proceedings of MT Summit II*, Munich, Germany, pp. 158–159.
Waldhör, Klemens (1998). "EPTAS: A Client/Server Based Translation Support System." In *Translating and the Computer 20*. London: The Association for Information Management.
Wheeler, Peter (1995). "Offering Large-system Machine Translation as a Bureau Service." *Proceedings of MT Summit V: Machine Translation Conference, Exhibition and Tutorial*, Luxembourg.
Zervaki, Thei (2002). "Online Free Translation Services." In *Translating and the Computer 24*. London: The Association for Information Management.

Translation Software

AAMT Internet Working Group (2004). "MT Software of Internet Service." *AAMT Journal*, No. 36.
Ananiadou, Sophie (1987). "A Brief Survey of Some Current Operational Systems." In Margaret King, ed., *Machine Translation Today: The State of the Art*. Edinburgh: Edinburgh University Press, pp. 171–191.
Cochard, Jean-Luc (1987). "A Brief Look at a Typical Software Architecture." In Margaret King, ed., *Machine Translation Today: The State of the Art*. Edinburgh: Edinburgh University Press, pp. 117–123.
Coughlin, Josette M. (1990). "MT or CAT: Criteria for the Independent Translator to Select a Computerized System." *Meta*, Vol. 35, No. 2, pp. 455–457.
Downs, Linn Hedwig (1985). "Selecting a Machine Translation Software

Vendor." In Catriona Picken, ed., *Translating and the Computer 7*. London: The Association for Information Management, pp. 75–84.

Edmonds, E. (1984). "A Software Tool for Implementing Machine Translation." *Proceedings of the International Conference on the Methodology and Techniques of Machine Translation*, Cranfield Institute of Technology, Cranfield, England.

Haynes, Colin (1998). "Installing and Using Translation Software." *Breaking Down the Language Barriers*. London: The Association for Information Management, pp. 159–168.

Haynes, Colin (1998). "MT Software around the World." *Breaking Down the Language Barriers*. London: The Association for Information Management, pp. 137–152.

Hutchins, W. John and Walter K. Hartmann (2002). "Compendium of Translation Software: Commercial Machine Translation Systems and Computer-aided Translation Support Tools." European Association for Machine Translation (http://www.eamt.org/compendium. html).

Johnson, Roderick L. and Michael A. Rosner (1984). "Machine Translation and Software Tools." *The Institute for the Study of Semantics and Cognition Tutorial on Machine Translation*, Lugano, Switzerland.

Johnson, Roderick L. and Michael A. Rosner (1987). "Machine Translation and Software Tools." In Margaret King, ed., *Machine Translation Today: The State of the Art*. Edinburgh: Edinburgh University Press, pp. 154–167.

Keil, G. C. (1979). "Machine Translation Software." *Proceedings of the British Computer Society* '79, London, England.

Miller, L. Chris (1994). "Commercial PC-based Machine Translation Software Packages." *Proceedings of the 1st Conference of the Association for Machine Translation in the Americas: Technology Partnerships for Crossing the Language Barrier* (*AMTA-1*), Columbia, Maryland, USA, pp. 242–243.

O'Sullivan, Siegrun (1990). "Problems in Software Translation and How to Avoid Them." In Catriona Picken, ed., *Translating and the Computer 11: Preparing for the Next Decade*. London: The Association for Information Management, pp. 20–23.

Petitpierre, Dominique (1987). "Software Background for Machine Translation: A Glossary." In Margaret King, ed., *Machine Translation Today: The State of the Art*. Edinburgh: Edinburgh University Press, pp. 111–116.

Richmond, Ian M. (1994). "Doing It Backwards: Using Translation Software to Teach Target-language Grammaticality." *Computer Assisted Language Learning*, Vol. 7, pp. 65–78.
Schubert, Klaus (1997). "Remote-access Translation Services: Software Design with the User in Focus." In *Translating and the Computer 19*. London: The Association for Information Management.
Scott, Donia R. (1996). "Computer Support for Authoring Multilingual Software Documentation." In *Translating and the Computer 18*. London: The Association for Information Management.
Wang, Shufeng 王樹峰 and Zhang Yongkui 張永奎 (2002). 〈基於英漢詞典和翻譯軟件的跨語言信息檢索實踐〉 (An Experiment on English-Chinese Cross-language Information Retrieval Using Bilingual Dictionaries and Machine Translation Software). 《第一屆學生計算語言學研討會論文集》 (*SWCL-2002: First Students' Workshop on Computational Linguistics: Proceedings*), Institute of Computational Linguistics, Peking University, Beijing, China, p. 151.

Translation Speed

Allen, Jeffrey (2004). "Translation Speed versus Content Management." *Multilingual Computing and Technology*, No. 62.
Booth, Andrew D. (1961). "Syntactic Processing in Machine Translation and Its Implications for Cost and Speed." In Allen Kent, ed., *Information Retrieval and Machine Translation*. New York: Interscience, Vol. 2, pp. 759–763.
Brown, Antony F. R. (1961). "Flexibility versus Speed." In Harold P. Edmundson, ed., *Proceedings of the National Symposium on Machine Translation*. London: Prentice-Hall, pp. 444–450.

Translation Strategy

Forcada, Mikel L. (2000). "Learning Machine Translation Strategies Using Commercial Systems: Discovering Word-reordering Rules." *Proceedings of MT 2000: Machine Translation and Multilingual Applications in the New Millennium*, Exeter, England, pp. 7–18.
Forcada, Mikel L. (2001). "Learning Machine Translation Strategies Using Commercial Systems: Discovering Word-reordering Rules." *Machine Translation Review*, No. 12, pp. 5–7.

Hutchins, W. John (1986). "Problems, Methods, and Strategies." *Machine Translation: Past, Present and Future*. Chichester: Ellis Horwood, pp. 40–60.

Hutchins, W. John (1986). "Strategies and Methods since the Mid-1960s." *Machine Translation: Past, Present and Future*. Chichester: Ellis Horwood, pp. 174–189.

Hutchins, W. John and Harold L. Somers (1992). "Basic Strategies." *An Introduction to Machine Translation*. London: Academic Press, pp. 69–80.

Kingscott, Geoffrey (1988). "Translator Strategies for Getting the Most out of Word Processing." In Muriel Vasconcellos, ed., *Technology as Translation Strategy*. New York: State University of New York at Binghamton, pp. 14–18.

Pause, Peter E. (1997). "Interlingual Strategies in Translation." In Christa Hauenschild and Susanne Heizmann, eds., *Machine Translation and Translation Theory*. Berlin and New York: Mouton de Gruyter, pp. 175–190.

Pérez-Ortiz, Juan Antonio, and Mikel L. Forcada (2001). "Discovering Machine Translation Strategies beyond Word-for-Word Translation: A Laboratory Assignment." In Bente Maegaard, ed., *Proceedings of MT Summit VIII: Machine Translation in the Information Age*, Santiago de Compostela, Spain, pp. 57–60.

Petzolt, Birte Prahl-Susanne (1997). "Translation Problems and Translation Strategies Involved in Human and Machine Translation: Empirical Studies." In Christa Hauenschild and Susanne Heizmann, eds., *Machine Translation and Translation Theory*. Berlin and New York: Mouton de Gruyter, pp. 123–144.

Tucker, Allen B. (1987). "Current Strategies in Machine Translation Research and Development." In Sergei Nirenburg, ed., *Machine Translation: Theoretical and Methodological Issues*. Cambridge: Cambridge University Press, pp. 22–41.

Vasconcellos, Muriel, ed. (1988). *Technology as Translation Strategy*. New York: State University of New York at Binghamton.

Translation Technology

Abaitua, Joseba (1999). "Is It Worth Learning Translation Technology?" *Proceedings of the 3rd Forum on Translation in Vic. Training*

Translators and Interpreters: New Directions for the Millennium, Universitat de Vic, Vic, Spain.

Abaitua, Joseba (2000). "Is It Worth Learning Translation Technology?" *International Journal of Translation*, Vol. 12, Nos. 1–2, pp. 21–39.

Abaitua, Joseba (2000–2001). "Is It Worth Learning Translation Technology?" *International Journal of Translation*, Vol. 13, Nos. 1–2, pp. 5–14.

Bennis, Michael (2005). "Tools of the Trade—Using Translation Technology to Meet Your Quality Agenda." *Programme of the Annual Conference of the Association of Translation Companies: Surviving and Prospering in a Changing Translation Market*, School of Oriental and African Studies, University of London, England.

Blatt, Achim (1998). "EURAMIS Alignment and Translation Memory Technology." *T&T*, Vol. 1, pp. 74–114.

Bowker, Lynne (2002). *Computer-aided Translation Technology: A Practical Introduction*. Ottawa: University of Ottawa Press.

Bowker, Lynne (2002). "Other New Technologies and Emerging Trends." *Computer-aided Translation Technology: A Practical Introduction*. Ottawa: University of Ottawa Press, pp. 129–140.

Budin, Gerhard (1999). "Integrating Translation Technologies Using SALT." In *Translating and the Computer 21*. London: The Association for Information Management.

Chan, Sin-wai (2004). *A Dictionary of Translation Technology*. Hong Kong: The Chinese University Press.

Chau, Kam Hong Carrie and Irene Ip Kwok Chun (2002). "Chinese IT Terminology Management in Hong Kong." In Chan Sin-wai, ed., *Translation and Information Technology*. Hong Kong: The Chinese University Press, pp. 155–163.

Freivalds, John (1999). "The Technology of Translation." *Management Review*, Vol. 88, No. 7, pp. 48–52.

Hunt, Timothy (2003). "Translation Technology: Failures and Future." *Globalisation Insider*, Vol. 12, No. 1.

Hutchins, W. John (1993). "Latest Developments in Machine Translation Technology: Beginning a New Era in MT Research." *Proceedings of MT Summit IV: International Cooperation for Global Communication*, Kobe, Japan, pp. 11–34.

Hutchins, W. John (1997). "Translation Technology and the Translator." In Catherine Greensmith and Marilyn Vandamme, eds., *Proceedings of the International Conference, Exhibition and AGM ITI Conference*. London: Institute of Translation and Interpreting, pp. 113–120.

Hutchins, W. John (1998). "Translation Technology and the Translator." *Machine Translation Review*, No. 7, pp. 7–19.

Kenny, Dorothy and Andy Way (2001). "Teaching Machine Translation and Translation Technology: A Contrastive Study." In Bente Maegaard, ed., *Proceedings of MT Summit VIII: Machine Translation in the Information Age*, Santiago de Compostela, Spain, pp. 13–17.

Khoutyz, Irina (2006). "Erasing Cultural Boundaries through Technology." *Proceedings of the 6th Portsmouth Translation Conference: Translation Technologies and Culture,* School of Languages and Area Studies, University of Portsmouth, England.

Kingscott, Geoffrey (1996). "The Impact of Technology and the Implications for Teaching." In Cay Dollerup and Vibeke Appel, eds., *Teaching Translation and Interpreting 3: New Horizons*. Amsterdam and Philadelphia: John Benjamins Publishing Company, pp. 295–300.

Korkas, Vassilis (2006). "The Impact of Technology on Translator Training: Translation Product v. Translation Process." *Proceedings of the 6th Portsmouth Translation Conference: Translation Technologies and Culture*, School of Languages and Area Studies, University of Portsmouth, England.

Lockwood, Rose, Jean Leston, and Laurent Lachal (1995). *Globalisation: Creating New Markets with Translation Technology*. London: Ovum Ltd.

Macklovitch, Elliott (2001). "Recent Trends in Translation Technology." *Proceedings of the 2nd International Conference: The Translation Industry Today—Multilingual Documentation, Technology, Market*, Bologna, Italy, pp. 23–47.

Mason, Jane and Adriane Rinsche (1995). *Ovum Evaluates: Translation Technology Products*. London: Ovum Ltd.

McCallum, Bob (2004). "Translation Technology at the United Nations." *Localisation Reader 2004–2005*.

Melby, Alan K. (1998). "Eight Types of Translation Technology." *Proceedings of the 39th Annual Conference of the American Translators Association*, Hilton Head Island, South Carolina, USA.

Murphy, Dawn (2000). "Keeping Translation Technology under Control." *Machine Translation Review*, No. 11, pp. 7–9.

O'Brien, Sharon (1999). "Translation Technology—The Next

Generation." In *Translating and the Computer 21*. London: The Association for Information Management.
O'Brien, Sharon and Dorothy Kenny (2001). "In Dublin's Fair City: Teaching Translation Technology at Dublin City University." *Language International*, Vol. 13, No. 5, pp. 20–23.
Pellet, Mercedes (2001). "Using Technology Wisely in Language Services." *Multilingual Computing and Technology*, Vol. 12, No. 4, pp. 55–56.
Rinschet, Adriane (1995). "Translation Technology—A Survey of Latest Product Developments." *Proceedings of MT Summit V: Machine Translation Conference, Exhibition and Tutorial*, Luxembourg.
Rohrer, Christian (1993). "The Future of MT Technology." *Proceedings of MT Summit IV: International Cooperation for Global Communication*, Kobe, Japan, pp. 195–196.
Samuelsson-Brown, Geoffrey (1996). "New Technology for Translators." In Rachel Owens, ed., *The Translator's Handbook*, 3rd ed. London: The Association for Information Management, pp. 279–293.
Schäfer, Ulrich and Daniel Beck (2006). "Automatic Testing and Evaluation of Multilingual Language Technology Resources and Components." *Proceedings of the 5th International Conference on Language Resources and Evaluation* (*LREC-2006*), Genoa, Italy.
Scherf, Willi G. (1992). "Training, Talent and Technology." In Cay Dollerup and Anne Loddegaard, eds., *Teaching Translation and Interpreting: Training, Talent and Experience*. Amsterdam and Philadelphia: John Benjamins Publishing Company, pp. 153–160.
Shih, Chung-ling (2006). "Modifying Current Translation Teaching with the Assistance of MT and TM Technologies." *Helpful Assistance to Translators: MT & TM*. Taipei: Bookman Books Ltd., pp. 344–360.
Shih, Chung-ling (2006). "Technological Turn and Its Effects upon Translation." *Helpful Assistance to Translators: MT & TM*. Taipei: Bookman Books Ltd., pp. 69–96.
Somers, Harold L. (2003). "Translation Technologies and Minority Languages." In Harold Somers, ed., *Computers and Translation: A Translator's Guide*. Amsterdam and Philadelphia: John Benjamins Publishing Company, pp. 87–103.
Vasconcellos, Muriel, ed. (1988). *Technology as Translation Strategy*. New York: State University of New York at Binghamton.
Yuste, Elia (2000). "Translation Instruction in the Y2K—Electronic

Corpora, Internet, and Translation Technology." *Proceedings of the 7th Conference of the International Society for the Study of European Ideas (ISSEI-2000), Workshop 501: Teaching Translation in the Information Age,* Bergen, Norway.

Translation Template

Auerswald, Marko (2000). "Example-based Machine Translation with Templates." In Wolfgang Wahlster, ed., *Verbmobil: Foundations of Speech-to-speech Translation*. Berlin: Springer Verlag, pp. 418–427.

Carl, Michael (1999). "Inducing Translation Templates for Example-based Machine Translation." *Proceedings of MT Summit VII: MT in the Great Translation Era*, Singapore, pp. 250–258.

Cicekli, Ilyas and H. Altay Güvenir (2003). "Learning Translation Templates from Bilingual Translation Examples." In Michael Carl and Andy Way, eds., *Recent Advances in Example-based Machine Translation*. Dordrecht: Kluwer Academic Publishers, pp. 255–286.

Güvenir, H. Altay and Ilyas Cicekli (1998). "Learning Translation Templates from Examples." *Information Systems*, Vol. 23, pp. 353–363.

Kaji, Hiroyuki, Yuuko Kida, and Yasutsugu Morimoto (1992). "Learning Translation Templates from Bilingual Text." *Proceedings of the 14th International Conference of Computational Linguistics* (*COLING-92*), Nantes, France, pp. 672–678.

Kinoshita, Satoshi, Akira Kumano, and Hideki Hirakawa (1994). "Improvement in Customizability Using Translation Templates." *Proceedings of the 15th International Conference on Computational Linguistics* (*COLING-94*), Kyoto, Japan, pp. 25–30.

Öz, Zeynep and Ilyas Cicekli (1998). "Ordering Translation Templates by Assigning Confidence Factors." In David L. Farwell, Laurie Gerber, and Eduard Hovy, eds., *Machine Translation and the Information Soup*. Berlin: Springer Verlag, pp. 51–61.

Qian, Yueliang 錢躍良 and Liu Kaiying 劉開瑛 (2001).〈農作物模板自動生成的技術研究〉(Research on the Automatic Generation of Agricultural Products Templates). In Huang Changning 黃昌寧 and Zhang Pu 張普, eds.,《自然語言理解與機器翻譯》(*Natural Language Understanding and Machine Translation*). Beijing: Tsinghua University Press, pp. 198–203.

Yao, Tianshun 姚天順, Yang Erbao 楊二寶, Zhang Le 張樂, and Lü Xueqiang 呂學強 (2002). "The Method of Similar Template for Spoken Language Chinese-English MT System." In Yu Shiwen, ed., *Proceedings of the 2nd China-Japan Natural Language Processing Joint Research Promotion Conference (CJNLP-2002)*. Beijing: Institute of Computational Linguistics, Peking University, pp. 96–103.

Zheng, Baoshan 鄭保山, Liu Qun 劉群, and Zhang Xiang 張祥 (1999).〈機器翻譯模板的建立原則和方法〉(Establishing Principles and Methods of the Templates for Machine Translation). In Huang Changning 黃昌寧 and Dong Zhendong 董振東, eds.,《計算機語言學文集》(*Essays on Computational Linguistics*). Beijing: Tsinghua University Press, pp. 299–304.

Translation Theory

Amtrup, Jan W. (1997). "Perspectives for Incremental MT with Charts." In Christa Hauenschild and Susanne Heizmann, eds., *Machine Translation and Translation Theory*. Berlin-New York: Mouton de Gruyter, pp. 211–222.

Hauenschild, Christa and Susanne Heizmann, eds. (1997). *Machine Translation and Translation Theory*. Berlin-New York: Mouton de Gruyter.

Riabtseva, Nadeshda K. (1987). "Machine Translation Output and Translation Theory." *Computers and Translation*, Vol. 2, No. 1, pp. 37–43.

Translation Tool

Adab, Beverly (2002). "The Internet and Other IT Resources: Tools for Translators within a Translation Programme." In Chan Sin-wai, ed., *Translation and Information Technology*. Hong Kong: The Chinese University Press, pp. 133–153.

Ahrenberg, Lars and Magnus Merkel (1996). "On Translation Corpora and Translation Support Tools: A Project Report." In Karin Aijmer, Bengt Alterberg, and Mats Johansson, eds., *Languages in Contrast*. Lund: Lund University Press, pp. 183–200.

Al-Shehari, Khalid (2006). "The Use of Electronic Tools in Solving Culturally-oriented Problems from the Perspective of Professional Translators." *Proceedings of the 6th Portsmouth Translation*

Conference: Translation Technologies and Culture, School of Languages and Area Studies, University of Portsmouth, England.

Amtrup, Jan W., Karine Megerdoomian, and Rémi Zajac (1999). "Rapid Development of Translation Tools." *Proceedings of MT Summit VII: MT in the Great Translation Era*, Singapore.

Amtrup, Jan W., Karine Megerdoomian, and Rémi Zajac (2000). "Rapid Development of Translation Tools: Application to Persian and Turkish." *Proceedings of the 18th International Conference on Computational Linguistics* (*COLING-2000*), Saarbrücken, Germany, pp. 982–986.

Amtrup, Jan W. and Rémi Zajac (2000). "A Modular Toolkit for Machine Translation Based on Layered Charts." *Proceedings of the 18th International Conference on Computational Linguistics* (*COLING-2000*), Saarbrucken, Germany.

Andersen, Paul (1999). "Tools for the CEEC Languages, An Overview." *Proceedings of the 4th Workshop of the European Association for Machine Translation: EU and the New Languages: Translation—Possibilities, Policies and Practicalities*, Prague, the Czech Republic.

Austermühl, Frank (2001). "Corpora as Translation Tools." *Electronic Tools for Translators.* Manchester: St. Jerome Publishing Company, pp. 124–133.

Austermühl, Frank (2001). *Electronic Tools for Translators.* Manchester: St. Jerome Publishing Company.

Austermühl, Frank (2001). "The World on a Disk—Translation Resources on CD-ROM." *Electronic Tools for Translators.* Manchester: St. Jerome Publishing Company, pp. 90–101.

Balkan, Lorna (1992). "Translation Tools." *Meta*, Vol. 37, No. 3, pp. 408–420.

Brace, Colin (1997). "Translation Tools: To Use or Not to Use?" *Proceedings of the 2nd Workshop of the European Association for Machine Translation: Language Technology in Your Organization?* University of Copenhagen, Copenhagen, Denmark, p. 33.

Cassar, Nigel (1990). "Computer Tools to Improve the Work of Translators." In Catriona Picken, ed., *Translating and the Computer 11: Preparing for the Next Decade.* London: The Association for Information Management, pp. 29–38.

Castellano, Lanna (1983). "The Practical Tools Employed." In Catriona Picken, ed., *The Translator's Handbook.* London: The Association of Information Management, pp. 47–49.

Chanod, Jean-Pierre (1998). "Multilingual Tools at the Xerox Research Centre." *Proceedings of the 3rd Workshop of the European Association for Machine Translation: Translation Technology: Integration in the Workflow Environment*, Geneva, Switzerland, pp. 73–84.

Civera, Jorge, Antonio L. Lagarda, Elsa Cubel, Francisco Casacuberta, Enrique Vidal, Juan M. Vilar, and Sergio Barrachina (2005). "A Computer-assisted Translation Tool Based on Finite-state Technology." *Proceedings of the 11th Workshop of the European Association for Machine Translation: Machine Translation/ Translation Aids—Tools to Increase Quality and to Save Money*, the University of Oslo, Norway.

Colson, Jean-Pierre (2005). "A New Computational Tool for Analyzing Translation Process: The TransCorrect Project." *Meta*, No. 50, No. 2, pp. 573–579.

de Gregorio-Godeo, Eduardo and Silvia Molina-Plaza (2006). "Exploring the Culture-technology Interface in the Design of Translation Tools: Creating an English-Spanish/Spanish-English Dictionary of Phaseological Units." *Proceedings of the 6th Portsmouth Translation Conference: Translation Technologies and Culture,* School of Languages and Area Studies, University of Portsmouth, England.

Dimitrakaki, Vasiliki (2006). "Google: A Powerful Tool in the Hands of the Translator or Just an Illusion?" *Proceedings of the 6th Portsmouth Translation Conference: Translation Technologies and Culture*, School of Languages and Area Studies, University of Portsmouth, England.

European Commission, Translation DG (2004). "Translation Tools and Workflow." Directorate-General for Translation of the European Commission.

Feng, Zhiwei 馮志偉 (2004).〈因特網上的翻譯工具〉(Translation Tools on the Internet).《機器翻譯研究》(*Studies on Machine Translation*). Beijing: China Translation and Publishing Corporation, pp. 750–772.

Feng, Zhiwei (2006). "The Role of Translation Tools in the Information Age." *Programme of an International Conference on Computer-aided Translation: Theory and Practice*, Department of Translation, The Chinese University of Hong Kong, Hong Kong.

Fersøe, Hanne (1997). "Why Don't They Use Translation Tools?" *Proceedings of the 2nd Workshop of the European Association for Machine Translation: Language Technology in Your Organization?* University of Copenhagen, Copenhagen, Denmark, pp. 42–52.

Flournoy, Raymond S. and Chris Callison-Burch (2001). "Secondary Benefits of Feedback and User Interaction in Machine Translation Tools." In Bente Maegaard, ed., *Proceedings of MT Summit VIII: Machine Translation in the Information Age*, Santiago de Compostela, Spain.

Fulford, Heather (2001). "Translation Tools: An Exploratory Study of Their Adoption by UK Freelance Translators." *Machine Translation*, Vol. 16, No. 4, pp. 219–232.

Gross, Alex (1992). "Limitation of Computers as Translation Tools." In John Newton, ed., *Computers in Translation: A Practical Appraisal*. London and New York: Routledge, pp. 96–130.

Hutchins, W. John (1999). "The Development and Use of Machine Translation Systems and Computer-based Translation Tools." *Proceedings of an International Conference on Machine Translation and Computer Language Information Processing*, Beijing, China.

Hutchins, W. John (2003). "The Development and Use of Machine Translation Systems and Computer-based Translation Tools." *International Journal of Translation*, Vol. 15, No. 1, pp. 5–26.

Isabelle, Pierre (1993). "Translation Analysis and Translation Support Tools." *Proceedings of the 13th International Conference on Artificial Intelligence, Expert Systems and Natural Language*, Avignon, France.

Kalantzi, Dimitra (2002). "Teaching MT/CAT Tools in Greece: The State of the Art." *Proceedings of the 6th EAMT Workshop Teaching Machine Translation*, Manchester, England, pp. 33–42.

Kenny, Dorothy (1999). "CAT Tools in an Academic Environment: What Are They Good for?" *Target*, Vol. 11, No. 1, pp. 65–82.

King, Margaret (1999). "TransRouter: A Decision Support Tool for Translation Managers." *Proceedings of MT Summit VII: MT in the Great Translation Era*, Singapore.

Kugler, Marianne, Khurshid Ahmad, and Gregor Thurmair, eds. (1991). "New Tools for Human Translators." Special Issue, *Machine Translation*, Vol. 12, Nos. 1–2.

Lawson, Veronica, ed. (1985). *Tools for the Trade: Translating and the Computer 5*. London: The Association for Information Management.

Lewis, Terence (1997). "When Not to Use MT and Other Translation Tools." *Proceedings of the 2nd Workshop of the European Association for Machine Translation: Language Technology in Your Organization?* University of Copenhagen, Copenhagen, Denmark, pp. 34–41.

Llitjós, Ariadna Font and Jaime G. Carbonell (2004). "The Translation Correction Tool: English-Spanish User Studies." *Proceedings of the Workshop on the Amazing Utility of Parallel and Comparable Corpora, the 4th International Conference on Language Resources and Evaluation* (*LREC-2004*), Lisbon, Portugal.

Maegaard, Bente (1997). "Evaluation of Language Tools." In *Translating and the Computer 19*. London: The Association for Information Management.

Macklovitch, Elliott and Marie-Louise Hannan (1998). "Line 'Em Up: Advances in Alignment Technology and Their Impact on Translation Support Tools." *Machine Translation*, Vol. 13, No. 1, pp. 41–57.

Merkel, Magnus (1996). "Checking Translations for Inconsistency—A Tool for the Editor." *Proceedings of the 2nd Conference of the Association for MMT in the Americas*, Montreal, Quebec, Canada, pp. 157–167.

Nogueira, Danilo (2002). "Translation Tools Today: A Personal View." *Translation Journal*, Vol. 6, No. 1.

O'Brien, Sharon (1998). "Practical Experience of Computer-aided Translation Tools in the Localization Industry." In Lynne Bowker, Michael Cronin, Dorothy Kenny, and Jennifer Pearson, eds., *Unity in Diversity? Current Trends in Translation Studies*. Manchester: St. Jerome Publishing, pp. 115–122.

Peters, Carol and Eugenio Picchi (1998). "Computational Tools for the Translator." *Netvaerk LSP SSP, Fagsprogsforskningen I Norden, Nyhedsbrev*, Vol. 1, pp. 1–10.

Poeiras, Fábio (2005). "Translation Tools—Translation Will Never Be the Same Again: An Overview of Current Translation Tool Technologies and New Trends in Translation." *Translating Today*, No. 2.

Rico Pérez, Celia (2001). "Reproducible Models for CAT Tools Evaluation: A User-oriented Perspective." In *Translating and the Computer 23*. London: The Association for Information Management.

Savourel, Yves (2000). "Ensuring Translation Tools Are TMX Compliant." *MultiLingual Computing and Technology*, Vol. 11, No. 31, Issue 3, pp. 47–49.

Shadbolt, David (2002). "Finding the Right Language Technology Tools." *Multilingual Computing and Technology*, Language Technology Supplement, Vol. 13, No. 7.

Sokolova, Svetlana (1995). "The Tools for Adapting a Machine

Translation System to Individual Needs." In *Translating and the Computer 17*. London: The Association for Information Management.
Stoeller, Willem (1997). "How Translation Tools Help." *MultiLingual Communications and Technology*, Vol. 14, No. 3, pp. 26–29.
Stoll, Cay-Holger (1988). "Translation Tools on PC." In Catriona Picken, ed., *Translating and the Computer 9: Potential and Practice*. London: The Association for Information Management, pp. 11–26.
Theologitis, Dimitri (1998). "Language Tools at the EC Translation Service: The Theory and the Practice." In *Translating and the Computer 20*. London: The Association for Information Management.
Thurmair, Gregor (1997). "Exchange Interfaces for Translation Tools." *Machine Translation Summit VI*, San Diego, CA, USA, pp. 74–93.
von Kleist-Retzow, Beate, Marianne Kugler, Gabriele Stallwitz, and Klemens Waldhör (1995). "Integrating Translation Resources and Tools." In Marianne Kugler, Khurshid Ahmad, and Gregor Thurmair, eds., *Translator's Workbench*. Berlin: Springer Verlag, pp. 157–167.
Zarechnak, Michael (1988). "The Tradition of MT as an Information Tool." *Proceedings of the 29th Annual Conference of the American Translators Association*, Seattle, Washington. Medford, New Jersey: Learned Information Inc., pp. 103–118.
Zetzsche, Jost (2003). "TMX Implementation in Major Translation Tools." *Multilingual Computing and Technology*, Vol. 14, No. 2, pp. 23–27.

Translation Unit

Bennett, Paul A. (1993). "The Translation Unit in Human and Machine." *Babel*, Vol. 40, No. 1, pp. 12–20.
Lewis, Amber L. (1997). "The Practical Implications of a Minimum Machine Translation Unit." *Babel*, Vol. 43, No. 2, pp. 138–150.
Yamamoto, Kaoru, Yuji Matsumoto, and Mihoko Kitamura (2001). "A Comparative Study on Translation Units for Bilingual Lexicon Extraction." *Proceedings of the Workshop on Data-driven Machine Translation, 39th Annual Meeting and 10th Conference of the European Chapter of the Association for Computational Linguistics*, Toulouse, France, pp. 87–95.

Translation Validation

Macklovitch, Elliott (1994). "Using Bi-textual Alignment for Translation Validation: The TransCheck System." *Technology Partnerships for Crossing the Language Barrier: Proceedings of the 1st Conference of the Association for Machine Translation in the Americas*, Columbia, Maryland, USA, pp. 157–164.

Macklovitch, Elliott (1995). "Can Terminology Consistency Be Validated Automatically?" *The IVes Journées Scientifiques, Lexicommatique et Dictionnairiques*, Lyon, AUPELF-UREF.

Translation Workflow

Attnäs, Mats, Pierre Senellart, and Jean Senellart (2005). "Integration of SYSTRAN MT Systems in an Open Workflow." *Proceedings of MT Summit X*, Phuket, Thailand.

Blatt, Achim (1998). "Workflow Using Linguistic Technology at the Translation Service of the European Commission." *Proceedings of the 3rd Workshop of the European Association for Machine Translation: Translation Technology: Integration in the Workflow Environment*, Geneva, Switzerland, pp. 7–18.

Brundage, Jennifer A., Susan McCormick, and Chris Pyne (1997). "Managing Distributed MT Projects Today—A New Challenge." *Proceedings of MT Summit VI*, San Diego, California, USA.

Calvert, David (2005). "Translation of Magazines and Brochures Using a Tagged RTF File Workflow." In *Translating and the Computer 27*. London: The Association for Information Management.

Carroll, Sarah (2000). "Introducing the TRADOS Workflow Development." In *Translating and the Computer 22*. London: The Association for Information Management.

Clarke, Anthony (2000). "MT within a Productive Translation Workflow." *Proceedings of the 5th Workshop of the European Association for Machine Translation: Harvesting Existing Resources*, Lubljana, Slovenia.

Drugan, Joanna (2004). "Multilingual Document Management and Workflow in the European Institutions." In *Translating and the Computer 26*. London: The Association for Information Management.

European Commission, Translation DG (2004). *Translation Tools and*

Workflow. Directorate-General for Translation of the European Commission.
Lafullarde, Anne (2006). "Deployment of a Translation Workflow at Fortis AG: The Hybrid MT-TM Translation Model at Work in a Down-to-earth Translation Department in an Insurance Company." *Proceedings of the Localization World Conference*, Barcelona, Spain.
Hartley, Tony and Klaus Schubert (1998). "From Testbench to Workflow: Relocating MT in Education and Training." In *Translating and the Computer 20*. London: The Association for Information Management.
Kaeser, Paul (1998). "Workflow Automation of Translation Projects." *Proceedings of the 3rd Workshop of the European Association for Machine Translation: Translation Technology: Integration in the Workflow Environment*, Geneva, Switzerland, pp. 41–44.
King, Maghi (1998). "Workflow, Computer Aids and Organizational Issues." *Proceedings of the 3rd Workshop of the European Association for Machine Translation: Translation Technology: Integration in the Workflow Environment*, Geneva, Switzerland, pp. 29–39.
Röthlisberger-Käser, Monika (2002). "CLS Workflow—A Translation Workflow System." In *Translating and the Computer 24*. London: The Association for Information Management.
Schubert, Klaus (1999). "Resource and Workflow Management Support in Teletranslation." In *Translating and the Computer 21*. London: The Association for Information Management.
Schütz, Jörg (1998). "Multilingual Human Language Technology in Automotive Documentation Workflows." In *Translating and the Computer 20*. London: The Association for Information Management.
Stadler, Hans-Udo (2005). "Lexicon-coding Workflow at CLS Communication." *Proceedings of the 10th Workshop of the European Association for Machine Translation: Practical Applications of Machine Translation*, Budapest, Hungary, pp. 255–261.
Yamamoto, Y. (2005). "Toward Translation Engineering—Introducing SATILA, an MT+TM Translation Workflow." *AAMT Journal*, Vol. 37.

❖ PART 36 ❖

Translation Memory

Translation Memory

Allen, Jeffrey (1999). "Adapting the Concept of TM to Authoring Memory for Controlled Language Writing Environment." In *Translating and the Computer 21*. London: The Association for Information Management.

Andrés Lange, Carmen and Winfield S. Bennett (2000). "Combining Machine Translation with Translation Memory at Baan." In Robert C. Sprung, ed., *Translating into Success: Cutting-edge Strategies for Going Multilingual in a Global Age*. Amsterdam and Philadelphia: John Benjamins Publishing Company, pp. 201–218.

Benis, Michael (1999). "Translation Memory from O to R." *ITI Bulletin*, April, pp. 4–19.

Benis, Michael (2003). "Much More Than Memories." *ITI Bulletin*, November-December.

Berry, Mark (1995). "Who Owns Translation Memory?" *MCB News*, No. 10.

Bowker, Lynne (2006). "Translation Memory and 'Text'." In Lynne Bowker, ed., *Lexicography, Terminology, and Translation: Text-based Studies in Honour of Ingrid Meyer*. Ottawa: University of Ottawa Press, pp. 175–187.

Brockmann, Daniel (1997). "TR06: Controlled Language and Translation Memory: A Perfect Match to Save Translation Cost." *TC-Forum Translation Issues,* No. 4.

Bruckner, Christine and Mirko Plitt (2001). "Evaluating the Operational Benefit of Using Machine Translation Output as Translation Memory Input." In Bente Maegaard, ed., *Proceedings of MT Summit VIII: Machine Translation in the Information Age*, Santiago de Compostela, Spain.

Bugel-Shunra, Dena (2002). "T-Remote Memory (New Framework for Sharing Translation Memory)." *Multilingual Computing and Technology*, Vol. 13, No. 6.

Callison-Burch, Chris (2004). "Searchable Translation Memories." In *Translating and the Computer 26*. London: The Association for Information Management.

Callison-Burch, Chris, Colin Bannard, and Josh Schroeder (2005). "A Compact Data Structure for Searchable Translation Memories." *Proceedings of the 10th Workshop of the European Association for Machine Translation: Practical Applications of Machine Translation*, Budapest, Hungary, pp. 59–65.

Calvert, David (2005). "Translation of Magazines and Brochures Using a Tagged RTF File Workflow." In *Translating and the Computer 27*. London: The Association for Information Management.

Carl, Michael and Silvia Hansen (1999). "Linking Translation Memories with Example-based Machine Translation." *Proceedings of MT Summit VII: MT in the Great Translation Era*, Singapore, pp. 617–624.

Champollion, Yves (2006). "Very Large Translation Memories: Is the Free Model Viable?" In *Translating and the Computer 28*. London: The Association for Information Management.

Cranias, Lambros, Harris Papageorgiou, and Stelios Piperidis (1997). "Example Retrieval from a Translation Memory." *Natural Language Engineering*, Vol. 3, pp. 255–277.

Cruz-Lara, Samuel, Nadia Bellalem, Julien Ducret, and Isabelle Kramer (2006). "Interoperability between Translation Memories and Localization Tools by Using the Multilingual Information Framework." *Proceedings of the 11th Workshop of the European Association for Machine Translation: Machine Translation/Translation Aids—Tools to Increase Quality and to Save Money*, the University of Oslo, Norway.

Fabricz, Karoly (2005). "Developing Translation Memories." *Translation Today*, No. 3, pp. 34–36.

Gordon, Ian (1997). "The TM Revolution—What Does It Really Mean?" In *Translating and the Computer 19*. London: The Association for Information Management.

Gow, Francie (2004). "Extracting Useful Information from TM Databases." *Localisation Reader 2004–2005*.

Grönroos, Mickel and Ari Becks (2005). "Bringing Intelligence to Translation Memory Technology." In *Translating and the Computer 27*. London: The Association for Information Management.

Heyn, Matthias (1996). "Integrating Machine Translation into Translation Memory Systems." *Proceedings of the 1st Workshop of the European Association for Machine Translation (TKE-96): Language Resources, Terminology, Economics, and User Needs*, Vienna, Austria, pp. 113–126.

Heyn, Matthias (1998). "Translation Memories: Insights and Prospects." In Lynne Bowker, Michael Cronin, Dorothy Kenny, and Jennifer Pearson, eds., *Unity in Diversity? Current Trends in Translation Studies*. Manchester: St. Jerome Publishing, pp. 123–136.

Hodász, Gábor, Balázs Kis, and Tamás Gröbler (2004). "Translation Memory as a Robust Example-based Translation System." *Proceedings of the 9th Workshop of the European Association for Machine Translation: Broadening Horizons of Machine Translation and Its Applications*, Foundation for International Studies, Malta, pp. 82–89.

Hummel, Jochen (2005). "TM, TRADOS and SDL. What's Next?" In *Translating and the Computer 27*. London: The Association for Information Management.

Humphreys, Lee (1996). "Use of Linguistic Resources Like Translation Memories in Machine Translation Systems." *Proceedings of the 1st Workshop of the European Association for Machine Translation (TKE-96): Language Resources, Terminology, Economics, and User Needs*, Vienna, Austria, pp. 101–110.

Iverson, Steve (2004). "Working with Translation Memory." *Localisation Reader 2004–2005*.

Jian, Jia-Yan, Yu-Chia Chang, and Jason S. Chang (2004). "Collocational Translation Memory Extraction Based on Statistical and Linguistic Information." *Proceedings of the International Conference on Research in Computational Linguistics (ROCLING-XVI)*, Taipei, Taiwan.

Lagoudaki, Elina (2006). "Translation Memories Survey 2006: Users' Perceptions around TM Usage." In *Translating and the Computer 28*. London: The Association for Information Management.

Lange, Carmen Andres and Winfield S. Bennett (2000). "Combining Machine Translation with Translation Memory at Baan." In Robert C. Sprung, ed., *Translating into Success: Cutting-edge Strategies for Going Multilingual in a Global Age*. Amsterdam and Philadelphia: John Benjamins Publishing Company, pp. 203–218.

Le Meur, André and Marie-Jeanne Derouin (2006). "Lemma-oriented Dictionaries, Concept-oriented Terminology and Translation Memories." *Proceedings of the 5th International Conference on Language Resources and Evaluation (LREC-2006)*, Genoa, Italy.

Leplus, Thomas, Philippe Langlais, and Guy Lapalme (2004). "Weather Report Translation Using a Translation Memory." In Robert E. Frederking and Kathryn B. Taylors, eds., *Machine Translation: From Real Users to Research*. Berlin: Springer Verlag, pp. 154–163.

Levitt, Garry (2004). "New Developments in TM Sharing." *Multilingual Computing and Technology*, Vol. 15, No. 7.

Macdonald, K. (2001). "Improving Automatic Alignment for Translation Memory Creation." In *Translating and the Computer 23*. London: The Association for Information Management.

Macklovitch, Elliott, Michel Simard, and Philippe Langlais (2000). "TransSearch: A Free Translation Memory on the World Wide Web." In Maria Gavrilidou, George Carayannis, Stella Markantonatou, Stelios Piperidas, and Gregory Stainhaouer, eds., *Proceedings of the 2nd International Conference on Language Resources and Evaluation*. Paris: ELRA, Vol. 3, pp. 1201–1208.

MacKlovitch, Elliott (2000). "Two Types of Translation Memory." In *Translating and the Computer 22*. London: The Association for Information Management.

Macklovitch, Elliott and Graham Russell (2000). "What's Been Forgotten in Translation Memory." In John S. White, ed., *Envisioning Machine Translation in the Information Future*. Berlin: Springer Verlag, pp. 137–146.

Mbaeyi, P. N. O. (1984). "What Is the Language of Memory?" *Proceedings of the International Conference on the Methodology and Techniques of Machine Translation*, Cranfield Institute of Technology, Cranfield, England.

McTait, Kevin and Arturo Trujillo (1999). "A Building Blocks Approach to Translation Memory." In *Translating and the Computer 21*, London: The Association for Information Management.

Musale, Shailendra (2004). "Getting More from Translation Memories." *Localisation Reader 2004–2005*.

O'Leary, Tara (2000). "Memory-based Translation: Using Translation Memory Tools, from a Freelancer's Perspective." In *Translating and the Computer 22*. London: The Association for Information Management.

Planas, Emmanuel and Osamu Furuse (1999). "Formalizing Translation Memories." *Proceedings of MT Summit VII: MT in the Great Translation Era*, Singapore, pp. 331–339.

Planas, Emmanuel (2000). "Extending Translation Memories." *Proceedings of the 5th Workshop of the European Association for Machine Translation: Harvesting Existing Resources*, Lubljana, Slovenia.

Planas, Emmanuel and Osamu Furuse (2003). "Formalizing Translation Memory." In Michael Carl and Andy Way, eds., *Recent Advances in*

Example-based Machine Translation. Dordrecht: Kluwer Academic Publishers, pp. 157–188.

Rapp, Reinhard (2002). "A Part-of-speech-based Search Algorithm for Translation Memories." *Proceedings of the 3rd International Conference on Language Resources and Evaluation* (*LREC-2002*), Las Palmas de Gran Canaria, Spain, pp. 466–472.

Rode, Tony (2000). "Translation Memory: Friend or Foe?" *International Journal for Language and Documentation*, pp. 12–13.

Schäler, Reinhard (1996). "Machine Translation, Translation Memories and the Phrasal Lexicon: The Localisation Perspective." *Proceedings of the 1st Workshop of the European Association for Machine Translation* (*TKE-96*)*: Language Resources, Terminology, Economics, and User Needs*, Vienna, Austria, pp. 21–33.

Schäler, Reinhard (2001). "Beyond Translation Memories." In Bente Maegaard, ed., *Proceedings of MT Summit VIII: Machine Translation in the Information Age*, Santiago de Compostela, Spain, pp. 49–55.

Shih, Chung-ling (2004).〈翻譯記憶系統訓練〉(Translation Memory Systems Training). In《電腦輔助翻譯》(*MT and TM*). Taibei: The Bookman Press, pp. 179–209.

Shih, Chung-ling (2006). *Helpful Assistance to Translators: MT & TM*. Taipei: Bookman Books Ltd.

Shih, Chung-ling (2006). "Theoretical Studies of MT and TM." In *Helpful Assistance to Translators: MT & TM*. Taipei: Bookman Books Ltd., pp. 2–34.

Shih, Chung-ling (2006). "TM, Technological Features, Pedagogical Benefits and Challenging Problems." In *Helpful Assistance to Translators: MT & TM*. Taipei: Bookman Books Ltd., pp. 35–68.

Shuttleworth, Mark (2002). "Combining MT and TM on a Technology-oriented Translation Masters: Aims and Perspectives." *Proceedings of 6th EAMT Workshop on Teaching Machine Translation*, Manchester, England, pp. 123–129.

Simard, Michel and Philippe Langlais (2001). "Sub-sentential Exploitation of Translation Memories." In Bente Maegaard, ed., *Proceedings of MT Summit VIII: Machine Translation in the Information Age*, Santiago de Compostela, Spain, pp. 335–339.

Simard, Michel (2003). "Translation Spotting for Translation Memories." *Proceedings of the Human Language Technology and North American*

Chapter of Association of Computational Linguistics 2003 (HLT/NAACL-2003), Edmonton, Alberta, Canada.

Somers, Harold L. and Gabriela Fernàndez Diaz (2004). "Translation Memory vs. Example-based MT: What Is the Difference?" *International Journal of Translation*, Vol. 16, No. 2, pp. 5–33.

Tardif, François and Anne Laugesen (2006). "Going Global with the TextBase Translation Memory." In *Translating and the Computer 28*. London: The Association for Information Management.

van Hoof, Antonius, Bernhard Keck, Renate Mayer, Marianne Kugler, and Cornelia Menzel (1995). "Translation Memory." In Marianne Kugler, Khurshid Ahmad, and Gregor Thurmair, eds., *Translator's Workbench*. Berlin: Springer Verlag, pp. 83–99.

Webb, Lynn E. (1999). "Advantages and Disadvantages of Translation Memory: A Cost/Benefit Analysis." MA Thesis. California: Monterey Institute of International Studies.

Wu, Hua, Wang Haifeng, Liu Zhanyi, and Tang Kai (2005). "Improving Translation Memory with Word Alignment Information." *Proceedings of MT Summit X*, Phuket, Thailand.

Zetzsche, Jost (2006). "TM and MT." *Proceedings of the 7th Biennial Conference of the Association for Machine Translation in the Americas (AMTA-2006): Visions for the Future of Machine Translation*, Boston Marriott, Cambridge, MA, USA.

Matching

Garside, Roger (1995). "Matching Words in a Bilingual Corpus." *Machine Translation Review*, No. 2, pp. 7–18.

Zhang, Kaizhong and Dennis Shasha (1997). "Tree Pattern Matching." In Alberto Apostolico and Zvi Galil, eds., *Pattern Matching Algorithms*. New York: Oxford University Press, pp. 341–371.

Fuzzy Match

Zheng, Fengbin 鄭逢斌, Jiang Baoqing 姜保慶, Chen Zhiguo 陳志國, Guo Zhengwei 郭拯危, and Qiao Baojun 喬保軍 (2002).〈語義校對系統中的句子語義骨架〉(Fuzzy Matching Technique by Sentence Skeleton in Semantic Collation System).《第一屆學生計算語言學研討會論文集》*(SWCL-2002: First Students' Workshop on Computational Linguistics:*

Proceedings), Institute of Computational Linguistics, Peking University, Beijing, China, pp. 346–350.

Translation Memory Database

Gow, Francie (2006). "An Evaluation Methodology for Comparing Two Approaches to Search and Retrieval in Translation Memory Databases." In Lynne Bowker, ed., *Lexicography, Terminology, and Translation: Text-based Studies in Honour of Ingrid Meyer*. Ottawa: University of Ottawa Press, pp. 189–199.

Shih, Chung-ling (2006). "The Use of TM Databanks as the Scaffold in Translation Teaching." *Helpful Assistance to Translators: MT & TM*. Taipei: Bookman Books Ltd., pp. 250–275.

Topping, Suzanne (2000). "Sharing Translation Database Information: Considerations for Developing an Ethical and Viable Exchange of Data." *Multilingual Computing and Technology*, Vol. 11, No. 5, pp. 59–61.

Translation Memory Exchange

Briggs, Brian (2000). "TMX Standard Offers Benefits." *MultiLingual Computing and Technology*, Vol. 30, No. 2, pp. 61–63.

Carroll, Sarah (1999). "The Technical Content of TMX 1.1." *MultiLingual Computing and Technology*. Vol. 22, No. 6, pp. 48–49.

Melby, Alan (2006). "Standard Formats for Sharing Terminology and Translation Memories: All You Ever Wanted to Know about the TMX and TBX Standards." *Proceedings of the Localization World Conference*, Barcelona, Spain.

Savourel, Yves (2000). "Ensuring Translation Tools Are TMX Compliant." *MultiLingual Computing and Technology*, Vol. 31, No. 3, pp. 47–49.

Zerfass, Angelika (2003). "Translation Memory Exchange: What It Is, What It Does and What Comes after the Data Exchange." *Proceedings of the Localization World Conference 2003*, Seattle, Washington, DC, USA.

Translation Memory System

Assenat-Falcone, Suzanne (1998). "Review of Four Translation Memory Programs." *Accurapid Translation Journal*, Vol. 1, No. 2.

Assenat-Falcone, Suzanne (2000). "More Translation Memory Tools (Not Many More, But Good Ones)." *Translation Journal*, Vol. 4, No. 2.

Bohm, Edgar (1997). "A Translation Memory System in the University Context—Practical Applications and Didactic Implications." In Eberhard Fleischmann, Wladimir Kutz, and Peter A. Schmitt, eds., *Translationsdidaktik*. Tübingen: Narr, pp. 361–367.

Bowker, Lynne (2002). "Translation-memory Systems." *Computer-aided Translation Technology: A Practical Introduction*. Ottawa: University of Ottawa Press, pp. 92–128.

Falcone, Suzanne (1998). "Translation Aid Software: Four Translation Memory Programs Reviewed." *Translation Journal*, Vol. 2, No. 1.

García, Ignacio (2003). "Standard Bearers: TM Brand Profiles at Lantra-L." *Translation Journal*, Vol. 7, No. 4.

Gerasimov, Andrei (2001). "An Effective and Inexpensive Translation Memory Tool." *Translation Journal*, Vol. 5, No. 3.

Gow, Francie (2003). "Metrics for Evaluating Translation Memory Systems." MA thesis, University of Ottawa.

Heyn, Matthias (1996). "Integrating Machine Translation into Translation Memory Systems." *European Association for Machine Translation: Workshop Proceedings*, Geneva, Switzerland, pp. 111–123.

Heyn, Matthias (1996). "Integrating Machine Translation into Translation Memory Systems." *Proceedings of the 1st Workshop of the European Association for Machine Translation (TKE-96): Language Resources, Terminology, Economics, and User Needs*, Vienna, Austria, pp. 113–126.

Hodász, Gábor (2006). "Evaluation Methods of a Linguistically Enriched Translation Memory System." *Proceedings of the 5th International Conference on Language Resources and Evaluation (LREC-2006)*, Genoa, Italy.

Huang, Jin-xia, Wang Wei, and Zhou Ming (2003). "A Unified Statistical Model for Generalized Translation Memory System." *Proceedings of MT Summit IX*, New Orleans, Louisiana, USA.

Planas, Emmanuel (1999). "Translation Memory Tools: Comparative Studies of Star, Trados, IBM TM2 and Shallow Translation." *Proceedings of the LISA Asia Forum Workshop*, Shanghai, China.

Planas, Emmanuel (2005). "SIMILIS Second-generation Translation Memory Software." In *Translating and the Computer 27*. London: The Association for Information Management.

Ray, Deborah S. and Eric J. Ray (1999). "Good, Fast, Cheap: Translation Memory Systems Offer the Potential for All Three." *Technical Communication*, Vol. 46, No. 2, pp. 280–285.

Shih, Chung-ling (2006). "Development of Multilingual Websites with the Aid of Machine Translation and Translation Memory Tools." *Helpful Assistance to Translators: MT & TM*. Taipei: Bookman Books Ltd., pp. 227–249.

Somers, Harold L. (2003). "Translation Memory Systems." In Harold L. Somers, ed., *Computers and Translation: A Translator's Guide*. Amsterdam and Philadelphia: John Benjamins Publishing Company, pp. 31–47.

Whyman, Edward K. and Harold L. Somers (1999). "Evaluation Metrics for a Translation Memory System." *Software—Practice and Experience*, Vol. 29, pp. 1265–1284.

Zerfass, Angelika (2000). "Evaluating Translation Memory Systems." *Proceedings of the 3rd International Conference on Language Resources and Evaluation* (*LREC-2002*), Las Palmas, Canary Islands, Spain.

Zerfass, Angelika (2002). "Comparing Basic Features of TM Tools." *Multilingual Computing and Technology*, Language Technology Supplement, Vol. 13, No. 7.

❖ PART 37 ❖

Translator's Workstation

Translator's Workbench

Ahmad, Khurshid, Paul Holmes-Higgin, Margaret Rogers, Monika Höge, Khai Le-Hong, Christine Huwig, Ralf Kese, and Renate Mayer (1993). "User-driven Software Development: Translator's Workbench—An Exemplar Case Study." In Michael Smith and Gavriel Salvendy, eds., *Proceedings of the 5th International Conference on Human-Computer Interaction (HCI International-93)*, Orlando, Florida, USA, Vol. 1, pp. 319–324.

Forsdick, Brian (1990). "Managing Translation Projects Using Project Manager Workbench." In Catriona Picken, ed., *Translating and the Computer 11: Preparing for the Next Decade*. London: The Association for Information Management, pp. 3–8.

Heyer, Gerhard (1995). "Introduction." In Marianne Kugler, Khurshid Ahmad, and Gregor Thurmair, eds., *Translator's Workbench*. Berlin: Springer Verlag, p. 3.

Ishida, R. (1994). "Future Translation Workbenches: Some Essential Requirements." *The LISA Forum Newsletter*, Vol. 3, pp. 3–12.

Kugler, Marianne, Gerd Heyer, Ralf Kese, Beate von Kleistretzow, and Guenter Winkelmann (1993). "The Translator's Workbench: An Environment for Multi-lingual Text Processing and Translation." In Sergei Nirenburg, ed., *Progress in Machine Translation*. Amsterdam: IOS and Tokyo: Ohmsha, pp. 185–189.

Kugler, Marianne, Khurshid Ahmad, and Gregor Thurmair, eds. (1995). *Translator's Workbench*. Berlin: Springer Verlag.

Kumar, Akshi (2005). "Design and Development of Translator's Workbench." *Translation Journal*, Vol. 9, No. 3.

Le-Hong, Khai, Monika Höge, and Andrea Hohmann (1992). "User's Point of View of the Translator's Workbench." In *Translating and the Computer*. London: The Association for Information Management, pp. 25–31.

Lewalle, Pierre (1998). "The Translator's Workbench and Beyond: Off-line Add-ons to On-line Tools." *Proceedings of the 3rd Workshop of the European Association for Machine Translation: Translation Technology: Integration in the Workflow Environment*, Geneva, Switzerland, pp. 71–72.

Rinsche, Adriane (1996). "Translator's Workbenches: A Practical Application." *Proceedings of the 1st Workshop of the European*

Association for Machine Translation (TKE-96): Language Resources, Terminology, Economics, and User Needs, Vienna, Austria, pp. 127–136.

Thomas, Patricia (1990). "The Translator's Workbench Project." In Catriona Picken, ed., *Translating and the Computer 11: Preparing for the Next Decade*. London: The Association for Information Management, pp. 9–19.

Thurmair, Gregor (1995). "TWB in the Documentation Context." In Marianne Kugler, Khurshid Ahmad, and Gregor Thurmair, eds., *Translator's Workbench*. Berlin: Springer Verlag, pp. 16–23.

Trujillo, Arturo (1999). "Translator's Workbench and Translation Aids." *Translation Engines: Techniques for Machine Translation*. Berlin and New York: Springer Verlag, pp. 57–82.

Translator's Workstation

Ashizaki, Tatsuo (1995). "Adaptation of JICST's MT System for Workstation and PC's." *Proceedings of MT Summit V: Machine Translation Conference, Exhibition and Tutorial*, Luxembourg.

Bashkansky, Guy and Uzzi Ornan (1998). "Monolingual Translator Workstation." In David L. Farwell, Laurie Gerber, and Eduard Hovy, eds., *Machine Translation and the Information Soup*. Berlin: Springer Verlag, pp. 136–149.

Cohen, A., P. Cousseau, Dean J. Grannes, C. McNeilly, Sergei Nirenburg, P. Shell, and Dieter Waltermann (1993). *Translators WorkStation: User's Manual*. Pittsburg: School of Computer Science, Carnegie Mellon University.

Fulford, Heather and Joaquin Granell-Zafra (2004). "The Freelance Translator's Workstation: An Empirical Investigation." *Proceedings of the 9th Workshop of the European Association for Machine Translation: Broadening Horizons of Machine Translation and Its Applications*, Foundation for International Studies, Malta, pp. 53–61.

Höge, Monika and E. Kroupa (1991). "Towards the Design of a Translator's Workstation—Organisational Background and User Implications." In H.-J. Bullinger, ed., *Human Aspects in Computing: Design and Use of Interactive Systems and Information Management*. Stuttgart: Elsevier, pp. 1036–1040.

Hutchins, W. John (1998). "The Origins of the Translator's Workstation." *Machine Translation*, Vol. 13, No. 4, pp. 287–307.

Jäppinen, Harri, K. Hartonen, Leo Kulikov, A. Nykänen, and Aarne H. Ylä-Rotiala (1993). "KIELIKONE Machine Translation Workstation." In Sergei Nirenburg, ed., *Progress in Machine Translation*, IOS Press.

Jäppinen, Harri, Leo Kulikov, and Aarne H. Ylä-Rotiala (1991). "KIELIKONE Machine Translation Workstation." *Proceedings of MT Summit III*, Seattle, Washington, DC, USA.

Levin, Lori S. (1993). "Translator's Workstations and Language Learner's Workstations." In Sergei Nirenburg, ed., *Progress in Machine Translation*. Amsterdam: IOS and Tokyo: Ohmsha, pp. 287–290.

Macklovitch, Elliott (1989). "An Off-the-shelf Workstation for Translators." In Deanna Lindberg Hammond, ed., *Coming of Age: Proceedings of the 30th Annual Conference of the American Translators Association*. Medford, New Jersey: Learned Information Inc., pp. 491–498.

Macklovitch, Elliott (1993). *PTT-3: A Third Version of the CITI's Workstation for Translators*. Laval, Canada: Centre d'innovation en technologies de l'information.

Melby, Alan K. (1984). "Recipe for a Translator Work Station." *Multilingua*, Vols. 3–4, pp. 225–228.

Melby, Alan K. (1987). "The Translator Workstation in 1987." In Karl Kummer, ed., *Across the Language Gap: Proceedings of the 28th Annual Conference of the American Translators Association*. Medford, New Jersey: Learned Information Inc., pp. 417–424.

Melby, Alan K. (1992). "The Translator Workstation." In John Newton, ed., *Computers in Translation: A Practical Appraisal*. London and New York: Routledge, pp. 147–165.

Melby, Alan K. (1994). "The Translator's Workstation." In Deanna Lindberg Hammond, ed., *Professional Issues for Translators and Interpreters*. Amsterdam and Philadelphia: John Benjamins Publishing Company, pp. 127–147.

Nedoma, Andrew and Jurek Nedoma (2005). "TROFFI—Comprehensive Management System Tailored for a Translation Agency." In *Translating and the Computer 18*. London: The Association for Information Management.

Scherf, Willi G. (1990). "Computer Assisted Translation, the Workstation and the Translator." In Hans Czap and Wolfgang Nedobity, eds.,

Proceedings of the Conference on Terminology and Knowledge Engineering (*TKE-90*). Frankfurt: INDEKS Verlag, pp. 574–578.

Somers, Harold L. (2003). "The Translator's Workstation." In Harold L. Somers, ed., *Computers and Translation: A Translator's Guide*. Amsterdam and Philadelphia: John Benjamins Publishing Company, pp. 13–30.

Tong, Loong-Cheong (1987). "The Engineering of a Translator Workstation." *Computers and Translation*, Vol. 2, No. 4, pp. 263–273.

Vaumoron, Jean A. (1988). "The Ideal Workstation? Perspective of the In-house Translator." In Muriel Vasconcellos, ed., *Technology as Translation Strategy*. New York: State University of New York at Binghamton, pp. 36–41.

Zajac, Rémi (1996). "Towards a Multilingual Analyst's Workstation: TEMPLE." *Proceedings of the 2nd Conference of the Association for Machine Translation in the Americas: Expanding MT Horizons* (*AMTA-2*), Montreal, Quebec, Canada, pp. 280–284.

Zajac, Rémi and Michelle Vanni (1997). "Glossary-based MT Engines in a Multilingual Analyst's Workstation Architecture." *Machine Translation*, Vol. 12, Nos. 1–2, pp. 131–151.

KIELIKONE

Arnola, Harri, Kaarina Hyvönen, Jukka-Pekka Juntunen, Tim Linnanvirta, and Petteri Suoranta (1996). "KIELIKONE Finnish-English MT System *TRANSMART* in Practical Use." In *Translating and the Computer 18*. London: The Association for Information Management.

Arnola, Harri (1996). "Kielikone Machine Translation Technology and Its Perspective on the Economics of Machine Translation." *Proceedings of the 1st Workshop of the European Association for Machine Translation* (*TKE-96*): *Language Resources, Terminology, Economics, and User Needs*, Vienna, Austria, pp. 73–88.

Hyvönen, Kaarina and Harri Arnola (1998) "Kielikone MT Takes User-Friendliness Seriously." In *Translating and the Computer 20*. London: The Association for Information Management.

Jäppinen, Harri, K. Hartonen, Leo Kulikov, A. Nykänen, and Aarne H. Ylä-Rotiala (1993). "KIELIKONE Machine Translation Workstation." In Sergei Nirenburg, ed., *Progress in Machine Translation*. Amsterdam: IOS and Tokyo: Ohmsha, pp. 173–184.

Jäppinen, Harri, Leo Kulikov, and Aarne H. Ylä-Rotiala (1991). "KIELIKONE Machine Translation Workstation." *Proceedings of MT Summit III*, Seattle, Washington, DC, USA.

Nuutila, Pertti (1996). "Roughlate Service for In-house Customers." In *Translating and the Computer 18*. London: The Association for Information Management.

❖ PART 38 ❖

Transliteration

Name Entity

Alegria, Iñaki, Nerea Ezeiza, and Izaskun Fernandez (2006). "Named Entities Translation Based on Comparable Corpora." *Proceedings of the 11th Conference of the European Chapter of the Association for Computational Linguistics (EACL-2006)*, Trento, Italy.

Al-Onaizan, Yaser and Kevin Knight (2002). "Translating Named Entities Using Monolingual and Bilingual Resources." *Proceedings of the 40th Anniversary Meeting of the Association for Computational Linguistics (ACL-2002)*, Philadelphia, PA, USA, pp. 400–408.

Amigó, Enrique, Anselmo Peñas, Julio Gonzalo, and Felisa Verdejo (2003). "Suggesting Named Entities for Information Access." *Proceedings of the 4th International Conference on Intelligent Text Processing and Computational Linguistics (CICLing-2003)*, Mexico City, Mexico, pp. 559–563.

Asahara, Masayuki and Yuji Matsumoto (2003). "Japanese Named Entity Extraction with Redundant Morphological Analysis." *Proceedings of the Human Language Technology and North American Chapter of Association of Computational Linguistics 2003 (HLT/NAACL-2003)*, Edmonton, Alberta, Canada.

Babych, Bogdan and Anthony F. Hartley (2003). "Improving Machine Translation Quality with Automatic Named Entity Recognition." *Proceedings of the 7th Workshop of the European Association for Machine Translation: Improving Machine Translation through Other Language Technology Tools: Resources and Tools for Building MT*, Budapest, Hungary, pp. 1–8.

Babych, Bogdan and Anthony F. Hartley (2004). "Disambiguating Translation Strategies in MT Using Automatic Named Entity Recognition." *Proceedings of the 9th Workshop of the European Association for Machine Translation: Broadening Horizons of Machine Translation and Its Applications*, Foundation for International Studies, Malta, pp. 18–25.

Bikel, Daniel, Scott Miller, Richard Schwartz, and Ralph Weischedel (1997). "Nymble: A High-performance Learning Name Finder." *Proceedings of the 5th Conference on Applied Natural Language Processing*, Seattle, Washington, DC, USA.

Bollegala, Danushka, Yutaka Matsuo, and Mitsuru Ishizuka (2006). "Extracting Key Phrases to Disambiguate Personal Names on the

Web." *Proceedings of the 7th International Conference on Intelligent Text Processing and Computational Linguistics* (*CICLing-2006*), Mexico City, Mexico.

Bunescu, Razvan and Marius Pasca (2006). "Using Encyclopedic Knowledge for Named Entity Disambiguation." *Proceedings of the 11th Conference of the European Chapter of the Association for Computational Linguistics* (*EACL-2006*), Trento, Italy.

Chen, Conrad and Hsi-Jian Lee (2004). "A Three-phase System for Chinese Named Entity Recognition." *Proceedings of the International Conference on Research in Computational Linguistics* (*ROCLING-XVI*), Taipei, Taiwan.

Chen, Hsin-Hsi, Sheng-Jie Huang, Ding Yung-Wei, and Tsai Shih-Chung (1998). "Proper Name Translation in Cross-language Information Retrieval." *Proceedings of the 36th Annual Meeting of the Association for Computational Linguistics and 17th International Conference on Computational Linguistics* (*COLING-ACL-98*), Montreal, Quebec, Canada, pp. 232–236.

Chen, Hsin-Hsi, Yang Changhua, and Lin Ying (2003). "Learning Formulation and Transformation Rules for Multilingual Named Entities." *Proceedings of the ACL Workshop on Multilingual and Mixed-language Named Entity Recognition*, Sapporo, Japan, pp. 1–8.

Chinchor, Nancy (1997). "MUC-7 Named Entity Task Definition." *Proceedings of the 7th Message Understanding Conference* (*MUC-7*), Fairfax, VA, USA.

Chung, Grace, Stephanie Seneff, and Chao Wang (2003). "Automatic Acquisition of Names Using Speak and Spell Mode in Spoken Dialogue Systems." *Proceedings of the Human Language Technology and North American Chapter of Association of Computational Linguistics 2003* (*HLT/NAACL-2003*), Edmonton, Alberta, Canada.

Collins, Michael and Yoram Singer (1999). "Unsupervised Models for Named Entity Classification." *Proceedings of the Joint SIGDAT Conference on Empirical Methods in NLP and Very Large Corpora* (*EMNLP/VLC-99*), University of Maryland, College Park, MD, USA.

Cowie, Jim, Sergei Nirenburg, and Hugo Molina-Salgado (2000). "Generating Personal Profiles." *Proceedings of the International Conference on Machine Translation and Multilingual Applications in the New Millenium* (*MT-2000*), University of Exeter, England.

Cucerzan, Silviu and David Yarowsky (1999). "Language Independent

Named Entity Recognition Combining Morphological and Contextual Evidence." *Proceedings of the Joint SIGDAT Conference on Empirical Methods in NLP and Very Large Corpora* (*EMNLP/VLC-99*), College Park, MD, USA.

Dalli, Angelo (2004). "An Internet-based Method for Verification of Extracted Proper Names." *Proceedings of the 5th International Conference on Intelligent Text Processing and Computational Linguistics* (*CICLing-2004*), Chung-Ang University, Seoul, Korea, pp. 165–168.

Danielsson, Pernilla and Katarina Mühlenbock (1998). "When Stålhandske Becomes Steelglove: A Corpus Based Study of Names in Parallel Texts." In David L. Farwell, Laurie Gerber, and Eduard Hovy, eds., *Machine Translation and the Information Soup*. Berlin: Springer Verlag, pp. 266–274.

Daum'e III, Hal and Daniel Marcu (2005). "A Large-scale Exploration of Effective Global Features for a Joint Entity Detection and Tracking Model." *Proceedings of Human Language Technology Conference and Conference on Empirical Methods in Natural Language Processing* (*HLT/EMNLP-2005*), Vancouver, BC, Canada.

Fang, Xiaoshan and Sheng Huanye (2002). "Pattern Extraction for Chinese Person Name Recognition Using an Example-based Approach."《第一屆學生計算語言學研討會論文集》(*SWCL-2002: First Students' Workshop on Computational Linguistics: Proceedings*), Institute of Computational Linguistics, Peking University, Beijing, China, pp. 90–97.

Favre, Benoit, Frédéric Bechet, and Pascal Nocéra (2005). "Robust Named Entity Extraction from Large Spoken Archives." *Proceedings of Human Language Technology Conference and Conference on Empirical Methods in Natural Language Processing* (*HLT/EMNLP-2005*), Vancouver, BC, Canada.

Federico, Marcello, Nicola Bertoldi, and Vanessa Sandrini (2002). "Bootstrapping Named Entity Recognition for Italian Broadcast News." *Proceedings of the 2002 Conference on Empirical Methods in Natural Language Processing* (*EMNLP-2002*), University of Pennsylvania, Philadelphia, PA, USA.

Filatova, Elena and John Prager (2005). "Tell Me What You Do and I'll Tell You What You Are: Learning Occupation-related Activities for Biographies." *Proceedings of Human Language Technology*

Conference and Conference on Empirical Methods in Natural Language Processing (*HLT/EMNLP-2005*), Vancouver, BC, Canada.

Florian, Radu, H. Hassan, A. Ittycheriah, Hongyan Jing, Nanda Kambhatla, X. Luo, Nicolas Nicolov, and Salim Roukos (2004). "A Statistical Model for Multilingual Entity Detection and Tracking." *Proceedings of the Human Language Technology Conference/North American Chapter of the Association for Computational Linguistics Annual Meeting* (*HLT/NAACL-2004*), Boston, MA, USA.

Freeman, Andrew, Sherri Condon, and Christopher Ackerman (2006). "Cross Linguistic Name Matching in English and Arabic." *Proceedings of the Human Language Technology Conference—Annual Meeting of the North American Chapter of the Association for Computational Linguistics* (*HLT-NAACL-2006*), New York, USA.

Fung, Pascale (1995). "A Pattern Matching Method for Finding Noun and Proper Noun Translations from Noisy Parallel Corpora." *Proceedings of the 33rd Annual Conference of the Association for Computational Linguistics*, Boston, MA, USA, pp. 226–233.

Hacioglu, Kadri, Benjamin Douglas, and Ying Chen (2005). "Detection of Entity Mentions Occurring in English and Chinese Text." *Proceedings of Human Language Technology Conference and Conference on Empirical Methods in Natural Language Processing* (*HLT/EMNLP-2005*), Vancouver, BC, Canada.

Hasegawa, Takaaki, Satoshi Sekine, and Ralph Grishman (2004). "Discovering Relations among Named Entities from Large Corpora." *Proceedings of the 42nd Annual Meeting of the Association for Computational Linguistics* (*ACL-2004*), Barcelona, Spain, pp. 415–422.

Hirschman, Lynette, Florence Reeder, John Burger, and Keith Miller (2000). "Name Translation as a Machine Translation Evaluation Task." *Proceedings of the 2nd International Conference on Language Resources and Evaluation* (*LREC-2000*), *Workshop Proceedings: Evaluation of Machine Translation*, Athens, Greece, pp. 21–28.

Huang, Fei and Stephan Vogel (2002). "Improved Named Entity Translation and Bilingual Named Entity Extraction." *Proceedings of the IEEE 4th International Conference on Multimodal Interfaces* (*ICMI-2002*), Pittsburgh, PA, USA, pp. 253–260.

Huang, Fei, Stephan Vogel, and Alex H. Waibel (2004). "Improving Named Entity Translation Combining Phonetic and Semantic

Similarities." *Proceedings of the Human Language Technology Conference/North American Chapter of the Association for Computational Linguistics Annual Meeting* (*HLT/NAACL-2004*), Boston, MA, USA.

Huang, Fei, Stephan Vogel, and Alex H. Waibel (2004). "Toward Named Entity Extraction and Translation in Spoken Language Translation." *Proceedings of the International Workshop on Spoken Language Translation* (*IWSLT-2004*), Kyoto, Japan.

Huang, Fei (2005). "Cluster-specific Named Entity Transliteration." *Proceedings of Human Language Technology Conference and Conference on Empirical Methods in Natural Language Processing* (*HLT/EMNLP-2005*), Vancouver, BC, Canada.

Ittycheriah, Abraham, Lucian Lita, Nanda Kambhatla, Nicolas Nicolov, Salim Roukos, and Margo Stys (2003). "Identifying and Tracking Entity Mentions in a Maximum Entropy Framework." *Proceedings of the Human Language Technology and North American Chapter of Association of Computational Linguistics 2003* (*HLT/NAACL-2003*), Edmonton, Alberta, Canada.

Jacquemin, Christian and Caroline Bush (2000). "Combining Lexical and Formatting Cues for Named Entity." *Proceedings of the Joint Sigdat Conference on Empirical Methods in Natural Language Processing and Very Large Corpora* (*EMNLP/VLC-2000*), Hong Kong University of Science and Technology, Hong Kong.

Ji, Heng 季姮 and Luo Zhensheng 羅振聲 (2001).〈基於反比概率模型和規則的中文姓名自動辨識系統〉(Inverse Name Frequency Model and Rules-based Chinese Name Identification System). In Huang Changning 黃昌寧 and Zhang Pu 張普, eds.,《自然語言理解與機器翻譯》(*Natural Language Understanding and Machine Translation*). Beijing: Tsinghua University Press, pp. 123–128.

Ji, Heng and Ralph Grishman (2006). "Analysis and Repair of Name Tagger Errors." *Proceedings of the Joint Conference of the International Committee on Computational Linguistics and the Association for Computational Linguistics* (*COLING/ACL-2006*), Sydney, Australia.

Jiang, Jing and Cheng Xiang Zhai (2006). "Exploiting Domain Structure for Named Entity Recognition." *Proceedings of the Human Language Technology Conference—Annual Meeting of the North American Chapter of the Association for Computational Linguistics* (*HLT-NAACL-2006*), New York, USA.

Jiménez, Marisa (2001). "Generation of Named Entities." In Bente Maegaard, ed., *Proceedings of MT Summit VIII: Machine Translation in the Information Age*, Santiago de Compostela, Spain.

Kazakov, Alexander and Andrei Maslianik (2002). "Web Mining for Proper Name Dictionary Acquisition." *International Journal of Translation*, Vol. 14, No. 2, pp. 51–54.

Kim, Seokhwan, Yu Song, Kyungduk Kim, Jeong-Won Cha, and Gary Geunbae Lee (2006). "MMR-based Active Machine Learning for Bio Named Entity Recognition." *Proceedings of the Human Language Technology Conference—Annual Meeting of the North American Chapter of the Association for Computational Linguistics (HLT-NAACL-2006)*, New York, USA.

Klementiev, Alexandre and Dan Roth (2006). "Named Entity Transliteration and Discovery from Multilingual Comparable Corpora." *Proceedings of the Human Language Technology Conference—Annual Meeting of the North American Chapter of the Association for Computational Linguistics (HLT-NAACL-2006)*, New York, USA.

Klementiev, Alexandre and Dan Roth (2006). "Weakly Supervised Named Entity Transliteration and Discovery from Multilingual Comparable Corpora." *Proceedings of the Joint Conference of the International Committee on Computational Linguistics and the Association for Computational Linguistics (COLING/ACL-2006)*, Sydney, Australia.

Krishnan, Vijay and Christopher Manning (2006). "An Effective Two-stage Model for Exploiting Non-local Dependencies in Named Entity Recognition." *Proceedings of the Joint Conference of the International Committee on Computational Linguistics and the Association for Computational Linguistics (COLING/ACL-2006)*, Sydney, Australia.

Kumano, Tadashi, Hideki Kashioka, Hideki Tanaka, and Takahiro Fukusima (2004). "Acquiring Bilingual Named Entity Translations from Content-aligned Corpora." *Proceedings of the 1st International Joint Conference on Natural Language Processing (IJCNLP-2004)*, Hainan Island, China.

Kumaran, Giridhar and James Allan (2005). "Using Names and Topics for New Event Detection." *Proceedings of Human Language Technology Conference and Conference on Empirical Methods in Natural Language Processing (HLT/EMNLP-2005)*, Vancouver, BC, Canada.

Lee, Chun-Jen, Jason S. Chang, and Jyh-Shing Roger Jang (2004).

"Bilingual Named-entity Pairs Extraction from Parallel Corpora." *Proceedings of IJCNLP-04 Workshop on Named Entity Recognition for Natural Language Processing Applications*, Hainan Island, China, pp. 9–16.

Li, Xin, Paul Morie, and Dan Roth (2004). "Robust Reading: Identification and Tracing of Ambiguous Names." *Proceedings of the Human Language Technology Conference/North American Chapter of the Association for Computational Linguistics Annual Meeting* (*HLT/NAACL-2004*), Boston, MA, USA.

Lin, Tracy, Wu Jian-Cheng, and Jason S. Chang (2004). "Extraction of Name and Transliteration in Monolingual and Parallel Corpora." In Robert E. Frederking and Kathryn B. Taylors, eds., *Machine Translation: From Real Users to Research*. Berlin: Springer Verlag, pp. 177–186.

Liu, Jimin, Xiao Jing, and Chua Tat-seng (2002). "Finding Names in Chinese Text Using a Hybrid Rule Induction Model."《第一屆學生計算語言學研討會論文集》(*SWCL-2002: First Students' Workshop on Computational Linguistics: Proceedings*), Institute of Computational Linguistics, Peking University, Beijing, China, pp. 112–117.

Liu, Kaiying 劉開瑛 (2001).〈專有名詞與網絡詞語識別軟件技術研究〉(A Study on Proper Noun and Network Terms Recognition Software Technology).《輝煌二十年——中國中文信息學會二十周年學術會議》(*Proceedings of Conference of the 20th Anniversary of CIPSC*). Beijing: Tsinghua University Press, pp. 7–13.

Miller, Keith J. and Sherri Condon (2006). "Name Translation." *Proceedings of the 7th Biennial Conference of the Association for Machine Translation in the Americas* (*AMTA-2006*)*: Visions for the Future of Machine Translation*, Boston Marriott, Cambridge, MA, USA.

Minkov, Einat, Richard C. Wang, and William W. Cohen (2005). "Extracting Personal Names from Email: Applying Named Entity Recognition to Informal Text." *Proceedings of Human Language Technology Conference and Conference on Empirical Methods in Natural Language Processing* (*HLT/EMNLP-2005*), Vancouver, BC, Canada.

Minkov, Einat, Richard C. Wang, Anthony Tomasic, and William W. Cohen (2006). "NER Systems That Suit User's Preferences: Adjusting the Recall-precision Trade-off for Entity Extraction." *Proceedings of the Human Language Technology Conference—Annual Meeting of the North American Chapter of the Association for Computational Linguistics* (*HLT-NAACL-2006*), New York, USA.

Mitsumori, Tomohiro, Sevrani Fation, Masaki Murata, Kouichi Doi, and Hirohumi Doi (2004). "Boundary Correction of Protein Names Adapting Heuristic Rules." *Proceedings of the 5th International Conference on Intelligent Text Processing and Computational Linguistics* (*CICLing-2004*), Chung-Ang University, Seoul, Korea, pp. 169–172.

Moore, Robert C. (2003). "Learning Translations of Named-entity Phrases from Parallel Corpora." *Proceedings of the 10th Conference of the European Chapter of the Association for Computational Linguistics* (*EACL-2003*), Budapest, Hungary, pp. 259–266.

Nenkova, Ani and Kathleen R. McKeown (2003). "References to Named Entities: A Corpus Study." *Proceedings of the Human Language Technology and North American Chapter of Association of Computational Linguistics 2003* (*HLT/NAACL-2003*), Edmonton, Alberta, Canada.

Niu, Cheng, Li Wei, and Rohini K. Srihari (2004). "Weakly Supervised Learning for Cross-document Person Name Disambiguation Supported by Information Extraction." *Proceedings of the 42nd Annual Meeting of the Association for Computational Linguistics* (*ACL-2004*), Barcelona, Spain, pp. 597–604.

Nobata, Chikashi, Satoshi Sekine, and Jun-ichi Tsujii (2000). "Difficulty Indices for the Named Entity Task in Japanese." *Proceedings of the 38th Annual Meeting of the Association for Computational Linguistics* (*ACL-2000*), Hong Kong.

Okanohara, Daisuke and Jun-ichi Tsujii (2006). "Improving the Scalability of Semi-Markov Conditional Random Fields for Named Entity Recognition." *Proceedings of the Joint Conference of the International Committee on Computational Linguistics and the Association for Computational Linguistics* (*COLING/ACL-2006*), Sydney, Australia.

Palmer, David and David Day (1997). "A Statistical Profile of the Named Entity Task." *Proceedings of the 5th Conference on Applied Natural Language Processing*, Seattle, Washington, DC, USA.

Paşca, Marius (2005). "Finding Instance Names and Alternative Glosses on the Web: WordNet Reloaded." *Proceedings of the 6th International Conference on Intelligent Text Processing and Computational Linguistics* (*CICLing-2005*), Mexico City, Mexico, pp. 272–283.

Pedersen, Ted, Anagha Kulkarni, Roxana Angheluta, Zornitsa Kozareva, and Thamar Solorio (2006). "An Unsupervised Language Independent Method of Name Discrimination Using Second Order Co-occurrence Features." *Proceedings of the 7th International Conference on Intelligent Text Processing and Computational Linguistics* (*CICLing-2006*), Mexico City, Mexico.

Pedersen, Ted, Anagha Kulkarni, Roxana Angheluta, Zornitsa Kozareva, and Thamar Solorio (2006). "Improving Name Discrimination: A Language Salad Approach." *Proceedings of the 11th Conference of the European Chapter of the Association for Computational Linguistics* (*EACL-2006*), Trento, Italy.

Peirsman, Yves (2006). "What's in a Name? The Automatic Recognition of Metonymical Location Names." *Proceedings of the 11th Conference of the European Chapter of the Association for Computational Linguistics* (*EACL-2006*), Trento, Italy.

Qu, Yan and Gregory Grefenstette (2004). "Finding Ideographic Representations of Japanese Names Written in Latin Script via Language Identification and Corpus Validation." *Proceedings of the 42nd Annual Meeting of the Association for Computational Linguistics* (*ACL-2004*), Barcelona, Spain, pp. 183–190.

Raghavan, Hema and James Allan (2005). "Matching Inconsistently Spelled Names in Automatic Speech Recognizer Output for Information Retrieval." *Proceedings of Human Language Technology Conference and Conference on Empirical Methods in Natural Language Processing* (*HLT/EMNLP-2005*), Vancouver, BC, Canada.

Rebholz-Schuhmann, Dietrich, Harald Kirsch, Sylvain Gaudan, Miguel Arregui, and Goran Nenadic (2006). "Annotation and Disambiguation of Semantic Types in Biomedical Text: A Cascaded Approach to Named Entity Recognition." *Proceedings of the 11th Conference of the European Chapter of the Association for Computational Linguistics* (*EACL-2006*), Trento, Italy.

Shen, Dan, Zhang Jie, Su Jian, Zhou Guodong, and Tan Chew Lim (2004). "Multi-criteria-based Active Learning for Named Entity Recognition." *Proceedings of the 42nd Annual Meeting of the Association for Computational Linguistics* (*ACL-2004*), Barcelona, Spain, pp. 589–596.

Shih, Cheng-Wei, Tzong-Han Tsai, Shih-Hung Wu, Chiu-Chen Hsieh, and Wen-Lian Hsu (2004). "The Construction of a Chinese Named Entity

Tagged Corpus: CNEC1.0." *Proceedings of the International Conference on Research in Computational Linguistics* (*ROCLING-XVI*), Taipei, Taiwan.

Soboroff, Ian and Donna Harman (2005). "Novelty Detection: The TREC Experience." *Proceedings of Human Language Technology Conference and Conference on Empirical Methods in Natural Language Processing* (*HLT/EMNLP-2005*), Vancouver, BC, Canada.

Solorio, Thamar and Aurelio López López (2004). "Learning Named Entity Classifiers Using Support Vector Machines." *Proceedings of the 5th International Conference on Intelligent Text Processing and Computational Linguistics* (*CICLing-2004*), Chung-Ang University, Seoul, Korea, pp. 155–164.

Solorio, Thamar (2005). "Exploiting Named Entity Taggers in a Second Language." *Proceedings of the 43rd Annual Meeting of the Association of Computational Linguistics* (*ACL-2005*), Ann Arbor, Michigan, USA.

Song, Rou 宋柔 and Benjamin K. Ts'ou 鄒嘉彥 (2001). 〈漢語專名的初步研究〉 (A Primary Study on Chinese Proper Noun). 《輝煌二十年──中國中文信息學會二十周年學術會議》 (*Proceedings of Conference of the 20th Anniversary of CIPSC*). Beijing: Tsinghua University Press, pp. 14–19.

Sproat, Richard, Tao Tao, and Cheng Xiang Zhai (2006). "Named Entity Transliteration with Comparable Corpora." *Proceedings of the Joint Conference of the International Committee on Computational Linguistics and the Association for Computational Linguistics* (*COLING/ACL-2006*), Sydney, Australia.

Stalls, Bonnie Glover and Kevin Knight (1998). "Translating Names and Technical Terms in Arabic Text." *Proceedings of the 36th Annual Meeting of the Association for Computational Linguistics and 17th International Conference on Computational Linguistics* (*COLING-ACL-98*), Montreal, Quebec, Canada.

Stevenson, Mark and Robert Gaizauskas (2000). "Using Corpus-derived Name Lists from Named Entity Recognition." *Proceedings of the 6th Applied Natural Language Processing Conference*, Seattle, Washington, DC, USA, pp. 290–295.

Sutton, Charles, Michael Sindelar, and Andrew McCallum (2006). "Reducing Weight Undertraining in Structured Discriminative Learning." *Proceedings of the Human Language Technology*

Conference—Annual Meeting of the North American Chapter of the Association for Computational Linguistics (*HLT-NAACL-2006*), New York, USA.

Tan, Hongye 譚紅葉, Zheng Jiaheng 鄭家彥, and Liu Kaiying 劉開瑛 (1999).〈中國地名的自動識別方法研究〉(Research on the Method of Automatic Recognition of Chinese Place Names). In Huang Changning 黃昌寧 and Dong Zhendong 董振東, eds.,《計算機語言學文集》(*Essays on Computational Linguistics*). Beijing: Tsinghua University Press, pp. 174–179.

Toole, Janine (2000). "Categorizing Unknown Words: Using Decision Trees to Identify Names and Misspellings." *Proceedings of the 6th Applied Natural Language Processing Conference*, Seattle, Washington, DC, USA, pp. 173–179.

Tsai, Tzong-Han, Shih-Hung Wu, and Wen-Lian Hsu (2003). "Mencius: A Chinese Named Entity Recognizer Using Hybrid Model." *Proceedings of the International Conference on Research in Computational Linguistics* (*ROCLING-XV*), Hsin-Chu, Taiwan.

T'sou, Benjamin K. Y. and Kwong Oi Yee (2001). "Evaluating Chinese-English Translation Systems for Personal Name Coverage." In Bente Maegaard, ed., *Proceedings of MT Summit VIII: Machine Translation in the Information Age*, Santiago de Compostela, Spain.

Uchimoto, Kiyotaka, Ma Qing, Masaki Murata, Hiromi Itoh Ozaku, and Hitoshi Isahara (2000). "Named Entity Extraction Based on a Maximum Entropy Model and Transformation Rules." *Proceedings of the 38th Annual Meeting of the Association for Computational Linguistics* (*ACL-2000*), Hong Kong.

Utsuro, Takehito, Manabu Sassano, and Kiyotaka Uchimoto (2002). "Combining Outputs of Multiple Japanese Named Entity Chunkers by Stacking." *Proceedings of the 2002 Conference on Empirical Methods in Natural Language Processing* (*EMNLP-2002*), University of Pennsylvania, Philadelphia, PA, USA.

van Halteren, Hans (2004). "Linguistic Profiling for Authorship Recognition and Verification." *Proceedings of the 42nd Annual Meeting of the Association for Computational Linguistics* (*ACL-2004*), Barcelona, Spain, pp. 199–206.

Wakao, Takahiro, Robert J. Gaizauskas, and Yorick Wilks (1996). "Evaluation of an Algorithm for the Recognition and Classification of Proper Names." *Proceedings from the 16th International Conference on Computational Linguistics* (*COLING-96*), Copenhagen, Denmark, pp. 418–423.

Wan, S. and C. Verspoor (1998). "Automatic English-Chinese Name Transliteration for Development of Multilingual Resources." *Proceedings of the 36th Annual Meeting of the Association for Computational Linguistics and 17th International Conference on Computational Linguistics* (*COLING-ACL-98*), Montreal, Quebec, Canada.

Wang, Houfeng and Shi Wuguang (2005). "A Simple Rule-based Approach to Organization Name Recognition in Chinese Text." *Proceedings of the 6th International Conference on Intelligent Text Processing and Computational Linguistics* (*CICLing-2005*), Mexico City, Mexico, pp. 757–760.

Wang, Xing 王省, Huang Degen 黃德根, and Yang Yuansheng 楊元生 (1999).〈基於統計和規則相結合的中文姓名識別〉(Identifying Chinese Names Based on Combination of Statistics and Rules). In Huang Changning and Dong Zhendong, eds.,《計算機語言學文集》(*Essays on Computational Linguistics*). Beijing: Tsinghua University Press, pp. 155–161.

Wolinski, Francis, Frantz Vichot, and Bruno Dillet (1995). "Automatic Processing of Proper Names in Texts." *Proceedings of the 7th Conference of the European Chapter of the Association for Computational Linguistics* (*EACL-95*), Dublin, Ireland, pp. 31–38.

Wu, Xuelun 吳雪軍, Zhu Jingbo 朱靖波, Chen Xueyao 陳學耀, and Zhuo Hongxia 卓紅霞 (2002).〈基於統計和規則的人名識別方法〉(Person Names Recognition Method Based on Statistics and Rules).《第一屆學生計算語言學研討會論文集》(*SWCL-2002: First Students' Workshop on Computational Linguistics: Proceedings*), Institute of Computational Linguistics, Peking University, Beijing, China, p. 117.

Wu, Youzheng, Jun Zhao, Bo Xu, and Hao Yu (2005). "Chinese Named Entity Recognition with Multiple Features." *Proceedings of Human Language Technology Conference and Conference on Empirical Methods in Natural Language Processing* (*HLT/EMNLP-2005*), Vancouver, BC, Canada.

Zhang, Yanli 張艷麗, Huang Degen 黃德根, Zhang Lijing 張麗靜, and Yang Yuansheng 楊元生 (2001).〈統計和規則相結合的中文機構名稱識別〉(Identification of Chinese Organization Names Based on Statistics and Rules). In Huang Changning 黃昌寧 and Zhang Pu 張普, eds.,《自然語言理解與機器翻譯》(*Natural Language Understanding and*

Machine Translation). Beijing: Tsinghua University Press, pp. 233–239.

Zheng, Jiaheng 鄭家恒 and Yang Xiaoyan 楊曉岩 (2001).〈英文譯名自動識別方法研究〉(Research on an Automatic Recognition Method for Translated Terms of English Language).《輝煌二十年——中國中文信息學會二十周年學術會議》(*Proceedings of Conference of the 20th Anniversary of CIPSC*). Beijing: Tsinghua University Press, pp. 171–178.

Zhou, Guodong, Su Jian, and Yang Lingpeng (2005). "Resolution of Data Sparseness in Named Entity Recognition Using Hierarchical Features and Feature Relaxation Principle." *Proceedings of the 6th International Conference on Intelligent Text Processing and Computational Linguistics* (*CICLing-2005*), Mexico City, Mexico, pp. 738–749.

Transliteration

Bilac, Slaven and Hozumi Tanaka (2005). "Direct Combination of Spelling and Pronunciation Information for Robust Back-transliteration." *Proceedings of the 6th International Conference on Intelligent Text Processing and Computational Linguistics* (*CICLing-2005*), Mexico City, Mexico, pp. 402–413.

Ekbal, Asif, Supid Kumar Naskar, and Sivaji Bandyopadhyay (2006). "A Modified Joint Source Channel Model for Transliteration." *Proceedings of the Joint Conference of the International Committee on Computational Linguistics and the Association for Computational Linguistics* (*COLING/ACL-2006*), Sydney, Australia.

Goto, Isao, Naoto Kato, Noriyoshi Uratani, and Terumasa Ehara (2003). "Transliteration Considering Context Information Based on the Maximum Entropy Method." *Proceedings of MT Summit IX*, New Orleans, Louisiana, USA.

Jung, Youngim, Aesun Yoon, and Hyuk-Chul Kwon (2006). "Disambiguation Based on Wordnet for Transliteration of Arabic Numerals for Korean TTS." *Proceedings of the 7th International Conference on Intelligent Text Processing and Computational Linguistics* (*CICLing-2006*), Mexico City, Mexico.

Knight, Kevin and Jonathan Graehl (1997). "Machine Transliteration." *Proceedings of the 35th Annual Meeting of the Association for*

Computational Linguistics and 8th Conference of the European Chapter of the Association for Computation Linguistics, Madrid, Spain, pp. 128–135.

Knight, Kevin and Jonathan Graehl (1998). "Machine Transliteration." *Computational Linguistics*, Vol. 24, No. 4, pp. 599–612.

Kuo, Jin-Shea, Haizhou Li, and Ying-Kuei Yang (2006). "Learning Transliteration Lexicons from the Web." *Proceedings of the Joint Conference of the International Committee on Computational Linguistics and the Association for Computational Linguistics* (*COLING/ACL-2006*), Sydney, Australia.

Lee, Chun-Jen and Jason S. Chang (2003). "Acquisition of English-Chinese Transliterated Word Pairs from Parallel-aligned Texts Using a Statistical Machine Transliteration Model." *Proceedings of the Human Language Technology and North American Chapter of Association of Computational Linguistics 2003* (*HLT/NAACL-2003*), Edmonton, Alberta, Canada, pp. 96–103.

Lee, Jason S. and K.-S. Choi (1997). "A Statistical Method to Generate Various Foreign Word Transliterations in Multilingual Information Retrieval System." *Proceedings of the 2nd International Workshop on Information Retrieval with Asian Languages* (*IRAL-97*), Tsukuba, Japan, pp. 123–128.

Li, Haizhou, Zhang Min, and Su Jian (2004). "A Joint Source-channel Model for Machine Transliteration." *Proceedings of the 42nd Annual Meeting of the Association for Computational Linguistics* (*ACL-2004*), Barcelona, Spain, pp. 159–166.

Lin, Ming-Shun, Chia-Ping Chen, and Hsin-Hsi Chen (2005). "An Approach of Using the Web as a Live Corpus for Spoken Transliteration Name Access." *Proceedings of the International Conference on Computational Linguistics and Speech Processing* (*ROCLING-XVII*), National Cheng Kung University, Tainan, Taiwan.

Lin, Tracy, Wu Jian-Cheng, and Jason S. Chang (2003). "Word Transliteration Alignment." *Proceedings of the International Conference on Research in Computational Linguistics* (*ROCLING-XV*), Hsin-Chu, Taiwan.

Lin, Tracy, Wu Jian-Cheng, and Jason S. Chang (2004). "Extraction of Name and Transliteration in Monolingual and Parallel Corpora." In Robert E. Frederking and Kathryn B. Taylors, eds., *Machine Translation: From Real Users to Research*. Berlin: Springer Verlag, pp. 177–186.

Lin, W.-H. and H.-H. Chen (2002). "Backward Transliteration by Learning Phonetic Similarity." *Proceedings of the 6th Conference on Natural Language Learning* (*CoNLL-2002*), Taipei, Taiwan.

Malik, M. G. Abbas (2006). "Punjabi Machine Transliteration." *Proceedings of the Joint Conference of the International Committee on Computational Linguistics and the Association for Computational Linguistics* (*COLING/ACL-2006*), Sydney, Australia.

❖ PART 39 ❖

Words

Word

Bédard, Claude (1996). "Juggling with Words: Some Insights from the Human Translation Process." *Proceedings of the 2nd Conference of the Association for Machine Translation in the Americas: Expanding MT Horizons* (*AMTA-2*), Montreal, Quebec, Canada, pp. 24–33.

Blanco, Xavier, Mikhail A. Alexandrov, and Alexander F. Gelbukh (2006). "Modified Makagonov's Method for Testing Word Similarity and Its Application to Constructing Word Frequency List." In Alexander F. Gelbukh, ed., *Advances in Natural Language Processing*, Special Issue of *Research in Computing Science*, No. 18, pp. 16–27.

Brown, Ralf D. (2002). "Corpus-driven Splitting of Compound Words." *Proceedings of the 9th International Conference on Theoretical and Methodological Issues in Machine Translation* (*TMI-2002*), Keihanna, Japan, pp. 12–21.

Fazly, Afsaneh, Ryan North, and Suzanne Stevenson (2006). "Automatically Determining Allowable Combinations of a Class of Flexible Multiword Expressions." *Proceedings of the 7th International Conference on Intelligent Text Processing and Computational Linguistics* (*CICLing-2006*), Mexico City, Mexico.

Galicia-Haro, Sofía N. and Alexander F. Gelbukh (2005). "Unsupervised Learning of P NP P Word Combinations." *Proceedings of the 6th International Conference on Intelligent Text Processing and Computational Linguistics* (*CICLing-2005*), Mexico City, Mexico, pp. 328–331.

Kondrak, Grzegorz (2003). "Identifying Complex Sound Correspondences in Bilingual Wordlists." *Proceedings of the 4th International Conference on Intelligent Text Processing and Computational Linguistics* (*CICLing-2003*), Mexico City, Mexico, pp. 434–445.

Makagonov, Pavel P. and Mikhail A. Alexandrov (2002). "Empirical Formula for Testing Word Similarity and Its Application for Constructing a Word Frequency List." *Proceedings of the 3rd International Conference on Intelligent Text Processing and Computational Linguistics* (*CICLing-2002*), Mexico City, Mexico.

Mihalcea, Rada F. (2002). "Diacritics Restoration: Learning from Letters versus Learning from Words." *Proceedings of the 3rd International Conference on Intelligent Text Processing and Computational Linguistics* (*CICLing-2002*), Mexico City, Mexico.

O'Hara, Tom and Janyce Wiebe (2003). "Classifying Functional Relations in Factotum via WordNet Hypernym Associations." *Proceedings of the 4th International Conference on Intelligent Text Processing and Computational Linguistics* (*CICLing-2003*), Mexico City, Mexico, pp. 349–361.

Pala, Karel and Radek Sedláèek (2005). "Enriching WordNet with Derivational Subnets." *Proceedings of the 6th International Conference on Intelligent Text Processing and Computational Linguistics* (*CICLing-2005*), Mexico City, Mexico, pp. 296–302.

Pan, Shimei and Kathleen R. McKeown (1999). "Word Informativeness and Automatic Pitch Accent Modeling." *Proceedings of the Joint SIGDAT Conference on Empirical Methods in NLP and Very Large Corpora* (*EMNLP/VLC-99*), University of Maryland, College Park, MD, USA.

Suzuki, Satoshi (2003). "Probabilistic Word Vector and Similarity Based on Dictionaries." *Proceedings of the 4th International Conference on Intelligent Text Processing and Computational Linguistics* (*CICLing-2003*), Mexico City, Mexico, pp. 564–574.

Torres, Marco A., Susumu Kuroyanagi, and Akira Iwate (1997). "Fast Lexical Post-processing on Cursive Script Recognition." *Proceedings of the International Conference on Research in Computational Linguistics* (*ROCLING-X*), Academia Sinica, Taipei, Taiwan.

Tsai, Jia-Lin, Gladys Hsieh, and Wen-Lian Hsu (2003). "Auto-discovery of NVEF Word-pairs in Chinese." *Proceedings of the International Conference on Research in Computational Linguistics* (*ROCLING-XV*), Hsin-Chu, Taiwan.

Tsai, Jia-Lin, Cheng-Lung Sung, and Wen-Lian Hsu (2003). "Chinese Word Auto-confirmation Agent." *Proceedings of the International Conference on Research in Computational Linguistics* (*ROCLING-XV*), Hsin-Chu, Taiwan.

Tsai, Jia-Lin, Tien-Jien Chiang, and Wen-Lian Hsu (2004). "Applying Meaningful Word-pair Identifier to the Chinese Syllable-to-word Conversion Problem." *Proceedings of the International Conference on Research in Computational Linguistics* (*ROCLING-XVI*), Taipei, Taiwan.

Collocation

Bolshakov, Igor A. and Alexander F. Gelbukh (2001). "A Large Database of Collocations and Semantic References: Interlingual Applications." *International Journal of Translation*, Vol. 13, Nos. 1–2, pp. 167–187.

Bolshakov, Igor A. and Sabino Miranda-Jiménez (2004). "A Small System Storing Spanish Collocations." *Proceedings of the 5th International Conference on Intelligent Text Processing and Computational Linguistics* (*CICLing-2004*), Chung-Ang University, Seoul, Korea, pp. 245–249.

Bolshakov, Igor A. (2004). "Getting One's First Million … Collocations." *Proceedings of the 5th International Conference on Intelligent Text Processing and Computational Linguistics* (*CICLing-2004*), Chung-Ang University, Seoul, Korea, pp. 226–239.

Bolshakov, Igor A. and Sofia N. Galicia-Haro (2006). "Web-based Measurements of Intra-collocational Cohesion in Oxford Collocations Dictionary." *Proceedings of the 7th International Conference on Intelligent Text Processing and Computational Linguistics* (*CICLing-2006*), Mexico City, Mexico.

Chen, Xiaohe 陳小荷 (1999).〈動賓組合的自動獲取與標注〉(Automatic Acquisition and Bracketing of Verb-object Collocations). In Huang Changning 黃昌寧 and Dong Zhendong 董振東, eds.,《計算機語言學文集》(*Essays on Computational Linguistics*). Beijing: Tsinghua University Press, pp. 215–221.

Echizen-ya, Hiroshi, Kenji Araki, Yoshio Momouchi, and Koji Tochinai (2003). "Effectiveness of Automatic Extraction of Bilingual Collocations Using Recursive Chain-link-type Learning." *Proceedings of MT Summit IX*, New Orleans, Louisiana, USA.

Fontenelle, Thierry (1994). "Towards the Construction of a Collocational Database for Translation Students." *Meta*, Vol. 39, No. 1, pp. 47–56.

Guo, Wenhong 郭文宏, Zhang Yongkui 張永奎, and Long Yifei 龍一飛 (1999).〈基於義類搭配的漢語文本特徵信息抽取研究〉(Research of Extraction of Chinese Text Information Based on Semantic Category Collocation). In Huang Changning and Dong Zhendong, eds.,《計算機語言學文集》(*Essays on Computational Linguistics*). Beijing: Tsinghua University Press, pp. 199–203.

Haruno, Masahiko, Satoru Ikehara, and Takefumi Yamazaki (1996). "Learning Bilingual Collocations by Word-level Sorting." *Proceedings from the 16th International Conference on Computational Linguistics* (*COLING-96*), Copenhagen, Denmark, pp. 525–530.

Ikehara, Satoru, Satoshi Shirai, and Hajime Uchino (1996). "A Statistical

Method for Extracting Uninterrupted and Interrupted Collocations from Very Large Corpora." *Proceedings from the 16th International Conference on Computational Linguistics* (*COLING-96*), Copenhagen, Denmark, pp. 574–579.

Joshi, Aravind K. and Sriram Venkatapathy (2004). "Recognition of Multi-word Expressions Using Machine Learning Techniques: A Study of Verb-Noun (V-N) Collocations." *Proceedings of the International Conference on Natural Language Processing* (*ICON-2004*), International Institute of Information Technology, Hyderabad, India.

Kenny, Dorothy (2001). "Two Left Eyes: Creative Collocations in GEPCOLT." *Lexis and Creativity in Translation: A Corpus-based Study*. Manchester: St. Jerome Publishing, pp. 189–211.

Kim, Seonho, Zooil Yang, Mansuk Song, and Jung-Ho Ahn (1999). "Retrieving Collocations from Korean Text." *Proceedings of the Joint SIGDAT Conference on Empirical Methods in NLP and Very Large Corpora* (*EMNLP/VLC-99*), University of Maryland, College Park, MD, USA.

Kim, Yuseop, Byoung-Tak Zhang, and Yung Taek Kim (2001). "Collocation Dictionary Optimization Using WordNet and K-Nearest Neighbor Learning." *Machine Translation*, Vol. 16, No. 2, pp. 89–108.

Li, Baoli, Lu Qin, and Li Yin (2003). "Building a Chinese Shallow Parsed TreeBank for Collocation Extraction." *Proceedings of the 4th International Conference on Intelligent Text Processing and Computational Linguistics* (*CICLing-2003*), Mexico City, Mexico, pp. 404–407.

Lü, Yajuan and Zhou Ming (2004). "Collocation Translation Acquisition Using Monolingual Corpora." *Proceedings of the 42nd Annual Meeting of the Association for Computational Linguistics* (*ACL-2004*), Barcelona, Spain, pp. 167–174.

Martinez, David and Eneko Agirre (2000). "One Sense per Collocation and Genre/Topic Variations." *Proceedings of the Joint Sigdat Conference on Empirical Methods in Natural Language Processing and Very Large Corpora* (*EMNLP/VLC-2000*), Hong Kong University of Science and Technology, Hong Kong.

Ohomori, Kumiko and Masanobu Higashida (1999). "Extracting Bilingual Collocations from Non-aligned Parallel Corpora." *Proceedings of the 8th International Conference on Theoretical and Methodological Issues in Machine Translation* (*TMI-99*), Chester, England, pp. 88–97.

Orliac, Brigitte and Mike Dillinger (2003). "Collocation Extraction for Machine Translation." *Proceedings of MT Summit IX*, New Orleans, Louisiana, USA.

Pecina, Pavel (2005). "An Extensive Empirical Study of Collocation Extraction Methods." *Proceedings of the 43rd Annual Meeting of the Association of Computational Linguistics* (*ACL-2005*), Ann Arbor, Michigan, USA.

Pecina, Pavel and Pavel Schlesinger (2006). "Combining Association Measures for Collocation Extraction." *Proceedings of the Joint Conference of the International Committee on Computational Linguistics and the Association for Computational Linguistics* (*COLING/ACL-2006*), Sydney, Australia.

Ritz, Julia (2006). "Collocation Extraction: Needs, Feeds and Results of an Extraction System for German." *Proceedings of the 11th Conference of the European Chapter of the Association for Computational Linguistics* (*EACL-2006*), Trento, Italy.

Sekine, Satoshi and Jun-ichi Tsujii (1995). "Automatic Acquisition of Semantic Collocation from Corpora." *Machine Translation*, Vol. 10, No. 3, pp. 219–258.

Seretan, Violeta and Eric Wehrli (2006). "Accurate Collocation Extraction Using a Multilingual Parser." *Proceedings of the Joint Conference of the International Committee on Computational Linguistics and the Association for Computational Linguistics* (*COLING/ACL-2006*), Sydney, Australia.

Sharoff, Serge, Bogdan Babych, and Anthony F. Hartley (2006). "Using Collocations from Comparable Corpora to Find Translation Equivalents." *Proceedings of the 5th International Conference on Language Resources and Evaluation* (*LREC-2006*), Genoa, Italy.

Shimohata, Sayori, Toshiyuki Sugio, and Junji Nagata (1997). "Retrieving Collocations by Co-occurrences and Word Order Constraints." *Proceedings of the 35th Annual Meeting of the Association for Computational Linguistics and 8th Conference of the European Chapter of the Association for Computational Linguistics*, Madrid, Spain, pp. 476–481.

Smadja, Frank Z. (1992). "How to Compile a Bilingual Collocational Lexicon Automatically." *Proceedings of the AAAI Workshop on Statistically-based NLP Techniques*, San Jose, CA, USA.

Smadja, Frank Z. (1993). "Retrieving Collocation from Text: Xtract." *Computational Linguistics*, Vol. 19, No. 1, pp. 143–177.

Smadja, Frank Z., Kathleen R. McKeown, and Vasileios Hatzivassiloglou (1996). "Translating Collocations for Bilingual Lexicons: A Statistical Approach." *Computational Linguistics*, Vol. 22, No. 1, pp. 1–38.

Song, Honglin 孫宏林 (2000). 〈詞語搭配在文本中的分佈特徵〉 (Distributional Property of Collocations in the Texts). In Yu Shiwen 俞士汶 and Zhu Xuefeng 朱學鋒, eds.,《計算語言學文集》(*Papers on Computational Linguistics*), Vol. 4. Beijing: Department of Computer Science and Technology and Institute of Computational Linguistics, Peking University, pp. 150–157.

Spohr, Dennis and Ulrich Heid (2006). "Modeling Monolingual and Bilingual Collocation Dictionaries in Description Logics." *Proceedings of the 11th Conference of the European Chapter of the Association for Computational Linguistics* (*EACL-2006*), Trento, Italy.

Teleoacă, Anca Irinel (2004). "Computer Collocations and Computer Metaphors." *Translation Journal*, Vol. 8, No. 3.

Vintar, Špela (2000). "Extracting Terms and Terminological Collocations from the ELAN Slovene-English Parallel Corpus." *Proceedings of the 5th Workshop of the European Association for Machine Translation: Harvesting Existing Resources*, Lubljana, Slovenia.

Wu, Chien-Cheng and Jason S. Chang (2003). "Bilingual Collocation Extraction Based on Syntactic and Statistical Analyses." *Proceedings of the International Conference on Research in Computational Linguistics* (*ROCLING-XV*), Hsin-Chu, Taiwan, pp. 33–55.

Xu, Ruifeng, Qin Lu, and Sujian Li (2006). "The Design and Construction of a Chinese Collocation Bank." *Proceedings of the 5th International Conference on Language Resources and Evaluation* (*LREC-2006*), Genoa, Italy.

Context

Black, Ezra, Andrew Finch, and Ruigiang Zhang (1999). "Applying Extrasentential Context to Maximum Entropy Based Tagging with a Large Semantic and Syntactic Tagset." *Proceedings of the Joint SIGDAT Conference on Empirical Methods in NLP and Very Large Corpora* (*EMNLP/VLC-99*), University of Maryland, College Park, MD, USA.

Booth, Andrew D. (1956). "Influence of Context on Translation." In Colin Cherry, ed., *Information Theory: Papers Read at a Symposium on Information Theory Held at the Royal Institution, London*. London: Butterworths, pp. 181–183.

Buscaldi, Davide, Paolo Rosso, and Manuel Montes-y-Gómez (2005). "Context Expansion with Global Keywords for a Conceptual Density-based WSD." *Proceedings of the 6th International Conference on Intelligent Text Processing and Computational Linguistics* (*CICLing-2005*), Mexico City, Mexico, pp. 256–259.

Eberle, Kurt, Walter Kasper, and Christian Rohrer (1992). "Contextual Constraints for MT." *Proceedings of the 4th International Conference on Theoretical and Methodological Issues in Machine Translation of Natural Languages: Empiricist vs. Rationalist Methods in MT* (*TMI-92*), Montreal, Quebec, Canada, pp. 213–224.

Fukumoto, Fumiyo, Yoshimi Suzuki, and Jun'ichi Fukumoto (1997). "An Automatic Extraction of Key Paragraph Based on Context Dependency." *Proceedings of the 5th Conference on Applied Natural Language Processing*, Seattle, Washington, DC, USA.

Gamon, Michael, Eric K. Ringger, Simon Corston-Oliver, and Robert C. Moore (2002). "Machine-learned Contexts for Linguistic Operations in German Sentence Realization." *Proceedings of the 40th Annual Meeting of the Association for Computational Linguistics* (*ACL-2002*), Philadelphia, PA, USA, pp. 25–32.

Harper, Kenneth E. (1956). "Contextual Analysis in Word-for-word MT." *Mechanical Translation*, Vol. 3, No. 2, pp. 40–41.

Hazez, Slim Ben (2001). "Modeling Textual Context in Linguistic Pattern Matching." *Proceedings of the 2nd International Conference on Intelligent Text Processing and Computational Linguistics* (*CICLing-2001*), Mexico City, Mexico.

Hermjakob, Ulf and Raymond J. Mooney (1997). "Learning Parse and Translation Decisions from Examples with Rich Context." *Proceedings of the 35th Annual Meeting of the Association for Computational Linguistics and 8th Conference of the European Chapter of the Association for Computational Linguistics* (*ACL/EACL-97*), Somerset, New Jersey, USA, pp. 482–489.

Kaplan, Abraham (1955). "An Experimental Study of Ambiguity and Context." *Mechanical Translation*, Vol. 2, No. 2, pp. 39–46.

Koch, Stephan, Uwe Küssner, and Manfred Stede (2000). "Contextual

Disambiguation." In Wolfgang Wahlster, ed., *Verbmobil: Foundations of Speech-to-speech Translation*. Berlin: Springer Verlag, pp. 466–477.

Lehmann, Winfred P. (1987). "The Context of Machine Translation." *Computers and Translation*, Vol. 2, No. 3, pp. 135–158.

Levin, Lori S., Oren Glickman, Yan Qu, Donna Gates, Alon Lavie, Carolyn P. Rosé, Carol Van Ess-Dykema, and Alex H. Waibel (1995). "Using Context in Machine Translation of Spoken Language." *Proceedings of the 6th International Conference on Theoretical and Methodological Issues in Machine Translation* (*TMI-95*), Leuven, Belgium, pp. 173–187.

Montes-y-Gómez, Manuel, Manuel Pérez-Coutiño, Luis Villaseñor-Pineda, and Aurelio López López (2004). "Contextual Exploration of Text Collections." *Proceedings of the 5th International Conference on Intelligent Text Processing and Computational Linguistics* (*CICLing-2004*), Chung-Ang University, Seoul, Korea, pp. 483–491.

Olteanu, Marian and Dan Moldovan (2005). "PP-attachment Disambiguation Using Large Context." *Proceedings of Human Language Technology Conference and Conference on Empirical Methods in Natural Language Processing* (*HLT/EMNLP-2005*), Vancouver, BC, Canada.

Pan, Shimei and Julia Hirschberg (2000). "Modeling Local Context for Pitch Accent Prediction." *Proceedings of the 38th Annual Meeting of the Association for Computational Linguistics* (*ACL-2000*), Hong Kong.

Patwardhan, Siddharth and Ted Pedersen (2006). "Using WordNet-based Context Vectors to Estimate the Semantic Relatedness of Concepts." *Proceedings of the 11th Conference of the European Chapter of the Association for Computational Linguistics* (*EACL-2006*), Trento, Italy.

Perera, Praharshana and René Witte (2005). "A Self-learning Context-aware Lemmatizer for German." *Proceedings of Human Language Technology Conference and Conference on Empirical Methods in Natural Language Processing* (*HLT/EMNLP 2005*), Vancouver, BC, Canada.

Roumen, Rob and Theo van der Ster (1993). "Context: A New Concept in Computer-aided Translation." In Klaus-Dirk Schmitz, ed., *Proceedings of the Conference on Terminology and Knowledge Engineering* (*TKE-93*). Frankfurt: INDEKS-Verlag, pp. 215–220.

Roussinov, Dmitri, Leon J. Zhao, and Weiguo Fan (2005). "Mining Context Specific Similarity Relationships Using the World Wide Web." *Proceedings of Human Language Technology Conference and Conference on Empirical Methods in Natural Language Processing* (*HLT/EMNLP-2005*), Vancouver, BC, Canada.

Sibanda, Tawanda, Ozlem Uzuner, and Ozlem Uzuner (2006). "Role of Local Context in Automatic Deidentification of Ungrammatical, Fragmented Text." *Proceedings of the Human Language Technology Conference—Annual Meeting of the North American Chapter of the Association for Computational Linguistics* (*HLT-NAACL-2006*), New York, USA.

Sierra, Gerardo and Rodrigo Alarcón (2002). "Recurrent Patterns in Definitory Context." *Proceedings of the 3rd International Conference on Intelligent Text Processing and Computational Linguistics* (*CICLing-2002*), Mexico City, Mexico.

Specia, Lucia, Maria das Graças Volpe Nunes, and Mark Stevenson (2006). "Translation Context Sensitive WSD." *Proceedings of the 11th Workshop of the European Association for Machine Translation: Machine Translation/Translation Aids—Tools to Increase Quality and to Save Money*, the University of Oslo, Norway.

Younger, Daniel H. (1967). "Recognition and Parsing of Context-free Languages in Time n^3." *Information and Control*, Vol. 10, No. 2, pp. 189–208.

Zhang, Hao 張浩, Liu Qun 劉群, and Bai Shuo 白碩 (2002).〈結構上下文相關的概率句法分佈〉(Structural Context Conditioned Probabilistic Parsing of Chinese).《第一屆學生計算語言學研討會論文集》(*SWCL-2002: First Students' Workshop on Computational Linguistics: Proceedings*), Institute of Computational Linguistics, Peking University, Beijing, pp. 46–51.

Neologism

Xu, Yanhua 徐艷華 and Kang Shiyong 亢世勇 (2002).〈基於數據庫的新造詞語的構詞法研究〉(A Study of Word-formation of New Words Based on Corpora).《第一屆學生計算語言學研討會論文集》(*SWCL-2002: First Students' Workshop on Computational Linguistics: Proceedings*), Institute of Computational Linguistics, Peking University, Beijing, China, pp. 286–291.

Synonym

de Jong, Franciska and Lisette Appelo (1987). *Synonymy and Translation.* Eindhoven: Philips Research Laboratories.

Siniakov, Peter (2006). "Recognition of Synonyms by a Lexical Graph." *Proceedings of the 11th Conference of the European Chapter of the Association for Computational Linguistics* (*EACL-2006*), Trento, Italy.

Temmerman, Rita (1990). "Terminography and Synonymy." In Marcel Thelen and Barbara Leeandowska-Tomaszczyk, eds., *Translation and Meaning, Part 1.* Maastricht: Euroterm, pp. 109–121.

Turcato, Davide, Fred Popowich, Janine Toole, Dan Fass, Devlan Nicholson, and Gordon Tisher (2000). "Adapting a Synonym Database to Specific Domains." *Proceedings of the ACL-2000 Workshop on Recent Advances in Natural Language Processing and Information Retrieval*, Hong Kong, pp. 1–11.

Unknown Word

Cartoni, Bruno (2006). "Dealing with Unknown Words by Simple Decomposition: Feasibility Studies with Italian Prefixes." *Proceedings of the 5th International Conference on Language Resources and Evaluation* (*LREC-2006*), Genoa, Italy.

Chen, Keh-Jiann and Ming-Hong Bai (1997). "Unknown Word Detection for Chinese by a Corpus-based Learning Method." *Proceedings of the International Conference on Research in Computational Linguistics* (*ROCLING-X*), Academia Sinica, Taipei, Taiwan.

Chiang, Tung-Hui, Jing-Shin Chang, Ming-Yu Lin, and Keh-Yih Su (1992). "Statistical Models for Word Segmentation and Unknown Word Resolution." *Proceedings of the Conference of the Association for Computational Linguistics and Chinese Language Processing* (*ROCLING-V*), National Taiwan University, Taipei, Taiwan.

Erk, Katrin (2006). "Unknown Word Sense Detection as Outlier Detection." *Proceedings of the Human Language Technology Conference—Annual Meeting of the North American Chapter of the Association for Computational Linguistics* (*HLT-NAACL-2006*), New York, USA.

Haruechaiyasak, Choochart, Chatchawal Sangkeettrakarn, Pornpimon Palingoon, Sarawoot Kongyoung, and Chaianun Damrongrat (2006).

"A Collaborative Framework for Collecting Thai Unknown Words from the Web." *Proceedings of the Joint Conference of the International Committee on Computational Linguistics and the Association for Computational Linguistics* (*COLING/ACL-2006*), Sydney, Australia.

Hung, Chen-Ming and Lee-Feng Chien (2004). "Finding Relevant Concepts for Unknown Terms Using a Web-based Approach." *Proceedings of the International Conference on Research in Computational Linguistics* (*ROCLING-XVI*), Taipei, Taiwan.

Lin, Ming-Yu, Tung-Hui Chiang, and Keh-Yih Su (1993). "A Preliminary Study on Unknown Word Problem in Chinese Word Segmentation." *Proceedings of the Conference of the Association for Computational Linguistics and Chinese Language Processing* (*ROCLING-VI*), Nantou, Taiwan.

Ling, Yih-Jeng, Ming-Shing Yu, Shyh-Yang Hwang, and Ming-Jer Wu (1998). "A Way to Extract Unknown Words without Dictionary from Chinese Corpus and Its Applications." *Proceedings of the International Conference on Research in Computational Linguistics* (*ROCLING-XI*), Hsin-Chu, Taiwan.

Lu, Xiaofei (2005). "Hybrid Methods for POS Guessing of Chinese Unknown Words." *Proceedings of the 43rd Annual Meeting of the Association of Computational Linguistics* (*ACL-2005*), Ann Arbor, Michigan, USA.

Nakagawa, Tetsuji and Yuji Matsumoto (2006). "Guessing Parts-of-speech of Unknown Words Using Global Information." *Proceedings of the Joint Conference of the International Committee on Computational Linguistics and the Association for Computational Linguistics* (*COLING/ACL-2006*), Sydney, Australia.

Pei, Tzusheng 貝子勝, Wei-Chuan Li 黎偉權, and Tung-Ming Koo 吳東明 (1990). "Acquisition of Syntactic Properties of English Unknown Words from a Corpus." *Proceedings of the Conference of the Association for Computational Linguistics and Chinese Language Processing* (*ROCLING-III*), Taipei, Taiwan.

Peshkin, Leonid, Avi Pfeffer, and Virginia Savova (2003). "Bayesian Nets for Syntactic Categorization of Novel Words." *Proceedings of the Human Language Technology and North American Chapter of Association of Computational Linguistics 2003* (*HLT/NAACL-2003*), Edmonton, Alberta, Canada.

Toole, Janine (2000). "Categorizing Unknown Words: Using Decision Trees to Identify Names and Misspellings." *Proceedings of the 6th Applied Natural Language Processing Conference*, Seattle, Washington, DC, USA, pp. 173–179.

Uchimoto, Kiyotaka, Satoshi Sekine, and Hitoshi Isahara (2001). "The Unknown Word Problem: A Morphological Analysis of Japanese Using Maximum Entropy Aided by a Dictionary." *Proceedings of the 2001 Conference on Empirical Methods in Natural Language Processing* (*EMNLP-2001*), Carnegie Mellon University, Pittsburgh, PA, USA.

Yu, Chuanwu 于傳武, Li Sheng 李生, Chen Yin 陳鄞, and Zhao Tiejun 趙鐵軍 (2002).〈基於混合策略的漢語未登錄詞整體識別〉(A Hybrid Method for Identification of Various Types of Unknown Words).《第一屆學生計算語言學研討會論文集》(*SWCL-2002: First Students' Workshop on Computational Linguistics: Proceedings*), Institute of Computational Linguistics, Peking University, Beijing, China, pp. 52–58.

Word Order

Lu, Chuan 魯川 (2001).〈信息處理用漢語句子語序的識知研究〉(A Cognitive Study on Chunk Order of Chinese Sentences for Information Processing).《輝煌二十年——中國中文信息學會二十周年學術會議》(*Proceedings of Conference of the 20th Anniversary of CIPSC*). Beijing: Tsinghua University Press, p. 186.

Word Processing

Amsler, Robert A. (1987). "Words and Worlds." *Proceedings of the 3rd International Workshop on Theoretical Issues in Natural Language Processing* (*TINLAP-3*), Las Cruces, North Mexico, USA, pp. 16–19.

Bower, David and Margaret Bowen (1988). "Introducing Future Translators to Word Processing." In Muriel Vasconcellos, ed., *Technology as Translation Strategy*. New York: State University of New York at Binghamton, pp. 42–47.

Wu, Dekai, Zhao Jun, and Sui Zhifang (1999). "An Information Theoretic Empirical Analysis of Dependency-based Feature Types for Word Prediction Models." *Proceedings of the Joint SIGDAT Conference on*

Empirical Methods in NLP and Very Large Corpora (*EMNLP/VLC-99*), University of Maryland, College Park, MD, USA.

Word Processor

Haynes, Colin (1998). "Translating with a Word-processor." *Breaking Down the Language Barriers*. London: The Association for Information Management, pp. 103–105.

Haynes, Colin (1998). "Word-processors Are Powerful Tools for Translation." *Breaking Down the Language Barriers*. London: The Association for Information Management, pp. 90–102.

Word Recognition

Wilpon, Jay G., Lawrence R. Rabiner, and A. Bergh (1982). "Speaker-independent Isolated Word Recognition Using a 129-word Airline Vocabulary." *The Journal of the Acoustical Society of America*, Vol. 72, No. 2.

Zheng, Jiaheng 鄭家恒 and Li Wenhua 李文花 (2001). 〈新詞語自動識別方法研究〉 (The Study of Automatic Recognition for New Words). In Huang Changning 黃昌寧 and Zhang Pu 張普, eds.,《自然語言理解與機器翻譯》(*Natural Language Understanding and Machine Translation*). Beijing: Tsinghua University Press, pp. 187–192.

Word-reordering Rule

Forcada, Mikel L. (2000). "Learning Machine Translation Strategies Using Commercial Systems: Discovering Word-reordering Rules." *Proceedings of the International Conference on Machine Translation and Multilingual Applications in the New Millenium* (*MT-2000*), University of Exeter, England.

Forcada, Mikel L. (2001). "Learning Machine Translation Strategies Using Commercial Systems: Discovering Word Reordering Rules." *Machine Translation Review*, No. 12, pp. 13–18.

Word Selection

Lee, Hyo-Kyung (2002). "Classification Approach to Word Selection in

Machine Translation." In Stephen D. Richardson, ed., *Machine Translation: From Research to Real Users*. Berlin and New York: Springer Verlag, pp. 114–123.

Word Sense

Amaro, Raquel, Rui P. Chaves, Palmira Marrafa, and Sara Mendes (2006). "Enriching Wordnets with New Relations and with Event and Argument Structures." *Proceedings of the 7th International Conference on Intelligent Text Processing and Computational Linguistics* (*CICLing-2006*), Mexico City, Mexico.

Bordag, Stefan (2006). "Word Sense Induction: Triplet-based Clustering and Automatic Evaluation." *Proceedings of the 11th Conference of the European Chapter of the Association for Computational Linguistics* (*EACL-2006*), Trento, Italy.

Kruengkrai, Canasai, Hitoshi Isahara, Thatsanee Charoenporn, and Virach Sornlertlamvanich (2004). "Mining Word Senses from Text for Corpus-based Lexicography." *Proceedings of the International Conference on Natural Language Processing* (*ICON-2004*), International Institute of Information Technology, Hyderabad, India.

Mohammad, Saif and Graeme Hirst (2006). "Determining Word Sense Dominance Using a Thesaurus." *Proceedings of the 11th Conference of the European Chapter of the Association for Computational Linguistics* (*EACL-2006*), Trento, Italy.

Pantel, Patrick and Dekang Lin (2003). "Automatically Discovering Word Senses." *Proceedings of the Human Language Technology and North American Chapter of Association of Computational Linguistics 2003* (*HLT/NAACL-2003*), Edmonton, Alberta, Canada.

Wiebe, Janyce and Rada F. Mihalcea (2006). "Word Sense and Subjectivity." *Proceedings of the Joint Conference of the International Committee on Computational Linguistics and the Association for Computational Linguistics* (*COLING/ACL-2006*), Sydney, Australia.

Word Translation

Bédard, Claude (1996). "Juggling with Words: Some Insights from the Human Translator." *Proceedings of the 2nd Conference of the*

Association for Machine Translation in the Americas (*AMTA-96*). Montreal, Quebec, Canada, pp. 24–33.

Bull, William, Charles Africa, and Daniel Teichroew (1955). "Some Problems of the 'Word'." In William N. Locke and Andrew D. Booth, eds., *Machine Translation of Languages: Fourteen Essays*. Cambridge, MA: Technology Press of the Massachusetts Institute of Technology, pp. 86–103.

Diab, Mona and Steve Finch (2000). "A Statistical Word-level Translation Model for Comparable Corpora." *Proceedings of the Conference on Content-based Multimedia Information Access* (*RIAO-2000*), Paris, France.

Echizen-ya, Hiroshi, Kenji Araki, Yoshio Momouchi, and Koji Tochinai (2004). "Acquisition of Word Translations Using Local Focus-based Learning in Ainu-Japanese Parallel Corpora." *Proceedings of the 5th International Conference on Intelligent Text Processing and Computational Linguistics* (*CICLing-2004*), Chung-Ang University, Seoul, Korea, pp. 297–301.

Even-Zohar, Yair and Dan Roth (2000). "A Classification Approach to Word Prediction." *Proceedings of the 1st Meeting of the North American Chapter of the Association for Computational Linguistics*, Seattle, Washington, DC, USA, pp. 124–131.

Fung, Pascale and Benfeng Chen (2006). "Robust Word Sense Translation by EM Learning of Frame Semantics." *Proceedings of the Joint Conference of the International Committee on Computational Linguistics and the Association for Computational Linguistics* (*COLING/ACL-2006*), Sydney, Australia.

Harkin, Duncan (1957). "The History of Word Counts." *Babel*, Vol. 3, No. 2, pp. 113–124.

Harper, Kenneth E. (1956). "Contextual Analysis in Word-for-word MT." *Mechanical Translation*, Vol. 3, No. 2, pp. 40–41.

Kenny, Dorothy (2001). "A Word about Words." *Lexis and Creativity in Translation: A Corpus-based Study*. Manchester: St. Jerome Publishing, pp. 73–104.

Kenny, Dorothy (2001). "Lonely Words: Creative Hapax Legomena and Writer-specific Forms." *Lexis and Creativity in Translation: A Corpus-based Study*. Manchester: St. Jerome Publishing, pp. 142–188.

Koehn, Philipp and Kevin Knight (2000). "Estimating Word Translation Probabilities from Unrelated Monolingual Corpora Using the EM

Algorithm." *Proceedings of the 17th National Conference on Artificial Intelligence and 12th Conference on Innovative Applications of Artificial Intelligence* (*AAAI-2000*), Austin, Texas, USA, pp. 711–715.
Köhn, Philipp and Kevin Knight (2001). "Knowledge Sources for Word-level Translation Models." *Proceedings of the 2001 Conference on Empirical Methods in Natural Language Processing* (*EMNLP-2001*), Carnegie Mellon University, Pittsburgh, PA, USA.
Korovina, T. I. (1982). "Multilingual Word-for-word Translation Using a Display." *Cybernetics*, Vol. 14, No. 2, pp. 282–283.
Mair, Victor H. and Liu Yongquan, eds. (1991). *Characters and Computers*. Amsterdam: IOS Press.
McNamee, Paul and James Mayfield (2006). "Translation of Multiword Expressions Using Parallel Suffix Arrays." *Proceedings of the 7th Biennial Conference of the Association for Machine Translation in the Americas* (*AMTA-2006*)*: Visions for the Future of Machine Translation*, Boston Marriott, Cambridge, MA, USA.
Oswald, Victor A. (1952). "Word-by-word Translation." *Proceedings of the M.I.T. Conference on Mechanical Translation,* Massachusetts Institute of Technology, Cambridge, MA, USA.
Pantel, Patrick and Dekang Lin (2000). "Word-for-word Glossing with Contextually Similar Words." *Proceedings of the 1st Annual Meeting of the North American Chapter of Association for Computational Linguistics* (*NAACL-2000*), Seattle, Washington DC, USA, pp. 78–85.
Rapp, Reinhard (1999). "Automatic Identification of Word Translations from Unrelated English and German Corpora." *Proceedings of 37th Annual Meeting of the Association for Computational Linguistics* (*ACL-99*), University of Maryland, College Park, MD, USA.
Reeder, Flo and Dan Loehr (1998). "Finding the Right Words: An Analysis of Not-translated Words in Machine Translation." In David L. Farwell, Laurie Gerber, and Eduard Hovy, eds., *Machine Translation and the Information Soup*. Berlin: Springer Verlag, pp. 356–363.
Richens, Richard H. and M. A. K. Halliday (1957). "Word Decomposition for Machine Translation." In Leon E. Dostert, ed., *Research on Machine Translation*. Washington, DC: Georgetown University, pp. 71–78.
Su, Jian, Guo Jin, and Tong Loong Cheong (1999). "Target Word Selection with Co-occurrence and Translation Information." *Proceedings of MT Summit VII: MT in the Great Translation Era*, Singapore.

Yu, Shiwen, Duan Huiming, and Zhu Xuefeng (2001).〈語言工程中同形及兼類詞語處理策略〉(The Processing of the Homograph and the Multi-category Words in Language Engineering). In Huang Changning 黃昌寧 and Zhang Pu 張普, eds.,《自然語言理解與機器翻譯》(*Natural Language Understanding and Machine Translation*). Beijing: Tsinghua University Press, pp. 211–218.

❖ GENERAL INDEX ❖

❖ AUTHOR INDEX ❖

❖ TITLE INDEX ❖